The
J.R.R. Tolkien
Companion
& Guide

The
J.R.R. Tolkien
Companion
& Guide

CHRISTINA SCULL
WAYNE G. HAMMOND

*

Chronology

HOUGHTON MIFFLIN COMPANY

BOSTON · NEW YORK

2006

For information about permission to reproduce selections
from this book, write to Permissions, Houghton Mifflin Company,
215 Park Avenue South, New York, New York 10003.

Visit our Web site: www.houghtonmifflinbooks.com.

Library of Congress Cataloging-in-Publication Data
Scull, Christina.
The J.R.R. Tolkien companion & guide / Christina Scull,
Wayne G. Hammond.
v.   cm.
Includes bibliographical references and indexes.
Contents: 1. Chronology — 2. Reader's guide.
ISBN-13: 978-0-618-39102-8 (v. 1)
ISBN-10: 0-618-39102-9 (v. 1)
ISBN-13: 978-0-618-39101-1 (v. 2)
ISBN-10: 0-618-39101-0 (v. 2)
1. Tolkien, J. R. R. (John Ronald Reuel), 1892–1973 — Encyclopedias.
2. Middle Earth (Imaginary place) — Encyclopedias. 3. Fantasy liter-
ature, English — Encyclopedias. I. Hammond, Wayne G. II. Title.
III. Title: J.R.R. Tolkien companion and guide.
PR6039.032Z833 2006
828'.91209 — dc22   2006025040

Set in Adobe Minion Pro and Gentium

Printed and bound in Italy by L.E.G.O SpA

1 2 3 4 5 6 7 8 9

In Memory of

RAYNER UNWIN

Mentor and Friend

Contents

Preface

THIS BOOK has been designed to serve as a reference of (at least) first resort for the study and appreciation of the works of J.R.R. Tolkien. It is meant to be a companion to his readers, and a basic guide to his writings and ideas, his life and times, his family, friends, and colleagues, and the places he knew and loved. It is not, despite a similarity of titles, a handbook of his invented lands and characters in the manner of Robert Foster's *Complete Guide to Middle-earth* or J.E.A. Tyler's *Complete Tolkien Companion*. Nor is it a substitute for standard works such as Humphrey Carpenter's *J.R.R. Tolkien: A Biography*, Christopher Tolkien's *History of Middle-earth*, and the present authors' *J.R.R. Tolkien: Artist and Illustrator* and *The Lord of the Rings: A Reader's Companion*, or for the vast body of critical literature about Tolkien. Although it often will be found useful by itself, in particular where it provides information newly gleaned from archives or collected from recent scholarship, its purpose is equally to point to other resources in which a subject is more fully considered or differing points of view are expressed.

The length of this work may surprise readers who, focused on *The Hobbit* and *The Lord of the Rings*, have been less aware of Tolkien's other writings, or who, perhaps misled by the biographies of our subject that have followed Carpenter (and are largely derived from his book), have thought that Tolkien lived in a simple circumscribed world in which little happened beyond his writing, his teaching, his immediate family, and the Inklings. In fact, his life was remarkably full, his circle of friends was wide and varied, and his tales of Bilbo and Frodo Baggins exist alongside other works of fiction and poetry, not least the vast 'Silmarillion' mythology, and next to significant contributions to Old and Middle English studies. In consequence, there is much to say about Tolkien, so much that we have had to divide our book into two volumes.

One of these is an extensive **Chronology** of Tolkien's life and works, which has allowed us reasonably to assemble – as a biographical essay would not have done, demanding more selection and brevity – many of the miscellaneous details about Tolkien we have gathered in the course of research, details which individually may be of little moment, but in relation to one another can be very illuminating. Altogether these form a picture of a extraordinarily busy man: Tolkien the scholar, Tolkien the teacher and administrator, Tolkien the husband and father, Tolkien the creator of Middle-earth. His critics have not always appreciated how busy he truly was – those who claim that he should have published more in his academic fields, and those who fault him for not completing *The Silmarillion* as if he had nothing else to do even in his retirement. One of our aims in this book is to show that Tolkien neither wasted his time nor shirked his responsibilities – to document how much, on a regular basis, duties in connection with his academic career (lectures, classes, supervision of postgraduate students, examinations, committee meetings, and so forth) occupied his waking hours; how often he and his family were beset by illness and injury; how, to pay doctors' bills in the years before the National Health Service was established (in 1948) and to provide for his children's education, he added to an already heavy workload; how he was almost constantly under the threat of deadlines, and if he did not meet them all it was not because he did too little, but because he did so much.

The Chronology also allows us to see when, as sometimes happened, Tolkien's many responsibilities came into collision. In April 1937, for instance, within the space of a day or two he received for correction proofs of both *The Hobbit* and his British Academy lecture, *Beowulf: The Monsters and the Critics*; while in the summer and autumn of 1953 he prepared simultaneously *The Lord of the Rings* for publication and his translation of *Sir Gawain and the Green Knight* for radio broadcast, and also wrote two talks to accompany the latter. We have not attempted, by any means (even if it were possible), a complete day-to-day reconstruction of Tolkien's complex life, but we have erred in the Chronology on the side of inclusion for the sake of a fuller picture. This is particularly so during the period from 18 January 1944 to early 1945, when Tolkien frequently described his daily chores, as well as the progress of *The Lord of the Rings*, in a series of letters to his youngest son, Christopher, then posted abroad in the Royal Air Force (see *Letters of J.R.R. Tolkien*, pp. 67 ff.).

Although the most private of Tolkien's surviving papers remain private, a great deal else has been open to us, published and unpublished, which we have found a rich mine of data. These papers have been useful not only in adding to our knowledge of J.R.R. Tolkien, but also in verifying details previously accepted as fact. We found, for instance, in assembling information for 1952 that there was no possible opportunity for Tolkien to travel to Kerry in Ireland that year, as authorities (even ourselves) have previously reported. This led, as we investigated further, to a vivid recollection by Tolkien's daughter Priscilla that the visit was, rather, in 1951, and that she herself had been a participant.

Sometimes, however, evidence has been lacking, and even when present is not always complete or clear-cut. To give only a few examples: we can say that Tolkien attended particular meetings of the Inklings because the facts are mentioned, chiefly in letters by his friend C.S. Lewis, in diaries kept by W.H. 'Warnie' Lewis, and in letters that Tolkien wrote to his son Christopher. We can list which lectures he was scheduled to give as an Oxford professor, because they were announced prior to each term in the *Oxford University Gazette*. We know that he was present at certain board and committee meetings because minutes are preserved, chiefly in the Oxford University archives. But we know about only some of the holidays he took, from a handful of letters and dated paintings and drawings, and about only some of the society meetings and other events he attended (or could have attended) at King Edward's School, Birmingham and at Oxford, through secretaries' minutes, magazine reports, and printed timetables. On occasion, his Oxford lectures were cancelled or rescheduled, but a published announcement of that fact has not always come to our attention; and as for the lectures Tolkien gave at Leeds, such schedules of these that survive in the Leeds University archives name only their subjects, not the lecturers themselves, in consequence of which we have indicated only those lectures that Tolkien seems likely to have given (based partly on the statement he wrote when he applied for the Rawlinson and Bosworth Professorship of Anglo-Saxon at Oxford in 1925). We know as well that Tolkien marked School Certificate papers for many years, to augment his professor's salary, and sometimes acted as an external university examiner, but these activities seem to be little documented.

We have also included in the Chronology references to some, but no more than a fraction (even of that portion known to us), of the personal and professional correspondence that consumed another large portion of Tolkien's time. He received many requests from colleagues for information, or for comments on their ideas; requests from colleagues or former students for references when applying for academic positions; and requests from publishers to give his opinion of books under consideration. He was often sent, in addition, offprints of scholarly papers and copies of books, most of which would have required at least an acknowledgement, if not reading and criticism: these amounted to hundreds of titles during his working life. And then, after the publication of *The Hobbit* and especially *The Lord of the Rings*, he received thousands of letters expressing appreciation, asking questions, or requesting his autograph. His publishers too were in frequent touch with him about various literary, financial, and legal matters. And all of this was in addition to letters he wrote to and received from his family and intimate friends.

Tolkien's correspondence with his publisher George Allen & Unwin in particular has been of immense value to us. In many of his letters he writes of his personal activities, of academic pressures, and of his or his family's health, as well as about business at hand. These documents, however, became less frequent in his later years, reflecting increased personal contact with publisher's staff and use of the telephone.

Perhaps our greatest difficulty in writing the Chronology has been to decide where to place events that cannot be firmly dated, such as the emergence of the Inklings. Many of Tolkien's works, moreover, can be placed only within a range of years, and only roughly in order of writing. In doing so, we have relied on internal as well as external evidence – on handwriting, paper, and typefaces, and on the state of development of the work in question. Where Christopher Tolkien as a result of his own extensive research into the history of his father's writings has been able to group works in a sequential order, we have placed the grouping at the start of the relevant time span, rather than insert the writings in question arbitrarily into the Chronology. We have also made use of dates of composition inscribed by Tolkien on his writings and art, keeping in mind that some of these were added after the fact, sometimes many years later, and that memory can err; but such statements by the creator of a work must hold weight, unless evidence is found to the contrary. In a few instances it is indeed the case that there is conflicting evidence for dates, most notably for the origin and writing of *The Hobbit*. In such cases we have made multiple entries in the Chronology, with cross-references, and have discussed the matter at greater length in the other part of our *Companion and Guide*.

That volume, which we have called the **Reader's Guide**, complements the Chronology and vice versa. An asterisk (*) before names, titles, words, or phrases in the Chronology indicates that a corresponding entry may be found in the Guide; and in using the Guide, the reader will often wish to consult the Chronology for a more detailed view of a particular segment of time.

The Reader's Guide comprises a 'What's What', a 'Where's Where', and a 'Who's Who' of Tolkien, arranged in alphabetical order and in a single sequence. *Inter alia* it includes entries for:

¶ Tolkien's academic writings and his works of poetry and prose fiction, with summaries, concise backgrounds or histories, brief surveys of reviews and criticism (in so far as these exist), and miscellaneous commentary.

¶ Key ideas in Tolkien's writings, such as *eucatastrophe* and *sub-creation*, and general topics such as his religion, his views towards women, his reading, and disputes over the American copyright of *The Lord of the Rings*.

¶ Places that Tolkien lived, worked, or visited, the colleges and universities with which he was associated, pubs and bookshops he frequented, and so forth. It should be assumed by the reader that the places named in this book are in England unless otherwise stated, that English counties are referred to generally according to the names and boundaries that existed in Tolkien's lifetime (before the reorganization of local governments in the later twentieth century), and that while coverage is full, it is not exhaustive: we have not attempted to list every place in which Tolkien set foot. Nor have we attempted to account for every claim by British towns and regions to Tolkien's presence, or as an inspiration for *The Lord of the Rings*, put forth in recent years with the rise in his popularity: some of these are exaggerated, others dubious at best. In all cases, we have preferred to rely on documentary evidence such as letters, guest books, and diaries, rather than on assumptions and reported 'tradition'. It should be noted also that while some of the places described in this book are open to the public, others are not. Readers therefore who wish to follow in Tolkien's footsteps should take care not to trespass on private property, including college grounds when not open to visitors.

¶ Members of Tolkien's family; colleagues at Leeds and Oxford; fellow members of the Inklings and other groups or societies to which he belonged; publishers and editors; notable teachers and students; and major correspondents. Here too, our coverage is selective. Tolkien had many friends and acquaintances, some of whom figured mainly, or wholly, in his private life, and do not appear in published letters or biographies. Our aim has been to give an individual entry to anyone whom we know to have been particularly significant in Tolkien's life or to the production of his works, or for whom a biographical note gives us the opportunity to describe, more fully than in the Chronology, an important or particularly interesting aspect of Tolkien or his writings. Other persons with whom Tolkien was concerned are mentioned in passing, in various contexts in the *Companion and Guide*: references to these may be found in the comprehensive index at the end of each volume.

In the Chronology volume are also genealogical charts of the Tolkien and Suffield families; a bibliographical list of Tolkien's published writings; a list of his poems, published and unpublished, by title and first line; a list of his published paintings, drawings, doodles, and maps; and a list of his works with the languages into which they have been translated.

A bibliography, with full citations, of the books, articles, media, electronic resources, and archives we have used in the writing of the *Companion and Guide*, is included for convenience in both the Chronology and the Reader's Guide. In this list of sources we have indicated simply which, in our opinion, are the most important or essential for an understanding of J.R.R. Tolkien – a personal choice, but one informed by decades of familiarity with the subject, and which we feel may be welcomed especially by newer readers.

*

A few general notes are in order. J.R.R. Tolkien is sometimes referred to in this book as 'Ronald', to distinguish him from other Tolkiens or when reference by his surname seemed inappropriate in construction, and also generally for the young Tolkien, before he went up to Oxford in 1911. Titles of works are always given as found, except that we have regularized the capitalization of hyphenated titles where variation occurs in practice, e.g. *On Fairy-Stories*, *The Sea-Bell*. Titles of discrete works by Tolkien, including poems, essays, and the individual tales of *The Book of Lost Tales*, are italicized following Christopher Tolkien's example in *The History of Middle-earth*, while titles of chapters or other subsections of text are expressed in quotation marks. But it is to be understood that 'The Silmarillion', so expressed, refers to Tolkien's mythology in general, and *The Silmarillion*, so italicized, generally to the book edited by Christopher Tolkien and first published in 1977, though in a few instances (understood in context) to the book that Tolkien wished to complete. All other titles are given in italics or in roman within quotation marks, as appropriate, following common conventions of style, except that we have preferred not to distinguish titles of books *within* titles of books by reversion to roman or by quotation marks. Direct quotations generally follow their source in spelling and punctuation; but we have silently emended the occasional misspelled word or other minor error.

Because of the multiplicity of editions, *The Hobbit* and *The Lord of the Rings* are cited here only by chapter and by book and chapter, respectively; where we have quoted from these works, it has been from current corrected texts. For most books by Tolkien we have used and cited the first editions, unless otherwise stated. The same is true for two invaluable books by Humphrey

Carpenter, his biography of Tolkien (1977) and his book on the Inklings (1978). *On Fairy-Stories* and *Leaf by Niggle*, however, have been quoted from the best edition of *Tree and Leaf*, first published by Unwin Hyman, London, in 1988, and works such as *Beowulf: The Monsters and the Critics* have been quoted most conveniently (as indicated) from *The Monsters and the Critics and Other Essays* (1983).

Contributions by Tolkien to books and periodicals, or discrete works by Tolkien otherwise contained in a larger work (for instance, as the *Ainulindalë* is contained within *The Silmarillion*), are cited in their separate entries in the Reader's Guide with inclusive page numbers according to (as a convenient point of reference) the first printing of the first edition.

We have assumed that our reader has some knowledge of *The Hobbit* and *The Lord of the Rings*, so that we may refer (say) to 'Bilbo' or 'Frodo' without further explanation. *The Silmarillion*, as the central work among Tolkien's writings on Middle-earth, should be as well known, but is not; nonetheless, it has not been feasible to gloss in the *Companion and Guide*, from entry to entry, every mention of every character or place in the mythology, these being legion. For assistance in this respect, we advise the reader to consult Robert Foster's invaluable *Complete Guide to Middle-earth*. We must also point out that in writing his stories Tolkien sometimes altered the names of characters, places, etc. from text to text, or applied multiple names within a story, e.g. *Melko* > *Melkor* > *Morgoth*, and that in our accounts of the history of Tolkien's fiction we refer to names as he used them in the particular text under discussion.

The titles of several books about Tolkien frequently referred to in the *Companion and Guide* are abbreviated for convenience:

J.R.R. Tolkien: Artist and Illustrator by Wayne G. Hammond and Christina Scull (1995; corrected edn. 1998) generally as *Artist and Illustrator*.

J.R.R. Tolkien: A Biography by Humphrey Carpenter (1977) as *Biography*.

Brothers and Friends: The Diaries of Major Warren Hamilton Lewis, edited by Clyde S. Kilby and Marjorie Lamp Mead (1982) as *Brothers and Friends*.

J.R.R. Tolkien: A Descriptive Bibliography by Wayne G. Hammond with the assistance of Douglas A. Anderson (1993) as *Descriptive Bibliography*.

The Inklings: C.S. Lewis, J.R.R. Tolkien, Charles Williams and Their Friends by Humphrey Carpenter (1978) as *The Inklings*.

Letters of J.R.R. Tolkien, selected and edited by Humphrey Carpenter, with the assistance of Christopher Tolkien (1981), as *Letters*.

J.R.R. Tolkien: Life and Legend by Judith Priestman for the Bodleian Library (1992) as *Life and Legend*.

Pictures by J.R.R. Tolkien, with a foreword and notes by Christopher Tolkien (1979; 2nd edn. 1992), as *Pictures*.

The Lord of the Rings: A Reader's Companion by Wayne G. Hammond and Christina Scull (2005) as *Reader's Companion*.

The Tolkien Family Album by John and Priscilla Tolkien (1992) as *The Tolkien Family Album*.

For all quotations, page references are given whenever possible. Although selected cross-references are provided in the main sequence of boldfaced headings in the Reader's Guide, for full direction to the many names, titles, and topics mentioned in this book the reader is advised to consult the index in either volume.

In general we have applied the recommendations of the *Oxford Style Manual*, with a few exceptions guided by personal bibliographic or typographic taste. Quotations correspond to original text in wording, spelling, capitalization, and interior punctuation, except that on occasion, to suit construction, we have begun a quotation at a point within the original sentence or paragraph and have capitalized the first word to form a complete sentence. Omissions from quoted matter, except for brief extracts, are indicated by three spaced points (. . .); but quotations that are complete sentences end with full stops, or another terminal mark of punctuation as appropriate, even though the original text might continue beyond that point. In lengthier quotations we have indicated omission between two paragraphs by three spaced points following the full stop at the end of the matter quoted in the first, but (for simplicity's sake, the present book not being a rigorous textual study) not also with a mark of ellipsis when the succeeding paragraph begins at some point other than that in the original.

Our friends, at least, and our publisher especially, will be aware of how long a gestation this book has had, long years since we were asked to write for Tolkien a work of reference similar to that which Walter Hooper wrote for C.S. Lewis (*C.S. Lewis: A Companion & Guide*, 1996). In that time it grew far beyond its expected bounds, as new information was discovered, and as more aspects of Tolkien's life and works demanded explanation and expression. Other responsibilities, and other writings more time-sensitive (such as our fiftieth anniversary edition of *The Lord of the Rings* and its *Reader's Companion*), have also delayed the present book. Given still more time, two volumes could easily have become three, but in the end there must be limits. The Reader's Guide, indeed, had to be restrained to accommodate binding machinery as much as publishing schedules. Inevitably, as the length of this book and the labour to produce it have increased, the possibility for typographical errors and inconsistencies of practice or form has also become greater; and although we have made every possible effort to avoid them, we have no doubt that some are lurking in the text. If (or rather, when) in the process of using this book readers find that we have made errors or serious omissions, we would be glad to learn about them, and will endeavour to acknowledge such *addenda* and *corrigenda* in a public venue.

Unless otherwise stated, the opinions expressed in this book are our own.

*

As always, we are grateful to members of the Tolkien family for their assistance and support. Christopher Tolkien once again has acted as our mentor, a greater task than could be imagined when this book was first proposed (as a single volume), and with his sister Priscilla has shared memories of their father. Priscilla Tolkien has also read parts of the *Companion and Guide* in draft, and suggested valuable additions and improvements. Joanna Tolkien, Michael George Tolkien, and Simon Tolkien have also been of assistance.

For suggesting that we write for J.R.R. Tolkien the equivalent of Walter Hooper's excellent *C.S. Lewis: A Companion & Guide*, and for patiently awaiting its completion (in a somewhat different and considerably enlarged form), we would like to thank David Brawn at HarperCollins U.K. We are indebted also to Chris Smith, the current director of Tolkien projects at HarperCollins, who has been remarkably patient and diplomatic as we have brought this book to a close, and who has given us sound advice on matters of production.

Thanks are due as well to Cathleen Blackburn of Manches LLP, legal representatives of the Tolkien Estate, who has guided us in matters related to copyright and permissions to quote from Tolkien's writings.

We owe special thanks to Arden R. Smith, who kindly read most of this book in typescript and advised us especially on matters concerning Tolkienian linguistics; to Douglas A. Anderson, for reading parts of the *Companion and Guide*, for sharing with us information about Tolkien's early poetry, and for supplying other useful details; and to John Garth, for allowing us to read an early draft of part of his *Tolkien and the Great War* (2003) and for saving us time during our own early research in the National Archives by supplying us with pertinent reference numbers.

We are deeply grateful to the highly knowledgeable staff of many libraries and archives, including: Owen Dobbs, Blackwell's Bookshops; Neil Somerville, BBC Written Archives Centre, Caversham Park, Reading; Philippa Bassett, University of Birmingham Archives; Sandy Botha, Bloemfontein Cathedral; Judith Priestman, Colin Harris, and other staff of the Department of Special Collections and Western Manuscripts, Bodleian Library, Oxford; the staff of Duke Humfrey's Library, Bodleian Library; the staff of the Bodleian Law Library; Angela Pusey, British Academy; the staff of the Department of Manuscripts, British Library, London; John Wells, Department of Manuscripts and University Archives, Cambridge University Library; the staff of the Centre for Oxfordshire Studies, Oxford Central Library; Richard Hamer, Vincent Gillespie, and Judith Curthoys of the library of Christ Church, Oxford, for the Early English Text Society archive; the staff of Christie's, South Kensington; Thomas Lecky and Francis Wahlgren of Christie's, New York; Christine Butler, archives of Corpus Christi College, Oxford; Susan Usher, the English Faculty Library, Oxford; Paul Cavill, the English Place-Name Society; Lorise Topliffe and John Maddicott, Exeter College Library, Oxford; Natalie Milne, Glasgow University Archive Services; the staff of HarperCollins, London; Ólöf Dagný, Hið íslenska bókmenntafélag (Icelandic Literary Society), Reykjavík; Kerry York, King Edward's School, Birmingham; Ann Farr, Brotherton Library, the University of Leeds; Mark Shipway, Leeds University archives; Charles Elston, Matt Blessing, and their staff in the Department of Special Collections and University Archives, Marquette University, Milwaukee, Wisconsin; Fiona Wilkes and Sarah Bendall, Merton College Library, Oxford; Tony Cadogan, National Sound Archives, British Library, London; John Foley, National University of Ireland; Simon Bailey and Alice Blackford, Oxford University Archives; Martin Maw and Jenny McMorris, Oxford University Press Archives; Rob Wilkes, Oxford Theses (Humanities), Bodleian Library; Naomi Van Loo and Ellena J. Pike, McGowin Library, Pembroke College, Oxford; the staff of the National Archives, Kew (formerly the Public Record Office); the staff of the Radcliffe Science Library, Oxford; Michael Bott, Department of Archives and Manuscripts, University of Reading; Meic Pierce Owen, University of St Andrews Library; David Smith, St Anne's College Library, Oxford; Carolyn Warne, St Leonard's School, Fife; Claire Goodwin, Simmons College Archives, Boston, Massachusetts; Roger Dalrymple, Society for the Study of Mediaeval Languages and Literature; Sister Helen Forshaw, archives of the Society of the Holy Child Jesus; Phillip Errington, Sotheby's, London; the staff of the Staffordshire Archives Service; Lucy Wright, the library of University College, London; Kirsten Williams, Viking Society for Northern Research; Christopher Mitchell, Marjorie Mead, and the staff of the Marion E. Wade Center, Wheaton College, Illinois; the staffs of the Chapin Library of Rare Books and the Williams College Libraries, Williamstown, Massachusetts; and Joanna Parker, Worcester College Library, Oxford.

For assistance in ways both large and small, we are grateful to David Bratman; Hugh Brogan; Marjorie Burns; Raymond Chang; Joe R. Christopher; Michaël Devaux; John Ellison; Matt Fisher; Steve Frisby; Pauline Gasch; Christopher Gilson; Diana Pavlac Glyer; Mark Hooker; Carl F. Hostetter; Charles A. Huttar; Julia Margretts; Jeremy Marshall; Ed Meskys; Gregory Miller; Peter Miskech; John D. Rateliff; Alan and Louise Reynolds; Paolo Romeo; René van Rossenberg; William A.S. Sarjeant; Richard Sturch; Makoto Takahashi; Paul Edmund Thomas; George H. Thompson; Johann Vanhecke; Richard C. West; Diana and Barry Willson; and Susan Wood.

Most especially, we are indebted to the dedicatee of this book, the late Rayner Unwin, for advice in the writing of the *Companion and Guide* and for many years of friendship and encouragement.

Christina Scull & Wayne G. Hammond
Williamstown, Massachusetts
July 2006

Chronology

IN ADDITION to events with which J.R.R. Tolkien was more directly concerned, the **Chronology** includes selected events from the wider history of the world, which we hope will serve as useful points of reference. Persons, writings, and other subjects marked with an asterisk (*), for the most part only at their first appearance, are treated more fully in the **Reader's Guide**.

Dates are given as precisely as possible, according to available evidence, and qualified as necessary to indicate if approximate (*c. = circa*) or uncertain (?).

Here it has seemed appropriate to address the young Tolkien as 'Ronald' before he went up to Oxford (October 1911), and thereafter usually as 'Tolkien'. Unless otherwise noted, 'Gilson' refers to Robert Q. (Rob) Gilson, 'Smith' to Geoffrey Bache (G.B.) Smith, and 'Wiseman' to Christopher Wiseman, Tolkien's three closest friends during his schooldays and the First World War.

1889

21 January 1889 Edith Mary Bratt (*Edith Tolkien) is born in Gloucester, England to Frances 'Fannie' Bratt of Wolverhampton and Alfred Frederick Warrilow of Handsworth. She will be brought up in that *Birmingham suburb together with her cousin *Jennie Grove.

1891

16 April 1891 *Arthur Reuel Tolkien (*b*. 1857), son of John Benjamin and Mary Jane Tolkien (see *Tolkien family), and *Mabel Suffield (*b*. 1870), daughter of John and Emily Suffield (see *Suffield family), both of Birmingham, England, are married in Cape Town Cathedral after a three-year betrothal. Arthur had emigrated to *South Africa in 1889, and in 1890 was appointed manager of the Bloemfontein (Orange Free State) branch of the Bank of Africa. Mabel had sailed to South Africa from England on the *Roslin Castle* in March 1891, only a few weeks after her twenty-first birthday.

1892

3 January 1892 John Ronald Reuel Tolkien is born to Arthur and Mabel Tolkien at Bank House, Maitland Street, in Bloemfontein.

4 January 1892 Arthur Tolkien writes to his mother that 'the baby is (of course) lovely. It has beautiful hands and ears (very long fingers) very light hair, "Tolkien" eyes and very distinctly a "Suffield" mouth. . . . The boy's first name will be "John" after its grandfather [John Benjamin Tolkien], probably John Ronald Reuel altogether. Mab wants to call it Ronald and I want to keep up John and Reuel . . .' (quoted in *Biography*, p. 12). It was the custom in the Tolkien family for the eldest son of the eldest son to be called 'John'; 'Reuel' apparently was taken from the surname of a family friend (see *Letters*, pp. 397–8, and *Names).

31 January 1892 John Ronald Reuel Tolkien is baptized in the Anglican Cathedral, Bloemfontein. *See note.* His godparents are Mabel's elder sister, Edith Mary 'May' Incledon (see *Incledon family), G. Edward Jelf, and Tom Hadley, the husband of Arthur's sister Florence.

15 November 1892 Arthur, Mabel, baby Ronald in the arms of his nurse, and two native household servants pose in the garden of Bank House for a photograph, which the Tolkiens send with Christmas greetings to friends and relatives (reproduced in *Biography*, pl. 1a, and in *The Tolkien Family Album*, p. 16; another photograph of Ronald from around this time appears in *The Tolkien Family Album*, p. 13). At some time in 1892 or 1893 the houseboy Isaak, shown in the photograph, steals baby Ronald for a time, to show off a white baby at his kraal. Despite the turmoil this causes, Isaak is not dismissed.

1893

Autumn (southern hemisphere) 1893 Mabel's elder sister May and her husband, Walter Incledon, a Birmingham merchant, with their daughter Marjorie, come to Bloemfontein. May and Marjorie stay at Bank House through the southern winter while Walter travels on business.

Summer (southern hemisphere) 1893–1894 Ronald spends the cooler parts of the day in the garden and often watches his father planting vines or trees. One day Ronald is bitten by a tarantula and runs away in terror; his nurse snatches him up and sucks out the poison. In later life he will recall running through the grass, but not the spider itself. – Ronald now shows an interest in drawing, often scribbling with pencil and paper when he visits his father's offices downstairs in Bank House. But his health suffers in the heat, and he is bothered by teething.

1894

17 February 1894 Ronald's younger brother, *Hilary Arthur Reuel Tolkien, is born.

November 1894 Mabel takes her sons on a long train journey to the coast near Cape Town so that Ronald can be in cooler air. He will retain a faint memory of running from the sea to a bathing hut across the sands. On their return to Bloemfontein preparations are made for the family to visit England. Although Arthur is happy in South Africa, Mabel is irritated with Bloemfontein life and dislikes the hot climate, which also poses a risk to Ronald's health.

Christmas 1894 'My first Christmas memory is of blazing sun, drawn curtains and a drooping eucalyptus' (Tolkien, letter to W.H. Auden, 7 June 1955, *Letters*, p. 213).

1895

1895 The heat of South Africa having affected Mabel and Ronald so badly, she and Arthur decide that, rather than wait until they can travel together to England on home-leave, she should go on ahead with the boys, and Arthur will join them later, when he feels able to leave the bank.

Late March or early April 1895 Ronald watches his father paint 'A.R. Tolkien' on the lid of a cabin trunk.

Beginning of April 1895 Mabel Tolkien, Ronald and Hilary, and the boys' nurse embark on the SS *Guelph* at Cape Town. Three weeks later they arrive in Southampton, England, where they are met by Mabel's younger sister Jane (*Emily Jane Neave). Together they travel to Birmingham. They stay with Mabel's parents, her sister Jane, and her brother William in their house at 9 Ashfield Road, Kings Heath (see *Birmingham and environs). Ronald now also meets his Tolkien relatives and becomes part of a much larger family circle, although throughout his life he will feel himself much more a Suffield than a Tolkien.

Spring–summer 1895 Ronald's health improves. Arthur Tolkien writes to say that he misses his wife and children, but his departure for England is always delayed.

November 1895 Arthur Tolkien, still in South Africa, contracts rheumatic fever. Although he seems to recover, he does not feel it wise to undertake the long journey home and then face an English winter.

Christmas 1895 Ronald enjoys his first wintry Christmas with a real Christmas tree.

1896

January 1896 Mabel hears that Arthur is still in poor health, and decides that she must return to Bloemfontein to take care of him. She books passage to South Africa for herself and the boys, to leave on 2 March.

14 February 1896 Ronald dictates to his nurse a letter to his father: 'I am so glad I am coming back to see you it is such a long time since we came away from you.... I am got such a big man now because I have got a man's coat and a man's bodice.... Auntie Gracie [Grace Mountain *née* Tolkien] has been to see us I walk every day and only ride in my mailcart a little bit' (quoted in *Biography*, p. 16). On that same day Mabel receives a telegram that Arthur has suffered a severe haemorrhage. Ronald's letter is never sent.

15 February 1896 Arthur Tolkien dies in the afternoon. The funeral service is held in the Cathedral in Bloemfontein, and he is buried in the Anglican cemetery. Arthur's estate will bring Mabel an income of only some thirty shil-

lings per week, from shares in South African mines; to this Walter Incledon
will add a little. She and the boys are unable to stay in the Suffield house permanently, and in any case Mabel thinks that country air will benefit her sons.

Summer 1896 Mabel Tolkien rents a cottage at 5 Gracewell Road in *Sarehole, a hamlet south of Birmingham. At the impressionable age of four and a
half, for the first time Ronald experiences life in a green countryside. He and
Hilary explore the surrounding area: Sarehole mill with its water-wheel, meadows, and a tree-lined sandpit; they paddle in the stream; they pick wildflowers
and mushrooms and gather blackberries, and are sometimes chased by irate
millers or farmers when they trespass. They also climb trees, including a willow which overhangs the mill pond; Ronald will not forget that one day this
tree was cut down and simply left lying on the ground. He and Hilary make
friends with some of the local children and learn a little of the local dialect, but
are sometimes mocked for their middle-class accents, long hair, and pinafores.
– John Benjamin Tolkien, Ronald's paternal grandfather, dies.

1896–1899 Mabel decides to teach her boys at home. Ronald had already
learned to read by the age of four. He now develops a decorative style of handwriting indebted to his mother's own, and an abiding interest in alphabets
and scripts (*Calligraphy). He also begins to learn Latin and German, which
he likes, and French which attracts him less. When he shows an aptitude for
*languages, and an interest in the sounds, shapes, and meanings of words,
his mother also begins to teach him etymology, in which she herself is interested. She tries to teach him to play the piano but has little success. He is more
interested in drawing, especially landscapes and trees. He will develop a great
interest in botany and come to know the subject well. The only subject that
Mabel does not teach him is geometry; this is taught by his Aunt Jane, Mabel's
sister. Ronald will later say that it was 'to my mother who taught me (until I
obtained a scholarship at the ancient Grammar School in Birmingham) that
I owe my tastes for philology, especially of Germanic languages, and for
romance' (*Letters*, p. 218). He will also remark, of early interests that remained
with him through the years: 'It has always been with me: the sensibility to
linguistic pattern which affects me emotionally like colour or music; and the
passionate love of growing things; and the deep response to legends (for lack
of a better word) that have what I would call the North-western temper and
temperature' (letter to W.H. Auden, 7 June 1955, *Letters*, p. 212). – It is probably
in this period that Mabel takes the boys on at least one seaside holiday, and
Ronald begins his first sketchbook: near the beginning is a childish drawing,
Sea Weeds and Star Fishes (*Life and Legend*, pp. 12–13). – At this time Mabel is
still a practising Anglican. Since her husband's death, she has taken her sons
with her every Sunday to a 'high' Anglican Church.

Ronald's early reading includes the *Alice* books by Lewis Carroll, which
amuse him; *The Princess and the Goblin* and *The Princess and Curdie* by
*George MacDonald; the fairy books of *Andrew Lang, in particular 'The
Story of Sigurd' in *The Red Fairy Book* which fires his interest in *dragons; and

Stories for my Children by E.H. Knatchbull-Hugessen, especially the tale of 'Puss Cat Mew' (*Fairy-stories). He also likes Red Indian tales and Arthurian legends (*Arthur and the Matter of Britain). In later life, he will note that he did not enjoy *Treasure Island* by Robert Louis Stevenson, the stories of Hans Christian Andersen, or *The Pied Piper* by Robert Browning; and that while he read fairy-stories he did not develop a real taste for and appreciation of them until he was about eight. Nor was it until he began to study Latin and Greek at school that he developed any appreciation of *poetry. Even in early childhood his interests are more factual or scientific (*Science): history, astronomy, natural history (especially botany and zoology), palaeontology (he liked pictures of prehistoric animals), geology, grammar, and etymology. He will note several times that he was not particularly interested in or proficient at mathematics.

1896–1900 Much later, Tolkien will write to a group of primary school children in *Acocks Green, some two miles north-east of Sarehole: 'I lived till I was 8 at Sarehole and used to walk to A[cocks] G[reen] to see my uncle. It was all "country" then . . .' (17 October 1966, quoted in Sotheby's, *English Literature, History, Children's Books and Illustrations*, London, 16 December 2004, p. 274).

1897

22 June 1897 Ronald will later recall walking through the river-meadows up the hill to the old college, Moseley Grammar School, which he saw illuminated with fairy-lights for Queen Victoria's Diamond Jubilee.

1898

1898–1899 Ronald will later recall that when he was about six or seven years old he wrote a story or poem about a dragon. 'I remember nothing about it except a philological fact. My mother said nothing about the dragon, but pointed out that one could not say "a green great dragon", but had to say "a great green dragon". I wondered why, and still do. The fact that I remember this is possibly significant, as I do not think I ever tried to write a story again for many years, and was taken up with language' (letter to W.H. Auden, 7 June 1955, *Letters*, p. 214). See note.

1899

9 October 1899 Beginning of the Boer War between Britain and the Boers of the Transvaal and the Orange Free State.

Mid-October 1899 Mafeking is besieged by the Boers. Because Ronald had been born in the Orange Free State, he and his mother would have a special interest in events occurring there. On 16 November 1914, not long after the First World War begins, he will write to his friend *Christopher Wiseman expressing patriotism and a fierce belief in nationalism, but denying that he is a militarist: 'I no longer defend the Boer War! I am a more & more convinced Home Ruler' (Tolkien Papers, Bodleian Library, Oxford).

November 1899 Ronald sits the entrance examination for *King Edward's School, Birmingham, which his father had attended, but fails to obtain a place.

Late 1899 or early 1900 Mabel Tolkien begins to take Ronald and Hilary on Sundays to St Anne's, a Roman Catholic church in Alcester Street, Birmingham.

1900

?1900 Late in life Tolkien will recall that when he was 'about 8 years old' he 'read in a small book (professedly for the young) that nothing of the language of primitive peoples (before the Celts or Germanic invaders) is now known, except perhaps *ond* – 'stone' (+ one other now forgotten)' (letter to Graham Tayar, 4–5 June 1971, *Letters*, p. 410). *See note.*

Spring 1900 Mabel and her sister May, having decided to convert to Roman Catholicism, begin to receive instruction at St Anne's.

16 May 1900 Mafeking is relieved after seven months of resistance. In England there are widespread celebrations on 18–19 May.

June 1900 Mabel is received into the Catholic Church. The Suffield family, especially Mabel's Unitarian father, and the Tolkiens who were mainly Baptists, are shocked. Mabel is now faced with hostility and the loss of financial help. Walter Incledon refuses to continue his support and forces his wife May to recant her decision to join the Church of Rome. Undeterred, Mabel begins to instruct her sons in the Roman Catholic faith.

26–28 June 1900 During this period Ronald sits the entrance examination for King Edward's School a second time and obtains a place.

Autumn term 1900 Ronald begins to attend King Edward's School. His fee of £12 per year is paid by a Tolkien uncle. He is placed in the Eleventh Class under W.H. Kirkby. The Thirteenth Class is the lowest at King Edward's School and the First Class the highest, but after the Eighth Class there are three unnumbered classes: Lower Remove, Upper Remove, and Transitus. Above Transitus the School is divided into a Classical Side and a Modern Side, with more classes on the latter (the Classical Side did not include a Seventh Class). Pupils do not necessarily pass through all classes, but might skip ahead; nor do they spend a set amount of time in each class. According to the School curriculum published in 1906,

> the nine Classes from the 13th upwards to the Transitus, inclusive, receive instruction in the ordinary elementary subjects of a liberal education, *viz*, Arithmetic and Elementary Mathematics, Scripture, English, History, Geography, French, Latin and Drawing. The boys are also (as far up as class 8) instructed in Botany, with the intention of training their powers of observation and evoking an interest in the objects and

phenomena of nature. . . . All boys throughout the School are required to take physical exercises in the Gymnasium, unless forbidden to do so by a medical man.

– For a while, Ronald walks most of the way to school, which is in the centre of Birmingham four miles from home, because Mabel cannot afford train fares, and the cheaper trams do not run as far as Sarehole. But before the end of September 1900 Mabel and her sons will move to 214 Alcester Road, Moseley, closer to King Edward's School and on a tram route. Ronald will find being in the city 'dreadful' after the peace and green of Sarehole (quoted in *Biography*, p. 25). During his first term, ill health will keep Ronald away from school on several occasions. – Hilary continues to be taught at home by his mother.

Late 1900 or early 1901 Mabel Tolkien and her sons move to a terrace house, 86 Westfield Road in Kings Heath, close to the new Roman Catholic church of St Dunstan's. The house is noisy since it backs onto the railway line, but for Ronald there are compensations. On the far side of the line are green fields, and flowers and other plants grow on the banks of the railway cutting. Ronald is not at all attracted by the trains themselves, but becomes fascinated by the strange Welsh names on the coal trucks they pull: the Welsh language will come to play an important part in his writings. He tries to learn more about it, but the only books available are still too advanced for him.

1901

22 January 1901 Queen Victoria dies. Edward VII succeeds to the throne.

Autumn term 1901 By now, Ronald has advanced to the Eighth Class, under A.W. Adams.

1902

Early 1902 Dissatisfied with the house in Kings Heath and with St Dunstan's, Mabel looks elsewhere. She finds the *Birmingham Oratory more to her taste, and is able to find a house to rent nearby, at 26 Oliver Road in Edgbaston. Ronald and Hilary now will be able to attend St Philip's, a Catholic grammar school attached to the Oratory. Ronald will not have to make the long journey into the centre of Birmingham, and the fees are lower than at King Edward's School. One of the Oratory Fathers, *Francis Xavier Morgan, who acts as parish priest soon becomes a close and sympathetic friend of the family.

31 May 1902 The Boer War ends with the Peace Treaty of Vereeniging. The Boers accept British sovereignty.

?Summer 1902 Ronald having outpaced his classmates, Mabel removes him and Hilary from St Philip's School and once again teaches the boys at home.

9 August 1902 Coronation of King Edward VII.

November 1902 Ronald sits the entrance examination at King Edward's School and is awarded a Foundation Scholarship; therefore no fees will have to be paid for his education. The Scholarship will be renewed in 1904, 1906, and 1908.

1903

1903 Frances Bratt dies. Edith is sent by her guardian, solicitor Stephen Gateley, to Dresden House School, a boarding school run by two sisters named Watts who place a particular emphasis on music. Here Edith will develop her talent for playing the piano.

Spring term 1903 Ronald re-enters King Edward's School. He is placed in the Lower Remove Class under R.H. Hume.

July 1903 Ronald is placed eleventh out of twenty-four in the Lower Remove.

Autumn term 1903 Ronald advances from the Lower Remove. After leaving one of the Removes or Transitus, pupils have a choice. The School Curriculum of 1906 states that

> above Transitus, the average age of which is about 14, though an able boy will usually pass through it quite a year earlier than that, the School is divided into a Classical or Literary, and Modern, or rather Scientific Side. The Modern Side do not learn Greek, nor (except in a Voluntary Class) do the Classical Side learn Science. The amount of time given to Mathematics on both sides is the same, and Modern Languages are also studied on both Sides. Boys who have any prospect of proceeding to Oxford or Cambridge should take the Classical Side, and it is especially desirable that boys who show mathematical promise should do so. All who contemplate a Degree in Arts at any University will naturally take this Side.

Ronald is on the Classical Side, and since there is no Seventh Class on that Side, he moves into the Sixth Class, under *George Brewerton. There he will begin to study Greek, he will be introduced also to Shakespeare (*Drama) and *Chaucer (and encouraged to read the latter in the original), and with the aid of a primer lent him by Brewerton, he will begin to learn Old English (*Languages).

Christmas 1903 Mabel Tolkien sends drawings made by Ronald and Hilary to the boys' Tolkien grandmother, and comments on how hard Ronald has worked on them since school broke up on 16 December:

> Ronald can match silk lining or any art shade like a true 'Parisian Modiste'. – Is it his Artist or Draper Ancestry coming out? – He is going along at a great rate at school – he knows far more Greek than I do Latin – he says he is going to do German with me these holidays – though at

present [with a lingering illness] I feel more like Bed. One of the clergy, a young, merry one, is teaching Ronald to play chess – he says he has read *too* much, everything fit for a boy under fifteen, and he doesn't know any single classical thing to recommend him. Ronald is making his First Communion this Christmas – so it is a very great feast indeed to us this year. [quoted in *Biography*, p. 28]

At his confirmation Ronald takes the additional name 'Philip' but will rarely use it. – At about this time, Ronald buys a copy of *Chambers's Etymological Dictionary*, 'the beginning of my interest in German Philology (& Philol[ogy]. in general)' (note by Tolkien, dated 1973, in his copy of the book, quoted in *Life & Legend*, p. 16).

1904

January 1904 Ronald and Hilary have measles followed by whooping cough. Hilary also develops pneumonia. The strain of nursing the boys proves too much for Mabel's health. – From 1 January, motor-cars in Britain have to be licensed and fitted with number plates; 23,000 cars are registered. The speed limit is 20 miles per hour. Tolkien will later remark on the spread of the motor-car with consequent noise and fumes (see *Environment; *Progress in Bimble Town*).

April 1904 By now, Mabel is in hospital, diagnosed with diabetes; at this time insulin treatment for diabetics is not yet available. Hilary is sent to stay with his Suffield grandparents, and Ronald to their Aunt Jane, now married to a former lodger in the Suffield home, Edwin Neave, and living in Hove on the south coast of England, near Brighton. Ronald will be absent from King Edward's School for the summer term.

27 April 1904 Ronald sends his mother a drawing on the back of a card posted in Brighton: it is inscribed *They Slept in Beauty Side by Side (Artist and Illustrator*, fig. 4) and apparently shows Jane and Edwin Neave in bed. This is one of several drawings Ronald makes for his mother at this time. Another, inscribed *Working Overtime S.P.Q.R.*, is of Edwin Neave, an insurance clerk, sitting at a tall desk with a Guardian Fire Insurance calendar on the wall. An even more humorous drawing, inscribed '*For Men Must Work*' as *Seen Daily at 9 am* depicts Ronald and Edwin striding along the promenade to the Guardian office. At some point Jane must have left her nephew and husband in order to visit Mabel in hospital, for in another drawing, *What Is Home without a Mother (or a Wife) (Life and Legend*, p. 14), on which is written 'Show Aunt Jane', Edwin Neave is darning a sock while Ronald is mending his trousers.

Late June 1904 Mabel has recovered sufficiently to leave hospital and must now undergo a lengthy convalescence. Father Francis Morgan arranges for her and the boys to stay at Woodside Cottage, *Rednal, Worcestershire, near the Oratory retreat and cemetery. They lodge with the local postman and his wife, Mr and Mrs Till. They have the freedom of the Oratory's grounds and can explore the adjoining Lickey Hills. Mabel writes to her mother-in-law: 'Boys look *ridiculously* well compared to the weak white ghosts that met me on train 4 weeks ago!!! Hilary has got tweed suit and his first Etons today! and looks *immense*. – We've had perfect weather. Boys will write first wet day but what with Bilberry-gathering – Tea in Hay – Kite-flying with Fr. Francis – sketching – Tree Climbing – they've never enjoyed a holiday so much' (quoted in *Biography*, pp. 29–30). Father Francis visits many times. Mabel and the boys attend Mass on Sundays at the Oratory retreat, if a priest is in residence, or they are driven to St Peter's Catholic church in nearby Bromsgrove with Mr and Mrs Church, the gardener and caretaker for the Oratory fathers.

8 August 1904 Ronald writes a three-page pictorial code letter to Father Francis, which ends in plain text with a limerick about the priest 'to pay you out for not coming!'

September 1904 Even when autumn term begins at King Edward's School, Mabel decides not to leave Woodside Cottage. Therefore Ronald has to rise early and walk over a mile from Rednal to the nearest station to catch a train into Birmingham; by the time he comes home at the end of the day it is growing dark, and Hilary sometimes meets him with a lamp.

8 November 1904 Mabel sinks into a diabetic coma.

14 November 1904 Mabel Tolkien dies in Woodside Cottage, with Father Francis Morgan and May Incledon at her bedside.

17 November 1904 Mabel Tolkien is buried in the churchyard of St Peter's, Bromsgrove, and her grave marked with a cross of the same design as that used for the graves of the Oratory fathers. In her will she has appointed Father Francis as Ronald and Hilary's guardian.

December 1904 Ronald is listed eleventh out of fifteen in the Sixth Class at King Edward's School.

Late 1904 Since Ronald and Hilary cannot live with him in the Oratory, Father Francis has to find them suitable lodgings, but he knows that both the Suffield and the Tolkien families had opposed Mabel's conversion and might try to contest her will to gain control of the boys. King Edward's School records list Ronald's address, immediately following his mother's death, as care of Laurence Tolkien (one of Arthur's brothers, an insurance manager) at Dunkeld, Middleton Hall Road, Kings Norton. By January 1905, however, Father Francis arranges for Ronald and Hilary to live with Beatrice Suffield, the widow of Mabel's youngest brother, William. This seems a good compromise, as Aunt Beatrice has no strong religious views, she is family, and she lives near the Oratory at 25 Stirling Road in Edgbaston. The boys are given a large room at the top of her house from which they have a view of the countryside in the distance. – During school holidays Ronald and Hilary often stay with other relatives. Among these are two of their father's sisters (see *Tolkien family), Aunt Grace who lives in Newcastle with her husband William Mountain and their children Kenneth and Dorothy, and Aunt Mabel who lives at Abbotsford, 69 Wake Green Road, Moseley, Birmingham with her husband Tom Mitton and their children. But most often they stay with the Incledons, who now live at *Barnt Green, Worcestershire, near Rednal. (A second daughter, Mary, had been born to May and Walter Incledon in 1895.) On one of his early visits to the Incledons Ronald discovers that Marjorie and Mary Incledon have constructed a language, 'Animalic', almost entirely out of English animal, bird, and fish names, and are able to converse in it fluently. He learns a little of Animalic and is amused by it. He does not admit to his cousins that he himself had already indulged a 'secret vice' of creating languages: he will later remark that he had been making up imaginary languages since he could write (see *Languages, Invented).

1905

1905 With the permission of the Oratory, for otherwise they would have to go to St Philip's, Ronald continues to attend King Edward's School, now together with Hilary. Father Francis will also allow Ronald to attend classes on the New Testament in Greek, offered by the Chief Master of King Edward's, *Robert Cary Gilson. Aunt Beatrice gives the boys board and lodging but little affection or consideration for their feelings; one day Ronald discovers that she has burnt their mother's personal papers and letters. In many ways the Oratory is Ronald and Hilary's real home. In the morning, they serve Mass for Father Francis, and they eat breakfast in the refectory before leaving for school, either on foot or by horse-bus or bicycle. Ronald will later describe this period in his life as having 'the advantage of a (then) first rate school and that of a "good Catholic home" – "in excelsis": [I was] virtually a junior inmate of the Oratory house, which contained many learned fathers (largely "converts")' (letter to *Michael Tolkien, begun after 25 August 1967, *Letters*, p. 395). – Having access to books in Spanish belonging to Father Francis Morgan (who is half Spanish), Ronald tries to teach himself that language.

6 and 8 July 1905 Athletic Sports are held at the King Edward's School Grounds.

2 August 1905 Speech Day and prize-giving at King Edward's School. Ronald, who has tied for first place in the Sixth Class, receives as a prize the book *Roman History* by W.W. Capes (1879).

Summer 1905 According to Humphrey Carpenter, Father Francis Morgan took Ronald and Hilary on holiday to *Lyme Regis, on the south coast of England, every summer after their mother's death; and 'later in childhood' Ronald went on a railway journey to *Wales (*Biography*, p. 26).

Autumn term 1905 Ronald is now in the Fifth Class at King Edward's School, under C.H. Heath. There he meets Christopher Wiseman, who becomes a close friend and friendly rival. At the end of term Ronald is placed first and Wiseman second in the class. Other pupils who also will become close friends are *Robert Q. 'Rob' Gilson, the son of the Chief Master, and *Vincent Trought.

1906

***c*. 1906–1907** On a later visit to his Incledon cousins, Ronald discovers that Marjorie has lost interest in Animalic. He and Mary begin to create a new and more sophisticated language, 'Nevbosh' or 'New Nonsense'.

Spring or summer term 1906 Ronald enters the Fourth Class under *R.W. Reynolds. He thinks that Reynolds makes Greek and Roman history boring, but likes him as a person. At the end of the summer term Ronald is placed second in the class (Christopher Wiseman is sixth) and is awarded a joint prize for Grammar.

28 and 30 June 1906 Athletic Sports are held at the King Edward's School Grounds.

27 July 1906 Speech Day and prize-giving at King Edward's School.

Summer 1906 Father Francis takes Ronald and Hilary on holiday to Lyme Regis. They stay at the Three Cups Hotel in Broad Street. Ronald enjoys exploring the countryside and shore, sketching, and searching for fossils in the cliffs; on one of his visits to Lyme Regis he finds a prehistoric jawbone and pretends that it came from a dragon. He draws a view of the harbour from the window of the hotel (*Lyme Regis Harbour from the Drawing Room Window of the Cups Hotel*, see *Artist and Illustrator*, fig. 8).

Autumn term 1906 Ronald enters the Third Class at King Edward's School, under A.E. Measures. At the end of term he is placed fourth out of twenty in the class (Christopher Wiseman is eighth).

1907

Spring term 1907 Ronald enters the Second Class at King Edward's School, under both Robert Cary Gilson, the Chief Master, and his assistant A.E. Measures.

4 April 1907 Field Marshal Earl Roberts visits King Edward's School to inspect the newly established Cadet Corps. At this date Ronald may not have been one of the cadets, but almost certainly was one of those who packed the school hall almost to suffocation to hear an address from Earl Roberts after the inspection.

9 May 1907 Ronald notes the date in a copy of W. Salesbury's *Dictionary in Englysche and Welshe* (London, 1877) and that the book came to him from T. Shankland.

27 and 29 June 1907 Athletic Sports are held at the King Edward's School Grounds.

31 July 1907 Speech Day and prize-giving at King Edward's School. Now at the end of the summer term, Ronald is placed fourth out of twenty in his class.

Summer 1907 Father Francis again takes Ronald and Hilary to Lyme Regis. He learns from them that they are not happy living with their Aunt Beatrice.

Autumn term 1907 Ronald enters the First or Senior Class, under Robert Cary Gilson and A.E. Measures. There are twenty-two boys in the class, listed by seniority rather than by term work or examination results; among these is *Wilfrid Hugh Payton, who will be one of the members of the *T.C.B.S. during Ronald's last term at school. Gilson is an inspiring teacher who tries to interest his pupils in classical linguistics and philology, but also encourages them to branch out in their studies. Ronald will later recall that on many occasions the Chief Master imposed on him the writing of lines, such as 'punctuality is the soul of business' and 'brevity is the soul of wit'. – Outside his official studies Ronald is already pursuing interests in Old English (Anglo-Saxon) and Middle English. He feels a special sympathy and even a sense of recognition for Middle English works such as *Sir Gawain and the Green Knight and *Pearl, written in the West Midlands dialect which he thinks was spoken by his mother's West Midlands ancestors. He even begins to learn Old Norse in order to read the story of Sigurd in the original. He also reads books on philology and the history of language, and begins to buy books secondhand. He is learning a lot, developing an interest in philology and a deep appreciation of the look and sound of words. He also discovers Esperanto and learns enough of its grammar and structure to be able to read works written in it. Probably at about this time he begins to create for himself a language to suit his own aesthetic tastes: Naffarin, influenced by Latin and Spanish. – He is not alone at King Edward's School in his unusual interests: Christopher Wiseman is studying Egyptian and its hieroglyphics, while *Geoffrey Bache Smith, who will later become a close friend, is interested in Welsh.

1908

Beginning of 1908 Ronald and Hilary move to 37 Duchess Road, Edgbaston, the home of Louis Faulkner, a wine merchant; his wife, Mrs Faulkner, holds musical evenings which some of the Fathers from the nearby Oratory attend. The boys' room is on the second floor; in the room beneath them is another lodger, Edith Bratt. The three young people become friends, and deeper feelings develop between Ronald and Edith. She conspires with the Faulkners' maid, *Annie Gollins, to smuggle extra food from the kitchen to the hungry boys upstairs, by means of a basket lowered from their window.

25 and 27 June 1908 Athletic Sports are held at the King Edward's School Grounds.

30 July 1908 Speech Day and prize-giving at King Edward's School. Ronald is awarded a prize for achievement in English.

Autumn term 1908 Christopher Wiseman has now joined Ronald and seventeen others in the First Class at King Edward's School. Rob Gilson and Vincent Trought are in the Second Class. – During the 1908–9 school year Ronald will present to the School library two books by *G.K. Chesterton, *Orthodoxy* (1908) and *Heretics* (1905).

1908 or 1909 One of Ronald's school-friends buys *A Primer of the Gothic Language* by *Joseph Wright at a missionary sale, thinking it a Bible Society product. When he realizes his error he sells the book to Ronald, who upon opening it is 'at least as full of delight as first looking into Chapman's Homer' (quoted in *Biography*, p. 37). The surviving fragments of Gothic (*Languages) give him aesthetic pleasure. He is fascinated by Gothic in itself, 'a beautiful language', and learns from the primer how to convert words of other Germanic languages into Gothic script. 'I often put "Gothic" inscriptions in books, sometimes Gothicizing my Norse name and German surname as Ruginwaldus Dwalakōnis' (letter to Zillah Sherring, 20 July 1965, *Letters*, p. 357). He inscribes 'Ermanaþiudiska Razda eþþau Gautiska tungō' ('Language of the Great People, or Gautish [Gothic] tongue') inside a notebook to be used for work dealing with Gothic, but only uses a few pages (the notebook will be used later for a Quenya phonology and lexicon). – He now abandons the Latin- and Spanish-influenced Naffarin and begins to develop an imaginary 'lost' Germanic language, trying to fit it into the historical development of the Germanic tongues.

1909

1909 Edwin Neave dies. – During 1909, Ronald is supposed to be working hard, as he is to sit for an *Oxford Scholarship at year's end, but he is distracted by linguistic interests and he begins to take an active part in school activities. One of these is rugby football, in which Ronald's slight form is a handicap. One day, however, 'I decided to make up for weight by (legitimate) ferocity, and I ended up a house-captain at end of that season, & got my colours the next' (letter to Michael Tolkien, 3 October 1937, *Letters*, p. 22). He will be described in the *King Edward's School Chronicle* as 'a light but hard-working forward who makes up for his lightness by his determined dash. Tackles well but his kicking is weak' ('Football Characters', n.s. 25, no. 180 (April 1910), p. 35). During one game his tongue will be badly damaged, an accident he will sometimes blame when people complain that they find his speech difficult to understand. On another occasion he will damage his nose. – His relationship with Edith now becomes more serious. They begin to meet in Birmingham tea-shops; they go on cycle-rides together; they have a private whistle-call by which one can summon the other to the window at Duchess Road. Ronald will later recall to Edith their first kisses and 'absurd long window talks' (quoted in *Biography*, p. 40). By summer 1909 they will decide that they are in love.

26 March 1909 Ronald takes part in one of the traditional Latin debates at King Edward's School, in the role of 'Spurius Vectigalius Acer, Haruspex'. (*Haruspex* = 'soothsayer, prophet'. The names of Tolkien's Latin debate personae always contain plays on his surname, here *vectigal* 'toll' and *acer* 'keen'.)

Summer term 1909 The King Edward's School Officers Training Corps (formerly the Cadet Corps) participates in field exercises, including one in the Clent Hills near Birmingham. As reported in the *King Edward's School Chronicle*, 'the corps went out five times with the 5th Battalion of the Royal Warwickshire Regiment, and took part in the training of a Battalion under the instruction of Lieut.-Col. [John] Barnsley' ('Officers' Training Corps', n.s. 24, no. 177 (November 1909), p. 80). Tolkien is almost certainly now a member of the Corps (see entry for 27 July–4 August 1909).

10 June 1909 Ronald writes this day's date (Corpus Christi 1909) on the title-page of a small notebook he calls *The Book of Foxrook* (*Writing systems). This

> contains the key to a secret code consisting of a rune-like phonetic alphabet and a sizable number of ideographic symbols called 'monographs' . . . each monograph representing an entire word. . . . The code in Foxrook is not only the earliest known example of an invented alphabet devised by Tolkien, it is also the only one of his writing systems that is primarily ideographic. The majority of Foxrook is in English, including most of the messages written in code and the glosses of the monographs, but one page is almost entirely in Esperanto. [Arden R. Smith and Patrick Wynne, 'Tolkien and Esperanto', *Seven* 17 (2000), pp. 29–30]

1 and 3 July 1909 Athletic Sports are held at the King Edward's School Grounds.

7 July 1909 King Edward VII and Queen Alexandra visit Birmingham. After a reception and luncheon at the Council House they drive to Edgbaston to open the New Buildings of the University of Birmingham. The cadets of the King Edward's School Officers Training Corps parade in the playground behind the School and then, preceded by a fife and drum band, march some distance by way of Bristol Road to the University to contribute to a Guard of Honour for the royal visitors.

26 July 1909 Speech Day and prize-giving at King Edward's School. Ronald is runner-up for the German prize.

27 July–4 August 1909 Ronald participates with seventy-one other cadets in the King Edward's School Officers Training Corps at the Public Schools' Camp, *Tidworth Pennings on Salisbury Plain. They travel there by special train on 27 July. Although it rains that day, the remaining days at camp have fine weather. The King Edward's School contingent are in one of four battalions given thorough training, culminating in 'a grand field day, known officially as the Battle of Silk Hill, wherein nearly 20,000 troops of all arms, Regulars and Territorials, took part' ('Officers' Training Corps', *King Edward's School Chronicle* n.s. 24, no. 177 (November 1909), p. 81). One of Ronald's contemporaries at King Edward's School will later recall that 'he and I and six others occupied one bell tent. One evening Tolkien came charging in, leapt up and clasped the central pole high up and slid down it to the ground, not having noticed that someone had fixed a candle to the pole with his clasp knife. Tolkien must still carry the scar of the very nasty cut that resulted' (William H. Tait, letter to the editor, *Old Edwardians Gazette*, June 1972, p. 17).

Summer 1909 Ronald spends part of the summer holidays at Rednal working for an Oxford scholarship.

Autumn term 1909 Ronald's friends Robert Gilson, *Ralph Stuart Payton ('the Baby'), and Vincent Trought have joined him, together with Christopher Wiseman, in the First Class at King Edward's School. There are now only fifteen pupils in the class.

8 October 1909 Now a member of the King Edward's School Debating Society, Ronald makes his maiden speech on the motion: 'That this house expresses its sympathy with the objects and its admiration of the tactics of the Militant Suffragette.' The *King Edward's School Chronicle* will report that he 'spoke of the Suffragette from a Zoological point of view and gave an interesting display of his paronomasiac powers [ability to play on words]. A good humourous speech' ('Debating Society', n.s. 24, no. 177 (November 1909), p. 84). The motion fails, 12 votes to 20.

26 October 1909 Ronald plays in the King Edward's School Rugby 1st XV for the first time, in a home match against Jesus College, Oxford. King Edward's School loses, 9 to 19. According to the *King Edward's School Chronicle*, the home team 'continued to keep their opponents well in hand, and were at length rewarded by a try by Tolkien, who had shown himself throughout the afternoon a keen forward, and fully deserved this success. The kick did not succeed. . . . At the close of the game J.R.R. Tolkien and H.N. Thompson received their 2nd Team Colours' ('Football', n.s. 24, no. 177 (November 1909), p. 88). (A photograph of the 1909–10 1st XV appears in *Biography*, pl. 5a, and in *The Tolkien Family Album*, p. 26.)

30 October 1909 Ronald plays in a 1st XV home match against the 2nd XV of Old Edwardians II. King Edward's School loses, 8 to 10.

6 November 1909 Ronald plays in a 1st XV away match at Oakham, Leicestershire, against Oakham School. King Edward's School loses, 13 to 14.

9 November 1909 Ronald plays in a 1st XV away match at The Reddings, Moseley, against Moseley II. King Edward's School loses, 0 to 17.

13 November 1909 Ronald plays in a 1st XV away match at Lifford, against Kings Norton. King Edward's School loses, 0 to 30.

19 November 1909 The King Edward's School Debating Society addresses the motion: 'That this house deplores the disappearance of the stocks as a form of punishment.' According to the *King Edward's School Chronicle*, 'J.R.R. Tolkien in a distinctly humorous speech, though somewhat marred by a faulty delivery, advocated the revival of the stocks as an admirable method for the training of the marksmen of this country. It would also benefit the grocers' trade' ('Debating Society', n.s. 24, no. 178 (December 1909), p. 96). The motion carries, 13 to 12.

26 November 1909 At a meeting of the Literary Society of King Edward's School the Reverend E.W. Badger, one of the Masters, reads a paper entitled *William Morris, Artist, Craftsman and Poet.*

Near the end of autumn term 1909 Ronald and Edith ride their bicycles to the Lickey Hills on an afternoon excursion. They leave and return separately so that no one will know they are seeing each other. At the end of the afternoon they have tea at the house in Rednal where Ronald had stayed in the summer, but the woman who provides the tea mentions Ronald's visit to the caretaker at the Oratory retreat, who mentions it to the cook at the Oratory, and so the news reaches Father Francis Morgan. Father Francis is worried that Ronald is not giving his full attention to work towards a university scholarship, and is shaken when further enquiries reveal more about Ronald and Edith's clandestine meetings. He demands that their relationship cease.

December 1909 Very soon after this turmoil Ronald goes to Oxford to sit the University scholarship examination, staying in Corpus Christi College. He fails to obtain an award but is young enough to be able to try again next year. He must win an award if he wants to attend the University of Oxford, since his small inheritance from his father's estate is not enough to pay the fees, nor can Father Francis afford to pay them.

1910

1 January 1910 Ronald writes in his earliest surviving diary: 'Depressed and as much in dark as ever. God help me. Feel weak and weary' (quoted in *Biography*, p. 42). His depression is due not only to his disappointment at Oxford, but also to the difficulty of his relationship with Edith. He is torn between his feelings for her and his duty to the guardian to whom he owes so much. Although Father Francis has not specifically ordered Ronald not to see Edith again, his wishes are clear. – During this month he finds new lodgings for Ronald and Hilary with a Mrs MacSherry at 4 Highfield Road, Edgbaston. Ronald will live at this address until going up to *Oxford in autumn 1911.

Spring term 1910 At King Edward's School Ronald gives a lecture to the First Class entitled *The Modern Languages of Europe: Derivations and Capabilities*. After he takes up three one-hour sessions and is still not finished, the master calls a halt.

20 January 1910 Ronald feels that he and Edith must discuss what they are to do. They meet without asking Father Francis for permission. They spend part of the day in the countryside discussing plans, but also visit E.H. Lawley & Sons, jewellers, at 24 New Street, Birmingham. Edith buys Ronald a pen for ten shillings and sixpence as a belated birthday present; he spends the same on a wrist watch as a twenty-first birthday present for Edith.

21 January 1910 Ronald and Edith celebrate her twenty-first birthday by having tea together. But their meeting is seen and reported to Father Francis: he now forbids Ronald to meet or even write to Edith. By now, in fact, she has decided to move to *Cheltenham to live with two elderly family friends, Mr and Mrs C.H. Jessop. Ronald may see her to say goodbye on the day she leaves Birmingham, and then there is to be no contact until he comes of age three years later.

23 January 1910 At King Edward's School Ronald takes part in a debate on the motion: 'That the vulgar are the really happy.' He argues that there is no reason why this should be true of the vulgar as a class, and the fact that vulgarity and happiness sometimes accompany one another is no proof.

12 February 1910 Ronald plays in a 1st XV home match against Kings Norton. King Edward's School wins, 11 to 8.

15 February 1910 Ronald plays in a 1st XV home match against Birkenhead School, Oxton, Cheshire. King Edward's School wins, 20 to 0.

16 February 1910 Ronald writes in his diary that he had prayed that he would see Edith by accident, and his prayer had been answered. 'Saw her at 12.55 at Prince of Wales. Told her I could not write and arranged to see her off on Thursday fortnight. Happier but so much long to see her just once to cheer her up. Cannot think of anything else' (quoted in *Biography*, p. 43).

19 February 1910 Ronald plays in 1st XV home match against the University of Birmingham. King Edward's School loses, 5 to 6.

21 February 1910 Ronald writes in his diary: 'I saw a dejected little figure sloshing along in a mac and tweed hat and could not resist crossing and saying a word of love and cheerfulness. This cheered me up a little for a while. Prayed and thought hard' (quoted in *Biography*, p. 43).

23 February 1910 Ronald and Edith meet again accidentally.

26 February 1910 Ronald plays in a 1st XV away match at Elmdon Road, against Bromsgrove School. King Edward's School loses, 8 to 21. – At least one of Ronald's unplanned meetings with Edith has been reported to Father Francis. Ronald writes in his diary that he has 'had a dreadful letter' from his guardian 'saying I had been seen with a girl again, calling it evil and foolish. Threatening to cut short my University career if I did not stop. Means I cannot see E[dith]. Nor write at all. God help me. Saw E. at midday but would not be with her. I owe all to Fr. F[rancis] and so must obey' (quoted in *Biography*, p. 43).

2 March 1910 Edith leaves Birmingham for Cheltenham, Ronald has a last glimpse of her as she rides her bicycle to the station. Although Edith will miss Ronald, she will now live in greater comfort, and she will be able to play the piano as much as she likes, a pleasure forbidden her by Mrs Faulkner.

4 March 1910 Ronald's friend W.H. Payton reads a paper on *The Ingoldsby Legends* at a meeting of the King Edward's School Literary Society.

11 March 1910 In another Latin debate at King Edward's School Ronald plays the part of a Greek ambassador, 'Eisphorides Acribus Polyglotteus', and speaks entirely in Greek. On another such occasion, according to Humphrey Carpenter, Ronald 'astonished his schoolfellows when, in the character of a barbarian envoy, he broke into fluent Gothic; and on a third occasion he spoke in Anglo-Saxon. These activities occupied many hours . . .' (*Biography*, p. 48).

12 March 1910 Ronald plays in a 1st XV away match at Elmdon Road, against the Old Edwardians II. King Edward's School wins, 30 to 6.

26 March 1910 (Easter Saturday) With the permission of Father Francis, Ronald writes a long letter to Edith. This ends with a poem, probably *Morning*, which he will later date to March 1910 – his earliest dated surviving verse. He encloses two devotional pamphlets, *The Stations of the Cross* and *The Seven Words of the Cross*. – At about this time Ronald begins to write original poems in English, in addition to translating poems into Latin as part of the classical curriculum at school. Much of his early poetry celebrates his appreciation of nature and landscape.

April 1910 Ronald sees a performance of J.M. Barrie's *Peter Pan* (first performed at Christmas 1904) in Birmingham. He writes in his diary: 'Indescribable but I shall never forget it as long as I live. Wish E[dith] had been with me' (quoted in *Biography*, pp. 47–8).

5 April 1910 Ronald plays in a 1st XV home match against the King's Shropshire Light Infantry. King Edward's School wins, 19 to 0.

6 April 1910 The King Edward's School Musical and Dramatic Society presents the Annual Open Concert at 7.30 p.m. in the Governors' Board Room. During the programme Ronald's friend Rob Gilson recites John of Gaunt's dying speech from Shakespeare's *Richard II*.

May 1910 Ronald writes a poem, *The Dale Lands*.

6 May 1910 King Edward VII dies. George V succeeds to the throne.

June 1910 Ronald writes a poem, *Evening*.

12 June 1910 Ronald inscribes his Greek edition of *The Fifth Book of Thucydides* with his name and a Gothic text which he later translated as: 'I read the words of these books of Greek history in the sixth month of this year; thousand, nine hundreds, ten, of Our Lord: in order to gain the prize given every year to the boy knowing most about Thucydides, and this I inscribed in my books on the twelfth of the sixth (month) after I had already first read through all the words carefully' (letter to Zillah Sherring, 20 July 1965, *Letters*, p. 357).

30 June and 2 July 1910 Ronald attends the King Edward's School Athletic Sports at the School Grounds. He comes third in the One Mile Flat Race, Open.

July 1910 Ronald takes the examinations for the Oxford and Cambridge Higher Certificate, passing in five subjects: Latin, Greek, Elementary Mathematics, Scripture Knowledge (Greek Text), and History, and also satisfies the examiners in English Essay. – He writes a poem, *Wood-sunshine*, noteworthy among his earliest verse for its references to 'fairy things tripping so gay' and 'sprites of the wood', a foreshadowing of later writings (*Biography*, p. 47). He will later date another poem, *The Sirens*, also to this month.

27 July 1910 Speech Day and Prize-giving at King Edward's School, followed by various performances. Ronald is awarded the prize for German, and plays the part of the Inspector in a performance in Greek of *The Birds* by Aristophanes, for which the *King Edward's School Chronicle* will single him out for special praise. His friends Rob Gilson and Christopher Wiseman appear in scenes from Shakespeare's *Henry V*. – Hilary Tolkien attends his final day at King Edward's School. He will be given a post in Walter Incledon's family business, but will soon decide that he would rather work on the land.

28 July–6 August 1910 Ronald attends camp with the King Edward's School Officers Training Corps. Sixty-four cadets parade at the School on the morning of 28 July under the command of Captain R.H. Hume before travelling by special train from Snow Hill Station, Birmingham, to *Aldershot in Hampshire. They and cadets from other schools pitch camp on Farnborough

Common and spend two days drilling in preparation for an inspection by the Duke of Connaught on the Saturday afternoon. During their field training the cadets are taken in groups to visit the depot of military airplanes and airships in the neighbouring Farnborough. A battery of field artillery is demonstrated to them. During the second week, the cadets are inspected by Field Marshals Lord Roberts and Lord Kitchener. 'The weather was on the whole good, but on two evenings the rain fell in torrents and nearly washed out the Camp' (R.H. Hume, 'O.T.C. Annual Camp, Aldershot, 1910', *King Edward's School Chronicle* n.s. 26, no. 183 (November 1910), p. 74).

Summer 1910 Ronald takes a holiday in *Whitby on the northeast coast of England. He makes at least seven drawings of the busy fishing port and the ruined abbey on the cliff above the town. – Either this summer or in 1911 he also visits St Andrews, Scotland and draws a view, *St Andrews from Kinkell Brae*. Evidence suggests that his Aunt Jane Neave is now warden of a women's college in St Andrews, or otherwise employed in that city. *See note for August– early September 1911.*

Autumn term 1910 At King Edward's School Ronald is now a Prefect, Secretary of the Debating Society, Football Secretary, House Football Captain, and a corporal in the Officers Training Corps, each of which posts has various duties. He is also, together with Christopher Wiseman and Rob Gilson, a Sub-Librarian. *See note.* Another future member of the T.C.B.S., *Sidney Barrowclough, is now among the twenty boys in the First Class. Despite these distractions, Ronald is (or is supposed to be) working hard for his second attempt to gain an Oxford scholarship. – During his last year at school Ronald will discover the Finnish *Kalevala* in the English translation by W.F. Kirby. Also during this year he will present two books to the School library: *The Lost Explorers: A Tale of the Trackless Desert* by Alexander Macdonald (1906, a novel about the Australian Outback), and *Scouting for Buller* by Herbert Hayens (1902, a novel about the Boer War).

7 October 1910 Ronald makes the opening speech at a meeting of the King Edward's School Debating Society, in favour of the motion: 'That this House considers that the Debating Society does more harm than good.' He accuses the Society of encouraging the growth of punning and draws 'a harrowing picture of the devastation wrought through this malpractice by members of the Society in Camp at Aldershot' ('Debating Society', *King Edward's School Chronicle* n.s. 26, no. 183 (November 1910), p. 69). The motion fails, 5 to 15.

14 October 1910 Rob Gilson reads a paper on John Ruskin at a meeting of the King Edward's School Literary Society.

15 October 1910 Ronald plays in a 1st XV home match against the Old Edwardians II. King Edward's School loses, 6 to 10. (A photograph of the 1st XV for the 1910–11 season is reproduced in Anthony Trott, *No Place for Fop or Idler: The Story of King Edward's School, Birmingham* (1992), p. 89.)

21 October 1910 The King Edward's School Debating Society addresses the motion: 'This House advocates State Endowment of the Drama.' Although Ronald is not reported to have made any direct contribution to the debate,

C.H. Richards 'regretted bitterly the weak moment in which he had capitulated to the highwaymanism of the Secretary' (Ronald) in persuading him to lead the opposition to the motion ('Debating Society', *King Edward's School Chronicle* n.s. 26, no. 183 (November 1910), p. 70). The motion fails, 9 to 14.

22 October 1910 Ronald plays in a 1st XV away match at Denstone, Staffordshire, against Denstone College. King Edward's School wins, 17 to 13. The *King Edward's School Chronicle* will report that 'Tolkien played a characteristic dashing game' ('Football', n.s. 26, no. 183 (November 1910), p. 83).

25 October 1910 Ronald plays in a 1st XV home match against Jesus College, Oxford. King Edward's School loses, 5 to 6.

29 October 1910 Ronald plays in a 1st XV home match against Oakham School. King Edward's School wins, 9 to 8.

November 1910 As Debating Society Secretary, Ronald almost certainly writes the report of the meetings of the Society on 7 and 21 October published in the *King Edward's School Chronicle* for November 1910. As Football Secretary, he possibly also writes the report of matches published in the same number.

1 November 1910 Ronald plays in a 1st XV away match against The Leys School, Cambridge. King Edward's School loses, 0 to 6. After the match, Ronald, Christopher Wiseman, and another player receive their first team colours.

4 November 1910 Ronald attends a meeting of the King Edward's School Debating Society; the motion is: 'This House deplores the occurrence of the Norman Conquest.' It will be reported in the *King Edward's School Chronicle* that

in a speech attempting to return to something of Saxon purity of diction, ('right English goodliness of speechcraft'?) [Ronald] deplored before 'the worshipful fellows of the speechguild,' the influx of polysyllabic barbarities which ousted the more honest if humbler native words. He finally appealed to the House's sentiment, recalling the deaths of Harold and Hereward, but lapsed regrettably in his enthusiasm into such outlandish horrors as 'famous' and 'barbarous.' ['Debating Society', n.s. 26, no. 184 (December 1910), p. 95]

The motion fails, 8 to 12.

5 November 1910 Ronald plays in a 1st XV home match against the University of Birmingham. King Edward's School loses, 6 to 20. It may be during this match that Ronald suffers injury to his tongue or nose, as he does not play for the rest of the term. (In playing rugby 'I got rather damaged – among things having my tongue nearly cut out': letter to Michael Tolkien, 3 October 1937, *Letters*, p. 22.) The *King Edward's School Chronicle* will note that several members on the 1st XV are now on the injured list.

11 November 1910 Ronald's friend Vincent Trought reads a paper, 'Romanticism', at a meeting of the King Edward's School Literary Society.

18 November 1910 At a meeting of the King Edward's School Debating Society Ronald speaks against the motion: 'A System of Arbitration would be in every way preferable to War.' The motion fails, 5 to 12.

December 1910 As Debating Society Secretary, Ronald almost certainly writes the report of the meeting of the Society on 4 November published in the *King Edward's School Chronicle* for December 1910. As Football Secretary, he possibly also writes the report of matches published in the same number. – The King Edward's School Musical and Dramatic Society presents the Annual Open Concert. During the evening Rob Gilson recites the abdication speech from Shakespeare's *Richard II*, and two scenes from Sheridan's *The Rivals* are performed.

2 December 1910 At a meeting of the King Edward's School Debating Society Ronald proposes the motion: 'We are Degenerating.' According to a report (presumably by Ronald himself) in the *King Edward's School Chronicle*, he 'based all his argument upon intellectual degradation, and inveighed against the artificiality and unwholesomeness of Our outlook. After appearing to proclaim himself a hedonist, he produced what proved to be the most unfortunately conspicuous part of the debate. This was his "Theory of Bumps." Men progressed in bumps, bumping low, but never bumping as low as they had bumped before' ('Debating Society', n.s. 26, no. 185 (February 1911), p. 5). This theory is taken up by succeeding speakers, and at the end of the debate 'the Hon. Opener thereupon adjusted his theory of bumps to one of contusions. He remained defiant in a lost cause. He knew the House had a delightful custom of invariably voting Negative. It did.' The motion fails, 10 to 16.

Mid-December 1910 Ronald goes to Oxford on his second attempt to win a scholarship.

16 December 1910 At a sparsely attended meeting of the King Edward's School Debating Society the Old Boys discuss the question of whether 'the evils of the Press have up to now exceeded its Benefits.' The motion fails, 3 to 16.

17 December 1910 Ronald learns that he has been awarded an Open Classical Exhibition at Exeter College, worth £60 a year. He immediately informs Edith, who telegraphs her congratulations on the same day. He ought to have won a more valuable scholarship, but as he later wrote: 'I was clever, but not industrious or single-minded; a large part of my failure was due simply to not working (at least not at classics) not because I was in love, but because I was studying something else: Gothic and what not' (letter to Michael Tolkien, 6–8 March 1941, *Letters*, p. 52). But this exhibition, together with a bursary from King Edward's School and some extra finance from Father Francis, makes it possible for him to attend Oxford. He can now enjoy his last two terms at King Edward's School with pressure removed and his future secure.

Christmas 1910 Ronald receives an unsigned Christmas card from Edith.

1911

20 January 1911 At a meeting of the King Edward's School Literary Society the Chief Master, Robert Cary Gilson, speaks about 'out of doors literature': mountaineering, *al fresco* in poetry, walking tours, and so forth.

27 January 1911 The King Edward's School Debating Society addresses the motion: 'This House considers that Holidays are in no way Beneficial, and demands their Abolition.' One speaker likens the desire to work our brains without rest to attempting to set the Koh-i-Noor diamond in a jelly. In the February 1911 *King Edward's School Chronicle* Ronald will report himself as taking this remark as a personal insult, since he was in the habit of wearing a yellow pencil in his mouth (i.e. a pencil with a yellow barrel, a feature of the Koh-i-Noor brand). The motion fails, 6 to 13.

February 1911 As Debating Society Secretary, Ronald almost certainly writes the report of the meetings of the Society on 18 November, 2 and 16 December, and 27 January published in the *King Edward's School Chronicle* for February 1911. As Football Secretary, he possibly also writes the report of matches published in the same number.

4 February 1911 Ronald plays in a 1st XV away match against the University of Birmingham, at the University Ground. King Edward's School loses, 0 to 14.

10 February 1911 The King Edward's School Debating Society addresses the motion: 'That Slavery is a desirable social condition and that this House deplores its disappearance.' (No reports of this or subsequent Debating Society meetings in February–March 1911 appear in the *King Edward's School Chronicle*.)

14 February 1911 Ronald plays in a 1st XV away match against Birkenhead School. King Edward's School loses, 6 to 14.

17 February 1911 At a meeting of the King Edward's School Literary Society Ronald reads a paper on the Norse sagas. According to the *King Edward's School Chronicle*, he considers the *Völsunga Saga* one of the best of the sagas, and though it is inferior to Homer in most respects, in some it excels: 'There is no scene in Homer like the final tragedy of Sigurd and Brynhild' ('Literary Society', n.s. 26, no. 186 (March 1911), p. 19). The paper concludes with a sketch of the Norse religion and quotations from various sagas.

24 February 1911 The King Edward's School Debating Society addresses the motion: 'This House would welcome the establishment of a Central Imperial Parliament.'

March 1911 Ronald writes a poem, **The Battle of the Eastern Field*, a humorous account of a football match. It will be published in the *King Edward's School Chronicle* for this month. As Football Secretary, he possibly also writes the report of matches published in the same number of the *Chronicle*.

3 March 1911 Ronald's friend W.H. Payton reads a paper on Richard Jefferies at a meeting of the King Edward's School Literary Society.

10 March 1911 Ronald takes part in a Latin debate, in the role of 'T. Porto-rius Acer Germanicus'. He will write a report in Latin entitled *Acta Senatus*, to be published in the *King Edward's School Chronicle* for March 1911. The edit-orial for this number will note that pupils 'are reminded by the ever active Secretary of the Debating Society', i.e. Ronald Tolkien, about the forthcoming Open Debate (p. 17).

15 March 1911 The King Edward's School Officers Training Corps partici-pates in a field exercise with cadets from other neighbouring schools and the University of Birmingham. The King Edward's School cadets go to Ley Hill and take part in an attack on another group's position on Griffin Hill. The weather is bitterly cold, indeed the exercise is halted for half an hour by a storm of sleet. Later the cadets have tea at the University refectory; the King Edward's School contingent is so cheered and warmed that it insists on marching back to the School instead of taking the train.

18 March 1911 Ronald takes part in a 1st XV away match at Bromsgrove, against Bromsgrove School. King Edward's School loses, 3 to 8. This is Ronald's last game for the school. In the *King Edward's School Chronicle* a report will sum up his contribution to the team during 1910–11: 'A light forward, who pos-sesses pace and dash, and is a good dribble. He has done much good individual work, especially in breaking away from the scrum to assist the three-quarters. His tackling is always reliable, and he follows up hard. Has been a most capa-ble and energetic Secretary. Captain of Measures" (n.s. 26, no. 187 (June 1911), p. 49). In addition to the games played against teams from other schools or colleges Ronald has also played in inter-house football matches: these are not reported in the *Chronicle* but in 1910–11 Measures' House played six games as well as a play-off when it tied with another house.

24 March 1911 The King Edward's School Debating Society holds an impromptu debate.

4 April 1911 Ronald takes part in the Annual Open Debate, the motion being: 'That the works attributed to William Shakespeare were written by Francis Bacon.' He speaks in favour, pouring

> a sudden flood of unqualified abuse upon Shakespeare, upon his filthy birthplace, his squalid surroundings and his sordid character. He declared that to believe that so great a genius arose in such circumstances commits us to the belief that a fair-haired European infant could have a woolly-haired prognathous Papuan parent. After adducing a mass of further detail in support of the Hon. Opener, he gave a sketch of Bacon's life and the manner in which it fitted into the production of the plays, and concluded with another string of epithets. ['Debating Society', *King Edward's School Chronicle* n.s. 26, no. 187 (June 1911), p. 43]

The motion fails, 37 to 52. As Debating Society Secretary Ronald thanks Mr Reynolds, the Vice President, for all that he has done for the Society.

27 April 1911 Christopher Wiseman writes to Ronald (addressing him as 'Gabriel', one of his nicknames) after hearing that he has been appointed Librarian at King Edward's School. Wiseman will be a Sub-Librarian, and intends to ask their friend Vincent Trought to become one too.

Summer term 1911 Much of this term is taken up by examinations spread over six weeks. Between the exams the pupils have much spare time, even allowing for revision. Some of the senior boys – Sidney Barrowclough, Rob Gilson, Ralph Payton, W.H. Payton, Ronald Tolkien, Vincent Trought, and Christopher Wiseman – form an unofficial group called the Tea Club. They make tea for themselves in the King Edward's School library cubby-hole and (against the rules) bring in food. Later and especially during vacation they meet in the Tea Room at Barrow's Stores in Corporation Street, Birmingham; they have a favourite secluded table between two settles which they name the Railway Carriage, and now call themselves the Barrovian Society after 'Barrow's'. The most important members of the 'T.C.B.S.' (Tea Club, Barrovian Society), as the group becomes, will be Ronald, Rob Gilson, Christopher Wiseman, and eventually G.B. Smith, who will remain closely associated when other members drift away. – As a member of the Officers Training Corps Ronald takes part in drills and in the House competition for the Drill Cup.

June 1911 Ronald edits the June number of the *King Edward's School Chronicle* and writes the editorial. As Debating Society Secretary, he almost certainly writes the report of the meeting of the Society on 4 April that appears in the same number. In an account of the members of the Debating Society Ronald is described as 'an energetic Secretary who does not consider that his duties excuse him from speaking. Has displayed great zeal in arranging meetings throughout the session and considerable ingenuity in advertising them. He is an eccentric humorist who has made many excellent speeches, at times rather burdened with anacolutha. Made one valiant effort to revive Beowulfic oratory' ('Debating Society', n.s. 26, no. 187 (June 1911), p. 45).

June or July 1911 Ronald writes a poem about King Richard I and the Crusaders, *A Fragment of an Epic: Before Jerusalem Richard Makes an End of Speech. See note.*

15 June 1911 The annual inspection of the King Edward's School Officers Training Corps takes place. The cadets exhibit their drilling abilities to Major W.L. Loring. Measures' House, of which Ronald is a member, comes third out of four in the competition for the House Drill Shield.

21 June 1911 Ronald travels to London as one of eight cadets from the King Edward's School Officers Training Corps chosen to line the route for the coronation of George V. At about 11.00 a.m. they arrive at Lambeth Park, adjoining Lambeth Palace, where they join other cadets in a camp. The cadets are then free until the evening when all the assembled corps are drilled by Major Ingram. Ronald will later recall that the year 1911 was 'the *annus mirabilis* of sunshine in which there was virtually no rain between April and the end of October, except on the eve and morning of George V's coronation' (letter to Michael Tolkien, *c.* 25 August 1967, *Letters*, p. 391). *See note.*

22 June 1911 Reveille is sounded at 4.45 a.m. At about 6.00 a.m. the cadets march to their position on Constitution Hill adjoining Buckingham Palace. They arrive at about 7.00. The various processions do not leave the Palace until 9.30; in the interim the cadets are able to watch various troops moving into position and to see Lord Roberts and Lord Kitchener passing by. The King's procession sets out at 10.30, but the cadets catch only a glimpse as it travels down the Mall and does not pass in front of them. They then have another long wait until, soon after 2.00 p.m., the procession returns from Westminster Abbey along Constitution Hill immediately in front of the cadets and provides them with 'a spectacle never to be forgotten' ('The Coronation', *King Edward's School Chronicle* n.s. 26, no. 188 (July 1911), p. 60). They are too far away to witness the Royal Family's appearance on the balcony of Buckingham Palace, and are then marched back to camp.

23 June 1911 The cadets help line the streets for a Royal Progress and are in position near Buckingham Palace soon after 8.00 a.m. At 11.00 a.m. the Royal Family leave the Palace. According to the reporter for the *King Edward's School Chronicle* – possibly Ronald Tolkien himself – the procession 'was even more gorgeous than that of the previous day'. The cadets do not wait for the return of the procession but march back to camp for dinner and then return to Birmingham, arriving at about 10.30 p.m. 'with the feeling that we had had the experience of our lives' ('The Coronation', July 1911, p. 60).

29 June and 1 July 1911 Ronald attends the King Edward's School Athletic Sports at the School Grounds. He comes third in the One Mile Open race.

July 1911 Ronald edits the July number of the *King Edward's School Chronicle* and writes at least the editorial. – King Edward's School awards Ronald the Milward Exhibition, worth £50.

2 July 1911 Seventy-six cadets from King Edward's School travel by special train to Windsor Great Park to participate in a review of the Officers Training Corps by King George V.

3 July 1911 547 officers, 17,440 non-commissioned officers and men, 470 horses, and 14 guns take part in a display of 'manly patriotism' (*The Times*, 3 July 1911, p. 7). A longer report in the *Times* of 4 July waxes eloquent about the event 'among the ancient oak trees' of Windsor Great Park 'in glorious summer foliage'. The massed Corps 'practically represented the entire intellectual reinforcement that the Military Services controlling the Empire will receive five or six years hence. It was no mummer's rabble that defiled before the King, it was no semi-organized collection of train bands; it was a force of young soldiers, led by seasoned soldiers, trained by seasoned soldiers, quitting themselves like men, like citizens of a great Empire' (p. 9).

26 July 1911 Summer term and Ronald's time at King Edward's School end with Speech Day and prize-giving, followed by musical and dramatic performances. Ronald is one of six recipients in the Classical First Class of the Chief Master's Leaving Prizes. The final item on the programme is a performance in Greek of Aristophanes' play *The Peace* in which Ronald takes the part of Hermes. The evening closes with the national anthem sung in Greek. Ronald will later recall that 'the school-porter was sent by waiting relatives to find me. He reported that my appearance might be delayed. "Just now," he said, "he's the life and soul of the party." Tactful. In fact, having just taken part in a Greek play, I was clad in a himation and sandals, and was giving what I thought a fair imitation of a frenzied Bacchic dance' (quoted in *Biography*, p. 49).

August–early September 1911 Ronald joins a walking tour in the Swiss Alps organized by the *Brookes-Smith family, along with his Aunt Jane Neave and his brother Hilary. *See note*. Both he and Colin Brookes-Smith, at that time a young boy, will later recount parts of the holiday, from which the following seems a reasonable reconstruction of events. The party apparently numbers twelve at the start. The Brookes-Smiths and their guests travel from England to Innsbruck, Austria by train and boat, and from there make their way to *Switzerland. They proceed mainly on foot, by mountain paths avoiding roads, carrying heavy packs, sometimes sleeping rough in barns, sometimes staying in inns or small hotels, often cooking and eating in the open. Their route takes them from Interlaken to Lauterbrunnen, Mürren, and the Lauterbrunnental, over the two Scheidegge to Grindelwald past the Eiger and the Mönch, and on to Meiringen where they have a fine view of the Jungfrau. They then cross the Grimsel Pass to reach the Rhône and Brig. – From there (according to Tolkien, though he does not name the village) they make their way upwards again and stay at a châlet inn in Belalp at the foot of the Aletsch glacier. Ronald will later recall several incidents while in Belalp, including the fun he and others had by temporarily damming a rill that ran down the hillside towards the inn. The party venture onto the glacier a few days later, where some of the members, including Ronald, pose for a photograph (*The Tolkien Family Album*, p. 31) and Ronald comes 'near to perishing' in an avalanche: 'the member of the party just in front of me (an elderly schoolmistress) gave a sudden squeak and jumped forward as a large lump of rock shot between us. About a foot at most before my unmanly knees' (letter to Michael Tolkien, after 25 August 1967, *Letters*, p. 393; Colin Brookes-Smith, however, will recall that an avalanche occurred when the party was returning to Arolla – see below – from a day trip to a high-altitude hut). – From Brig (according to Colin Brookes-Smith) the party travels to Visp and Stalden, over a high pass from St-Niklaus to Gruben, over the Forcletta Pass to Grimentz, and on to Haudères, Arolla, and eventually Sion. Ronald will recall 'our arrival, bedraggled, one evening in Zermatt and the lorgnette stares of the French bourgeoises dames. We climbed with guides up to [a] high hut of the Alpine Club, roped (or I should have fallen into a snow-crevasse), and I remember the dazzling whiteness of the tumbled snow-desert between us and the black horn of the Matterhorn some miles away' (*Letters*, p. 393). – Probably during, or soon after, this holiday Ronald makes a drawing with the self-descriptive title *The Misty Mountains* (*Artist and Illustrator*, fig. 200) and inserts it in his first sketchbook. – For Ronald this holiday will be a seminal experience. In later years he will often remark (like Bilbo in *The Lord of the Rings*) that he would like to see mountains again, or say that some of his experiences on his trip to Switzerland were incorporated into his writings, for instance the 'thunder-battle' in *The Hobbit*, Chapter 4. He will also note that the Silverhorn in the Alps is 'the Silvertine (*Celebdil*) of my dreams' (*Letters*, p. 392). The scenery around the Lauterbrunnental and Mürren almost certainly will influence how he visualizes and draws Rivendell and Dunharrow in Middle-earth, while the Alps will appear as the Misty Mountains in pictures such as *Bilbo Woke up with the Early Sun in His Eyes* for *The Hobbit* (*Artist and Illustrator*, fig. 113).

17 August 1911 Christopher Wiseman writes to thank Ronald for postcards he sent from Switzerland.

September 1911 Ronald writes a poem, *The New Lemminkäinen*, a parody on Kirby's translation of the *Kalevala*.

4 October 1911 Rob Gilson writes to Ronald, pointing out that the latter has not returned two books, including the first volume of the *Kalevala*, to the King Edward's School library, nor has he handed over the keys to the tea closet or the fine box. He thinks it a pity that Ronald, who is to play Mrs Malaprop in a performance of *The Rivals* by Richard Brinsley Sheridan at King Edward's School in December will not return to Birmingham until 7 October, the day after their friend *Thomas Kenneth ('Tea-Cake') Barnsley (who is to play Bob Acres) leaves, so they will not be able to rehearse together. Gilson asks Ronald to read his part with him on the evening of 9 October.

End of the second week in October 1911 Ronald and L.K. Sands, another former pupil of King Edward's School, are driven by R.W. Reynolds to Oxford in a car, then a novelty. Ronald will later recall that the weather was still hot, and everyone seemed to be dressed in flannels and punting on the river. He takes up residence in Exeter College; his rooms (no. 9 on the no. 7 staircase, in a building known as Swiss Cottage) overlook the Turl. He settles in quickly and makes friends.

15 October 1911 Michaelmas Full Term begins at Oxford University.

17 October 1911 Tolkien matriculates at Oxford.

Michaelmas Term 1911 Tolkien begins to read *Literae Humaniores* or Classics, mainly Greek and Latin authors but also Philosophy and Classical History. During his first five terms at Oxford he will attend lectures and classes to prepare himself for his first examination, Honour Moderations (popularly 'Hon. Mods'), which he will take in February 1913. During this term he almost certainly attends lectures by *L.R. Farnell on *Agamemnon* by Aeschylus in translation, a set text, on Wednesdays and Fridays at 10.00 a.m. at Exeter College, beginning 18 October. For lectures on the other books set for Honour Moderations – Demosthenes, Homer, Plato, Sophocles, Euripides, Cicero, Tacitus, Virgil – he has a wide choice. Having chosen Comparative Philology as his Special Subject, he attends lectures by *Joseph Wright on Gothic Grammar with Translation of the Gospel of St Mark, at 12.15 p.m. on Tuesdays and Thursdays in the Taylor Institution, beginning 19 October. But he also takes advantage of other aspects of Oxford life: clubs and societies, and entertainments, sometimes to the detriment of his studies.

Second half of October 1911 Tolkien writes a poem, *From Iffley* (**From the Many-Willow'd Margin of the Immemorial Thames*), describing Oxford as seen from the river at a village south-east of the city.

31 October 1911 Tolkien attends the Annual Freshman's Wine at Exeter College. This begins at 8.45 p.m. with an entertainment, mainly of songs, and continues at 10.00 p.m. with a dance in the hall. Tolkien collects many signatures on his souvenir programme.

6 November 1911 Tolkien writes a poem, *Darkness on the Road*.

7 November 1911 Tolkien writes a poem, *Sunset in a Town*.

10 November 1911 Tolkien is granted a certificate by the University Registry, Oxford, exempting him from the preliminary examination (Responsions). He had already passed the relevant subjects in the Oxford and Cambridge Higher Certificate in July 1910. *See note.*

21 November 1911 Tolkien attends a Smoking Concert at Exeter College. The programme includes an orchestra playing selections by Sullivan, Tchaikovsky, Monckton, and Lehar, banjo solos, songs, and humorous recitations.

24 November 1911 Tolkien attends a Smoking Concert at Exeter College at 8.00 p.m. The programme includes the orchestra playing Sullivan, Offenbach, Bizet, Gounod, Suppé, and Herold, songs, and a piano solo.

25 November 1911 Tolkien first borrows *A Finnish Grammar* by C.N.E. Eliot (1890) from the Exeter College library. Having already read the *Kalevala* in translation, he wants to know something of the language in which it was written. He will later recall that

> it was like discovering a complete wine-cellar filled with bottles of an amazing wine of a kind and flavour never tasted before. It quite intoxicated me; and I gave up the attempt to invent an 'unrecorded' Germanic language, and my 'own language' [the 'Elvish' language Qenya, later *Quenya*, which he begins to devise, see *Languages, Invented] – or series of invented languages – became heavily Finnicized in phonetic pattern and structure. . . . I never learned Finnish well enough to do more than plod through a bit of the original. [letter to W.H. Auden, 7 June 1955, *Letters*, p. 214].

He also now has access to books which help him to study the Welsh language, which has fascinated him since childhood. These interests will take up much time which Tolkien should be devoting to his classical studies, and they will be at least partly responsible for his unsatisfactory performance when he takes Honour Moderations at Oxford in February 1913. In late 1914 or early 1915 he will write in a paper on the *Kalevala*: 'When [Honour Moderations] should have been occupying all my forces I once made a wild assault on the stronghold of the original language and was repulsed with heavy losses' (Tolkien Papers, Bodleian Library, Oxford).

28 November 1911 Tolkien joins the King Edward's Horse, a territorial cavalry regiment, similar to the Officers Training Corps (*Societies and clubs). Its membership limited to colonials, Tolkien qualifies because he was born in the Orange Free State. If he has not learned to ride before, he does so now.

December 1911 Tolkien continues to play rugby football. The *Stapeldon Magazine* of Exeter College for December 1911 will note (p. 110) that 'the Freshmen produced some very sound forward material. . . . Tolkien is a winger pure and simple and might have had some consideration had he been but one in eight.'

?Last part of Michaelmas Term 1911 Tolkien and other students, mainly freshmen, form a new society, the Apolausticks (*Societies and clubs). He is its first President. The eleven members draw up a programme of meetings for Hilary Term 1912: these will be mainly discussions of various literary figures. Later programmes will include elaborate dinners and debates.

9 December 1911 Michaelmas Full Term ends.

Early to mid-December 1911 Tolkien returns to Birmingham. Early in the vacation he spends much of his time rehearsing for the performance of Sheridan's *The Rivals* to be given on 21 December by members of the King Edward's School Musical and Dramatic Society, augmented by himself and T.K. Barnsley. Other T.C.B.S. members are also prominent in the cast and organization: Christopher Wiseman as Sir Anthony Absolute, Rob Gilson as Captain Absolute, and G.B. Smith as Faulkland. (By now, Smith has become an accepted member of the T.C.B.S.) After the dress rehearsal, the cast march in full costume up Corporation Street to have tea in Barrow's Stores.

14 December 1911 Tolkien attends the Oxford and Cambridge Old Edwardians Society Annual Dinner at the Midland Hotel, Birmingham, eight courses plus coffee.

15 December 1911 Tolkien takes part in the Old Boys' Debate at King Edward's School on the motion: 'That this house approves the principle of gratuitous public service.' Speaking in favour, he 'declared that he felt so deeply on the subject that he had written a brochure upon it. The House requested him to read it, but it had unfortunately been left at home. Of the few magnificent quotations which were given from memory, none have survived. The Hon. gentleman then attacked the practicability of the scheme for payment of members, and applied it by analogy to school officers. The result would be financial and moral ruin' ('Debating Society', *King Edward's School Chronicle* n.s. 27, no. 191 (March 1912), p. 14). The motion fails, 12 to 14.

21 December 1911 Sheridan's *The Rivals* is performed under the auspices of the King Edward's School Musical and Dramatic Society at 7.30 p.m. in Big School. According to the *King Edward's School Chronicle*,

> the performance was a thorough success both artistically and financially. . . . J.R.R. Tolkien's *Mrs Malaprop* was a real creation, excellent in every way and not least so in make-up. Rob Gilson as *Captain Absolute* made a most attractive hero, bearing the burden of what is a very heavy part with admirable spirit and skill; and as the choleric old *Sir Anthony*, C.L. Wiseman was extremely effective. Among the minor characters,

G.B. Smith's rendering of the difficult and thankless part of *Faulkland* was worthy of high praise. ['The Musical and Dramatic Society', n.s. 27, no. 191 (March 1912), p. 10]

Christmas 1911 Tolkien probably spends part of the vacation with his Incledon relatives at Barnt Green. They have the custom of performing theatrical entertainments during the holiday, including the farce *Cherry Farm*, probably written by Tolkien.

1911–1912 Drawings by Tolkien from this period reveal an interest in abstract ideas. *Silent, Enormous, and Immense* is dated December 1911. *Firelight Magic, Sleep*, and a 'male caricature' are dated to 1911–1912. *Thought* (*Artist and Illustrator*, fig. 33; and probably also *Convention* on its verso) and *A Wish* are dated to 1912. Other drawings which probably date from this time are *Before* (*Artist and Illustrator*, fig. 30), *Ark!!!*, and *Afterwards* (*Artist and Illustrator*, fig. 31).

1912

21 January 1912 Hilary Full Term begins at Oxford.

Hilary Term 1912 Tolkien again has a choice of lectures on the various Greek and Latin authors set for Honour Moderations, and will attend Joseph Wright's lectures on Comparative Greek Grammar on Tuesdays and Thursdays at 12.15 p.m. in the Taylor Institution, beginning 24 January. During his time as an undergraduate he will have tutorials which Wright gives in his house in the Banbury Road; he will later recall 'the vastness of Joe Wright's dining room table (when I sat alone at one end learning the elements of Greek philology from glinting glasses in the further gloom)' (*Valedictory Address to the University of Oxford*, in *The Monsters and the Critics and Other Essays*, p. 238). Tolkien will be invited on some Sunday afternoons to huge Yorkshire teas given by Wright and his wife Elizabeth. Wright is both a demanding and an inspiring teacher, and when he learns that Tolkien is interested in the Welsh language he encourages him to pursue it. – Christopher Wiseman informs Tolkien by letter that Vincent Trought died suddenly early on 20 January while convalescing in Cornwall. Although King Edward's School will probably send a wreath, Wiseman wants to send one from the T.C.B.S. and asks if Tolkien would like to subscribe.

22 January 1912 It seems likely that when Tolkien receives Wiseman's letter of 21 January he telegraphs in reply, asking for details of Trought's funeral as he wishes to attend, and saying that he wishes to subscribe to the wreath. Wiseman replies this day by letter (which does not leave until the 5.45 a.m. collection on 23 January) that the funeral is to be at Gorran, near Falmouth in Cornwall, on 23 January, but he does not know the time. Even if Wiseman had telegraphed, Tolkien would not have had time to get to Cornwall, a train journey of some eight hours from Oxford. – The Apolausticks meet at 4.30 p.m. in C.A.H. Fairbank's rooms.

25 January 1912 Wiseman writes to thank Tolkien for sending a postal order for Trought's wreath.

27 January 1912 The Apolausticks meet at 8.00 in M.W.M. Windle's rooms to discuss Lewis Carroll.

3 February 1912 The Apolausticks meet at 4.30 p.m. in R.H. Gordon's rooms.

10 February 1912 The Apolausticks meet at 8.00 p.m. in H.G.L. Trimingham's rooms to discuss the nineteenth-century poets C. Stuart Calverley and J.K. Stephen.

17 February 1912 The Apolausticks meet at 4.30 p.m. in *Colin Cullis's rooms.

20 February 1912 Tolkien attends the London Old Edwardians' Seventh Annual Dinner at the Holborn Restaurant, ten courses plus coffee. Tolkien is one of the two named to respond to the toast 'The Old Edwardian Association'. At this or an unrecorded meeting of the Old Edwardians in 1912 he meets some members who remembered his father.

24 February 1912 The Apolausticks meet at 8.00 p.m. in O.O. Staples' rooms to discuss G.K. Chesterton and George Bernard Shaw.

2 March 1912 The Apolausticks meet at 4.30 p.m. in W.W.T. Palmer's rooms.

4 March 1912 At a meeting of the Stapeldon Society (*Societies and clubs) Tolkien speaks in favour of the motion: 'This House deplores the signs of degeneracy in the present age.' The motion fails, 4 votes to 8. The Stapeldon Society is technically the Exeter College debating organization, but also deals with general interests of the students.

9 March 1912 The Apolausticks meet at 8.00 p.m. in Tolkien's rooms to discuss Maurice Maeterlinck.

16 March 1912 Hilary Full Term ends.

19 March 1912 Christopher Wiseman writes to Tolkien, agreeing to a T.C.B.S. meeting at Barrow's Stores. He suggests a date of 22 March, and that Tolkien might play for the Old Edwardians against King Edward's School on 23 March. (In the event, Tolkien does not play, but possibly attends the match.)

2 April 1912 Tolkien returns to King Edward's School to take part in the Annual Open Debate. He speaks against the motion: 'That it is better to be Eccentric than Orthodox.' According to the *King Edward's School Chronicle*, he 'began by denying the true opposition between the orthodox and the eccentric, and maintained the possibility of a man's being both at the same time. He made, however, a number of interesting points: in particular, the parallel to the rules which govern Society which he drew from a game of cricket, where eccentricity would be obviously intolerable' ('Debating Society', n.s. 27, no. 193 (June 1912), p. 38). The motion fails, 23 to 22.

28 April 1912 Trinity Full Term begins at Oxford.

Trinity Term 1912 Tolkien attends Joseph Wright's continuing lectures on Comparative Greek Grammar on Tuesdays and Thursdays at 12.15 p.m. in the Taylor Institution, beginning 2 May. He attends lectures on the authors set for Honour Moderations, probably including those given by L.R. Farnell at Exeter College: the Private Orations of Demosthenes, on Wednesdays and Fridays at 10.00 a.m., beginning 1 May; and Annals I and II of Tacitus (set texts), on Wednesdays and Fridays at 12.00 noon, beginning 1 May. He also attends classes and tutorials with the newly appointed Classics tutor at Exeter College, E.A. Barber. – Tolkien continues to devote much of his time to social occasions, and to his interest in Finnish, Welsh, and Germanic languages. College records show that he was considered lazy, and that during the summer term he was warned that he might lose his exhibition, a warning that led him to improve. At the same time, he becomes less regular in performing his religious duties.

30 April 1912 The Apolausticks meet at 8.00 p.m. in Colin Cullis's rooms. Cullis has succeeded Tolkien as President of the society for Trinity Term.

May 1912 Tolkien poses with other members of the Apolausticks for a group photograph (reproduced in *Biography*, pl. 6b).

11 May 1912 The Apolausticks meet at 8.00 p.m. in G.S. Field's rooms. Tolkien gives a paper (subject not recorded).

28 May 1912 Tolkien attends the Summer Concert of the Exeter College Music Society. The programme includes songs as well as *The Death of Minnehaha* by Samuel Coleridge Taylor, performed by the Choir and Orchestra and two guests, Frederick Ranalow and Bessie Tyas. Among the accompanists is Adrian Boult, President of the Oxford Musical Club, later a renowned conductor.

1 June 1912 The Apolausticks meet at 7.30 p.m. for an elaborate dinner at the Randolph Hotel in Oxford. Tolkien proposes the toast 'The Club'. He and nine other members sign his menu card.

15 June 1912 The Apolausticks meet in M.W.M. Windle's rooms. Tolkien proposes the motion: 'That a belief in ghosts is essential to the welfare of a people'. It is carried by one vote.

22 June 1912 Trinity Full Term ends.

27 July–?10 August 1912 Tolkien camps with the King Edward's Horse on Dibgate Plateau near *Folkestone. His regiment is inspected by Lieutenant General Sir James Grierson (in charge of the Eastern Command), Major-General Allenby (Inspector of Cavalry), and Brigadier-General Bingham. The historian Lieutenant-Colonel Lionel James will report that

it was an altogether boisterous fortnight. The south-westerly gales were so severe, and the camping area so exposed, that on two nights the tents and marquees were nearly all levelled. The work done, however, was of quite a high standard for an irregular unit. For one night the Regiment practised billetting during field operations. The outpost scheme that necessitated the billetting was a foretaste of the actual service conditions which were soon to become the daily life of so many who were training that summer. There was not an officer or man out that night who was not drenched to the skin. [*The History of King Edward's Horse* (1921), p. 52]

Summer vacation 1912 Tolkien goes walking in *Berkshire, sketching the villages and the scenery. He begins a new sketch book, perhaps buying it while on tour. He is near Lambourn on 21 and 23 August, in Eastbury 27–28 August, and once more in Lambourn 30–31 August. He paints three watercolours of the Lambourn countryside, makes three ink drawings at Eastbury, mainly of picturesque thatched cottages, and devotes two pages to ink drawings of details of the church at Lambourn (see *Artist and Illustrator*, figs. 11–13). – Tolkien will visit St Andrews again in 1912, probably in the summer vacation but possibly at Easter. While there he writes a short poem, *The Grimness of the Sea*. He will later inscribe this manuscript 'Original nucleus of "The Sea-song of an Elder Day"' (*The Horns of Ylmir*).

13 October 1912 Michaelmas Full Term begins.

Michaelmas Term 1912 Tolkien probably attends Joseph Wright's lectures on Comparative Latin Grammar on Tuesdays and Thursdays at 12.15 p.m. in the Taylor Institution, beginning 17 October. He also probably attends lectures by L.R. Farnell on the *Odyssey* (Homer is a set author) on Mondays, Wednesdays, and Fridays at 12.00 noon at Exeter College, beginning 14 October. If he did not attend Farnell's lectures on *Agamemnon* by Aeschylus (in translation) in Michaelmas Term 1911, he probably does so this term, on Wednesdays and Fridays at 10.00 a.m. at Exeter College, beginning 16 October. He possibly attends Gilbert Murray's lectures on Aeschylus' *Agamemnon* and Euripides' *Electra* on Tuesdays and Thursdays at 12.00 noon in the Examinations School, beginning 15 October. – 'Oxoniensis', the writer of 'Oxford Letter' in the *King Edward's School Chronicle* for December 1912, remarks that 'Tolkien, if we are to be guided by the countless notices on his mantelpiece, has joined all the Exeter Societies which are in existence, and has also done well to get an occasional place in an exceptionally strong College "pack"' (n.s. 28, no. 196, p. 85).

18 October 1912 The Apolausticks meet at 8.00 p.m. in R.H. Gordon's rooms . Gordon is President of the society for this term.

25 October 1912 The Apolausticks meet at 8.00 p.m. in A. Barnett's rooms. The refreshments include Swedish punch.

30 October 1912 The Apolausticks meet at 4.30 p.m. in L.L.H. Thompson's rooms.

31 October 1912 Christopher Wiseman sends Tolkien news of himself and Rob Gilson, both of whom are now at Cambridge University.

3 November 1912 Tolkien is elected to the Exeter College Essay Club (*Societies and clubs).

6 November 1912 The Apolausticks meet at 8.00 p.m. in Tolkien's rooms for a debate, according to the date printed on the society's schedule for this term. It is possible, however, that the date or the time was changed, as in the evening of 6 November Tolkien certainly attends the Exeter College Freshman's Wine, which includes songs, a piano solo, and a humorous recitation. While there he collects signatures from the performers on his printed programme.

11 November 1912 At a meeting of the Stapeldon Society Tolkien tells a funny story about the Sub-Rector and a Mr Pickop.

13 November 1912 The Apolausticks meet at 4.30 p.m. in W.W.T. Massiah-Palmer's rooms.

18 November 1912 At a meeting of the Stapeldon Society Tolkien is elected to serve on a committee to investigate College charges.

19 November 1912 Tolkien attends the College Smoking Concert and collects signatures of friends on his printed programme. The first half of the concert consists of music by Suppé, Sullivan, *et al.* played by an orchestra and songs performed by some of the students. The second half consists of dance music.

20 November 1912 The Apolausticks meet at 4.30 p.m. in H.G.L. Trimingham's rooms.

25 November 1912 The Stapeldon Society meets.

27 November 1912 The Apolausticks meet at 8.00 p.m. in W.E. Hall's rooms.

2 December 1912 The Stapeldon Society meets.

4 December 1912 The Apolausticks meet at 8.00 p.m. in R.H. Gordon's rooms.

7 December 1912 Michaelmas Full Term ends.

December 1912 Tolkien makes the drawings *Other People* (with *Undertenishness* on the verso, *Artist and Illustrator*, fig. 34) and *Back of Beyond* (with *End of the World* on the verso, *Artist and Illustrator*, fig. 36). The drawing *Wickedness* probably also dates from around this time (*Artist and Illustrator*, fig. 32).

Christmas 1912 Tolkien spends at least part of his vacation with his Incledon relatives at Barnt Green. He has written a play for them, *The Bloodhound, the Chef, and the Suffragette*. In its performance he plays the leading part of 'Professor Joseph Quilter, M.A., B.A., A.B.C., alias world-wide detective Sexton Q. Blake-Holmes, the Bloodhound' (*Biography*, p. 59). The play concerns a lost heiress who has fallen in love with a penniless student living in the same lodging house, and whom she would be free to marry on her twenty-first birthday in two days' time if her father does not discover her first. The play is obviously much influenced by Tolkien's own circumstances with his twenty-first birthday approaching, when he will be free of his promise to Father Francis Morgan not to contact Edith Bratt.

1913

1913 Probably during this year, Tolkien makes the drawing *Xanadu* (*Artist and Illustrator*, fig. 37).

3 January 1913 At midnight, as Tolkien reaches the age of twenty-one, he begins a letter to Edith Bratt, telling her that his feelings for her have not changed and that he wants to marry her. A few days later he receives a reply from Edith that she is engaged to George Field, the brother of one of her school-friends, Molly Field; but the letter also makes it clear that she had done this because she had not expected that Ronald would still care for her, and George was kind and someone she felt she could accept as a husband. Tolkien writes again, and they arrange to meet.

8 January 1913 Tolkien goes to Cheltenham to see Edith. She meets him at the station. They walk into the country to be alone and undisturbed while discussing their situation; there they sit under a railway viaduct. Edith agrees to break her engagement to George and to marry Ronald, but they decide to keep their engagement secret for a while. The only exception is Father Francis, whom Tolkien feels it is his duty to inform.

First part of 1913 When Father Francis learns of Tolkien's engagement, he is not enthusiastic, but accepts the inevitable. Tolkien promises Edith that he will work hard to gain a good degree to ensure their future together. But if their marriage is to be blessed by the Catholic Church, Edith must convert to Roman Catholicism. Although she has become an active member of the Church of England while living in Cheltenham with her family friends the Jessops, she is willing to convert, but prefers to delay this step until closer to their marriage, or at least until they are officially engaged. Tolkien insists that she not delay, however, and as a consequence, as expected, the Jessops order her to leave their house. Edith manages to find lodgings in *Warwick, not far from Oxford, and moves there with her cousin Jennie Grove. She begins to take instruction from the Roman Catholic parish priest, Father Murphy.

January 1913 Tolkien begins to keep a diary in which, under the heading 'JRRT and EMB in account together, AMDG [ad maiorem Dei gloriam]', he notes the number of hours he works (quoted in *Life and Legend*, p. 27). He also records, in red ink, his now more assiduous performance of religious duties.

12 January 1913 Hilary Full Term begins.

Hilary Term 1913 Tolkien works hard, but he has to take Honour Moderations at the end of February, and now has only a few weeks to make up for the four terms in which he has not devoted enough time to his studies. From 14 January he will attend Joseph Wright's continuing lectures on Comparative Latin Grammar on Tuesdays and Thursdays at 12.15 p.m. in the Taylor Institution, and perhaps also E.A. Barber's lectures on Virgil (questions and translations) on Tuesdays, Thursdays, and Saturdays at 10.00 a.m. at Exeter College, or those by Gilbert Murray on Euripides' *Bacchae* (a set text) on Tuesdays and Thursdays at 10.00 a.m. in the Examination Schools. – Tolkien continues to play an active role in the Stapeldon Society; his participation in other societies or clubs during this term is not clear. Three meetings of the Exeter College Essay Club are held in Hilary Term, at which papers are presented on (at least) the poetry of Oscar Wilde, and Dante Gabriel Rossetti as a poet and artist. *See note.*

20 January 1913 At a meeting of the Stapeldon Society Tolkien is elected to the Kitchen Committee together with Mr Price. The minutes record that Mr Price said that he considered quantity of food more important than quality, but Mr Tolkien 'expressed his capacity for discrimination and guaranteed the suppression of Mr Price's tendencies' (Exeter College archives). During a debate at the same meeting Tolkien speaks against the motion: 'The Pipe is better than the Cigarette.' The motion fails, 5 to 8. In fact, Tolkien usually smokes a pipe, only occasionally cigarettes.

27 January 1913 At a meeting of the Stapeldon Society the College charges committee, of which Tolkien is a member, presents its report. This is amended and carried for first reading.

1 February 1913 Tolkien sends Edith a picture postcard of the dining hall at Exeter College, with an 'X' marking the place where he sits (reproduced in *The Tolkien Family Album*, p. 35). He tells her that he has been to Holy Communion that morning and will go again the next day (Sunday), and that he is about to go to a meeting of the Old Edwardians.

3 February 1913 The Stapeldon Society meets.

10 February 1913 The Stapeldon Society meets.

17 February 1913 The Stapeldon Society meets. The minutes record that 'Mr Gordon was censured for appearing on the towpath in a large overcoat and carrying a stick or cane borrowed from Hookham and tripping Mr Hoffman up and almost causing him to fall into The River. After the House had unanimously agreed in condemning Mr Gordon, Mr Tolkien rose and said it was he who tripped Mr Hoffman but even then the House remained adamant in its hostile attitude towards Mr Gordon' (Exeter College archives).

24 February 1913 The Stapeldon Society meets.

27 February 1913 The First Public Examination for the Honour School of Greek and Latin Literature (Honour Moderations) begins. Tolkien takes probably twelve written papers, each of three hours' duration, one in the morning and one in the afternoon over a period of several days. He is required to translate passages from Homer and Demosthenes, and from Virgil and Cicero (the *Orations*); and to translate, without preparation, passages from Greek authors other than Homer and Demosthenes, and from Latin authors other than Virgil and Cicero. He is also examined on four Greek plays, *Œdipus Tyrannus* and *Elektra* by Sophocles, *Agamemnon* by Aeschylus, and the *Bacchae* by Euripides, with special attention to *Œdipus Tyrannus*; on Plato, his choice of two of the *Gorgias*, *Protagoras*, and *Phædo*; on *Annals I–IV* by Tacitus; and on Latin prose composition, on Greek prose composition, and on Greek and Latin verse composition. In addition he takes a general paper on Greek and Latin grammar, literary criticism, and antiquities, including questions on Homer, Virgil, Demosthenes, and Cicero; and a paper on a subject of his choice, the elements of Comparative Philology as applied to Greek and Latin, with a special knowledge of Greek philology.

28 February 1913 Tolkien resigns from the King Edward's Horse. His discharge certificate, dated 28 February 1913, certifies that Trooper no. 1624, who enlisted to serve in the Territorial Force of the County of London on 28 November 1911, is discharged in consequence of his own request, and that his claims have been properly settled. *See note.*

March 1913 Tolkien's efforts to make up for lost time prove insufficient to achieve a First Class in Honour Moderations. He is placed in the Second Class, though the examiners give his paper on Comparative Philology an 'alpha' (*see note*). One examiner notes in the mark book (Oxford University Archives EX 2/2/23) that Tolkien's Latin Prose paper was 'largely illegible' and his Greek Verse paper was written in 'filthy script!' His lowest marks are for the translation of Virgil, for the paper on Tacitus, and for Latin verse composition. His tutors having noted his success in the Comparative Philology paper, and at least Professor Joseph Wright knowing of his interest in Germanic languages, suggest that Tolkien change from Classics to the English Honour School in the following (Trinity) term. Exeter College very generously allows Tolkien to keep his Classics exhibition when he agrees to this suggestion; he will learn that this was due to the influence of his tutor, L.R. Farnell, at that time Sub-Rector of the College, who had a great respect for Philology.

3 March 1913 The Stapeldon Society meets.

End of Hilary Term or beginning of Trinity Term 1913 L.R. Farnell writes about Tolkien to *A.S. Napier, the Merton Professor of English Language and Rawlinson Professor of Anglo-Saxon. Tolkien visits Napier at his house in Headington, east of the centre of Oxford. 'I recall that I was ushered into a very dim room and could hardly see Napier. He was courteous, but said little. He never spoke to me again. I attended his lectures, when he was well enough to give them' (letter to *Neil Ker, 22 November 1970, *Letters*, p. 406).

8 March 1913 Hilary Full Term ends.

18 March 1913 Tolkien returns to Birmingham to take part in the annual Open Debate at King Edward's School. The motion 'That modern life is prosaic' is introduced by Sidney Barrowclough ('only the educated classes . . . would choose to discuss a motion of such a kind; any other class would take its truth for granted'), then argued by G.B. Smith in the negative ('no life could be prosaic, which was lived in an age of problems as great and as interesting as those of the present day'), G.H. Bonner in the affirmative ('The question before the House was, not whether romance was dead or not, but whether there was enough of it in modern life to make that life other than prosaic'), and R.S. Payton in the negative ('The object of modern life . . . was universal knowledge. But the actual importance of this search has made it far more romantic than the mythical quest of the ancient demi-god'). The discussion being thrown open to all,

> Mr J.R.R. Tolkien rose to oppose the motion. After to some extent criticising the speakers on both sides, he declared that romance did not mean megalomania, and was far more likely to be found in an age of small and limited efforts, than in one of boasting, and of excessive ambition. Finality was essential to it; what was not essential was, that there should be any knowledge or realisation of its existence before a romantic life could be lived.

Tolkien 'considered that the proof of the motion would be found in the lives of the poor, and instanced their taste for exciting literature' ('Debating Society', *King Edward's School Chronicle* n.s. 28, no. 199 (May 1913), pp. 34–6). The motion fails, 19 to 52.

21 March 1913 Rob Gilson sends a postcard to Tolkien at Exeter College; on 25 March it will be forwarded to Tolkien at Phoenix Farm, Gedling, near Nottingham, where his brother Hilary has come to live.

7 April 1913 Honour Moderations results are issued; they will be published in *The Times* on 8 April (p. 6). Tolkien's name is in the Second Class.

17 April 1913 Honour Moderations results are published in the *Oxford University Gazette*. In the same issue Tolkien is listed as a student in both English Language and Literature and Medieval and Modern European Languages and Literature other than English.

Over the next seven terms Tolkien will need to become familiar with a range of literary and philological subjects and set texts as prescribed in the Oxford *Regulations of the Board of Studies*, knowing that he may be examined on them in ten papers at the end of Trinity Term 1915:

Old English texts, especially *Beowulf, The Fight at Finnesburg, Deor's Complaint*, the *Wife's Complaint, Waldere, The Ruin, The First Riddle*, the Old English *Exodus, Elene*, Gregory's *Dialogues* bks. 1 and 2 (MSS. C and O), and selections 1–34 from the *Anglo-Saxon Reader*, 8th edn., ed. Henry Sweet. The latter comprises 'Cynewulf and Cyneheard' from the *Saxon Chronicle*; 'On the State of Learning in England' from King Alfred's preface to the West-Saxon version of Gregory's *Cura Pastoralis (Pastoral Care)*; Chapter 21 of Alfred's translation of the *Cura Pastoralis*; 'The Voyages of Ohthere and Wulfstan' and 'The Amazons (I, 10)' from Alfred's version of the *Compendious History of the World* by Orosius; 'The Battle of Ashdown', 'Alfred and Godrum', and 'Alfred's Wars with the Danes' from the *Saxon Chronicle*; a selection from Alfred's translation of *De Consolatione Philosophiae* by Boethius; 'Account of the Poet Caedmon' from Alfred's translation of the *Ecclesiastical History* by the Venerable Bede; extracts from the Laws of Ine; a selection of charters; two homilies by Ælfric, 'The Assumption of St John the Apostle' and 'The Nativity of the Innocents'; the 'Life of King Oswald' from Ælfric's *Lives of the Saints*; Wulfstan's address to the English, a homily; 'The Martyrdom of Ælfeah' and 'Eustace at Dover, and the Outlawry of Godwine' from the *Saxon Chronicle*; a selection of charms; 'Beowulf and Grendel's Mother' from *Beowulf; The Battle of Maldon; The Fall of the Angels*, a biblical poem once attributed to Caedmon; *Judith*; 'The Happy Land' from *The Phœnix; The Dream of the Rood; The Wanderer*; a selection of riddles; gnomic verses; *The Seafarer*; Northumbrian fragments; Mercian hymns; Kentish charters; the *Codex Aureus* inscription; and a Kentish psalm.

Middle English texts, especially *Havelok; Pearl; The Owl and the Nightingale; The Taill of Rauf Coolyear*; selections from *Specimens of Early English, Part 1*, 2nd edition, nos. 5, 6, 8, 9, 11, 13, 15, 17, 19, and *Part II*, 4th edn., nos. 1, 7,

9, 10, 15, 16, ed. Richard Morris and Walter W. Skeat; and selections from *An Old English Miscellany* ('old' in the sense of 'early', not Anglo-Saxon), ed. Richard Morris, pp. 1–138. The selections from Morris and Skeat comprise 'Jewish and Christian Offerings' from the *Ormulum*; 'Hengist and Horsa' from Layamon's *Brut*; two texts from *The Life of St Juliana*; 'The Seven Deadly Sins' and 'Directions How a Nun Should Live' from the *Ancrene Riwle*; *A Good Orison of Our Lady* (a short rhyming poem); two Old Kentish sermons, *Sermo in Die Epiphaniae* and *Dominica Secunda post Octavam Epiphaniae*; passages in the life of Joseph, from the English version of Genesis and Exodus; two versions of *A Moral Ode*; *King Horn*; the *Reign of William the Conqueror* and the *Life of St Dunstan* by Robert of Gloucester; 'The Visit of the Magi' and 'The Flight into Egypt' from *Cursor Mundi* (*Cursur o Werld*); sermon on Matthew XXIV:43 and the Paternoster, Ave Maria, and Credo from the Middle Kentish of Dan Michael of Northgate; extracts from *The Pricke of Conscience* by Richard Rolle of Hampole; extracts from *Piers the Plowman* (A text); and extracts from bk. 7 of *The Bruce* by John Barbour. The selections from *An Old English Miscellany* comprise a bestiary ('The Lion', 'The Eagle', 'The Serpent', 'The Ant', 'The Hart', 'The Fox', 'The Spider', 'The Whale', 'The Elephant', 'The Panther', 'The Dove'); Old Kentish sermons; and miscellaneous items mainly from Jesus College (Oxford) MS I. Arch. I. 29.

The works of Geoffrey Chaucer, especially his *Troilus and Criseyde*, the Prologue to the *Canterbury Tales*, 'The Pardoner's Tale', 'The Franklin's Tale', and 'The Clerk's Tale'.

The works of Shakespeare, especially *Love's Labour's Lost*, *Henry IV Part 1* and *Part 2*, *Hamlet*, and *Antony and Cleopatra*.

The history of English literature in general.

The history of the English language.

Gothic and Germanic philology.

In addition, Tolkien will have to choose a Special Subject on which he will be examined separately. He will choose Scandinavian Philology, which according to the *Regulations* will have special reference to Icelandic, together with a special study of the *Snorra Edda* (i.e. the *Prose* or *Younger Edda*), *Gylfaginning* (Chapters 20–54); the *Völsunga Saga* (Chapters 13–31); *Hallfreðar Saga*; *Þorfinns Saga Karlsefnis*; and *Hrafnkels Saga*.

20 April 1913 Trinity Full Term begins.

Trinity Term 1913 *Kenneth Sisam, Professor Napier's assistant, becomes Tolkien's tutor. Tolkien will later write: 'I think I certainly derived from [Sisam] much of the benefit which he attributes to Napier's example and teaching. . . . His teaching was, however, spiced with a pungency, humour and practical wisdom which were his own. I owe him a great debt and have not forgotten it. . . . He taught me not only to read texts, but to study second-hand book catalogues, of which I was not even aware. Some he marked for me' (letter to Neil Ker, 22 November 1970, *Letters*, p. 406). During this term Kenneth Sisam gives the following classes: on Sweet's *Anglo-Saxon Reader* (prose), on

Mondays at 10.00 a.m. in the Examination Schools, beginning 28 April; Elementary Historical Grammar, on Tuesdays at 10.00 a.m. in the Examination Schools, beginning 22 April; *Havelok*, on Thursdays at 10.00 a.m. in the Examination Schools, beginning 24 April; and Sweet's *Anglo-Saxon Reader* (verse), on Fridays at 10.00 a.m. in the Examination Schools, beginning 25 April. He will give these classes at the same times every term while Tolkien is an undergraduate in the English School, and in one term or another (excepting Michaelmas Term 1914, see below) Tolkien probably attends them all. In Trinity Term 1913 Sisam also gives a class on Morris and Skeat's *Specimens of Early English* on Wednesdays at 10.00 in the Examination Schools, beginning 23 April; he will repeat it in Michaelmas Term 1913, Michaelmas Term 1914, and Hilary and Trinity Terms 1915. – Tolkien's tutor for Scandinavian Philology is *W.A. Craigie, the Taylorian Lecturer in the Scandinavian Languages. During this term Craigie lectures on Scandinavian Philology, with special reference to Old and Middle English, on Tuesdays at 5.00 p.m. in the Taylor Institution, beginning 22 April. Tolkien probably also attends Joseph Wright's lectures on Gothic Grammar on Tuesdays and Thursdays at 12.15 p.m. in the Taylor Institution, from 24 April. – Tolkien already knows some of the relevant texts and a fair amount of Old English and Old Norse. He works much harder than he had at Classics, for he finds the texts more interesting, and he begins to develop a special interest in the dialect of Middle English peculiar to the West Midlands, the area from which his Suffield ancestors came. When he reads the Old English poem *Crist* with its reference to 'Earendel' it strikes resonances that will endure in future writings. – At a meeting of the Exeter College Essay Club, Tolkien shares one of his growing enthusiasms by reading a paper on the Norse sagas. The *Stapeldon Magazine* for June 1913 will report (p. 276) that

> the reader proved himself an able and enthusiastic champion, and by adopting a somewhat unconventional turn of phrase, suiting admirably with his subject and the quotations with which he ended, he added a spirit and freshness to an already admirable paper. It is therefore no disparagement to say that the quotations were enjoyed perhaps even more than the criticism of the reader. The subsequent discussion revealed a wide cleavage of taste.

21 April 1913 Tolkien probably speaks with Kenneth Sisam, following the instruction printed in the *Oxford University Gazette* for 17 April that anyone wishing to attend Sisam's classes should call on him at Merton College between 10.00 and 11.00 a.m.

27 April 1913 Rob Gilson replies to a letter from Tolkien in which the latter apparently had written of his Second Class in Honour Moderations and of his decision to change to the English School. Gilson had seen the Honour Moderations results announced in the papers but had not known whether to send congratulations or commiserations. His comments suggest that Tolkien might have earlier expressed an interest in the English School or a growing lack of interest in Classics. Gilson reports his father's opinion that Tolkien ought to have got a First. He also remarks that a postcard he sent to Tolkien at Barnt Green had missed him, and refers to Tolkien having darted to and fro during the vacation.

28 April 1913 At a meeting of the Stapeldon Society Mr Mackarness is appointed to the post of Jester, with Tolkien as his deputy. The minutes note that 'Mr Mackarness in thanking the house remarked that he was afraid that his repertoire was somewhat unfitted to the high standard of morals pertaining in the Society and Mr Tolkien to the general surprise endorsed the remark' (Exeter College archives). Tolkien probably finishes his term of duty on the Kitchen Committee, as new members are elected.

1 May 1913 Tolkien acquires a copy of the Everyman edition of the *Mabinogion*, translated by Lady Charlotte Guest.

12 May 1913 At a meeting of the Stapeldon Society Tolkien describes confrontations between Town and Gown with which he had been involved the previous night. The Society minutes note that 'the Deputy Public Orator [Tolkien] then went on to describe his arrest and subsequent release and told how on returning to college he had delighted the spectators by a magnificent, if unavailing, attempt to scale the Swiss Cottage and had spent the rest of the evening in climbing in and out of Mr Barnett's window' (Exeter College archives).

26 May 1913 At a meeting of the Stapeldon Society Tolkien, as Deputy Public Orator, is called upon to propose a vote of censure against the President of the Society for being absent from a meeting without giving notice.

31 May 1913 The Apolausticks meet for a six-course dinner at an unnamed venue. Tolkien's menu card shows that Mr A. Barnett is now President. (This is the last record of the Apolausticks in the Tolkien Papers preserved in the Bodleian Library, but the group may have continued to exist and to meet regularly.)

5 June 1913 Christopher Wiseman writes to Tolkien, who has mentioned in a letter some injury to his foot. Wiseman wants Tolkien to get better so that they can both take part in King Edward's School Sports as Old Edwardians.

9 June 1913 At a meeting of the Stapeldon Society R.H. Gordon and J.R.R. Tolkien are elected President and Secretary of the Society for the next term. Tolkien also proposes a vote of censure against the outgoing President for having attended only two meetings during his tenure of office. – G.B. Smith, still at King Edward's School, replies to a letter from Tolkien he received that morning. Smith, who will go up to Oxford in Michaelmas Term 1913, having been awarded an exhibition at Corpus Christi College, asks Tolkien about obtaining furniture, etc. for his college rooms.

10 June 1913 Rob Gilson writes to Tolkien from his home at Marston Green near Birmingham, mentioning a long letter in which Tolkien has said how much he is enjoying the Oxford English School. Gilson asks him to play tennis on Saturday, 14 June, and if he will be in Birmingham for the King Edward's School Sports on 28 June, and for Speech Day on 28 July. – Tolkien replies immediately, informing Gilson that he will be in Warwick until 28 June or 1 July.

12 June 1913 Gilson writes again to encourage Tolkien to visit him on 14 June, and sends him train times to Warwick from Marston Green.

14 June 1913 Trinity Full Term ends. – Tolkien probably travels to Marston Green to attend a tennis party at the Gilsons. Rob Gilson and other school friends are present. – In the evening, Tolkien probably travels to Warwick to visit Edith and Jennie Grove.

?14 June–28 June or 1 July 1913 Tolkien stays in Warwick. A suitable house is found for Edith and Jennie to rent at 15 Victoria Road, Warwick, and they deal with many domestic details. Tolkien and Edith attend Benediction in the Catholic church together for the first time.

18 June 1913 Tolkien sketches the gardens of Pageant House, Warwick (*Pageant House Gardens, Warwick*, see *Artist and Illustrator*, fig. 14).

28 June–1 July 1913 Tolkien possibly takes up Gilson's invitation of 12 June that they attend the King Edward's School Sports. If so, he may have spent the weekend and perhaps the beginning of the next week with the Gilson family at Marston Green before going to Barnt Green.

At least 2–12 July 1913 Tolkien stays at Barnt Green with the Incledons. He makes several drawings and watercolours, including views of the Incledons' cottage and garden and of foxgloves in a nearby wood (*Artist and Illustrator*, figs. 17–18). He also paints the view *King's Norton from Bilberry Hill* (*Artist and Illustrator*, fig. 16). Tolkien now begins to use a large sketchbook, at the beginning of which he copies, probably from postcards, views of Broad Street, Oxford and the Dining Hall at Exeter College, and makes a sketch of the cottage at Barnt Green.

?Late July 1913 Tolkien visits Phoenix Farm. He draws *Phoenix Farm from Gedling*, a view seen from a distance. Possibly at this time, though more likely in 1914, he draws another, closer view of the farm (*Phoenix Farm, Gedling*, see *Artist and Illustrator*, fig. 15). – Tolkien is hired by a Mr Killion to accompany two Mexican boys, Ventura del Rio and José del Rio, to *France to join a third boy, Eustaquio, and their aunts, Angela Martinez del Rio de Thomas and Julia Gonzalez, and while in France to act as their escort and tutor.

29 July 1913 At Charing Cross station Tolkien speaks with Mr Killion, but there seem to be no plans to govern the work he is about to do. He is introduced to Ventura and José, who attend the Roman Catholic school at *Stonyhurst in Lancashire. 'They are quite jolly & good & most submissive and quiet especially little José who never speaks' (letter to Edith Bratt, 29 July 1913, courtesy of Christopher Tolkien).

30 July 1913 Tolkien, Ventura, and José arrive in Paris. They are met by the boys' aunts at the Gare du Nord, who weep and greet the boys so volubly that Tolkien must lose his temper to get them into a taxi. Their intended hotel, the Hôtel de l'Athenée, being closed, they go to the Hôtel Plaza. Later they will move to the Hôtel des Champs-Elysées. 'The boys really are most excellent & the smallest one [Eustaquio] . . . who has just come from Mexico, is the nicest child I have ever met, I think' (letter to Edith Bratt, 30 July 1913, courtesy of Christopher Tolkien).

31 July–12 August 1913 While in France and with the Mexican boys, Tolkien has to speak mainly Spanish or French, in neither of which is he proficient. Although he enjoys seeing Paris, the visit reinforces his pre-existing dislike for the inhabitants of France and their language. He feels a deep grudge against the Norman Conquest, which he thinks has done so much to destroy Anglo-Saxon culture and to adulterate the English language. On 5 or 6 August the aunts decide to go to Brittany, and Tolkien looks forward to visiting that Celtic area with its close ties to Wales and the Welsh language. But on 10 August Tolkien, the boys, and the elder of the aunts, Madame Angela, go only to Dinard, a fashionable seaside resort. Tolkien writes to Edith: 'Brittany! And to see nothing but trippers and dirty papers and bathing machines' (quoted in *Biography*, p. 67).

13 August 1913 Madame Angela is struck by a car and dies soon afterward. Her last wish is to be returned to her native Mexico. Tolkien sends the news to Mr Killion by telegram, and presumably also contacts Madame Julia.

14 August 1913 Madame Julia arrives in Dinard in the morning; Tolkien meets her at the station. Although the owners of the hotel in which they have been staying are kind at first, their attitude changes when they learn that the party are all Roman Catholics. Tolkien and Ventura return to Paris on the night train to make mortuary arrangements.

15 August 1913 Tolkien writes from the Hôtel des Champs-Elysées to Mr Killion regarding the problems he is encountering following the death of Madame Angela. Madame Julia wishes to return to Mexico at once with the boys. Tolkien speculates that if the boys go Mr Killion (apparently their guardian) may need someone to bring Ventura and José back from Mexico in time for January term at Stonyhurst, in which case he offers his 'hypothetical services' (private collection).

16 August 1913 Tolkien and Ventura dine with Madame Cervantes, a helpful friend resident in Paris.

17 August 1913 Tolkien writes again to Mr Killion, noting that he and Ventura have been to Mass and Communion at the English church in Paris, and to Mass at the Spanish church. He and Ventura again dine with Madame Cervantes.

18 August 1913 Tolkien and Ventura rise at 3.00 a.m. in order to meet Madame Angela's coffin at Montparnasse on the 4.00 a.m. train. They reach the station at 3.45, but the train is late, and in fact the coffin arrives on a still later train at 5.15 a.m., and conveyances for it at 6.45. Madame Julia arrives in Paris with José and Eustaquio. Tolkien writes to Mr Killion, convinced that the boys should not return to Mexico but continue their education at Stonyhurst. – Tolkien writes to Edith: 'There is no fear of my going to Mexico. Mr Killion will not, I am confident, allow the two elder boys – nor if possible the younger boy – to go back: & in any case I shall not go' (courtesy of Christopher Tolkien).

20 August 1913 Tolkien writes to Mr Killion, concerned with mourning clothes for the boys and with their education while abroad.

> Rushing about sight-seeing or any obvious form of enjoyment is of course out of the question for a while so I have tried to find out what of the best, most readable, and least palpably 'instructive' of boys books they haven't read. Many of these I have got in cheap editions . . . such as *King Solomon's Mines*, *Kim* and so forth. José, the most thoughtful of the three, was very anxious to have a huge tome that he caught sight of . . . 'Mexico the Land of Unrest' a meticulous history (by an Englishman I think) of the revolution – but I thought it a little too hard for his digestion yet.
>
> He is now reading *The White Company*.
>
> There is no accommodation in this hotel for children so at their earnest entreaties I also got them some draughts of which they are very fond. [private collection]

He has had a long talk with José on top of the Arc de Triomphe on the merits of returning to Stonyhurst, and otherwise has tried to lead the boys to 'take the sensible view with content, in order not to upset next term with pinings'. He appraises each boy's character. Tolkien and the boys are to return to England on 30 August, unless Mr Killion has other plans. He has spent 'a long day in steamship companies' offices, banks and so forth'.

29 August 1913 Tolkien writes to Edith that he and the boys are to leave France on the following day. They are to arrive at Southampton on 1 September, and that same day to go to *Bournemouth in Hampshire, where they are to stay (c/o Fisher, Devonshire House) for two weeks. On 15 September they are to go to London, and from there the boys are to return to Stonyhurst on 16 September. – Tolkien will tell Edith concerning his experience in France: 'Never again except I am in the direst poverty will I take any such job' (quoted in *Biography*, p. 68).

30 August–1 September 1913 Tolkien and the boys return to England.

16 September 1913 Christopher Wiseman writes to Tolkien from Grenoble, France, where he is taking a holiday course at the university. He has heard from Gilson of Tolkien's experiences in France. He urges Tolkien to visit Birmingham towards the end of September, and suggests T.C.B.S. meetings on the evening of Saturday, 27 September (when Gilson will be absent) and on Wednesday, 1 October (when Gilson should be able to participate).

Last half of September 1913 Tolkien visits Warwick (from ?17 September), Birmingham, and Norwich.

Early October 1913 Tolkien again stays in Warwick; a postcard from Gilson is forwarded there from Exeter College.

10 October 1913 Tolkien writes to Edith. By now, he has returned to Oxford.

12 October 1913 Michaelmas Full Term begins.

Michaelmas Term 1913 Kenneth Sisam offers the same five classes as in Trinity Term 1913. Tolkien probably attends lectures by W.A. Craigie on Old Icelandic Grammar on Tuesdays at 5.00 p.m. in the Taylor Institution, beginning 14 October, and on *Gylfaginning* on Thursdays at 5.00 p.m. in the Taylor Institution, beginning 16 October, and lectures by A.S. Napier on Morris and Skeat's *Specimens of Early English* on Mondays at 12.00 noon in the Examination Schools, beginning 20 October. He definitely attends Napier's lectures on English Historical Grammar on Tuesdays and Fridays at 12.00 noon in the Examination Schools, beginning 21 October, and on Old English Dialects on Thursday at 12.00 noon in the Examination Schools, beginning 23 October; lectures by *D. Nichol Smith, Goldsmiths' Reader in English, on (Samuel) Johnson and His Friends on Wednesdays and Fridays at 11.00 a.m. in the Examination Schools, beginning 15 October; and G.K.A. Bell's course on Chaucer's Prologue to the *Canterbury Tales* and the 'Franklin's Tale' on Wednesdays at 5.45 p.m. at Christ Church, beginning 15 October. – G.B. Smith goes up to Oxford as an exhibitioner at Corpus Christi. A closer friendship develops between Smith and Tolkien, perhaps because Smith too is reading English, and he is the only other inner member of the T.C.B.S. to attend Oxford. Nonetheless the four (Tolkien, Smith, Gilson, and Wiseman) share ideas of what they might do in the world, how they might make an impact.

Academic year 1913–1914 Probably at some time during this year Tolkien takes part in a university rag against the town, the police, and the proctors. 'Geoffrey [? G.B. Smith] and I "captured" a bus and drove it up to Cornmarket making various unearthly noises followed by a mad crowd of mingled varsity and 'townese'. It was chockfull of undergrads before it reached the Carfax. There I addressed a few stirring words to a huge mob before descending, and removing to the "maggers memugger" or the Martyrs' Memorial where I addressed the crowd again' (quoted in *Biography*, p. 54).

13 October 1913 At an extraordinary meeting of the Stapeldon Society a scheme for the redecoration of the Junior Common Room at Exeter College is discussed. Tolkien attends and, as Secretary, takes minutes.

20 October 1913 The Stapeldon Society meets. Tolkien takes the minutes. In accordance with a motion which is carried unanimously, the Secretary (Tolkien) is instructed to inform the Bursar that the house viewed with apprehension and jealousy his removal of hall breakfast on Sundays without notice given to the Society's committee. Later in the meeting Tolkien proposes the motion for discussion: 'This House believes in ghosts.' He is opposed wittily by *T.W. Earp. The motion fails, 6 to 8.

27 October 1913 The Stapeldon Society meets. Tolkien takes the minutes. In a debate following Society business he speaks in favour of the motion: 'Living in college is preferable to living in diggings [i.e. lodgings].' The motion carries, 16 to 5.

28 October 1913 Tolkien attends the Exeter College Freshman's Wine. The evening includes a programme of songs, piano and English horn solos, a performance by the Exeter Brass Band, and at 10.00 p.m., a dance.

3 November 1913 The Stapeldon Society meets. As Secretary, Tolkien takes the minutes. The main business of the meeting is discussion of a report by the Kitchen Committee.

10 November 1913 The Stapeldon Society meets. Tolkien takes the minutes. In a debate following Society business he speaks against the motion: 'This House would welcome the greater play of the Democratic Factor in foreign policy.' The motion fails, 7 to 10.

17 November 1913 The Stapeldon Society meets. Tolkien takes the minutes. In a debate following Society business he speaks against the motion: 'This House considers the failure of the Olympic Games Fund a satisfactory sign of the healthy state of British sport.' The motion carries, 10 to 8.

19 November 1913 Tolkien attends the Exeter College Smoker, for which he has designed the programme cover: depicting merry undergraduates in evening dress dancing along the Turl, it is similar to his (presumably contemporaneous) drawing *Turl Street, Oxford* (*Life and Legend*, p. 26; *Artist and Illustrator*, fig. 19). The first part of the Smoker includes songs, piano and banjo solos, and character sketches; the second part consists of dance music played by the orchestra. Tolkien collects several signatures on his printed programme, including those of E.A. Barber and L.R. Farnell, friends, and performers.

24 November 1913 The Stapeldon Society meets. Tolkien takes the minutes. Congratulations are voted to those who had organized the Smoker, and to Tolkien 'for covering the outside of the card in black and white' (Exeter College archives). Tolkien as Secretary is instructed to convey the Society's congratulations to a Balliol student for placing an 'article of common domestic utility' upon the Martyrs' Memorial. In a debate that follows, Tolkien speaks against the motion: 'Europe is destined soon to lose its position of pre-eminence in world politics'. The motion carries, 9 to 1.

December 1913 An untitled poem by Tolkien (*From the Many-Willow'd Margin of the Immemorial Thames*) is published in the *Stapeldon Magazine* for December 1913. This is the first verse of the poem *From Iffley* which he wrote in October 1911 (the second verse is lost by the editor of the magazine).

1 December 1913 The Stapeldon Society meets, riotously, at 8.00 p.m. Tolkien takes the minutes, which he will later write up at length in a very graphic style: 'At the 791st meeting . . . one of the world's great battles between democracy and autocracy was fought and won, and as usual in such conflicts the weapons of democracy were hooliganism and uproar, and an unyielding pertinacity only excelled by that of the chair. . . .' The meeting is packed, and long before the officers enter, 'the ominous sounds of a gigantic house athirst for their blood could be heard . . . to the sound of wild and impartial ululation the Pres. announced the candidates for office in Hilary Term; and the House simmered audibly while voting papers were distributed and counted.' Tolkien is elected President for Hilary Term; he and the other successful candidates make brief speeches. But objections are made as to whether certain actions of the current President were constitutional, and later in the meeting

> all bounds, all order, and all else was forgotten; and in one long riot of raucous hubbub, of hoarse cries, brandished bottles, flying matchstands, gowns wildly fluttered, cups smashed and lights extinguished the House declared its determination to have its will and override the constitution. For precisely one calendar hour did the House battle with noise and indignation for its desire. It was at one time on the point of dissolving and becoming another Society; at another it was vociferating for Rule 40; at another for Rule 10; at another no rule at all or for the President's head or his nether-garments.

The evening ends with the customary vote of thanks to the outgoing officers, and a 'vote of admiration for the rock-like constancy with which the President [the main target] had withstood this unparalleled storm or rebellious and insubordinate riot' (Exeter College archives). The House is too exhausted to hear Mr Macdonald and Mr Blomfield debate whether they should wash themselves or take exercise, and adjourns.

5 December 1913 Tolkien writes a letter (*Oxford Letter*), apparently in response to a request from the editor of the *King Edward's School Chronicle*, giving an account of Old Edwardians at Oxford. It will be published as by 'Oxon' in the December 1913 issue.

6 December 1913 Michaelmas Full Term ends.

12 December 1913 Christopher Wiseman, who with his family has moved to Wandsworth Common, London, invites Tolkien to join him and G.B. Smith for a T.C.B.S. meeting at his home on 19 December. In the event, Tolkien does not attend (nor is there clear evidence that the other members met in his absence).

15 December 1913 Tolkien is scheduled to open the Annual Old Boys Debate at King Edward's School, Birmingham, but is suddenly taken ill. Rob Gilson therefore introduces the motion: 'That the World is becoming over-civilised'. G.B. Smith also speaks in favour.

16 December 1913 Apparently having recovered from his illness, Tolkien captains the Old Edwardians in a rugby match against King Edward's School. Gilson, Smith, and Wiseman also play. King Edward's School wins, 14 to 10.

Late December 1913–early January 1914 Tolkien visits Barnt Green. He writes a poem, *Outside*, suggested by a tune heard in 1912, and apparently is again involved in amateur theatricals (on 4 January 1914 Rob Gilson will write that his letter will probably arrive on the morning of Tolkien's 'production').

?17–?19 December 1913 Tolkien informs his T.C.B.S. friends that he is engaged, but gives no details about Edith, not even her name. He possibly tells G.B. Smith in person (no letter of congratulations from Smith is in Tolkien's T.C.B.S. correspondence file) and writes to Wiseman and Gilson. *See note.*

20 **December 1913 (postmark)** Christopher Wiseman sends congratulations to Tolkien on his engagement, on a postcard addressed to him at Barnt Green.

1914

4 January 1914 Rob Gilson writes to Tolkien, sending congratulations on his engagement. G.B. Smith has asked him to attend a T.C.B.S. meeting next week, and Gilson hopes that Tolkien will be there too (in the event, he does not attend).

Later in 1914 Tolkien visits Cromer in Norfolk, a seaside resort on the north-east coast of England. The occasion will later inspire a poem, *The Lonely Harebell* (see entry for 10 November–1 December 1916).

6 January 1914 Tolkien apparently decides that the new sketchbook he began the previous summer should be devoted henceforth to imaginative subjects. Probably at this time he tears out the three topographical drawings he had already made in it and writes on its cover: *The Book of Ishness*. He inserts (now or later) an undated drawing, *Ei uchnem: Russian Boatmen's Song*, a stylized view of a boat on a river. This is followed in the book by a sketch of a fantastic house in an apparently northern landscape ('Northern House', *Artist and Illustrator*, fig. 38), dated 'Jan[uary] 6 1914'. This is followed in the book by three undated works, *An Osity or Balliol College Unmasked*, *Eeriness* (*Artist and Illustrator*, fig. 40), and *Childhood Memories of My Grandmother's House*.

8 January 1914 Tolkien is in Warwick at the end of Christmas vacation. Today, the anniversary of their reunion, Edith is received into the Catholic Church, and she and Tolkien are formally betrothed in the church at Warwick by Father Murphy. To celebrate the occasion, probably on this date but certainly during January, Tolkien writes a poem, *Magna Dei Gloria (Warwick)* dedicated 'To EMB' (Edith Mary Bratt).

12 January 1914 Tolkien paints another watercolour, *Beyond* (*Artist and Illustrator*, fig. 19) in *The Book of Ishness*, and probably also the closely related drawings that follow, *There* and *Here*.

18 January 1914 Hilary Full Term begins.

Hilary Term 1914 Kenneth Sisam continues to teach the *Anglo-Saxon Reader* (Prose), Elementary Historical Grammar, *Havelok*, and the *Anglo-Saxon Reader* (Verse). Tolkien almost certainly attends Sisam's two new classes, *Beowulf* on Wednesdays at 10.00 a.m. in the Examination Schools, beginning 21 January, and *The Pearl* on Saturdays at 10.00 a.m. in the Examination Schools, beginning 24 January. He probably also attends A.S. Napier's continuation of his lectures on English Historical Grammar, on Mondays, Tuesdays, and Fridays at 12.00 noon in the Examination Schools, beginning 23 January; on Morris and Skeat's *Specimens*, on Thursdays at 12.00 noon in the Examination Schools; and on Old English Dialects, on Saturdays at 12.00 noon in the Examination Schools, beginning 24 January. Tolkien also attends this year (or, less probably, in 1915) W.A. Craigie's lectures on *Hrafnkel's Saga* on Thursdays at 5.00 p.m. in the Taylor Institution, beginning 22 January, and probably Craigie's continuation of his lectures on Old Icelandic Grammar on Tuesdays at 5.00 p.m. in the Taylor Institution, beginning 20 January. He possibly attends as well lectures by Sir John Rhys on Welsh: *The Mabinogion* on Tuesdays and Fridays at 6.00 p.m. at Jesus College, beginning 23 January, and by *E.E. Wardale on the Literature of the Old English Period on Mondays at 11.00 a.m. in the Old Ashmolean, beginning 26 January. – Tolkien and Colin Cullis, President and Secretary of the Stapeldon Society for Hilary Term, examine the Society's rules before they are reprinted. Cullis writes two pages of possible amendments, which they both sign. Tolkien uses the versos of these sheets to make a list of unusual English words, with a note to look them up in the *Oxford English Dictionary*. – During this term, Tolkien is also a member of a committee to draw up a new constitution for the Exeter College Essay Club; he signs the new rules in January 1914. He is Secretary of the Club for Hilary Term, but no minutes survive until those for the meeting of 4 March. – Probably during this term, Tolkien plays a football match with the Exeter College Rugby XV versus the Boat Club. (A photograph of the combined teams is reproduced in the *Exeter College Association Register 1992*, p. 33.)

26 January 1914 Tolkien chairs a meeting of the Stapeldon Society. The new Secretary records that 'the memory and imagination of the House was stirred by the cinematographically vivid minutes of the last meeting', written by Tolkien as the previous Secretary (Exeter College archives).

30 January 1914 The Sub-Rector signs a note giving Tolkien and Colin Cullis leave 'to have supper for nine on Sat. nights in the rooms of one or the other this term' (Tolkien Papers, Bodleian Library, Oxford). Tolkien will later write on this note: 'Germ of the Chequers', i.e. the beginning of the Chequers Club. The only recorded meeting of this club is on 18 June 1914, but it may be supposed that Tolkien and Cullis host at least some dinners during Hilary Term. Many of the members who will sign Tolkien's menu on 18 June were also members of the Apolausticks, which suggests that the Chequers Club was a successor to that group.

Early February 1914 Christopher Wiseman and T.K. Barnsley form a delegation from Cambridge to the Oxford Wesley Society; Rob Gilson accompanies them. They have 'a splendid weekend. . . . I saw lots of [his Birmingham friend Frederick] Scopes and Tolkien and G.B. Smith, all of whom seem very contented with life' (Gilson, letter to Marianne Cary Gilson, 17 February 1914, quoted in John Garth, *Tolkien and the Great War* (2003), p. 32).

2 February 1914 Tolkien chairs a meeting of the Stapeldon Society, although he is suffering from 'gastric influenza' contracted the previous evening.

9 February 1914 Tolkien chairs a meeting of the Stapeldon Society. A committee is elected, consisting of the President of the Junior Common Room, the President of the Stapeldon Society (Tolkien), and Mr R.C. Gordon, to consider the question of a College Dinner in Trinity Term as part of celebrations marking the sexcentenary of the founding of Exeter College.

16 February 1914 Tolkien chairs a meeting of the Stapeldon Society. His eagle eye or keen sense of smell detecting the presence of a glass of intoxicating liquor, he orders its immediate removal. The members later debate the motion: 'Flirting is a reprehensible past-time'. The votes at the end being equal, Tolkien as President casts the deciding vote in favour of the motion.

23 February 1914 Tolkien chairs a meeting of the Stapeldon Society. Someone having upset a bath in the room above, Tolkien is reported to have remarked: 'Zeus thunders on the right' (Exeter College archives).

2 March 1914 Tolkien chairs a meeting of the Stapeldon Society. In a debate he speaks in favour of the motion: 'The cheap cinema is an engine of social corruption'. The motion fails, 9 to 10.

4 March 1914 At a meeting of the Exeter College Essay Club in the rooms of E.W. Marshall, Tolkien is elected President of the Club for Trinity Term. He reads a paper on Francis Thompson which begins with biographical details, then justifies Tolkien's opinion that Thompson should be ranked among the very greatest of poets. Supporting his views with many quotations, he praises Thompson's metrical power, the greatness of his language, and the immensity of his imagery and its underlying faith.

9 March 1914 Tolkien chairs a meeting of the Stapeldon Society. He replies as departing President to a vote of thanks to officers at the end of their term of office. He remains however on the Sexcentenary Dinner committee.

Spring 1914 Exeter College awards Tolkien the Skeat Prize for English. He uses the £5 to buy *The Life and Death of Jason* and *The House of the Wolfings*, both by William Morris, as well as the Morris translation of the *Völsunga Saga* and *A Welsh Grammar* by Sir John Morris Jones. He will later remark: 'My college, I know, and the shade of Walter Skeat, I surmise, was shocked when the only prize I ever won (there was only one other competitor) . . . was spent on Welsh' (*English and Welsh*, in *The Monsters and the Critics and Other Essays*, p. 192).

14 March 1914 Hilary Full Term ends.

15 March 1914 Tolkien adds to *The Book of Ishness* a watercolour of the sea, or possibly of the Great Wave which sometimes haunts his dreams, 'towering up, and coming in ineluctably over the trees and green fields' (letter to W.H. Auden, 7 June 1955, *Letters*, p. 213).

21 April 1914 Tolkien adds to *The Book of Ishness* a simple, diagrammatic drawing entitled *Everywhere*, and a strange design of bells and dancing lamp-posts entitled *Tarantella* (?).

26 April 1914 Trinity Full Term begins.

Trinity Term 1914 Tolkien very likely attends the conclusion of A.S. Napier's lectures on English Historical Grammar, on Tuesdays, Thursdays, and Fridays at 12.00 noon in the Examination Schools, beginning 30 April. He probably attends Kenneth Sisam's classes on *Beowulf* and *Pearl*, and perhaps one or more of Sisam's four recurring classes on the *Anglo-Saxon Reader*, on *Havelok*, and on Elementary Historical Grammar. He probably also attends (more likely now than in Trinity Term 1915, immediately before final examinations) W.A. Craigie's lectures on Outlines of Scandinavian Philology on Tuesdays at 5.00 p.m. in the Taylor Institution, beginning 28 April, and on the *Hallfreðar Saga* on Thursdays at 5.00 p.m. in the Taylor Institution, beginning 30 April; and perhaps D. Nichol Smith's lectures on English Literature from Caxton to Milton on Wednesdays and Fridays at 11.00 a.m. in the Examination Schools, beginning 29 April. He possibly attends lectures by Sir John Rhys on Welsh: *The Mabinogion* (White Book Text) on Tuesdays and Fridays at 5.00 p.m. at Jesus College, beginning 1 May.

4 May 1914 The Stapeldon Society meets.

16 May 1914 Tolkien rewrites his poem *Wood-sunshine* (first composed in July 1910). – G.K. Chesterton gives a lecture, *Romance*, at 5.30 p.m. in the Oxford Examination Schools.

18 May 1914 Tolkien rewrites his poem *The Dale Lands* (first composed in May 1910), now with the slightly emended title *The Dale-lands*. – At a meeting of the Stapeldon Society Tolkien is given the task of writing to various people to ask if they would propose toasts at the Sexcentenary Dinner. In a debate following Society business he proposes the motion: 'That Oxford was made for Eights Week and not Eights Week for Oxford'. The motion carries, 6 to 3.

20 May 1914 Tolkien chairs a meeting of the Exeter College Essay Club in Colin Cullis's rooms. J.F. Huntington reads a paper on George Borrow. In the discussion afterwards, Tolkien confesses to having no great admiration for Borrow.

26 May 1914 Tolkien attends a performance by the Exeter College Musical Society. The programme includes songs by members of the Society and guests Miss Dora Arnell and Mr Stewart Gardner, as well as flute and pianoforte solos.

1 June 1914 At a meeting of the Stapeldon Society the members 'listened with breathless interest to the respectively frolicsome, frivolous and fearful adventures which had befallen Messrs. Tolkien, Robinson and Wheway' (Society minutes, Exeter College archives).

3 June 1914 Tolkien chairs a meeting of the Exeter College Essay Club in Mr Huntington's rooms. He is elected Critic for Michaelmas Term. A visiting speaker, Cyril Bailey, reads a paper, *Signs of the Times*. (This is the last meeting recorded in the Society minutes book until Michaelmas Term 1918, but that there were meetings during 1914–18 is evident from references in the *Stapeldon Magazine* and elsewhere.)

6 June 1914 The Junior Common Room entertains the Senior Common Room (i.e. the Rector and Fellows of the College) with a ten-course dinner in the Hall to celebrate the sexcentenary of the foundation of Exeter College. Tolkien proposes the toast to the College Societies. He collects twenty-three signatures on his menu.

15 June 1914 Tolkien attends a meeting of the Stapeldon Society. The members pass a vote of congratulation for the committee that arranged the Sexcentenary Dinner.

18 June 1914 Tolkien attends the 'Chequers Clubbe Binge', a five-course dinner. Its printed menu has a cover designed by Tolkien and lists twelve members of the Club including himself. He and seven others sign his copy of the menu.

20 June 1914 Trinity Full Term ends.

23 June 1914 A Sexcentenary Ball is held at Exeter College.

June–July 1914 Tolkien spends the early part of his vacation visiting Edith in Warwick. Probably on this visit he draws a view of Warwick Castle seen from under a bridge, apparently made from a punt or boat on the river. He will later date it '1913–14?'

August 1914 Tolkien explores the Lizard Peninsula in *Cornwall on foot with Father Vincent Reade of the Birmingham Oratory. Their visit extends from at least 5 August to 18 or 19 August, a period fixed by letters written by Tolkien to Edith on 5, 8, 11, 14, and 16 August (in the latter 'only three days till I see you'; quoted by Christopher Tolkien in private correspondence). During the visit Tolkien makes several drawings: *Cadgwith, Cornwall, Cove near the Lizard* (*Artist and Illustrator*, fig. 21), and *Caerthilian Cove & Lion Rock* (*Artist and Illustrator*, fig. 20, a mistitled view of the sea off Pentreath Beach), as well as a rough sketch for the Lion Rock. On 8 August Tolkien will write to Edith:

We walked over the moor-land on top of the cliffs to Kynance Cove. Nothing I could say in a dull old letter would describe it to you. The sun beats down on you and a huge Atlantic swell smashes and spouts over the snags and reefs. The sea has carved weird wind-holes and spouts into the cliffs which blow with trumpety noises or spout foam like a whale, and everywhere you see black and red rock and white foam against violet and transparent seagreen. [quoted in *Biography*, p. 70]

After exploring some of the villages inland from the Lizard promontory, they walk

through rustic 'Warwickshire' scenery, dropped down to the banks of the Helford river (almost like a fjord), and then climbed through 'Devonshire' lanes up to the opposite bank, and then got into more open country, where it twisted and wiggled and wobbled and upped and downed until dusk was already coming on and the red sun just dropping. Then after adventures and redirections we came out on the bare bleak 'Goonhilly' downs and had a four mile straight piece with turf for our sore feet. Then we got benighted in the neighbourhood of Ruan Minor, and got into the dips and waggles again. The light got very 'eerie'. Sometimes we plunged into a belt of trees, and owls and bats made you creep: sometimes a horse with asthma behind a hedge or an old pig with insomnia made your heart jump: or perhaps it was nothing worse than walking into an unexpected stream. The fourteen miles eventually drew to an end – and the last two miles were enlivened by the sweeping flash of the Lizard Lights and the sounds of the sea drawing nearer. [quoted in *Biography*, p. 71]

4 August 1914 Germany invades Belgium. Britain, one of the nations that had guaranteed the neutrality of Belgium by treaty in 1839, gives Germany an ultimatum that if its forces have not been withdrawn by midnight, Germany and Britain will be at war. – George Allen & Unwin Ltd. (*Publishers) is formed out of the assets of George Allen & Co. Ltd.

7 August 1914 Units of the British Expeditionary Force cross to France.

12 August 1914 Britain declares war on Austria-Hungary.

At least 23–30 August 1914 Tolkien stays at The White House, Northgate, Warwick. While there he writes to his Aunt May Incledon on 23 August, and to a Mrs Stafford in Oxford on 30 August. Possibly Tolkien stays in Warwick beyond 30 August, to be near Edith.

Late September 1914 Tolkien visits Phoenix Farm, Gedling, which by now his Aunt Jane Neave is running with the Brookes-Smiths and his brother Hilary. By this time too, Hilary has enlisted in the Royal Warwickshire regiment. Tolkien having decided to finish his studies at Oxford before himself enlisting, he faces considerable family disapproval. It is probably during this visit that he makes an undated drawing of Phoenix Farm in the same sketchbook that he used in Cornwall.

24 September 1914 While at Phoenix Farm, Tolkien writes the poem *The Voyage of Éarendel the Evening Star* (**Éalá Éarendel Engla Beorhtast*), inspired by the word or name *Earendel* in the Old English *Crist*. The mariner Éarendel (later *Eärendel*, *Eärendil*) will become a key figure in the mythology or *legendarium* (*'The Silmarillion') whose invention and revision will occupy Tolkien for the rest of his life. When, however, at some time in the autumn or early winter 1914, Tolkien shows his poem to G.B. Smith, he will admit that he does not yet know what it is really about, and will promise to 'try to find out' (quoted in *Biography*, p. 75). This may take him some time, as shown by an early attempt to recast the poem in a classical setting with 'Phosphorus' replacing 'Éarendel' as the protagonist. The poem is the germ from which the mythology evolved, rather than the first consciously written poem of the mythology.

11 October 1914 Michaelmas Full Term begins.

Michaelmas Term 1914 When Tolkien returns to Oxford, he finds that many of his friends have chosen to enlist. The Examination Schools having been commandeered, lectures are given elsewhere. Tolkien attends A.S. Napier's lectures on *Pearl* on Tuesdays at 12.00 noon in the Ashmolean Museum, beginning 20 October, and on *Beowulf* on Thursdays and Saturdays at 12.00 noon in the Ashmolean, beginning 15 October; lectures by *Sir Walter Raleigh, the Professor of English Literature, on Chaucer and His Contemporaries on Tuesdays and Thursdays at 11.00 a.m. at Magdalen College, beginning 13 October; and W.A. Craigie's lectures on the *Völsunga Saga* on Thursdays in the Taylor Institution, beginning 15 October – at 5.00 p.m., according to the

Oxford University Gazette, but Tolkien records it in a manuscript schedule for Michaelmas Term as from 2.00 to 4.00 p.m. This schedule suggests that Tolkien is no longer attending Kenneth Sisam's classes (during the war, held at 40 Broad Street) or repeating those he had already attended; but he has weekly tutorials with Sisam, on Mondays for an hour at midday, at each of which he is to read an essay. If he has not done so already in Trinity Term 1914, he possibly attends lectures by Sir John Rhys on Welsh: *The Mabinogion* (White Book Text) on Tuesdays and Fridays at 5.00 p.m. at Jesus College, beginning 16 October. – Tolkien and Colin Cullis, the latter prevented from enlisting by poor health, decide to live in 'digs' rather than in college, and find rooms at 59 St John Street (*see note*).

Mid-October 1914–June 1915 Although there will be no conscription until late in the war there is considerable pressure on all young men to join up, and great disapproval of those who do not. Tolkien is therefore pleased to discover the existence of a scheme by which he can prepare for the Army with the Officers Training Corps at Oxford while continuing to study, and need not go on active service until he has taken his degree. In this context, Tolkien drills in the University Parks from 9.00 to 10.00 a.m. on Mondays, 9.00–10.00 a.m. and 2.00–4.30 p.m. on Wednesdays and Fridays, and 2.00–4.30 p.m. on Saturdays. He also usually attends one lecture per week, and classes in signalling and map-reading on free afternoons.

Mid-October 1914 At about this time, Tolkien begins to retell the story of Kullervo from the *Kalevala* 'somewhat on the lines of [William] Morris's romances with chunks of poetry in between' (letter to Edith Bratt, [October 1914], *Letters*, p. 7). He briefly drafts variant outlines of the story, then writes in full, filling just over twenty-one sides of foolscap paper; but when the story is about three-quarters complete he leaves it unfinished and drafts its conclusion only in outline. (Later Tolkien will transform the story of Kullervo into the tale of Túrin Turambar, one of the most important episodes in his mythology; see **'Of Túrin Turambar'.) Among these papers, on the opposite side of a sheet containing a rough re-working of one of the poems in his *Story of Kullervo*, is the earliest extant version of Tolkien's poem *May Day*, already considerably developed; but see entry for 20–21 April 1915.

19 October 1914 At a meeting of the Stapeldon Society a hearty vote of confidence in all Exonians serving with His Majesty's Forces is enthusiastically passed. When the issue of electing representatives for the Central Committee is raised, Tolkien points out that their election by the Stapeldon Society is, strictly speaking, out of order, but as there is no larger body left in the College due to the war the Society should arrogate to itself the right. The members discuss the redecoration of the Junior Common Room, and Tolkien is deputed to refer the matter to Reginald Blomfield, architect of the scheme.

***c.* 23 October 1914** Despite occasionally having to drill in the rain and to clean his rifle afterwards, the extra duty suits Tolkien. He writes to Edith: 'Drill is a godsend. I have been up a fortnight nearly, and have not yet got a touch even of the real Oxford "sleepies"' (quoted in *Biography*, p. 73).

27 October 1914 Tolkien is very active at a meeting of the Stapeldon Society, proposing a vote of censure, reporting a talk he had with the Sub-Rector concerning entertainment, and giving a warning to prospective officers. The Rector and Dr Marett lead a discussion of 'Superman and International Law' to which Tolkien also contributes.

3 November 1914 At a meeting of the Stapeldon Society Tolkien gives the House interesting statistics from a pamphlet entitled *A Bathman's Memoirs*. Three members of the Society, including Tolkien, recount the narrow escapes they have had from a freshman on a cyclometer. In a debate that follows, Tolkien proposes the motion: 'This House approves of spelling reform.' The motion carries, 7 to 6.

5 November 1914 Britain declares war on Turkey.

10 November 1914 At a meeting of the Stapeldon Society Tolkien tells a story, according to the minutes, 'which could not possibly have offended the tender feeling of the House. It also had the merits of being true' (Exeter College archives). In a debate that follows he speaks against the motion: 'This House deprecates an ideal of nationalism.' The motion carries, 12 to 7. – Christopher Wiseman writes to Tolkien, asking him to set aside a few days in the Christmas vacation to stay with him in London, when Gilson and Smith will also be able to come.

11 November 1914 Tolkien again borrows *A Finnish Grammar* by C.N.E. Eliot from the Exeter College library, presumably in conjunction with the essay he will read on 22 November, or with his work on *The Story of Kullervo*.

Before 15 November 1914 Tolkien writes to Wiseman, commenting on the power of the T.C.B.S. to shake the world.

15 November 1914 Wiseman writes to Tolkien, expressing a fear that the members of the T.C.B.S. – some now at Oxford, some at Cambridge – have been growing apart and no longer have the same interests. Nonetheless he does not think that either institution 'can really have destroyed what made you and me the Twin Brethren in the good old school days before there was a T.C.B.S. apart from us and V[incent] T[rought].' He is unhappy, but not judgemental, that Tolkien still has not told his friends the name of his fiancée.

16 November 1914 Tolkien writes an eight-page letter to Wiseman. He has read parts of a letter from Wiseman to Smith, and makes it clear that he too considers the friendship between himself and Wiseman to be 'the great twin brotherhood . . . the vitality and fount of energy from which the T.C.B.S. derived its origin.' He thinks that Wiseman's feeling of growing apart has arisen partly because the four members have not been able to meet without other, less sympathetic people present, but also because he and Wiseman (unlike Gilson and Smith) have always discussed more fundamental matters with each other, and for both of them religion is at once their moving force and their foundation. He suggests that they discuss what unifies them, what is of supreme importance to them, and what are 'allowable' differences. For himself, religion, human love, the duty of patriotism, and a fierce belief in nationalism are of vital importance. He is 'not of course a militarist, and 'more & more [a] convinced Home Ruler' (Tolkien Papers, Bodleian Library, Oxford). Some old college friends may be coming up next weekend, but he does want to see Wiseman, so the latter should come to Oxford when he can. – Also on this date, Wiseman writes again to say that Rob Gilson can attend a T.C.B.S. meeting on 12 December. He thinks that Gilson disagrees with Tolkien about the worldshaking power of the T.C.B.S., a point which should be fought out when they meet on the 12th.

17 November 1914 At a meeting of the Stapeldon Society Tolkien takes part in a debate, on the motion: 'This House disapproves of a system of stringent economy in the present crisis.' The motion carries, 11 to 5. The Society minutes do not record on which side of the issue Tolkien spoke.

22 November 1914 Tolkien reads an essay on the *Kalevala, The Finnish National Epic*, to a meeting of the Sundial Society at Corpus Christi College, in Mr Water's rooms. When he first came upon the *Kalevala*, he said, he 'crossed the gulf between the Indo-European-speaking peoples of Europe into the smaller realm of those who cling in quiet corners to the forgotten tongues and memories of an elder day'. The 'mythological ballads' that comprise the *Kalevala* 'are full of that very primitive undergrowth that the literature of Europe has on the whole been cutting away and reducing for centuries with different and earlier completeness in different peoples' (Tolkien Papers, Bodleian Library, Oxford). *See note.* At the same meeting, G.B. Smith is elected president of the society for the coming term.

24 November 1914 The Stapeldon Society meets.

27 November 1914 Tolkien works in the morning, drills and attends a lecture in the afternoon, has dinner with T.W. Earp (then Secretary of the Exeter College Essay Club), and attends a meeting of the Essay Club in Mr Bedwell's rooms. At the latter the Reverend G.H. Fendick reads a paper on T.E. Brown, reviewing his activities as a schoolmaster and poet; a keen discussion follows. Several members then read poems they themselves have written; Tolkien reads his *Voyage of Éarendel*. Later that evening, Tolkien writes to Edith, describing his day. The Essay Club meeting was 'an informal kind of last gasp' (the Club has been meeting only intermittently, due to the war). He found the Essay Club paper 'bad' but the discussion interesting. 'It was also composition meeting and I read "Earendel" which was well criticised' (*Letters*, p. 8). – Probably inspired by his visit to Cornwall in August, Tolkien begins to rewrite and greatly extend his poem *The Grimness of the Sea* (first composed in 1912).

28 November 1914 R.Q. Gilson joins the Cambridgeshire (11th) Battalion, Suffolk Regiment as a second lieutenant.

?Late 1914 Tolkien writes in his St John Street rooms a long poem concerning Eärendel (now so spelt), in which Eärendel is a mariner who wanders earthly seas, a figure of ancient lore whose tales are bound up with those of the fairies (or Elves, as the poem will be later emended). On the back of one of the earliest workings of the poem is an outline of a great voyage by Eärendel to all points of the compass on earth, but also to 'a golden city' later identified as the Elvish city Kôr, before setting sail in the sky as in *The Voyage of Éarendel* *the Evening Star.* Tolkien's mythology is rapidly developing in his imagination, becoming broad and deep and taking on enduring features. Later he will divide the first part of the long poem, **The Bidding of the Minstrel*, from its second part, to be entitled *The Mermaid's Flute.*

Late 1914 Tolkien begins to create, or continues to work on, his 'nonsense fairy language' (Qenya), as he will later refer to it (letter to Edith Bratt, 2 March 1916, *Letters,* p. 8).

December 1914 Tolkien rewrites his poem *Outside* (first composed in December 1913). – The *Stapeldon Magazine* for December 1914 comments on changes the war has brought to Oxford. Bugles are heard in the morning; many undergraduates wear uniform to lectures; colleges have been partly taken over as barracks; many rooms are empty since their occupants have enlisted; the Parks are full of troops drilling, and there are convalescent soldiers and Belgian refugees in the streets. All who able to do so have joined the Officers Training Corps. Regular or organized games are impossible. 'All other games have been neglected in preparation for the "Greater Game"' (p. 104). – G.B. Smith joins the Oxfordshire and Buckinghamshire Light Infantry.

2 December 1914 The Stapeldon Society meets.

4 December 1914 Tolkien continues to rewrite his poem *The Grimness of the Sea,* now giving it a new title, *The Tides.* He inscribes the current manuscript 'On the Cornish Coast'.

5 December 1914 Michaelmas Full Term ends.

12–13 December 1914 Tolkien attends a T.C.B.S. meeting or 'council' at the Wiseman family home in London. The friends know that they will soon be involved in the war and want to regain their former closeness. They spend much of the weekend sitting around a gas fire, smoking and talking. They all have ambitions in literature, art, or music, and feel that they gain inspiration from each other. Tolkien will later refer to the 'hope and ambitions . . . that first became conscious at the Council of London. That Council was . . . followed in my own case with my finding a voice for all kind of pent up things and a tremendous opening up of everything for me: – I have always laid that to the credit of the inspiration that even a few hours with the four always brought to us' (letter to G.B. Smith, 12 August 1916, *Letters,* p. 10).

16 December 1914 The German navy bombards the English coast, attacking Scarborough, Whitby, and Hartlepool.

21 December 1914 Tolkien writes a poem, *Dark.*

22 December 1914 Tolkien writes a poem, *Ferrum et Sanguis: 1914* (i.e. 'Iron and Blood').

27 December 1914 Tolkien paints in *The Book of Ishness* an elaborate watercolour, *The Land of Pohja (Artist and Illustrator,* fig. 41), inspired by the *Kalevala* story of the magician Väinämöinen whose music entices the Moon to settle in a birch-tree and the Sun in a fir-tree; when the Moon and Sun are captured by Louhi, the evil Mistress of Pohja (or Pohjola), darkness and frost descend on the world. This episode foreshadows, perhaps, Tolkien's pivotal tale in **'The Silmarillion'* of the destruction of the Two Trees, the theft of the

Silmarils, and the Darkening of Valinor. *The Land of Pohja* continues the theme of darkness already expressed by Tolkien in the poems *Dark* and *Ferrum et Sanguis*.

1915

January 1915 Tolkien writes a poem, *As Two Fair Trees*, perhaps to celebrate the anniversary of his reunion with Edith. – He revises his poem *The Tides*, now called *Sea-Chant of an Elder Day*.

17 January 1915 Hilary Full Term begins.

Hilary Term 1915 Tolkien attends the continuation of A.S. Napier's lectures on *Pearl* on Tuesdays at 12.00 noon in the Ashmolean Museum, beginning 26 January, and on *Beowulf* on Thursdays and Saturdays at 12.00 noon in the Ashmolean, beginning 21 January. He also attends Sir Walter Raleigh's lectures on Drama in the Sixteenth and Seventeenth Centuries on Tuesdays and Thursdays at 11.00 a.m. at Magdalen College, beginning 19 January. If he has not done so already in 1914, he now attends W.A. Craigie's lectures on *Hrafnkel's Saga* on Thursdays at 5.00 p.m. in the Taylor Institution, beginning 21 January. He probably continues to have a weekly tutorial with Kenneth Sisam, and probably attends Sisam's lectures on English Poetry before the Norman Conquest on Saturdays at 11.00 a.m. in the Ashmolean, beginning 23 January. He possibly attends lectures by Sir John Rhys on Welsh on Tuesdays and Fridays at 6.00 p.m. at Jesus College, beginning 22 January.

Hilary and Trinity Terms 1915 Tolkien is President of the Junior Common Room.

25 January 1915 At a meeting of the Stapeldon Society a member proposes that a key to the baths at Exeter College should be placed in a glass case to provide for the possibility of Zeppelin raiders (presumably, so that the baths can be used for shelter). Tolkien is among those who oppose the motion, which fails. The members strongly disapprove of the curtailment of baths as a method of economy. Tolkien tells the House that the Bursar believes that half the College is unwashed, and if the baths were closed down the other half might become likewise. The minutes record that 'Class II O.T.C. [Officers Training Corps] in the person of Mr Tolkien then gave Class I and others valuable hints on drilling a boy entitled "Jones best ever ready word of command, always useful, will never wear out, Hip hop!"' (Exeter College archives).

February 1915 Tolkien reads to the Exeter College Essay Club the essay on the *Kalevala* he had earlier read to the Sundial Society (22 November 1914).

1 February 1915 The Stapeldon Society meets.

8 February 1915 Tolkien attends a meeting of the Stapeldon Society. The members discuss the tearing up of troublesome tram lines by the Oxford Town Clerk. They decide that the Secretary should write to applaud his actions, and ask for the gift of a tram rail or even a portion of one.

15 February 1915 The Stapeldon Society meets.

22 February 1915 Tolkien attends a meeting of the Stapeldon Society. The Town Clerk has given them a seven-foot length of tram rail. The minutes of the meeting will read:

On the motion of Mr Tolkien it was carried (a) that it should be present at the last meeting in every term (b) that it should be carried in procession to the new Pres[ident]'s rooms by the first year [i.e. the first-year members] (c) that every Pres[ident]'s name should be engraved upon it. The House then adjourned to the quad and a procession was formed headed by the officers, who were followed by the tram line supported by selected members of the first year followed by the rest of the house in order of precedence, slowly and *steadfastly* round the quad, the first year stentoriously breathing, the rest all singing a mournful dirge alternating with Tipperary [the song 'It's a long way to Tipperary']. When they reached the foot of the staircase enthusiasm grew apace and the line was soon safely deposited under the Pres[ident]'s bed. [Exeter College archives]

March 1915 At a meeting of the Exeter College Essay Club Tolkien reads a further revised version of his poem *Sea-Chant of an Elder Day*; but when sending a typed copy of the work to G.B. Smith during this month, the title becomes *Sea-Song of an Elder Day*. Possibly at the same time, he paints in *The Book of Ishness* a watercolour entitled *Water, Wind & Sand* (*Artist and Illustrator*, fig. 42) and inscribes on the facing page 'Illustration to Sea-Song of an Elder Day'. The small figure enclosed in a white sphere in the foreground of the painting may be the seed from which the 'Silmarillion' frame-story emerged, that the poem was the song that Tuor sang to his son Eärendel in their exile after the fall of Gondolin. – Tolkien writes a poem for Edith, *Sparrow-song (Bilink)* (later simply *Sparrow Song*). The word *bilink* will later occur in a lexicon of his invented language Gnomish, in the form *bilin, bilinc* 'a small bird, esp. sparrow'.

1 March 1915 The Stapeldon Society meets. – Rob Gilson writes to Tolkien, urging him to attend a T.C.B.S. meeting at Cambridge on the weekend of 6–7 March.

2 March 1915 Christopher Wiseman writes to Tolkien, urging him to come to the T.C.B.S. meeting. He is sure that he can get him rooms in college. G.B. Smith is to attend, and if they do not take this opportunity Wiseman does not know when the four will be able to gather together again.

6 March 1915 Tolkien having failed to reply to their letters, Gilson and Wiseman send him a telegram, in jest claiming his resignation from the T.C.B.S. unless he appears at the weekend. – In the event, he does not go to Cambridge.

8 March 1915 Tolkien rewrites his poem *Dark* (first composed in December 1914), now with the alternate title *Copernicus v. Ptolemy* or *Copernicus and Ptolemy*. He shares it with Wiseman and Smith, who will mention it in letters of 15 April and ?25 March respectively. – Tolkien attends a meeting of the Stapeldon Society. He is recorded as making criticisms of the minutes.

?10 (possibly, less likely 17) March 1915 G.B. Smith writes to Tolkien (*see note*) from Magdalen College, Oxford, where he is billeted with the Oxfordshire and Buckinghamshire Light Infantry. Tolkien has sent him either the whole poem concerning Eärendel that he wrote late in 1914, or the first part to which he will later give the title *The Bidding of the Minstrel*. Smith thinks that it is very good, except that it tails off at the end. He asks Tolkien to send him typewritten copies of his poems, which after reading he will send on to Gilson if Tolkien wishes. He is having typed the poem he intends to enter for the annual Newdigate Prize for poetry (established 1806; the set topic in 1915 was 'Glastonbury').

10–11 March 1915 Tolkien writes a poem, *Why the Man in the Moon Came Down Too Soon (An East Anglian Phantasy)*, later prefixed *A Faërie*.

11 March 1915 Wiseman writes to Tolkien, adding comments from Gilson as they reread one of Tolkien's letters. Tolkien seems to have explained that his failure to reply immediately to their letters of 1 and 2 March was due to the fact that he has set a specific day in the week for answering letters. They wonder why Tolkien is so often the one absent from T.C.B.S. meetings, and describe what he missed in Cambridge the previous weekend. Tolkien has evidently suggested a three-day meeting on a weekend early in Trinity Term. Wiseman explains that as his mother is recovering from an operation he does not think that they can meet at his home in London; they might meet instead at a hotel in the Cotswolds. Gilson adds a postscript that in order to obtain leave from the Army he needs to know early to plan his weekend leaves.

13 March 1915 Hilary Full Term ends.

Easter Vacation 1915 Tolkien spends most or possibly all of his vacation in Warwick. He probably adds another watercolour, *Tanaqui*, to *The Book of Ishness*: this seems to depict Kôr, in Tolkien's mythology the shining city of the Elves in Eldamar, about which he will write a poem on 30 April. The painting agrees with the poem, but also shows details such as the slender silver tower of the house of Inwë 'shooting skyward like a needle' which Tolkien will not describe in writing until several years later in *The Book of Lost Tales*.

?15 (possibly, less likely, 22) March 1915 Smith writes to Tolkien. He is very glad to have received Tolkien's typed verses, and comments on *The Sea-Song of an Elder Day*, *Outside*, *As Two Fair Trees*, and *Why the Man in the Moon Came Down Too Soon*.

17–18 March 1915 Tolkien reworks the latter part of the Eärendel poem of ?late 1914 as an independent work entitled *The Mermaid's Flute*. This may be in response to comments made by Smith in his letter of ?10 March.

?Spring 1915 Probably no earlier than spring 1915 Tolkien begins to make a systematic record of his invented language Qenya in a small notebook previously used for notes on Gothic, which he will now continue to use for several years. He will call this *Qenyaqetsa*. Eventually the book will contain a phonology and a lexicon, both heavily worked.

22 March 1915 Gilson writes to Tolkien, explaining that he can get leave only every other week, and cannot keep holding weekends open for a meeting of the T.C.B.S. He asks Tolkien to let him know at once, if possible, which weekends are best for him.

?25 March 1915 Smith writes to Tolkien. He has shown Tolkien's verses to their friend and fellow Oxford poet *H.T. Wade-Gery, who thinks *Why the Man in the Moon Came Down Too Soon* and *As Two Fair Trees* very good, but that *Sea-Chant of an Elder Day* though good in places is too exaggerated. He also approves of *Copernicus and Ptolemy (Dark)*. Smith sends Tolkien the poem he intends to submit for the Newdigate Prize, 'Glastonbury'. He will send Tolkien's poems and his own to Gilson as soon as he can. He cannot arrange a meeting of the T.C.B.S. unless Tolkien comes to Oxford for Easter (Easter Sunday 1915 was on 4 April). He thinks that his battalion will be leaving before 12 April, and he cannot get leave before then.

26 March 1915 (postmark) Wiseman replies to a postcard from Tolkien. He thinks it doubtful that he can attend a T.C.B.S. meeting on 11 or 17 April.

30 March 1915 (postmark) Wiseman, now at Cleeve Hill, Cheltenham, writes to Tolkien, proposing a T.C.B.S. meeting on 18 April in Tolkien's St John Street rooms. He relies on Tolkien to arrange this with his landlady.

31 March 1915 Gilson writes to Tolkien that he has received his poems safely (via Smith) but has not yet read them. Wiseman has told him that a T.C.B.S. meeting on 18 April at Oxford has been settled.

April 1915 Tolkien writes in a notebook, which he dates to this month, notes on *The Owl and the Nightingale*, chiefly about its vocabulary.

?3 April 1915 Smith writes to Tolkien. He is unwell and sick at heart, but finds consolation in Tolkien's letters and his comments on Smith's Newdigate Prize entry. He has now forwarded to Gilson Tolkien's poems, except the '"Earendel" things'. He thinks that Tolkien's verse 'is very apt to get too complicated and twisted and to be most damned difficult to make out'; *The Mermaid's Flute* is rather bad in this respect (Tolkien Papers, Bodleian Library, Oxford). He would like Tolkien to make his verse more lucid without losing its luxuriance, and suggests that he read shorter lyrics by William Blake as an example of the clear and simple. He does not know if he will be in Oxford on 18 April.

4 April 1915 Tolkien writes to Wiseman (letter not seen).

5 April 1915 (postmark) Wiseman again writes to Tolkien, repeating his message of 30 March.

6 April 1915 Tolkien sends a postcard to Wiseman (not seen).

10 April 1915 Tolkien writes to Wiseman, possibly giving news about Smith (letter not seen). Wiseman replies at once that he now received Tolkien's messages of 4, 6, and 10 April. He has advised Smith to ask for leave next week.

12 April 1915 Smith writes to Tolkien from his home in West Bromwich that he is on sick leave, and will not be able to attend the T.C.B.S. meeting on 18 April. He is trying to arrange a transfer into a battalion which Tolkien could also join after his examinations. Before Tolkien receives this letter, he sends a telegram (contents unknown) to Wiseman, who finds it disturbing.

13 April 1915 Wiseman sends a telegram to Tolkien in Warwick, asking what arrangements he has made for their Oxford 'council' as problems have arisen. In a letter written the same day, he explains that Gilson has been ill since 6 April and it will be very difficult for him to get leave the next weekend. If Gilson cannot attend, Wiseman's mother would welcome the smaller group at Cleeve Hill; if Smith also cannot attend, the meeting will not take place.

14 April 1915 Gilson writes to Tolkien from Marston Green, where he has been on sick leave. He will return to his battalion on Friday, 16 April, and there is no possibility of getting leave for the weekend. He believes that Wiseman is now trying to arrange a meeting in Cambridge.

15 April 1915 Wiseman writes to Tolkien. The 'Council of Oxford' must be abandoned. He has received Tolkien's poems via Gilson and has nearly finished a musical setting for *Wood-sunshine*. He asks Tolkien to spend the next weekend with him and his family.

15–16 April 1915 Tolkien writes a poem, *Courage Speaks with the Love of Earth*. The title will be changed to *Courage Speaks with a Child of Earth*, and later to *Now and Ever* and *The Two Riders*.

16 April 1915 Wiseman receives a postcard from Tolkien indicating that the latter will not be able to visit the Wisemans at the weekend.

?19 April 1915 Smith replies to a note from Tolkien. He is soon to join the 8th Oxfordshire and Buckinghamshire regiment at No. 1 Camp, Sutton Veny, Wiltshire. By now, he has applied to transfer to the 19th Battalion of the *Lancashire Fusiliers, but is not yet able to join them at their training camp in Wales. He is not sure if he can get Tolkien a commission in the battalion he hopes to join, but will do his best. Apparently in response to doubts expressed by Tolkien, he gives arguments in favour of Tolkien enlisting as soon as he has taken his degree in June: these include better prospects for choosing a battalion, and Army pay.

20–21 April 1915 Tolkien writes this date on a manuscript of his poem *May Day* (later called *May Day in a Backward Year* and *May-day*).

22 April 1915 Tolkien rewrites his poem *Evening* (first composed in March 1910). Later he will give it a new title, *Completorium*.

25 April 1915 Trinity Full Term begins.

Trinity Term 1915 Tolkien probably attends the conclusion of A.S. Napier's lectures on *Beowulf* on Thursdays and Saturdays at 12.00 noon in the Ashmolean Museum, beginning 1 May, and on *Pearl* on Tuesdays at 12.00 noon in the Ashmolean Museum, beginning 4 May. He possibly attends *H.F.B. Brett-Smith's lectures on Shakespeare on Tuesdays at 11.00 a.m. at Corpus Christi College, beginning 27 April; D. Nichol Smith's lectures on Dryden on Wednesdays and Fridays at 12.00 noon in the Ashmolean Museum, beginning 28 April; and Percy Simpson's lectures on Elizabethan Drama on Mondays at 11.00 a.m. in Oriel College, beginning 26 April. He probably continues to have a weekly tutorial with Kenneth Sisam. Although his final examinations are fast approaching he will find time to write several poems in the early part of the term. – Wiseman writes to Tolkien with comments on his poems, which

Wiseman has discussed with Gilson this afternoon. He says that Smith is enthusiastic about them, while he himself is 'wildly braced.... I can't think where you get all your amazing words from' (Tolkien Papers, Bodleian Library, Oxford). He refers to *Copernicus and Ptolemy, Earendel, Why the Man in the Moon Came Down Too Soon, From Iffley (From the Many-Willow'd Margin of the Immemorial Thames), As Two Fair Trees,* and *Wood-sunshine.* – British, Australian, and New Zealand troops land on the Gallipoli peninsula.

27–28 April 1915 In his rooms at 59 St John Street, Tolkien writes two poems, *You & Me and the Cottage of Lost Play* (**The Little House of Lost Play: Mar Vanwa Tyaliéva*) and **Goblin Feet.* The first, evidently influenced by thoughts of Edith, introduces the 'Cottage of Lost Play' which will be the setting of much of the story-telling in *The Book of Lost Tales. Goblin Feet* seems to have been merely a fairy poem written to please Edith. Later Tolkien will come to dislike it, with its images of tiny fairies (rejected in his mythology), and wish that it could be buried and forgotten, but now he submits it (with *You & Me and the Cottage of Lost Play*) to the annual volume of *Oxford Poetry*, co-edited by T.W. Earp. Of the two poems, only *Goblin Feet* will be chosen for publication.

29–30 April 1915 Tolkien writes a poem, *Tinfang Warble,* only eight lines long. He will later rewrite and lengthen it.

30 April 1915 Tolkien writes the poem *Kôr: In a City Lost and Dead* (**The City of the Gods*). Its 'sable hill' and 'marble temples white' (**The Book of Lost Tales, Part One,* p. 136) agree with the watercolour *Tanaqui* painted during Easter Vacation 1915.

2 May 1915 Tolkien revises his poem *Darkness on the Road* (first composed in November 1911). He also makes a fair copy of his poem *The Mermaid's Flute.*

3 May 1915 Tolkien writes a poem, *Morning Song,* a revision of *Morning* (composed in March 1910). – At about this time he has several of his poems typed by the copying office of William Hunt at 18 Broad Street, Oxford, and the typescripts stapled in a booklet. – The Stapeldon Society meets.

10 May 1915 On one page of *The Book of Ishness* Tolkien paints a watercolour, another view of the Elvish city Kôr (*Artist and Illustrator,* fig. 44). The city is framed by two dying trees from whose branches grow a crescent Moon and a blazing Sun – an early, visual expression of the Two Trees which will become an essential feature in Tolkien's mythology – while in the sky is a single star. On the opposite blank (verso) page of the book Tolkien writes 'The Shores of Faery'. (See further, entry for 8–9 July 1915 and related note.)

?Mid-May 1915 Probably at about the same time, on the next opening in *The Book of Ishness* Tolkien paints a watercolour described on the facing page as 'Illustr[ation]: To "Man in the Moon"' (*Artist and Illustrator,* fig. 45), and underneath this inscription he writes out four lines of the poem he had composed in March: *Why the Man in the Moon Came Down Too Soon.* When he comes to describe the vessel of the Moon in *The Book of Lost Tales* some four years later, he apparently will look back to this picture for inspiration ('Rods there were and perchance they were of ice, and they rose upon it like aëry masts, and sails were caught to them by slender threads', *The Book of Lost Tales, Part One* (1983), p. 192).

?14 May 1915 G.B. Smith writes to Tolkien. He is now in the 19th Battalion of the Lancashire Fusiliers, temporarily at the Grand Hotel, Penmaenmawr, Wales. Needing a Welsh grammar, he asks Tolkien to send his (Smith's) copy if he has it, or to buy him a new one, or to sell him Tolkien's own Welsh grammar. He expects that Tolkien will send him *Georgian Poetry*, and asks Tolkien to show some of Smith's verses to the editor of *Oxford Poetry 1915*.

17 May 1915 Tolkien apparently is absent from a meeting of the Stapeldon Society, since T.W. Earp will be reported as having spoken on his behalf.

22 May 1915 Tolkien attends an eight-course dinner given by a fellow student at Exeter College, E.E. St L. Hill, for friends before the latter joins the 19th Battalion of the Lancashire Fusiliers as a second lieutenant. Tolkien obtains many signatures on his printed menu.

23 May 1915 Italy declares war on Austria-Hungary.

28 May 1915 The Psittakoi, an Oxford student society of which T.W. Earp is President, meets in R.H. Barrow's rooms at Exeter College. Tolkien gives a paper on *The Quest of Beauty and Other Poems* by H.R. Freston. (Freston, *b.* 1891, had been a student at Exeter, probably one or two years senior to Tolkien. *The Quest of Beauty and Other Poems*, the first of his two books of verse, was published by Blackwell in 1915. By April 1915 he had joined the Royal Berkshire Regiment. He was killed in action at La Boiselle on 24 January 1916.)

?29 May (?5 June) 1915 Smith writes to Tolkien. He has been reading *Georgian Poetry* as well as another book Tolkien has sent him, apparently on medieval scripts.

31 May 1915 Zeppelins bomb London for the first time.

?10 June 1915 Smith writes to Tolkien, who has asked advice on being posted to Smith's regiment. Smith suggests that Tolkien write to Colonel Stainforth of the 19th Lancashire Fusiliers, and ask if Stainforth will consider his application for a commission. If he is successful, Smith will do his best to get Tolkien into his hut and company.

> I think it is quite on the cards that I shall be in Birmingham next week, because I have toothache like Satan himself, and must see my dentist. I am strongly in favour of your going to Allports', Cotmore Row for your clothing. They are no dearer and far and away better than anybody out-side London, or perhaps inside it. I have worn these clothes hard and solid ever since I had them, and there are no signs of wearing out. Now you have one uniform, and the most you want is another tunic, a pair of slacks, perhaps a pair of breeches, and perhaps a British Warm. If you can get slacks under 35/- you will be a genius; and breeches are Allports' extra special article. If you could manage to be in Birmingham during the next week we might visit that distinguished emporium together. . . . It is most important to buy only the darkest stuffs for breeches and Warm, because the [Commanding Officer] here hates anything light. . . .

As to Camp Kit. You want a bed, bath & washstand (they can be dispensed with), a sleeping-bag (preferably Jaeger, 35/- also) a blanket or two, and a kit-bag. Avoid a 'valise'. But don't get these until I let you know the best place, as to wh[ich] I will enquire. . . . [Tolkien Papers, Bodleian Library, Oxford]

Smith confirms, apparently in reply to a query, that Tolkien's copy of a book on Keats which he now cannot find was mistakenly included in the parcel of books he sent to Smith.

10 June 1915 Examinations for the Honour School of English Language and Literature at Oxford begin with papers set at 9.30 a.m. and 2.00 p.m. in the Sheldonian Theatre. Each paper lasts three hours. According to the Oxford *Regulations of the Board of Studies* all candidates in the English School are to take papers 1–4, and those specializing in English Language also take papers A5–9, as well as a tenth paper chosen from a list of Special Subjects. On 10 June at 9.30 a.m. Tolkien sits Paper 1: Beowulf and Other Old English Texts. There is no choice of question. The first two questions require translation of extracts, with comments sought on six of the seven extracts in the first question and one of the four extracts in the second question. In addition, there are seven questions on topics such as the historical background of *Beowulf*, metrical types, and Old English grammar. – At 2.00 p.m. Tolkien sits Paper 2: Middle English Authors. There is no choice of question. The first three questions require translation of extracts, with comments sought on two of the five extracts in the first question, one of the six extracts in the second question, and one of the six extracts in the third question. There are also five questions mainly expanding upon the extracts.

11 June 1915 The Examinations continue. At 9.30 a.m. Tolkien sits Paper 3: Chaucer. There are ten miscellaneous questions about Chaucer's poetry and prose, with no restriction on the number to be answered. – At 2.00 p.m. Tolkien sits Paper 4: Shakespeare. There are eleven very miscellaneous questions on Shakespeare's life, times, and writings, with no restriction on the number to be answered. – Smith replies to a letter from Tolkien. He is delighted about 'a notable achievement' (Tolkien Papers, Bodleian Library, Oxford), and asks if they should keep it secret from Gilson and Wiseman until it can be shown to them in concrete form. (His meaning, probably, is that both Tolkien and Smith have poems being considered for publication in *Oxford Poetry 1915*.) He urges Tolkien to write at once to Colonel Stainforth. Smith will be in Birmingham from 16 to 18 June if Tolkien wants to see him.

12 June 1915 The Examinations continue. At 9.30 a.m. Tolkien sits Paper A5: History of English Literature. There are twelve questions, with no limit as to the number to be answered: one each on Old English poetry; Langland and Chaucer; William Caxton as writer and translator; Christopher Marlowe; Milton's *Comus* and *Paradise Lost*; John Dryden; the heroic couplet; the periodical essay; Thomas Gray; Sir Walter Scott as a novelist; and Wordsworth's influence on his contemporaries. – At 2.00 p.m. Tolkien sits Paper A6:

Historical English Grammar. There are seventeen questions, and candidates are asked not to attempt more than ten. While most of the questions are philological, some are about general influences on the development of the English language.

14 June 1915 The Examinations continue. At 9.30 a.m. Tolkien sits Paper A7: Gothic and Germanic Philology. The first question requires the translation of four of six extracts from the Gothic Gospel of St Mark. Candidates are asked to attempt no more than nine of the thirteen questions that follow, all strictly philological. – At 2.00 p.m. Tolkien sits Paper A8: Old English and Middle English Set-Books. (See the list of set texts above, preceding the entry for 20 April 1913.) There is no choice of question. The first three questions require translation of extracts, with comments sought on four of the five extracts in the first question, and on the single extract in the second question. The third question requires the translation of four extracts, to which questions 4–6 are related.

15 June 1915 The Examinations continue. At 9.30 a.m. Tolkien sits Paper A9: Old English and Middle English Unseen Translations. The first question requires the translation of five Old English extracts, and a short note on the class of poetry to which one of the extracts belongs. The second question asks for five Middle English extracts to be turned into Modern English, and for comments on two of them. The third question asks for a comparison of the language of an early Middle English extract with late Old English, and comments on the chief differences. – At 2.00 p.m. Tolkien sits Paper A10: Scandinavian Philology, his Special Subject. There is no choice of question. The first question requires four passages to be translated into English; the second question, three passages with explanatory notes. Ten further questions are mainly philological, but one is on Old Icelandic metre and poetic diction, and another asks the candidate to contrast Icelandic saga-writing of the classical period with Middle English literature of the same date. – At some date after the papers are completed, Tolkien will also have to face a viva (oral examination).

19 June 1915 Trinity Full Term ends.

?20 June 1915 G.B. Smith replies to a letter from Tolkien, who apparently has written to Colonel Stainforth. Tolkien is sure to get through the medical examination. Smith had an excellent time in Birmingham, during which he made enquiries on Tolkien's behalf. He writes further about camp kit:

You will want a bed, bath-and-washstand, sleeping-bag, and at least two blankets or rugs; also a hair (*not* an air) or down pillow, and I rather advise a mattress (cork), and a few other things.

Thus:
Bed
Bath-and-washstand
Sleeping-bag

2 rugs
Down pillow
Mattress
Soap-box
Hooks for tent-pole
Ground-sheet (optional)

To carry these I should get:
1 good sized canvas kit-bag, of the *sack* shape (the others, like a cricket-bag, are nicer but dear).

1 tin box for underclothes, but don't spend too much on it, or get too large an one, as they are allowed only within these islands. Do not get a valise, until you are obliged to. I hate them, and mine cost me the hell of a sum. Also bring a small bag or suit-case.

Add 1 steel shaving mirror (price 1/6). All else seems to me unnecessary. My table and chairs I intend to be soap-boxes bought on the spot, also I mean to bring an honest tin bucket.

Now you might get all this very cheap at the Birmingham Household Supply Assn. in Carpatian Street. I should perhaps get a Jaeger sleeping-bag at Allports, if you want a nice article. Don't forget towels and a Burberry. I think I would get everything as cheap as you can: I mean beds, etc. The B.H.S.A. did me quite well.

I think this is all I need tell you at present. Except to keep perfectly calm, and correspond with me as much as possible. By the way, make Allports get you the same buttons as they got me: they will know which they are. And do be careful not to get bright breeches or a bright British Warm. The breeches I have just ordered from them are light-weight Bedford cord, rather nice I think.

I don't know how you are off for boots. I don't know a good place in B[irming]ham either. I always buy shoes at Day's, and they are good enough, but their boots feed me. I have tried Manfield but don't think much. Maybe you know better than I do. The best pair I have had are a good pair I believe to be K5. I think unless you can find a good make these much-advertised makes are not bad. You don't want more than 2 or at most 3 pairs, and a pair of shoes.

If you want a wrist-watch, I strongly advise Greaves. They are like Allports, of an assured reputation, and prodigious age. My grandfather went there, which always means that they are rather dear and very reliable. I got a very good 40/- silver watch: I shouldn't pay less. You may get a gold one for £3 or so: they are very nice. But I wouldn't worry about luminous things.

Binoculars and prismatic compasses, very dear, may be obtained, unless you decide to wait, which you may quite well do, at Lucking's. Straight-through Lemaire glasses are supposed to be as good as binoculars, and are less expensive.

Get your Sam Browne made with D rings at the back if you can, so as to carry your mackintosh. And get a mackintosh-carrier fitted with swivels, *not* a sling. The shops will know what I mean, if you don't. Get a haversack (a thin and light one) fitted with ditto, to hand on the belt, also a water-bottle; I should get these at the B.H.S.A. also, if possible. The water-bottle is not strictly essential: I've lost mine! The idea is you see to attach all these things to the belt when one goes on marches etc. by swivels: not to have them slung independently over the shoulders. But don't worry if you can't get these in B[irming]ham: just leave it, and don't get any at all. Except of course your Sam Browne, which can be altered afterwards. . . . [Tolkien Papers, Bodleian Library, Oxford]

28 June 1915 Tolkien applies for a temporary commission in the regular Army for the period of the war. He lists his service in the Oxford University Officers Training Corps since October 1914, and in the King Edward's Horse from October 1911 to January 1913. He requests to be posted to the 19th Battalion of the Lancashire Fusiliers, though the form makes it clear that there is no guarantee of appointment to a particular unit. – Smith, now at Brough Hall Camp, Catterick Bridge, near Richmond in Yorkshire, writes to Tolkien. Colonel Stainforth evidently has offered Tolkien a place in his battalion, and Smith urges him to write again to Stainforth, to learn if he wants Tolkien to join the unit at once or wait until gazetted (i.e. until his commission is made official by announcement in *The Times*). He pledges again that he will try to get Tolkien into his company, but doubts that he will succeed. Tolkien can bring a book or two and some paints with him when he enters the Army, as long as they are portable.

29 June 1915 Tolkien has his Army medical examination. He declares that he has never suffered from any serious illness or injury.

30 June 1915 Captain Whatley of the Oxford University Officers Training Corps certifies Tolkien's Army application. Tolkien is accepted and given £50 to buy a uniform and equipment. He has to wait a few days before his commission is gazetted.

July 1915 Tolkien spends time in Warwick and visits his relatives at Moseley and Barnt Green. He probably also visits Father Francis Morgan in Birmingham. – Tolkien writes to Rob Gilson. In the event, he will not receive a reply until September.

2 July 1915 A list of candidates for the *Literis Anglicis* examination, Trinity Term 1915, includes 'Tolkien, Joannes R.R.' under Classis I (First Class). The list is signed by A.S. Napier, *C.H. Firth, D. Nichol Smith, and *H.C. Wyld. An announcement of Tolkien's First Class Honours will appear in the *Times* for 3 July.

4 July 1915 Smith sends congratulations to Tolkien at 57 Emscot Road, Warwick on 'one of the highest distinctions an Englishman can obtain' (Tolkien Papers, Bodleian Library, Oxford).

8–9 July 1915 Tolkien writes (or possibly revises) a poem, *The Shores of Faery*, putting into words the scene he had painted two months earlier in *The Book of Ishness* (see entry for 10 May). It refers to 'the two Trees naked are / That bear Night's silver bloom, / That bear the globed fruit of Noon', and to Eärendel, 'one lone star / That fled before the moon'. The ship of Eärendel (spelled thus) and the Two Trees appear, as well as significant names such as *Taniquetil, Valinor,* and *Eglamar*. Possibly around the same time, certainly not much later, Tolkien writes the poem into *The Book of Ishness,* on the page facing the painting, blank except for the words 'The Shores of Faery'. Probably soon afterward he makes slight changes to the manuscript, then records the poem in emended form in a notebook of fair copies, with the date 'July 8–9 1915'. With the latter manuscript is a prose preface in which Tolkien describes Eärendel as 'the Wanderer who beat about the Oceans of the World' and eventually launched his ship on 'the Oceans of the Firmament' but was hunted by the Moon and fled back to Valinor where he gazed at the Oceans of the World from the towers of Kôr. Tolkien will later inscribe typescripts of the poem 'Moseley & Edgb[aston] July 1915 (walking and on bus). Retouched often since – esp[ecially] 1924' and 'First poem of my mythology Valinor [?thought of about] 1910'. *See note.*

9 July 1915 Tolkien writes a poem, *The Princess Ní*. He will inscribe a later typescript 'Moseley B'ham [Birmingham] Bus between Edgb[aston]. and Moseley July 1915'. – G.B. Smith writes to Tolkien at Abbotsford, Moseley, Birmingham (the home of Tolkien's Aunt Mabel and her husband Tom Mitton), again suggesting that he ask Stainforth what he wants him to do, and giving him more advice about equipment. The War Office will write to him when he is gazetted. He is very pleased that Tolkien got a First at Oxford. He suggests books that Tolkien should bring with him: one on oriental painting; *1914 and Other Poems* by Rupert Brooke, and anything else by Brooke; *Georgian Verse*; Browne's *Religio Medici* and *Urn Burial*; Sir Philip Sidney's *Defence of Poesie*; and Sir Francis Bacon's *Essays*. He should get the earlier books in editions with old spelling. – The War Office writes to Tolkien c/o Father Francis Morgan at the Birmingham Oratory. Tolkien has been appointed a temporary second lieutenant in the New Army and has been posted to the 13th Battalion of the Lancashire Fusiliers, a reserve training unit; but prior to joining his battalion he is to attend a class of instruction at *Bedford, and is to report to a Colonel Tobin at 20 de Parys Avenue, Bedford on 19 July between 2.00 and 4.00 p.m. He is to provide himself with bedding and to join in uniform (if ready). He should apply to his Army agents for his outfit allowance but must pay his own travelling expenses. – When he receives this letter Tolkien is very disappointed that he has not been posted to the same battalion as Smith. He writes to Smith to inform him, and also to Christopher Wiseman, telling him of his posting and that he will be visiting relatives in Moseley and Barnt Green.

11 July 1915 Tolkien drafts and probably sends a letter from Abbotsford to a Mr How at Exeter College. He has to report to Bedford on 19 July so will be unable to receive his degree on 20 July. He will be sending a cheque to cover what he owes for battels and asks what 'caution money' he needs to pay to keep his name on the College's books and eventually receive an M.A. He also asks how he should authorize the transfer of the Junior Common Room bank account to the new President of the JCR when one is elected; uncertainty as to who might be in College next term or whether such an official would be needed had made it impossible for him to settle the matter before he left. – Christopher Wiseman writes to Tolkien. Having seen a notice that the Navy wants mathematicians as instructors, he is now awaiting the formal notice of his appointment from the Admiralty. He asks to see more of Tolkien's poems.

13 July 1915 Smith writes to Tolkien at Abbotsford, Moseley, Birmingham (forwarded on 15 July to Tolkien at the Incledons, Barnt Green). He advises Tolkien to write to the Colonel of the 13th Battalion, and to Colonel Stainforth of the 19th, asking if his posting to the 13th is a mistake.

c. **13–14 July 1915** Wiseman writes to Tolkien. Wiseman and his mother will be staying in Bromsgrove for about a week; he and Tolkien must spend some time together, and his mother insists that Tolkien and Edith join them for tea at Barrow's Stores, possibly on 15 July. He asks if Tolkien can shorten his visit to Moseley and go to Barnt Green earlier, so that they can go walking for a day. He will ring Tolkien the next evening. (There is no evidence that Tolkien and Wiseman were able to meet as Wiseman suggests, though it would have been possible before Tolkien had to leave for Bedford on 19 July.)

13–14 July 1915 Now at Barnt Green, Tolkien writes a poem, *The Trumpets of Faery* (later *The Trumpets of Faerie*), describing a procession of Elves winding its way through woods. He probably also begins to work on the first version of another poem, **The Happy Mariners*, using in part the verso of his draft letter to Mr How written on 11 July.

16 July 1915 The War Office issues Tolkien's commission as a temporary second lieutenant in the Infantry.

17 July 1915 Tolkien's commission is announced in the *Times*' 'London Gazette' column.

18 July 1915 G.B. Smith, who has heard nothing further from Tolkien, writes to him at Abbotsford, Moseley, to cheer him up.

19 July 1915 Tolkien begins Army training at Bedford. He is billeted in a house with other trainee officers. – R.W. Reynolds writes to Tolkien. He comments on poems Tolkien has sent him: *You & Me and the Cottage of Lost Play*, *The Shores of Faery*, *Kôr: In a City Lost and Dead*, and *The Princess Nî* are mentioned. He finds in them echoes of Icelandic sagas, William Morris, Rudyard Kipling, and Walter de la Mare. – Probably after he begins training at Bedford, Tolkien writes a poem, *Thoughts on Parade*.

?23 July 1915 Smith writes to Tolkien, probably in reply to a letter. Tolkien can still try to get a transfer after his training, if both commanding officers agree.

24 July 1915 Tolkien completes the first version of his poem *The Happy Mariners*, which he dates to 24 July. He will inscribe a later version 'Barnt

Green July 1915 and Bedford and later', which suggests that he began the poem when he was at Barnt Green earlier in July and continued to work on it after reporting for duty at Bedford. Elements and imagery of *The Happy Mariners*, such as the white tower in the Twilit Isles that 'glimmers like a spike of lonely pearl' and 'Night's dragon-headed doors' (*Stapeldon Magazine*, June 1920), will come to figure in Tolkien's mythology.

26 July 1915 Wiseman writes to Tolkien, in reply to a card. He suggests that Tolkien and Edith visit the Wisemans in London on some weekend after about 14 August.

August 1915 While still at Bedford Tolkien revises his poem *The Trumpets of Faery*. – After his initial instruction he joins the rest of the 13th Battalion in Lichfield, *Staffordshire. He apparently is billeted in an encampment outside the city. He does not feel much affinity with his fellow officers, or share their taste for ragtime music; nor does he enjoy the constant drilling and lectures. He will later write of 'these grey days wasted in wearily going over, over and over again, the dreary topics, the dull backwaters of the art of killing' (quoted in *Biography*, p. 78). He spends some time reading Old Icelandic so as not to forget his studies. He will recall being in a dirty wet marquee 'crowded with (mostly) depressed and wet creatures ... listening to somebody lecturing on map-reading, or camp-hygiene, or the art of sticking a fellow through ... [when] the man next to me said suddenly in a dreamy voice: "Yes, I think I shall express the accusative case by a prefix!"' (*A Secret Vice*, in *The Monsters and the Critics and Other Essays*, p. 199) – someone else interested in inventing languages. – At some point during his training Tolkien specializes in signalling. By the beginning of 1916 he will study various ways of transmitting messages by flag, heliograph, and lamp, using codes such as Morse code. Also he has to learn how to use signal-rockets and field-telephones, and carrier-pigeons. One of the books he uses in his studies is *Signalling: Morse, Semaphore, Station Work, Despatch Riding, Telephone Cables, Map Reading*, ed. E.J. Solano (1915).

2 August 1915 R.W. Reynolds writes to thank Tolkien for sending him another poem (possibly *The Happy Mariners*). In response to a request from Tolkien he sends advice about publishing a book of poems. In normal times, Reynolds would have advised Tolkien to first publish single poems in magazines, to establish his name; but as 'the odds are against your being able to have the leisure for some time to come to go bombarding editors and publishing verses' (Tolkien Papers, Bodleian Library, Oxford), Tolkien should go ahead with his book, though he should not be disappointed if it fails. Fairy poems, Reynolds thinks, are Tolkien's strong suit. He is not altogether happy with a title Tolkien has proposed for his book. – Tolkien has also consulted Smith on this point, who (in an undated letter) thinks it worthwhile for Tolkien to publish his poems.

4 August 1915 Tolkien rewrites his poem *Thoughts on Parade*, now called *The Swallow and the Traveller on the Plains*.

?Mid–late August 1915 Christopher Wiseman urges Tolkien and Edith to spend one of the next two weekends at the Wiseman home in London. He will try to get Smith to come as well. (There is no evidence that the visit occurred.)

9 September 1915 Tolkien rewrites *The Happy Mariners*, now linked explicitly with Eärendel.

12 September 1915 Tolkien writes a poem, *A Song of Aryador*, while at Whittington Heath camp near Lichfield. Later, in *The Book of Lost Tales*, it will be said that when Men entered Hisilómë which they called *Aryador*, some of the Elves who were lost on the march to Valinor still dwelt there and were feared by Men who called them the Shadow Folk.

13 September 1915 After a long silence Rob Gilson, temporarily in the 3rd Durham Temporary Hospital, Sunderland, writes to Tolkien at Exeter College, forwarded to Whittington Heath. He is annoyed that he has not taken up Tolkien's invitation to criticize his poems, as he feels that one of the best things the T.C.B.S. can do at present is to help its members with their creative work.

14 September 1915 At Whittington Heath, Tolkien writes a poem, *Dark Are the Clouds about the North*.

17 September 1915 Gilson writes from the 3rd Durham Temporary Hospital, Sunderland, to Tolkien at Whittington Heath. He has received a number of T.C.B.S. letters in the past few days, including one from Tolkien enclosing some of his poems. Gilson is about to be released from hospital and will have a week of sick leave at Marston Green; if Tolkien cannot visit him there, Gilson will travel to Lichfield.

19 September 1915 R.W. Reynolds writes to Tolkien at Whittington Heath and thanks him for sending his poems. He likes all of them, though he makes some criticisms. He wonders if Tolkien has thought of a new title for his book.

Autumn 1915 Tolkien and a fellow officer buy a motor cycle. Tolkien will use it to visit Edith and friends when he has leave.

21 September 1915 Gilson writes from Marston Green to Tolkien at Whittington Heath. He has sent telegrams to Wiseman and Smith asking them to come to Lichfield on Saturday (25 September) if possible.

23 September 1915 Wiseman, now at the Royal Naval College, Greenwich, writes to Tolkien at Whittington Heath. He intends to be present at the 'Council of Lichfield' on 25–26 September. – Gilson, who has heard from Smith, writes to Tolkien that all four T.C.B.S. members can be in Lichfield on 25 September, and asks if Tolkien can find three beds there for the night. He suggests that they have lunch the following day at the Gilsons' home at Marston Green and a quiet afternoon in the garden.

24 September 1915 Gilson informs Tolkien by telegram that he and Smith will arrive in Lichfield at 10.34 am on the 25th and make the George Hotel their headquarters.

25 September 1915 At 11.00 a.m. Gilson and Smith write to Tolkien from the George Hotel, Lichfield. They hope to meet him at the hotel when they return from sightseeing just before 1.00 p.m., if not sooner.

25–26 September 1915 The T.C.B.S. 'Council of Lichfield'. This is the last time that Tolkien, Gilson, Smith, and Wiseman meet together before being separated by war, and apparently the last time that Tolkien sees Gilson.

5 October 1915 Gilson, now with his battalion at No. 2 Camp, Sutton Veny, writes to Tolkien. He and Smith have decided that Tolkien should send his book of poems to the publisher Sidgwick & Jackson. Tolkien should not forget the proposed 'Council of Bath', and should try to keep both 16 and 23 October as possible dates.

6 October 1915 Smith writes to Tolkien from the York House Hotel, Bath. Smith and Gilson are making a preliminary excursion to Bath and have practically engaged inexpensive rooms in the South Parade for a T.C.B.S. 'council' on 23 October.

9 October 1915 Smith writes to Tolkien that he is sorry he has not had time to reply to Tolkien's impressive postcard. He recommends that Tolkien send his poems to the publisher Hodder and Stoughton, or to Sidgwick & Jackson, and asks for copies of Tolkien's later poems so that he can show them to H.T. Wade-Gery.

19 October 1915 Smith, now at No. 6 Camp, Codford St Mary, Wiltshire, writes to Tolkien. Tolkien should let him know as soon as possible if he is coming to Bath, and inform Gilson by telegram so that he can book rooms. – Gilson writes from No. 3 Camp, Sutton Veny, to Tolkien at Brocton Camp, *Staffordshire, forwarded to him at Penkridge, Rugeley (i.e. Rugeley Camp on Cannock Chase). *See note.* Gilson is likely to be sent to the front very soon, and if at all possible would like the T.C.B.S. to meet the next weekend.

24 October 1915 Smith writes to Tolkien at Whittington Heath from the Wisemans' house in London. He has heard from Tolkien that he cannot join them for the weekend. Tolkien seems to have been depressed about various matters, one of which is that Edith is ill. Smith thanks Tolkien for sending more poems and is particularly impressed with *The Happy Mariners* and *Dark Are the Clouds about the North*. Smith and Gilson have not gone to Bath, but on impulse have joined Wiseman in London. There they have reaffirmed the principles of the T.C.B.S. and have decided 'once again on the work it will have to do after the war is over: to drive from life, letters, the stage and society that dabbling in and hankering after the unpleasant sides and incidents in life and nature which have captured the larger and worser tastes in Oxford, London and the world: ... to reestablish sanity, cleanliness, and the love of real and true beauty in everybody's breast' (Tolkien Papers, Bodleian Library, Oxford).

27 October 1915 Wiseman writes to Tolkien, giving an account of the previous weekend.

31 October 1915 Gilson writes to Tolkien at Whittington Heath, giving his account of the weekend 23–24 October. He was very sorry that Tolkien could not come; he feels that the T.C.B.S. is not complete unless all four are present.

November 1915 Tolkien moves with the 13th Battalion to Rugeley Camp in Staffordshire. – G.B. Smith goes to France with the 19th Lancashire Fusiliers.

November 1915–early 1916 While stationed at Cannock Chase Tolkien takes the opportunity to visit Phoenix Farm, Gedling. Colin Brookes-Smith will later recall that Tolkien arrived on an AJS motor cycle, and one morning allowed Colin to ride it up the road and back. Probably during this period Tolkien also participates in the cutting up of a poached deer, an event to which he will later refer during lectures on *Sir Gawain and the Green Knight* at Oxford. *See note.*

?21–28 November 1915 Tolkien writes a poem, *Kortirion among the Trees* (**The Trees of Kortirion*); one of its earliest copies will be inscribed 'dedicated to Warwick'. A fair copy will be dated 'Nov. 21–28', and a later typescript inscribed 'Warwick, a week's leave from camp – written largely in a house in Victoria Street [where Edith and Jennie Grove live] and in [mine?] in Northgate St.' In fact Tolkien is in camp on 25 and 26 November, from which he writes on each date to Edith (see below), and in the second letter says that he has 'written out a pencil copy of "Kortirion"' (*Letters*, p. 8). This suggests that Edith knows about the work already, that Tolkien may have begun the poem during a visit to Warwick and continued to work on it when he returned to camp, and that after writing out the pencil copy on 26 November he made further alterations (27–28 November) before making the dated fair copy. – To a fair copy of the poem Tolkien will append a prose introduction which explains that Kortirion was a city of the fairies (later Elves) in the Lonely Isle 'after the great wars with Melko and the ruin of Gondolin', built 'in memory of their ancient dwelling of Kôr in Valinor' (*The Book of Lost Tales, Part One*, p. 25). It is clear that he intends Warwick to be the site where earlier had stood Kortirion, whose memory still lingers, and his mythology to be particularly connected with England (the 'Lonely Isle'). Although the date of this prose introduction is uncertain, its sentimental yet hopeful tone, so like that of the poem, suggests that both were written at roughly the same time. If that is so, several very notable elements have been added by Tolkien to his rapidly growing mythology. On one early copy he gives the poem a subsidiary (but not entirely legible) title in Qenya, *Narqelion la . . tu y aldalin Kortirionwen*, 'Autumn (among) the Trees of Kortirion'. On one of the surviving working sheets he drafts four lines of a poem in Qenya on a similar theme (**Narqelion*). By now, Tolkien has developed his invented language to the extent that he is able to use it in composition.

21 November 1915 Gilson writes to Tolkien that the last he has heard from him is a letter Smith showed him in London. He hopes that Tolkien is no longer depressed and that Edith is now better.

25 November 1915 Tolkien writes to Edith from Rugeley Camp.

26 November 1915 Tolkien writes to Edith from Rugeley Camp, giving an account of his day:

The usual kind of morning standing about and freezing and then trotting to get warmer so as to freeze again. We ended up by an hour's bombthrowing with dummies. Lunch and a freezing afternoon. All the hot days of summer we doubled about at full speed and perspiration, and now we stand in icy groups being talked at! Tea and another scramble – I fought for a place at the stove and made a piece of toast on the end of a knife: what days! [*Letters*, p. 8]

He has written out a pencil copy of *Kortirion among the Trees*; he first intends to send it to the T.C.B.S. as he owes them all letters, then decides that he will send it to Edith and make another copy for the T.C.B.S.

28 November–4 December 1915 Tolkien writes a poem, *The Pool of the Dead Year (and the Passing of Autumn)*.

December 1915 Tolkien moves with the 13th Battalion to Brocton Camp on Cannock Chase.

1 December 1915 Tolkien's poem *Goblin Feet* is published in *Oxford Poetry 1915*. The volume also includes 'Songs on the Downs' by G.B. Smith and three poems by H.T. Wade-Gery.

2 December 1915 Smith, now in the trenches in France, writes to Tolkien in care of the 13th Lancashire Fusiliers, 3rd Reserve Brigade, Officers Company, Brocton Camp. He asks for the long letter Tolkien promised in his last postcard that he would send.

20 December 1915–9 January 1916 British and allied troops evacuate Gallipoli.

22 December 1915 Smith writes to Tolkien, thanking him for various letters and commenting on *Oxford Poetry 1915* and *Goblin Feet*. Smith and Wade-Gery agree that they and Tolkien are the best contributors to the volume.

26 December 1915 Gilson writes to Tolkien in care of the 3rd Reserve Brigade, Officers Company, P Lines, Brocton Camp. Tolkien has written to him about some problems, as Gilson remarks on 'the extra blackness of your fate in these dark days' (Tolkien Papers, Bodleian Library, Oxford). He has just forwarded *Kortirion among the Trees* to Wiseman, and has made a copy for Smith. He likes the poem very much though he makes one or two criticisms.

30 December 1915 Wiseman writes to Tolkien at Brocton Camp. He has been posted to the *HMS Superb*. He has received *Kortirion among the Trees* from Gilson, and will write about it later.

1916

1916 Tolkien paints a watercolour, *The Day after the Day after Tomorrow*. On the verso of the sheet is another picture, *Wrenching a Slow Reluctant Truth*, presumably done at same time.

?January–February 1916 Tolkien writes *Over Old Hills and Far Away*, another 'fairy' poem about the piper Tinfang Warble. The manuscript has an apparently contemporaneous note, 'Jan[uary]–Feb[ruary] 1916'. A later typescript of the poem will be inscribed 'Brocton Camp, Christ[mas]–Jan[uary] 1915–16'.

7 January 1916 Gilson writes to inform Tolkien that he is leaving for the front on 8 January.

12 January 1916 Smith writes to Tolkien at Brocton Camp, full of praise for *Kortirion among the Trees*: 'it is a great and a noble poem' (Tolkien Papers, Bodleian Library, Oxford). He finds life dreary and thinks he is not a success in the Army. He wishes it were possible to hold another T.C.B.S. Council.

19 January 1916 Dora Owen, who has seen *Goblin Feet* in *Oxford Poetry 1915*, writes to ask Tolkien if she may include it in a collection of fairy poetry she is compiling for publication by Longmans (*The Book of Fairy Poetry*, 1920). On receiving the letter Tolkien will send her several of his poems to read and consider.

c. 26 January–22 March 1916 Knowing that he will soon be ordered to the front, Tolkien and Edith set the date for their wedding. Tolkien informs his T.C.B.S. friends (his pertinent letter to Gilson is dated 26 January) and sets his affairs in order to provide for Edith in case the worst happens. He sells his share in the motor cycle, and goes to Birmingham to arrange with Father Francis Morgan the transfer of his modest inheritance into his own name. He intends to tell Father Francis of his forthcoming marriage, but recalling the latter's past disapproval he finds it impossible to raise the subject. The wedding is arranged to take place in Warwick on 22 March despite the fact that it will be Lent and therefore the marriage service cannot be followed by a nuptial Mass. Tolkien and Edith may have chosen this date because they feared that his departure was imminent, or Tolkien may have chosen it to combine his return to Oxford for his degree ceremony, his wedding, and his honeymoon into one period of leave. He does eventually manage to write of his plans to Father Francis, who replies wishing Tolkien and Edith 'every blessing and happiness' (quoted in *Biography*, p. 78) and saying that he would like to conduct the ceremony himself in the Oratory Church, Birmingham; but it is too late to change the arrangements.

2 February 1916 Dora Owen writes to Tolkien to say how much she has enjoyed his poems. She mentions especially *The Trumpets of Faerie, The Princess Nî, A Song of Aryador, Sea-Song of an Elder Day, The Shores of Faery, You & Me and the Cottage of Lost Play*, and *Outside*. She praises them for 'a certain haunting quality in their music' and feels that he ought to get them published; she suggests that he send them to Sidgwick & Jackson, or Elkin Matthews, or John Lane. She suggests placing *The Trumpets of Faerie* first.

3 February 1916 Smith writes to Tolkien at M Lines, Brocton Camp, thanking him for a letter. Tolkien probably mentioned a training course, as Smith says that he too has returned to his regiment after time spent on instruction. He encourages Tolkien to try to get his poems published, to write to Sidgwick & Jackson or anyone else. He greatly admires Tolkien's work,

and my chief consolation is, that if I am scuppered to-night . . . there will still be left a member of the great T.C.B.S. to voice what I dreamed and what we all agreed upon. For the death of one of its members cannot,

I am determined, dissolve the T.C.B.S. Death is so close to us now that I feel – and I am sure you feel, and all the three other heroes feel, how impuissant it is. Death can make us loathsome and helpless as individuals, but it cannot put an end to the immortal four!

He urges Tolkien to publish, as 'you I am sure are chosen. . . . Make haste, before you come out to this orgy of death and cruelty' (quoted in *Biography*, p. 86).

4 February 1916 Wiseman writes to Tolkien, praising *Kortirion among the Trees* which he returns.

9 February 1916 Smith writes to Tolkien at Brocton Camp about what friendship with the other T.C.B.S. members means to him, and probably in response to Tolkien expressing worry that he is taking up too much of the time of the T.C.B.S. with his poetry. Smith says that they believe in his work and feel that in some way they contribute. He has had a letter in which Tolkien told him that he and Edith are getting married and that he has sent his poems to Sidgwick & Jackson. – The Military Service Act introduces conscription for unmarried men between 18 and 41.

22 February 1916 Smith writes to Tolkien at M Lines, Brocton Camp, urging him to send *Kortirion among the Trees* to a publisher. He has mentioned it to R.W. Reynolds and asks Tolkien to send him a copy if he has not already done so.

March 1916 Tolkien completes his Qenya poem *Narqelion*, inspired by *Kortirion among the Trees*. It is a song to autumn with passing references to Eldamar and the Gnomes (a kindred of the Elves in Tolkien's mythology, later the Noldoli or Noldor).

1 March 1916 Wiseman writes to Tolkien at Brocton Camp, in reply to a letter telling Wiseman of the forthcoming wedding and perhaps also rebutting one of Wiseman's comments on *Kortirion among the Trees*. Wiseman defends his views, and says that while Tolkien is fascinated by night and stars and 'little, delicate, beautiful creations', he is 'more thrilled by enormous, slow-moving, omnipotent things' and scientific discoveries, 'the wonderful secrets that man is continually digging out . . . of the great sun, the great stars, the amazing greatness of mountains' (Tolkien Papers, Bodleian Library, Oxford).

2 March 1916 Tolkien writes to Edith. He has spent a miserable wet afternoon re-reading old military lecture-notes 'and getting bored with them after an hour and a half. I have done some touches to my nonsense fairy language [Qenya] – to its improvement. I often long to work at it and don't let myself 'cause though I love it so it does seem such a mad hobby!' (*Letters*, p. 8).

4 March 1916 Smith sends Tolkien part of his long poem 'The Burial of Sophocles'.

5 March 1916 (postmark) Smith writes to Tolkien at M Lines, Brocton Camp, sending the whole of a poem (presumably the last section of 'The Burial of Sophocles'). He asks Tolkien to read it and then post it in the addressed envelope to a place of safe keeping unless he wants to keep it himself. He mentions that he has just received a long letter from Tolkien.

9 March 1916 Gilson writes to Tolkien at M Lines, Brocton Camp, sending him his good wishes, prayers, and blessings for his approaching marriage.

10 March 1916 R.W. Reynolds writes to Tolkien, thanking him for a letter and for the poem *Kortirion among the Trees* which he likes. He asks to see more poems.

14, 17, 26 March and 16 April 1916 Wiseman sends to Tolkien at Brocton Camp, forwarded to the School of Signalling, a long letter written in stages. He writes at great length about the T.C.B.S. and his present hopes, and reminisces about the past. He defends his position concerning *Kortirion among the Trees*, feeling that Tolkien has not grasped what he was trying to express, and notes differences in their tastes. He, Gilson, and Smith have been corresponding about what to give Tolkien and Edith as a wedding present, but have decided to ask them what they want. He would like to hear about the wedding. Tolkien has written to him that 'the Eldar, the Solosimpe, the Noldoli [different kindreds of Elves in his mythology] are better, warmer, fairer to the heart than the mathematics of the tide, or the vortices that are the winds . . .' (Tolkien Papers, Bodleian Library, Oxford).

16–18 March 1916 Tolkien writes, or continues to write, a poem, originally called *The Wanderer's Allegiance*, concerning Warwick and Oxford (**The Town of Dreams and the City of Present Sorrow*). Subsequently this is divided into three parts in a manuscript dated 'March 16–17–18 1916' with subtitles 'Prelude', 'The Inland City', and 'The Sorrowful City'. A later manuscript will be inscribed in part 'March 1916, Oxford and Warwick'.

16 March 1916 Tolkien attends his delayed degree ceremony in Oxford.

22 March 1916 Tolkien and Edith are married by Father Murphy after early Mass, in the Church of St Mary the Immaculate in Warwick. After the ceremony they travel by train to *Clevedon in Somerset for a week's honeymoon; while in the train they doodle on the back of a greetings telegram versions of Edith's new name. During their honeymoon they visit the *Cheddar Gorge and Caves which make a great impression on Tolkien.

31 March 1916 Sidgwick & Jackson rejects the volume of poems, *The Trumpets of Faerie*, that Tolkien had submitted for publication.

April 1916 Edith gives up the house in Warwick she had been renting with Jennie Grove. Tolkien finds lodgings for them in the Staffordshire village of *Great Haywood, which is near his camp and has a Catholic Church. The priest, Father Augustine Emery, welcomes Edith and gives the couple a special nuptial blessing at Sunday Mass.

6 April 1916 Smith writes to Tolkien at M Lines, Brocton Camp. He says that it is a long time since he has heard from Tolkien. He mentions, but cannot yet recommend, a literary agent to whom he has sent some of his poems, the Authors' Alliance in London.

Mid-April–mid-May 1916 Tolkien takes a course of instruction at the Northern Command and Ripon Training Centre Signalling School, Farnley Park, *Otley, Yorkshire.

28 April 1916 Acting Captain L.K. Sands, the fellow King Edward's School student with whom Tolkien travelled to Oxford in October 1911, dies of machine-gun wounds received the previous day in France.

8 May 1916 Tolkien applies to the Adjutant, 13th Battalion, for leave from 13 to 17 May on completion of his signalling course. If leave is granted, his address will be 26 Hamilton Terrace, Leamington.

10 May 1916 A.S. Napier dies.

11 May 1916 The Adjutant, 13th Battalion, replies to Tolkien that no leave is being granted, but then strikes this order and grants him leave until the first train on 15 May.

13 May 1916 Tolkien's '(Provisional) Instructor's Certificate of Signalling (For Officers)' is so dated, and signed by the Commandant at Farnley Park. This certifies that Tolkien has qualified, and states that he has obtained 95% accuracy in Written Examination, Examination in Telephony etc. (Oral and Practical), and Knowledge of Map Reading; and speeds for disc of 4 words per minute, for lamp of 6 words per minute, for buzzer of 10 words per minute, and for semaphore of 8 words per minute. – Tolkien presumably now takes his leave, returning to camp on 15 May.

23 May 1916 Smith sends Tolkien at Brocton Camp a telegram from West Bromwich saying that he is on leave until 29 May and asking if they can meet.

24 May 1916 Smith, presumably having received a reply from Tolkien, sends another telegram saying that he proposes to come to Great Haywood on Saturday afternoon and will stay one night.

26 May 1916 Smith sends a telegram to Tolkien c/o Mrs Kendrick (Edith's landlady) in Great Haywood, giving the arrival time of his train.

27–28 May 1916 Smith visits the Tolkiens in Great Haywood. In a later letter he mentions having met both Edith and Jennie Grove.

?End of May 1916 Smith writes to thank Tolkien for a 'splendid two days' (Tolkien Papers, Bodleian Library, Oxford).

2 June 1916 Army Headquarters, Cannock Chase, informs Tolkien by telegram that he is to join the British Expeditionary Force in France, but first will report to the Embarkation Staff Officer at Folkestone on 5 June. He is granted 48 hours leave.

3 June 1916 Tolkien and Edith spend the night at the Plough and Harrow Hotel in Hagley Road, Edgbaston.

4 June 1916 In the afternoon, Tolkien and Edith say farewell. He goes to London by train.

5 June 1916 Tolkien takes the 11.05 a.m. train from Charing Cross Station to arrive at Folkestone at 1.00 p.m. There he reports to the Embarkation Staff Officer and spends the night.

6 June 1916 Tolkien crosses the English Channel to Calais and travels to camp No. 32 at Étaples. Equipment he had bought – including a camp bed, sleeping bag, mattress, and spare boots – having failed to arrive, he begs, borrows, or buys replacements. – Possibly on this date he writes or begins to write a poem expressing his feelings for the land he has left, ending with 'O lonely, sparkling isle, farewell.' The earliest, undated version has the Qenya title *Tol Eressëa*, but later the poem will be called *The Lonely Isle* (a literal translation from the Qenya) and will bear the dedication 'For England'. Tolkien's mythology is now closely tied to England, and the reference in the poem to a 'fair citadel' is to both Warwick and Kortirion. – On or after this date Tolkien probably also writes the poem *Habbanan beneath the Stars*. He will later note on a revised manuscript of the work 'Insp[ired] Brocton [Camp] Dec[ember] [19]15, written Étaples June 1916'.

7 June 1916 Tolkien moves to camp No. 25 at Étaples. There newly arrived soldiers are given final training and toughening up before being sent to the front. *See note.* Tolkien dislikes the hardened professional officers above him, who treat him like a schoolboy, but he will come to respect the ordinary enlisted men. Although as an officer he cannot make friends among them, he appreciates their qualities and will have closer contact with those who serve as his batman. He will soon be assigned from the reserve 13th Battalion to the active 11th Battalion, part of the 74th Infantry Brigade of the 25th Division of the British Expeditionary Force.

June–October 1916 It is now difficult for Tolkien to find the time or suitable conditions to write at length. But he manages to write or revise some poems, and he can develop his stories in his mind and continue to connect their strands so that when eventually he does have leisure to write them down, his stories are almost fully formed. He will later say in an interview that one could not write in the trenches: 'You might scribble something on the back of an envelope and shove it in your back pocket but that's all. You couldn't write. You'd be crouching down among fleas and filth' (Philip Norman, 'The Hobbit Man', *Sunday Times Magazine*, 15 January 1967, p. 36). But he will also say to his son Christopher in 1944: 'Lots of the early parts of [the mythology] (and the languages) – discarded or absorbed – were done in grimy canteens, at lectures in cold fogs, in huts full of blasphemy and smut, or by candle-light in bell-tents, even some down in dugouts under shell fire' (*Letters*, p. 78). By now he may have already begun to use a small notebook to jot down ideas, brief notes, and single sentences and names. – Since 5 June he has kept a concise diary, recording where he sleeps each night and when, in the coming months, he sees G.B. Smith: for this he uses a small, thin notebook, inscribed after Smith's death 'Diary of brief time in France and of the last seven times I saw G.B.S.' The entries are marked with two symbols which may mark when Tolkien is able to attend Mass, and perhaps when he makes confession. *See note.* – He sends frequent letters to Edith, but as these are read by the censor Tolkien cannot say too much. He and Edith, however, have devised a secret code of dots which enables her to know roughly where he is.

?18 (possibly 11) June 1916 Smith, having returned to France, writes to Tolkien 'attached 11th [Battalion] Lancashire Fusiliers, 25th I.B.D., 25 A.P.O. (S) 17,

B.E.F.' (Tolkien Papers, Bodleian Library, Oxford). He is sorry that Tolkien's summer at Great Haywood had been cut short, and also that Tolkien has not been assigned to the same battalion as Smith.

22 June 1916 Gilson replies to a letter from Tolkien received the previous day on Gilson's return from a night working party. He is cheered to receive letters from the T.C.B.S. (This seems to be Gilson's final letter to Tolkien.)

25 June 1916 Smith writes to Tolkien, wishing him the very best of luck 'in all that may happen to you within the next few months, and may we live beyond them to a better time' (Tolkien Papers, Bodleian Library, Oxford).

27–28 June 1916 Tolkien with other reinforcements travels to join his battalion at the front. After a slow train journey via Abbeville, having taken twenty-four hours to reach Amiens, he marches to the hamlet of Rubempré ten miles away. Gunfire can be heard in the distance.

28 June 1916 The war diary of the 11th Battalion, Lancashire Fusiliers notes the arrival of Second Lieutenant J.R.R. Tolkien.

29–30 June 1916 The 11th Battalion, as usual when not in the trenches, spends much of the day drilling and at bayonet practice, but Tolkien as an officer trained for signal duties will also spend time in specialist training.

30 June–1 July 1916 On 30 June, departing at 9.15 p.m., the battalion marches to billets in the village of Warloy-Baillon, arriving at about 1.00 a.m. on 1 July.

1 July 1916 The lengthy Battle of the Somme begins: the Allies aim to overcome strong German defences in the Somme River valley in north-west France. Prior to the battle (actually a series of sub-battles), British and French artillery have heavily bombarded German positions in preparation for a grand infantry assault. But when Allied troops climb out of their trenches at 7.30 a.m. this day and go 'over the top' they find that barbed wire has not been cut as expected, that the strongly built German defences have survived the shelling, and that the enemy is ready with deadly cross-fire. On the first day of the Somme the British casualties alone are 19,240 killed, 35,493 wounded, and 2,152 missing. Tolkien and the 11th Lancashire Fusiliers are in reserve, but he hears the thunder of the artillery and no doubt sees dead and wounded brought back behind the lines. – Among those killed in action this day is Lieutenant R.Q. Gilson, with the 11th Suffolks near La Boiselle.

2 July 1916 The 11th Battalion waits in readiness. – At 9.30 a.m. Tolkien attends Mass in a field at Warloy-Baillon.

3–5 July 1916 At 8.30 p.m. on 3 July the 11th Battalion parades and marches to Bouzincourt with the rest of the 74th Infantry Brigade, reaching it at midnight. Captain Lionel Ferguson of the 13th Cheshires, who followed the same route on this day, will write in his diary: 'We left Warloy at dusk, meeting a very tired Highland Division coming out of the show. It was a sight new to me to see really tired men, they were just walking along in twos and threes, holding each other up for support, unshaved, covered with mud, and war worn, in fact never have I seen troops in worse condition' (quoted in Malcolm Brown, *The Imperial War Museum Book of the Somme* (1996; reissued 2002), p. 118).

Tolkien is able to sleep in a hut for the rest of that night and the two following nights. The 11th Battalion remains in reserve at Bouzincourt until 6 July and is kept occupied with drilling, training, and inspections.

?3–8 July 1916 During this period Tolkien writes two poems, *A Dream of Coming Home* and *A Memory of July in England*. The earliest manuscript of the first, dedicated 'To my wife', is dated 'Bouzincourt July 4–8 1916' and refers to 'a vision of Great Haywood in May'. A later inscription on another manuscript assigns it to 'Bouzincourt during the British barrage July 3 (?) 1916'. The manuscript of *A Memory of July in England* is dated 'Bouzincourt July 7–8 1916'.

6 July 1916 At 1.00 p.m. A and C companies of the 11th Battalion parade and move to Usna Hill, arriving at about 4.00 p.m. At 11.00 p.m. they proceed to the trenches at La Boiselle. Two companies, including Tolkien, remain with the brigade at Bouzincourt to act as carrying parties for rations and ammunition. He re-reads 'Edith's letters with news from home and glance[s] once again at his collection of notes from the other members of the T.C.B.S.' (Humphrey Carpenter, *Biography*, p. 83).

6–8 July 1916 G.B. Smith arrives in Bouzincourt on 6 July. When free from duties he and Tolkien meet on 6, 7, and 8 July, before Smith returns to the front. They talk as often as they can, 'discussing poetry, the war, and the future. Once they walked in a field where poppies still waved in the wind despite the battle that was turning the countryside into a featureless desert of mud' (*Biography*, p. 83).

7 July 1916 Companies A and C relieve the 2nd Battalion, Royal Irish Rifles in the trenches at 1.00 a.m., and are later sent over the top to help consolidate a position in some newly-captured German trenches near Ovillers. Enemy defensive fire is constant, and losses are heavy. In the afternoon, A Company is pulled back.

8–10 July 1916 C Company of the 11th Battalion overshoots the German trench that is its objective and finds itself in an exposed position. Although carrying parties from B and D Companies bring them supplies of wire and tools and help with the work during the night of 8–9 July, their position remains too exposed, and at 3.00 p.m. on 9 July they withdraw to the front line trenches held by A Company, having suffered heavy casualties. A and C Companies are relieved during the night of 9–10 July. Tolkien writes in his diary: 'Battalion went into action between Ovillers and La Boiselle on Thursday [6th], coming out on Sunday night [9th] – I was in "B" team remained in Bouzincourt' (Tolkien Papers, Bodleian Library, Oxford). *See note.*

10–13 July 1916 A and C Companies arrive at Bouzincourt at 7.00 a.m. on 10 July. At 4.00 p.m. the whole battalion parades and marches to Senlis-le-Sec, arriving about 6.00 p.m. There, over the next few days, it will be re-equipped and reorganized to fill gaps after the losses of 7–10 July: these include 2 officers and 10 other ranks killed, 3 officers and 112 other ranks wounded, 1 officer and 43 other ranks missing. On 12 July, after company training, the battalion marches at 10.00 a.m. to Albert to make room for the 9th Loyal North Lancashires, but are then recalled to Senlis-le-Sec.

12 July 1916 Smith sends Tolkien a field postcard on which he has ticked 'I am quite well'.

14 July 1916 The 11th Battalion parades at 10.20 a.m. and moves to Usna Hill, where it bivouacks from 1.00 p.m. At 8.20 p.m. it proceeds to the front line trenches at La Boiselle. The men have to stumble through the long communications trenches to reach the front line, passing corpses 'horribly torn by the shells. Those that still had faces stared with dreadful eyes' (*Biography*, p. 83). Tolkien will find the communications system in chaos, and that many of the systems in which he has been carefully trained cannot be used since the Germans have succeeded in tapping field telephones, Morse code buzzers might be heard by the enemy, and visual signals might be seen by the Germans on higher ground. An attack by the 7th Infantry Brigade at 11.00 p.m. fails.

15 July 1916 A and B Companies of the 11th Lancashire Fusiliers take part in a second attack, going over the top at 2.00 a.m. 'No Man's Land' between the opposing lines is now a sea of mud marked by barriers of barbed wire and scattered with bloated, decaying bodies it has been too dangerous to recover. The Lancashire Fusiliers suffer heavy losses from machine-gun fire and have to withdraw to the front line trenches. Later that day they move back to dugouts around La Boiselle to serve as support troops for their own 74th Infantry Brigade, who are preparing for another attack on Ovillers. Tolkien will note in his diary that he saw action at Ovillers on 15 July but slept in a dugout at La Boiselle. It is not clear whether, as a Signalling Officer, he would have gone over the top or remained in the front line trenches to manage communications. – Smith writes to Tolkien about Gilson's death; see further, entry for 17 July 1916.

16 July 1916 Men from the 74th Infantry Brigade attack Ovillers at 1.30 a.m. with some success, but at about noon three bombing squads of the 11th Lancashire Fusiliers are ordered to reach a battalion of the 5th Royal Warwickshire Regiment which has been cut off. They attack so strongly that the Germans are driven back to their trenches and eventually surrender at about 7.30 p.m. At 8.00 p.m. the Lancashire Fusiliers reach the beleaguered Warwickshires, and eventually Ovillers is captured. Tolkien will note in his diary that he was in action until relieved during the night.

17 July 1916 The 74th Infantry Brigade is relieved during the night of 16–17 July and arrives at Bouzincourt at 6.00 a.m. Tolkien sleeps during the morning. At 4.30 p.m. the 11th Battalion parades and marches to bivouacs at Forceville, arriving at 6.30 p.m. – Today Tolkien probably receives a letter written by Smith on 15 July (postmarked 16 July): 'I saw in the paper this morning that Rob has been killed. I am safe but what does that matter. Do please stick to me, you and Christopher. I am very tired and most frightfully depressed at this worst of news. Now one realises in despair what the T.C.B.S. really was. Oh my dear John Ronald what ever are we going to do?' (quoted in *Biography*, p. 84). Although Gilson was killed early on 1 July his body was not recovered for some time, and he was at first listed only as missing.

18 July 1916 At 7.45 a.m. the 11th Battalion parades and marches to Beauval for a few days' rest, arriving at 1.30 p.m. The men spend the rest of the day cleaning up.

19 July 1916 After physical training by company, the 11th Battalion parades at 10.00 a.m. for reorganization. At 2.30 p.m. the 74th Infantry Brigade is inspected by Major-General E.G.T. Bainbridge, General Officer Commanding the 25th Division. – Tolkien records in his diary the expenses of a dinner for himself and five other officers of A Company.

20 July 1916 The 11th Battalion spend the day in training at Beauval. At midnight Lieutenant W.H. Reynolds, to this point the Battalion Signalling Officer, takes over command of Brigade Signals. Tolkien succeeds him as Signalling Officer of the 11th Battalion.

21 July 1916 At 10.00 a.m. the 74th Infantry Brigade parades and marches to billets at Bus-lès-Artois, arriving at 4.00 p.m., having had dinner on the way. Tolkien will note in his diary that he slept in huts in a wood this night and the two following nights.

22 July 1916 Lieutenant R.S. Payton, one of Tolkien's friends from King Edward's School, is killed on the Somme while leading his machine gunners into action.

22–23 July 1916 The 11th Battalion is kept busy with more training at Bus-lès-Artois.

23 July 1916 In the morning, Tolkien attends a Roman Catholic service.

24 July 1916 At 10.00 a.m. the 74th Infantry Brigade, including the 11th Battalion, parades and marches to Mailly-Maillet. They arrive around noon and are served dinner. The 74th is to relieve the 87th Infantry Brigade. The large wood south-west of the village is often used for troop encampments. At 1.30 p.m. each platoon of the 11th Battalion is guided from the wood to the front line trenches at Beaumont-Hamel by a member of the 1st Border Regiment, whom the battalion is relieving. The relief is completed at about 5.00 p.m. The Battalion diary will note: 'Trenches very good + a good supply of deep dugouts for men'. A, B, and D Companies are in the front line, with C Company in support.

25 July 1916 Smith writes to Tolkien, praising his poem *The Lonely Isle*.

25–29 July 1916 Except for occasional shelling which causes six deaths, the 11th Battalion spends much of this relatively quiet period repairing and strengthening existing trenches as well as digging new ones and a headquarters area for the battalion and the brigade. At night men excavate forward dugouts and set up wire barriers. The communications system is mended and strengthened. An armoured cable is laid between battle headquarters and the battalions in line. On the night of 28–29 July patrols sent out to examine enemy wire are unable to do so because of hostile fire. On 29 July two German aeroplanes circle for from 5.00 to 7.00 p.m. until driven away by anti-aircraft fire. During this period Tolkien spends his nights in trenches near Auchonvillers and Beaumont-Hamel.

30 July 1916 The 11th Battalion is relieved at 4.00 a.m. by the 9th Loyal North Lancashire Regiment and returns to Mailly-Maillet as part of the Division reserve. Tolkien will note in his diary that he slept in the wood at Mailly-Maillet on the nights of 30 July to 4 August.

31 July 1916 The men of the 11th Battalion take baths. New men are trained on Lewis Guns and bombing.

1 August 1916 Minden Day. At 9.30 a.m., following physical drill, the 11th Battalion commemorates with a ceremonial parade the Lancashire Fusiliers' part in the Battle of Minden on 1 August 1759, a famous victory against the French during the Seven Years' War. In late morning there is training, and in the afternoon sporting competitions are held: Inter-Company Drill Competition, Blindfold Boxing, Potato Race, Inter-Company Relay Race, and Inter-Company Tug-of-War. At 6.00 p.m. the 74th Infantry Brigade Troupe gives a concert. The officers dine with staff captain Major G.C.S. Hodgson. During the night working parties from the battalion help to repair trenches.

2–4 August 1916 The 11th Battalion, still in reserve, is occupied with drilling and training. Working parties assist day and night in work on dugouts and trenches for the 74th Infantry Brigade headquarters.

4 August 1916 (postmark) Smith writes to Tolkien, probably enclosing a letter Wiseman had written to Smith on hearing of Gilson's death, in which Smith has underlined parts. When Tolkien receives it he too marks certain parts and adds his comments.

5 August 1916 The 11th Battalion, relieved of reserve duties at Mailly-Maillet by the 1st Leicestershires, marches to a camp between Acheux and Bertrancourt, arriving at 2.00 p.m. Tolkien will note in his diary that he slept in a tent at Bertrancourt on the nights of 5 and 6 August.

6 August 1916 At 10.00 a.m. Tolkien attends a Roman Catholic service in the church at Bertrancourt. In the afternoon, the 11th Battalion undergoes more training.

7 August 1916 In the morning, the 11th Battalion is given physical training. Lieutenant-Colonel L.G. Bird, Commanding Officer of the 11th Battalion, orders an advance party consisting of 2nd Lieutenant G.A. Potts, 2nd Lieutenant Tolkien, the Battalion Sergeant Major, and four Company Sergeant Majors to report to battalion headquarters in the trenches at 11.00 am. The rest of the battalion is to parade at 1.00 pm, then at 1.30 p.m. to proceed to the trenches. The Headquarters Signallers are to leave first, followed by D and C Companies, the Battalion Bombers, and A and B Companies. Officers' kits for the trenches are to be handed in to the Quartermaster by noon, carefully and legibly labelled. By 5.30 p.m. the battalion arrives at its destination, opposite Beaumont-Hamel with the villages of Colincamps and Mailly-Maillet to the rear. On arrival it immediately begins to repair trenches damaged by enemy action. *See note.* Tolkien will note in his diary that he slept in the *sucrérie* at Mailly-Maillet, south-east of Colincamps, on the nights of 7 to 9 August; in fact the ruined sugar refinery is nearer to Colincamps.

8–9 August 1916 The 11th Battalion proceeds with trench repairs, interrupted only when under fire; four men are killed and four wounded.

10 August 1916 Relieved by the 1st Welsh Guards in the afternoon, the 11th Battalion marches to Bus-lès-Artois. Lieutenant-Colonel Bird's orders for this operation instruct companies to report completion of relief by wire to battalion headquarters, and specify that all officers' kits and other stores for transport are to be at the Dump at the end of Cheeroh Avenue (the main communication trench to the front line) no later than 3.00 p.m., with officers' servants in attendance. If required, some of the signalling personnel are to stay in the line until 11 August to ensure the smooth working of communications; but Tolkien will record that he slept that night, and the following four nights, in the 'same billets as before at Bus[-lès-Artois]'. In the evening he goes into a nearby wood, thinks about Gilson, and considers Wiseman's letter (see entry for 4 August).

11–14 August 1916 The 11th Battalion remains at Bus-lès-Artois, occupied with drills, training, inspections, and boxing competitions, and on 13 August with baths. The 25th Divisional Engineers conduct training in visual signalling, and in office wiring and cable joining.

11 August 1916 Smith writes to Tolkien, thanking him for a letter (probably written before Tolkien received Wiseman's letter from Smith) and commenting, presumably in response to something Tolkien wrote, that he thinks 'there are still a great many sober men and true' (Tolkien Papers, Bodleian Library, Oxford). – In the evening, Tolkien again goes into the wood to sit and think.

12–13 August 1916 Tolkien writes a letter to Smith, thanking him for sending Wiseman's letter. Tolkien has thought much since receiving it, and finds that he no longer agrees with the comments he made on it:

What I meant, and thought Chris meant, and am almost sure you meant, was that the T.C.B.S. had been granted some spark of fire – certainly as a body if not singly – that was destined to kindle a new light, or, what is the same thing, rekindle an old light in the world; that the T.C.B.S. was destined to testify for God and Truth in a more direct way even than by laying down its several lives in this war (which is for all the evil of our own side in the large view good against evil). So far my chief impression is that something has gone crack. I feel just the same to both of you – nearer if anything and very much in need of you – I am hungry and lonely of course – but I don't feel a member of a little complete body now. I honestly feel that the T.C.B.S. has ended – but I am not at all sure that it is not an unreliable feeling that will vanish – like magic perhaps when we come together again. Still I feel a mere individual at present – with intense feelings more than ideas but very powerless. [*Letters*, p. 10]

He hopes that those who are left will be able to continue its work. He ends by saying that if the letter seems incoherent it was 'due to its being written at different sittings amongst the noise of a very boring Company mess'. He wishes that he could write more but has much to do (now on the 13th, a Sunday): 'The Bde Sig. Offr. [Brigade Signalling Officer] is after me for a confabulation, and I have two rows to have with the QM [Quartermaster] and a detestable 6.30 parade – 6.30 p.m. of a sunny Sabbath' (*Letters*, pp. 9–10).

14 August 1916 Robert Cary Gilson, Chief Master of King Edward's School, replies to a letter of sympathy Tolkien sent to him on the death of his son. Rob Gilson's will directs that Tolkien should have some of his books or drawings.

15 August 1916 At 10.00 a.m. the 11th Battalion parades and marches to 'hutments' in the wood at Acheux-en-Amiénois, arriving at 1.00 p.m. They will remain there, occupied with training and drilling, until 19 August, when they will march to Hédauville and then on to the trenches at Thiepval on 20 August; Tolkien however will be on a signalling course (see below). – Smith writes to Tolkien, not yet having received his letter of 12–13 August. He cannot sleep for memories of Rob Gilson and of the last time he saw him. He thinks that in some ways Rob is to be envied: 'After all he is out of the great struggle of life, and it often seems that rest and peace are a great boon. . . . I wish I could find you – I search for you everywhere' (Tolkien Papers, Bodleian Library, Oxford).

16–23 August 1916 Tolkien attends a course for Battalion Signalling Officers in the 25th Division. The rest of the 11th Battalion is involved in other activities. Tolkien will note in his diary that he slept in the wood at Acheux on the nights of 15 to 17 August, at battalion headquarters at Acheux on 18 August, and at 'billet 89 Acheux' from 19 to 23 August.

19–22 August 1916 Smith writes to Tolkien on 19 August that he received his long letter (of 12–13 August) the day before and disagrees with much of it:

> The idea that the T.C.B.S. has stopped is for me entirely impossible. . . . The T.C.B.S. is not so much a society as an influence on the state of being. I never for two consecutive seconds believed in the four-ideal-friends theory except in its very widest sense as a highly important and very worthy communion of living souls. That such an influence on the state of being could come to an end with Rob's loss is to me a preposter-ous idea. . . . The T.C.B.S. is not finished and never will be.

He returns Tolkien's letter with 'some rather curt and perhaps rude comments'. He had hoped to see Tolkien on 19 August as both Tolkien's battalion and Smith's are in Hédauville, but found that Tolkien was away on a course; but they are sure to meet soon, and 'I am not quite sure whether I shall shake you by the hand or take you by the throat, so enormously do I disagree with your letter and agree with myself!' (Tolkien Papers, Bodleian Library, Oxford). In fact he sees Tolkien later that day, and again each day on 20, 21, and 22 August.

22 August 1916 Tolkien, Smith, and H.T. Wade-Gery have dinner at Bou-zincourt, and are shelled while eating. This is the last time that Tolkien will see G.B. Smith.

23 August 1916 The signalling course ends.

24 August 1916 Tolkien leaves Acheux, travels by way of Hédauville, and rejoins his battalion who are occupying trenches at the edge of a wood near Thiepval, a German stronghold and the focus of an Allied assault.

24–26 August 1916 The 11th Battalion spends most of this time constructing new trenches while other units take a more active role, but even so there are casualties due to shelling. – Tolkien writes two poems. He dates the manuscript of the first, *The Thatch of Poppies*, to 'Acheux Hédauville Thiepval Aug[ust] 24–25 1916'. He dedicates the second, *The Forest Walker*, 'To Bus-lès-Artois Wood', and in it obliquely refers to his feelings when he had gone to that wood on 10 and 11 August to think about Rob Gilson's death. He will later write on one manuscript of *The Forest Walker*: 'HQ [headquarters] dugout Thiepval Wood Aug[ust] 25–26'. He will note in his diary having slept in a dugout at Thiepval on the nights of 24 and 25 August.

26–27 August 1916 From about 5.00 to 10.45 p.m. on 26 August the 11th Battalion is relieved by the 1/5 West Yorkshire Regiment, under shelling. The battalion marches to Bouzincourt, arriving at about 1.00 a.m. on 27 August. The men rest and clean up.

28–31 August 1916 At 4.00 a.m. on 28 August the 11th Battalion parades and marches to relieve the 4th Royal Berkshire and 5th Gloucester Regiments in trenches north of Ovillers, near the Leipzig Salient. The battalion works day and night to repair and strengthen the trenches, ankle-deep in water, hindered by heavy rain and shelling. Although the Battalion diary will describe each of these days as 'quiet', five men are killed and thirty wounded. Tolkien as Battalion Signalling Officer helps to install, or supervises the installation of, a new system of cables connecting the front line with Brigade headquarters. He will note in his diary that he spent the night of 28 August in 'Specialist mess 88', and the nights of 29 to 31 August at Ovillers-La-Boiselle. – Close to the trenches is Authuille Wood, described by John Masefield as 'a romantic and very lovely wood, pleasant with the noise of water. But at its north-eastern end it runs out in a straggling spinney along the Leipzig's east flank . . Here the enemy fearing for his safety kept up a terrible barrage. The trees are burnt, ragged, unbarked, topped and cut off short, the trenches are blown in and jumbled, and the ground blasted and gouged' (*The Old Front Line* (1917), p. 65).

1–5 September 1916 On 1 September the 11th Battalion leaves the front line, exchanging places with the 9th Loyal North Lancashires who have been in support. The 11th Battalion spends the next few days cleaning up the relief trenches, but also sends working parties to the front line and communications trenches to aid the Royal Engineers. Tolkien is probably involved with the laying of more cables between each battalion and Brigade headquarters. He will note in his diary that he spent the nights of 1 to 5 September at Ovillers-La-Boiselle.

6 September 1916 The 11th Battalion is relieved by the 6th South Staffordshires and marches to bivouacs 500 yards east of Bouzincourt. *See note.* The men spend the day cleaning and reorganizing. Probably at about this time a letter written on 25 August by the mother of Thomas Gaskin, asking for information about the death of her son, is passed to Tolkien for reply. *See note.*

7–12 September 1916 The men of the 11th Battalion proceed in stages to Franqueville for a long training session. They are carefully ordered to march, on their way from Bouzincourt, through the southern outskirts of Beauquesne, not through the centre; that four companies, each with its signallers, Lewis Gun teams, and bombers will leave at five-minute intervals, followed by transport, with the first company leaving at 8.20 a.m.; that at 8.00 a.m. the battalion's second in command will inspect the billets they are leaving to be sure they are perfectly clean; that all officers' kits and company stores are to be at the quartermaster's stores no later than 6.00 a.m., with officers' servants in attendance; and that care is to be taken when observing the regulation halt of ten minutes each hour, to prevent closing up of the column. The battalion reaches Léalvillers on 7 September (Tolkien spends the night in a billet), Puchevillers on the 8th (Tolkien sleeps two nights in a bivouac; 9 September is spent in drilling and reorganizing), Beauval on the 10th, Candas on the 11th, and Franqueville on the 12th. Tolkien will note in his diary that he spent the nights of 10, 11, and 12 September in billets.

10 September 1916 Smith writes to Tolkien, asking him to send a field postcard telling how he is. He has heard from R.W. Reynolds but has had nothing from Wiseman for ages. – Tolkien will note in his diary that he attended Mass this day, presumably at Beauval.

13–24 September 1916 In Franqueville the 11th Battalion, with the rest of the 74th Brigade, spends time with drills, parades, and inspections, and in physical, company, and specialist training. On 17 September the men are given a demonstration of drill and guard mounting by staff of the 4th Army School. On 22 September there is a battalion competition in bayonet fighting and assaulting. On 24 September the officers of the 74th Brigade take part in a staff ride held by their Commanding Officer, Brigadier-General Armytage. During this period the Divisional Engineers train six men for each battalion in visual signalling. A second trained signalling officer is now posted to the 11th Battalion, 2nd Lieutenant Leslie Risdon Huxtable. – Tolkien revises his poem *The Mermaid's Flute* (first composed in March 1915), and probably writes a new poem, later dated 'Franqueville? Sept[ember].' The latter, beginning 'O Lady Mother throned amid the stars', will be called *Consolatrix Afflictorum* and *Stella Vespertina*.

16 September 1916 Smith writes to Tolkien, enclosing a letter from Wiseman. Wiseman has sent copies of the letters Smith and Tolkien had sent Wiseman in the winter of 1914, and while reading them Smith realizes that Tolkien was right when he said that they have changed. Smith apparently has had a letter from Tolkien letting off steam, as he says: 'I am intensely sorry to hear of your frictions with others. I know how one officer can make a beast of himself to his junior, if he is a swine enough to do so' (Tolkien Papers, Bodleian Library, Oxford). Wiseman, writing from *HMS Superb* on 30 August and

4 September, says that he has been reading through his 'TCBSian' archive of correspondence and can see the changes and development in the group.

25–27 September 1916 The 11th Battalion makes its way back to the front line, mainly on foot, but on 25 September partly by motor bus. The men spend the night of the 25th at Forceville and of the 26th at Hédauville. They reach bivouacs near Bouzincourt on the 27th. On that evening they make their way through the communication trenches and relieve the 1/7 West Yorkshire Regiment at the front near Thiepval Wood. The battle for Thiepval Ridge having begun on 26 September, the village itself has just fallen, and the Joseph, Schwaben, Zollern, and Hessian Trenches have been captured, but beyond is a German strongpoint, the Schwaben Redoubt. Tolkien will note in his diary that on the night of 26 September he shared a tent with 2nd Lieutenant Huxtable, and on the night of the 27th he slept in a dugout at Thiepval.

26 September 1916 One of the tanks just introduced into the war by the British Army sticks fast and cannot be moved. It will be one of the sights of Thiepval for months to come.

28–29 September 1916 For much of 28 September the men of the 11th Battalion, in the front line trenches on the edge of Thiepval Wood, have a good view of the attack by the 18th Division on Schwaben Redoubt. At about 6.00 p.m. three patrols from the 11th Battalion, each consisting of thirty men and a Lewis Gun detachment and led by an officer, are sent to occupy trenches the enemy is believed to have abandoned. By 6.45 p.m. they have achieved their objective and taken twenty-one prisoners. They explore the communication trenches leading to the enemy's close-support line, and during the night take twenty more prisoners and find a quantity of maps and an unopened mailbag. A signaller from the 11th Battalion, Lance-Corporal A. Fletcher, later will be awarded the Distinguished Conduct Medal for using a discarded German torch to communicate with the front line when his own lamp is smashed, and for rescuing a wounded man. Early on the morning of 29 September, with the enemy still strongly holding its support line, an advance position is moved back slightly to consolidate and strengthen the front line. Tolkien will note in his diary that he was in action at Thiepval during the nights of 28 and 29 September. – The prisoners taken at the Schwaben Redoubt include men from a Saxon regiment which had fought alongside the Lancashire Fusiliers against the French at Minden in 1759. Tolkien speaks in German to one of the captured officers and offers him a drink of water; the officer corrects his pronunciation. In a moment of calm while the guns are silent, Tolkien's hand is on the receiver of a trench telephone when a field-mouse runs across his fingers.

30 September 1916 The 11th Battalion is relieved by the 7th Royal West Kents during the early morning and marches to Englebelmer, arriving at 8.00 a.m. The men spend the day cleaning up and resting.

1–5 October 1916 At 11.00 a.m. on 1 October the 11th Battalion parades and marches to a camp at W8 Central, near Bouzincourt, arriving at about 12.30 p.m. The men spend the next few days in company and specialist training, including a battalion attack practice on 2 October.

3 October 1916 Smith writes to Tolkien, saying he has not heard from him for a very long time.

6–9 October 1916 On 6–7 October the 74th Brigade relieves the 75th Brigade at Mouquet Farm, a fortified position recently captured from the Germans. The 11th Lancashire Fusiliers relieve the 11th Cheshires and take up position in the front line in the recently captured Zollern and Hessian Trenches and in the Fabeck support trench east of Thiepval. Although the Germans have lost their forward trenches they are holding out in parts of the Schwaben and Stuff Redoubts. During the next few days and nights the men of the 11th Battalion spend much of their time under heavy shelling, repairing and deepening old trenches, digging new trenches to gunpits in No Man's Land, and laying and burying new communication lines. – On 7 October the signal office of the 74th Brigade is moved two hundred yards from its original site, entailing extra cable-laying for the signals engineers. On 9 October two shells hit the signals dugout, and communications have to be repaired. The Stuff Redoubt is finally taken on this date. – Tolkien will note in his diary that he spent the nights of 6 to 12 October at Battalion headquarters in front of Mouquet Farm.

10–12 October 1916 On 10 October B Company of the 11th Battalion stays in the front line in Zollern Trench while A, C, and D companies are relieved by the 9th Loyal North Lancashires and the 13th Cheshires and retire to Fabeck and Midway support trenches near Mouquet Farm. The men continue to dig and improve trenches. On 10 October 2nd Lieutenant Huxtable is wounded. Throughout this period at the front Tolkien is probably kept very busy, as the new buried communication lines are difficult to install and some are damaged by shelling.

13–16 October 1916 On 13 October the 11th Battalion relieves the 13th Cheshires and returns to the front line in Zollern and Hessian Trenches. They again spend time digging and rewiring. Battalion headquarters is moved to Zollern Redoubt, where Tolkien spends the nights of 13 to 16 October. On 14 October the Schwaben Redoubt is finally taken.

16–17 October 1916 The 11th Cheshires relieve A and B Companies of the 11th Battalion on 16 October and D Company on 17 October; these retire to support trenches near Mouquet Farm while C Company stays in the front line. In the afternoon of 16 October three German planes fly overhead. In the evening of 17 October the 11th Lancashire Fusiliers move to Ovillers Post, where Tolkien spends the night at Battalion headquarters. – The British generals are planning another major assault, hoping to capture the German Regina Trench and the high ground held by the enemy before winter comes. The attack will be made from Hessian Trench, which faces Regina Trench and is separated from it by a space varying from two hundred to five hundred yards. Every effort is made to obtain as much information about the terrain and enemy positions as possible. A map issued to Tolkien shows 'information obtained from prisoners [and] Trenches corrected from air photos taken

17-10-16'; at some point he adds to it the position of a 'phone' and 'WF', code letters for the 11th Lancashire Fusiliers (a reproduction of the map appears in *Life and Legend*, p. 32).

18 October 1916 The 11th Battalion receives Operation Order No. T26 (*see note*) and spends the day preparing for battle. At 10.30 p.m. the men march towards the front line. A patrol consisting of a captain and a second lieutenant examines the enemy wire. Tolkien will note in his diary that he spent that night at Battalion headquarters near 'Lancs Trench' (Zollern Trench).

19 October 1916 The 11th Battalion reaches Hessian Trench at 4.00 a.m. The attack is meant to take place this day, but constant heavy rain has damaged the trenches, the saturated ground makes movement difficult, the lines of communication between Brigade and Division headquarters have gone down during the night, and the rain, together with mist, makes visual signals impossible. The assault postponed for forty-eight hours, the battalion returns to Ovillers Post, where Tolkien spends the night at Battalion headquarters.

20 October 1916 In the afternoon, the 11th Battalion is drawn up at Ovillers Post, organized into groups to proceed up the narrow trenches, and issued bombs, sandbags, and other stores from 'K' Dump at Ovillers on the way to Hessian Trench. 74th Infantry Brigade Signals will complain that Battalion Signalling Officers did not keep them informed about the progress of units moving into the front line. Tolkien spends the night at Battalion headquarters, again near 'Lancs Trench'.

21 October 1916 The last members of the 11th Battalion reach their position in Hessian Trench at about 3.00 a.m. The men spend the rest of the night improving the trenches and the means of leaving them quickly at the start of the attack. The Brigade signal report centre has been set up unusually close to the front line, and the various battalion headquarters are in dugouts in the front line of Hessian Trench. Tolkien is presumably stationed at 11th Battalion headquarters, at the position he marked as 'WF' on his map; he will record in his diary that on the nights of 21 and 22 October he was in action in Hessian Trench. The 11th Lancashire Fusiliers have been set the task of taking a five hundred-yard section of Regina Trench where it is at its closest to Hessian Trench. Just after noon the British artillery begin heavy firing, and three waves of assault troops go over the top at short intervals, trying to synchronize their movements with the barrage. When men of the 11th Battalion rush into Regina Trench they find the enemy unprepared, though there is resistance at one or two points, and they manage to link up with other regiments to their left and right. The 25th Division Engineers will report that communications throughout the attack were very satisfactory, though information did not always get back to Division headquarters as well as might have been expected. The 11th Battalion achieves its objective by 12.50 p.m. News of its success is sent to Division headquarters by carrier pigeon. But the battalion has paid heavily for its success with 15 killed, 26 missing, and 117 wounded. *See further, note.* The survivors spend the rest of the day consolidating their position in Regina Trench, digging connecting trenches back to Hessian Trench, laying communication lines, and destroying the German communication trenches to Regina Trench.

22 October 1916 The Germans shell Regina Trench heavily. At 4.00 p.m. the 11th Battalion is relieved by the 7th Queen's Royal West Surrey Regiment. When the battalion reaches Ovillers Post the men are given hot soup and then marched to a camp north of the Albert-Bouzincourt road. Tolkien will note in his diary having slept this night at a camp 'near Albert'.

23 October 1916 The 11th Battalion is inspected by Brigadier-General Bethell, commander of the 74th Brigade. The men then travel to Vadencourt Wood by motor-bus, where they are inspected by Major-General Bainbridge, commanding the 25th Division. Tolkien spends the night in hutments at Vadencourt.

24 October 1916 The 11th Battalion marches in the rain to Beauval. The men spend the rest of day cleaning up. Tolkien will note in his diary that he spent the nights of 24 to 27 October in a billet at Rue de L'Epinette, Beauval.

25 October 1916 The 11th Battalion is inspected by General Sir Hubert Gough, commanding the 5th Army, who compliments the men on their work. During the day, Tolkien begins to feel ill.

26 October 1916 In the morning, the men of the 11th Battalion have baths. In the afternoon, they are inspected by Field-Marshal Sir Douglas Haig, the Commander-in-Chief. In the evening there is a concert in Beauval Mairie.

27 October 1916 Tolkien reports sick with a temperature of 103 degrees. Nevertheless he spends the night in his billet at Beauval.

28 October 1916 By evening at the latest, Tolkien is in the Officers' Hospital at Gézaincourt. He is suffering from 'trench fever', a highly infectious disease carried by lice. The crowded and squalid conditions in the trenches mean that some 97 per cent of the soldiers are infested by lice, and trench fever is common. The sickness usually begins with a headache, giddiness, and muscular pain especially in the shins, and lasts a few days, followed by a remission and then a relapse, or often a series of relapses and remissions. It is only after the war ends that the louse will be found to be the carrier.

29 October 1916 Tolkien is put on the sick train at Candas and travels via Étaples to Le Touquet. He is admitted to No. 1 British Red Cross Hospital, also known as the Duchess of Westminster's Hospital.

30 October–7 November 1916 Tolkien remains in hospital in Le Touquet. He writes to his Commanding Officer, Lieutenant-Colonel Bird, apparently expressing his regret at leaving the 11th Battalion and his hope that when he returns to the front it will be to the same battalion. – He also writes a poem, *Morning Tea*. Although its manuscript includes the (later?) note 'Duch[ess] of Westminster's Hospital Le Touquet Nov[ember] 8 1916', it must have been composed no later than the morning of the 7th, if in fact it was written in hospital at Le Touquet.

7 November 1916 Tolkien travels by train via Étaples to Le Havre, spending the night en route.

8 November 1916 At Le Havre Tolkien embarks on the hospital ship *HMHS Asturias*. Later he will note in his diary that the *Asturias* was torpedoed by the Germans the following year (20 March 1917), but although badly damaged, she was not sunk.

9 November 1916 The *Asturias* leaves Le Havre, possibly during the night, and arrives at Southampton on the same day. Tolkien then travels by train to Birmingham and is admitted to the 1st Southern General Hospital, set up in the grand arched halls and corridors of the University of Birmingham at Edgbaston. *See note.* – Captain E. Munday, Adjutant of the 11th Lancashire Fusiliers, replies to Tolkien's letter to Lieutenant-Colonel Bird. The Commanding Officer cannot ensure that Tolkien will be posted to the same battalion when he returns to the front, but suggests that he write at once when he is posted to a battalion depot, and the 11th Battalion will request him. He encloses a separate letter dated 9 November (the letter to Tolkien is dated 8 November) which Tolkien should submit to the authorities as soon as he is passed fit to return to duty. This letter requests that Tolkien be returned to the 11th Battalion as soon as possible. Lieutenant-Colonel Bird 'values the services of Lt. Tolkien very highly'; in his absence his signallers are under a non-commissioned officer, and his services are badly needed. The battalion is very short of officers. The envelope in which these letters are sent is postmarked 'Field Post Office, 10 Nov. 1916' and addressed to Tolkien at 'D. Ward, No. 1 Red Cross Hospital, Le Touquet', but the address is struck through and the envelope redirected to Great Haywood.

10 November–1 December 1916 During the next few weeks Tolkien is probably visited by Edith, Father Francis, and relatives who live in the Birmingham area. He is also visited by, or manages himself to visit, R.W. Reynolds. On a War Office form dated 22 November he gives his temporary address as c/o T.E. Mitton Esq., Moseley, Birmingham (i.e. Tom Mitton, husband of Tolkien's paternal Aunt Mabel), but since a later medical report will indicate at least two more weeks before his temperature returns to normal, it is unlikely that he actually leaves the hospital by the 22nd. – Tolkien writes at once to Smith and Wiseman to let them know that he has been shipped home and is in hospital. He encloses his letter to Smith in one to Smith's mother (Mrs Ruth A. Smith), telling her that her son was safe when he last heard from him, and asking her to forward his message. – During November, but after he has returned to Birmingham, Tolkien revises *The Town of Dreams and the City of Present Sorrow* (see entry for 16–18 March 1916). He also writes the poem *The Lonely Harebell*, the manuscript of which he will inscribe 'hospital Birmingham Nov[ember] 1916 (part [?from matter] near Lichfield Sep[tember] 1915 insp[ired] *Cromer 1914)'.

13 November 1916 Mrs Smith writes to thank Tolkien for his news and says that she will forward his letter to her son.

16 November 1916 Smith, having received Tolkien's letter, replies to him at '3 South General Hospital, Edgbaston, Birmingham'. He is delighted to hear that Tolkien is 'still alive, if weak and ill as you are bound to be. From your letter I see plainly that you have been through it' (Tolkien Papers, Bodleian Library, Oxford). He hopes to get leave soon and will visit Tolkien and Edith. For the moment he is the Adjutant of his battalion (now camped near the village of Souastre on the Doullens-Arras road). – Christopher Wiseman, on *HMS Superb*, replies to Tolkien's letter. He wishes that he could get leave to visit Tolkien in Birmingham, but leave is given only in special circumstances. He suggests that if Tolkien is granted extended sick leave he might visit Wiseman in the north where his ship is based; or if Tolkien and Edith were to visit Wiseman's mother in Wandsworth, she would welcome them both. Now that Tolkien is free of the censor, Wiseman asks to be told as much as Tolkien knows about Gilson's death, what engagements he himself has been in, where Smith is, and any news about him. Since their 'skirmish' in the spring Tolkien has not sent him any of his poetry.

18 November 1916 Smith writes to Tolkien at the General Hospital. He forgot to say in his last letter that he is sure that his mother would be glad to get Tolkien books or anything else he wants, and to visit him. – The Battle of the Somme officially ends.

29 November 1916 Smith is hit by shrapnel when his battalion is shelled. Although wounded in his right arm and thigh, he is able to walk to the dressing station to wait for an ambulance. He writes to his mother that his wounds are not serious.

2 December 1916 Tolkien is examined by a Medical Board at the 1st Southern General Hospital. Although his temperature has been normal for a week, he is still suffering from headaches and pains in the leg and is very weak. The Board declares him unfit for any service for the next six weeks and grants him leave from 9 December 1916 to 12 January 1917. By this date he has been attached to the 3rd (Reserve) Battalion of the Lancashire Fusiliers, based at Thirtle Bridge on the east coast of England near Hull. – By now, Smith's wounds are considered dangerous. Gas gangrene has set in.

3 December 1916 G.B. Smith dies at 3.30 a.m.

8 December 1916 Wiseman writes a long letter to Tolkien, mainly about politics and the war. He thanks Tolkien for his letter and for his latest poems. He hopes that Tolkien will begin to publish, and is convinced that 'if you do come out in print you will startle our generation as no one has yet' (Tolkien Papers, Bodleian Library, Oxford). He knows that R.W. Reynolds thought Tolkien much influenced by Francis Thompson, and that Tolkien has studied Thompson deeply, but Wiseman cannot see any obvious connection. Tolkien apparently having expressed a wish to join the Royal Engineers, Wiseman suggests that he write to Brigadier-General Sir John Barnsley (T.K. Barnsley's father), who might be able to help.

9 December 1916 Between now and mid-December Tolkien travels to Great Haywood to spend his leave with Edith.

16 December 1916 (postmarked 18 December) Wiseman writes a brief letter to Tolkien to say that he has just received news from home that G.B. Smith died on 3 December. His letter is addressed to Tolkien at the 1st Southern General Hospital but is redirected to Great Haywood. Soon after Tolkien receives this letter, he sends his condolences to Smith's mother.

22 December 1916 Mrs Smith responds to Tolkien's message with details of her son's last days. Since Smith had asked that his poetry be published if he fell, his mother asks Tolkien for any of her son's verses that might be included. – Upon receipt of her letter, Tolkien replies at once. Around this time he also writes to R.W. Reynolds.

?c. 25 December 1916 Tolkien writes a poem, *GBS* (later *G.B.S.*) in memory of G.B. Smith. He will later note on a typescript copy 'Great Haywood Christ[mas] 1916–17'.

26 December 1916 Mrs Smith writes to thank Tolkien for the copy of her son's verses, and tells him to keep the original.

28 December 1916 R.W. Reynolds replies to a letter from Tolkien. Reynolds is glad that Tolkien has found a congenial spot to convalesce. Mrs Smith has been in touch with him too about her son's wish that a book of his poems should be published; Reynolds asks if Tolkien knows anything of Smith's wishes in this matter. He understands that Mrs Smith has also written to H.T. Wade-Gery.

End of 1916–first half of 1917 Tolkien begins to write the first prose version of his mythology, *The Book of Lost Tales*, either while still in the 1st Southern General Hospital or after going on sick leave to Great Haywood on 9 December 1916. One of the first parts to be written is *The Cottage of Lost Play*, which introduces the framework of the tales: a mariner, Eriol, reaches the island of Tol Eressëa and hears from the fairies (or elves) who dwell there stories of the creation of the world and its subsequent history. In the mythology as originally conceived, Tol Eressëa will be eventually uprooted and moved across the sea to become England. – Another part written at this time is a story from near the end of the mythology, *Tuor and the Exiles of Gondolin* (*'Of Tuor and the Fall of Gondolin'*), which Tolkien will tend to call simply *The Fall of Gondolin. See note.* – Tolkien also continues to work on his invented languages. He makes additions to the *Qenyaqetsa*, and traces the 'development' of the language from an earlier form, Primitive Eldarin. He begins to develop another 'Elvish' language, Gnomish or Goldogrin, also with roots in Primitive Eldarin; eventually this will become 'Sindarin'. Possibly as early as the end of 1916, but no later than early 1917, Tolkien begins work on a Gnomish grammar, *Lam na nGoldathon* ('Tongue of the Gnomes', *Gnomish Grammar*) and a Gnomish lexicon, *i·Lam na·Ngoldathon 'Goldogrin'* (*Gnomish Lexicon*). – It is perhaps during his time of convalescence at Great Haywood that Tolkien draws heraldic devices for three places in England of great significance to himself and Edith, the village of Great Haywood and the towns of Warwick and Cheltenham, to which he gives names in Goldogrin: Tavrobel, Kortirion, and Celbaros.

1917

?1917–?1919 While working on *The Book of Lost Tales* Tolkien keeps a note-book, originally inscribed 'Names and Lang[uage] to Book of Lost Tales' (later 'Notebook B'). This includes a list of words in Eldarissa (i.e. Qenya), a chart of races of beings, and a table comparing two forms of the proper names in the story of Tuor (see *The Poetic and Mythologic Words of Eldarissa*, *Early Chart of Names*, *Official Name List*). Associated with this notebook are various tables and lists on loose sheets (see *The Creatures of the Earth*, *'Matar and Tulir'*, *'Names of the Valar'*, and *'Otsan and Kainendan'*). – Probably in this period Tolkien also writes *'Name-list to The Fall of Gondolin'*, derived from the *Official Name List*; a parallel list of Qenya names from *The Cottage of Lost Play* with Gnomish (Goldogrin) equivalents (*Names and Required Alterations*); and, related to the *Qenyaqetsa*, a description of the conjugation of the verb in Qenya (*The Qenya Verb Forms*).

2 January 1917 Tolkien writes to the War Office from Great Haywood, reporting himself for further orders and giving his address from 12 January as 185 Monument Road, Edgbaston, Birmingham.

18 January 1917 Wiseman writes to Tolkien. He apologizes for not sending a letter before, explaining that this is the fifth he has written and has torn up his earlier attempts. He is glad to hear that Tolkien is ill again (because it keeps him from the front) and asks what exactly is wrong with him. He comments: 'As you said, it is you and I now . . . the old and original. The whole thing is so ineffably mysterious. To have seen two of God's giants pass before our eyes, to have lived and laughed with them, to have learnt of them, to have found them something like ourselves, and to see them go back again into the mist whence they came out.' He understands that R.W. Reynolds has been in touch with Tolkien about publishing Smith's poems, and says though he thinks Reynolds will do justice to Smith as a poet, he will see him 'as a poet and not a man, as something like a successful protégé . . . as a genius, as a prodigy, anything but a soul who is saying what it feels and how it thinks.' He asks Tolkien if he can do anything; he feels that the T.C.B.S. should have a hand in the matter, but if they do they must be 'cruelly honest and not allow sentiment to cloud judgement'. He does not think that Smith's last poems were his best, but they should probably go into a collection. He has never seen Smith's poem *The Burial of Sophocles* and asks Tolkien to make a copy for him. He returns Tolkien's own poems with comments on a separate sheet, possibly those on the back of an unused telegram form preserved among the Tolkien Papers; in these he mentions *The Pool of the Dead Year*, *Tinfang Warble*, *The Forest Walker*, and *A Dream of Coming Home*, and says that Tolkien ought to start 'the epic' (Tolkien Papers, Bodleian Library, Oxford).

21 January 1917 Mrs Smith writes to Tolkien at Great Haywood, forwarded to Abbotsford, Wake Green Road, Moseley (the home of his Aunt Mabel and Uncle Tom Mitton). She has heard from R.W. Reynolds and is grateful to him and to Tolkien for the trouble they are taking over her son's poetry.

23 January 1917 Tolkien is examined by a Medical Board at the 1st Southern General Hospital. Although his condition has improved, he is still pale and weak, his appetite is poor, he has experienced two slight returns of fever, and he still has occasional pains in his knees and elbows. The Board declares him unfit for general service for two months, and unfit for home and light duty for one month. His leave is extended to 22 February.

12 February 1917 Tolkien writes to the War Office from Great Haywood to report that at the expiration of his leave on 22 February his address will be Great Haywood, Staffordshire. – Edith Tolkien either begins to make a fair copy of Tolkien's first version of *The Cottage of Lost Play* or finishes doing so: she writes her initials and today's date on the cover of the school exercise book used for the purpose.

27 February 1917 Tolkien is examined by a Medical Board at the Military Hospital, Lichfield. He is still debilitated and has pains in his legs and occasional fever. The Board declares him unfit for general or home service for two months or even light duty for one month, and recommends one month's treatment in an officers' convalescent hospital. His address on the completed form is changed from Great Haywood to Abbotsford, Moseley, Birmingham (the Mittons). He is sent to Furness Auxiliary Hospital in Harrogate, Yorkshire, probably at once. *See note.*

Beginning of March 1917 Having heard that G.B. Smith's brother Roger, also serving in the Army, died in Mesopotamia on 25 January, Tolkien writes from Harrogate to Smith's mother.

4 and 9 March 1917 Wiseman replies to a letter from Tolkien sent a month earlier. He is pleased to have set Tolkien off on his great work: 'The reason why I want you to write the epic is because I want you to connect all these [poems and tales] up properly, & make their meaning & context tolerably clear' (Tolkien Papers, Bodleian Library, Oxford). With his letter Tolkien had sent some poems, on which Wiseman now comments. He asks for news of G.B. Smith's poems and whether Tolkien is doing anything to get his own work published. He has received another letter from Tolkien and is glad that Edith is now with him at Harrogate. Wiseman addresses the letter to Tolkien at 95 Valley Drive, Harrogate, Yorkshire, presumably where Edith and Jennie Grove are staying.

6 March 1917 G.B. Smith's mother replies to Tolkien at Furness Auxiliary Hospital to thank him for his sympathy.

28 March 1917 Tolkien is examined by a Medical Board at Furness Auxiliary Hospital. He is improving but still has pains in his knees and elbows. The Board declares him unfit for general and home service for one month, but fit for one month's light duty at home, and recommends a further three weeks of sick leave, until 18 April. His address on the completed form is given as 95 Valley Road, Harrogate.

6 April 1917 The United States declares war on Germany.

14 April 1917 Wiseman, on leave in London, informs Tolkien by telegram that he will visit him on 18 April.

15 April 1917 (postmark) Wiseman writes to Tolkien at 95 Valley Drive, Harrogate, confirming what he has already telegraphed, that he is on leave and wants to visit Tolkien and Edith in the morning of 18 April. According to his present orders, he needs to catch a train from Leeds in the afternoon, but if his leave is extended he might not come until 19 April. On receiving this, Tolkien probably telegraphs that he has to report for duty on the latter date.

17–?18 April 1917 In the circumstances, Wiseman arrives in Harrogate on 17 April, at 6.51 p.m. according to a telegram he sends that afternoon. Tolkien lends him manuscripts of Smith's poems and a typewritten copy.

19 April 1917 At the expiration of his leave Tolkien joins the 3rd (Reserve) Battalion of the Lancashire Fusiliers at Thirtle Bridge Camp on the Holderness peninsula, near Withernsea, part of the Humber Garrison. The battalion has two duties: to train new recruits for the front, and to guard against any assault from the sea. The camp houses some 1,600 soldiers. Probably around this time, Edith and Jennie Grove move into furnished lodgings in Hornsea. *See note.*

Spring 1917 For a brief time early in Tolkien's posting to the Humber Garrison he is put in charge of an outpost and given quarters which allow Edith to live with him for a while. This arrangement lasts, perhaps, through late May or early June. – Tolkien will annotate a later version of his poem *Sea-Song of an Elder Day* (after 31 August–2 September 1917, see below): 'Present shape due to rewriting and adding introd[uction] & ending in a lonely house near Roos, Holderness (Thirtle Bridge Camp) Spring 1917' (quoted in *The Shaping of Middle-earth* (1986), p. 215). The 'lonely house' is probably to be identified with the officer's quarters provided to Tolkien as commander of the outpost. The extant manuscript of the poem as written out in March 1915 (as *Sea-Chant of an Elder Day*) includes a later addition, a short prose introduction which connects the poem to the story of the fall of Gondolin (see entry for End of 1916–early 1917): it becomes 'the song that Tuor told to Eärendel his son what time the Exiles of Gondolin dwelt awhile in Dor Tathrin the Land of Willows after the burning of their city' (quoted in *The Shaping of Middle-earth*, p. 214). – Tolkien also continues to work on his Gnomish lexicon, rewriting in ink over an earlier pencil layer. An inscription indicates that this stage at least is written at 'Tol Withernon', almost certainly a Gnomish reference to 'Withernsea'.

1 May 1917 Tolkien is examined by a Medical Board at Humber Garrison headquarters in Hull. 'He is improving but requires hardening' (Public Record Office). The Board declares him fit for home service but unfit for general service. His address is recorded as HQ3, Thirtle Bridge.

19 May 1917 Wiseman writes to Tolkien, returning the manuscripts of Smith's poems. He will keep the typed copy until he can send Tolkien his suggestions. He thinks that they should not aim at publishing 'Opera Omnia, but a good book of verse' (Tolkien Papers, Bodleian Library, Oxford).

?Late May–?early June 1917 Tolkien and Edith visit a wood near Roos. There she dances for him, a seminal event in the development of his mythology. As he will describe it in 1964 in a letter to Christopher Bretherton: 'the original version of the "Tale of Lúthien Tinúviel and Beren" . . . was founded on a small wood with a great undergrowth of 'hemlock' (no doubt many other related plants were also there) near Roos in Holderness, where I was for a while on the Humber Garrison' (*Letters*, p. 345); and in a letter to his son Christopher in 1972: 'I never called Edith *Lúthien* – but she was the source of the story that in time became the chief part of the *Silmarillion*. It was first conceived in a small woodland glade filled with hemlocks at Roos in Yorkshire. . . . In those days her hair was raven, her skin clear, her eyes brighter than you have seen them, and she could sing – and *dance*' (*Letters*, p. 420). *See note.*

1 June 1917 Tolkien is examined by a Medical Board at Humber Garrison headquarters in Hull. The Board declares him fit for general service, and orders him to remain with his unit at Thirtle Bridge until further notice.

?Late June–early July 1917 Christopher Wiseman writes to Tolkien and returns the typewritten copies of Smith's poems, with a suggested arrangement. He is convinced that only a selection of Smith's best work should be published, and it should be arranged most effectively rather than by strict order of writing. He suggests that some of the poems might be accompanied by explanatory notes of the circumstances in which they were written. He also comments at length on the political situation. He has not heard from Tolkien since he saw him in Harrogate.

31 July 1917 Captain T.K. Barnsley, one of Tolkien's friends at King Edward's School, is killed near Ypres while consolidating a captured position.

1 August 1917 Tolkien attends the elaborate dinner with which the 3rd Battalion of the Lancashire Fusiliers celebrates Minden Day. He signs his menu card and obtains the signatures of twenty-three others at the dinner, including L.R. Huxtable. – Tolkien writes a poem, *Companions of the Rose*, dedicated 'For RQG [R.Q. Gilson] Suffolk Regiment GBS [G.B. Smith] Lancashire Fusiliers'. On Minden Day, roses are worn by all ranks in the Lancashire Fusiliers, and a toast is drunk to those who fell at Minden. (Gilson's regiment had also fought in that battle.)

Mid-August 1917 Tolkien is admitted to 'Brooklands', an officers' hospital in Cottingham Road, Hull, and for six weeks runs a fever. He finds congenial company among the other patients, including a friend from the Lancashire Fusiliers, and continues his writing, including *The Tale of Tinúviel*. – The hospital is visited by nuns of the order of the Sisters of Mercy who have a house in Hull. One of these, Mother Mary Michael, becomes a lifelong correspondent and friend, and godmother to Tolkien's second son, Michael.

?Mid- to late August or ?September 1917 Tolkien writes a poem, *The Grey Bridge of Tavrobel*. At a later date he will write on the manuscript: 'Brooklands Red [Cross] hosp[ital] Cottingham Road, Hull Sept or Aug 1917?'

22 August 1917 In the early hours German Zeppelins attack the Yorkshire coast, including the mouth of the Humber, with high-explosive and incendiary bombs.

31 August–2 September 1917 Tolkien again rewrites his poem *Sea-Song of an Elder Day*, now with an added title, *The Horns of Ulmo* (> *The Horns of Ylmir*), to fit it explicitly within his mythology. He writes on the manuscript

'Aug[ust] 31 Sep[tember] 2 1917 Hospital Hull'. Later he will write out a fair copy of the poem, incorporating emendations, with the annotation described above (see entry for Spring 1917).

September 1917 Tolkien further revises his poem *The Mermaid's Flute*.

1 September, 7 and 10 October 1917 Wiseman replies in stages to a letter by Tolkien, who has heard about the death of Wiseman's mother. Wiseman apologizes for not sending an earlier letter, and provides details. He has heard from Tolkien that he and Edith are expecting a baby and says it is great news. He agrees with Tolkien's arrangement of G.B. Smith's poems for publication. He has heard from Mrs Incledon that Tolkien is still in hospital in Hull. He approves of the poem *Companions of the Rose* which Tolkien had enclosed with his last letter, and says that he is 'sorry it is the only one [presumably, the only entirely new poem] this year'. But the Muse 'has not been entirely idle because you have spent a good time on the mythology' (Tolkien Papers, Bodleian Library, Oxford). He discusses at length an anonymous leader he has read in the *Times Literary Supplement* (20 September 1917, pp. 445–6) entitled *Creation and Invention*, on the distinction between 'invention' and 'imagination'. Wiseman sees the former in Tolkien's poem *Copernicus and Ptolemy* and the latter in his mythology.

25 September 1917 German Zeppelins attack the Lincolnshire and Yorkshire coasts between midnight and 3 am. Although they are unable to penetrate far inland because of defensive gunfire, they drop sixteen bombs on Hull, with little material damage.

?Late September 1917 Edith and Jennie Grove are not happy in their lodgings in Yorkshire, and unable to visit Tolkien in hospital often because of the difficult journey to Hull. With Edith now in an advanced state of pregnancy, the women return to Cheltenham until the birth of the child.

16 October 1917 Tolkien is examined by a Medical Board at Humber Garrison headquarters in Hull. He has been in hospital for nine weeks, and though his temperature returned to normal three weeks ago, he still has not recovered his strength, he suffers from debility and pain in his arms and shins, and he looks delicate. The Board declares him 30 per cent disabled, unfit for general and home service for one month but fit for light duty at home, and orders him to rejoin the 3rd Lancashire Fusiliers at Thirtle Bridge. He leaves the hospital on this date.

16 November 1917 Tolkien is examined by a Medical Board at Humber Garrison headquarters in Hull. He is slowly recovering, and in the intervening month has suffered only one slight attack of fever. The Board declares him 20 per cent disabled, unfit for general service for two months but fit for home service, including active duty with troops. He is ordered to continue service with the 3rd Lancashire Fusiliers at Thirtle Bridge. – Edith gives birth to a son in a Cheltenham nursing home. It is a difficult delivery, and for a while her life is in danger. Tolkien cannot get leave for some days, but May Incledon visits Edith and writes to reassure Tolkien.

19 November 1917 R.W. Reynolds writes to thank Tolkien for a parcel and for a poem or poems which he will read aloud to his wife. He is very interested 'in the book of tales you are at work on' (*The Book of Lost Tales*) and hopes to see it 'when it is in a state to travel' (Tolkien Papers, Bodleian Library, Oxford). Sidgwick & Jackson have been considering G.B. Smith's poems for publication for three weeks.

c. 22 November 1917 Tolkien goes to Cheltenham to see Edith and the baby. Father Francis comes from Birmingham. The baby is baptized *John Francis Reuel Tolkien. His godparents are Hilary Tolkien and Mary Incledon (who has become a Roman Catholic). To pay the costs of Edith's medical care, Tolkien sells the last few shares in South African mines remaining from his inheritance. According to Humphrey Carpenter, after the christening of John Tolkien 'Edith brought the child back to Yorkshire, moving into furnished rooms at Roos' (*Biography*, p. 97). *See note.*

24 November 1917 Tolkien's promotion from Second Lieutenant to full Lieutenant from 1 July is listed in the *London Gazette*. It will be printed in *The Times* on 26 November (p. 2).

Late November–December 1917 Tolkien returns to duty. At some time in December he is transferred to the 9th Battalion, Royal Defence Corps, based at Easington, some ten miles south of Thirtle Bridge near the tip of the Holderness peninsula. Tolkien resides, however, a few miles still further south, at Kilnsea. The Royal Defence Corps had been formed in August 1917 from the Home Service Garrison Battalions of eighteen regiments to provide a home guard for ports, railways, and the like.

December 1917–March 1918 Tolkien revises part of *The Town of Dreams and the City of Present Sorrow* (see entry for 10 November–1 December 1916) as *The Song of Eriol*, referring to the wandering mariner in *The Book of Lost Tales*. One of the manuscripts of the poem includes a later note, 'Easington 1917–18'.

?10 (?17 ?20) December 1917 Wiseman replies to a letter in which Tolkien told him of the safe birth of his son. He insists on being considered as an uncle. He has received several letters from Tolkien, in one of which Tolkien asked for more about the article in the *Times Literary Supplement* (see entry for 1 September 1917). Wiseman now writes at great length what he remembers about it, and replies to Tolkien's comments on what Wiseman had written in his earlier letter.

1918

1918 Tolkien probably spends much of his leisure time during 1918 writing the first version of a third story for *The Book of Lost Tales*: *The Tale of Turambar* (see *The Book of Lost Tales*; *'Of Túrin Turambar'*).

1918–1919 An influenza pandemic kills between twenty and forty million people around the world. Among the dead (in 1919) will be Tolkien's friend Colin Cullis.

January–March 1918 Tolkien rewrites the poem *The Lonely Harebell* (first composed in November 1916). On a later manuscript, in which the poem is called *Elf Alone*, he will add a note: '1915–1916 rewr[itten] 1918 | Cromer, Hosp[ital] Birm[ingham] | farmhouse near Easington, Yorks'.

19 January 1918 Tolkien is examined by a Medical Board at Humber Garrison headquarters in Hull. Although he has had two slight attacks, with a temperature reaching 100 degrees Fahrenheit, which required bed rest for five days, he is gradually improving. The Board declares him 20 per cent disabled, unfit for general service for one month but fit for active duty with troops on home service for one month. He is ordered to continue service with the 9th Royal Defence Corps at Easington, and treatment by the regimental medical officer.

19 February 1918 Tolkien is examined by a Medical Board at Humber Garrison headquarters in Hull. He is improving slowly but 'still looks weak & is unable for much exertion . . . & requires hardening' (National Archives, Kew WO 339/34423). The Board declares him 20 per cent disabled, unfit for general service but fit for active duty with troops on home service. He is ordered to continue service with the 9th Royal Defence Corps at Easington and treatment by the regimental medical officer.

Late February–early March 1918 At some time in this period Tolkien returns to the 3rd Lancashire Fusiliers at Thirtle Bridge, and for five days is confined to bed by an attack of influenza.

10 March 1918 In the evening, German Zeppelins attack Hull and Hornsea.

19 March 1918 Tolkien is examined by a Medical Board at Humber Garrison headquarters in Hull. His general tone is improving but he still needs hardening. The Board declares him 20 per cent disabled, unfit for general service but fit for active duty with troops on home service. He is ordered to continue service with the 3rd Lancashire Fusiliers at Thirtle Bridge.

10 April 1918 A Medical Board at Humber Garrison headquarters declares Tolkien recovered and fit for general service.

Spring (?May) 1918 Tolkien is posted again to Penkridge, Rugeley Camp, Staffordshire. Edith, John, and Jennie Grove find rooms in a nearby house at Gipsy Green (*Staffordshire). Tolkien is able to stay with them occasionally. The name of Gipsy Green may be reflected in *Fladweth Amrod* (Gnomish, 'Nomad's Green'), a place in Tol Eressëa associated with Eriol and mentioned in *The Book of Lost Tales. See note.*

May–June 1918 Tolkien makes some drawings at Gipsy Green (*Artist and Illustrator*, figs. 22–23). One is a view of the house, another a series of vignettes: Edith washing herself, fixing her hair, playing the piano, carrying John in the garden; John in his cot; cats that dance when Edith plays the piano; and Tolkien himself in uniform, riding a bicycle to the camp timed '8.25 a.m.' and '8.27 a.m.', and standing erect at '9 a.m.' Another sheet includes a portrait of Jennie Grove, a view of Edith from behind, and John in his cot. Probably at about this time Tolkien also draws other views of a garden, and *Road near Stafford.*

?June 1918 Tolkien is transferred to Brocton Camp.

June or July 1918 The firm of Erskine Macdonald publishes *A Spring Harvest* by Geoffrey Bache Smith, with a short introductory note by 'J.R.R.T.'

29 June 1918 Tolkien contracts gastritis at Brocton Camp. Now or soon thereafter he is admitted to hospital in Hull, probably 'Brooklands' officers' hospital (he is recorded as resident there by 4 September). – Although she is once again separated from her husband by a long distance, Edith decides to stay for the time being at Gipsy Green. She is happy there, finds looking after the baby tiring, and is still not fully recovered from John's difficult birth.

17 July 1918 A Medical Board in Hull declares Tolkien unfit in any category for one month. While in hospital he will learn a little Russian and work to improve his Spanish and Italian.

Late July–August 1918 Tolkien loses nearly two stone (28 lbs) as a result of his illness.

26 July 1918 The War Office, apparently unaware of Tolkien's medical condition, orders him to return to France via Boulogne on 27 July.

31 July 1918 The War Office cancels its order of 26 July.

4 September 1918 Tolkien is examined by a Medical Board at Humber Garrison headquarters in Hull. He is improving and beginning to regain the weight he had lost. The Board declares him 100 per cent disabled, unfit in any category for two months, and recommends that he be transferred to a convalescent hospital.

11 September 1918 Tolkien is transferred to Savoy Convalescent Hospital in Blackpool on the west coast of England.

12 September 1918 The War Office instructs its Northern Command, in charge of the Humber Garrison, to ascertain whether Tolkien is fit for Class C(ii), sedentary employment only. It is now nearly two years since illness forced his return from France, and for most of this time he has been ill or able to carry out only restricted duties.

28 September 1918 Tolkien's medical records are reported transferred to Western Command, as he is now under its jurisdiction in Blackpool.

1 October 1918 The War Office authorizes Tolkien to take up sedentary employment, apparently having concluded that he is eligible for Class C(ii) even in advance of another examination. Tolkien himself, or perhaps the War Office on his behalf, now applies to the Ministry of Labour in this regard.

5 October 1918 The Ministry of Labour, Appointments Department, Officers' University and Technical Classes (OUTC), Professional and Business Register acknowledges Tolkien's application for employment under the Ministry, and informs him that his services have been requested from the War Office.

13 October 1918 Tolkien is present at a special dinner featuring Italian food, probably sponsored by Italians for patients at the Savoy Hospital and the King's Lancashire Military Convalescent Hospital in Blackpool. (Italy at this time is ruled by the House of Savoy.) Tolkien obtains five signatures, including those of at least two Italians, on his printed menu card.

14 October 1918 A Medical Board at the King's Lancashire Military Convalescent Hospital, Blackpool, declares Tolkien unfit for six months in any category except sedentary employment, and recommends that he be given one month's leave. He is ordered to report in writing to the Controller, OUTC, Gresham House, Oxford.

Late October 1918 Although officially on leave, Tolkien returns to Oxford by the end of the month.

1 November 1918 Tolkien reports for duty at the Ministry of Labour Appointments Department in Oxford. He gives as a contact address the OUTC office in University College.

Early November 1918 With little hope of an academic post, Tolkien accepts an offer from his former tutor in Old Icelandic, William Craigie, to join the staff of the *New English Dictionary*, later and more widely known as the **Oxford English Dictionary*.

11 November 1918 The Armistice is signed.

29 November 1918 Tolkien writes notes on possible ways to work Watling Street, Wéland (Wayland), and the Romans into his mythology.

Late 1918 Tolkien, Edith, John, and Jennie Grove move into rooms at 50 St John Street, Oxford, let by a Miss Mahon.

16 December 1918 Christopher Wiseman, on leave in London, replies to a letter from Tolkien which took seven weeks to reach him, having followed his ship to Sevastopol and back. He had heard just before that letter arrived that Tolkien is now in Oxford. Wiseman, still on active service in the Navy, describes his future movements.

27 December 1918 Wiseman replies to a message from Tolkien. He is sorry to have been unable to visit Oxford. He must now return to *HMS Monarch* for a short time, then take up an appointment at Cambridge teaching junior officers. He assumes that Tolkien is now settled at 50 St John Street.

1919

1919 Tolkien marks the new year by beginning to record in a diary principal events in his life and his thoughts about them. He writes in English, at first with Roman letters, but later in a phonetic alphabet of his own invention. Eventually he attaches this to his mythology and names it the 'Alphabet of Rúmil' after the Elvish sage in his stories who devised letters to record Qenya texts (*Writing systems). From 1919 to the mid-1920s he will make constant alterations to the alphabet, so that even he will have difficulty reading it, and will rarely use it after 1930.

1919–1920 Tolkien revises his poem *The Pool of the Dead Year* (first composed in November–December 1915), now entitled *The Pool of Forgetfulness*. Probably during this period he also writes the poems *The Brothers in Arms* (later reworked as *The Brothers-in-Arms*), and *Nursery Rhymes Undone* (later revised as *The Cat and the Fiddle*, see **The Man in the Moon Stayed Up Too Late*).

c. **1919–*c.* 1923** Tolkien writes a series of tables of Qenya pronouns and pronominal prefixes and suffixes (*'Early Qenya Pronouns'). Later he reuses some of these sheets, with other discarded papers (including a letter dated 4 June 1920), in compiling a partial English–Old English dictionary.

?January–?June 1919 Tolkien writes a cosmogonical myth, *The Music of the Ainur* (*Ainulindalë), and otherwise continues work on *The Book of Lost Tales*, but largely abandons it, apparently by the end of June 1919. (See further, entry for *The Book of Lost Tales* in **Reader's Guide**.) The tales written in this period tell of the conflicts between the renegade Melko and the rest of the Valar (guardians or angelic powers) when he tried to seize the rule of the world; Melko's destruction of the Two Trees which gave light to Valinor, home of the Valar and of many Elves; his theft of precious jewels from the Elves and his flight into Middle-earth (not yet so-called); and the long and bitter war of the Elves with Melko in the hope of recovering their jewels. Some tales are left only in the form of rough notes and outlines which suggest that the author is undecided about many things in his mythology. – Probably during this period Tolkien extensively re-writes *The Fall of Gondolin* in ink over the original pencil version, and Edith makes a fair copy of the revision. – A list, **Corrected Names of Chief Valar*, and a brief Qenya text associated with *The Nauglafring: The Necklace of the Dwarves* (*The Book of Lost Tales*), *'Si Qente Feanor', may also date from this period. – At this time Tolkien also writes revisions to his Gnomish lexicon on the backs of *Oxford English Dictionary* proof slips.

January 1919 Tolkien begins work as an assistant at the *Oxford English Dictionary* in the Old Ashmolean building in Broad Street, Oxford, a short walk from the Tolkien home in St John Street. Under the supervision of *Henry Bradley, he will work on words beginning with 'W'. Most of those on the *Dictionary* staff also teach in the University, and their hours are flexible: Oxford University Press records at the end of March 1919 show that up to that date Tolkien was paid only one and one-half months' salary. – Tolkien will also accept tutorial work, and will come to find his services increasingly sought, particularly by the Oxford women's colleges, where English is one of the more popular subjects. He tutors students from Lady Margaret Hall, St Hugh's, Somerville, and St Hilda's, mainly in small groups. It is an advantage that he is married, as Edith's presence means that the colleges do not need to send a chaperone when their young ladies are tutored by Tolkien at his home.

19 January 1919 Hilary Full Term begins at Oxford.

Hilary Term 1919 Tolkien is noted as an Honorary Member of the Exeter College Essay Club, but is not recorded as present at any meetings during this term.

14 February 1919 Tolkien is examined by the Standing Medical Board, Merton Street, Oxford. The Board declares him unfit for general service or service abroad for six months, and unfit for active duty with troops on home service for three months, but fit for sedentary employment.

21 February 1919 Tolkien reads part of William Blake's prophetic books, which he has never seen before, and discovers to his astonishment several similarities in the nomenclature (though not necessarily the function) between Blake's beings and those in his own mythology.

15 March 1919 Hilary Full Term ends.

3 April 1919 The first slips prepared by Tolkien for the *Oxford English Dictionary* with editorial text and illustrative quotations, after emendation and approval by Bradley, are sent to Oxford University Press for typesetting. As Tolkien becomes more proficient, Bradley makes fewer alterations. Some of Tolkien's later work on the *Dictionary* will be under the editorship of *C.T. Onions.

27 April 1919 Trinity Full Term begins.

14 May 1919 In the evening, Tolkien attends a meeting of the Exeter College Essay Club at which C.A.R. Radford reads a paper on Rupert Brooke.

4 June 1919 In the evening, Tolkien attends a meeting of the Exeter College Essay Club at which *Wilfred R. Childe, an honorary visitor, reads a paper on modern poetry.

7 June 1919 Tolkien is examined by the Standing Medical Board, Merton Street, Oxford. The Board declares him unfit for general service or service abroad for six months, but fit for active duty with troops on home service. Tolkien is ordered 'to return to O.U.T.C. [Officers' University and Technical Classes] Oxford to complete his course' and the Ministry of Labour is to be informed.

21 June 1919 Trinity Full Term ends.

28 June 1919 The Treaty of Versailles with Germany is signed. Germany cedes Alsace-Lorraine to France, the larger part of Posen and West Prussia to Poland, and other territory to Belgium. The German army is not to exceed 100,000 men in number, and the size and number of its guns are restricted. Its navel power is also limited. An area thirty miles on the east side of the Rhine is to be demilitarized.

Summer–autumn 1919 Probably during this period Tolkien is commissioned by Oxford University Press to write the glossary (*A Middle English Vocabulary*) for the collection *Fourteenth Century Verse & Prose*, edited by his former tutor, Kenneth Sisam. Much research will be required for this, his first academic publication; and it may be for this reason that after June 1919 he largely abandons *The Book of Lost Tales*. Although he (apparently) now begins to retell the tale of Túrin Turambar in alliterative verse, he does not proceed very far with it, and is not occupied with any other major work on his mythology for the rest of the year. – Around this time, he also ceases to do much, if any, work on the *Qenyaqetsa* and the *Gnomish Lexicon*.

8 July 1919 The War Office informs Tolkien that his release from military service has been approved. He is to call at the Dispersal Unit at Fovant, near Salisbury in Wiltshire, on 15 July; his Army pay will cease on 16 July. The district OUTC office of the Ministry of Labour will issue him a Railway Warrant for the journey.

15 July 1919 Tolkien travels to Fovant to receive documents officially discharging him from military service, though he is still obliged to return to duty in the event of an emergency. His demobilization papers include a Protection Certificate (Officer) which states that he is released with effect 16 July; that he has the rank of Temporary Lieutenant; that the last unit in which he served was OUTC Oxford; that his Medical Category is C(i); that his occupation in civilian life is 'tutor'; and that his permanent address is 'Exeter College, Oxford'. He is also given a Demobilization Ration Book, valid for a fortnight, after which he will need a civilian ration book.

19 July 1919 Britain celebrates peace with victory parades.

4 September 1919 The Ministry of Pensions writes to Tolkien that in respect of his disability he has been awarded temporary retired pay at the rate of £35 a year from 16 July 1919 to 6 December 1919, and encloses a form for Tolkien to send to the Paymaster General. If his disability continues at the end of the period he can request a medical examination for further consideration of his case.

17 September 1919 Tolkien's combined income from the *Oxford English Dictionary* and from tutoring allows him to rent a small house at 1 Alfred Street (now called Pusey Street); the family moves on this date. Edith is able to bring her piano out of storage. The Tolkiens can also afford to engage a cook-housemaid to help Edith.

?Late summer 1919–?September 1920 Tolkien begins to write, or writes the earliest version of, **Light as Leaf on Lindentree*, an expression in verse of the story of Beren and Lúthien. He will note on a later version that the poem had its 'first beginnings' in 1919–20 at his home in Alfred Street.

12 October 1919 Michaelmas Full Term begins.

Michaelmas Term 1919 Tolkien holds the office of Critic to the Exeter College Essay Club.

30 October 1919 Tolkien receives his Master of Arts degree at Oxford in a Congregation.

?November 1919 Tolkien begins to keep a notebook in which he records his two-year-old son's pronunciation and use of words. He will later do the same for his second son, Michael.

11 November 1919 The Ministry of Pensions writes to Tolkien, who seems to have informed the authorities that he is still suffering some disability. The Ministry directs him to enter a hostel or colony for treatment and training, and also raises his retired Army pay to the maximum disabled rate, though he will be expected to use part of this to cover the costs of care. In the event, Tolkien seems not to have followed this directive, but used the verso of the letter to write part of a new poem, *The Ruined Enchanter: A Fairy Ballad*.

12 November 1919 In the evening, Tolkien attends a meeting of the Exeter College Essay Club at which C.H.B. Kitchin reads a paper, *World Progress and English Literature*. As Critic, Tolkien opens the discussion, touching upon the obsession with antiquity in art and ascribing the lure of the past to its familiarity. But he holds that the 'widening of modern knowledge of the universe &

consequent opening up of new fields of ideas, should more than compensate for any blunting of our capacity for imaginative appreciation of certain aspects of nature, as compared with the ancients' (Exeter College archives).

26 November 1919 In the evening, Tolkien attends a meeting of the Exeter College Essay Club at which E.C. Dickinson reads a paper, *The Aesthetic Value of the Ballad*. As Critic, Tolkien opens the discussion, touching on the origin of the ballad, and maintains that because of a different origin, the so-called modern ballad is not really a ballad at all.

6 December 1919 Michaelmas Full Term ends.

Winter 1919 Tolkien will later write in his diary that this winter 'found me still pegging away at tutoring in Oxford, still with the glossary [to *Fourteenth Century Verse & Prose*] hanging over me' (quoted by Christopher Tolkien in private correspondence).

1920

1920s or 1930s Tolkien writes a poem, *Vestr um haf* (Old Norse 'west over sea'). Much later, he will revise it as *Bilbo's Last Song (at the Grey Havens)*.

c. 1920–c. 1924 On one or more occasions during this period Tolkien revises the first section of the Eärendel poem he had written in ?late 1914. In the latest text he gives it the title *The Bidding of the Minstrel, from the Lay of Eärendel*.

18 January 1920 Hilary Full Term begins.

10 March 1920 In the evening, Tolkien attends a meeting of the Exeter College Essay Club and reads a shortened version of *The Fall of Gondolin*. Present in the audience are *Nevill Coghill (*see note*) and *H.V.D. 'Hugo' Dyson, who will become friends and fellow members of the *Inklings. Tolkien has worked hard on an introduction: his notes have many deletions and hesitations. In one deleted passage he mentions that his 'cycle' (mythology) concerns 'the coming of the mariner Eriol to the Lonely Island'. He declares that

the conventional apology of readers for their papers was never more due to the Club than tonight; but I must plead circumstances and a Secretary too strong for me. Circumstances have prevented me writing a critical paper; and the Secretary who had somehow entrapped me into 'reading something' this term, would not release me from my promise. Therefore I must read something already written, and in desperation I have fallen back on this Tale. It has, of course, never seen the light before but it was not written maliciously for your annoyance but in past days for my own amusement. A complete cycle of events in an Elfinesse of my own imagining has for some time past grown up (rather than been constructed) in my mind. Some of the episodes have been scribbled down (at great length – a length due to their interest for myself which can hardly be shared). This tale is not the best of them but it is the only one that has so far been revised at all and insufficient as that revision has been, I dare read aloud. It will take a longish time – please depart when you want to: perhaps (I may console myself by reflecting) too long for anyone to be left to tear me to pieces at the end. I have not the time or cheek to give a resume of the cycle so that you must please bear with the incidental allusions to other tales. [courtesy of, and corrected by, Christopher Tolkien; cf. *Unfinished Tales*, p. 5]

But the members of the Essay Club enjoy the reading. The Club Secretary will record in the minutes:

As a discovery of a new mythological background Mr Tolkein's [sic] matter was exceedingly illuminating and marked him out as a staunch follower of tradition, a treatment indeed in the manner of such typical Romantics as William Morris, George Macdonald, de la Motte-Fouquet [*sic, for* Fouqué] etc. We gathered likewise that the reader's acquaintanceship with Scandinavian saga and legend was not a little. . . . The battle of the contending forces of good and evil as represented by the Gongothlim [*sic, for* Gondothlim] and the followers of Melco [*sic, for* Melko] was very graphically and astonishingly told, combined with a wealth of attendance to detail interesting in extreme. At the conclusion as the hour had grown very late the president moved the omission of discussion, and the society adjourned after the customary vote of thanks to host and reader. [Exeter College archives; cf. *Letters*, pp. 445–6]

Although Tolkien's 'apology' states that *The Fall of Gondolin* is the only one of his tales 'that has so far been revised at all', this is not strictly true: the tales of Beren and Lúthien and of Túrin Turambar had also been rewritten. It may be that Tolkien means *recently* revised; an extant slip giving directions for the shortening of *The Fall of Gondolin* when delivered orally is almost certainly related to this reading, and alterations on similar slips show developments in the mythology subsequent to the work apparently completed in June (*The Book of Lost Tales*).

?March or later 1920 Tolkien writes a short prose work, *Ælfwine of England* (*Eriol and Ælfwine), in part reusing the paper of letters sent to him in February 1920. 'Ælfwine' ('Elf-friend') now, for a time, is the name of the mariner of his tales, who was still called 'Eriol' in the deleted introductory remark to *The Fall of Gondolin* mentioned above (10 March 1920). A related plot-outline for the work dates from around the same time, and not long after writing the first version of *Ælfwine of England* Tolkien rewrites it, introducing much new matter. 'It seems likely that *Ælfwine of England* was to be the beginning of a complete rewriting of the *Lost Tales*' (Christopher Tolkien, *The Book of Lost Tales, Part Two*, p. 322). Two outline schemes for *The Book of Lost Tales*, in both of which the mariner is called Ælfwine, apparently also belong to this time: one scheme is cursory though not without additions, while the other seems to be a projected (but unrealized) revision of the *Lost Tales*, preserving their general plan but with notes that some tales should be abridged or recast, with the names of certain characters changed and Tol Eressëa no longer identified with England, and with the role of the mariner diminished.

13 March 1920 Hilary Full Term ends.

17 March 1920 Tolkien replies to a request from a Miss Duncan at Somerville College, Oxford for guidance on questions that she might face in the Old English paper of her examination. He sends her fifty possible questions, many taken from past papers. He remarks that he hopes some time to produce a select bibliography, but will have no time to do so in the forthcoming vacation.

25 April 1920 Trinity Full Term begins.

Trinity Term 1920 Tolkien teaches a class on *Sir Gawain and the Green Knight*, Saturdays at 10.00 a.m. at 40 Broad Street, beginning 1 May. – He is an honorary member of the Exeter College Essay Club.

11 May 1920 Oxford University grants women full membership. They are now eligible for all degrees except the Bachelor of Divinity and the Doctor of Divinity. Attempts to exclude women dons from faculty boards and from acting as examiners are overwhelmingly defeated.

End of May 1920 Tolkien ceases to work for the *Oxford English Dictionary*.

June 1920 Tolkien's poem *The Happy Mariners* (first composed in July 1915) is published in the *Stapeldon Magazine* for June 1920, with only a few minor changes from the version rewritten on 9 September 1915. – Probably some time this month, informed of the opening by Kenneth Sisam, Tolkien applies for the post of Reader in English Language at the University of *Leeds.

Late June 1920 Tolkien goes to Leeds to be interviewed for the Readership. He is met at the station by *George S. Gordon, the Professor of English. While travelling by tram to Gordon's house they talk about Sir Walter Raleigh, Professor of English Literature at Oxford. 'As (still) a stiff-necked young philologist, I did not in fact think much of Raleigh – he was not, of course, a good lecturer; but some kind spirit prompted me to say that he was "Olympian". It went well; though I only really meant that he reposed gracefully on a lofty pinnacle above my criticism' (Tolkien, draft letter to R.W. Chapman, 26 November 1941, *Letters*, p. 56). The Committee on the Readership, consisting of the Vice-Chancellor, Professor Gordon, and Professor Strong, consider Tolkien as well as three other candidates.

?Second half of 1920–?1921 Either while in Oxford or not long after he moves to Leeds in the autumn, Tolkien writes prose fragments which postdate *The Book of Lost Tales*. One such fragment, *Turlin and the Exiles of Gondolin*, appears to be the beginning of a new version of *The Fall of Gondolin*. Another, describing the return of the Gnomes to the Great Lands, fills in part of the gap in *The Book of Lost Tales* which should contain the (unwritten) tale told by Gilfanon (earlier Ailios), *The Travail of the Noldoli* (see *'The Gnomes Come to the Great Lands'*). Both fragments show some development in the evolution of the mythology, the emergence of new characters, and inevitably changes of name (*'Flight of the Gnomes'*). On a slip of paper Tolkien makes brief notes developing *The Flight of the Noldoli*. But then he seems to give up any idea of continuing the mythology in prose. He begins *The Lay of the Fall of Gondolin* in rhyming couplets, but abandons it after writing 130 lines.

1 July 1920 Tolkien's appointment as Reader in English Language is recommended at a meeting of the Committee at Leeds.

21 July 1920 Tolkien's appointment is ratified at a meeting of the University of Leeds Council.

27 July 1920 Tolkien has lunch with George S. Gordon in Oxford.

Summer 1920 The Tolkien family go on holiday to a cottage in Trywn Llanbedrog on the coast of Cardigan Bay in North Wales. Edith Tolkien, now in the later stages of her second pregnancy, is upset by spiders that fall on her bed; she and her husband will later tell their second son, Michael, that Michael's fear of spiders might be due to this incident. – Tolkien draws two views of the Welsh coast.

October 1920 Tolkien's poem *Goblin Feet* is included, with a colour illustration by Warwick Goble, in *The Book of Fairy Poetry*, ed. Dora Owen.

1 October 1920 Tolkien takes up the Readership in English Language at the University of Leeds at a salary of £600 per year (*see note*). Edith will stay in Oxford for the birth of their second child, due very soon, and until Tolkien can find a suitable place for them to live in Leeds. With George S. Gordon's help, Tolkien finds a place to stay during the week in Leeds, at 21A St Michael's Road, Headingly; otherwise he spends as much time as he can in Oxford with his family. The staff of the School of English Language and Literature at Leeds, in addition to Gordon and Tolkien, consists of only two Assistant Lecturers and one Tutor in English Composition.

Autumn term 1920 Tolkien applies, by invitation, for two professorships of English Language: the Baines Chair at the University of Liverpool, and the new De Beers Chair at the University of Cape Town, South Africa. – Beginning this term, Tolkien actively assembles a personal library related to his teaching and studies. In addition to works concerned with Old English, Middle English, Icelandic, and other Germanic languages, he acquires many books on the various Celtic languages and literatures (Gaelic, Welsh, Breton, and Irish).

Late 1920–1923 At some time during this period Tolkien rewrites the poem *Tinfang Warble* (first composed in April 1915), doubling its length from the original eight lines. He will later note on a typescript: 'Rewritten Leeds 1920–23'.

Late 1920–1925 While at Leeds Tolkien writes an untitled, unfinished alliterative poem ('Lo! the flame of fire // and fierce hatred'), almost certainly a lay of Eärendel (see *'Lay of Eärendel'), which begins with the destruction of Gondolin and breaks off with refugees in the Land of Willows. – He also produces a typescript *Qenya Phonology* and a manuscript Qenya grammar (*Qenya: Descriptive Grammar of the Qenya Language*). He begins to make a typescript fair copy of the grammar, which he expands in the process but does not complete.

4 October 1920 University of Leeds term begins.

Leeds academic year 1920–1921 George S. Gordon, not long retired from military service, is just beginning to revise the English syllabus at Leeds by adopting that of Oxford, according to which undergraduates are offered specialized courses in medieval English language and literature or post-Chaucerian literature. He has been given a free hand to do so, and in turn gives Tolkien a free hand to develop the linguistic side of the school. Gordon will later recall that Tolkien began with only five linguistic specialists out of more than sixty honour students of the second and third years. – The *University of Leeds Calendar* for 1920–1 lists several lectures or classes to take place during the year for which Tolkien may have responsibility: History of English Language to the Close of the Fourteenth Century, and the special study of West Saxon Texts and the Language of Chaucer, on Mondays and Fridays at 3.00 p.m. and Thursdays at 11.30 a.m.; Old English Verse with a special study of *Beowulf, The Fight at Finnesburg, Widsith, Waldere,* and *Deor's Lament* on Mondays at 10.00 a.m.; The History of Modern English: Old and Middle English Texts on Wednesdays at 10.00 a.m.; Old and Middle English Dialects on Fridays at 12.00 noon; Gothic on Tuesdays at 2.00 p.m.; Early English Literature on Mondays at 12.00 noon; and Chaucer, weekly at an hour to be arranged. Tolkien might also be responsible for the first few lectures in an introductory course on English Literature which begins with the Prologue to the *Canterbury Tales,* the *Second Shepherd's Play, Everyman,* and *Morte d'Arthur,* and then moves on to Shakespeare, etc., Mondays and Wednesdays at 11.00 a.m. A Third Year Essay Class is also offered, involving discussions following upon papers read by students to the class, and chiefly concerned with Early English Literature and Civilization, weekly at an hour to be arranged; and there are weekly tutorial groups. – While at Leeds Tolkien will produce various duplicated or mimeographed pages to give to his students. (He will later use spare copies of some of these to write notes and drafts.) The topics of such pages include the *Ancrene Riwle* (October 1920); Phonology, and the Grammar of Layamon's *Brut* (November 1920); Kentish Dialect (Middle English) (27 January 1923); and the Development of Old English to Middle English (14 October 1923).

22 October 1920 Ronald and Edith Tolkien's second child, Michael Hilary Reuel Tolkien, is born at home in Oxford. His godparents are Monsignor Augustine Emery, the priest the Tolkiens knew at Great Haywood, and Mother Mary Michael of the Sisters of Mercy in Hull, whom Tolkien met when she visited him in hospital.

21 December 1920 Term ends at Leeds.

Christmas 1920 The Tolkien family spend Christmas in Oxford. John, now three years old, asks his father what Father Christmas is like, and where he lives. Tolkien responds by writing a letter to John as from Father Christmas, the first in a series (the *'Father Christmas' letters) which will continue until 1943. A double picture of Father Christmas trudging through a snow storm, and the house in which Father Christmas lives, accompanies the letter, enclosed in an envelope addressed with decorative writing and with a painted 'North Pole' stamp and postmark.

?End of 1920 Tolkien notes in a résumé of the year 1920 that 'the glossary [*A Middle English Vocabulary*] hardly got touched again' (quoted by Christopher Tolkien in private correspondence).

1921

?1921–?1924 Tolkien begins a typescript of his essay '*The Kalevala' or Land of Heroes* (read to Oxford societies in November 1914 and February 1915), but leaves it unfinished after nineteen pages, probably close to the end. He makes minor changes to the text throughout and reworks some sections. It is only in this typescript that, after referring to the *Kalevala* as 'mythological ballads' full of a 'primitive undergrowth' now cut away and reduced in other European literature, he adds: 'I would that we had more of it left – something of the same sort that belonged to the English.' He probably makes this typescript in preparation for still another reading of the paper, perhaps near Christmas: at one point he refers to 'our present holiday mood' (Tolkien Papers, Bodleian Library, Oxford).

?1921–summer 1924 Tolkien begins or continues work on the first version of *The Children of Húrin*, the story of Túrin Turambar, a long work in alliterative verse (cf. entry for Summer–autumn 1919). He begins a first version in manuscript and emends it; he also makes and emends a typescript, possibly in stages as the manuscript progresses. The manuscript has no title, but the typescript is called *The Golden Dragon*, changed to *Túrin Son of Húrin & Glórund the Dragon*. By summer 1924 Tolkien will have written 2201 lines but covered only half the story of Túrin. – During this period he also writes an index of names in the poem (*Index of Names for *The Lay of the Children of Húrin*').

After 3 January 1921 Tolkien draws up a synoptic table of the varieties of the Alphabet of Rúmil he has used in his diary. During January he will also draw up another table of this alphabet, with the title 'Gondolic Script'.

8 January 1921 By now, Tolkien has been consulted regarding a proposed series of Middle English texts designed for teaching. He is strongly in favour of normalization of texts, that is, making them consistent in spelling, etc., while Kenneth Sisam and David Nichol Smith are just as strongly opposed.

11 January 1921 Term begins at Leeds.

18 January 1921 Kenneth Sisam suggests to the authorities of the Oxford University Press that an edition of *Sir Gawain and the Green Knight* for students is badly needed.

End of January 1921 Tolkien is offered the De Beers Chair in Cape Town. He decides not to accept because Edith and baby Michael are not fit to travel, and he does not want to be separated from his family.

12 February 1921 Tolkien hands over to John Johnson, Assistant Secretary to the Delegates of the Oxford University Press, material for *A Middle English Vocabulary*. Johnson asks his opinion of a report made by Kenneth Sisam which argues firmly against normalization in the proposed Middle English text series.

14 February 1921 Tolkien writes to John Johnson from St Michael's Road, Leeds, enclosing a revised slip for the glossary. Although he could write an essay on the ethics and objects of normalization, which he supports at least for the sake of students whose approach to a text is literary, Tolkien feels that 'before even poking my nose into other matters I must knock down this mole-hill glossary (grown into a mountain by accumulated domestic distractions)'. He remarks however, surely with his own glossary for *Fourteenth Century Verse & Prose* in mind, that in non-normalized texts most of the trouble 'then falls on the "glossarist", who spends endless time (and space) recording forms that could be eliminated and still leave the printed text perfectly Middle English (and intelligible to the scribes and editors if resuscitated)' (Oxford University Press archives). But by mid-August he will have agreed that normalization of the text of *Sir Gawain and the Green Knight* is ill-advised.

March 1921 Tolkien finds furnished rooms for himself, Edith, and their sons at 5 Holly Bank, Leeds, which they will rent from a Miss Moseley, a niece of Cardinal Newman. (A photograph of the house, as 'Hollybank', appears in *The Tolkien Family Album*, p. 44.) *See note.*

16 March 1921 Tolkien is appointed a member of the Board of the Faculty of Arts at Leeds.

23 March 1921 Term ends at Leeds.

21 April 1921 Term begins at Leeds.

?Late April 1921 Following the Leeds spring vacation, Tolkien and his family move into 5 Holly Bank. Jennie Grove moves to Birmingham.

Early May 1921 Oxford University Press sends Tolkien corrected page proofs of *Fourteenth Century Verse & Prose*.

25 May 1921 Tolkien attends a meeting of the Board of the Faculty of Arts at Leeds.

2 July 1921 Term ends at Leeds.

?August 1921–1925 Tolkien continues to work on his invented languages. He begins a new Gnomish or Noldorin grammar entitled *Lam i·Ngolthor* (changed to *Lam na·NGoluith*), mainly in manuscript (*'Early Noldorin Grammar'*). He also types lists of Noldorin words and names taken from *The Book of Lost Tales* and the Noldorin grammar (*'Noldorin Word-lists'*). These are not all made at the same time and are extensively emended.

16 August 1921 C.T. Onions writes that he hopes to see Tolkien and Edith on 19 August when they come to Oxford, apparently to complete business regarding their move to Leeds. By now, Onions has suggested to Tolkien in correspondence that the latter should prepare, or help to prepare, an edition of *Sir Gawain and the Green Knight*, and agrees with Tolkien that normalization is not desirable for that work.

Late August 1921 Tolkien and his family move to a leased house at 11 St Mark's Terrace, Woodhouse Lane, in Leeds near the University. John and Priscilla Tolkien will later remark, regarding the pollution then common in Leeds, that 'chemicals in the air rotted the curtains within six months, and baby Michael was covered in smuts if he was left outside in his pram for any length of time; and Ronald found that he had to change his collar three times a day!' (*The Tolkien Family Album*, p. 45, with a photograph).

3 October 1921 Term begins at Leeds.

Leeds academic year 1921–1922 The *University of Leeds Calendar* for 1921–1922 lists several lectures or classes to take place during the year for which Tolkien may have responsibility: History of the English Language to the Close of the Fourteenth Century, and the special study of West Saxon Texts and of the Language of Chaucer, on Mondays and Fridays at 3.00 p.m.; Old English Verse with a special study of *Beowulf, The Fight at Finnesburg, Widsith, Waldere, Deor's Lament* on Mondays at 10.00 a.m.; The History of English on Wednesdays at 10.00 a.m.; Old and Middle English Texts on Mondays at 12.00 noon; Old and Middle English Dialects, fortnightly on Fridays at 12.00 noon; Introduction to Germanic Philology, with special reference to Old English, on Wednesdays at 11.00 a.m.; Gothic on Tuesdays at 2.00 p.m.; Early English Literature on Thursdays at 11.00 a.m.; and Chaucer, weekly at an hour to be arranged. A Third Year Essay Class is also offered, involving discussions following upon papers read by students to the class, and chiefly concerned with Early English Literature and Civilization, fortnightly on Fridays at 12.00 noon; and there are weekly tutorial groups.

16 October 1921 Tolkien draws up a table of 'Rúmil's Alphabet'.

18 October 1921 Tolkien attends a meeting of the Board of the Faculty of Arts at Leeds.

21 October 1921 Tolkien hears that *Fourteenth Century Verse & Prose* has been published, without his glossary which is still not finished. – He makes revisions to his table 'Rúmil's Alphabet'. During this month he will also begin another table of the alphabet, which he will complete in December.

26 October 1921 Tolkien remarks in his diary that he has 'practically done nothing but slave at the Glossary since last Friday' (quoted by Christopher Tolkien in private correspondence).

29 October 1921 George S. Gordon writes to David Nichol Smith to ask his opinion of *E.V. Gordon, a B.Litt. student Tolkien has recommended to fill one of two staff positions Gordon hopes to add to the Leeds English School.

15 November 1921 Tolkien attends a meeting of the Board of the Faculty of Arts at Leeds.

22 December 1921 Term ends at Leeds.

1922

?1922–1925 Tolkien creates several varieties of Valmaric script (*Writing systems), which he uses in addition to the Alphabet of Rúmil. – Tolkien writes approximately 120 entries for an English–Qenya dictionary (*'English–Qenya Dictionary'), primarily in Valmaric script.

Early 1922 Tolkien sends the completed manuscript of *A Middle English Vocabulary* to Oxford University Press. – George S. Gordon discusses with David Nichol Smith the idea of a book of selections from the works of Geoffrey Chaucer for use by students, and probably in this period talks to Tolkien about it also. This will develop into the *'Clarendon Chaucer', edited by Gordon and Tolkien, and ultimately abandoned.

January 1922 Tolkien draws up an untitled table of a variety of the Alphabet of Rúmil.

12 January 1922 Term begins at Leeds. E.V. Gordon takes up the post of Assistant Lecturer in English.

?January 1922–1925 Tolkien and E.V. Gordon work together to develop the language side of the Leeds English School. To make it more accessible they form a 'Viking Club' (*Societies and clubs) for past and present students of Old Icelandic, who meet to drink beer, read sagas, and sing comic songs and nonsense verses containing linguistic jokes, and popular songs or nursery rhymes translated into Old English, Gothic, or Old Norse. Most of the latter are written by Gordon or Tolkien, and circulated as stencilled sheets (see further, *Songs for the Philologists*). The Old English version of *The Mermaid* ('It was in the broad Atlantic') proves particularly popular. Tolkien even composes at least one Old English crossword puzzle to amuse his students.

20 January 1922 Tolkien gives a talk on the *Oxford English Dictionary* to a poorly attended joint meeting of the Yorkshire Dialect Society and the English Association, held at the University of Leeds. He is probably a member of both organizations by this time (*Societies and clubs).

8 February 1922 C.T. Onions writes to John Johnson to ask the position of Oxford University Press concerning their proposed student's edition of *Sir Gawain and the Green Knight*. He notes that Tolkien and E.V. Gordon have decided to produce such an edition, and that the University of Leeds is helping to pay for a rotographed facsimile of the original manuscript for the editors' use. Later in February he will pledge, on behalf of Tolkien and Gordon, that their book will not exceed 160 pages in length.

Beginning of March 1922 Edith and Michael Tolkien have bad colds. Edith records in her account book for the week 27 February–4 March (reproduced in *The Tolkien Family Album*, p. 46) that of a total expenditure of £8 9s 6d, 4s 3d are for medical costs, £2 5s 1d for food, and £4 11s 8d for wages for Mary (the maid?) and the children's nurse. – Tolkien becomes ill with influenza. – He receives proofs of *A Middle English Vocabulary*.

11 March 1922 Tolkien returns the bulk of the proofs of *A Middle English Vocabulary*, heavily corrected, to John Johnson at Oxford University Press. He apologizes for not sending them by return of post due to illness. He has just recovered from influenza.

22 March 1922 Term ends at Leeds.

20 April 1922 Term begins at Leeds.

25 April 1922 Tolkien attends a meeting of the Board of the Faculty of Arts at Leeds.

11 May 1922 *A Middle English Vocabulary* is published as a separate volume.

13 May 1922 Sir Walter Raleigh dies.

23 May 1922 Tolkien attends a meeting of the Board of the Faculty of Arts at Leeds.

8 June 1922 *A Middle English Vocabulary* is published in one volume with *Fourteenth Century Verse & Prose.*

26 June 1922 Tolkien sends a postcard to Henry Bradley, with whom he had worked on the *Oxford English Dictionary*, hoping that he has recovered from an illness. Tolkien includes a riddle in Old English verse based on a nursery rhyme, 'Enigma Saxonicum nuper "inventum".'

1 July 1922 Term ends at Leeds.

Summer 1922 The Tolkien family go on holiday for some weeks at *Filey on the Yorkshire coast. Tolkien spends much of his time marking School Certificate examination papers, an annual chore which he will undertake for many years to earn extra money to support his family. – While at Filey, Tolkien draws in *The Book of Ishness* a picture of his son John standing on a cliff looking out to sea.

Late July 1922 George S. Gordon resigns his chair at Leeds, having been elected Merton Professor of English Literature at Oxford. Tolkien will unsuccessfully apply for the Leeds chair, to which *Lascelles Abercrombie is elected. Michael Sadler, the Vice-Chancellor at Leeds, will inform Tolkien that the University hopes to create a new Professorship of English Language for him.

28 July 1922 By this date Tolkien has agreed to review, for the *Times Literary Supplement, Beowulf: An Introduction to the Study of the Poem* by *R.W. Chambers. He will make several pages of notes, but not complete the task.

2 October 1922 Term begins at Leeds.

Leeds academic year 1922–1923 In the absence of a *University of Leeds Calendar* for 1922–3 (not published), one assumes that Tolkien gives many of the same lectures as in earlier years, but he now shares the burden of Language instruction with E.V. Gordon.

?October 1922 Tolkien writes a poem, *The Clerke's Compleinte*, playing on the General Prologue to Chaucer's *Canterbury Tales*, about the chaos of registration at the start of the academic year at Leeds.

17 October 1922 Tolkien attends a meeting of the Board of the Faculty of Arts at Leeds. He is appointed to two sub-committees, one to decide what modifications of intermediate courses and examinations should be made for holders of Higher School Certificates, and one to review and report upon degrees in Arts, Commerce, and Law.

25 October 1922 Tolkien gives a talk on 'Watling Street' at a meeting of the Language Colloquium at the University, Leeds, held at 12 Beech Grove Terrace at 4.10 p.m.

21 November 1922 Tolkien attends a meeting of the Board of the Faculty of Arts at Leeds.

December 1922 Tolkien's poem *The Clerke's [sic] Compleinte* is published in *The Gryphon*, a Leeds University magazine, for December 1922.

14 December 1922 Tolkien attends a meeting of the Board of the Faculty of Arts at Leeds.

20 December 1922 Term ends at Leeds.

Christmas 1922 John and Michael Tolkien attend a party for children of University of Leeds staff. Michael Sadler, the Vice-Chancellor, plays Father Christmas but becomes stuck coming down the chimney; for a while, all those present can see is a pair of waving legs, until Sadler and a pile of parcels crash to the ground. It is probably at this party that both John and Michael catch measles, and in turn infect Edith and their nurse. Tolkien will write on 13 February: 'By the beginning of January I was the only one in the house left up. . . . The vacation work lay in ruins; but they (not the work) are all better now and not much the worse. I escaped' (letter to Elizabeth M. Wright, *Letters*, p. 11).

?End of 1922 Tolkien writes a poem, *Iumonna Gold Galdre Bewunden* (see *The Hoard*), inspired by line 3052 in *Beowulf* ('the gold of men long ago enmeshed in enchantment').

1923

?1923–1926 A revised version of Tolkien's poem *Tinfang Warble* (first composed in 1914) appears in the *Inter-University Magazine*, published by the University Catholic Societies' Federation of Great Britain. – Another poem by Tolkien, *The Grey Bridge of Tavrobel* (written in ?1917), is published in the same magazine, though not in the same issue.

?1923 Tolkien translates a prophecy by Gerald of Wales (Giraldus de Barri, Giraldus Cambrensis, *c.* 1146–1223) into late twelfth-century English of the South-west Midlands for W. Rhys Roberts, Professor of Classics at Leeds (retired 1923) to include in a paper, 'Gerald of Wales on the Survival of Welsh' (published 1925).

1923 Tolkien rewrites his poem *May Day* (first composed in April 1915) and makes the first of three typescripts of his poem *Light as Leaf on Lindentree*. – Tolkien first becomes acquainted with a manuscript glossary of the dialect of the Huddersfield District in South Yorkshire, prepared by Walter E. Haigh. Tolkien will urge Haigh to continue to work on it, and will later contribute a foreword; see entry for 12 January 1928.

January 1923 Tolkien's poem *Iumonna Gold Galdre Bewunden* is published in *The Gryphon* for January 1923.

10 January 1923 Term begins at Leeds.

13 February 1923 Tolkien writes to Elizabeth Wright, the wife of his former teacher Joseph Wright and herself a scholar (see *Joseph Wright), to thank her for an offprint of an article by her about *Sir Gawain and the Green Knight*. He notes that 'Philology is making headway' at Leeds. 'The proportion of "language" students is very high, and there is no trace of the press-gang!' (*Letters*, p. 11).

20 February 1923 Tolkien attends a meeting of the Board of the Faculty of Arts at Leeds.

20 March 1923 Tolkien attends a meeting of the Board of the Faculty of Arts at Leeds.

21 March 1923 Term ends at Leeds.

Spring 1923 Tolkien's poem *The City of the Gods* (composed in April 1915 with the title *Kôr*) is published in the Leeds magazine *The Microcosm* for Spring 1923.

19 April 1923 Term begins at Leeds.

20 April 1923 Tolkien attends a meeting of the Board of the Faculty of Arts at Leeds.

26 April 1923 A review by Tolkien of *Hali Meidenhad: An Alliterative Prose Homily of the Thirteenth Century*, ed. F.J. Furnivall, is published in the *Times Literary Supplement* for 26 April under the title *Holy Maidenhood*. *Hali Meidenhad* belongs to a group of works (*Katherine Group) to which Tolkien will devote a great deal of attention in his career.

May 1923 Tolkien catches a severe cold, which turns into pneumonia. He is gravely ill, his life in danger; but he will begin to recover by 12 June. His grandfather, John Suffield, aged 90, stays with Tolkien and his family at this time.

23 May 1923 Henry Bradley, Tolkien's former supervisor on the *Oxford English Dictionary*, dies.

June 1923 Three of Tolkien's poems are published in *A Northern Venture: Verses by Members of the Leeds University English School Association*: *Enigmata Saxonica Nuper Inventa Duo* ('two Saxon riddles newly discovered'), comprising two original riddles in Old English, one of which Tolkien sent to Henry Bradley in June 1922; *Tha Eadigan Saelidan: The Happy Mariners* (see *The Happy Mariners*), previously published with slight differences in June 1920; and *Why the Man in the Moon Came Down Too Soon*, first composed in March 1915 and retouched in 1923.

Early June 1923 George S. Gordon discusses the Clarendon Chaucer with Tolkien, perhaps while Gordon is at Leeds as an external examiner.

14 June 1923 Tolkien is first mentioned (in extant correspondence) as co-editor of the Clarendon Chaucer, in a letter by George S. Gordon to Kenneth Sisam, now an official at Oxford University Press. By now, the Press has agreed to publish the book in its Clarendon English Series of student texts. It is to emphasize Chaucer's works other than the *Canterbury Tales*, together with selections from critical literature and a glossary. Although Gordon and Tolkien had originally proposed to prepare a fresh text, they are required to use the existing edition of Chaucer by Professor Skeat (also published by Oxford).

30 June 1923 Term ends at Leeds.

Late June or July 1923 Once Tolkien has recovered from his illness, he and his family travel on holiday: the University of Leeds has instructions to forward his post to various addresses. One of these is Evesham (*West Midlands) where Tolkien's brother Hilary now owns a market garden and a plum and apple orchard. The visitors help Hilary with chores, and he and his brother amuse John and Michael by flying giant kites.

27 July 1923 George S. Gordon writes to Kenneth Sisam that Tolkien has agreed, or will soon agree, to provide a glossary for the Clarendon Chaucer. Gordon optimistically thinks that Tolkien will be ready to begin work as soon as he receives the texts, and will be able to finish in September.

?August 1923–1925 Tolkien begins to combine the list of Noldorin words and names compiled earlier at Leeds into a Noldorin dictionary (see *'Noldorin Dictionary'). – Around this time he also begins to compile an English–Qenya dictionary, with Qenya words given in Valmaric script (*'English–Qenya Dictionary').

October 1923 *Henry Bradley, 3 December 1845–23 May 1923,* an appreciation by Tolkien, is published in the *Bulletin of the Modern Humanities Research Association* for October 1923.

October–November 1923 Tolkien's poem *The Cat and the Fiddle: A Nursery Rhyme Undone and Its Scandalous Secret Unlocked* (*The Man in the Moon Stayed Up Too Late,* first composed probably in 1919–20) is published in *Yorkshire Poetry* for October–November 1923.

1 October 1923 Term begins at Leeds.

Leeds academic year 1923–1924 The *University of Leeds Calendar* for 1923–4 lists several lectures or classes to take place during the year for which Tolkien (or E.V. Gordon) may have responsibility: History of the English Language to the Close of the Fourteenth Century, and the special study of West Saxon Texts and of the Language of Chaucer, on Mondays and Fridays at 3.00 p.m. and Thursdays at 12.00 noon; Chaucer on Thursdays at 12.00 noon; Old English Verse with a special study of *Beowulf, The Fight at Finnesburg, Widsith, Waldere,* and *Deor's Lament* on Mondays at 10.00 a.m.; The History of English on Wednesdays at 10.00 a.m.; Old and Middle English Texts on Mondays at 12.00 noon; Old and Middle English Dialects, fortnightly on Fridays at 12.00 noon; Introduction to Germanic Philology, with special reference to Old English, on Wednesdays at 11.00 a.m.; and Early English Literature on Thursdays at 11.00 a.m. A Third Year Essay Class is also offered, involving discussions following upon papers read by students to the class, and chiefly concerned with Early English Literature and Civilization, fortnightly on Fridays at 12.00 noon, as well as a Special Subject (Gothic, Old Icelandic, etc.) on Tuesdays at 2.00 p.m. or at hours to be arranged. – The pressure of academic duties on Tolkien and Gordon by now has delayed completion of their edition of *Sir Gawain and the Green Knight.* On 10 November 1923 Gordon will inform Kenneth Sisam that he and Tolkien each have to conduct about fifteen hours of lectures and classes per week at Leeds, which leaves them little leisure. They are also hampered by the lack of good library facilities.

16 October 1923 Tolkien attends a meeting of the Board of the Faculty of Arts at Leeds. – George S. Gordon forwards to Kenneth Sisam a letter he has received from Tolkien, raising many points about the text for the Clarendon Chaucer, especially in relation to the Prologue to the *Canterbury Tales.* Sisam will reply that although he agrees with Tolkien, to put all of his suggestions into effect would be too costly.

17 October 1923 Tolkien's annual salary at the University of Leeds is raised from £600 to £700.

10 November 1923 E.V. Gordon writes to Kenneth Sisam regarding *Sir Gawain and the Green Knight*. He hopes that Oxford University Press will allow it to be longer than 160 pages. He and Tolkien will cut its glossary as much as possible, as glossaries are expensive to set in type, but even so they feel that they need another forty pages. If Oxford University Press insists, they will cut to 160 pages, but it will not be as good or as lively as they would like. Tolkien has agreed to submit the complete copy by 23 April, and the text in two weeks' time.

13 November 1923 Kenneth Sisam writes to E.V. Gordon, agreeing to 200 pages for *Sir Gawain and the Green Knight*, but the copy must be so good that there will be few proof corrections. He must receive some of the copy before 23 April, or it might be difficult to publish in time for the following university year.

15 November 1923 E.V. Gordon replies to Kenneth Sisam, accepting his conditions. He and Tolkien will try to reduce the glossary to fifty pages, though *Sir Gawain and the Green Knight* is different from most Middle English works and needs more glossing. In regard to a question asked by Gordon in an earlier letter, if Oxford University Press would be interested in a Modern English translation of *Sir Gawain and the Green Knight*, Sisam has asked for a sample of the text, suggesting lines 2000–2200; Gordon now notes that Tolkien made a translation of these lines some time ago, which they will revise and send to Sisam.

20 November 1923 Tolkien attends a meeting of the Board of the Faculty of Arts at Leeds. He is appointed to a committee to make arrangements for the entertaining of members of other faculties.

Late November–early December 1923 The Tolkien house is ransacked by burglars. Among the items stolen (and never recovered) are Edith's engagement ring and her best coat, but none of Tolkien's books. The family discover that their new maid, hired that autumn, is a member of a gang of thieves.

8 December 1923 E.V. Gordon writes to Kenneth Sisam. Despite Tolkien's misfortunes, they will soon be able to send Sisam the text for *Sir Gawain and the Green Knight*. Gordon has more or less completed the notes, but Tolkien will have to go through them, and some material must be transferred from the glossary to the notes.

Last half of December 1923 Tolkien receives and corrects proofs of text for the Clarendon Chaucer.

14 December 1923 E.V. Gordon sends Kenneth Sisam a clean copy of the text of *Sir Gawain and the Green Knight*. He adds that Tolkien has been lucky enough to acquire a copy of Thorkelin's *Beowulf* (the first full edition of that poem) for seven shillings.

19 December 1923 Term ends at Leeds.

Christmas 1923 Tolkien writes a letter to John as from Father Christmas, dated Christmas Eve. He is sending Lotts Bricks to John and Michael for Christmas.

1924

?1924–?1936 Tolkien writes out a declensional paradigm for *entu*, *ensi*, *enta* in his invented language Qenya.

?1924–1925 Tolkien begins to make an alliterative translation of *Beowulf*. Probably while still at Leeds he also works on a prose translation of that poem (apparently complete by spring 1926; see entry for ?26 April 1926).

1924 Tolkien revises his poem *The Forest Walker* (first composed 25–6 August 1916). – He retouches his poem *The Shores of Faëry* (first composed in July 1915) and possibly makes a new version in typescript. – He rewrites the penultimate verse of his poem *Light as Leaf on Lindentree*, and to precede it adds fifteen lines of alliterative verse. At the time of this writing or soon after, he inserts the poem and most of the alliterative lines into *The Children of Húrin*. – Possibly at this time he revises his poem *The Voyage of Éarendel the Evening Star* (first composed in September 1914).

5 January 1924 Tolkien returns corrected proofs of the first twenty-one pages of text of the Clarendon Chaucer. He has found only three misprints but has marked alterations to Skeat to which Kenneth Sisam had agreed, and justifies other changes he has made, especially in regard to punctuation. Tolkien also makes some queries about the setting of the glossary in *Sir Gawain and the Green Knight*, and asks if at some time Oxford University Press would be interested in publishing an *Introduction to German Philology* he would prepare.

8 January 1924 Kenneth Sisam writes to Tolkien, agreeing with most of the changes he has made to the first pages of proofs of the Clarendon Chaucer, but mainly on grounds of cost hopes that Tolkien will limit changes to punctuation. He gives him some advice about the glossary to *Sir Gawain and the Green Knight*, and expresses interest in an *Introduction to German Philology* if it were not too long or too unreadable.

10 January 1924 Term begins at Leeds.

14 January 1924 Tolkien writes to R.W. Chambers, thanking him for a copy of his inaugural lecture as Quain Professor of English Language and Literature at University College, London, 'Concerning Great Teachers of the English Language', which Tolkien has enjoyed reading. He has only just received it 'a day or two ago', as it was 'not forwarded while I was away' (reproduced in Caroline Chabot, 'Raymond Wilson Chambers (1874–1942)', *Moreana* 24, no. 93 (February 1987), p. 80).

15 January 1924 Tolkien attends a meeting of the Board of the Faculty of Arts at Leeds.

Mid-January 1924 Michael Tolkien is ill with appendicitis, but miraculously recovers on the eve of an operation.

1 February 1924 Tolkien sends Kenneth Sisam more corrected proofs of the Clarendon Chaucer text, with as little alteration as possible. He thanks Sisam for two extra copies of proofs of *Sir Gawain and the Green Knight*, for specimens of its glossary printed in two different ways, and for a copy of *Religious Lyrics of the Fourteenth Century*, edited by Carleton Brown. – By now, the Tolkiens have found a new maid.

26 February 1924 Kenneth Sisam writes to George S. Gordon that he is alarmed at the slow progress of the Clarendon Chaucer. Tolkien is carrying on with the text, but there is still the glossary to complete, and he is also still occupied with *Sir Gawain and the Green Knight*. Sisam asks Gordon for the introduction and notes he was to provide. He has heard from E.V. Gordon that he too is worried about the progress of *Sir Gawain*. On 28 February George S. Gordon will reply to Sisam in Tolkien's defence.

5 March 1924 Kenneth Sisam writes to Tolkien that he is patiently expecting the Clarendon Chaucer, and asks him to check some corrections in *A Middle English Vocabulary*, presumably for the 1924 reprint.

17 March 1924 Tolkien and his family move to a three-storey house they have purchased at 2 Darnley Road, West Park, in the outskirts of Leeds with open fields nearby. – Here, when his son John cannot sleep, Tolkien will sit on his bed and tell him stories. These include a tale of 'Carrots', a boy with red hair who climbs into a cuckoo clock and has a series of adventures. Tolkien seems not to have written this down, nor indeed most of the stories he tells his children. An exception is *The Orgog*, the strange, convoluted tale of an odd creature travelling through a fantastic landscape. A watercolour by Tolkien, *A Shop on the Edge of the Hills of Fairy Land* (*Artist and Illustrator*, fig. 71), later inscribed 'Drawn for John, Darnley Road, Leeds 1924', seems to relate to *The Orgog*, but does not illustrate the part of the story that survives.

20 March 1924 Term ends at Leeds.

21 March 1924 Kenneth Sisam writes to David Nichol Smith, complaining that Tolkien is holding up not only the Clarendon Chaucer but the edition of *Sir Gawain and the Green Knight* with E.V. Gordon, and that this state of affairs cannot be allowed to continue.

24 April 1924 Term begins at Leeds.

May 1924 Tolkien writes a poem, **The Nameless Land*, at his home in Darnley Road, inspired by reading the Middle English poem *Pearl* for examination papers. – Three of Tolkien's poems are published in the anthology *Leeds University Verse 1914–24*, compiled and edited by the English School Association, Leeds: *The Lonely Isle* (composed in June 1916); *The Princess Ní* (composed in July 1915); and **An Evening in Tavrobel*, a revision of *Two Eves in Tavrobel* (composed in July 1916).

15 May 1924 George S. Gordon informs Kenneth Sisam that Tolkien has agreed to retire from the Clarendon Chaucer. (In the event, Tolkien does not retire, or no replacement for him is found. He will be recorded as still at work on the project in October 1924.)

20 May 1924 Tolkien attends a meeting of the Board of the Faculty of Arts at Leeds.

12 June 1924 English Final Honour School examinations begin at Oxford; Tolkien is an external examiner. Other examiners are H.F.B. Brett-Smith, H.C. Wyld, and Oliver Elton. There are ninety candidates. The examiners' statement of results will be dated 11 July 1924. Later in the year the examiners' report will note that 'the general impression conveyed by the papers was that many of the candidates had neglected the linguistic part of the work until towards the end of their time, in the belief that they could "get it up" hurriedly in a few weeks', an impression confirmed in the *viva voce* examinations (Oxford University Archives FA 4/10/2/3).

17 June 1924 Tolkien attends a meeting of the Board of the Faculty of Arts at Leeds.

?Summer 1924–early 1925 Tolkien adds another 75 lines to the first version of *The Children of Húrin*. Now or possibly while still working on the first version, he begins a second, expanded version, at first called *Túrin*, changed to *The Children of Húrin*. Again he works both in manuscript and typescript, with revisions and emendations. By summer 1925, after writing 817 lines, he leaves the second version unfinished. – Tolkien develops various elements from *The Children of Húrin* into an independent poem, originally untitled ('The high summer / waned to autumn'). Each of three versions is much developed from its predecessor; the second version is entitled *Storm over Narog*, and the third *Winter Comes to Nargothrond*. – In another untitled poem ('With the seething sea // Sirion's waters'), Tolkien develops a section from *The Children of Húrin* describing the river Sirion meeting the sea.

5 July 1924 Term ends at Leeds.

16 July 1924 Tolkien's appointment to a new Professorship of English Language from 1 October 1924 is confirmed at a meeting of the University of Leeds Council. By virtue of this appointment he becomes a member of the University Senate. His annual salary is now £800.

***c.* 20 July 1924** Tolkien dines at the Randolph Hotel in Oxford with George S. Gordon and three men from Canada: R.S. Knox and Herbert Davis, both former lecturers in the Leeds English School, and E.J. Pratt, who will become one of Canada's best-known poets. Knox will recall that during the evening Gordon played the piano, leading the others in song. – Tolkien possibly dines at Gordon's house a day or two later, again with the visitors from Canada.

21 August 1924 Tolkien retouches his poem *The Trumpets of Faery* (originally composed in July–August 1915) and gives it a new title, *The Horns of the Host of Doriath*.

1 October 1924 Term begins at Leeds. Tolkien is now Professor of English Language.

Leeds academic year 1924–1925 The *University of Leeds Calendar* for 1924–1925 lists several lectures or classes for which Tolkien may have responsibility; later his application for the Rawlinson and Bosworth Professorship of Anglo-Saxon at Oxford (25 June 1925) will indicate courses he taught at Leeds during this academic year. These include: History of English on Mondays and Wednesdays at 12.00 noon; Introduction to Germanic Philology on Thursdays at 10.00 a.m.; Essays and Discussions on Fridays from 9.30 to 11.00 a.m.; Linguistic Study of Old and Middle English Texts on Fridays at 11.00 a.m.; Old Icelandic (Second Year) on Fridays at 2.00 p.m.; and Medieval Welsh, an optional subject on a day and hour to be arranged personally with Tolkien. He also teaches one or more of the following: Old and Middle English Readers on Mondays at 10.00 a.m.; either Middle English Texts (*Sir Gawain and the Green Knight*) or Chaucer on Thursdays at 12.00 noon; and either Early English Literature or Middle English Texts (*Layamon's Brut*: Selections) on Thursdays at 11.00 a.m. Tolkien conducts as well a voluntary reading class for the study of additional Old and Middle English texts, on Fridays at 12.00 noon; he will later note that this attracted more than fifteen students, not all from the linguistic side of the English department.

3 October 1924 Tolkien attends a meeting of the Senate of the University of Leeds.

?18 (received 19) October 1924 George S. Gordon writes to Kenneth Sisam, enclosing the text and notes for the essays for the Clarendon Chaucer. He reports that Tolkien has finished the glossary and has written a first draft of the notes on the text, which he is working to abbreviate when he can find the time.

21 October 1924 Tolkien attends a meeting of the Board of the Faculty of Arts at Leeds.

22 October 1924 Tolkien works on the glossary for the Clarendon Chaucer; it is not finished, despite George S. Gordon's claim of *c.* 19 October.

23 October 1924 Tolkien writes to thank Kenneth Sisam for sending a proof of the frontispiece for *Sir Gawain and the Green Knight* and two sets of proofs of the Clarendon Chaucer together with comments by George S. Gordon. He promises to work on the Chaucer in any cracks of free time.

5 November 1924 Tolkien attends a meeting of the Senate of the University of Leeds. He is appointed to the Library Committee.

16 November 1924 Tolkien attends a meeting of the Senate of the University of Leeds.

21 November 1924 Ronald and Edith Tolkien's third child, Christopher Reuel Tolkien, is born at home in Leeds. His godparents are Wilfred R. Childe, Lecturer in the Leeds English School, and Mrs E.M. Spilmont, apparently the former Miss Moseley from whom Tolkien had rented 5 Holly Bank in Leeds.

Early December 1924 Tolkien and at least some of his family are ill. He informs Kenneth Sisam that this has delayed his work on the Clarendon Chaucer.

5 December 1924 Kenneth Sisam writes to Tolkien, asking to have the glossary for the Clarendon Chaucer by 31 December 1924, and the notes by 31 January 1925. He advises Tolkien that the book cannot stand the cost of a long glossary, and that it is not aimed at readers interested in philology.

8 December 1924 George S. Gordon informs Kenneth Sisam that Tolkien has sent him the manuscript of his glossary for the Clarendon Chaucer, with a preface, for Gordon to examine. – Tolkien attends a meeting of the Senate of the University of Leeds.

20 December 1924 Term ends at Leeds.

22 December 1924 George S. Gordon sends with approval to Kenneth Sisam the manuscript of Tolkien's glossary and preface for the Clarendon Chaucer.

23 December 1924 Kenneth Sisam writes to George S. Gordon. Tolkien has been warned about the cost of excess proof correction. He will have to pay this himself if he makes as many corrections to the proofs of the Clarendon Chaucer as he did to those of *A Middle English Vocabulary*. – Tolkien, as 'Father Christmas', writes two short letters to his sons John and Michael. Among other things, he is bringing John a station, and Michael an engine (the boys are model train enthusiasts).

1925

?1925–?1926 Tolkien begins to make a Modern English translation of the Middle English poem *Pearl*. – Possibly around this time, he and E.V. Gordon plan to produce a joint edition of *Pearl* similar to their edition of *Sir Gawain and the Green Knight*. Tolkien, however, will make little or no contribution by June 1937.

1925 'Gerald of Wales on the Survival of Welsh', an essay by W. Rhys Roberts, former Professor of Classics at Leeds, is published in the *Transactions of the Honourable Society of Cymmrodorion: Session 1923–1924*. It contains, among other versions of a prophecy by Gerald of Wales (Giraldus Cambrensis), one in late twelfth-century English of the South-west Midlands prepared by Tolkien.

?Early 1925 Tolkien writes, but does not finish, an alliterative poem. Each of its three manuscripts has a different title: *The Flight of the Gnomes as Sung in the Halls of Thingol*; *Flight of the Gnomes* (added later); and **The Flight of the Noldoli from Valinor*.

5 January 1925 Kenneth Sisam writes to George S. Gordon that the glossary for the Clarendon Chaucer must be cut by ten pages. He leaves it to Gordon to discuss with Tolkien how this might be done. – Sisam also writes to Tolkien, returning the glossary and advising him to abandon all easy words and practically all references as a way of reducing its length. He asks how Tolkien is progressing with *Sir Gawain and the Green Knight* – evidently Tolkien is now correcting proofs.

8 January 1925 A review-essay by Tolkien, *Philology: General Works*, is published in **The Year's Work in English Studies*, vol. 4 (1924, for 1923). He discusses at length some fifteen works (mainly books, some in French or German), and refers to many others in passing.

13 January 1925 Term begins at Leeds.

20 January 1925 Tolkien attends a meeting of the Board of the Faculty of Arts at Leeds.

21 January 1925 Tolkien attends a meeting of the Senate of the University of Leeds.

24 January 1925 Tolkien attends a meeting of the Senate of the University of Leeds.

26 January 1925 Tolkien writes a letter of appreciation to Joseph Wright on his retirement.

4 February 1925 Tolkien attends a meeting of the Senate of the University of Leeds. He is appointed to a committee on the terms of appointment of junior staff.

5 February 1925 Kenneth Sisam reminds Tolkien that he is supposed to have completed the notes for the Clarendon Chaucer by 31 January. *Sir Gawain and the Green Knight* is progressing well through the press.

17 February 1925 Tolkien attends a meeting of the Board of the Faculty of Arts at Leeds.

Late February or early March 1925 Tolkien sends George S. Gordon a revised glossary for the Clarendon Chaucer.

4 March 1925 George S. Gordon sends Tolkien's revised glossary to Kenneth Sisam, saying that it is now the right length. Gordon feels, however, that Tolkien's preface is too curt and professional for the school audience at which the book is aimed. He sends Sisam a 'chattier' version, which the latter will prefer. – Tolkien attends a meeting of the Senate of the University of Leeds.

17 March 1925 Tolkien attends a meeting of the Board of the Faculty of Arts at Leeds.

23 March 1925 Kenneth Sisam sends Tolkien an advance copy of *Sir Gawain and the Green Knight*. Oxford University Press are to change the binding and add guard sheets to protect the collotype plates. Since he can send only one copy, Sisam asks Tolkien to show it to E.V. Gordon and to let him know of any faults as soon as possible.

25 March 1925 Term ends at Leeds.

April 1925 An article by Tolkien, **Some Contributions to Middle-English Lexicography*, is published in the *Review of English Studies* for April 1925.

23 April 1925 Term begins at Leeds. – *Sir Gawain and the Green Knight*, edited by Tolkien and E.V. Gordon, is published.

May 1925 Tolkien receives proofs of the glossary to the Clarendon Chaucer probably in mid-May. George S. Gordon seems to have corrected galley proofs of the text: these and probably Tolkien's corrected glossary are set in page proof and sent to Gordon and Tolkien later in May.

6 May 1925 Tolkien attends a meeting of the Senate of the University of Leeds.

19 May 1925 Tolkien attends a meeting of the Board of the Faculty of Arts at Leeds.

28 May 1925 Tolkien attends a meeting of the Board of the Faculty of Arts at Leeds.

June 1925 Tolkien's poem *Light as Leaf on Lindentree* (composed 1919–20 and later) is published in *The Gryphon* for June 1925.

5 June 1925 Tolkien attends a meeting of the Senate of the University of Leeds.

11 June 1925 English Final Honour School examinations begin at Oxford; Tolkien is an external examiner. Other examiners are George S. Gordon, Oliver Elton, and Edith Wardale. There are 154 candidates.

12 June 1925 W.A. Craigie having decided to leave the Rawlinson and Bosworth Professorship of Anglo-Saxon, it is announced in the *Oxford University Gazette* that candidates for the chair must submit their names to the Registrar by 4 July, together with no fewer than eight copies of any statement, references, and testimonials. The notice states that the Professor will be required to lecture on Old English language and literature, and may also lecture on other Old Germanic languages, especially Icelandic. He must give no fewer than forty-two lectures during the academic year, and must reside within the University during six months at least between 1 September and the following 1 July. The stipend is to be £1,000 a year. – If he has not done so already, having heard that Craigie, his former tutor, is leaving Oxford, Tolkien now writes to several of his colleagues for letters testifying to his qualifications for the Rawlinson and Bosworth chair.

Mid-June 1925 By now, Tolkien and George S. Gordon finish correcting page proofs of the Clarendon Chaucer.

Summer 1925 By now, Tolkien has abandoned *The Children of Húrin* and now begins a new poem, the **Lay of Leithian*, in octosyllabic couplets. He will continue to work on this for six years, abandoning it in its turn unfinished in September 1931. Tolkien will write in his diary that he began 'the poem of Tinúviel' during the period of the summer examinations of 1925 (quoted in **The Lays of Beleriand* (1985), p. 150).

23 June 1925 Oxford University Press produces revised page proofs of the Clarendon Chaucer. These however do not include the notes, which Tolkien has not yet written, nor George S. Gordon's introduction and notes on the critical essays.

End of June 1925 Tolkien submits a formal printed application for the Rawlinson and Bosworth Professorship of Anglo-Saxon at Oxford, dated 25 June 1925 but with a covering letter dated 27 June. The application includes letters of support from distinguished colleagues, all but one of which Tolkien by now has solicited: L.R. Farnell, Rector of Exeter College, Oxford (23 June); Joseph Wright, the retiring Professor of Comparative Philology (22 June); the late Henry Bradley (7 June 1920, a letter undoubtedly written in support of Tolkien's readership at Leeds); M.E. Sadler, former Vice-Chancellor at Leeds, now Master of University College, Oxford (17 June); George S. Gordon, Merton Professor of English Literature, Oxford (28 June); Allen Mawer, Professor of English Language and Philology in the University of Liverpool (25 June); and Lascelles Abercrombie, Professor of English Literature, Leeds (June 1925).

July 1925 An article by Tolkien, **The Devil's Coach-horses*, is published in the *Review of English Studies* for July 1925.

4 July 1925 Term ends at Leeds.

14 July 1925 Tolkien writes out the examiners' statement for the English Final Honour School at Oxford. Later in the year, the examiners' report will note 'signs . . . that the candidates were beginning to combine their literary and linguistic knowledge, and that the modern unnatural division between Literature and Philology was beginning to break down' (Oxford University Archives FA 4/10/2/3).

21 July 1925 The electors to the Rawlinson and Bosworth Professorship of Anglo-Saxon meet: they are H.M. Chadwick, Elrington and Bosworth Professor of Anglo-Saxon at Cambridge; R.W. Chambers, Quain Professor of English Language and Literature, University College, London; Hermann G. Fiedler, Taylorian Professor of the German Language and Literature, Oxford; C.T. Onions, Lecturer in English, Oxford; the Rev. Charles Plummer, Fellow of Corpus Christi College, editor of medieval texts; Joseph Wells, Vice-Chancellor of Oxford University; and H.C. Wyld, Merton Professor of English Language and Literature, Oxford. Professor Allen Mawer of Liverpool having decided not to apply, and Professor Chambers having declined a direct offer of the chair, the electors consider three applications: two of these are from Tolkien and his former tutor, Kenneth Sisam. Tolkien is elected by four votes to three. – E.S. Craig, the University Registrar, writes to Tolkien with his congratulations, and sends him an undertaking to sign.

22 July 1925 Tolkien's election to the Rawlinson and Bosworth chair is announced in *The Times*. – He returns the signed undertaking to E.S. Craig at once. He assumes that the statutes governing the chair can be mitigated during Michaelmas Term 1925, as he has to give six months' notice to Leeds. – He informs the Vice-Chancellor at Leeds that he has been elected to the Rawlinson and Bosworth Professorship, and resigns his Leeds chair 'only with feelings of great regret at this sudden severance, in spite of this unexpected turn of fortune for myself' (*Letters*, p. 13). – Tolkien is in the process of marking School Certificate examination papers, having read two hundred answers on 'Caesar's ghost', when he writes to H.F.B. Brett-Smith at Oxford. Brett-Smith has sent Tolkien congratulations on his election to the Rawlinson and Bosworth Professorship. Tolkien encloses a poem with his reply.

24 July 1925 Oxford Registrar E.S. Craig replies that Tolkien should be able to arrange his schedule, in consultation with his colleagues, so that he can teach at both Leeds and Oxford during Michaelmas Term. He sends Tolkien a schedule of lectures for Michaelmas Term, the proposed lecture list, and the corresponding list for Michaelmas Term 1924.

7 August 1925 In a letter to R.W. Chambers Tolkien mentions that he has only just finished marking School Certificate examination papers, which he must do in order to pay doctor's bills.

8 August 1925 Tolkien replies to a letter from H.F.B. Brett-Smith. He promises to send more of his poetry, and remarks on the tedious labour of correcting examination papers.

23 August 1925 Tolkien works on the *Lay of Leithian*, marking this date on the manuscript page that begins with line 557.

Late August 1925 The Tolkiens have professional family photographs taken in Leeds. A comb in the photographer's waiting room is used to tidy John and Michael's hair; some weeks later, they will develop ringworm.

30 or 31 August 1925 Partly to celebrate his new appointment, Tolkien and his family take a three-week holiday at Filey. They stay in a cottage on a cliff overlooking the sea.

2 September 1925 When the Tolkiens look out of the window for several nights, they see the full moon rise and make a silver 'path' across the sea.

3 or 4 September 1925 Tolkien takes John and Michael for walks on the shingle beach and shows them how to skim stones into the sea. Michael carries his favourite toy, a miniature dog, made of lead and painted black and white, which he normally refuses to let go even to have his hand washed. Now, in his excitement, he puts it down on the shingle, and when he looks for it later it cannot be found. Tolkien and the boys will search for two days with no success.

5 September 1925 In the afternoon, the east coast of England is struck by a severe storm which continues into the night. The Tolkiens' cottage is shaken by the winds so severely that they fear the roof might blow off. Tolkien calms his sons by telling them a story, which is also intended to comfort Michael for the loss of his toy dog. In *Roverandom* a real dog is turned into a toy, taken to the moon along a silver 'moon path', and (returned to earth) brought under the sea where he disturbs a great serpent, causing a terrible storm. Tolkien does not write down this story at once, but at some time before the end of 1925 he will draw the lunar landscape described in it, titling it in a variety of his Valmaric alphabet (*Artist and Illustrator*, fig. 72).

6 September 1925 The Tolkiens go down to the beach at Filey. The high tide, blown inland by the storm, has destroyed beach huts and swept over the promenade. There is now even less hope of finding Michael's lost toy.

Mid-September 1925 On one day during their holiday at Filey the Tolkiens walk a long way to see the remains of a German submarine sunk in the First World War near Flamborough Head. – Tolkien writes lines 649–757 of the *Lay of Leithian*.

1 October 1925 Term begins at Leeds; Tolkien takes up his appointment as Rawlinson and Bosworth Professor of Anglo-Saxon at Oxford. To fulfil the notice required by his contract, he will not vacate his chair at Leeds until 31 December 1925, but will continue to live and teach there during the autumn term as well as undertake his new duties at Oxford. His lectures and classes at Leeds are presumably similar to those of the previous year, but necessarily rescheduled to allow him to travel four times (fortnightly) to Oxford, where he lectures on Fridays and Saturdays. – Probably at some time after his return to

Oxford, Tolkien makes a manuscript copy of his poem *The Clerke's Compleinte*, using letterforms of Chaucer's time and with emendations from the text published in December 1922. Later still, he will further emend the poem, replacing Leeds with Oxford as the place to which students travel in October.

6 October 1925 Tolkien attends a meeting of the Senate of the University of Leeds.

7 October 1925 The Vice-Chancellor of Oxford delivers a speech in Latin to Convocation reviewing the past academic year and welcoming newcomers to positions in the University, including Tolkien as Professor of Anglo-Saxon.

11 October 1925 Michaelmas Full Term begins at Oxford. Tolkien's scheduled lectures for this term are: *Anglo-Saxon Reader* (Selected Extracts, for those who have already acquired the elements of Old English), fortnightly on Fridays and Saturdays at 10.00 a.m. in the Examination Schools, beginning 16 October; and *Beowulf* (Text), fortnightly on Fridays and Saturdays at 11.00 a.m. in the Examination Schools, also beginning 16 October.

20 October 1925 Tolkien attends a meeting of the Board of the Faculty of Arts at Leeds.

21 October 1925 The University of Leeds Council notes Tolkien's resignation as of 31 December 1925.

30 October 1925 Tolkien attends a meeting of the Board of the Faculty of Medieval and Modern Languages and Literature (of which, at this date, the Oxford English School is still a part) at 3.30 p.m. in the Board Room of the Clarendon Building, Oxford. He is elected a member of the English Fund Committee for three years, and also a member of a committee 'to consider the conduct of and regulations for the Examination in the Honour School of English and report to the Board' (Oxford University Archives FA 4/10/1/1). He is appointed supervisor of M.G. Last of the Society of Oxford Home-Students, a probationer B.Litt. student wishing to study an Old English subject; and also supervisor of Julia Maud Keays-Young, also of the Society of Oxford Home-Students, who is working on a B.Litt. thesis, *England and the English in the Icelandic Sagas*. – At one of the Faculty Board meetings in Michaelmas Term 1925 Tolkien will be appointed an elector to the Merton Professorship of English Language and Literature for three years. Later he will be reappointed at intervals for further terms, but is never called upon to serve.

4 November 1925 Tolkien attends a meeting of the Senate of the University of Leeds.

12 November 1925 The University of Leeds Committee on the Chair of English Language discuss a successor to Tolkien and agree unanimously that E.V. Gordon should be appointed to the Chair from 1 January 1926. Tolkien, George S. Gordon, and Allen Mawer of Liverpool have written in support of E.V. Gordon's application. The Committee also agree to accept an offer of occasional assistance that Tolkien made at some point in 1925, and that he should be paid accordingly.

17 November 1925 Tolkien attends a meeting of the Board of the Faculty of Arts at Leeds.

21 November 1925 The committee (including Tolkien) appointed to consider the examination in the Honour School of English at Oxford completes work on its report for the Board of the Faculty of Medieval and Modern Languages and Literature. It will be presented to a meeting of the Board, in Tolkien's absence, on 3 December.

12 December 1925 Michaelmas Full Term ends at Oxford.

End of autumn term 1925 or early 1926 Students of the English School at Leeds take up a collection to pay for a photograph of Tolkien to be hung in the staff-house of the Department of English. They make a present to Tolkien of a print of a rejected version.

19 December 1925 Term ends at Leeds.

Christmas 1925 Tolkien, as 'Father Christmas', writes to John and Michael. He explains that he can write only one letter to them this year as he has been busy moving house (as the Tolkiens themselves will do very soon), his old home having been accidentally damaged by the North Polar Bear. But Tolkien also encloses a postscript as from the North Polar Bear, and a double illustration of the accident and of Father Christmas below his new house high on a cliff.

End of 1925 Tolkien resumes correspondence with R.W. Reynolds, who is now retired from King Edward's School.

1926

?1926–?1930 At some time in this period, Tolkien makes the first 'Silmarillion' map, incorporating the much greater geographical detail included in *The Children of Húrin* and the *Lay of Leithian* (relative to *The Book of Lost Tales*). It will remain his working map until at least 1932, during which time he will make many additions and emendations. The map is originally only one sheet, but two supplementary sheets extend the area covered to the east and west.

1926–1933 Tolkien keeps a diary written in a proto-Fëanorian alphabet (see *Writing systems).

Early 1926 Tolkien writes a prose manuscript of twenty-eight pages entitled 'Sketch of the Mythology with especial reference to "The Children of Húrin"' (*Sketch of the Mythology*) to explain the background of the poem to R.W. Reynolds. This is the first text to cover the whole of Tolkien's mythology from the rebellion of Morgoth to the age of Men and 'the last end of the tales'. The story has advanced since *The Book of Lost Tales*, apparently (to judge by the lack of intervening texts) only in Tolkien's mind while he was at Leeds. He will revise the *Sketch*, in places heavily, between 1926 and 1930.

First part of 1926 Tolkien sends R.W. Reynolds many of his poems, including the unfinished *Lay of Leithian* and part of *The Children of Húrin*. In August 1926, having received Reynolds' comments in return, Tolkien will write in his diary: '[*The Tale of*] *Tinúviel* meets with qualified approval [by Reynolds], it is too prolix, but how could I ever cut it down, and the specimen I sent of *Túrin* with little or none' (quoted in *The Lays of Beleriand*, p. 3).

4 January 1926 Tolkien and his family leave their house in Leeds.

7 January 1926 The Tolkiens move to 22 Northmoor Road, Oxford. *Basil Blackwell, the publisher and bookseller, lives next door at no. 20. John and Michael are not able to attend school immediately, as they still have ringworm. After a lengthy and expensive treatment they will attend the Dragon School in Bardwell Road, a few minutes' walk from Northmoor Road.

?1926–?1930 For some years after the move to 22 Northmoor Road a series of Icelandic *au pair* girls will live with the Tolkien family and entertain the boys with tales about trolls. Tolkien himself will continue to tell his children stories, most of which are never written down: some concern the characters Bill Stickers, Major Road Ahead, Timothy Titus, and Tom Bombadil. The latter is inspired by a Dutch doll (i.e. a jointed wooden doll) which belonged to the Tolkien children (according to some sources; according to *Biography* it belonged to Michael).

13 January 1926 Term begins at Leeds. E.V. Gordon succeeds to Tolkien's chair, but as the successor to his own readership will not take up office until October 1926, Tolkien will undertake some teaching or lecturing at Leeds during the spring term. His last recorded payment by Leeds will be in April 1926.

17 January 1926 Hilary Full Term begins at Oxford. Tolkien's scheduled lectures for this term are: Introduction to Germanic Philology on Tuesdays at 10.00 a.m. in the Examination Schools, beginning 19 January; *Beowulf* (Text) on Tuesdays and Thursdays at 11.00 a.m. in the Examination Schools, beginning 19 January; and *Anglo-Saxon Reader* on Thursdays at 10.00 a.m. in the Examination Schools, beginning 21 January.

Hilary Term 1926 Tolkien founds the Kolbítar (*Societies and clubs), an informal reading club for dons interested in the Icelandic sagas and eddic writings. They will meet regularly and translate sections in turn, the length of the section varying from a paragraph for the least skilled reader, to several pages for Tolkien; and they will discuss over drinks what has been translated. Sometimes they will meet in pubs, but often in the rooms of *John Bryson, at this time a Tutor and Lecturer at Merton College. *See note.*

5 February 1926 Tolkien attends a meeting of the Board of the Faculty of Medieval and Modern Languages and Literature at 3.30 p.m. in the Board Room of the Clarendon Building.

4 March 1926 A review-essay by Tolkien, *Philology: General Works*, is published in *The Year's Work in English Studies*, vol. 5 (for 1924). He discusses some fifteen works (mainly books) at length, and mentions many others in the course of forty pages.

11 March 1926 Tolkien attends a meeting of the Board of the Faculty of Medieval and Modern Languages and Literature at 3.30 p.m. in the Board Room of the Clarendon Building. He is appointed to a committee to draft a reply to a letter from the Hebdomadal Council on the duties and payments of examiners. He and C.T. Onions are appointed examiners of the B.Litt. thesis of Joseph Reeves, a non-collegiate student, *An Edition of the Vernon Text of the Ancrene Riwle and a Study of Its Relation to the Other MSS.*

13 March 1926 Hilary Full Term ends at Oxford.

24 March 1926 Term ends at Leeds.

21 April 1926 Term begins at Leeds.

25 April 1926 Trinity Full Term begins at Oxford. Tolkien's scheduled lectures for this term are: *Beowulf* (Text, continued) on Tuesdays and Fridays at 11.00 a.m. in the Examination Schools, beginning 27 April; *Anglo-Saxon Reader* (selected extracts) on Thursdays at 10.00 a.m. in the Examination Schools, beginning 29 April; and Introduction to Germanic Philology on Thursdays at 11.00 a.m., in the Examination Schools, beginning 29 April.

?26 April 1926 Tolkien writes to Kenneth Sisam. He has made a complete Modern English translation of *Beowulf* and will send him a specimen. He encloses his Modern English translation of *Pearl*, which he has made in spare moments and wonders if it could be published by itself. He is laid up with shingles, so that he does not know if he will be able to lecture this week.

4–12 May 1926 General Strike in support of miners. The miners will stay on strike until 19 November.

?9 May 1926 Tolkien, Edith, and their children visit Kenneth Sisam in the afternoon for tea.

11 May 1926 Tolkien attends a meeting of the English Faculty in the afternoon at Merton College, Oxford. Also present is *C.S. Lewis, recently elected Fellow and Tutor in English Language and Literature at Magdalen College, who will write in his diary:

> In to Merton for the 'English tea' at 4.... Discussion turned on [*R. F.W.] Fletcher's proposal to co-ordinate the lecture list with the ordinary course of tutorial work. Everyone agreed, tho' [George] Gordon spoke of the danger of making the thing too much of 'an easy running engine which can give no pleasure to anyone except the engineer'. Miss [Margaret Lucy] Lee [tutor in English for the Society of Oxford Home-Students] talked a lot of nonsense about the need for lessons in pronunciation and beginners' 'outlines of literature'.
>
> Tolkien managed to get the discussion round to the proposed English Prelim[inary examination, see entry for 9 December 1926]. I had a talk with him afterwards. He is a smooth, pale, fluent little chap – can't read Spenser because of the forms – thinks the language is the real thing in the school – thinks all literature is written for the amusement of *men* between thirty and forty.... His pet abomination is the idea of 'liberal' studies. Technical hobbies are more in his line. [*All My Road Before Me: The Diary of C.S. Lewis 1922–1927* (1991), pp. 392–3]

12 May 1926 Tolkien is prevented by ill health from reading a paper on the *Elder Edda* to the Exeter College Essay Club.

14 May 1926 Tolkien attends a meeting of the Board of the Faculty of Medieval and Modern Languages and Literature at 3.30 p.m. in the Board Room of the Clarendon Building. He and Joseph Wright are appointed examiners of the

B.Litt. thesis of Huntington Brown of University College, *Varieties of Pronunciation in the Standard English of the Sixteenth Century (The Vowels of Stressed Syllables)*.

5 June 1926 Tolkien and Joseph Wright examine Huntington Brown *viva voce* on his B.Litt. thesis at 11.30 a.m. in the Examination Schools. Tolkien will write out their undated report. *See note.*

10 June 1926 English Final Honour School examinations begin.

12 June 1926 Tolkien and C.T. Onions examine Joseph Reeves, a non-collegiate student, *viva voce* on his B.Litt. thesis, *An Edition of the Vernon Text of the Ancrene Riwle and a Study of Its Relation to the Other* [*Manuscripts*], at 10.00 a.m. in the Examination Schools.

16 June 1926 Onions and Tolkien sign their report on the examination of Joseph Reeves.

17 June 1926 Tolkien attends, for the last time, a meeting of the Board of the Faculty of Medieval and Modern Languages and Literature at 3.30 p.m. in the Board Room of the Clarendon Building. From Michaelmas Term 1926 he will attend meetings of the newly separate English Faculty Board.

19 June 1926 Trinity Full Term ends at Oxford.

23 June 1926 Encaenia (an annual procession to the Sheldonian Theatre at Oxford to hear an oration in Latin, to commemorate founders and benefactors, and to witness the conferring of honorary degrees). During his years at Oxford, Tolkien will usually attend Encaenia, and with his wife (while her health permitted) also the garden party following the ceremonies.

25 June 1926 Tolkien replies to an enquiry from Willard G. Harding, about the word *gemowe*, which Tolkien has not encountered before.

End of June 1926 Tolkien attends a dinner at Leeds for departing senior members of the Faculty.

3 July 1926 Term ends at Leeds.

16 August 1926 Tolkien writes in his diary that he has done 'a little typing of part of *Tinúviel*' (quoted in *The Lays of Beleriand*, p. 150). This is the first mention of the typescript (by this date already in progress) of the *Lay of Leithian*, here called in full *The Gest of Beren Son of Barahir and Lúthien the Fay Called Tinúviel the Nightingale or The Lay of Leithian, Release from Bondage*. The typescript incorporates emendations made on the earlier manuscript and includes further changes. It is not clear if he has done any more work on the poem since he reached line 757, the end of Canto III in September 1925. The manuscript of Canto IV is completed in March 1928.

?Summer 1926 While the Tolkien family are having a picnic on the banks of the Cherwell, Michael trips over willow roots and falls into the river. Tolkien, wearing his best tennis flannels, jumps in to rescue his son. – Summer 1926 is the earliest date, if probably the least likely, among several considered for the moment when Tolkien, in the midst of marking School Certificate examination papers, wrote the opening words of *The Hobbit* ('In a hole in the ground there lived a hobbit'). See further, the entry for *The Hobbit* in **Reader's Guide**.

October 1926 Tolkien is admitted to a non-stipendiary professorial fellowship at Pembroke College.

17 October 1926 Michaelmas Full Term begins. Tolkien's scheduled lectures and classes for this term are: the Old English *Exodus* on Tuesdays at 10.00 a.m. in the Examination Schools, beginning 19 October; Gothic on Tuesdays at 5.30 p.m., place to be arranged, beginning 19 October; The Verse of Sweet's *Anglo-Saxon Reader* on Thursdays at 10.00 a.m. in the Examination Schools, beginning 21 October; Old English Philology on Thursdays at 11.00 a.m. in the Examination Schools, beginning 21 October; Old Icelandic Texts (Class) on Thursdays at 5.30 p.m., place to be arranged, beginning 21 October; *King Horn* on Fridays at 11.00 a.m. in the Examination Schools, beginning 22 October; and Icelandic Discussion Class on Fridays at 5.30 p.m., place to be arranged, beginning 22 October.

Michaelmas Term 1926 Tolkien is nominated to serve as an examiner in the Honour School of English Language and Literature from Hilary Term 1927 to Hilary Term 1929.

5 November 1926 Tolkien attends an English Faculty Board meeting. Meetings are usually held in the Board Room of the Clarendon Building, and in this period (when scheduled) at 3.30 p.m. on Fridays. Tolkien is appointed an elector to the Jesus Professorship of Celtic until Michaelmas Term 1928. (He will be reappointed continuously until Michaelmas Term 1963, but only in 1947 will he take part in an election.) – English Faculty Board meetings are always preceded by a meeting of the Applications Committee, which deals with matters concerning research students and presents their decisions for approval by the full Board. *See note for 4 November 1927.* The Applications Committee has appointed Tolkien supervisor of Ruth A. Crook of Somerville College, a probationer B.Litt. student who wishes to work on a Middle English subject.

10 November 1926 Tolkien attends a Pembroke College meeting.

16 November 1926 Tolkien, now a member of the English Faculty Library Committee, attends a special meeting held in the Library, with George S. Gordon, David Nichol Smith, Edith Wardale, and the Librarian. They discuss the mixed response of the colleges to a proposal that there be an annual £1 subscription for use of the Library from undergraduates reading for the School of English.

17 November 1926 Tolkien attends a meeting of the Exeter College Essay Club at 8.30 p.m. in the Rector's lodgings. He reads a paper on the *Elder Edda*, postponed from 12 May. According to a report in the *Stapeldon Magazine* for December 1926, 'the reader, after sketching the character and historical background of the *Edda*, described certain of the poems. He also gave a number of translations and readings from the Icelandic which demonstrated the peculiar poetic and musical qualities of the language' ('Essay Club', p. 96).

9 December 1926 Tolkien attends an English Faculty Board meeting. He is appointed, with George S. Gordon, David Nichol Smith, *F.P. Wilson, and Edith Wardale, to a committee to draft a lecture schedule for the academic year 1927–8, to be reported to the Board at the first meeting in Trinity Term

1927. (Tolkien will be re-appointed to this committee until at least 1931.) He is also appointed, with George S. Gordon, H.F.B. Brett-Smith, David Nichol Smith, and Edith Wardale, to a committee to consider the question of a Preliminary Examination in the English School. The Applications Committee has appointed Tolkien and Gordon examiners of the B.Litt. thesis of *Mary Lascelles of Lady Margaret Hall, *Alexander and the Earthly Paradise in Medieval English Literature.*

11 December 1926 Michaelmas Full Term ends.

20 December 1926 Tolkien, as 'Father Christmas', writes a letter to his sons. He tells how the North Polar Bear turned on the taps for the Aurora Borealis, producing a splendid display. He also sends a picture showing the scene with the lights filling the sky, and an envelope with a stamp and inscription written by the Snow Man, Father Christmas's gardener.

1927

?1927–early 1928 Tolkien draws the attention of C.T. Onions to the use in *The Owl and the Nightingale* of a phrase about which Onions is writing an article for the *Review of English Studies* ('Middle English (i) *Wite God, Wite Crist,* (ii) *God It Wite*', July 1928).

1927 Edith Tolkien gives her husband the desk on which he will later write *The Hobbit* and *The Lord of the Rings.* – Tolkien's poem *The Nameless Land* (composed in May 1924) is published in *Realities: An Anthology of Verse,* ed. G.S. Tancred. – Tolkien rewrites his poem *Over Old Hills and Far Away* (originally composed ?January–February 1916). – Tolkien possibly writes the first version of his poem *Knocking at the Door* (*The Mewlips*). – In his preface to *An Introduction to Old Norse,* published in 1927, E.V. Gordon acknowledges his debt to Tolkien in preparing the apparatus of the book, for reading proof of its Grammar, and for making valuable suggestions and corrections. – Tolkien plants two trees in front of 22 Northmoor Road; one is a red leaved *prunus* which flowers very early, and the other a variety which flowers later.

23 January 1927 Hilary Full Term begins. Tolkien's scheduled lectures and classes for this term are: the Old English *Exodus* on Tuesdays at 10.00 a.m. in the Examination Schools, beginning 25 January; Gothic (Class, continued) on Tuesdays at 5.30 p.m. in Pembroke College, beginning 25 January; The Verse of Sweet's *Anglo-Saxon Reader* on Thursdays at 10.00 a.m. in the Examination Schools, beginning 27 January; Old English Philology (Morphology and Vocabulary) on Thursdays at 11.00 a.m. in the Examination Schools, beginning 27 January; Old Icelandic: *Völsunga Saga* on Thursdays at 5.30 p.m. in Pembroke College, beginning 27 January; *King Horn* (Textual and Dialectical Comparisons of the Manuscripts) on Fridays at 11.00 a.m. in the Examination Schools, beginning 28 January; and Discussion Class (continued) on Fridays at 5.15 p.m. in the Examination Schools, beginning 28 January.

Hilary Term 1927–Hilary Term 1929 Tolkien is an examiner in the English Final Honour School.

?Late 1920s or 1930s Tolkien writes two companion poems, *Völsungakviða en nýja* ('The New Lay of the Völsungs') and *Guðrúnarkviða en nýja* ('The New Lay of Gudrún'), of 339 and 166 eight-line stanzas respectively. After the Second World War he will have an amanuensis typescript made of them; otherwise each survives only in a fair copy manuscript. On 29 March 1967 Tolkien will write to *W.H. Auden, who had sent him part of the *Elder Edda* translated into Modern English: 'In return again I hope to send you . . . a thing I did many years ago when trying to learn the art of writing alliterative poetry: an attempt to unify the lays about the Völsungs from the *Elder Edda*, written in the old eight-line *fornyrðislag* stanza' (*Letters*, p. 379). *See note*.

1 February 1927 Tolkien attends an English Faculty Library Committee meeting at 2.30 p.m. in the Library.

10 February 1927 Tolkien and George S. Gordon examine Mary Lascelles of Lady Margaret Hall *viva voce* on her B.Litt. thesis, *Alexander and the Earthly Paradise in Medieval English Literature*, at 2.00 p.m. in the Examination Schools.

11 February 1927 Tolkien attends an English Faculty Board meeting. The Applications Committee has approved the B.Litt. thesis subject of Ruth Anna Crook, 'an edition of the prose life of Seinte Margharete, based on MS Bodley 34 and MS Roy 17 A XXVII, with a grammar and glossary which will consider parallels on other texts of the same group'. Tolkien is to continue as her supervisor. The Committee also assigns him to supervise A.C. Corlett of St Edmund Hall, who has applied for admission to a course of special study preparatory to research for a B.Litt. – Tolkien and George S. Gordon sign their report on the examination of Mary Lascelles.

18 February 1927 The Kolbítar meet at Exeter College and begin to read the *Völsunga Saga*.

24 February 1927 A review-essay by Tolkien, *Philology: General Works*, is published in *The Year's Work in English Studies*, vol. 6 (for 1925). He discusses some twenty-four books, many of them lengthy *Festschriften*, and articles of varying length, in the course of forty-six pages.

2 March 1927 The *Oxford University Gazette* announces that Tolkien will be chairman of the examiners of the Final Honour School of English Language and Literature for 1927–8.

16 March 1927 Tolkien attends a Pembroke College meeting.

17 March 1927 At an English Faculty Board meeting, in Tolkien's absence, the Committee on a Preliminary Examination in the Honour School of English Language and Literature (of which he is a member) recommends that the examination should cover the outlines of a period of English social and political history; the elements of Old English, and prescribed portions of Chaucer; prescribed Greek or Latin books; and unprepared translation from not less than two or more than three of Greek, Latin, French, German, Italian, or Spanish.

19 March 1927 Hilary Full Term ends.

1 May 1927 Trinity Full Term begins. Tolkien's scheduled lectures for this term are: *Judith* and *Beowulf* (lines 1251–1650) on Thursdays at 10.00 a.m. in the Examination Schools, beginning 5 May; Old English Philology (concluded) on Thursdays at 11.00 a.m. in the Examination Schools, beginning 5 May; and The Heroic Poems of the *Elder Edda* on Fridays at 11.00 a.m. in the Examination Schools, beginning 6 May.

12 May 1927 Tolkien attends an English Faculty Library Committee meeting at 2.15 p.m. in the Library.

June 1927 Two poems by Tolkien, **Fastitocalon* and **Iumbo, or ye Kinde of ye Oliphaunt* (composed probably in the 1920s), are published in the *Stapeldon Magazine* for June 1927, as by 'Fisiologus', under the general title *Adventures in Unnatural History and Medieval Metres, Being the Freaks of Fisiologus*.

15 June 1927 Tolkien attends a Pembroke College meeting.

16 June 1927 English Final Honour School examinations begin. Tolkien is chairman of the examiners. There are 127 candidates.

23 June 1927 At a meeting of the English Faculty Board, in Tolkien's absence, he is elected a member of the Committee for Nomination of Public Examiners in the Honour School of English Language and Literature and in the Pass School, Group B6, to Hilary Term 1931. He and H.C. Wyld are appointed examiners of the B.Litt. thesis of G.W. Small of Merton College (but according to the *Oxford University Gazette*, Small is later examined not by Tolkien and Wyld but by W.A. Craigie and C.T. Onions). Tolkien is also appointed an examiner of the B.Litt. thesis of Daniel Ferguson Aitken of Balliol College, *A Study of the English Romance of Sir Tristrem in Relation to Its Sources*.

25 June 1927 Trinity Full Term ends.

26 June 1927 So far, the Kolbítar have read the *Younger* (or *Prose*) *Edda* and the *Völsunga Saga*. In Michaelmas Term they plan to read the *Laxdæle Saga*.

28 June 1927 The English Faculty Library Committee, in Tolkien's absence, authorizes a collotype facsimile of *Sir Gawain and the Green Knight* to be made from plates lent by Tolkien.

30 June 1927 Encaenia.

September 1927 The Tolkien family take a holiday in Lyme Regis. They stay in a lodging house. Either during this visit or in 1928, Tolkien, curious about its workings, breaks a cuckoo-clock in the lodging house to the annoyance of the landlady. While at Lyme Regis Tolkien takes up drawing and painting again, and adds several works to *The Book of Ishness*: some are topographical (*Golden Cap from Langmoor Garden*; an unidentified house; *Boats, Lyme Regis*; and *Oh To Be in Oxford (North) Now That Summer's There* (*Artist and Illustrator*, fig. 25)); two are scenes from his mythology (*Mithrim* and *Glórund Sets Forth to Seek Túrin* (*Artist and Illustrator*, figs. 46–47)); and one, a coiled dragon, is related to *Beowulf* by its caption, 'hringboga heorte gefysed' (*Artist and Illustrator*, fig. 48). – He also makes at least three illustrations for *Roverandom*, which he probably retells at this time: a drawing, *The White Dragon Pursues Roverandom and the Moondog*, and two watercolours, *The Gardens of the Merking's Palace* and *House Where 'Rover' Began His Adventures*

as a 'Toy' (*Artist and Illustrator*, figs. 73, 75–76). A related, untitled drawing
('Rover Arrives on the Moon', *Artist and Illustrator*, fig. 74) is dated '1927–8'.
– Around this time Tolkien makes three drawings on a single page (*Artist and
Illustrator*, fig. 77), one of 22 Northmoor Road, one of a seated (giant?) figure,
and one of an ogre and child.

16 October 1927 Michaelmas Full Term begins. Tolkien's scheduled lectures and classes for this term are: *Beowulf* and *The Fight at Finnesburg* on
Tuesdays and Thursdays at 11.00 a.m. in the Examination Schools, beginning
18 October; The Prose of Sweet's *Anglo-Saxon Reader* on Thursdays at 10.00
a.m. in the Examination Schools, beginning 20 October; and Germanic Philology (Class) on Fridays at 12.00 noon at Pembroke College, beginning 21
October.

19 October 1927 Tolkien attends a Pembroke College meeting.

21 October 1927 Tolkien writes to Willard G. Harding about the etymology
of *sag*.

27 October 1927 Tolkien attends an English Faculty Library Committee
meeting at 2.00 p.m. in the Library. The Committee decides to strengthen and
complete the philological section of the Library, and officially adopts for this
purpose a list of works in Old and Middle English and Icelandic prepared by
Tolkien.

4 November 1927 Tolkien attends an English Faculty Board meeting. He is
elected to the Applications Committee officially for one year, but in practice for
the rest of his working life at Oxford. *See note.* He is also elected to the Library
Committee, and appointed supervisor of advanced student E. Olszewska of
Lady Margaret Hall, whose D.Phil. thesis is *A History of the Scandinavian Influence on the English Language*. He proposes that the General Board be asked to
initiate legislation for a Diploma in Comparative Philology (as suggested during summer 1927 by the Boards of Faculties of Literae Humaniores, of English
Language and Literature, of Medieval and Modern Languages, and Oriental
Languages). The English Faculty Board is to be represented on the Commit-
tee for Comparative Philology by two members, including the Rawlinson and
Bosworth Professor of Anglo-Saxon. The Board endorses Tolkien's proposal.
Also during this meeting Tolkien presents the report of the examiners in the
1927 English Honour School, written by himself on behalf of the committee
(Tolkien, Ernest de Selincourt, A.O. Belfour, and F.P. Wilson).

5 November 1927 Tolkien certifies that Julia Maud Keays-Young has completed course work towards her B.Litt.

9 November 1927 Tolkien attends a Pembroke College meeting.

16 November 1927 Tolkien and Eugène Vinaver examine Daniel Ferguson
Aitken of Balliol College *viva voce* on his B.Litt. thesis, *A Study of the English
Romance of Sir Tristrem in Relation to Its Sources*, at 11.00 a.m. in the Examina-
tion Schools.

21 November 1927 Tolkien and Vinaver sign their report on the examination of D.F. Aitken.

23 November 1927 Tolkien attends a Pembroke College meeting.

27 November 1927 The Arthurian Society is formed (*Societies and clubs), with Eugène Vinaver as its first Honorary President. Tolkien will become a member.

2 December 1927 Tolkien certifies that A.C. Corlett of St Edmund Hall is qualified to be a full B.Litt. student, with the thesis *The Phonology of the Vowels in the Poems of B. Mus. MS Nero Ax (Sir Gawain, Pearl, Patience, Purity) with Special Reference to the Treatment of Middle English.*

9 December 1927 Tolkien attends an English Faculty Board meeting. The Applications Committee has appointed Tolkien and E.V. Gordon examiners of the B.Litt. thesis of Julia Maud Keays-Young, *England and the English in the Icelandic Sagas.* It has also appointed Tolkien supervisor of B.Litt. student A.C. Corlett, and of advanced student H.M. Buckhurst of St Hugh's College. Miss Buckhurst's thesis to be *The Historical Grammar of Old Icelandic.* – Tolkien also attends a Pembroke College meeting.

10 December 1927 Michaelmas Full Term ends.

21 December 1927 Tolkien, as 'Father Christmas', writes a letter dated 21 December to the entire Tolkien family as well as Aslaug (one of the Icelandic *au pair* girls) and Jennie Grove, who usually spends Christmas with the Tolkiens. Father Christmas has heard from Michael and Christopher but not John, whom he assumes will soon be too big to hang up a stocking. He tells how the Man in the Moon came to visit him on 7 December, fell asleep, and was pushed under the sofa by the North Polar Bear. With the Man absent from the moon, dragons came out and obscured its light (surely a reference to the lunar eclipse that occurred on 8 December). With this is an illustration of the North Pole with no moon or Northern Lights, lit only by a comet and stars.

Christmas 1927 Tolkien probably writes out the first manuscript of *Roverandom* during the holidays.

1928

c. **1928** In or around 1928 Tolkien begins to write a series of poems which he calls collectively *Tales and Songs of Bimble Bay.* These include *The Bumpus* (see *Perry-the-Winkle*), *The Dragon's Visit*, *Glip, Poor Old Grabbler* (later *Old Grabbler*), *Progress in Bimble Town*, and *A Song of Bimble Bay.* – Tolkien also makes many paintings and drawings (see also entries for July through September), including *The Wood at the World's End* (in two versions; *Artist and Illustrator*, fig. 60); a decorative frieze with a peacock; a flowering tree with a bird (*Pictures*, no. 42); a page with drawings of realistic flowers, possibly to precede a 'Tree of Amalion' drawing (see entry for July–August 1928); and *Maddo*, a gloved hand crawling down a curtain, and *Owlamoo*, a sinister owl-like creature, both drawn to exorcise bogeys imagined by young Michael Tolkien (*Artist and Illustrator*, figs. 78–79). The preceding are all dated '1928'. An undated drawing of three friezes in *The Book of Ishness*, incorporating favourite motifs of waves, clouds, mountains, moons, and stars (*Artist and Illustrator*, fig. 59), is probably also made around this time, as are two unusual drawings in a geometric style, one entitled *Moonlight on a Wood*, accompanying but not part of *The Book of Ishness* (*Artist and Illustrator*, fig. 61; *Life and Legend*, p. 5).

1928 The new Committee for Comparative Philology begins to meet this year. As Rawlinson and Bosworth Professor of Anglo-Saxon, Tolkien is a member of the Committee, and will continue to be a member until Michaelmas Term 1960. – Tolkien reads a paper, *The Chill Barbarians of the North*, at a meeting of the Newman Society in Oxford. – Evidently at some time this year Tolkien hands over notes he has written for the Clarendon Chaucer to George S. Gordon, so that Gordon can assist in their reduction. – *Poetic Diction: A Study in Meaning* by *Owen Barfield is published. It will come to have a profound influence on Tolkien. Barfield and Tolkien had became acquainted earlier in the 1920s through their mutual friend C.S. Lewis. – Otto Jespersen invents an artificial language, 'Novial'. Tolkien will refer to it as 'ingenious, and easier than Esperanto, but hideous' (*The British Esperantist*, May 1932, p. 182).

12 January 1928 *A New Glossary of the Dialect of the Huddersfield District* by Walter E. Haigh, which includes a foreword by Tolkien, is published on 12 January.

22 January 1928 Hilary Full Term begins. Tolkien's scheduled lectures and classes for this term are: *Beowulf* and *The Fight at Finnesburg* on Tuesdays and Thursdays at 11.00 a.m. in the Examination Schools, beginning 24 January; The Prose of Sweet's *Anglo-Saxon Reader* on Thursdays at 10.00 a.m. in the Examination Schools, beginning 26 January; and Germanic Philology (Class) on Fridays at 12.00 noon in the Examination Schools, beginning 27 January.

2 February 1928 Tolkien attends an English Faculty Library Committee meeting at 2.15 p.m. in the Library. The members discuss the purchase of new books and decide for the moment to concentrate on Philology, and to acquire the books recommended by Professor Tolkien.

10 February 1928 At a meeting of the English Faculty Board, in Tolkien's absence, he is appointed to a committee 'to consider the position of language teaching for men undergraduates', i.e. whether it is 'desirable that male candidates in the English School should receive special tuition in the linguistic branch of their studies' (Oxford University Archives FA 4/5/1/1). – Tolkien and E.V. Gordon examine Julia Maud Keays-Young of the Society of Oxford Home-Students *viva voce* on her B.Litt. thesis, *England and the English in the Icelandic Sagas*, at 10.00 a.m. in the Examination Schools. Tolkien writes out their report.

29 February 1928 Tolkien attends a Pembroke College meeting.

14 March 1928 Tolkien attends a Pembroke College meeting.

16 March 1928 Tolkien attends an English Faculty Board meeting. He is appointed to a committee to draft a scheme of lectures for 1928–9.

17 March 1928 Hilary Full Term ends.

Late March–early April 1928 During the Easter vacation Tolkien returns to the *Lay of Leithian* and probably writes Cantos IV–IX and part of Canto X. He notes the following dates on the manuscript: line 1161 (Canto IV), 27–8

March; line 1736 (Canto VI), 29 March; line 1943 (Canto VII), 30 March; line 2114 (Canto VII), 31 March; line 2385 (Canto VIII), 2 April; line 2423 (Canto VIII), 3 April; line 2769 (Canto IX), 4 April; line 2877 (Canto X), 5 April; line 2929 (Canto X), 6 April (i.e. 1768 lines since in the nine days since 28 March); line 2998 (Canto X), 27 April. He probably writes the outlines before beginning Cantos IV (line 758), VI (line 1584), IX (line 2566), and X (line 2856). He apparently reaches line 3030 by the end of the vacation, and writes no more until November 1928.

29 April 1928 Trinity Full Term begins. Tolkien's scheduled lectures for this term are: The Legendary Traditions in *Beowulf* and *Deor's Lament* on Tuesdays and Thursdays at 11.00 a.m. in the Examination Schools, beginning 1 May; *The Fight at Finnesburg* and the 'Finn Episode' on Thursdays at 10.00 a.m. in the Examination Schools, beginning 3 May; and The Mythological Poems of the *Elder Edda* on Fridays at 12.00 noon in the Examination Schools, beginning 4 May.

May 1928 Tolkien paints in *The Book of Ishness* a small watercolour sketch of a warrior fighting a dragon (*Artist and Illustrator*, fig. 49). Possibly at about the same time he draws a dragon coiled around a tree, dated only '1928' (*Pictures*, no. 40).

18 May 1928 Tolkien attends an English Faculty Board meeting. The Committee on Tuition in Linguistic Subjects in the English School presents a report, typed by Tolkien and signed by H.F.B. Brett-Smith, George S. Gordon, C.T. Onions, Tolkien, and H.C. Wyld, stating that neither the University nor the colleges are able to provide for male candidates

> special tuition in the linguistic subjects of the English School that is comparable in range or thoroughness to that given in literature, or sufficient in amount or quality to enable these candidates to satisfy the minimum requirements of the statutes. . . . The committee wish to record, also, the view that the linguistic and literary subjects of the curriculum are intended to be simultaneous and complementary studies, and that it is very undesirable that candidates should be allowed to relegate either the one or the other (according to their specialization) to a brief portion only of the period of their reading, whatever may be, now or in the future, the practical necessities of tutorial arrangements. [Oxford University Archives FA 4/5/2/1]

The Board resolves that the Committee, with Tolkien as convenor, should consider the best means of acting on the report.

20 May 1928 The English Faculty Library Committee agrees, at a meeting in Tolkien's absence, that under his guidance the Philology section of the Library has been greatly strengthened.

14 June 1928 English Final Honour School Examinations begin. Tolkien is an examiner.

22 June 1928 At a meeting of the English Faculty Board, in Tolkien's absence, changes in the regulations for special subjects (Gothic, Old Norse, Old Icelandic) that Tolkien has proposed are discussed and adopted with minor modifications.

23 June 1928 Trinity Full Term ends.

27 June 1928 Encaenia.

July 1928 Tolkien draws in pencil and black ink two views of Grendel's mere as in *Beowulf*, called *Wudu Wyrtum Fæst* (*Artist and Illustrator*, figs. 50–51), plus a preparatory sketch, and a sketch of a gnarled tree (*Artist and Illustrator*, fig. 129). The first two are dated 'Vivas July 1928'.

?Summer 1928 Probably during this summer, Tolkien writes and illustrates a picture book, **Mr. Bliss*. Although little more than the finished book now survives, it seems certain to have been preceded by a draft text, drawings, and layout. *See note*. – In Summer 1928 he possibly also writes the first words of *The Hobbit* ('In a hole in the ground there lived a hobbit'), while in the midst of marking School Certificate examination papers. (This, at least, is one of the most likely dates for the origin of *The Hobbit*. Summer 1929 is also possible; but Tolkien himself will later recall that he did not write the first words of *The Hobbit* until 1930 at the earliest, after which there was a gap of time before he proceeded with the story. On 7 June 1955 he will write to W.H. Auden: 'I did nothing about it [*The Hobbit*], for a long time [after writing its first words], and for some years I got no further than the production of Thror's Map' (*Letters*, p. 215). This, however, is only one account; see further, entry for *The Hobbit* in **Reader's Guide**.)

July–August 1928 The Tolkiens again take a holiday in Lyme Regis. Father Francis Morgan joins them there. Tolkien spends part of his time drawing and painting. He makes three topographical drawings: *View from Mr Wallis' Broad Street, Lyme* (*Artist and Illustrator*, fig. 26); *Tumble Hill near Lyme Regis* (*Artist and Illustrator*, fig. 27); and a rough sketch of roofs and chimneys. But subjects from his mythology predominate: a watercolour of Nargothrond, the underground stronghold of the Noldorin Elves (*Pictures*, no. 33); *Taur-na-Fúin* (*Artist and Illustrator*, fig. 54); *Halls of Manwë on the Mountains of the World above Faerie* (also known as *Taniquetil*; *Artist and Illustrator*, fig. 52); a pencil drawing of Nargothrond (*Artist and Illustrator*, fig. 56); *The Vale of Tol Sirion* (*Artist and Illustrator*, fig. 55); and probably also a very rough sketch of Hirilorn and Lúthien's hut. He also draws a small mountain landscape (*Artist and Illustrator*, fig. 53) after *Halls of Manwë*, and what will become the best known of several drawings of the 'Tree of Amalion', a stylized tree bearing a variety of flowers and leaves (*Artist and Illustrator*, fig. 62).

17 August 1928 Tolkien attends the Oxford dinner of the Eighth Pax Romana Congress, an international organization founded in 1921 for Catholic students. His menu card is signed by some of the attendees, including an Austrian and a German who express their gratitude to him for acting as their guide in Oxford.

September 1928 Tolkien draws *Gondolin & the Vale of Tumladin from Cristhorn*, another picture related to his mythology (*Artist and Illustrator*, fig. 58).

14 October 1928 Michaelmas Full Term begins. Tolkien's scheduled lectures for this term are: *The Battle of Maldon*, *Brunanburh*, and verse from the *Chronicle* on Tuesdays at 10.00 a.m. in the Examination Schools, beginning 16 October; the Old English *Exodus* on Tuesdays at 11.00 a.m. in the Examination Schools, beginning 16 October; Old English Verse (Miscellaneous Pieces) on Thursdays at 11.00 a.m. in the Examination Schools, beginning 18 October; The *Völsunga Saga* and Related Lays on Fridays at 12.00 noon in the Examination Schools, beginning 19 October; and The Germanic Verb on Thursdays at 10.00 a.m. in the Examination Schools, beginning 18 October.

17 October 1928 Tolkien attends a Pembroke College meeting.

2 November 1928 At a meeting of the English Faculty Board, in Tolkien's absence, he is re-elected to the Applications Committee. David Nichol Smith presents the report of the examiners (including Tolkien) for the English Final Honour School. The Applications Committee has appointed Tolkien as supervisor of R. Tuve of Somerville College, a probationer B.Litt. student who will work in medieval English literature. It has also appointed Tolkien and Kenneth Sisam examiners of the D.Phil. thesis of Peter Haworth of University College, *An Edition of British Museum MS Harley 2257*.

4 December 1928 Tolkien and Kenneth Sisam examine Peter Haworth of University College *viva voce* on his D.Phil. thesis at 11.30 a.m. in the Examination Schools.

5 December 1928 Tolkien and Kenneth Sisam sign their report on the examination of Peter Haworth. – Tolkien attends a Pembroke College meeting.

7 December 1928 Tolkien attends an English Faculty Board meeting., at which he raises the question of payment of examiners in the Final Honour School. He is appointed to a committee to consider the matter.

8 December 1928 Michaelmas Full Term ends.

11 December 1928 Tolkien attends an English Faculty Library Committee meeting at 2.15 p.m. in the Library.

Christmas 1928 Tolkien, as 'Father Christmas', writes to his sons. Although his letter is dated 20 December, it is probably not finished in time for Christmas Day, as an added note dated Boxing Day (26 December) states that the North Polar Bear failed to post it earlier. The letter proper tells how the North Polar Bear fell down stairs while carrying Christmas parcels. It is accompanied by a picture of the accident. Father Christmas brings paints for John and 'railway things and a farm and animals' to Michael and Christopher. – If Tolkien conceived *The Hobbit* in summer 1928, he possibly now begins to tell the story to his children, and to add to the tale (while retelling previous parts) each successive Christmas until *c*. 1932. Once he begins to write it down, he also makes a few illustrations and maps for the story to keep in the 'home manuscript'. See further, entry for *The Hobbit* in **Reader's Guide**.

1929

?1929–1930 At the request of R.E.M. Wheeler (later Sir Mortimer Wheeler), during 1928–9 director of excavation at a site at Lydney Park, Gloucestershire with prehistoric, Roman and post-Roman remains including a temple to Nodens, Tolkien writes a note on the name *Nodens*. – During this period Tolkien and C.S. Lewis become allies in a campaign to reform the Oxford English School syllabus.

1929 Hilary Tolkien marries Magdalen Matthews in Evesham. After the wedding, the bride and groom travel to Oxford to spend the rest of the day with Ronald and Edith. – Tolkien becomes a member of the Philological Society (*Societies and clubs).

9 January 1929 The committee appointed at the 7 December meeting of the English Faculty Board meets to consider the question of the remuneration of examiners in the Final Honour School. The members agree that there is a need for some adjustments, but think it would be advisable for the chairman to take the matter up informally with the appropriate authorities.

17 January 1929 An article by Tolkien, *Ancrene Wisse and Hali Meiðhad*, is published in *Essays and Studies by Members of the English Association*, vol. 14.

20 January 1929 Hilary Full Term begins. Tolkien's scheduled lectures for this term are: the Old English *Exodus* (continued), Tuesdays at 11.00 a.m. in the Examination Schools, beginning 22 January; Old English Verse (Miscellaneous Pieces), Thursdays at 10.00 a.m. in the Examination Schools, beginning 24 January; *Völsunga Saga* and Related Lays, Fridays at 12.00 noon in the Examination Schools, beginning 25 January; Legends of the Goths, Tuesdays at 10.00 a.m. in the Examination Schools, beginning 22 January; and The Germanic Verb (continued), Thursdays at 11.00 a.m. in the Examination Schools, beginning 24 January.

23 January 1929 Tolkien attends a Pembroke College meeting.

28 January 1929 Tolkien gives a public lecture at Leeds, *Celts and the Teutons in the Early World*. A report in *The Gryphon*, February 1929, p. 146, will note that

> the English School owes a very great debt to Professor Tolkien; but it is not only for academic reasons that his old students remember him, and some of them were glad to share again his obvious regret that the lecture must somehow be terminated at the end of the allotted period, though the subject is nowhere near exhausted; to be flattered by the assumption that they could instantly recognise Old Welsh and [Proto-Germanic] forms; to know that on some minute point all the world's available learning was placed before them; to plunge down a remote and devious path, and emerge in the old familiar fashion at "our old friend Vortigern, of Hengist and Horsa fame". ['Professor Tolkien on Celts and Teutons', *The Gryphon* n.s. 10, no. 4 (February 1929), p. 146]

8 February 1929 Tolkien attends an English Faculty Board meeting. The committee on the payment of examiners in the Final Honour School presents a report written out by Tolkien.

20 February 1929 Tolkien attends a Pembroke College meeting.

15 March 1929 Tolkien attends an English Faculty Board meeting. The Board resolves that George S. Gordon and Tolkien should draw up a memorandum, to be submitted to the General Board, on the need for the appointment of a Lecturer in English Language. – Tolkien also attends a Pembroke College meeting.

16 March 1929 Hilary Full Term ends.

28 April 1929 Trinity Full Term begins. Tolkien's scheduled lectures for this term are: Old English Verse (Miscellaneous Pieces) on Thursdays at 10.00 a.m. in the Examination Schools, beginning 2 May; and (Old Norse) *Carmina Scaldica* on Tuesdays and Thursdays at 11.00 a.m. in the Examination Schools, beginning 30 April.

9 May 1929 Tolkien attends an English Faculty Library Committee meeting at 2.15 p.m. in the Library.

14 May 1929 Tolkien attends a Pembroke College meeting.

17 May 1929 At a meeting of the English Faculty Board, in Tolkien's absence, he is appointed to a committee to consider the annual scheme of lectures.

20 May 1929 Tolkien, with H.C. Wyld and C.T. Onions, signs a letter to the Secretary of Faculties asking the University to consider appointing a lecturer to teach 'English Language'. The draft of the letter is in Onions' hand, but the typescript appears to have been made by Tolkien. The submission points out that there are three official teachers of English Language: the Merton Professor of English Language and Literature (Wyld), the Rawlinson and Bosworth Professor of Anglo-Saxon (Tolkien), and the Reader in English Philology (Onions), and that 'the two Professors normally give from two to three times the amount of public instruction required by statute, not infrequently dealing with elementary parts of their subjects. . . . All three, if they are to consider the needs of the School, are obliged to neglect considerable sections of the subjects which ought to be adequately represented in the University, and still the linguistic syllabus of the School is not covered' (Oxford University Archives FA 4/5/2/2).

31 May 1929 Tolkien certifies that R.A. Crook of Somerville College has completed course work towards her B.Litt.

5 June 1929 Tolkien attends a Pembroke College meeting.

12 June 1929 Tolkien certifies that A.C. Corlett of St Edmund Hall has completed course work towards his B.Litt.

13 June 1929 English Final Honour School Examinations begin. There are 105 candidates. E.V. Gordon should be an external examiner, but is granted a leave of absence; Tolkien serves in his place.

18 June 1929 Priscilla Mary Reuel Tolkien is born at home in Oxford, the fourth and last child, and only daughter, of Ronald and Edith Tolkien. Her godparents are Francis de Zulueta, Regius Professor of Civil Law at Oxford, and Helen Buckhurst, former Fellow and English language tutor at St Hugh's College, Oxford.

21 June 1929 Tolkien is elected to represent the Faculties of Theology, Law, Literae Humaniores, Modern History, English Language and Literature, Medieval and Modern European Languages and Literature, and Oriental Languages on the General Board for three years until Michaelmas Term 1932.

22 June 1929 Trinity Full Term ends.

26 June 1929 Encaenia.

6 October 1929 Michaelmas Full Term begins. Tolkien's scheduled lectures for this term are: The Common Germanic Consonant-Changes on Tuesdays at 10.00 a.m. in the Examination Schools, beginning 15 October; *Beowulf* on Tuesdays and Thursdays at 11.00 a.m. in the Examination Schools, beginning 15 October; *Baldrs Draumar, Guðrúnarkviða en forna*, and *Atlakviða* on Thursdays at 10.00 a.m. in the Examination Schools, beginning 17 October (listed also as *Old Norse Texts* under the School of Medieval and Modern Languages).

16 October 1929 Tolkien attends a Pembroke College meeting.

22 October 1929 Tolkien attends an English Faculty Library Committee meeting at 2.15 p.m. in the Library.

25 October 1929 Tolkien attends a General Board meeting.

November 1929 Tolkien returns to the *Lay of Leithian*. Beside line 3031 in the manuscript he writes 'Nov. 1929'.

1 November 1929 At a meeting of the English Faculty Board, in Tolkien's absence, he is re-elected to the Library Committee, and appointed to a committee to consider the regulations for Responsions and Pass Moderations.

6 November 1929 Tolkien attends a Pembroke College meeting.

8 November 1929 Tolkien attends a General Board meeting.

Mid-November 1929 Until they reach a certain age, the Tolkien boys usually write to Father Christmas in late autumn to tell him what they would like as presents. In 1929 they receive an early reply, as from the North Polar Bear, who tells them that he hurt his paw cutting Christmas trees, and that his real name is Karhu. He sends love to John for his birthday.

22 November 1929 Tolkien attends a General Board meeting.

?11 (?18 ?25) November 1929 Tolkien and C.S. Lewis attend a society meeting, then retire to Lewis's rooms in Magdalen College and sit for three hours until 2.30 am talking of the gods and giants and Asgard.

Late November or early December 1929 By 6 December, Tolkien lends the typescript of the *Lay of Leithian* to C.S. Lewis to read.

30 November 1929 Michaelmas Full Term ends.

6 December 1929 Tolkien attends a General Board meeting. – He also attends an English Faculty Board meeting. The report of the committee appointed on 1 November to consider the regulations for Responsions and Pass Moderations is presented, and with a few changes is adopted by the Board. The archived report includes a manuscript page written by Tolkien on the requirements for candidates offering Old English. Tolkien is appointed to a committee to draft a letter to be sent to the colleges on tuition in English Language.

7 December 1929 C.S. Lewis writes to Tolkien that he sat up the previous night reading the *Lay of Leithian* and is delighted. He has not yet finished, and will send more detailed criticism later. It is clear that he has read as far as about line 2017, and that he has received more, perhaps as far as line 3031 (see entry for November 1929).

Christmas 1929 Tolkien, as 'Father Christmas', writes to his children. He tells how the residents of the North Pole celebrated the coming of winter with a bonfire and fireworks, and how the North Polar Bear opened a window during a gale, scattering the lists and letters on Father Christmas's desk. He also sends an illustration in three tiers, of Father Christmas and Polar Bear at work in the office, the bonfire and fireworks, and the office with papers blown into the air. Father Christmas says that he was very pleased with Christopher's card, and sends him a fountain pen and a picture just for himself, of Father Christmas flying in his sleigh above the sea on the upper North wind, with a South West gale raising big waves below.

?End of 1929 or early 1930 C.S. Lewis sends Tolkien at least fourteen pages of detailed criticism of the *Lay of Leithian*, to line 1161. Tolkien apparently considers Lewis's comments carefully, for almost all the verses criticized are marked for revision in the typescript, and many of the proposed emendations, or modifications of these, are incorporated into rewritten and retyped versions of Canto I and the beginning of Canto IV.

1930

1930 By now Tolkien has become an ordinary member of the Council of the Philological Society. – During this year Tolkien writes all or most of another prose version of the 'Silmarillion' mythology, the *Quenta* (or *Qenta*) *Noldorinwa* or *Pennas-na-Ngoelaidh*, largely a reworking and expansion of the *Sketch of the Mythology*, and apart from the *Sketch* the only prose 'Silmarillion' that he will ever complete. The major part of the *Quenta Noldorinwa*, at least as far as the end of the story of Beren and Lúthien, is finished prior to the last week of September 1930. Tolkien produces two overlapping typescripts, the second of which expands upon the latter part of the first. – Probably at about the same time Tolkien translates a short piece from the beginning of the *Quenta Noldorinwa* into Old English, later entitled *Pennas*. He also makes several lists of Old English versions of Elvish names. – Possibly while working on the *Quenta Noldorinwa*, Tolkien writes quickly the first version of the 'earliest' **Annals of Beleriand* to provide a chronology of events. Its manuscript will be heavily emended. – Perhaps also as an aid at about the same time, he produces a series of genealogical tables of the Elvish princes, of the three houses of the Fathers of Men, and of the Houses of Eastern Men; a table of the divisions of the Qendi (Elves); and a list of the many names by which the Lindar, Noldor, and Teleri (three kindreds of the Elves) were known.

1930s Tolkien writes the first version of his poem *Shadow-Bride*. – Tolkien writes a seven-page essay, *The Feanorian Alphabet* (see *Writing systems).

Early 1930s Tolkien writes a substantial part of a long poem, *The Fall of Arthur* (*Arthur and the Matter of Britain). It progresses through different versions and narrative outlines, but is abandoned unfinished after 954 lines. Tolkien will send one version to his friend R.W. Chambers for comment (see entry for 9 December 1934). – Like-minded members of the Oxford English School, led by Tolkien and C.S. Lewis, form a group called The Cave (*Societies and clubs), named after the Cave of Adullam (Samuel 22:1–2). Their aim is to seek reform of the English School, but The Cave is also a social group which has informal dinners together, especially after the members have achieved many of their aims. The Cave will survive into the 1940s.

12 January 1930 Hilary Full Term begins. Tolkien's scheduled lectures and classes for this term are: Problems of Old English Philology on Tuesdays at 10.00 a.m. in the Examination Schools, beginning 21 January; *Beowulf* on Tuesdays and Thursdays at 11.00 a.m. in the Examination Schools, beginning 21 January; *Baldrs Draumar, Atlakviða, Bandamanna Saga, Hænsaþóris Saga*, and *Hávarðs Saga Halta* on Thursdays at 10.00 a.m. in the Examination Schools, beginning 23 January; and Old Norse Texts (Class), at an hour and place to be arranged.

14 January 1930 Tolkien and his family move into 20 Northmoor Road, which he has bought from Basil Blackwell, from their smaller house next door. Much of their furniture is moved over the fence dividing the properties.

22 January 1930 Tolkien attends a Pembroke College meeting.

28 or 29 January 1930 Tolkien attends a meeting of the Kolbítar. Among those present are C.S. Lewis, John Bryson, and *R.M. Dawkins.

31 January 1930 Tolkien attends a General Board meeting.

7 February 1930 Tolkien attends an English Faculty Board meeting. The Board approves a regulation that before being accepted as a full B.Litt. student, a probationer must pass a written examination in set subjects unless exempted by the Board. Draft regulations for Pass Moderations are presented, and changes made.

27 February 1930 Joseph Wright dies. Tolkien is named executor of his estate.

28 February 1930 Tolkien attends a General Board meeting.

3 March 1930 A memorial service for Joseph Wright is held in the University Church of St Mary the Virgin.

8 March 1930 Hilary Full Term ends.

11 March 1930 Tolkien attends a Pembroke College meeting.

14 March 1930 Tolkien attends an English Faculty Board meeting. The Board records its sense of loss on the death of Joseph Wright. Tolkien is appointed to the committee on the annual scheme of lectures. He presents proposals for alteration of the regulations governing examinations in the English Honour School, with regard to papers on the medieval period. Some of his proposals are adopted, and he is appointed to a committee to consider the remaining proposals. Tolkien and David Nichol Smith are asked to draft, for submission to the General Board, a statement of the Faculty Board's reasons for appointing *C.L. Wrenn as University Lecturer in English Philology and *Dorothy Everett as University Lecturer in Middle English. – Tolkien also attends a General Board meeting. The Board accepts a benefaction from Charles James O'Donnell to promote the study of the British or Celtic element in the English language (see *English and Welsh*).

25 April 1930 Tolkien is listed in the *Oxford University Gazette* as a Moderator in Literis Graecis et Latinis (Pass School) from the first day of Michaelmas Term 1930 to the first day of Michaelmas Term 1931.

27 April 1930 Trinity Full Term begins. Tolkien's scheduled lectures for this term are: Finn and Hengest: The Problem of the Episode in *Beowulf* and the Fragment (i.e. the 'Finnesburg Fragment'; see *Finn and Hengest*) on Tuesdays at 11.00 a.m. in the Examination Schools, beginning 29 April; the Germanic Numerals on Tuesdays at 12.00 noon in the Examination Schools, beginning 29 April; and *Deor's Lament*, *Waldere*, and *Runic Poem* on Thursdays at 11.00 a.m. in the Examination Schools, beginning 1 May.

30 April 1930 Tolkien attends a Pembroke College meeting.

9 May 1930 Tolkien attends a General Board meeting.

16 May 1930 Tolkien attends an English Faculty Board meeting. The committee (including Tolkien) appointed at the last meeting submits proposed revised regulations for the Final Honour School, regarding examination papers to be taken. The Applications Committee has appointed Tolkien and C.L. Wrenn examiners for the B.Litt. thesis of Evan Clifford Llewellyn of Jesus College, *The Influence of Middle Dutch and Middle Low German on English Speech*.

23 May 1930 Tolkien attends a General Board meeting. The Board appoints C.L. Wrenn as University Lecturer in English Philology for one year from 1 October 1930, and Dorothy Everett as University Lecturer in Middle English for five years. Wrenn is to deliver intercollegiate lectures and carry on advanced study or research, which will relieve Tolkien of some of his academic burden. He and his wife Agnes will become friends of Tolkien and Edith.

29 May 1930 An article by Tolkien, *The Oxford English School*, is published in the *Oxford Magazine* for 29 May.

By June 1930 Tolkien records two short segments, 'At the Tobacconist's' and 'Wireless', for a Linguaphone English course.

c. 8 June 1930 (Whitsunday) Tolkien's eldest son, John, is confirmed and takes the additional name Joseph.

11 June 1930 Tolkien attends a Pembroke College meeting.

12 June 1930 English Final Honour School examinations begin.

17 June 1930 Tolkien chairs an English Faculty Library Committee meeting at 2.15 p.m. in the Library. It is decided in future to have only one meeting per term on the Thursday of the fourth week of term.

20 June 1930 At an English Faculty Board meeting, in Tolkien's absence, C.T. Onions replaces him on the Committee for the Nomination of Public examiners in the Honour School of English Language and Literature. The Applications Committee has appointed Tolkien and Onions examiners of the B.Litt. thesis of L.E. Jones of Lady Margaret Hall, *An Edition of British Museum MS Harley 2372.*

25 June 1930 Encaenia.

21 June 1930 Trinity Full Term ends.

16 July 1930 Tolkien and C.L. Wrenn examine E.C. Llewellyn of Jesus College *viva voce* on his B.Litt. thesis, *The Influence of Middle Dutch and Middle Low German on English Speech*, at 11.00 a.m. in the Examination Schools.

18 July 1930 Tolkien and Wrenn sign their report (written out by Tolkien) on the examination of E.C. Llewellyn.

29 July 1930 Tolkien attends an extraordinary meeting of the English Faculty Library Committee in the Board Room of the Clarendon Building to elect an Assistant Librarian. He also chairs a special meeting of the English Faculty Board at 12.15 p.m..

2–9 August 1930 The Universal Congress of Esperanto is held in Oxford; Tolkien will later refer to it in *A Secret Vice*.

Summer 1930 In later years Tolkien will distinctly recall having written the first words of *The Hobbit* ('In a hole in the ground there lived a hobbit'), while in the midst of marking School Certificate examination papers in his study at 20 Northmoor Road, thus not before summer 1930. But cases can also be made for an earlier origin; see the entry for *The Hobbit* in **Reader's Guide**. – During summer 1930 Tolkien and his sons dig up the tennis court at 20 Northmoor Road to make a vegetable garden.

September–October 1930 Tolkien continues to write the *Lay of Leithian*. He writes a fifth plot outline, which takes up the story around line 3117. He notes the following dates on the manuscript: lines 3076–84 (Canto X), September 1930; line 3220 (Canto X), 25 September; line 3267 (Canto XI), 26 September; line 3478 (Canto XI), 27 September; line 3650 (Canto XII), 28 September; line 3790 (Canto XII), 30 September; line 3840 (Canto XIII), 1 October. Possibly at this time he continues as far as line 3860, where a typescript copy ends (before continuing in manuscript to the end of Canto XIII).

September 1930 Kenneth Sisam writes to Tolkien, asking if he would be interested in cooperating in an edition of the *Ancrene Riwle*.

23 September 1930 Tolkien completes a fair copy manuscript of his poem **The Lay of Aotrou and Itroun*, following a good but incomplete manuscript of some earlier date.

12 October 1930 Michaelmas Full Term begins. Tolkien's scheduled lectures for this term are: *Elene* on Tuesdays and Thursdays at 11.00 a.m. in the Examination Schools, beginning 14 October; and Old English Minor Poems (including *The Wanderer*, *The Seafarer*, *The Dream of the Rood*, and *The Battle of Maldon*) on Tuesdays and Thursdays at 12.00 noon in the Examination Schools, beginning 14 October.

Michaelmas Term 1930 Edward Tangye Lean matriculates at University College, Oxford. At some time during his undergraduate years he will found a literary society or club called *'The Inklings', which meets in his rooms. It will last only a few terms at most, and not after Tangye Lean graduates in 1933. Tolkien will later write that Tangye Lean 'was, I think, more aware than most undergraduates of the impermanence of their clubs and fashions, and had an ambition to found a club that would prove more lasting. Anyway, he asked some "dons" to become members. C.S. L[ewis] was an obvious choice, and he was probably at that time Tangye-Lean's tutor. . . . In the event both C.S.L. and I became members' (letter to William Luther White, 11 September 1967, *Letters*, pp. 387–8).

24 October 1930 Tolkien attends a General Board meeting. He is elected to the Standing Committee on Responsions, Holy Scripture, and Pass Moderations.

25 October 1930 Tolkien and C.T. Onions examine L.E. Jones of Lady Margaret Hall *viva voce* on her B.Litt. thesis, *An Edition of British Museum MS Harley 2372*, at 11.00 a.m. in the Examination Schools.

31 October 1930 Onions and Tolkien sign their report of the examination of L.E. Jones. They recommend that she resubmit her work after revision. – Tolkien attends an English Faculty Board meeting. He is elected to the Applications Committee with C.T. Onions. He is appointed to a committee 'to consider the number and emoluments of the Readers' (Oxford University Archives FA 4/5/1/1). Probably at this meeting the printed proposed revised regulations for the Final Honour School are presented; these include a note that they are to be circulated to the Faculty, and that comments should be sent to Tolkien no later than 22 November 1930. The Applications Committee has appointed Tolkien the supervisor of E.V. Williams of Jesus College, a probationer B.Litt. student who wishes to work on a Middle English subject.

5 November 1930 Tolkien attends a Pembroke College meeting.

14 November 1930 Tolkien attends a General Board meeting.

21 November 1930 Tolkien replies at last to Kenneth Sisam's letter of September 1930. He would like to cooperate in an edition of the *Ancrene Riwle*, and already has rotographs of one of its most important manuscripts (Corpus Christi College, Cambridge MS 402). He believes that he could produce a plain text, with a limited glossary, in a short time, once he completed work on the Clarendon Chaucer; but a full text, with a complete glossary and grammar, would better serve the study of Middle English. He points out that the Oxford English syllabus is going to be altered to include a special study of the (West Midlands) language of that manuscript, and of a related manuscript in the Bodleian Library. He does not feel that he is solely responsible for the delay in completing the Clarendon Chaucer; he complains that all of the work done so far on the book has been done by him. George S. Gordon has not returned draft notes Tolkien sent him two years earlier, and Tolkien will do no more unless he is given some help in the difficult task of selecting notes and reducing them to the limits Sisam requires.

25 November 1930 Kenneth Sisam replies to Tolkien, approving his decision to try to finish the Clarendon Chaucer.

28 November 1930 Tolkien, as 'Father Christmas', writes to his children in reply to their letters. The North Polar Bear has had whooping cough.

5 December 1930 Tolkien attends a General Board meeting. – He also attends an English Faculty Board meeting. The report (dated 28 November) of the committee (including Tolkien) appointed to consider the question of Readers' and Lecturers' emoluments is presented.

6 December 1930 Michaelmas Full Term ends.

Christmas 1930 Tolkien, as 'Father Christmas', writes to his children. His letter, dated 23–24 December, tells how the North Polar Bear came to have whooping cough after being lost in a snowstorm. An enclosed picture shows Father Christmas finding Polar Bear in the snow, and Polar Bear sitting with his feet in mustard and hot water; the party to celebrate Polar Bear's recovery; and Snow Boys and Polar Cubs pulling a giant Christmas cracker. – If Tolkien conceived *The Hobbit* in summer 1930, he possibly now begins to tell the story to his children.

28 December 1930 George S. Gordon writes to Tolkien, returning his notes for the Clarendon Chaucer, praising them and commenting on various points.

1931

Early 1930s from ?1931 Tolkien writes various undated texts closely associated with but later than the *Quenta Noldorinwa* and the first version of the 'earliest' *Annals of Beleriand*. These are the 'earliest' *Annals of Valinor*, a chronological record of events during 3000 Valian Years (30,000 of our years) from the time the Valar entered the World until the return of the Elves to Middle-earth and the rising of the Sun and the Moon; two texts of the same work in Old English; and a second version of the 'earliest' *Annals of Beleriand*, virtually a new work but unfinished.

?1931 Tolkien writes several manuscripts in an invented 'Elvish' script, *Tengwar* (*Writing systems). Among these are versions of his poems *Errantry* and *The Adventures of Tom Bombadil* (see reproductions, *Pictures by J.R.R. Tolkien* (1979; 2nd edn. 1992), no. 48), both apparently composed around this time.

18 January 1931 Hilary Full Term begins. Tolkien's scheduled lectures and classes for this term are: Old English Minor Poems (continued): *Judith*, Riddles, and *The Battle of Brunanburh* on Tuesdays at 11.00 a.m. in the Examination Schools, beginning 20 January; the Old English *Exodus* on Tuesdays at 12.00 noon in the Examination Schools, beginning 20 January; Gothic Traditions, Thursdays at 11.00 a.m. in the Examination Schools, beginning 22 January; *Carmina Scaldica*: Introduction to Reading of Scaldic Poetry, at an hour and place to be arranged; and Old English Textual Criticism, at an hour and place to be arranged.

?1931–Trinity Term 1933 The members of Edward Tangye Lean's 'Inklings' society, including Tolkien and C.S. Lewis, read aloud unpublished compositions and receive criticism. Among those works is an early version of *Errantry*. – Using the verso of an early manuscript of *Errantry*, Tolkien works on a version of his verse drama **The Homecoming of Beorhtnoth Beorhthelm's Son*.

22 January 1931 Tolkien writes to Kenneth Sisam. He has done as much work as possible on the Clarendon Chaucer despite a 'shattered vac[ation]' (Oxford University Press archives), and Pass Moderations and external examining at four universities will now leave him no leisure before August. He asks for guidance on the permitted length of the book and the audience at which it is aimed, to avoid wasted labour. He has been unable to do any research, though 'obscurities and unsatisfactory explanations' remain. Further work on the Chaucer will have to be extracted from time normally given to sleep or study, but Tolkien vows to complete the book before the summer if physically possible. Then he will think about an edition of the *Ancrene Riwle* on the lines that Sisam has indicated.

30 January 1931 Tolkien attends a General Board meeting.

6 February 1931 Tolkien attends an English Faculty Board meeting. He is appointed to a committee on proposed new regulations for the Honour School. The Applications Committee has readmitted L.E. Jones of Lady Margaret Hall as a B.Litt. student, with Tolkien as her supervisor.

12 February 1931 Tolkien attends an English Faculty Library Committee meeting at 2.15 p.m. in the Library. The Committee will now have two meetings per term, to be held on the second and seventh Thursdays.

13 February 1931 Tolkien attends a General Board meeting.

24 February 1931 Tolkien and thirteen others sign a letter to the General Board, requesting that the Chair of Comparative Philology be raised from Grade B to Grade A.

25 February 1931 Tolkien attends a Pembroke College meeting.

26 February 1931 Tolkien attends an English Faculty Library Committee meeting at 2.15 p.m. in the Library. The Committee discuss what might be read only in the Library and what might be borrowed. Tolkien raises the question of making the bulk of the Napier Collection (the Library's Old and Middle English holdings, based on the personal library of A.S. Napier) open to circulation.

27 February 1931 Tolkien attends a General Board meeting.

13 March 1931 Tolkien attends a General Board meeting. – He also attends an English Faculty Board meeting. The Faculty Board regrets the refusal of the General Board to provide for another Reader in English Literature. David Nichol Smith and Tolkien undertake to prepare for the next meeting of the Board a draft reply on the needs of the Faculty. – Tolkien also attends a Pembroke College meeting.

14 March 1931 Hilary Full Term ends.

16 March 1931 First Public Examination (Pass Moderations) begins. Tolkien is an examiner.

April 1931 The Tolkien family take a holiday in Milford-on-Sea, the home of Michael Tolkien's godfather, Father Augustine Emery, formerly parish priest at Great Haywood. John Tolkien will remember walking with his father along the shingle spit to Hurst Castle where Charles I had been imprisoned, a fort jutting out into the Solent (conversation with the authors).

7 April 1931 Kenneth Sisam writes to Tolkien, explaining that the Clarendon Chaucer should have fewer notes than an ordinary school edition, as it is not to be for beginners, and that the notes should be concerned only with major difficulties.

9 April 1931 Kenneth Sisam writes to Tolkien, forwarding a query from a correspondent about a possible connection between Middle English *aliri* and the word *aleary* in a children's rhyme.

26 April 1931 Trinity Full Term begins. Tolkien's scheduled lectures for this term are: *The Battle of Brunanburh* on Tuesdays at 11.00 a.m. in the Examination Schools, beginning 28 April; the Old English *Exodus* (continued) on Thursdays at 10.00 a.m. in the Examination Schools, beginning 30 April; and Old English Textual Criticism (continued) on Thursdays at 11.00 a.m. in the Examination Schools, beginning 30 April. *See note.* – C.L. Wrenn replaces Tolkien as the supervisor of E.V. Williams.

29 April 1931 Tolkien attends a Pembroke College meeting.

5 May 1931 Tolkien attends an English Faculty Library Committee meeting at 2.15 p.m. in the Library. He again proposes that the Napier books, except the most valuable, be allowed to circulate. With the Committee's agreement he is left to obtain the necessary permission from the Faculty Board.

8 May 1931 Tolkien attends a General Board meeting.

15 May 1931 Tolkien attends an English Faculty Board meeting. He proposes that C.L. Wrenn be appointed to the University Lectureship in English Language for a period of five years from the first day of Michaelmas Term 1931. David Nichol Smith and Tolkien present a draft reply to the General Board on the needs of the Faculty, which the English Faculty Board approves. The report of the Committee on the Regulations is presented, but the Board decides to consider it at an adjourned meeting on 22 May. The Applications Committee has appointed Tolkien and C.T. Onions examiners of the B.Litt. thesis of *Alistair Campbell of Balliol College, *The Production of Diphthongs by 'Breaking' in Old English from 700 to 900.*

16 May 1931 Tolkien reads a paper, *Chaucer's Use of Dialects* (*Chaucer as a Philologist: The Reeve's Tale*), to the Philological Society in Oxford.

22 May 1931 Tolkien attends a General Board meeting. This deals with, among other matters, the constitution of the Board of Faculty of English Language and Literature, and a statement asking the Board its policy in regard to the Honour School of English. – Tolkien attends an adjourned meeting of the English Faculty Board at 3.00 p.m. The new regulations for the syllabus of the English School are amended and adopted to come into force with examinations in 1933. Among documents discussed is one which considers whether 'English Literature from 1850 till Present Time' should be an A Paper. Tolkien submits a typescript, based on a statement provided possibly by H.F.B. Brett-Smith and probably representing the views of several members of the Faculty, which does not approve the compulsory inclusion of Literature after 1800 in the work of all candidates taking the Modern Literature Course III, and which recommends that the existing papers be retained. To this Tolkien adds a manuscript note: 'Professor Tolkien would agree to the modification but considers it a matter primarily for the decision of those mainly concerned with the direction of the work in modern literature' (Oxford University Archives FA 4/5/2/3).

5 June 1931 Tolkien attends a General Board meeting.

10 June 1931 Tolkien attends a Pembroke College meeting.

11 June 1931 English Final Honour School examinations begin.

12 June 1931 Tolkien and C.T. Onions examine Alistair Campbell of Balliol College *viva voce* on his B.Litt. thesis, *The Production of Diphthongs by 'Breaking' in Old English from 700 to 900*, at 2.30 p.m. in the Examination Schools.

15 June 1931 Tolkien and Onions sign their report (written by Tolkien) on their examination of Alistair Campbell.

17 June 1931 Tolkien is listed in the *Oxford University Gazette* for 17 June as a member of the Committee for Comparative Philology, concerned with Section D (Germanic), and 'will see Diploma Students by appointment and direct their work in the respective Sections offered by them' (p. 680).

19 June 1931 Tolkien attends a General Board meeting. – He also attends an English Faculty Board meeting, at which he is appointed to a committee to consider the memorandum of the General Board on the Final Pass School.

20 June 1931 Trinity Full Term ends.

24 June 1931 Encaenia.

28 July 1931 Tolkien attends a meeting of the English Faculty Board at 12.15 p.m.

September 1931 Tolkien continues to write the *Lay of Leithian*, which may have reached line 3860 at the beginning of the previous October. He notes the following dates on the manuscript, all in Canto XIII: line 3881, 14 September; line 3887, 15 September; line 3962, 16 September; line 4029, 14 September (*sic*); line 4045, 16 September (*sic*); line 4085, 17 September. He will write no further dates in the manuscript, but will continue it to line 4223, Canto XIV. He apparently abandons the poem, leaving it unfinished, in September 1931. – Tolkien's eldest son, John, begins to attend the Oratory School, a Catholic boarding school at Caversham, near Reading in Berkshire.

19–20 September 1931 Tolkien dines with C.S. Lewis and their friend *H.V.D. 'Hugo' Dyson at Magdalen College, Oxford. After dinner they stroll along Addison's Walk in the college grounds, discussing metaphor and myth. But they are 'interrupted by a rush of wind which came so suddenly on the still, warm evening and sent so many leaves pattering down that we thought it was raining. We all held our breath, the other two appreciating the ecstasy of such a thing almost as you would' (C.S. Lewis, 18 October 1931, *They Stand Together: The Letters of C.S. Lewis to Arthur Greeves (1914–1963)*, p. 421). They retire to Lewis's rooms in Magdalen to talk further. They discuss Christianity, the difference between love and friendship, poetry, and books. Tolkien goes home at 3.00 a.m.; Lewis and Dyson talk a while longer. The evening is a seminal moment for Lewis, who had abandoned atheism for theism, and now will move from believing in God to accepting Christ.

7 October 1931 Tolkien attends a special meeting of the English Faculty Library Committee at 2.15 p.m. in the Library. J.L.N. O'Loughlin of St Edmund Hall, Oxford is nominated to succeed to the post of Assistant Librarian. There is further discussion of opening the Napier Collection to readers.

11 October 1931 Michaelmas Full Term begins. Tolkien's scheduled lectures for this term are: *Beowulf* on Tuesdays and Thursdays at 11.00 a.m. in the Examination Schools, beginning 13 October; *Guðrúnarkviða en forna* on Tuesdays at 12.00 noon in the Examination Schools, beginning 13 October; Problems of Old English Philology on Thursdays at 12.00 noon in the Examination Schools, beginning 15 October.

Michaelmas Term 1931 Tolkien is nominated to serve as an examiner in the Honour School of English Language and Literature from Hilary Term 1932 to Hilary Term 1934.

14 October 1931 Tolkien attends a Pembroke College meeting.

15 October 1931 A poem by Tolkien, **Progress in Bimble Town*, one of the *Tales and Songs of Bimble Bay*, probably written *c.* 1927–8, is published as by 'K. Bagpuize' in the *Oxford Magazine* for 15 October 1931.

22 October 1931 Tolkien attends an English Faculty Library Committee meeting at 2.15 p.m. in the Library.

23 October 1931 Tolkien attends a General Board meeting. He is re-elected to the Standing Committee on Responsions, Holy Scripture, and Pass Moderations.

30 October 1931 Tolkien attends an English Faculty Board meeting. He is re-elected to the Library Committee. The report of the committee (including Tolkien) appointed to consider a memorandum for the General Board relating to the reform of the Final Pass School is presented, and adopted with minor amendments. The Applications Committee has appointed Tolkien supervisor of probationer B.Litt. students **E.O.G. Turville-Petre of Christ Church and A.F. Colburn of St Edmund Hall.

31 October 1931 Tolkien, as 'Father Christmas', writes to his children in reply to early letters. He says that he has not begun to think about Christmas.

?Autumn 1931 Tolkien delivers an essay (**A Secret Vice*), apparently at a meeting of a philological society. The 'vice' is the creation of languages for personal enjoyment.

5 November 1931 Tolkien attends a Pembroke College meeting.

6 November 1931 Tolkien attends a General Board meeting.

22 November 1931 C.S. Lewis writes to his brother **Warren H. 'Warnie' Lewis that it has become a regular custom for Tolkien to call on him at Magdalen College on Monday mornings for conversation and to drink a glass.

2 December 1931 R.E.M. Wheeler writes to Tolkien. The Society of Antiquaries is to publish a report on the excavations at Lydney Park, Gloucestershire. Wheeler returns a note that Tolkien had written some time earlier, on the name *Nodens* (**The Name 'Nodens'), together with a proof. – The governing committee of the Early English Text Society (*Societies and clubs) commissions its Secretary, *Mabel Day, to inquire whether Professors C.T. Onions and J.R.R. Tolkien contemplate editing the *Ancrene Riwle.*

3 December 1931 Tolkien attends a meeting of the Committee for Comparative Philology at 4.15 p.m. in the Delegates Room of the Clarendon Building.

Between c. 3 and 8 December 1931 Tolkien replies to R.E.M. Wheeler, speculating about connections between the names *Nuada, Lludd,* and *Lydney.*

Between c. 3 and 11 December 1931 Tolkien writes to Allen Mawer, a noted scholar of English place-names, about *Lydney.*

4 December 1931 Tolkien attends a General Board meeting. – He also attends an English Faculty Board meeting. Now, or at the meeting on 5 February 1932, the Board considers an undated report on the section of the General Board's paper *Revision of Needs of Faculties* which relates to the English School. The report identifies the need to establish a statutory University Lectureship in English Literature; to endow a readership or lectureship in medieval Scandinavian languages; and to erect a new building with more space for the English Library. – The Applications Committee has admitted A.F. Colburn as a B.Litt student under Tolkien's supervision. His thesis is to be *A Critical Text of Hali Meiðhad Together with a Grammar and Glossarial Note.* Tolkien and C.L. Wrenn are appointed examiners of the B.Litt. thesis of Allan McIntyre Trounce of St Catherine's Society, *An Edition of the Middle English Romance of 'Athelstan' with Historical, Literary and Linguistic Introduction, Notes and a Glossary.*

5 December 1931 Michaelmas Full Term ends.

9 December 1931 R.E.M. Wheeler writes to thank Tolkien for his note. The idea that Tolkien proposes is one which he himself had long considered. Wheeler suggests that Tolkien keep the proof of his note on *Nodens* while he decides whether or not to rewrite it to include the *Nuada-Lludd-Lydney* association. (In the event, Tolkien will discuss *Nuada* and *Lludd* but not *Lydney.*)

12 December 1931 Allen Mawer replies to Tolkien that he himself had looked into the name *Lydney* some time ago, but came to no clear conclusions.

Christmas 1931 Tolkien, as 'Father Christmas', writes to his children. The letter is dated 23 December, but a note on the envelope as from the North Polar Bear apologizes for forgetting to post it. The letter is very elaborate, in green and red ink and with many decorative letters, and with comments as by the North Polar Bear in the margins. Father Christmas apologizes for not being able to send the children all that they asked for, but they must remember that there are many poor and starving people in the world. Since the children are most interested in railways, he sends them 'mostly things of that sort'. Most of the letter tells of the consequences when the North Polar Bear let a candle fall in the cellar in which firework crackers and sparklers were stored, and the tricks played by Polar Bear's nephews who have been staying with him. The letter is accompanied by three pictures: one, roughly drawn (with an apology that Father Christmas had no time to do a proper picture), depicts both the firework explosion and Father Christmas and Polar Bear in the kitchen; a second, inscribed 'My latest portrait', shows Father Christmas packing parcels, with a pencil sketch of Father Christmas in his sleigh on the verso; and the third, attributed to the North Polar Bear, is both a self-portrait and a stylized landscape of the sun rising or setting behind mountains.

?1931–?1932 At about the time that Tolkien abandons the *Lay of Leithian*, he returns again briefly to the story of Túrin and begins a poem in rhyming couplets, entitled *The Children of Húrin*. This is based on the second version of the alliterative lay of the same title, but is abandoned in turn after only 170 lines.

1932

?1932 or 1933 Tolkien writes a poem, *Looney* (later revised as *The Sea-Bell*).

1932 Tolkien buys his first car, a Morris Cowley which the family nicknames 'Jo' after the first letters of its registration. Soon after acquiring it, Tolkien and his family visit his brother Hilary in Evesham. The car has two punctures on the way and an encounter with a stone wall near Chipping Norton. It will give the family more freedom to explore the countryside around Oxford (see *Oxford and environs).

2 January 1932 R.E.M. Wheeler asks Tolkien to return the proof of his note, as the publisher is pressing for it. But Tolkien evidently has already done so, as Wheeler writes another letter on the same day, thanking him for the proof. Probably in response to a statement by Tolkien that he intends to continue his inquiries into the name *Nodens*, Wheeler says that he would like to see the results when ready.

13 January 1932 Tolkien and C.L. Wrenn examine A.M. Trounce of St Catherine's Society *viva voce* on his B.Litt. thesis, *An Edition of the Middle English Romance of 'Athelstan' with Historical, Literary and Linguistic Introduction, Notes and a Glossary*, at 11.00 a.m. in the Examination Schools.

17 January 1932 Hilary Full Term begins. Tolkien's scheduled lectures for this term are: *Beowulf* (continued) on Tuesdays and Thursdays at 11.00 a.m. in the Examination Schools, beginning 19 January; *Atlakviða* and *Baldrs Draumar* on Thursdays at 12.00 noon in the Examination Schools, beginning 21 January; The Language of the Vespasian Psalter Glosses on Tuesdays at 12.00 noon in the Taylor Institution, beginning 19 January; and Problems of Old English Philology on Fridays at 12.00 noon in the Taylor Institution, beginning 22 January.

20 January 1932 Tolkien attends a Pembroke College meeting.

21 January 1932 Tolkien and Wrenn sign their report (written by Tolkien) on the examination of A.M. Trounce.

28 January 1932 Tolkien chairs an English Faculty Library Committee meeting at 2.15 p.m. in the Library. He, C.L. Wrenn, and the Assistant Librarian,

J.L.N. O'Loughlin, by now have completely reorganized the philological part of the Library's collections.

29 January 1932 Tolkien attends a General Board meeting.

5 February 1932 Tolkien attends an English Faculty Board meeting. The Applications Committee has appointed Tolkien supervisor of *S.R.T.O. (Simonne) d'Ardenne of the Society of Oxford Home-Students, a probationer B.Litt. student who wants to work on a Middle English subject.

15 February 1932 Tolkien attends the inaugural meeting of the Society for the Study of Mediæval Languages and Literature (successor to the Arthurian Society; *Societies and clubs) at 5.30 p.m. in the Taylor Institution. He becomes one of five ordinary members on the first Executive Committee, to serve a two-year term (but apparently serves until 1936). Also on the committee are Eugène Vinaver and *Dorothy Everett. C.T. Onions is appointed editor of the Society journal, *Medium Ævum*.

26 February 1932 Tolkien attends a General Board meeting.

3 March 1932 Tolkien chairs an English Faculty Library Committee meeting at 2.15 p.m. in the Library.

4 March 1932 Tolkien certifies that E.O.G. Turville-Petre has pursued a course of study preparatory to research, and recommends him as a B.Litt. student. His thesis is to be *An Edition of Víga-Glúms Saga from the Manuscripts, with Introduction and Notes.*

11 March 1932 Tolkien attends an English Faculty Board meeting. The Applications Committee has appointed Tolkien supervisor of E.O.G. Turville-Petre. – Tolkien attends a General Board meeting. – He also attends a Pembroke College meeting.

12 March 1932 Hilary Full Term ends.

24 April 1932 Trinity Full Term begins. Tolkien's scheduled lectures for this term are: Finn and Hengest: The Fragment and the Episode (Textual Study and Reconstruction) on Tuesdays and Thursdays at 11.00 a.m. in the Examination Schools, beginning 26 April; *Deor's Lament* and *Waldere* on Tuesdays at 12.00 noon in the Examination Schools, beginning 26 April; and *Völundarkviða* on Thursdays at 12.00 noon in the Examination Schools, beginning 28 April.

27 April 1932 Tolkien attends a Pembroke College meeting.

May 1932 Extracts from a letter by Tolkien to the magazine *The British Esperantist* are published in the number for May 1932, as *A Philologist on Esperanto*. By now he has become a member of the Board of Honorary Advisors of the British Esperanto Association's Education Committee. – The May 1932 number of the journal *Medium Ævum* notes that an article by Tolkien about the phrase 'Sigelwara Land' (Old English *Sigelhearwan*) is among those 'in hand or . . . promised for publication' (see *Sigelwara Land).

5 May 1932 Tolkien attends an English Faculty Library Committee meeting at 2.15 p.m. in the Library.

6 May 1932 Tolkien attends a General Board meeting.

13 May 1932 Tolkien attends an English Faculty Board meeting. Proposals for the remuneration of examiners are considered. David Nichol Smith and

Tolkien are authorized to draw up the Board's observations for submission to the General Board. The Applications Committee has appointed Tolkien and C.L. Wrenn examiners of the D.Phil. thesis of D.J. Rogers of Jesus College, *The Syntax of Cursor Mundi.*

20 May 1932 Tolkien attends a General Board meeting.

3 June 1932 Tolkien attends a General Board meeting.

9 June 1932 English Final Honour School examinations begin. Tolkien is an examiner.

?June 1932–June 1933 Tolkien writes the first version of a poem, *Mythopoeia*, rejecting the notion that myth and fairy-story are lies, and declaring that Man creates in imitation of the Creator. He will write at least seven versions. At the end of the final manuscript he will later inscribe: 'Written mainly in the Examination Schools during Invigilation', i.e. while acting as an examiner.

17 June 1932 Tolkien attends an English Faculty Board meeting, a General Board meeting, and a Pembroke College meeting.

18 June 1932 Trinity Full Term ends.

22 June 1932 Encaenia.

July 1932 Tolkien's note *The Name 'Nodens'* is published as Appendix A in *Report on the Excavation of the Prehistoric, Roman, and Post-Roman Site in Lydney Park, Gloucestershire* by R.E.M. Wheeler and T.V. Wheeler.

2 August 1932 Tolkien and C.L. Wrenn examine D.J. Rogers of Jesus College *viva voce* on his D.Phil. thesis, *The Syntax of Cursor Mundi*, at 2.30 p.m. in the Examination Schools. Tolkien will later write the examiners' report.

Late August–?early September 1932 The Tolkien family take a holiday at Lamorna Cove in Cornwall with C.L. Wrenn, his wife Agnes, and their daughter Carola. Tolkien and Wrenn amuse the children by having a swimming race while wearing panama hats and smoking pipes. The cove is isolated, unlike popular tourist resorts such as Filey. The Tolkien and Wrenn families go on long walks, even as far as Land's End. They are amused by one of the local characters, an old man who, Tolkien will later write, 'used to go about swapping gossip and weather-wisdom and such like. To amuse my boys I named him Gaffer Gamgee, and the name became part of family lore to fix on old chaps of that kind' (letter to Christopher Bretherton, 16 July 1964, *Letters*, p. 348). The name will be given to Sam's father in *The Lord of the Rings*.

30 August 1932 Kenneth Sisam replies to a letter from Tolkien, who had asked whether the Old English *Exodus* might have been influenced by early Gallican Psalters.

9 October 1932 Michaelmas Full Term begins. Tolkien's scheduled lectures for this term are: *Elene* on Tuesdays and Thursdays at 11.00 a.m. in the Examination Schools, beginning 11 October; Introduction to Old English Philology on Tuesdays at 12.00 noon in the Examination Schools, beginning 11 October; Old English Prosody on Thursdays at 12.00 noon in the Examination Schools, beginning 13 October; and *Völuspá* on Fridays at 12.00 noon in the Examination Schools, beginning 14 October.

12 October 1932 Tolkien attends a Pembroke College meeting.

18 October 1932 Tolkien certifies that S.R.T.O. d'Ardenne of the Society of Oxford Home-Students has pursued a course of study preparatory to research, and recommends her acceptance as a B.Litt. student with the thesis *An Edition of the Liflade ant te Passiun of Seinte Iuliene (MS Bodley 34)*. At about this time Simonne d'Ardenne begins to stay (for about a year) with the Tolkien family at 20 Northmoor Road. Together Tolkien and d'Ardenne will also begin to prepare an edition of *Seinte Katerine*, another work in the 'Katherine Group' contained in MS Bodley 34.

20 October 1932 Tolkien attends an English Faculty Library Committee meeting at 2.15 p.m. in the Library.

25 October 1932 Tolkien replies to a letter from R.W. Chapman of Oxford University Press, noting that he must complete the Clarendon Chaucer or 'lose for ever the goodwill of the Clarendon Press' (i.e. the distinguished imprint of Oxford University Press which is to publish the book). Its glossary has been written and corrected, but needs to be collated with the notes, which are also complete except for the selection from the Prologue to the *Canterbury Tales* and the 'Monk's Tale' but are nearly all too long. 'If I could send in the notes after drastic cuts and have the bits back again typed fairly quickly I think I could soon complete the job, in spite of the burdens of the day and the night.' Once the Chaucer is out of the way Tolkien would like to work on other books, indeed feels that he ought to, not only in deference to what is expected of professors but because during the past few years, through research and teaching, he has learned a good deal worth writing about. He has done much work on the Old English matter of Finn and Hengest, though more would be needed to make it suitable for publication. He suggests his prose translation of *Beowulf*, but feels that it should be preceded by introductory matter on the diction of Old English verse, its metre, and so forth, and include notes concerning particularly difficult problems in the text. 'All this stuff is in existence as lectures or papers to societies and if only I could free my mind and conscience of the Chaucerian incubus might soon be sufficiently polished up to hand over' (Oxford University Press archives). He asks if Oxford University Press have thought about a cheap edition of *Beowulf* aimed at the non-specialist, who under the new English syllabus has to read the entire poem. He points out the need for editions of *Elene* and *Exodus* which will remain set books in the English School; he has existing commentaries to both.

27 October 1932 R.W. Chapman writes to Tolkien, offering help with typing and urging him to get the Chaucer off his mind so that he can move on to other things. He thinks a prose *Beowulf* a good idea provided that it is not too long. Kenneth Sisam is already working on *Elene*.

28 October 1932 Tolkien attends an English Faculty Board meeting. He is re-elected to the Applications Committee. The Applications Committee has approved S.R.T.O. d'Ardenne as a full B.Litt. student; Tolkien is to continue as her supervisor.

2 November 1932 Tolkien attends a Pembroke College meeting.

30 November 1932 Tolkien, as 'Father Christmas', writes to his children in response to early letters. He tells them that the North Polar Bear has disappeared, and that the 'snowbabies holidays' begin on 1 December.

December 1932 The first of two parts of Tolkien's essay *Sigelwara Land* is published in *Medium Ævum* for December 1932.

2 December 1932 Tolkien attends an English Faculty Board meeting. The report of the English Faculty Library Committee is presented. The Applications Committee has appointed Tolkien and Dorothy Everett examiners of the B.Litt. thesis of Mary Elizabeth Carroll of St Hilda's College, *The Phonology of Hampshire Place-Name Forms, Particularly as Found in Documents of the Thirteenth and Fourteenth Centuries, Compared with That of the Usages of Winchester, and of Other Texts for Which a Hampshire Origin Has Been Suggested.* – Tolkien attends a Pembroke College meeting.

3 December 1932 Michaelmas Full Term ends.

18 December 1932 Tolkien writes to Kenneth Sisam, informing him that *Sigelwara Land* will run through three numbers of *Medium Ævum* (in the event, it will appear in only two). He thanks Sisam, probably for information about Gallican psalters, and says that he must check the exact spelling of a passage in the Paris Psalter for the last instalment of his essay. He is putting the last touches to his paper on the 'Reeve's Tale', which Sisam had seen, for the *Transactions of the Philological Society* (**Chaucer as a Philologist: The Reeve's Tale*). He will then turn to the Clarendon Chaucer and hopes to be rid of that burden soon. David Nichol Smith is helping him to 'curtail my overwhelming mass of notes'. He hopes that his *Beowulf* translation might come next, 'but life is short, & so is the day. I am obliged to examine Oxford (complete new syllabus), Manchester and Reading, for the meeting of ends, the coming year; and probably P. Mods [Pass Moderations] at the end of it. Also there are lectures & B.Litts and goodness knows what' (Oxford University Press archives). If he can find any free time from children and work, he would like to visit Sisam either at home or at the Oxford University Press.

Christmas 1932 Tolkien, as 'Father Christmas', writes four pages to his children, dated 23 December, significantly expanding the 'mythology' of the Father Christmas letters. He tells how the North Polar Bear became lost in caves decorated long ago with paintings of animals and other figures, and in which he found goblins, 'to us very much what rats are to you, only worse'. Having rescued Polar Bear with the help of the Cave Bear, Father Christmas found his storerooms disturbed by goblins, which he drove away with the help of Red Gnomes. He apologizes for not being able to carry as many toys this year: the goblins have smashed some of them, and he is taking 'useful stuff' (food and clothes) to people who are hungry and cold. Enclosed with the letter is an elaborate picture of Father Christmas in his sleigh drawn by eight pair of reindeer above the Oxford skyline; of the North Pole; of Father Christmas, the North Polar Bear, and the Cave Bear looking at cave paintings while goblins lurk around corners; and of the party that Father Christmas will have on St Stephen's Day. A second picture, mainly copied from reproductions of real prehistoric cave paintings, purports to show some of the art found in the goblin caves. In addition, Tolkien sends, as from the North Polar Bear, a letter written in an alphabet he has made up from marks in the caves.

End of 1932–beginning of 1933 Tolkien lends *The Hobbit* in typescript to C.S. Lewis; at this stage (it seems) the story ends with the death of Smaug, near the end of the chapter 'Fire and Water' as finally published in 1937. (See further, entry for *The Hobbit* in **Reader's Guide**.) During the next three years the same typescript will be lent to other friends, including *M.E. (Elaine) Griffiths, a B.Litt. student under Tolkien's supervision, and the *Reverend Mother St Teresa Gale, Mother Superior at Cherwell Edge in St Cross Road in Oxford, a convent of the Order of the Holy Child Jesus to which was attached a hostel for Catholic women in the Society of Oxford Home-Students.

1933

15 January 1933 Hilary Full Term begins. Tolkien's scheduled lectures for this term are: *Elene* (continued) and *The Vision of the Cross* (i.e. *The Dream of the Rood*) on Tuesdays and Thursdays at 11.00 a.m. in the Examination Schools, beginning 17 January; Old English Textual Criticism on Tuesdays at 12.00 noon in the Examination Schools, beginning 17 January; *Völsunga Saga* on Thursdays at 12.00 noon in the Examination Schools, beginning 19 January; and The Language of the Vespasian Psalter Glosses on Fridays at 12.00 noon in the Examination Schools, beginning 20 January.

18 January 1933 Tolkien attends a Pembroke College meeting.

25 January 1933 C.S. and Warnie Lewis are Tolkien's guests for dinner at high table at Pembroke College. After dinner they retire to the Common Room for dessert and wine, then stand around the fire talking mainly about Samuel Johnson and Anthony Trollope. Tolkien and the Lewis brothers go to C.S. Lewis's rooms in Magdalen College for more conversation until 11.00 p.m., when Tolkien drives Warnie Lewis most of the way home.

26 January 1933 Tolkien attends an English Faculty Library Committee meeting at 2.15 p.m. in the Library.

30 January 1933 Adolf Hitler becomes Chancellor of Germany.

3 February 1933 At an English Faculty Board meeting, in Tolkien's absence, the Applications Committee reports that it has appointed Tolkien and Kenneth Sisam examiners of the B.Litt. thesis of *N.R. Ker of Magdalen College, *A Study of the Additions and Alterations in MSS Bodley 340 and 342.*

4 February 1933 C.S. Lewis writes: 'Since term began [15 January] I have had a delightful time reading a children's story Tolkien has just written [presumably *The Hobbit*]. . . . Whether it is really *good* (I think it is until the end) is of course another question' (*They Stand Together: The Letters of C.S. Lewis to Arthur Greeves (1914–1963)*, p. 449).

9 February 1933 The Oxford Union Society debates the motion 'that this House will in no circumstance fight for its King and Country'. The motion is carried 275 votes to 153 and is widely discussed in the press.

14 February 1933 Tolkien and Dorothy Everett examine M.E. Carroll of St Hilda's College *viva voce* on her B.Litt. thesis, *The Phonology of Hampshire Place-Name Forms*, at 2.30 p.m. in the Examination Schools. – The Society for the Study of Mediæval Languages and Literature holds its second meeting.

17 February 1933 Tolkien attends a Pembroke College meeting. – He and Dorothy Everett sign their report (written by Tolkien) on the examination of M.E. Carroll.

2 March 1933 Tolkien certifies that S.R.T.O. d'Ardenne has completed course work towards her B.Litt.

8 March 1933 Tolkien attends a Pembroke College meeting.

10 March 1933 Tolkien attends an English Faculty Board meeting.

11 March 1933 Hilary Full Term ends.

16 March 1933 Tolkien writes to Kenneth Sisam that he hopes to see him at his home at Boar's Hill, Oxford, on 18 March. Tolkien is very pleased because he has been given a complete set of the *Oxford English Dictionary*. He has been reading the thesis of N.R. Ker and finds it hard going.

21 March 1933 Tolkien and Kenneth Sisam examine N.R. Ker of Magdalen College *viva voce* on his B.Litt. thesis, *A Study of the Additions and Alterations in MSS Bodley 340 and 342*, at 2.30 p.m. in the Examination Schools.

c. 25 March 1933 Tolkien and C.S. Lewis discuss the latter's response to *The Three Musketeers* by Alexandre Dumas as a work with no background behind the plot. They remark on how the word *romance* is used to describe works by authors as different as Dumas and William Morris, and agree 'that for what *we* meant by romance there must be at least the hint of another world – one must "hear the horns of elfland"' (C.S. Lewis, 25 March 1933, *They Stand Together: The Letters of C.S. Lewis to Arthur Greeves (1914–1963)*, p. 452).

1 April 1933 In Germany the Nazis begin to persecute the Jews. Jewish businesses will be boycotted – most are soon liquidated – and Jewish lawyers and doctors barred from their professions.

23 April 1933 Trinity Full Term begins. Tolkien's scheduled lectures for this term are: Old English Verse Texts (for those beginning the Honour Course) on Tuesdays and Thursdays at 11.00 a.m. in the Examination Schools, beginning 25 April; The Germani on Tuesdays at 12.00 noon in the Examination Schools, beginning 25 April; and Prolegomena to the Study of Old English and Old Norse Poetry on Thursdays at 12.00 noon in the Examination Schools, beginning 27 April. E.O.G. Turville-Petre is to teach a class in Old Norse on behalf of Tolkien.

26 April 1933 Tolkien attends a Pembroke College meeting.

24 May 1933 The *Oxford University Gazette* reports that Tolkien has been appointed a Moderator in Literis Graecis et Latinis (Pass Moderations) from the first day of Michaelmas Term 1933 to first day of Michaelmas Term 1934.

12 May 1933 Tolkien attends an English Faculty Board meeting.

8 June 1933 Tolkien chairs an English Faculty Library Committee meeting at 2.15 p.m. in the Library. – English Final Honour School examinations begin. Tolkien is chairman of the examiners.

11 June 1933 At a board meeting of Hið íslenzka bókmenntafélag (the Icelandic Literary Society), Sigurður Nordal nominates Tolkien as an honorary member.

16 June 1933 Tolkien attends an English Faculty Board meeting. He is appointed to the Committee for the Nomination of Public Examiners in the Honour School of English Language and Literature and in the Pass School, Group B.6, to Hilary Term 1937. – He also attends a Pembroke College meeting.

17 June 1933 Trinity Full Term ends. – The annual general meeting of Hið íslenzka bókmenntafélag confirms with applause Tolkien's honorary membership.

20 June 1933 Tolkien attends a Pembroke College meeting.

21 June 1933 Encaenia.

?Summer 1933 John Tolkien and his father erect a trellis in front of 20 Northmoor Road to screen their garden from the eyes of passers-by.

26 July 1933 Tolkien and Hugo Dyson entertain the Lewis brothers at dinner in Exeter College. Dyson and Tolkien are in exuberant form, especially Dyson. As it is vacation they dine in the Common Room with various members of Exeter and their guests. Nevill Coghill is among those present. They eat a dinner of cold soup and lobster salad served with cider, then retire to another room to drink sauterne, and to deck chairs in the garden for coffee. After some conversation Tolkien, Dyson, the Lewis brothers, and a clergyman walk to Magdalen College and stroll in the deer park. At about 10.00 p.m. they adjourn to the Magdalen Common Room for drinks. The party breaks up about 10.20.

?August–early October 1933 Probably during the summer vacation Tolkien begins to write lectures on 'Beowulf: General Criticism' which he will give during Michaelmas Term 1933. These may be the work first called Beowulf with Critics and later Beowulf and the Critics (see *Beowulf: The Monsters and the Critics). Tolkien will later produce a revised and enlarged version of the lectures, presumably for 'Beowulf: General Criticism' as delivered in Michaelmas Term 1934 or 1936.

14 September 1933 While driving with his family to visit relatives in Birmingham, Tolkien passes through Hall Green, formerly the hamlet of Sarehole. He finds that most of the scenery and buildings he remembers from his boyhood have been destroyed or much altered. He will record in his diary that Sarehole had become 'a huge tram-ridden meaningless suburb where I actually lost my way' (quoted in Biography, p. 124).

?October 1933 Tolkien submits, probably by invitation, a poem, Firiel (*The Last Ship), for publication in the Chronicle of the Convents of the Sacred Heart, the journal of a Roman Catholic order which has an Oxford branch (established 1929) at 11 Norham Gardens. Firiel dates from the early 1930s, and is possibly written at this time. Tolkien is in close contact with the Oxford convent: Priscilla Tolkien will recall going there for children's parties in the summer and also at Christmas when her father provided entertainment.

8 October 1933 Michaelmas Full Term begins. Tolkien's scheduled lectures for this term are: *Beowulf*: General Criticism on Tuesdays at 11.00 a.m. in the Examination Schools, beginning 10 October; The Origins of the English Language on Tuesdays at 12.00 noon in the Examination Schools, beginning 10 October; Old English Prose Pieces (Cynewulf and Cyneheard, Ohthere and Wulfstan, *Sermo Lupi ad Anglos*) on Thursdays at 11.00 a.m. in the Examination Schools, beginning 12 October; and The Historical and Legendary Traditions in *Beowulf* and Other Old English Poems on Thursdays and Fridays at 12.00 noon in the Examination Schools, beginning 12 October. He will continue to supervise B.Litt. students A.F. Colburn, L.E. Jones (later L.E. Rogers), and E.O.G. Turville-Petre. *See note.*

?Michaelmas Term 1933 Edward Tangye Lean having graduated from Oxford, the name of his literary club, 'The Inklings', is transferred (not earlier than this term) to an ultimately more famous group of friends which by now has already formed around C.S. Lewis. The new group, informal and of varying composition, will usually meet in a pub, often the Eagle and Child (or 'Bird and Baby', see *Oxford and environs) in St Giles', for an hour or two before lunch on Tuesdays to talk and drink together; and in Lewis's rooms in Magdalen College after dinner on Thursdays, where they will read compositions for the criticism or acclaim of those present, otherwise letting conversation wander where it will. These meetings will become an important part of Tolkien's life for almost twenty years. *See note.*

10 October 1933 The future novelist Barbara Pym, then an undergraduate at Oxford, notes in her diary that Tolkien gave an amusing lecture on *Beowulf* this morning.

11 October 1933 Tolkien attends a Pembroke College meeting.

19 October 1933 By this date Tolkien, as chairman, has written a six-page report of the examiners in the Honour School for 1933.

20 October 1933 Tolkien attends a special meeting of the Committee on Comparative Philology at 4.15 p.m. in the Music Lecture Room of the Clarendon Building.

27 October 1933 Tolkien attends an English Faculty Board meeting. He is re-elected to the Library Committee. The report of the examiners in the English Honour School for 1933 (of which Tolkien is chairman) is presented. The Applications Committee has appointed Tolkien supervisor of probationer B.Litt. students J.E. (Joan) Blomfield (see *E.O.G. Turville-Petre) of Somerville College and M.E. Griffiths of the Society of Oxford Home-Students, who are interested in Old English and Middle English philology respectively.

2 November 1933 A member of the Convents of the Sacred Heart in Oxford writes to Tolkien, acknowledging receipt of his poem *Firiel*.

3 November 1933 Tolkien attends a Pembroke College meeting.

9 November 1933 Tolkien's poem *Errantry* is published in the *Oxford Magazine* for 9 November 1933.

15 November 1933 The Early English Text Society Committee votes to publish the English, French, and Latin texts of the *Ancrene Riwle*, edited under the auspices of the Society in conjunction with American scholars.

23 November 1933 Tolkien chairs an English Faculty Library Committee meeting at 2.15 p.m. in the Library. – Later he has tea with the Lewis brothers and an ex-pupil of C.S. Lewis.

28 November 1933 Tolkien completes the application forms for J.E. Blomfield and M.E. Griffiths to be accepted as full B.Litt. students. Blomfield's thesis is to be *The Origins of Old English Orthography, with Special Reference to the Representation of the Spirants*, and Griffiths' thesis is to be *Notes and Observations on the Vocabulary of Ancrene Wisse MS CCCC 402*.

30 November 1933 Tolkien attends an English Faculty Board meeting. The Applications Committee has accepted J.E. Blomfield and M.E. Griffiths as full B.Litt. students; Tolkien is to continue as their supervisor.

1 December 1933 Tolkien attends a Pembroke College meeting.

2 December 1933 Michaelmas Full Term ends.

Early December 1933 Tolkien, as 'Father Christmas', writes a short letter to his children, dated 2 December. He has had 'a good many letters' from them.

4 December 1933 Tolkien goes for a walk with C.S. Lewis.

21 December 1933 Tolkien gives to R.W. Chambers an elaborately calligraphic and illuminated copy of a poem he has written, **Doworst*, a satirical account of the vivas at Oxford, written in the style and metre of the fourteenth-century poem *Piers Plowman*.

Christmas 1933 Tolkien, as 'Father Christmas', writes to his children. The letter is dated 21 December, and the envelope 'postmarked' 22 December. Father Christmas tells how goblins invaded his house, and were fought by elves and gnomes and the North Polar Bear as well as himself. Enclosed is a triple illustration in an elaborate frame, depicting Father Christmas awakened by goblins riding on bats, a snowy landscape with the Northern Lights, and the North Polar Bear and gnomes in battle with goblins.

Mid-1930s C.S. Lewis and some of his students meet in his rooms in Magdalen College to read and discuss *Beowulf*. One of Lewis's students, E.L. Edmonds, will later recall that Tolkien came quite often to these 'beer and *Beowulf*' evenings. 'It was very obvious that [Tolkien and Lewis] were great friends – indeed, they were like two young bear cubs sometimes, just happily quipping with one another' ('C.S. Lewis, the Teacher', *In Search of C.S. Lewis*, (1983), p. 45).

Mid-1930s–end of 1937 Tolkien revises some components of his 'Silmarillion' mythology and writes new texts. He does not necessarily finish one work before starting another, and makes changes to previously written texts to conform with new story elements or changed names as they emerge. Works from this period include, in the probable order in which they are begun: the 'later' *Annals of Beleriand*, a fuller and more finished version of the 'earliest' *Annals*; the **Ambarkanta: The Shape of the World*, a list of cosmographical words and explanations and a description of the world of the mythology, accompanied by three diagrams and two maps; the 'later' *Annals of Valinor*, a development of the 'earliest' *Annals*; the first version of *The Tale of Years*, as an accompaniment to the *Annals* as they become fuller; the *Lhammas* or 'Account of Tongues', in three versions (the third entitled *Lammasethen*), which describes the development and interrelationships of the various Elvish languages and also includes information about the speech of the Valar, Men, and Orcs, with summaries of the history of the Elves and two 'genealogical tables', *The Tree of Tongues* and *The Peoples of the Elves*; a substantial work on Noldorin phonology, and a five-page exposition of Elvish runes; two brief texts (see *Writing systems), *The Elvish Alphabets*, which describes the Noldorin alphabets of Rúmil and Fëanor and the Runic alphabet of Dairon, and *The 'Alphabet of Dairon'* which includes more information about runes; the *Ainulindalë*, the first retelling of the Creation myth since *The Music of the Ainur* in *The Book of Lost Tales*; and the *Quenta Silmarillion*, in which the mythology is told as a narrative at much greater length than in the *Quenta Noldorinwa* and which incorporates much new material. In the latter Tolkien has great difficulty in compressing the tale of Beren and Lúthien which he had told at great length in the *Lay of Leithian*, and rejects drafts that are disproportionate to the rest of the work; while he is writing another version of this story, he sends a fair copy of the *Quenta Silmarillion* to George Allen & Unwin to be considered for publication (see entry for 15 November 1937). – Probably contemporary with his work on the *Lhammas* and the *Quenta Silmarillion*, Tolkien prepares the *Etymologies* (or *Beleriandic and Noldorin Names and Words*), 'an etymological dictionary of word-relationships: an alphabetically-arranged list of primary stems, or "bases", with their derivatives' (Christopher Tolkien, *The Lost Road and Other Writings* (1987), pp. 342–3). This is apparently compiled progressively through the alphabet, but changes are made in the course of composition.

1934

c. **1934–1935** Tolkien writes a review of the Devonshire volumes published by the English Place-Name Society in 1931 and 1932. This also mentions the Northampton and Surrey volumes, which appeared in 1933 and 1934, but not the 1935 Essex volume. In the event, the review is never published.

14 January 1934 Hilary Full Term begins. Tolkien's scheduled lectures for this term are: *Waldere* and *Deor's Lament*, together with the Old Norse *Völundarkviða*, on Tuesdays at 11.00 a.m. in the Examination Schools, beginning 16 January; and The Historical and Legendary Traditions in *Beowulf* and Other Old English Poems (continued) on Tuesdays and Thursdays at 12.00 noon in the Examination Schools, beginning 16 January. Tolkien will continue to supervise B.Litt. students J.E. Blomfield, A.F. Colburn, M.E. Griffiths, and E.O.G. Turville-Petre.

18 January 1934 Tolkien's poem *Looney* is published in the *Oxford Magazine* for 18 January 1934.

19 January 1934 Tolkien attends a meeting of the Committee for Comparative Philology at 5.15 p.m. in the Delegates Room of the Clarendon Building. In the absence of the usual chairman, he is asked to take the chair. He is made a member of the Committee for the Nomination of Examiners for the Diploma in Comparative Philology for two years from the beginning of Hilary Term 1934.

25 January 1934 Tolkien chairs an English Faculty Library Committee meeting at 2.15 p.m. in the Library.

31 January 1934 Tolkien attends a Pembroke College meeting.

15 February 1934 Tolkien's poem *The Adventures of Tom Bombadil* is published in the *Oxford Magazine* for 15 February 1934.

21 February 1934 Tolkien attends a Pembroke College meeting.

23 February 1934 By this date Priscilla Tolkien has been ill for five weeks, and doctors have been unable to diagnose the cause. Tolkien's own and his family's ill health in the past few years, with consequent doctors' bills, and the expense of sending his sons to school, have made it difficult for him to make ends meet, even by undertaking tasks such as marking examination papers.

1 March 1934 Tolkien certifies that E.O.G. Turville-Petre has completed course work towards his B.Litt.

9 March 1934 Tolkien attends an English Faculty Board meeting. The Applications Committee has appointed Tolkien and E.V. Gordon examiners of the B.Litt. thesis of E.O.G. Turville-Petre, *An Edition of Víga-Glúms Saga from the Manuscripts, with Introduction and Notes.*

10 March 1934 Hilary Full Term ends.

12 March 1934 First Public Examination (Pass Moderations) begins. Tolkien is an moderator.

25 March 1934 Tolkien's poem *Firiel* is published in the *Chronicle of the Convents of the Sacred Heart* 4 (1934).

26 March 1934 Tolkien goes to C.S. Lewis's rooms in Magdalen College at 4.00 p.m. After tea, he and the Lewis brothers read Wagner's *Die Walküre*, Warnie in English, the others in German. *See note.* – Soon after 6.00 p.m. Tolkien goes home, but later meets the Lewises at the Eastgate Hotel for dinner. They then return to Magdalen to finish the reading and to drink whiskey. The reading leads to a discussion about Wotan, and to long and interesting conversation on religion. The meeting breaks up at about 11.30 p.m.

28 March 1934 L.R. Farnell dies.

18 April 1934 Elaine Griffiths, the B.Litt. student working on aspects of the Cambridge manuscript of the *Ancrene Riwle* (*Ancrene Wisse*), writes to Tolkien, sending references in the manuscript for which he had asked. By now Tolkien has been preparing an edition of the *Ancrene Wisse*, and Griffiths is his *de facto* assistant.

22 April 1934 Trinity Full Term begins. Tolkien's scheduled lectures for this term are: Old English Verse (for those beginning the Honour Course) on Tuesdays at 11.00 a.m. in the Examination Schools, beginning 24 April; *Völundarkviða, Atlakviða,* and *Atlamál* on Tuesdays at 11.00 a.m. in the Examination

Schools; and *The Fight at Finnesburg* (continued; probably a further continuation of The Historical and Legendary Traditions in *Beowulf* and Other Old English Poems) on Tuesdays and Thursdays at 12.00 noon in the Examination Schools, beginning 24 April. (Thus announced in the *Oxford University Gazette*, without correction for the listing of two lectures scheduled for Tuesdays at 11.00 a.m.) Tolkien will continue to supervise B.Litt. students J.E. Blomfield and M.E. Griffiths.

25 April 1934 Tolkien attends a Pembroke College meeting.

3 May 1934 Tolkien attends an English Faculty Library Committee meeting at 2.15 p.m. in the Library.

11 May 1934 Tolkien attends an English Faculty Board meeting. The Applications Committee has appointed Tolkien and *M.R. Ridley examiners of the B.Litt. thesis of Mary M. McEldowney of the Society of Oxford Home-Students, *The Fairy Tales and Fantasies of George MacDonald*.

26 May 1934 Tolkien and E.V. Gordon examine E.O.G. Turville-Petre of Christ Church *viva voce* on his B.Litt. thesis, *An Edition of Víga-Glúms Saga from the Manuscripts, with Introduction and Notes*, at 12.00 noon in the Examination Schools.

28 May 1934 Tolkien and E.V. Gordon sign their report (written by Tolkien) on the examination of E.O.G. Turville-Petre.

June 1934 The second part of Tolkien's essay *Sigelwara Land* is published in *Medium Ævum* for June 1934.

7 June 1934 Tolkien attends an English Faculty Library Committee meeting at 2.15 p.m. in the Library. – English Final Honour School examinations begin.

12 June 1934 Tolkien and M.R. Ridley examine Mary M. McEldowney of the Society of Oxford Home-Students *viva voce* on her B.Litt. thesis, *The Fairy Tales and Fantasies of George MacDonald*, at 10.00 a.m. in the Examination Schools. Later they sign their report of the examination.

15 June 1934 Tolkien attends an English Faculty Board meeting at 3.30 p.m. – Tolkien attends a meeting of the Committee for Comparative Philology at 5.15 p.m. in the Delegates Room of the Clarendon Building. – Tolkien also attends a Pembroke College meeting.

16 June 1934 Trinity Full Term ends.

19 June 1934 There is a Gaudy at Pembroke College. The Master and Fellows entertain guests in the Hall.

20 June 1934 Encaenia.

19 July 1934 Hugo Dyson, who has been an examiner in the English Honour School, gives a dinner at Exeter College to celebrate the end of exams. He, the Lewis brothers, Tolkien, H.F.B. Brett-Smith, C.T. Onions, C.L. Wrenn, and Nevill Coghill dine in rooms there. Warnie Lewis will recall in his diary that 'everyone was in uproarious spirits – the reaction I suppose after examining. In fact the evening was just a little too high-spirited – too much farce and too little real talk' (Marion E. Wade Center, Wheaton College, Wheaton, Illinois). After the dinner they adjourn to Coghill's rooms in Exeter.

Second half of 1934 Tolkien's paper *Chaucer as a Philologist: The Reeve's Tale* is published in the *Transactions of the Philological Society* for 1934. Although delivered three years earlier, its publication has been delayed 'principally due to hesitation in putting forward a study, for which closer investigation of words, and more still a much fuller array of readings from [manuscripts] of the *Reeve's Tale*, were so plainly needed. But for neither have I had opportunity, and dust has merely accumulated on the pages. The paper is therefore presented . . . practically as it was read, though with the addition of a "critical text", and accompanying textual notes, as well as of various footnotes, appendices, and comments naturally omitted in reading' (p. 1).

September 1934 From 1934 the Tolkien family usually spend two weeks at the beginning of September, before the boys return to school, at *Sidmouth on the southern coast of Devon. On this occasion Tolkien drives there with the family luggage, including many of Priscilla's bears and other soft toys which she refuses to leave behind. As there is no room in the car for anyone else, Edith, Christopher, and Priscilla travel by train, and John and Michael cycle down in the course of two or three days. The family stays at a house called 'Aurora'. They enjoy themselves on the beach but also explore the surrounding countryside and other beaches in the car. – Later in the month Michael Tolkien begins to attend the Oratory School at Caversham.

21 September 1934 Tolkien attends the funeral of Francis Fortescue Urquhart, Senior Fellow of Balliol College, a requiem Mass at the Church of St Aloysius, and burial at Wolvercote Cemetery.

Between late summer and early autumn 1934 Tolkien, as 'Father Christmas', writes to Christopher in reply to a telegram and letters from Christopher and Priscilla. Father Christmas tells them that his post office does not open until Michaelmas Term.

14 October 1934 Michaelmas Full Term begins. Tolkien's scheduled lectures for this term are: *Beowulf*: General Criticism on Tuesdays at 11.00 a.m. in the Examination Schools, beginning 16 October; *Elene* and *The Vision of the Cross* on Tuesdays and Thursdays at 12.00 noon in the Examination Schools, beginning 16 October; and Outlines of the History of English (Old English Period) on Tuesdays at 12.00 noon in the Examination Schools, beginning 16 October. (Thus announced in the *Oxford University Gazette*, without correction for the listing of two lectures scheduled for Tuesdays at 12.00 noon.) Tolkien will continue to supervise B.Litt. students J.E. Blomfield and M.E. Griffiths.

17 October 1934 Tolkien attends a Pembroke College meeting.

18 October 1934 At a dinner attended by members of The Society (*Societies and clubs), men who meet generally to discuss Oxford education, Tolkien is among those suggested for election.

23 October 1934 Robin Flower of the British Museum Department of Manuscripts reports to a meeting of the Early English Text Society Committee that Professor Tolkien will allow the Society to use his text of the Corpus

Christi College, Cambridge manuscript of the *Ancrene Riwle*. Dr Flower has called on Tolkien at some time before this date.

25 October 1934 Tolkien attends an English Faculty Library Committee meeting at 2.15 p.m. in the Library.

2 November 1934 Tolkien attends a Pembroke College meeting. – At an English Faculty Board meeting, in Tolkien's absence, he is re-elected to the Applications Committee.

20 November 1934 Tolkien, as 'Father Christmas', sends Christopher birthday greetings, and says that he is sorry that Priscilla has not been well.

23 November 1934 Tolkien certifies that J.E. Blomfield of Somerville College has completed course work towards her B.Litt.

7 December 1934 Tolkien attends an English Faculty Board meeting. He is appointed to a committee to draft regulations for English Literature in Pass Moderations. – He also attends a Pembroke College meeting.

8 December 1934 Michaelmas Full Term ends.

9 December 1934 R.W. Chambers, having been lent a copy of *The Fall of Arthur*, writes to Tolkien, praising the poem and urging him to finish it.

Christmas 1934 Tolkien, as 'Father Christmas', writes letters dated Christmas Eve to Christopher and Priscilla. He apologizes for not having time to write as long a letter as in 1932 and 1933. The letter to Christopher tells of the Polar Bear's nephews and the Cave cubs, and of the Christmas tree that Father Christmas brought from Norway and planted in a pool of ice. He sends love to Mick (Michael) and John. In a shorter letter to Priscilla, he hopes that she will be well soon, and comments on her toy bear, Bingo. He sends a picture for both children, showing the Christmas tree with its magic lights.

1935

1935 Probably early this year, Tolkien is invited to give the 1936 Sir Israel Gollancz Memorial Lecture to the British Academy, on a subject of his choice. – Priscilla Tolkien begins to attend Rye St Antony, a small private school for girls run by two lay Catholic women.

20 January 1935 Hilary Full Term begins. Tolkien's scheduled lectures for this term are: *Elene* (concluded) and the Old English *Exodus* on Tuesdays and Thursdays at 11.00 a.m. in the Examination Schools, beginning 22 January; Grammar of the Vespasian Psalter Glosses on Tuesdays at 12.00 noon in the Examination Schools, beginning 22 January; The Principal Problems of Old English Phonology on Thursdays at 12.00 noon in the Examination Schools, beginning 24 January. He will continue to supervise B.Litt. student M.E. Griffiths.

23 January 1935 At a dinner of The Society its Secretary, R.W. Chapman, is instructed to write to Tolkien offering membership. By 28 January Tolkien will happily accept.

25 January 1935 Tolkien attends a Pembroke College meeting.

31 January 1935 Tolkien chairs an English Faculty Library Committee meeting at 2.15 p.m. in the Library.

8 February 1935 Tolkien attends an English Faculty Board meeting. The report of the committee (including Tolkien) appointed to draft regulations for English Literature in Pass Moderations is presented. The Applications Committee has appointed Tolkien and C.T. Onions examiners of the B.Litt. thesis of E.V. Williams of Jesus College, *The Phonology and Accidence of the [Old English] Glosses in MS Cotton Vespasian A.1 (Vespasian Psalter)*.

27 February 1935 Tolkien attends a Pembroke College meeting.

13 March 1935 Tolkien attends a Pembroke College meeting. – The Early English Text Society Committee agrees to print the French text of the *Ancrene Riwle* line by line, while the other manuscripts of that work (including the Cambridge manuscript, *Ancrene Wisse*) are to be set up in EETS editions with their own paragraph divisions, with modernized capitals and punctuation (but see entry for 11 December 1935), and with the page numbers of Morton's edition (1853) included in the margin. The EETS editions to be published include the Cambridge manuscript 'from the loan of Dr Tolkien's transcript' (Early English Text Society archive).

15 March 1935 Tolkien attends an English Faculty Board meeting.

16 March 1935 Hilary Full Term ends. – Germany formally denounces the terms of the Treaty of Versailles restricting the size and armed strength of the Germany army, and at once begins to build its forces.

28 April 1935 Trinity Full Term begins. Tolkien's scheduled lectures for this term are: Introduction to the *Poetic Edda* on Thursdays at 11.00 a.m. in the Examination Schools, beginning 2 May; 'Grimm's Law' on Thursdays at 12.00 noon in the Examination Schools, beginning 2 May; and Introduction to Old English Verse (for those beginning the Honours Course) on Fridays at 12.00 noon in the Examination Schools, beginning 30 April. He will continue to supervise B.Litt. student M.E. Griffiths.

1 May 1935 Tolkien attends a Pembroke College meeting. – In the evening, Tolkien attends a dinner of The Society hosted by John Sparrow at All Souls College, Oxford. Sparrow gives an account of the election of the Rector of Lincoln in 1851. The sixteen members present decide to alter the customary day of their dinners from Wednesday to Friday, despite a last-minute protest by Tolkien (who nonetheless attends the next meeting, on Friday, 18 October).

6 May 1935 George V celebrates his Silver Jubilee. The Vice-Chancellor, Proctors, and graduates of the University assemble in academic garb in the Divinity School, and at 9.40 a.m. walk in procession to a special service in the Cathedral at 10.00 a.m. There is a celebration dinner at Pembroke College in the evening.

15 May 1935 Tolkien attends a Pembroke College meeting.

17 May 1935 Tolkien attends an English Faculty Board meeting. The Applications Committee has appointed Tolkien and C.L. Wrenn examiners of the B.Litt. thesis of A.M. Morton of St Hugh's College, *William Morris's Treatment of His Icelandic Sources*.

11 June 1935 Father Francis Morgan dies. Tolkien receives formal notification from the Birmingham Oratory. *See note.* – Tolkien attends a Pembroke College meeting.

13 June 1935 Tolkien attends an English Faculty Library Committee meeting at 2.15 p.m. in the Library. – English Final Honour School examinations begin.

14 June 1935 Tolkien attends a Pembroke College meeting.

21 June 1935 Tolkien attends an English Faculty Board meeting, a Pembroke College meeting, and possibly a meeting of the Committee for Comparative Philology (at 5.15 p.m. in the Delegates Room of the Clarendon Building).

22 June 1935 Trinity Full Term ends.

26 June 1935 Encaenia.

9 August 1935 Tolkien writes to R.W. Chambers. The latter having sent a copy of his biography of Sir Thomas More – in fact, two copies by mistake – and evidently a letter as well, Tolkien belatedly expresses gratitude. Despite the press of examinations at the end of term, he has been able to read *Thomas More* twice, and finds it 'overwhelmingly moving: one of the great sagas, those rarely felicitous events produced by the meeting of the great subject and the uniquely fitted author'. Since his son John has the work available to him at school, Tolkien has given the spare copy to Simonne d'Ardenne, 'a Catholic in origin'. He wonders how Chambers knows 'that I was this year foisted upon the University Education council. . . . Not that I am likely to be of any use. I meet other more able and more apostolic men. But I never can make head or tail of "public buiness" even of a minor sort' (quoted in Caroline Chabot, 'Raymond Wilson Chambers (1874–1942)', *Moreana* 24, no. 94 (June 1987), pp. 85–6).

Beginning of September 1935 The Tolkien family take a two-week holiday at Sidmouth. They stay again at 'Aurora'.

15 September 1935 In Nazi Germany the Nürnberg Laws deprive Jews of rights of citizenship. Intermarriage of Jews and non-Jews is forbidden.

17 September 1935 Tolkien and C.L. Wrenn examine A.M. Morton of St Hugh's College *viva voce* on her B.Litt. thesis, *William Morris's Treatment of His Icelandic Sources*, at 12.00 noon in the Examination Schools. Tolkien writes out their undated report.

27 September 1935 Oxford University Press sends Simonne d'Ardenne, and possibly Tolkien, proofs of *An Edition of the Liflade ant te Passiun of Seinte Iuliene*. To obtain a degree from the University of Liège, d'Ardenne has to present her B.Litt. thesis as a published work.

3 October 1935 Italy invades Ethiopia.

13 October 1935 Michaelmas Full Term begins. Tolkien's scheduled lectures for this term are: *Beowulf*: Text on Tuesdays at 11.00 a.m. in the Examination Schools, beginning 15 October; Finn and Hengest on Tuesdays and Thursdays at 12.00 noon in the Examination Schools, beginning 15 October; and Old English Texts (Paper B2) on Thursdays at 11.00 a.m. in the Examination

Schools, beginning 17 October. He will continue to supervise B.Litt. student M.E. Griffiths.

17 October 1935 Tolkien attends a Pembroke College meeting.

18 October 1935 In the evening, Tolkien attends a dinner of The Society hosted by R.W. Chapman at Oriel College, Oxford. Fifteen members are present. Chapman speaks about Oxford and Cambridge.

Autumn 1935 *A.H. Smith, on behalf of the Early English Text Society, invites Tolkien to prepare an edition of the Cambridge manuscript of the *Ancrene Riwle* (MS CCCC 402). Tolkien indicates that he is interested, but will have to rely on the assistance of Elaine Griffiths. He is given until the end of the year to reply formally.

24 October 1935 Tolkien attends an English Faculty Library Committee meeting at 2.15 p.m. in the Library.

1 November 1935 Tolkien attends a Pembroke College meeting.

28 November 1935 Tolkien attends an English Faculty Library Committee meeting at 2.15 p.m. in the Library.

29 November 1935 Tolkien and C.T. Onions examine E.V. Williams of Jesus College *viva voce* on his B.Litt. thesis, *The Phonology and Accidence of the O.E. Glosses in MS Cotton Vespasian A.1 (Vespasian Psalter)*, at 2.30 p.m. in the Examination Schools.

30 November 1935 Tolkien and Onions sign their report (written by Tolkien) on the examination of E.V. Williams.

4 December 1935 Tolkien attends a Pembroke College meeting.

6 December 1935 Tolkien attends an English Faculty Board meeting. – He possibly attends a meeting of the Council for Comparative Philology at 5.15 p.m. in the Delegates Room of the Clarendon Building.

7 December 1935 Michaelmas Full Term ends.

11 December 1935 The Early English Text Society Committee decides that all except the Latin texts of the *Ancrene Riwle* are to be printed in EETS editions with the capitals and punctuation of the original.

Christmas 1935 Tolkien, as 'Father Christmas', writes a four-page letter to 'My dear children' (Christopher and Priscilla), dated 24 December. He comments on the cold weather, on the difficulty of the North Polar Bear in returning home from a visit to the Polar Cubs, and on giving his elves magic sparkler spears to frighten the goblins if they should reappear. He sends love to all the children and to Priscilla's bears, and hopes that they will enjoy the pantomime they are going to see. The letter is interspersed with small illustrations. – Tolkien spends almost the whole of the Christmas vacation until 4 January, except Christmas Day itself, putting into shape the proofs of *Seinte Iuliene* on behalf of Simonne d'Ardenne, working against a deadline as the work must be printed by a fixed date.

Late December 1935 Mabel Day, Secretary of the Early English Text Society, writes to Tolkien, asking him to confirm his interest in preparing an edition of the *Ancrene Riwle* (*Ancrene Wisse*).

1936

?1936–?1937 Probably in 1936 Tolkien and C.S. Lewis agree that there are too few stories of the kind they like to read, and that they will try to write some themselves. They further agree that Lewis should write a 'space-travel' story, and Tolkien one on 'time-travel'. The effort by Lewis will result in his *Out of the Silent Planet*, finished by October 1937. Tolkien on his part draws upon his still developing mythology, and upon a dream he has had since early child-hood, of a great wave coming out of the sea and towering over the land: his 'Atlantis-haunting' (*Atlantis). He produces, first, a brief outline for the story of Atalantë (*Númenor), an island created as a gift to Men who aided in the defeat of the evil Morgoth, but engulfed by the sea when the Númenóreans dare to assail the land of the Gods. Tolkien follows this with a full narrative in manuscript, hastily written and much corrected in the course of composition, and that in turn with a more finished manuscript with the title (added later) *The Last Tale: The Fall of Númenor*, and with an amanuensis typescript. After the sketch and first version of *The Fall of Númenor*, but contemporary with the second and intimately connected, Tolkien also begins to work on *The Lost Road*, 'of which the end was to be the presence of my hero in the drowning of Atlantis. This was to be called *Númenor*, the Land in the West' (letter to Christopher Bretherton, 16 July 1964, *Letters*, p. 347). He writes two chapters of *The Lost Road*, introducing a father and son who are to appear and reappear in different phases of Germanic and Celtic legend, and then nearly two chapters of the Númenórean episode before deciding that this should come last. He makes rough notes of what might be included in the intervening parts, but does not write them except for a fragment of an Anglo-Saxon episode which includes prose and alliterative versions of the legend of King Sheave. At some time in 1936 or 1937, however, he abandons *The Lost Road* altogether, while *The Fall of Númenor* will evolve ultimately into the *Akallabêth*.

It is probably in association with *The Lost Road* that Tolkien rewrites his poem *The Nameless Land* (first composed in May 1924), entitling it *Ælfwine's Song Calling upon Eärendel* and *The Song of Ælfwine (on Seeing the Uprising of Eärendel)*.

1936 Thirteen poems by Tolkien written for the amusement of his students at Leeds are published, without Tolkien's knowledge or approval, in *Songs for the Philologists*, a booklet privately printed by students in the Department of English at University College, London. The poems are *From One to Five*; *Syx Mynet*; *Ruddoc Hana*; *Ides Ælfscyne*; *Bagme Bloma*; *Eadig Beo Þu!*; *Ofer Widne Garsecg*; *La, Huru*; *I Sat upon a Bench*; *Natura Apis*; *The Root of the Boot*; *Frenchmen Froth*; and *Lit' and Lang'*. Some are printed with errors, or altered to remove references to Leeds. The poems had been given to the students by A.H. Smith, who had been a student of Tolkien at Leeds.

?By early 1936 Tolkien offers his Modern English translation of *Pearl* to the London publisher J.M. Dent. It is not accepted, but is seen by Guy Pocock, who in 1936 joins the staff of the British Broadcasting Corporation (BBC) and recommends that part of the translation be read on radio.

?Early 1936 Tolkien is asked by the publisher George Allen & Unwin if he would be interested in producing a revised edition of John R. Clark Hall's Modern English translation of *Beowulf* and *The Fight at Finnesburg*. He replies that he does not have the time to spare, but suggests that Elaine Griffiths is qualified to undertake the work, and offers to read what she produces and to write a preface or introduction. *Susan Dagnall, a member of the Allen & Unwin staff who had been a student in the English School at Oxford, is sent to discuss the project with Griffiths and probably also with Tolkien. While there Dagnall learns of the existence of *The Hobbit* and borrows a typescript. *See note.* Upon reading *The Hobbit* she urges Tolkien to finish the book and to submit it for publication. Tolkien agrees to do so. Returning to the story at the point he seems to have left off some three years earlier, he writes 'Not at Home', originally as Chapter 14, and the first part of 'The Gathering of the Clouds' (published Chapter 15), but then decides that the structure of the story would be improved if 'Not at Home' preceded 'Fire and Water'. In the course of several months, he works out the remaining text in a new manuscript.

5 January 1936 Tolkien writes to Mabel Day of the Early English Text Society. He apologizes for not having given a firm decision about *Ancrene Wisse* by 31 December. He explains that Elaine Griffiths, on whose assistance he relies and who has been preparing a diplomatic transcription of MS CCCC 402 and a complete index and glossary, had to go home early in December and has only just resumed her work; while he himself has been busy with *Seinte Iuliene*. He can now offer to produce an edition of *Ancrene Wisse* for the Society, but feels that he must explain about work he has already done. He has transcribed 75 of the 117 folios of the manuscript and has almost completed a verbal index. He has also spent time preparing a complete vocabulary and grammar of 'AB' (a variant of Middle English related to MS CCCC 402 and MS Bodley 34). Because he has been working from rotographs, he will need to collate his transcriptions with the original manuscript in Cambridge, and intends to begin that work soon. He can let the Society have four requested specimen pages in the following week. He asks what format and what accompanying material will be required for the Society edition. He suggests that the text be printed line by line, as Elaine Griffiths' glossary is keyed to folio and line as in the original manuscript. As an example of what he would like, he sends a specimen proof of *Seinte Iuliene*. He inquires also if, after *Ancrene Wisse*, the EETS would be interested in an edition of the Middle English life of St Katherine (*Seinte Katerine*), for which he and Simonne d'Ardenne have already prepared the text.

14 January 1936 Tolkien writes to Mabel Day. Because he has not had time to type the promised specimen pages, he sends pages of manuscript transcription, from which printed specimens may be produced. He asks again about the general editorial policy of the Early English Text Society, and about matters of presentation.

15 January 1936 Mabel Day writes to Tolkien, acknowledging his two letters. She has sent the first to A.W. Pollard, Honorary Director of the Early English Text Society. She explains some points of the Society's editorial policy, which will be better developed once all of the specimens for proposed editions of *Ancrene Riwle* manuscripts have been set up. She promises to send Tolkien specimens of the edition of the French manuscript of the *Ancrene Riwle*. – A.W. Pollard writes to Tolkien. While he can see advantages of reproducing a (prose) text in print line by line, he prefers a uniformity of style in printing editions of the five or six *Ancrene Riwle* texts, of which the Cambridge manuscript will be only one. It is still to be decided what editorial matter should accompany the texts.

16 January 1936 Tolkien replies to Mabel Day, thanking her for answering his queries and arguing against altering texts, for the sake of future editors who often will be obliged to reconstruct what has been altered, if not driven back to the original manuscripts. He will proceed with an edition of *Ancrene Wisse* as quickly as he can. – Probably on or soon after this date Tolkien also writes to A.W. Pollard; two versions of a letter survive, one certainly a draft. *See note.* Although he will bow to the Early English Text Society Committee's decision, Tolkien puts forward a long and detailed argument in favour of line-by-line transcription. Such a transcription, preserving the arrangement in the original manuscript, has enormous advantages to the scholar. Also, as he has already transcribed most of the Cambridge manuscript by folio and line, and has prepared a nearly complete glossary and index according to this plan, he is reluctant to see this work upset. To follow the EETS plan would require a great deal of labour in recasting references already in being, and would set back other work on *Ancrene Wisse* and related texts.

19 January 1936 Hilary Full Term begins. Tolkien's scheduled lectures for this term are: The Legend of Wayland the Smith, followed by a study of the text of *Deor's Lament* and of *Völundarkviða* on Tuesdays and Thursdays at 11.00 a.m. in the Examination Schools, beginning 21 January; and *Atlakviða* on Tuesdays and Thursdays at 12.00 noon in the Examination Schools, beginning 21 January. These are probably cancelled, however, after Tolkien injures his leg on 1 February; he will offer them as classes at his home in Northmoor Road in Trinity Term 1936. He will continue to supervise B.Litt. student M.E. Griffiths.

20 January 1936 Death of George V. Edward VIII succeeds to the throne.

22 January 1936 Tolkien attends a Pembroke College meeting.

23 January 1936 Members of Convocation (see *Oxford, University of) meet in the Sheldonian Theatre at 12.00 noon to hear the proclamation of Edward VIII, and then walk in procession, led by the Vice-Chancellor and the Proctors, to St Mary's Church to witness the proclamation there by the City authorities. Lectures which would interfere with attendance at the ceremony are cancelled.

27 January 1936 A.W. Pollard writes to Tolkien. Robin Flower has been asked by the Early English Text Society Committee to take special charge of the *Ancrene Riwle* editions. Tolkien's specimens are being forwarded to him.

28 January 1936 Day of mourning for the funeral of George V. Lectures are cancelled. The Vice-Chancellor, Proctors, and graduates, in academic dress, meet in the Divinity School by 11.35 a.m. and process to a Memorial Service at noon in the Church of St Mary the Virgin.

1 February 1936 Warnie Lewis notes in his diary that Tolkien has torn a ligament in his leg playing squash and will be in bed for ten weeks. – C.S. Lewis visits Tolkien after tea.

7 February 1936 The Faculté de Philosophie et Lettres, Liège, authorizes publication of Simonne d'Ardenne's thesis on *Seinte Iuliene*. Oxford University Press will print one thousand copies by early March. Librairie E. Droz of Paris will publish it under d'Ardenne's name only, to satisfy requirements of her degree at Liège; but for this, the book would appear as a joint work by d'Ardenne and Tolkien. Simonne d'Ardenne herself privately refers to it as a joint effort, and some of Tolkien's colleagues will recognize his contribution. The *Seinte Iuliene* probably contains more of his views on early Middle English than anything he will ever publish under his own name.

19 February 1936 C.H. Firth dies.

26 February 1936 Mabel Day sends Tolkien a list of possible amendments for *A Middle English Vocabulary*. She thinks that Robin Flower has seen Tolkien in Oxford to discuss the specimen pages for *Ancrene Wisse*.

Early March 1936 Tolkien reads *The Place of the Lion* by *Charles Williams, which C.S. Lewis has recommended.

1 March 1936 By this date Tolkien must have submitted his application for a Leverhulme Research Fellowship, which he will be granted from October 1936 for two years.

7 March 1936 Germany reoccupies the Rhineland.

9 March 1936 Simonne d'Ardenne writes to Tolkien, asking how he is recovering from his leg injury, and referring to his surgeon. She will tell him the date of her *viva* at Liège when she knows it. A copy of *Seinte Iuliene* has gone to Tolkien. She regrets that 'our profit' will be smaller than they had thought, because of the percentage demanded by Droz (Tolkien Papers, Bodleian Library, Oxford).

14 March 1936 Hilary Full Term ends.

26 April 1936 Trinity Full Term begins. Tolkien's scheduled lectures for this term are: Outlines of Old English Phonology and Grammar on Tuesdays and Thursdays at 12.00 noon in the Examination Schools, beginning 28 April; and Introduction to Old English Poetry on Thursdays at 11.00 a.m. in the Examination Schools, beginning 30 April. But because Tolkien is still recovering from his squash injury, his lectures are cancelled, and instead he reads Old Norse and Old English texts with small classes at home in 20 Northmoor Road: *Atlakviða* on Tuesdays at 11:00 a.m.; *Völundarkviða* and *Deor's Lament* on Thursdays at 11.00 a.m.; and *Andreas* with other Old English texts on Thursdays at 5.00 p.m. Undergraduates wishing to attend are required to inform Tolkien in advance, if possible before 28 April. – Tolkien will continue to supervise B.Litt. student M.E. Griffiths, who is required to apply for a certificate during this term (but apparently abandons her thesis, as she is no longer listed in Michaelmas Term 1936).

April or May 1936 The Rev. Adrian Morey writes to Tolkien. He has discovered an Anglo-Saxon version of the Lord's Prayer ('Our Father') in a manuscript in the British Museum, and asks if it is worth publishing. Tolkien suggests that Morey write an article, which would be useful to students.

?May–?June 1936 C.S. Lewis lends Tolkien his copy of *The Silver Trumpet* by Owen Barfield. It is much appreciated by the Tolkien children.

1 May 1936 In the evening, Tolkien, on crutches, attends a dinner of The Society hosted by Sir Francis Wylie at Brasenose College, Oxford. Nineteen members are present; no paper being presented, they give themselves up to conversation.

9 May 1936 Italy formally annexes Ethiopia. The King of Italy assumes the title 'Emperor of Ethiopia'.

13 May 1936 The Rev. Adrian Morey acknowledges Tolkien's reply. Tolkien will later recall that he

> once (lightheartedly) began to collect material for the history of the "Our Father" in English – inspired by some correspondence with Dom Adrian Morey. I thought it would mainly concern minor changes in syntax (as *which, who*), and the variants used for *temptation* and *trespass(es)*; but I soon found that it was a much more complicated matter, not only because of the divergence between the use as a prayer and the translations of the Gospels, but because of the difficulties in the Greek and Latin texts. Also there have been a very large number of divergent versions in English, and there are still several in use. . . . [Tolkien Papers, Bodleian Library, Oxford]

E.O.G. Turville-Petre will send him copies of two Icelandic versions in April 1943.

15 May 1936 Tolkien attends an English Faculty Board meeting. He submits manuscript and mimeographed proposals for a revision of texts prescribed or cited in the regulations for the English Honour School. – He also attends a Pembroke College meeting.

17 May 1936 The Catholic Archbishop of Birmingham, Dr Williams, comes to Oxford to commemorate the seventh centenary of the death of the Blessed Agnellus of Pisa, sent to England by St Francis to found a province of the Franciscan Order. The Archbishop visits the site of the first Franciscan church in the country. *The Times* of 19 May will list Tolkien among those 'who took part in the procession from Campion Hall to the site of the church' and that 'during the morning a Mass was sung in the church of [St] Edmund and St Frideswide, near the new Greyfriars Friary, in the presence of the Archbishop' (p. 28).

21 May 1936 *The Allegory of Love: A Study in Medieval Tradition* by C.S. Lewis is published. In his preface Lewis notes that 'the first chapter was read and commented upon by Mr. B. Macfarlane and Professor Tolkien so long ago that they have probably forgotten the labour, but I do not therefore forget the kindness.'

June 1936 The June number of *Medium Ævum* no longer lists Tolkien as a member of the Executive Committee of the Society for the Study of Mediæval Languages and Literature, but he is now on its Editorial Board with C.T. Onions, Eugène Vinaver, and others. He will continue to be on the Editorial Board until his retirement from academic duties in 1959.

2 June 1936 Tolkien has apparently undertaken to act as one of the examiners for the M.A. degree at the University of London for four years. He receives some M.A. papers to mark on this date, from E.V. Gordon who seems to have acted as liaison.

3 June 1936 E.V. Gordon, having realized that he had said nothing about the marking system when he sent the papers, writes to explain it. He has read the edition of *Seinte Iuliene* and is 'grieved that your name is not attached to it, because . . . practically all that is especially valuable in it is recognisably yours. There is really no other piece of Middle English editing to touch it. And the financial interest in it is really not sufficient reward or return for the wealth of new material you have given' (Tolkien Papers, Bodleian Library, Oxford).

Between 3 and 11 June 1936 Tolkien writes to E.V. Gordon with queries about the London M.A. papers.

11 June 1936 Tolkien attends an English Faculty Library Committee meeting in the Library. It is noted that Professor Tolkien, Dr Onions, and the Librarian have been requested to act as the Bodleian committee for the purchase of foreign books on English. – English Final Honour School examinations begin. – E.V. Gordon writes in response to Tolkien's queries. Vivas will be held in London on 12 June, before which date the marked scripts are required. Tolkien will not be concerned with vivas until the last two years of his appointment. The papers from overseas candidates will arrive for marking later. Gordon, the Smith Professor of English Language and Germanic Philology at the University of Manchester since autumn 1931, discusses the viva date for Manchester, where Tolkien is also an external examiner; Tolkien had hoped to be able to change it, but that will not be possible. Gordon hopes that Tolkien can be in Manchester on 26 June, as the relevant documents must be signed by both external examiners to be legal. He is sorry that Tolkien cannot stay for the weekend. As a result of the publication of *Seinte Iuliene* several scholars are revising their works in progress.

14 June 1936 G.K. Chesterton dies.

19 June 1936 Tolkien attends an English Faculty Board meeting. – He also attends a Pembroke College meeting.

20 June 1936 Trinity Full Term ends.

24 June 1936 Encaenia.

18 July 1936 The Spanish Civil War begins.

21 July 1936 Tolkien receives a letter from the BBC asking for permission to broadcast part of his translation of the Middle English poem *Pearl* in the late evening during August. Tolkien replies on the same day, authorizing the reading.

7 August 1936 Part of Tolkien's translation of *Pearl* is read on London regional radio from 11.40 p.m. to midnight.

10 August 1936 Tolkien writes to his son Christopher. 'The Hobbit is now nearly finished, and the publishers clamouring for it' (quoted in *Biography*, p. 180).

?Summer 1936 Tolkien learns that he has been awarded a Leverhulme Research Fellowship from October 1936 for two years. – He engages his son Michael to help in making a fresh typescript of *The Hobbit*. In the event, Tolkien completes this himself.

?September 1936 The Tolkien family have two weeks' holiday at Sidmouth.

13 September 1936 The Rev. Adrian Morey writes to Tolkien. He has decided to include the text of the Anglo-Saxon 'Our Father' in a book, and asks Tolkien to write out a version to send to Cambridge University Press. The text will be published in *Bartholomew of Exeter, Bishop and Canonist: A Study in the Twelfth Century* (1937), in which Morey thanks Tolkien for his assistance.

25 September 1936 Simonne d'Ardenne writes to Tolkien. As soon as she finishes an article on the Brussels Cross she will send it to him as he had asked. She is sending him three versions of *Seinte Katerine*; in these she has noted the illuminated capitals and thinks that the printer might represent each of these with a larger capital letter. She has made rough notes on the various manuscript readings, which will be useful if they succeed in getting the texts printed. She wishes him success in his forthcoming British Academy Lecture.

3 October 1936 Tolkien has finished retyping *The Hobbit*, but sends Allen & Unwin its earlier typescript with the final chapters added.

5 October 1936 Allen & Unwin receive the *Hobbit* typescript, as well as one illustration for that work, presumably *Thror's Map*. – Stanley Unwin writes to Tolkien, acknowledging receipt of the typescript. Both Unwin and his ten-year-old son *Rayner will read it before 20 October. Unwin expresses an interest in publishing Tolkien's translation of *Pearl* and asks if he can see it.

10 October 1936 The typescript of *The Hobbit* is read by Stanley Unwin.

11 October 1936 Michaelmas Full Term begins. Tolkien's scheduled lectures for this term are: *Beowulf*: General Criticism on Tuesdays at 11.00 a.m. in the Examination Schools, beginning 13 October; *Elene* on Tuesdays and Thursdays at 12.00 noon in the Examination Schools, beginning 13 October; and Alliterative Verse on Thursdays at 11.00 a.m. in the Examination Schools, beginning 15 October. – Tolkien's eldest son, John, is now a student at his father's old college, Exeter.

16 October 1936 In the evening, Tolkien attends a dinner of The Society hosted by Nevill Coghill at Exeter College, Oxford. Fifteen members are present. Coghill speaks about the making of good Europeans by an exchange of schoolboys.

21 October–2 November 1936 The children's author Rose Fyleman, also a free-lance reviewer for Allen & Unwin, reads the *Hobbit* typescript.

22 October 1936 Tolkien attends an English Faculty Library Committee meeting in the Library.

26 October 1936 R.W. Chapman of Oxford University Press writes to George S. Gordon. He is pleased to learn that Tolkien has received an increase in salary, which he hopes will relieve him of drudgery, and that he has been given a Leverhulme Research Fellowship; but the type for the Clarendon Chaucer has been standing for more than ten years, and Chapman does not think there is much chance that Tolkien will finish his part of the work. Kenneth Sisam has suggested E.V. Gordon or Oxford D.Phil. student *J.A.W. Bennett to replace Tolkien on the project.

27 October 1936 Formation of the Berlin-Rome Axis.

28 October 1936 George S. Gordon replies to R.W. Chapman. He thinks that Tolkien finished most of his annotation years ago, but on too large a scale, and found it too tedious to abbreviate. He will speak to Tolkien about making another effort to finish his work.

30 October 1936 Tolkien attends an English Faculty Board meeting. He is re-elected to the Applications Committee. It is resolved that the Standing Committee on Applications should meet at 3.30 p.m. on the Thursday preceding the day of the Board's meeting. – Rayner Unwin writes a favourable review of *The Hobbit*, for which he is paid one shilling.

***c*. November 1936** Tolkien writes out a chart of Quenya noun inflections (the 'Bodleian declensions').

4 November 1936 Tolkien attends a Pembroke College meeting.

5 November 1936 George S. Gordon has spoken to Tolkien about completing the Clarendon Chaucer. He informs Oxford University Press that Tolkien will try again to do so.

11 November 1936 Tolkien attends a Pembroke College meeting.

17 November 1936 Agreement of the German-Japanese Pact.

25 November 1936 Tolkien delivers the Sir Israel Gollancz Memorial Lecture, *Beowulf: The Monsters and the Critics*, to the British Academy in London, setting a new standard in *Beowulf* criticism.

26 November 1936 Tolkien chairs an English Faculty Library Committee meeting in the Library. He successfully proposes that the Library house the *Bibliographia Oxoniensis*, for which the Bodleian Library cannot not find room.

28 November 1936 Susan Dagnall visits Tolkien in Oxford. They certainly discuss *The Hobbit*, and possibly also the Clark Hall *Beowulf*. On being shown a specimen page for *The Hobbit*, Tolkien suggests changes. It is perhaps at this point that he hands over five maps to be included in *The Hobbit*: *Thror's Map*, to be tipped in at its first mention in Chapter 1 or at a later mention in Chapter 3, with its 'moon-letters' so printed on the verso of the sheet as to be visible when held up to the light (*Artist and Illustrator*, fig. 85); *Wilderland*, a more general map of the lands in which the story takes place; and lesser maps of the land between the Misty Mountains and Mirkwood, of the area east of Mirkwood to just east of the River Running, and of the Long Lake combined with a view of the Lonely Mountain (*Artist and Illustrator*, fig. 128). Having been asked by Allen & Unwin to submit any other children's stories he has written, to be considered for publication, Tolkien gives Susan Dagnall *Farmer Giles of Ham* and *Roverandom*, both of which he has retyped and revised, and his picture book, *Mr. Bliss*. He hands over his translation of *Pearl* as well. Tolkien and Dagnall also discuss a 'prolegomena' by C.S. Lewis which Allen & Unwin are interested in publishing as a text for students (probably his celebrated lectures 'Prolegomena to Medieval Poetry' begun in January 1932, much later partly the basis of his book *The Discarded Image*). Tolkien promises to ask Lewis about it.

2 December 1936 Stanley Unwin sends Tolkien a signed duplicate contract for *The Hobbit*.

4 December 1936 Tolkien attends an English Faculty Board meeting. – He also attends a Pembroke College meeting. – Susan Dagnall sends Tolkien a revised specimen page of *The Hobbit* for approval. She asks him to write a short paragraph describing the book, for Allen & Unwin to use in their forthcoming announcements list and for publicity.

5 December 1936 Michaelmas Full Term ends. – Simonne d'Ardenne again writes to Tolkien that she will send him her article on the Brussels Cross as soon as it is finished, and asks him to give her English prose some 'Tolkienian' flavour.

8 December 1936 Tolkien writes to Susan Dagnall. He does not like a star ornament placed at the beginning of the chapter on the revised *Hobbit* specimen. He also queries the margins as set. He encloses a paragraph describing the book as requested, and an alternative text by C.S. Lewis. Lewis does not like the idea of his 'prolegomena' being used as a 'cram' text.

9 December 1936 Tolkien delivers his lecture *Beowulf: The Monsters and the Critics* to the Manchester Medieval Society. He is delayed travelling to Manchester from Oxford; in the meantime, to entertain the audience, E.V. Gordon gives an impromptu account of the Norse settlements in Greenland.

10 December 1936 Susan Dagnall writes to Tolkien. His *Hobbit* maps need to be redrawn: they contain too many colours, and their shading would require reproduction by the more elaborate halftone process. Dagnall suggests that *Thror's Map* and *Wilderland* be printed as endpapers in red and blue, or any other two colours, and that the other three maps be printed with the text in a single colour. She asks if the 'moon-runes' on *Thror's Map* are very important, as they will be difficult to reproduce. She has told the Allen & Unwin production department to begin typesetting *The Hobbit* and to submit proofs to Tolkien; but they will need to know where to place the three smaller maps. The star ornament to which he objects will be removed. – Abdication of Edward VIII. George VI succeeds to the throne.

14 December 1936 Members of Convocation meet in the Sheldonian Theatre at 12.00 noon to hear the proclamation of George VI, and then process, led by the Vice-Chancellor and the Proctors, to St Mary's Church to witness the proclamation there by the City authorities. Lectures which would interfere with attendance at the ceremony are cancelled.

Christmas 1936 Tolkien, as 'Father Christmas', writes a letter dated 23 December, addressed only to Christopher and Priscilla. He apologizes for not being able to send a long letter, but hopes that his picture will explain why. In fact the letter from Father Christmas is accompanied by another letter in a different script, as from the elf Ilbereth: this tells how the North Polar Bear worked hard to give each child an individual number to help in packing and record keeping, and then fell asleep in the bath with the taps running, with the result that water poured into the English Delivery Room below. The picture, drawn in tiers, shows the North Pole and the Northern Lights; Polar Bear in the bath; water pouring through the ceiling; and Polar Bear explaining his numbering system to the elves. Also enclosed with the letters and picture are a copy of a goblin alphabet as by Polar Bear. – During the holidays members of the Tolkien family one by one are laid low with influenza, brought back from school by one of the boys. – Tolkien redraws some of his pictures for *The Hobbit*.

31 December 1936 Tolkien himself contracts influenza.

1937

1937 Tolkien revises his poem *Kortirion among the Trees* (first composed in November 1915).

4 January 1937 Tolkien writes to Susan Dagnall, enclosing six pictures. He has redrawn *Thror's Map* and *Wilderland* and has decided that the other three maps are not necessary. He has also redrawn 'one or two of the amateur illustrations of the "home manuscript" [of *The Hobbit*, probably the master typescript], conceiving that they might serve as endpapers, frontispiece or what not' (Tolkien-George Allen & Unwin archive, HarperCollins). These are *Mirkwood*, *The Elvenking's Gate*, *Lake Town*, and *The Front Gate*. He intends *Mirkwood* (*Artist and Illustrator*, fig. 88) to be used as the front endpaper. The final *Elvenking's Gate* has evolved through a series of drawings made from various perspectives, and has inspired (probably at the same time) a similar view of Nargothrond (*Artist and Illustrator*, fig. 57). *Lake Town* is based on an earlier drawing, *Esgaroth* (*Artist and Illustrator*, fig. 126).

7 January 1937 Tolkien returns a 'slip' to Allen & Unwin, probably a proof of the publicity paragraph he has written about *The Hobbit*. He has made some corrections. – C.A. Furth of the Allen & Unwin production department writes to Tolkien. The publishers think that his line drawings for *The Hobbit* are admirable, and are having reproduction blocks made. *Mirkwood*, shaded with ink wash, 'will present a little difficulty in reproduction – unless it were to be printed separately on glossy paper, which we think would be disturbing', and since (except for *The Front Gate*) the drawings are horizontal, they will have to be turned parallel with the spine of the book (Tolkien-George Allen & Unwin archive, HarperCollins). Allen & Unwin will try a cunning method to deal with the 'moon-letters' on *Thror's Map* (probably they mean to print the runes in a grey tone). Furth asks Tolkien where the interior illustrations should be placed in the book. In regard to *Mr. Bliss*, the manuscript of which Furth is returning, Allen & Unwin would like to publish it but are concerned about the cost of printing. Furth asks Tolkien to redraw his lavishly coloured pictures in only three colours and black, to make them easier and cheaper to reproduce. He is willing to call on Tolkien in Oxford to explain better what is needed. He also discusses the calligraphy or type that might be used in place of Tolkien's original lettering. – Rayner Unwin enthusiastically reports on *Farmer Giles of Ham* and *Roverandom*. He thinks that both books need illustrations, and suggests that they might be published together.

14 January 1937 Tolkien visits the British Museum in London, perhaps to do research in its manuscript or book collections. He also calls on George Allen & Unwin in nearby Museum Street, hoping to discuss *The Hobbit*, but C.A. Furth and Susan Dagnall are not in the office due to illness.

17 January 1937 Hilary Full Term begins. Tolkien's scheduled lectures and classes for this term are: The *Elder Edda* on Tuesdays at 12.00 noon in the Examination Schools, beginning 19 January; The Vespasian Hymns: Grammar and Phonology on Thursdays at 11.00 a.m. in the Examination Schools, beginning 21 January; Fundamental Problems of Old English Phonology on Thursdays at 12.00 noon in the Examination Schools, beginning 21 January; and Old English Verse Texts (Class), at an hour and place to be arranged. Tolkien is also listed as one of a series of lecturers (with Nevill Coghill, H.V.D. Dyson, C.S. Lewis, and C.L. Wrenn) on *Hamlet*, Fridays at 5.00 p.m. in the Examination Schools, beginning 22 January. – Tolkien writes to C.A. Furth. He is endeavouring to earn a grant for 'research' in addition to his ordinary duties, but might find odd moments to redraw *Mr. Bliss*, especially as he is free from the burden of examining for two years. He would welcome Furth's advice. Regarding *The Hobbit*, he had not intended *Thror's Map* to be used as an endpaper. He discusses the placement of *Wilderland* and of the four drawings (other than maps) he sent on 4 January. He now sends six more, probably drawn after his earlier drawings were accepted: *The Hill: Hobbiton across the Water, The Trolls, The Mountain-path, The Misty Mountains Looking West from the Eyrie towards Goblin Gate, Beorn's Hall*, and *The Hall at Bag-End, Residence of B. Baggins Esquire*. The final pen and ink version of *The Hill* has evolved through several sketches and drawings. For *The Trolls* Tolkien has abandoned an earlier drawing, *Trolls' Hill*, and an intermediate illustration, *The Three Trolls Are Turned to Stone*, instead adapting a picture by Jennie Harbour for a retelling of 'Hansel and Gretel'. *The Misty Mountains Looking West* has been redrawn from a similar version. *Beorn's Hall* is adapted from an earlier picture by Tolkien, *Firelight in Beorn's House*, which had been inspired by a drawing of a Norse hall in a book by E.V. Gordon. (See *Artist and Illustrator*, ch. 4.)

22 January 1937 In the evening, Tolkien attends a dinner of The Society hosted by Michael Holroyd in the new Common Rooms at Brasenose College, Oxford. Twelve members are present. Holroyd speaks about careers for undergraduates, referring to the declining birth rate and the experience of foreign universities.

23 January 1937 Susan Dagnall asks Tolkien if he could see her and C.A. Furth in Oxford on either Saturday or Sunday, 13 or 14 February, to discuss the problem of illustrations for *Mr. Bliss*. Allen & Unwin can include at least four of the six additional *Hobbit* drawings without increasing the price of the book, and perhaps will use a fifth on the dust-jacket. (In the event, all are printed in the book.) She asks Tolkien to send them again the original drawing of *Thror's Map*, as the blockmaker omitted the 'moon-letters'. Fresh blocks will have to be made, but the map will be folded and tipped in at the point Tolkien wants. – Tolkien replies to Susan Dagnall that he will keep 13 and 14 February open, but the afternoons or evenings are best for him to receive visitors. He sends Allen & Unwin the original of *Thror's Map*, hoping that they can print the runes on the back as intended. He has drawn a copy of the runes in mirror-reverse, so that if viewed through the sheet when held up to the light, they will read the right way around. He returns proofs of the earlier illustrations he has been sent and notes defects in the reproductions of *Mirkwood* and *Wilderland*. Elaine Griffiths has been appointed to a position in the Society of Oxford Home-Students from next term, but Tolkien hopes that they will both finish their work on the Clark Hall *Beowulf* before the present term ends.

1 February 1937 Susan Dagnall writes to Tolkien, to correct a misstatement in her letter of 23 January. *Thror's Map* will have to be printed as an endpaper in *The Hobbit* after all for reasons of cost, but the runes will be printed so that they do not appear 'so blatantly on the front' (Tolkien-George Allen & Unwin archive, HarperCollins). The defects Tolkien noted on the proofs of *Mirkwood* and *Wilderland* will be corrected. Dagnall sends rough proofs of the four drawings to be included in the book from the second group; Allen & Unwin still hope to squeeze in the remaining two at the ends of chapters.

2 February 1937 R.W. Chambers writes to Tolkien, urging him not to delete a single word from *Beowulf: The Monsters and the Critics* when it is prepared for publication.

4 February 1937 Tolkien's poem *The Dragon's Visit*, one of the *Tales and Songs of Bimble Bay*, written probably *c.* 1928, is published in the *Oxford Magazine* for 4 February 1937.

5 February 1937 Tolkien attends an English Faculty Board meeting. The minutes will record:

A Standing Order was made that no application for admission as a Pro-bationer B.Litt. Student or Advanced Student should be considered by the Applications Committee unless the applicant had previously been in communication with a person or persons appointed by the Board to interview such candidates. The Board appointed Professor Nichol Smith and Professor Tolkien for this purpose. [Oxford University Archives FA 4/5/1/1]

– Tolkien writes to Susan Dagnall, confirming their appointment for 13 February. In regard to *Thror's Map*, he relents: 'Let the Production Dept. do as it will'. He approves the rough proofs of the four drawings, but marks two defects in the block for *The Trolls*. He comments that he should not have put in a wash shadow by the door in *The Hall at Bag-End*, which in the line-block has come out black, obscuring detail. He would have written sooner, but has had 'three desperately crowded days' (Tolkien-George Allen & Unwin archive, Harper-Collins).

8 February 1937 Tolkien writes to R.W. Chambers. He sends information about A.L. Rowse which Chambers had requested, and tells him about the forthcoming publication of *The Hobbit*.

13 February 1937 Susan Dagnall visits Tolkien in Oxford at 3.00 p.m. *See note.*

18 February 1937 A revised version of Tolkien's poem *Knocking at the Door: Lines Induced by Sensations when Waiting for an Answer at the Door of an Exalted Academic Person* (first composed in 1927) is published in the *Oxford Magazine* for 18 February 1937 as by 'Oxymore'.

19 February 1937 Tolkien attends a Pembroke College meeting.

20 February 1937 Tolkien attends a Pembroke College meeting. – He receives from Allen & Unwin proofs of signatures A–H of *The Hobbit*.

21 February 1937 Tolkien writes to Allen & Unwin. He has corrected the first proofs of *The Hobbit* but would like to keep them until he has the complete set, since he has noticed some minor discrepancies in the text, and between the text and the illustrations, though few printers' errors. He wishes to learn when the rest of the proofs will arrive, and notes that he will deal with them quickly as he can correct a batch of about eight signatures within twenty-four hours of receipt. He notes that the defects he had pointed out in *The Trolls* still appear in proof, and supposes that it has not been possible to correct them.

24 February 1937 C.A. Furth writes to Tolkien. The fine lines in *The Trolls* have broken when reduced, but there is no room to enlarge the illustration. They plan to meet on Saturday, 27 February, and can discuss the point further at that time. – Tolkien receives the rest of the *Hobbit* proofs. He is asked to replace unavoidable alterations and deletions with words taking up as nearly as possible the same amount of space. With these, or soon afterward, he is sent rough proofs of the remaining two drawings, which are to be included in *The Hobbit*.

27 February 1937 C.A. Furth visits Tolkien in Oxford. Tolkien will remark in his letter of ?10 March that he was a poor host, too concerned with his own troubles. Probably at this meeting Furth asks Tolkien to produce a design for the dust-jacket of *The Hobbit*.

March 1937 In the preface to his edition of *The Battle of Maldon* (1937) E.V. Gordon thanks Tolkien for reading proof and making 'many corrections and contributions. . . . Professor Tolkien, with characteristic generosity, gave me the solution to many of the textual and philological problems discussed in the following pages' (p. vi).

2 March 1937 The typescripts of *Farmer Giles of Ham* and *Roverandom* are returned to Tolkien by Allen & Unwin.

4 March 1937 Tolkien attends an English Faculty Library Committee meeting. – A revised version of Tolkien's poem *Iumonna Gold Galdre Bewunden* (first composed perhaps at the end of 1922) is published in the *Oxford Magazine* for 4 March 1937.

?10 March 1937 Tolkien returns to Allen & Unwin corrected proofs of *The Hobbit* with the two additional illustrations in position, as well as marked proofs of the two endpapers and the original drawing of *Thror's Map*. He suggests that the endpapers would be best printed in black and red. In a letter to C.A. Furth he apologizes for sending them a week later than expected, but other matters suddenly became urgent, and also for the many alterations he has made. He realizes that he should have re-read *The Hobbit* before it went for typesetting. While proofreading he found considerable confusions of narrative and geography. He has had to alter about sixteen pages considerably, though he has tried as far as possible to ensure that the revisions occupy the same space as the text that was set. He thinks it advisable to see revised proofs of the most heavily altered sections. He asks if Allen & Unwin have decided when *The Hobbit* will be published; if at an early date, he will try to produce a dust-jacket design at once.

12 March 1937 Tolkien chairs a meeting of the English Faculty Board. C.S. Lewis asks that four representatives of the Board meet the joint committee of the English and Classical Associations to consider Greek and English studies. He, Tolkien, M.R. Ridley, and possibly C.T. Onions are willing to do so.

13 March 1937 Hilary Full Term ends.

23 March 1937 C.A. Furth writes to Tolkien, confirming that he certainly will be sent proofs of the most heavily corrected sections of *The Hobbit*, though the printers might prefer to reset the entire book. Tolkien's corrections may exceed an author's usual allowance. It is unfortunate that Allen & Unwin had not realized that the typescript 'which Miss Dagnall persuaded you to send us was never really intended for printing without further revision' (Tolkien-George Allen & Unwin archive, HarperCollins). The same colours must be used on both endpapers (Tolkien would prefer *Wilderland* to appear in black and blue); he agrees with Tolkien that black and red would be best. The runes, indistinct in the proof (in a failed attempt to suggest 'moon-letters'), will be replaced with the more carefully drawn version Tolkien has returned to them, and will be printed in black rather than red and without a halftone effect. The book will be published when it is ready. Allen & Unwin hope that Tolkien will be able to design a dust-jacket for *The Hobbit*, but this is not urgent as he still has to see revised proofs.

30 March 1937 Tolkien writes to C.A. Furth. He hopes that revised proofs of *The Hobbit* will come to him during vacation, which ends on 24 April. He will try to produce a dust-jacket design for the book.

31 March 1937 C.A. Furth writes to Tolkien, belatedly returning a *Hobbit* drawing. The printers are revising the typesetting of the whole book. They hope to send Tolkien some of the revised proofs the weekend of 3–4 April, and all of the proofs by about 7 April.

7 April 1937 Oxford University Press sends Tolkien proofs of his essay *Beowulf: The Monsters and the Critics.*

13 April 1937 Revised proofs for *The Hobbit* apparently having arrived as promised, Tolkien now returns them together with proofs of the endpapers. He writes to Allen & Unwin, pointing out that he has altered eight words to correct narrative errors he missed before, and he has marked a few other corrections, some of errors made in the revised typesetting. He takes note of the cost of excess correction, and 'must pay what is just, if required; though I shall naturally be grateful for clemency' (*Letters*, p. 16). He passes the endpapers but regrets that *Wilderland* is not being printed in black and blue as he had wished. He wonders if both endpapers would not be better in black and blue, which would mean changing 'red' to 'blue' on p. 30 of the text; but on second thought he decides to accept red. He is sorry that it has proved impossible (as it seems) to substitute better drawn runes he has supplied for *Thror's Map*. He thinks some of the illustrations badly placed, but is unable to judge how they will fall on the finished page. He sends a draft design for the dust-jacket, but foresees objections: it has too many colours (blue, green, red, black); it needs simplifying; the lettering could be improved. He explains the runic inscription in the border. He would be glad to hear as soon as possible if the design is of any use, as he has little time left before the beginning of term in which to make a new drawing.

15 April 1937 C.A. Furth writes to Tolkien. The margins around the *Hobbit* illustrations will be adjusted before printing. He apologizes for not including Tolkien's more careful drawing of the 'moon-letters' for *Thror's Map*, and cannot understand how this happened. He thinks the dust-jacket design 'admirable', but suggests that the red colouring be omitted, which would improve the clarity of the title and remove a 'flush on the central mountain, which makes it look to our eyes just a trifle like a cake' (Tolkien-George Allen & Unwin archive, HarperCollins). He suggests that the runes in the border should be against a green background. He returns Tolkien's original art for redrawing, and to ensure a jacket of correct proportions he will send Tolkien a dummy of the book.

15–?17 April 1937 Tolkien takes a walking holiday in the *Quantock Hills in Somerset with C.S. Lewis and Owen Barfield. He finds it hard going to walk more than twenty miles a day in rough country while carrying a pack.

25 April 1937 Trinity Full Term begins. Tolkien's scheduled lectures and classes for this term are: Outlines of Old English Phonology and Grammar on Tuesdays and Thursdays at 12.00 noon in the Examination Schools, beginning 27 April; and Old English Verse Texts (Class), at an hour and place to be arranged. – Tolkien writes to C.A. Furth. He has redrawn the *Hobbit* dust-jacket, but does not think it much improved. It is now the exact size of the book. Tolkien has omitted the 'offending pink icing on the mountainous cake' (which his children like) but has left the sun and dragon red; if effect alone is considered rather than cost, he thinks red 'very desirable' and suggests other places on the jacket where it might be applied. The rest of the design is now in blue, black, and green; but it would be improved also by using a second, dark shade of green here and there. He leaves such questions, however, for Furth to decide. 'The design is probably too complicated already.' He is returning separately the dummy, with the (now tattered) paper model of the jacket, and a brown paper model of the same size as the enclosed design. He worries in a long postscript that he has drawn the jacket too wide, with too much space allowed for the back and hinges. If it is wrong 'I cannot do anything more about it, as term is now in full blast' (Tolkien-George Allen & Unwin archive, HarperCollins).

28 April 1937 C.A. Furth writes to Tolkien. The red colour on the dust-jacket will have to be omitted. The sun on the upper jacket will be distinguished by an outline. 'Otherwise everything seems straightforward and we are proceeding with the reproduction' (Tolkien-George Allen & Unwin archive, HarperCollins).

30 April 1937 Tolkien attends a Pembroke College meeting. – In the evening, Tolkien attends a dinner of The Society hosted by G.F. Hudson in the hall of All Souls College, Oxford. Seventeen members are present. Hudson speaks about the entertainment of foreign visitors.

6 May 1937 Tolkien attends an English Faculty Library Committee meeting.

11 May 1937 C.A. Furth writes to Tolkien. An American publisher is interested in *The Hobbit*, wants to add four colour illustrations to the book, and have suggested employing a good American artist. 'It occurred to us, however, that it would be better if all the illustrations were from your hand', and Furth recalls (presumably from his visit of 27 February) having seen some pictures that Tolkien has tucked away in a drawer (Tolkien-George Allen & Unwin archive, HarperCollins). He asks if Tolkien could send five or six of them, which Allen & Unwin will forward to the American publisher.

12 May 1937 Coronation of King George VI and Queen Elizabeth. There are no lectures or classes at Oxford. The Vice-Chancellor, Proctors, and graduates, in academic dress, assemble at 9.40 a.m. in the Divinity School and process to a special service in the Church of St Mary the Virgin.

13 May 1937 Tolkien writes to C.A. Furth. He asks the name of the American publisher interested in *The Hobbit*. 'As for the illustrations: I am divided between knowledge of my own inability and fear of what American artists (doubtless of admirable skill) might produce. In any case I agree that all the illustrations ought to be by the same hand: four professional pictures would make my own amateurish productions look rather silly.' He does have some pictures, but they illustrate 'The Silmarillion'. He would have to draw new ones for the American *Hobbit*. He will try to do so, but does not have much time in the middle of term, and it might be some time before he can produce anything. 'Perhaps the matter does not allow of much delay? It might be advisable, rather than lose the American interest, to let the Americans do what seems good to them – as long as it was possible (I should like to add) to veto anything from or influenced by the *Disney studios (for all whose works I have a heartfelt loathing). I have seen American illustrations that suggest that excellent things might be produced – only too excellent for their companions' (*Letters*, p. 17). He asks how much time he would have to produce samples for the Americans; and again, when the English edition of *The Hobbit* is to be published.

14 May 1937 Tolkien attends an English Faculty Board meeting. – C.A. Furth writes to Tolkien. The American publisher interested in *The Hobbit* is the Houghton Mifflin Company. Allen & Unwin will probably publish the book themselves in October 1937. They have no information yet as to when the American edition will be published, so there might be time for Tolkien to make coloured drawings to submit to them. Furth thinks that it would be best to forward Tolkien's letter to Houghton Mifflin, so that they will know his mind, and that he might be able to send them some (finished) drawings by the end of June. He will ask them to cable if they cannot wait so long. Allen & Unwin have already suggested that if Houghton Mifflin decide to use an American artist, Tolkien should be allowed to see specimens of his work.

22 May 1937 Allen & Unwin send Tolkien for his approval a proof of the *Hobbit* dust-jacket.

26 May 1937 Allen & Unwin send Tolkien for his approval sample binding cases for *The Hobbit*.

28 May 1937 Tolkien writes to Allen & Unwin. He approves the proof dust-jacket for *The Hobbit*, though he thinks that the sun would be improved if it had a slightly finer outline. Of the sample binding cases, he prefers the one in green. He agrees that 'The Hobbit' in the title would be best centred; but he does not like the italic lettering Allen & Unwin have used, or a wavy line at the edges and under the title. Either there should be no line, or it should be straight. He thinks that 'a small design would be an improvement' and will try to produce something. (Tolkien-George Allen & Unwin archive, Harper-Collins). – Tolkien also writes a second letter to Allen & Unwin, noting that 'this is the most busy time of the year in every way. A week later and a time of relative peace will arrive' (Tolkien-George Allen & Unwin archive, Harper-Collins). He discusses how the publication date of *The Hobbit* might affect its sales in Oxford. He would prefer it to come out sooner than later, lest people assume that it is the major fruit of his Leverhulme Research Fellowship. He mentions the possibility of reviews in the *Oxford Magazine*, and by C.S. Lewis in the *Times Literary Supplement*. He encloses three 'Silmarillion' pictures as examples of his work in colour. If Houghton Mifflin like them, he could probably improve his standard for *The Hobbit* pictures. He will see what he can do as soon as he has time. He asks if there is any chance that Houghton Mifflin might use *Mirkwood* as an endpaper in their *Hobbit*, and put the maps in the text in the original colours, with *Thror's Map* and the runes redrawn?

31 May 1937 Tolkien writes to Lionel Salt, the Bursar at Pembroke College. He will have to miss a play this evening, as one of his sons (Christopher) is being operated on for appendicitis.

June 1937 Tolkien spends much of his time caring for one of his children who is seriously ill (presumably Christopher, while recovering from appendicitis), and is ill himself. – He draws an ornamental wraparound design for the *Hobbit* binding, featuring mountains, moons, suns, and winged dragons.

1 June 1937 C.A. Furth writes to Tolkien. Allen & Unwin have written to Houghton Mifflin regarding Tolkien's letter of 28 May and have sent them the three 'Silmarillion' drawings. Furth asks Tolkien to return the approved *Hobbit* binding case. He agrees to remove the wavy line from underneath the title on the binding, but feels that something is needed at the edge; perhaps Tolkien's small design will change the effect. They will change the lettering from italic to roman. Publication is now planned for September. Allen & Unwin will send unbound advance copies to C.S. Lewis and to the editor of the *Oxford Magazine*.

2 June 1937 Mabel Day reports to the Early English Text Society Committee that their *Ancrene Riwle* subcommittee met on 27 May and recommended that the texts of that work to be published by EETS should be printed line by line as in the original manuscripts. The main Committee, unconvinced of the need for this approach, asks that the printer prepare specimen pages from several of the manuscripts, and instructs Mabel Day to ask Professor Tolkien what would be the precise benefits of line-by-line transcription relative to the expense involved. She does so on the same day.

10 June 1937 Tolkien attends an English Faculty Library Committee meeting. – English Final Honour School examinations begin.

15 June 1937 Tolkien attends a Pembroke College meeting.

18 June 1937 Tolkien attends an English Faculty Board meeting at 3.30 p.m. in Oriel College Lecture Room No. 4. – Tolkien possibly attends a meeting of the Committee for Comparative Philology at 5.15 p.m. in the Delegates Room of the Clarendon Building.

19 June 1937 Trinity Full Term ends.

23 June 1937 Encaenia.

June or July 1937 A.H. Smith calls on Tolkien in regard to his *Ancrene Riwle* edition for the Early English Text Society.

1 July 1937 Tolkien's Sir Israel Gollancz Memorial Lecture, *Beowulf: The Monsters and the Critics*, is published. In the weeks to follow he will receive several letters of appreciation and praise: correspondents include R.W. Chambers, Allen Mawer (1 July), David Nichol Smith (4 July), F.E. Harmer (5 July), George S. Gordon (8 July), F. Molina (29 July), and Oliver Elton (3 August). At least Chambers and Harmer, as well as Elaine Griffiths and Kenneth Sisam, receive copies personally from the author.

8 July 1937 C.A. Furth writes to Tolkien. He is sending a new *Hobbit* sample binding case with different lettering and without the lines under the title, which he agrees is an improvement. But unless Tolkien feels strongly about it, Allen & Unwin would like to leave the wavy lines at top and bottom.

?9 July 1937 Tolkien belatedly writes to C.A. Furth, sending the *Hobbit* binding design 'at far as it had got a month ago, rather as evidence that I did do something. I thought the wavy line might be transformed into something significant; and tried to find an ornamental dragon-formula' (Tolkien-George Allen & Unwin archive, HarperCollins). But he thinks that the revised cover will do, and returns the sample case. He asks what the Americans think of the specimens he sent. He says that he has not yet drawn any new *Hobbit* illustrations but will start to do so if they are still wanted. – In the event, he evidently does not wait for confirmation of the latter, and will soon begin to produce five new pictures in pen and watercolour, some of which will evolve through a series of preliminary sketches. *See note.*

?22 July 1937 In reply to a request from Susan Dagnall, Tolkien writes to Allen & Unwin, enclosing the most recent photograph of himself that exists. He asks again if Houghton Mifflin are likely to require colour illustrations for *The Hobbit* from him, as he does 'not want to labour in vain.' Since he has to be in London on 28 July, he would like to call at Allen & Unwin's offices and submit what he has done. 'Your production dep[artmen]t might perhaps kindly advise me as to whether the efforts are passable, and in any case suitable for reproduction' (Tolkien-George Allen & Unwin archive, HarperCollins). – By now Tolkien has made four colour illustrations for *The Hobbit*: *Rivendell, Bilbo Woke Up with the Early Sun in His Eyes, Bilbo Comes to the Huts of the Raft-elves,* and *Conversation with Smaug.*

23 July 1937 A.W. Rablen, an undergraduate at Oxford for the past few years, writes to Tolkien, listing misprints Rablen has found in the 1930 impression of the Tolkien-Gordon edition of *Sir Gawain and the Green Knight.*

24 July 1937 Stanley Unwin writes to Tolkien. He and C.A. Furth would be pleased to see Tolkien on 28 July, and suggests that they meet at 12.20 p.m. Allen & Unwin will cable Houghton Mifflin if they have not had a reply by 26 July. Unwin asks if Tolkien owns the copyright to the photograph he sent.

25 July 1937 Tolkien writes to Stanley Unwin. He will arrive at Allen & Unwin's offices at about 12.30 p.m., if his train is on time. He does not think that it will take long to tell him whether what he has done is suitable, or if not suitable, what is wrong. The photograph he has supplied was paid for by the students in his department when he left Leeds; he is not sure of the copyright position.

28 July 1937 Tolkien goes to London, arriving probably on the 12.05 p.m. train. Around 12.30 p.m. he visits Allen & Unwin's offices in Museum Street, taking with him the four finished colour illustrations for *The Hobbit*. These are approved and left to be forwarded to Houghton Mifflin. He is scheduled to be at a meeting in Curzon Street from 3.00–4.30 p.m.

29 July 1937 Tolkien is in London again. Although Stanley Unwin had invited him to lunch, apparently when he next came down from Oxford, Tolkien felt that 29 July was 'too soon . . . to bother you again' (Tolkien-George Allen & Unwin archive, HarperCollins).

6 August 1937 Mabel Day writes to Tolkien. Although most members of the Early English Text Society Committee are in favour of publishing the texts of the *Ancrene Riwle* line-by-line, A.W. Pollard considers it unnecessary and not advisable. Pollard is disappointed that Tolkien still has not provided detailed evidence of the advantages of retaining line-endings as in the original manuscripts. She asks Tolkien for copy to set up thirty-two pages so that the Committee can see how a line-by-line treatment would work. Since the point of view has also been extended that if the line-endings are kept, so too should contractions, Day asks for two pages with contractions not expanded, and which includes a passage in Latin. She requests the material in time to be printed by November.

?7–?21 August 1937 Tolkien and his family take a holiday in Sidmouth.

10 August 1937 C.A. Furth writes to Tolkien. He is sending him an advance copy of *The Hobbit* and offering more. He reports that Houghton Mifflin think that Tolkien's dust-jacket design has a 'British look', and that they have assumed that the drawings Tolkien sent merely as examples of his work are illustrations for *The Hobbit*.

13 August 1937 Tolkien writes to C.A. Furth. He asks that copies of *The Hobbit* be sent to George S. Gordon and R.W. Chambers, enclosing notes that Tolkien has written. Allen & Unwin may also use the colour illustrations if they wish. Tolkien suggests that they 'keep them in "cold storage"' when they are returned from America (Tolkien-George Allen & Unwin archive, Harper-Collins). He has now completed a colour version of the frontispiece, *The Hill: Hobbiton-across-the Water*. – Tolkien also writes to Stanley Unwin, hoping to be able to have lunch with him when he is next in London, probably in November. He had time only to glance at Elaine Griffiths' work on the Clark Hall *Beowulf* before going to Sidmouth, but will correct or help in correcting it, and write his 'small bit', as soon as he returns to Oxford (Tolkien-George Allen & Unwin archive, HarperCollins).

16 August 1937 C.A. Furth writes to Tolkien. He has sent the copies of *The Hobbit* as requested. He returns the drawing of a dragon that Tolkien had made for the binding. Furth agrees that the colour illustrations may be stored in the Allen & Unwin safe.

28 August 1937 Tolkien writes to Mabel Day. He is working on the specimens she requested in her letter of 6 August. He had hoped to complete work by now on his transcription and collation of *Ancrene Wisse*, but because of the death of the librarian at Corpus Christi College, Cambridge, and other difficulties, he has not been able to see the original manuscript; and possible library repairs at Cambridge may make consultation impossible for some time. He asks if the Early English Text Society has formally asked for permission to publish the text of the manuscript, as the acting librarian knows of no such permission. Tolkien feels that he said all that he could about the advantages of line-by-line presentation in a letter long ago to A.W. Pollard (he believes) and in conversation with Robin Flower and A.H. Smith. He thanks Day for valuable notes on *A Middle English Vocabulary*, sent long ago, and will make what use he can of them under the severe limitations of plate-correction, if an opportunity for another reprint arises – though he now has no control over the glossary.

30 August 1937 Mabel Day writes to Tolkien. She will ask Corpus Christi College, Cambridge for permission to publish MS CCCC 402. She informs Tolkien that A.W. Pollard seems never to have received a letter from him regarding line-by-line presentation. Pollard is anxious to receive examples of scribal errors occurring generally at line-ends, which has been put forward as the reason for presenting a manuscript line by line.

31 August 1937 Tolkien sends C.A. Furth *The Hill: Hobbiton-across-the Water* to forward to Houghton Mifflin if Allen & Unwin think it good enough. He chose the colour subjects for *The Hobbit* so that they would be evenly distributed throughout the book, especially when taken in conjunction with the black and white drawings. He asks if there is any chance of remuneration, as these colour illustrations were made specially for Houghton Mifflin and involved considerable labour. 'At the moment I am in such difficulties (largely owing to medical expenses) that even a very small fee would be a blessing' (*Letters*, p. 20). He does not expect Allen & Unwin to pay if they should decide to use the colour pictures, however: he appreciates that 'production costs have been excessive (and that I have been hard on proofs)'. They 'are most welcome at any time to anything you think I can do, in the way of drawing or redrawing, that is fit to use on *The Hobbit*' (*Letters*, p. 20). He hopes that Mr Baggins will eventually come to his rescue. He has had letters of appreciation from George S. Gordon, R.W. Chambers, and Russell Meiggs, the editor of the *Oxford Magazine*. He encloses comments on the dust-jacket flap copy for *The Hobbit*, pointing out various errors and inaccuracies and sends a revised version of the blurb that they might wish to use.

1 September 1937 and later By summer 1937 E.V. Gordon, having given up hope of any contribution from Tolkien, has completed by himself work on an edition of *Pearl*, though he tells Kenneth Sisam at Oxford University Press that he would still welcome any contribution by Tolkien, which would certainly be for the good of the edition. But he does not want any long delays, as he has other commitments, and *Pearl* is replacing *Sir Gawain* on the Oxford English syllabus in 1938. Therefore by the beginning of September 1937 he sends his complete manuscript to Tolkien for him to revise and criticize, and suggests a date by which the work should be done. – By 20 November 1937 Tolkien will write at least one letter to Gordon, expressing the opinion that some parts are too long.

4 September 1937 C.A. Furth writes to Tolkien. He has asked Houghton Mifflin to return the specimen pictures, and has put forward Tolkien's claim for a fee. If Allen & Unwin need to reprint *The Hobbit*, they will include the new colour art and will make some remuneration for their use. In regard to Tolkien's criticism of the dust-jacket blurb, Allen & Unwin will substitute his wording on any reprint, but much of it by then will be crowded out by quotations from reviews. They may, however, be able to use some of what Tolkien wrote in their press material. Furth sends him a copy of a full-page pre-publication advertisement in the trade paper.

5–7 September 1937 Tolkien writes to C.A. Furth. He apologizes for the length of his letter regarding the jacket blurb: 'I am afraid that, when I don't neglect letters, I am apt to write ones much too long' (Tolkien-George Allen & Unwin archive, HarperCollins). He thinks that he is still owed five copies of *The Hobbit* but will need twelve in all, to go to Leeds, Birmingham, Manchester, Cambridge, etc. He will have no immediate opportunity to rework *Mr. Bliss* as his research fellowship is rather exigent, but there might be a few odd moments if he was sure what was needed. In a postscript dated 7 September he suggests reviewers of *The Hobbit*, including W.R. Childe at Leeds, and personal connections which might promote sales in Britain and elsewhere. His wife has asked for the return of the photograph of Tolkien he sent to Allen & Unwin, as it is her property.

6 September 1937 Stanley Unwin writes to Tolkien, offering him an advance on royalties. He sends a cheque for £25.

?Early September 1937 Around this time, Tolkien replaces his first car with another second-hand car.

8 September 1937 C.A. Furth writes to Tolkien. He is sending a complimentary copy of *The Hobbit* to W.R. Childe. Tolkien's remaining author's copies will be posted around 20 September, and he has asked that Tolkien be sent another dozen complimentary copies for publicity purposes.

17 September 1937 Tolkien writes to C.A. Furth. He needs only five outstanding author's copies of *The Hobbit*, and seven more 'to give to one or two people who for reasons of age or finance cannot buy' (Tolkien-George Allen & Unwin archive, HarperCollins). He has gone through a great deal of the Clark Hall *Beowulf* but cannot pass it without seeing Elaine Griffiths. He confesses that he has not yet written his own part. – Tolkien writes to Stanley Unwin, thanking him for the cheque which arrived at a very convenient moment.

21 September 1937 *The Hobbit* is published by George Allen & Unwin. Tolkien probably receives the twelve copies he has requested only on or just before 21 September. He spends much of publication day, and possibly the next few days, inscribing copies to family, friends, colleagues, and former students, writing letters, and presumably wrapping and posting books. Known recipients are Helen Buckhurst, Simonne d'Ardenne, E.V. Gordon, Elaine Griffiths, Jennie Grove, the Jennings family, K.M. Kilbride (whom he also sends a copy of *Beowulf: The Monsters and the Critics*), Stella Mills, Dorothy Moore, Jane Neave, and Hilary Tolkien. Tolkien is not sure of Jane Neave's current address and asks Hilary for it. In the coming days and weeks he will receive many letters of thanks and praise for *The Hobbit*.

22 September 1937 Tolkien writes to his Aunt Jane Neave, intending to send the letter with a copy of *The Hobbit* (but see entry for 6 October 1937). He looks forward to seeing her at Christmas, and will fetch her in his new car.

24 September 1937 Hilary Tolkien sends his brother their Aunt Jane's address.

27 September 1937 Christopher Tolkien begins to attend the Oratory School at Caversham, joining his brother Michael. Tolkien drives the boys to the school and sees some of the new 'flats'. – C.A. Furth informs Tolkien that Houghton Mifflin will pay him $100 for his illustrations to *The Hobbit*.

30 September 1937 Susan Dagnall asks Tolkien if he can recommend someone to write a book, to be called *The Loom of Language*, based on a synopsis she encloses.

1 October 1937 Tolkien writes to Susan Dagnall, asking for more information about *The Loom of Language*. – Jane Neave writes to Tolkien. She has heard about *The Hobbit* from Hilary, but has not yet received a copy. She asks for more information, and suggests that she might get a copy from the Times Book Club.

2 October 1937 Susan Dagnall writes to Tolkien. The idea for *The Loom of Language* originated apparently at a weekend party by a group including one of Allen & Unwin's authors, and the synopsis was passed to them for possible development. *See note.* – C.S. Lewis anonymously reviews *The Hobbit* in the *Times Literary Supplement*. He points out that both *The Hobbit* and *Alice's Adventures in Wonderland* 'belong to a very small class of books which have nothing in common save that each admits us to a world of its own – a world that seems to have been going on before we stumbled into it but which, once found by the right reader, becomes indispensable to him' (p. 714).

3 October 1937 Tolkien writes to his son Michael at school. He thanks Michael for keeping an eye on Christopher, and commiserates with him on not yet being in the school rugby football team. 'Mummy seems to have taken to car-riding . . . and I have now got to take her', Priscilla, and a family friend out this afternoon (*Letters*, p. 23).

5 October 1937 Tolkien writes to Susan Dagnall. He thinks the scheme of *The Loom of Language* bad, in fact he had wondered if it was a leg-pull.

6 October 1937 After receiving Jane Neave's letter of 1 October Tolkien realizes that even though Hilary has sent him her address, he has not yet sent her the copy he signed and the letter he wrote on 22 September. Apparently he is unable to find these, and therefore signs and dates another copy on 6 October, and writes another letter in which he asks about the Times Book Club. When he finds the original copy he keeps it in his own collection with the earlier letter.

7 October 1937 Mary St John, OSB, of Oulton Abbey, the sister of Christopher Wiseman, writes to ask Tolkien if he would send her a copy of *The Hobbit*. Since she has taken a vow of poverty she offers to pay with prayers for him and his family.

8 October 1937 C.S. Lewis anonymously reviews *The Hobbit* for the London *Times*. He compares it to *The Wind in the Willows* and remarks that 'in this book a number of good things, never before united, have come together: a fund of humour, an understanding of children, and a happy fusion of the scholar's with the poet's grasp of mythology' (p. 20).

9 October 1937 Jane Neave writes to Tolkien enthusiastically about *The Hobbit*, the signed copy of which she has now received. She cannot find the reply from the Times Book Club.

10 October 1937 Michaelmas Full Term begins. Tolkien's scheduled lectures and classes for this term are: *Beowulf*: Text on Tuesdays at 11.00 a.m. in the Examination Schools, beginning 12 October; Finn and Hengest on Tuesdays and Thursdays at 12.00 noon in the Examination Schools, beginning 12 October; Old English Texts (Class) on Tuesdays at 5.15 p.m. at Pembroke College, beginning 12 October.

11 October 1937 Stanley Unwin writes to Tolkien. His son Rayner is rereading *The Hobbit* now that it is in print. He sends Tolkien an appreciative letter from Richard Hughes, and warns him 'that *The Hobbit* has come to stay and that a large public will be clamouring next year to hear more from you about Hobbits' (Tolkien-George Allen & Unwin archive, HarperCollins). Bumpus, the important London bookseller, has taken fifty copies on the basis of the *Times* review.

13 October 1937 Jane Neave is scheduled to pass through Oxford on her way to London by coach. Tolkien possibly meets her during a stop from 11.50 a.m. to 12.30 p.m. – Tolkien attends a Pembroke College meeting.

15 October 1937 Tolkien writes to Stanley Unwin, commenting on reviews of *The Hobbit* and the letter from Richard Hughes. He notes that no reviewer has mentioned his use of *dwarves* rather than *dwarfs*; he himself became aware of his usage only through reading reviews. He is perturbed at the idea of a sequel: he cannot think of anything more to say about hobbits, but he has a great deal to say about the world (of 'The Silmarillion') into which Bilbo Baggins intruded. He would like to show this material to Allen & Unwin and get an independent opinion of it. But if it is more about the hobbit that is wanted, he will start to think what can be done. He wonders if possibly such works will be successful enough to allow him to write, rather than spend vacations on examining and such things in order to pay medical and education bills, as he has done for seventeen years. 'Writing stories in prose or verse has been stolen, often guiltily, from time already mortgaged, and has been broken and ineffective. I may perhaps now do what I much desire to do, and not fail of financial duty. Perhaps!' (*Letters*, p. 24). He comments on the reception of *The Hobbit* in Oxford. 'The attitude is (as I foresaw) not unmixed with surprise and a little pity. My own college [Pembroke] is I think good for about six copies, if only in order to find material for teasing me' (*Letters*, p. 24). He asks if 27 October would be a suitable day for him to have lunch with Unwin. He could bring *Mr. Bliss* with him to get advice on how to redraw it to make it reproducible. He acknowledges the return of the specimen drawings lent to Houghton Mifflin.

19 October 1937 Stanley Unwin writes to Tolkien. He thinks that Tolkien might well hope for an income from writing. He confirms a lunch appointment for 27 October.

?20 or 27 October 1937 C.S. Lewis reads part of *Out of the Silent Planet* at a meeting of the Inklings.

21 October 1937 Tolkien attends an English Faculty Library Committee meeting.

23 October 1937 Tolkien writes to Stanley Unwin, confirming their lunch appointment on 27 October. He will try to start writing a sequel to *The Hobbit* soon, and will submit it to Rayner Unwin at the earliest opportunity. – Tolkien attends a Pembroke College meeting.

27 October 1937 Tolkien travels to London, probably on the 12.05 train, for a 12.45 lunch with Stanley Unwin. Unwin asks him to submit various writings for consideration. After their meeting Unwin makes a rough list of material that Tolkien has mentioned. These include 'a volume of short fairy stories in various styles practically ready for publication ... (Sil Marillion) [*sic*]'; 'the typescript of a History of the Gnomes, and stories arising from it'; *Mr. Bliss*; *The Lost Road*, 'a partly written novel of which we could see the opening chapters'; 'a great deal of verse of one kind and another which would probably be worth looking at'; a translation of *Beowulf* 'upon which he has as yet done very little'; and the 'Father Christmas' letters (Tolkien-George Allen & Unwin archive, HarperCollins). Unwin also notes that Tolkien spoke enthusiastically of *The Marvellous Land of Snergs* by E.A. Wyke-Smith (1927). – Tolkien had planned to travel to London this day in order to attend a lecture by Professor Joseph Vendryes at the British Academy later in the day. But he is tired, and has 'a worrying business on mind awaiting me at 3 o'clock' which, in the event, takes 'so long that I only just managed to squeeze in [an appointment] in Elliott & Fry [the photographers] before my train. But, though I rather rushed them, they were very polite and expeditious, so that I hope the results will be satisfactory' (letter to Stanley Unwin, 29 October 1937, Tolkien-George Allen & Unwin archive, HarperCollins). Tolkien has been sent to Elliott & Fry by Allen & Unwin, so that they can have photographs for publicity purposes.

28 October 1937 Stanley Unwin writes to Tolkien. He hopes that by their next meeting, on 17 November, Tolkien 'will have put together the volume of short fairy stories in various styles. I hope you will also bring with you the *History of the Gnomes* and such chapters as you have written of *The Lost Road*' (Tolkien-George Allen & Unwin archive, HarperCollins). He would also like to see *Out of the Silent Planet* by C.S. Lewis, which Tolkien apparently has mentioned.

29 October 1937 Tolkien attends an English Faculty Board meeting. He is elected to the Standing Committee on the Library, and is appointed (as convenor) to a committee 'to consider and report on the whole question of the First Public Examination as affecting the English scheme' (Oxford University Archives FA 4/5/1/1), together with *Helen Darbishire, C.S. Lewis, M.R. Ridley, and David Nichol Smith. The Applications Committee has appointed Tolkien the supervisor of advanced student K.R. Brooks of Merton College, who is preparing an edition of the Old English poem *Andreas*. – Tolkien writes to Stanley Unwin, suggesting dates in November for their next meeting. If 10 November, he would prefer the afternoon, for tea rather than lunch, so as not to miss a meeting in Oxford in the morning. 12 or 15 November would be free all day. He has seen C.S. Lewis, whose contract for *Out of the Silent Planet* obliges him to submit it first to the publisher J.M. Dent. – Tolkien writes again to Unwin, after receiving his letter of 28 October which suggests a meeting on Wednesday, 17 November. Tolkien can meet him on that date but 'unless urgent matters intervene I work with Mr. Lewis each W[ednesday] morning and dine in College (my only night in the week). Mondays and Saturdays are my only days left empty (supposedly dedicated to my own study)' (Tolkien-George Allen & Unwin archive, HarperCollins). He asks if he should borrow a copy of *Out of the Silent Planet* for Unwin to read, so that he would already have an opinion should Dent refuse to publish it. – J.N.L. Myres, a History scholar of Christ Church, Oxford writes to Tolkien regarding a bone object with a runic inscription found in an Anglo-Saxon cemetery at Caister-by-Norwich. The inscription is legible, but other authorities can make no sense of it.

30 October 1937 Stanley Unwin writes to Tolkien, apparently having received only his first letter of 29 October. He suggests meeting on 10, 12, or 15 November.

31 October 1937 Tolkien writes to Stanley Unwin, leaving it to him to choose between 15 or 17 November for their meeting.

1 November 1937 Stanley Unwin writes to Tolkien, setting their meeting for Monday, 15 November. He would like to see *Out of the Silent Planet* if there is a spare typescript Tolkien can provide.

3 November 1937 Tolkien attends a Pembroke College meeting.

5 November 1937 Tolkien writes to Stanley Unwin. He has received proofs of his photographs from Elliott & Fry. Edith has chosen one for them to send to Unwin. – F.E. Harmer, Lecturer in English at the University of Manchester, writes to Tolkien, asking if he can cite an instance of the use of *(ge-)frith* as an adjective in Middle English or Old English. She has sent *The Hobbit* to her nephews.

10 November 1937 Tolkien probably attends a meeting in Oxford this morning. – Stanley Unwin writes to Tolkien in reply to his comments about Elliott & Fry. He sends him a complimentary ticket for the *Sunday Times* Book Fair.

15 November 1937 Tolkien meets Stanley Unwin in London. He hands over for consideration the *Lay of Leithian* (recorded by Unwin as 'Long Poem'), the *Quenta Silmarillion*, the *Ainulindalë*, the *Ambarkanta*, and *The Fall of Númenor* (which Unwin calls collectively 'The Gnomes Material'), *The Lost Road*, and again, *Farmer Giles of Ham* and *Mr. Bliss* (George Allen & Unwin archive, University of Reading). They discuss the revised edition of the Clark Hall *Beowulf*, and Unwin explains exactly what is wanted. Tolkien shows him some of Elaine Griffiths' work, with heavy corrections to the text. Later in the day Tolkien visits the *Sunday Times* Book Fair at Dorland Hall in south-west London, and will wish that he could have stayed there longer: 'Russian books, book-cases, American juveniles, all sorts of things. As a mere author I could not escape the feeling that there are already too many (let alone the dead whose works yet live)' (letter to Stanley Unwin, 17 November 1937, Tolkien-George Allen & Unwin archive, HarperCollins). – After this meeting Tolkien will tell Elaine Griffiths what the publisher wants regarding the Clark Hall volume.

15 November–19 December 1937 Tolkien continues to work on the *Quenta Silmarillion* while the fair copy manuscript is with Allen & Unwin, and probably also in the brief time between its return from the publisher and the start of composition of *The Lord of the Rings*. In two less carefully written and slightly overlapping manuscripts, he extends the story of the *Quenta Silmarillion* from the point at which Beren cuts a Silmaril from Morgoth's crown, to the flight of Túrin from Thingol's court. As he writes, Tolkien decides to change certain names; on 20 November he makes a note to remind himself to make these alterations in the fair copy manuscript when it returns.

16 November 1937 Since Allen & Unwin have already looked at *Farmer Giles of Ham*, Stanley Unwin returns the typescript to Tolkien. He comments that 'if there were sufficient material of a like character to put with it, it would make a most excellent book' (Tolkien-George Allen & Unwin archive, Harper-Collins). – C.V. Salmon of the BBC writes to Tolkien. He would like to discuss the possibility of a broadcast on *Beowulf*, with a reading in the original Old English.

17 November 1937 Tolkien writes to Stanley Unwin. He sends a letter from a Mlle Tardivel asking about a possible French translation of *The Hobbit*. He has sent her an interim reply that he would pass the proposal to Allen & Unwin. He mentions that Simonne d'Ardenne has translated *Farmer Giles of Ham* into French and might be considered as a translator of *The Hobbit*. – Tolkien replies to C.V. Salmon. He would be pleased to discuss a *Beowulf* broadcast. If Salmon can come to Oxford, he can see him almost any day if he is not lecturing; but if they are to meet in London Mondays (especially) and Wednesdays are the most convenient for Tolkien.

***c.* 20 November 1937** E.V. Gordon writes to Tolkien. Like Tolkien, Kenneth Sisam also thinks that Gordon's edition of *Pearl* needs cutting. Gordon will write to Sisam that as it is much easier to cut someone else's work than to reduce one's own, he hopes that Tolkien will be willing to prune *Pearl*.

20 November 1937 Stanley Unwin writes to Tolkien. Allen & Unwin are trying to arrange German, Scandinavian, and other rights for translations of *The Hobbit*. He will write to both Simonne d'Ardenne and Mlle Tardivel.

23 November 1937 C.V. Salmon of the BBC writes to Tolkien. He asks if Tolkien can see him in Oxford on Monday, 29 November. – Tolkien is appointed a Governor of King Edward's School, Birmingham, as the representative of Oxford University on the governing body. He will be reappointed in 1940 to act until 1947, but will resign on 1 January 1941. Although the Governors meet once a month, Tolkien will attend only four meetings during his term of office.

26 November 1937 Tolkien replies to C.V. Salmon that he can see him at any time in the morning of the 29th.

27 November 1937 Tolkien's Aunt Mabel Mitton (*née* Tolkien) dies.

28 November 1937 G.E. Selby, a friend, writes to Tolkien, querying discrepancies between the runes on *Thror's Map* and the way they are reported in the text of *The Hobbit*.

29 November 1937 Tolkien writes to E.V. Gordon. He is travelling to Birmingham for the funeral of Mabel Mitton. – C.V. Salmon visits Tolkien in Oxford. Tolkien agrees to undertake the *Beowulf* broadcast. (In the event, the programme will consider Old English verse in general.) – Allen & Unwin give the manuscript of the *Lay of Leithian* to one of their readers, Edward Crankshaw, for comment.

30 November 1937 Stanley Unwin returns the manuscript of *The Lost Road*. He has had a typescript made, which he will send to Tolkien. – C.V. Salmon informs Tolkien that the broadcast date on which they had agreed the previous day is no longer available. He suggests instead 14 January, from 10.45 to 11.00 p.m. He will write again to suggest another time for rehearsal.

?1 December 1937 Tolkien writes to E.V. Gordon. He is willing to attempt to reduce the length of the edition of *Pearl*, but is opposed to any drastic reduction (perhaps as suggested by Kenneth Sisam).

2 December 1937 E.V. Gordon writes to Kenneth Sisam. He is willing to undertake the reduction of *Pearl* together with Tolkien, but he fears that it will take a long time.

3 December 1937 Tolkien attends an English Faculty Board meeting. He is appointed to a committee 'to consider the list of Lecturers and Grants' (Oxford University Archives FA 4/5/1/1). The report of the committee (including Tolkien) on the First Public Examination, dated 16 November 1937, is presented; after discussion, further consideration is postponed until the next meeting. – Tolkien also attends a Pembroke College meeting. – Tolkien writes to C.V. Salmon, apologizing for the delayed reply. 14 January will suit him as a broadcast date. He politely objects to the loss of five minutes from their original plan, leaving only fifteen which Tolkien feels is rather short, and will require him to change his incipient ideas. He thinks that even the highbrow minority need adequate hints of what to listen for.

4 December 1937 Michaelmas Full Term ends.

7 December 1937 C.V. Salmon writes to Tolkien. He apologizes for the loss of five minutes and agrees that it would be better to cut down on quotation (from *Beowulf*) rather than introductory matter.

***c.* 8 December 1937** Tolkien falls ill with influenza, from which he will recover very slowly.

13 December 1937 Noted children's author *Arthur Ransome writes to Tolkien, pointing out the latter's use of *men* in *The Hobbit* when referring to hobbits or dwarves.

14 December 1937 R.W. Chambers writes to Tolkien. He has written a review of *Beowulf: The Monsters and the Critics*, and again expresses his appreciation. He will soon be sending Tolkien a copy of his Shakespeare lecture (*The Jacobean Shakespeare and Measure for Measure*, 1937). – Edward Crankshaw returns the *Lay of Leithian* to Allen & Unwin.

14–15 December 1937 Tolkien writes to G.E. Selby. He remarks that he has been ill and still feels unwell. He comments at length on *The Hobbit*, of which he does not much approve, preferring his mythology with its consistent nomenclature and organized history. He had hoped that Allen & Unwin would be interested in his history of the Elves, but they want more hobbits instead. Selby is correct in what he wrote (28 November) about the runes in *The Hobbit*.

15 December 1937 Tolkien writes to Arthur Ransome. He was delighted to receive a letter from him; his children have retained the books by Ransome they read when young. He will make the suggested corrections in *The Hobbit*, and sends Ransome a list of other errors he has discovered. He amuses himself by transcribing part of Ransome's letter and his reply into Tengwar. – Stanley Unwin writes to Tolkien. The first printing of *The Hobbit* has sold out, but a reprint with four colour illustrations will be available almost immediately. He is returning under separate cover the manuscripts Tolkien had submitted. As Tolkien had surmised, it would be difficult to do anything with the verse *Lay of Leithian*, but their reader (Edward Crankshaw) was impressed with some pages of a prose version that accompanied it, 'in spite of its eye-splitting Celtic names'. *See note.* Unwin thinks that 'The Silmarillion' 'contains plenty of wonderful material' which might be mined to produce 'further books like *The Hobbit* rather than a book in itself' (Tolkien-George Allen & Unwin archive, HarperCollins). What Allen & Unwin badly need is another *Hobbit*, and failing that, a volume of stories like *Farmer Giles of Ham*. – Tolkien will assume that all of the material he gave to Stanley Unwin has been read, and that Unwin's mention of the brief prose version accompanying the *Lay of Leithian* refers to the whole *Quenta Silmarillion* and accompanying material. In fact the 'Silmarillion' papers have been found too disordered, or peculiar and difficult, and not given to a reader. Apparently only Stanley Unwin at Allen & Unwin has looked at 'The Gnomes Material'. – C.V. Salmon writes to Tolkien. He asks if Tolkien will be in London after 3 January to rehearse the *Beowulf* programme, and looks forward to seeing the script.

16 December 1937 Tolkien writes to Stanley Unwin. Readers of *The Hobbit* having given the book 'a flatteringly close scrutiny', pointing out errors or discrepancies, he sends a list of emendations (Tolkien-George Allen & Unwin archive, HarperCollins). He has also received several queries concerning runes, and wonders if a runic alphabet should be added to the book. He comments on reviews of *The Hobbit*; asks to receive four more copies at author's rates to use as Christmas presents; asks which four colour illustrations Allen & Unwin are using in the second printing; and asks if they can send him a spare print of the picture *Conversation with Smaug* which shows the dragon on his hoard within the Lonely Mountain. Tolkien is to give a lecture on dragons at the University Museum in Oxford, and wants to show a slide of the picture. He notes that he has not yet written his annual letter to his children as from 'Father Christmas'. He expresses joy that 'The Silmarillion' 'is not rejected with scorn. I have suffered a sense of fear and bereavement, quite ridiculous, since I let this private and beloved nonsense out; and I think if it had seemed to you to be nonsense I should have felt really crushed.' Although he hopes that one day 'The Silmarillion' will be published, and refutes some of the publisher's reader's comments, he had not thought that anything he submitted was what Allen & Unwin wanted. 'But I did want to know whether any of the stuff had any exterior non-personal value. I think it is plain that quite apart from it, a sequel or successor to *The Hobbit* is called for. I promise to give this thought and attention.' But it is difficult with 'the construction of elaborate and consistent mythology (and two languages)' occupying his mind, and the Silmarils in his heart; also he is not sure what more he can do with hobbits. He asks if 'Tom Bombadil, the spirit of the (vanishing) Oxford and Berkshire countryside, could be made into the hero of a story' (*Letters*, p. 26). He encloses a copy of his poem *The Adventures of Tom Bombadil* from the *Oxford Magazine*. – Stanley Unwin writes to Tolkien about W.G. Le Tall of Geoffrey Tyndale's Bookshop in Bath, who is offering prizes to schoolchildren for pictures of Bilbo, essays on *The Hobbit*, and answers to a long list of questions.

17 December 1937 C.A. Furth writes to Tolkien. He gives more details about the reprint of *The Hobbit*, which Allen & Unwin have rushed through to meet demand in the Christmas trade. In order to include the new colour art in their second printing, they had to retrieve the original pictures from Houghton Mifflin, and then send them back again for the American edition. 'At the last minute the crisis was so acute, that we fetched part of the reprint from our printers at Woking in a private car, in order to avoid the delay of half a day between two of the printers' vans' (Tolkien-George Allen & Unwin archive, HarperCollins). They will keep Tolkien's corrections for use in the third printing. They are sending him two copies of the reprint. – C.V. Salmon asks Tolkien how he would like his talk to be billed in the *Radio Times*. – W.G. Le Tall writes to Tolkien. He gives details of the bookshop competition and asks Tolkien to sign his personal copy of *The Hobbit*. In reply Tolkien will offer to sign copies of *The Hobbit* for the winners of the competition, and provide copies of his runic alphabet if the bookseller cannot get them made.

18 December 1937 Tolkien writes to C.V. Salmon. After being ill for ten days with influenza he is now suffering from severe 'pink eye' and laryngitis. He can hardly see, is not supposed to write, and cannot talk. He hopes that he will be recovered in time for the broadcast on 14 January, and suggests that the rehearsal date be made as late as possible. He will send his script when he is fit enough to write it. He makes some changes to the proposed announcement in the *Radio Times*.

19 December 1937 Tolkien writes to C.A. Furth. He has received six copies of the new impression of *The Hobbit* but needs two more. (He will send copies at least to Mrs Ruth Smith, the mother of G.B. Smith, and his Aunt Florence Hadley *née* Tolkien.) He thinks that the colour pictures have come out well, though he is sorry that *Bilbo Woke* has not been included (it will be present in the American edition in 1938, which however will exclude *Bilbo Comes to the Huts of the Raft-elves*). He sends a few more corrections. Most significantly, he has 'written the first chapter of a new story about Hobbits – "A long expected party"' (*Letters*, p. 27).

Mid-December 1937–beginning of February 1938 Tolkien writes in quick succession four versions of the opening of the work that will become *The Lord of the Rings*. The first of these is a five-page manuscript in which the party is given by Bilbo. In a second manuscript, closely based on the first, Tolkien introduces much new material, including the arrival of Gandalf in Hobbiton; this will be heavily emended, but abandoned unfinished. In the third version the party is given instead by Bilbo's son, Bingo. And in the fourth, finished by 1 February 1938, it is given by Bilbo's nephew, Bingo Bolger-Baggins. – Once Tolkien begins work on *The Lord of the Rings* he more or less abandons new writing of the *Quenta Silmarillion*. But he corrects the manuscript of the latter returned from Allen & Unwin in accordance with the note he made on 20 November. At about the same time, he also makes these changes in the *Etymologies*. At some date before 3 February 1938 he begins a typescript of the *Quenta Silmarillion* with an alternative title, *I·Eldanyárë* ('The History of the Elves'), but abandons it after describing the Elves in Valinor.

20 December 1937 Stanley Unwin sends Tolkien a set of the colour plates for *The Hobbit*, as well as his son Rayner's report on *The Adventures of Tom Bombadil*. Rayner likes the poem but thinks that a sequel to *The Hobbit*, featuring Bullroarer Took (mentioned in Chapter 1), would make a better story. – With a second letter of this date Unwin sends Tolkien the typescript he has had made of *The Lost Road*. He finds it is difficult to judge from the fragment if the work would have any popular appeal. He would like to see it complete, but 'cannot hold out any hope of commercial success', whereas another book on the lines of *The Hobbit* would surely succeed. Later Tolkien will correct errors in *The Lost Road* made by the typist.

22 December 1937 K.M. Kilbride, one of Tolkien's students at Leeds with whom he keeps in touch and to whom he sent a copy of *The Hobbit*, writes to him, commenting on the book and sending news and Christmas wishes. She asks if Tolkien will sign a replacement copy (second printing) of *The Hobbit* if she sends it to him after Christmas. Her original copy has been destroyed after she lent it to a child who developed scarlet fever. *See note.*

24 December 1937 C.V. Salmon writes to Tolkien, suggesting that the rehearsal for his broadcast be at noon on 12 January. – Separately the BBC send Tolkien a contract for his talk.

Christmas 1937 Tolkien, as 'Father Christmas', writes a long letter to Christopher and Priscilla. It is begun as by Father Christmas, and completed as by the elf Ilbereth with interruptions by the North Polar Bear. It is accompanied by a large illustration, drawn in coloured inks as by Ilbereth, with nine scenes describing the year at the North Pole. – Probably both Jane Neave and Jennie Grove spend this Christmas with the Tolkien family.

27 December 1937 Tolkien writes to C.V. Salmon. He is not recovering very fast, but thinks that he will have his voice back soon. Since he has to attend a meeting in London on 10 January at 3.00 p.m. it would be convenient if he could rehearse on that day. – Ruth Smith writes to Tolkien, thanking him for sending a copy of *The Hobbit* and his annual letter.

30 December 1937 *Beowulf: The Monsters and the Critics* is reprinted in the *Proceedings of the British Academy*, vol. 22.

1938

c. **1938–1939** At a meeting of The Cave the members hold a competition for the best reading, the prize to be a copy of the worst book that can be found. The winner is *Leonard Rice-Oxley, and the book is *Would I Fight?* essays by Oxford undergraduates and recent graduates edited by Keith Briant and Lyall Wilkes (1938). The prize copy is signed by the members present: Joan Blomfield, H.F.B. Brett-Smith, Dorothy Everett, Elaine Griffiths, F.C. Horwood, C.S. Lewis, C.L. Morrison, Rice-Oxley, Tolkien, *Dorothy Whitelock, and C.L. Wrenn.

1938–early 1939 Invited to deliver the Andrew Lang Lecture for 1938–9 at the University of St Andrews (*On Fairy-Stories*), Tolkien spends considerable time in research and composition. He writes many pages of manuscript, in at least two versions, most of which are heavily revised.

1938 Tolkien is appointed to the Committee for Nomination of Examiners for the Diploma in Comparative Philology, until Hilary Term 1941.

January 1938 In addition to writing his talk for the BBC, working on the sequel to *The Hobbit*, and making some progress with 'The Silmarillion', Tolkien prepares *Farmer Giles of Ham* to read to the Lovelace Society at Worcester College. Lacking time to write a paper on fairy-stories as requested, he rewrites his children's story, increasing its length by about half and adding philological and historical allusions that would appeal to an audience of undergraduates and dons. – Christopher Tolkien, having come home from school at Christmas feeling unwell, is x-rayed and found to have irregularities of the heart. He will spend much of the year lying on his back in bed. In the summer he will have a bed on a swing in the garden from which he watches the stars with a telescope his father buys for him.

1 January 1938 Tolkien gives an illustrated lecture on dragons at 2.30 p.m. at the University Museum, Oxford. This is one of a series of six Christmas lectures for children, 30 December 1937–10 January 1938, sponsored by the Ashmolean Natural History Society of Oxfordshire, but the only one given by Tolkien. (The others are on 'Birds of Oxford', 'Whales and Whaling', 'Pack Horses, Coaches, and Highwaymen', 'Coral Reefs', and 'Electric Sparks'.) He shows slides of dinosaurs and of his own drawings of dragons.

3 January 1938 C.V. Salmon informs Tolkien that he has booked a studio for rehearsal on 10 January at 11.00 a.m.

?6 January 1938 Tolkien writes to C.V. Salmon. If the 9.12 train on 10 January is on time, he should arrive at the BBC studio by 11.00 a.m. He is still unwell, but now more normal. He has found it difficult to keep his talk within the time-limit, and will not be able to post his script until the following day.

?7 January 1938 Tolkien sends his script to C.V. Salmon with a cover note. He hopes that he has timed it accurately for thirteen minutes.

10 January 1938 Tolkien goes to London to rehearse his talk at the BBC. He presumably also attends the meeting referred to in his letter of 27 December.

13 January 1938 Tolkien sends C.V. Salmon a revised script of his broadcast talk, evidently incorporating amendments Salmon has suggested. One of his children has 'suddenly developed a bad heart, & I have had doctors in and out, and have been generally perturbed' (BBC Written Archives Centre).

14 January 1938 Tolkien presumably records his talk at the BBC studio in London. Entitled *Anglo-Saxon Verse*, the sixth in the series *Poetry Will Out: Studies in National Inspiration and Characteristic Forms*, it is broadcast on the National Programme from 10.45 to 11.00 p.m.

16 January 1938 Hilary Full Term begins. Tolkien's scheduled lectures and classes for this term are: *Beowulf*: Text (continued) on Tuesdays at 11.00 a.m. in the Examination Schools, beginning 18 January; the Old English *Exodus* on Tuesdays and Thursdays at 12.00 noon in the Examination Schools, beginning 18 January; Old English Texts (Class: second year, Courses I and II) on Tuesdays at 5.15 p.m. at Pembroke College, beginning 18 January; and Old Norse Texts (Class) on Thursdays at 5.15 p.m. at Pembroke College, beginning 20 January. Tolkien will continue to supervise D.Phil. student K.R. Brooks. – A letter from 'Habit' is published in the *Observer*, asking about sources for *The Hobbit*.

18 January 1938 G.H. White of the Examination Schools writes to Tolkien, sending him a cutting of the 'Habit' letter in the *Observer*. He conveys the hope of everyone at the Schools that Tolkien will soon be well.

Between 18 January and 18 February 1938 Tolkien writes to the *Observer* in response to 'Habit'.

21 January 1938 The Committee for Comparative Philology, in Tolkien's absence, elects him a member of the Committee for the Nomination of Examiners for three years from Hilary Term 1938.

25 January 1938 Tolkien attends an English Faculty Library Committee meeting.

1 February 1938 Tolkien asks C.A. Furth to send him four more copies of *The Hobbit*. Furth has forwarded a letter from Houghton Mifflin with a cheque for the colour pictures. He asks Furth to 'ask Mr. Unwin whether his son, a very reliable critic, would care to read the first chapter of the sequel to *The Hobbit*? I have typed it. I have no confidence in it, but if he thought it a promising beginning, could add to it the tale that is brewing' (*Letters*, p. 28). Tolkien seems not to have proceeded beyond the several versions of the first chapter of *The Lord of the Rings*, but is considering how that story might develop.

4 February 1938 Tolkien attends an English Faculty Board meeting. The report of the committee on the First Public Examination is discussed, and after some amendment is referred to the original committee (including Tolkien) for re-drafting, for submission to the General Board. The committee (including Tolkien) set up on 3 December 1937 'to consider the list of Lecturers and Grants' presents its report; after amendment it is adopted and sent to the General Board. – Having heard from Stanley Unwin that Rayner would like to read the first chapter of *The Lord of the Rings*, Tolkien sends it to C.A. Furth. After receiving from a young reader a list of errata in *The Hobbit*, he has offered Christopher, while he is in bed with a bad heart, twopence each for any further errors he can find. Tolkien encloses a list from both sources in case they should be needed.

8 February 1938 W.G. Le Tall of Geoffrey Tyndale's Bookshop sends Tolkien his personal copy of *The Hobbit* to sign, and reports that his bookshop competition has had few entries. He asks Tolkien for six copies of the runic alphabet.

11 February 1938 Stanley Unwin writes to Tolkien, returning the first chapter of the *Hobbit* sequel. Rayner is delighted with it, but having publisher blood in him, he is concerned that a child who has not read *The Hobbit* and who picks up the sequel would be able to follow it and to appreciate it as much as he himself has. But that is easily dealt with, and Tolkien should proceed with his work.

13 February 1938 Tolkien's Aunt Florence Hadley in British Columbia writes to thank him for a copy of *The Hobbit*.

14 February 1938 Tolkien reads his revised version of *Farmer Giles of Ham* at a meeting of the Lovelace Society at Worcester College, Oxford in the evening. It is well received. Tolkien will later write that 'the audience was apparently not bored – indeed they were generally convulsed with mirth' (letter to C.A. Furth, 24 July 1938, *Letters*, p. 39). The meeting adjourns at 10.30 p.m. *See note.*

15 February 1938 C.A. Furth writes to Tolkien, returning the manuscript of *Mr. Bliss* with a sheet of instructions to show Tolkien the best procedure for redrawing its pictures. These are to be in three colours and black only.

17 February 1938 Tolkien writes to C.A. Furth. He wishes that Allen & Unwin could find someone to draw the pictures for *Mr. Bliss* properly. He does not think that he is capable of it himself. At any rate he is unlikely to be able to do anything before the Long Vacation, or the end of his 'research fellowship'. He is not sure what he can do with only three colours, and wonders why his pictures cannot be reproduced in full colour like those in Beatrix Potter's books. Is it too costly? He has done no more on the *Hobbit* sequel, which 'is still where it was, and I have only the vaguest notions of how to proceed' (*Letters*, p. 29). – In a separate letter he informs Allen & Unwin that Houghton Mifflin have not yet returned to him his five original watercolour paintings for *The Hobbit*.

18 February 1938 Tolkien writes to Stanley Unwin. He is encouraged by Rayner's approval, but at the moment the *Hobbit* sequel 'is not unfolding'. He has very little time to spend on it, and 'squandered so much on the original *Hobbit* (which was not meant to have a sequel) that it is difficult to find anything new in that world' (*Letters*, p. 29). C.S. Lewis has submitted *Out of the Silent Planet* to Allen & Unwin. Tolkien comments on it favourably.

?Late February–4 March 1938 Tolkien writes two more chapters of his *Hobbit* sequel: 'Three's Company and Four's More' (later to evolve into published bk. I, ch. 3), and an untitled chapter 'III' which brings the hobbit travellers to Buckland. Probably he also makes at this time the first (or earliest surviving) map of the Shire, and a rough sketch of the hobbits crossing the Brandywine (*Artist and Illustrator*, fig. 146). His manuscript drafts for the new chapters, written after 18 February, are rough and incomplete, with several versions of parts. He makes a typescript but immediately begins to revise 'Three's Company and Four's More', retyping some pages. In the draft manuscript for this chapter he includes a conversation about the Ring between Bingo and the elves the hobbits meet on the road, but omits it in the typescript; he decides that Gandalf should tell Bingo about the Ring and its history, and that this would be best placed in a foreword or separate chapter. He writes an early version of this new (but unnumbered and untitled) chapter, possibly even before writing 'III' but certainly before continuing the story at the end of August 1938.

19 February 1938 C.A. Furth writes to Tolkien. The present drawings for *Mr. Bliss* could be reproduced by the same process as Beatrix Potter's (colour halftone blocks), but would have to be printed on glossy paper. If Tolkien really finds that children do not mind glossy paper, he should return the manuscript of *Mr. Bliss*, and Allen & Unwin will work out costings for that process.

20 February 1938 Tolkien's reply to 'Habit' is printed in the *Observer*.

23 February 1938 Tolkien attends a meeting of the Governors of King Edward's School in Birmingham.

25 February 1938 Tolkien attends a Pembroke College meeting.

26 February 1938 Mabel Day, Secretary of the Early English Text Society, writes to remind Tolkien that he still has not sent the specimen pages asked for six months earlier.

1 March 1938 *The Hobbit* is published in the United States.

2 March 1938 Stanley Unwin sends Tolkien an extract from the first (unfavourable) reader's report on *Out of the Silent Planet*.

4 March 1938 Tolkien writes a long letter to Stanley Unwin in support of *Out of the Silent Planet*, though not without noting faults. In passing he mentions having read *Land under England* by Joseph O'Neill (1935) and *A Voyage to Arcturus* by David Lindsay (1920). He comments on the copy of the American edition of *The Hobbit* he has received: he is glad that they have included *Bilbo Woke* but cannot imagine why they have spoiled the picture of Rivendell 'by slicing the top and cutting out the ornament at the bottom.' He has now finished the third chapter of his *Hobbit* sequel, which has taken an 'unpremeditated turn' (probably that the hobbits are overtaken on the road not, as at first, by Gandalf, but by a Black Rider; *Letters*, p. 34). Both C.S. Lewis and Christopher Tolkien have read the story in serial form, and approve. Tolkien asks if Rayner would like to read it as well.

5 March 1938 Allen & Unwin having received from Houghton Mifflin the five colour illustrations for *The Hobbit*, now return them to him.

11 March 1938 At an English Faculty Board meeting, in Tolkien's absence, the Applications Committee reports that it has appointed Tolkien and David Nichol Smith examiners of the D.Phil. thesis of J.A.W. Bennett of Merton

College, *The History of Old English and Old Norse Studies in England from the Time of Junius till the End of the Eighteenth Century.*

12 March 1938 Hilary Full Term ends. – The Houghton Mifflin Company asks Tolkien for black and white drawings of hobbits for use in advertising, and one in colour for a poster. After trying out a rough sketch of a hobbit, Tolkien will reply: 'I am afraid, if you will need drawings of hobbits in various attitudes, I must leave it in the hands of someone who can draw' (*Letters*, p. 35). In this letter he will describe how he pictures hobbits, and explain that the text should include some mention of Bilbo acquiring boots, which he is shown wearing in some of illustrations in *The Hobbit.*

12–13 March 1938 Germany invades and annexes Austria.

16 March 1938 Stanley Unwin writes to Tolkien. He now has three readers' reports on *Out of the Silent Planet* and is waiting for a fourth. Rayner would love to read the *Hobbit* sequel in serial form.

Late March–?early April 1938 The Tolkien family take an early holiday at 'Aurora' in Sidmouth.

1 April 1938 Stanley Unwin writes to Tolkien. Only one out of five readers of *Out of the Silent Planet* thinks that it could be successful, but he is showing the work to John Lane at The Bodley Head (another publisher, of which Unwin is part owner).

24 April 1938 Trinity Full Term begins. Tolkien's scheduled lectures and classes for this term are: Outlines of Old English Phonology on Tuesdays and Thursdays at 12.00 noon in the Examination Schools, beginning 26 April; and Old Norse Texts (Elementary Class) on Wednesdays at 5.15 p.m. at Pembroke College, beginning 27 April. Tolkien will continue to supervise D.Phil. student K.R. Brooks. – During this term Tolkien is elected by the Faculty of English Language and Literature to serve on the General Board till Michaelmas Term 1941; he will be reappointed for further three-year terms in 1941 and 1944, and will be on the Board until Michaelmas Term 1947.

25 April 1938 Houghton Mifflin notify Tolkien by cablegram that *The Hobbit* has won the *New York Herald Tribune* prize of $250 for the best book for younger children published (in the United States) that spring. The award will be announced formally on 28 April.

?26 April 1938 Tolkien forwards to Stanley Unwin the cablegram from Houghton Mifflin. He also sends the first three typed chapters of the *Hobbit* sequel for Rayner to read. Both Rayner Unwin and Susan Dagnall will read them.

29 April 1938 Stanley Unwin writes to Tolkien. Allen & Unwin will use the cablegram from Houghton Mifflin for publicity purposes. Unwin asks Tolkien to expedite Elaine Griffiths' return of the Clark Hall *Beowulf* proofs, with the minimum corrections necessary for its use as a good crib. He looks forward to publishing Tolkien's own translation of *Beowulf* when it is ready. – In the evening, Tolkien attends a dinner of The Society hosted by J.R.H. Weaver at Trinity College, Oxford. Eleven members are present. Weaver discusses inconsistencies and anomalies in the awarding of honorary degrees.

3 May 1938 Stanley Unwin sends Tolkien a report by Rayner on the *Hobbit* sequel: 'I like the first chapter, the second and third have I think a little too much conversation and "hobbit talk" which tends to make it lag a little. Otherwise it seems very good, although it does not start as quickly as *The Hobbit*. But the black riders seem all right! What will it be called?' (Tolkien-George Allen & Unwin archive, HarperCollins). – Kenneth Sisam at Oxford University Press writes to Tolkien. They have E.O.G. Turville-Petre's edition of *Víga-Glúms Saga*, based on his 1934 B.Litt. thesis, in hand for publication in the *Oxford English Monographs* series (of which Tolkien is one of three general editors), but there will be a delay in printing as the Press needs to obtain a set of special characters for printing Icelandic. Sisam belatedly thanks Tolkien for a copy of his *Beowulf* lecture, which he praises.

13 May 1938 Tolkien attends an English Faculty Board meeting. He is appointed an elector to the Merton Professorship of English Literature until Michaelmas Term 1943; he will be reappointed for further terms or will serve *ex officio* until Michaelmas Term 1958, and will take part in elections in 1946 and 1957. He is also appointed an elector to the Taylorian Professorship of German Language and Literature until Michaelmas Term 1943, and will be reappointed until Michaelmas Term 1958; no election will take place during this period.

17 May 1938 The *New York Herald Tribune* awards are presented at a luncheon during the American Booksellers Association convention in New York City. A representative from Houghton Mifflin accepts the award for *The Hobbit* on Tolkien's behalf. When Tolkien receives the *Herald Tribune* cheque in the morning post, he will immediately pass it to his wife to pay an outstanding doctor's bill.

25 May 1938 Tolkien attends a meeting of the Governors of King Edward's School in Birmingham.

1 June 1938 Stanley Unwin informs Tolkien that Houghton Mifflin have sold three thousand copies of *The Hobbit* to date. He asks for news of the Clark Hall *Beowulf*. – Tolkien attends a Pembroke College meeting.

2 June 1938 The Reverend *Adam Fox, one of the Inklings, is elected Professor of Poetry at Oxford, having been nominated and supported by Tolkien and C.S. Lewis.

4 June 1938 Tolkien writes to Stanley Unwin. Rayner's opinion on 'hobbit talk' agrees with that of C.S. Lewis, though such talk privately amuses Tolkien himself 'and to a certain degree also my boy Christopher'. He says that he has been unable to work on the *Hobbit* sequel since 'the Christmas vacation' (probably an error for 'Easter vacation', see entry for 4 March 1938). He has 'three works in Middle English and Old English going to or through the press [probably the *Ancrene Wisse*, *Pearl*, and the Clark Hall *Beowulf*], and another in Old Norse in a series of which I am an editor under my hand [*Víga-Glúms Saga*]. ....' Also he has students coming from Belgium and Canada to work under his direction in July until the middle of August. When his Leverhulme Research Fellowship ends in September he will 'have to return to the examination treadmill to keep the boat afloat' (*Letters*, p. 36). He apologizes at length for the state of the Clark Hall *Beowulf*. Having declined Allen & Unwin's invitation to edit it himself, knowing that he would not have the time, he now realizes that he should have looked more carefully at Elaine Griffiths' proofs and not approved her work so hastily. He feels that she is capable of doing the work, but for various reasons she is unable to finish it. Tolkien could quickly write his own brief introductory note once he saw the book complete. He still has neither the time nor the inclination to undertake the revision himself (but see entry for 24 July 1938).

7 June 1938 Tolkien and David Nichol Smith examine J.A.W. Bennett of Merton College *viva voce* on his D.Phil. thesis, *The History of Old English and Old Norse Studies in England from the Time of Junius till the End of the Eighteenth Century*, at 2.30 p.m. in the Examination Schools.

9 June 1938 Tolkien and David Nichol Smith sign their report (written by Tolkien) on the examination of J.A.W. Bennett. – English Final Honour School examinations begin.

10 June 1938 Stanley Unwin writes to Tolkien. He regrets that Tolkien is unlikely to find much time for story-writing. He will write to Elaine Griffiths concerning the Clark Hall volume.

17 June 1938 Tolkien attends an English Faculty Board meeting. – He also attends a Pembroke College meeting. – He possibly attends a meeting of the Committee for Comparative Philology at 5.15 p.m. in the Board Room of the Clarendon Building.

18 June 1938 Trinity Full Term ends.

21 June 1938 A gaudy is held at Pembroke College. The Master and Fellows entertain guests in the Hall.

22 June 1938 Encaenia. – Tolkien attends a Pembroke College meeting.

29 June 1938 C.A. Furth of George Allen & Unwin writes to Tolkien. Elaine Griffiths has asked to be released from her contract for the Clark Hall *Beowulf*. Furth asks Tolkien to suggest a student to finish the work.

July–13 August 1938 Tolkien works at pressure with Simonne d'Ardenne, presumably on their edition of *Seinte Katerine*, and with *W. Meredith Thompson from Winnipeg on *Wohunge* and related Middle English manuscripts (see *Katherine Group).

22 July 1938 Rütten & Loening Verlag of Potsdam, who are interested in publishing a German translation of *The Hobbit*, write to Tolkien. They ask if he is of 'arisch' origin – by which they mean, not of Jewish descent.

24 July 1938 Tolkien writes to C.A. Furth. He cannot recommend another student to complete work on the Clark Hall *Beowulf*. He is now inclined to feel that this is not a student's job after all. He suggests that he should visit Furth after about 13 August to discuss this and other matters. 'My suggestion will probably be that you allow me to put the thing into such order as is now possible, for such remuneration as seems good to you, with a title to be devised. I should prefer on the whole not to be mentioned, or to put too much new stuff into it, to the prejudice of my own "translation"' (Tolkien-George Allen &

Unwin archive, HarperCollins). – After going to Reading on business, Tolkien writes again to C.A. Furth. Pressure of research under the Leverhulme Grant 'has taken all my time, and also dried up invention. The sequel to *The Hobbit* has remained where it stopped. It has lost my favour, and I have no idea what to do with it' (Tolkien-George Allen & Unwin archive, HarperCollins). He offers Allen & Unwin his rewritten *Farmer Giles of Ham* instead, although this now has a more adult and satiric flavour, and he has not written any stories to accompany it. There is also *Mr. Bliss* but he does not think he can do anything to improve it.

25 July 1938 Tolkien sends the letter from Rütten & Loening to Stanley Unwin. 'Do I suffer this impertinence because of the possession of a German name, or do their [Germany's] lunatic laws require a certificate of "arisch" origin from all persons of all countries? . . . I do not regard the (probable) absence of all Jewish blood as necessarily honourable; and I have many Jewish friends, and should regret giving any colour to the notion that I subscribed to the wholly pernicious and unscientific race-doctrine' (Tolkien-George Allen & Unwin archive, HarperCollins). But for Allen & Unwin's sake he will not jeopardize a German translation without their approval. He sends two drafts of a reply to Rütten & Loening, and leaves it to Unwin to choose which to post. In the first he vents his true feelings, though feigns confusion as to the publisher's meaning:

> I regret that I am not clear as to what you intend by *arisch*. I am not of *Aryan* extraction: that is Indo-Iranian; as far as I am aware none of my ancestors spoke Hindustani, Persian, Gypsy, or any related dialects. But if I am to understand that you are enquiring whether I am of *Jewish* origin, I can only reply that I regret that I appear to have *no* ancestors of that gifted people. My great-great-grandfather came to England in the eighteenth century from Germany: the main part of my descent is therefore purely English, and I am an English subject – which should be sufficient. I have been accustomed, nonetheless, to regard my German name with pride, and continued to do so throughout the period of the late regrettable war, in which I served in the English army. I cannot, however, forbear to comment that if impertinent and irrelevant enquiries of this sort are to become the rule in matters of literature, then the time is not far distant when a German name will no longer be a source of pride. [*Letters*, pp. 37–8]

Unwin will choose to send the second letter, which is probably shorter and more temperate.

27 July 1938 Tolkien replies to a letter from *John Masefield, who has invited him to impersonate Geoffrey Chaucer and recite the 'Nun's Priest's Tale' (from the *Canterbury Tales*) in the 1938 *'Summer Diversions' in Oxford. In regard to lines of verse with which Masefield proposes to introduce him, Tolkien comments that they seem 'to allude to the erroneous imagination that Chaucer was the first English poet, and that before and except for him all was dumb and barbaric' (*Letters*, p. 39). He will do his best to recite the 'Nun's Priest's Tale' in a supposed fourteenth-century pronunciation, though he thinks 'that a modified modern pronunciation (restoring rhymes but otherwise avoiding archaism) is the best – such as I once heard you use on the Monk's Tale a good many years ago' (*Letters*, p. 40).

28 July 1938 Stanley Unwin writes to Tolkien. Tolkien's letters of 25 July 'have been a source of much merriment and satisfaction at this office' (Tolkien-George Allen & Unwin archive, HarperCollins). He explains that under law a German publisher must produce a certificate that the author of the work to be published is not Jewish. He has sent to Rütten & Loening Tolkien's second letter, which he thinks most suitable.

29 July 1938 E.V. Gordon dies. Tolkien now begins to help in the settling of Gordon's affairs and academic obligations. He will finish setting the papers for the 1938 New Zealand Honours examinations, and will make some revisions to the edition of *Pearl* in Middle English with which he was collaborating with Gordon to some extent, and which Gordon had nearly completed.

3 August 1938 Tolkien takes part in the Summer Diversions organized by John Masefield and Nevill Coghill at the Oxford Playhouse. In the first half of the programme he recites, from memory, Chaucer's 'Nun's Priest's Tale' in the guise of the fourteenth-century poet, wearing a green robe, turban, and liripipe, and with a centrally parted beard. The *Oxford Mail* of 4 August 1938 will report that

Prof. Tolkien, wearing a beard and the resplendent robes of the 14th century and speaking into a 20th-century microphone, was a spectacle in himself.

One can only stand amazed at his bravery in reciting without manuscript a Canterbury Tale, slightly cut, it is true, but still fraught with endless perils and difficulties for the speaker.

The audience were at first a little scared of Chaucer's Middle English, but not for long. Prof. Tolkien spoke his lines magnificently, and there can have been none present who were unable to enjoy the beauty and the subtlety and the wit of the first Poet Laureate's work. ['"Gammer Gurton" at Oxford Diversions: With Chaucer's "Nonnes Preestes Tale," Spoken in Middle English by Prof. J.R.R. Tolkien', p. 6]

– C.A. Furth writes to Tolkien. Allen & Unwin would be happy to accept Tolkien's offer to work on the Clark Hall *Beowulf*, and suggests a possible remuneration.

8 August 1938 C.A. Furth writes to Tolkien. It seems that *Mr. Bliss* will have to be the next book by Tolkien that is published by Allen & Unwin, but it is now too late to do so for Christmas 1938. They will ask him for the manuscript next spring.

9 August 1938 Tolkien writes to C.A. Furth. He has to go to Walthamstow on 10 August, and will call on Allen & Unwin in the afternoon on the chance that he can talk with Furth. He was summoned to Walthamstow 'on a melancholy errand to the Connaught Hospital' only a few hours earlier, so could not give more notice (Tolkien-George Allen & Unwin archive, HarperCollins). He has had a reply from Rütten & Loening which he would like help in answering.

10 August 1938 Tolkien visits the Connaught Hospital, Walthamstow, and C.A. Furth at George Allen & Unwin in London.

11 August 1938 Tolkien writes to John Masefield. He enjoyed hearing his *Letter from Pontus* which Masefield read in the Summer Diversions, as well as the prologue and epilogues. He asks for a copy of them.

12 August 1938 John Johnson of Oxford University Press sends Tolkien, at Mabel Day's request, specimen pages for the Early English Text Society edition of the Corpus Christi College manuscript of the *Ancrene Riwle*.

14 August 1938 Simonne d'Ardenne writes to Tolkien, commenting on the various lives of St Katherine she has read in the British Museum.

Last half of August 1938 Tolkien is unwell, so depressed by troubles that he reaches the edge of a nervous breakdown. He is ordered to rest by his doctor and unable to do anything for a week or two.

c. **28–30 August 1938** Tolkien resumes work on *The Lord of the Rings*, beginning apparently with manuscript additions to the typescript of the third chapter, and extending as far as the seventh chapter, which begins with the hobbits' arrival at Bree. He has little difficulty (as it seems from the extant manuscripts) in writing at least the first three of these new chapters, though the story continues to change and evolve, and new ideas come to Tolkien in the process. When he reaches the point at which the hobbits have been captured by the Barrow-wight, he makes a rough plot outline for the story as far as their arrival at Rivendell, with a brief mention of the discussions to be held there, and already foresees a journey to the Fiery Mountain (Mount Doom). At this time he possibly also makes the finished drawing *Old Man Willow* (*Artist and Illustrator*, fig. 147).

31 August 1938 Tolkien writes to C.A. Furth about his illness since 10 August and his period of enforced rest. He is now beginning to feel better. He asks about German and French translations of *The Hobbit*, and encloses a cutting about actress Shirley Temple's interest in that book. He sends a copy of the enlarged version of *Farmer Giles of Ham*, which he has had typed by the Academic Copying Office in Oxford, though he realizes that it is not long enough to be published alone. He has planned a sequel, though the story 'does not need one', and he has 'an unfinished pseudo-Celtic fairy-story of a mildly satirical order . . . called the *King of the Green Dozen*' (see *Celtic influences) which he might complete if *Farmer Giles* seems to Allen & Unwin 'worthy of print and companionship'. 'In the last two or three days,' he adds, 'after the benefit of idleness and open air, and the sanctioned neglect of duty, I have begun again on the sequel to the "Hobbit" – The Lord of the Ring [*sic*]. It is now flowing along, and getting quite out of hand. It has now reached Chapter VII and progresses towards quite unforeseen goals' (*Letters*, p. 40). He asks Furth's indulgence concerning the Clark Hall *Beowulf* for a while; he would relinquish it if he knew anyone who could do the job properly.

1–15 September 1938 The Tolkien family take a holiday at Sidmouth. Tolkien evidently is able to work a great deal on *The Lord of the Rings*, and probably finishes what Christopher Tolkien will later call the 'First Phase', breaking off in the middle of Bingo's conversation with the dwarf Glóin during the feast at Rivendell. He has more difficulty in writing the original seventh chapter (later 'At the Sign of the Prancing Pony', 'Strider', and the beginning of 'A Knife in the Dark', bk. I, ch. 9–11 as published), crossing out sections, overwriting pencil in ink, and adding riders. As he is undecided whether the landlord or Trotter is to give Gandalf's letter to Bingo, and uncertain of the movements of the Black Riders, he writes two versions of part of the chapter. He drafts the eighth chapter in pencil (to the end of 'A Knife in the Dark' and 'Flight to the Ford', bk. I, ch. 11–12 as published), then three beginnings of the ninth chapter (later 'Many Meetings', published bk. II, ch. 1) in ink and pencil, the first before overwriting all or most of the pencil draft of the eighth chapter in ink, much of it close to the published text. Tolkien probably writes all of this at Sidmouth and then falters, making notes considering what might follow and writing two pages headed *Queries and Alterations*. He has doubts about some of the story he has written and is considering possible changes. He is beginning to query the character Trotter and his history; and as he ponders the powers and history of Bingo's ring the idea that it is the Ruling Ring begins to emerge. He will decide to revise or rewrite as necessary the chapters already written. Within the eighth chapter he makes a small sketch plan of Bree and the East Road (*The Return of the Shadow*, p. 335), and he rewrites the poem *Light as Leaf on Lindentree* for Trotter to recite under Weathertop.

3 September 1938 C.A. Furth writes to Tolkien. Allen & Unwin have not yet been able to arrange for a French translation of *The Hobbit*, but the German contracts are signed and the German publisher is awaiting permission to remit the advance payment. He offers to send Tolkien his share of the advance immediately, anticipating the arrival of payment from Germany.

?Late September–?early October 1938 Tolkien revises *The Lord of the Rings* (the 'Second Phase' as later described by Christopher Tolkien) as far as the end of the chapter in which the hobbits stay with Tom Bombadil. He makes changes to the story and alters his cast of hobbits, now introducing Sam Gamgee. He substantially rewrites the first three chapters of the book, some sections more than once or with variant texts; elsewhere changes are fewer, and he cannibalizes pages earlier produced. He adds a new second chapter, 'Ancient History' (later 'The Shadow of the Past', published bk. I, ch. 2), in which Gandalf tells Bingo about the Ring and Gollum, and advises Bingo to leave the Shire. Tolkien subdivides the original third chapter, with the titles 'A Short Cut to Mushrooms' and 'A Conspiracy Unmasked' (bk. I, ch. 4–5 as published). For the fourth and fifth chapters he merely emends the original text and inserts a section about the Black Riders' attack on Crickhollow.

28 September 1938 Tolkien attends a Pembroke College meeting.

28–30 September 1938 The British Prime Minister Neville Chamberlain attends the Munich Conference with Hitler, Mussolini, and Deladier of France. On his return to Britain he declares that an agreement he has signed with Hitler will mean 'peace in our time'.

7 October 1938 Tolkien attends a meeting of the General Board. He is elected to the Standing Committee on Pass Examinations.

9 October 1938 Michaelmas Full Term begins. Tolkien's scheduled lectures for this term are: *Beowulf*: Historical and Legendary Allusions on Tuesdays at 11.00 a.m. in the Examination Schools, beginning 11 October; Language of the Vespasian Hymns on Tuesdays at 12.00 noon in the Examination Schools, beginning 11 October; *Atlakviða* on Thursdays at 11.00 a.m. in the Examination Schools, beginning 13 October; and Outlines of Old Icelandic Phonology on Thursdays at 12.00 noon in the Examination Schools, beginning 13 October. Tolkien will continue to supervise D.Phil. candidate K.R. Brooks.

10 October 1938 Simonne d'Ardenne writes to Tolkien. She complains about Hitler but is hoping for the best. She is sending him her copy of Sweet's *Anglo-Saxon Primer* which Tolkien has promised to emend for her students. She encloses a copy of her review of *Les poèmes mythologiques de l'Edda*, translated by Félix Wagner (1936) and asks if Tolkien approves of it. She also asks him (once more) to read for comment her article on the Brussels Cross when she has finished it ('The Old English Inscription on the Brussels Cross', *English Studies* (Amsterdam) 21 (1939)).

12 October 1938 Tolkien attends a Pembroke College meeting.

13 October 1938 Tolkien writes to Stanley Unwin that because of other commitments and ill health he has not been able to work on the Clark Hall *Beowulf*. He suggests that the task be passed to C.L. Wrenn, the University Lecturer in English Language at Oxford, who is willing to tackle it at once and who is known for his punctuality.

14 October 1938 In the evening, Tolkien attends a dinner of The Society hosted by G.R.G. Mure at Merton College, Oxford. Eleven members are present. Mure begins a conversation on the University and the European situation, some of which the members find unsettling.

Mid-October–December 1938 Probably at about this time Tolkien returns to the beginning of the story once more (the 'Third Phase' as later described by Christopher Tolkien), making a new fair copy manuscript of the whole work as far as the conversation between Frodo (replacing Bingo) and Glóin at Rivendell from the chaotic existing texts: this incorporates many small changes and moves generally closer to the published text. There are only a few important narrative changes, mainly concerning the cast of hobbits, in particular the part played by Odo Bolger (much of which will be later discarded). In places Tolkien tries out several versions of new or revised material before he is satisfied. He writes a new text to provide background information about Hobbits, which he calls the 'Foreword' (precursor of the Prologue in the published book), into which he moves some material already written. Soon after its completion, he changes its conclusion and adds an account of Bilbo's encounter with Gollum in *The Hobbit*, and then makes a typescript copy. By this point, as he will write to C.A. Furth of Allen & Unwin on 2 February 1939, the work had 'reached Chapter 12 (and had been re-written several times), running to over 300 [manuscript] pages of the same size as this paper and written generally as closely' (*Letters*, pp. 41–2). During this phase Tolkien also draws family trees of the Bagginses, Tooks, Bolgers, and Brandybucks among the Hobbits, and makes a sketch plan of Bree, the Greenway, and the East Road.

18 October 1938 Stanley Unwin writes to Tolkien. He understands and sympathizes with his problems. Allen & Unwin have written to C.L. Wrenn concerning the Clark Hall *Beowulf*.

21 October 1938 Tolkien attends a General Board meeting.

27 October 1938 Lascelles Abercrombie dies.

28 October 1938 Tolkien attends an English Faculty Board meeting. Tribute is paid to Lascelles Abercrombie. Tolkien is re-elected to the Standing Committee on Applications.

November 1938 *The Coloured Lands* by G.K. Chesterton is published. Tolkien will immediately make use of it for his lecture *On Fairy-Stories*.

2 November 1938 Tolkien attends a Pembroke College meeting.

4 November 1938 At a General Board meeting, in Tolkien's absence, the report of the Standing Committee on Pass Examinations (including Tolkien) is presented.

9 November 1938 Tolkien attends a Pembroke College meeting.

18 November 1938 Tolkien attends a General Board meeting.

19 November 1938 Tolkien adds a note to a page of the early ('First Phase') manuscript of *The Lord of the Rings* where Trotter hands Bingo a letter from Gandalf. Presumably Tolkien has now reached this point in revising and rewriting the existing texts.

22 November 1938 F.E. Harmer of the University of Manchester writes to Tolkien, sending an offprint of her article 'Anglo Saxon Charters and the Historian' for the *Bulletin of the John Rylands Library* (October 1938). She likes Tolkien's *Beowulf* lecture more every time she reads it.

24 November 1938 Tolkien attends an English Faculty Library Committee meeting.

2 December 1938 Tolkien attends an English Faculty Board meeting at which he is appointed to a committee on the needs of the Faculty. He also attends a General Board meeting.

3 December 1938 Michaelmas Full Term ends.

6 December 1938 The Early English Text Society Committee appoints Tolkien to that body, his membership having been proposed by the Director. The *Ancrene Riwle* subcommittee has agreed to have a sample of the Corpus Christi College text printed in a line-by-line transcription and with expanded abbreviations. The Committee gives permission to Professor Tolkien and Simonne d'Ardenne to submit an edition of *Seinte Katerine*.

Christmas 1938 Tolkien, as 'Father Christmas', writes a short letter to 'My dear Priscilla and all others at your house'. He apologizes that he has not had time to draw a large picture, but instead sends some rhymes. These are accompanied by decorations in the margins and added comments as from the North Polar Bear, and a drawing of Father Christmas in his sleigh entitled *Setting Out*, all of which surely took no little time to complete. In fact they are not finished by Christmas Day. In another short letter, dated Boxing Day (26 December), Father Christmas writes that by mistake, his letter as well as a book for Priscilla had not been sent. The accompanying envelope is inscribed 'Deliver Xmas Day if possible', 'despatched 8 pm 26 December', and 'Sorry I forgot, FC [Father Christmas]'. – Tolkien spends much of his Christmas vacation marking New Zealand Honours examination papers in place of E.V. Gordon.

?End of 1938–January 1939 Tolkien is ill with influenza.

1939

1939 Tolkien becomes a vice-president of the Philological Society, a position he will hold until 1970–1. – C.S. Lewis twice sees the animated film *Snow White and the Seven Dwarfs* in the cinema (premiered in Britain in 1938). On the second occasion he is accompanied by Tolkien, who finds Snow White to be beautiful but dislikes the Disney Studio's treatment of the dwarfs.

January 1939 Invited to do so, Tolkien agrees to work in the cryptography department of the Foreign Office in the event of war.

4 January 1939 C.L. Wrenn sends to Allen & Unwin the introduction and first 450 lines of the Clark Hall *Beowulf*. Noting the chaotic state of the work and proofs he has inherited, he asks for more time to complete his task.

6 January 1939 C.A. Furth of George Allen & Unwin replies to Wrenn, agreeing that he should have more time. Furth wonders if it might not be cheaper to reset the Clark Hall volume entirely, and asks if Tolkien has made any progress with the preface he is still expected to write for it.

7 January 1939 Wrenn tells C.A. Furth that he will mention the preface to Tolkien.

13 January 1939 Tolkien attends a General Board meeting. The Board votes to ask the Standing Committee on Pass Examinations (of which Tolkien is a member) to reconsider the regulations for examinations under the supervision of the Board.

15 January 1939 Hilary Full Term begins. Tolkien's scheduled lectures for this term are: *Andreas* on Tuesdays and Thursdays at 11.00 a.m. in the Examination Schools, beginning 17 January; and *Deor's Lament, Völundarkviða* on Tuesdays at 12.00 noon in the Examination Schools, beginning 17 January. Tolkien had been scheduled to lecture on Old English Historical Grammar (Inflexions) on Thursdays at 12.00 noon in the Examination Schools, but is replaced by C.E. Bazell. He will continue to supervise D.Phil. student K.R. Brooks.

18 January 1939 Tolkien attends a Pembroke College meeting.

24 January 1939 C.A. Furth writes to Tolkien, suggesting that if little progress with the *Hobbit* sequel has been made during the Christmas vacation, Allen & Unwin ought now to try to solve the technical problems that have prevented publication of *Mr. Bliss*.

20 January 1939 In the evening, Tolkien attends a dinner of The Society hosted by John Sparrow at All Souls College, Oxford. Twelve members are present. Sparrow describes an 'Oxford accident' in 1830–1, involving Mark Pattison, later Rector of Lincoln College.

2 February 1939 Tolkien replies to C.A. Furth. He estimates that *The Lord of the Rings* will require at least another 200 manuscript pages to complete, and asks the latest date by which the completed manuscript ought to reach Allen & Unwin. 'I am at the "peak" of my educational financial stress, with a second son [Michael] clamouring for a university and the youngest [Christopher] wanting to go to school (after a year under heart-specialists), and I am obliged to do exams and lectures and what not.' He has just recovered from influenza. He wonders if Allen & Unwin should consider *Mr. Bliss* or *Farmer Giles of Ham* as his next work to be published. He finds *The Lord of the Rings* 'in itself a good deal better than *The Hobbit*, but it may not prove a very fit sequel. It is more grown-up – but the audience for which *The Hobbit* was written has done that also.' Although his eldest son is enthusiastic about the new work, 'it would be a relief to me to know that my publishers were satisfied. . . . The writing of *The Lord of the Rings* is laborious, because I have been doing it as well as I know how, and considering every word. . . . In spare time it would be easier and quicker to write up the plots already composed of the more lighthearted stories of the Little Kingdom to go with *Farmer Giles*. But I would rather finish the long tale, and not let it go cold' (*Letters*, p. 42).

3 February 1939 Tolkien attends an English Faculty Board meeting. The committee, including Tolkien, appointed on 2 December 1938 to consider the needs of the Faculty presents its report (dated 26 January 1939). The report is adopted, and Tolkien is appointed to a committee to draft 'a reasoned statement' on it for submission to the General Board (Oxford University Archives FA 4/5/1/1).

8 February 1939 C.A. Furth writes to Tolkien. The middle of June 1939 is the latest date that Allen & Unwin can receive the *Hobbit* sequel for Christmas publication. They would prefer to publish *The Lord of the Rings* before *Mr. Bliss* and *Farmer Giles of Ham*, and would like to see what Tolkien has written so far. He sends accounts and a royalty payment for 1938, and offers Tolkien an advance on royalties for *The Hobbit* due from Houghton Mifflin.

10 February 1939 Tolkien attends a General Board meeting. – He replies to C.A. Furth that the advance 'was rather a welcome tonic'. Influenza has not damaged him much, 'though it caught me in a state of exam-exhaustion; but my throat seems to be getting worse, and I don't feel very bright'. He vows to 'make a special effort, at the expense of other duties', to finish off *The Lord of the Rings* before 15 June, and to have it typed to send to his publisher. He asks if Allen & Unwin have heard from the German publisher who had promised to let him read their translation of *The Hobbit*: he is concerned that odd things will happen to it, especially alterations of nomenclature. He asks also for comments on the enlarged *Farmer Giles of Ham*. Should he complete its sequel, or write other stories of the Little Kingdom? 'I just wonder whether this local family game played in the country just round us is more than silly' (*Letters*, p. 43). *See note.*

11 February 1939 C.A. Furth writes to Tolkien. He has told the German publisher of *The Hobbit* that Tolkien would like to see a proof of the translation. Although personally Furth likes *Farmer Giles of Ham* very much, it presents marketing problems because it does not fall into any firm category, neither a 'juvenile' nor 'fiction'. He thinks that such a 'sport' would do better after the *Hobbit* sequel is published and Tolkien is a more established author (Tolkien-George Allen & Unwin archive, HarperCollins). – Furth's remark about the difficulty of categorizing *Farmer Giles of Ham* possibly inspires Tolkien to include a comment in the second manuscript of *On Fairy-Stories*: 'Grown-ups writing fairy-stories for grown-ups are not popular with publishers or book-sellers. They have got to find a niche. To call their works *fairy-tales* places them at once as *juvenilia*; but if a glance at their contents shows that that *will* not do, then where are you?' (Tolkien Papers, Bodleian Library, Oxford).

15 February 1939 Tolkien attends a Pembroke College meeting.

16 February 1939 Tolkien attends an Early English Text Society Committee meeting at University College, London.

18 February 1939 C.A. Furth writes to Tolkien. The Germans will not publish *The Hobbit* until the autumn, but have promised to let Tolkien see a proof. – R. Cary Gilson dies.

24 February 1939 Tolkien attends a General Board meeting.

25 February 1939 Tolkien attends a Pembroke College meeting.

8 March 1939 In the evening, Tolkien delivers the Andrew Lang Lecture, *On Fairy-Stories*, in the United College Hall at the University of St Andrews, Scotland. While in St Andrews he enjoys the hospitality of educator T.M. Knox.

10 March 1939 Tolkien attends an English Faculty Board meeting. The Board approves a statement submitted by Tolkien on the needs of the Faculty, for submission to the General Board. This includes requests for the establishment of a statutory lectureship in English Literature and a lectureship in Icelandic. – Tolkien also attends a General Board meeting.

11 March 1939 Hilary Full Term ends.

?Mid-March 1939 Tolkien visits Cambridge, probably to see the manuscript of the *Ancrene Wisse*. While there he amuses the children of *H.S. (Stanley) Bennett of the Cambridge English School with *Farmer Giles of Ham*.

27 March 1939 Tolkien begins a four-day training course in cryptography at the Foreign Office.

31 March 1939 Britain and France pledge their support to Poland in the event of war.

21 April 1939 Tolkien attends a Pembroke College meeting. – He also attends a General Board meeting.

23 April 1939 Trinity Full Term begins. Tolkien's scheduled lectures and classes for this term are: Outlines of Old English Phonology on Tuesdays and Thursdays at 12.00 noon in the Examination Schools, beginning 25 April; and Old Norse (Elementary Class) on Wednesdays at 5.30 p.m. at Pembroke College, beginning 26 April. He will continue to supervise D.Phil. student K.R. Brooks.

26 April 1939 Tolkien attends a Pembroke College meeting.

28 April 1939 In the evening, Tolkien attends a dinner of The Society hosted by Kenneth Sisam at Merton College, Oxford. Fourteen members are present. Sisam speaks about the Oxford University Press.

29 April 1939 Britain reintroduces conscription for men from age twenty.

5 May 1939 Tolkien attends a General Board meeting.

6 May 1939 Tolkien writes to R.W. Chambers, who has sent a copy of *Man's Unconquerable Mind*, a collection of Chambers' essays and lectures. Tolkien's bookshelves are now 'well-endowed with your generous gifts, yet there are I think 2 studies in the volume that I do not possess, and have not read ...' (reproduced in Caroline Chabot, 'Raymond Wilson Chambers (1874–1942)', *Moreana* 24, no. 94 (June 1987), p. 93).

12 May 1939 Tolkien attends an English Faculty Board meeting.

19 May 1939 Tolkien attends a General Board meeting.

June 1939 From at least this month Tolkien is again on the Executive Committee of the Society for the Study of Mediæval Languages and Literature, until some time in 1948–9.

8 June 1939 English Final Honour School examinations begin. Among the successful candidates is Tolkien's eldest son, John.

12–13 June 1939 A single candidate for the Diploma in Comparative Philology sits his examinations. Tolkien, *G.E.K. Braunholtz (Professor of Comparative Philology), and C.L. Wrenn are the examiners.

14 June 1939 Tolkien attends a Pembroke College meeting.

16 June 1939 Tolkien attends an English Faculty Board meeting. The Board accepts the resignation of C.L. Wrenn from his University Lectureship in English Language as from 31 December 1939; Tolkien is appointed to a committee to recommend an appointment at the next meeting of the Board. Probably at this meeting he is also appointed to the Committee for Nomination of Examiners in the Honour School of English Language and Literature and Pass School Group B until Michaelmas Term 1942. – The Committee for Comparative Philology meets at 5.15 p.m. in the Delegates Room of the Clarendon Building. The members decide that in the future they will meet at 2.00 p.m. on the third and eighth Thursdays in term. Tolkien will write up the minutes for this meeting.

17 June 1939 Trinity Full term ends.

21 June 1939 Encaenia. – Stanley Unwin writes to Tolkien, asking about the progress of *The Lord of the Rings*.

28 June 1939 Tolkien attends a meeting of the governors of King Edward's School in Birmingham.

Summer 1939 W. Meredith Thompson visits Oxford to continue work with Tolkien on *Wohunge* and related manuscripts.

7 July 1939 Tolkien receives a letter from John Masefield, inviting him to take part again in the 'Summer Diversions'.

14 July 1939 Tolkien replies to John Masefield. He has considered several of the *Canterbury Tales* for suitability and adaptability to the right length, and has also looked at some of the works of John Gower (1325?–1408), but was interrupted by the urgent task of marking Civil Service examination papers. He has come to the conclusion that either he should repeat the 'Nun's Priest's Tale' that he read in 1938, or he should recite a reduced version of the *'Reeve's Tale'. He suggests how the latter might be reduced and recited in the Northern dialect on which he once remarked (see *Chaucer as a Philologist: The Reeve's Tale*).

Second half of July 1939 Masefield decides in favour of Tolkien reciting the 'Reeve's Tale'. Tolkien prepares the text for his reading, which is published as a pamphlet, presumably for the audience on 28 July.

26 July 1939 Tolkien attends a meeting of the governors of King Edward's School in Birmingham.

28 July 1939 Tolkien takes part in the 'Summer Diversions' in the Cooperative Hall, Oxford, again appearing as Chaucer in full costume and beard, but this year speaks without a microphone. In addition to Tolkien's recitation of the 'Reeve's Tale' (from memory), the programme includes performances by the Legat School of Dancing and a prologue, poems, and epilogue spoken by John Masefield. The *Oxford Mail* will report on 29 July (final page) that Tolkien performed

> superbly, and it is a lasting tribute to him that he barely once faltered. One can only deeply regret the abbreviations that were made in the text. It seems an unjust criticism of an Oxford audience to indicate with such bluntness that they are not broadminded enough to accept the distinctly broad humour of Chaucer in a story of his which can least afford to be cut because of the amazingly ingenious way in which the plot is worked out. Nobody would deny that the 'Reeve's Tale' loses by abbreviation. ['Canterbury Tale and Ballet: Oxford Performances of Summer Diversions', final page]

?August 1939 Tolkien has an accident, resulting in concussion and requiring stitches. (Priscilla Tolkien has suggested to us that this occurred while her family was visiting an old school friend of Edith Tolkien on a farm in Worcestershire.)

August–autumn 1939 Tolkien's accident leaves him unwell for a long time, 'and that combined with the anxieties and troubles that all share [with the outbreak of war], and with the lack of any holiday, and with the virtual headship of a department in this bewildered university have made me unpardonably neglectful' (letter to Stanley Unwin, 19 December 1939, *Letters*, p. 44). Edith Tolkien is also ill through summer and autumn 1939. Nonetheless, Tolkien now continues to work on *The Lord of the Rings*.

In August he produces rough and sometimes confusing papers containing 'plot-outlines, questionings, and portions of the text' which show the author temporarily 'at a halt, even at a loss, to the point of a lack of confidence in radical components of the narrative structure that had been built up with such pains' (Christopher Tolkien, *The Return of the Shadow* (1988), p. 370). He considers, *inter alia*, a version once more with Bilbo as the hero, that the hobbit Trotter is actually Bilbo's cousin Peregrin Boffin, that a dragon should invade the Shire, and that Frodo should meet the 'Giant Treebeard'; and he accurately foresees final elements of the story yet to be written: a snowstorm in the pass over the mountains, the Mines of Moria, the loss of Gandalf, a siege, that Frodo will find himself unable to destroy the Ring, that Gollum will seize it and fall, the devastation of the Shire.

Tolkien now (*see note*) picks up the story from the point at which he had abandoned it in earlier workings: Bingo/Frodo's conversation with Glóin at the feast in Rivendell. After several false starts he completes a version of 'The Council of Elrond' (published bk. II, ch. 2), still far from its final form, in which the Fellowship consists of Gandalf, Boromir, and five hobbits, one of whom is Peregrin Boffin (alias Trotter). Following on from this he writes a first version of 'The Ring Goes South' (published bk. II, ch. 3), at great speed and probably *ab initio* as a full narrative, without making any preliminary notes or sketches, not even bothering to strike through rejected passages, though not long after this is finished he emends it in pencil; and then with equal speed he writes a two-page sketch of the episode in Moria (foreseeing the loss of Gandalf, and his return), followed by a first draft of 'The Mines of Moria' (published bk. II, ch. 4, 'A Journey in the Dark'). On the final page of the manuscript he draws the inscription on Balin's tomb, first in the Old English runes used in *The Hobbit*, then in his own runic alphabet, the *Cirth* (*Writing systems); and on the verso of the sheet he makes the first sketch of 'A Page of Balin's Book' (the book from which Gandalf reads in the Chamber of Mazarbul). At the same time, he draws a working map of the lands south of the Carrock to Rohan and Fangorn Forest (*The Return of the Shadow*, p. 439), and probably also a sketch of the West Gate of Moria with the Misty Mountains behind, and a finished drawing of a more distant view (*Artist and Illustrator*, figs. 148–149), neither of which agrees with any surviving text.

In this phase of writing Tolkien also substantially revises his account of the journey to Rivendell told in Book I of *The Lord of the Rings*. He wishes to clarify Gandalf's part in events, especially his delayed reappearance, and to this end makes many outlines, notes, and time-schemes co-ordinating events and the movements of Gandalf, the Black Riders, and Frodo and his companions. He heads one note 'Final decisions. Oct. 8 1939', but emends, and in the writing rejects, much of it. Another page of rough notes, much emended, dated

'Autumn 1939' and headed 'New Plot', explains that Gandalf was delayed by Black Riders who besieged him in a 'Western Tower'. In both of these dated notes, Tolkien decides that Trotter is not a Hobbit but a Man, and subsequently makes the necessary changes in Book I.

Tolkien now emends his earlier manuscript with corrections, additions, and inserted riders, and makes drafts for new or replacement sections of the text (the 'Fourth Phase' as later described by Christopher Tolkien). He writes out fair copies of those parts of the manuscript that are most altered, and combines these with portions that are unrevised. A fair copy of a long chapter, 'At the Sign of the Prancing Pony' (encompassing bk. I, ch. 9–10 as published), is dated 'Revised Version Oct. 1939'. At this time Tolkien writes at least the first four lines of Bilbo's verse about Aragorn (the true name of 'Trotter') which appears in Gandalf's letter, and Sam's song about Gil-galad; and he revises the poem *Light as Leaf on Lindentree* and the 'Troll Song' (*The Stone Troll*) to be sung by Sam in Book I, Chapter 11. When Tolkien finishes this work the text for Book I of *The Lord of the Rings* is substantially that which eventually will be published. It is possibly in connection with this rewriting that Tolkien makes new versions of the Baggins, Brandybuck, and Took family trees, and the first version of the Boffin family tree.

23 August 1939 Britain warns Germany that it will support Poland if the latter is attacked. Germany and Russia sign a non-aggression pact.

24 August 1939 The Emergency Powers Defence Act gives 'defence regulations' issued by the government the power of law.

29 August 1939 Tolkien attends a Pembroke College meeting.

31 August 1939 Britain begins to evacuate schoolchildren from London.

1 September 1939 At dawn Germany attacks Poland. Britain sends an ultimatum to Germany to withdraw. British armed forces are mobilized. Blackout is imposed throughout Britain, enforced by Air Raid Patrol wardens: households, shops, and businesses are required to ensure that no light escapes their windows after a designated time of day, by putting up black fabric or paper. Putting up such material, and taking it down again in the morning, will prove to be a tedious chore for most families.

3 September 1939 Britain sends a second ultimatum to Germany at 9.00 a.m. At 11.00 a.m. Britain declares war on Germany. At 11.15 a.m. the Prime Minister, Neville Chamberlain, announces this act by radio. Priscilla Tolkien will retain a vivid memory of the declaration of war: 'I had gone to Mass with my father and Christopher at St Gregory's Church in the Woodstock Road. *Father Douglas Carter, the parish priest and a friend of the family, offered to anyone who wanted to stay to hear the announcement on his wireless, but my father, visibly upset to be at war, said we should go home to my mother who was listening to the wireless in the kitchen' (private correspondence). – The Tolkien family cancel a planned holiday in Sidmouth.

During the Second World War, 1939–1945 The Examination Schools in Oxford become a military hospital. English School lectures are given elsewhere, mainly in the Taylor Institution. Pembroke College is partly taken over by the Army and the Ministry of Agriculture. Tolkien is amused by a notice on the College Lodge which reads: 'PESTS: FIRST FLOOR'. The Fellows and undergraduates have to retreat into the remaining spaces.

September 1939 Michael Tolkien, having left the Oratory School at the end of the summer term, volunteers for Army service but is instructed to spend one year at university. He enters Trinity College, Oxford to read History. Tolkien is grateful that Trinity College offers him reduced fees.

4 September 1939 The staff of the London offices of Oxford University Press move to Oxford. Among them is Charles Williams, who had met C.S. Lewis some years earlier and will now become a member of the Inklings.

5 September 1939 The first air raid warning of the Second World War sounds in Oxford. Priscilla Tolkien will 'vividly remember the chaos this caused quite early in the morning with traffic at its height and police stopping the traffic with the Air Raid Wardens out in the streets. If there *had* been an air raid it would have been catastrophic' (private correspondence).

8 September 1939 During a conversation with C.S. Lewis, Tolkien explains the origin of his surname. – Philip Unwin of George Allen & Unwin writes to consult Tolkien about the likely demand for the Clark Hall *Beowulf* in the present circumstances. Since the outbreak of war probably will mean paper shortages, unless Tolkien thinks that there would be a demand, Unwin suggests that it would be wise of Tolkien to delay his work on the volume for a couple of months.

9 September 1939 British troops begin to cross into France.

15 September 1939 Tolkien replies to Philip Unwin. He understands that universities will continue to function despite the war, and that there will still be a demand (though reduced) for *Beowulf*. The Clark Hall volume needs only a brief preface by him, if any, since its reviser, C.L. Wrenn, 'is now the professor of English at King's College, London [i.e. no longer a mere Lecturer], and his name alone should be ample guarantee for the new "crib".' He apologizes for his long silence regarding *The Lord of the Rings*, which he supposes no longer interests Allen & Unwin greatly, though 'I still hope to finish it eventually. It is only about 3/4 written. I have not had much time, quite apart from the gloom of approaching disaster, and have been unwell most of this year . . .' (Tolkien-George Allen & Unwin archive, HarperCollins).

16 September 1939 Tolkien attends a special meeting of the General Board 'to consider regulations for examinations in Honour Moderations in Greek and Latin Literature, Mathematics, and Natural Science' (Oxford University Archives FA 1/1/4).

24 September 1939 Petrol rationing is introduced. Before long, Tolkien will sell his car.

29 September 1939 Tolkien attends a meeting of the General Board, which issues emergency decrees to deal with the war situation: these concern, for instance, lapses of time allowed in attending studies and excuses from oral examination.

30 September 1939 The population of Britain is required to register with the Government. Everyone is to be issued an identity card.

October 1939 Tolkien is informed that he will not be required to work as a cryptographer for the present (in the event, he is never called upon to do so).

3 October 1939 Tolkien attends a Pembroke College meeting.

6 October 1939 W.N. Beard, of the George Allen & Unwin production staff, writes to Tolkien. C.L. Wrenn has completed his revision of the Clark Hall *Beowulf*, which is now ready for press except for Tolkien's preface. Beard will send Tolkien a complete set of uncorrected proofs.

9 October 1939 Tolkien chairs an English Faculty Board meeting at 3.30 p.m. in the Board Room of the Clarendon Building, having been elected chairman for 1939–40.

13 October 1939 Tolkien attends a General Board meeting.

15 October 1939 Michaelmas Full Term begins. Tolkien possibly lectures on the Old English *Exodus. See note.* He will continue to supervise D.Phil. student K.R. Brooks.

Michaelmas Term 1939–Hilary Term 1945 During the war the student population at Oxford changes. There are fewer male students, and many of those matriculate younger so that they can study for at least a brief period before being called up for war service (Christopher Tolkien, for one, will matriculate when only seventeen). University faculties are asked to provide courses which will allow such students to gain credits, leading to a full degree if they return to Oxford after the war, and to devise special examinations for them. Later the faculties are also asked to provide six-month courses for Navy and Air Force cadets. Faculty members are called up or volunteer for other duties. Tolkien will write to Stanley Unwin on 19 December 1939: 'I have lost both my chief assistant and his understudy' (Tolkien-George Allen & Unwin archive, HarperCollins). – Shortened honours courses leading to a special certificate are now introduced at Oxford. As first proposed in autumn 1939, each course consists of three 'sections', examined at the end of each term, in which it is possible to obtain either a 'pass' or 'distinction', and students are allowed to count the first public examination as one section. The holder of a certificate (or 'war degree') will later be entitled to return to Oxford to convert it into a full honours degree. This scheme, however, is immediately controversial: some argue that three terms of work are too few, compared with the number at other universities.

20 October 1939 In the evening, Tolkien attends a dinner of The Society hosted by Roger Mynors in the Massey Room at Balliol College, Oxford. Thirteen members are present. *Lord David Cecil is elected to their ranks. Secretary R.W. Chapman will record in his minutes that 'notwithstanding the Precedent of 1914–1919 the Society *highly resolved* to go on meeting eating drinking and defying the King's Enemies, as providence may allow' (MS Eng. d.3529, Bodleian Library, Oxford).

27 October 1939 Tolkien chairs an English Faculty Board meeting. Since, as chairman, he is on the Applications Committee and the Library Committee

ex officio, he is replaced as an ordinary member on these by Helen Darbishire and David Nichol Smith respectively. He is now presumably also on the
Lecture List Committee. He undertakes to discuss dates with Sir Edmund
Chambers, who has agreed to lecture at Oxford in Hilary Term 1940. As a
result of the war, recruitment and replacement of staff are suspended, which
affects the University Lectureship in English Language from which C.L.
Wrenn had resigned. The Board agrees to extend the present Lecturer's period
of office, or otherwise to provide for the continuation of teaching in the subject. Tolkien undertakes to consult with the Secretary of Faculties and to make
any necessary representation to the General Board. It is probably at this meeting that he is nominated to serve as examiner in the English Honour School
from Hilary Term 1940 to Hilary Term 1943. – Tolkien also attends a General
Board meeting.

November 1939–early May 1940 Tolkien's son John is in Rome to study
for the priesthood at the Venerable English College. Although Italy has not yet
entered the war, she is allied with Germany and there are many German troops
in the capital.

2 November 1939 The Committee for Comparative Philology meets at 2.00
p.m. in the Delegates Room of the Clarendon Building. – According to C.S.
Lewis, he, Tolkien, Charles Williams, and C.L. Wrenn have a pleasant evening
during which they discuss 'the most distressing text in the Bible ("narrow is
the way and few they be that find it") and whether one really could believe in
a universe where the majority were damned and also in the goodness of God'
(letter to W.H. Lewis, 5 November 1939, *Collected Letters*, vol. 2 (2004), p. 283).

8 November 1939 Tolkien attends a Pembroke College meeting.

9 November 1939 Tolkien chairs an English Faculty Library Committee meeting at the Taylor Institution. A note in Tolkien's hand, added to the
Committee minutes book at this point (but dated 24 May 1945), recalls that
when, during the autumn of 1939, the Government took over the Examination
Schools where the English Faculty Library was also housed, most of the books
belonging to the Library were transferred to the Taylor Institution. Some volumes, estimated at approximately 2,000 in number, were deposited in the
basement of the Bodleian Library. – In the evening, Tolkien attends a meeting
of the Inklings, which begins with dinner at the Eastgate Hotel. Later he reads
part of *The Lord of the Rings*, Charles Williams reads a nativity play, and C.S.
Lewis reads from his book *The Problem of Pain* (published 1940). In a letter to
his brother, Lewis will note that Hugo Dyson was exceptionally exuberant at
the meeting, and that 'the subject matter of the three readings formed almost
a logical sequence, and produced a really first rate evening's talk of the usual
wide-ranging kind – "from grave to gay, from lively to severe"' (11 November
1939, *Collected Letters*, vol. 2 (2004), p. 289).

10 November 1939 Tolkien attends a General Board meeting.

14 November 1939 W.N. Beard writes to Tolkien, reminding him that his
reply is still needed to Beard's letter of 6 October.

21 November 1939 Stanley Unwin writes to Tolkien. He would like his eldest son, David, currently working in Blackwell's Bookshop in Oxford, to meet Tolkien.

23 November 1939 In the evening, Tolkien attends a meeting of the Inklings. The members finish reading *Irene Iddesleigh* by Amanda M'Kitterick Ros, a novel written in excessively flowery prose with much alliteration, first published in 1897. *See note.*

30 November 1939 Tolkien chairs an English Faculty Library Committee meeting at the Taylor Institution. – Since Charles Williams and other Inklings are away, instead of holding their usual Thursday meeting in his rooms, C.S. Lewis spends the evening with Tolkien at 20 Northmoor Road. They drink gin and lime juice and read to each other, Tolkien from *The Lord of the Rings*, Lewis from *The Problem of Pain*. Edith Tolkien is in the Acland Hospital, Oxford, recovering from an operation.

6 December 1939 Tolkien attends a Pembroke College meeting.

8 December 1939 Tolkien chairs an English Faculty Board meeting. C.L. Wrenn has agreed to postpone his resignation as University Lecturer in English Language until 31 March 1940. – Tolkien also attends a General Board meeting.

9 December 1939 Michaelmas Full Term ends.

11 December 1939 W.N. Beard again reminds Tolkien that the Clark Hall *Beowulf* is ready for press except for the brief foreword that Tolkien has promised to write.

13 December 1939 Members of The Cave meet at Balliol College, hosted by M.R. Ridley who reads poems by Swinburne and Kipling.

18 December 1939 Tolkien replies to W.N. Beard's second reminder (11 December) asking for the preface to the Clark Hall *Beowulf*. He hopes to have time to write it in the next few days. – Tolkien visits David Unwin in Blackwell's Bookshop, Oxford, and admires a display he has arranged. The two apparently have met before this time, as on the same day, Stanley Unwin writes to Tolkien that he is distressed to hear from David of Tolkien's troubles, and hopes that Mrs Tolkien is better.

19 December 1939 Tolkien replies to Stanley Unwin. Edith is 'an invalid but apparently mending at last'. Tolkien thinks it unlikely that he will be called for war service as he is carrying a heavy administrative load at Oxford. He apologizes for having done nothing about the foreword to the Clark Hall *Beowulf*; he promises to 'try and collect my weary wits' and write one at once, though he finds writing of any kind very difficult. He has read part of the new translation and thinks it greatly improved. As for *The Lord of the Rings*, he has 'never quite ceased work' on it. 'It has reached Chapter XVI ['The Mines of Moria'].' He fears, though, that it is growing too large, and he is unsure whether it will please the same audience who enjoyed *The Hobbit*, 'except in so far as that has grown up too'. He asks if there is any chance of publication of *The Lord of the Rings* if he could finish it before spring. 'If you would like to try it on anyone as a serial I am willing to send in chapters. But I have only one fair copy. I have had to go back and revise early chapters as the plot and plan took firmer shape and so nothing has yet been sufficiently definitive to type.' But he has little time to spend on it, and wishes that Allen & Unwin would publish *Farmer Giles of Ham* which is at least finished. He has seen copies of *The Hobbit* in several shop windows and hopes that it will continue to sell; even apart from taxation, his income has seriously decreased, and 'in the general ruin of academic life there is no way of making up the deficit. Outside lectures are cancelled, and exams do not take place or yield very little. . . . Surgeons and hospitals brook no delays.' The health of his invalid son Christopher is improved, however, and his daughter's school having been commandeered, she is 'both better in health and more advanced in knowledge for the change to the old-fashioned governess system. So with my wife's return we ought to have something like Christmas' (Tolkien-George Allen & Unwin archive, Harper-Collins, partly printed in *Letters*, p. 44). (Since 1935 Priscilla has attended the small Catholic school Rye St Antony. In 1939 her piano teacher, a friend of the family, becomes her governess, an arrangement which will last until 1942.)

24 December 1939 Tolkien, as 'Father Christmas', writes to Priscilla. He has had two letters from her. He comments on her family of toy bears and on 'this horrible war'. With the letter is a drawing of Father Christmas walking down a path between Christmas trees; both this and the accompanying envelope are less elaborate than in previous years.

28 December 1939 Stanley Unwin writes to Tolkien. It would be a relief to Allen & Unwin, he says, to have the foreword to the Clark Hall *Beowulf*, which need only be a few hundred words. His son Rayner would be delighted to read the *Hobbit* sequel (as it has progressed). Unwin still thinks that *Farmer Giles of Ham* should be published after *The Lord of the Rings*. He offers to pay in advance royalties of just over £100 due to Tolkien on 30 April 1940.

1940

Early 1940s Tolkien writes a story, *Sellic Spell*, an attempt to reconstruct the Anglo-Saxon tale that lies behind the folk- or fairy-tale element in *Beowulf*. He makes a version of part of the story in Old English, and at least four manuscripts and typescripts of a text in Modern English. (See **Beowulf*.) – At some time during the war, Edith's aviary in the garden at 20 Northmoor Road is turned into a hen-house so that the family can have fresh eggs. This will mean more work for Tolkien: his daughter will remember him cleaning out the poultry den while smoking a large and pungent pipe. It is now difficult to get any domestic help, and Edith's health is not good. – During part of the war, Rosemary Mitton, daughter of Tolkien's cousin Eric (eldest son of Mabel and Tom Mitton), lives with the Tolkien family in Northmoor Road.

?1940 Tolkien revises his poem *The Happy Mariners*. – By January ?1941, and probably during 1940, Tolkien becomes an air raid warden. Usually there are two men on duty at the various posts, one of whom is on 'key duty' and responsible for locking and unlocking the post and staying awake all night, while the other may sleep and is called if necessary. The wardens are supposed to wear a uniform when on duty. Tolkien's post is in Park Town, only a few minutes from Northmoor Rood, where he goes regularly on night duty and comes back to breakfast in the morning. He always shares duty: one of his companions is the Jewish scholar and historian Cecil Roth.

1940 *Víga-Glúms Saga*, edited by Tolkien's former B.Litt. student E.O.G. Turville-Petre (as G. Turville-Petre), is published at last, the first title in the *Oxford English Monographs* series.

January 1940 Edith and Priscilla visit *Weston-super-Mare in Somerset, presumably as part of Edith's convalescence.

3 January 1940 Tolkien writes to R.W. Chapman. He has been having problems arranging a venue for the dinner of The Society that Tolkien is to host on 26 April. Also he is suffering from bronchitis.

8 January 1940 Rationing of bacon, butter, and sugar is introduced in Britain. Later, other foods will be added to the list.

12 January 1940 Tolkien attends a General Board Meeting. A report from the Committee on Advanced Studies is presented.

14 January 1940 Hilary Full Term begins. Tolkien's scheduled lectures and classes for this term are: *Exodus* (2), a continuation of a course on the Old English *Exodus*, on Tuesdays and Thursdays at 11.00 a.m. in the Taylor Institution, beginning 16 January; and Grimm's Law and Verner's Law on Tuesdays at 12.00 noon in the Taylor Institution, beginning 16 January. He will continue to supervise D.Phil. student K.R. Brooks.

Hilary Term 1940 Damage caused by burst water pipes in 20 Northmoor Road forces Tolkien to spend most of Hilary Term in a hotel attic (possibly Linton Lodge in the next road).

17 January 1940 Tolkien attends a Pembroke College meeting.

19 January 1940 In the evening, Tolkien attends a dinner of The Society hosted by J.R.H. Weaver at Trinity College, Oxford. Nine members are present. They discuss difficulties and possible solutions to their continuing to meet in wartime, and whether to elect new members likely to remain in Oxford.

25 January 1940 Tolkien chairs an English Faculty Library Committee meeting in the Taylor Institution. – In the evening, he attends a meeting of the Inklings in C.S. Lewis's rooms in Magdalen College. He reads a chapter of *The Lord of the Rings*.

29 January 1940 Charles Williams writes to his wife that he is to go to Magdalen College at 10.45 a.m. 'where Lewis and Tolkien will put on their gowns and escort me to the Divinity School' (*To Michal from Serge* (2002), p. 42). There he gives the first of a series of lectures on John Milton. Later, Williams drinks sherry in the bar of the Mitre Hotel with Lewis, Tolkien, and Gerald Hopkins from the Oxford University Press.

?Early February 1940 Tolkien and C.S. Lewis attend a performance of *A Midsummer Night's Dream* by William Shakespeare at the Oxford Playhouse.

1 February 1940 The Inklings meet in C.S. Lewis's rooms in Magdalen College. *R.E. 'Humphrey' Havard, a medical doctor, reads a short paper concerning his clinical experience of pain, which he has written for C.S. Lewis to use in his *Problem of Pain*. Lewis will write to his brother on 3 February: 'We had an evening almost equally compounded of merriment, piety, and literature' (*Collected Letters*, vol. 2 (2004), p. 343).

5 February 1940 Tolkien probably attends Charles Williams' second lecture, on Milton's *Comus*, which pays special attention to chastity. – A member of the Allen & Unwin staff writes to Tolkien, reminding him that the Clark Hall *Beowulf* is only awaiting his preface before going to press.

9 February 1940 Tolkien attends a General Board meeting.

22 February 1940 In the evening, Tolkien attends a meeting of the Inklings in C.S. Lewis's rooms in Magdalen College. The members argue furiously about cremation, with Tolkien and Havard (both Roman Catholics) objecting strongly to the practice.

23 February 1940 Tolkien attends a General Board meeting.

29 February 1940 Tolkien attends a meeting of the Inklings in C.S. Lewis's rooms in Magdalen College.

5 March 1940 W.N. Beard again reminds Tolkien that the Clark Hall *Beowulf* is awaiting his preface.

6 March 1940 Tolkien attends a Pembroke College meeting.

8 March 1940 Tolkien chairs a meeting of the English Faculty Board. He is appointed to a committee to report at the first Board meeting in Trinity Term 'whether any changes in the present system of special Examinations in English should be made for 1940–1' (Oxford University Archives FA 4/5/1/1). The Board agrees that C.L. Wrenn should be asked to postpone his resignation until the end of Trinity Term 1940, that the University should be asked to allow a new appointment, and that an election be made in time for the new Lecturer to be in the post by the beginning of Michaelmas Term 1940. – Tolkien also attends a General Board meeting.

9 March 1940 Hilary Full Term ends.

13 March 1940 Tolkien attends a meeting of The Cave in the Golden Cross in Cornmarket Street, Oxford. H.F.B. Brett-Smith, Hugo Dyson, C.S. Lewis, and Leonard Rice-Oxley are also present.

Spring 1940 Tolkien draws *Spring 1940*, a view of his garden at 20 Northmoor Road, with a Victoria plum tree covered with blossom and daffodils growing in the lawn (*Artist and Illustrator*, fig. 3).

25 March 1940 In the afternoon, Tolkien meets C.S. Lewis at Magdalen College. As the committee meeting they had expected to attend is cancelled, they stroll along Addison's Walk in the grounds of Magdalen and beside the river Cherwell.

27 March 1940 Stanley Unwin writes to Tolkien, asking when his preface to the Clark Hall *Beowulf* will be finished: it needs only a word or two.

28 March 1940 Tolkien attends a postponed committee meeting at Pembroke College (a meeting probably of the committee formed on 8 March). He provides sherry for the members.

30 March 1940 Tolkien replies to Stanley Unwin. He sends apologies for 'vexatious and uncivil behaviour', noting his wife's illness, that he himself has been ill, and that his University duties have trebled, among other troubles. He knew that 'a word or two' would suffice for his contribution to the Clark Hall volume, 'but I believed that more was hoped for. . . . For a fairly considerable "preface" is really required', as the edition contained

> no reference whatever to either a translator's or a critic's problems. I advised originally against any attempt to bring the apparatus of the old book up to date – it can be got by students elsewhere. But I did not expect a reduction to 10 lines, while the "argument" (the least useful part) was re-written at length. That being so I laboured long and hard to compress (and yet enliven) such remarks on *translation* as might both be useful to students and of interest to those using the book without reference to the original text. But the result ran to 17 of my [manuscript] pages (of some 300 words each) – not counting the metrical appendix, the most original part, which is as long again. I was in this stage early in March, and trying to make up my mind what to jettison, when your letter of March 27th reached me yesterday.

He sends what he has done, suggesting that it might be considered in a future edition, or, retouched, as 'a suitable booklet for students'; but 'to meet the immediate emergency' he suggests '(with grief, reluctance, and penitence) that the passages marked in *red* (?1400 words), or those in *blue* (750–800?) might serve' (*Letters*, pp. 45–6).

April 1940 The Tolkien family, except for John, take almost a fortnight's holiday at Weston-super-Mare, near Clevedon where Tolkien and Edith spent their honeymoon years before. They revisit the caves in the nearby Cheddar Gorge, which will inspire the Glittering Caves of Aglarond in *The Lord of the Rings*.

2 April 1940 Stanley Unwin writes to Tolkien. Regardless of commercial considerations, he wants to include the whole of Tolkien's introductory preface in the Clark Hall *Beowulf* as it will add enormously to interest in the book and its value to students.

5 April 1940 Stanley Unwin writes to Tolkien. His preface to the Clark Hall volume will need thirty-six pages; if Tolkien agrees, Unwin intends to have it typeset immediately. He sends a stamped, addressed telegraph form for Tolkien's reply. Since Tolkien has provided more than the publisher expected, Unwin offers to pay five guineas at once and a further five guineas if the book is reprinted.

6 April 1940 Tolkien sends a telegram to Allen & Unwin, agreeing to the publication of his preface to the Clark Hall *Beowulf*, and accepting Unwin's offer of payment.

8 April 1940 Allen & Unwin send Tolkien a cheque for his preface, and inform him that he will be sent proofs as soon as they arrive from the printer.

13 April 1940 A new Control of Paper order comes into force in Britain, reducing (partly retrospectively) the amount of paper and paper board supplied by mills to customers during March, April, and May 1940 from 60% to 30% of the amount supplied or manufactured in the same period last year, except under licence. Licences already issued to supply or convert paper are reduced by 50%. Paper supply will continue to be strictly controlled until 1949. The publishing industry also will suffer losses from bombing and from the call-up of important members of staff.

19 April 1940 Tolkien attends a General Board meeting. – W.N. Beard sends Tolkien rough proofs of his preface to the Clark Hall *Beowulf* and asks for their return as soon as possible.

21 April 1940 Trinity Full Term begins. Tolkien's scheduled lectures and classes for this term are: Old Norse (Elementary Class) on Thursdays at 11.00 a.m. in the Taylor Institution, beginning 25 April; and Outlines of Old English Phonology on Tuesdays and Thursdays at 12.00 noon in the Taylor Institution, beginning 23 April. He will continue to supervise D.Phil. student K.R. Brooks.

24 April 1940 Tolkien attends a Pembroke College meeting. – Tolkien writes to Stanley Unwin, returning marked proofs of his preface to the Clark Hall *Beowulf*. He introduces few alterations to his text, but notes many errors, especially with Old English words. He encloses a page of copy for the revision of p. xxxvi (containing lines 210–28 of *Beowulf* in the original).

25 April 1940 W.N. Beard writes to Tolkien, assuring him that corrections to the Clark Hall *Beowulf* will be made with care. – Beard informs C.L. Wrenn that Tolkien has suggested (presumably on the returned proof) that 'Finnsburg' in the title *Beowulf and the Finnsburg Fragment* be changed to 'Finnesburg', subject to Wrenn's approval. – In the evening, Tolkien attends a meeting of the Inklings. R.E. Havard reads an account of a mountain climb in which he had taken part.

26 April 1940 In the evening, Tolkien hosts a dinner of The Society in the Senior Common Room and Parlour at Pembroke College. Only four members are present. In the absence of the Secretary, Tolkien himself writes the minutes. 'No business was performed other than eating and drinking in moderation (both meritable and suitable), and conversation – which the smallness of the party prevented from becoming sectional.' One of the topics discussed is 'the rewards of picture-collecting and the sorrows of dealers', inspired by the absence of pictures in the room (stored away during the war) and the presence of K.T. Parker, Keeper of the Department of Fine Art at the Ashmolean Museum. 'The host did not read a paper, explaining that the remarks he had contemplated making (but had not arranged in suitable form) were primarily intended for heads of houses – and none were present' (MS Eng. d.3529, Bodleian Library, Oxford).

2 May 1940 Charles Williams reads his play *Terror of Light* at a meeting of the Inklings in C.S. Lewis's rooms in Magdalen College.

3 May 1940 Tolkien chairs an English Faculty Board meeting at 3.30 p.m. in the Board Room of the Clarendon Building. The members discuss the report of the committee on changes that may be needed to the system of special examinations in English (see entry for 8 March 1940). The Board agrees to revisions. It also resolves to inform the Hebdomadal Council that it would welcome the conferment of the Degree of M.A. by Decree on Alistair Campbell, B.Litt., Balliol College.

8 May 1940 Tolkien chairs a special meeting of the English Faculty Board at 2.15 p.m. in the Board Room of the Clarendon Building. *G.V. Smithers is appointed to the Statutory Lectureship in English Language for three years from 1 October 1940, and emergency examinations in 1940–1 are discussed.

10 May 1940 Neville Chamberlain resigns as Prime Minister; he is replaced by a coalition government led by Winston Churchill. Germany invades Belgium and the Netherlands.

15 May 1940 Tolkien writes to Stanley Unwin, asking for payment of monies due him as of 30 April, as he is 'in certain difficulties' (Tolkien-George Allen & Unwin archive, HarperCollins).

16 May 1940 In the evening, Tolkien attends a meeting of the Inklings in C.S. Lewis's rooms in Magdalen College. Also present are R.E. Havard, Charles Williams, and C.L. Wrenn. After the meeting, they walk through the College grounds. – Italy having become too dangerous for the Venerable English College to remain in Rome, its priests and students, including John Tolkien, depart on this date, dressed in civilian clothes. They will journey by train for five days, and only just manage to board the last boat to leave Le Havre. John's family will be much relieved to hear that he is safe. After a short stay at Ambleside in the Lake District, the Venerable English College will spend six years in Stonyhurst, Lancashire.

17 May 1940 Tolkien attends a General Board meeting.

27 May–3 June 1940 British and French troops, surrounded by Germans at Dunkirk on the north coast of France, are evacuated in a fleet of small boats.

31 May 1940 Tolkien attends a General Board meeting.

6–12 June 1940 English Final Honour School examinations take place. Tolkien is one of five examiners, also including Nevill Coghill, E. Llewellyn, C.S. Lewis, and Leonard Rice-Oxley. The number of candidates is much reduced this year because of the war: only twenty-two men and fifty-three women, plus one man in the United States of America. Three of the examiners are suffering illness; one conference has to be held in a nursing home. The Divinity School in which the examinations are chiefly held is found, on the whole, an improvement on the commandeered Examination Schools, except that there is no artificial light. During one morning, it becomes so overcast that nothing can be read or written, but the invigilator's request for seventy-six candles is refused, presumably because of the fear of fire in the historical building. Then 'after an expert fowler among the candidates had captured a terrified refugee thrush, and returned it (protesting) to Exeter College Garden, light slowly returned' (report by Tolkien, 14 March 1941, Oxford University Archives FA 4/5/2/7). *See note.* The candidates are allowed extra time to complete the examination. Because of the war, vivas are temporarily discontinued.

10 June 1940 Italy declares war on Britain and France.

10 and 11 June 1940 Three candidates for the Diploma in Comparative Philology sit their examination. Tolkien, G.E.K. Braunholtz, and Alfred Ewert (Professor of Romance Languages) are the examiners.

12 June 1940 Tolkien attends a Pembroke College meeting.

14 June 1940 Tolkien chairs a meeting of the English Faculty Board. – He also attends a General Board meeting.

15 June 1940 Trinity Full Term ends. – Michael Tolkien leaves Trinity College to become an anti-aircraft gunner.

19 June 1940 Encaenia.

10 July–31 October 1940 The Battle of Britain takes place, in which the Royal Air Force opposes attempts by the German Luftwaffe to destroy airfields and industries and demoralize the population. Michael Tolkien will be awarded the George Medal 'for his action as an anti-aircraft gunner defending aerodromes' during the battle (Humphrey Carpenter, *Biography*, p. 158).

13–14 July 1940 The English Final Honour School examiners have meetings, 'involving many meals at the Golden Cross and pints in the courtyard' (C.S. Lewis to W.H. Lewis, 20 July 1940, *Collected Letters*, vol. 2 (2004), p. 424).

15 July 1940 The examiners of the English Final Honour School for 1940 complete their statement of results.

16 July 1940 The new edition of the Clark Hall *Beowulf* with Tolkien's preface is published.

5 August 1940 The Registrar of Oxford University writes to Tolkien, sending papers submitted by a candidate in the English Honour School who has been allowed to sit his examinations in America. Tolkien is to mark those with which he is concerned as an examiner. Later, having acquired most or all of this candidate's scripts, he will use their blank versos and covers in writing *The Lord of the Rings*.

?9 August 1940 The Inklings meet, breaking up at nearly 1.00 a.m. Around this time the regular Thursday Inklings meetings are changed to Fridays.

16 August 1940 In lieu of a regular Inklings meeting in C.S. Lewis's rooms in Magdalen College, as most members cannot attend this evening, Lewis and R.E. Havard visit Tolkien at home after dinner and stay until nearly 1.00 a.m.

17 August 1940 Germany proclaims a total blockade of Britain. During the next two years, many merchant ships as well as escorting military vessels will be sunk by U-boats and other ships of the German navy. Loss of life at sea will be great, and in Britain food and raw materials will be in short supply.

19 August 1940 Tolkien signs alone, as chairman of the examiners for the Honour School of English Language and Literature, a supplementary list of one candidate, the American whose papers have been received later than the rest.

24 August 1940 German aircraft begin to bomb central London.

Late August 1940–?late 1941 Tolkien now, as it seems, in late August 1940 returns to *The Lord of the Rings* after a long pause, continues to work probably until the beginning of Michaelmas Term in October, picks up the story again during the Christmas vacation, and works on it at times during 1941 (*see note*). It is not possible to date his writing or revision during this period more precisely, except for a narrative outline, headed 'New Plot. Aug. 26–27, 1940': in this Tolkien decides that Gandalf's unexplained absence in Book I was caused by the wizard Sarumond/Saramund/Saruman, who betrays Gandalf to the Black Riders. Tolkien also writes an account of Gandalf and the hobbit Hamilcar Bolger (later Fredegar 'Fatty' Bolger) telling Frodo in Rivendell of their adventures, and of Gandalf's rescue of Hamilcar from Black Riders. He adds other passages to agree with this account, but then rejects the episode.

The various decisions Tolkien now makes entail considerable emendation and rewriting, especially of the second part of 'At the Sign of the Prancing Pony' (published bk. I, ch. 10, 'Strider'). He also revises 'Many Meetings' (published bk. II, ch. 1), with an addition in which Bilbo tells Frodo of Aragorn's background, and the third of ultimately fifteen versions of the poem Bilbo recites at Rivendell (evolved in stages from the poem *Errantry*); already, though not so named, the 'Merry Messenger' of the poem is being transformed into Earendel. At least three new versions of 'The Council of Elrond' (published bk. II, ch. 2) date from this time as well, as Tolkien works out additional material to be discussed, mainly arising from the position of Aragorn as the heir of Elendil. He leaves the third and fourth incomplete, and in the latter incorporates pages from the second version. Possibly at this time (*see note*), Tolkien makes some notes for reorganizing the order of speeches at the Council, then uses the fourth version of the chapter as the basis of a fifth. Probably not long after this is completed he has an amanuensis typescript made. At this stage the chapter includes material that later will be removed to the Appendices of *The Lord of the Rings*, or will become the basis of the separate work, *Of the Rings of Power and the Third Age*.

At some point at 'a relatively early stage in the writing of *The Lord of the Rings*' (Christopher Tolkien, *Sauron Defeated* (1992), p. 331), perhaps while he is revising 'The Council of Elrond' and considering the role Elendil of Númenor played in the Last Alliance, Tolkien also takes up the amanuensis typescript of *The Fall of Númenor* from the period 1936–?1937. He emends it, and in a related manuscript he drafts new passages. He then writes a fine new manuscript of *The Fall of Númenor*, incorporating changes made to the typescript, but omitting a new conclusion concerning Beleriand and the Last Alliance of Elves and Men against Sauron.

Having settled most of his doubts and made necessary changes in Book I and the beginning of Book II of *The Lord of the Rings*, Tolkien now revises the account he had written a year earlier of the journey of the Company of the Ring from Rivendell as far as Balin's tomb. He writes a fresh manuscript of 'The Ring Goes South' (published bk. III, ch. 3), advancing confidently and making changes in the process, and including two versions of the conversation in Bilbo's room at the beginning of the chapter. Not long after its completion he has an amanuensis typescript made from the manuscript, probably by his son Christopher. The original workings for Bilbo's song 'I sit beside the fire and think' also belong to this time; and it seems likely as well that while Tolkien is writing the second version of 'The Ring Goes South', he draws the first of several small-scale maps of the western part of Middle-earth: two sheets glued together, it is drawn with great care and delicacy, using pencil and coloured chalks to distinguish features such as mountains, rivers, marshes, and woods. Tolkien will use this map for a long time, making additions and alterations as his ideas of the geography change, sometimes gluing new sheets over old, sometimes adding them to the edges. Probably also at about this time, he draws an aerial view of the Mountains of Moria and Dimrill Dale (*Artist and Illustrator*, fig. 158), and a plan of the area.

Tolkien next rewrites the first part of the Moria episode, 'The Mines of Moria (i)' (corresponding to published bk. II, ch. 4, 'A Journey in the Dark'). Within the manuscript he first draws the Doors of Durin as they were originally conceived; later he will erase parts of the drawing and revise it according to his changed description of the doors (*The Treason of Isengard*, p. 182; *Artist and Illustrator*, fig. 150). He replaces the first version of the inscription on Balin's tomb, and evidently at about the same time prepares a table of 'Dwarf-runes for writing English (phonetic)'.

At last he moves the story beyond the discovery of Balin's tomb, where he had abandoned it (as it appears) in autumn 1939, based in part on sketches he made at that time. He writes a new chapter, 'The Mines of Moria (ii)' (corresponding to published bk. II, ch. 5, 'The Bridge of Khazad-dûm'), still using the examination paper acquired in August 1940, at first in pencil, then partly overwriting in ink, then continuing in ink or pencil. The story develops as he writes and revises at great speed, until the surviving members of the Fellowship emerge from Moria. At once, he makes a fair copy of the chapter, now subtitled 'The Bridge', polishing and elaborating the draft. Probably at this time he also makes a second version of the first page of the book of Mazarbul, in the form of a 'facsimile' of the damaged page showing tears and stains, and the first (or possibly first surviving) 'facsimiles' of the other two pages. *See note.*

Possibly at this point, or at least before he begins to write of Lothlórien (see entry for Late 1941–early 1942), Tolkien very quickly produces an elaborate outline, *Sketch of Plot*, of the story foreseen from Moria.

Late summer 1940 Two women evacuees are billeted for a short time in the Tolkien household (see also entry for 29 September).

Autumn 1940 Christopher Tolkien returns to the Oratory School.

7 September–27 October 1940 Germany focuses its attempt to bomb Britain into submission with heavy raids on London. Although parts of the city are devastated and over 14,000 civilians are killed, the Luftwaffe also suffers heavy losses, and Hitler postpones plans to invade Britain.

27 September 1940 Germany, Italy, and Japan form an alliance.

29 September 1940 Tolkien writes to his son Michael. The evacuees that had been billeted with the Tolkiens left 'this morning, back home to Ashford. . . . I have never come across more simple, helpless, gentle and unhappy souls (mother and daughter-in-law). They had been away from their husbands for the first time in their married lives, and found they would prefer to be blown to bits' (*Letters*, p. 46).

6 October 1940 Tolkien writes to Michael. He is sorry that Michael's time at university has been interrupted, but 'I still hope you will be able to come back again. And certainly you will learn a lot, first!' (*Letters*, p. 46).

11 October 1940 Tolkien attends a General Board meeting.

13 October 1940 Michaelmas Full Term begins. Tolkien's scheduled lectures and classes for this term are: *Beowulf* (text) on Tuesdays at 11.00 a.m. in the Taylor Institution, beginning 15 October; Old Norse (Class) on Tuesdays at 12.00 noon in the Taylor Institution, beginning 15 October; and Kentish on Thursdays at 11.00 a.m. in the Taylor Institution, beginning 17 October. He will continue to supervise D.Phil. student K.R. Brooks. – Requirements for the war degree at Oxford are refined. Sections are incorporated into two 'parts', which vary in the amount of work prescribed and are examined at intervals of a year or more. Students who complete both parts are to obtain a classified honours degree, but in general, undergraduates will have time to complete only the first part before entering national service, and will have to return to university after the war if they wish to complete the entire course of study.

16 October 1940 Tolkien attends a Pembroke College meeting.

18 October 1940 *The Problem of Pain* by C.S. Lewis, dedicated to the Inklings, is published.

24 October 1940 Tolkien chairs an English Faculty Library Committee meeting at 3.30 p.m.

25 October 1940 Tolkien chairs a meeting of the English Faculty Board. He is re-elected chairman for 1940–1. The Applications Committee has appointed Tolkien as supervisor of M.Y. Pickard of Lady Margaret Hall, a probationer B.Litt. student who wishes to work on a Middle English subject.

November 1940 Winifred Husbands of University College, London writes to Tolkien regarding *Songs for the Philologists*, apparently the first that he has heard of the existence of that unauthorized booklet (see entry for 1936). Although most copies of it have been destroyed in a fire, Tolkien is asked to give retrospective permission for the publication of his poems. Later, Winifred Husbands will send Tolkien two of the surviving copies, in which he will correct textual errors.

7 November 1940 The remaining stock of the second printing of *The Hobbit* is destroyed in a bombing raid on London, a blow to sales until Allen & Unwin can put another reprint in hand two years later. (A single bomb destroyed 1,400,000 books in a binder's warehouse, affecting 2,100 titles on the Allen & Unwin list.)

14 November 1940 Working late, Tolkien sees an ever-increasing fiery glow on the horizon. On 15 November he will learn that Coventry, only forty miles away, has been devastated by German incendiary raids and 1,000 people killed. The bombing of London and other major cities in Britain will continue into 1942.

20 November 1940 Birmingham suffers in a heavy air raid.

22 November 1940 Tolkien attends a General Board meeting.

27 November 1940 Tolkien certifies that M.Y. Pickard is qualified to be a B.Litt. student. Her thesis will be an edition of *The Parlement of the Thre Ages*.

28 November 1940 Tolkien chairs an English Faculty Library Committee meeting at 2.30 p.m. The report of the English Library for 1939–40 records that by the courtesy of the Taylorian authorities, the working library and the more valuable books were transferred in October 1939 to the Taylor Institution. In order to provide sufficient assistance for those working for the Special Examinations, some of the books most in request have been acquired in duplicate.

December 1940 Congregation, the legislative body of Oxford University, approves a revised scheme for the war degree. Those students who matriculate from Hilary Term 1941 will need to complete five terms of residence and four sections, rather than three sections in three terms. This makes it more likely that candidates for the degree will have to return to Oxford after the war to fulfil the requirements.

6 December 1940 Tolkien chairs an English Faculty Board meeting at 3.30 p.m. in the Board Room of the Clarendon Building. He is appointed to a committee 'to report next Term on the whole question of the Special Examinations and Shortened Final Honour School' (Oxford University Archives FA 4/5/1/1). The report of the English Faculty Library Committee is presented. The Board approves M.Y. Pickard as a full B.Litt. student and appoints Tolkien as her supervisor. – Tolkien also attends a General Board meeting.

c. **7 December 1940** Michael Tolkien is in the Worcester Royal Infirmary, having been injured in an accident with an Army vehicle during night training.

7 December 1940 Michaelmas Full Term ends.

13 December 1940 Tolkien, as 'Polar Bear', writes a short note dated '2 am. Dec. 13th' to Christopher and Priscilla, and as 'Father Christmas' adds a comment.

c. **21 December 1940** At some time near Christmas, Tolkien, and presumably Edith, Christopher, and Priscilla, stay at the Hopmarket in Worcester in order to visit Michael in the Worcester Royal Infirmary.

23 December 1940 Tolkien, as 'Polar Bear', writes to Priscilla. He is glad that she has returned home (from Worcester). 'Message came on Saturday that your house was empty.'

24 December 1940 Tolkien, as 'Father Christmas', writes a short letter to Priscilla. He tells of penguins who came north to help Father Christmas, and encloses a drawing of them dancing with the North Polar Bear. He notes that 'this horrible war is reducing all our stocks, and in so many countries children are living far from their homes.'

Late December 1940–early 1941 Tolkien takes care of family members while they are ill in bed. – After an apparent hiatus during Michaelmas Term, he returns to work on *The Lord of the Rings* (see entry for Late August 1940–late 1941).

1941

1941 Tolkien becomes *ex officio* an elector to the new Vigfússon Readership in Ancient Icelandic Literature and Antiquities. He will remain an elector until his change of chair in 1945, and then will be an elector either appointed or *ex officio* from 1948 until Michaelmas Term 1965. The term of office is seven years. He will take part in elections in 1941, 1948, 1955, and 1961.

2 January 1941 Tolkien writes to his son Michael. He has been 'clearing up arrears of correspondence' and has 'at last got as far as getting out my story [*The Lord of the Rings*] again; but as soon as I get really started, term will be casting its shadow ahead, and I shall have to think of lectures and committees' (*Letters*, p. 47).

7 January 1941 In the evening, R.E. Havard drives Tolkien and the Lewis brothers to a pub in Appleton, a village a few miles south-west of Oxford. Tolkien offers the locals some snuff which had been given him as a birthday present. Since Basil Blackwell now lives in Appleton, the locals appreciate a humorous story Warnie Lewis tells about Hugo Dyson in Blackwell's Bookshop.

12 January 1941 Tolkien writes to Michael, describing the excursion to Appleton. Otherwise 'life has been rather dull, and much too full of committees and legislative business, which has kept me up late several nights' (*Letters*, p. 47). Although there have been several air raid warnings in Oxford, so far there have been no actual raids.

17 January 1941 Tolkien attends a General Board meeting.

19 January 1941 Hilary Full Term begins. Tolkien's scheduled lectures and classes for this term are: *Beowulf* (text, continued) on Tuesdays and Thursdays at 11.00 a.m. in the Taylor Institution, beginning 21 January; Kentish (Middle English) on Thursdays at 12.00 noon in the Taylor Institution, beginning 23 January; and Old Norse (Class), time and place to be arranged. He will continue to supervise B.Litt. student M.Y. Pickard and D.Phil. student K.R. Brooks. – Around this time, Tolkien contracts influenza.

20 January 1941 The Secretary of King Edward VI Schools, Birmingham, informs Tolkien, the governor for King Edward's School appointed by Oxford University, of the death of two other governors. It is hoped that as many governors as possible will be able to attend the funerals on 21 and 23 January.

28 January 1941 Michael Tolkien leaves the Worcester Royal Infirmary to convalesce.

30 January 1941 Tolkien chairs an English Faculty Library Committee meeting.

31 January 1941 Tolkien chairs an English Faculty Board meeting. The report of the Committee on Special Examinations and Shortened Final Honour School is presented, a lengthy document in the writing of which Tolkien has played a major part. The Board has to further consider courses and examinations for the shortened war degree. – Tolkien also attends a General Board meeting.

6 February 1941 Tolkien chairs an English Faculty Library Committee meeting. As the Librarian expects to leave at half-term to take up government work, the Committee must consider a replacement.

14 February 1941 Tolkien attends a General Board meeting.

28 February 1941 Tolkien attends a General Board meeting.

1 March 1941 Tolkien chairs an English Faculty Library Committee and also takes the minutes.

4 March 1941 Tolkien certifies that K.R. Brooks has completed the number of terms for submission of his D.Phil.

6–8 March 1941 Tolkien writes a long letter to Michael about marriage and relations between the sexes. By now Michael evidently has informed his parents of his attachment to Joan Griffiths, a nurse at the Worcester Royal Infirmary.

12 March 1941 Tolkien attends a Pembroke College meeting.

14 March 1941 Tolkien chairs an English Faculty Board meeting. As chairman of the examiners in the Honour School for 1940 he presents their report, a three-page manuscript. The Applications Committee has appointed Tolkien and C.T. Onions examiners of the D.Phil. thesis of K.R. Brooks, *Edition of the Old English Poem 'Andreas'*. N.R. Ker is appointed University Lecturer in Palaeography for five years from 1 October 1941. – Tolkien also attends a General Board meeting.

15 March 1941 Hilary Full Term ends. – Tolkien, Edith, and Priscilla go to Worcester to visit Michael who has returned to hospital for treatment, and to meet Joan Griffiths. They stay again at the Hopmarket. During the war they will stay there also at other times, to see Walter and Marjorie Incledon who moved to Worcester from their home near the south-east coast of England.

18 March 1941 Tolkien writes to Michael, stressing that he feels himself to be a Suffield and that any corner of Worcestershire is 'home' to him (*Letters*, p. 54).

21 March 1941 Tolkien writes to John Waller, editor of the Oxford literary magazine *Kingdom Come*, in reply to a solicitation. He has nothing for the April issue; until the 'long vac' begins in July he will be too busy setting papers and reading theses to write anything.

22 March 1941 Ronald and Edith celebrate their Silver Wedding anniversary with a modest supper party. Among the guests are Hugo Dyson and C.S. Lewis. Priscilla is the only one of the Tolkien children able to attend.

25 April 1941 Tolkien attends a General Board meeting.

27 April 1941 Trinity Full Term begins. Tolkien's scheduled lectures for this term are: Legend of Wayland (*Deor's Lament* and *Völundarkviða*) on Tuesdays at 10.00 a.m. in the Taylor Institution, beginning 29 April; and Outlines of Old English Phonology on Tuesdays and Thursdays at 12.00 noon in the Taylor Institution, beginning 29 April. He will continue to supervise B.Litt. student M.Y. Pickard.

Trinity Term 1941 Tolkien drafts regulations for the final examination for the Shortened Honour School in English (Parts I and II), to be taken in Trinity Term 1942, for those who expect to be able to stay at the University until then.

30 April 1941 Tolkien attends a Pembroke College meeting.

4 May 1941 In the afternoon, Priscilla is playing with friends in the garden next to 20 Northmoor Road, and Christopher is tracking with his telescope a bomber flying above, when they notice black smoke pouring from its engines and realize that it is going to crash. There is an explosion and a ball of fire as the plane comes down in the estate belonging to Professor Haldane (see *Naomi Mitchison) at the end of Linton Road. Tolkien, as an air raid warden, goes to the scene. He will tell his children of great acts of heroism by local people who brave the fire before official help arrives, including one who climbed into the burning house to rescue a boy trapped in an upstairs room.

9 May 1941 Tolkien chairs an English Faculty Board meeting. He queries whether an election to the Vigfússon Readership should be made at once, or deferred until the end of the war. The Board decides in favour of an immediate election, if a suitable candidate can be found. Tolkien is authorized to report this, together with the Board's reasons for the decision, to the Vice-Chancellor for submission to the Hebdomadal Council. – Tolkien also attends a General Board meeting.

12 May 1941 Tolkien attends a Pembroke College meeting.

23 May 1941 Tolkien attends a General Board meeting.

By June 1941 Michael Tolkien has become an officer cadet at the Royal Military College, Sandhurst.

1 June 1941 Clothes begin to be rationed in Britain.

4 June 1941 Tolkien is re-elected to the General Board until Michaelmas Term 1944.

6 June 1941 Tolkien attends a General Board meeting.

9 June 1941 Tolkien writes to Michael. When lectures ended on 5 June Tolkien hoped to be able to rest and to put some order into the family garden before 'Schools' begin on 12 June, but 'the everlasting rain has prevented my outdoor work, and lots of extra business prevented any rest'. He adds: 'I have spent most of my time of late drafting rules and regulations, only to find all kinds of loopholes as soon as they are in print, and only to be cursed and criticized by those who have not done the work, and won't try to understand the aims and objects!' (*Letters*, p. 54). He discusses his own war experience and his feelings for Michael, and comments on war news.

12 June 1941 Tolkien attends an English Faculty Library Committee meeting. – English Final Honour School examinations begin. Tolkien is an examiner with Nevill Coghill, Dorothy Everett, C.S. Lewis, and Leonard Rice-Oxley, . There are 56 candidates in the Honour School, 15 men and 41 women. The examiners will sign their statement on 21 July. In the report he will present on 5 December, Tolkien notes that the examinations were held in the Sheldonian Theatre, which proved 'an admirable place for the purpose except for the unevenness of the floor. But there was plenty of spare room, and those whose tables and chairs rocked unduly were able to migrate.' The examiners have to judge the work of candidates offering 'papers of Honours standard' (Oxford University Archives FA 4/5/2/7), and of those taking Honours papers in lieu of Sections. Vivas are again suspended.

18 June 1941 B.E.C. Davis, Westfield College, University of London writes to thank Tolkien for arranging for Westfield College students to use the English Faculty Library for the same fee as Oxford students.

19 June 1941 Tolkien attends a Pembroke College meeting.

20 June 1941 Tolkien chairs an English Faculty Board meeting. – He also attends a General Board meeting.

21 June 1941 Trinity Full Term ends.

22 June 1941 Germany invades Russia.

25 June 1941 Encaenia.

13 July 1941 Britain and Russia agree a mutual aid pact.

19 July 1941 Tolkien attends a preliminary meeting of the electors to the Vigfússon Readership in Ancient Icelandic Literature and Antiquities. The other electors are Professor Boyd (presumably James Boyd, a Goethe scholar), R.W. Chambers, George S. Gordon, C.S. Lewis, C.T. Onions, and David Nichol Smith.

27 July 1941 In the morning, Tolkien visits C.S. Lewis at Magdalen College; Charles Williams and other friends from the Inklings are also present. *See note.*

26 August 1941 The electors to the Vigfússon Readership in Ancient Icelandic Literature and Antiquities meet at 10.00 a.m. Present are Tolkien, Boyd, Chambers, Gordon, Nichol Smith, and Onions. They elect E.O.G. Turville-Petre to the post for a period of seven years from 1 October 1941.

10 October 1941 Tolkien attends a General Board meeting.

12 October 1941 Michaelmas Full Term begins. Tolkien's scheduled lectures for this term are: William Morris: *The Story of Sigurd and the Fall of the Nibelungs* on Tuesdays at 11.00 a.m. in the Taylor Institution, beginning 14 October; *Beowulf*: Heroic and Legendary Matter on Tuesdays and Thursdays at 12.00 noon in the Taylor Institution, beginning 14 October; and Old English Historical Grammar (Inflexions) on Thursdays at 11.00 a.m. in the Taylor Institution, beginning 16 October. He will continue to supervise B.Litt. student M.Y. Pickard.

17 October 1941 Tolkien attends a Pembroke College meeting. – In the evening, Tolkien attends a dinner of The Society, the first to be held after an interval of eighteen months, hosted by R.W. Chapman at Magdalen College, Oxford. Six members are present. They discuss the difficulties of meeting during wartime.

24 October 1941 Tolkien chairs an English Faculty Board meeting. He is re-elected chairman for the next year. *M.B. (Mary) Salu of Lady Margaret Hall is admitted as a probationer B.Litt. student, with Tolkien as her supervisor. – Tolkien also attends a General Board meeting.

Autumn 1941 Tolkien replies to queries from W.J.B. Owen, University College, Bangor, North Wales, about the Old English *Wanderer*.

5 November 1941 Tolkien attends a Pembroke College meeting.

7 November 1941 Tolkien attends a General Board meeting.

11 November 1941 Michael Tolkien and Joan Griffiths are married. Tolkien is not present at the wedding.

21 November 1941 Tolkien attends a General Board meeting.

26 November 1941 Tolkien writes some reminiscences of George S. Gordon at the request of R.W. Chapman, Secretary to the Delegates of the Oxford University Press. Gordon is known to be terminally ill, and Tolkien's words are perhaps wanted for an obituary.

1 December 1941 Tolkien and C.T. Onions submit a report approving the D. Phil. thesis by K.R. Brooks. As Lt. Brooks is now serving overseas, his viva is waived.

5 December 1941 Tolkien chairs an English Faculty Board meeting. He presents his report as chairman of the examiners in the Honour School for 1941. – He also attends a General Board meeting.

6 December 1941 Michaelmas Full Term ends.

Late 1941–?January 1942 Probably towards the end of 1941 Tolkien writes the Lothlórien episode in *The Lord of the Rings*, originally as one chapter (published as bk. II, ch. 6–7, 'Lothlórien' and 'The Mirror of Galadriel'). (*See note*; also see entry for Late August 1940–late 1941, and related *note*.) As he proceeds, he overlaps 'draft and fair copy, often writing the preliminary draft in pencil on the fair copy manuscript and then erasing it or overwriting it in ink' (Christopher Tolkien, *The Treason of Isengard*, p. 238). The story evolves as he writes, requiring many emendations to earlier parts of the chapter. He spends much effort drafting the song of Nimrodel by Legolas, and writes early versions of the lament for Gandalf. He interrupts the text with outlines for narrative yet to come, and draws a small plan of Caras Galadon. His picture *The Forest of Lothlorien in Spring* (*Artist and Illustrator*, fig. 157) probably also dates from this time, when he first describes the golden wood (*see note*). When he has finished the chapter, he makes a fair copy, and further emendations as he writes.

In like fashion, revising in the course of composition, Tolkien continues the story with the chapter 'Farewell to Lórien' (published bk. II, ch. 8). 'By this time,' Christopher Tolkien has said, 'it had become my father's method to begin making a fair copy before a new stretch of the narrative had proceeded very far' (*The Treason of Isengard*, p. 267): the fair copy is built up in stages, as different parts of the draft text are completed. During the writing of the chapters set in Lothlórien Tolkien temporarily rejects *Aragorn* as Trotter's true name in favour first of *Elfstone* (and replaces the name *Aragorn* with *Elfstone* haphazardly in earlier text as far back as the chapter at Bree and the fifth version of the Council of Elrond), then rejects *Elfstone* for *Ingold*, before returning to *Elfstone*. He works on the two songs sung by Galadriel; the one she sings on the swan-boat is already close to the published text, but *Namárië* still differs considerably.

Before he writes the conclusion of 'Farewell to Lórien', Tolkien drafts a substantial outline of subsequent chapters. He imagines Boromir's encounter with Frodo, his attempt to seize the Ring, Frodo's flight, and Frodo and Sam's journey in Mordor. The last of these becomes actual narrative for much of its length. Within the draft Tolkien draws a small sketch of the gate of Minas Morgul (*Artist and Illustrator*, fig. 170; *The Treason of Isengard*, p. 342). On the back of the first leaf of this outline he makes rough workings for a revision of his *Lay of Aotrou and Itroun* (completed in its original form in 1930), to which he also turns at this time.

Tolkien then continues *The Lord of the Rings* with a new chapter, 'The Scattering of the Company' (later divided into 'The Great River' and 'The Breaking of the Fellowship', published bk. II, ch. 9–10). Due to the wartime paper shortage he scribbles some of the initial rough draft of the first part of the chapter between the lines of candidates' writing on examination scripts. Having made a fair copy, he emends it heavily and rewrites a section on inserted slips. Uncertain as to whether time moved at a different pace, or no time passed at all, while the Company was in Lothlórien, he writes several versions of the conversation on the subject (ultimately in 'The Great River'), and devises variant time-schemes. On one of the latter he notes, or will note at a later date, that the phases of the moon given in the scheme relate to those in our world for 1941–2, plus six days (altered to five days).

For the first part of 'The Breaking of the Fellowship' (as it became) Tolkien achieves a text in fair copy manuscript only after much experimentation and correction; for the second he has much less difficulty. Probably at this time he draws the related aerial view *Rauros Falls & the Tindrock* (*Artist and Illustrator*, fig. 159). While writing an outline for the end of the chapter and the beginning of Book III, evidently in December 1941 or January 1942, he doodles references to the Muar River and the Japanese attack on Malaya that occurred at that time. Tolkien hesitates about Aragorn's actions at the beginning of 'The Departure of Boromir', the first chapter of Book III, but parts of this are already close to the published text. Within the draft he draws a sketch of the area near Amon Hen (*The Treason of Isengard*, p. 383). He continues the draft without a break into 'The Riders of Rohan' (published bk. III, ch. 2), but finds it necessary to rewrite the first part when he decides to make a radical alteration in the story. In this chapter, as in those that follow, Tolkien adopts 'the practice, occasionally found earlier, of erasing his primary draft, or substantial portions of it, and writing a new version on the pages where it had stood' (Christopher Tolkien, *The Treason of Isengard*, p. 390). The next section, however (published as bk. III, ch. 3–4, 'The Uruk-hai' and 'Treebeard'), almost writes itself, with both draft and fair copy manuscripts close to the final text. Around this time Charles Williams queries a phrase in the chapter, which Tolkien probably has read to the Inklings.

7 December 1941 Japanese forces attack Pearl Harbor, Hawaii.

8 December 1941 The United States and Great Britain declare war on Japan.

11 December 1941 Germany and Italy, as allies of Japan, declare war on the United States.

18 December 1941 A National Service Act in Britain provides for conscription of unmarried women between the ages of 20 and 30, to work in factories, nursing, transport, and other key occupations. Later in the war, conscription was extended also to married women, unless pregnant or with young children.

22 December 1941 Tolkien, as 'Father Christmas', writes to Priscilla. Fewer children write to him because of the 'horrible war', and his stores are getting low: 'I have now to send what I can instead of what is asked for'. He describes another invasion by Goblins and how they were routed, but has not had time to draw a picture this year. He could not find a copy of *Moldy Warp, the Mole* by Alison Uttley, so is sending Priscilla other books he hopes she will like.

End of 1941 Michael Tolkien transfers into the Royal Air Force and trains to become a rear-gunner in bomber aircraft. He sees action over France and Germany.

1942

7 January 1942 The sixty-fifth birthday of place-name scholar Eilert Ekwall is marked by the publication of *A Philological Miscellany Presented to Eilert Ekwall* (Uppsala: A.-B. Lundequistska Bokhandeln, 1942). This includes a statement of mutual respect signed by Tolkien, colleagues at Oxford, and other English scholars.

18 January 1942 Hilary Full Term begins. Tolkien's scheduled lectures for this term are: Old English Verse: Metre, Style, and Diction on Tuesdays and Thursdays at 11.00 a.m. in the Taylor Institution, beginning 20 January; and the Old English *Exodus* on Tuesdays and Thursdays at 12.00 noon in the Taylor Institution, beginning 20 January. He will continue to supervise B.Litt. student M.Y. Pickard and probationer B.Litt. student M.B. Salu. – Christopher Tolkien matriculates at Trinity College, Oxford when only seventeen. Like many others, he has entered university early, in order to complete some of his studies before being called up for war service.

21 January 1942 Tolkien attends a Pembroke College meeting.

25 January 1942 In the evening, Tolkien attends a dinner of The Society hosted by Lord David Cecil in the common room of New College, Oxford. Five members are present.

30 January 1942 Tolkien chairs an English Faculty Board meeting. – He also attends a General Board meeting.

?February–?Midsummer 1942 Continuing work on *The Lord of the Rings*, Tolkien writes 'The White Rider' (published bk. III, ch. 5): 'initial drafting not erased or overwritten, more developed but discontinuous drafting, and a "fair copy" that itself underwent constant correction in the act of composition' (Christopher Tolkien, *The Treason of Isengard*, p. 425). In the midst of this process he makes two outlines of the course of the story foreseen from Fangorn, though he still has not conceived many significant parts of the story yet to be told. One of the outlines is very extensive, with significant changes to the overall chronology. He then continues the draft of 'The White Rider' into 'The King of the Golden Hall' (published bk. III, ch. 6) – certainly after 9 February 1942, as the name *Gondor* now appears – and writes at least half of the new chapter before stopping to revise the conclusion of 'The White Rider'. *See note.*

February 1942 *The Screwtape Letters* by C.S. Lewis, dedicated to Tolkien, is published.

2 February 1942 Tolkien certifies that M.B. Salu is qualified to undertake research for a B.Litt. Her thesis is to be a *Grammar of Ancrene Wisse (Phonology and Accidence)*, supervised by Tolkien.

5 February 1942 Tolkien chairs an English Faculty Library Committee meeting. The question of War Damage Insurance for the Library is discussed, and Tolkien is asked to make preliminary inquiries about it.

9 February 1942 Soap is rationed in Britain. – Tolkien writes a note recording his decision to alter some place names in *The Lord of the Rings*, including *Ondor* to *Gondor*.

13 February 1942 Tolkien attends a General Board meeting.

27 February 1942 Tolkien attends a General Board meeting.

5 March 1942 Tolkien chairs an English Faculty Library Committee meeting. Having investigated the question of insurance for the Library against war damage, he explains that the University has not taken out a specific policy, but is prepared to cover the cost of a basic working library should the need arise.

11 March 1942 Tolkien attends a Pembroke College meeting.

12 March 1942 George S. Gordon dies.

13 March 1942 Tolkien chairs an English Faculty Board meeting. He is asked to write to Mrs George S. Gordon on behalf of the Board, and to express to her the members' sense of loss to English studies by the death of her husband. The Board agrees to changes to qualifications for candidates to the Final Honour School to take effect in Trinity Term 1942 and in 1943.

14 March 1942 Hilary Full Term ends. – A funeral service for George S. Gordon is held in Magdalen College Chapel.

?April 1942 Tolkien writes the story **Leaf by Niggle*. He will later recall that he 'woke up one morning . . . with that odd thing virtually complete in my head. It took only a few hours to get down, and then copy out' (letter to Stanley Unwin, *c.* 18 March 1945, *Letters*, p. 113). *See note.*

23 April 1942 R.W. Chambers dies.

24 April 1942 Tolkien attends a General Board meeting.

26 April 1942 Trinity Full Term begins. Tolkien's scheduled lectures and classes for this term are: Anglo-Saxon Reader (class) on Tuesdays and Thursdays at 11.00 a.m. in the Taylor Institution, beginning 28 April; and Old English Sounds and Inflexions on Tuesdays and Thursdays at 12.00 noon in the Taylor Institution, beginning 28 April. He will continue to supervise B.Litt. students M.Y. Pickard and Mary Salu.

29 April 1942 Tolkien attends a Pembroke College meeting.

7 May 1942 Tolkien chairs an English Faculty Library Committee meeting. The Taylor Reading Rooms are being made available for the consultation of English Library books. – Tolkien chairs an English Faculty Board meeting, held unusually on a Thursday rather than a Friday. He is elected to the Nominating Committee for Pass Moderations for three years from 1 October 1942.

8 May 1942 Tolkien attends a General Board meeting.

15 May 1942 Tolkien chairs a special meeting of the English Faculty Board at 3.30 p.m. in the Board Room of the Clarendon Building. Kenneth Sisam is elected a member of the electors to the Rawlinson and Bosworth Professorship of Anglo-Saxon, replacing the late R.W. Chambers. The Board approves changes in requirements for papers and special studies in different sections of the School.

9 June 1942 Tolkien attends a General Board meeting.

11 June 1942 The English Faculty Library Committee, in Tolkien's absence, decides to buy books from the collection of the late George S. Gordon. – English Final Honour School examinations begin. Tolkien is an examiner with H.F.B. Brett-Smith, Leonard Rice-Oxley, Dorothy Everett, and C.S. Lewis. There are 125 candidates. The examiners will submit a statement dated 17 July.

19 June 1942 At an English Faculty Board meeting, in Tolkien's absence, a regulation is made that 'the Shortened Final Honour School will be open to candidates of 5–7 Terms' standing who have previously passed in two Sections of the Special Examination, of which Section E1 must be one. They must offer five papers from one of the three Courses presented in the regulations for the full Honour School . . . and will be permitted to include in their choice the subjects of their Sections' (Oxford University Archives FA 4/5/1/1). Probably in relation to this, Tolkien will prepare for discussion a draft paper on the regulations for Shortened Honours: he will suggest either that there be no compulsory preliminary examination, and after two years of continuous study the candidate should take six papers of the full Honour School (equivalent to not less than two-thirds of the full requirement); or that the candidate should take six papers or subjects, two in reduced form in sections which they must pass, and four other papers in full form in the Honour School in Trinity Term.

20 June 1942 Trinity Full Term ends.

24 June 1942 Encaenia.

Summer–?autumn 1942 Tolkien writes a long portion of *The Lord of the Rings*, eventually divided into five chapters ('Helm's Deep', 'The Road to Isengard', 'Flotsam and Jetsam', 'The Voice of Saruman', and 'The Palantír', published bk. III, ch. 7–11), apparently working on it as a whole rather than bringing each part to a developed state before beginning work on the next. 'Passages of very rough and piecemeal drafting' are 'built into a completed manuscript that was in turn heavily overhauled, the whole complex advancing and changing at the same time' (Christopher Tolkien, *The War of the Ring*, p. 3). Tolkien occasionally pauses to write an outline of the story to come or changes to be made. He writes some early drafting for 'The Road to Isengard' on the back of a letter he has received, dated 31 July 1942.

The story of Helm's Deep is developed in successive drafts in which the fortifications become more elaborate and the account of its defence more complex. At this time Tolkien probably redraws the pertinent section of his working map, and also makes a small aerial view and map of Helm's Deep, as well as a more elaborate picture, *Helm's Deep and the Hornburg* (*Artist and Illustrator*, figs. 160, 161). He completes 'The Road to Isengard' only after writing seven versions of Théoden and Gandalf's conversation about riding to Isengard, and four of Merry's lecture on pipeweed, besides much other preliminary drafting. Apparently satisfied, he makes a fair copy, but removes most of the material on pipeweed into the Prologue of *The Lord of the Rings*; then he rejects much of what he has written and begins to draft again, with a different time scheme and changes in the route to Isengard. Finally he makes a fair copy of this second version. It takes him a long time to decide on the appearance of the tower of Orthanc, developing ideas in draft text and in a series of fifteen drawings. The most elaborate of these, which fits the preliminary draft and shows the tower within the circle of Isengard and with the mountains behind (*Artist and Illustrator*, fig. 162; see also figs. 163–4, *The War of the Ring*, p. 33, and *Sauron Defeated* (1992), pp. 138–9), is drawn on the back of an examination script of a candidate who took final examinations in June 1942.

In 'The Voice of Saruman' the interview with Saruman is completed only after several drafts. When he comes to 'The Palantír' the appearance of that object is unexpected, and he is not immediately certain how to use it in the story. As he later wrote: 'I knew nothing of the *Palantíri*, though from the moment the Orthanc-stone was cast from the window, I recognized it, and knew the meaning of the "rhyme of lore" that had been running through my mind: *seven stars and seven stones and one white tree*' (letter to W.H. Auden, 7 June 1955, *Letters*, p. 217). Later in the year he will read this section to C.S. Lewis and, based on his criticism, delete some 'passages of light-hearted hobbit conversation' (letter to Charlotte and Denis Plimmer, 8 February 1967, *Letters*, p. 376).

It is possibly now that Tolkien drafts in succession two brief openings to the first chapter of Book IV, 'The Taming of Sméagol', but does no further work on this section until spring 1944.

4 July 1942 In the evening, Tolkien attends a dinner of The Society hosted by Nevill Coghill in the New Room at Magdalen College. Six members are present. They dine on clear soup; salmon with frozen peas; gooseberry meringues; sherry, hock, port, and madeira; strawberries, cherries, etc.

c. **4 August 1942** Christopher Tolkien completes a typescript copy of the fair copy of the *Lord of the Rings* chapter 'Galadriel'. Christopher will also make copies of 'Farewell to Lórien' and 'The Scattering of the Company' (later 'The Great River' and 'The Breaking of the Fellowship').

27 August 1942 Basil Blackwell, to whom Tolkien apparently has lent his translation of *Pearl*, writes to express his delight in it. He asks if Tolkien would write an introduction aimed at the lay reader rather than the student, and offers to purchase the copyright to the translation, the sum to be placed against

Tolkien's outstanding account at Blackwell's Bookshop. Tolkien seems already, or around this same time, to have offered translations of Middle English works also to Kenneth Sisam at Oxford University Press, but will give *Pearl* to Blackwell for setting in type.

6 September 1942 The German advance into the U.S.S.R. is halted at Stalingrad.

Autumn Term 1942 Priscilla begins to attend the Oxford High School for Girls.

19 September 1942 Tolkien attends a General Board meeting.

9 October 1942 Tolkien attends a General Board meeting.

11 October 1942 Michaelmas Full Term begins. Tolkien's scheduled lectures for this term are: *Beowulf* (text, lines 1–1650) on Tuesdays and Thursdays at 10.00 a.m. in the Taylor Institution, beginning 13 October; and Language of the Vespasian Hymns on Tuesdays and Thursdays at 11.00 a.m. in the Taylor Institution, beginning 13 October. He will continue to supervise B.Litt. students M.Y. Pickard and Mary Salu. – Possibly in connection with the present lectures, Tolkien compiles a chart of vowel-changes which map 'Normal Development of "A" in Vespasian Ps[alter] & Ancrene Wisse'.

14 October 1942 Tolkien attends a Pembroke College meeting.

17 October 1942 In the evening, Tolkien attends a dinner of The Society hosted by G.F. Hudson at New College, Oxford. Five members are present. They dine on soup, mutton, and a sweet, with sherry and Burgundy wine, and do not break up until midnight.

23 October–13 November 1942 General Montgomery's 8th Army attacks the Germans under General Rommel at El Alamein in North Africa, achieving victory on 4 November and recapturing Tobruk on 13 November.

23 October 1942 Tolkien chairs an English Faculty Board meeting. He is re-elected chairman for 1942–3. – He also attends a General Board meeting.

4 November 1942 Tolkien attends a Pembroke College meeting.

6 November 1942 Tolkien attends a General Board meeting.

26 November 1942 Tolkien chairs an English Faculty Library Committee meeting.

1 December 1942 Sir William Beveridge, in a report on social insurance, advocates for Britain a comprehensive scheme of welfare 'from the cradle to the grave'.

4 December 1942 Tolkien chairs an English Faculty Board meeting. He and David Nichol Smith are appointed examiners of the B.Litt. thesis of *R.G.L. (Roger Lancelyn) Green of Merton College, *Andrew Lang as a Writer of Fairy Tales and Romances.* – Tolkien also attends a General Board meeting. – Stanley Unwin writes to Tolkien. The London bookseller Foyles is to publish *The Hobbit* in its Children's Book Club, which will enable a reprint of the Allen & Unwin edition in the same press run.

5 December 1942 Michaelmas Full Term ends.

7 December 1942 Tolkien writes to Stanley Unwin. He wonders if, because of the war, it is 'of any use, other than private and family amusement, to endeavour to complete the sequel to *The Hobbit*. I have worked on it at intervals since 1938, all such intervals in fact as trebled official work, quadrupled domestic work, and "Civil Defence" have left. It is now approaching completion.' He hopes to have free time to work on *The Lord of the Rings* during the Christmas vacation, and thinks that he might finish the book early in 1943. It has now reached Chapter 31 (as it then was numbered, i.e. 'The Palantír'), and Tolkien believes that it needs at least six more chapters to be finished; these are already sketched. It is in typescript up to about Chapter 23, and has been approved by his sons and C.S. Lewis. In regard to *The Hobbit*, Tolkien asks if all of the corrections he has sent for that work (he encloses a list) have been incorporated in the 1942 reprint (not published until 1943). He also asks if Unwin would consider the publication of 'a volume, containing three or four shorter "Fairy" stories and some verses? "Farmer Giles" which I once submitted to you, has pleased a number of children and grown-ups. If too short, I could add to it one or two similar tales, and include some verse on similar topics, including "Tom Bombadil"' (*Letters*, p. 58). If a reprint of the Clark Hall *Beowulf and the Finnesburg Fragment* should become possible, he would correct a serious misprint in his part and make some corrections in Wrenn's part of the book.

16 December 1942 Stanley Unwin writes to Tolkien. He is trying to find out if all of the corrections had been made in the reprint of *The Hobbit* before moulds of the type were made (for the production of printing plates). The new edition of *The Hobbit* is delayed at the binders. He would be happy to consider a volume of shorter fairy-stories, and would like to look at *Mr. Bliss* again. There is no possibility of a reprint of the Clark Hall volume for some time.

24 December 1942 Tolkien, as 'Father Christmas', writes to Priscilla. He has not had a letter from her, but expects that she has been very busy at her new school. His stocks are very low (except for books, which he is sending her), and 'deliveries too are more difficult than ever this year with damaged houses and houseless people and all the dreadful events going on in your countries.' The North Polar Bear sends a mysterious parcel for one of Priscilla's toy bears, apparently something to eat.

1943

1943 or 1944 Tolkien prepares an edition of the Middle English poem *Sir Orfeo*.

1943 Tolkien revises a talk on Old English Verse, probably to give at the Oxford High School for Girls. – Ronald and Edith Tolkien are almost the only guests at the wedding of Gabriel Turville-Petre and Joan Blomfield, both former B.Litt. students of Tolkien. – Christopher and Priscilla Tolkien assist their father in typing *The Lord of the Rings*. Christopher also makes a map of Middle-earth based on his father's working map, and a similar map of the Shire.

Early 1943 Tolkien becomes godfather to R.E. Havard's son, David.

January–mid-March 1943 Some Navy and Air Force cadets are to be drafted to Oxford to take six-month academic courses at the same time that they train to be officers. Tolkien works on a scheme of English courses and consults prospective tutors and lecturers. Special lectures and courses are needed to suit the less academically trained audience.

?January–?August 1943 Tolkien revises and enlarges his lecture *On Fairy-Stories* and makes a fair copy.

11 January 1943 Tolkien's first grandchild is born: Michael George Reuel, son of *Michael and Joan Tolkien.

15 January 1943 Tolkien attends a General Board meeting.

17 January 1943 Hilary Full Term begins. Tolkien's scheduled lectures for this term are: *Beowulf* (lines 1–1650) on Tuesdays and Thursdays at 10.00 a.m. in the Taylor Institution, beginning 19 January; the Old English *Exodus* on Tuesdays and Thursdays at 11.00 a.m. in the Taylor Institution, beginning 19 January; *Beowulf* (lines 1651–end) on Fridays at 10.00 a.m. in the Taylor Institution, beginning 22 January; and Sweet's *Anglo-Saxon Reader* (nos. i, x, xvi, xxvi) on Fridays at 11.00 a.m. in the Taylor Institution. He will continue to supervise B.Litt. students M.Y. Pickard and M.B. Salu.

20 January 1943 Tolkien attends a Pembroke College meeting.

23 January 1943 In the evening, Tolkien attends a dinner of The Society hosted by Mark Van Oss in the Chaplain's dining room at Magdalen College. Seven members are present. They dine on soup, chicken, a sweet, Welsh rarebit, sherry, claret, and port. Conversation is sustained until about 11.30.

26 January 1943 Tolkien sprains his ankle.

29 January 1943 Tolkien writes to J.L.N. O'Loughlin. Because he is organizing courses for Navy and Air Force cadets, he probably will have no vacations in the near future. – At an English Faculty Board meeting, in Tolkien's absence, he is appointed chairman of a committee 'to reconsider the regulations for Examinations (other than Emergency Examinations) under the supervision of the Board' (Oxford University Archives FA 4/5/1/1).

31 January 1943 The German 6th Army surrenders at Stalingrad.

4 February 1943 Tolkien chairs an English Faculty Library Committee meeting.

12 February 1943 Tolkien attends a General Board meeting.

17 February 1943 In the evening, *E.R. Eddison, author of *The Worm Ouroboros*, dines at Magdalen College with C.S. Lewis. It is not clear if Tolkien, Warnie Lewis, and Charles Williams are also present, but certainly they join Lewis and Eddison afterwards for a meeting of the Inklings in Lewis's rooms.

26 February 1943 Tolkien attends a General Board meeting.

27 February 1943 Tolkien almost certainly attends the ceremony at which Charles Williams is given an honorary M.A. degree, and possibly has helped to arrange its conferment. – Edith Wardale dies.

8 March 1943 Tolkien and David Nichol Smith examine Roger Lancelyn Green of Merton College *viva voce* on his B.Litt. thesis, *Andrew Lang as a Writer of Fairy Tales and Romances*, at 11.30 a.m. at Merton.

12 March 1943 Tolkien chairs an English Faculty Board meeting. He, C.S. Lewis, and Leonard Rice-Oxley are appointed to be examiners of Allied prisoners of war in German and Italian camps who have worked at the Board's set syllabus. Tolkien submits a scheme for an English course for Navy and Air Force cadets he has drawn up after consultation with tutors. This is approved, and he is appointed director of the course. He will hold this office until March 1944. – Tolkien also attends a General Board meeting.

13 March 1943 Hilary Full Term ends.

16 March 1943 Tolkien types for reproduction his scheme of an English course for cadets. In the first half of the course all cadets must study the general history of English Literature from its beginnings to the present; outlines of the history of the English Language; and Modern English, including the writing of English and the criticism of contemporary examples of written English. Exercises in the writing of English will continue during the second half of the course, when each cadet will also choose one of a group of optional subjects for which appropriate works will be selected for reading and study; in the course to begin on 8 April, these subjects will be English Poetry, or Drama, or the English Novel, or Essays, Letters, and Biography. It is proposed that during the first half of the first course general lectures on the optional subjects will be provided, and cadets should attend the lectures on two of these subjects.

From ?mid-March 1943 Probably in mid-March Tolkien sends a letter to those who are to be directors and tutors of cadets at Oxford, asking them to indicate which of 25, 26, 27 March would be the best date for a meeting. In addition to any lecturing to cadets that he may undertake, as director of the course he is responsible for general administration. Among his duties he must personally interview the cadets, keep in touch with all of those concerned with the programme, chair meetings, and arrange substitutes for lecturers who are indisposed. At least once, it seems, he himself substitutes for C.S. Lewis: in a surviving draft lecture he says that although Lewis probably would have talked about the matter of King Arthur and its relation to medieval literature in English, Tolkien thinks that he had better talk about Language.

25 March 1943 Basil Blackwell sends Tolkien proofs of *Pearl* and asks him to correct them at his leisure. He still hopes that Tolkien will write an introduction.

April 1943 *Christian Behaviour* by C.S. Lewis is published; it includes a chapter on 'Christian Marriage'. Tolkien writes and keeps in his copy of the book a lengthy draft letter to Lewis commenting on and disagreeing with many of Lewis's views on the subject.

8 April 1943 The first course for cadets begins.

20 April 1943 Tolkien lunches with the Air Squadron, invited probably because of his work with Air Force cadets. – Tolkien writes to C.S. Lewis, who has been ill and unable to teach. '[M.R.] Ridley was so astounded at the ignorance of all 22 cadets, revealed in his first class, that he leaped at the chance of another hour [as a substitute for Lewis], esp[ecially] since otherwise there was no "Use of E[nglish]" class next week at all' (*Letters*, p. 59).

21 April 1943 Tolkien writes to the poet Alan Rook, thanking him for sending a copy of his book *These Are My Comrades* (1943). Tolkien recalls pleasant days when he and Rook met before the war; he has heard news of Rook occasionally through Mrs Joseph Wright. He promises to send Rook a story to read, almost certainly *Leaf by Niggle*.

22 April 1943 E.O.G. Turville-Petre writes to Tolkien. Presumably at Tolkien's request, Turville-Petre sends him two texts of the Lord's Prayer, probably both in Old Icelandic, and says that he thinks that one of them is the oldest Icelandic version preserved. He promises to send more in a few days.

30 April 1943 Tolkien attends a General Board meeting.

2 May 1943 Trinity Full Term begins. Tolkien's scheduled lectures for this term are: Old English Texts on Tuesdays and Thursdays at 10.00 a.m. in the Taylor Institution, beginning 4 May; and Outlines of Old English Phonology on Tuesdays and Thursdays at 11.00 a.m. in the Taylor Institution, beginning 4 May. He will continue to supervise B.Litt. students M.Y. Pickard and M.B. Salu.

4 May 1943 Tolkien and David Nichol Smith sign their report (written by Tolkien) of their examination of Roger Lancelyn Green. Although they are impressed with his thesis, they recommend that it be referred back for correction and more work on its central chapters on fairy tales. – In the evening, Tolkien dines at the George Restaurant (one of the finest restaurants in Oxford) with R.E. Havard, the Lewis brothers, and Charles Williams. After dinner they probably go to Lewis's rooms in Magdalen College for a meeting of the Inklings.

12 May 1943 The Allies' North African campaign ends.

13 May 1943 Tolkien attends an English Faculty Library Committee meeting. The University Chest (the committee dealing with University finances) has written to say that the University Auditor has noted some informality in the system of registering students as readers of the Library. Tolkien is asked to explain to an official of the Chest that under war conditions it is difficult to impose a more complicated practice than that currently in use. – Allen & Unwin send Tolkien a royalty statement for 1942. Binding problems have delayed release of the new printing of *The Hobbit*.

14 May 1943 Tolkien chairs an English Faculty Board meeting. Roger Lancelyn Green is granted leave to re-submit his B.Litt. thesis within the statutory period. The Board discusses changes in set books for 1943–4. The committee appointed on 29 January, of which Tolkien is a member, is asked 'to report on the establishment of a Part III in the Shortened Honour School for candidates who return to Oxford after war-service' (Oxford University Archives FA 4/5/1/1). – Tolkien also attends a General Board meeting.

28 May 1943 Tolkien attends a General Board meeting.

17 June 1943 English Final Honour School examinations begin.

24 June 1943 Tolkien meets Warnie Lewis and Charles Williams for a drink, probably in the late morning.

25 June 1943 Tolkien chairs an English Faculty Board meeting. The Board approves a scheme for a Part III of the Honour School for candidates who return after war service. – Tolkien also attends a General Board Meeting. He is named to the electors to the Goldsmiths' Readership in English Language until Michaelmas Term 1948. (No election will be held during the time he holds office.) – The cadets attending the Oxford course begin a break, ending 5 July.

26 June 1943 Trinity Full Term ends.

30 June 1943 Encaenia.

July 1943 Christopher Tolkien is called up into the Royal Air Force, 'in the midst of typing and revising the Hobbit sequel and doing a lovely map' (Tolkien, letter to Stanley Unwin, 29 June 1944, *Letters*, p. 86).

7 July 1943 Basil Blackwell writes to Tolkien, reminding him that he has not yet returned the proofs of *Pearl*, and asking again about an introduction to the work.

10 July 1943 The Allies invade Sicily.

12 July 1943 Allen & Unwin send Tolkien two complimentary copies of Foyles' Children's Book Club edition of *The Hobbit*.

3 August 1943 Tolkien writes a long letter to schoolgirl *Hobbit* enthusiasts Leila Keane and Patricia Kirke, in reply to their questions about runes. He tells them about runes in our world, in *The Hobbit*, and in the forthcoming *Lord of the Rings*, and about different writing systems and languages in Middle-earth and how he has represented these in his stories.

By 5 August 1943 Charles Williams, on Tolkien's behalf, asks Margaret Douglas, who types material for him, to make a typescript of *On Fairy-Stories*. She will find Tolkien's handwriting difficult to read.

September 1943 At the beginning of this month the first group of cadets take examinations (one paper is dated 6 September). – A second group of cadets arrives probably towards the end of September.

3 September 1943 The Allies land in southern Italy.

8 September 1943 Italy capitulates.

16 September 1943 The first course for cadets ends.

17 September 1943 Basil Blackwell sends Tolkien another reminder about *Pearl*. He needs to set something on the credit side of Tolkien's account with Blackwell's Bookshop.

c. 18 September 1943 Tolkien replies to Basil Blackwell, sending him a cheque. He apparently offers an excuse for not completing his work on *Pearl*.

22 September 1943 Tolkien writes to Christopher. He has heard C.S. Lewis read his 'new translation in rhymed alexandrines of the *Aeneid*' in his rooms in Magdalen College (quoted by Christopher Tolkien in private correspondence).

24 September 1943 Basil Blackwell acknowledges Tolkien's cheque and hopes that he will be able to deal with *Pearl* in the coming term.

29 September 1943 Tolkien discusses with Charles Williams the lectures Williams will be giving during Michaelmas Term.

10 October 1943 Michaelmas Full Term begins. Tolkien's scheduled lectures for this term are: *Beowulf* (text, lines 1–1650) on Tuesdays and Thursdays at 10.00 a.m. in the Taylor Institution, beginning 12 October; and Old English Texts on Tuesdays and Thursdays at 11.00 a.m. in the Taylor Institution, beginning 12 October. He will continue to supervise B.Litt. students M.Y. Pickard and M.B. Salu.

12 October 1943 Tolkien possibly attends a lecture given by Charles Williams. Certainly he meets Williams during the day, and reassures him that the restlessness of his audience was probably because the Queen was in Oxford.

13 October 1943 Tolkien attends a Pembroke College meeting. – Italy declares war on Germany, with which it previously had been allied. Germany occupies most of Italy.

14 October 1943 The Queen of the Netherlands receives a Doctor of Civil Law degree by Diploma in the Sheldonian Theatre, Oxford at 2.30 p.m.

22 October 1943 Tolkien chairs an English Faculty Board meeting. He reports that the scheme for a Part III of the Honour School for candidates who return after war service, approved at the previous meeting, does not seem to fit with any general scheme proposed, and that he has therefore withdrawn it. The Board refers the scheme back to the original committee (of which Tolkien is a member) for further consideration. Tolkien is re-elected chairman of the Board for another year, and is appointed supervisor of Roger Lancelyn Green's B.Litt. thesis, replacing David Nichol Smith. – Tolkien also attends a General Board meeting.

Michaelmas Term 1943 Once each week during this term Roger Lancelyn Green spends an hour with Tolkien to discuss the revision of Green's B.Litt. thesis. Green will later recall that Tolkien admitted: 'It was my fault that your thesis was referred back – you must blame me! But I wanted to know more about the Fairies!' In consequence of which, Green now writes an additional chapter, 'of which I treasure the original draft written all over by Tolkien with comments and suggestions' (Green, 'Recollections', *Amon Hen* 44 (May 1980), p. 7). – Possibly during this time, Green confesses to Tolkien that he has written a fairy-story himself, *The Wonderful Stranger*. Tolkien insists on reading and criticizing it (Green will think that he did not care for it much), and in return he lends Green *Farmer Giles of Ham* (then called *The Lord of Thame*).

26 October 1943 In the evening, Tolkien visits C.S. Lewis in his rooms in Magdalen College. There he meets C.E.M. Joad, the philosopher and broadcaster, who had been dining with Lewis. Tolkien and Joad find that they agree on many fundamental points, and Joad talks about Russia which he has visited.

29 October 1943 Tolkien sleeps at the air raid wardens' area headquarters.

?November 1943 Tolkien writes a poem, *A Closed Letter to Andrea Charicoryides Surnamed Polygrapheus, Logothete of the Theme of Geodesia in the Empire, Bard of the Court of Camelot, Malleus Malitiarium, Inclinga Sum Sometimes Known as Charles Williams*.

2 November 1943 Tolkien attends, and probably chairs, a meeting of tutors concerned with courses for the cadets, and produces some notes of decisions.

3 November 1943 Tolkien attends a Pembroke College meeting.

5 November 1943 Tolkien attends a General Board meeting.

10 November 1943 In the morning, Tolkien hears Charles Williams read two chapters of his new novel *All Hallows' Eve*.

28 November–1 December 1943 The leaders of Great Britain, the United States, and the Soviet Union meet in Teheran.

29 November 1943 Tolkien writes to Christopher, then in a training camp in Manchester, on his feelings about politics and those who govern.

1 December 1943 Tolkien attends a Pembroke College meeting.

4 December 1943 Michaelmas Full Term ends.

9 December 1943 Tolkien writes to Christopher. Life has been a rush, and he has not seen C.S. Lewis or Charles Williams for weeks. 'The daily round(s) and the common task + + [*sic*] which furnish so much more than one actually asks. No great fun, no amusements; no bright new idea; not even a thin small joke. Nothing to read – and even the papers with nothing but Teheran Ballyhoo.' He finds 'Americo-cosmopolitanism very terrifying', i.e. the introduction of American ways throughout the world, and expresses his love for England '(not Great Britain and certainly not the British Commonwealth (grr!))' (*Letters*, p. 65). He may have to go to Cardiff on 15–16 December to hold a *viva* (in the event, postponed until January).

16 December 1943 The first half of the English course for the second group of Navy and Air Force cadets ends.

Christmas 1943 Tolkien writes his final letter as 'Father Christmas'. He supposes that Priscilla will hang up her stocking just once more, and has sent nearly all of the books she asked for. Although it is a 'grim' year 'I am still very much alive, and shall come back again soon, as merry as ever.'

29 December 1943 The second half of the English course for Navy and Air Force cadets begins.

Late December 1943 Tolkien receives a message from Simonne d'Ardenne in Belgium through the International Red Cross.

Late 1943 or early 1944 Consulted by a Polish military officer named Poptawski about devising a new technical vocabulary, Tolkien undertakes some study of the Polish language.

1944

1944 Tolkien's edition of *Sir Orfeo*, prepared for the use of cadets, is reproduced by mimeograph. Possibly around this time, he also makes a Modern English translation of the poem. – Michael Tolkien is judged medically unfit for further military service, and returns to his studies at Trinity College, Oxford. – *Robert Murray, grandson of Sir James A.H. Murray of the *Oxford English Dictionary*, becomes a friend of the Tolkien family. An undergraduate at Corpus Christi College, Oxford, he is introduced to the Tolkiens by his aunt

Rosfrith, a friend of the family. Between now and 1954 he will read *The Lord of the Rings* in manuscript and proof.

6 January 1944 Tolkien sends a notice to those involved with the Oxford courses for cadets. He details the lectures and classes arranged thus far for the second half of the academic year, and asks to receive offers of other lectures and to know if those who took part in the 'Use of English' classes (in the first half) wish to arrange any further work. He himself is possibly involved with 'History of English' on Mondays at 11.00 a.m., the only class or lecture for which the notice names no member of the Faculty.

8 January 1944 Tolkien writes to Christopher, urging him to remember his guardian angel and to make a habit of saying the 'praises', which Tolkien often does himself (in Latin).

12 January 1944 Tolkien certifies that Roger Lancelyn Green has completed course work for his B.Litt.

14 January 1944 Tolkien attends a General Board meeting. – He telephones Charles Williams to ask him to speak to the Navy cadets.

16 January 1944 Hilary Full Term begins. Tolkien's scheduled lectures for this term are: *Beowulf* (lines 1651–end) on Mondays at 10.00 a.m. in the Taylor Institution, beginning 17 January; the Old English *Exodus* on Tuesdays and Thursdays at 11.00 a.m. in the Taylor Institution, beginning 18 January; *Beowulf* (lines 1–1650) on Wednesdays at 10.00 a.m. in the Taylor Institution, beginning 19 January; and Language of the Vespasian Hymns on Thursdays at 12.00 noon in the Taylor Institution, beginning 20 January. He will continue to supervise B.Litt. students M.Y. Pickard and M.B. Salu.

17 January 1944 Tolkien gives two lectures, one of them possibly 'History of English' for the cadets. – Later he confers with E.O.G. Turville-Petre about a *viva* to be held in Cardiff. – That night he sleeps at the air raid wardens' headquarters. He shares the duty with Cecil Roth, with whom he stays up talking until after midnight. Tolkien finds it hard to sleep. – By this date, Christopher Tolkien is being sent to South Africa to train as a pilot.

18 January 1944 Cecil Roth wakes Tolkien at 6.50 a.m. so that he can attend Communion. Tolkien arrives at St Aloysius' at 7.15 in time for Confession before Mass. – Later he shops at the fishmonger before lecturing at 11.00 a.m. After the lecture he meets the Lewis brothers and Charles Williams in the White Horse pub. – Tolkien writes to Christopher, the first of at least eighty letters he will send to his son overseas in the next thirteen months, each letter and each page numbered 'so that if any go awry you will know – and the bare news of importance can be made up.' These provide, for this period, a picture of Tolkien's life in close (if often mundane) detail: e.g., for 18 January 1944, 'the *fouls* [hens] do not lay, but I have still to clean out their den' (*Letters*, p. 67).

19 January 1944 Tolkien attends a Pembroke College meeting. – Between now and 3 March, he writes four more letters to Christopher.

?24 or 25 January 1944 Tolkien meets the Lewis brothers and Charles Williams in the White Horse pub. Williams reads comments on Milton sent to him by his friend Lois Lang-Sims.

27 January 1944 Tolkien chairs an English Faculty Library Committee meeting.

28 January 1944 Tolkien chairs an English Faculty Board meeting. He is appointed to a committee to draft a statement for submission to the Hebdomadal Council by 3 February, giving the views of the Board about a recommendation in the Norwood Report (the report of the Committee on the Curriculum and Examinations in Secondary Schools, chaired by Sir Cyril Norwood) on the teaching of English in English Schools 'which, if adopted, would result in fewer students reading English Literature at the Universities' (Oxford University Archives FA 4/5/1/1). Tolkien also presents the report signed by all of the examiners, which he has written and typed, of the work of Allied prisoners of war who have been candidates in the Oxford examination for prisoners of war in English Language and Literature. Tolkien and David Nichol Smith are appointed examiners of Roger Lancelyn Green's resubmitted B.Litt. thesis. – Tolkien also attends a General Board meeting.

28 January–3 February 1944 During this period the committee established to draft a statement on the Norwood Report on behalf of the English Faculty Board completes its work quickly. Tolkien signs the statement as committee chairman. The Board 'unanimously protests against the dichotomy made in the Report . . . between "training in the use of the English language" and "the study of English literature". Teachers and pupils alike can best learn how to use English from those who have used it best. These writers are collectively called English Literature. . . . For some years past many teachers and examiners have been labouring to secure that the study of English shall yield its full value in a scheme of humane education; but their efforts are now threatened with frustration by the proposals of the Report, which on this topic are reactionary and ill-informed' (Oxford University Archives FA 4/5/2/7).

18 February 1944 Tolkien attends a General Board meeting.

26 February 1944 The second half of the English course for the second group of cadets ends.

1 March 1944 In the morning, Tolkien meets C.S. Lewis in a pub. – In a letter to Christopher, Tolkien says that he has been partly instrumental in R.E. Havard being recalled from a Navy posting on the other side of the world and re-posted to a Malaria Research Board in Oxford.

2–29 March 1944 During this period Tolkien writes five more letters to Christopher.

6 March 1944 Tolkien and David Nichol Smith re-examine Roger Lancelyn Green of Merton College *viva voce* on his B.Litt. thesis at 11.00 a.m. at Merton College. The examiners now feel that Green's thesis is well balanced.

8 March 1944 Tolkien attends a Pembroke College meeting.

10 March 1944 Tolkien chairs an English Faculty Board meeting. The Board agrees to support a General Preliminary Examination for admission to any Final Honour School, and that Latin should be compulsory for all Arts candidates. The Board recommends that C.T. Onions should continue in office as University Reader, as his teaching is essential and he cannot be replaced at present. M.R. Ridley is appointed to succeed Tolkien as director of the English course for Navy and Air Force cadets (though Tolkien will continue to be involved with the programme). – Tolkien also attends a General Board meeting.

11 March 1944 Hilary Full Term ends.

29 March 1944 Tolkien sees the Lewis brothers and lunches with C.S. Lewis, who reads him part of a new story, probably *The Great Divorce*. Lewis is pressuring Tolkien to finish *The Lord of the Rings*.

30 March 1944 Tolkien writes to Christopher that 'the "vac[ation]" is already half over & the exam. wood only just cleared', probably setting examinations for the University of Wales (*Letters*, p. 68).

31 March 1944 Tolkien spends much of the morning shopping and queuing, obtaining only one slab of pork pie. – He has a 'dreadfully bad and lugubriously dull dinner' in Pembroke College (letter to Christopher Tolkien, 3 April 1944, *Letters*, p. 69) and is glad to get home before 9.00 p.m.

April 1944 The third English course for cadets begins. It consists of 'Modern English (including the writing of English and criticism of contemporary examples of written English), to be taken by all cadets throughout the course; English Literature; Outlines of the History of English (optional)' (Oxford University Archives FA 4/5/1/1).

1 April 1944 Tolkien leaves 20 Northmoor Road at about 9.00 a.m., travels to Pembroke College where he leaves his bicycle, walks to the railway station, and catches the 9.30 a.m. train to Birmingham. He shares a railway carriage with an R.A.F. officer and a young American officer from New England, with whom Tolkien has lively conversation trying to enlighten the American about 'feudalism', English class distinctions and social behaviour, and accents. They have coffee in the refreshment room at Snow Hill station before parting. Tolkien then strolls through Birmingham and thinks that it has been more damaged by the growth of 'flat featureless modern buildings' than by enemy action. He takes a tram to Edgbaston Park Road where King Edward's School is now located, arriving at 12.15 p.m. to attend a lunch for Old Boys. He is not impressed by the 'ghastly utterly third-rate new school buildings' (letter to Christopher Tolkien, 3 April 1944, *Letters*, p. 70).

3 April 1944 Tolkien writes to Christopher that he has begun 'to nibble at [the] Hobbit again' (i.e. *The Lord of the Rings*) and has 'started to do some (painful) work on the chapter which picks up the adventures of Frodo and Sam again; and to get myself attuned have been copying and polishing the last written chapter (Orthanc-Stone [i.e. 'The Palantír', published bk. III, ch. 11])' (*Letters*, p. 69).

5 April 1944 Tolkien writes to Christopher that he is 'seriously embarked on an effort to finish my book, & have been sitting up rather late: a lot of re-reading and research required. And it is a painful sticky business getting into swing again. I have gone back to Sam and Frodo, and am trying to work out their adventures. A few pages for a lot of sweat: but at the moment they are just meeting Gollum on a precipice' (*Letters*, p. 70). – Tolkien takes up again the more developed of the two brief texts written in ?1942 for the beginning of the chapter that will become 'The Taming of Sméagol' (bk. IV, ch. 1), and continues the narrative. Through a series of drafts he tries to devise a way that is not too complicated for Frodo and Sam to descend from the Emyn Muil to the lands below. After he has drafted part of the chapter he begins a fair copy, but rejects parts of it and writes replacement pages; he completes the fair copy in stages. Towards the end of the chapter he seems to be moving forward more confidently. At the point where Frodo remembers his conversation with Gandalf about Bilbo's pity for Gollum, Tolkien decides that Gandalf should have said more, and alters the text of 'Ancient History' ('The Shadow of the Past', published bk. I, ch. 2). In the course of the work he makes two brief time-schemes, one of which synchronizes a passing storm with a storm at Helm's Deep in Book III.

?7 April 1944 Tolkien spends part of the day and night struggling with *The Lord of the Rings*.

8 April 1944 Tolkien writes to Christopher of the previous 'beautiful night with high moon. About 2 a.m. I was in the warm silver-lit garden, wishing we two could go for a walk' (quoted in *Biography*, p. 197).

12 April 1944 In the morning, Tolkien sees C.S. Lewis and Charles Williams for almost two hours. He reads them the completed chapter 'The Taming of Sméagol', which they approve. – He meets Edith and Priscilla for lunch, but they are unable to find anywhere to eat, and return home.

13 April 1944 Tolkien helps with admission of the new group of cadets; among the Navy cadets, though Tolkien does not realize it, is Rayner Unwin. – Later that day he begins to write a letter to Christopher (now in the Transvaal), and Mrs Connaughton, a family friend, arrives from Carmarthen with gifts of food. – In the evening, Tolkien attends a meeting of the Inklings in C.S. Lewis's rooms in Magdalen College. He is very impressed with the chapter Warnie Lewis reads from the book he is writing (*The Splendid Century: Some Aspects of French Life in the Reign of Louis XIV*, not published until 1953), even though Tolkien is not interested in its subject. He does not think so well of the concluding chapter of *The Great Divorce* read by C.S. Lewis. Charles Williams and R.E. Havard are also present at the meeting, which lasts until after midnight.

13–18 April 1944 Tolkien writes another chapter of *The Lord of the Rings*, which will become 'The Passage of the Marshes' (published bk. IV, ch. 2), begun by 13 April. He starts with rough preliminary drafting written at speed for one section, then makes a clearer manuscript which he corrects and changes as he writes, repeating the procedure for successive sections. The completed manuscript closely approaches the published text. At some point Tolkien makes a rough map of part of Gondor and Mordor, and on this plots Frodo's journey from Rauros to the Morannon. During the writing of the chapter he also makes a brief chronology of Frodo's movements in the early chapters of Book IV.

While writing 'The Passage of the Marshes' Tolkien looks ahead and changes his mind about the position of the pass of Kirith (later *Cirith*) Ungol by which Frodo and Sam are to enter Mordor. He draws a series of sketches showing its position (*The War of the Ring*, pp. 108, 114), first close to the Morannon in the north, and then, when he decides that this area would be heavily guarded, near Minas Morghul (later *Morgul*) in the mountains west of Mordor.

14 April 1944 In the morning, Tolkien works for 'an hour or two' on his new chapter of *The Lord of the Rings* and brings 'Frodo nearly to the gates of Mordor' (letter to Christopher Tolkien, 13–15 April 1944, *Letters*, p. 71). – In the afternoon, he mows the lawns at 20 Northmoor Road. – In the evening he is occupied with an air raid exercise until 10.00 p.m., when he has supper with his family. – During the night he is on air raid warden duty at area headquarters, and gets little sleep because of noise from traffic.

15 April 1944 Tolkien continues his letter of 13 April to Christopher. Although term is about to begin and proofs of University of Wales examination papers have arrived, he is 'going to continue "Ring" in every salvable moment' (*Letters*, p. 71). He is currently an external examiner for the University of Wales, evidently with the responsibility of setting papers as well as marking them and consulting with other examiners. – Later he and Edith have tea with David Nichol Smith and his wife. – Tolkien has supper with Elaine Griffiths and other dons.

16 April 1944 Tolkien replies to a letter from the Eighth Army, one of many of this sort that he often receives, which asks the 'Regius Professor of English' to adjudicate in a mess dispute as to the correct pronunciation of the surname of the poet William Cowper. – Either today or on 17 April, Tolkien writes again to Christopher.

17 April 1944 In the morning, Tolkien is visited by Frank Pakenham (later Lord Longford), who is organizing an interdenominational Christian Council for Oxford. Tolkien joins the Council but declines to act as secretary. – Later he tutors his B.Litt. student Mary Salu for one hour. – He spends the afternoon dealing with a plumbing emergency and cleaning out the hen-house.

18 April 1944 Several letters from Christopher arrive. Tolkien writes a long reply. The trees are coming into leaf and the flowers are blooming; but the grass is growing quickly too, and Tolkien finds mowing a never-ending job. – Apparently he completes 'The Passage of the Marshes' on this day.

19 April 1944 In the morning, Tolkien reads 'The Passage of the Marshes' to C.S. Lewis and Charles Williams, which they approve.

19–30 April 1944 Tolkien works on another chapter of *The Lord of the Rings*, 'Gates of the Land of Shadow', later divided in two as 'The Black Gate Is Closed' and 'Of Herbs and Stewed Rabbit' (bk. IV, ch. 3–4 as published). Less hesitant at this point, after some initial drafting he writes a continuous legible draft extending for the whole of 'The Black Gate Is Closed', and follows with a fair copy. He continues the draft with a brief outline of the story ahead as far as the stairs of Kirith Ungol; he still has little idea of how the story will develop. He then carries on into 'Of Herbs and Stewed Rabbit' which he writes in stages with initial drafting and outlines both preceding and interspersed with the writing of the completed manuscript. This includes several rejected passages and fresh starts, and in places is itself the vehicle of primary composition. Even in the completed manuscript of the chapter the Rangers of Ithilien are led by Falborn, a kinsman of Boromir.

21 April 1944 Tolkien attends a General Board meeting.

23 April 1944 Trinity Full Term begins. Tolkien's only scheduled lecture series for this term is Old English Texts on Tuesdays and Thursdays at 11.00 a.m. in the Taylor Institution, beginning 25 April. He will continue to supervise B.Litt. students M.Y. Pickard and M.B. Salu. – Tolkien writes to Christopher. He has now nearly finished 'Gates of the Land of Shadow'. The story 'takes me in charge, and I have already taken three chapters over what was meant to be one! And I have neglected too many things to do it. I am just enmeshed in it now, and have to wrench my mind away to tackle exam-paper proofs and lectures' (*Letters*, pp. 73–4). – That night, he sits up on air raid warden duty until 1.30 a.m., when he decides to retire, as it is warm enough to leave the window open to hear alerts; but as he is about to do so, the air raid siren wails. He does not get to bed until 3.30, or to sleep until 4.00.

24 April 1944 Tolkien wakes at 8.45 a.m. He stays in bed another hour reading a letter from Christopher which has just arrived, as he eats a breakfast of toast and home-made marmalade. He spends the rest of the morning in town on errands. – He begins a letter to Christopher, then works on the lecture he is to give the next day.

25 April 1944 Tolkien still feels the effects of his lack of sleep on Sunday night. He goes into central Oxford early to deal with some business for Mrs Joseph Wright, as executor for her late husband's estate. He gives what he considers a poor lecture, then meets the Lewis brothers and Charles Williams in the White Horse pub for half an hour. – He spends the rest of the day mowing three lawns, writing to his son John, and struggling with a passage in *The Lord of the Rings*. 'At this point', he tells John, 'I require to know how much later the moon gets up each night when nearing full, and how to stew a rabbit!' (*Letters*, p. 74).

26 April 1944 Tolkien attends a Pembroke College meeting which (unusually) lasts only twelve and a half minutes. – Later he continues his letter of 24 April to Christopher, commenting on sermons and asking Christopher, if he should ever get to Bloemfontein, to see if the old bank house is still standing and to look for Arthur Tolkien's grave. One of the family hens having broken an egg, 'I have spent an agreeable time catching her, . . . cleaning her, trimming her and disinfecting her – and then disinfecting myself. Grr! The fourth lawn will have to wait' (*Letters*, p. 74).

27 April 1944 After giving two lectures and attending to some troublesome business in town, Tolkien is too tired to attend an Inklings meeting in the evening.

29 April 1944 Tolkien spends the day working on *The Lord of the Rings*.

30 April 1944 Tolkien writes to Christopher about the stupidity of war and resulting human misery. 'It is full Maytime by the trees and grass now. But the heavens are full of roar and riot' (*Letters*, p. 77). The noise of aircraft makes conversation in the garden impossible. In *The Lord of the Rings* 'Sam has gratified a life-long wish to see an Oliphaunt, an animal about which there was a hobbit nursery-rhyme', which Tolkien quotes. Apparently he has finished 'Of Herbs and Stewed Rabbit', and has only just written the poem **Oliphaunt* which he adds to the end of 'The Black Gate Is Closed'.

1 May 1944 Tolkien reads another chapter of *The Lord of the Rings* to C.S. Lewis, probably 'The Black Gate Is Closed' and 'Of Herbs and Stewed Rabbit' not yet separated.

?1–?7 May 1944 Tolkien writes the chapter of *The Lord of the Rings* called at this time 'Faramir', later 'The Window on the West' (bk. IV, ch. 5). The work is intense, concentrated, and complex. A new character comes on the scene: '(I am sure I did not invent him, I did not even want him, though I like him, but there he came walking into the woods of Ithilien): Faramir, the brother of Boromir', a development of Falborn (letter to Christopher Tolkien, 6 May 1944, *Letters*, p. 79). Falborn does not become Boromir's brother until the second of three drafts of the beginning of the chapter, and his name is not changed to 'Faramir' until the third of the drafts. When the story reaches part of the way through Faramir's questioning of the hobbits, Tolkien makes a fair copy, followed by several outline sketches and short drafts: at first he is uncertain how to use Faramir in the tale. Then he continues to the end of the chapter with 'characteristic "over-lapping" – when the narrative takes a wrong direction or is in some respect unsatisfactory, collapses into a scrawl, and is replaced by a new page beginning at an earlier point (thus producing sections of near repetition)' (Christopher Tolkien, *The War of the Ring*, p. 152). Finally he makes another fair copy.

4 May 1944 Tolkien writes to Christopher. He is 'busy now with the next' chapter of *The Lord of the Rings*; 'we shall soon be in the shadows of Mordor at last. I will send you some copies, as soon as I can get them made' (*Letters*, p. 77).

5 May 1944 Tolkien spends the morning working on *The Lord of the Rings*. – In the afternoon, he chairs an English Faculty Board meeting. – He also attends a General Board meeting. – In the evening, he returns to *The Lord of the Rings* while Edith and Priscilla attend a performance at the Playhouse, and has supper with them at 9.00 p.m.

6 May 1944 Tolkien writes to Christopher, sympathizing with complaints the latter had made about conditions in camp. – In the evening, Tolkien attends a dinner of The Society hosted by K.T. Parker in the New Room at Magdalen College. Six members are present. They dine on soup, salmon, salad, peaches and junket, cider, port, and beer.

8 May 1944 In the morning, Tolkien reads 'Faramir' to C.S. Lewis and Charles Williams to their great approval. – He lunches in Oxford with Edith.

?8–?11 May 1944 Tolkien writes another chapter of *The Lord of the Rings*, 'Journey to the Cross Roads', later divided into 'The Forbidden Pool' and 'Journey to the Cross-roads' (bk. IV, ch. 6–7 as published). In the first part he makes an initial continuous draft with little hesitation despite new elements entering as he writes; the second part gives him more difficulty, and some of the overlapping drafts become outlines. Finally he makes a fair copy.

9 May 1944 In the morning, Tolkien meets C.S. Lewis. – In the evening, he dines in Pembroke College with Leonard Rice-Oxley as his guest, but finds the occasion dull. The Master of Pembroke tactlessly remarks on his pleasure that a Roman Catholic has not been elected to the Rectorship of Lincoln College.

11 May 1944 Tolkien writes to Christopher. His time is filled mostly with 'lectures, house, garden (very exigent just now: lawns, hedges, marrow-beds, weeding) & what can be spared for "Ring"' (*Letters*, p. 79).

12 May 1944 Tolkien spends the morning writing, and the afternoon gardening in sultry heat. – Later he writes to Christopher. In *The Lord of the Rings* Frodo and Sam 'are now in sight of Minas Morghul' (*Letters*, p. 79). He has not yet had copies of the recent chapters made to send to Christopher, as he wants to get on with the story.

?12–21 May 1944 For most of this period Tolkien takes 'advantage of a bitter cold grey week (in which the lawns have not grown in spite of a little rain)' to work on *The Lord of the Rings*, but strikes a difficult patch. 'All that I had sketched or written before proved of little use, as times, motives etc., have all changed. However at last with v. great labour, and some neglect of other duties, I have now written or nearly written all the matter up to the capture of Frodo in the high pass on the very brink of Mordor' (letter to Christopher Tolkien, 21 May 1944, *Letters*, p. 81). 'The matter' comprises the final three chapters of Book IV ('The Stairs of Cirith Ungol', 'Shelob's Lair', and 'The Choices of Master Samwise', ch. 8–10 as published), at this point considered a single unit, and at first a continuation of the draft for 'Journey to the Cross-roads' before it becomes only a sketch. He writes a new outline for the rest of Book IV, making changes as new ideas come to him, then continues to draft. He builds up a fair copy in stages, part of it written on new sheets, and part over a pencil draft (partly erased); in this he replaces multiple spiders with one great spider, and in the middle of the text makes a drawing (*Shelob's Lair*, see *Artist and Illustrator*, fig. 171) which shows the sequence of events as originally conceived (stair, tunnel, stair). The underlying pencil draft stops at the point at which Sam sees Frodo lying bound; the ink fair copy continues, but soon declines into initial drafting. Tolkien now apparently realizes that the narrative demands a change in sequence (to stair, stair, tunnel), and writes a note to this effect, a brief outline, and a longer note which includes a plan of the tunnels (*The War of the Ring*, p. 201). At this point also, perhaps, he draws a map of Minas Morghul and the Cross-roads which shows a track and not a tunnel at the top of the first stair (*The War of the Ring*, p. 181).

13 May 1944 Tolkien spends some time clearing up his study, 'which had got into the chaos that always indicates literary or philological preoccupation' (letter to Christopher Tolkien, 14 May 1944, *Letters*, p. 80), and attending to business. When he can turn his mind again to *The Lord of the Rings* he realizes that he has not paid enough attention to the phases of the moon in his story. He spends the afternoon rewriting parts of earlier chapters to put this right.

14 May 1944 Tolkien begins a letter to Christopher, commenting on the 'pretty stirring little sermon, based on Rogation Days' given by Father Douglas Carter that morning at the Church of St Gregory and St Augustine in Oxford (*Letters*, p. 80). He has had an idea for a short story (apparently never written) in which a man sees from a high window the changes in a small piece of land from the Palaeolithic era until the present day.

15 May 1944 Tolkien sees C.S. Lewis from 10.45 a.m. to 12.30 p.m. Lewis reads him two chapters from *The Great Divorce*, and Tolkien reads his new (double) chapter 'Journey to the Cross-roads'. – In the late afternoon Tolkien continues his letter to Christopher begun on 14 May. He thinks that so far his writing of *The Lord of the Rings* has gone well, 'but I am now coming to the nub, when the threads must be gathered and the times synchronized and the narrative interwoven; while the whole thing has grown so large in significance that the sketches of concluding chapters (written ages ago) are quite inadequate, being on a more "juvenile" level' (*Letters*, pp. 80–1).

21 May 1944 Tolkien begins a letter to Christopher on a cold day. 'I worked very hard at my chapter – it is most exhausting work; especially as the climax approaches and one has to keep the pitch up: no easy level will do; and there are all sorts of minor problems of plot and mechanism. I wrote and tore up and rewrote most of it a good many times' (*Letters*, p. 81). He is referring to 'The Stairs of Cirith Ungol' which, following his decision that its sequence of events should be stair, stair, tunnel, needs considerable rewriting and emendation. He begins to draft from the point where he has changed the story, and makes a sketch of the tower of Kirith Ungol seen in the distance. After he completes a draft to his satisfaction, he makes a fair copy, on one page of which he draws a sketch of Kirith Ungol seen from the path at the top of the second stair (*Artist and Illustrator*, fig. 172; *The War of the Ring*, p. 204). – During the night he is on key duty at air raid warden headquarters. He retires at 3.30 a.m. on 22 May.

22 May 1944 Tolkien reads to C.S. Lewis and Charles Williams 'The Stairs of Kirith Ungol', which they approve. – Later he continues his letter to Christopher of 21 May. – He again spends the night at air raid warden headquarters, but is unable to sleep, partly because of traffic noise.

c. 22–28 May 1944 Tolkien to work on the final two chapters of Book IV of *The Lord of the Rings*. He continues the new draft and emends the unfinished fair copy or inserts replacement pages to bring it into agreement with the changes he has decided to make. He is uncertain of events at the end of 'Shelob's Lair' and writes two versions. He then continues the rough drafting into which the first fair copy deteriorated, to the end of 'The Choices of Master Samwise', rewriting parts several times. Within the draft he draws two sketches of the final approach to the Cleft (for one, see *Artist and Illustrator*, fig. 173) and a plan of the tunnel (*The War of the Ring*, p. 225). Even when he finishes a fair copy he is not satisfied, but changes and rewrites. He is spending all the time he can spare in a 'desperate attempt to bring "The Ring" to a suitable pause, the capture of Frodo by the Orcs in the passes of Mordor, before I am obliged to break off by examining', and achieves this 'by sitting up all hours' (letter to Christopher Tolkien, 31 May 1944, *Letters*, p. 83).

23 May 1944 At 6.00 a.m. Tolkien gives up trying to sleep. He is not very bright at the lecture he gives that morning, partly because of the bad night, but also because of his 'absorption in Frodo, which now has a great grip and takes a lot out of me: chapter on Shelob and the disaster in Kirith Ungol has been written several times. Whole thing comes out of the wash quite different to any preliminary sketch!' (letter to Christopher Tolkien, 25 May 1944, *Letters*, p. 82). – At home he spares some time from writing to make a hen-coop and chick-run to replace an untidy box and jumbled net on the lawn.

25 May 1944 In the morning, Tolkien gives two lectures, one of them probably to cadets. – Later he writes to Christopher. 'I was disposed, at last, to envy you a little; or rather to wish I could be with you "in the hills". There is something in nativity, and though I have few pictorial memories, there is always a curious sense of reminiscence about any stories of Africa, which always move me deeply' (*Letters*, p. 82). – In the evening, he dines at Pembroke College, then goes to a meeting of the Inklings in C.S. Lewis's rooms in Magdalen College. Lewis reads more from *The Great Divorce*, and his brother reads another chapter from his book on the times of Louis XIV. Hugo Dyson is also present. Tolkien does not return home until after midnight.

29 May 1944 In the morning, Tolkien reads to C.S. Lewis the final two chapters of Book IV of *The Lord of the Rings*. Lewis approves, and is moved to tears by 'The Choices of Master Samwise'.

30 May 1944 Tolkien has to walk into town to deliver lectures, his bicycle having had a puncture. – He spends the afternoon repairing the tyre.

31 May 1944 Tolkien begins a letter to Christopher. 'Until midday today I was sweating at Section Papers: & took my [manuscripts] to the Press at 2 p.m. today – the last possible day.' He is 'not really satisfied with the surname Gamgee [in *Samwise Gamgee*] and sh[oul]d change it to Goodchild if I thought you would let me' (*Letters*, p. 83).

1 June 1944 Tolkien dines in Pembroke College, then walks home with Edith and Priscilla who have been to a performance of *Emma*, a dramatization of the Jane Austen novel, with Anna Neagle in the title role.

2 June 1944 Tolkien attends a General Board Meeting.

3 June 1944 Tolkien continues his letter to Christopher begun 31 May. Having finished setting papers, during the gap before examination scripts arrive he is typing the new chapters of *The Lord of the Rings* so that they can be duplicated and sent to Christopher at intervals. He types slowly at first, as he is out of practice, but so far has finished two chapters.

6 June 1944 D-Day: the Allies land in Normandy. – Tolkien writes again to Christopher.

7 June 1944 Tolkien types more of *The Lord of the Rings*, except (apparently) for the chapter 'The Black Gate Is Closed', for which he writes out a clear manuscript. *See note.*

8 June 1944 Tolkien wakes at 5.00 a.m. (or 7.00 a.m. British Double Summer Time) to attend Mass on the Feast of Corpus Christi. – English Final Honour School examinations begin. – In the evening, Tolkien dines in Pembroke College, followed by a meeting of the Inklings in C.S. Lewis's rooms in Magdalen College. Also present are Warnie Lewis, Charles Williams, and a special guest, E.R. Eddison. The time from 9.00 p.m. to 12.30 a.m. is occupied by readings. Tolkien particularly appreciates a chapter from *The Splendid Century* by Warnie Lewis, and the chapter Eddison reads from his uncompleted romance *The Mezentian Gate*.

10 June 1944 In the morning, Tolkien is occupied with examinations. In a letter to Stanley Unwin of 29 June he will mention being 'drowned in an abyss of exams' (Tolkien-George Allen & Unwin archive, HarperCollins). – In the afternoon, he attends 'a mass-meeting at Rhodes House in favour of a local Christian Council', which he describes later this day in a letter to Christopher (see *Letters*, p. 84). – 'Four of the new eight chapters' of *The Lord of the Rings* (Book IV will have ten chapters when finally subdivided) are now 'in the typist's hands [Margaret Douglas, a friend of Charles Williams] and when they return I will send them to you' (courtesy of Christopher Tolkien).

11 June 1944 Tolkien continues his letter to Christopher begun on 10 June. He comments on his childhood memories of South Africa and England.

12–26 June 1944 During this period Tolkien writes another two letters to Christopher.

13 June 1944 V-1 (flying bomb) attacks on London begin. These will last until the end of August.

16 June 1944 Tolkien chairs an English Faculty Board meeting. The Board approves revised regulations for Old Norse, to come into force in Michaelmas Term 1946. – Tolkien also attends a General Board meeting.

17 June 1944 Trinity Full Term ends.

21 June 1944 Encaenia.

22 June 1944 Stanley Unwin sends Tolkien a cheque for royalties earned by *The Hobbit*. He would like Tolkien to meet Rayner while the latter is at Oxford as a Navy cadet.

23 June 1944 The *Oxford University Gazette* for 23 June announces that the Vice-Chancellor and Proctors have nominated Tolkien to serve two further years on the General Board from the first day of Michaelmas Term 1944.

27 June 1944 Tolkien finishes marking examination scripts, and writes again to Christopher.

28 June 1944 In the evening, Tolkien attends a meeting of the Inklings, at which Hugo Dyson, Charles Williams, and presumably the Lewis brothers are also present.

29 June 1944 Tolkien writes to Stanley Unwin. He will be delighted to see Rayner. He asks that Rayner let him know how they could meet: 'whether I can roll into his rooms, and whether he would care at any time to wander up here to my house and have tea (meagre) in my garden (untidy)'. He apologizes for not having realized that Rayner was now among the cadets, and explains that he ceased to be director of the courses for cadets in March, because he had not had 'a day or night off or away from this town for two years' (Tolkien-George Allen & Unwin archive, HarperCollins). He notes that Rayner did very well in the half-course exam and was one of the few whose work compared favourably even with the normal university students. The new director has implemented the idea of not having a special examination for cadets, but of putting them through a genuine university preliminary examination. Tolkien thanks Unwin for the cheque: he still labours 'under debts, mainly due to trying to complete a family's education after war has taken most of one's means'. Having been released from organizing the cadets' courses, he has brought *The Lord of the Rings* to 'within sight of conclusion, and am now about to conclude it, disregarding all other calls, as far as is possible' (*Letters*, p. 85–6). He hopes that Allen & Unwin are still interested in the work, despite a shortage of paper. He has never received a copy of the last Allen & Unwin reprint of *The Hobbit*. Agnes Wrenn is staying at his house for rest and respite from V-1 attacks on London.

3 July 1944 Tolkien writes again to Christopher.

4–6 July 1944 During this period Tolkien writes another letter to Christopher.

7 July 1944 Tolkien spends the morning shopping and, apparently, lecturing to cadets. – Later, while riding to town for the second time, the rear tyre on his bicycle blows out. Tolkien consoles himself at the Gardeners' Arms pub while the tyre is repaired. – After lunch he makes a third journey into central Oxford. – From 5.00 p.m. he spends three hours enlarging the hen-house with bits of old wood and salvaged nails. – On this day also, Tolkien begins a letter to Christopher using a 'midget' font on his typewriter (a 'Hammond' machine with interchangeable fonts) to fit more words on a page. He describes his day and the antics of a family of bullfinches which have nested in or near the Tolkiens' garden. – Stanley Unwin writes to Tolkien. He has forwarded to Rayner Tolkien's suggestion for a meeting. Tolkien should not hesitate to visit him in his rooms. Allen & Unwin would reprint *The Hobbit* if they had enough paper to do so. Unwin apologizes for not having sent Tolkien a copy of the latest reprint; he does not have a copy but will try to find one.

Between mid-July and mid-September 1944 Tolkien visits Rayner Unwin in his rooms at Trinity College, Oxford. Rayner will later recall:

I was somewhat abashed: a professor was a revered figure in Oxford in those days. But Tolkien was considerate and quite prepared to do most of the talking. The difficulty was to follow the thread of his conversation. His pipe, constantly being lit, with matches burning his fingers and clouds of smoke; then the quick half-swallowed words of some story that often ended in a spasm of chuckles and an enquiring look to see if the joke had pleased me too. [*George Allen & Unwin: A Remembrancer* (1999), pp. 87–8]

9 July 1944 Tolkien continues his letter to Christopher begun on 7 July. He mentions a connection (according to the *Kalevala*) of bullfinches with brewing ale, and discusses 'machinery' and its 'attempts to actualize desire, and so to create power in this World' (*Letters*, p. 87).

10 July 1944 Stanley Unwin writes to Tolkien. A copy of the latest reprint of *The Hobbit* has been found and sent to him.

12 July 1944 Tolkien telephones Charles Williams to suggest that during the morning they visit C.S. Lewis, who is in a nursing home after a minor operation. They do so, and find Lewis well enough to return home the next day.

14 July 1944 Tolkien, with his daughter Priscilla, attends a performance of *Hamlet* at the Oxford Playhouse, a production of the Oxford University Dramatic Society. It makes a great impression on him: 'It was played fast without cuts; and came out as a very exciting play . . . to my surprise, the part that came out as the most moving, almost intolerably so, was the one that in reading I always found a bore: the scene of mad Ophelia singing her snatches' (letter to Christopher Tolkien, 28 July 1944, *Letters*, p. 88).

Mid-July 1944 Tolkien sends Christopher typescripts of the first three chapters of Book IV of *The Lord of the Rings*.

17 July 1944 Tolkien writes again to Christopher.

24 July 1944 Tolkien attends a Pembroke College meeting. – Possibly on this date, certainly between 18 and 27 July, Tolkien writes to Christopher.

28 July 1944 Tolkien writes to Christopher. He will not alter Sam Gamgee's name without his approval.

29 or 30 July 1944 Tolkien writes again to Christopher.

31 July 1944 Tolkien begins a letter to Christopher. He has been neglecting other duties to proceed with the typing of new chapters of *The Lord of the Rings*, has nearly finished, and will send them to Christopher soon. He mentions that Priscilla has just read *Out of the Silent Planet* and *Perelandra* by C.S. Lewis and finds it hard to accept that Ransom, the principal character of those novels, is not meant to be a portrait of her father. Tolkien comments on good war news and wonders what the world will be like when the war is over. He expresses pessimism about 'further growth in the great standardised amalgamations with their mass-produced notions and emotions' (*Letters*, p. 89).

1 August 1944 Tolkien continues the letter to Christopher begun on 31 July. He wants to obtain *First Whisper of 'The Wind in the Willows'*, edited by Kenneth Grahame's widow, which has just been published. – A member of the Allen & Unwin staff writes to Tolkien. Two more copies of *The Hobbit* have been found.

8 August 1944 Tolkien writes again to Christopher.

12 August 1944 Tolkien replies to Christopher's comments about South Africa and life in the Royal Air Force. He is 'absolutely dry of any inspiration for the Ring [*The Lord of the Rings*] and am back where I was in the Spring, with all the inertia to overcome again. What a relief it would be to get it done' (*Letters*, p. 91). He thinks that Christopher should soon receive the chapters sent him about a month ago; he will not send any more until he has Christopher's next address.

Between 13 and 21 August 1944 Tolkien writes another letter to Christopher.

22 August 1944 Tolkien lectures in the morning. Finding the 'Bird and Baby' closed (presumably because of lack of supplies), he joins the Lewis brothers and Charles Williams for ale at the King's Arms. – He writes to Christopher that he 'hopes to see the lads [Inklings] tomorrow; otherwise life is as bright as water in a ditch' (*Letters*, p. 92).

1 September 1944 Basil Blackwell writes to Tolkien, who still has not returned proofs of his translation of *Pearl*. Blackwell wonders if the reason Tolkien still has not done so is that he thinks that Blackwell is trying to take advantage of his financial difficulty by suggesting the purchase of the copyright. Blackwell now suggests that they proceed on the basis of a royalty, with an advance to be set against Tolkien's bookshop account. Blackwell has had to pay for setting the type, which the printer cannot keep standing indefinitely. Tolkien will reply at once, evidently to the effect that he does not think that Blackwell is trying to take advantage, and mentions the introduction that Blackwell has hoped that Tolkien will write.

3 September 1944 Tolkien writes to Christopher. Priscilla has been wading through G.K. Chesterton's *The Ballad of the White Horse* for several evenings, while Tolkien has tried to explain its obscure parts.

4–22 September 1944 During this period Tolkien writes four more letters to Christopher.

6 September 1944 Basil Blackwell writes to Tolkien. Tolkien's reply has set his mind at ease. He would value a full introduction, but will leave it to Tolkien's judgement. – T.S. Gregory, editor of the *Dublin Review*, writes to Tolkien, seeking a contribution.

8 September 1944 Germany begins to attack London with V-2 rockets; other cities in England will be attacked later. The attacks will continue until 27 March 1945.

9 September 1944 Margaret Douglas receives via Charles Williams several more chapters of *The Lord of the Rings* to type, but does not begin to type these until 19 September.

17 September 1944 Dim-out replaces blackout in Britain, loosening restrictions on lights.

19 September 1944 Tolkien writes to G.E. Selby, agreeing to act as referee in his application for a post. He congratulates Selby on his marriage and on the birth of a daughter. His own daughter, Priscilla, at present is typing parts of *The Lord of the Rings*. These apparently do not include Book IV; Priscilla will later recall in *The Tolkien Family Album* 'when she was about fourteen and only able to type with two fingers, typing out early chapters of *The Lord of the*

Rings, her intense excitement at the outset of the story and her terror of the Black Riders' pursuit of the hobbits as they left the Shire' (p. 72). – In the afternoon, Rayner Unwin visits Tolkien at 20 Northmoor Road after 'passing out' as a cadet and before leaving Oxford on 21 September. He will later recall that he met Edith and, he thought, Priscilla on this occasion, had tea, and inspected hens in the garden. He tells Tolkien that he wants to return to Oxford to read English when the war is over. Tolkien apparently lends him a copy of his translation of *Pearl*.

20 September 1944 Tolkien writes to Stanley Unwin. He is sorry that, as he no longer directs the English programme for cadets and only teaches a specialist class, he could not be of more assistance to Rayner while he was at Oxford.

21 September 1944 In the evening, Tolkien cycles to Magdalen College for an Inklings meeting in almost peacetime light: it is no longer necessary to maintain the blackout, streets are being lit again and windows uncovered. Both the Lewis brothers and Williams attend. In addition to pleasant talk, Warnie Lewis reads the last chapter of *The Splendid Century*, and C.S. Lewis reads an article and part of his translation of the *Aeneid*. Tolkien does not leave until midnight, when he walks part of the way home with Williams while discussing 'the difficulties of discovering what common factors if any existed in the notions associated with *freedom*, as used at present' (letter to Christopher Tolkien, 23–5 September 1944, *Letters*, p. 93)

23 September 1944 Tolkien begins a reply to Christopher, who has read and approved of 'The Taming of Sméagol', 'The Passage of the Marshes', and 'The Black Gate Is Closed'. Tolkien promises to send Christopher more chapters as soon as they have been typed. He comments on war news and on the attitude in the media towards all Germans. He has to try to get on with *Pearl* to satisfy Basil Blackwell, but would really like to go walking in the country. The Inklings have agreed that if they survive the war they will celebrate victory by taking 'a whole inn in the country for a least a week, and spend it entirely in beer and talk' (*Letters*, p. 94).

26 September 1944 Stanley Unwin writes to Tolkien. He comments on the proof of an interesting poem, presumably *Pearl*, that Tolkien lent to Rayner.

27 September 1944 In the morning, Tolkien meets Warnie Lewis and Charles Williams for about half an hour.

30 September 1944 Tolkien, Edith, and Priscilla attend a performance of *Arms and the Man* by George Bernard Shaw at the Oxford Playhouse. He thinks the production poor, and that the play does not wear well. Also at the theatre are Charles Williams and Margaret Douglas. – Later Tolkien writes to Christopher. He hopes to have more chapters of *The Lord of the Rings* to send him soon. Tolkien is revising the work as 'I can't get on without having back stuff fresh in mind. Do you remember chapter "King of the Golden Hall"? Seems rather good, now it is old enough for a detached view' (*Letters*, p. 94).

End of September or beginning of October 1944 A fourth group of cadets arrives at Oxford. The English Course is described in the *Oxford University Gazette* as including (1) Modern English (all cadets); (2) English Literature;

(3) Outlines of the History of English (optional). Among the Air Force cadets in this group is Anthony Curtis, who will later recall that he wore his air squadron uniform for three days each week, and his academic gown another three. Sessions with Lewis on *Paradise Lost* made him feel an ignoramus, and 'if you did venture to challenge one of his theories the ground was cut from beneath your feet with lightning speed'; but Tolkien, who taught the cadets medieval English,

> was the soul of affability. He did all the talking, but he made you feel you were his intellectual equal. Yet his views beneath the deep paternal charm were passionately held. At the first of these classes he handed round some sample passages of medieval English he had had typed out. One of them was an English translation of the first verses of the Gospel According to John. 'You see,' he said triumphantly, 'English was a language that could move easily in abstract concepts when French was still a vulgar Norman patois'. ['Remembering Tolkien and Lewis', *British Book News*, June 1977, p. 429]

Between 30 September and 5 October 1944 Tolkien writes another letter to Christopher.

First half of October 1944 Margaret Douglas types more chapters of *The Lord of the Rings*.

3 October 1944 At 12.00 noon Tolkien goes to the 'Bird and Baby' with Charles Williams. They find the Lewis brothers already there and have lively conversation. Tolkien notices 'a strange tall gaunt man half in khaki half in mufti with a large wide-awake hat, bright eyes and a hooked nose sitting in the corner' and taking an interest (letter to Christopher Tolkien, 6 October 1944, *Letters*, p. 95): the poet *Roy Campbell, whom C.S. Lewis had recently lampooned in the *Oxford Magazine*. The conversation becomes fast and furious, and Tolkien is late for lunch.

5 October 1944 In the evening, Tolkien attends a meeting of the Inklings in C.S. Lewis's rooms in Magdalen College. Roy Campbell is present by invitation. Under the influence of port, Lewis is 'a little belligerent' and insists 'on reading out his lampoon again' to Campbell's amusement; 'but we were mostly obliged to listen to the guest' (letter to Christopher Tolkien, 6 October 1944, *Letters*, p. 95). Campbell talks about his life, including his participation in the Spanish Civil War, and recounts picaresque stories about poets and musicians. Tolkien does not leave Magdalen until midnight, when he and Campbell walk together to Beaumont Street.

6 October 1944 Tolkien writes to Christopher. He has earned about £51 from his vacation labours on the cadets. He describes his meetings and conversation with Roy Campbell, and C.S. Lewis's odd reactions to him.

10 October–?end of October 1944 Tolkien returns to *The Lord of the Rings* but strikes 'a most awkward error (one or two days) in the synchronization, v[ery] important at this stage, of movements of Frodo and the others [possibly the relative positions of the characters at the time of the full moon on 6 February], which has cost labour and thought and will require tiresome small alterations in many chapters; but at any rate I have actually begun Book Five' (letter to Christopher Tolkien, 12 October 1944, *Letters*, p. 97). *See note.* He makes two brief time-schemes which include events in Book IV as already written, and some at the beginning of Book V which take place at the same time. (It is not clear if he discovers the chronological problem as a result of making these schemes, or makes the schemes to help solve the problem.) The second scheme is later emended.

Tolkien makes several draft openings for both 'Minas Tirith' and 'The Muster of Rohan'. Some of those for the latter begin as clear manuscripts but deteriorate into scribbles as Tolkien finds himself uncertain of events and even of the relevant geography. Among the drafts are three sketches of Dunharrow (*The War of the Ring*, p. 239); probably at the same time, he makes a fine coloured drawing of Dunharrow (*Artist and Illustrator*, fig. 166) which fits the description in the latest draft. He makes typescripts of the beginning of both chapters. In successive drafts he makes many changes to the appearance of Dunharrow and the surrounding terrain, as well as at least seven further working sketches of the topography. One of these shows a conception for which no written description is made (or appears to survive).

Probably interspersed with these abortive beginnings, Tolkien makes a page of notes about the story to come, and six rough outlines for the development of Book V, not all extending to the end of the work. Some note the contents of each chapter, and all pay special attention to the chronology; one includes a sketch map of Harrowdale (*The War of the Ring*, p. 258), another the earliest sketch of Minas Tirith (*Artist and Illustrator*, fig. 167; *The War of the Ring*, p. 261), and the latest a map of the White Mountains and South Gondor drawn rapidly in pencil, with rivers in blue crayon. A larger and more elaborate drawing of Minas Tirith, *Stanburg* or *Steinborg* (*Artist and Illustrator*, fig. 168), seems to be based on the sketch but is unfinished.

On 16 October Tolkien writes to Christopher that he has 'been struggling with the dislocated chronology of the Ring, which has proved most vexatious, and has not only interfered with other more urgent and duller duties, but has stopped me getting on. I think I have solved it all at last by small map alterations, and by inserting an extra day's Entmoot, and extra days into Trotter's chase and Frodo's journey' (*Letters*, p. 97). He writes out the chronological alterations needed in *The Lord of the Rings* chapter by chapter and makes the changes: quite substantial rewriting of 'The Riders of Rohan'; expansion of the end of 'The Uruk-hai'; and not only adds a day to Entmoot but also changes the Entish song. It is probably now that he makes a new, elaborate time-scheme which shows the actions of all the major characters synoptically from 19 January, the fifth day of the voyage of the Fellowship down the Anduin, until 8 February. This scheme includes changes to Book III, advances the breaking of the Fellowship by one day, and adds a day to Frodo and Sam's journey to the Morannon. Tolkien will use this as a working chronology, which will be much emended and overwritten. At this point it still shows no time passing while the Fellowship is in Lórien.

A short, clearly written narrative entitled 'Fall of Théoden in the Battle of Osgiliath' also may belong to this time, perhaps a draft for a scene that Tolkien imagined vividly and wanted to set down even though he had not yet reached that point in the story.

12 October 1944 Tolkien writes to Christopher. He wrongly thinks that Book V of *The Lord of the Rings* will be the final part. – He submits his story *Leaf by Niggle* to the *Dublin Review*.

13 October 1944 Tolkien attends a General Board meeting.

14 October 1944 Tolkien sends Christopher copies of three chapters of *The Lord of the Rings*: 'Of Herbs and Stewed Rabbit', 'Faramir' (i.e. 'The Window on the West'), and 'The Forbidden Pool'.

15 October 1944 Michaelmas Full Term begins. Tolkien's scheduled lectures for this term are: Outlines of Old English Phonology on Tuesdays and Thursdays at 10.00 a.m. in the Taylor Institution, beginning 17 October; and *Beowulf* (lines 1–1650) on Tuesdays and Thursdays at 11.00 a.m. in the Taylor Institution, beginning 17 October. He will continue to supervise B.Litt. students M.Y. Pickard and M.B. Salu.

16 October 1944 Tolkien writes to Christopher. He has been struggling with *The Lord of the Rings*, but now must give his attention to lectures and to his translation of *Pearl*.

23 October 1944 Tolkien writes to Christopher. He has just been out to look up at a 'skywide Armada' of Allied aircraft. 'There seems to be no time to do anything properly; and I feel tired all the time, or rather bored' (*Letters*, p. 97).

25 October 1944 Tolkien writes a long letter to Christopher. He also writes a second letter, accompanying two more chapters of *The Lord of the Rings*, 'Journey to the Cross-roads' and 'The Stairs of Cirith Ungol'. He comments on a fan letter about *The Hobbit* written by a twelve-year-old American boy, of a sort he receives occasionally.

27 October 1944 At an English Faculty Board meeting, in Tolkien's absence, he is appointed to a committee 'to report whether any changes were desirable in the regulations for emergency examinations in and after 1945–6' (Oxford University Archives FA 4/5/1/1).

28 October 1944 Tolkien writes to Christopher. 'This empty year is fading into a dull grey mournful darkness: so slow-footed and yet so swift and evanescent' (*Letters*, p. 98).

Between 29 October and 7 November 1944 Tolkien writes again to Christopher.

?Late 1944 Now that an end of war seems to be in sight and the prospect that Charles Williams will soon return to London, C.S. Lewis and Tolkien plan a *Festschrift* for Williams to honour his work for Oxford University. Tolkien decides that his contribution will be a revised version of *On Fairy-Stories*.

1 November 1944 The British Council forwards a letter from a Swedish scholar, Ragnar Furuskog (dated 16 October). Furuskog wants to work on the phonology of manuscript B of the Katherine Group (i.e. MS Bodley 34) and manuscript A of the *Ancrene Riwle* (MS CCCC 402) as a thesis for his doctorate. He asks if Tolkien's edition of the latter (*Ancrene Wisse*), announced as 'at press' in 1936, will soon be published, or if he could obtain a photostat copy of the manuscript; if Tolkien or one of his students plans to work, or is already working, on a similar investigation; and if Tolkien has any objection to Furuskog's choice of topic or knows of any work in progress with which it would collide. Having received this letter, Tolkien will make enquiries and carefully consider a reply.

5 November 1944 Tolkien and Priscilla cycle in wind and rain to St Gregory's, where they hear a good sermon from Father Douglas Carter on healings by Christ and modern miracles. This makes Tolkien think of the word *eucatastrophe* which he had coined to describe 'the sudden happy turn in a story which pierces you with a joy that brings tears' (letter to Christopher Tolkien, 7–8 November 1944, *Letters*, p. 100). As Tolkien and Priscilla leave the church they see an old tramp on the porch who makes Tolkien think of St Joseph.

6 November 1944 Tolkien buries a hen that has died: Biddy, considered almost a friend of the family, and an outstanding layer of double-yolk eggs. – He sees C.S. Lewis and Charles Williams from about 10.40 a.m. to 12.50 p.m. He will 'recollect little of the feast of reason and flow of soul, partly because we all agree so. It was a bright morning , and the mulberry tree in the grove just outside C.S.L.'s window shone like fallow gold against [a] cobalt blue sky.' – In the afternoon 'the weather worsened again' and he does 'one of the foulest jobs. I grease-banded all the trees (apple) tying 16 filthy little pantelettes on. It took 2 hours, and nearly as long to get the damned stuff off hands and implements. I neglected it last year, and so lost ½ a glorious crop to "moth"' (letter to Christopher Tolkien, 7–8 November 1944, *Letters*, p. 102).

7 November 1944 After lecturing Tolkien sees the Lewis brothers and Charles Williams briefly in the 'Bird and Baby'. The pub is now 'gloriously empty, with improved beer, and a landlord wreathed in welcoming smiles! He lights a special fire for us!' (*Letters*, p. 102).

7–8 November 1944 Tolkien writes to Christopher. He describes a vision or apperception of a ray of light and a mote which he had had not long ago while praying in St Gregory's when the *Quarant' Ore* (Forty Hours' Devotion) was being held there. He mentions having attended *Hamlet* with John Gielgud at the New Theatre in Oxford, apparently in recent weeks.

8 November 1944 Tolkien attends a Pembroke College meeting.

Between 9 and 23 November 1944 Tolkien writes three letters to Christopher.

10 November 1944 Tolkien attends a General Board meeting. – He writes a long reply to Ragnar Furuskog, polite and accommodating but with the underlying hope (made clear in other correspondence) that Furuskog will be discouraged and take up another topic. Tolkien explains that he and Simonne d'Ardenne before the war had done most of the preliminary work for an edition of *Seinte Katerine*, and had intended to proceed to a full investigation of the 'AB' language; but in the present uncertainty of war he cannot stand in the way of other investigators prepared to do immediate work. His B.Litt. student Mary Salu has completed the index of all words and forms in the Cambridge manuscript of the *Ancrene Riwle* begun by Elaine Griffiths, and is preparing a thesis, now nearly completed, on its grammar and phonology. If Furuskog feels that this is an obstacle to his project, Tolkien has other suggestions. He also discusses the difficulty of obtaining photographs or transcripts, when many original manuscripts have been sent to safe places for the duration of the war and are not presently available for consultation or photography. But he might be able to arrange for the Academic Copying Office in Oxford to make Furuskog a copy of Tolkien's own transcript of the Cambridge manuscript.

11 November 1944 Tolkien writes a covering letter to the British Council and sends it with his reply to Furuskog of 10 November, which is to be forwarded to Sweden. He remarks that Furuskog and the professor who suggested his research topic must surely have realized from Tolkien and Simonne d'Ardenne's published work that they are working on the proposed subject and have already covered most of the ground. Tolkien hopes that if he does let Furuskog see his transcripts for use in his studies, the latter will not use them as the basis of an edition. He asks the British Council for help in contacting d'Ardenne in Belgium (of whom he has had no news since Christmas 1943). – Tolkien also writes to Mabel Day at the Early English Text Society, to whom Furuskog evidently also sent a letter, about which Day subsequently wrote to Tolkien. Since photography of the original Cambridge manuscript is not possible at present, he has only to sit on his transcripts to put an end to Furuskog's project, 'but that seems hardly the attitude to take up'. He hopes that when Furuskog hears of Mary Salu's work he will turn as Tolkien has suggested, to an investigation of 'the collateral and closely related languages' which 'might prove useful' (Early English Text Society archive).

14 November 1944 The British Council informs Tolkien that his reply to Furuskog has been forwarded to their representative in Sweden, whom they have asked to ensure that Tolkien's offer of a copy of his transcript is not exploited. They are making enquiries about d'Ardenne.

23 November 1944 Tolkien gives two lectures and spends time re-drafting the findings of the Committee on Emergency Exams (see entry for 27 October 1944). – In the evening, he goes to the Mitre at about 8.00 p.m., where he meets Charles Williams and R.E. Havard for drinks before they join the Lewis brothers and Owen Barfield for a meeting of the Inklings in C.S. Lewis's rooms in Magdalen College. Barfield 'is the only man who can tackle C.S.L[ewis] making him define everything and interrupting his most dogmatic pronouncements with subtle *distinguo's*. The result was a most amusing and highly contentious evening, on which (had an outsider eavesdropped) he would have thought it a meeting of fell enemies hurling deadly insults before drawing their guns' (letter to Christopher Tolkien, 24 November 1944, *Letters*,

p. 103). In addition to a discussion of ghosts and the special nature of hymns, the Inklings hear two excellent sonnets sent by a young poet to C.S. Lewis, and take parts in a reading of Barfield's play *Medea*. Tolkien leaves about 12.30 a.m. and gets to bed at about 1.00 a.m.

24 November 1944 Tolkien attends a General Board meeting. – He writes to Christopher, pleased that his son has seen and remembered a quotation from the *Exeter Book*. 'It cheered me a lot to see a bit of Anglo-Saxon, and I hope indeed that you'll soon be able to return and perfect your study of that noble idiom. . . . I have to teach or talk about Old English to such a lot of young persons who simply are not equipped by talent or character to grasp it or profit by it' (*Letters*, pp. 102–3).

Between 24 November and 17 December 1944 Tolkien writes two or three letters to Christopher.

?27 November 1944 Tolkien joins C.S. Lewis and Charles Williams in Magdalen College at 11 a.m. and stays for two hours. They talk about prosody, and about Charles Lamb, an author Tolkien does not like. *See note.*

29 November 1944 Tolkien writes to Christopher. He sends him typescripts of 'Shelob's Lair' and 'The Choices of Master Samwise', 'the last two chapters that have been written' of *The Lord of the Rings*. 'Book Five and Last' will open 'with the ride of Gandalf to Minas Tirith. . . . Some of this is written or sketched.' Tolkien summarizes how the story will continue, though he is still not certain of the exact manner of the destruction of the Ring. He comments that 'all these last bits were written ages ago, but no longer fit in detail, nor in elevation (for the whole thing has become much larger and loftier). . . . It will probably work out very differently from this plan when it really gets written, as the thing seems to write itself once I get going, as if the truth comes out then, only imperfectly glimpsed in the preliminary sketch' (*Letters*, p. 104).

December 1944 Mabel Day writes to Tolkien concerning the health of Robin Flower of the British Museum. She apparently asks Tolkien's opinion about a possible successor to Dr Flower on the Early English Text Society Committee.

8 December 1944 Tolkien chairs an English Faculty Board meeting. He is re-elected chairman for the rest of the academic year. The committee set up on 27 October 1944, of which Tolkien is a member, presents its report on whether changes are needed in the regulations 'for emergency examinations in and after 1945–6' (Oxford University Archives FA 4/5/1/1). – Tolkien also attends a General Board meeting.

9 December 1944 Michaelmas Full Term ends. – Joan Anne (Joanna), daughter of Michael and Joan Tolkien, is born.

?Christmas vacation 1944 On a sunny Monday morning at about 10.00, Charles Williams reads the first two chapters of his *The Figure of Arthur* to Tolkien and C.S. Lewis in Lewis's rooms in Magdalen College. Lewis will later describe himself and Tolkien on this occasion as seated on a chesterfield smoking their pipes and stretching their legs, while Williams sat in the armchair opposite. *See note.*

12 December 1944 At an Early English Text Society Committee meeting, in Tolkien's absence, the Secretary is requested to write to Tolkien and ask how his work on the *Ancrene Riwle* is progressing.

13 December 1944 Around this time Tolkien continues to develop Bilbo's song in Rivendell (*The Lord of the Rings*, bk. II, ch. 2). The next version is a clear manuscript written on four slips of paper, probably followed by five typescripts in which Tolkien progressively makes changes to produce the final version beginning 'There was a merry messenger'. After this there is probably another long gap before Tolkien returns to the poem (see *Errantry*).

18 December 1944 In the morning, Tolkien sees C.S. Lewis. – Later he writes to Christopher that Lewis's 'fourth (or fifth?) novel is brewing, and seems likely to clash with mine (my dimly projected third) [possibly by now he has conceived *The Notion Club Papers*]. I have been getting a lot of new ideas about Prehistory lately (via Beowulf and other sources of which I may have written) and want to work them into the long-shelved time-travel story I began [*The Lost Road*].' He and Lewis are considering 'writing a book in collaboration on "Language" (Nature, Origins, Functions). Would there were time for all these projects!' (*Letters*, p. 105).

19–23 December 1944 Tolkien writes another letter to Christopher during this period.

23 December 1944 Ragnar Furuskog writes to Tolkien. He intends to work on the phonology (and possibly accidence) of MS Bodley 34 only for his thesis. He accepts Tolkien's offer to arrange for the Academic Copying Office to make a copy of Tolkien's transcript of MS CCCC 402, but he would prefer, to begin with, a copy of Simonne d'Ardenne's transcript of MS Bodley 34. Tolkien apparently never replies.

24 December 1944 Tolkien writes to Christopher, who has commented on the second group of chapters of *The Lord of the Rings* he has received. Tolkien remarks that Charles Williams, who is reading all of *The Lord of the Rings* written thus far, says that 'the great thing is that its *centre* is not in strife and war and heroism (though they are all understood and depicted) but in freedom, peace, ordinary life and good liking' (*Letters*, p. 105).

26 December 1944 Tolkien rises late. After doing some chores, from about 11.30 a.m., wrapped up well in old rags, he spends time hewing old brambles and making a fire to burn them.

27 December 1944 The rime today, Tolkien will observe, is 'even thicker and more fantastic. When a gleam of sun (about 11) got through it was breathtakingly beautiful: trees like motionless fountains of white branching spray against a golden light and, high overhead, a pale translucent blue. It did not melt. About 11 p.m. the fog cleared and a high round moon lit the whole scene with a deadly white light: a vision of some other world or time. It was so still that I stood in the garden hatless and uncloaked without a shiver, though there must have been many degrees of frost' (letter to Christopher Tolkien, 28 December 1944, *Letters*, p. 107).

28 December 1944 Tolkien writes to Christopher. 'We are getting lots of letters from you, and v[ery] quickly' (*Letters*, p. 106).

29 December 1944–17 January 1945 Tolkien writes four more letters to Christopher during this period.

1945

January 1945 *Leaf by Niggle* is published in the *Dublin Review*.

9 January 1945 Tolkien writes to *Hobbit* enthusiasts Leila Keane and Patricia Kirke, giving them news of *The Lord of the Rings* and telling them about himself and his children.

18 January 1945 Tolkien writes to Christopher. He has been 'browsing through the packed and to me enthralling pages of [F.M.] Stenton's *Anglo-Saxon England*. A period mostly filled with most intriguing Question Marks. I'd give a bit for a time machine' (*Letters*, p. 108).

Between 19 and 29 January 1945 Tolkien writes another letter to Christopher.

21 January 1945 Hilary Full Term begins. Tolkien's scheduled lectures for this term are: *Beowulf* (lines 1651–end) on Tuesdays and Thursday at 10.00 a.m. in the Taylor Institution, beginning 23 January; and the Old English *Exodus* on Tuesdays and Thursdays at 11.00 a.m. in the Taylor Institution, beginning 23 January. He will continue to supervise B.Litt. students M.Y. Pickard and M.B. Salu.

26 January 1945 H.C. Wyld, the Merton Professor of English Language and Literature, dies.

29 January 1945 Tolkien spends much of the morning dealing with a leaking scullery tap and a blocked sink. At nearly 11.00 a.m. he leaves for Magdalen College to meet C.S. Lewis. The only wood Lewis has to put on the fire in his rooms is elm, which burns badly; and as this provides little heat, Lewis and Tolkien go to the Mitre for warmth and beer. – Later in the day, Tolkien hears of Wyld's death.

30 January 1945 Following a heavy storm during the night, Tolkien spends part of the morning digging coal, coke, and fowls out of the snow. Clad in oilskins, he cycles into town over treacherous roads, arriving late to lecture. – After his lectures he adjourns to the 'Bird and Baby' where he meets C.S. Lewis and R.E. Havard. – The snow is thawing, and on his way home he falls off his bicycle three times and is drenched by passing cars. It takes him until 3.30 p.m. to finish clearing the snow and drains. He then settles down to read letters from Christopher. – He begins a long letter to Christopher. Tolkien must make up his mind whether to apply for Wyld's Merton chair.

31 January 1945 Tolkien continues his letter to Christopher begun on 30 January. He discusses the Eden 'myth,' *The Lord of the Rings* (Christopher has received and read more chapters), and war news. Towards the end he says that 'it is 9 p.m., and I have some letters of necessity to write, and 2 lectures tomorrow' (*Letters*, p. 111).

Between 1 and 10 February 1945 Tolkien writes another letter to Christopher.

2 February 1945 Tolkien chairs an English Faculty Board meeting. He undertakes to draft an explanation of why a candidate who has taken Part II, and then been absent on approved war service, need only take eight instead of nine papers to qualify for full honours in the Final Honour School of English Language and Literature. He also undertakes to write to Mrs Wyld expressing the Board's sympathy on the death of her husband. The Registrar has asked the Board for its observations on the vacancy in the Merton Professorship of English Language and Literature. The Board defers its reply to the next meeting. – Tolkien also attends a General Board meeting.

10–11 February 1945 Tolkien writes a lengthy letter to the *Catholic Herald*, correcting a correspondent who had erroneously derived the name *Coventry* from *convent*.

11 February 1945 Tolkien writes to Christopher, concerning *Coventry*.

13 February 1945 Tolkien writes to Mabel Day, in reply to her letter of December 1944 and a later message in early 1945. He admits that he does not answer letters promptly, 'yet I seem always at my desk when not doing housework'. He cannot attend an Early English Text Society Committee meeting on Friday, 16 January: it is impossible from him to come to London on Fridays, because his wife is unwell, but also because on Fridays he customarily has important board meetings in Oxford, and duties involving the cadets. His only free days in term are Wednesdays and Sundays. He was sorry to hear the news about Dr Flower; when he received her December letter he had thought of C.T. Onions as a possible successor but had done nothing. She now mentions W.A. Craigie, and although Tolkien would prefer Onions 'as a man to get things done' he has 'the warmest personal' feelings for Craigie. In regard to his edition of the *Ancrene Wisse*:

> My text is all transcribed, and typed except for the first few folios ... transcribed in a v[ery] careful hand. Some still need checking against the rotographs I have [one or two pages have been lent to Dr Flower], and if that is sufficient they could be set up soon. There are a number of points where the actual [manuscript] ought to be looked at: the corrections in the early folios, and a few cases of doubtful readings; but I don't know whether that is possible at present. [Early English Text Society archive]

16 February 1945 Tolkien attends a General Board Meeting.

20 February 1945 Tolkien is elected to membership in the Oxford Dante Society (*Societies and clubs). Other members at the time include Maurice Bowra (Warden of Wadham College), *Father Martin D'Arcy, R.M. Dawkins, *Colin Hardie, C.S. Lewis, and Charles Williams. The Society meets once a term, to be entertained to dinner by each member in turn, and to hear a paper read by a member.

23 February 1945 A letter by Tolkien on place-name origins and the derivation and use of *convent* is published in the *Catholic Herald* for 23 February as *The Name Coventry*.

24 February 1945 Stanley Unwin writes to Tolkien: 'Is it not time that we had a new book from you?' (Tolkien-George Allen & Unwin archive, Harper-Collins). Although paper is still short, they are planning for the future.

March or April 1945 Tolkien introduces Robert Murray to Father Douglas Carter.

2 March 1945 Tolkien attends a General Board meeting.

8 March 1945 Tolkien chairs an English Faculty Library Committee meeting.

14 March 1945 Tolkien attends a Pembroke College meeting.

15 March 1945 Stanley Unwin writes to Tolkien. *Leaf by Niggle* in the *Dublin Review* has come to his attention, and he has shown it to his elder son, David, who writes children's books as 'David Severn'. He sends Tolkien a copy of David's comments in which he praises the story highly, and says that even four such pieces would make a small book worth printing. He hopes that this will encourage Tolkien to show Allen & Unwin more of his work. Unwin asks if he can borrow *Farmer Giles of Ham* again, as David would like to read it.

16 March 1945 Tolkien chairs an English Faculty Board meeting at 3.30 p.m. The Board discusses qualifications for the Honours degree. Since the Secretary of Faculties has agreed to Tolkien's submission made as a result of the meeting on 2 February, the Board resolves that candidates who have previously obtained Honours in the Shortened School (other than Part I in 1942) should be permitted, beginning with the examination in 1946, to omit one paper in the Full Final Honour School. The needs of the Faculty are also discussed, and Tolkien and David Nichol Smith are authorized to draw up a statement for submission to the Secretary of Faculties. Tolkien reports on preliminary discussions which have been held 'on a proposed tripartite arrangement with Cambridge and London for the teaching of Scandinavian languages' (Oxford University Archives FA 4/5/1/1), and he is authorized, with E.O.G. Turville-Petre, to continue them. – Tolkien also attends a General Board meeting.

17 March 1945 Hilary Full Term ends.

?18 March 1945 Tolkien writes to Stanley Unwin, apologizing for his 'unproductiveness and (seeming) neglect' in not providing works for Unwin to publish. He has been worried about Christopher, his 'real primary audience' for *The Lord of the Rings*, and during his absence in South Africa (he will return to England this month) has spent much of his spare time writing to him. Since writing Book IV last autumn 'I have been more than ever burdened, or the ratio between duty and weariness has been more unfavourable'. He describes his time as occupied with

> endless unrelated jobs, from the most menial ones about the house to correcting cadet-essays, and all the complexities of departmental administration in these difficult days. Not to mention the problems of other

universities. My opposite numbers or colleagues in all the 'chairs' about Britain are dying or retiring, and I seem in danger of becoming universal 'adviser' to puzzled faculties, and unofficial employment exchange to young men and women trying to get into or out of or back into jobs.

He describes how he came to write *Leaf by Niggle*, and says that he has never written anything else of its kind that might be published with it: 'two others, of that tone and style, remain mere budding leaves'. He suggests that he send to Allen & Unwin for consideration a bundle of those works that he can find. He asks if they are considering *Farmer Giles of Ham* for inclusion. Since the 'corrected and properly typed copy' of *Farmer Giles* has been lent to someone, he promises to send David Unwin 'a tolerable home-made copy' (evidently the original typescript of the revised version of 1938, from which the Academic Copying Office in Oxford made a professional copy; in the event, Tolkien does not send the story to Unwin until 1946). He has plotted a sequel, but it is likely to remain unwritten as 'the heart has gone out of the Little Kingdom, and the woods and plains are aerodromes and bomb-practice targets'; but he suggests as a companion piece 'another comic fairy story', *The King of the Green Dozen*, which is half-written and 'could be finished without much pain, if "Farmer Giles" is approved' (in the event, it will remain unfinished). His 'only real desire is to publish "The Silmarillion"'. He estimates that 'three weeks with nothing else to do – and a little rest and sleep first – would probably be sufficient' to finish *The Lord of the Rings*, but 'I don't see any hope of getting them', and it is not the kind of writing that can be fitted into odd moments. He remembers that he had promised to let Unwin see part of what was written, but

it is so closely knit, and under a process of growth in all its parts, that I find I have to have all the chapters by me – I am always, you see, hoping to get at it. And anyway only one copy (home-typed or written by various filial hands and my own), that is legible by others, exists, and I've feared to let go of it; and I've shirked the expense of professional typing in these hard days, at any rate until the end, and the whole is corrected.

But if Unwin would really like to see it, he could send it part at a time, 'with all its present imperfections on it – riders, alternatives, variable proper names' (Tolkien-George Allen & Unwin archive, HarperCollins, partly printed in *Letters*, pp. 112–14).

He might find a few weeks during the year for this work, but in the immediate future he has 'special exams' until Easter (presumably for the cadets), and some trouble with the University of Wales (he is again an examiner); during the Easter vacation he will have to spend time considering a successor to H.C. Wyld; he is in trouble with Basil Blackwell, who wants him to proofread his translation of *Pearl* and provide an introduction; E.V. Gordon's widow wants him to put her husband's edition of *Pearl* in order as he had promised; he is also in serious trouble with the Clarendon Press (probably about the Clarendon Chaucer); and Simonne d'Ardenne has arrived in Oxford, having survived the German occupation of Belgium, with the manuscript of *Seinte Katerine* that they began together before the war and promised the Early English Text Society; while the EETS is also inquiring after his own edition of the *Ancrene Riwle*.

22 March 1945 Stanley Unwin writes to Tolkien. Tolkien should send anything that he thinks might make a volume with *Leaf by Niggle*. They have not yet received from Tolkien the typescript of *Farmer Giles of Ham*. Unwin would prefer to wait until *The Lord of the Rings* is complete before seeing that work, especially as at present Allen & Unwin do not have the paper to print such a lengthy book.

26 March 1945 Tolkien attends a General Board meeting. – He drafts a letter to the Secretary of Faculties and types a statement on the needs of the English Faculty as requested at the last Board meeting, either with David Nichol Smith or for discussion with him. He points out that the English School

beside its principal field of literary and linguistic history from AD 700, is either responsible for, or shares largely in the maintenance of other allied subjects, notably Icelandic language and antiquities, comparative philology, Germanic philology, English palaeography and bibliography.

It receives small support in the way of fellowships from the men's colleges as a whole, least of all in linguistic and mediaeval subjects; and it can never count on reappointment in the same subject, if one of its few male teachers that hold fellowships either retires or dies. An important part of the lecturing has in recent years been provided without fee or emolument.

In spite of this shortage the tendency appears to be to reduce the number of men supported either by fellowship or university appointment, and those that remain are over-worked. In order to conduct a cadet course all the resident men, fellows and professors (with the exception of the late Professor Wyld, whose sight and health were failing), had to take part, and most of these have now had no break in teaching and examining since January 1943.

At present there are not enough men and women with a fellowship or appointment to provide for the proper relief and change of examiners in those examinations of which the English Board has charge. The Lecturer in English Language is absent, but even if he were not, the position in this respect would be unsatisfactory. It has long been so. The Professor of Anglo-Saxon [Tolkien himself] has for years been obliged to take a large share in the examination of Pass Moderations and Sections. [Oxford University Archives FA 4/5/2/7]

4 April 1945 Stanley Unwin writes to Tolkien, reminding him again to send the typescript of *Farmer Giles of Ham*.

27 April 1945 Tolkien attends a General Board meeting.

28 April 1945 Trinity Full Term begins. Tolkien's scheduled lectures for this term are: *Beowulf* (lines 1–1650) on Tuesdays and Thursdays at 11.00 a.m. in the Taylor Institution, beginning 30 April; and The Language of the Vespasian Psalter Gloss on Thursdays at 12.00 noon in the Taylor Institution, beginning 2 May. He will continue to supervise B.Litt. students M.Y. Pickard and M.B. Salu.

2 May 1945 Tolkien attends a Pembroke College meeting.

5 May 1945 Field Marshal Montgomery on Lüneburg Heath accepts the surrender of German forces in North Germany, Holland, and Denmark.

7 May 1945 German envoys sign terms of surrender at Reims. In the evening the Prime Minister, Winston Churchill, announces to the British people the end of the war in Europe.

8 May 1945 Britain celebrates VE day, the end of the war in Europe.

10 May 1945 Charles Williams is taken ill. – Tolkien entertains the air raid wardens with whom he has shared duty with an 'A.R.P. R.I.P. sherry party' at 20 Northmoor Road (according to Malcolm Graham and Melanie Williams, *When the Lights Went Out: Oxfordshire 1939 to 1945*, p. 6).

11 May 1945 Tolkien chairs an English Faculty Board meeting. He is elected to the Nominating Committee for the Honour School and Group B 6 until Michaelmas Term 1948. He is appointed to a committee to report on a communication from the General Board about the payment of Examiners for Prizes, etc. – He also attends a General Board meeting.

14 May 1945 Charles Williams undergoes surgery in the Radcliffe Infirmary.

15 May 1945 Charles Williams dies in the Radcliffe Infirmary. C.S. Lewis is told of his death when he arrives to visit. Lewis then goes to the 'Bird and Baby' and breaks the news to his friends there, presumably including Tolkien. One of the subjects of conversation is almost certainly that the proposed *Festschrift* in honour of Charles Williams should now be a memorial volume, with royalties going to Williams' widow. By this date, Tolkien's revision of *On Fairy-Stories* is already completed. – On the same day, Tolkien writes a letter of sympathy to Charles Williams' widow.

17 May 1945 Edith Tolkien writes to Christopher that his father will be attending Charles Williams' funeral on 18 May.

18 May 1945 The funeral of Charles Williams takes place in St Cross, Holywell, Oxford. He is buried in the adjoining churchyard.

19 May 1945 *Father Gervase Mathew says a Mass at Blackfriars for Charles Williams, with Tolkien serving.

23 May 1945 Tolkien attends a Requiem Mass for John Fraser, Jesus Professor of Celtic, said by Father Douglas Carter at the Church of St Gregory and St Augustine, and probably also is present at the interment at Wolvercote Cemetery.

24 May 1945 Tolkien chairs an English Faculty Library Committee meeting.

25 May 1945 Tolkien attends a General Board meeting. – The electors to the Merton Professorship of English Language and Literature meet for the first time. Those present are the Vice-Chancellor, the Warden of Merton, F.M. Powicke (the Regius Professor of Modern History at Oxford), C.T. Onions, David Nichol Smith, and Kenneth Sisam. Tolkien, though also an elector, does not attend, presumably because he has been approached as a candidate. No notice requesting applications for the Chair has been published, but the electors evidently have had discussions among themselves. Those present at the meeting agree that the most suitable person to elect to the Professorship is Tolkien, and it is understood that he is willing to stand. They also agree to ask the Hebdomadal Council to appoint an elector in Tolkien's place to take part in the actual election on 23 June.

26 May 1945 Margaret Douglas writes to Tolkien, returning *On Fairy-Stories* which she had typed for him in 1943 and which she found among Charles Williams' papers.

29 May 1945 Tolkien writes to Christopher, who is now stationed with the R.A.F. in Shropshire and hopes to be transferred to the Fleet Air Arm. Tolkien says that it would be a comfort to him if the transfer takes place, and expresses his dislike of both British and American imperialism in the Far East.

June 1945 Tolkien visits Wales as an examiner for the University of Wales. He lends some of his unpublished works, including *The Lay of Aotrou and Itroun* and *Sellic Spell*, to his friend *Gwyn Jones, Professor of English Language and Literature at Aberystwyth. – Jones writes to Tolkien that he thinks *Sellic Spell* should be prescribed reading for all university students of *Beowulf*.

2 June 1945 Tolkien writes to an Oxford acquaintance named Maegraith, who has sent several stories he has written and asked for Tolkien's opinion. Tolkien apologizes for not having acknowledged their receipt earlier; he has been busy with endless jobs and examinations, and due to the death or retirement of professors everywhere he is an elector or advisor in half a dozen places and consequently has many letters to write. He now provides three and a half pages of comments on Maegraith's stories.

3 June 1945 Tolkien writes to Christopher. He will probably attend a stand-down parade of the Civil Defence in the University Parks in the afternoon.

8 June 1945 Tolkien attends a General Board meeting.

14 June 1945 English Final Honour Examinations begin.

22 June 1945 Tolkien chairs an English Faculty Board meeting. – He also attends a General Board meeting.

23 June 1945 Trinity Full Term ends. – The electors to the Merton Professorship of English Language and Literature meet: the roster is the same as on 25 May, less Professor Powicke but with the addition of C.S. Lewis in place of Tolkien. They formally elect Tolkien as Merton Professor of English Language and Literature, with effect from October 1945. In this chair he will have special responsibility for Middle English up to 1500. The position also gives him a seat on the English Faculty Board *ex officio*. He will no longer be an *ex officio* member of the Committee on Comparative Philology, but will be co-opted or appointed, and will serve as chairman of that committee from 1945 to 1960.

27 June 1945 Encaenia.

7 July 1945 Tolkien attends a General Board Meeting.

10 July 1945 Tolkien attends an Early English Text Society Committee meeting at Magdalen College, Oxford. The *Ancrene Riwle* sub-committee is reorganized to consist of C.T. Onions as chairman, Mabel Day, Dorothy Everett, Tolkien, and C.L. Wrenn. It is agreed that Tolkien should approach Professor d'Ardenne about submitting *Seinte Katerine* to the Society for publication. A motion by Tolkien and Wrenn that the Director should approach A.H. Smith to ask if he wishes to retire from the Committee, and to ask him to return the Treasurer's books and papers in his possession, is carried.

16 July 1945 Mabel Day sends Tolkien 'A[ncrene] R[iwle] instructions', either (or both) for use with his edition or for his reference as a member of the *Ancrene Riwle* sub-committee.

26 July 1945 The Labour Party, led by Clement Attlee, wins the first postwar election in Great Britain. Polling at home takes place on 5 July, but the votes are not counted for three weeks to enable those from the armed services abroad to be included.

6 August 1945 The atomic bomb is dropped on Hiroshima.

9 August 1945 The atomic bomb is dropped on Nagasaki. – Tolkien writes to Christopher, expressing his horror at the atomic bombs and the 'utter folly of these lunatic physicists to consent to do such work for war-purposes: calmly plotting the destruction of the world!' (*Letters*, p. 116).

15 August 1945 Japan surrenders. Britain celebrates VJ Day.

18 August 1945 E.R. Eddison dies.

7 September 1945 Tolkien attends his final Pembroke College meeting.

11 September 1945 Tolkien sends a postcard from Whitby, Yorkshire, to his grandson Michael George. While at Whitby Tolkien probably visits Mother Mary Michael of the Sisters of Mercy, now living there, who had befriended him in hospital in Hull in 1917.

13 September 1945 Ragnar Furuskog writes to Tolkien. He has not received a reply to his letter of 23 December 1944, and repeats some of its contents. Although it is now possible for him to come to England to work on the manuscripts, he would still like copies of the transcripts of the *Ancrene Wisse* and *Seinte Katerine*. Professor d'Ardenne has now written to Furuskog's supervisor welcoming his proposed study.

9 October 1945 Tolkien writes to Christopher, informing him that the Inklings propose to consider him a permanent member.

10 October 1945 At 10.00 a.m. Tolkien is elected and admitted as a Fellow of Merton College. (Hugo Dyson is also elected a Fellow at this time.) Tolkien then takes part in a College meeting which lasts until 1.30 p.m. and breaks up in disorder. He lunches in Merton, and puts his name on the housing list at the Estates Bursary. – No longer a Fellow of Pembroke College, Tolkien writes to its Bursar, L.E. Salt, settling his account and thanking Salt for his kindness. Tolkien expresses his satisfaction that he will remain a member of the College and also an honorary member of the Senior Common Room.

11 October 1945 Tolkien walks around Merton College in the afternoon with Hugo Dyson (who has been allotted the rooms Tolkien had wanted, overlooking the meadows). – Later he writes to Christopher, describing his first experiences at Merton. 'It is incredible belonging to a real college (and a very large and wealthy one)' (*Letters*, p. 116). He plans to go to an Inklings meeting that evening.

12 October 1945 Tolkien attends a General Board meeting.

14 October 1945 Michaelmas Full Term begins. Tolkien's scheduled lectures for this term are: Old English prescribed texts, excluding *Beowulf* and *Exodus*, on Tuesdays and Thursdays at 11.00 a.m. in the Taylor Institution, beginning 16 October; and History of the English Language to AD 1100 on Thursdays and Fridays at 12.00 noon in the Taylor Institution, beginning 18 October. Tolkien not only has to prepare and deliver new lectures on subjects which are the responsibility of the Merton Professor of English Language and Literature – the history of the English language, and English Literature down to and during the period of Chaucer – but until his successor to the Rawlinson and Bosworth chair is elected, he also has to continue to lecture on Old English. In 1963 he will write to his son Michael: 'I was never obliged to teach anything except what I loved (and do) with inextinguishable enthusiasm. (Save only for a brief time after my change of chair in 1945 – that was awful)' (*Letters*, pp. 336–7). For this term Tolkien also will continue to supervise B.Litt. students M.Y. Offord (*née* Pickard) and M.B. Salu.

15 October 1945 Mabel Day writes to Tolkien, informing him of a change in the Early English Text Society rules for editors.

18 October 1945 Tolkien dines for the first time at Merton high table and finds it

> very agreeable; though odd. For fuel-economy the common room is not heated, and the dons meet and chat amiably on the dais, until someone thinks there are enough there for grace to be said. After that they sit and dine, and have their port, and coffee, and smoke and evening newspapers all at high table in a manner that if agreeably informal is rather shocking to one trained in the severer ceremonies and strict precedence of medieval Pembroke. [letter to Christopher Tolkien, 22 October 1945, *Letters*, pp. 116–17]

At about 8.45 p.m. he and Hugo Dyson stroll through the Merton grounds to Magdalen College and visit Warnie Lewis and R.E. Havard. They break up at about 10.30.

22 October 1945 Tolkien writes to Christopher.

26 October 1945 At an English Faculty Board meeting, in Tolkien's absence, he is re-elected chairman for 1945–6. He is also elected to the Standing

Committee on the Sidney Lee Bequest with C.S. Lewis and H.F.B. Brett-Smith; and to the electors to the Rawlinson and Bosworth Professorship in Anglo-Saxon. He will continue to be an elector until Michaelmas Term 1958, and will takes part in the 1946 election of his successor. – Elaine Griffiths is now a Lecturer in the Oxford English School.

3 November 1945 The British Council write to Tolkien on behalf of Ragnar Furuskog, who has complained to them that he has not yet received a reply to his letters to Tolkien of December 1944 and September 1945.

9 November 1945 Tolkien attends a General Board meeting.

14 November 1945 A notice in the *Oxford University Gazette* states that anyone who wishes to be admitted as an advanced student or a probationer B.Litt. student in the School of English Language and Literature must communicate with one of the persons appointed by the Board for an interview, either David Nichol Smith or Tolkien.

17 November 1945 Tolkien writes to Roger Sharrock, who has sought his support for applications to posts at various universities. Tolkien mentions that there are not enough tutors at Oxford, and the present tutors are overworked.

21 November 1945 Tolkien attends a Merton College meeting.

23 November 1945 Tolkien attends a General Board Meeting.

29 November 1945 Tolkien chairs an English Faculty Library Committee meeting. – The report of the Committee on the Payment of Examiners for Prizes, Scholarships, and Research Degrees is signed by the members, including Tolkien. The original draft of the report is in his handwriting.

December 1945 Tolkien's poem *The Lay of Aotrou and Itroun* is published in the December issue of the *Welsh Review*, edited by Gwyn Jones.

7 December 1945 Tolkien chairs an English Faculty Board meeting. He is appointed to a committee to report to the Board at its first meeting next term on the additional needs of the Faculty for 1946–7. Tolkien is empowered as chairman, 'during the present emergency', to authorize each Lecturer to increase his teaching hours up to twenty a week if necessary' (Oxford University Archives FA 4/5/1/1). The Applications Committee has appointed Tolkien (in place of David Nichol Smith) supervisor of T.J.A. Monaghan, Exeter College, an advanced student for a D.Phil. working on Thomas Tyrwhitt (1730–1786) and his contributions to English Scholarship. – Tolkien also attends a General Board meeting.

8 December 1945 Michaelmas Full Term ends.

10 December 1945 Tolkien attends a Merton College meeting.

11 December 1945 In the morning, Tolkien and Warnie Lewis leave Oxford by the 9.35 train and travel to *Fairford, Gloucestershire, for a 'Victory Inklings' gathering to celebrate the end of the war. – In the afternoon, Tolkien and Warnie take a two-hour walk west of Fairford by Sunhill and Meysey Hampton, calling at the White Hart pub which they find full of Polish soldiers. – They stay at the Bull inn and spend the evening reading: Warnie lends Tolkien his copy of the letters of Dr John Brown, the Scottish physician and essayist.

12 December 1945 C.S. Lewis arrives in Fairford by train, and R.E. Havard by car. Owen Barfield is ill and cannot join them. After lunch Tolkien, Havard, and the Lewis brothers take a long walk north of Fairford via Quenington; Warnie is struck by the exquisite subdued colours of sky and landscape.

13 December 1945 The assembled friends visit the church in Fairford, where Tolkien points out a gilded helmet on the wall with a bird's nest. – In the afternoon, they walk through Horcott and Whelford, southeast of Fairford; in Whelford they are impressed by the atmosphere of the simple church, where Tolkien says a prayer.

14 December 1945 In the morning, the friends walk north from Fairford to the Coln St Aldwyn, picturesque but with a small war factory; there they drink beer at the Pig and Whistle, which opens at 10.00 a.m. – They then pass through nearby Hatherop and Quenington; in the latter village the landlady at The Keepers gives them each a home-baked ginger biscuit. – They arrive back in Fairford for lunch, and return to Oxford by the 2.12 pm train.

Christmas vacation 1945–August 1946 Tolkien writes during 'a fortnight of comparative leisure' around Christmas 1945 'three parts of another book, taking up in an entirely different frame and setting what little had any value in the inchoate *Lost Road*': *The Notion Club Papers* (letter to Stanley Unwin, 21 July 1946, *Letters*, p. 118). He hopes to complete this in a rush, but after Christmas his health gives way. *See note.* Tolkien later divides the work in two, then rejects the division but never completes the second part.

He writes a rough but complete manuscript of Part One, 'The Ramblings of Michael Ramer: *Out of the Talkative Planet*', which presents the 'reports' of two successive meetings at which the problems of space-travel, and the possibility of travelling in one's dreams, are discussed. This is followed by a second, fuller manuscript, an incomplete fair copy, and a typescript. Tolkien subsequently emends the second manuscript to foreshadow events and discussions in Part Two, 'The Strange Case of Arundel Lowdham': in that part he records further meetings of the Club, continuous with those of Part One, and introduces the 'Atlantis story', the story of Númenor. He begins with discontinuous drafting and then makes a manuscript; he follows this with a typescript, and in the course of typing replaces a large section. Possibly because the conception has become too complicated, he leaves both manuscript and typescript unfinished at the same point: only two brief texts give some idea of how the work was to develop.

At this time Tolkien also produces several 'artifacts' associated with *The Notion Club Papers*: 'facsimiles' of Númenórean script, and of Lowdham's transcriptions of texts he has heard in a dream, and of title-pages for 'published' books. At some time (or times) in 1946, before 22 August, Tolkien reads *The Notion Club Papers* to the Inklings.

Tolkien now also writes the poem *The Death of Saint Brendan* (*Imram), producing much initial working, four finished manuscripts, and a typescript. He includes the alliterative verse retelling of the legend of King Sheave, previously associated with *The Lost Road*, but writes it out as if it were prose. At some later time, he will develop the poem (as *Imram*) in three further type-scripts.

Probably at this time, with his renewed interest in Númenor, Tolkien makes some alterations and additions to the fine manuscript of *The Fall of Númenor* written *c.* 1940–1, which tells the story of Númenor as it might be remembered by Elves. After writing three texts or sketches, he begins the first version of **The Drowning of Anadûnê*; these show rapidly evolving ideas about the history of Númenor and how it might be remembered in Mannish rather than Elvish tradition. The primary draft for *The Drowning of Anadûnê* is composed on a typewriter rather than in manuscript (apparently the first time Tolkien takes this approach). He makes three further typescripts incorporating emendations, changes, and replacement passages. He becomes increasingly interested in Adunaic, the language of Númenor, and begins (but does not finish) a detailed account of Adunaic and its phonology which extends for seventeen typed pages.

Later workings by Tolkien of his poem *The Song of Ælfwine* (*The Nameless Land*, first composed in 1924) and a prose note may date from this time.

End of 1945–early 1946 At the end of 1945 Simonne d'Ardenne comes to Oxford on a British Council grant to continue her work with Tolkien on *Seinte Katerine*. During her visit she probably stays with the Tolkien family. But neither she nor Tolkien is in sufficiently good health to do extensive work, and d'Ardenne has to break off her stay also to return to her university duties in Belgium. They manage, however, '(most of it by Mlle d'A[rdenne]) a good deal of up-picking of threads, and some work, so far as that is now or at present possible on the difficult Catherine-legend; besides some subsidiary lexical enquiries. The whole of B ([MS] Bodley 34) has been re-collated against the printed texts, which do not stand the test very well. But the collation of CCCC [MS CCCC 402, the *Ancrene Wisse*] has not been done' (letter to Mabel Day, 17 July 1946, Early English Text Society archive).

1946

1946 Much influenced by Tolkien and by other friends, Robert Murray joins the Roman Catholic Church. – Although the war is over, shortages continue; the ration allowance for butter, margarine, and cooking fat is reduced in February; bread and flour are rationed in July.

?Early 1946 Probably at this time, while Tolkien is considering the cosmology of his legendarium in relation to *The Notion Club Papers*, he makes a new version of the *Ainulindalë*, based on the version written in the 1930s but introducing radical changes (e.g. the Sun in existence from the beginning of Arda). He probably begins with a rough pencil draft of which only half a page survives, then makes a typescript on which he later (probably in 1948) writes 'Round World Version'.

18 January 1946 Tolkien attends a General Board meeting.

20 January 1946 Hilary Full Term begins. Tolkien's scheduled lectures for this term are: *Beowulf* on Fridays at 11.00 a.m. in the Taylor Institution, beginning 25 January; and History of English Language: Middle English on Wednesdays and Fridays at 12.00 noon in the Taylor Institution, beginning 23 January. He will continue to supervise B.Litt. students M.Y. Offord and M.B. Salu, and D. Phil. student T.J.A. Monaghan.

1 February 1946 Tolkien chairs an English Faculty Board meeting. The report of the committee appointed 7 December 1945 to consider the additional needs of the Faculty, 1946–7, and the question of University Lectureships, is presented, based on a manuscript version by Tolkien and signed by him and other members. As a result, Tolkien is appointed to a committee to report on 'the question of appointing one or more intercollegiate lecturers as University Lecturers as from 1 October 1946' (Oxford University Archives FA 4/5/1/1). He and David Nichol Smith undertake to submit draft amendments for the Syllabus for the Final Honour School for consideration at the next meeting. – Tolkien also attends a General Board meeting.

2 February 1946 Tolkien attends the first meeting of the electors to the Rawlinson and Bosworth Professorship of Anglo-Saxon, at 11.15 a.m. in the Delegates Room of the Clarendon Building. The electors agree that the vacant chair should be advertised, and applications received should be circulated to the electors after 30 March 1946.

6 February 1946 Tolkien attends a Merton College meeting.

10 February 1946 Tolkien's eldest son, John, is ordained a Roman Catholic priest in the Church of St Gregory and Augustine, Oxford.

11 February 1946 Tolkien serves at Father John's first Mass, in the Church of St Aloysius, Oxford.

15 February 1946 Tolkien attends a General Board meeting. He is elected a member of the Standing Committee on Examinations.

End of February–March 1946 Tolkien is ill, the result of various worries.

15 March 1946 Tolkien chairs an English Faculty Board meeting. The Board considers changes in the syllabus for the Final Honour School suggested by Tolkien and David Nichol Smith; it makes small changes, and agrees that *Sir Gawain and the Green Knight* should be permitted as an alternative to *Pearl* in the examination in 1947. The committee on 'the question of appointing one or more intercollegiate lecturers as University Lecturers as from 1 October 1946', set up on 1 February with Tolkien among its members, submits a report (dated 6 March) which suggests that lecturerships be distributed widely among tutors; the report is referred back to the committee for further considera-tion. The Applications Committee has accepted J.J. (John) Lawlor, Magdalen College, as a B.Litt. student to work on 'The Revelations of Dame Juliana of Norwich edited from the Manuscripts with Introduction, Notes, and Glossary' with Tolkien as his supervisor. Lawlor will later comment about Tolkien as his supervisor: 'My first and abiding impression was one of immediate kindness. Tutored [as an undergraduate] by [C.S.] Lewis I had expected to be tested with a few falls, so to speak. But the gentle creature who sucked his pipe and gazed meditatively along its stem seemed interested only in what he could do to help' (Lawlor, *C.S. Lewis: Memories and Reflections* (1998), pp. 30–1).

16 March 1946 Hilary Full Term ends.

18 March 1946 Tolkien attends a Merton College meeting. – C.A. Furth of George Allen & Unwin writes to ask Tolkien's opinion on whether it would be worthwhile to issue a revised edition of *Outlines of the History of the English Language* by Ernest Classen. He offers Tolkien a consultancy fee of 2 guineas.

20 March 1946 Tolkien writes to the Oxford University Registrar in connection with the election to the Rawlinson and Bosworth chair. He is unwell, and although his doctor has ordered him to apply for a term's leave, he realizes that this is impossible in the present academic plight, short of a complete collapse. He is, however, going away for a while, and will return for the weekend of the election, but hopes that the other electors will excuse him from preparing a number of formal documents, and be content with an oral statement made at the meeting from notes. Five prospective applicants have asked his permission to give his name as a reference. He asks that the candidates' statements and applications be sent to Northmoor Road (evidently so that he may read them on his return).

25 March 1946 Stanley Unwin writes to Tolkien. *The Hobbit* is being reprinted in a press run of 4,000 copies. – Mabel Day, Early English Text Society, writes to Tolkien. She has had a letter from Ragnar Furuskog asking questions about the proposed editions of *Seinte Katerine* and the *Ancrene Wisse*.

25 March–1 April 1946 Tolkien stays at New Lodge in Stonyhurst, Lancashire, where his son John had stayed several times in the period 1942–5. In the register Tolkien firmly declares himself 'English' rather than (as in other entries) 'British'. In a letter to Stanley Unwin on 21 July 1946 he will say that he came 'near to a real breakdown' around this time, and went away and 'ate and slept and did nothing else, by orders, but only for three weeks, and not for the six months that my doctor prescribed . . . but I came back to a term so troublous that it was all I could do to get through it' (Tolkien-George Allen & Unwin archive, HarperCollins).

2 April 1946 In the morning, Tolkien and Christopher meet R.E. Havard and Warnie Lewis in the 'Bird and Baby'. Warnie thinks that Tolkien looks wonderfully improved by his rest at Stonyhurst. Tolkien is now staying with Christopher at the Bear inn at Woodstock, while Edith is away. – Havard drives Warnie and the Tolkiens back to the Bear, and over lunch they argue about the morality of the Nuremburg trials. In the afternoon, they drive into the Cotswolds, until they come to the valley of the Evenlode, where they sit 'for a long time on the bank of the river in a rank neglected piece of meadow, backed by neglected wood' (*Brothers and Friends*, p. 189). – C.A. Furth of George Allen & Unwin writes to Tolkien, who has not yet replied to Furth's letter of 18 March.

11 April 1946 R.E. Havard and the Lewis brothers join Tolkien and Christopher for an Inklings dinner to celebrate their last night at the Bear.

12 April 1946 Tolkien presumably returns to 20 Northmoor Road on this date.

13 April 1946 The electors to the Rawlinson and Bosworth Professorship of Anglo-Saxon, including Tolkien, meet at 11.15 a.m. in the Delegates Room of the Clarendon Building. They discuss nine applications. The meeting is adjourned to 16 April.

14 April 1946 *Research v. Literature*, a review by Tolkien of *English Literature at the Close of the Middle Ages* by E.K. Chambers, is published in the London *Sunday Times* for 14 April.

16 April 1946 The electors to the Rawlinson and Bosworth Professorship of Anglo-Saxon meet again at 3.45 p.m., and elect C.L. Wrenn to the chair, with effect from 1 October. The time taken to make this election means that for the entire academic year 1945–6 the chair of Anglo-Saxon is vacant, and Tolkien has to continue to lecture on the subject.

25 April 1946 Tolkien attends a Merton College meeting.

26 April 1946 Tolkien attends a General Board meeting. He is appointed to a committee to consider 'the question of scarcity of books' (Oxford University Archives FA 1/1/5).

28 April 1946 Trinity Full Term begins. Tolkien's scheduled lectures for this term are: *Beowulf* (continued) on Wednesdays and Fridays at 11.00 a.m., place to be arranged, beginning 1 May; and History of English Language (continued) on Wednesdays at 12.00 noon and Fridays at 10.00 a.m. in the Taylor Institution, beginning 1 May. He will continue to supervise B.Litt. students J.J. Lawlor, M.Y. Offord, and M.B. Salu, and D. Phil. student T.J.A. Monaghan. – Christopher Tolkien returns to Trinity College, Oxford to continue his studies interrupted by the war.

9 May 1946 Tolkien chairs an English Faculty Library Committee meeting. The Committee considers a change in Library hours, which Tolkien has temporarily sanctioned, and the new hours are provisionally adopted. Tolkien will cease to be a member of the Library Committee once he ceases to be chairman of the English Faculty Board at the start of Michaelmas Term 1946.

10 May 1946 Tolkien chairs an English Faculty Board meeting. The Committee on the University Lecturerships, of which Tolkien is a member, reports to the Board, and it is agreed, subject to the approval of the General Board, to appoint Lord David Cecil and Dorothy Whitelock to Lecturerships for five years from 1 October 1946. Tolkien undertakes to draw up statements for direct submission to the General Board. It is decided that the Committee should remain in being for any further consideration of the conditions of tenure of new Lecturerships that might become available. – Tolkien also attends a General Board meeting.

11 May 1946 Tolkien attends a Merton College meeting.

13 and 20 May 1946 The British Council write to Tolkien, probably one of many such requests he receives. They ask him to look at papers supporting an application for a grant as a British Council Scholar for 1946, and to say whether he thinks it would be a profitable award.

14 May 1946 In the evening, Tolkien attends a dinner of The Society hosted by Nevill Coghill at Exeter College, Oxford. Ten members are present. They dine on soup, fish, and a sweet, with beer, cider, port, and sherry.

21 May 1946 Tolkien's manuscript statement for the General Board promised at the English Faculty Board meeting of 10 May 1946, of the Reasons of the Board of the Faculty of English Language and Literature for the Appointment of University Lecturers, is stamped 'received 21 May 1946' (probably by the printers).

1 June 1946 Tolkien attends a Merton College meeting.

Early June 1946 Tolkien writes to University College, London about a planned meeting of the Board of Advisors to choose an occupant for the Quain Chair. He asks if the meeting fixed for 6 June is still to take place, since one candidate (presumably C.L. Wrenn) has accepted an Oxford chair, leaving only one candidate to be considered. Tolkien thinks that the Advisors should seek to widen the field. He is unwell and also heavily engaged with an extremely difficult term, and does not want to waste a day if it is not necessary.

7 June 1946 Tolkien attends a General Board meeting. The Committee on the Scarcity of Books is asked to deal with a lack of philosophical books.

13 June 1946 English Final Honour School Examinations begin.

21 June 1946 Tolkien chairs an English Faculty Board meeting. The Board expresses its deep regret at the departure after thirty-eight years of David Nichol Smith, who has resigned the Merton Chair of English Literature. Tolkien is appointed to a committee to draw up regulations for the Vaughan Morgan Scholarship, for consideration at the next meeting. A report of the committee on University Lecturerships, of which Tolkien is a member (and who wrote out the original manuscript of the report), is adopted for presentation to the General Board.

22 June 1946 Trinity Full Term ends.

25 June 1946 Tolkien attends a Merton College meeting, and is appointed to its library committee until 1949.

26 June–4 July 1946 Tolkien and his wife stay at New Lodge, Stonyhurst. Edith signs the visitors' book first and dittoes from the previous entry 'British' as her nationality; Tolkien does the same. Edith writes in the 'Remarks' column 'A very enjoyable visit', which Tolkien dittoes in agreement. This is the first holiday they have had alone together for over twenty years.

4 July 1946 Tolkien returns from Stonyhurst. He receives a note by G.E. Selby.

7 July 1946 Tolkien writes to G.E. Selby, expressing the hope that with Wrenn as Oxford Professor of Anglo-Saxon, and 'a new and vigorous colleague' in the Merton chair of English Literature, he will be relieved of some of his academic duties and have time to write again (quoted in Maggs Bros., *Autograph Letters & Historical Documents*, Catalogue 1086 (1988), item 168).

17 July 1946 Tolkien writes to Mabel Day. Since the end of term he has been trying to deal with neglected business, and is about half way through a mountain of letters. His rotograph of the *Ancrene Wisse* manuscript is on loan to his student Mary Salu, except for the first leaf, lent long ago to Dr Flower and presumably lost. Tolkien's irritation with Ragnar Furuskog's enquiries has increased his 'natural disinclination to answer letters'; he takes them 'to be no more than a declaration of academic war', when it was obvious that Furuskog's planned research would collide with work Tolkien and his colleagues had already begun. He has not seen Salu's work recently, but expects to see her in the Long Vacation, and by early next year she should be almost ready to present her thesis. The original manuscripts in which Furuskog is interested will soon be returned from the places of safe-keeping to which they were moved during the war, and then it should be possible for Furuskog to get his own copies. Tolkien remarks: 'I hardly feel that international courtesy compels us to supply him with collation made on the spot, or with the time-taking information regarding "all books papers or reviews bearing on the subject", which he will require "as my work progresses", he says. I daresay. And I need a secretary' (Early English Text Society archive).

18 July 1946 Tolkien attends an Early English Text Society Committee meeting at Magdalen College, Oxford. He reports that Simonne d'Ardenne's edition of *Seinte Katerine* will probably not be ready until 1947.

20 July 1946 Tolkien attends a Merton College Meeting.

21 July 1946 Tolkien writes to C.A. Furth. He apologizes for not answering Furth's letters about Classen's *Outlines*, and admits to having neglected many things in the spring while he was unwell:

> I could, if letters did not so quickly bury themselves and become a mound, when one has no secretary, not even an amateur member of the household, to write so much as a postcard, have sent a polite refusal at once. . . . I would have done what you asked gladly, except that this kind of small task, which tends to multiply indefinitely, till the total becomes a great labour, is precisely the kind of thing that I am now sternly refusing from all sources, in the desperate hope of at last getting a little time to write in.

He does not know Classen's book, but gives his opinion of its sort, for which 'there should be a rising demand . . . in future'. He has received a letter from Horus Engels about a German translation of *The Hobbit*, and has replied that 'all questions of translation and copyright are in the hands of the publishers' (Tolkien-George Allen & Unwin archive, HarperCollins). He wonders if anything is known about Rütten & Loening, the prospective German publisher of *The Hobbit* before the war, and what might be the prospects for translations into other languages. He asks also for news of Susan Dagnall. – Tolkien writes another belated letter, to Stanley Unwin (now Sir Stanley).

> I have been ill, worry and overwork mainly, but am a good deal recovered; and am at last able to take some steps to see that at least the overwork, so far as it is academic, is alleviated. For the first time in 25

years, except the year I went on crutches (just before *The Hobbit* came out, I think), I am free of examining, and though I am still battling with a mountain of neglects . . . and with a lot of bothers in this time of chaos and 'reconstruction', I hope after this week actually to – write.

But after a long gap since he last worked on *The Lord of the Rings* 'I shall now have to study my own work in order to get back into it. But I really do hope to have it done before the autumn term, and at any rate before the end of the year.' He will no longer 'be left all alone to try and run our English School' as C.L. Wrenn will take Anglo-Saxon off his shoulders in October, and a new Merton Professor of Literature will be elected. 'It ought to be C.S. Lewis, or perhaps Lord David Cecil, but one never knows.' He is trying to find a job for his son Michael, which 'is more difficult than I hoped – for a man with a George Medal, a good service record, a little business experience, and a year as a temporary Civil servant, and a good degree [a Second in History from Oxford].'

He wonders if David Unwin is still interested in *Farmer Giles of Ham*, which Tolkien is now sending after more than a year's delay. If he 'could have a little leisure' Tolkien might be able to 'add a few things of the same sort, still not finished. But [*Leaf by*] *Niggle* has never bred any thing that consorts with himself at all.' He mentions *The Notion Club Papers*; 'but I am putting *The Lord of the Rings* . . . before all else, save duties that I cannot wriggle out of' (Tolkien-George Allen & Unwin archive, HarperCollins, partly printed in *Letters*, pp. 117–18). He continues, however, to concern himself to some degree with *The Drowning of Anadûnê*, which he reads to the Inklings and to his son Christopher this summer.

23 July 1946 The typescript of *Farmer Giles of Ham* (in the form as read to the Lovelace Society in 1938) is received at Allen & Unwin. By 26 July it will be read or looked at by Stanley Unwin, David Unwin, and W.N. Beard. Another reader will return it to the publisher on 19 August.

24 July 1946 C.A. Furth writes to Tolkien. The situation regarding the German translation of *The Hobbit* is uncertain: the last address of Rütten & Loening was bombed during the war, they have not been licensed to resume publishing by any of the three Western occupying powers (Furth does not know about Russia), so Allen & Unwin need an official ruling on whether the contract is still binding. At present a German publisher cannot negotiate directly with an English firm. Allen & Unwin's efforts to arrange translations are hampered by a lack of copies to send out, but Spanish, Danish, and Czech translations of *The Hobbit* are being considered. A Dutch publisher has turned it down. Susan Dagnall married shortly before the war and now has one or two children. – Stanley Unwin writes to Tolkien. The reprint of *The Hobbit* is moving slowly due to problems at the printers and binders, but he sends Tolkien £50 in anticipation of royalties. He looks forward to seeing *The Lord of the Rings*, though paper shortages and production difficulties, currently worse than during the war, will make it difficult to publish.

27 and 29 July 1946 The electors to the Merton Professorship of English Literature, including Tolkien, meet and agree to publish a notice of the forthcoming election in the *Oxford University Gazette*.

Summer 1946 Christopher Tolkien will later 'remember my father, in his study in the house in North Oxford [20 Northmoor Road], reading me *The Drowning of Anadûnê* on a summer's evening: this was in 1946. . . . Of this reading I recall with clarity that the tents of Ar-Pharazôn were as a field of tall flowers of many colours', a passage which entered with the final version of the work: therefore Tolkien read from either the third manuscript or the subsequent typescript. 'I have the strong impression that the Adunaic names were strange to me, and that my father read *The Drowning of Anadûnê* as a new thing that he had written' (Christopher Tolkien, *Sauron Defeated*, pp. 389–90).

8 August 1946 In the evening, Tolkien attends an Inklings meeting in C.S. Lewis's rooms in Magdalen College. Also present are Hugo Dyson, R.E. Havard, Warnie Lewis, and Gervase Mathew, as well as Stanley Bennett of Cambridge, who has been dining with C.S. Lewis. Warnie Lewis will note in his diary that it was not the sort of evening he much enjoyed: 'mere noise and buffoonery: though Hugo as improvisatore was very funny at times' (*Brothers and Friends*, p. 193).

15 August 1946 Tolkien dines at Queen's College, Oxford with J.A.W. Bennett, then takes him to a meeting of the Inklings in C.S. Lewis's rooms in Magdalen College. R.E. Havard and Warnie Lewis are also present. During the evening they discuss the historical and literary works of Robert Sencourt.

20 August 1946 In the morning, Tolkien meets the Lewis brothers in the 'Bird and Baby'.

22 August 1946 Tolkien dines at Merton College with Warnie Lewis as his guest. Warnie will note in his diary that they dined in the 'common room by candle light, a party of seven . . . a good dinner, and a glass of better port than Magdalen gives one'. – After dinner they collect Christopher Tolkien, and walk to C.S. Lewis's rooms in Magdalen College for an Inklings meeting. J.A.W. Bennett also attends. C.S. Lewis reads a new poem, 'The True Nature of Gnomes', and Tolkien (according to Warnie) 'a magnificent myth which is to knit up and concludes his Papers of the Notions Club', i.e. *The Drowning of Anadûnê* (Marion E. Wade Center, Wheaton College, Wheaton, Illinois, partly printed in *Brothers and Friends*, p. 194).

?Late August 1946 Tolkien has a ten-day holiday away from Oxford.

3 September 1946 The electors to the Merton Professorship of English Literature, including Tolkien, meet at 2.00 p.m. They elect F.P. Wilson to the chair with effect from 1 January 1947. Tolkien will write to Stanley Unwin on 30 September that it has been a 'tiresome business which has gone far to destroy my chance of "writing" this summer' (Tolkien-George Allen & Unwin archive, HarperCollins). He is referring, perhaps, to the fact that neither C.S. Lewis nor David Cecil, whom he thought the most suitable candidates, was chosen. Lewis is unpopular with many members of the English Faculty for his overt Christianity and Evangelism, and was rejected by the electors despite the quality of his academic writings. There is nothing that Tolkien can do against the majority opinion, but he surely feels it personally, and it may be that Lewis's failure to obtain the chair slightly sours relations between them for a while. – One of the electors, C.H. Wilkinson, a member of the Lovelace Society who was present when Tolkien read *Farmer Giles of Ham* to them on 14 February 1938 and has urged its publication, again speaks to Tolkien about it.

19 September 1946 Tolkien attends a meeting of the Inklings in C.S. Lewis's rooms in Magdalen College. R.E. Havard, Warnie Lewis, and Christopher Tolkien are also present. According to Warnie Lewis, they discuss Hugo Dyson's 'figityness which Tollers [Tolkien] attributes to his harness galling; at Reading, having practically no work to do, he could live by whim, but here he has to work and doesn't like it' (*Brothers and Friends*, p. 195). They also discuss the morality of atom bombs and total war in general. –Stanley Unwin writes to Tolkien. Allen & Unwin are considering the publication of *Farmer Giles of Ham*. Unwin asks if Tolkien has made any illustrations for it, or has anyone in mind who might illustrate it.

c. **23 September 1946–?October 1947** Tolkien returns again to *The Lord of the Rings*. On 30 September he tells Stanley Unwin that the 'tiresome business' of the election to the Merton chair on 3 September has 'gone far to destroy my chances of "writing" this summer', but that he picked up *The Lord of the Rings* 'again last week and wrote (a good) chapter, and was then drowned with official business' (*Letters*, p. 118). He begins probably by writing in pencil a synopsis of the proposed contents of the chapters of Book V, which he partly overwrites in ink, then makes a precise outline with dates. His ideas for the continuation of the story are much developed since he last worked on it in autumn 1944. He begins but does not complete a draft for 'Minas Tirith'; he bases its beginning on a short text made in 1944, and towards the end he stops and redrafts the last part. Then he makes a typescript of the entire chapter.

In the draft he draws sketch plans of the city with its circles and gates, and of the city in relation to Mount Mindolluin (the out-thrust pier of rock is not yet present; see *The War of the Ring*, p. 280). On the verso of one leaf of the typescript he draws another plan of Minas Tirith (*The War of the Ring*, p. 290).

At this stage, Tolkien's plan for the next chapter, which he entitles 'Many Roads Lead Eastward', is that its first part should concern the ride to the Hornburg and the separate departures of Théoden and Aragorn (the beginning of bk. V, ch. 2, 'The Passing of the Grey Company'), while its second part should follow Théoden and Merry to Dunharrow (bk. V, ch. 3, 'The Muster of Rohan'). Tolkien makes three drafts for the first part, which include the earliest forms of the prophetic verse about Erech. On the verso of an outline for the continuation of the first draft he draws a contour map of the White Mountains, and at the end of the second draft, where it leads into what becomes 'The Muster of Rohan', he makes a sketch of Starkhorn.

He begins a new draft of Théoden's ride to Dunharrow, following one made in 1944, and in this makes two pencil sketches which show his final conception of Harrowdale and Dunharrow (*The War of the Ring*, p. 314). After this draft peters out into a brief outline, he begins a clearly written manuscript which deteriorates into a scrawl; then after a short gap of text in the extant drafts, he hurriedly reaches the end of the chapter. At this stage Merry is to ride openly with the Rohirrim to Minas Tirith.

Tolkien now types a fair copy of the chapter, based on his latest versions of the two parts. That part which became 'The Muster of Rohan' is now close to the published text.

For the next chapter, 'The Siege of Gondor' (published bk. V, ch. 4), Tolkien writes a brief, rough pencil text, then revises it by overwriting in ink. On the first page of this he writes some notes with the first appearance of the final calendar of *The Lord of the Rings*; by now Tolkien has abandoned the idea that no time passed while the Fellowship were in Lórien. He then begins a new draft in soft pencil, ink over pencil, and ink with pencil corrections: he tries a new, shorter opening in which some of the events of the day are told briefly in retrospect. In the middle of this Tolkien stops to write a brief outline before continuing ever more roughly, until he is writing little more than an outline as the siege begins. He then makes a fair copy manuscript which proceeds to the end of the chapter, still with the shorter opening and in which Denethor's relationship with Faramir differs from that in the published text. But in a marginal note Tolkien writes that this must be changed, and on a slip of paper he writes a brief statement of how and why. The last part of the fair copy, describing the sortie to rescue Faramir and the siege, is based on more drafting and probably completed in sections.

Before beginning 'The Ride of the Rohirrim' (published bk. V, ch. 5) – probably developed simultaneously with 'The Siege of Gondor' (*see note*) – Tolkien writes two outlines for the chapter, the first in pencil overwritten in ink, and calculates the distances covered. His first ideas differ considerably from those that emerge later. He is uncertain where the chapter should begin, whether Merry should go openly to Minas Tirith, and how much to tell in direct narrative and how much in retrospect. He drafts and abandons two openings to the chapter; then he writes a new opening in which Merry accepts an invitation to ride with the disguised Éowyn, but decides to move this to the end of 'Many Roads Lead Eastward' (later 'The Muster of Rohan') with the addition of an alliterative song, *From Dark Dunharrow in the Dim Morning*. He writes a fine manuscript of this and attaches it to the end of the typescript of the previous chapter.

Tolkien then writes 'The Ride of the Rohirrim' mainly from Merry's point of view and the early part in retrospect, in a series of overlapping stages in which as he rejects parts already written he returns to an earlier point in the story, in places overwriting an earlier version in ink. He begins a fair copy of the chapter based on this draft to begin with, then on other texts and miscellaneous drafts. On an inserted page he draws a map of the Druadan Forest, Stonewain Valley, and environs.

Tolkien now prepares a brief outline of future events from the arrival of the Rohirrim at the Pelennor Wall as far as the Host of the West reaching the Morannon, but immediately rejects it and writes the fuller outline which Christopher Tolkien will call (in *The War of the Ring*) 'The Story Foreseen from Forannest': this extends as far as the destruction of the Ring but still differs in many respects from the final story. Probably about the same time, Tolkien writes outlines concerning Aragorn's ride to the Stone of Erech and the summoning of the Dead, entitled 'The march of Aragorn and defeat of [the] Haradrim'. It is already clear that he intends at least part of the story to be told in brief later, probably at Minas Tirith by Gimli or Legolas. He also makes outlines for the continuation of the story of Frodo and Sam.

Tolkien originally intends 'The Battle of the Pelennor Fields' (published bk. V, ch. 6) to be part of 'The Ride of the Rohirrim'. He writes the narrative as a continuous draft, makes many emendations, and adds or replaces passages before making a fair copy. The draft includes the alliterative song *The Mounds of Mundburg*. For a brief moment Tolkien considers placing 'The Houses of Healing' (bk. V, ch. 8) next in sequence, and writes a short draft for the beginning of the chapter before changing his mind. He begins a draft for 'The Pyre of Denethor' (bk. V, ch. 7), but stops and makes several outlines before beginning successive drafts, the last interrupted by an outline, and writing alternate texts of Gandalf's rescue of Faramir and his conversation with Denethor. He then makes a fair copy, but not until he has written at least part of the draft of the following chapter.

Tolkien apparently begins to work on 'The Houses of Healing' by writing a short text to precede the beginning already drafted, and making an outline for the chapter, followed by another looking further ahead. He then writes a complete draft of the chapter which still differs considerably from the published text. He cannibalizes some pages from the draft in the fair copy that follows, but also makes changes, and replaces part of what he writes with new text. At one point he overwrites in ink some abandoned pencil drafting with early forms of speeches made at the debate of the commanders in the 'The Last Debate' (published bk. V, ch. 9). Presumably he wants to record ideas as they come into his mind.

As originally written, the next chapter, entitled 'The Parley at the Black Gate', includes the entry of Gimli and Legolas into Minas Tirith, the debate of the commanders, and the account by Gimli and Legolas of their journey with Aragorn from the Hornburg to Minas Tirith, and extends to the opening of battle before the Morannon. But after making many drafts and experiments to organize this material, Tolkien decides not only to divide 'The Parley at the Black Gate' into two chapters (eventually 'The Last Debate' and 'The Black Gate Opens', published bk. V, ch. 9-10), but also to move the first part of the journey of the Grey Company to the end of 'Many Paths Lead Eastward' (later 'The Passing of the Grey Company', published bk. V, ch. 2). Tolkien has Gimli and Legolas describe the journey of the Grey Company from the Hornburg in both the draft and a more finished manuscript. At the point when the Company reaches Erech the second version becomes the primary draft, and Tolkien begins a revised version with the departure from Erech; both continue into the beginning of what becomes 'The Black Gate Opens'. Tolkien originally intends that both Merry and Pippin should remain in Minas Tirith, then decides that Pippin should accompany the Host of the West: he begins a new draft, then writes a fair copy which reaches the end of the (combined) chapter and of Book V.

But Tolkien is not satisfied, and experiments with various arrangements. First he places the telling of the journey of the Grey Company before the debate, and moves the debate into the final chapter; to achieve this, he alters the pagination on most of the original pages, rewrites some passages, and provides a new opening for the second chapter. He makes a typescript of this rearrangement of the two chapters, which he revises, and replaces two sections with manuscript. He then writes an experimental version of the first part of the journey of the Grey Company as far as their entry into the Paths of the Dead, told as narrative to be placed at the end of 'Many Paths Lead Eastward', but he is still uncertain. He makes a second typescript of the chapter of Gimli and Legolas telling the story in Minas Tirith, incorporating various revisions but making no structural change; and writes a rough manuscript of the journey of the Grey Company as far as the departure from the Stone of Erech written as direct narrative instead of being told by Gimli, though still mainly seen through his eyes, to be placed at the end of 'The Passing of the Grey Company'. Then he makes a typescript of 'The Last Debate' beginning with the telling of the rest of the journey of the Grey Company, followed by the debate of the commanders, moved back into the shortened chapter.

Probably near the beginning of this period Tolkien makes a new map of Middle-earth, drawn on a single sheet of paper ruled in squares and lettered and numbered according to the first map. His execution is rough, 'contour lines' are impressionistic, and features such as the Nindalf and the Dead Marshes are shown by rough pencil hatching. Tolkien uses this as a working map while writing Book V.

30 September 1946 Tolkien writes to Stanley Unwin. He thanks Unwin for the advance on *The Hobbit* reprint, which 'came at a very useful moment'. Referring to a note appended to the typescript of *Farmer Giles of Ham* he sent to Allen & Unwin, he remarks:

I think I once planned a volume of 'Farmer Giles' with (say) three other probably shorter stories interleaved with such verse as would consort with them from the *Oxford Magazine*: *Errantry*, *Tom Bombadil*, and possibly *The Dragon's Visit*. Of the stories one only is written [*Sellic Spell*] – and might not seem so suitable though I have been urged to publish it. I send you a copy. The other 'The King of the Green Dozen' would exactly consort, but is only half-written. The third an actual sequel to 'Farmer Giles' is a mere plot.

My verse story [probably *The Lay of Aotrou and Itroun*], which I also enclose . . . might not be felt to go with it. As 'Leaf by Niggle' certainly would not?

He has never tried to illustrate *Farmer Giles of Ham* and does not know anyone
to suggest. With leisure he could provide other works to accompany *Farmer
Giles*, 'but I am in a tough spot academically and domestically, and see no hope
of leisure until the various new professors come along. I could not promise to
complete anything soon. At least I suppose I could, but it would be difficult –
and really the Hobbit sequel is so much better (I think) than these things, that
I should wish to give it all spare hours.' He must now 'hastily turn to departmental estimates for the quinquennium 1947–52!' (Tolkien-George Allen &
Unwin archive, HarperCollins, partly printed in *Letters*, p. 118). – On the same
day Tolkien also writes a brief note to Stanley Unwin, to accompany poems to
consider for publication with *Farmer Giles of Ham*: *The Hoard*; *Errantry*; *Tom
Bombadil*; *The Dragon's Visit*; *The Man in the Moon* (*sic*); and *The Bumpus*.

1 October 1946 C.L. Wrenn takes up his duties as Rawlinson and Bosworth
Professor of Anglo-Saxon at Oxford.

3 October 1946 Tolkien attends a special meeting of the English Faculty
Board at 11.00 a.m. in the Board Room of the Clarendon Building. He begins in
the chair, but relinquishes it to R.F.W. Fletcher when the latter is elected chairman for 1946–7. This relieves Tolkien of considerable administrative duties.
The report of the committee (of which Tolkien is a member) on the needs of
the Faculty for 1947–1952 (to be submitted to the General Board for discussion
of the Quinquennial grant) is adopted with amendments. The report begins:
'The immediate and pressing need of the School of English is for an increase in
teaching staff. This has never been adequate; it is now gravely deficient. There
are not enough teaching members of the Faculty to cover the linguistic and literary tuition, or the supervision of advanced students, or the requisite changes
of examiners in the preliminary and final examinations' (Oxford University
Archives FA 4/5/2/8). (See further, *Oxford English School.) It then gives
a brief history of the staffing of the Faculty since its establishment in 1926,
showing no increase in staff (and for much of the time a decrease) despite an
increase in students, especially postgraduates. It also points out the need for a
central building for the School and its library, and for a full-time librarian.

9 October 1946 Tolkien attends a Merton College Meeting.

10 October 1946 In the evening, Tolkien attends a meeting of the Inklings
in C.S. Lewis's rooms in Magdalen College. Warnie Lewis records in his diary
that Tolkien 'continued to read his new Hobbit [*The Lord of the Rings*]' (*Brothers and Friends*, p. 195).

11 October 1946 Tolkien attends a General Board meeting. He is elected to
the Standing Committee on Examinations. – Philip Unwin writes to Tolkien.
He is seeking a reader's opinion of the matter Tolkien sent on 7 September.

13 October 1946 Michaelmas Full Term begins. Tolkien's scheduled lectures for this term are: *Ormulum* and *Ancrene Wisse* on Wednesdays at 12.00
noon in the Examination Schools, beginning 16 October; and *Sir Gawain and
the Green Knight* on Fridays at 12.00 noon in the Examination Schools, beginning 18 October. He will continue to supervise B.Litt. students J.J. Lawlor,
M.Y. Offord, and M.B. Salu, and D.Phil. student T.J.A. Monaghan.

16 October 1946 Tolkien is listed in the *Oxford University Gazette* as the sole interviewer for prospective advanced students in the English School.

18 October 1946 Tolkien attends a General Board meeting.

24 October 1946 King George VI and Queen Elizabeth visit Oxford to open the New Bodleian Library. The ceremony is preceded by a meeting of Members of Convocation in full academic dress in the Sheldonian Theatre, at which a Loyal Address is presented. Tolkien is present on the occasion and takes part in the subsequent procession to the Sheldonian for the actual opening. Priscilla Tolkien will recall her father saying that the ceremonial key broke in the lock, and someone had to open the door from the other side. – In the evening, Tolkien attends a meeting of the Inklings. Also present are R.E. Havard, the Lewis brothers, Christopher Tolkien, and Gervase Mathew who tells 'an immensely long and complicated story about the net of jealousy and intrigue in which Mrs Charles Williams is entangled.' Tolkien reads 'a couple of exquisite chapters' from *The Lord of the Rings* (W.H. Lewis, *Brothers and Friends*, p. 196).

25 October 1946 Tolkien attends an English Faculty Board meeting. He is elected to the Standing Committee on Applications together with F.P. Wilson, and is replaced on the Standing Committee on the Sidney Lee Bequest. He is also appointed to two committees which are to report at the next meeting: one to make recommendations on additional University Lecturers, and one to consider a communication from the General Board about the First Public Examination. The committee established on 25 June 1946 to draw up regulations for the Vaughan Morgan Scholarship is reconstituted, with Tolkien still a member, and asked to report at the next meeting. The Applications Committee has accepted *A.J. (Alan Joseph) Bliss as a probationer B.Litt. student to work on a Middle English subject, with Tolkien as his supervisor. – Tolkien also attends a General Board meeting.

1 November 1946 Horus Engels writes an illustrated letter to Tolkien in appreciation of *The Hobbit* (see *The Annotated Hobbit*, rev. and expanded edn. 2003, colour plate between pp. 178 and 179). He thanks Tolkien for a letter, and hopes that there will be a German translation of *The Hobbit*.

8 November 1946 Tolkien attends a General Board meeting.

11 November 1946 Simonne d'Ardenne sends to Tolkien for his comments a draft article on the word *losenge* she has written; she knows that it needs recasting. Having dealt with it, she will now spend her spare time on *Seinte Katerine*. She is looking forward to resuming her work with Tolkien in 1947. She has heard from Edith and Priscilla that they have a smaller house: presumably Tolkien has already heard that a house owned by Merton College will be available soon (see entry for 14 March 1947). – Stanley Unwin writes to Tolkien. He thinks that *Farmer Giles of Ham* would be better published by itself, rather than in a miscellaneous collection. He again asks if Tolkien has any suggestion for an illustrator, stressing that it is important to find an artist who will enter thoroughly into the spirit of the book.

15 November 1946 Tolkien attends a General Board meeting.

16 November 1946 In the evening, Tolkien attends a dinner of The Society hosted by G.R.G. Mure at Merton College. Six members are present. They have a three-course meal, with drinks.

21 November 1946 Philip Unwin writes to Tolkien. Cadbury's, the chocolate and cocoa manufacturer, wants to include a riddle from *The Hobbit* in an advertisement. Unwin asks Tolkien how he would like Allen & Unwin to reply.

22 November 1946 Tolkien attends a General Board meeting.

23 November 1946 Tolkien replies to Philip Unwin. He would prefer not to be associated with advertisements.

c. **27 November 1946** By this date Priscilla Tolkien has suggested a young artist, Milein Cosman, as a possible illustrator for *Farmer Giles of Ham*. After some difficulty in arranging a meeting, Cosman visits Tolkien in Oxford ten days before he writes to Stanley Unwin on 7 December 1946. She shows him some of her work, and he lends her a spare copy of *Farmer Giles of Ham*.

28 November 1946 Tolkien probably attends a meeting of the Inklings this evening at which Roy Campbell reads some of his translations of Spanish poems. On this occasion *John Wain, a Fellow of St John's, Oxford, and recent addition to the Inklings, wins a bet by reading a chapter of *Irene Iddesleigh* without a smile (see entry for 23 November 1939).

6 December 1946 Tolkien attends an English Faculty Board meeting. Three committees of which Tolkien is a member – to make recommendations on additional University Lecturers; to consider a communication from the General Board about the First Public Examination; and to draw up regulations for the Vaughan Morgan Scholarship – submit reports; all are approved after emendation. The Board agrees 'to apply for a grant (if possible in conjunction with the Board of the Faculty of Medieval and Modern Languages), for a course of eight lectures on Celtic by W.J. Gruffydd to be given in Trinity Term 1947'; Tolkien undertakes to submit a reasoned statement. He also gives notice that, at the next meeting, he will 'raise the question of a B.Phil. degree for students of English' (Oxford University Archives FA 4/5/1/2). – Tolkien also attends a General Board meeting.

7 December 1946 Michaelmas Full Term ends. – Tolkien writes to Stanley Unwin. He believes that the matter of illustrations for *Farmer Giles of Ham* is best left in the publisher's hands, but Priscilla has suggested Milein Cosman. Tolkien has seen her and judges her an artist of merit, though he doubts that she is an illustrator. If Allen & Unwin would like to look at her work, he will tell her to call. He tells Unwin about the letter from Horus Engels (1 November 1946), and comments that the illustrations Engels sent were too 'Disnified' for his taste (i.e. in the style of the Walt Disney Studio). He hopes that his move in the near future to a smaller house (at 3 Manor Road, Oxford) will alleviate 'the intolerable domestic problems' which take up so much of his spare time. He hopes to finish *The Lord of the Rings* soon, and will let Unwin see it 'before long, or before January. I am on the last chapters' (*Letters*, p. 119). – Tolkien also writes to Miss M. Standeven, who once attended his lectures on Old English poetry, apologizing for the delay in answering her letter of 8 October expressing her appreciation of *The Hobbit*. University life at present leaves little energy or time even for keeping up with his professional learning, let alone the writing of fantasy fiction which takes much time and thought, and he can no longer steal as much time from the night as he used to. He tells her that the sequel to *The Hobbit* is nearly finished.

11 December 1946 C.A. Furth writes to Tolkien. Milein Cosman should call on Allen & Unwin with her portfolio. The German translation rights to *The Hobbit* have reverted to Allen & Unwin, who are negotiating with a Swiss publisher.

18 December 1946 Oxford University Press sends Tolkien galley proofs of *On Fairy-Stories*. He is asked to send them with any corrections to C.S. Lewis, the editor of the *Festschrift* entitled *Essays Presented to Charles Williams*.

28 December 1946 Tolkien attends an Early English Text Society Committee meeting at Magdalen College.

1947

1947 or 1948 A joint article by Tolkien and Simonne d'Ardenne, *MS Bodley 34: A Re-Collation of a Collation, is published in *Studia Neophilologica* (Uppsala) for 1947–8. It is a response to an article by Ragnar Furuskog, 'A Collation of the *Katherine Group* (MS Bodley 34)' in the same journal for 1946–7.

Early 1947 Britain experiences the coldest weather since 1883, leading to a fuel crisis. Coal is rationed.

10 January 1947 Tolkien types an eight-page letter to A.W. Riddle in response to a request received the previous August. Riddle had evidently asked for his comments on a paper he had written on contemporary speech, which included a discussion of the use of the split infinitive and criticism of the grammarian H.W. Fowler who objected to the usage. As Professor of English Language and Literature Tolkien receives many letters like the one from Riddle. After discussing the origin and nature of the infinitive in English and its various usages, Tolkien characterizes the split infinitive as 'an innovation, a disturbance of received pattern' (quoted in Christie's, *20th-Century Books and Manuscripts*, London, 6 December 2002, p. 20). He thinks that Riddle is unfair to Fowler, and argues against pedantry in linguistic matters. The final sentence of his letter deliberately contains four split infinitives.

12 January 1947 Tolkien replies to Gilbert Murray, retired Regius Professor of Greek at Oxford, who has written to him on behalf of a colleague who wants to obtain an academic post in Britain rather than return to India. Tolkien expresses his sympathy and explains that he had interested himself in the case as chairman of the English Faculty Board with no success. He is no longer chairman, and has no influence since the scholar's expertise lies outside his field. He will show Murray's letter to F.P. Wilson, who is to visit him on Wednesday (15 January), but positions of the kind wanted become available only infrequently.

17 January 1947 Tolkien attends a General Board meeting. He is appointed a member of the Standing Committee on University Lecturers (CUF). An application (presumably written by Tolkien) from the Board of English Language and Literature for a grant for eight lectures on Celtic is discussed and approved.

19 January 1947 Hilary Full Term begins. Tolkien's scheduled lectures for this term are: *Sir Gawain and the Green Knight* (continued) on Wednesdays at 11.00 a.m. in the Examination Schools, beginning 22 January; and *Ancrene Wisse [and] Ormulum* on Wednesdays at 12.00 noon in the Examination Schools, beginning 22 January. He will continue to supervise B.Litt. students J.J. Lawlor, M.Y. Offord, and M.B. Salu, and D.Phil. student T.J.A. Monaghan.

22 January 1947 Tolkien certifies the acceptance of A.J. Bliss as a full B.Litt. student. His thesis is to be *Sir Orfeo: Introduction, Text, Commentary and Glossary*, supervised by Tolkien.

23 January 1947 Gwyn Jones writes to Tolkien. He has enjoyed Tolkien's translation of *Sir Gawain and the Green Knight*, which had been lent to him. He sends Tolkien a sample translation of his own.

31 January 1947 Tolkien attends an English Faculty Board meeting. The Board approves the suggestion of the General Board for a standing committee to which questions referred by the General Board can go immediately for report at the next meeting, and appoints a committee which includes Tolkien. (He apparently will remain on this committee, elected or *ex officio*, until Michaelmas Term 1952.) He is also appointed to a committee to consider and report on the present and immediate future of the B.Litt. course. The Board postpones consideration of a B.Phil. degree for students of English for the present. – Tolkien also attends a General Board meeting. The Board agrees 'to ask the Boards of the Faculties of Modern History, English Language and Literature, and Social Studies to appoint representatives to consult together, and report through their respective Faculty Boards to the General Board, on a suggestion that there might be a joint Preliminary Examination for Modern History, English Language and Literature, and P[olitics], P[hilosophy, and] E[conomics]' (Oxford University Archives FA 1/1/6).

1 February 1947 Tolkien attends a Merton College meeting. He is appointed to the wine committee, on which he will serve until his retirement in 1959.

5–6 February 1947 Tolkien takes part in the election to the Jesus Professorship of Celtic. The electors consider seven applications and agree to take up various references.

6 February 1947 In the evening, Tolkien attends an Inklings meeting in C.S. Lewis's rooms in Magdalen College. Also present are Colin Hardie, Warnie Lewis, Gervase Mathew, Christopher Tolkien, and John Wain. Hardie reads a paper on Vergil, and Christopher a chapter from *The Lord of the Rings*.

7 February 1947 Tolkien attends a General Board meeting.

10 February 1947 Tolkien attends a Merton College meeting.

20 February 1947 Gwyn Jones writes to Tolkien. He hopes that Tolkien has not been offended by his reworking of a passage of Tolkien's translation of *Gawain*.

28 February 1947 Tolkien attends a General Board meeting. The report of a Committee on Advanced Studies is adopted.

12 March 1947 The electors to the Jesus Professorship of Celtic, including Tolkien, meet at 11.30 a.m. They elect Idris Llewellyn Foster to the chair with effect from 1 October 1947.

14 March 1947 Tolkien, Edith, and Priscilla move to a house rented from Merton College at 3 Manor Road, Oxford. Many of Tolkien's papers go missing during the move. 20 Northmoor Road has become too large for the family, now that John, Michael, and Christopher are no longer living at home. Tolkien will tell Stanley Unwin on 5 May 1947 that the move was 'forced on me by taxation, and lack of all domestic aid'. But almost immediately the family find 3 Manor Road too small; there is no room that Tolkien can use as a study. Tolkien will tell Stanley Unwin that he now lives 'in a minute house near the centre of this town, and all my workshop is in college' (5 May 1947, Tolkien-George Allen & Unwin archive, HarperCollins). Merton College has agreed that when a larger house becomes available, it will be offered to Tolkien. – At a meeting of the English Faculty Board, in Tolkien's absence, the report of the committee (of which Tolkien is a member) appointed to consider the course for B.Litt. students is adopted after amendment. Since the several faculties concerned have been unable to agree on a joint Preliminary Examination, the Board decides to consider at the next meeting its previous proposals for an English Preliminary Examination.

15 March 1947 Hilary Full Term ends. – Tolkien attends a Merton College meeting.

17 March 1947 Tolkien attends a Merton College meeting. – A 'great gale' blows down 'nearly all the mighty trees of the Broadwalk in Christchurch Meadows' and devastates Magdalen deer park (letter to Jane Neave, 8–9 September 1962, *Letters*, p. 321).

31 March 1947 Tolkien attends a Merton College meeting.

2 April 1947 Milein Cosman accepts the commission from George Allen & Unwin to illustrate *Farmer Giles of Ham*.

3 April 1947 Ronald Eames, art editor for Allen & Unwin, writes to Milein Cosman. Allen & Unwin would like a specimen illustration for *Farmer Giles of Ham* not only for them to approve the style, but also for submission to Tolkien for approval.

24 April 1947 Tolkien attends a Merton College meeting. – In the evening, he attends an Inklings meeting, presumably in C.S. Lewis's rooms in Magdalen College, accompanied by his guest, Gwyn Jones. Also present are R.E. Havard, Warnie Lewis, Gervase Mathew, and Christopher Tolkien. Hugo Dyson arrives just as they start to listen to another part of *The Lord of the Rings*, and (as Warnie Lewis will record) 'as he now exercises a veto on it – most unfairly

I think – we had to stop'. Jones reads a Welsh tale 'of his own writing, a bawdy humorous thing told in a rich polished style' (*Brothers and Friends*, p. 200).

25 April 1947 Tolkien attends a General Board meeting.

27 April 1947 Trinity Full Term begins. Tolkien's scheduled lectures and classes for this term are: Middle English (Seminar) on Tuesdays at 5.30 p.m. at Merton College, beginning 29 April; *Ormulum* on Wednesdays at 11.00 a.m. in the Examination Schools, beginning 30 April; Germanic Philology (Seminar) on Thursdays at 5.30 at Merton College, beginning 1 May; and another series of lectures to be arranged on Fridays at 11.00 a.m. in the Examination Schools, beginning 2 May. He will continue to supervise B.Litt. students A.J. Bliss, M.Y. Offord, and M.B. Salu, and D.Phil. student T.J.A. Monaghan.

30 April 1947 Stanley Unwin writes to Tolkien. Allen & Unwin intend to publish *Farmer Giles of Ham* even though the cost of the illustrations, two of them in colour, will make it appear expensive for its size. But Unwin thinks that the book will still sell because of its merit. Once Milein Cosman has submitted a specimen illustration and the publisher and Tolkien have approved it, Allen & Unwin will commission her to proceed. The reprint of *The Hobbit* is still held up at the binders.

May 1947 Tolkien and Rayner Unwin meet twice.

2 May 1947 Tolkien attends a General Board meeting.

5 May 1947 Tolkien writes to Stanley Unwin. He signs and returns the agreement for the publication of *Farmer Giles of Ham*, acknowledges 30 June as the delivery date for the text, and comments on the apparently small size of the initial royalty. He asks Unwin to return the typescript of *Farmer Giles*, along with other, rejected material he had sent to the publisher, as Milein Cosman has his only other copy. 'I ought to give it a look-over before passing [it] for press, and avoid the many (yet insufficient) alterations in proof suffered by *The Hobbit*.' The pressure he is under at the moment, 'in the whirl of term', should relax in about a month, and as he is not an examiner this summer he promises to return *Farmer Giles* in good time. His move to a smaller house dislocated all of his work in February and March, but he hopes that he will now have more time. *Farmer Giles of Ham* 'is hardly a worthy sequel to *The Hobbit*, but on the real sequel [*The Lord of the Rings*], life hardly allows me any consecutive time to work. It slowly nears completion but won't reach it until the autumn' (Tolkien-George Allen & Unwin archive, HarperCollins). He is pleased to hear that Rayner has returned to his studies at Trinity College, Oxford, and would love to see him but does not want to obtrude. Since Tolkien occasionally has to visit London on University of London business, he asks if Unwin would be bored if he were to call with due notice; or if Unwin should visit Oxford, he would be delighted to see him.

8 May 1947 Tolkien attends a Merton College meeting. – Stanley Unwin returns Tolkien's signed copy of the agreement for *Farmer Giles of Ham*, together with a cheque as an advance on royalties, the typescript of *Farmer Giles*, and the other material requested. He explains why the royalty for *Farmer*

Giles is low, and asks Tolkien to supply a brief descriptive paragraph about the work for Allen & Unwin's announcement list.

9 May 1947 Tolkien attends an English Faculty Board meeting. The question of making recommendations to the General Board for additional appointments to University Lecturerships is referred to a committee which includes Tolkien, and which is to report at next meeting. The Board decides that it would prefer to devise its own Preliminary Examination, and that general proposals for this should be submitted to a meeting of the Faculty. Tolkien is a member of the committee that is to draft an outline of these proposals. – Tolkien also attends a General Board meeting.

16 May 1947 Tolkien attends a General Board meeting. – A member of staff in the translations department of Allen & Unwin informs Tolkien that the Swedish publisher to whom they have sold translations rights for *The Hobbit* wants to know if he would object if some of his drawings were replaced with illustrations by a well-known Swedish painter. – Tolkien will reply, in an undated postcard, that he has no objection, but thinks it best if all of his illustrations were replaced, excepting only the maps: 'the mixture would be unpleasing, and hard on the amateur, who would look all the worse' (Tolkien-George Allen & Unwin archive, HarperCollins).

24 May 1947 Stanley Unwin visits Oxford. He attempts to see Tolkien at Merton College, but does not find him there.

25 May 1947 Mlle S. Mansion, a colleague of Simonne d'Ardenne, whom Tolkien has assisted with introductions to scholars, calls on Tolkien. She tells him that her sister would like to make a French translation of *The Hobbit*. Tolkien will refer her to Allen & Unwin.

28 May 1947 Tolkien writes to Stanley Unwin. He is sorry to have missed Tolkien (on the 24th), but seldom goes to Merton on Sundays. 'I have not had a chance to do any writing, nor even to do more than glance at "Giles". I am afraid he is what he is and no more than a few verbal adjustments are possible.' He has now seen Rayner twice; 'he is free to call on me as he will. I shall be a good deal freer, for a while, after June, when I am relieved of numerous offices that I have held too long' (Tolkien-George Allen & Unwin archive, Harper-Collins).

29 May 1947 Tolkien attends a Merton College meeting.

30 May 1947 Tolkien attends a General Board meeting.

June 1947 C.S. Lewis reviews Eugène Vinaver's edition of *The Works of Sir Thomas Malory* (i.e. *Le Morte Darthur*) for the *Times Literary Supplement*. Since he has already bought this three-volume set, he sells his review copies to Tolkien.

2 June 1947 Stanley Unwin writes to Tolkien, inviting him to lunch on 24 July.

6 June 1947 Tolkien attends a General Board meeting.

7 June 1947 The Faculty committee (of which Tolkien is a member) set up to draft proposals for a Preliminary Examination meets at 5.00 p.m. at Corpus Christi College, Oxford.

9 June 1947 Tolkien approves an application by T.J.A. Monaghan to supplicate for the D.Phil.

12 June 1947 English Final Honour School Examinations begin.

17 June 1947 The English Faculty meet to consider the proposals of the committee for a Preliminary Examination for the English School.

18 June 1947 The committee for considering proposals for the Preliminary Examination revises its work, incorporating amendments approved at the Faculty meeting.

20 June 1947 Tolkien attends an English Faculty Board meeting. The members discuss revised proposals regarding the Preliminary Examination. After making some amendments, the Board accepts the proposals for submission to the General Board. The report of the committee (of which Tolkien is a member) set up on 9 May to recommend appointments to University Lecturerships is submitted to the Board, which votes to submit eight names, and asks the committee to arrange them in order of priority. – Tolkien also attends a General Board meeting.

21 June 1947 Trinity Full Term ends. – Tolkien attends an Early English Text Society Committee meeting at Magdalen College, Oxford.

24 June 1947 Tolkien attends a Merton College meeting. He is appointed the Fellow to attend the estates progress. – Tolkien is assigned new rooms, part of set 6, staircase 4 in the Fellows' Quadrangle.

25 June 1947 Encaenia.

30 June 1947 Tolkien writes to Warnie Lewis, who is in hospital in Ireland. Tolkien is praying for Warnie's recovery, and is sending him typescripts of Book IV of *The Lord of the Rings* to read. – Allen & Unwin write to Tolkien, to remind him that he has not sent the descriptive paragraph asked for in the letter of 8 May.

5 July 1947 Tolkien writes to Allen & Unwin. He returns *Farmer Giles of Ham* revised for press. He found time to look at it only after term ended. He has now 'gone through it carefully, making a good many alterations, for the better (I think and hope) in both style and narrative.' He encloses a rough copy of a preface to the work; if Allen & Unwin do not find it suitable, he will try again. He also encloses a short draft for a publicity paragraph. He points out that *Farmer Giles of Ham* (in its enlarged form) 'was *not* written *for* children', though they might enjoy it. 'I think it might be well to emphasize the fact that this is a tale specially composed for reading aloud: it goes very well so, for those that like this kind of thing at all' (*Letters*, p. 119). He would like to dedicate it to C.H. Wilkinson of Worcester College. He asks if Stanley Unwin can see him when he visits London on 9 July.

7 July 1947 Mary Salu writes to Tolkien, sending him references he wanted related to her glossary of the *Ancrene Riwle*.

8 July 1947 Stanley Unwin sends a telegram inviting Tolkien to lunch on 9 July. Tolkien replies with his acceptance the same day.

9 July 1947 Tolkien takes the 10.15 a.m. train from Oxford to London, to lunch with Stanley Unwin at the Reform Club. They agree that Rayner should read *The Lord of the Rings* in sections. – Tolkien then has a 2.30 p.m. appointment at Westminster. – Warnie Lewis receives from Tolkien 'a long interesting' and 'mainly theological' letter (diary entry for 9 July, *Brothers and Friends*, p. 205).

11 July 1947 Stanley Unwin writes to Tolkien. Copies of *The Hobbit*, held up at the binder for over a year, should be available in about three months.

***c.* 22 July 1947** Tolkien sends Ida Gordon, widow of E.V. Gordon, a revised introduction to her late husband's edition of *Pearl*, which she is preparing for publication.

24 July 1947 Tolkien attends a meeting in London at 2.30 p.m. at Senate House, the University of London. – While in London he leaves a typescript of Book I of *The Lord of the Rings* at Allen & Unwin's offices in Museum Street. It is recorded in the publisher's register as delivered by 'hand to SU', i.e. Stanley Unwin (George Allen & Unwin archive, University of Reading). It will be passed to Rayner Unwin, who will later recall that he put all else aside to read and report on it. He will find it 'a weird book' but 'a brilliant and gripping story'. He will praise it highly, but sometimes

> the struggle between darkness and light (sometimes one suspects leav-
> ing the story proper to become pure allegory) is macabre and intensified
> beyond that in *The Hobbit.* . . . Converting the original Ring [in *The Hob-
> bit*] into this new and powerful instrument [in *The Lord of the Rings*]
> takes some explaining away and Gandalf is hard put to it to find reasons
> for many of the original Hobbit's actions. But the linking of the books is
> well done on the whole though a knowledge of the earlier book is almost
> presupposed.

He is not sure who will read it: 'children will miss something of it but characters like Tom Bombadil . . . will delight them and if grown ups will not feel infra dig to read it many will undoubtedly enjoy themselves' (*George Allen & Unwin: A Remembrancer* (1999), pp. 91–2).

25 July 1947 Ida Gordon writes to Tolkien, thanking him for his letter and the introduction to *Pearl*. She expresses her pleasure and relief that, after all, he has been able to revise it.

28 July 1947 Stanley Unwin writes to Tolkien, addressing him as 'Tolkien', a more familiar form of address than 'Professor Tolkien' which he had been using, and in return asks to be called 'Unwin' (rather than 'Sir Stanley'). He sends a copy of Rayner's report on Book I of *The Lord of the Rings*, and says that Rayner would like the second instalment after their return from a visit to Switzerland on about 23 August. The typescript is being returned by registered post.

31 July 1947 Tolkien writes to Stanley Unwin, as 'Unwin'. He welcomes the more familiar terms of address. Rayner having read Book I so quickly, Tolkien has 'now another urgent reason, in addition to the clamour of the circle [of his friends], for finishing [*The Lord of the Rings*] off, so that it can be finally judged.' He comments at length on Rayner's report, noting especially that Rayner should not think that the work is *allegory. 'There is a "moral", I suppose, in any tale worth telling. But that is not the same thing.' Tolkien notes that *The Lord of the Rings* has been read and approved by C.S. Lewis; Charles Williams; Christopher Tolkien; a solicitor (Owen Barfield); a doctor (probably R.E. Havard); an elderly army officer (W.H. Lewis); an elementary school-mistress (possibly, Priscilla Tolkien has suggested in correspondence, 'a charming American high school teacher called Dorothy, whose surname I have forgotten, who sent us food parcels during the war and came to visit us . . . between 1947 and 1953 . . . we took her to the St Cross churchyard as she wanted to photograph the grave of Kenneth Grahame'); an artist (Marjorie Incledon); and a farmer (according to Priscilla Tolkien in private correspondence, 'a pork farmer from Wiltshire, who was an occasional visitor to the Inklings and was known affectionately as Little Pig Robinson [after the character by Beatrix Potter]'). Rayner has spotted a weakness in the link between *The Hobbit* and *The Lord of the Rings*, the problem of Gollum offering Bilbo the Ring as a present (in the first edition of *The Hobbit*): the proper way to deal with this, Tolkien says, would be to revise Chapter 5 of *The Hobbit* – though 'any alteration of any radical kind is of course impossible, and unnecessary' beyond the correction of misprints. 'Also: it is inevitable that the knowledge of the previous book should be presumed; but there is in existence a Foreword, or opening chapter, "Concerning Hobbits"' which gives necessary information from *The Hobbit* and explains many points that fans of that book have enquired about. He now wishes to finish *The Lord of the Rings* 'as devised and then let it be judged. But forgive me! It is written in my life-blood, such as that is, thick or thin; and I can no other' (*Letters*, p. 122). He states that he is enclosing a list of misprints in *The Hobbit*, but in fact does not, nor does he send this letter until 26 September.

Summer 1947 Simonne d'Ardenne stays with the Tolkien family in Oxford, leaving before 21 September. On that date Tolkien will write to Stanley Unwin that during August and most of September 'I have been obliged to devote myself mainly to philology, especially as my colleague from Liège, with whom I had been embarking on "research" before the war, was staying here to help get our work ready for press' (*Letters*, p. 124). – Even so, perhaps influenced by Rayner's comments, Tolkien also considers how *The Hobbit* might be altered to bring it into accord with *The Lord of the Rings*. He now writes a new account of Bilbo's encounter with Gollum. He also makes revisions to the first two books of *The Lord of the Rings*, though he cannot find time to do as much revision as he would like. On 21 September he will tell Stanley Unwin, on sending him the typescripts of Book II and a Foreword 'Concerning Hobbits', that

Chapter XIV ['The Council of Elrond'] has been re-written to match the re-writing of Chapter II 'Ancient History' which [Rayner] has read. Chapter II is now called 'The Shadow of the Past' and most of its 'historical' material has been cut out, while a little more attention is paid to

Gollum. So that if XIV seems repetitive, it is not actually so; practically nothing now in XIV will appear in II. [*Letters*, p. 124]

Beginning of August 1947 Tolkien receives a letter from Milein Cosman about *Farmer Giles of Ham*, but forgets to answer it.

?Early August 1947 Tolkien sends linguistic material related to *Pearl* to Ida Gordon.

2 August 1947 Tolkien attends a Merton College meeting.

4 August 1947 Tolkien intends to join C.S. and Warnie Lewis for supper at Magdalen College, but cannot get away.

5–9 August 1947 On 5 August Tolkien and the Lewis brothers travel to Malvern on the 11.28 a.m. train. They eat a sandwich lunch en route, and at about 2.00 p.m. they arrive at No. 4, the Lees, the home of Leonard and Maureen Blake, with whom the Lewises have temporarily exchanged houses. On 19 August Warnie Lewis will record that

> Tollers looked a little blank at the idea of sleeping on the divan, but we soon had him fixed up by taking Maureen's bed out of her room and set-ting it up in the nursery. Tollers fitted easily into our routine, and I think he enjoyed himself. His one fault turned out to be that he wouldn't trot at our pace in harness; he will keep going all day on a walk, but to him, with his botanical and entomological interests, a walk, no matter what its length, is what we would call an extended stroll, while he calls us 'ruth-less walkers'. [*Brothers and Friends*, p. 207]

During their visit they climb to the British Camp (said to have been defended by Caractacus against the Romans in 75 AD) on the Herefordshire Beacon or Camp Hill (1,114 feet high). They are accompanied by *George Sayer, a former pupil of C.S. Lewis, now a master at Malvern College. Sayer will later recall that C.S. Lewis asked him to walk with Tolkien while they went ahead because 'he's a great man, but not our sort of walker. He doesn't seem able to talk and walk at the same time. He dawdles and then stops completely when he has some-thing interesting to say.' Sayer finds that Tolkien likes 'to stop to look at the trees, flowers, birds and insects', and is a fount of curious information about plants, while 'some of the names of the places we saw from the hills produced philological or etymological footnotes'.

> He talked so well that I was happy to do nothing but listen, though even if one was by his side, it was not always easy to hear all that he said. He talked faster than anyone of his age that I have known, and in a curious fluttering way. Then he would often spring from one topic to another, or interpolate remarks that didn't seem to have much connection with what we were talking about. He knew more natural history than I did, certainly far more than the Lewises, and kept coming out with pieces of curious information about the plants that we came across. ['Recol-

lections of J.R.R. Tolkien', *Proceedings of the J.R.R. Tolkien Centenary Conference 1992* (1995), p. 22]

The holiday also includes visits to pubs for refreshment and meals, but in Tolkien's opinion they find only one really good inn, The Unicorn. Tolkien returns to Oxford on the morning train on 9 August; the Lewis brothers stay longer in Malvern.

8 August 1947 Ida Gordon writes to Tolkien, thanking him for sending the linguistic material for *Pearl*, and for his general comments and suggestions. She asks him for advice and guidance in preparing the work for publication.

12–21 August 1947 Tolkien and Priscilla stay at New Lodge, Stonyhurst. In the guest book they sign their nationality as 'English' (not 'British'). During the visit Tolkien makes a drawing, *New Lodge, Stonyhurst*, which he gives to the owner of the establishment. On 21 September Tolkien will write to Stanley Unwin: 'For a few days my daughter and I had there blazing sun, a rare commodity in those parts, and abundant food, less rare there than in some other places' (Tolkien-George Allen & Unwin archive, HarperCollins).

?Early September 1947 Tolkien stays for a few nights with Marjorie and Walter Incledon in Rottingdean, Sussex. – Michael Tolkien takes up a post as master at the Oratory School, Woodcote in southern Oxfordshire. (The school moved from Caversham to Woodcote in 1942.)

2 September 1947 Philip Unwin writes to Tolkien, asking whether the riddles in *The Hobbit* were invented by him or taken from common folklore. Houghton Mifflin want to include two poems and five riddles from *The Hobbit* in an anthology, and are disputing the fee Allen & Unwin want to charge, alleging that the riddles are taken from common folklore.

16 September 1947 In the morning, Tolkien meets the Lewis brothers in the 'Bird and Baby'.

18 September 1947 Stanley Unwin sends to Tolkien printed specimen pages for *Farmer Giles of Ham*, and asks if they should abandon Milein Cosman as illustrator since she has not yet sent a specimen drawing. He reminds Tolkien that he had promised to send another instalment of *The Lord of the Rings* for Rayner to read.

20 September 1947 Tolkien replies to Philip Unwin that all of the riddles in *The Hobbit* are his own work except two, which are traditional. Although his riddles are in the style and method of old literary (not 'folk-lore') riddles, they have no models as far as he is aware, except the egg-riddle which is derived from a longer literary riddle.

21 September 1947 Tolkien writes to Stanley Unwin, enclosing his letter of 31 July which he failed to post earlier. 'Most of August and September have for me flitted fast with much work broken by various short holidays and journeys.' He encloses 'some notes on *The Hobbit* [i.e. corrections]; and (for the possible amusement of yourself and Rayner) a specimen of a re-writing of Chapter V of that work, which would simplify, though not necessarily improve, my present task' (*Letters*, p. 124). Although Tolkien makes light of the re-writing, Unwin will take it as another correction and hand it on to his production department. Tolkien is sending Book II of *The Lord of the Rings* for Rayner to read. He likes the specimen pages for *Farmer Giles of Ham*, and encloses Milein Cosman's letter of early August. 'I am replying [to Cosman] that I should like to see the proposed illustrations, but in the meanwhile ... it would be satisfactory if she would get into touch with you.' He notes that the announcement slips for *Farmer Giles of Ham* still identify him as the Professor of Anglo-Saxon, two years after he vacated that chair; in modesty he would prefer not to have his title attached, 'unless you think it would really affect [increase] sales' (Tolkien-George Allen & Unwin archive, HarperCollins, partly printed in *Letters*, p. 124). He mentions also that he has been invited to give two lectures in Boston, Massachusetts in February 1948, and asks Unwin if the offered $1,500, for his fee and expenses for a fortnight, would allow him to bring back any money.

22–25 September 1947 As designated Fellow to attend the estates progress, Tolkien spends four days with the Warden and Bursar of Merton inspecting the College's extensive estates in Cambridge, Leicestershire, and Lincolnshire. On 30 September he will write to Stanley Unwin:

> I was much instructed and very interested by my estates tour, in which I did 500 miles in four days not including the tramping around, and saw some very high-powered farming and some of other sort. I also managed to visit Merton House and Pythagoras Hall in Cambridge, antiques that I had never seen before, and to visit the great minster at Lincoln which also I had failed to see before. [Tolkien-George Allen & Unwin archive, HarperCollins]

23 September 1947 In Stanley Unwin's absence, a member of staff at Allen & Unwin writes to Tolkien, stating that a $1,500 fee for the American visit would leave him a reasonable margin beyond his fare and living expenses.

26 September 1947 Tolkien writes a letter to Jennifer Brookes-Smith, daughter of Colin Brookes-Smith (see *Brookes-Smith family). She hopes to come up to Oxford to read English, and evidently has written to Tolkien for advice. He tells her that the priority given to ex-service people leaves fewer places for others, and advises her on the choice of a college. He also explains the runes and various errors in *The Hobbit*, about which she has also asked.

27 September 1947 Stanley Unwin writes to Tolkien. Rayner is reading the further instalment of *The Lord of the Rings* and will return it to Tolkien at the beginning of term. Unwin is relieved to know that Milein Cosman is making progress. He has sent the corrections to *The Hobbit* to the Allen & Unwin production department; any that have not been incorporated in the present reprint will go in the next.

30 September 1947 Tolkien writes to Stanley Unwin. He hopes that Rayner enjoyed the second instalment and will not hesitate to say what he thinks about it. – On the same day he replies to a letter from a young fan named Rosemary, and tells her about *The Lord of the Rings*.

1 October 1947 W.J.B. Owen of University College, Bangor, North Wales, sends notes (possibly on *The Wanderer*) to Tolkien to look over before they are put into print.

2 October 1947 Tolkien replies to a letter from A.W. Riddle written on 29 March. He apologizes for the long delay; even now he cannot give a full answer, as professors have no secretarial or office help. He then writes nearly six pages discussing such matters as 'to overthrow' which Riddle has asked about. He says that 'language has both a logical and an historical (or habitual) aspect' and that 'history will discover that the adverbial element *over* became agglutinated to *throw* (forming a new word with specialized meaning) before the peculiar use of *to* as a sign of the (originally) inflected infinitive was ever thought of' (quoted in Christie's, *20th-Century Books and Manuscripts*, London, 6 December 2002, p. 20).

4 October 1947 Tolkien and Hugo Dyson collect Warnie Lewis at his home, the Kilns in Headington, Oxford, and they go to the 'Bird and Baby' for a drink. Tolkien talks about the early history of Sweden, and Dyson reports college gossip. Tolkien has suggested that the Inklings establish 'cellarettes', or small holdings of wine, for themselves at Merton and Magdalen. Warnie says that his brother agrees with the plan.

7 October 1947 Tolkien buys six or seven bottles of wine for the Merton 'cellarette' before arriving at the 'Bird and Baby', where he meets Warnie Lewis.

8 October 1947 Tolkien attends a Merton College meeting.

9 October 1947 Tolkien hosts a meeting of the Inklings at Merton College. Also present are David Cecil, Colin Hardie, C.S. and Warnie Lewis, Christopher Tolkien, and John Wain. Cecil reads from his forthcoming book *Two Quiet Lives* (published in 1948), a study of the poet Thomas Gray and Dorothy Osborne, wife of Sir William Temple. Tolkien or Christopher reads a chapter from *The Lord of the Rings*.

12 October 1947 Michaelmas Full Term begins. Tolkien's scheduled lectures and classes for this term are: Seminar (Middle English) on Tuesdays and Thursdays at 5.30 p.m. at Merton College, beginning 14 October; Outline of the History of English on Wednesdays at 11.00 a.m. in the Examination Schools, beginning 15 October; and Chaucer: the 'Clerke's Tale' and the 'Pardoner's Tale' on Wednesdays and Fridays at 12.00 noon in the Examination Schools, beginning 15 October. He will continue to supervise B. Litt. students A.J. Bliss, M.Y. Offord, and M.B. Salu.

Michaelmas Term 1947 At the beginning of term Rayner Unwin returns Book II of *The Lord of the Rings* to Tolkien. He will later write:

> I do not seem to have made any written report on it, but I recollect, if not on this then on subsequent occasions when I visited him at his home, discussing and taking off batches of text to comment on as best I could. I found this difficult because I had no map and no ability to refer back to check on characters or situations, but I never doubted the power of the story. My comments were, I hope, encouraging but they could not

have been very specific. Tolkien did not seem to mind. I was a trusted
audience, not an incipient publisher. . . . [*George Allen & Unwin: A Remembrancer* (1999), p. 92]

In regard to these occasions, until Rayner left Oxford at the end of the Trinity
Term 1949:

> Over tea, fussed over by Edith, and subjected to cheerful monologues by
> the Professor on cruxes and variations that sometimes referred to what
> I had been reading, and sometimes to the totally unknown *Silmaril-
> lion*, I assumed that everything was proceeding slowly but in the right
> direction. We scarcely mentioned my academic work. . . . I did not even
> attend his lectures. He had adopted me as a friendly young initiate to
> Middle-earth, and I was unimaginatively content in that role. [*George
> Allen & Unwin: A Remembrancer*, p. 92]

Elsewhere Rayner will recall that Tolkien always assumed in conversation that
Rayner was familiar with every detail of the invented world, but 'I must have
said the right, tactful things, because I know that I was puzzled by these odd
chapters despite their undoubted narrative power' ('An At Last Finished Tale:
The Genesis of *The Lord of the Rings*', *Lembas Extra* 1998, p. 78).

?Michaelmas Term 1947 Possibly during this term, Tolkien reads a paper
at a meeting of the Oxford Dante Society.

14 October 1947 In the morning, Tolkien meets *James Dundas-Grant (a
new addition to the Inklings), Colin Hardie, and Warnie Lewis at the 'Bird and
Baby'. Dundas-Grant recounts a story illustrating second sight. Tolkien con-
fides in Warnie that he has an internal pain and is to be x-rayed.

23 October 1947 Tolkien dines at Merton College with Warnie Lewis as his
guest. They discuss 'the insoluble problem of children in very poor districts:
how to combine a real education with the recognition of a parent's rights in
their children' (Marion E. Wade Center, Wheaton College, Wheaton, Illinois).
– Tolkien then hosts a meeting of the Inklings at Merton, providing green
tea and a bottle of commanderia, a sweet wine from Cyprus. Also present are
R.E. Havard and the Lewis brothers. C.S. Lewis reads a new poem, 'Donkey's
Delight', and Tolkien reads a chapter of *The Lord of the Rings*. Warnie Lewis
suggests *C.E. ('Tom') Stevens (a History tutor at Magdalen College) as a new
member of the Inklings, and those present agree.

24 October 1947 Tolkien attends an English Faculty Board meeting. The
Secretary of Faculties having queried the proposed Preliminary Examination,
the matter is discussed again, concerns are answered, and changes are made.
Tolkien is appointed supervisor of three probationer B.Litt. students: J.J.I. Graf
of Lincoln College, to work on a subject connected with English language syntax; Celia Sisam of Lady Margaret Hall, Kenneth Sisam's daughter, to work on
a subject connected with Middle English philology; and Auvo Kurvinen, a
Finnish student at St Anne's, also to work on a Middle English subject.

30 October 1947 Tolkien attends a meeting of the Inklings in C.S. Lewis's rooms in Magdalen College. Also present are R.E. Havard and Warnie Lewis. In a long discussion about the ethics of cannibalism only Tolkien feels 'that no circumstances – death or the consent of the victim included – can justify it'. This leads to a discussion of 'the possible confusion which exists in our minds between aesthetic distaste and hatred of sin'. Warnie Lewis records that Tolkien 'then read us the last chapter of the Hobbit [*The Lord of the Rings*], that is to say the last he has written: so I fear this toothsome standing dish will be off for some time to come' (*Brothers and Friends*, p. 212). C.S. Lewis pleads illness just as a bottle of wine is to be opened; Warnie observes that there has yet to be a bottle of wine opened at an Inklings meeting at Magdalen.

5 November 1947 Tolkien attends a Merton College meeting. – Allen & Unwin write to Tolkien. The reprint of *The Hobbit* has arrived at last, and a copy is being sent to him.

11 November 1947 In late morning Tolkien meets James Dundas-Grant, Colin Hardie, R.E. Havard, and the Lewis brothers in the 'Bird and Baby'. One of the topics of conversation is *Essays Presented to Charles Williams*, at least one advance copy of which is now in hand. Warnie Lewis is shocked by a story Tolkien repeats about dishonest behaviour by Clement Attlee, the (Labour) Prime Minister.

13 November 1947 Tolkien hosts an Inklings meeting at Merton College. Also present are Colin Hardie, C.S. and Warnie Lewis, and Christopher Tolkien. Tolkien reads 'a rich melancholy poem on autumn' (W.H. Lewis, *Brothers and Friends*, pp. 214–15; possibly a revised version of *The Trees of Kortirion*), and displays a facsimile of the Ellesmere Chaucer manuscript (of *The Canterbury Tales*) he has bought for £55. The Inklings also discuss public schools, including the Oratory School which Christopher Tolkien attended, and the psalms. C.S. Lewis again shows reluctance to the opening of a bottle of wine, though he had agreed to 'cellarettes' at Merton and Magdalen.

18 November 1947 Tolkien, James Dundas-Grant, Colin Hardie, R.E. Havard, C.S. and Warnie Lewis, and Father John Tolkien gather in the 'Bird and Baby'. Father John talks of his slum parish in Coventry, and when conversation moves to second sight recounts a story he has been told about it.

19 November 1947 Ronald Eames of George Allen & Unwin writes to Tolkien, asking if Milein Cosman has yet shown him a specimen drawing.

24 November 1947 Tolkien and his wife probably dine with Austin and *Katharine Farrer, neighbours in Manor Road.

27 November 1947 Tolkien hosts a meeting of the Inklings at Merton College. Also present are R.E. Havard, C.S. and Warnie Lewis, and for the first time, C.E. Stevens. Warnie Lewis will note that they 'talked of B[isho]p Barnes, of the extraordinary difficulty of interesting the uneducated indifferent in religion; savage and primitive man and the common confusion between them; how far pagan mythology was a substitute for theology; bravery and panache'. C.S. Lewis demands that the Inklings give up 'clubbing for wine'; 'as we were in process of consuming a bottle of Tollers' port and half a bottle of his rum, it was perhaps not the happiest moment at which to come to such a decision!' (*Brothers and Friends*, p. 216).

28 November 1947 The standing committee (of which Tolkien is a member) on matters referred by the General Board prepares a report on a communication concerning the Quinquennial Grant for discussion at the next English Faculty Board meeting. The committee would like the Grant to provide for two lecturerships in English Literature, the lecturership in Old and Middle English, the Goldsmiths' Professorship in English Literature, and readerships in English Language and Textual Criticism.

30 November 1947 Tolkien replies, in runes, to a request from Katharine Farrer, also written in runes, that he sign her copy of *The Hobbit*. He agrees, and says that his next book will contain more about runes and other alphabets. In the meantime, he asks if she 'would like a proper key to the special Dwarvish adaptation of the English runic alphabet only part of which appears in *The Hobbit*' (*Letters*, pp. 124, 441). Farrer will reply, again in runes, that she would prize such a key.

December 1947 A scholarly note, *"iþþlen' in Sawles Warde* by Tolkien and S.R.T.O. d'Ardenne, commenting on the correct interpretation of a word in *Sawles Warde* in MS Bodley 34, is published in *English Studies* for December 1947.

Before 15 December 1947 Tolkien sends Katharine Farrer several examples of Dwarvish writings in different styles, including one written as by Thorin Oakenshield of *The Hobbit*.

2 December 1947 Tolkien meets Warnie Lewis at the 'Bird and Baby'. They discuss the behaviour of undergraduates, the landlord having remarked that poorly-behaved students keep respectable customers out of the house.

4 December 1947 *Essays Presented to Charles Williams*, including a revised version of Tolkien's lecture *On Fairy-Stories*, is published.

5 December 1947 In the morning, Tolkien meets Warnie Lewis in the King's Arms for a beer. One topic of conversation is the late Cardinal Arthur Hinsley. – Tolkien attends an English Faculty Board meeting. The Board decides to revive its Monographs Committee (not to be confused with the editorial board for the *Oxford English Monographs*). The members of the Monographs Committee are the chairman of the Faculty Board plus two elected members, and sometimes co-opted members. Tolkien will be a member, elected, *ex officio*, or co-opted from 1947 until his retirement in 1959. The standing committee's report on the Quinquennial Grant is discussed. The Board also approves the insertion in the lecture list of a course on *Sir Orfeo* by Tolkien's B.Litt. student A.J. Bliss. A draft statute for the Preliminary Examination in English Language and Literature and draft decree (which Tolkien has helped to compose) are approved; and Tolkien is appointed to a committee to draw up regulations for the Examination for the Board's consideration. (Soon after this Board meeting the committee will circulate the drafts to the English Faculty and ask for comments by 9 January 1948.)

6 December 1947 Michaelmas Full Term ends.

8 December 1947 Tolkien attends a Merton College meeting.

13 December 1947 Stanley Unwin sends Tolkien a letter from the Swedish publisher of *The Hobbit* and asks him to deal with its last paragraph (not seen by the present authors). Five copies of the Swedish *Hobbit* are being sent to Tolkien.

15 December 1947 Katharine Farrer writes to Tolkien, thanking him for the key to Dwarvish runes and enclosing her copy of *The Hobbit* to be signed.

17 December 1947 Tolkien sends a copy of *Essays Presented to Charles Williams* to T.M. Knox at the University of St Andrews, and probably on the same date, another to Simonne d'Ardenne. In a letter sent with Knox's copy Tolkien thanks him for his hospitality when Tolkien delivered his lecture *On Fairy-Stories* at St Andrews in 1939. He suspects that Knox was instrumental in the choice of Tolkien as the 1939 Andrew Lang Lecturer, and notes that he took Knox's advice (evidently in intervening correspondence) to publish *On Fairy-Stories* in full and without reference to the University.

18 December 1947 Warnie Lewis records 'a well attended Inklings [meeting] which began with a good dinner at the Royal Oxford [Hotel]' (Marion E. Wade Center, Wheaton College, Wheaton, Illinois).

23 December 1947 Tolkien writes to Ronald Eames at Allen & Unwin. He has heard nothing more from Milein Cosman.

Christmas 1947 The Tolkien family receive a parcel, probably containing food, from J.L.N. O'Loughlin, who is now in the United States. – On Christmas Day Tolkien is stricken with gastric influenza and has to spend two days in bed. He takes time to recover fully.

30 December 1947 Ronald Eames writes to Tolkien. Allen & Unwin may withdraw the commission to Milein Cosman.

1948

?1948–?1950 Probably at this time Tolkien reworks his lecture *A Secret Vice* (first given ?autumn 1931) for a new delivery. He makes some minor changes: 'more than 20 years ago' in relation to his invented language Nevbosh become 'almost 40 years ago'. Other changes show that Tolkien is no longer so sure that an artificial language is a good thing.

1948 or 1949 Tolkien becomes President of the Society for the Study of Mediæval Languages and Literature in 1948 or early in 1949. He will hold this office until 1952 or 1953.

1948 Tolkien is appointed to the Merton College stipends committee, on which he will serve until 1959. – Priscilla Tolkien visits Simonne d'Ardenne in Belgium, and is struck that the choice of clothing there is much wider than in post-war Britain.

1 January 1948 Tolkien hosts a meeting of the Inklings at Merton College. Also present are R.E. Havard, C.S. and Warnie Lewis, C.E. Stevens, and Christopher Tolkien. They discuss different versions of the Bible and the Collects, A.E. Housman and the ferocity of his prefaces, and the *Chanson de Roland*.

2 January 1948 Probably in the morning, Tolkien meets Hugo Dyson and Warnie Lewis in the King's Arms. They are later joined by C.E. Stevens.

5 January 1948 Mother Mary Agnes of Maryfield College, Dublin, writes to Tolkien wondering if he recalls her as one of his students at Leeds, and expressing her pleasure in *The Hobbit*.

14 January 1948 Tolkien attends a Merton College meeting.

16 January 1948 Ronald Eames writes to Tolkien. He is sending roughs and a finished specimen drawing by Milein Cosman for *Farmer Giles of Ham*. He asks if Tolkien would like Cosman to visit him in Oxford to discuss the work. Allen & Unwin are planning for twelve one-colour illustrations, two in colour, and possibly decorative endpapers.

17 January 1948 Tolkien certifies the acceptance of Auvo Kurvinen as a full B.Litt. student. Her thesis is to be an edition of *Syre Gawene and the Carle of Carelyle*, supervised by Tolkien.

18 January 1948 Hilary Full Term begins. Tolkien's scheduled lectures and classes for this term are: Outline of the History of English (continued) on Wednesdays at 11.00 a.m. in the Examination Schools, beginning 21 January; Chaucer's *Parlement of Foules* on Wednesdays and Fridays at 12.00 noon in the Examination Schools, beginning 21 January; and Seminar (Middle English) on Thursdays at 5.30 p.m. at Merton College, conducted by Tolkien and Angus McIntosh. The lecture list also includes *Sir Orfeo* on Saturdays at 11.00 a.m. in the Examination Schools, given by A.J. Bliss for the Merton Professor of English Language and Literature. Tolkien will continue to supervise B.Litt. students A.J. Bliss, Auvo Kurvinen, M.Y. Offord, and Mary Salu, and probationer B.Litt. students J.I. Graf (until 30 January) and Celia Sisam. – Tolkien writes to J.L.N. O'Loughlin, thanking him for his parcel. He comments on the situation in the Oxford English School, which now has three more or less active professors and should move ahead; 'but I am either tired or disgruntled and think Oxford would be a grand place to get away from!' (Paul C. Richards Autographs, *Catalogue 228*, item 210). – Tolkien writes again to his young fan Rosemary, who has evidently sent him a drawing she has made of Gollum. He is sorry that he has not yet finished *The Lord of the Rings*, but he has been unwell and very busy. He thinks that her drawing is much more like his own idea of Gollum than most people's, and that the picture of Gollum in the Swedish edition of *The Hobbit* makes him look huge.

25 January 1948 Tolkien writes to C.S. Lewis, part of a larger correspondence arising from criticisms Tolkien made of a work by Lewis read aloud to the Inklings (apparently part of his *English Literature in the Sixteenth Century*, not published until 1954), but he does not send this letter for a week. He regrets pain he has caused Lewis, and comments on the function of a critic, and then on confession, repentance, and forgiveness. 'My verses and my letter [among the correspondence preceding this, apparently the only extant letter in the series] were due to a sudden very acute realization ... of the pain that may enter into authorship, both in the making and in the "publication", which is an essential part of the full process' (*Letters*, p. 126). He explains that his recent absences from Inklings meetings are not connected to his disagreement with Lewis: 'I have missed three [meetings]: one because I was desperately tired, the others for domestic reasons – the last because my daughter (bless her! always mindful of Thursdays) was obliged to go out that evening' (*Letters*, p. 129).

30 January 1948 Tolkien attends an English Faculty Board meeting. It is agreed that the Applications Committee (of which Tolkien is a member) should serve also as the Lecture List Committee. The Board decides to invite Professor Kemp Malone to deliver some lectures; Tolkien is to make preliminary enquiries in the matter. Tolkien is appointed to a committee to report direct to the General Board on the approximate number of CUF (Common University Fund) Lecturerships the English Faculty Board wishes to have over the next three years. The General Board presumably has seen the draft documents for the Preliminary Examination and made some suggestions; the Faculty Board now makes some amendments, for a reply to be sent to the General Board on 31 January.

31 January 1948 Ronald Eames writes to Tolkien, noting that Tolkien has not yet replied to Eames' letter of 16 January, and informing him that Milein Cosman will be in Oxford at the end of the week.

3 February 1948 Tolkien certifies that M.Y. Offord has pursued the required course of research for a B.Litt.

5 February 1948 Priscilla Tolkien writes to Ronald Eames on her father's behalf. He has been advised for health reasons to go away for the next week or so, and therefore cannot see Milein Cosman. Tolkien will leave the decision to Allen & Unwin, but thinks that the style of Cosman's drawings is not suitable for *Farmer Giles of Ham*.

8 February 1948 Priscilla Tolkien writes to Ronald Eames again. Her father has been able to see Milein Cosman after all, and has returned her work to her. He is willing for her to continue with *Farmer Giles of Ham* if Allen & Unwin agree.

12 February 1948 At a meeting of the University of Oxford Visitatorial Board, the Vice-Chancellor reports that he has given a leave of absence to Tolkien for three weeks in the present (Hilary) term, presumably for the health reasons mentioned by Priscilla Tolkien on 5 February. Tolkien subsequently spends some time away from Oxford.

26 February 1948 Tolkien and Christopher attend a meeting of the Inklings, 'both looking the better for their trip to Brighton' (*Brothers and Friends*, p. 218). Also present is *R.B. McCallum, a Tutor in History at Pembroke College, whom Tolkien has introduced to the Inklings.

4 March 1948 Tolkien certifies that A.J. Bliss has pursued the required course of research for a B.Litt. – In the evening, Tolkien hosts a meeting of the Inklings at Merton College. Also present are the Lewis brothers and Christopher Tolkien. Warnie Lewis records that they talk 'of philology, various ways of saying "farewell", and of the inexplicable problem of why some children are allowed to die in infancy' (*Brothers and Friends*, p. 218). Tolkien has a bad cold.

5 March 1948 Tolkien attends a special meeting of the English Faculty Board at 2.15 p.m. in the Board Room of the Clarendon Building. The General Board has suggested that the English Preliminary Examination might be broadened by including subjects such as Philosophy and Modern Languages as options to the existing subjects. The Committee on the English Preliminary Examination (of which Tolkien is a member) has drafted a reply which, after amendment, is accepted by the Faculty Board. They consider that the English Preliminary Examination is already as wide as any examination of its kind can be, and it should be a test, critical as well as linguistic, of the capacity of candidates to read in that School; and that the inclusion of the options suggested by the General Board would destroy its essential character.

11 March 1948 The English Faculty Library Committee decides to ask Tolkien about the possibility of securing another copy of Simonne d'Ardenne's edition of *Seinte Iuliene*. – In the evening, Tolkien attends a meeting of the Inklings at Magdalen College. Warnie Lewis will describe it as a 'red letter Inkling'. Dr Warfield M. Firor of Baltimore has sent C.S. Lewis a ham, and Lewis has arranged a dinner for eight: sherry, soup, fillet of sole, the ham, and a pâté as savoury. Tolkien and Hugo Dyson contribute bottles of a 1923 Burgundy from Merton College, and David Cecil two bottles of port. Also present are Colin Hardie, R.E. Havard, and Christopher Tolkien. They all drink a toast to Firor, and sign a letter to him expressing their appreciation for the ham (see *The Inklings*, pl. 9). After dinner they go to C.S. Lewis's rooms where they hold 'the great Tuxedo raffle – for an American dinner jacket suit' (*Brothers and Friends*, p. 218–19), sent to C.S. Lewis by an American admirer. Hardie is the winner, but as the suit does not fit him he gives it to Christopher. The party does not break up until 1.00 a.m. (The letters of C.S. Lewis show that, in this period when England still suffered strict food rationing, the food parcels he frequently received from correspondents in America often included hams, and that he entertained the Inklings to ham-feasts more frequently than the few occasions that can be dated.)

12 March 1948 Tolkien attends an English Faculty Board meeting. The Board approves the report of the committee (of which Tolkien is a member) appointed to report to the General Board on the approximate number of CUF Lecturerships the English Faculty Board would like approved in the next three years. The Board agree to approach the General Board about inviting Simonne d'Ardenne to give three or four lectures on Medieval English. If she can do so, Tolkien will be responsible for detailed arrangements and the most suitable dates. A draft advertisement for a University Lecturer in Medieval English is also approved: applications are to be made by 1 June 1948, and Tolkien is appointed to the committee to consider them and to make recommendations.

13 March 1948 Hilary Full Term ends.

15 March 1948 Tolkien attends a Merton College meeting. He is appointed a member of a committee to recommend a suitable inscription for a tablet commemorating Idris Deane Jones, Fellow of Merton 1921–47, to be placed in the College Chapel.

16 March 1948 In the morning, at the 'Bird and Baby', Tolkien 'insisted on talking reminiscently and joyously of the Inklings dinner across [James] Dundas Grant, who of course had not been asked' (W.H. Lewis, *Brothers and Friends*, p. 219).

18 March 1948 Tolkien attends a meeting of the Inklings. Also present are Colin Hardie, C.S. and Warnie Lewis, C.E. Stevens, and Christopher Tolkien. The talk is largely philological.

19 March 1948 In the morning, Tolkien meets Warnie Lewis in the King's Arms. They discuss Douglas Hyde, the former editor of the *Daily Worker*, who has thrown up his job, has renounced Communism, and is about to be received into the Roman Catholic Church. Warnie records that Tolkien told him that 'the obvious joke about Jekyll and Hyde is already going the rounds of Oxford. He is, I think rightly, not pleased at the splash the R[oman] C[atholic] papers are making over the news' (Marion E. Wade Center, Wheaton College, Wheaton, Illinois).

20 March 1948 Tolkien writes a letter to Mabel Day of the Early English Text Society, who apparently has written to ask what progress he has made on the *Ancrene Wisse*. He tells her he has 'been unwell for some time, espec[ially] since October, and though X-ray exams revealed nothing immediately serious beyond 19 poisonous teeth, I was obliged, for the first time, to take part of last term off and go away. I still feel far from well, though possibly if I can find time and money for the removal of all my teeth, I may improve. They are said at any rate to account for perhaps 10% of my debility!' The manuscript of the *Ancrene Wisse* is completely copied, and the transcription typed except for a few early folios that were copied with such care that typing is not necessary; but it needs collation with the original. Tolkien realizes that he is 'being a nuisance and holder-up', and if anyone can be found to take over the work he would 'gracefully and gratefully' hand over the transcriptions; but not the photostats, which are his and in use. In any case, he cannot go to Cambridge to do the collation until the end of the summer term. He also mentions that he has seen C.T. Onions 'fairly often of late' (Early English Text Society archive).

31 March 1948 *Hugh Brogan, a young *Hobbit* enthusiast, writes to Tolkien, asking for more information about the Necromancer, Moria, etc.

7 April 1948 Tolkien replies to Hugh Brogan, telling him about the forthcoming *Lord of the Rings* which will give him more information about the world of *The Hobbit*. 'Only the difficulty of writing the last chapters, and the shortage of paper have so far prevented its printing. I hope at least to finish it this year, and will certainly let you have advance information' (*Letters*, p. 129). But what Brogan really needs to answer his questions is 'The Silmarillion'. If Tolkien can find time and a way of reproducing some of the associated maps, chronological tables, and elementary information about the Eldarin language, he will send these to Brogan. Tolkien also mentions a 'Professor's "conference"' in which he is taking part.

8 April 1948 Hugh Brogan writes to Tolkien, thanking him for the information and the offer of documents.

10 April 1948 Tolkien attends an Early English Text Society Committee meeting at Magdalen College, Oxford. He reports that Simonne d'Ardenne's edition of *Seinte Katerine* is almost ready for submission. – Tolkien writes to the Academic Registrar of the University of London, as a member of its Board of Advisors, to ask what is the University's policy with reference to extension of the age of retirement.

12 April 1948 The Academic Registrar of the University of London replies to Tolkien's query, and also informs him that five candidates have been nominated to the Chair of Education at the Institute of Education and been asked to attend interviews with the Board of Advisors at Senate House on 20 April.

15 April 1948 C.S. Lewis has received two more parcels from Dr Firor, one containing another ham, and the other various items, including a fruit cake. When the Inklings meet in the evening, they enjoy the cake and discuss a future ham-feast. Lewis will tell Firor that one decision made by the members was that each participant in the feast is to provide his own bread (which is still rationed).

17 April 1948 In the morning, Tolkien meets Hugo Dyson and Warnie Lewis in the King's Arms. They have an 'idiotic but amusing' time, during which Dyson is rude to an Oxford Councillor (*Brothers and Friends*, p. 220).

20 April 1948 Tolkien presumably attends a meeting of the Board of Advisors at 2.30 p.m. at the Senate House, University of London, to consider candidates for the Chair of Education. – He certifies the acceptance of Celia Sisam as a full B.Litt. student. Her thesis is to be 'a text of the "Lambeth Homilies" with a select glossary, critical notes and a linguistic introduction', supervised by Tolkien.

22 April 1948 Tolkien attends a Merton College meeting.

25 April 1948 Trinity Full Term begins. Tolkien's scheduled lectures for this term are: Outline of the History of English Language (cont.) on Thursdays and Fridays at 12.00 noon in the Examination Schools, beginning 28 April. The lecture list also includes: The West Saxon Dialect in Middle English on Wednesdays at 12.00 noon in the Examination Schools, given by A.J. Bliss for the Merton Professor of English Language and Literature. Tolkien will continue to supervise B.Litt. students Auvo Kurvinen, M.B. Salu, and Celia Sisam.

28 April 1948 Tolkien attends a meeting of the electors to the Vigfússon Readership in Ancient Icelandic Literature and Antiquities. E.O.G. Turville-Petre is re-elected for seven years from 1 October 1948. – Tolkien probably works on one of his lectures on 'Outlines of the History of English'.

29 April 1948 Tolkien attends a Merton College Meeting.

6 May 1948 At an English Faculty Library Committee meeting it is reported that Tolkien has kindly offered to try to obtain from Belgium copies of Simonne d'Ardenne's *Seinte Iuliene*.

7 May 1948 Tolkien attends an English Faculty Board meeting. The General Board has approved the Preliminary Examination syllabus submitted by the Faculty Board and agreed to convert the Goldsmiths' Readership in English Language into a Professorship of English Literature, and to establish

Readerships in English Language and in Textual Criticism. Tolkien, as Merton Professor of English Language and Literature, becomes an elector to these readerships *ex officio*. It is agreed that Tolkien will propose and F.P. Wilson will second a recommendation to be sent to the General Board about the conditions under which Mr Leishman, a Tutor at St John's College, should hold a University Lecturership.

11 May 1948 Alan Bliss writes to Tolkien. He has been able to lecture that day and does not anticipate any more problems (presumably he has been ill). He asks for Tolkien's opinion of a new reading of a bestiary which has occurred to him.

24 May 1948 C.S. Lewis telephones Tolkien to say that Charlie Blagrove, the landlord of the 'Bird and Baby', died the previous day.

25 May 1948 The University of Oxford confers the honorary degree of Doctor of Civil Law on Princess Elizabeth. Tolkien is almost certainly present in the Sheldonian Theatre for the ceremony at 3.00 p.m., and he and Edith are probably among the 1,600 guests at a garden party given to entertain the Princess at St John's College later in the afternoon.

27 May 1948 Tolkien attends a Merton College meeting.

12 June 1948 In the evening, Tolkien attends a dinner of The Society hosted by Lord David Cecil at New College, Oxford. Eight members are present.

15 June 1948 Tolkien makes several drafts of a letter to Katharine Farrer (possibly begun a few days before) in reply to a letter she has sent expressing an interest in 'The Silmarillion'. He has 'spent what time I could spare since you wrote in collecting out of the unfinished mass such things as are more or less finished and readable (I mean legible)' and promises to bring her some manuscripts later the same day. (He probably puts this letter through her letterbox, nearby on Manor Road.) He apparently lends her the *Quenta Silmarillion* and two versions of the *Ainulindalë*, a 'Flat World' version (probably one from the 1930s) and a 'Round World' version (probably one written in 1946). But he is 'unable to find the "Rings of Power" which with the "Fall of Númenor" is the link between 'The Silmarillion' and the Hobbit world. But its essentials are included in Ch. II of *The Lord of the Rings*' i.e. Book II, Chapter 2 (*Letters*, p. 130). By this time, therefore, background material has been removed from 'The Council of Elrond' and developed as a separate text with the title *The Rings of Power* (*Of the Rings of Power and the Third Age*), even if it has not yet reached its final form.

18 June 1948 Tolkien attends an English Faculty Board meeting. C.T. Onions having decided to retire from the Board, Tolkien expresses the Board's regret on the loss and its high appreciation of Onions' long service to the Board and to the English School. The committee (including Tolkien) appointed to consider applications for the Lecturership in Medieval English recommends a candidate, but after discussion the appointment is deferred for further consideration.

19 June 1948 Trinity Full Term ends.

22 June 1948 Tolkien attends a Merton College meeting.

23 June 1948 Encaenia.

25 June 1948 Tolkien attends a special meeting of the English Faculty Board at 2.00 p.m. in the Board Room of the Clarendon Building, to discuss an appointment to the Lecturership in Medieval English. The report of the committee (of which Tolkien is a member) appointed to recommend a Lecturer in Medieval English is referred back to the committee for further consideration; and it is agreed 'to draw the committee's attention to the order of the Lecturer's duties as stated in the advertisement' (Oxford University Archives FA 4/5/1/2).

5 July 1948 The British National Health Service begins.

12 July 1948 Tolkien attends a special meeting of the English Faculty Board at 3.00 p.m. in the Board Room of the Clarendon Building. The Board decides to appoint *Norman Davis of Oriel College, Oxford as University Lecturer in Medieval English.

22 July 1948 Ronald Eames of Allen & Unwin writes to Tolkien. Milein Cosman has submitted further drawings in two different styles for *Farmer Giles of Ham*. Eames asks Tolkien for the address to which the drawings should be sent.

24 July 1948 Tolkien replies to Ronald Eames that until 14 August he will be dividing his time between Oxford and Payables Farm in Woodcote, 'where I have a hiding place', i.e. the home of his son Michael (Tolkien-George Allen & Unwin archive, HarperCollins). He suggests that the drawings should be sent to Merton College, or he could collect them in London. From 14 August till 14 September his address will be c/o the Oratory School, Woodcote, near Reading.

25 July 1948 Bread rationing ends in Britain.

27 July 1948 Ronald Eames sends Milein Cosman's drawings to Tolkien and comments on the two styles, one freer than the other. He thinks the freer style more successful, and in a sense more fashionable, resembling the work of Feliks Topolski and Edward Ardizzone. The drawings are rough at present but would receive more finish.

29 July 1948 At the request of Mabel Day, Oxford University Press send Tolkien a specimen page of her Early English Text Society edition (1946) of the *Ancrene Riwle* from MS Cotton Nero.

5 August 1948 Tolkien returns Milein Cosman's drawings to Ronald Eames and writes a long detailed criticism. He is 'not much interested in the fashionableness of these drawings', but is more concerned about 'their lack of resemblance to their text'. But if Eames really thinks that 'illustrations of this sort, wholly out of keeping with the style or manner of the text, will do, or will for reasons of contemporary taste be an advantage' (*Letters*, pp. 130–1) then go ahead; though he wonders how long it will take Cosman to finish the job, and if the book, long delayed, will ever be published.

10 August 1948 Ronald Eames writes to Tolkien. In view of his letter of 5 August, Allen & Unwin have decided to dispense with Milein Cosman's services and are inviting other artists to submit their work. Allen & Unwin were under the impression that Tolkien was genuinely satisfied with Cosman's earlier roughs. – Eames now writes to other artists, including *Pauline Diana Baynes, asking for specimen drawings to show to Tolkien. In his letter to Pauline Baynes, Eames notes that the illustrations need not be juvenile, as the book could best be described as 'an adult fairy story (complete with dragon and giant!)' requiring 'some historical and topographical (Oxford and Wales) realism' in its setting (George Allen & Unwin archive, University of Reading).

14 August–14 September 1948 Tolkien retires to the quiet of Payables Farm, Woodcote, vacated by his son Michael and his family while they are on holiday. There he completes *The Lord of the Rings*, at least in draft. *See note.*

Tolkien makes two drafts for 'The Tower of Kirith [later Cirith] Ungol' (bk. VI, ch. 1 as published). He soon abandons the first, which includes a sketch of the Tower with four tiers, as he first conceived it (*Artist and Illustrator*, fig. 174; *Sauron Defeated*, p. 19); he makes significant changes and additions in the second, which as he proceeds becomes rough and in places only an outline. He then writes a fair copy, stopping to make drafts for some sections, which reaches to the end of the chapter. He includes in the manuscript a small diagram of the space on the roof of the topmost tier of the tower. At some point he makes a second fair copy manuscript, and places with it the page from the first draft with the drawing of the Tower (even though in the later text the tower has only three tiers). The text of Sam's song in the second fair copy still differs from the published version.

Tolkien writes 'The Land of Shadow' and 'Mount Doom' (bk. VI, ch. 2–3 as published) as one chapter swiftly and with little hesitation. For the part that became 'The Land of Shadow' he makes a series of rough drafts, only rarely changing significantly the story first drafted, then copies it section by section, incorporating some emendations, into a continuous complete manuscript. He continues this manuscript as a primary text for the whole of 'Mount Doom'. Christopher Tolkien comments on 'Mount Doom' that it

> is remarkable in that the primary drafting constitutes a completed text, with scarcely anything in the way of preparatory sketching of individual passages, and while the text is rough and full of corrections made at the time of composition it is legible almost throughout; moreover many passages underwent only the most minor changes later. It is possible that some more primitive material has disappeared, but it seems to me ... that the long thought which my father had given to the ascent of Mount Doom and the destruction of the Ring enabled him, when at last he came to write it, to achieve it more quickly and surely than almost any earlier chapter in *The Lord of the Rings*. [*Sauron Defeated*, p. 37]

On the reverse of one of the draft pages of 'The Land of Shadow' Tolkien makes a sketch map of the geography of Mordor, and while writing 'Mount Doom' he makes a small sketch of the mountain in the original draft, and two more views on a separate page used for drafting (*Sauron Defeated*, p. 42). Perhaps also at this time Tolkien makes a finished drawing of Barad-dûr with

Mount Doom in the distance (*Artist and Illustrator*, fig. 145), but at any rate later than October 1944, as on the verso is a discarded unfinished beginning of the drawing *Stanburg* or *Steinborg*.

Tolkien seems to write the next few chapters without much difficulty, perhaps because he is now following a single thread. He writes a first draft for 'The Field of Cormallen [originally *Kormallen*]' (bk. VI, ch. 4 as published) with little preliminary drafting, and comes remarkably close to the final text for much of its length. He will later recall that when he finished the first rough writing (which he will wrongly date to 1949): 'I remember blotting the pages (which now represent the welcome of Frodo and Sam on the Field of Cormallen) with tears as I wrote' (letter to Jane Neave, 8–9 September 1962, *Letters*, p. 321). It is probably only after writing this draft that he makes a fair copy of 'The Land of Shadow' and 'Mount Doom', and then of 'The Field of Cormallen'.

On the back of a rejected page for the draft of 'The Field of Kormallen', before completing the chapter, Tolkien writes an outline (called by Christopher Tolkien 'The Story Foreseen from Kormallen') in his most difficult handwriting, in which he looks ahead to the end of *The Lord of the Rings* at the Grey Havens, and introduces some previously unmentioned episodes such as the marriage of Faramir and Éowyn. The first draft of the next chapter, 'The Steward and the King' (bk. VI, ch. 5), also comes close to the final version, and the fair copy even closer. Tolkien probably does not make the fair copy of this chapter until after he has drafted 'Many Partings' (bk. VI, ch. 6) or possibly even with the fair copies of the following chapters after completing *The Lord of the Rings* in draft.

Tolkien paginates his first draft for what became 'Many Partings' continuously with that of 'The Steward and the King', and into what becomes 'Homeward Bound' (bk. VI, ch. 7). But not far into 'Homeward Bound' he begins a new pagination in the draft which continues to the end of an (ultimately omitted) Epilogue. He apparently decides to complete the story as a continuous draft (based on preliminary drafting) from 'Many Partings' to the Epilogue, rather than revise and make a fair copy of each chapter before working on the next. Today it is thus often impossible to know at what stage he made corrections or additions to the draft: at the time of writing or soon after, several chapters later, or after the whole was complete. Tolkien does not include Arwen's gift to Frodo, or the verses at Théoden's funeral, in the first version of 'Many Partings'. Material which he later inserts into the earlier part of the draft, including the visit to Isengard and the meeting with Saruman on the road, is probably added while he is working on 'The Scouring of the Shire' (bk. VI, ch. 8). Christopher Tolkien has said that 'as far as the Battle of Bywater . . . [the manuscript] gives the impression of having been written in one long burst, and with increasing rapidity. Ideas that appear in earlier reaches of the text are contradicted later without correction of the former passages' (*Sauron Defeated*, p. 75).

Tolkien seems to be feeling his way as to the content of 'The Scouring of the Shire': this involves much rewriting, with significant changes made both in the story and the order of events. He writes several accounts of what happened at Farmer Cotton's house, and draws a sketch plan and view of the house to aid him (*Artist and Illustrator*, fig. 175). Although he realizes that Saruman is behind the troubles in the Shire, it is only after several false starts that the character is actually present in the Shire. Christopher Tolkien comments that 'it is very striking that here, virtually at the end of *The Lord of the Rings* and in an element in the whole that my father had long meditated, the story when he first wrote it down should have been so different from its final form (or that he so signally failed to see "what really happened"!)' (*Sauron Defeated*, p. 93). After the Battle of Bywater Tolkien begins to write in a much clearer hand which continues into 'The Grey Havens' (bk. VI, ch. 9), probably starting afresh after a break or because he is much clearer in his mind about the course of events. He continues the draft into the Epilogue: in this version, the Epilogue takes place some fifteen years later, with Sam reading to his children from the Red Book and telling them of the forthcoming visit of the King to the North.

?August 1948–?end of August 1950 Tolkien makes fair copies of these last chapters and the Epilogue, but possibly some (or all) are not made until after he has begun work on the Prologue and Appendices. In writing the fair copies Tolkien not only incorporates changes and additions he has already made to the draft, but makes more changes, approaching the published text closely. In the fair copy of 'Many Meetings' he changes the names of Elrond's daughter from Finduilas to Arwen Evenstar, and writes the first account of her gift to Frodo. On a page of drafting associated with a change he sketches a plan of the citadel at Minas Tirith. Probably around this time he also makes a quick sketch of the front of the city, showing its seven circles, great gate, and 'keel' (*Artist and Illustrator*, fig. 169).

Tolkien's second manuscript of 'The Scouring of the Shire' seems to be as much a working document as a fair copy. He still seems uncertain of some events: he replaces some pages when a new version of a fight at Farmer Cotton's house does not work out, inserts the pages with the account of the Battle of Bywater, begins to describe the encounter with Saruman, stops, and starts again. When he writes these last chapters he still views Frodo as taking a more active part in events and having great fame and honour in the Shire. When he decides later that Frodo's role is more passive, he makes changes and transfers many of Frodo's words and actions to Merry.

Tolkien probably has been long considering what background material should accompany *The Lord of the Rings*, either by addition to the Prologue begun long before, or as Appendices. He certainly has written some of this material by 31 October 1948: in a letter to Hugh Brogan on that date, he promises to lend 'a good deal of explanatory matter, alphabets, history, calendars, and genealogies' (*Letters*, p. 131).

After finishing the draft for Book VI, Tolkien probably begins to work on the ancillary material by revising the second version of the Foreword or Prologue written in 1938. Through five successive versions of all or part of this he makes alterations, rewrites part of the story of Bilbo's encounter with Gollum (though this remains the version told in the first edition of *The Hobbit*), and adds sections on the early history of Hobbits, on the founding of the Shire and its organization, and on pipeweed. He appears to write the third of these five versions close to the draft of 'The Scouring of the Shire', and possibly before the fair copy of that chapter.

Christopher Tolkien describes another text, typed on small scrap paper, 'very obviously set down by my father very rapidly *ab initio* without any previous drafting, following his thoughts as they came: sentences were abandoned before complete and replaced by new phrasing, and so on' (**The Peoples of Middle-earth* (1996), p. 19), which dates probably from after the narrative of *The Lord of the Rings* has been completed, at about the same time that Tolkien is working on the Prologue. Tolkien possibly intends it as a personal 'preface', in which he dedicates the work to the Inklings; he will later reuse one or two phrases in the published Foreword. But in this he also discusses the peoples of Middle-earth, their languages and scripts, and how he has represented the different languages in the story. Eventually he will use some of this material instead in published Appendices E and F.

Also in this period, while working on the Prologue, Tolkien makes two lengthy manuscripts from which Appendix F on 'The Languages and Peoples of the Third Age' will ultimately derive, but with much material omitted from the published book, including more about the interrelationships of the languages of Middle-earth and the development of the Common Speech, a long explanation of his decision to 'translate' names in different Middle-earth languages by names from different languages in our world, and explanation of Hobbit names as they 'really were' and as 'translated'. In the second manuscript, Tolkien includes a long section on the distinction between the familiar and the courteous second person, and his use of it in conversations between Faramir and Éowyn (later omitted in revision). He also writes and then removes twenty pages with an analysis of phonological and grammatical features of the Common Speech. He concludes the second manuscript with eight pages on pronunciation, with sections on consonants, vowels, and accents, which he will subsequently remove to become (in much developed form) the first part of Appendix E. Tolkien then makes in typescript a reduced version of this matter, incorporating other material and including a section on scripts which will also eventually become part of Appendix E. Probably in the course of typing, he changes the origin of the Common Speech.

Tolkien also makes new Hobbit family trees (Baggins, Bolger, Boffin, Brandybuck, Took, and Gamgee-Cotton) with the dates in Shire-reckoning, in different versions and variants.

He begins work on the calendars of Middle-earth (Appendix D in the published *Lord of the Rings*) with a brief rough manuscript probably written immediately following the two manuscripts on languages. He then makes a fair copy incorporating substantial alterations to the first text but which still differs in many respects from the published version. In association with these Tolkien writes two versions of a statement on the Gondorian Calendar in the

Fourth Age; he draws up tables comparing the dates of the New Era with those of the Shire Reckoning and the Steward's Reckoning; he lists the Quenya and Noldorin (Sindarin) names of the months and seasons; and he makes a manuscript table from which the Shire Calendar at the beginning of Appendix D will ultimately derive, including names of the days of the week to the left of each month which are omitted in the published version.

The material concerning the Second Age which appears in 'The Tale of Years' in *The Lord of the Rings* is closely related to the *Akallabêth*, a text which Tolkien begins at this time but which is apparently intended for and eventually published in *The Silmarillion*. Although he does not write the title *Akallabêth* on any of the texts, he always refers to the work by that name. He makes a list of thirteen kings of Númenor who followed Elros, with brief notes of a few significant events, and refers to it when writing the first text of the *Akallabêth*, and for the Second Age in early versions of 'The Tale of Years' (see below). He incorporates much of *The Drowning of Anadûnê* (1946) in the first version of the *Akallabêth*, a clear manuscript of twenty-three pages, after he replaces several of the original pages. After emending this manuscript, he makes a typescript introducing few further changes.

Tolkien also begins work on what will become 'The Tale of Years' with two brief texts: a 'Time Scheme', a summary of the Second and Third Ages, and 'The Second Age and the Black Years', which includes dates from the Great Battle to the loss of the One Ring. After emending and correcting the second text extensively, Tolkien makes a manuscript copy headed 'Of the Tale of Years in the Latter Ages', which has many similarities with the list of kings for the history of Númenor associated with the *Akallabêth*, but which differs considerably from the published Appendices of *The Lord of the Rings*. This text is closely associated with the earliest chronology of the Third Age, entitled 'Of the History of the Third Age little is known', in which Elrond's daughter is 'Finduilas', not 'Arwen': these precede the fair copy of 'Many Meetings' and belong with Tolkien's earliest work on the Appendices. Having emended these two documents, he combines them in a new manuscript 'Tale of Years', expanding entries and adding new material, especially for the Third Age. He then makes further additions to the new text for both the Second and Third Ages, and includes these in yet another, much expanded version, a clear manuscript probably intended as a final text. When Tolkien decides to change a date, rather than altering the original document he writes two new pages to replace them exactly.

Tolkien also includes much of the information which appears in 'The Tale of Years' for the Third Age in a different form in a series of texts concerning the Heirs of Elendil, from which 'The Realms in Exile' in Appendix A will derive. He writes an untitled account of the Northern Line, and a manuscript entitled *The Heirs of Elendil: The Southern Line of Gondor*, which lists the kings and some events in their reigns and gives details of the Stewards. He then writes a new text of the material dealing with Gondor, which begins as a fair copy but deteriorates towards the end as he develops and expands it. To this he attaches the untitled account of the Northern Line. After emending the composite text heavily, he makes a fair copy which he emends in turn especially in the part dealing with the Northern Line. He also draws a family tree showing the line of Dol Amroth, with a note on the origins of the house, and attaches it to the third, fair copy, manuscript of *The Heirs of Elendil* near the mention of Denethor's marriage to Finduilas.

Having listed the names of the Kings of the Mark when writing 'The Last Debate' in 1946, Tolkien now writes, probably in close succession, three brief texts on 'The House of Eorl'. The first two are primarily lists of kings, the second a fair copy of the first, while the third is a finely written manuscript which begins with a brief account of the origins of the Rohirrim and includes notes on Théoden and Éomer.

When Tolkien ceases work on this material in mid-1950, he has a series of fair copy texts which fill out the background to the actual narrative and seem intended to be included with it, if and when it is published.

Some time after he finishes *The Lord of the Rings* proper and has already written much of its background material, Tolkien makes new, very fine (third) manuscripts of four chapters: 'The Steward and the King', 'Many Partings', Homeward Bound', and 'The Scouring of the Shire'. It is only in these, by emendation, that he abandons the name 'Trotter', and Aragorn finally becomes 'Strider'. These now approach the published work closely, but Tolkien will continue to emend succeeding typescripts and, as with the whole of *The Lord of the Rings*, even in the galley and page proofs.

21 August 1948 Ronald Eames writes to Tolkien (at Merton College). He has specimens from five possible illustrators for *Farmer Giles of Ham*. He is unwilling to entrust them to the post, and wonders if there is any likelihood of Tolkien coming to London.

30 August 1948 Ronald Eames sends a copy of his previous letter to Tolkien (presumably to the Oratory School), having realized that Tolkien is away from Merton.

Late September 1948 Tolkien probably visits Cambridge to see the manuscript of the *Ancrene Wisse* at Corpus Christi College.

28 September 1948 Since he has had no reply to his letters, Ronald Eames writes again to Tolkien. The prospective artists for *Farmer Giles of Ham* are asking if a decision has been made, and want their work returned.

End of September–early October 1948 Tolkien probably telephones Ronald Eames in reply to his letters, and arranges to visit Allen & Unwin in London to look at specimen drawings. He chooses Pauline Baynes to illustrate *Farmer Giles of Ham* on the strength of ink and watercolour cartoons she has drawn after medieval manuscript illuminations, whose character perfectly complements his mock-medieval story.

October 1948 Katharine Farrer writes to Tolkien about the manuscripts he has lent her, expressing her enthusiasm and saying that she likes the 'Flat World' version best. Perhaps it is her opinion that leads Tolkien to abandon, for a time, any attempt to alter the cosmology of 'The Silmarillion' to that of a Round World with the Sun existing from the beginning.

?Late 1948 and by 1951 Tolkien drastically revises the *Ainulindalë* on the fair copy manuscript made in the 1930s, keeping a 'Flat World' but incorporating much of the new writing of the 'Round World' typescript made in 1946. The extent of the revision, not all of which is carried out at the same time, is such that he has to write much new material on the blank versos of the manuscript. In so doing he uses Anglo-Saxon letterforms, which he uses also in a final manuscript version, probably contemporary, no later than 1951. He writes this last manuscript in a calligraphic script with illuminated capitals and provides it with a title-page. He begins by following the revised manuscript closely, but diverges from it towards the end, and subsequently makes emendations.

2 October 1948 Tolkien attends an Early English Text Society Committee meeting at Magdalen College, Oxford. M.Y. Offord, his former B.Litt. student, is given permission to submit her B.Litt. thesis, *The Parlement of the Thre Ages*, for consideration. (It will be published in 1959.)

6 October 1948 Tolkien attends a Merton College meeting.

7 October 1948 Tolkien sends Ronald Eames his spare (uncorrected) copy of *Farmer Giles of Ham* to be sent on to Pauline Baynes. He thinks that it will suffice 'to give Miss Baynes an idea what she is in for' (Tolkien-George Allen & Unwin archive, HarperCollins). He has not kept a copy of the preface or of the revisions on the typescript he finally sent to Allen & Unwin on 5 July 1947, and asks if the publisher could make a copy of the text, or return it to him so that he can make a note of the revisions. – Ronald Eames informs Pauline Baynes that Tolkien was most impressed with her work.

10 October 1948 Michaelmas Full Term begins. Tolkien's scheduled lectures and classes for this term are: The Influence of Latin upon English on Wednesdays at 12.00 noon in the Examination Schools, beginning 13 October; *Sir Gawain and the Green Knight* on Fridays at 12.00 noon in the Examination Schools, beginning 15 October; and Middle English Philology (Seminar) on Fridays at 5.30 p.m. at Merton College, beginning 15 October. Tolkien is also scheduled to deliver a lecture entitled 'Language and Literature' for the course 'The Study of Literature' on 20 November at 11.00 a.m. in the Examination Schools. He will continue to supervise B.Litt. students Auvo Kurvinen, Mary Salu, and Celia Sisam. – Priscilla Tolkien matriculates at Lady Margaret Hall, Oxford, to read English. Since she is resident, her parents now live alone for much of the year. Priscilla will attend her father's lectures on *Sir Gawain and Green Knight*, and will later recall that he would point out with glee where the editors of the standard edition (Tolkien and Gordon) had made mistakes which he was now happy to correct.

12 October 1948 Ronald Eames sends the uncorrected typescript of *Farmer Giles of Ham* to Pauline Baynes, so that she may read it and decide if she wants to illustrate it.

13 October 1948 Ronald Eames sends the corrected typescript of *Farmer Giles of Ham* to Tolkien, and asks for its return as soon as possible.

20 October 1948 Tolkien takes part in the election to the Readership in Textual Criticism. The electors consider two applications and a name put forward by one of their number. The meeting is adjourned to 21 October.

21 October 1948 The electors to the Readership in Textual Criticism (including Tolkien) choose Herbert Davis of St John's College, Oxford for the position.

22 October 1948 Tolkien attends an English Faculty Board meeting. The Applications Committee has appointed him and Alistair Campbell examiners of the B.Litt. thesis of Rosemary Woolf of St Hugh's, *An Edition of the Old English Juliana*. The Board decides to accept in future the recommendations of the Applications Committee (of which Tolkien is a member) for the admission of probationer B.Litt. students without considering the details of each particular application.

23 October 1948 Tolkien takes part in the election to the Readership in English Language. The electors consider three applications and adjourn the meeting to 25 October.

25 October 1948 The electors to the Readership in English Language (including Tolkien) choose Dorothy Everett, Fellow of Lady Margaret Hall, for the position.

31 October 1948 Tolkien writes to Hugh Brogan.

> I managed to go into 'retreat' in the summer, and am happy to announce that I succeeded at last in bringing the 'Lord of the Rings' to a successful conclusion. . . . If only term had not caught me on the hop again, I should have revised the whole – it is astonishingly difficult to avoid mistakes and changes of name and all kinds of inconsistencies of detail in a long work, as critics forget, who have not tried to make one – and sent it to the typists. I hope to do so soon. . . .

As soon as he has a spare copy he will lend it to Brogan, 'plus a good deal of explanatory matter, alphabets, history, calendars, and genealogies reserved for the real "fans"'. He hopes that he might be able to send it for the Christmas holidays, but 'this university business of earning one's living by teaching, delivering philological lectures, and daily attendance at "boards" and other talk-meetings, interferes sadly with serious work' (*Letters*, p. 131).

Autumn 1948 Nathan C. Starr, an American correspondent of C.S. Lewis visiting Oxford, is invited to join Lewis and his friends one morning in the 'Bird and Baby'. When he arrives he is directed to the parlour set aside for the Inklings. Lewis, who is already there, tells him that by custom, as the latest comer, he should sit nearest the fire, and give that seat up when someone else arrives. Starr will later recall about eight or ten in attendance, but besides Lewis, only Tolkien, David Cecil, and perhaps Gervase Mathew by name; and that the conversation was casual and general, entirely informal.

1 November 1948 Tolkien sends Ronald Eames a new typescript of *Farmer Giles of Ham*, corrected for press. He has a copy from which an identical typescript can be typed if needed. He suggests that if Allen & Unwin do not immediately need the typescript, they might send it to Pauline Baynes, if she has accepted the commission, as the new text has some pictorial details which might catch her eye.

3 November 1948 Ronald Eames sends the new typescript to Pauline Baynes. – He writes to thank Tolkien for the typescript. Miss Baynes is keen to illustrate the story. The old typescript, sent to Baynes on 12 October, has not reached her; either it was packed in the wrong parcel or is temporarily lost in the post. Baynes will now suggest subjects to be illustrated and submit a specimen drawing. She aims to complete her part of the work early in 1949.

10 November 1948 Tolkien attends a Merton College meeting.

11 November 1948 Kenneth Sisam writes to Ida Gordon. He is glad that Tolkien is giving time to the edition of *Pearl*. He advises Mrs Gordon that Tolkien's weakness is a desire for perfection, which leads to delay.

17 November 1948 Tolkien writes this date on a draft headed 'Latin and English', presumably in preparation for one of his lectures this term on 'The Influence of Latin upon English'.

20 November 1948 Tolkien presumably delivers his lecture *Language and Literature* for the course 'The Study of Literature' at 11.00 a.m. in the Examination Schools. – Ronald Eames writes to Tolkien that Pauline Baynes enjoyed *Farmer Giles of Ham* very much. He lists subjects she has suggested for some of the one-colour illustrations and for the two colour plates. He asks Tolkien if these seem to be suitable. Also, the missing typescript has turned up.

21 November 1948 Tolkien writes to Ronald Eames. He thinks that Pauline Baynes is on the right track.

4 December 1948 Michaelmas Full Term ends.

6 December 1948 Tolkien attends a Merton College meeting. Ronald Eames sends Tolkien the first group of Pauline Baynes' line drawings for *Farmer Giles of Ham*. She intends to provide a considerable number of drawings throughout the text, and the author and publisher can reject any they do not like or for which there is no room. Eames asks for Tolkien's opinion of the drawings.

10 December 1948 Tolkien writes to Ronald Eames. He is delighted with the drawings he received last night: 'They seem to me the perfect counterpart to the text (or an improvement on it) and to accord exactly in mood. Put in freely they would give something of an air of a [manuscript] to the pages. My only difficulty will be to reject any without sorrow if they are all so good' (Tolkien-George Allen & Unwin archive, HarperCollins). Presumably he returns the drawings with this letter.

11 December 1948 Hugh Brogan writes to Tolkien. He hopes that the holidays will afford Tolkien some relief.

15 December 1948 Ronald Eames writes to thank Tolkien for returning the drawings. They have asked Pauline Baynes to proceed with the book. If Tolkien could let them have a copy of the corrected typescript, Allen & Unwin would send it to the printers, and the uncorrected copy could be returned to him.

Christmas 1948 Tolkien sends a calligraphic autograph note in blue and red ink to his grandson Michael George. – It is probably at this Christmas that he sends greetings to Hugh Brogan written in runes and Tengwar, with explanations of the scripts. He also sends him a letter saying that he hopes to visit Cambridge (where Brogan lives with his parents) in 1949, arriving on 19 March.

1949

Before June 1949 Tolkien obtains a passport to travel to the Republic of Ireland in June to act as the Extern Examiner for English examinations held by the National University of Ireland (Ollscoil na hÉireann). He encounters bureaucratic problems despite the fact that both his parents were British and he has lived in England since 1895, because he was born in the Orange Free State and some of his family papers have been lost.

Early 1949 Tolkien hears C.S. Lewis read *The Lion, the Witch and the Wardrobe*. Lewis will later remark that Tolkien disliked it intensely.

Early January 1949 Tolkien and Alistair Campbell examine Rosemary Woolf of St Hugh's College *viva voce* on her thesis *An Edition of the Old English Juliana*.

6 January 1949 Tolkien and Alistair Campbell sign their report on the examination of Rosemary Woolf.

13 January 1949 Tolkien attends a Merton College meeting.

16 January 1949 Hilary Full Term begins. Tolkien's scheduled lectures and classes for this term are: The Language of the *Ayenbyte of Inwit* on Wednesdays at 12.00 noon in the Examination Schools, beginning 19 January; *Sir Gawain and the Green Knight* on Fridays at 12.00 noon in the Examination Schools, beginning 21 January; and English Philology (Seminar) on Fridays at 5.30 p.m. at Merton College, beginning 21 January. He will continue to supervise B.Litt. students Auvo Kurvinen, M.B. Salu, and Celia Sisam.

25 January 1949 A schoolmistress sends Tolkien letters on *The Hobbit* and its runes written by some of her pupils. Tolkien receives many such letters from young readers.

27 January 1949 Tolkien certifies that Mary B. Salu has pursued the required course of research for her B.Litt.

28 January 1949 Tolkien attends an English Faculty Board meeting. The Board appoints Tolkien as an interviewer of prospective advanced and probationer B.Litt. students in the areas of Medieval Literature and Linguistic Studies. Tolkien is also appointed to a committee 'to consider alterations in the regulations of examinations under the supervision of the Board, particularly in respect of the withdrawal, after Trinity Term, of the English Sections' (Oxford University Archives FA 4/5/1/2). The Applications Committee has accepted

Anne Wakefield of St Hilda's College as a probationer B.Litt. student to work on an English Language subject, with Tolkien as her supervisor. Christopher Tolkien is among other probationer B.Litt. students accepted.

9 February 1949 Tolkien attends a Merton College meeting.

10 February 1949 Tolkien writes to Douglas Veale, the Oxford University Registrar. He asks how he should present a request for a period of leave (including Trinity Term), and points out that in all his years as a professor he has had no leave except for an 'emergency' fortnight a year earlier on medical grounds. 'Apart from the minor medical object of having all my teeth, which are said to be poisoning me, removed, my main object would be to complete a number of writings I have on hand' (Oxford University Archives FA 9/2/875).

11 February 1949 Douglas Veale replies that he will submit Tolkien's application to the Visitatorial Board when it meets on 18 February.

18 February 1949 Ronald Eames writes to Tolkien. He has not had a reply to his letter to Tolkien of 15 December 1938. If Allen & Unwin could have the duplicate corrected copy of *Farmer Giles of Ham*, they could proceed with typesetting.

19 February 1949 Tolkien, R.F.W. Fletcher, and F.P. Wilson, probably as the committee on matters referred by the General Board, draft a report for the English Faculty Board, apparently in response to a query from the General Board whether the English Faculty Board wished to reappoint the seven existing CUF Lecturers. They recommend reappointment of the existing Lecturers, but regret that the General Board is not allowing an increase in their number. The committee asks that the number of Lecturers allotted to the English Faculty be increased by six on 1 October 1949, and a further six as soon as possible.

23 February 1949 Douglas Veale informs Tolkien that the Visitatorial Board has agreed to grant him a leave of absence for Trinity Term 1949. He will enquire if the English Faculty Board thinks that a deputy should be appointed.

28 February 1949 Towards the end of February Tolkien has a brief rest and break at Downside Abbey, Stratton-on-the Fosse, near Bath, and replies to Ronald Eames from that address on 28 February. He explains that he does not have a duplicate corrected copy of *Farmer Giles of Ham* fit for the printers, only a copy on which he has entered all of the corrections and alterations, and he has no time to make another typescript. Allen & Unwin should retrieve from Pauline Baynes the copy he had retyped especially for the printers, and send her the unrevised copy. He adds: 'I am finding the labour of typing a fair copy of the "Lord of the Rings" v[ery] great, and the alternative of having it professionally typed prohibitive in cost. . . . I believe that after 25 years service I am shortly going to be granted a term of "sabbatical" leave, partly on medical grounds. If so, I may really finish a few things' (*Letters*, p. 132). He will later write to his Aunt Jane Neave, regarding *The Lord of the Rings* at this time: 'I then myself typed the *whole* of that work all VI books out, and then *once again* in revision (in places many times), mostly on my bed in the attic of the tiny terrace-house to which war had exiled us from the house in which my family had grown up' (8–9 September 1962, *Letters*, pp. 321–2). During this year Tolkien will spend much time in making a complete typescript of *The Lord of the Rings*, finishing only at the beginning of October. Inevitably he will make changes and additions as he proceeds.

Early March 1949 C.S. Lewis receives a parcel from one of his American correspondents on which Tolkien is noted as an alternative recipient. Assuming that it contains only items of food, he sends it to Tolkien, whose wife has been in poor health, and who, unlike Lewis, is not a frequent recipient of food parcels from the United States. Lewis will later discover that the parcel also contains headed notepaper for his own use, which he retrieves from Tolkien.

1 March 1949 Ronald Eames writes to Tolkien. He will ask Pauline Baynes to return her copy of *Farmer Giles of Ham*, and he will check it with the other copy to be sure it is the corrected one, then pass the latter to the printers.

2 March 1949 Tolkien, R.F.W. Fletcher, and F.P. Wilson sign Temporary Regulations for the Shortened Final Honour School for the years 1949–51. (The Shortened Final Honour School is for students whose studies were interrupted by the war, and who wish to acquire a degree. Changes are needed as English Sections will no longer be offered after Trinity Term 1949, nor unclassified Honour School passes.)

6 March 1949 From this date paper for books in Britain is no longer subject to licences or quotas, though is still not in ample supply.

Mid-March 1949 During Hilary term, for the first time, undergraduates in the English School are required to sit a Preliminary Examination in English Language and Literature.

11 March 1949 Tolkien attends an English Faculty Board meeting, during which he takes over the chair from R.F.W. Fletcher. The report of the committee (of which Tolkien is a member) on changes in the regulations for examinations under the supervision of the Board as a result of the withdrawal after Trinity Term 1949 of the English sections (of the war degree) is presented and agreed with emendations. Tolkien tells the Board that he does not propose to take sabbatical leave in Trinity Term, so there is no need to consider whether a deputy is needed in his stead. The Applications Committee has appointed Tolkien and Alistair Campbell examiners of the B.Litt. thesis of Ursula Mary Brown (later Ursula Dronke) of Somerville College, *An Edition of Þorgils and Haflið (from Stirlinga Saga)*. – Tolkien replies to a Miss R. Turnbull, who has sent him a fan letter. He remembers meeting her in the rooms of John Beckwith (presumably the John Beckwith who read Modern and Medieval History' at Exeter College before the Second World War). He will send her copies of *Farmer Giles of Ham* and *The Lord of the Rings* when they are published. He asks her, as a favour, to arrange for flowers to be sent at his expense to Mother Mary Michael to mark her diamond jubilee as a nun: she had befriended Tolkien when he was in hospital in 1917, and is now in a nursing home in Whitby. – Ronald Eames sends Tolkien forty-four illustrations by Pauline Baynes for *Farmer Giles of Ham*, twelve more than required. He asks for Tolkien's comments, and suggestions for which pictures might be omitted. Baynes has suggested which incidents in the story the colour plates should depict, referring to page numbers in the typescript. He hopes that Tolkien can deal with the matter quickly, so that Allen & Unwin can produce the book for Christmas.

12 March 1949 Hilary Full Term ends.

14 March 1949 Tolkien attends a Merton College meeting. He is appointed to a committee on research fellowships.

15 March 1949 Clothes rationing ends in Britain.

16 March 1949 Tolkien writes to Ronald Eames. He is pleased with Pauline Baynes' illustrations for *Farmer Giles of Ham* 'beyond even the expectations aroused by the first examples. They are more than illustrations, they are a collateral theme. I showed them to my friends whose polite comment was that they reduced my text to a commentary on the drawings' (*Letters*, p. 133). So far he can bear to think of losing only two of the forty-four pictures. He cannot work out the subjects suggested for colour illustrations, since the typescript he has retained has a different pagination; but he has every confidence in Baynes' selection. He will try to return the originals to Allen & Unwin the following day.

?17 March 1949 Tolkien posts Pauline Baynes' art for *Farmer Giles of Ham* to Allen & Unwin, and asks for her address.

18 March 1949 Hugh Brogan's mother writes to Tolkien, evidently in response to a letter Tolkien wrote suggesting that he visit Hugh while he is in Cambridge. Mrs Brogan replies that he will be welcome at any time, but suggests tea on Sunday.

19–20 March 1949 Tolkien visits Cambridge, presumably on business.

20 March 1949 Tolkien has tea with Hugh Brogan and his family. A letter written by Hugh Brogan several years later refers to Tolkien falling down the stairs during his visit.

21 March 1949 Ronald Eames writes to Tolkien. He is glad that Tolkien is satisfied, and gives him Pauline Baynes' address. They can leave for a while the question of which drawings to omit; they might be able to find ways of reducing production costs so that most can be included.

26 March 1949 In the evening, Tolkien attends a dinner of The Society hosted by John Sparrow in the hall of All Souls College, Oxford. Twelve members and one guest are present.

End of March 1949 C.S. Lewis lends *The Lion, the Witch and the Wardrobe* to Roger Lancelyn Green. Shortly after this, Tolkien meets Green and remarks: 'I hear you've been reading Jack's children's story. It really won't do you know! I mean to say: "*Nymphs and their Ways. The Love-Life of a Faun*". Doesn't he know what he's talking about?' (quoted in Roger Lancelyn Green and Walter Hooper, *C.S. Lewis: A Biography* (rev. edn. 2002), p. 307).

Beginning of April 1949 Tolkien attends a conference of English professors in Edinburgh. His daughter Priscilla accompanies him. They stay at the Invertiel Hotel in Blacket Place, Edinburgh, but are entertained by Tolkien's former student Angus McIntosh and his family.

?4 April 1949 Hugh Brogan writes to Tolkien, giving personal and family news. The letter is forwarded to Tolkien in Edinburgh.

8 April 1949 Ronald Eames sends Tolkien two sets of galley proofs of *Farmer Giles of Ham* and the typescript of the work, and asks him to return the printer's marked set with his own corrections as quickly as possible.

21 April 1949 Tolkien attends a Merton College meeting.

23 April 1949 Tolkien sends his apologies for not attending an Early English Text Society Committee meeting. At the meeting it is agreed that the Committee should henceforward be called the Council, and the *Ancrene Riwle* sub-committee should be the *Ancrene Riwle* Committee.

24 April 1949 Trinity Full Term begins. Tolkien's only scheduled lecture series for this term is on *Sawles Warde* on Wednesdays at 11.00 a.m. in the Examination Schools, beginning 27 April. He will continue to supervise B.Litt. students Auvo Kurvinen and Celia Sisam, and probationer B.Litt. student Anne Wakefield.

25 April 1949 Ronald Eames sends Tolkien the first of two coloured illustrations for *Farmer Giles of Ham* for his approval. Pauline Baynes has said that she can change the colours if Tolkien does not like the blue and brown she has used. Eames hopes that the proofreading is not proving difficult; the line blocks for the text are being made and as soon as he has the block pulls he will prepare a complete paste-up so that page proofs can be made.

27 April 1949 D.M. Davin, Assistant Secretary and Academic Publisher at Oxford University Press, writes to Kenneth Sisam. Davin will try to find a tactful way to approach Tolkien about his promised work on the E.V. Gordon edition of *Pearl*. Tolkien has not yet answered a letter about the Tolkien-Gordon edition of *Sir Gawain and the Green Knight*: if he does not reply in the next few days with any corrections he may have, the Press will proceed with a reprint without them. Davin has recently read the file on the Clarendon Chaucer and sympathizes with Sisam's struggles over that still unfinished project. He thinks that it would be best to meet with Tolkien to talk about these matters.

2 May 1949 Tolkien certifies that Auvo Kurvinen has pursued the required course of research for her B.Litt.

4 May 1949 Tolkien writes to Ronald Eames.

It is unfortunate that 'Farmer Giles' should come to the boil at the most impossible time of the year (for a professor). The Spring 'Vacation' is normally fully occupied: it is the period not only of professorial conferences, but of the industry of setting the papers for all the great network of exams, in which examinee and examiner alike struggle entoiled.

The galley-proofs arrived while I was away (conference), and when I returned I returned to papers and a situation made worse by being ill: I picked up a germ somewhere. [Tolkien-George Allen & Unwin archive, HarperCollins]

He has been able to look at the proofs only in the last day or two, and now returns the marked set. He has made few corrections, one of them the alteration of 'boots' in referring to the giant, which has bare feet in Pauline Baynes' illustrations. He notes that the dedication, title-page, and foreword are not included. He approves the colour illustration, though he had hoped it would have more colour. If it has to be limited to only two colours, he prefers the existing brown and blue scheme to other suggestions.

11 May 1949 Ronald Eames writes to thank Tolkien for returning the galley proofs. He will do a paste-up with the illustrations in the next few weeks and submit it to Tolkien for his approval. Allen & Unwin cannot afford more colours, but by using only two in the two plates, they can include most of Pauline Baynes' line drawings, which will make the book longer.

12 May 1949 Tolkien writes to Douglas Veale. His letter of 10 February had been only an enquiry, not an application. He had hoped to apply for two terms of leave, including Trinity Term, but it has proved impossible to drop or transfer his various duties and commitments so quickly. He would now like to apply for leave of absence during Michaelmas Term 1949 and Hilary Term 1950. He states: 'I have been for some time in indifferent health, but I do not apply primarily on medical grounds, since the treatment recommended me could, I hope, be taken during that part of the Long Vacation not occupied by examinations. I should hope to spend the period of leave, here and in other universities of Great Britain, mainly in writing and the completion of certain pieces of unfinished work' (Oxford University Archives FA 9/2/875). – Tolkien also writes a personal letter to Veale, thanking him for his kindness in regard to the earlier applications and explaining more fully why he has not been able to take the leave in Trinity Term granted by the Visitatorial Board: 'At the end of last term, when the matter came before the English Board, it had become clear that I could not get free; there were many duties and commitments that could not be dropped or transferred so quickly: teaching, supervision of research-students, theses and other examinations, and departmental matters (made more urgent by the pillaging of the linguistic staff to supply the universities of Scotland)' (Oxford University Archives FA 9/2/875; Norman Davis resigned his Oxford lectureship for a chair at Glasgow).

18 May 1949 Tolkien attends a Merton College meeting. – A Cambridge don writes to tell Tolkien that he will not be attending an Ad Eundem dinner on 9 July (*Societies and clubs).

19 May 1949 Ronald Eames sends Tolkien a paste-up of *Farmer Giles of Ham* and asks if he has any suggestions. He requests Tolkien to return the paste-up as soon as possible.

26 May 1949 Douglas Veale writes to Tolkien. The Visitatorial Board has granted his request for leave.

27 May 1949 Ronald Eames sends Tolkien Pauline Baynes' original art for the frontispiece to *Farmer Giles of Ham*. He asks for Tolkien's comments and the immediate return of the drawing, as there is an opening to have the two plates reproduced at a reasonable price if they put the job in hand almost at once. He gently reminds Tolkien that he has not yet commented on the paste-up.

28 May 1949 In the evening, Tolkien hosts a dinner of The Society at Merton College. Five members are present.

1 June 1949 Tolkien returns the paste-up to Ronald Eames and apologizes for holding it so long. He thinks that the illustrations have suffered from reduction. He is delighted with the design for the second colour plate, which he is returning under separate cover.

2 June 1949 Ronald Eames writes to thank Tolkien for returning the paste-up and the illustration.

4 June 1949 Tolkien writes to Pauline Baynes to express his great pleasure in her illustrations for *Farmer Giles of Ham*, and his regret that they suffer greatly in being drastically reduced for publication. He has a 'long romance in sequel to "The Hobbit"' which he has just completed and is being typed (i.e. *The Lord of the Rings*). It is held up at the moment, while he deals with examinations and other business, but he hopes that she will agree to look at it when the typing is done, presumably with a view to providing illustrations (courtesy of Mrs Pauline Gasch). (Tolkien is not an Examiner for the Oxford English School this year, but is acting as an external examiner for various other universities.)

7 June 1949 Tolkien recommends Anne Wakefield as a full B.Litt. student. The subject of her thesis is to be 'some new words and word patterns in early Modern English'.

8 June 1949 Tolkien signs the report of the Committee on Invitations to Lecture.

9 June 1949 English Final Honour School Examinations begin.

13 June 1949 Tolkien visits D.M. Davin at Oxford University Press. He feels that would be a great relief if he could hand over the Clarendon Chaucer, if someone could be found to take it on. Not much remains to be done with it, mainly the finishing off of notes. Tolkien intends to use sabbatical leave to clear up his obligations, including a revision of the Tolkien-Gordon *Sir Gawain and the Green Knight* and completion of E.V. Gordon's *Pearl*, of which only half of the glossary remains to do. Davin welcomes the idea of Tolkien handing over the Chaucer, while Tolkien promises to gather together the materials for the book and send them to the Press together with a list of people who might be able to carry the book through.

16 June 1949 Ronald Eames sends to Tolkien Pauline Baynes' design for the dust-jacket for *Farmer Giles of Ham*, with a few sketches of possible alternatives. He suggests the colours and lettering that might be used on the jacket, and perhaps a design of small repeated dragons on the endpapers.

17 June 1949 Tolkien attends an English Faculty Board meeting. J.A.W. Bennett is appointed Anne Wakefield's supervisor during Tolkien's sabbatical leave. No substitute is appointed for Celia Sisam: either Tolkien will continue to supervise her, or she works without supervision. The Board decides that it would be desirable to appoint deputies during Tolkien's leave of absence, and it is agreed to suggest that C.T. Onions (if possible) should be appointed to deal with Medieval Texts, and *E.J. Dobson for Modern English. The Board does not realize, however, that the cost of official deputies according to statute would have to be deducted from Tolkien's salary. After this becomes known in July, R.F.W. Fletcher, as chairman, will withdraw the request for deputies and inform Tolkien, asking him to inform Onions and Dobson in turn.

18 June 1949 Trinity Full term ends. – Tolkien writes to Ronald Eames that he is 'in the last throes of exams', and will be leaving in a few days to examine the colleges of the National University of Ireland (Ollscoil na hÉireann), so has not had time to ponder the various suggestions made by Pauline Baynes. But he does not think that they could improve on her dust-jacket design, and he would like a pattern of small dragons for the endpapers (produced by Baynes for the published book). He is returning the dust-jacket design separately to Allen & Unwin.

22 June–5 July 1949 Tolkien visits the Republic of Ireland for the first time, acting as Extern Examiner for the Summer Examinations at the National University of Ireland. The candidates' papers are presumably sent to him in Oxford for marking, while the visits are to conduct vivas and to consult with other examiners. (In years in which he is Extern Examiner, i.e. 1949–51, 1954, ?1956, and 1958–9, Tolkien will make two journeys to Ireland each year, usually in late June or July, and in late September to early October, and while there visits University Colleges in Dublin, Cork, and Galway, and Saint Patrick's College, Maynooth. On some of these visits he is accompanied by his son Christopher, and on more than one by his wife and his cousin Marjorie Incledon.)

27 June 1949 Ronald Eames sends to Tolkien two sets of page proofs of *Farmer Giles of Ham* with the corrected galley proofs. If Tolkien can return these in the next few weeks, it should be possible to publish the book in good time for Christmas.

9 July 1949 Tolkien returns the page proofs to Ronald Eames and apologizes for his delay. He returned from Ireland only on 5 July, and immediately had to deal with more examinations (presumably for another institution). He has found little to correct in the page proofs, but it has occurred to him that the King's letters set in italics on pp. 20 and 54 would look better in black letter; 'but it is not a point of sufficient importance to bother about' (Tolkien-George Allen & Unwin archive, HarperCollins). He sees that *Farmer Giles of Ham* will be a very slim book, and wishes that he had the time and inspiration to write other legends of the Little Kingdom, especially one about Giles' son George and the 'pig boy' Suet. – In the evening, Tolkien probably attends an Ad Eundem dinner at Exeter College.

11 July 1949 Tolkien and Alistair Campbell examine Ursula Mary Brown *viva voce* at 11.00 a.m. in the Examination Schools on her B.Litt. thesis *An Edition of Þorgils and Haflið (from Stirlinga Saga)*.

12 July 1949 Ronald Eames writes to thank Tolkien for returning the corrected proofs. It had already occurred to Allen & Unwin that the passages in italics would be better in black letter, and as Tolkien's corrections are so few they have instructed the printer to make the change. He sends proofs of the dust-jacket and asks Tolkien to inform the publisher of any corrections or changes as soon as possible. They will use thick paper for the book to make it seem more substantial.

13 July 1949 Tolkien returns one of the dust-jacket proofs with his academic details corrected: 'I was "translated" to the see of Merton in 1945. I do not myself feel convinced that these academic titles are really in place; and I wonder whether some simpler statement such as *"is a professional philologist and student of the northern tongues"* would not be more in keeping.' He put a reference to further 'legends of the Little Kingdom' in the foreword to *Farmer Giles of Ham* 'in case they should ever come to anything, or a manuscript of the fragmentary legend come to light. But Georgius and Suet remains only a sketch, and it is difficult now to recapture the spirit of the former days when we used to beat the bounds of the L[ittle] K[ingdom] in an ancient car' (Tolkien-George Allen & Unwin archive, HarperCollins; partly printed in *Letters*, p. 133). When he is finally free of *The Lord of the Rings*, of which he has nearly completed a final fair copy, he might find himself able to do something.

15 July 1949 Tolkien and Alistair Campbell sign their report on Ursula Mary Brown's B.Litt. thesis.

16 July 1949 Ronald Eames writes to thank Tolkien for his approval of the dust-jacket. Allen & Unwin agree with his suggested change to the biographical details.

22 July 1949 Evidently Tolkien still has not informed C.T. Onions that he will not be required as a deputy lecturer. R.F.W. Fletcher writes to the Registrar that he will remind Tolkien to do so.

23 July 1949 Tolkien sends apologies to the Early English Text Society for not attending a meeting.

1 August 1949 Tolkien attends a Merton College meeting.

13 August 1949 Hugh Brogan writes to Tolkien from France about problems on the Brogan family holiday.

Summer 1949 Tolkien takes a holiday at Sidmouth or nearby Budleigh. While there he meets Miss R.W. How, probably Ruth Winifred How, author of *Friendly Farm* (1946), *Adventures at Friendly Farm* (1948), etc.

13 September 1949 Stanley Unwin sends Tolkien an advance copy of *Farmer Giles of Ham* and the £25.00 due him on publication.

?Late September–?early October 1949 Tolkien visits Ireland again to act as Extern Examiner in the Autumn Examinations of the National University.

October 1949 Tolkien finishes typing *The Lord of the Rings* and gives the complete typescript to C.S. Lewis to read.

6 October 1949 T.S. Gregory of the Talks Department, BBC, writes to Tolkien, asking him to speak on the Third Programme about the fourteenth-century author Richard Rolle. He asks if he may call on Tolkien to discuss the matter. Sent to Tolkien at 20 Northmoor Road, the letter will be returned to the BBC, sent to Pembroke College on 10 October, and a third time on 19 October to 3 Manor Road (but there is no reply from Tolkien in the BBC files).

9 October 1949 Michaelmas Full Term begins. Tolkien is on sabbatical leave.

10 October 1949 The letter from the BBC sent to Tolkien's old address on 6 October is returned and the same letter is sent again, this time addressed to Tolkien at Pembroke College.

20 October 1949 *Farmer Giles of Ham* is published by George Allen & Unwin.

24 October 1949 D.M. Davin writes to remind Tolkien that he had agreed to deliver to Oxford University Press his material for the Clarendon Chaucer.

27 October 1949 C.S. Lewis, having read *The Lord of the Rings*, writes a letter of appreciation to Tolkien. He comments that once the book 'really gets under weigh the steady upward slope of grandeur and terror (not unrelieved by green dells, without which it would indeed be intolerable) is almost unequalled in the whole range of narrative art known to me'. He thinks that it excels in sub-creation, construction, and *gravitas*. There are 'many passages I could wish you had written otherwise or omitted altogether. If I include none of my adverse criticisms in this letter that is because you have heard and rejected most of them already (*rejected* is perhaps too mild a word for your reaction on at least one occasion!)' but he feels that the splendour of the tale can carry these faults (quoted in *Biography*, p. 204; *see note*). Lewis has now passed the typescript to his brother Warnie to read. – At a meeting of the English Faculty Board, in Tolkien's absence, C.L. Wrenn is appointed to interview prospective advanced and probationer B.Litt. students while Tolkien is on leave.

?Autumn 1949 *Milton Waldman, a senior editor at the publisher Collins, who has been introduced to Tolkien by Gervase Mathew, expresses an interest in *The Lord of the Rings* and 'The Silmarillion'. Tolkien lends him legible parts of the latter, and Waldman says that he would like to publish it, if Tolkien would finish it. Although *The Lord of the Rings* has been written for publication by Allen & Unwin, Tolkien has begun to resent their rejection of 'The Silmarillion' in 1937, and has come increasingly to feel that *The Lord of the Rings* and 'The Silmarillion' should be published together; indeed, that the former needs the latter to make its full impact. He therefore looks favourably on the possible publication of both books by Collins.

2 November 1949 Tolkien attends a Merton College meeting.

12 November 1949 Tolkien sends a letter and an inscribed copy of *Farmer Giles of Ham* to Miss How, whom he had met on holiday during the summer. He mentions that he has two 'very large scale works accepted and nearly finished' (Sotheby's, *Catalogue of Valuable Autograph Letters, Literary Manuscripts and Historical Documents*, London, 21–22 July 1980, p. 338). These must be *The Lord of the Rings* and 'The Silmarillion': Tolkien's discussions with Milton Waldman, therefore, are presumably far advanced. – Warnie Lewis finishes reading *The Lord of the Rings*. 'Golly, what a book! The inexhaustible fertility of the man's imagination amazes me. . . . How the public will take the book I can't imagine; I should think T[olkien] will be wise to prepare himself for a good deal of misunderstanding, and many crit[ic]s on the lines that "this political satire would gain greatly by compression and the excision of such irrelevant episodes as the journey to Lothlorien"' (*Brothers and Friends*, p. 231).

?Late autumn 1949–?early 1950 Katharine Farrer writes to Tolkien. Both she and her husband are delighted to hear, as Tolkien has told them, that 'The Silmarillion' is to be published. She asks him about the origins of the name *Pantucker* and forwards a fan letter about *The Hobbit* from Oxford professor of religion L.W. Grensted.

Early December 1949 Tolkien writes to Stanley Unwin, expressing his approval of the appearance of *Farmer Giles of Ham* and praising Pauline Baynes. He sends his best wishes to Rayner Unwin, now attending Harvard University.

2 December 1949 At a meeting of the English Faculty Board, in Tolkien's absence, F.P. Wilson reports on behalf of the Monographs Committee (of which Tolkien is a member). Christopher Tolkien is accepted as a full B.Litt. student, with E.O.G. Turville-Petre as his supervisor.

3 December 1949 Michaelmas Full Term ends.

5 December 1949 Tolkien attends a Merton College meeting.

12 December 1949 For Christmas Tolkien sends his grandson, Michael George, two books 'written by a very nice lady that I met at Sidmouth' (British Library MS Add. 71657). These are probably the two *Friendly Farm* books by Miss R.W. How.

13 December 1949 Tolkien writes to Milton Waldman, discussing *The Lord of the Rings*.

18 December 1949 Tolkien writes to *Naomi Mitchison, who has praised *Farmer Giles of Ham* and apparently asked him about some Icelandic and Irish names. He comments on *Farmer Giles of Ham*: 'it was I fear written very light-heartedly, originally of a "no time" in which blunderbusses or anything might occur'. He hopes to give her soon two long books, one a sequel to *The Hobbit*, the other 'pure myth and legend of times already remote in Bilbo's days', i.e. *The Lord of the Rings* and 'The Silmarillion' (*Letters*, pp. 133–4).

19 December 1949 Stanley Unwin writes to Tolkien. He asks when the typescript of *The Lord of the Rings* will be ready.

20 December 1949 Tolkien writes to Pauline Baynes, wishing her a Happy Christmas and apologizing for not replying earlier to a letter she sent him in June. He has heard from C.S. Lewis, who is impressed with her work for *Farmer Giles of Ham*, and has been in touch with her (about illustrating *The Lion, the Witch, and the Wardrobe*). He himself has 'two (large) books of mythical, legendary, or elvish kind that should in 1950 actually becoming production problems; and I very much hope that some illustration or decorations will be part of the programme. In which case I hope we shall meet' (Marion E. Wade Center, Wheaton College, Wheaton, Illinois). He asks her to let him know if she is ever in Oxford.

?21–?24 December 1949 Pauline Baynes probably writes to Tolkien to say that she will be having lunch with C.S. Lewis in Oxford on 31 December.

25 December 1949 Tolkien writes to Pauline Baynes. If she has a moment to spare during her visit to Oxford on 31 December, not only he but his wife and daughter would like to meet her. He suggests that she cross the road from Magdalen College (where Lewis has rooms) to Merton College and have tea in Tolkien's room.

31 December 1949 Pauline Baynes has lunch with C.S. Lewis at Magdalen College. She has written to Tolkien, saying that she is not sure what time she would have and does not want to cause Tolkien any trouble. Tolkien leaves a letter for her with Lewis: he realizes that it might be difficult to fit in a visit if she has to drive home that afternoon, but 'of course if you do find yourself adrift with time to spare before you drive away, we shall be pleased to see you. Round the corner to my house is just as near as to my room in Merton. But you are not to feel in any way tied' (Marion E. Wade Center, Wheaton College, Wheaton, Illinois). – Stanley Unwin sends Tolkien a query he has received from G.E. Selby at the College of the Venerable Bede, Durham, about the 'Authentic history of Faery' which Tolkien is supposed to have written (but did not).

?Late 1949–1950 Tolkien returns to work on the *Lay of Leithian*, which he had left unfinished in 1931 and which had been rejected for publication by Allen & Unwin in 1937. He has received encouraging criticism from someone to whom he lent the work as it stands. The (unidentified) critic has noted that it is difficult to avoid monotony when writing in octosyllabic couplets, and that while Tolkien has been astonishingly successful in this regard, he had not been consistently so. Among other matters criticized is Tolkien's use of 'archaisms so archaic they needed annotation' and 'distorted order' (quoted in *The Lays of Beleriand*, p. 2). Tolkien now takes up the typescript and begins to revise the poem, but by the time he reaches Canto II he is virtually writing a new poem based on much preliminary drafting. The rewritten Canto II is about two-thirds longer than the original, and is divided in two. Tolkien continues this work a short way into the original Canto III. He writes out a fine decorated manuscript of almost the whole of this new version of the poem, making further changes in the process. He is still working on the poem in the spring of 1950: on one of the preliminary draft pages he draws a plan of 99 Holywell Street, the house to which he will move in May 1950. – At about this same time, Tolkien begins to write a prose version of the story of Beren and Lúthien, told at length, but so closely based on the new version of the *Lay of Leithian* that in places it is almost a prose paraphrase of the verse. He writes it on the verso pages of the 'later' *Annals of Beleriand*, but stops at the point where Dairon tells Thingol of Beren's presence in Doriath.

1950

1950s Tolkien translates five Catholic prayers (*'Words of Joy') into Quenya. He makes six texts of the *Pater Noster*, four of the *Ave Maria*, and one of the *Sub Tuum Praesidium*, and single unfinished texts of the *Gloria Patri* and the Litany of Loreto. On the verso of the postcard on which he writes one of the later versions of the Quenya *Pater Noster* Tolkien also writes a partial translation of the same prayer in Sindarin (*Ae Adar Nín: The Lord's Prayer in Sindarin*).

Early 1950s Tolkien writes the beginning of a story, *Tal-Elmar, which extends to only six typewritten pages, plus a rejected page of manuscript and typescript, before it is set aside.

?1950–May 1951 Now that Tolkien has hope for the publication of 'The Silmarillion' he turns his attention to that work. It is still in an unfinished state, and exists in various forms. He needs to decide what the published work should contain: whether he should include the tales of Beren and Lúthien, Túrin, and the Fall of Gondolin told at length as well as in the shorter versions included in the *Quenta Silmarillion*; and the *Annals of Aman* as well as the *Quenta Silmarillion*. During this period Tolkien works at various times on all of these texts, not necessarily consecutively, and has to transfer changes and developments made in one text into other texts covering the same material. As usual, Tolkien has difficulty in keeping the shorter forms, such as the entries in the *Annals*, within bounds; his entries tend to expand and grow towards the *Quenta Silmarillion* in length. One brief document headed 'Alterations in last revision 1951' contains a short list of names and their definitions.

Tolkien begins work on the *Quenta Silmarillion* by making corrections and additions to the original manuscript and the typescript (entitled *Eldanyárë*) which he had left unfinished c. 1937–8. The amount of work varies from chapter to chapter, according to how much his ideas have evolved. Throughout he makes subtle changes in events and wording; he rewrites some parts several times before he is satisfied. He revises most heavily, usually making new manuscripts or typescripts, the chapters 'Of Valinor and the Two Trees', 'Of the Coming of the Elves' (which still includes what became 'Of Thingol and Melian'), and 'Of Men and Dwarves' (with a new title, 'Of the Naugrim and the Edain'). By 10 May 1951 he revises the *Quenta Silmarillion* as far as the end of the chapter 'The Wolf-hunt of Carcharoth'. It is probably at this time that he copies into the earlier manuscript of the *Quenta Silmarillion* the material from the two manuscripts he had written while the main *Quenta Silmarillion* was being considered by Allen & Unwin (see entry for 15 November–19 December 1937). He makes no addition to continue the story of Túrin from where he had abandoned it in 1937. In 1951–2 an amanuensis typescript will be made of the revised *Quenta Silmarillion*, paginated continuously with the rewritten *Ainulindalë*. – Probably also in this period Tolkien makes a few pencil corrections on the two *Ambarkanta* diagrams of 'Ilu' to reflect changes in cosmology and terminology.

1950–1951 At some time during these years the Tolkiens are visited in Oxford by Marjorie Hadley, Tolkien's cousin from British Columbia (daughter of Florence Hadley, *née* Tolkien).

Early January 1950 Milton Waldman writes to Tolkien, expressing delight in *The Lord of the Rings*. Although he is worried by its length, he would like to publish it if Tolkien has 'no commitment either moral or legal to Allen & Unwin' (quoted in *Letters*, p. 134).

10 January 1950 Tolkien's Oxford colleague *Helen Gardner writes to him, enclosing a message from an admirer, Richard Duncan-Jones, whose sister's autograph book Tolkien inscribed at a party held by Gardner.

15 January 1950 Hilary Full Term begins. Tolkien is on sabbatical leave.

28 January 1950 Tolkien receives a fan letter about *The Hobbit* from a child relative of Marjorie Incledon.

5 February 1950 Tolkien writes to Milton Waldman explaining his position in regard to *The Lord of the Rings*. In a draft of the letter he says that he believes that he has

> no *legal* obligation to Allen & Unwin, since the clause in *The Hobbit* contract with regard to offering the next book seems to have been satisfied either (a) by their rejection of *The Silmarillion* or (b) by their eventual acceptance and publication of *Farmer Giles*. I should . . . be glad to leave them, as I have found them in various ways unsatisfactory. But I have friendly personal relations with Stanley (whom all the same I do not much like) and with his second son Rayner (whom I do like very much).

And since *The Lord of the Rings* has always been considered a sequel to *The Hobbit*, he thinks that he may have a moral obligation to Allen & Unwin. But he will try to extricate himself from that publisher 'or at least the *Silmarillion* and all its kin' (*Letters*, p. 135).

8 February 1950 Tolkien attends a Merton College meeting.

11 February 1950 In the evening, Tolkien attends a dinner of The Society hosted by R.W. Chapman at Magdalen College. Fifteen members are present. Chapman reads an account of his stewardship of The Society from 1924 to 1949.

14 February 1950 The Oxford Dante Society meets. After dinner in the Oscar Wilde Room at Magdalen College, Sir Cyril Hushwood reads a paper, 'The Mighty World of Eye and Ear'.

16 February 1950 Tolkien possibly attends a meeting of teachers concerned with linguistic and medieval subjects at 2.00 p.m. in the Examination Schools, to discuss special subjects in the Final Honour syllabus of the English School.

24 February 1950 Tolkien writes to Stanley Unwin. He is 'at present "on leave", and away off and on; though the effort to cope with a mass of literary and "learned" debts, that my leave was supposed to assist, has proved too much for me, especially as I have been troubled with my throat and have felt often far from well.' For eighteen months he has been hoping for the day when he could call *The Lord of the Rings* finished; 'but it was not until after Christmas that this goal was reached at last. It is finished, if still partly unrevised, and is, I suppose, in a condition which a reader could read, if he did not wilt at the sight of it.' Because he cannot afford a professional typist, he has typed nearly all of it himself.

And now I look at it, the magnitude of the disaster is apparent to me. My work has escaped from my control, and I have produced a monster: an immensely long, complex, rather bitter, and very terrifying romance, quite unfit for children (if fit for anybody); and it is not really a sequel to *The Hobbit*, but to *The Silmarillion*. My estimate is that it contains, even without certain necessary adjuncts, about 600,000 words. . . . I can see only too clearly how impracticable this is. But I am tired. It is off my chest, and I do not feel that I can do anything more about it, beyond a little revision of inaccuracies. Worse still: I feel that it is tied to the *Silmarillion*. . . .

Ridiculous and tiresome as you may think me, I want to publish them both – *The Silmarillion* and *The Lord of the Rings* – in conjunction or in connexion . . . that is what I should like. Or I will let it all be. I cannot contemplate any drastic re-writing or compression. . . . But I shall not have any just grievance (nor shall I be dreadfully surprised) if you decline so obviously unprofitable a proposition. . . .

He wonders how 'little *Farmer Giles* [is] doing' (*Letters*, pp. 135–7).

?Early March 1950 Merton College offers Tolkien 99 Holywell Street, an old house with a secluded garden bounded by part of the old city wall, which divides it from New College.

6 March 1950 Stanley Unwin writes to Tolkien. To publish both *The Silmarillion* and *The Lord of the Rings* would be difficult, especially with the costs of book production three times what they were before the war. Unwin asks if there is any possibility of 'breaking the million words into, say, three or four to some extent self-contained volumes' (Tolkien-George Allen & Unwin archive, HarperCollins; quoted by Tolkien, *Letters*, p. 139). Over 2,000 copies of the first printing of 5,000 of *Farmer Giles of Ham* have been sold, but it has not yet done as well as they hoped.

7 March 1950 The Society of Authors invites Tolkien to become a member.

9 March 1950 Tolkien begins to have his diseased teeth removed.

10 March 1950 Tolkien replies to Stanley Unwin's suggestion of 6 March. He explains that 'a work of great length can, of course, be divided artificially'.

But the whole Saga of the Three Jewels and the Rings of Power has only one natural division into two parts . . . : *The Silmarillion* and other legends; and *The Lord of the Rings*. The latter is as indivisible and unified as I could make it.

It is, of course, divided into sections for narrative purposes (six of them), and two or three of these, which are of more or less equal length, could be bound separately, but they are not in any sense self-contained. [*Letters*, p. 138]

He wonders if many beyond his friends would read, or purchase, so long a work. He realizes the financial difficulties, and would not feel aggrieved should Allen & Unwin decline. He would be more encouraged if *Farmer Giles of Ham* had sold better; it does not seem to him to have been well promoted. 'I have not at the moment anything else completed to submit; but I am quite prepared to make something simpler and shorter soon. I feel, at the end of my leave of absence, a return of energy, and when the present time of trial is over (the process of removing all my teeth began yesterday, and that of removing my household goods begins shortly) I hope to feel still more' (*Letters*, p. 138). – Later Tolkien writes to Milton Waldman of Collins, telling him of Unwin's letter and his own reply. He hopes that Unwin will abandon *The Lord of the Rings* and 'The Silmarillion' without asking for the manuscripts 'and two months for "reading". . . . But time runs short. I shall soon be plunged back into business – I already am involved, as I find things getting very out of hand during my absence; and I shall not be free again for writing until I return from Ireland at the beginning of July' (*Letters*, pp. 139–40). He will be moving to 99 Holywell Street as soon as repairs to that house are finished, but he does not expect to be settled in before St George's Day (23 April). – At a meeting of the English Faculty Board, in Tolkien's absence, proposals for a review of the regulations governing linguistic and medieval studies are presented. The Applications Committee has admitted E.J. Stormon of Campion Hall as an advanced student to work on a D.Phil., with Tolkien as his supervisor. Stormon's thesis is *A Study of the Symbolism of Spiritual Renewal with Special Reference to The Pearl and The Final Plays of Shakespeare*.

11 March 1950 Hilary Full Term ends.

13 March 1950 Tolkien attends a Merton College meeting.

2 April 1950 Tolkien writes to Stanley Unwin, asking for a reply to his letter of 10 March. He would like to have a decision about *The Lord of the Rings* and 'The Silmarillion' before he enters 'a period of absorbing business and examination-preparation' (Tolkien-George Allen & Unwin archive, HarperCollins). He comments on a letter by Unwin published in the *Sunday Times*. He is afraid that his fantasies seem very remote and unimportant. (This will cross with a letter from Unwin to Tolkien written the following day.)

3 April 1950 Stanley Unwin writes to Tolkien, calling his attention to an article about *The Hobbit* and its author in the magazine *Junior Bookshelf*. Unwin is still studying the problem of how *The Lord of the Rings* might be published. To print 2,500 copies in two large volumes, each of 1392 pages, 'would involve an outlay of well over £5,000, and each volume would actually cost for paper, printing, and binding, without allowing anything for overheads, author or publisher, about 22/-' (Tolkien-George Allen & Unwin archive, Harper-Collins). He has asked his son Rayner, who is now at Harvard, for his opinion on the matter, and now sends Tolkien a copy of Rayner's reply, pointing out that it had not been intended for Tolkien's eyes, and that Tolkien should bear in mind that Rayner has never seen 'The Silmarillion' or the reader's report on it. Rayner had written:

The Lord of the Rings is a very great book in its own curious way and deserves to be produced somehow. *I* never felt the lack of a *Silmarillion* when reading it. But although he claims not to contemplate any drastic rewriting, etc., surely this is a case for an editor who would incorporate any *really* relevant material from *The Silmarillion* into *The Lord of the Rings* without increasing the enormous bulk of the latter and, if feasible, even cutting it. Tolkien wouldn't do it, but someone whom he would trust and who had sympathy (one of his sons?) might possibly do it. If this is not workable I would say publish *The Lord of the Rings* as a prestige book, and after having a second look at it, drop *The Silmarillion*. [quoted in *Biography*, p. 210]

When Tolkien reads this, he is furious, though he cannot understand why it was been sent to him since it seemed to reveal Allen & Unwin's real intentions.

4 April 1950 In the morning, Tolkien rings Warnie Lewis and asks him to meet at the 'Bird and Baby' after Tolkien has visited his dentist to be fitted with a set of false teeth. *See note.* – Stanley Unwin replies to Tolkien's letter of 2 April. He considers Tolkien's fantasies to be important and likely to endure, but taxation has deprived Allen & Unwin of the reserves they had once used to finance commercially difficult but worthwhile books like Tolkien's.

14 April 1950 Tolkien drafts a reply to Stanley Unwin's letter of 3 April. As he understands the situation, Allen & Unwin are willing to take *The Lord of the Rings*,

> but that is more than enough, and you do not want any trimmings; certainly not *The Silmarillion* which you have no intention of genuinely reconsidering. A rejection is after all a rejection, and remains valid. But the question of 'dropping' *The Silmarillion*, after a discreet feint, and taking *The Lord of the Rings* (edited) just does not arise. I have not offered, am not offering *The Lord of the Rings* to you, or anyone else, on such conditions – as surely I made plain before. I want a decision, yes or no: to the proposal I made: and not to any imagined possibility. [quoted in *Biography*, p. 210]

He then writes a less confrontational letter, but still includes an ultimatum as in the draft. He is puzzled why Unwin sent him Rayner's letter since it seems 'to reveal policy a little nakedly'. He has concluded that Unwin agrees with Rayner's opinion, and thinks that sending it 'was a good way of telling me what is the most I can hope for'. He apologizes for his delay in replying: 'I have been troubled by dentist and doctors since you wrote. I do not yet know the full report of the specialist and X-ray; but I gather that my throat is in a bad way. Still when all my teeth are at last out (four more went today) it may improve a little, and I may hope to escape any immediate operation. That is at any rate a more cheerful prospect than I had begun to envisage' (Tolkien-George Allen & Unwin archive, HarperCollins; partly printed in *Letters*, p. 141).

15 April 1950 Tolkien attends an Early English Text Society Council meeting at Magdalen College.

17 April 1950 Stanley Unwin writes to Tolkien. He is sorry that Tolkien felt it necessary to present an ultimatum, 'particularly one in connection with a manuscript which I have never seen in its final and complete form. We have not even had an opportunity of checking whether it does in fact run to one million, two hundred thousand words. . . . As you demand an *immediate* "yes" or "no" the answer is "no"; but it might well have been yes given adequate time and the sight of the complete typescript.' He regrets having sent Rayner's letter, and points out that Rayner has no say in decision-making and will be very disappointed. He personally admires and believes in Tolkien's genius, and

> had settled in my own mind that some way would be found of carrying out your wishes, and am bitterly disappointed to find myself pushed into such an embarrassing position with regard to it. But as Goethe remarked, 'it is the property of true genius to disturb all settled ideas'. So with sorrow I must perforce leave it at that, except to say how sincerely I pray that you may have a speedy and complete recovery from your present ailments, and invite you to remember that I am always ready to renew the search for 'ways and means'. [Tolkien-George Allen & Unwin archive, HarperCollins; partly quoted in *Biography*, p. 210]

?Second half of April 1950 Tolkien is able to tell Milton Waldman that *The Lord of the Rings* is free of any entanglements. Waldman arranges for Tolkien to visit Collins' offices in London to discuss publication.

20 April 1950 Tolkien attends a Merton College meeting. He is appointed a member of a committee to devise an inscription for a memorial tablet to A.B. Burney.

23 April 1950 Trinity Full Term begins. Tolkien's only scheduled lecture series for this term is Outlines of English Linguistic History on Wednesdays and Fridays at 11.00 a.m. in the Examination Schools, beginning 26 April. He will continue to supervise B.Litt. students Celia Sisam and Anne Wakefield, and will begin to supervise D.Phil. student E.J. Stormon.

29 April 1950 Tolkien signs the interim report of the standing committee for matters referred by the General Board on the Quinquennial Grant 1952–7, together with the other two committee members.

May 1950–end of 1950 Staff at the publisher Collins consider *The Lord of the Rings*. Milton Waldman visits Tolkien in Oxford to tell him that the work must be cut. Tolkien is dismayed; he says that he will try to comply, but appears never even to have begun such work. Soon after his visit, Milton Waldman leaves for Italy where he lives much of the year, and then falls ill, leaving *The Lord of the Rings* and the still unfinished 'Silmarillion' in the hands of someone at Collins who does not have Waldman's enthusiasm for them. By the end of 1950 nothing is settled about their publication.

May 1950 Tolkien, Edith, and Priscilla move into 99 Holywell at some time between 1 May, when they were still at Manor Road, and 28 May. But for much of the year, Priscilla is resident at Lady Margaret Hall. – Celia Sisam writes to Tolkien to thank him for seeing her while in the midst of moving into his new house. She sends him proof sheets of an article related to her B.Litt. thesis, 'The Scribal Tradition of the Lambeth Homilies', to appear in the *Review of English Studies*. Tolkien will write detailed corrections and annotations on the proof, but he will not be acknowledged in the article when it is published in April 1951.

5 May 1950 Tolkien attends an English Faculty Board meeting. The Board appoints Tolkien and F.P. Wilson to be its representatives in any discussions with the General Board about the Special Faculties Library. The report on the Quinquennial Grant 1952–7 is presented and discussed, and changes suggested. The Applications Committee has appointed Tolkien supervisor of the D.Phil. thesis of R. Vleeskruyer of St Catherine's College, *The Old English Life of St Chad*, and of Peter Goolden of Trinity College, a probationer B.Litt. student.

17 May 1950 Tolkien attends a Merton College meeting.

20 May 1950 In the evening, Tolkien attends a dinner of The Society hosted by J.R.H. Weaver at Trinity College, Oxford. Fourteen members are present. Weaver introduces a discussion on the preservation and exhibition of college treasures.

26 May 1950 Petrol rationing ends in Britain.

?June 1950 Tolkien completes further revisions to E.V. Gordon's edition of *Pearl*. He returns the work to Ida Gordon, who will now prepare it for publication.

5 June 1950 Tolkien, R.F.W. Fletcher, and F.P. Wilson sign an amended application for the Quinquennial Grant 1952–7 for the Board of the Faculty of English Language and Literature.

8 June 1950 In reply to a memorandum by C.L. Wrenn presented to the English Faculty Board concerning the Quinquennial Grant, Tolkien produces a typescript of four and one-half pages. Wrenn has proposed the establishment of a Chair of General Linguistics and the English Language, the establishment, or revival, of a Readership in Phonetics, and the provision of capital and grants to make Oxford University one of the centres of the Dialect Survey of Great Britain; and he seeks the provision of secretarial help, lacking at Oxford, for professors and faculty board chairmen who ought to be employed in research and teaching rather than clerical duties. Tolkien replies that if there is a need for a Chair of General Linguistics at Oxford it should not be

> attached to any one department that is primarily concerned with a literary language. Our school, the main business of which is the history of written and cultivated English (in periods antecedent to the student's life-time), could not, without a revolution which I would resist, accommodate as a professor a person who, by definition, is not to be concerned

with historical philology, and will use current English merely as his 'illustrative material', on the assumption that it is the common possession of 'all the relevant faculties'.

He supports a Readership in Phonetics 'as long as it is clear that it has no special connection with the English School; and as long as the case is not supported by assertions that misrepresent its intrinsic importance, and its usefulness to literary and philological studies.' As to the Dialect Survey, he thinks that

as we have spent some hundreds of years in raising our language out of the cow-byres and hedgerows, I have no special desire to see members of the School of English Language and Literature spending their time in what is left of those primitive haunts. I would not, of course, bar the way home for those who are seized with a *nostalgie de la boue*; but I should prefer them to be offered some education first. . . . Nothing could be more improper than the intrusion of dialectology and its field-work into an honours school of language and letters. When this has occurred it has proved highly deleterious. One result is to drive a wedge between the partnership of language and literature; another is that the students on the 'language' side are stinted of their proper education (even philologically considered), and while studying what is fugitive, barbarous, or vestigial, cease to be directed to the more humane parts of their own curriculum. . . . [Oxford University Archives FA 4/5/2/10]

He thinks that such matters should be supported by the Philological Society, not the University. – Tolkien approves the admission of Peter Goolden as a B.Litt. student to work on the thesis on the Old English version of the story of Apollonius of Tyre. – English Final Honour School Examinations begin.

16 June 1950 Tolkien attends an English Faculty Board meeting. Wrenn's memorandum and Tolkien's observations thereon are considered. It is agreed to reply to the General Board that the Faculty Board does not approve of a Chair of General Linguistics and the English Language as outlined in Wrenn's memorandum, but thinks that an appointment for the study of linguistics, especially on the philosophic side, is desirable but should not be attached to any one school; that a Readership in Phonetics is desirable but should not be attached to any one school; and that the Dialect Survey undertaken by the English Philological Society should not be a concern of the Board or the University. The standing committee (of which Tolkien is a member) on matters referred from the General Board is asked to discuss with the General Board the Quinquennial Grant application. The Applications Committee has approved Peter Goolden as a B.Litt. student and appointed C.L. Wrenn as his supervisor. It has also appointed Tolkien and Wrenn examiners of the D.Phil. thesis of E.J. Dobson of Merton College, *English Pronunciation 1500–1700 According to the Evidence of the English Orthoepists*.

17 June 1950 Trinity Full Term ends.

20 June 1950 Tolkien attends a Merton College meeting.

21 June 1950 Encaenia.

24 June 1950 Tolkien attends an Early English Text Society Council meeting at Magdalen College, Oxford.

25 June 1950 Forces from North Korea enter South Korea. Great Britain will soon become involved with other members of the United Nations in pushing back the invaders.

Late June–early July 1950 Tolkien probably travels to Ireland, where he is again Extern Examiner for the National University of Ireland.

21 July 1950 Ida Gordon writes to Tolkien, asking him to help with one or two points in the notes to *Pearl*, in some cases because she is unsure if she has read his handwriting correctly. The Secretary of the Clarendon Press (Oxford University Press) would like to have the completed work in hand before the beginning of October.

Late July or early August 1950 Tolkien replies to Ida Gordon.

26 July 1950 W.N. Beard of George Allen & Unwin writes to Tolkien. In order to fill an order from the Houghton Mifflin, Allen & Unwin need to reprint *The Hobbit* quickly. The corrections Tolkien sent some time ago have been incorporated. Beard is sending him proofs to check.

28 July 1950 Tolkien writes to inform Beard that he is about to go away until 31 July, but will try to deal with the proofs and send them off the day he returns.

1 August 1950 Tolkien returns the proofs of *The Hobbit* to W.N. Beard. There was little to correct in them, but they needed some consideration.

> It is now a long while since I sent in the proposed alteration of Chapter V, and tentatively suggested this slight remodelling of the original *Hobbit*. I was then still engaged in trying to fit on the sequel, which would have been a simpler task with the alteration, besides saving most of a chapter in that overlong work. However, I never heard any more about it at all; and I assumed that alteration of the original book was ruled out. The sequel now depends on the earlier version; and if the revision is really published, there must follow some considerable rewriting of the sequel. I must say that I could wish that I had had some hint that (in any circumstances) this change might be made, before it burst on me in page-proof. However, I have now made up my mind to accept the change and its consequences. The thing is now old enough for me to take a fairly impartial view, and it seems to me that the revised version is in itself better, in motive and narrative – and certainly would make the sequel (if ever published) much more natural. . . . Also, will it be noted in any way that this is a *revised* ed[itio]n or reprint? I take it that this alteration will at first only be on sale in the USA? But any subsequent reprintings for sale in G.B. [Great Britain] will follow suit? [Tolkien-George Allen & Unwin archive, HarperCollins; partly printed in *Letters*, p. 141]

On the verso of the beginning of a draft of this letter, Tolkien works out changes that will be needed in Chapter 6 of *The Hobbit* if the changed text is accepted, carefully fitting them to the existing spaces. Underneath this he writes a note about Thráin and Thrór, and draws a version of Durin's family tree which seems to precede that published by Christopher Tolkien in *The Peoples of Middle-earth* (p. 277).

August 1950 It seems likely that Tolkien does not begin work on the section 'Durin's Folk' in Appendix A of *The Lord of the Rings* until this month at the earliest, after having looked at *The Hobbit* again, which led him to think about the line of Durin. He now writes the first brief version of what became 'Durin's Folk' in a clear hand on a scrap of paper, and gives it the title 'Of Durin's Line'. He includes a genealogy which seems later than that associated with the draft reply to Beard, and is certainly later than the expanded 'Tale of Years' (see entry for ?August 1948–?end of August 1950). After making some emendations and additions, he writes a second clear manuscript, making very few changes, entitled 'Of Durin's Race', which is similar to the third version of 'The House of Eorl' and is probably made at the same time, and like other fair copies is intended for publication. He does not leave enough space to write the family tree clearly, and makes another copy.

9 August 1950 Stanley Unwin writes to Tolkien, in reply to Tolkien's letter of 1 August to W.N. Beard. He is disturbed to learn that the proof of *The Hobbit* with revised Chapter 5 came as a surprise. He reminds Tolkien that he had promised to incorporate the revisions when they were submitted to Allen & Unwin in September 1947. The revised text of *The Hobbit* will at first be on sale only in the United States, but any subsequent printings for sale in Britain will contain the new text. He asks Tolkien to suggest wording for a note to explain the revision.

11 August 1950 Harman Grisewood, Controller of the Third Programme, BBC, writes to Tolkien. He has heard from John Bryson that Tolkien has completed part of a translation of *Sir Gawain and the Green Knight*, and would like to know if Tolkien would allow the BBC to consider it for broadcast.

17 August 1950 Tolkien replies to Grisewood that his translation of *Sir Gawain* is far advanced and he is willing that the BBC consider it.

19 August 1950 Ida Gordon sends *Pearl*, now completed except for the introduction, to Oxford University Press. Tolkien has been through the glossary carefully. Mrs Gordon has incorporated his suggestions and corrections as well as notes left by her husband, and has put the material in order. She has made three emendations to the text and restored one reading at Tolkien's suggestion. Tolkien has also suggested two alterations in punctuation, and has written one note she cannot read.

Late August 1950 Tolkien is present at a conference of university professors of English held at Magdalen College. It is attended by scholars from some thirty countries, including Simonne d'Ardenne, and will lead to the formation of the International Association of University Professors of English. On 10 September Tolkien will write to Stanley Unwin that he has been away for most of August 'and returned to a rather frightful International Conference, and to exam work' (Tolkien-George Allen & Unwin archive, HarperCollins). – During the conference, at the request of D.M. Davin of Oxford University Press, Norman Davis asks Tolkien how much work he has done on *Pearl* and whether he thinks it fit for publication. Tolkien replies that he has done a great deal to the glossary and notes and has made some emendations in the text. He thinks the book ready for publication.

?30 August 1950 D.M. Davin speaks to Tolkien at lunch. Tolkien suggests that he visit Davin when he has the complete copy of *Pearl* so that they may go through it together. (It is not known if this event ever occurred. When Kenneth Sisam sees the manuscript, however, he suggests drastic cuts.)

September 1950 Tolkien is occupied with examination papers to be marked, probably for the National University of Ireland.

?Early September 1950 Tolkien replies to queries about *Pearl* he has received from Ida Gordon.

7 September 1950 Harman Grisewood of the BBC writes to Tolkien. He asks to see part of the text of Tolkien's *Sir Gawain and the Green Knight* to judge its suitability for broadcasting.

9 September 1950 Stanley Unwin writes to Tolkien. Correcting stereo plates of *The Hobbit* is proving a lengthy job and holding up an urgently needed reprint for Houghton Mifflin. Unwin asks if Tolkien would mind if the present reprint were made without waiting for the plates to be altered, assuming that the printers have not gone too far. He encloses an addressed postcard for Tolkien to reply by striking out one of two alternatives.

10 September 1950 Before receiving Stanley Unwin's letter of 9 September Tolkien writes to him about the revisions to *The Hobbit*: 'Please, do not be disturbed. I was surprised, and remain so; though I may be delighted, if and when I have time to consider properly the effects of the alteration in the original Hobbit.' He had sent his proposal for rewriting *The Hobbit*, and the list of corrections, on different paper, with different headings. He had assumed that Unwin's reply about incorporation in the next reprint referred only to the corrections, and that Unwin's silence on the rewriting was a rejection. Obviously they had not understood each other. The change has been made, however, and some friends Tolkien has consulted think that the rewriting an improvement. He is not finding it easy to write an explanatory note. He has to decide whether the first version should be ignored as a miswriting,

> or the story as a whole must take into account the existence of two versions and use it. The former was my original simpleminded intention, though it is a bit awkward (since the Hobbit is fairly widely known in its older form) if the literary pretence of historicity and dependence on record is to be maintained. The second can be done convincingly (I think), but not briefly explained in a note. In the former case, or in doubt, the only thing to do, I fancy, is just to say nothing . . . though I do not like it. There is, in any case, I take it, no question of inserting a note

into the American reprint. And you will no doubt warn me in good time when an English one will become necessary. [Tolkien-George Allen & Unwin archive, HarperCollins; partly printed in *Letters*, p. 142]

He encloses specimens of the sort of note that will be needed if he decides to recognize both versions as authentic, and suggestions as to how it might be shortened. – R.E. Havard's wife dies.

11 September 1950 Tolkien returns to Allen & Unwin the postcard sent him on 9 September, agreeing that the reprint of *The Hobbit* may go ahead without the plates being altered. He also writes a short note to Stanley Unwin that the only important corrections are those on pp. 30 and 64, to bring the runes and the text in line. 'I am constantly being bothered about the discrepancy – even at the International Conference colleagues from abroad raised the point with me!' (Tolkien-George Allen & Unwin archive, HarperCollins).

12 September 1950 In the morning, Tolkien meets Warnie Lewis, James Dundas-Grant, R.B. McCallum, and C.E. Stevens in the 'Bird and Baby'.

13 September 1950 Ida Gordon writes to Tolkien. She is still worried about the introduction to *Pearl*, though a section that Tolkien has rewritten has simplified the task considerably. She thinks that there may be some unnecessary detail in other sections, which she will try to reduce and simplify unless Tolkien thinks it inadvisable. – Stanley Unwin writes to Tolkien. It is evident that there were misunderstandings on both sides in regard to *The Hobbit*. The printers have gone too far with the corrections to revert to the earlier text. For economic reasons the reprint will include copies for Houghton Mifflin as well as Allen & Unwin, though the British copies will not be bound until needed. If Tolkien decides in favour of both versions of the text and wants to include a prefatory note in the British copies at a later date, Unwin thinks that his suggested shorter version is suitable. If, however, Tolkien were to let Allen & Unwin know immediately, this note could be included on the back of the contents page in the current reprint.

Between 13 and 18 September 1950 Tolkien writes to Ida Gordon, supplying additional notes for *Pearl*.

14 September 1950 Tolkien writes to Stanley Unwin. He has decided to accept both versions of Chapter 5 in *The Hobbit* as authentic in *The Lord of the Rings*, though at present he has no time to do the necessary rewriting. He encloses a copy of the briefest form of the prefatory note to be included in the reprint. In addition to dealing with the changed text of Chapter 5 and the corrections on pages 30 and 64, he takes the opportunity to explain an apparent discrepancy in the first edition noted by several of his correspondents, explaining that the Thrain who (according to *Thror's Map*), was of old King under the Mountain, is not the same as Thrain, the son of Thror the last King.

19 September 1950 In the morning, Tolkien meets the Lewis brothers, James Dundas-Grant, and Colin Hardie in the 'Bird and Baby'. Warnie Lewis will note in his diary that Tolkien was 'very confidential and "in the know" about the details of the Communist plot [probably the invasion of South

Korea, which was widely seen as a plot controlled by Moscow]. A good and quite unintentional *gaffe* by J [i.e. Jack = C.S. Lewis]: the question was propounded whether Tollers's voice production or Hugo's hand writing gave more trouble to their friends. J. "Well, there's this to be said for Hugo's writing, there's less of it'" (*Brothers and Friends*, p. 235). – Ida Gordon writes to Tolkien, thanking him for his letter and notes which solved most of her difficulties. She mentions various points that still worry her. When she has finished work on *Pearl* she intends to return to *The Wanderer* and *The Seafarer* and would be grateful if Tolkien could send her the material he had mentioned. – Stanley Unwin writes to Tolkien. The prefatory note for *The Hobbit* has been sent to the printers. Tolkien will receive a proof. – In the evening, Tolkien attends a ham supper in C.S. Lewis's rooms in Magdalen College. Also present are the Lewis brothers, James Dundas-Grant, Colin Hardie, and C.E. Stevens.

21 September 1950 W.N. Beard sends Tolkien a proof of his prefatory note to *The Hobbit*.

22 September 1950 Tolkien returns the proof to Allen & Unwin.

25 September 1950 Tolkien replies to Harman Grisewood's letter of 7 September. He has not had time to concentrate on *Sir Gawain*, and has been unable to make a fair copy of the translation of the whole, but sends a portion which he thinks should be sufficient for a preliminary decision. He has considered possible cuts, though with few exceptions the poem cannot be cut without destruction. – P.J. Spicer of the Clarendon Press writes to Tolkien. Penguin Books would like to reprint part of the Tolkien-Gordon edition of *Sir Gawain and the Green Knight* in a history of English Literature series, with modern spelling. The Press thinks that this might affect hardcover sales and ask Tolkien if he can suggest any non-copyrighted text for Penguin to use. Tolkien's reply is not extant, but J. proposal was turned down flat.

26 September–5 October 1950 Tolkien is in Ireland as Extern Examiner for the National University.

2 October 1950 *Farmer Giles of Ham* is published in the United States.

8 October 1950 Michaelmas Full Term begins. Tolkien's scheduled lectures and classes for this term are: Philology: Discussion Class on Tuesdays at 5.30 p.m. at Merton College, beginning 17 October; *Sir Gawain and the Green Knight* on Wednesdays at 11.00 a.m. in the Examination Schools, beginning 11 October; and Outlines of English Linguistic History (continued): The Foreign Elements on Fridays at 11.00 a.m. in the Examination Schools, beginning 13 October. Tolkien will continue to supervise B.Litt. students Celia Sisam and Anne Wakefield, and D. Phil. students E.J. Stormon and R. Vleeskruyer.

13 October 1950 R.F.W. Fletcher dies.

16 October 1950 Tolkien attends Fletcher's funeral at St Peter-in-the-East church, Oxford.

19 October 1950 Allen & Unwin send Tolkien ten copies of the Houghton Mifflin edition of *Farmer Giles of Ham*.

20 October 1950 Tolkien attends an English Faculty Board meeting and is asked to take the chair in place of R.F.W. Fletcher. He is deputed to write letters of condolence to Mrs Fletcher and to the Principal of St Edmund Hall, where Fletcher had been Senior Tutor; and he is elected chairman of the Board until Michaelmas Term 1951. Appointments are made to replace Tolkien as an ordinary member on various committees, such as the Library Committee, of which he is now a member *de facto*. He is also asked to invite Professor Kökeritz of Yale to give two lectures during a stay in Oxford. The Report of the Special Library Committee (of which Tolkien is a member) is amended and approved for submission to the General Board. It is agreed that Tolkien and C.L. Wrenn 'should submit agreed proposals for alterations in the regulations governing linguistic and medieval subjects at a later meeting' (Oxford University Archives FA 4/5/1/2). The Applications Committee has accepted as probationer B.Litt. students G.M.G. Evans of St Hugh's College, to work on a Middle English subject, and D.R. (Daphne) Castell of St Anne's College, to work on Thomas Chatterton, and has appointed Tolkien as their supervisor.

23 October 1950 Stanley Unwin has heard that Tolkien is having problems with Collins, and writes to let him know that the door is not closed for him at Allen & Unwin. He asks if Tolkien could lend Rayner a copy of 'The Silmarillion' which he has never seen, and continues: 'I gather that you have not made other arrangements for the publication of *The Lord of the Rings* so there is still hope that some day we may solve the publishing problem it presents and have privilege of being connected with its publication' (Tolkien-George Allen & Unwin archive, HarperCollins).

26 October 1950 Harman Grisewood writes to Tolkien. His *Sir Gawain and the Green Knight* is considered suitable for broadcasting.

30 October 1950 D.G. Bridson, Assistant Head of Features for the BBC, writes to Tolkien. *Sir Gawain and the Green Knight* will have to be split into four separate readings for broadcast, but the question of how to do so can be left until the complete script is available. When Tolkien has sent the rest of the work, Bridson will write again; but he would like to meet with Tolkien in London to discuss various matters of production.

1 November 1950 Tolkien attends a Merton College meeting. – 'S' (probably Susan Dagnall) writes a minute to Stanley Unwin about a visit made to Elaine Griffiths in Oxford concerning work she is doing for Allen & Unwin. 'She showed me *Tolkien's* "brilliant version of 'Exodus'" – introduction, text and notes. Apparently Tolkien has a drawer full of such texts, which in the name of scholarship and for the sake of students ought to be published' (Tolkien-George Allen & Unwin archive, HarperCollins).

4 November 1950 K.C. Turpin, Secretary of Faculties, writes to Tolkien as chairman of the English Faculty Board, querying which papers a (?war) candidate needs to take to complete his degree.

6 November 1950 Stanley Unwin writes to Tolkien to ask if he has ever made any arrangements to publish his translation of *Sir Gawain and the Green Knight*. He hopes that Tolkien would allow Allen & Unwin the privilege of considering it for publication. He also asks about *Pearl* which his son Rayner saw in Blackwell's galley proofs *c.* 1944.

7 November 1950 Tolkien replies to the Secretary of Faculties.

8 November 1950 *R.W. Burchfield, a Rhodes Scholar at Oxford, writes to Tolkien about a word in *Sir Gawain and the Green Knight*.

10–12 November 1950 Tolkien attends the first of two conferences in Liège to celebrate the sixtieth anniversary of the Departments of Germanic and Romance Philology at the University of Liège, the Congrès du LXe anniversaire des sections de Philologie romane et de Philologie germanique. Tolkien may have intended to participate in any event, but extant letters suggest rather that he went to replace R.F.W. Fletcher as the representative of the Oxford English School. He gives an address in English explaining the Oxford syllabus and the aims of the School (summarized in *Revue des langes vivantes* (1951–2), pp. 111–12, as *Les études d'anglais a l'Université d'Oxford*).

13–16 November 1950 Tolkien visits Simonne d'Ardenne in Solwaster, Belgium.

13 November 1950 Tolkien writes to Stanley Unwin, apologizing for treating his two kind letters with silence.

> But the calamitous death of the Chairman of our Faculty, in the first week of term and in the midst of much business, threw a mass of work on to me; and then I suddenly found it necessary to go to Liège. I am resting in the woods after an exhausting conference; and return home shortly. . . . I sent out *The Silmarillion* some little while ago; but maybe it will return ere long. As for other things I will dig in my drawers, as soon as I have a moment.

He had been surprised to find that at Liège they use *Farmer Giles of Ham* in the preliminary seminar 'as a whetstone of the appetite for more genuine documents of early England, as well as a specimen itself of English' (Tolkien-George Allen & Unwin archive, HarperCollins). – Tolkien also writes to D.G. Bridson at the BBC. He has no other reason to come to London, but might be able to arrange a meeting there once term is over on 2 December. He asks for the sample text of *Sir Gawain and the Green Knight* to be returned for revision. He offers, if it would be useful, to indicate parts which might be cut and to supply a brief narrative to replace them.

17 November 1950 Tolkien returns to Oxford.

20 November 1950 D.G. Bridson returns the sample of *Sir Gawain and the Green Knight* to Tolkien. A meeting after 2 December would suit him. It would be invaluable for Tolkien to suggest cuts, but he should do nothing until they have discussed the presentation.

30 November 1950 Tolkien attends an English Faculty Library Committee meeting.

1 December 1950 Tolkien chairs an English Faculty Board meeting. He reports that he has received appreciative replies to his letters to Mrs Fletcher and the Principal of St Edmund Hall, and that Professor Kökeritz would be pleased to lecture in Trinity Term if he returns to Oxford. The report of the

Special Library Committee on the need for an increased grant for the English Faculty Library is approved and forwarded to the General Board. It is agreed to apply to the General Board to increase to seven the examiners for the Final Honour School in Trinity Term 1951. It is also agreed that in Trinity Term 1951 the examiners could excuse candidates from being examined *viva voce*. Tolkien makes a statement on the proposals which have been agreed by himself and C.L. Wrenn for alterations in the regulations governing linguistic and medieval subjects. It is agreed that a memorandum on the issue should be circulated and considered at a Faculty meeting in Hilary Term. Tolkien reports that the examiners for the Preliminary Examination wish to apply for the appointment of an assessor, because of the eight set books only two are in French and neither of them is to be studied in detail. The Applications Committee has appointed Tolkien to replace Gervase Mathew as supervisor of the B.Litt. thesis of I.B. Bishop of Queen's College on *Pearl* considered in relation to thirteenth- and fourteenth-century ideals of poetry.

2 December 1950 Michaelmas Full Term ends.

4 December 1950 Tolkien attends a Merton College meeting.

11 December 1950 Tolkien and C.L. Wrenn examine E.J. Dobson of Merton College *viva voce* at 11.00 a.m. in the Examination Schools on his D.Phil. thesis *English Pronunciation 1500–1700 According to the Evidence of the English Orthoepists.*

14 December 1950 Tolkien and C.L. Wrenn sign and date a memorandum suggesting changes in the Final Honour School regulations, presumably for circulation to the Faculty in Hilary Term 1951 as agreed at the last Board meeting. The four-page manuscript is in Tolkien's hand, and a printed mimeo has the same date as the manuscript. For linguistic and medieval papers he and Wrenn suggest the addition of mediaeval Welsh as a subject, under Subsidiary Languages, in the hope that it will 'encourage some English candidates to take the first steps in Celtic philology'. The Vigfússon Reader suggests that suitable candidates might be allowed to take three papers on Icelandic and Old Norse subjects within the nine papers of Course I, since 'Old Norse is expressly attached to our faculty and it is not any longer possible to study it at all in any other School. Course I has in fact, as one function, necessarily to serve as a nursery (the chief one) of Icelandic scholarship in this country' (Oxford University Archives FA 4/5/2/10). This seems to be based on suggestions made by the Faculty earlier in the year while Tolkien was on leave.

19 December 1950 Tolkien meets Warnie Lewis, probably in a pub and with others also present, and tells a story about the writer Henry Seton Merriman (1862–1903).

1951

1951 *Elizabethan Acting* by B.L. Joseph is published in the series *Oxford English Monographs*, of which Tolkien is one of three general editors. He is acknowledged in Joseph's preface for comment and encouragement. This is the first volume in the series to be published since 1940. – Tolkien subscribes to *Mixed Feelings: Nineteen Poems* by John Wain, published by the University of Reading School of Art.

11 January 1951 Tolkien attends a Merton College meeting.

14 January 1951 Hilary Full Term begins. Tolkien's scheduled lectures and classes for this term are: *Sir Gawain and the Green Knight* (continued) on Wednesdays at 12.00 noon in the Examination Schools, beginning 17 January; Philology: Discussion Class on Thursdays at 5.15 p.m. at Merton College, beginning 18 January; and Philology: Middle English on Fridays at 12.00 noon in the Examination Schools, beginning 19 January. He will continue to supervise B.Litt. students Celia Sisam and Anne Wakefield, D.Phil. students E.J. Stormon and R. Vleeskruyer, and probationer B.Litt. students D.R. Castell and G.M.G. Evans.

18 January 1951 Tolkien chairs a meeting of the English Faculty Library Committee at which members discuss new books to buy and subscriptions to enter. He agrees to approach the Oxford University Press on the possibility of a discount on books bought for the Library. Tolkien proposes to write to the widow of his former colleague H.F.B. Brett-Smith, expressing the Committee's sympathy on his recent death.

26 January 1951 Tolkien chairs an English Faculty Board meeting. The proposals for the revision of the regulations for the Final Honour School are received, and it is agreed that these should be considered at a Faculty meeting on Monday in the fifth week of term and be reconsidered at the next meeting of the Board. The Applications Committee has appointed Tolkien to be supervisor of recognized student N.J. Peltola of the University of Helsinki. *See note.* – The meat ration is reduced in Great Britain.

7 February 1951 Tolkien attends a Merton College meeting.

8 February 1951 Tolkien takes part in the election of the Oxford Professor of Poetry, and presumably votes for C.S. Lewis. The successful candidate, however, is C. Day Lewis.

12 February 1951 The English Faculty meet to discuss the proposed changes in the Final Honour School regulations.

13 February 1951 Tolkien meets friends in the 'Bird and Baby'. Among those present are Roger Lancelyn Green, Colin Hardie, the Lewis brothers, R.B. McCallum, Gervase Mathew, John Wain, and C.L. Wrenn. The main topic of discussion is C. Day Lewis. Tolkien recalled years later that 'Lewis was not "cut to the quick" by his defeat in the election to the professorship of poetry: he knew quite well the cause. I remember that we had assembled soon after in our accustomed tavern and found C.S.L. sitting there, looking (and since he was no actor at all probably feeling) much at ease. "Fill up!" he said, "and stop looking so glum. The only distressing thing about this affair is that my friends seem to be upset"' (letter to Anne Barrett, 30 August 1964, *Letters*, p. 351).

8 March 1951 Tolkien attends a meeting of the English Faculty Library Committee. He reports that a letter has been sent to Mrs Brett-Smith as promised, but he has not yet been able to approach Oxford University Press about a discount.

9 March 1951 Tolkien chairs an English Faculty Board meeting. The proposals of the Faculty for the revision of the regulations of the Final Honour School are received and discussed. Some of the proposals are accepted, others not. It is agreed there should be a Faculty meeting at 2.30 p.m. on 21 May to consider the compilation of Lecture Lists. The Applications Committee has accepted G.M.G. Evans of St Hugh's College as a B.Litt. student, her thesis to be on 'an edition of the fable of "The Fox and the Wolf" from MS Digby 86' with Tolkien as her supervisor. The Committee has also admitted V.M. Martin of St Hilda's College as a probationer B.Litt. student, to work on a Middle English subject, with Tolkien as her supervisor; while Hugo Dyson has been appointed to replace Tolkien as supervisor of E.J. Stormon.

10 March 1951 Hilary Full Term ends.

12 March 1951 Tolkien attends a Merton College meeting. – Hugh Brogan writes to Tolkien, noting that it is almost two years since they met, and that if Tolkien ever comes to Cambridge again he would be welcome at Brogan's home.

?Spring 1951 The revised text of *The Hobbit* is published in the United States by the Houghton Mifflin Company.

2 April 1951 Christopher Tolkien marries Faith Faulconbridge.

14 April 1951 Tolkien attends an Early English Text Society Council meeting at Magdalen College, Oxford.

22 April 1951 Trinity Full Term begins. Tolkien's scheduled lectures for this term are: *Ormulum* and *Ayenbite of Inwit* on Wednesdays and Fridays at 12.00 noon in the Examination Schools, beginning 25 April; and *Sir Gawain and the Green Knight* on Fridays at 11.00 a.m. in the Schools, beginning 27 April. He will continue to supervise B.Litt. students I.B. Bishop, G.M.G. Evans, and Anne Wakefield, D.Phil. student R. Vleeskruyer, and probationer B.Litt. students D.R. Castell and V.M. Martin.

28 April 1951 Tolkien dines with C.S. and Warnie Lewis.

4 May 1951 Tolkien chairs an English Faculty Board meeting.

10 May 1951 Tolkien adds a note to the pre-*Lord of the Rings Quenta Silmarillion* at the end of the story of Beren and Lúthien 'revised so far, 10 May 1951'. Since little rewriting is done beyond this point in the narrative, he probably ceases work on the *Quenta Silmarillion* soon after this.

?Mid-May–?summer 1951 Tolkien probably begins work on the *Annals of Aman* after ceasing work on the *Quenta Silmarillion*, though some overlap is possible. After making some emendations and additions to the early entries in the 'later' *Annals of Valinor* written many years before, Tolkien decides to make a new clear manuscript, copying the part already emended and continuing, apparently with little preliminary drafting, to the end, making some changes at the time of writing or soon after. He adds much material. Eventually the annal form gives way to a narrative much longer than that in the *Quenta Silmarillion* and covering the same events. Most of the rewriting of the *Quenta Silmaril-*

lion corresponding to the period covered by the *Annals of Aman* seems to have preceded the rewriting of that work, but in some cases Tolkien apparently makes additions to the *Quenta Silmarillion* at the same time that he is writing entries in the *Annals of Aman*, notably material relating to Míriel, Fëanor, and the Silmarils. Tolkien writes lengthy entries in the *Annals of Aman* for chapters that he hardly touched in this period in the *Quenta Silmarillion*, notably 'Of the Flight of the Noldor' and 'Of the Sun and the Moon and the Hiding of Valinor'. Possibly he deliberately stops work on the *Quenta Silmarillion* and begins to write the *Annals* to provide a firmer framework for the developing narrative, then continues the main composition in that work. Probably not long after finishing work on the *Annals of Aman* he begins, but does not complete, a typescript, introducing changes as he proceeds.

?Mid-May 1951–?early 1952 In association with the *Annals of Aman* and the *Grey Annals* (see below) Tolkien makes a new version of *The Tale of Years*, which he uses as a working chronology during this period, making many corrections, rewriting, and interpolating material into the originally clear text. When he first writes *The Tale of Years* its dates agree with those in the *Annals of Aman* as originally written, and the same changes are made to both. In the later part it agrees closely with the *Grey Annals*, which reached only as far as 499. For the period beginning 500, Tolkien first copies the pre-*Lord of the Rings* version of *The Tale of Years*, but then makes so many corrections, additions, and alterations that he makes a replacement manuscript from the year 400, writing longer entries for 400–499 so that it begins to approach the 'Annals' format. He then begins to make a typescript which he continues (possibly some time later) as a rough manuscript and finally abandons with the entry for 527.

Later, but probably in the early years of the decade, Tolkien will make two very fine manuscripts, almost identical in form, of a text removed from the *Annals of Aman* entitled 'Of the Beginning of Time and Its Reckoning', intended to precede the chronological entries of *The Tale of Years*. Possibly at about this time too, Tolkien writes the **Dangweth Pengoloð: The Answer of Pengoloð to Aelfwine Who Asked Him How Came It that the Tongues of the Elves Changed and Were Sundered*. His first version is a clear manuscript which he emends only lightly; probably soon afterward, he rewrites it as a fine illuminated manuscript. **Of Lembas*, a two-page manuscript similar to the *Dangweth Pengoloð* but less fine, may date from the same time, if not later in the decade.

Probably in this same period, Tolkien also begins work on a lengthy prose version of the story of Túrin, the **Narn i Chîn Húrin* (or *Narn i Hîn Húrin*), perhaps to use as a basis for that story in the *Grey Annals* and (presumably) eventually in the *Quenta Silmarillion*. It is perhaps for that reason that he starts not at the beginning, which he told at length years earlier in the alliterative lay *The Children of Húrin*, but as Túrin rushes north to Dor-lómin after the destruction of Nargothrond, though this means that there is no detailed account of the sack of Nargothrond. Although Tolkien seems to base most of the entries about Túrin in the *Grey Annals* on the *Narn*, it is possible that he works on some passages in both texts at the same time. For the section of the *Narn* dating to this time he begins with scribbled drafting on slips of paper, from which he then writes a manuscript; but from the point where the men of Brethil discuss what action to take against Glaurung, Tolkien seems uncertain of events, trying out ideas in rough draft notes, and rewriting so much in the draft manuscript that it becomes chaotic. At last he makes a fair copy.

16 May 1951 Tolkien attends a Merton College meeting.

21–25 May 1951 Tolkien meets with D.M. Davin of Oxford University Press. They agree that Tolkien will hand over his material for the Clarendon Chaucer. Probably on this occasion they also discuss the Tolkien-Gordon edition of *Sir Gawain and the Green Knight*: Tolkien says that he has been rewriting part of the introduction and hopes to finish it this summer.

21 May 1951 The English Faculty meet at 2.30 p.m. to consider compilation of Lecture Lists.

29 May 1951 Tolkien attends a performance of Shakespeare's *Twelfth Night* at New College at 8.00 p.m.

30 May 1951 D.M. Davin writes to Tolkien. He will send a car to pick up the Clarendon Chaucer material from the lodge at Magdalen College at 11.30 a.m. on 8 June, if Tolkien will leave it there. Tolkien has suggested that Dorothy Everett might complete the book, but Davin does not want to distract her from another project.

2 June 1951 Tolkien attends an Ad Eundem Dinner.

6 June 1951 Ida Gordon writes to D.M. Davin at Oxford University Press. Although she can understand some of the suggestions he has sent her in regard to *Pearl*, she feels that the work would suffer if its associated matter were cut by half as Davin has asked (on Kenneth Sisam's advice). She notes that the section Davin has targeted in particular, including a discussion of problems involved with the work, was contributed by Tolkien, a reduced rewriting of the original version. (In the event, this will be published.)

7 June 1951 English Final Honour School Examinations begin. Priscilla Tolkien is among those being examined. (She will pass her examinations and be awarded her B.A.)

8 June 1951 Tolkien writes to D.M. Davin. He has sent Oxford University Press all that might be useful of his material for the Clarendon Chaucer:

(1). Working copy made of galleys of the *text*, with 2 copies of the resultant *revises* in page-proof (not themselves, I think, again corrected throughout). (2). The correct[?ed] proofs of the *glossary*. (3). The draft of notes for *all* pieces but the last two (from *Monk's Tale* and *Nun's Priest's Tale*): the earlier items revised and reduced, the rest progressively in need of revision, and those for the *Reeve's Tale* possibly too illegible. . . . I deeply regret the whole affair. The material contains much that is fresh and a prodigious amount of labour – sp. in the construction, reduction, and revision of the glossary. But I was given the very sticky end of the stick, and need say no more. [Oxford University Press Archives]

He knows nothing about George S. Gordon's material.

c. **8 June 1951** After receiving Ida Gordon's letter of 6 June, D.M. Davin discusses it with Tolkien. Tolkien is happy to give Mrs Gordon a free hand to condense or omit any parts of his contribution to *Pearl* in the interests of brevity.

11 June 1951 D.M. Davin writes to thank Tolkien for the Chaucer material. At present all suitable editors are occupied, but the material will be retained until they can find a solution.

14 June 1951 Tolkien attends a meeting of the English Faculty Library Committee.

15 June 1951 Tolkien chairs an English Faculty Board meeting.

16 June 1951 Trinity Full Term ends.

19 June 1951 Tolkien attends a Merton College meeting.

20 June 1951 Encaenia.

Late June–early July 1951 Tolkien presumably travels to Ireland where he is again Extern Examiner for the National University of Ireland.

9 July 1951 The second edition of *The Hobbit* is published in Britain.

By 18 July 1951 Tolkien has submitted to the organizers of the Congrès International de Philologie Moderne in Liège the title of a paper he plans to give in September. Simonne d'Ardenne is trying to get him regarded as a Guest of Honour. The organizing committee will prefer 'About the Etymology of *Lozenge*' to Tolkien's suggested 'Lozenge: An Etymology'.

Late July–15 August 1951 Tolkien, Edith, and Priscilla, who had just had her Oxford viva, holiday in Ireland. They travel to North Wales and take the ferry from Fishguard to Cork where they are met by Bridget McCarthy, Professor of English at University College, Cork, whom Tolkien has met when examining in Ireland, and who has become a friend as well as a colleague. The Tolkiens stay for a few days in Cork with Bridget and her aunt, then are driven by Bridget to Castle Cove, a remote village in the west part of Kerry on the north bank of the Kenmare River, near the point where it flows into the Atlantic. They stay in a hotel run by the Misses O'Flaherty. Castle Cove having no public transport, an O'Flaherty brother, who runs the local taxi service, drives them to Mass in the church in the village of Derrynan about five miles away. Castle Cove is quiet and unspoilt, with almost deserted strands and miles of sand.

During this holiday, Tolkien turns again to topographical drawing, using a new sketchbook. He draws nine views of the Kerry landscape (not all finished), in a more impressionistic style than his earlier works. *See note.* He is particularly interested in depicting the sky and the varying weather.

After the holiday, the Tolkiens return to Cork, and as the bells of the cathedral are ringing, sail for Wales on the *Innisfallen* on the evening of 15 August, the Feast of the Assumption.

?Summer 1951–?early 1952 Tolkien probably begins to write the *Grey Annals* during the summer vacation of 1951. He is certainly working on the latter part of these in October–November 1951, when he writes 'Oct. 13', 'Oct. 25' and 'Nov. 1' against entries for the year 495 (the story of Túrin). He begins by revising a considerable part of the 1930s manuscript of the 'later' *Annals of Beleriand*, then writes a new and fuller manuscript version, partly on blank verso pages of the 'later' *Annals* and partly on new paper. After this he makes a fair copy entitled *The Annals of Beleriand or the Grey Annals*. He writes two versions from part way through the Annal for 463 to that for 466 (mainly concerned with the story of Beren and Lúthien), and bases the latter part of the story of Túrin directly on the recently written *Narn i Chîn Húrin*. Among new material added to the annals is a record of Melian's conversations with Galadriel (the latter character introduced from *The Lord of the Rings*). He abandons the *Grey Annals* at the death of Túrin (499) during this stage of writing, though he will make brief additions later at various times.

2 September 1951 R. Massart, secretary of the Liège conference, writes to Tolkien. He asks Tolkien to send by the end of the week a short synopsis of his paper for inclusion in the conference programme. He also asks if Tolkien would permit the inclusion of his paper in a proceedings of the conference, if it is decided to publish one.

10–13 September 1951 Tolkien attends the Congrès International de Philologie Moderne, the second of two conferences to celebrate the sixtieth anniversary of the Departments of Germanic and Romance Philology at the University of Liège. He gives a paper entitled on its publication in 1953 *Middle English 'Losenger': Sketch of an Etymological and Semantic Enquiry*.

10 September 1951 The Congrès begins at 10.30 a.m. in the salle académique of the University with 'une séance solennelle, à laquelle assistaient, outre les congessistes, de nombreuses personalités universitaires et des représentants des corps consitués'. Professor Maurice Delbouille gives the welcoming speech. At 11.30 a.m., 'M. le pro-recteur Fredericq' receives the guests of the University in 'la grande salle des professeurs'. John Orr of Edinburgh University makes a speech of thanks. At 2.30 p.m., the participants meet in plenary session and form 'la constitution du bureau du Congrès'. Mario Roques is chosen as President, to be assisted by vice-presidents and 'présidents de séance' Angelo Monteverdi (Rome), John Orr (Edinburgh), Cornelis De Boer (Leiden), Mgr Antonio Griera (Barcelona), John Ronald R. Tolkien (Oxford), Heinrich Hempel (Cologne), Louis Hjelmsley (Copenhagen), and Jean Fourquet (Strasbourg). At 3.00 p.m. the first session begins, with three presentations. At 8.00 p.m. there is 'une soirée de gala' organized by the Théâtre Communal Wallon du Trianon, and some members of the Congrès are able to take part in 'la représentation de deux pièces en dialect liégeois'.

11 September 1951 At the Liège Congrès there are two parallel programmes of presentations during the day. At 17.00 p.m. there is a visit to the Musée de la Vie Wallonne, guided by M. André, conservateur du Musée, and Élisée Legros, chargé du cours de folklore à l'Université, and a performance 'des marionnettes liégeoises'. In the evening, Paul Gruselin, the Mayor of Liège, receives the Congrès participants at a reception in the Hôtel de Ville.

12 September 1951 Most of those attending the Congrès join in an excursion through le pays de Herve, the Ardennes, and the valley of the Meuse, to the borders of the area where a romance language is spoken. At the end of the tour the participants are entertained to dinner by the province and town of Namur, at the casino of Namur.

13 September 1951 At the Congrès there are two parallel programmes of presentations during the day. At 6.00 p.m. participants are received at the Palais provincial by Joseph Leclercq, the Governor of the Province. At 8.00 p.m. there is a banquet at Hôtel d'Angleterre.

21 September 1951 Maurice Delbouille, one of the organizers of the Liège Congrès writes to Tolkien. He is sorry that his duties had prevented him talking to Tolkien at the Congrès. He asks Tolkien's opinion of an idea he has about the origin of the name *Jauvain* for one of King Arthur's knights, and discusses various theories that have been put forward. He seems to think that it is connected with the place name *Galloway* and 'roie de Galvoie'. Tolkien will reply before 21 November.

Late September–early October 1951 Tolkien presumably travels to Ireland where he is again Extern Examiner for the National University of Ireland.

October 1951 Tolkien has 'a terrible bout of fibrositis and neuritis of the arm' and cannot 'write at all (or bear myself) for a month' (letter to Rayner Unwin, 22 June 1952, *Letters*, p. 163).

10 October 1951 Tolkien attends a Merton College Meeting.

13 October 1951 Tolkien writes this date against an entry for the year 495 in the *Grey Annals*.

14 October 1951 Michaelmas Full Term begins. Tolkien's scheduled lectures for this term are: the 'Pardoner's Tale' by Chaucer on Wednesdays at 12.00 noon in the Examination Schools, beginning 17 October; Philology: Outlines of History of English Accidence on Fridays at 12.00 noon in the Examination Schools, beginning 19 October; and another lecture subject to be arranged. He will continue to supervise B.Litt. students I.B. Bishop, G.M.G. Evans, and Anne Wakefield, and probationer B.Litt. student V.M. Martin.

25 October 1951 Tolkien writes this date written against an entry for the year 495 in the *Grey Annals*.

26 October 1951 At an English Faculty Board meeting, in his absence, Tolkien is elected chairman until Michaelmas Term 1952. The Applications Committee has accepted R.W. Burchfield of Magdalen College as a B.Litt. student for a subject in Middle English philology, with Tolkien as his supervisor. It has also appointed Tolkien and Nevill Coghill examiners of the D.Phil. thesis of T.J. Grace of Campion Hall, *A Study of the Ascetical Elements in Piers Plowman and Their Bearing on the Structure and Meaning of the Poem: with Special Reference to the B Text. See note*. – A representative of Merton College writes to ask Tolkien if it is convenient to begin to alter the gutters on the back of his house at 99 Holywell.

27 October 1951 In the evening, Tolkien attends a dinner of The Society hosted by J.T. Christie, the Principal of Jesus College, Oxford, in his lodgings. Eleven members are present.

1 November 1951 Tolkien writes this date against an entry for the year 495 in the *Grey Annals*.

7 November 1951 Tolkien attends a Merton College meeting.

8 November 1951 Tolkien chairs a meeting of the Committee for Comparative Philology.

15 November 1951 Tolkien writes to Humphry House, a member of the English Faculty at Wadham College, Oxford, that Thursday 22 November would be the best date for him for a meeting. He knows the contents of the 'pamphlet' and approves the 'R H-D' proposals, but wonders if they should not print the larger number as R H-D means to make the thing wider known. (This probably refers to the Clark Lectures on Coleridge given by House in 1951 and published by Rupert Hart-Davis in 1953.)

19 November 1951 W.L. Kinter of New York writes to Tolkien, asking about 'Numenor', having seen a reference to it by C.S. Lewis.

21 November 1951 Maurice Delbouille writes to thank Tolkien for his reply to his query on *Gauvain* and *Galloway*, and discusses further variant forms and what Tolkien has replied about the etymology of *Galloway*. Tolkien has also drawn his attention to the form *Walgannius*. – Tolkien probably attends a Merton College Common Room meeting.

22 November 1951 Tolkien possibly attends a meeting with Humphry House regarding the Clark Lectures on Coleridge (see entry for 15 November 1951).

24 or 25 November 1951 Tolkien collapses, suffering from influenza.

25 November 1951 In response to a series of letters on *Faynights* which he has seen in the *Sunday Times*, including one published on 25 November from Iona and Peter Opie explaining the use of the word, Tolkien writes a long letter to the Opies which he sends to the *Sunday Times* to forward. He discusses the etymology of the word and its sources, and comments that he read their letter 'today, just as I had been puzzling over a curious Chaucer usage' which must be connected (Tolkien Papers, Bodleian Library, Oxford).

29 November 1951 Rayner Unwin, having tried to contact Tolkien a few days earlier and been told by Edith of her husband's illness, writes to Tolkien that he hopes he has recovered and is sorry not to have seen him. He asks again to see 'The Silmarillion'. 'Believe it or not I am still quite certain that you have something most important for publication in this book and *The Lords of the Ring*!' [*sic*] (quoted in *Letters*, p. 443).

?Late 1951 No definite arrangements for publishing 'The Silmarillion' and *The Lord of the Rings* have been made by Collins, partly because of the illness and absence of Milton Waldman, but also because the publisher is worried about their length. Evidently at Waldman's suggestion, Tolkien now writes a very long letter (about 10,000 words) explaining the two works, intended to demonstrate that they are interdependent and indivisible. He again mentions

The Rings of Power as a separate document, which by this time probably has been further developed towards the final form in which it appears as *Of the Rings of Power and the Third Age* in *The Silmarillion*.

?Late 1951–?early 1952 In a new version of the chapter 'Of the Silmarils and the Darkening of Valinor' in the *Quenta Silmarillion* Tolkien introduces many changes and gives it the new title 'Of Fëanor and the Silmarilli and the Darkening of Valinor'. At the same time, he probably introduces the same changes into the *Annals of Aman*. He continues to work on the *Grey Annals* and further on the *Quenta Silmarillion*, making changes and additions, often similar, to both works. He adds details of the foundation of Gondolin and Nargothrond, and a new chapter, 'Of Turgon and the Building of Gondolin', to the *Quenta Silmarillion*. He writes the story of Isfin, Eöl, and their son Meglin at length as a clear twelve-page manuscript (later entitled *Of Meglin*; see *Of Maeglin: Sister-son of Turgon, King of Gondolin*), but makes many emendations during and after the writing and adds riders based on it to the *Quenta Silmarillion* and the *Grey Annals*. He adds an entry to the *Grey Annals* describing the visit of Húrin and Huor to Gondolin in 458 to replace an earlier version of the story. He writes some of the riders added to the *Grey Annals* on pages from an engagement calendar with dates from August to December 1951, and rewrites the opening passage of the *Quenta Silmarillion* chapter 'Of the Siege of Angband' on the verso of a letter to him dated 14 November 1951.

Tolkien now begins to write, as well and at great length, a new account of *The Fall of Gondolin* with the title *Of Tuor and the Fall of Gondolin* (later published in *Unfinished Tales* with the title *Of Tuor and His Coming to Gondolin* to distinguish it from other versions). Tolkien retains many details from the version written for *The Book of Lost Tales* over thirty years earlier, which (it may be) he has just reread or has before him as he writes. But he also incorporates the substantial changes in the story of the First Age which evolved during those years, and writes in a style which owes much to his experience in writing *The Lord of the Rings*. He abandons the writing, however, at the point where Tuor first sees Gondolin across the plain of Tumladen. There are variant readings, and one section is rewritten several times. The carefully-written but much emended manuscript ends just before the narrative, and the last paragraphs are scribbled on a page from an engagement calendar for September 1951. Only a few hasty notes indicate the course of the story.

Probably at some time in or just after 1951 Tolkien makes some changes on one of the Old English versions of the 'earliest' *Annals of Valinor* from the early 1930s, then makes a new manuscript of part of another, rewriting it in the ninth-century Mercian form of Old English, with similarities to the interlinear glosses of the Vespasian Psalter. *See note.*

After completion of *The Lord of the Rings* and while working on 'The Silmarillion' Tolkien introduces a radical change to the history and inter-relationships of the Elvish languages: 'Noldorin' (with relationships to Welsh) has been the language of the Noldor in Aman, but now becomes (after much experimentation with other ideas) 'Sindarin', the language of the Elves who stayed in Beleriand and which the exiled Noldor adopted for general use in place of the Quenya they had spoken in Aman. Tolkien's changing ideas on the subject are reflected in emendations and additions he makes to his various narrative texts and annals, in particular successive versions of an 'excursus' near the beginning of the *Grey Annals*. But the change is not just theoretical, and entails much work on the linguistic materials. Tolkien will also revise Appendix F of *The Lord of the Rings* accordingly.

6 December 1951 Tolkien attends a meeting of the English Faculty Library Committee.

7 December 1951 Tolkien chairs an English Faculty Board meeting. The Committee on Monographs (of which Tolkien is a member) reports that both Dr Joseph's book *Elizabethan Acting* and Miss Brown's edition of the 'Saga of Thorgils and Hazli' are in the press. Tolkien reports that he has received a communication from the Secretary of the Faculties concerning appointments during the new quinqennium. This is referred to the Standing Committee on Matters Referred by the General Board. It is agreed that a standing committee on the Lecture List should be established; Tolkien as chairman is appointed one of its three members. The Applications Committee has reappointed him supervisor of D.Phil. student E.J. Stormon of Campion Hall, in place of Hugo Dyson; has accepted R.W. Burchfield as a D.Phil. (instead of B.Litt.) student to work on *The Vocabulary and Phonology of the Ormulum* with Tolkien as his supervisor; and has accepted V.M. Martin as a B.Litt. student to work on *An Edition of the Minor Pieces of MS Nero A 14* with Tolkien as her supervisor.

Burchfield will later recall that during his postgraduate work he saw Tolkien

at weekly intervals in the academic years 1951–2 and 1952–3, sometimes in Merton College, sometimes at his home in Holywell. He puffed at his pipe while I told him of my work. He made many acute observations. I followed them all up. He beamed when I made some discoveries. Now and then he mentioned the hobbits, but he didn't press them on me, spotting that my interest lay in the scraped out o's and doubled consonants of the *Ormulum* rather than in the dwarves . . . Orcs, and Mr Bilbo Baggins. The two years passed all too quickly and then I was swept into full-time teaching at Christ Church and afterwards into lexicography. My work on the *Ormulum* had to be put aside. [*The Independent Magazine*, 4 March 1989, p. 50; but *see note*]

8 December 1951 Michaelmas Full Term ends.

10 December 1951 Tolkien attends a Merton College meeting.

14 December 1951 The Standing Committee on Matters Referred by the General Board, with Tolkien as chairman, prepares some draft regulations, probably in response to the communication noted at the last Board meeting.

19 December 1951 Iona and Peter Opie write to Tolkien. They would like to include an extract from his letter on *Faynights* as a footnote in a forthcoming work. (Extracts will be included in their *Lore and Language of Schoolchildren*, published in 1959.)

1952

1952 or 1953 After having served as its president for several years, Tolkien becomes vice-president of the Society for the Study of Medieval Languages and Literature, a post he will hold until his death in 1973.

1952 Priscilla Tolkien leaves Oxford to take up secretarial work in Bristol. Her parents now live alone, with none of their children at home. – *Þorgils Saga ok Hafliða*, edited by Ursula Brown, is published in the *Oxford English Monographs* series. In her preface she thanks Tolkien for valuable criticism and advice.

15 January 1952 At the University of Glasgow the committee of the W.P. Ker Lecturership meets to consider the appointment of the W.P. Ker Lecturer for 1952–3, and recommends to the University Court that Tolkien be invited. The Lecture, established in 1938, is to be 'on some branch of literary or linguistic studies'.

17 January 1952 Tolkien attends a Merton College meeting.

20 January 1952 Hilary Full Term begins. Tolkien's scheduled lectures for this term are: the 'Pardoner's Tale' by Chaucer (continued) on Wednesdays at 12.00 noon in the Examination Schools, beginning 23 January; and Philology: Outlines of the History of English Accidence (continued) on Fridays at 12.00 noon in the Examination Schools, beginning 25 January. He will continue to supervise B.Litt. students I.B. Bishop, G.M.G. Evans, V.M. Martin, and Anne Wakefield; D.Phil. students R.W. Burchfield and E.J. Stormon; and now also supervise probationer B.Litt. student B.D.H. Miller.

24 January 1952 Tolkien attends a meeting of the English Faculty Library Committee.

?31 January 1952 Tolkien writes to the Secretary of the University Court, Glasgow, agreeing to be the W.P. Ker Lecturer for 1952–3. He hopes to arrange a date between October 1952 and March 1953, and suggests as a topic for the lecture *Sir Gawain and the Green Knight*.

1 February 1952 Tolkien chairs an English Faculty Board meeting. During vacation Tolkien has changed an appointed examiner: the Board now confirms his action and that the chairman can do this if necessary between meetings. The Applications Committee has appointed Tolkien and G.V. Smithers examiners of the B.Litt. thesis of A.W. Ward of St Edmund's Hall, *Some Problems in the English Orthoepists*.

6 February 1952 Death of King George VI.

7 February 1952 Tolkien attends another feast given by C.S. Lewis in Magdalen College to consume a ham sent by Dr Firor of John Hopkins University in the United States. Tolkien will write to his son John on 10 February that 'it was like a glimpse of old times: quiet and rational (since Hugo [Dyson] was not asked!). C.S.L. asked [C.L.] Wrenn and it was a great success, since it pleased him, and he was very pleasant: a good step towards weaning him from "politics" (academic)' (*Letters*, p. 161).

9 February 1952 Convocation meets in the Sheldonian Theatre at noon for the Proclamation of the Accession of Elizabeth II, and then walks in Procession to St Mary's Church to hear the Proclamation to the City of Oxford.

13 February 1952 Tolkien attends a Merton College meeting.

15 February 1952 Oxford lectures are cancelled on the day of George VI's funeral. There is a memorial service in St Mary's Church at 2.00 p.m.

16 February 1952 In the evening, Tolkien attends a dinner of The Society hosted by John Bryson at Balliol College, Oxford. Nine members are present. Bryson presents a paper on the Pre-Raphaelite Brotherhood as Oxford undergraduates.

21 February 1952 Identity cards, instituted in 1939, are abolished in Britain.

?March 1952 Milton Waldman has Tolkien's long exposition on 'The Silmarillion' and *The Lord of the Rings* typed, and presumably shows it to various people in Collins, but it does not achieve the desired effect. – Tolkien writes to Collins, saying that his time has been wasted and that they must publish *The Lord of the Rings* immediately, or he will send the manuscript again to Allen & Unwin.

13 March 1952 Tolkien attends a meeting of the English Faculty Library Committee.

14 March 1952 Tolkien chairs an English Faculty Board meeting. He reads a letter from a Mr Alton thanking the Board for a grant of £50 in recognition of his service in re-organizing the English Faculty Library. The General Board has sent out information to all faculty boards concerning plans for new buildings; Tolkien as chairman is authorized to act on behalf of the English Faculty Board when necessary. He reports that he is negotiating college affiliation for Professors L.A. Landa and E.V.K. Dobbie who have been granted Fulbright Awards for 1952–3. The Board agrees that in future it will meet at 2.15 p.m. on the first and eighth Fridays of term. It also agrees that the time has come 'to review the regulations governing the Preliminary Examination, and that the matter should be raised at the Faculty meeting in Trinity Term' (Oxford University Archives FA 4/5/1/2). Members of the Board are asked to submit to the chairman (Tolkien) their recommendations on the British Council scheme for the interchange of University Lecturers, in time for the recommendations to be circulated with the agenda for the first meeting in Trinity Term. – D.M. Davin, Oxford University Press, writes to Tolkien, noting that the latter does not wish his name to appear on the title-page of *Pearl*. Davin therefore assumes that royalties should be paid to Mrs Gordon. In consideration of the good deal of work Tolkien has done on the book, however, Davin suggests that he receive an outright payment, and asks for his views on the matter.

15 March 1952 Hilary Full Term ends.

17 March 1952 Tolkien attends a Merton College meeting.

18 April 1952 Collins are frightened by the great length of the book Tolkien has proposed, which with the present cost of paper would mean a very big outlay by the publisher. Tolkien's hope of seeing 'The Silmarillion' published now collapses. He abandons, unfinished, most of the writing and rewriting he has done for his mythology during the period *c.* 1949–52 and will do little or no work on 'The Silmarillion' for several years.

19 April 1952 Tolkien attends an Early English Text Society Council meeting at Magdalen College, Oxford. It is agreed that in future the *Ancrene Riwle* sub-committee should be incorporated into the ordinary meetings of the Council, and that all the texts of the *Ancrene Riwle* should include an introduction by N.R. Ker.

24 April 1952 Tolkien attends a Merton College meeting. He is appointed a member of a junior research fellowship committee.

27 April 1952 Trinity Full Term begins. Tolkien's scheduled lectures for this term are: Philology: Outlines of the History of English Accidence (concluded) on Wednesdays at 12.00 noon in the Examination Schools, beginning 30 April; and *Ayenbite of Inwit* on Fridays at 12.00 noon in the Examination Schools, beginning 2 May. He will continue to supervise B.Litt. students I.B. Bishop (with the title of his thesis changed to *The Structure of Pearl: The Interrelationship of Its Liturgical and Poetic Elements*), G.M.G. Evans, and V.M. Martin, D.Phil. students E.J. Stormon and R.W. Burchfield, and probationer B.Litt. student B.D.H. Miller.

2 May 1952 Tolkien chairs an English Faculty Board meeting at 2.15 p.m. in the Board Room of the Clarendon Building. He submits a list of recommendations for the interchange of University Lecturers as suggested by the British Council; three names are approved. In an amended report the Applications Committee has approved B.D.H. Miller of New College as a full B.Litt. student working on 'Dame Sirith', and has appointed Tolkien as his supervisor.

10 May 1952 J.E.A. Joliffe accepts an invitation from Tolkien to dine with the Oxford Dante Society on 27 May. Tolkien evidently is to be the host on this occasion, and has sent invitations to the Society's members.

21 May 1952 Tolkien attends a Merton College meeting.

27 May 1952 Tolkien evidently acts as host to the Oxford Dante Society.

?June 1952 Tolkien replies to a letter from Mrs Irene Roberts about his poem *Errantry*, which has reached her in roundabout way, passed on by word of mouth. She understood that the poem is connected in some way with English universities, and has written to various vice-chancellors; Maurice Bowra, the Vice-Chancellor of Oxford, apparently has recognized the poem or the style and directed her to Tolkien. She would like to illustrate *Errantry*. Tolkien sends her two copies of the poem, the 'Authorized Version' as printed in the *Oxford Magazine* in 1933 and a 'Revised Version' (as he will call them in his letter to Rayner Unwin of 22 June). He suggests that Mrs Roberts visit him and Edith if she is in Oxford.

11 June 1952 Tolkien and G.V. Smithers examine A.W. Ward of St Edmund's Hall *viva voce* at 2.30 p.m. in the Examination Schools on his B.Litt. thesis *Some Problems in the English Orthoepists*.

12 June 1952 English Final Honour School Examinations begin. Tolkien is chairman of the examiners with David Cecil, E.J. Dobson, F.C. Horwood, Kathleen M. Lea, *J.I.M. Stewart, and Dorothy Whitelock. There are 211 candidates (in a letter to George Sayer, Tolkien will give the figure 222). The examiners' statement of results will be issued on 30 July 1952.

17 June 1952 Mrs Irene Roberts replies to Tolkien. She has just been given a copy of *The Hobbit* and feels ashamed to have mentioned the word 'illustrations' to such a brilliant artist. She discusses the two versions of *Errantry* Tolkien has sent her, and some discrepancies with the version that reached her by oral transmission. She asks if the 'Flammifer' (presumably the 'Revised Version' of the poem) was written before the *Errantry* of the *Oxford Magazine*, as the former does not have quite the same liquid flow. Mrs Roberts' mention of 'Flammifer' shows that she has received one of the versions of Bilbo's song at Rivendell in *The Lord of the Rings*.

19 June 1952 At a meeting of the English Faculty Library Committee, in Tolkien's absence, it is agreed that Tolkien should be asked to write a letter of thanks to Mrs D. Plowman for her loan to the Library of the William Blake Trust edition of *Jerusalem*.

20 June 1952 Tolkien chairs an English Faculty Board meeting. It is agreed that a special meeting of the Board should be held on 24 October to consider suggestions by Helen Gardner and Humphry House for the revision of the syllabus in literature for the Preliminary Examination. Members of the Board are asked to send their comments to the chairman (Tolkien) so that these can be circulated in time for the special meeting. The Applications Committee has appointed Tolkien supervisor of the B.Litt. thesis of J.C. Haworth of St Hilda's College, *The Icelandic Episode in the Life and Work of William Morris*. – Rayner Unwin writes to Tolkien. Allen & Unwin have received an inquiry about Tolkien's poem *Errantry* from someone who has seen it somewhere and is anxious to trace it again. Rayner says that he has never seen it himself, and would like to see it. He also asks to see 'The Silmarillion' again. 'I would truly love to read it . . . and I do not yet despair of seeing it published together with many other choice things from your pen' (Tolkien-George Allen & Unwin archive, Harper-Collins).

21 June 1952 Trinity Full Term ends. – Judith, daughter of Michael and Joan Tolkien, is born.

22 June 1952 Tolkien writes to Rayner Unwin. He apologizes for not having answered his letter of 29 November. 'I am chairman again of the English examiners, and in the midst of a 7-day week, and a 12-hour day, of labour that will last right on to July 31st, when I shall be cast up exhausted on the shoals of August.' (In a later letter to Rayner, on 29 August, he will say that he no longer has the resilience to cope with examining and was utterly exhausted by 31 July.) He tells of the letter he himself has received about *Errantry* and gives an account of the writing and transmission of the poem. With the present letter he sends a copy of the 'Revised Version' of *Errantry*. He also writes:

As for *The Lord of the Rings* and *The Silmarillion*, they are where they were. The one finished (and the end revised), the other still unfinished (or unrevised), and both gathering dust. I have been both off and on too unwell, and too burdened to do much about them, and too downhearted. Watching paper-shortages and costs mounting against me. But I have rather modified my views. Better something than nothing! Although to me all are one, and the 'L[ord] of the Rings' would be better far (and eased) as part of the whole, I would gladly consider the publication of any part of this stuff. Years are becoming precious. And retirement (not far off) will, as far as I can see, bring not leisure but a poverty that will necessitate scraping a living by 'examining' and such like tasks.

When I have a moment to turn round I will collect the *Silmarillion* fragments in process of completion – or rather the original outline which is more or less complete, and you can read it. My difficulty is, of course, that owing to the expense of typing and the lack of time to do my own (I typed nearly all of *The Lord of the Rings*!) I have no spare copies to let out. But what about *The Lord of the Rings*? Can anything be done about that, to unlock gates I slammed myself? [*Letters*, pp. 162–3, corrected from the Tolkien-George Allen & Unwin archive, HarperCollins]

24 June 1952 Tolkien attends a Merton College meeting. He is appointed to the Library Committee for the period 1952–3.

25 June 1952 Encaenia.

1 July 1952 Rayner Unwin replies to Tolkien's letter of 22 June. He praises *Errantry* and says that when the examinations are over, and Tolkien has perhaps had a holiday, he would like to visit Tolkien and find out what else he has been hiding all these years. He asks if Tolkien could send him one of his copies of *The Lord of the Rings* by registered post, as 'it would give us a chance to refresh our memories and get a definite idea of the best treatment for it'. The capital outlay will be great, but it would help if they did not publish *The Lord and the Rings* and *The Silmarillion* all at once. 'We do *want* to publish for you – it's only ways and means that have held us up. So please let us have the Ring now, and when you are able the Silmarillion too (I've never read it at all you see) and by the time you are freer we shall be ready to discuss it' (Tolkien-George Allen & Unwin archive, HarperCollins; partly quoted in *Letters*, pp. 163–4). – Susan Dagnall dies.

4 July 1952 Tolkien writes a postcard to a student, saying that he forgot to note the date to which her viva has been changed. He believes it to be on 30 July but will keep whatever date has been set.

7 August 1952 Tolkien writes to George Sayer and his wife Moira, in response to letters from them. At the urging of C.S. Lewis he has lent them the typescript of the first half of *The Lord of the Rings*. He tells them that Allen & Unwin now want to reconsider it for publication, so the sooner the Sayers can finish reading it, the better; but he won't leave them in the middle of the story, and would like to hear their opinions of the whole book. In response to an invitation to stay with them in Malvern, he says that he will be free after 18 August.

8 or 9 August 1952 George Sayer drives to Oxford, returns the first half of *The Lord of the Rings*, and collects the second half.

10 August 1952 Tolkien replies to a letter from Moira Sayer. He hopes that George returned home safely and that they will enjoy the second half of *The Lord of the Rings*. 'It's pretty well a crescendo until at least Chap. 4 of the last "book". It is on the rallentando and coda [i.e. the winding down of the story, and the hobbits' return to the Shire] that I am specially anxious for your opinion' (Christie's, *20th-Century Books and Manuscripts*, London, 16 November 2001, p. 25). – An Australian reader writes to Tolkien that he thinks the Gollum of the old version of *The Hobbit* a much more interesting character.

11–18 August 1952 Tolkien stays in Cambridge, where he spends much of his time working in the library at Corpus Christi College on their manuscript of the *Ancrene Wisse*. Although Tolkien has told Moira Sayer that he would be staying at Peterhouse, Priscilla Tolkien will later recall that she and her mother accompanied him for at least part of the time, and that they all stayed at the Garden House Hotel.

Late August 1952 Tolkien stays with George and Moira Sayer at Malvern while Edith is with friends in Bournemouth. He and Sayer walk in the Malvern Hills, and drive to the Black Mountains on the borders of Wales where they pick bilberries and climb through the heather. They picnic on bread, cheese, and apples, washed down with perry, beer, or cider. Tolkien often compares the scenery to places in *The Lord of the Rings*, or pollution to the work of orcs.

Tolkien having asked the Sayers if he can do anything to help them, they suggest that he work in the garden. Sayer will recall that Tolkien 'chose an area of about two square yards, part flower border and part lawn and cultivated it perfectly: the border meticulously weeded and the soil made level and exceedingly fine; the grass cut with scissors closely and evenly. It took him quite a long time to do the job, but it was beautifully done. He was in all things a perfectionist' ('Recollections of J.R.R. Tolkien', *Proceedings of the J.R.R. Tolkien Centenary Conference 1992* (1995), p. 23).

One evening, to entertain his guest, Sayer produces a tape recorder. Tolkien 'had never seen one before and said whimsically that he ought to cast out any devil that might be in it by recording a prayer, the Lord's Prayer in Gothic' (Sayer, sleeve notes to the LP record *J.R.R. Tolkien Reads and Sings His The Hobbit and The Fellowship of the Ring* (1975)). When this is done and played back to Tolkien, he is delighted, and subsequently records on Sayer's machine some of the poems from *The Lord of the Rings*, an extract from 'The Ride of the Rohirrim' (bk. V, ch. 5), and the riddle scene from *The Hobbit* (ch. 5). These recordings, or some of them, will be issued by Caedmon Records of New York in 1975. *See note.*

When they attend Mass on Sunday, 24 August, Tolkien leans over to help some children in the pew in front of him, who are trying to follow the service in a simple picture book missal. Sayer will recall that when we came out of the church we found that he was not with us. I went back and found him kneeling in front of the Lady Altar with the young children and their mother, talking happily and I think telling stories about Our Lady. I knew the mother and found out later that they were enthralled. This again was typical: he loved children and had the gift of getting on well with them. 'Mummy, can we always go to church with that nice man?' ['Recollections of J.R.R. Tolkien', *Proceedings of the J.R.R. Tolkien Centenary Conference 1992* (1995), p. 24]

– When Tolkien returns home to Oxford, he will send Moira Sayer a charming bread-and-butter letter in Elvish, with a translation.

29 August 1952 Tolkien writes to Rayner Unwin. He is anxious to publish *The Lord of the Rings* 'as soon as possible. I believe it to be a great (though not flawless) work.' The expense of having it typed having proved prohibitive, he has had to do it himself, and as 'there is only one (more or less) fair copy' he does not want to trust it to the post, 'and in any case I am now going to devote some days to correcting it finally. For this purpose I am retiring tomorrow from the noise and stench of Holywell to my son's [Michael] cottage on Chiltern-top while he is away with his children.' Tolkien suggests that he then bring *The Lord of the Rings* to Rayner in London, or if Rayner could collect it in Oxford Tolkien could show him other material, and they could discuss 'matters relative to the production of *The Lord* (*maps*, possible additions and subtractions etc.)'. He describes the tape recordings he made with George Sayer and wonders if the BBC might be interested. He will not attend even the International Congress of Linguists on 1 September, of which he is an official: 'time is so miserably short, and I am tired. I have on my plate not only the "great works", but the overdue professional work I was finishing up at Cambridge (edition of the *Ancrene Wisse*); the W.P. Ker lecture at Glasgow; *Sir Gawain*; and new lectures!' (Tolkien-George Allen & Unwin archive, HarperCollins; mostly published in *Letters*, p. 164). He has constant fan mail (concerning *The Hobbit*) from all over the English-speaking world, asking for 'more', especially about the Necromancer.

30 August–10 September 1952 Tolkien stays at Michael Tolkien's cottage (Chapel Cottage, at the Oratory School, Woodcote) while Michael and his family are away, to read through and correct *The Lord of the Rings*. Tolkien's eldest son, John, is with him at least part of the time. Since he has written *The Lord of the Rings* over such a long span of years, some elements in the story need to be changed, and even in later parts Tolkien needs to ensure that all of the adjustments consequent upon changes in the story's chronology have been made. It is possibly at this time that he inserts riders in the typescript, adding an extra day and night to Sam and Frodo's journey between the Morannon and the stewing of the rabbits, and another day into 'Journey to the Cross-roads' (bk. IV, ch. 7). As a result of his work on the history of the realms in exile in *The Heirs of Elendil*, possibly at this time Tolkien also makes some alterations and additions in a late typescript to *The Lord of the Rings*.

He may do no more than read through and check the narrative at this time, but undoubtedly as he reads he has to do much cross-checking. If he has not made them already, he must now make the alterations to *The Lord of the Rings* consequent upon his decision to accept as valid both versions of Bilbo's encounter with Gollum. He writes replacement pages to insert in the Prologue, giving the 'true' (second version) account, but hesitates whether he should explain here or in 'The Shadow of the Past' (bk. I, ch. 2) the 'false' version related in the first edition of *The Hobbit*. He writes the necessary new material for both alternatives. In a separate 'Note' he works out an explanation of the different story in the two editions of *The Hobbit*; and on the verso of this makes a new, third version of the Gamgee and Cotton family trees. It is probably at this time that he writes the Foreword that will appear in the first edition of *The Lord of the Rings*.

It is possibly at this time as well, perhaps as a result of Mrs Roberts' criticism sent to him the previous June, that Tolkien further develops Bilbo's song at Rivendell in Book II, Chapter 2. He begins the first, manuscript text of this new group with the phrase 'Eärendel was a mariner'. He then makes a typescript which he uses as the basis for massive rewriting, and follows this with a second typescript which with a few amendments is the text that will be published. Nonetheless, he will begin a divergent line of development in a new typescript based on the first typescript of the song, with the title *The Short Lay of Eärendel*, in which he introduces new elements, and later will begin to make a fine manuscript with elaborate initials, *The Short Lay of Eärendel: Eärendillinwë*. He will abandon the latter after only one page, probably because he already had begun further emendation, and then begin another, similar manuscript which is brought to completion.

Tolkien's first account of *The Tale of Aragorn and Arwen* may also belong to this period of revision, if it was not already in existence. His first version, *Of Aragorn and Arwen Undómiel*, part manuscript and part typescript, is longer than the eventual published text and includes a long passage summarizing the War of the Ring. He then makes a full typescript, introducing only a few minor changes, but strikes through the account of the War of the Ring, rewrites the work at even greater length, and attaches it to the main typescript as riders. He then makes a new typescript incorporating the additions and changes.

Early September 1952 Priscilla Tolkien takes up a job in Bristol.

1 September 1952 Rayner Unwin writes to Tolkien. He will come to Oxford on 18 or 19 September to collect *The Lord of the Rings*, and to discuss ways and means, and if anything can be done with the tape recordings.

10 September 1952 Rayner Unwin writes to Tolkien, to confirm that he and his wife will call on Tolkien on Friday 19 September.

19 September 1952 Rayner and Carol Unwin visit Tolkien at Oxford. Rayner collects *The Lord of the Rings* and some 'Silmarillion' material.

?20 September–late September or early October 1952 Tolkien and Edith stay for at least a week at the Highcliffe Hotel, Clevedon, Somerset. Edith visits Priscilla in Bristol.

22 September 1952 Rayner Unwin writes to Tolkien. He has begun to obtain a cost estimate for *The Lord of the Rings*, and to learn what problems its production will entail.

24 September 1952 Tolkien writes to his grandson Michael George from Clevedon. He sends a map of the area and a drawing of the view from his window.

27 September 1952 Priscilla Tolkien visits her parents while they are staying at Clevedon.

Early October 1952 Around this time Tolkien is consulted by a Mr Burns, probably of the publisher Burns & Oates, concerning some proposed work with which a Miss Kirchberger is concerned (possibly Clare Kirchberger, editor and translator of religious works by early writers). Burns promises to send Tolkien a complimentary copy of '*The Cloud*' on 7 October (probably *The Cloud of Unknowing and Other Treatises by an English Mystic of the Fourteenth Century*, 6th and rev. edn., Burns & Oates, 1952).

3 October 1952 Britain explodes an atomic bomb in the Pacific.

5 October 1952 Tea rationing ends in Britain.

8 October 1952 Tolkien attends a Merton College meeting.

12 October 1952 Michaelmas Full Term begins. Tolkien's scheduled lectures for this term are: *Sir Gawain and the Green Knight* on Wednesdays at 12.00 noon in the Examination Schools, beginning 15 October; Philology: English Orthography on Fridays at 11.00 a.m. in the Schools, beginning 17 October; and *Ayenbite of Inwit* on Fridays at 12.00 noon in the Examination Schools, beginning 17 October. He will continue to supervise B.Litt. students G.M.G. Evans, J.C. Haworth, V.M. Martin, and B.D.H. Miller, and D.Phil. students E.J. Stormon and R.W. Burchfield.

16 October 1952 Tolkien chairs a meeting of the English Faculty Library Committee.

17 October 1952 Tolkien chairs an English Faculty Board meeting. J.N. Bryson of Balliol is elected the new chairman. Tolkien ceases to be an *ex officio* member of committees such as the Library Committee, the Lecture List Committee, and the committee to deal with matters referred by the General Board, but is made an ordinary member of the Applications Committee. It is reported that during the vacation Tolkien had to appoint two replacement examiners. The Applications Committee has appointed Tolkien the supervisor of recognized student T.P. Dunning for his thesis on early English homiletic literature, and Tolkien and Mary Lascelles examiners of the B.Litt. thesis of F.M. Whalley of St Anne's College, *The Rise of the English Original Fairy-Story 1800–1865*.

23 October 1952 Tolkien finishes drafting a statement for Board of the Faculty of English Language and Literature on the O'Donnell Lecture Trust, giving its history. – Rayner Unwin writes to Tolkien, enclosing a sheet which shows three different calculations for the cost of publishing *The Lord of the Rings*. The best so far would mean a publication price of 70 shillings for a single volume, and two volumes would be more expensive because of double binding costs. But he is obtaining another estimate from a different printer.

24 October 1952 Tolkien attends an English Faculty Board special meeting at 2.15 p.m. in the Board Room of the Clarendon Building at which Helen Gardner and Humphry House's proposals for the Preliminary Examination are discussed. The only change agreed which affects the early period is that the Old English *Battle of Maldon* will replace 'Aelfric's Homilies on *St Oswald* and *The Assumption of St John*'. – Tolkien replies to Rayner Unwin. He cannot follow the estimates, but is grateful for the trouble Rayner is taking with *The Lord of the Rings*, and hopes that he will be able to make a definite decision soon. 'The thing weighs on my mind, for I can neither dismiss it as a disaster and turn to other matters, nor get on with it and things concerned with it (such as the maps).' He agrees that £3.10.0 is expensive for a book, asks how many Allen & Unwin would print, and comments on the likely sales. He continues:

> I am at last after three weeks incessant labour of the most exacting and dreariest sort, getting into rather calmer water. I have shuffled off the Chairmanship of the Board, and concluded a number of tasks, and now, barring lecturing and teaching, have only to face (before preparation for Schools begins in February) examination of a tiresome thesis (on Fairy Tales!), reading and editing a monograph for a series, producing a contribution to 'Essays and Studies' by December 2nd [*The Homecoming of Beorhtnoth Beorhthelm's Son*], completing my edition of *Ancrene Wisse*, and writing the W.P. Ker Lecture for Glasgow. And also (if I can) finding somewhere else to live and moving! This charming house has become uninhabitable – unsleepable-in, unworkable-in, rocked, racked with noise, and drenched with fumes. Such is modern life. Mordor in our midst.

He also comments on the British atomic bomb: the resulting cloud was produced by 'persons who have decided to use the Ring for their own (of course most excellent) purposes' (*Letters*, p. 165). – In the evening, Tolkien attends a dinner of The Society hosted by K.T. Parker at Oriel College, Oxford. Twelve members are present. Parker initiates a discussion on fine arts in the university.

?Late October–early November 1952 Tolkien again visits Cambridge, presumably to work on the *Ancrene Wisse*. – On his return home he finds two packets sent him by Mr Burns, assumes that they are duplicate copies of the book promised him, and returns one packet without opening either.

Early November 1952 Rayner Unwin, having looked at the cost estimates for *The Lord of the Rings*, sends a telegram to his father, who is on a business trip in the Far East. He admits that publication of *The Lord of the Rings* will be a big risk, and believes that Allen & Unwin might lose up to a thousand pounds, but in his opinion Tolkien has written a work of genius. He asks if he may offer Tolkien a contract. Stanley Unwin cables in reply: '*If* you believe it is a work of genius, *then* you may lose a thousand pounds' (quoted in Rayner Unwin, *George Allen & Unwin: A Remembrancer* (1999), p. 99).

5 November 1952 Tolkien attends a Merton College Meeting.

9 November 1952 Wilfred Childe dies.

10 November 1952 Rayner Unwin writes to Tolkien that Allen & Unwin would like to publish *The Lord of the Rings* under a profit-sharing agreement (i.e. no royalties will be paid until all costs have been recovered, but thereafter the author will receive half-profits; if the book does badly, the author will receive nothing and the publisher will suffer a loss, but less of a loss than if he had to pay royalties, but if the book is successful the author will earn a substantially better return than under the usual royalty arrangements). Allen & Unwin are still considering whether to publish it in one expensive volume or in three reasonably sized (and priced) volumes.

12 November 1952 Tolkien replies to Rayner Unwin's letter of 10 November, which has cheered him immensely. He will lose no time in spreading the news.

13 November 1952 C.S. Lewis writes to congratulate Tolkien.

15 November 1952 Tolkien receives a letter from Mr Burns. He only just reads it when, at 9.00 a.m., he is rung up by Miss Kirchberger, ostensibly to ask his advice about her work, but (Tolkien thinks) mainly concerned to learn what has occurred in regard to the book about which Tolkien is being consulted. – Tolkien replies to Burns. He mentions his views about 'modernization' or 'semi-translation' in regard to Miss Kirchberger's work. By now he has opened the other packet sent by Mr Burns, not the expected *Cloud*, but a gift from a Professor Kennedy (probably Charles W. Kennedy's *Early English Christian Poetry, Translated into Alliterative Verse with Critical Commentary*, published 1952), about which Tolkien writes a lengthy commentary and negative criticism. He explains that he has written at length due to

> unexpected freedom and exhilaration. I was 'cut' by two researchers this morning who normally occupy between them over two hours every Saturday morning: freedom. I also heard both that a dramatic dialogue in real alliterative verse (of various styles) on chivalry and common sense (in the mouths of two fictitious Anglo-Saxons) had been accepted [*The Homecoming of Beorhtnoth Beorhthelm's Son*]; and more remarkable, a 'romance' of at least 500,000 words [*The Lord of the Rings*]: exhilaration. [private collection]

He refers to 'the Salu', probably the translation of *The Ancrene Riwle* into Modern English by his former student Mary Salu, which Burns & Oates will publish in 1955 and for which Tolkien will write a brief preface.

17 November 1952 Rayner Unwin writes to Tolkien. Allen & Unwin have decided to publish *The Lord of the Rings* in three volumes at a price not exceeding 25*s* each. As they now have all the information they need for estimates, Rayner thinks that he should return the manuscript to Tolkien so that the author can put the final polish on the first two books (mentioning, for instance, that he knows that Tolkien wants to do some work on the Council of

Elrond). Since Tolkien does not like to trust the post, and he, Rayner, cannot spare a day to come to Oxford in the near future, he asks if Tolkien knows of anyone who might be travelling from London to Oxford who could be trusted with the manuscript.

25 November 1952 Tolkien writes to thank a Mr (Christopher) Sandford for the gift of the Golden Cockerel Press *Sir Gawain and the Green Knight: A Prose Translation*, with an introductory essay by Gwyn Jones (1952), which he received at the beginning of a troubled term. He apologizes for his delay in acknowledging it.

26 November 1952 Rayner Unwin sends Tolkien two forms of agreement for the publication of *The Lord of the Rings*, and asks him to sign one copy and return it. The contract specifies that the manuscript is to be ready for the printer by 25 March 1953. Rayner again mentions the problem of returning the manuscript to Tolkien.

27 November 1952 Tolkien writes to Rayner Unwin. He would like to see Rayner on Wednesday 3 December and collect the manuscript. He could come up by 10.15 a.m. train which arrives at 11.30 a.m., and would be free until 4.45 p.m.

28 November 1952 Rayner Unwin replies to Tolkien. 3 December will be fine. He invites Tolkien to have lunch with him and his wife.

3 December 1952 Some problem (either physical or public transport) prevents Tolkien's planned visit to Allen & Unwin in London.

5 December 1952 Tolkien attends an English Faculty Board meeting. A memorandum on the O'Donnell Lecture Trust (probably from Tolkien) is received. The appointment of the chairman and Professor Tolkien as the Board's representatives on the Trust is confirmed. They are asked to report to the Board after they have met the representatives of the other universities concerned. The Applications Committee has recommended that the application for the admission of S. Jakobsdottir of Somerville College as an advanced student should be deferred until she has been interviewed by Professor Tolkien.

6 December 1952 Michaelmas Full Term ends.

8 December 1952 Tolkien attends a Merton College meeting.

?9 December 1952 Tolkien writes to Rayner Unwin. 'I intend to come tomorrow by the 10.15 and since it is possible, I hope, to move about again, should reach you about noon' (Tolkien–George Allen & Unwin archive, HarperCollins). He says that he will bring the contract with him.

10 December 1952 Tolkien takes the contract to London, lunches with Rayner and Carol Unwin in their flat above Allen & Unwin's offices in Museum Street, and collects the typescript of *The Lord of the Rings*.

Christmas vacation 1952 Tolkien spends time revising *The Lord of the Rings*, but the work is hindered by various problems, including bronchitis.

1953

10 January 1953 Tolkien attends a meeting of the O'Donnell Trustees and representatives of the Universities of Edinburgh, Wales, and Oxford at Senate House, the University of London, to discuss the O'Donnell Lecture scheme. He will write a report of the meeting for the boards of the Oxford faculties of English Language and Literature and of Mediaeval and Modern Languages.

18 January 1953 Hilary Full Term begins. Tolkien's scheduled lectures for this term are: *Sir Gawain and the Green Knight* (continued) on Wednesdays at 11.00 a.m. in the Examination Schools, beginning 21 January; The Language of the *Ayenbite of Inwit* (continued) on Fridays at 11.00 a.m. in the Examination Schools, beginning 23 January; and the 'Pardoner's Tale' by Chaucer on Fridays at 12.00 noon in the Examination Schools, beginning 23 January. He will continue to supervise B.Litt. students G.M.G. Evans, J.C. Haworth, V.M. Martin, and B.D.H. Miller, D.Phil. student R.W. Burchfield, and recognized student T.P. Dunning.

21 January 1953 Tolkien, once again chairman of the examiners in the English Honour School, in that capacity writes to K.C. Turpin, Secretary of Faculties, the University Registry. He gives an estimated number of candidates in the Honour School for 1953 at 225. The five examiners already in office wish to apply for the nomination of two extra examiners, one mainly in Modern English and another mainly on medieval and linguistic subjects.

23 January 1953 Tolkien attends an English Faculty Board meeting. His report of the meeting of the O'Donnell Trustees and representatives of the Universities of Edinburgh, Wales, and Oxford is presented and its recommendations approved. The Applications Committee has appointed Tolkien supervisor of the D.Phil. thesis of A.D. Horgan of New College, *The Vocabulary of the Cursor Mundi; with Principal Reference to MS Cotton Vesp. A3*.

27 January 1953 Philip Unwin of George Allen & Unwin writes to Tolkien. The publisher has received a request from a teacher at St Margaret's School, Edinburgh, who wishes to stage, privately for the school and parents, a dramatic adaptation of *The Hobbit* she has made. Unwin asks if Tolkien wants the publisher to grant free permission or to charge a nominal fee, and if he would like Allen & Unwin to ask to see a copy of the script.

30 January 1953 In the evening, Tolkien hosts a dinner of The Society at Merton College. Eleven members are present. According to the minutes, Tolkien 'tossed *in medium* a sack of paradoxes and problems on the Retiring Age for professors and others, which detonated an explosive discussion. The conversation later switched to the more agreeable topic of the illiteracy of undergraduates' (MS Eng. d.3529, Bodleian Library, Oxford).

?February or March 1953 Tolkien completes his alliterative translation of *Sir Gawain and the Green Knight*, passes proofs of the talk he gave in Liège in 1951 (*Middle English 'Losenger'*), and sends *The Homecoming of Beorhtnoth Beorhthelm's Son* with the essay on 'ofermod' to *Essays and Studies*, a publication of the English Association.

3 February 1953 Tolkien replies to Philip Unwin's letter of 27 January, telling him to give free permission for the performance.

11 February 1953 Tolkien attends a Merton College meeting.

18 February 1953 Ida Gordon writes to D.M. Davin of Oxford University Press. She suggests that they ask Tolkien's opinion if the title of her late husband's book should be *Pearl* or *The Pearl*.

25 February 1953 D.M. Davin writes to Tolkien. He asks if Tolkien thinks £50 a reasonable payment for his services in connection with *Pearl*.

1 March 1953 Tolkien replies to D.M. Davin. He would be grateful for a fee of £50. He hopes that the book will sell well, and will try to ensure this by inducing authorities to retain or re-insert *Pearl* in the syllabi.

8 March 1953 Tolkien writes to George Sayer. He asks for suggestions for titles for the individual volumes of *The Lord of the Rings*, and refers to his omission of the Epilogue to the final book, on Sayer's advice, though he would like some other device for conveying its information. (By now, some time after his letter to Milton Waldman in ?late 1951, Tolkien has written a second version of the Epilogue.)

13 March 1953 Tolkien attends an English Faculty Board meeting. He is asked to draft for the chairman's approval a statement in support of the Board's application for the designation of Alistair Campbell as a Senior Lecturer. The draft statute concerning the O'Donnell Lecturer, as amended at the meeting, is approved for submission to the General Board.

14 March 1953 Hilary Full Term ends.

16 March 1953 Tolkien attends a Merton College meeting.

18 March 1953 Rayner Unwin writes to Tolkien, asking if he has completed revision of the first two books of *The Lord of the Rings*, which by contract are to be finished by 25 March.

?Mid-March 1953 L.G. Smith, a publicist for George Allen & Unwin, writes to Tolkien, asking him to prepare for publicity purposes a description of *The Lord of the Rings* in not more than one hundred words, and biographical details about the author.

24 March 1953 Tolkien writes to Rayner Unwin. He will not be able to meet the required delivery date for *The Lord of the Rings*. His wife is in increasing ill health, and for her sake, on doctor's orders, he has had to spend most of his spare time 'in finding and negotiating for the purchase of a house on high dry soil and in the quiet', and is now on the point of moving. Also he himself was ill during the 'vital Christmas Vacation', and 'I am now still involved as chairman in controlling the setting of all the honours English papers for June, and a week behind at that. I am afraid I must ask for your lenience in the matter of the date.' But he notices that Rayner has asked only for the first two books, the revision of which he had practically completed before disaster overtook him. He could send both by the end of the month, or the first book, which is ready and for which he has a spare corrected copy, immediately. He hopes that between 23 April and June 17 he will have enough leisure to deal with 'the bulk of the later books (which need little revision). . . . But I go into a tunnel of examinations from 17 June to 27 July which will give me 12 hours work a day. After that I shall lift my battered head, I hope. I am resigning from Exams anyway; but I could not get out of it this year' (*Letters*, p. 166). He asks if Rayner can advise him how to deal with the request from the Allen & Unwin publicity department, wondering how it is possible to describe *The Lord of the Rings* in a hundred words; but he might get help from someone else who has read it, such as C.S. Lewis. Having discussed with Rayner at some point possible titles for the three volumes of *The Lord of the Rings*, Tolkien has been giving thought to the matter, but since the two books in the second volume are not related, he thinks that it might be best to have volume numbers, and to give titles to the six books: in Volume 1, *The Ring Sets Out* and *The Ring Goes South*; in Volume 2, *The Treason of Isengard* and *The Ring Goes East*; and in Volume 3, *The War of the Ring* and *The End of the Third Age*. If this is not possible, he suggests that the three volumes have the titles *The Shadow Grows*, *The Ring in the Shadow*, and *The War of the Ring* (or *The Return of the King*). – Tolkien replies to L.G. Smith. He is in the midst of moving house, but after 1 April will do what he can in response to the publicity department's request. He can supply biographical details if his entry in *Who's Who* is not sufficient, but feels that it is impossible to describe *The Lord of the Rings* in only 100 words. 'The briefest possible statement, which must also make clear the relation of *The Lord of the Rings* to *The Hobbit* will take, according to my first sketch, 300/400. I will send it along in a few days' (Tolkien-George Allen & Unwin archive, HarperCollins).

?Late March 1953 Tolkien writes to George Sayer, asking for help in writing a publicity blurb for *The Lord of the Rings*. He finds himself unable to think of anything that is not too apologetic for the purpose.

27 March 1953 Rayner Unwin writes to Tolkien. 'As I said when we signed the contract, the date for delivery of the manuscript was not finally binding though of course we would like it as soon as we can have it' (Tolkien-George Allen & Unwin archive, HarperCollins). He sends sample paragraphs of what is needed for publicity purposes.

30 March 1953 Tolkien and Edith move into 76 Sandfield Road in the Oxford suburb of Headington. Christopher Tolkien and his wife Faith move into the house his parents had occupied in Holywell Street. The move is more disruptive than Tolkien expects, as he will tell Rayner Unwin on 11 April: 'In spite of every care the move proved disastrously dislocating, and instead of two days I have spent ten in endless labour; and still cannot lay my hands on many papers and notes that I need [for completion of *The Lord of the Rings*]. In addition things have gone wrong with the examination business which is under my unhappy charge; and I leave on Tuesday morning for Glasgow to deliver a W.P. Ker Lecture which is still only half prepared' (*Letters*, p. 167).

11 April 1953 Tolkien writes to Rayner Unwin. He has at last revised for press Books I and II of *The Lord of the Rings* and plans to send them to Allen & Unwin in two packets on 13 April. He deals with various matters which he and Rayner presumably discussed at one of their meetings. He will also send his original Foreword to *The Lord of the Rings* which of course need not be printed yet, since I cannot find my note of the additions or alterations which you thought would be required in view of the publication of the work in three volumes. Also, the matter of 'appendices' at the end of volume III, after the final and rather short sixth 'book', has not been decided. It is no good promising things that are not going actually to appear; but I very much hope that precisely what is here promised, in however reduced a form, will in fact prove possible.

He is not returning the design he has made for the Doors of Durin (bk. II, ch. 4), since he has not had time to re-draw it, but will deal with it when it is needed. He points out that this picture should appear in white line on a black background, since it represents a silver line in the darkness, and asks what the Allen & Unwin production department thinks about that idea. Rayner has already rejected the reproduction in colour of Tolkien's 'facsimiles' of the burned and torn pages of the Dwarves' 'Book of Mazarbul' and suggested line-blocks instead. Tolkien thinks that the omission of these facsimiles is regrettable, and that line-blocks are not suitable for the purpose. He hopes that it might be possible to include the facsimiles in the 'appendix' (in the event, they will be omitted from the book, as published in English, until the edition of 2004). He expects to find revision of the rest of *The Lord of the Rings* easier than of the first two books, which 'were written first a very long time ago, have been often altered, and needed a close consideration of the whole to bring them into line'. He wants to know when he is likely to be asked to give his attention to proofs or anything else, as 'I shall have a little elbow-room until about the 20th of June; after that no time at all for anything but exam-scripts until about August 1. I shall then be tired, but my time will be free (more or less) during August and September' (*Letters*, p. 168). He decides that three different maps are needed, some appearing in more than one volume, and explains that these already exist, as in writing such a story one must make the map first, but they are not fit for reproduction. He asks if he should try to redraw them as soon as he can and send them for the consideration of the Allen & Unwin production department. He asks Rayner to pass to the publicity department a description of *The Lord of the Rings* he has written in 300 words, and a blurb of 95 words which George Sayer has written at Tolkien's request.

12 April 1953 Tolkien prepares his typescript for posting, and writes a note for enclosure with it.

13 April 1953 Tolkien sends a postcard to George Allen & Unwin. He has sent the first volume of *The Lord of the Rings* by registered post in one packet rather than two.

14 April 1953 Tolkien travels to Glasgow to give the W.P. Ker Memorial Lecture. His attention to *The Lord of the Rings* having left him with only a few days to work on his lecture, it is still unfinished, or unpolished, when he leaves Oxford. – Rayner Unwin writes to Tolkien, acknowledging safe receipt of the typescript of *The Lord of the Rings* and dealing with various points. Galley proofs of Book I should be ready in about two months; the Foreword can follow later. White lines on black for the Doors of Durin picture would present no technical difficulty, 'but in the middle of the text of a book it is rather a black lump and the shadow of this block page tends to go through and mar other pages. There is a way, I gather, of using a tint instead of solid black and using a half tone screen but we could experiment with this when we have a drawing and let you see more precisely the alternatives' (Tolkien-George Allen & Unwin archive, HarperCollins). He apologizes about the 'Book of Mazarbul' pictures: Tolkien may have a full-page line drawing for each, or they can go into the Appendices. Rayner agrees that three maps are needed, but they must not be too large or with too many folds. He suggests that the small-scale map of the whole field of action might be spread across a double page, and the smaller maps of the Shire and Gondor might be fitted on a page each. He sends Tolkien a specimen page to show how much room he would have and the scale of the page.

15 April 1953 Tolkien delivers the W.P. Ker Memorial Lecture, on *Sir Gawain and the Green Knight*, to an audience of 300 at the University of Glasgow. When quoting the text of the poem he uses his own recently completed Modern English translation, which is well received. He will think the lecture less good than it might have been because he had not given it enough attention in writing, though it might be improved when prepared for publication. (It will not published until 1983, in *The Monsters and the Critics and Other Essays*.)

?16 or 17 April 1953 Tolkien returns to Oxford from Glasgow by train. En route,

> I travelled all the way from Motherwell to Wolverhampton with a Scotch mother and a wee lassie, whom I rescued from standing in the corridor of a packed train, and they were allowed to go 'first' without payment since I told the inspector I welcomed their company. My reward was to be informed ere we parted that (while I was at lunch) the wee lassie had declared: 'I like him but I canna understand a word he says.' To which I could only lamely reply that the latter was universal but the former was not so usual. [quoted in *Biography*, p. 127]

19 April 1953 Tolkien attends an Early English Text Society Council meeting at Magdalen College, Oxford. The editorial secretary states that there is little further to report on the Cleopatra, Titus, and Corpus texts of the *Ancrene Riwle*. It is agreed that all of the editions of the English version of the *Ancrene Riwle* should contain an introductory note giving a history of the edition.

23 April 1953 Tolkien chairs the final papers meeting of the English examiners. He is now deeply involved in organizing the examinations, so much so that he himself becomes the only examiner behind with his papers.

26 April 1953 Trinity Full Term begins. Tolkien's scheduled lectures for this term are: *Sir Gawain and the Green Knight* (concluded) on Wednesdays at 12.00 noon in the Examination Schools, beginning 29 April; and The Language of the *Ancrene Wisse* on Fridays at 12.00 noon in the Examination Schools, beginning 1 May. He will continue to supervise B.Litt. students G.M.G. Evans, J.C. Haworth, V.M. Martin, and B.D.H. Miller, D.Phil. students R.W. Burchfield and A.D. Horgan, and recognized student T.P. Dunning. E.J. Stormon's D.Phil. thesis has been referred back, and he is now again working under Tolkien's supervision. The title of his thesis has been changed to *A Study of the Symbolism of Spiritual Renewal, with Special Reference to The Pearl*.

27 April 1953 L.G. Smith of George Allen & Unwin sends Tolkien a draft publicity blurb for *The Lord of the Rings*, evidently derived from the material Tolkien and George Sayer have written, and asks Tolkien to return it to the publisher with any alterations he would like made.

28 April 1953 Tolkien writes to George Sayer. He tells of his lecture in Glasgow and his work on *The Lord of the Rings* with Allen & Unwin. He is worried about C.S. Lewis, who is not well. He hopes to visit Sayer again, and to make a two-voice tape recording with him.

29 April 1953 Adrien Bonjour of Lausanne University sends Tolkien, as a token of gratitude and admiration, an offprint of an article he has written, probably 'Monsters Crouching and Critics Rampant, or the *Beowulf* Dragon Debated' in *PMLA* 68 (1953).

?May 1953 Tolkien writes to Adrien Bonjour with his thanks for the offprint and comments.

1 May 1953 Tolkien attends an English Faculty Board meeting. It is agreed to apply to the General Board for the conferment of the title of Professor upon E.O.G. Turville-Petre while he holds the Vigfússon Readership in Icelandic Literature. Tolkien and Wrenn are asked to draft a statement in support of the application.

4 May 1953 In the evening, Warnie and C.S. Lewis visit R.E. Havard at home, where they find Tolkien. Warnie will record in his diary that the friends considered whether to listen to a broadcast of *The Man Who Was Thursday* by G.K. Chesterton, but decided not to do so. Instead they enjoyed 'two bottles of Burgundy between the four of us, and some good talk: much of it on translation in general, and on Ronnie Knox's bible in particular [*The Holy Bible, Abridged and Re-arranged* by Monsignor Ronald Knox, 1936], which was torn in pieces by Tollers. Ronnie, he said, had written so much parody and pastiche that he had lost what little ear for prose he had ever had. Humphrey [Havard] defended Ronnie' (*Brothers and Friends*, p. 242).

5 May 1953 Tolkien returns the draft blurb to L.G. Smith with emendations.

7 May 1953 L.G. Smith writes to thank Tolkien for the revised blurb. He will send a proof in a few days.

20 May 1953 Tolkien attends a Merton College meeting.

27 May 1953 Adrien Bonjour writes to Tolkien. He has read Tolkien's remarks concerning the *Beowulf* dragon with great interest.

31 May 1953 An Oxford City and University Service to mark the coronation of Elizabeth II is held in St Mary's Church at 11.00 a.m. Heads of Houses,

Doctors, and Masters of Art of the University assemble in the Divinity School by 10.40 a.m. and walk in procession to the Church.

2 June 1953 Coronation of Queen Elizabeth II. No lectures or classes are given today at Oxford.

4 June 1953 L.G. Smith sends Tolkien a proof of the blurb for *The Lord of the Rings*.

5 June 1953 Tolkien writes to Rayner Unwin to ask the state of progress of *The Lord of the Rings*. He now has a lull of a few days, but 'on Thursday next, 11 June, Schools begin, and from 17th. until the Vivas, beginning on July 16, I shall be submerged under scripts, requiring anything up to 14 hours a day. The Vivas only occupy about 6 hours a day, but the chairman has to put in a good deal of evening work.' But he does not want to hold matters up, and if he knows when proofs are to arrive he might be able to get help with them. In the time before 17 June he will try to deal with the maps and the Doors of Durin drawing. He asks Rayner when the printer will need more manuscript; he sees no chance of getting away for more than a day or two in the vacation, and he will be too tired to attend the big 'Anglistic' conference in August in Paris, 'so that I hope to be able to put the whole of the rest of *The Lord of the Rings* in final form before next term. Only at one point is there in fact much to do to it; it was the earlier, and by now pretty ancient "books" that needed most attention' (Tolkien-George Allen & Unwin archive, HarperCollins). – Tolkien returns the proof of the blurb to L.G. Smith with no changes, and asks to have a fair number of copies to send to numerous correspondents to whom he has promised early information. He asks if there is any way of ensuring that a reviewer will get a chance to review the book. Both he and C.S. Lewis think that a sympathetic review of the first volume by Lewis, who has read the whole, would be of value.

11 June 1953 Tolkien and Mary Lascelles (his former student, now teaching at Oxford) examine F.M. Whalley of St Anne's College *viva voce* at 2.15 p.m. in the Examination Schools on her B.Litt. thesis *The Rise of the English Original Fairy Story*. – The English Final Honour School examinations begin. Tolkien is chairman of the examiners, who also include David Cecil, E.J. Dobson, F.C. Horwood, Kathleen M. Lea, J.I.M. Stewart, and Dorothy Whitelock. There are 164 candidates. – *Pearl*, edited by E.V. Gordon and prepared for publication by Ida L. Gordon with assistance and contributions by Tolkien, is published. – Rayner Unwin writes to Tolkien. The printers are being slower than anticipated with *The Fellowship of the Ring*, but proofs should be ready by the end of the month. Allen & Unwin will need 'the odds and ends of the First Volume (illustrations, maps, etc.) ready fairly soon and we will have the next 2 books (which constitute the Second Volume) as soon as you have them prepared' (Tolkien-George Allen & Unwin archive, HarperCollins).

19 June 1953 Tolkien attends an English Faculty Board meeting at 2.15 p.m. in the Board Room of the Clarendon Building. It is reported that the General Board has agreed to confer the title of Professor on E.O.G. Turville-Petre.

20 June 1953 Trinity Full Term ends.

Late June 1953 Tolkien visits his son Michael at the Oratory School, on the occasion of their prize day.

22 June 1953 Tolkien writes to the Controller, Third Programme, BBC, that some time ago he had been negotiating for the broadcast of his translation of *Sir Gawain and the Green Knight*. The translation had been approved, but he had not been able to complete it owing to other demands on his time. It is now finished, and he asks if the BBC is still interested. If they do not want to broadcast the whole he could suggest a suitable selection, but he thinks that some brief, non-technical introductory remarks and comment would be necessary. – Dorothy Everett dies.

23 June 1953 Tolkien attends a Merton College meeting. He is appointed Sub-warden with effect from 1 August 1953. The promotion of one of the Fellows has brought his turn for office a year earlier than he expected. He will hold the office until 21 June 1955. As Sub-warden he is also a member of the Finance Committee and serves on various *ad hoc* committees. One of his duties as Sub-warden is to send out advance notices and agenda for meetings.

24 June 1953 Encaenia. – Tolkien writes to George Sayer. He is having trouble with his hand, and busy with examinations scripts: these must be finished by 14 July, and he has over 300 still to read. Regarding another visit to Malvern, with Priscilla no longer at home Tolkien cannot travel unless someone stays with Edith, or Edith herself is away; and as Sub-warden of Merton College he now has additional duties. Their new house is pleasant, but Edith still suffers from rheumatism and arthritis.

25 June 1953 Rayner Unwin writes to Tolkien. The printers will not able to complete the galley proofs of *The Lord of the Rings* by 30 June, but could send them piecemeal from then as finished, or they could wait and send when they are complete.

26 June 1953 Tolkien replies to Rayner Unwin. As he is already behind with examination scripts and will have no time at all for *The Lord of the Rings* until 16 July, Rayner should collect galley proofs as they arrive and send them on later.

27 June 1953 In the evening, Tolkien attends a dinner of The Society hosted by Mark Van Oss at Magdalen College. Nine members are present. Their summer dinner is complemented by white wine and prolonged with brandy. Van Oss speaks about college gardens and especially trees.

30 June 1953 Tolkien attends a Merton College meeting. – P.H. Newby, of the Talks Department at the BBC, writes to Tolkien, asking him to send the BBC for consideration his translation of *Sir Gawain and the Green Knight*.

6 July 1953 Tolkien writes to the Secretary of Faculties, Oxford, asking for a grant towards the purchase of a tape recording machine. 'For seminars or small classes,' he writes, such machines 'are extraordinarily effective in the exhibition of phonetics and of linguistic change; and for "practical philology", the reconstruction of past forms of speech and literary modes (a department in which I have long been especially interested and active) they have become an indispensable assistant.' He is fairly familiar with such machines, and has made a number of recordings, 'some of which are in use for instructional purposes elsewhere' (Oxford University Archives FA 4/5/1/2 E(53)24). He has in mind a portable machine primarily for his professorial use, to be housed in his room at college, but which could be transported easily to lecture rooms, or lent to other members of the School. (There is no reply preserved in the University archives, but probably Tolkien is told that he needs approval of the Faculty Board. The matter will be discussed at the first meeting in Michaelmas Term.)

8 July 1953 Tolkien sends the typescript of his translation of *Sir Gawain and the Green Knight* to P. H. Newby at the BBC.

10 July 1953 P. H. Newby writes to Tolkien, acknowledging receipt of *Sir Gawain* and suggesting a meeting in Oxford on 17 July to discuss it. – D.M. Davin of Oxford University Press writes to remind Tolkien that they would like to see his Middle English translations whenever they are ready.

12 July 1953 Tolkien writes to P. H. Newby. He will be conducting *viva voce* examinations every day except Sundays from 16 to 29 July, from 10.00 a.m. onwards, but should be free at about 3.30 p.m. on Friday 17 July, or immediately after lunch on Saturday 18 July. He invites Newby to have tea with him on Friday.

15 July 1953 P. H. Newby writes to Tolkien to suggest that their meeting be postponed until 11.00 a.m. on Friday 31 July. The BBC would like to broadcast Tolkien's translation of *Sir Gawain and the Green Knight* around Christmas 1953. They think that it should be read by one voice, possibly by Dylan Thomas. Newby discusses the need to spread the work over several readings, and how it might be divided. This is the main problem he would like to discuss with Tolkien, but he is also concerned about the best way to read the poem aloud, and about a talk to introduce the readings.

17 July 1953 W.N. Beard of George Allen & Unwin writes to Tolkien. Galley proofs 1–82 of the first volume of *The Lord of the Rings* are being sent to him. He asks Tolkien to return the typescript with the galleys, as they still have to make blocks.

18 July 1953 Tolkien writes to W.N. Beard. He has not received any galley proofs of *The Fellowship of the Ring*, and hopes that they have not been sent to his old address, 99 Holywell.

20 July 1953 W.H. Beard writes to Tolkien. The proofs had indeed been sent to 99 Holywell by mistake. When the Post Office returns them, they will be forwarded immediately to Tolkien in Headington. In the meantime, Beard encloses an uncorrected set of galley proofs 1–83 and marked galleys 84–100 with the corresponding typescript.

22 July 1953 Tolkien writes to W.H. Beard. He has managed to retrieve the galley proofs from Holywell, and after 29 July will be able to settle down to check them. He has noticed, however, and objects to it strongly, that the compositors have taken it upon themselves to make certain alterations: *dwarves* to *dwarfs*, *elven* to *elfin*, *further* to *farther*, etc. He has also noticed that the pages from which blocks are to be made are missing.

24 July 1953 W.N. Beard writes to Tolkien. He is appalled that the printers have made such radical deviations from the author's copy; they have been informed that they must bear the expense of corrections. If possible, they would like the galley proofs returned in small instalments so that they can start to produce page proofs.

27 July 1953 Tolkien having failed to reply to P.H. Newby's letter of 15 July, Newby writes again, asking if Friday, 31 July at 11.00 a.m. would be convenient to meet. Tolkien will telex back that he would be pleased to see Newby at 11.00 a.m. on Friday at Merton College.

28 July 1953 Rayner Unwin writes to Tolkien. They need to decide on titles for *The Lord of the Rings* soon. Allen & Unwin are keen to have a completely separate title for each of the published volumes, even at the expense of no overall title. After looking at Tolkien's letter of 24 March he suggests *The Lord of the Rings* on the spine and title-page of Volume 1, with book titles *The Ring Sets Out* and *The Ring Goes South*; *The Ring in the Shadow* (or *The Shadow and the Ring*) on the spine and title-page of Volume 2, with book titles *The Treason of Isengard* and *The Ring Goes East*; and *The War of the Ring* on the spine and title-page of Volume 3, with *The End of the Third Age* as the title of Book VI, and the title of Book V to be arranged later.

29 July 1953 The examiners in the English Honour School, including Tolkien as chairman, sign a statement of results.

31 July 1953 Tolkien attends a Merton College meeting. – At 11.00 a.m. he meets P.H. Newby at Merton College to discuss BBC broadcasts of *Sir Gawain and the Green Knight*. By now Tolkien has divided the poem for six readings, and suggests that the first should be prefaced by a five-minute talk to introduce the listener to what is to follow; Tolkien wants to do the reading himself, and performs for Newby's benefit. Newby thinks that Tolkien read quite well, but not well enough for the BBC to let him read the entire poem. Newby offers to audition Tolkien in a studio, but thinks that he can persuade him to let the BBC go ahead with a different reader.

?August 1953–?first half of 1954 Tolkien begins to compile a glossary-index to *The Lord of the Rings*, promised in the Foreword to *The Fellowship of the Ring*, but does not complete it. He will write to a correspondent in 1956 that 'an index of names was to be produced, which by etymological interpretation would also provide quite a large Elvish vocabulary. . . . I worked at it for months, and indexed the first two vols. (it was the chief cause of the delay of vol. iii) until it became clear that size and cost were ruinous' (letter to H. Cotton Minchin, April 1956, *Letters*, pp. 247–8). In fact he indexes all of *The Lord of the Rings*, but only names of places. (Cf. entry for 31 August 1953.)

4 August 1953 Tolkien writes to Christopher Tolkien that the *Lord of the Rings* 'galleys are proving rather a bore! There seem such an endless lot of them; and they have put me very much out of conceit with parts of the Great Work. . . . But the printing is very good, as it ought to be from an almost faultless copy. . . .' He complains about the alterations made by 'impertinent compositors' (*Letters*, p. 169). – W.N. Beard of George Allen & Unwin sends proofs of the Foreword, contents page, and galley proofs 120–132 of *The Lord of the Rings*. The printers who altered Tolkien's spellings had followed the *Oxford English Dictionary* for style, but Allen & Unwin pointed out that the copy had stated that the style of the author was to be followed, and the printers have agreed to be responsible for the expense of correction.

5 August 1953 Kathleen Lea of Lady Margaret Hall, who has been one of Tolkien's fellow examiners, writes to thank him for the gift of a calligraphic copy of *Doworst* (see entry for 21 December 1933). Miss Lea sends Tolkien some sherry 'to go with the galleys' of *The Lord of the Rings* (Tolkien-George Allen & Unwin archive, HarperCollins). She mentions having seen Tolkien at a performance of Shakespeare's *Henry VIII*. – P.H. Newby writes to Tolkien. He is glad that it has been possible to divide *Sir Gawain and the Green Knight* into suitable lengths for reading. He asks Tolkien to come, at BBC expense, to Broadcasting House in London at 2.00 p.m. on 1 September to be recorded. The recording could be played back immediately, and the matter of a reader discussed further.

6 August 1953 W.N. Beard writes to Tolkien. After an exhaustive search, the printers cannot find p. 7 of the *Lord of the Rings* typescript with drawings of blocks to be made (probably the G *tengwa* and elf-rune on the fireworks). Allen & Unwin hope that Tolkien has a rough of the designs which could be redrawn for reproduction. But the printers do have the title-page designs, and Tolkien will be sent proofs shortly.

8 August 1953 Tolkien replies to Rayner Unwin's letter of 28 July. 'In spite of the official end of Schools last week I have been involved in the usual aftermath of enquiries, and other business. Also I have found the proofs exacting without a break, and it has not been easy to get a grip on the "saga" again.' He is 'opposed to having separate titles for each volume, and no over-all title', and thinks *The Lord of the Rings* a good general title, not just for the first volume. He suggests as titles for the three volumes *The Return of the Shadow*, *The Shadow Lengthens*, and *The Return of the King*. He does not really like the subtitles for the individual books. He has now received the rest of the proofs, but has 'an uncomfortable feeling that when I came to see you at the end of last year you wished for some alteration or clarification of the *Foreword*, which I undertook to see to, but took no note of.' Tolkien asks if Allen & Unwin intend to fulfil the promises for appendices made at the end of the Foreword, but, since the work is to be published in three parts, at least some note on spelling and pronunciation should be included in the first volume. (Rayner will bracket the last two queries, and note in the margin 'rewrite Foreword to break the reader gently to the strangeness of names and situations'.) Tolkien also asks the publisher's position in regard to the 'Book of Mazarbul' pages. (Rayner will write in the margin: 'expense as with fire writing: we left it as half tone'.) Tolkien will attempt to redraw the Doors of Durin as soon as possible, as well as the maps needed in the first volume. In regard to the latter, 'the minimum requirements are, I think it was agreed, a larger scale map of the Shire; a small scale map of the whole country; and another map of the southern country

(Gondor and Mordor). . . . If I draw them to scale, and see that the distances referred to in the text are observed with reasonable accuracy, will it be possible to have them re-drawn and made prettier? Or do you wish me to make them for reproduction in my amateurish way? I wish I had more skill – and more time!' (Tolkien-George Allen & Unwin archive, HarperCollins; partly printed in *Letters*, pp. 169–70). – Tolkien also writes to W.N. Beard at Allen & Unwin, noting more instances of the printers not following his copy, agreeing to return the galley proofs in instalments, making some query about the designs for blocks, and suggesting a separate table of contents for each book. – Tolkien writes a third letter to Allen & Unwin this day. A friend in Canada has informed him that *The Hobbit* has been dramatized on Canadian radio. No one has contacted him about this. He asks to be sent a copy of *The Hobbit* with the revised text, which he needs for working on *The Lord of the Rings*.

Mid-August 1953 During the next few weeks Tolkien probably draws at least two versions of the Doors of Durin, in which trees are shown on the doors with many crescent moons. The typescript for the printer had read 'two trees each bearing a crescent moon'; this will be altered in page proof to 'each bearing crescent moons'.

9 August 1953 Tolkien writes to P. H. Newby. He will come to Broadcasting House at 2.00 p.m. on 1 September. He has been considering the presentation of *Sir Gawain and the Green Knight*, but work on proofs of *The Lord of the Rings* has not allowed him to think further about the best divisions of *Sir Gawain*. He asks about payment for broadcast of the translation and for any talk or reading.

11 August 1953 Tolkien returns corrected galley proofs 1–16 of *The Lord of the Rings* together with two pages of copy required for line blocks (galleys 6 and 15). – Ronald Eames of George Allen & Unwin acknowledges Tolkien's letter to W.N. Beard, who is on holiday. He asks Tolkien to indicate in the galley proofs the position of the blocks. – Philip Unwin sends Tolkien a copy of the revised *Hobbit*. He is investigating the matter of the Canadian broadcast. – P. H. Newby's secretary at the BBC writes that Newby is away, and will answer Tolkien's letter when he returns on 24 August. In the meantime she is arranging for Tolkien's travel expenses to be paid. – Tolkien receives a letter from the BBC Accounts Department, who have been asked to send him the cost of a first-class railway fare to London.

12 August 1953 Rayner Unwin writes to Tolkien. He thinks it best to discuss in person the points raised in Tolkien's letter of 8 August, and would like to see Tolkien in Oxford on Monday, 17 August at about 11.00 a.m.

13 August 1953 Tolkien writes to Rayner Unwin. He would be delighted to see him at the desired date and time, and tells him how to get to Sandfield Road. – Tolkien returns to Allen & Unwin in two packets corrected galley proofs 17–69 for Book I of *The Lord of the Rings*, along with two pages of copy for galley 54.

14 August 1953 Ronald Eames writes to Tolkien, acknowledging the return of the corrected galley proofs and the typescript of the pages from which blocks are to be made. But he asks to have the complete typescript again, as this will help the printers to understand the corrections and to follow Tolkien's spelling more closely. Having seen Tolkien's first examples of lettering for *The Lord of the Rings*, 'we do feel that more accurate and larger drawings are desirable. Alternatively, your drawings will have to be copied by the block-maker's artist, and you may not find this satisfactory. The printers have already ventured to re-draw the inscription for the title-page, and we send these specimens herewith to show you the kind of result we may expect by leaving this work to them' (Tolkien–George Allen & Unwin archive, HarperCollins).

15 August 1953 Tolkien replies to Ronald Eames. He will give the typescript to Rayner Unwin when he sees him on Monday, but is not sure whether he has entered on it all of the corrections of errors and the few alterations he has made to the galley proofs. He has just noticed that the printer has changed his 'nasturtians' to 'nasturtiums'. He asks for his spelling to be restored, commenting at length on usage and citing the opinion of the Merton College gardener. His drawings of Cirth and Tengwar, including those on the title-page, were not intended as exact specimens to be copied: he had hoped that someone with more skill than he might improve them. The fibrositis he suffered two years earlier has affected his ability to draw such lettering. But he has redrawn the inscription for Balin's tomb, adapting it to the page size: it is supposed to have been the work of a skilled mason. He commends the printers' drawings for the title-page, so close to those he sent that he thought they had returned his own work. But as his work had not been intended as a model, he will make new versions of the Cirth and Tengwar lettering for the title-page, to fit the proposed layout. He suggests that the height of the runes be reduced. He asks if another drawing of the 'fire-letters' in Book I, Chapter 2 is required.

17 August 1953 Rayner Unwin visits Tolkien at Sandfield Road. They discuss the matters raised in Tolkien's letter of 8 August. Tolkien gives Rayner a letter to be given to Ronald Eames, insisting on 'nasturtians', together with corrected galley-proofs (presumably for Book II) and sketches (probably for the Doors of Durin). – Later in the day, Tolkien writes to Rayner Unwin. Only after he had seen Rayner to the bus did he realize that he had not offered his guest any refreshment. Tolkien suggests as the overall title of his book *The Lord of the Rings*, with volume titles *The Fellowship of the Ring*, *The Two Towers*, and *The War of the Ring* or *The Return of the King*.

> The Fellowship of the Ring will do, I think; and fits well with the fact that the last chapter of the Volume is The Breaking of the Fellowship. The Two Towers gets as near as possible to finding a title to cover the widely divergent Books 3 and 4; and can be left ambiguous [as to which towers are meant]. . . . On reflection I prefer for Vol. III The War of the Ring, since it gets in the Ring again; and also is more non-committal, and gives less hint about the turn of the story: the chapter titles have been chosen also to give away as little as possible in advance.

Apparently he has argued during their meeting that the Ring inscription in Chapter 2 should be printed in red; he now writes that on reflection, red is not sufficiently important to be worth the expense. But he urges that the last runic page of the 'Book of Mazarbul' should be used as a frontispiece. He promises to bring the copy for the second volume to London on 1 September, and to endeavour to send all copy by the end of September. He is now turning his attention to the maps and the Foreword. He apologizes for using a red ribbon to type his letter – for economy, as he now types a lot 'for my hand's sake', and the red part of the ribbon is hardly used (*Letters*, pp. 170–1).

19 August 1953 Rayner Unwin writes to Tolkien. He thinks that they covered the ground very successfully during his visit. He likes Tolkien's suggested titles, except that he prefers *The Return of the King* to *The War of the Ring*. The printers' artist will do all of the necessary re-drawing of the runes and will submit them to Tolkien before the blocks are made. The corrected galleys are being put into page proof. Rayner asks if Tolkien has any particular feelings about the placing of the maps in the text.

20 August 1953 Ronald Eames writes to Tolkien. The galley proofs have been passed to the printers.

22 August 1953 Tolkien attends the wedding in Evesham of his nephew Gabriel, son of Hilary Tolkien. Tolkien's son John officiates.

26 August 1953 P. H. Newby writes to Tolkien. He is looking forward to seeing Tolkien, and gives details of the fees paid by the BBC.

31 August 1953 Tolkien writes to Rayner Unwin. He reminds Rayner that he will be in London on the following day, and hopes that Rayner will have lunch with him. He will come to Museum Street in any case just before noon, bringing the copy for press of the second volume of *The Lord of the Rings*. He apologizes that he has 'not yet completed the required maps. I found that it needed a complete re-reading of the whole, and the making of a rough index of place-names (and distances); also I am bothered about shape and scale.' He would like some advice about these, and thinks that it would help if he could have at least two colours in the printing. His revision of 'Part II', i.e. Volume 2, has been so thorough that they might dispense with galley proofs, if that would be an advantage. 'But I am a bit shaken in my faith in my own accuracy. In revising the text for place-names I have come across about 22 errors and inconsistencies unnoted in the proofs passed by me of Part I. However, they do not affect the line numbering, and can, I suppose be left to page-proof.' He offers to send a list, and would be grateful if the printers would keep an eye open for inconsistencies; 'and I hope that the severity of some of my remarks have not wholly obscured the fact that many of their queries were very useful' (Tolkien-George Allen & Unwin archive, HarperCollins). – Tolkien writes to P. H. Newby to confirm their appointment at Broadcasting House on the following day. Despite being snowed under with proofs, he has spent a couple of days conducting experiments with *Sir Gawain* on a tape recorder, 'which have suggested various points to me. Among them, that the translation, as reading copy, needs smoothing and easing a bit at some points, even if it neglects the accuracy required in a printed form for use (largely) together with the original text.... I am still not happy ... about the placing of the divisions.... However, that and other points can be dealt with tomorrow, or later' (BBC Written Archives Centre). – Tolkien writes to George Sayer. He has had 'to work day and (especially) night at the seemingly endless galleys of the Great Work that had piled up during Vivas, at drawings and runes and maps; and now at the copy of Vol. II.' The BBC will broadcast his translation of *Sir Gawain and the Green Knight* but are not so keen to have him as a performer, though he is going to London for an audition. He hired an old tape recorder, the best he could get locally, to work on *Sir Gawain*, which was 'very helpful in matters of timing and speed. With the help of Christopher and Faith [Tolkien]' he 'made some three voice experiments, and recordings of the temptation scenes. An enormous improvement – and assistance to the listener. Chris was making an extremely good (if slightly Oxonian ...) Gawain, before we had to break off' (George Sayer, 'Recollections of J.R.R. Tolkien', *Proceedings of the J.R.R. Tolkien Centenary Conference 1992* (1995), p. 24, emended with reference to the original letter).

1 September 1953 Tolkien meets P.H. Newby at Broadcasting House in London, and reads from his translation of *Sir Gawain and the Green Knight*.

2 September 1953 P.H. Newby writes to Tolkien, expressing pleasure at seeing him on 1 September and hearing him read. He notes the six original divisions of the poem that Tolkien has suggested. Tolkien has not been approved to read the poem himself, as Newby says that he is going to study the work again with Tolkien's suggestions in mind, that it might be read by several actors. When the division of the poem has been decided, the BBC Copyright Department will arrange for Tolkien's fee (based on the number of lines read in each programme).

3 September 1953 Tolkien writes to P.H. Newby. He does not think that the division of *Sir Gawain and the Green Knight* can be improved if they decide on six readings. Since his visit on 1 September, he has made the same divisions again. But after careful consideration, he thinks that such a division is 'destructive of the natural form of the poem', and explains why. He suggests instead a division into five parts, with the Third (and longest) Fit divided in two. He thinks that he should say a few preliminary words before the First Fit, and then speak the opening lines in Middle English as representing the voice of the medieval poet, after which the modern narrator should take over. In regard to his audition, he writes:

> It was very good for an elderly professor, who has been too long and too often in the position of critic, to be put through it. You are not very easy to please! If one can assume that the record you played back to me would, on an average [radio] set, come through with anything like the clarity that it had in the studio, I can only say that it sounded to me better than most things I have listened to of the sort – more *interesting* (more variable and unexpectable [*sic*]). It could be improved, of course, quite

apart from my voice-quality. I deliberately selected a passage that I had not practiced, and had seldom read aloud before; and I made one or two mistakes in the Middle English that pained me! [BBC Written Archives Centre]

He discusses the idea of using more than one voice, stating that there are 1,790 narrative lines in the poem and 740 of direct speech, for which at least four voices would be needed, calculating the number of lines for each character, and noting which parts could be doubled. He thinks that the use of different voices would enliven and clarify the poem, and that he could increase the dialogue a little by making slight alterations.

8 September 1953 P.H. Newby writes to Tolkien. After discussion at a Third Programme meeting, it has been agreed to have his translation of *Sir Gawain and the Green Knight* read by different voices, and since this will provide variety even for the lengthy Third Fit, the work could be read in four programmes, with Tolkien giving a twenty-minute talk as a fifth programme. He asks for Tolkien's comments.

9 September 1953 W.N. Beard of George Allen & Unwin sends Tolkien for approval copies of the redrawn illustrations for *The Lord of the Rings*, and asks for any corrections to be made lightly in pencil. The blockmaker can insert tints to fill in the trees in the Doors of Durin picture, and a slightly different tint for the background, if Tolkien wishes.

13 September 1953 Tolkien writes to P.H. Newby. He thinks the new proposal for *Sir Gawain and the Green Knight* excellent. He is going away on 15 September for a week, but will take the text and a copy of the translation with him 'in the hope of finding a little time to look over it with the idea of smoothing the version in places so as to ease the task of the voices, if possible. Though the "gnarled knobbly" passages in the version are usually a reflection of the original. I might also occasionally increase the lines put into direct speech . . .' (BBC Written Archives Centre). He will be busy on his return, but near and after the end of October should be less so, and, he hopes, will be able to do anything required by the BBC to assist in rehearsal and recording.

14 September 1953 Philip Unwin writes to Tolkien. Thomas Nelson & Sons, the Canadian publisher sublicensed by George Allen & Unwin, gave permission for the free use of brief extracts from *The Hobbit* on Canadian radio. Though the permission in this case seems reasonable, Allen & Unwin will ask Nelson's to consult them in any future instance.

15–22 September 1953 Tolkien takes Edith for a week's holiday, probably to Bournemouth. It is not known if he had time to review *Sir Gawain and the Green Knight* as promised to P.H. Newby; he certainly takes with him the various sketches for the first volume of *The Lord of the Rings*, but finds himself 'in circumstances of great discomfort, in which it was not possible to do more than look at them' (letter to W.N. Beard, 23 September 1953, Tolkien-George Allen & Unwin archive, HarperCollins).

21 September 1953 Tolkien not having replied to his letter of 9 September, W.N. Beard writes to say that the printers are waiting for Tolkien's approval before they can proceed with blockmaking.

22 September 1953 The BBC Copyright Department writes to offer Tolkien a fee of 200 guineas for the use of his translation of *Sir Gawain and the Green Knight*, and sends him the relevant forms to sign, returning one copy.

23 September 1953 Tolkien replies to W.N. Beard, apologizing for not sending his comments on the drawings sooner. They are 'not altogether satisfactory': he 'should have done the original sketches more carefully, and given more explanations; but the execution of the copies is not in places very good.' He had not expected that a block would be made from the sketches for the Doors of Durin he sent: he was awaiting comments on them, indicating preferences or queries for technical reasons.

> Otherwise I should have said at once that only the inscription on version B was correct, and given such helps and explanations for the copier as I now enclose. To copy a rather scratchy inscription without knowing the purport, or the normal forms of the individual letters, was asking too much.
>
> I am afraid that this will have to be done again. When this is done: I agree to the alteration of the original sketches, making the outer arms of the trees curve outside the pillars; but the third major leaf-curve on the right hand tree needs refining. The inscription, and the explanatory matter at the bottom (now in script italics) will need re-writing.
>
> I have provided explanations of the inscription – basic forms, and hooked forms for this particular purpose, and placing on the arch – which should be sufficient.

He does not like italics generally, and these, he argues, are not good.

> The italics, no doubt, have come in because of the note in red in my hand on the margin of version B. But this relates to a suggestion that I made to Mr Rayner Unwin that the drawing should stop at the foot of the pillars; and that the explanation, being virtually part of the text, should be printed in italics below. If the words are to be made part of the block, then I think an upright form is in every way preferable; and I provide an example of the style and arrangement that I should like.
>
> You note in your letter of 9 Sept. that tints can be inserted; and I should like this to be done according to the arrangement in version B: that is, a grey tint and a very light grey tint, noting especially that the leaves and 'moon-curves' on the trees should be left white.

The 'red letters' in Galley 15 (the Ring inscription, bk. II, ch. 2) are 'not good enough'. He supplies a revision to the same scale, then realizes that he has been criticizing his own original drawing, not a version redrawn by a printer's artist.

He considers the Cirth and Tengwar inscriptions at the head and foot of the title-page satisfactory, though 'a little of the lightness and style has gone in the process of regularizing the elvish letters at the foot', and two corrections need to be made to the Tengwar. He thinks the inscription on Balin's tomb unsatisfactory: 'it is neater and firmer than the original', but 'the style of the original has not been caught. The heavy strokes are now *far too heavy*, and irregularly so.' He discusses the inscription in detail. 'In placing and weight the copy remains, to my mind, much to be preferred, in spite of its slight unsteadiness, which I hoped that a younger hand might have removed with more delicacy' (Tolkien-George Allen & Unwin archive, HarperCollins).

25 September 1953 P.H. Newby writes to Tolkien. The recording of the four parts of *Sir Gawain and the Green Knight* will take place on 20, 22, and 27 October and 3 November, rehearsals to begin each day at 10.30 a.m., with the actual recording at 2.30 p.m. He invites Tolkien to join them at the BBC for any or all of these sessions. Tolkien's expenses will be paid, and on one of those days they could record his introduction and twenty-minute talk. He asks for a reply by return.

26 September 1953 Sugar rationing ends in Britain.

29 September 1953 W.N. Beard writes to Tolkien. He has asked the printers to revise the drawings for *The Fellowship of the Ring* in light of Tolkien's letter of 23 September, and will send the revised art for approval. He is sending page proofs under separate cover together with the corrected galleys. The title-page is not as requested, but Tolkien will be sent revised proofs.

October 1953 Tolkien's dramatic dialogue, *The Homecoming of Beorhtnoth Beorhthelm's Son*, is published in *Essays and Studies 1953*.

4 October 1953 Tolkien returns the signed copyright permission form to the BBC. – Tolkien writes to P.H. Newby. He had been unable to answer Newby's letter of 25 September until he knew his unavoidable term-time engagements. While none of the dates given by Newby is impossible, Tuesdays are inconvenient for him. He will endeavour to be present on each occasion, but cannot guarantee his presence, though he will definitely come on 22 October and 3 November and would like to be present for the reading of the Third Fit on 27 October. He can only arrive at 10.30 a.m. by catching the 8.40 a.m. train which involves some domestic difficulty, but at least on 22 October and 3 November he will try to arrive by that time. He will aim to have his introductory remarks, including the reading of a stanza in Middle English, written before the first rehearsal. He asks Newby to confirm that these together should last five minutes. He will try to have the twenty-minute concluding talk ready by 22 October, but it might have to wait until 3 November. He asks who will be the readers. He sends a copy of the First Fit with minor corrections, and will deal with the rest as soon as he can. He asks, if the BBC are having copies of the text made for the performers, if he could have one as he has used his only spare copy for the corrections.

5 October 1953 Philip Unwin writes to Tolkien. It has been learned that Thomas Nelson & Sons also gave permission for readings on Canadian radio from *Farmer Giles of Ham*.

7 October 1953 Tolkien attends a Merton College meeting. – W.N. Beard sends Tolkien revised *Lord of the Rings* drawings for his approval. The printers estimate the length of the second volume at about 352 pages, compared with 424 for the first volume. Beard asks to borrow the typescript for the third volume for a short time to prepare an estimate of length, and thus estimate the published price of all three volumes. – P.H. Newby writes to thank Tolkien for his letters and corrections. He sends him a typed script of the First Fit which includes the names of the readers. He hopes that Tolkien will be able to be present at the first of the programmes, but it does not matter if he is not there by 10.30 a.m. Newby will proceed with the rehearsal, and when Tolkien arrives he can put a gloss on the readers' interpretation. The recording Tolkien made will be played to the readers to give them an idea of the way he wants the poem read. Newby confirms that Tolkien's introductory remarks and reading in Middle English should last five minutes. They can record this when it is convenient to Tolkien; Newby suggests 3.45–4.30 p.m. on 22 October for rehearsal and recording. Tolkien's twenty-minute talk will involve an hour's rehearsal, so probably should be done separately, perhaps some time in December. He has asked the BBC Talks Booking Manager to arrange for payment of Tolkien's expenses and fees for attendance at the rehearsals, and for giving the talks.

8 October 1953 Ronald Boswell, BBC Talks Booking Manager, writes to Tolkien, informing him of the fees payable for his two talks and for each attendance at rehearsal, plus first class return fares between Oxford and London.

9 October 1953 Tolkien writes to P.H. Newby. He will try to send any corrections or improvements on the remainder of the script as soon as possible. On Thursday 22 October he must be back in Oxford by 7.00 p.m., so must catch a train no later than 4.50 p.m.; this would be desirable on the other days also. He asks if he could rehearse his introduction on 20 October. It suits him to leave the longer talk until early in December. – Tolkien writes to W.N. Beard. The page proofs of *The Fellowship of the Ring* have arrived at a busy time, with term about to begin. His son (?Christopher) is reading them, and Tolkien will look at them himself as soon as he has time. He passes the much improved drawings. He asks if it would unduly delay matters if he delivered the typescript of the third volume in person on 20 October. He does not want to entrust it to the post, since he does not have a completely revised second copy, and

> what is to appear in it is not quite settled – in points that would materially affect length and cost: e.g. whether to omit the last chapter or 'epilogue'; and what form or length the appendices, promised in the Foreword, should take. By the 20th I might hope to have these points clearer.

The Maps. I am stumped. Indeed in a panic. They are essential; and urgent; but I just cannot get them done. I have spent an enormous amount of time on them without profitable result. Lack of skill combined with being harried. Also the shape and proportions of 'The Shire' as described in the tale cannot (by me) be made to fit into [the] shape of a page; nor at that size be contrived to be informative.

Do you think I could consult you on this matter on the 20th? I could bring some stuff that one more skilled might reduce to respectable form.

He feels that it is important to have proper maps, especially as the 'Book of Mazarbul' pages will not be included. 'Even at a little cost there should be picturesque maps, providing more than a mere index to what is said in the text. I could do maps suitable to the text. It is the attempt to cut them down and omitting all their colour (verbal and other) to reduce them to black and white bareness, on a scale so small that hardly any names can appear, that has stumped me' (Tolkien-George Allen & Unwin archive, HarperCollins; partly printed in *Letters*, p. 171). – Tolkien writes to Philip Unwin, thanking him for his two letters about the Canadian broadcasts. Tolkien's informant about these, Professor W. Meredith Thompson, will be arriving in Oxford shortly.

10 October 1953 Tolkien returns the revised drawings for *The Lord of the Rings* by registered post to George Allen & Unwin. – Tolkien writes to Ronald Boswell, BBC Talks Booking Manager, that the terms offered for *Sir Gawain and the Green Knight* are satisfactory. He will inform Mr Boswell if he has to miss any of the rehearsals.

11 October 1953 Michaelmas Full Term begins. Tolkien's scheduled lectures for this term are: the 'Pardoner's Tale' and Prologue by Chaucer on Mondays at 11.00 a.m. in the Examination Schools, beginning 12 October; and *The Owl and the Nightingale* on Mondays and Wednesdays at 12.00 noon in the Examination Schools, beginning 12 October. He will continue to supervise B.Litt. students G.M.G. Evans, J.C. Haworth, V.M. Martin, and B.D.H. Miller, and D.Phil. students R.W. Burchfield and E.J. Stormon. A.D. Horgan has a leave of absence for Michaelmas Term. (Although R.W. Burchfield continues to be listed as a D.Phil student of Tolkien in the *Oxford University Gazette*, by now he has ceased to see Tolkien regularly, and has become involved full-time in teaching and ultimately lexicography.)

12 October 1953 Ronald Boswell sends Tolkien a contract for his first introductory talk on *Sir Gawain and the Green Knight*. A second contract will be sent when the date is fixed. – P.H. Newby writes to Tolkien. He will arrange to record the introductory talk for *Sir Gawain* earlier on 22 October so that Tolkien can catch the 4.50 p.m. train from London to Oxford. He asks for a copy of Tolkien's introductory remarks, with a promised stanza in Middle English, to type out for the benefit of the engineers and other technicians concerned in the recording. He suggests that the longer talk be recorded in the afternoon on 3 December. – W.N. Beard writes to Tolkien. He will be pleased to see Tolkien and the typescript of *The Return of the King* on 20 October. He is sure that he can help Tolkien with the maps.

By 13 October 1953 Tolkien's paper *Middle English 'Losenger'* is published in *Essais de philologie moderne (1951)*.

15 October 1953 Tolkien writes to P.H. Newby. He is 'laid up at the moment, afflicted simultaneously with laryngitis, lumbago, and (worst) sciatica. The last is very immobilizing and not improving very rapidly. The first is improving, but my voice such as it is, is in poor shape . . . at the moment even sitting is not a comfortable process' (BBC Written Archives Centre). He still hopes to be present at the BBC on 20 October, but warns Newby that this might not be possible. He has drafted his introductory remarks, but they need cutting to fit into five minutes. He hopes to put the introductory talk in final shape, timed, and to send it with a copy of the Middle English stanza by 19 October. He agrees to the afternoon of 3 December for recording the concluding talk.

16 October 1953 At a meeting of the English Faculty Board, in Tolkien's absence, the members note the death of Dorothy Everett. Tolkien is elected to replace her on the Nominating Committee until Michaelmas Term 1954. He is also appointed to be the Board's representative on the board of electors to the O'Donnell Lecturership in Celtic Studies until Michaelmas Term 1958. (He will remain an elector until 1963.) His application for a grant for the purchase of a tape recorder is forwarded to the General Board with the English Faculty Board's strong support. The Applications Committee has accepted T.P. Dunning of Campion Hall as a probationer B.Litt. student with Tolkien continuing as his supervisor. *See note.* The Applications Committee is asked by the English Faculty Board to appoint supervisors in place of Dorothy Everett for one advanced and one B.Litt. student after consultation with Professor Tolkien. Christopher Tolkien is issued a B.Litt. certificate. – P.H. Newby writes to Tolkien. 19 October will be early enough for the BBC to receive his introductory remarks. If he cannot come on Tuesday, they will do their best and receive his criticism later.

18 (?19) October 1953 Tolkien writes to W.N. Beard. He is laid up and cannot keep his engagements in London 'tomorrow', i.e. those scheduled for 20 October (letter dated 18 October, Tolkien-George Allen & Unwin archive, HarperCollins). He asks to postpone his appointment with Beard until 27 October.

20 October 1953 W.N. Beard writes to Tolkien. He and Rayner Unwin are sorry to learn of Tolkien's illness. Tolkien should call at Allen & Unwin on 27 October.

21 October 1953 Ronald Boswell writes to Tolkien. Since, as he understands from P.H. Newby, Tolkien is unable to record his introductory talk for the BBC Third Programme on 22 October, his contract will have to be adjusted.

22 October 1953 Tolkien attends the rehearsal at Broadcasting House, London, but does not record his talk: this is rescheduled for 3 November between 3.30 and 4.00 p.m. – Ronald Boswell writes to Tolkien. The BBC have altered the date on his contract for recording his introductory remarks, and ask him to alter his copy. Boswell thinks it best to wait until the final rehearsal before calculating his fees and fares, based on his attendance.

26 October 1953 Tolkien writes to W.N. Beard. He is recovering, but has had no time to deal with more than arrears of local duties and cannot come to Allen & Unwin on 27 October. He will try to fix another day. – Rayner Unwin writes to Tolkien, asking if he could suggest any 'people who have some fame in the world and who are known to be favourably disposed towards *The Hobbit*, who could be persuaded to read a proof of *The Fellowship of the Ring* and give a good quotable opinion on it', such as C.S. Lewis. Allen & Unwin have 'a few spare proofs' (Tolkien-George Allen & Unwin archive, HarperCollins).

27 October 1953 W.N. Beard writes to Tolkien. They will see him at Allen & Unwin when he is fit. – Tolkien does, however, attend the rehearsal of *Sir Gawain* at the BBC.

28 October 1953 Ronald Boswell writes to Tolkien, enclosing a contract for recording his longer talk on *Sir Gawain and the Green Knight* on 3 December. Boswell asks Tolkien to sign and return a reply sheet.

31 October 1953 In the evening, Tolkien attends a dinner of The Society hosted by G.R.G. Mure at Merton College. Ten members are present. Mure discusses the century 1851–1951.

1 November 1953 Tolkien is drenched in a sudden downpour, setting back his recovery from illness. On 30 November he will write to Rayner Unwin that he recovered from health problems only to fall a victim to 'gastric flu'.

2 November 1953 Probably on this day Tolkien telephones P.H. Newby and gives him alterations to the script.

3 November 1953 Illness prevents Tolkien from going to London for the BBC rehearsal or to record his introductory talk on *Sir Gawain and the Green Knight*. The BBC Talks Booking Manager writes to him again, asking that he amend the contract for a third time. He is arranging payment of fees and fares for Tolkien's attendance at rehearsals on 22 and 27 October.

5 November 1953 P.H. Newby writes to Tolkien. He is sorry that Tolkien has been ill again, and suggests that he record the five-minute introduction to *Sir Gawain* and the Middle English stanza on 3rd December, when he is due to record his longer talk. If Tolkien could arrive by 11.00 a.m., they could rehearse the introduction, then record it between 12.15 and 12.30. After lunch, they could begin to rehearse the talk at 2.00 p.m. and record it from 3.30 to 4.00.

6 November 1953 Tolkien writes to P.H. Newby. He has been very disappointed to miss the rehearsals. 'The germ renewed its assault on my throat at the end of last week, and my attempt to disregard it and carry on was ill-advised. . . .' He agrees that it would be wise to postpone his recording until 3 December. If he catches the 9.12 a.m. train he should arrive at Broadcasting House at about 11.00 a.m. 'All this ought to have been great fun, and for me the crown of a good many years' work, and not a matter of tired effort' (BBC Written Archives Centre). – He also writes to the BBC Talks Booking Manager, apologizing for being unreliable.

9 November 1953 P.H. Newby writes to Tolkien. He is glad that 11.00 a.m. on 3 December will suit Tolkien, and looks forward to receiving the 2,800-word script of his talk on *Sir Gawain* in due course.

10 November 1953 The BBC Talks Booking Manager sends Tolkien an amended contract for the short talk.

18 November 1953 Lionel Simmons, Assistant to the Literary Editor of the *Radio Times*, writes to Tolkien, asking if he would write a short article for the magazine to introduce the broadcast of *Sir Gawain and the Green Knight*. If Tolkien is interested, he should ring Simmons on 20 November in the morning, reversing the charges, so that they can discuss the matter.

19 November 1953 Tolkien writes to Stanley Unwin (in reply to a letter not preserved in the Allen & Unwin archive). Unwin seems to have informed Tolkien that the Houghton Mifflin Company will publish *The Lord of the Rings* in the U.S.A., and passed on appreciative comments about *The Hobbit* from Paul Brooks, editor-in-chief at Houghton Mifflin. Tolkien says that Unwin's letter was very welcome, and a tonic that contributed to his recovery. He has been much cheered by Paul Brooks's approval. –Tolkien also writes to Rayner Unwin, noting that he has struggled with ill health all term, and only this week has been able to attend to various business matters. C.S. Lewis would be glad to help in the matter of preliminary opinion on *The Lord of the Rings*, and might suggest some other names. Tolkien suggests a few other persons who might be asked to give an opinion of *The Fellowship of the Ring*, but is not sure how some of them will react. If there are enough spare proofs of that volume, he would like another copy.

20 November 1953 Tolkien presumably rings Lionel Simmons of the *Radio Times* to discuss an article on *Sir Gawain*.

25 November 1953 Stanley Unwin writes to thank Tolkien for his letter of 19 November. Unwin has just read the proofs of *The Fellowship of the Ring* and 'should like to be able to congratulate you in person upon a really outstanding piece of work' (Tolkien-George Allen & Unwin archive, HarperCollins).

26 November 1953 Rayner Unwin writes to Tolkien. He will approach some of the people Tolkien suggested for opinions. He has sent Tolkien a second proof copy of *The Fellowship of the Ring*. The maps for the book are needed most urgently. The news that Houghton Mifflin will publish *The Lord of the Rings* is 'most cheering, it will enable us to produce a larger edition at I hope a more reasonable price' (Tolkien-George Allen & Unwin archive, Harper-Collins). – P.H. Newby's secretary writes to Tolkien, to confirm a telephone conversation she has just had with him. The BBC will record on 3 December between 2.00 and 4.00 p.m. the introductory piece which is to be broadcast with the First Fit of *Sir Gawain and the Green Knight* on 6 December, and will arrange a date to record the final talk when Tolkien has had time to write it.

27 November 1953 The BBC Talks Booking Manager writes to Tolkien. They will cancel the contract (which Tolkien has not returned) for his twenty-minute talk on *Sir Gawain*, which they have learned that he cannot record on 3 December as illness has prevented him from finishing it. They will issue a new contract when a new date is fixed. They ask him to return the amended contract for the five-minute talk he will be recording on 3 December, and will add his fare. He can be paid after making the recording. – W.N. Beard, Allen & Unwin, sends to Tolkien galley proofs 1–118 of *The Two Towers* in duplicate, with the corresponding manuscript.

30 November 1953 Tolkien writes to Rayner Unwin. He will bring the typescript of Books V and VI of *The Lord of the Rings* to Allen & Unwin on 3 December. 'I am pressed by business or I would promise to bring in at least such material as the needed maps could be made from' (Tolkien-George Allen & Unwin archive, HarperCollins). He hopes that galley proofs of *The Two Towers* will arrive during the Christmas vacation. – Tolkien writes as well to the BBC Talks Booking Manager, returning the amended contract. – Rayner Unwin writes to Tolkien in reply to his letter of the same day. He asks Tolkien to have lunch with him on 3 December, and mentions that he has been reading the galley proofs of *The Two Towers*.

1 December 1953 Tolkien writes to Rayner Unwin. He expects to reach Allen & Unwin in Museum Street, London at about noon on 3 December, and will bring the third volume of *The Lord of the Rings*. 'I must say I thought Volume Two read rather well . . . also I think there seem to be very few errors, in the first book at any rate' (Tolkien-George Allen & Unwin archive, Harper-Collins). He accepts Rayner's invitation to lunch. – W.N. Beard sends Tolkien proofs of preliminaries to *The Fellowship of the Ring*, and hopes that Tolkien likes the appearance of the title- and facing pages. He asks if the same should be done for the title-page of *The Two Towers*.

2 December 1953 Tolkien, who has lent proofs and a typescript of *The Lord of the Rings* to Robert Murray and asked his opinion of the work, receives a letter from Murray with comments and criticism. Tolkien immediately replies, apologizing for a typed rather than handwritten letter: 'My typing does not improve. Except in speed. I am now much faster than with my laborious hand, which has to be spared as it quickly gets tired and painful' (*Letters*, p. 173).

3 December 1953 Tolkien delivers the typescript of *The Return of the King* to Rayner Unwin in London. They have lunch together and discuss various matters, apparently including maps, dust-jackets, and how to inform writers of fan letters for *The Hobbit* about the forthcoming *Lord of the Rings*. – In the afternoon, Tolkien records his introductory talk to his translation of *Sir Gawain and the Green Knight* at Broadcasting House. He and P.H. Newby agree that he will record the longer talk on 29 December between 3.15 p.m. and 4.00 p.m. after rehearsing from 2.00 p.m., and that he will send Newby the script by 21 December. – Rayner Unwin writes to Tolkien. Proofs of the first two volumes of *The Lord of the Rings* (presumably requested during their meeting that day), as well as the unused Epilogue and some other papers, are being sent to Tolkien.

4 December 1953 *A Fourteenth-Century Romance*, an article by Tolkien on *Sir Gawain and the Green Knight*, is published in the *Radio Times* for this date. – Tolkien attends an English Faculty Board meeting. The Monographs

Committee (of which Tolkien is a member) reports that *Sir Orfeo*, edited by A.J. Bliss, is in press, and that the next volume in the *Oxford English Monographs* series will probably be *The Peterborough Chronicles* by Miss C. Clark. It is reported that the General Board 'has agreed to a grant of £100 from the fund of the Committee on Advanced Studies for the purchase of a tape recording machine as requested by Professor Tolkien'; the machine is to be lent to Tolkien 'on the understanding that when it is not in use it will be kept in the English Faculty Library' (Oxford University Archives FA 4/5/1/2). Tolkien is authorized to purchase the machine. It is also noted that the O'Donnell Lecture for 1954–5 will be given by Professor Tolkien. The Applications Committee has appointed J.A.W. Bennett to replace Tolkien as supervisor of T.P. Dunning. – The BBC Talks Booking Manager sends Tolkien a new contract for 29 December, and asks him to sign and return it, and disregard or destroy the earlier contract.

5 December 1953 Michaelmas Full Term ends.

6 December 1953 Tolkien's translation of the First Fit of *Sir Gawain and the Green Knight* is broadcast on the Third Programme from 10.25 to 11.00 p.m., preceded by a short introduction written and delivered by Tolkien.

7 December 1953 Tolkien attends a Merton College meeting at 10.00 a.m. in the Common Room. As Sub-warden he is a member of a committee appointed to consider the purposes of the 'Master Fund' and of another committee to consider alterations and improvements in common rooms. – Norman Davis, who heard the broadcast of 6 December, writes to Tolkien praising the translation and Tolkien's introductory remarks. – Jane Neave writes to Tolkien. She too heard the broadcast, and asks if the translation has been published, and Tolkien's opinion of the BBC readers.

?8–?11 December 1953 Tolkien replies to Jane Neave, evidently saying that he was not happy with the broadcast, though others seem to have enjoyed it.

8 December 1953 Tolkien returns the new contract, signed, to the BBC Talks Booking Manager. Tolkien writes that he received his fee but not his fare after the recording on 3 December.

9 December 1953 Tolkien writes to Rayner Unwin. He has found a case of cuttings and letters about *The Hobbit*. He suggests that Arthur Ransome and George Sayer might be asked to write something to promote *The Lord of the Rings*. Tolkien apparently also suggests that the BBC might be persuaded to do something on the lines of the tape recordings he had made in 1952. (This letter is not in the Tolkien-George Allen & Unwin files at HarperCollins. It has been reconstructed from Rayner Unwin's reply of 14 December.)

10 December 1953 The BBC Talks Booking Manager thanks Tolkien for returning the contract. He is asking the firm's accounts department to pay Tolkien's fare for 3 December. – P.H. Newby writes to Tolkien. He thinks that Tolkien sounded splendid in his reading, and hopes that he had not thought too badly of the first broadcast, which Tolkien had been unable to supervise himself. Newby asks how Tolkien is getting on with the script for his longer talk; Tolkien should send his talk to Newby's home address if it cannot reach him at the BBC by 17 December, when he is to go on holiday. – The First Fit of *Sir Gawain and the Green Knight* is broadcast again on the Third Programme, 7.35–8.15 p.m.

12 December 1953 Jane Neave writes to Tolkien. She suggests that Tolkien's ill health accounted for his gloom over the broadcast of *Sir Gawain*. She had enjoyed it, but understood that it must be difficult for Tolkien to feel satisfied when he, as the translator or the work, knew better than anyone else exactly what should be done with it.

13 December 1953 The Second Fit of *Sir Gawain and the Green Knight* is broadcast from 10.00 to 10.35 p.m. on the BBC Third Programme.

Between 14 and 20 December 1953 Marjorie Incledon writes to Tolkien. She tells him how much she has enjoyed the two broadcasts, and sends him socks for Christmas.

14 December 1953 Rayner Unwin writes to Tolkien. The case of cuttings and letters mentioned on 9 December sounds a heavy burden; Rayner asks if he should collect it by car. He will be in Museum Street on 29 December and would love to see Tolkien if he has a moment to drop in. He will follow up with Arthur Ransome and has already sent a proof to George Sayer. – Stanley Unwin sends a proof copy of *The Fellowship of the Ring* to Arthur Ransome and asks if he would write a few sentences about it. At about the same time, a copy is sent also to Naomi Mitchison, who will reply with enthusiasm on 29 December that she has asked the *New Statesman* if she can review the complete *Lord of the Rings* (in the event, she will review only *The Fellowship of the Ring*), and has written to Tolkien for help with Elvish. Extracts from her letter will be quoted on the original dust-jackets of *The Lord of the Rings* ('it's really super science fiction . . . but it is timeless and will go on and on. It's odd you know. One takes it completely seriously: as seriously as Malory').

16 December 1953 Rayner Unwin writes to Tolkien. 'The Americans [Houghton Mifflin] are getting restless and are anxious to have cut and dried facts and figures. We have temporarily staved them off but would be glad if, when you come down on the 29th, you would be in a position to drop in on us the finally corrected press proof of *The Fellowship of the Ring* and also the relevant pages of typescript to guide the printers when placing the blocks' (Tolkien-George Allen & Unwin archive, HarperCollins).

17 December 1953 The Second Fit of *Sir Gawain and the Green Knight* is broadcast again.

20 December 1953 The Third Fit of *Sir Gawain and the Green Knight* is broadcast on the BBC Third Programme from 8.10 to 8.55 p.m. – Jane Neave listens to the broadcast, following a script Tolkien has sent, and immediately writes to him criticizing some of the readers. She hopes that he was not disappointed.

21 December 1953 Jane Neave writes again to Tolkien, having listened to the second broadcast of the Third Fit, this time without following the script. She cannot not think what made her critical of the readers in her previous letter.

23 December 1953 Tolkien writes to P.H. Newby, sending the script for his longer talk on *Sir Gawain and the Green Knight*. He apologizes: 'I have been involved in every kind of bother getting more and more frantic, and spoiling more and more paper. In the end the resulting script is I think poor, but as good as I can make it in the circumstances. I had to drop most of what I had written (incl. the Chaucer connexion): it was too fine-drawn to argue over the air' (BBC Written Archives Centre). The broadcast was picked up by a friend in Liège (presumably Simonne d'Ardenne); he has just heard that he is to receive a doctorate from the University of Liège. – A.P. Rossiter, Jesus College, Cambridge, writes to Tolkien, enclosing a copy of a letter he sent to *The Listener*. He begs Tolkien to persuade the BBC readers not to ruin the last fit of *Sir Gawain*. He praises Tolkien's translation but thinks the BBC production bad.

28 December 1953 Tolkien writes to Rayner Unwin. He hopes to reach Allen & Unwin in Museum Street just before noon on 29 December, 'with proofs of Vol. I [of *The Lord of the Rings*] and map', presumably marked page proofs and the general map of Middle-earth redrawn by Christopher Tolkien. Tolkien hopes to carry back from Allen & Unwin the typescript of Volume 3. He must be at Broadcasting House at 2.00 p.m., but 'should be able to get away again about 4 p.m. if there is more to do' (Tolkien-George Allen & Unwin archive, HarperCollins). – Also on this date (postmark), Nevill Coghill sends Tolkien a card, saying that he enjoyed Tolkien's *Sir Gawain and the Green Knight*.

29 December 1953 Tolkien visits Allen & Unwin in London and talks with Rayner Unwin. Among other things, they discuss whether to use the blank page at the end of *The Fellowship of the Ring* to publicize the other volumes of *The Lord of the Rings*. Probably now, Tolkien is asked to suggest a dust-jacket design. – Later Tolkien rehearses and records his talk on *Sir Gawain* for the BBC at Broadcasting House.

30 December 1953 Tolkien writes to Rayner Unwin, sending further corrections to *The Lord of the Rings*. – The Fourth Fit of *Sir Gawain* is broadcast in the BBC Third Programme from 9.35 to 10.05 p.m.

31 December 1953 B.H. Alexander of the BBC Copyright Department writes to Tolkien, offering a fee for the use of twenty-four lines from his translation of *Pearl* in his talk on *Sir Gawain and the Green Knight* to be broadcast on 3 January and 7 January. – The Fourth Fit of *Sir Gawain and the Green Knight* is rebroadcast in the BBC Third Programme at 10.20 p.m.

1954

1954 Tolkien becomes a Fellow of the Royal Society of Literature. – *Sir Orfeo*, edited by A.J. Bliss, is published in the *Oxford English Monographs* series (of which Tolkien is an editor). In his preface Bliss records his debt to Tolkien 'whose penetrating scholarship is an inspiration to all who have worked with him'.

3 January 1954 Jane Neave writes to Tolkien. She enjoyed hearing his translation of *Sir Gawain*. – Tolkien's talk on *Sir Gawain and the Green Knight* is broadcast on the Third Programme from 5.55 to 6.16 p.m. He speaks on the meaning of the poem and its place in the literature of the Chaucerian period. (In 1975 a slightly reduced version of the talk will be published as part of the introduction to *Sir Gawain and the Green Knight, Pearl and Sir Orfeo*, edited by Christopher Tolkien.)

4 January 1954 Tolkien writes to the BBC Copyright Department, accepting the fee offered on 31 December. – Rayner Unwin writes to thank Tolkien for his message of 30 December. The corrections have been sent to the printers. Rayner sends a suggested text for the note at the end of *The Fellowship of the Ring*, as discussed on 29 December, though he now has doubts whether one of the 'two towers' is not Minas Tirith. (Rayner suggests: 'The title of the second book in this story is *The Two Towers* – Orthanc and Barad-dûr, where Saruman and Sauron dwell. The company of the Ring, now separated, pursue their hazardous journeys under the shadow of these dark fortresses, and no reader will fail to await the final outcome of their mission in the third volume, *The Return of the King*, with impatience. While awaiting for these books to appear many readers will want to refresh their memory of *The Hobbit*, which tells of Bilbo's early encounters with Gandolf [*sic*] and Gollum.') He asks for Tolkien's comments on this as soon as possible, and for the Shire map and a suggested dust-jacket design, so that the first volume can be printed. – Angus McIntosh and Jane Neave each write to Tolkien, praising his talk on *Sir Gawain*.

7 January 1954 Tolkien's talk on *Sir Gawain and the Green Knight* is re-broadcast in the BBC Third Programme at 10.50 p.m..

13 February 1954 In the evening, Tolkien attends a dinner of The Society hosted by L.J. Witts at Magdalen College. Ten members are present. Witts reads a paper about sabbaticals, exchanges, etc.

14 January 1954 Tolkien attends a Merton College adjourned General Meeting in the Common Room at 10.00 a.m. The Master Fund Committee (of which he is a member) reports. – Tolkien puts this date on a signed typescript discussing the burden on examiners, suggesting that the period of office be reduced from three to two years. – W.N. Beard, Allen & Unwin, writes to ask Tolkien when he will be returning the corrected galley proofs of *The Two Towers*. The printers are anxious to start work on them.

17 January 1954 Hilary Full Term begins. Tolkien's scheduled lectures for this term are: *The Owl and the Nightingale* on Mondays at 11.00 a.m. in the Examination Schools, beginning 18 January; and the 'Pardoner's Tale' by Chaucer on Wednesdays at 11.00 a.m. in the Examination Schools, beginning 20 January. He will continue to supervise B.Litt. students G.M.G. Evans, J.C. Haworth, V.M. Martin, and B.D.H. Miller, and D.Phil. students R.W. Burchfield, A.D. Horgan, and E.J. Stormon.

19 January 1954 The Rector of the University of Liège writes to Tolkien, officially informing him that he is to be awarded an honorary doctorate.

22 January 1954 Tolkien writes to Rayner Unwin. He is sending under separate cover corrected galley proofs 1–68 (for Book III, the first half of volume 2). He expects to post Book IV, nearly finished, on 25 January. (His emendations to Book IV probably include changes in the timing and passage of the great storm seen by Sam and Frodo as they descend from the Emyn Muil, and to Frodo's cry in Shelob's lair.) He has also revised volume 3 to the end of the story, and could let Allen & Unwin have the manuscript of that portion as soon as Rayner wishes. But he is not yet able to produce 'the extra fifty pages' (Appendices). He is not happy with the title *The Two Towers*: 'it must if there is any real reference in it to Vol. ii refer to *Orthanc* and the *Tower of Cirith Ungol*. But since there is so much made of the basic opposition of the Dark Tower and Minas Tirith, that seems very misleading' (Tolkien-George Allen & Unwin archive, HarperCollins). – At an English Faculty Board meeting, in Tolkien's absence, F.W. Wilson reports that the Monographs Committee (of which Tolkien is a member) is also considering the publication of Mr Dobbs' thesis on Elizabethan prisons and prison literature. After discussing Tolkien's memorandum of 14 January on examining in the Honour School, it is agreed to apply to the General Board for an amendment of the statute reducing the period of appointment of examiners from three to two years. (This change will be approved in February.) The Faculty Board also agrees to consider at its next meeting the desirability or otherwise of making Paper B12, 'English from 1830 to 1920', a main paper of the Honour School.

25 January 1954 W.N. Beard sends Tolkien a proof of the general Middle-earth map and acknowledges receipt of galleys 1–68 of *The Two Towers*.

27 January 1954 Rayner Unwin writes to Tolkien. In order to complete *The Fellowship of the Ring* Allen & Unwin still need from Tolkien his suggested dust-jacket design, map of the Shire, and approval or disapproval of Rayner's draft for a paragraph on the final page. Rayner thinks *The Two Towers* a good title: the reader could speculate which two towers are intended. He also thinks that the proof of Christopher Tolkien's map of Middle-earth looks highly successful. – W.N. Beard sends Tolkien at least eighty-six pages of proofreader's queries on *The Fellowship of the Ring*. Tolkien will answer some simply with a tick, 'stet', or 'yes', but for others will carefully explain the reasons for his decision. At the beginning of the pages, and again in his letter to Allen & Unwin of 29 January, he will express deep gratitude to the proofreader for his queries, even those that were not accepted, because they reflect careful attention paid to the work.

29 January 1954 Tolkien returns corrected galley proofs 69–118 of *The Two Towers* to Allen & Unwin, along with the queries sent with the page proofs of *The Fellowship of the Ring* with his comments. He has completed the revision of Books V and VI, and asks if it would be useful for him to send these to Allen & Unwin at once. – Tolkien replies to the Rector of the University of Liège (see entry for 19 January), thanking him, the Conseil Académique, and the Faculty of Philosophy and Letters at Liège, for their high esteem. He will make every effort to be present in Liège on 2 October to receive his honorary degree.

1–18 February 1954 Tolkien is resident at Merton College; presumably Edith is not at home.

1 February 1954 W.N. Beard writes to Tolkien. Tolkien's replies to the proofreader's queries have been passed to the printer. Allen & Unwin would like the typescript of *The Return of the King* which will enable them to confirm their estimates of length and proceed with typesetting.

2 February 1954 W.N. Beard sends Tolkien more proofreader's queries about *The Fellowship of the Ring*, and reminds him Allen & Unwin still need the Shire map, jacket design, and approval of the wording at the end of the volume. Beard sends proofs of pages which contain line-blocks, together with the original drawings.

6 February 1954 Tolkien takes part in the election of a Reader in English Language at Oxford. E.J. Dobson of Merton College is elected for seven years with effect from 1 March 1954. Later the electors take lunch together.

7 February 1954 Tolkien dines with Angus McIntosh, probably at Merton College.

10 February 1954 Tolkien attends a Merton College meeting.

22 February 1954 W.N. Beard writes to remind Tolkien that the printers are still waiting for the map of the Shire, and for his approval of the note at the end of *The Fellowship of the Ring* and of proofs of the line-blocks.

23 February 1954 Tolkien writes to W.N. Beard. He has been having 'numerous troubles and distractions that have made it impossible to deal with any of the matters outstanding' and asks him to 'pity a harassed man quite unable to enjoy or give proper attention to what should be a most exhilarating task'. He returns the 'eagle-eyed' proofreader's queries for which he is grateful, though he has accepted only a few suggestions. He provides an alternative text to that suggested by Rayner Unwin for the final page of *The Fellowship of the Ring*, remarking that he always finds that 'such expressions as "no reader will fail etc." rather cool any impatience I have than excite it; but I may be peculiar'. He also sends a brief note on pronunciation, to 'go in somewhere. I have now received many requests for more information on linguistic matters, but these will be satisfied later. I have also received enquiries about pronunciation, and the note is an answer (boiled down to the briefest) to those points most frequently asked.' (The note in question will be included in the first edition of *The Fellowship of the Ring* at the end of the Foreword, but omitted in the second edition (1965) when the Foreword is replaced in its entirety. See *Reader's Companion*, pp. lxix–lxx.) He has not been able to produce a suitable map of the Shire to fit in the space provided; his son, Christopher, has offered to draw one but cannot do so until Tolkien provides the material. Tolkien hopes to be able to do that during the week, and Christopher probably will draw the map during the weekend. Tolkien also has found himself without time or inspiration for a dust-jacket design, but might be able to do something if the matter could wait a week. He approves all of the blocks, though he thinks that the one for p. 59 (the Ring inscription, in Book I, Chapter 2) is 'disappointing ... and sadly lacks any elvish precision or finesse. It would look better in *red* (as designed and intended)', but he blames his original art. He thinks the proof of Christopher's general map of Middle-earth 'looks very well, and (except that a closer examination reveals that it has gone out of scale in places) is good enough.' He suggests that it include a scale (intended to be '2 cm to 100 miles') and points out that 'the *red* is a little out of register (a fraction low) and so obscures lettering by often cutting into black configurations'. In particular 'the most important name of *Minas Tirith* is illegible' (Tolkien-George Allen & Unwin archive, HarperCollins). He has decided to look through *The Return of the King* once more before sending it for typesetting. – M.R. Snowden, Oxford University Press, writes to Tolkien, asking his opinion of Peter Goolden's B.Litt. thesis on *Apollonius of Tyre* which he proposes to reduce and modify for publication. Kenneth Sisam has suggested that it might be accommodated in the *Oxford English Monographs* of which Tolkien at this time is chief editor.

26 February 1954 W.N. Beard writes to Tolkien. Allen & Unwin are looking carefully at the block for p. 59 of *The Fellowship of the Ring* to see if it can be improved. They will add a scale to the general map and see if it is technically possible to make 'Minas Tirith' more legible. Beard and Rayner Unwin have discussed the matter for the final page, and think it best for the note on pronunciation to appear as a footnote at the end of the Foreword. They will send proofs of pp. 8 and 423 to Tolkien soon.

4 March 1954 W.N. Beard sends Tolkien complete page proofs of *The Two Towers*. At Rayner Unwin's suggestion, two pages have been left at the beginning of the volume for a synopsis of *The Fellowship of the Ring* and a mention of *The Return of the King*.

Between 4 March and 5 April 1954 Tolkien corrects the page proofs of *The Two Towers*. On the title-page he writes transliterations of the Cirth and Tengwar inscriptions.

11 March 1954 An entry on a page from Tolkien's engagement diary (later reused for other purposes) reads: 'Horgan 11 a.m. Merton, 2 periods'. Horgan, one of Tolkien's D.Phil. students, presumably spends two hours with Tolkien.

12 March 1954 Tolkien attends an English Faculty Board meeting. The question of making paper B12, 'English from 1830 to 1920', a main paper of the English Honour School is referred to a committee consisting of Tolkien, J.N. Bryson (chairman), Lord David Cecil, Humphry House, and F.P. Wilson. Tolkien is asked to draft a statement supporting the English Faculty Board's application to the General Board for the conferment of a personal readership on G.V. Smithers.

13 March 1954 Hilary Full Term ends.

15 March 1954 Tolkien attends a Merton College meeting at 10.00 a.m. As Sub-warden he is automatically a member of a committee to consider what research fellowships should be offered for election in October 1954.

16 March 1954 Tolkien writes to W.N. Beard. He has returned that morning by registered post the proof of the general map of Middle-earth, together with a drawing for the small map 'A Part of the Shire' made by his son Christopher, drawn to scale twice that of the actual space available in the book. But he finds himself 'both without inspiration and time for doing a jacket design; but I hope perhaps to find a little of both in the next few days – at least enough to give a more skilled craftsman something to go on' (Tolkien-George Allen & Unwin archive, HarperCollins).

18 March 1954 W.N. Beard writes to Tolkien, approving the Shire map. By printing it 'landscapewise' they can 'make it larger than half scale', which will make the smaller lettering clearer. Rayner Unwin agrees, and 'is equally anxious that [the name] Minas Tirith in the large map should be completely legible' (Tolkien-George Allen & Unwin archive, HarperCollins).

19 March 1954 W.N. Beard sends Tolkien proofs of pp. 8 and 423 and of six blocks for approval.

23 March 1954 Tolkien writes to W.N. Beard, enclosing 'notions' for dust-jackets of the first two volumes of *The Lord of the Rings*. 'I can hardly call them more, owing to their technical deficiencies. But someone might be able to rectify them or produce something on their lines. (I have indicated the precise form and significance of the "elvish lettering")' (Tolkien-George Allen & Unwin archive, HarperCollins). These include different versions of the same basic design for *The Fellowship of the Ring*. (Five designs for the dust-jacket of *The Fellowship of the Ring* survive, and three for *The Two Towers*; probably Tolkien sends all of these on 23 March, but at any rate he draws all of them, and one for *The Return of the King*, between 23 and 26 March. Sketches also survive for various elements in *The Two Towers* and *The Return of the King* jackets, including the lettering, a crown, a ship, and the hand and arm of Sauron reaching threateningly across mountains.) – In the evening, Tolkien dines with Nevill Coghill, probably at Merton or Exeter.

24 March 1954 Tolkien writes to W.N. Beard, returning the proofs sent by Allen & Unwin on 19 March. He approves the proofs of blocks, except for the *tengwa* G on p. 33 of *The Fellowship of the Ring*, and the Ring inscription on p. 59 'where as I have said before, the "elvish script" is bad. It looks crooked, but that is because it is ill-written (I think). It is too large and sprawling and that effect is much increased by being in black and not in red as intended. Also, alas! at this eleventh (or twelfth) hour I have discovered an error in it – one that seems serious to me. I cannot think how I came to make it (in many successive versions) and to pass it' (Tolkien-George Allen & Unwin archive, HarperCollins); and unfortunately the inscription was transliterated on p. 267. Tolkien asks if anything can be done about it. Although he is reluctant to hold up production, apart from the error, the block is poor, and he would prefer if possible that another block be made on the lines of the two specimens he now encloses. If this cannot be done, on p. 267 *agh* should be emended to *akh*. (The block will be replaced as Tolkien wishes; but when *The Lord of the Rings* is reset for the edition of 2004, the rejected art will be mistakenly substituted for the approved Ring inscription. See further, *Reader's Companion*, p. 83.)

25 March 1954 Rayner Unwin writes to Tolkien. Allen & Unwin like the central theme of his *Fellowship of the Ring* design (a device incorporating the One Ring surrounded by the Ring inscription in Elvish script), especially a variation on dark brown paper; but Tolkien has used too many colours. Rayner suggests that the same device be used on all three volumes of *The Lord of the Rings*, with a different background colour for each volume and the title set in type rather than hand-drawn.

26 March 1954 Tolkien writes to Rayner Unwin. He has sketched a dust-jacket design for *The Return of the King*, but will not bother to send it. He agrees that 'the same device for each volume is, quite apart from expense, desirable: the whole thing is one book really, and it would be a mistake to over-emphasize the mechanically necessary divisions'. He is not sure which variant of his designs Rayner has chosen, but hopes that it is the one with three subsidiary rings, 'since the symbolism of that is more suitable to the whole story, than the one with a black centre and only the opposition of Gandalf indicated by the red-jewelled ring' (see *Artist and Illustrator*, fig. 177). He suggests that the titling be set 'in a simple form of Black Letter type, which accords better (I think) with the design and the elvish script than Roman'. Rayner's approval of the central device makes it more urgent that the Ring inscription on the jacket and that on p. 59 of *The Fellowship of the Ring* correspond exactly. He hopes that Allen & Unwin can persuade the Houghton Mifflin Company to adopt the same jacket design: 'Their taste in such matters is, left to themselves, deplorable. It would be difficult to find anything more horrible than their jackets to *The Hobbit* and *F[armer] Giles*' (Tolkien-George Allen & Unwin archive, HarperCollins). He asks Rayner for a spare page proof of *The Two Towers*.

29 March 1954 W.N. Beard writes to Tolkien, agreeing to the replacement of the blocks on pp. 33 and 59. – Tolkien probably attends an Ad Eundem dinner at Cambridge.

1 April 1954 Rayner Unwin writes to Tolkien. An extra proof of *The Two Towers* has been sent. Rayner has selected Tolkien's jacket design with only one elven-ring in addition to the One Ring, partly because Allen & Unwin staff like the look of it, but also because they cannot introduce another colour to distinguish the three rings one from another. Rayner suggests that the titling be set in a bold typeface which 'doesn't look too Roman but at the same time has a better display value than black letter' (Tolkien-George Allen & Unwin archive, HarperCollins). He reminds Tolkien that the latter is supposed to be dealing with *Hobbit* fan mail.

5 April 1954 Tolkien returns the marked page proofs of *The Two Towers* 1–192 to Allen & Unwin.

9 April 1954 D.M. Davin, Oxford University Press, writes to Tolkien in regard to the letter of 23 February sent by M.R. Snowden in Davin's absence. Davin has now written to Peter Goolden, explaining that his *Apollonius of Tyre* might be suitable for the *Oxford English Monographs* series.

Between 9 April and 3 May 1954 Peter Goolden writes to Tolkien in regard to the *Old English Apollonius of Tyre*. Tolkien replies that the thesis may be suitable for the *Oxford English Monographs*, but it would have to wait until another work being considered for the series is published.

12 April 1954 W.N. Beard writes to Tolkien. He is sending proofs of revised proofs for pp. 1–32 of *The Fellowship of the Ring* (including the Shire map) and for the blocks on pp. 33 and 59.

13 April 1954 Ronald Eames, Allen & Unwin, writes to Tolkien. He has had professional drawings made of the 'Ring and Eye' device following Tolkien's sketch for the dust-jacket, but the lettering does not conform with that of the revised block for p. 59 (the Ring inscription). He sends the drawings, separated for three-colour printing, and asks Tolkien to return them carefully packed.

15 April 1954 Tolkien writes to Ronald Eames and returns the drawings for the dust-jacket. He notes that the lettering for the central device is correct, but the vowel marks have been omitted. This needs to be corrected, and the 'flames' at the top of the inscription, he feels, could be improved. – Tolkien also writes to W.N. Beard. He approves the revised block for p. 33, and thinks the new block for p. 59 (the Ring inscription) improved, but hopes that the latter will come out better in the printed book than in the proof, where 'the fine lines are blurred and shaggy'. The notes on pronunciation at the end of the Foreword 'now look very crowded and rather forbidding. . . . I have indicated in red deletions which would relieve the crowding and the repetition. . . . I wish that in the past twelve months I had even the time to give more than half a hurried mind to these interesting details!' He has discovered two or three errors in the runes (Cirth) on the title-page, but is afraid they must remain. He will 'bear the brunt of any later explanations or apologies to decipherers. If the runes on the *Hobbit* jacket are any criterion, there will be not a few.' He thinks the Shire map 'looks very well indeed' (Tolkien-George Allen & Unwin archive, HarperCollins).

20 April 1954 Ronald Eames writes to Tolkien. The dust-jacket drawing will be revised. – P.H. Newby, BBC, writes to ask Tolkien if he thinks that an attractive Third Programme talk could be made out of an examination of the eighteenth-century Grammarians. He remembers that in conversations between rehearsals for *Sir Gawain and the Green Knight* Tolkien was critical of 'Grammarian's English' and wonders how far Tolkien would defend usage as the only arbiter of what is correct.

21 April 1954 Tolkien attends an Early English Text Society Council meeting at Magdalen College. – W.N. Beard writes to Tolkien. He will ask the printers to make sharper impressions of the blocks on pp. 33 and 59. The map of Middle-earth has been corrected to show 'Minas Tirith' more clearly. – In a second letter of the same date, Beard asks if Allen & Unwin can assume that Tolkien does not want them to print the transliterations he added to the proof of the title-page.

22 April 1954 Tolkien attends a Merton College meeting.

25 April 1954 Trinity Full Term begins. Tolkien's scheduled lectures for this term are: the 'Pardoner's Tale': The Legend on Wednesdays at 11.00 a.m. in the Examination Schools, beginning 28 April; and *The Owl and the Nightingale* on Fridays at 11.00 a.m. in the Examination Schools, beginning 30 April. He will continue to supervise B.Litt. students G.M.G. Evans, J.C. Haworth, V.M. Martin, and B.D.H. Miller, and D.Phil. students R.W. Burchfield, A.D. Horgan, and E.J. Stormon. – Naomi Mitchison, who has been reading page proofs of *The Fellowship of the Ring* and *The Two Towers*, has written to Tolkien asking questions about the work. Tolkien now writes a seven-page reply to her questions, including information about languages and translation, geography, dragons, Bombadil, Entwives, the name *Gamgee*, Wizards, Balrogs, Shelob, Galadriel, etc. Her questions will guide him

> in choosing the kind of information to be provided (as promised) in an appendix, and strengthen my hand with the publishers. . . . My problem is not the difficulty of providing it, but of choosing from the mass of material I have already composed. . . .
>
> I am giving what fragments of time I have to making compressed versions of such historical, ethnographical, and linguistic matter as can go in the Appendix. If it will interest you, I will send you a copy (rather rough) of the matter dealing with Languages (and Writing), Peoples and Translation. . . .
>
> I have a long historical table of events from the Beginning to the End of the Third Age. It is rather full; but I agree that a short form, containing events important for this tale would be useful. If you would care for typed copies of some of this material: e.g. The Rings of Power; The Downfall of Númenor; the Lists of the Heirs of Elendil; the House of Eorl (Genealogy); Genealogy of Durin and the Dwarf-lords of *Moria*; and The Tale of the Years (esp[ecially] those of the Second and Third Ages), I will try and get copies made soon. [*Letters*, pp. 174, 177]

Between 25 April and 8 May 1954 Naomi Mitchison visits Tolkien unexpectedly. Tolkien will write to Rayner Unwin on 8 May: 'Mrs Mitchison has been bombarding me; and she finally ran me to earth in Oxford' (Tolkien-George Allen & Unwin archive, HarperCollins). Probably soon after her visit, Tolkien sends her on loan a copy of his latest text on languages and writing. On 25 September 1954 he will write to her: 'I was sorry to find, when it was returned, that the screed on "languages" etc. had been sent uncorrected, and with lots of words and phrases unerased, so that parts were hardly intelligible' (*Letters*, p. 199). He also has a copy made of his chronology of the Second and Third Ages, which he will offer to send Mitchison in his letter of 25 September.

27 April 1954 Ronald Eames writes to Tolkien. Allen & Unwin suggest for the bindings of *The Lord of the Rings* a deep red cloth, stamped on the spine with the volume title within a ring. – Stanley Unwin writes to Tolkien, sending a copy of an appreciative letter from Richard Hughes, who has read proofs of *The Fellowship of the Ring*. Hughes's comments will lighten a despondency into which Tolkien feels he has fallen, because he has not been able to give proper attention to *The Lord of the Rings* during 1953 and 1954.

29 April 1954 Tolkien writes to Ronald Eames. He approves the binding design, and asks Eames to tell W.N. Beard that he does not want a transliteration of the Cirth and Tengwar inscriptions to appear on the title-pages of *The Lord of the Rings*.

30 April 1954 Tolkien attends an English Faculty Board meeting. The chairman reports that Tolkien's draft statement about G.V. Smithers has been forwarded to the General Board. C.L. Wrenn is elected to succeed Tolkien as a member of the Nominating Committee. The chairman makes a verbal report on behalf of the committee (of which Tolkien is a member) on the question of making Paper B12 a main paper in the Honour School. It is agreed that the proposal of the committee should be laid before the Faculty as a proposal of the Board at a meeting at 2.00 p.m. on 18 May in the Board Room. Appointed as CUF Lecturers are Christopher Tolkien, Tolkien's postgraduate students R.W. Burchfield and A.D. Horgan, and Peter Goolden and J.E. Turville-Petre (*née* Blomfield), whom Tolkien supervised briefly as probationer B.Litt. students. The Applications Committee has appointed Tolkien and G.V. Smithers examiners of the B.Litt. thesis of F.W. Watt, Queen's College, *Dialogue in Chaucer*. – Tolkien writes to Stanley Unwin, thanking him for the copy of Richard Hughes's letter. – W.N. Beard writes to Tolkien. Ronald Eames is pleased to have Tolkien's approval of the *Lord of the Rings* binding.

3 May 1954 Tolkien writes to D.M. Davin, apologizing for neglecting his and Snowden's letters. Since he was not an examiner for Goolden's thesis, he will have to consider it when he has time. – Tolkien writes to P.H. Newby. The eighteenth-century Grammarians would be a suitable subject for a broadcast talk, but 'a murderous spirit may well be aroused by any controversy about English grammar or usage'. He himself is 'in many ways an opponent of Grammarian English, and a defender of Usage: mainly because the grammarians, being largely ignorant of the history of English, have so often introduced an artificial discrepancy between the rules and what is natural' (BBC Written Archives Centre). He is not learned in the work of modern writers on the subject, and is too busy to take part. He suggests a debate. Also he asks Newby if the BBC would be interested in more alliterative verse: many people had shown an interest in it after his translation of *Sir Gawain and the Green Knight* was broadcast. He has written a dialogue concerning the Battle of Maldon (*The Homecoming of Beorhtnoth Beorhthelm's Son*), which might suitably be broadcast in August on the anniversary of the battle. He has made a recording of the dialogue and thinks it sounds very good. – W.N. Beard writes to Tolkien, asking when he will return the rest of the page proofs of *The Two Towers*.

4 May 1954 W.N. Beard writes to Tolkien. He is sending the final proofs of the general map of Middle-earth. Enough copies of the map will be printed to include one in each volume.

6 May 1954 Tolkien writes to W.N. Beard. He approves the maps for *The Lord of the Rings*. He likes the idea of having the map of Middle-earth in each volume, but hopes that it will be possible to have as well, in the final volume, a large-scale map of the area around Minas Tirith. – P.H. Newby writes to Tolkien. He had hoped that Tolkien would take part in the debate on Grammarian's English, and asks him to suggest some names to speak for and against. He would like to read Tolkien's dialogue on the Battle of Maldon. He intends to persuade the Third Programme to rebroadcast Tolkien's translation of *Sir Gawain and the Green Knight*. He asks, in regard to Tolkien's mention of alliterative verse on 3 May, and misunderstanding that Tolkien was referring to his 'dialogue' *The Homecoming of Beorhtnoth*, if Tolkien has a talk or another poem (besides *Sir Gawain*) in mind.

7 May 1954 Tolkien sends a postcard to Rayner Unwin with the rest of the corrected page proofs of *The Two Towers*. 'There are only a very few corrections not in copy, introduced for consistency, or geography, or emendation of my English and Elvish. I have abandoned *hath doth* etc. as marks of the archaism of the language of the South, since I had used them so inconsistently and sporadically' (Tolkien-George Allen & Unwin archive, HarperCollins). He also sends a synopsis of *The Fellowship of the Ring* to appear at the beginning of *The Two Towers*.

8 May 1954 In the morning, Tolkien writes a note to Rayner Unwin and prepares a parcel to send to him, before leaving for Cambridge. Tolkien posts the parcel, containing the manuscript of *The Return of the King* to the end of the narrative, from Cambridge, and later that day writes to Rayner again, from the Garden House Hotel. He has not yet written a synopsis of the previous volumes of *The Lord of the Rings* or the Appendices. He has been giving attention to the latter 'but cannot put it into final form until I know more or less precisely what room there is. Also I shall have to decide what is most advisable or required of the accumulated matter. Some readers no doubt will want little, others a lot' (Tolkien-George Allen & Unwin archive, HarperCollins). Houghton Mifflin need a studio portrait of Tolkien urgently, but he has not had one taken since *The Hobbit* was published. He asks when *The Fellowship of the Ring* will be published. (It is probably during his final work on *The Return of the King* that Tolkien changes the description of Minas Tirith to include a 'keel' dividing the city. He draws two views of Minas Tirith showing this feature on the backs of circulars dating from the early part of 1954, and probably also at this time makes a plan showing the same feature.) – A brief notice of a Merton College meeting to be held on 19 May is issued in Tolkien's name, as Sub-warden.

8–15 May 1954 Tolkien is in Cambridge as an elector for the newly established chair of Medieval and Renaissance English. The other electors are H.S. Bennett, Professor Basil Willey, Sir Henry Willink (the Vice-Chancellor of Cambridge), and Professor F.P. Wilson. Their first and unanimous choice for the chair is C.S. Lewis, even though he apparently has not applied. Willink will write to Lewis offering him the chair on 11 May. On 12 May Lewis will decline for domestic reasons, because he has led G.V. Smithers (a candidate for the chair) to believe that he (Lewis) was not in the field, and because he doubts that he has the energy and vigour the holder needs. On 14 May Willink will write to Lewis again, saying that the electors will not write to their second choice until June to give him time to reconsider the matter. But in a letter of 15 May Lewis will seem to make it clear that he will not change his mind.

10 May 1954 W.N. Beard writes to Tolkien. Allen & Unwin will consider 'a small map for the third volume showing the vital area around Minas Tirith, but enlarged to something like the map of the Shire in the first volume' (Tolkien-George Allen & Unwin archive, HarperCollins). – Nevill Coghill writes to Tolkien from Michigan State College, East Lansing. He cannot be at the Ad Eundem dinner on 22 May. The members are evidently going to vote on two new members; Coghill tells Tolkien whom he wishes to vote for.

12 May 1954 Rayner Unwin writes to Tolkien. Houghton Mifflin have verified their order for *The Fellowship of the Ring*. Rayner sends drafts of blurbs for both the Houghton Mifflin and the Allen & Unwin dust-jackets. *The Fellowship of the Ring* has now gone to press.

13 May 1954 Tolkien writes to Rayner Unwin. He thinks the blurb by Houghton Mifflin for their dust-jacket of *The Fellowship of the Ring* to be poor, and sends a page of suggested improvements, 'though without much more hope of effect than in the case of the appalling jacket they produced for *The Hobbit*'. He insists that at any rate Houghton Mifflin must correct their error of deriving the Ring from the dragon's hoard in *The Hobbit*. In regard to the Allen & Unwin blurb, Tolkien feels 'that comparisons with Spenser, Malory, and Ariosto (not to mention super Science Fiction) are too much for my vanity! I showed your draft notice to Geoffrey Mure (Warden) [of Merton], who was being tiresome this morning and threatening to eject me from my room in favour of a mere tutor. He was visibly shaken.... Anyway my stock went up sufficiently to obtain me an even better room, even at the cost of ejecting one so magnificent as the Steward' (*Letters*, p. 181–2, corrected from Tolkien-George Allen & Unwin archive, HarperCollins). Tolkien is having second thoughts about his synopsis of the first volume to be printed at the beginning of *The Two Towers*. He hopes that *The Fellowship of the Ring* can be published in July for various reasons, mainly because he would like it to be available when he goes to Dublin to be granted a D.Litt. on 20 July.

15 May 1954 Tolkien writes to P.H. Newby. He thinks that the only way the BBC would 'get a reasonably large audience for [a radio programme on] Grammar would be a debate'. He suggests C.L. Wrenn and Norman Davis as two experts who would be able to talk; 'anybody who knows enough about it could take either side'. The alliterative poem to which Tolkien referred in his letter of 3 May is his own on the Battle of Maldon (*The Homecoming of Beorhtnoth Beorhthelm's Son*); he is sending a copy to Newby under separate cover (i.e. the volume of *Essays and Studies* in which it was published). He encloses a copy of Rayner Unwin's blurb for *The Lord of the Rings*, which makes him blush. 'You should hear me read some of the scenes!' (BBC Written Archives Centre).

17 May 1954 Tolkien talks to C.S. Lewis, and convinces him that he would not have to give up his Oxford home if he were to accept the Cambridge chair, but could divide his time between Oxford and Cambridge. He also convinces Lewis that the electors will not consider G.V. Smithers, since they do not want a philologist for the post. – Tolkien writes to both Sir Henry Willink and H.S.

Bennett about his talk with Lewis. If Lewis could be assured that Cambridge would provide him with the equivalent of the rooms he has in Magdalen College at Oxford in which to live during term, then he would accept the chair. Tolkien realizes that this would depend upon Lewis's election to a fellowship, and asks if that would be difficult. He adds in his letter to Willink that he thinks that Magdalene College, Cambridge would be very attractive to Lewis.

18 May 1954 Tolkien attends an English Faculty meeting at 2.00 p.m. in the Board Room, Clarendon Building. The English Faculty Board's proposal to make Paper B12 (English from 1830 to 1920) a main paper in the Honour School is laid before the Faculty, who reject the change. *See note.* – P.H. Newby writes to Tolkien. He thanks him for suggesting names, but is surprised at the suggestion that the experts could take either side: he had imagined setting a linguist and a grammarian against each other. He has read *The Homecoming of Beorhtnoth*, but as it would need dramatic treatment in broadcasting, with sound effects, a choir of monks, etc., he is sending it to the Controller of the Third Programme, hoping that he in turn will persuade the Features Department to use it. – Rayner Unwin writes to Tolkien. He has forwarded Tolkien's remarks on the *Lord of the Rings* blurb to Houghton Mifflin. He does not know if they will use all or even part of the Allen & Unwin jacket design. He believes that delays in printing the jacket will make it impossible for Allen & Unwin to publish before 20 July, though he hopes that they will be able to publish on 29 July. He does not think that the synopsis in *The Two Towers* needs to be changed. He writes also of a bookseller in Belgium, Paul Gothier, who carries *The Hobbit* and might be convinced to sell *The Fellowship of the Ring*.

19 May 1954 Tolkien attends a Merton College meeting in the Common Room at 2.00 p.m. – C.S. Lewis writes to Sir Henry Willink. If certain conditions can be satisfied, he is interested in the Cambridge chair.

20 May 1954 Sir Henry Willink writes to Tolkien. Having had two letters from Lewis declining the Cambridge chair, and before receiving Tolkien's letter of 17 May, he had offered the chair to Helen Gardner, the second choice. He has now had a letter from Lewis accepting on the terms he had discussed with Tolkien. He is writing to Lewis to keep the matter open in case Miss Gardner refuses. – Rayner Unwin writes to ask if Tolkien could let Allen & Unwin look through his *Hobbit* fan mail as soon as possible.

22 May 1954 Tolkien probably attends an Ad Eundem dinner.

25 May 1954 W.N. Beard sends Tolkien a specimen binding case for *The Fellowship of the Ring*.

26 May 1954 Tolkien writes to W.N. Beard. He likes the binding case. He has not seen proofs of the dust-jacket, but he is chiefly anxious that the work be published. He would like his drawings for the dust-jackets to be returned. Since he is harassed with exams, he asks Beard to forward various messages to departments of Allen & Unwin. In regard to Rayner Unwin's request for *Hobbit* fan mail, he has found a box of miscellaneous cuttings and letters, but in a jumbled state; he will send them to the publisher to look through and decide what is useful, but wants them returned eventually.

29 May 1954 W.N. Beard writes to Tolkien. He hopes to have proofs of the dust-jacket by 31 May. The printing of the final map has caused some delay.

31 May 1954 Tolkien, having changed his mind, has looked through the *Hobbit* fan material himself. He writes to Rayner Unwin:

> I had to go through the case of cuttings and letters: it was in such a muddle, and a casual glance showed that it contained a lot of stuff referring to quite other matters of mine; or else correspondence with 'A and U' about poor 'Mr. Bliss' and other forgotten things.
>
> I am afraid the gleanings are disappointing. I have mislaid (or lost or put somewhere else) many letters that I had: but most of them were juvenile. Of what remains I have extracted those from people now dead, from members of my family, and from people already fully posted about *The Lord of the Rings*: e.g. Richard Hughes, and Mrs Mitchison. It does not leave much. To the names represented I might add those of my friends and fans: Professor Geoffrey Bullough of King's College London; and Professor Bernard Wright of Southampton.

Before sending the parcel he will look in college for more material. He asks about the progress of *The Return of the King*: 'Alas! for attempts at revision amid distractions' (Tolkien–George Allen & Unwin archive, HarperCollins). He encloses a slip for a correction he feels necessary, in Book V, Chapter 2 (presumably in the account of Aragorn and the Grey Company coming to Dunharrow and taking the Paths of the Dead). – Ronald Eames writes to Tolkien. He returns the drawings for the *Lord of the Rings* dust-jackets, and sends proofs of the jacket for *The Fellowship of the Ring* on green paper. The jackets for the other volumes are planned to be on blue and grey paper.

1 June 1964 Tolkien and G.V. Smithers examine F.W. Watt of Queens College *viva voce* on his B.Litt. thesis, *Dialogue in Chaucer*, at 2.30 p.m. in the Examination Schools.

2 June 1954 Tolkien sends letters and cuttings relating to *The Hobbit* in a registered parcel to Rayner Unwin.

3 June 1954 Tolkien writes to Ronald Eames, returning the jacket proofs. He wishes that he could approve them, but he thinks them 'very ugly indeed'. He should have been consulted earlier, but 'what the jacket looks like is ... of much less importance now than issuing the book as soon as possible; and if I had had nothing to do with it, I should not much mind. But as the Ring-motif remains obviously mine (though made rather clumsier), I am likely to be suspected by the few who concern me of having planned the whole.' He thinks the lettering 'unusually ugly': it has no affinity to Black Letter, 'not decorative but brutally emphatic'. He would prefer 'a normal serifed uncial (capital) type'. 'I also think that the balance of the whole is wrong. The centre of the Eye should be at or above the centre of the page (as in the drafts). And the colours chosen are to my taste both ugly and unsuitable. To be effective, of course, the background should be black or very dark, and the same as the filling of the Ring.

But at any rate I hope that something other than the blue, and especially the sick-green [paper] can be found.' He would rather have the jacket as it is than any more delay, but if it can be altered without delay he 'would like a different type for the title-lettering at least (on the page; the spine is passable)' (Tolkien-George Allen & Unwin archive, HarperCollins, partly printed in *Letters*, p. 182).

4 June 1954 Ronald Eames writes to Tolkien. Allen & Unwin will replace the lettering on the *Lord of the Rings* dust-jacket with 'a much lighter Old Face type called Perpetua' and will have revised proofs made. Allen & Unwin now propose to print the jackets for all three volumes on grey paper. – C.S. Lewis accepts the chair of Medieval and Renaissance English at Cambridge, which Helen Gardner has declined.

7 June 1954 Tolkien writes to Rayner Unwin, asking if the parcel of *Hobbit* letters and cuttings has arrived safely. He needs to know what space he will have at the end of *The Return of the King*, so that he can prepare the Appendices.

8 June 1954 Rayner Unwin writes to Tolkien. He confirms that the *Hobbit* material arrived, and thanks him for his corrections to *The Return of the King*. He cannot give him an accurate number of pages available for the Appendices until he has a proof of the final volume, but he estimates that about 44 pages would make the volume the same length as *The Two Towers*.

9 June 1954 W.N. Beard writes to Tolkien. He sends duplicate printers' proofs of *The Two Towers* with the printers' reader's queries on loose pages.

10 June 1954 Tolkien writes to W.N. Beard. He returns the reader's queries, nearly all of which he has accepted: for instance, 'tobacco' is changed to 'pipeweed', and Tolkien agrees that the sentence 'Wonder came into the man's eyes, and he laid them hastily by the wall' might be misread. Tolkien is 'very grateful and astonished at the reader's close attention not only to ordinary detail, but to the story and its idiom' (Tolkien-George Allen & Unwin archive, HarperCollins). – English Final Honour School examinations begin.

11 June 1954 W.N. Beard writes to Tolkien. He is sending a second set of queries by the same proofreader.

12 June 1954 Tolkien writes to W.N. Beard, returning the further queries. He has noticed a few more errors in *The Fellowship of the Ring* which had escaped both him and the reader, and lists them. – W.N. Beard writes to Tolkien. He is sending an advance copy of *The Fellowship of the Ring* wrapped in a proof of the altered dust-jacket printed on grey paper, and proofs of the dust-jackets of the other two volumes. He is having white endpapers replaced with cream paper to match the text pages.

14 June 1954 W.N. Beard writes to Tolkien, thanking him for returning the new queries. Allen & Unwin will correct the errors noted in *The Fellowship of the Ring* when reprinting.

15 June 1954 Tolkien writes to W.N. Beard. 'It was a great moment yesterday when I received the advance copy of *The Fellowship of the Ring*. The book itself is very presentable indeed. I think the jacket is now much improved, and is rather striking. I like the grey paper used, and much prefer it to the other colours' (*Letters*, p. 183). But he feels that there should be some differentiation between the volumes, which might be achieved by varying the colour of the lettering. He notes two errors in the text on the lower jacket.

18 June 1954 Tolkien attends an English Faculty Board meeting. The chairman reports the resignation of C.S. Lewis from the Board, on his appointment to the Cambridge professorship.

19 June 1954 Trinity Full Term ends.

21 June 1954 W.N. Beard writes to Tolkien. Allen & Unwin will vary the colour of the lettering on *The Two Towers*. Beard encloses revised page proofs of the preliminaries for that volume.

22 June 1954 Tolkien attends a Merton College meeting.

23 June–3 July 1954 Tolkien is in Ireland again as an Extern Examiner for the National University. He goes first to Cork, and on 25 June to Dublin, where he stays until at least 28 June. He presumably also visits Galway and Maynooth. Christopher Tolkien accompanies him.

30 June 1954 L.G. Smith, Allen & Unwin, writes to Tolkien. He is preparing a list of reviewers for *The Fellowship of the Ring* and asks if Tolkien has any suggestions.

2 July 1954 All food rationing ends in Britain.

3–15 July 1954 For the most part after he returns from Ireland, Tolkien is away from home.

5 July 1954 W.N. Beard sends Tolkien two complete sets of galley proofs of *The Return of the King* and the original typescript.

7 July 1954 W.N. Beard writes to Tolkien. Allen & Unwin have just reprinted 3,500 copies of *The Hobbit*, mainly to supply an order from the Houghton Mifflin Company for 1,000, but also because Allen & Unwin themselves will need more copies soon. Unfortunately the published price will have to rise from 8s. 6d. to 9s. 6d.

14 July 1954 L.G. Smith sends Tolkien the review list for *The Fellowship of the Ring*.

16 July 1954 Tolkien writes to Allen & Unwin, replying to various communications from his publisher in one letter before he leaves again for Dublin. He returns the marked proof of the title-page, synopsis, etc. for *The Two Towers*. 'The corrections of the unfortunate errors in the Runes etc. on the title-page may be (and at this stage I suppose must be) disregarded' (Tolkien-George Allen & Unwin archive, HarperCollins). He suggests that the *Dublin Review*, the *Oxford Times*, and any paper in Liège be added to the review list for *The Fellowship of the Ring*, and that review copies should be sent to Richard Hughes and C.S. Lewis. He has corrected the galley proofs of *The Return of the King*, but would like to have someone else read them before sending them back. He has mislaid the copy of *The Two Towers* with his corrections, and would like Allen & Unwin to ensure that he has corrected the Elvish invocation on p. 329 (*Aiya Eärendil Elenion Ancalima!*). There is also one correction which needs to be made, if possible, in the reprint of *The Hobbit*.

18–22 July 1954 Tolkien attends the centenary celebrations of the National University of Ireland in Dublin.

20 July 1954 Tolkien is awarded an Hon. D.Litt. by the National University of Ireland in a ceremony in Iveagh House. The address is given by Professor Jeremiah J. Hogan, who heard Tolkien's first lecture as Rawlinson and Bosworth Professor at Oxford. – W.N. Beard writes to Tolkien. Allen & Unwin are able to correct the errors on the title-page of *The Two Towers*, and will repeat the correction in *The Return of the King*. They have asked the printers to check the wording of the invocation in *The Two Towers*. They have rushed the correction to *The Hobbit* to the printers.

22 July 1954 W.N. Beard writes to Tolkien. The *Hobbit* correction arrived too late, but will be included in the next reprint. The printers have reported the corrected invocation in Elvish.

23 July 1954 (postmark) P.H. Newby writes to Tolkien. *Sir Gawain and the Green Knight* is to be broadcast again in September.

Late July–early September 1954 For a long while after his return from Ireland, Tolkien feels ill, 'with an appalling throat, a symptom, I think, rather than a cause of being run nearly out' (letter to Rayner Unwin, 9 September 1954, Tolkien-George Allen & Unwin archive, HarperCollins).

29 July 1954 *The Fellowship of the Ring* is published. Tolkien spends some time this day or soon afterwards inscribing and posting presentation copies. Recipients include friends K.M. Kilbride and Sarah Connaughton.

31 July 1954 Tolkien attends a Merton College meeting.

?August 1954–?early 1955 Tolkien works on the Appendices to *The Lord of the Rings*. Later he will write to Colonel Worskett: 'There are, of course, quite a lot of links between *The Hobbit* and The L.R. that are not clearly set out. They were mostly written or sketched out, but cut out to lighten the boat: such as Gandalf's exploratory journeys, his relations with Aragorn and Gondor; all the movements of Gollum, until he took refuge in Moria, and so on' (draft, 20 September 1963, *Letters*, p. 334). Some of this material will be published eventually in *Unfinished Tales* as *The Hunt for the Ring, a compilation of several variant accounts, also concerning Sauron's reluctance to use the Ringwraiths to search for the Ring, Saruman's jealousy of Gandalf which led him to take an interest in the Shire, and his scoffing at Gandalf for the use of pipe-weed during a meeting of the White Council. – At this time Tolkien also writes, first as a working manuscript and then in a revised version, a briefer account of the line of Dol Amroth than that made in 1948, followed by the dates of twenty-four rulers, not all of them named; and he produces further texts of 'Durin's Folk' in Appendix A. A partial draft typescript of the latter becomes a rough manuscript, with much retyping and rewriting as it progresses, but comes close to the published text as far as the point where the Dwarves have settled east of the Ered Luin. Tolkien then draws a line under what he has written, and in rougher manuscript tells the story of Thrain's ring, of the capture of Thrain by Sauron, and of Thorin until his meeting with Gandalf, which also appears in Appendix A but considerably rewritten. Tolkien also writes an account of Thorin's meeting with Gandalf and of subsequent events as Frodo and the other hobbits heard it from Gandalf in Minas Tirith and as Frodo recorded in the Red Book (see *The Peoples of Middle-earth*, pp. 279–84): this is the first version of what became **The Quest of Erebor*. Associated with it are various notes which Tolkien makes as he ponders the course of events, what Gandalf actually knew and planned, and which dates were already fixed. He then makes a moderately fair copy of the latter part, rewriting parts as he proceeds but making no essential changes in the story; and a ten-page typescript with many further minor emendations.

4 August 1954 Tolkien writes to P.H. Newby. He is pleased to hear about the rebroadcast of *Sir Gawain*, but has heard no more about *The Homecoming of Beorhtnoth*, nor has his copy of *Essays and Studies* been returned.

6, 8 August 1954 Tolkien writes to a Miss Perry, who had earlier written to him about *The Hobbit*, and has now commented on *The Fellowship of the Ring* even before she has finished reading it. Hers is the first letter he has received about the new book. He expresses his anxiety about reviews. On 8 August he adds comments on the *Sunday Times* review. This is the first of many letters sent by enthusiastic readers to the author of *The Lord of the Rings*. Early on, Tolkien enjoys receiving them and does not find replying an excessive burden, though he often begins his replies with an apology for not writing sooner.

7 August 1954 Tolkien writes to Katharine Farrer. The printers of *The Fellowship of the Ring* 'appear to have a highly educated pedant as a chief proof-reader' who began to 'correct' Tolkien's spelling and was rebuked by the author. 'It has been (and continues to be) a crushingly laborious year! So many things at once, each needing exclusive attention.' Allen & Unwin are 'clamouring' for his translation of *Sir Gawain and the Green Knight*, which they wish to publish. 'And I am struggling to select from all the mass of private stuff about the languages, scripts, calendars and history of the Third Age, what may prove interesting to those who like that sort of thing, and will go into the space (about 40 pages) [as appendices to *The Lord of the Rings*]' (*Letters*, pp. 183–4).

17 August 1954 Tolkien inscribes a copy of *The Fellowship of the Ring* to his son Michael, and adds a brief note pointing out that Michael is included in the printed dedication ('to all admirers of Bilbo, but especially to my sons and my daughter, and to my friends the Inklings', original Foreword, p. 7). He thinks that Michael's son, Michael George, may be old enough to enjoy the book. – W.N. Beard writes to Tolkien. He wishes to know when Tolkien will return the corrected proofs of *The Return of the King* with copy for the Appendices and the remaining map. He also needs a synopsis of the first two volumes of *The Lord of the Rings*.

25 August 1954 Rayner Heppenstall, BBC, writes to Tolkien. He hopes to broadcast *The Homecoming of Beorhtnoth Beorhthelm's Son* in the autumn. It would be an advantage if Tolkien could add a line or two to the dialogue to indicate visual stage directions, such as 'the lights disappear'. He anticipates the use of Gregorian chant, specially recorded, and asks if Tolkien knows of monks in Oxford 'whose grounds are not plagued by the sound of motor horns'. He asks also if the two principal speakers in *Beorhtnoth* should have 'some East-Anglian rural quality of speech' (BBC Written Archives Centre).

26 August 1954 Rayner Unwin sends congratulations to Tolkien on the publication of *The Fellowship of the Ring*. Repeat orders are already coming in, and inquiries about the other two volumes. 'The reviews (with the honourable exception of C.S. Lewis's magnificent essay in *Time and Tide*) have been equivocal but on the whole seem to have served their purpose by exciting curiosity about the book. . . .' With luck, Allen & Unwin will publish *The Two Towers* in November (Tolkien-George Allen & Unwin archive, HarperCollins).

28 August 1954 The Rector of the University of Liège writes to Tolkien. He sends details of the ceremony to be held on 2 October, and invites Tolkien and his wife to attend a lunch following the event.

?September 1954 Some time before Tolkien's letter to Rayner Unwin on 9 September, Simonne d'Ardenne arrives from Belgium to (as Tolkien writes) 'harass me with philological work on which we are supposed to be engaged' (*Letters*, p. 185).

September 1954 Peter Hastings, manager of a Catholic bookshop in Oxford, who must have read at least *The Two Towers* as well as *The Fellowship of the Ring* and had some conversation with Tolkien about the work, writes to Tolkien expressing his enthusiasm for *The Lord of the Rings*, but asks if Tolkien had not 'over-stepped the mark in metaphysical matters' (quoted in *Letters*, p. 187). Tolkien drafts a long reply defending his position and answering questions, but in the end does not send the letter, writing on it: 'It seemed to be taking myself too importantly' (*Letters*, p. 196). – Tolkien's translation of *Sir Gawain and the Green Knight* is broadcast again on BBC radio during September, prompting new letters from listeners. One, from an external student of the University of London, asks if the translation has been published; and one from British Nylon Spinners asks for permission to quote part of it in their house magazine.

4 September 1954 L.G. Smith, Allen & Unwin, sends Tolkien a draft press release about *The Lord of the Rings* for Belgian newspapers. He asks the date of Tolkien's degree ceremony at Liège so that it can be included.

7 September 1954 Tolkien writes to L.G. Smith, returning the draft press release with the date inserted.

8 September 1954 L.G. Smith replies to Tolkien. He is sorry to hear of Tolkien's recent illness.

9 September 1954 Tolkien writes to Rayner Unwin. He is still not feeling much better after his return from Ireland, and 'August, vital to my arrangements, has escaped me, ineffectually, without either real rest or accomplishment. . . . I have found myself in a drained and nervous state, in which it was impossible to think. Medical advice, of course, is admirable: drop everything, go away and sleep. Quite impossible to follow, alas!' He has subscribed to a London cuttings service and so has seen many of the reviews of *The Fellowship of the Ring*; he asks Rayner for advice on how to obtain copies of American reviews when the book is published in the United States. Houghton

Mifflin have sent him a 'backjacket' (presumably a blurb for the dust-jacket) for approval. He comments on reviews of the Allen & Unwin edition at length (see *Letters*, pp. 184–5), and says that he has been interviewed for the *Oxford Mail* but that the article will not appear until the following week as the paper is waiting for a photograph. (This is presumably the long review by Anthony Price of *The Fellowship of the Ring*, 'Fairy Story for Grown Ups Too', which will appear on 16 September 1954 with a photograph.) Tolkien has had two long letters from Nevill Coghill, and a request from Iceland to set some of the verse in *The Fellowship of the Ring* to music.

He would like Allen & Unwin to send copies of *The Fellowship of the Ring*, with a slip reading 'with the author's compliments', to Miss Helen M. Buckhurst, Professor B.G. McCarthy of Cork, Professor J.J. Hogan of Dublin, and the Reverend Mother Mary St John, St Mary's Abbey, Oulton (headmistress of a school, and sister of Christopher Wiseman); these are also to have the other volumes of *The Lord of the Rings* when they are published. When the second volume is published, a copy should go to Miss Margaret Douglas, a friend of Charles Williams who, Tolkien says, typed that volume gratis in 1944 (but *see note*).

He encloses various notes, requests, queries, and answers which he asks Rayner to pass to the appropriate departments of Allen & Unwin (*see note*). He has not finished correcting galley proofs of *The Return of the King*, but will try to do so and post them on 13 September: it is 'chiefly a matter of transferring corrections of my own and others from the rough copy', but he is 'troubled by the bottom of galley 95' (the 'title-page' of Bilbo and Frodo's book, in Book VI, Chapter 9), which should be 'rehandled' typographically. He regrets that he still does not have 'any copy to send in for the Appendices' but will try to produce it before the end of the month. 'My trouble is indecision (and conflicting advice) in selection from the too abundant matter. I have spent much ineffectual time on the attempt to satisfy the unfortunate promises of Vol I. p. 8' (to provide additional information at the end of the third volume; see *Reader's Companion*, p. lxix). He has produced a rough index as far as the middle of Volume 2. The 'alphabets' (Tengwar and Cirth to be reproduced in Appendix E) will need line-blocks made; he is hoping that Christopher will produce the large-scale map of Rohan, Gondor, and Mordor as soon as possible.

One correspondent has noted the errors in the Cirth and Tengwar writing on the title-page of *The Fellowship of the Ring*, but Tolkien does not feel it necessary to correct the title-page of *The Two Towers* if it would hold up publication. The correction to the text on p. 329 of *The Two Towers* should be *Aiya Eärendil Elenion Ancalima!* (Tolkien-George Allen & Unwin archive, HarperCollins; partly printed in *Letters*, p. 185). – Tolkien writes to the Rector of the University of Liège. He himself will attend the ceremony on 2 October, but for health reasons his wife will not be able to accompany him.

15 September 1954 Tolkien sends corrected galley proofs 1–97 for *The Return of the King* to Allen & Unwin with a draft synopsis for the beginning of the volume.

17 September 1954 Allen & Unwin send a telegram to Tolkien, asking for corrections to *The Fellowship of the Ring* which is being reprinted at once. – Tolkien replies that he will send corrections the following day. – W.N. Beard writes to Tolkien. He acknowledges receipt of the galley proofs and synopsis, lists the corrections to *The Fellowship of the Ring* that Allen & Unwin already have, and notes that the Cirth and Tengwar inscriptions on the title-page of that volume also will be corrected. Allen & Unwin are urging the printers to complete the reprint as soon as possible: the paper for it is already on its way to them, so they cannot wait more than a few days for any corrections.

18 September 1954 Tolkien writes to W.N. Beard, enclosing a list of seven further corrections to *The Fellowship of the Ring*. The Appendices and map are still not complete. – Tolkien replies to Hugh Brogan, who has written about *The Fellowship of the Ring*.

20 September 1954 Tolkien sends another correction to Allen & Unwin. – Rayner Unwin writes to Tolkien. *The Fellowship of the Ring* is selling well. Allen & Unwin have had an enquiry from a Swedish publisher about the work. Rayner has sent copies to those persons that Tolkien asked to have them, and will charge them to Tolkien's account. Rayner will ask Houghton Mifflin about obtaining American reviews.

22 September 1954 Tolkien replies to Rayner Heppenstall, BBC. The 'visual directions' in *The Homecoming of Beorhtnoth* can be disregarded, 'though I am considering some additional lines. I have tested this by recording the whole thing on tape'. He will make enquiries about the chant. He discusses how the Latin should be pronounced, and explains at length why 'no "dialect" tone or rural quality' is required for the two speakers' (BBC Written Archives Centre; partly printed in *Letters*, p. 187). Apart from dealing with galley proofs, he is involved in much examination work (probably for Ireland).

24 September 1954 W.N. Beard sends Tolkien a revised sketch for the title-page of *The Two Towers*, presumably correcting the Cirth and Tengwar inscriptions.

?24–?27 September 1954 Tolkien returns the sketch to W.N. Beard.

25 September 1954 Tolkien writes a six-page letter (preceded by a longer draft) to Naomi Mitchison in response to her 'generous and perceptive' review of *The Fellowship of the Ring* (*Letters*, p. 196) and to a letter from her in August. He comments in great detail on his *legendarium*.

27 September 1954 Rayner Heppenstall writes to Tolkien. He suggests that it may be better not to have any music for *The Homecoming of Beorhtnoth*.

28 September 1954 Tolkien writes to Daphne Castell, probably in response to a letter commenting on *The Fellowship of the Ring*. – W.N. Beard acknowledges receipt of the revised title-page sketch.

?1 October 1954 Tolkien travels to Belgium.

2 October 1954 In the morning, Tolkien receives an Honorary D.Litt. (Doct. en Lettres et Phil.) at the University of Liège. After the ceremony, he and the five other recipients of honorary degrees lunch with University dignitaries. – During this visit, Tolkien gives Simonne d'Ardenne corrected galley proofs of *The Return of the King* and a proof dust-jacket of *The Fellowship of the Ring*.

4 October 1954 Tolkien returns to Oxford. – W.N. Beard writes to Tolkien. The printers will wait until they have copy for the Appendices before transforming the galley proofs of *The Return of the King* into page form. They need the drawing of the remaining map. Rayner Unwin will be visiting Oxford early next week, and will call on Tolkien.

6 October 1954 Tolkien attends a Merton College meeting.

8 October 1954 E.H. Wakeham, Copyright Department, BBC, writes to Tolkien, asking him to sign and return a form giving permission for the broadcast of *The Homecoming of Beorhtnoth*, and stating the fee to be paid.

10 October 1954 Michaelmas Full Term begins. Tolkien's scheduled lectures for this term are: *Sir Gawain and the Green Knight* on Wednesdays at 11.00 a.m. in the Examination Schools, beginning 13 October; the *Ayenbite of Inwit* on Wednesdays at 12.00 noon in the Examination Schools, beginning 13 October; and Philology: Outline of the History of English Accidence on Fridays at 11.00 a.m. in the Examination Schools, beginning 15 October. He will continue to supervise B.Litt. students G.M.G. Evans, J.C. Haworth, V.M. Martin and B.D.H. Miller, and D.Phil. students R.W. Burchfield, A.D. Horgan, and E.J. Stormon.

11 October 1954 Tolkien writes to W.N. Beard. He asks when Rayner Unwin will be in Oxford: Tolkien is anxious to see him, but is going to Ireland on 16 October, and before then will have little free time except evenings. He requests another set of galley proofs of *The Return of the King*. – Later that day W.N. Beard replies to Tolkien that Rayner Unwin has had to postpone his visit for a week. Since Allen & Unwin are anxious that *The Return of the King* should be published in February 1955, they hope that Rayner will be able to collect the Appendices and map when he visits Tolkien.

12 October 1954 Rayner Unwin writes to Tolkien. Having received Tolkien's letter of 11 October, he will visit Oxford on 14 October, bringing another set of galley proofs of *The Return of the King*.

14 October 1954 Rayner Unwin visits Tolkien in Oxford. He is able to take away some material for the Appendices, family trees and *The Tale of Years*. By now Tolkien has made many emendations to the fourth Baggins and Took, the third Bolger and Boffin, and the fifth Brandybuck family trees, bringing them close to their final forms; of these he has made copies, of which the last were carefully drawn for the printer. The fourth Gamgee-Cotton family tree, entitled 'The Genealogy of Master Samwise, showing the rise of the family of Gardner of the Hill', also incorporates many changes and may belong to this time; on this Tolkien emends some of the birthdates of Sam's children, which appear *ab initio* in the fifth and final version, 'The Longfather-Tree of Master Samwise'. The index of names is now abandoned.

15 October 1954 Tolkien attends an English Faculty Board meeting. C.L. Wrenn is elected to replace J.N. Bryson as chairman. Tolkien is co-opted to the Standing Committee for the Lecture List (he was no longer on it when he ceased to be chairman of the Board two years earlier). The Applications Committee has appointed him supervisor of his former B.Litt. student, Auvo Kurvinen of St Anne's College, now returned as an advanced student concerned with 'the life of St Catherine of Alexandria in Middle English prose', and of probationer B.Litt. student L. Glanville of Somerville College for a medieval English literature subject.

16 October 1954 Tolkien travels to Dublin, probably in his capacity as Extern Examiner for the National University of Ireland, and probably also visits colleges in Cork, Galway, and Maynooth. While there he writes to E.H. Wakeham, BBC, that he believes that he owns all of the rights to *The Homecoming of Beorhtnoth*, but will check with Professor Bullough of King's College (the editor of *Essays and Studies*). He points out that the drama is not a translation but an original work, which may require alteration of the permissions form.

18 October 1954 Tolkien writes from Dublin to the Rector of the University of Liège, expressing gratitude for the honour conferred on him and the hospitality he received during his visit to Liège.

21 October 1954 *The Fellowship of the Ring* is published in the United States.

22 October 1954 Tolkien returns to Oxford. – Rayner Unwin writes to Tolkien. The printers are setting the family trees of *The Lord of the Rings* in type, but Rayner is returning *The Tale of Years*, which needs to be shortened. He suggests that considerable reduction be made in the accounts of events already told in *The Lord of the Rings*, and that a somewhat staccato style be adopted. The map is particularly urgent. – W.N. Beard writes to Tolkien. There has been a query about whether a change is needed on the title-page for the reprint of *The Fellowship of the Ring*. He sends a proof and asks Tolkien to indicate his answer on it and return it direct to the printers.

Late October 1954–first months of 1955 After receiving Rayner Unwin's letter of 22 October, Tolkien heavily emends one of the typescript copies of *The Tale of Years*. Most of the changes are aimed at shortening it by the omission of phrases, but Tolkien also makes alterations in the part dealing with the final years of Númenor, consequent on changes made to the typescript of the *Akallabêth*. In the process *The Tale of Years* is not much shortened after all. Tolkien then attempts to reduce it much more drastically in a series of typescript pages which apparently comprise at least two successive versions or parts of versions, with many changes and revisions of dates. Under pressure, Tolkien types rapidly and makes many errors. As he types one version he breaks off the entry for Second Age 2250–3000 (concerning the Númenóreans) in mid-sentence and follows it with a long account (more than 2,000 words) of the Númenóreans, their origin and division, the coming of Sauron, and the Downfall of Númenor. Christopher Tolkien will later speculate that as his father attempts to shorten *The Tale of Years* he became more aware of the fact that very little Númenórean history is given in *The Lord of the Rings*, and decided that something must be included apart from the brief entries in *The Tale of Years*.

Tolkien now makes a second typescript version of the account of Númenor, with the addition of a list of kings and queens, and omissions or abridgments of material dealing with Tar-Palantir, Míriel's marriage to Pharazôn ('by force'), and Sauron's policy in his attack on the coastal fortresses and harbours of the Númenóreans, printed in Appendix A as 'The Númenórean Kings'. This work is probably not done all at once, some of it perhaps after the number of pages allocated by Allen & Unwin for the Appendices was increased, probably at the beginning of February 1955.

Following on his manuscripts of 1948–9 entitled *The Heirs of Elendil*, which contained much information in common with *The Tale of Years*, Tolkien makes a rough typescript, also entitled *The Heirs of Elendil*, in which he tries to fit a great deal of information into a small space. He begins, 'There is no space here to set out the lines of kings and lords of Arnor and Gondor', then reduces the history of Arnor almost to vanishing point, and for Gondor briefly summarizes the three great evils beginning with the Kin-strife. Tolkien abandons this typescript unfinished after Eärnil's victory, possibly realizing that a text so abbreviated is of little value. He then makes a second typescript, expanding on the first in places, sometimes at considerable length.

It is also possibly at this time that Tolkien returns to the typescript of the *Akallabêth*. He makes some emendations, rewrites some passages and removes others, and inserts a long rider with a detailed account of the last rulers of Númenor, including the repentance of Tar-Palantir and the forced marriage of his daughter Míriel to Ar-Pharazôn. Associated with the rider are several other versions of the story, some written very roughly; these possibly predate the rider, but it may be that for a while Tolkien considers changing the story so that Míriel married Ar-Pharazôn for love.

25 October 1954 E.H. Wakeham, BBC, writes to Tolkien that the permissions form will indeed need altering. She asks whether Tolkien regards *The Homecoming of Beorhtnoth* as a poem or a play in verse, so that she can send the correct form, though in this case it will make little difference to the fee.

?Early November 1954 Rayner Heppenstall visits Tolkien in Oxford. They agree (as far as Tolkien will recall) to drop any reference to the 'Voice in the Dark' in *The Homecoming of Beorhtnoth*. Tolkien suggests that a few lines from the *Dies Irae* would be a better conclusion to the broadcast than the *Dirige*.

3 November 1954 Tolkien attends a Merton College meeting.

4 November 1954 Tolkien drafts a long letter to Robert Murray on points that Murray has raised about *The Lord of the Rings*. Tolkien has time to reply because he has finished 'ordering all the minutes and resolutions of a long and argumentative College-meeting yesterday (there being no fellow of ill-will, and only 24 persons of the usual human absurdity. I felt rather like an observer at the meeting of Hobbit-notables to advise the Mayor on the precedence and choice of dishes at a Shire-banquet)', and he has half an hour to spare before going into Oxford 'for a session with the College secretary' (*Letters*, p. 201).

6 November 1954 Tolkien writes to R.W. Burchfield, in reply to a card. Burchfield evidently has offered to lecture in the Oxford English School; Tolkien feels sure that the English Faculty Board would welcome this. Tolkien is pleased that Burchfield has purchased *The Fellowship of the Ring* and has enjoyed it. Some of his 'other philological colleagues . . . regard it as a regrettable waste of time better spent on other stuff' (quoted in Christie's, *Valuable Manuscripts and Printed Books*, London, 7 June 2006, p. 236).

9 November 1954 Roger Lancelyn Green notes in his diary that he went on this date to the 'Bird and Baby' (Eagle and Child pub, Oxford) to meet C.S. Lewis, and that W.H. Lewis, R.B. McCallum, Gervase Mathew, and Tolkien were also present. There was 'very good talk, about Tolkien's book [*The Lord of the Rings*], horror comics, who is the most influential and important man in various countries: decided Burke for Ireland, Scott for Scotland, Shakespeare for England – but there difficulties arose, Pitt and Wellington also being put forward' (quoted in Roger Lancelyn Green and Walter Hooper, *C.S. Lewis: A Biography*, rev. and expanded edn. 2002, p. 178).

10 November 1954 E.H. Wakeham, BBC, writes to remind Tolkien that he has not answered her letter of 25 October. – Rayner Unwin writes to Tolkien. Unless Allen & Unwin receive the rest of the Appendices soon, the publication of *The Return of the King* will be delayed. He sends Tolkien a copy of W.H. Auden's review of *The Fellowship of the Ring* in *Encounter* ('A World Imaginary but Real', November 1954).

11 November 1954 *The Two Towers* is published. – Tolkien possibly spends some time this day inscribing and posting presentation copies.

15 November 1954 Rayner Heppenstall's secretary writes to Tolkien. Rehearsals and recording of *The Homecoming of Beorhtnoth* at the BBC will take place on 3 December from 2.15 to 7.00 p.m. The work will be broadcast at 10.15 p.m. that evening.

16 November 1954 In the morning, Tolkien telephones Miss Wakeham to say that *The Homecoming of Beorhtnoth* is a play in verse. She will send the correct form to Tolkien later this day. – L.G. Smith writes to Tolkien. Allen & Unwin had sent details of *The Fellowship of the Ring* to persons who wrote to Tolkien about *The Hobbit*, but had omitted to keep a copy of a list of them. Smith asks Tolkien if he can send Allen & Unwin his copy of it.

17 November 1954 Tolkien returns the signed form to E.H. Wakeham. – He writes to Rayner Heppenstall that he will be unable to attend the rehearsals and recording of *The Homecoming of Beorhtnoth* on 3 December. He remains 'rather in the dark as to how you propose to treat the thing, and what part – if any; but some hint of "background" seems necessary – of the historical notes [included with the verse-drama in *Essays and Studies*] is to be included (as preface)' (BBC Written Archives Centre). He asks if it would be helpful if he went through the text and made any notes that occurred to him. He encloses a few lines of the *Dies Irae* to replace the *Dirige* as the conclusion. He asks for the return of the volume of *Essays and Studies* lent earlier in the year to P.H. Newby, as it is Tolkien's only printed copy. Also he would be grateful if the BBC could spare him a copy of the script for *The Homecoming of Beorhtnoth*.

18 November 1954 W.N. Beard sends Tolkien proofs of the family trees for *The Lord of the Rings*. That for 'Took of Great Smials' has been a tight fit. He asks for the return of the proofs of *The Return of the King*, and for the rest of the copy for the Appendices quickly.

22 November 1954 Rayner Heppenstall writes to inform Tolkien that *The Battle of Maldon* in Gavin Bone's translation, read by Michael Hordern, is to be broadcast at the beginning of the same week in which *The Homecoming of Beorhtnoth* will be transmitted, and will be preceded by an extract from the *Anglo-Saxon Chronicle*. This, Heppenstall thinks, will make it unnecessary to say anything before *The Homecoming of Beorhtnoth* other than that the work is set at night and there has been a battle. They can include a half-page of introductory scene-setting if Tolkien thinks it a good idea, but they would need that text very soon. They have an actor booked for the 'Voice in the Dark', and are considering different recordings of the *Dies Irae*. It would indeed be helpful for Tolkien to go through the text and make notes.

26 November 1954 Rayner Heppenstall's secretary sends Tolkien a copy of the script for *The Homecoming of Beorhtnoth*.

27 November 1954 Tolkien writes to Katharine Farrer, apologizing for not writing or calling when he knew that she and her husband had both been ill and troubled. He offers, if no other source is available, to help pay for a holiday for them, as Trinity (Austin Farrer's College) was very kind to him when he himself was in difficulties, offering reduced fees for Michael and Christopher's tuition. He returns a copy of a work by C.S. Lewis which Farrer had lent him, and a copy of *Encounter* with W.H. Auden's review of *The Fellowship of the Ring*. Tolkien is 'hopelessly behind with the "Appendices" to Vol. III; but I have been be-bothered with many things; and Chris[topher] too overwhelmed to help with maps' (*Letters*, p. 208). – On the same day, Ronald Eames writes to say that Allen & Unwin will reprint *The Two Towers* immediately. He asks about the proofs of the family trees, and the rest of the Appendices.

29 November 1954 Rayner Unwin sends Tolkien a proof of the Houghton Mifflin dust-jacket for *The Two Towers*. Allen & Unwin are still waiting anxiously for the Appendices. He asks if there is any way he can help with the Appendices.

December 1954 Hugh Brogan writes to Tolkien. He criticizes the archaic style used in parts of *The Lord of the Rings*.

1–2 December 1954 Tolkien writes to Rayner Heppenstall. The latter had not mentioned the broadcast of Bone's translation of *The Battle of Maldon* when he visited Tolkien in Oxford. Tolkien does not think that that would serve to make *The Homecoming of Beorhtnoth* comprehensible 'even to such readers as heard it. *I do earnestly hope that it may even now be possible to include such a* brief addition to the preliminary announcement as I have appended on the *enclosed* copy' (italics Tolkien's). He thought that they had agreed that it would be best to omit the 'Voice in the Dark'. The lines he selected from the *Dies Irae* 'make sense, are apt, and preserve the rhyme-scheme. They are either recited in speaking voice, or sung to simple tone or tune (which preserves the metre and emphasizes the rhyme)' (BBC Written Archives Centre). He adds several pages of notes on stress, speaking alliteration, the pronunciation of names, etc.

2 December 1954 Tolkien writes to Rayner Unwin. He has had time to only glance at the Houghton Mifflin dust-jacket. The description of the book 'must have been written by someone who has not read the book, but relied on hearsay inaccurately remembered. The "giving away of the plot" is, of course, a silly (and unnecessary) procedure; but at least the plot given away might be that of the book described.' He lists some of the inaccuracies in the blurb, but prefers to leave it to Allen & Unwin to decide whether to ask that it be altered. He does not know quite how Rayner 'can help in the task of putting the additional matter into form', as he had offered. 'Possibly you could have copies made of the items I am about to submit whether for this purpose you think them useful or not?' (Tolkien-George Allen & Unwin archive, HarperCollins; partly printed in *Letters*, p. 208).

3 December 1954 Tolkien attends an English Faculty Board meeting. The Committee on Monographs (of which Tolkien is a member) submits a report, and it is agreed 'to apply to the General Board, through the Committee on Advanced Studies, for a grant of £600 for the publication of two monographs'. Mr Robson gives notice that at the next meeting of the Board he will 'propose the appointment of a committee to consider the revision of the Final Honour School syllabus' (Oxford University Archives FA 4/5/1/2). – *The Homecoming of Beorhtnoth Beorhthelm's Son* is broadcast in the BBC Third Programme, 10.15–10.45 p.m., described in the *Radio Times* for 26 November 1954 (p. 43) as an 'epilogue' to the fragmentary Anglo-Saxon poem *The Battle of Maldon*.

4 December 1954 Michaelmas Full Term ends.

6 December 1954 Tolkien attends a Merton College meeting.

7 December 1954 Tolkien inscribes a copy of *The Two Towers* for his son Michael for a Christmas present, and writes a brief note. – Rayner Unwin writes to Tolkien. He has sent Tolkien's revisions of the American blurb for *The Two Towers* to Houghton Mifflin with a strong plea that they accept them. Tolkien's corrections for the first two volumes of *The Lord of the Rings* went straight to the printers to be incorporated in forthcoming new impressions. The reprint of *The Fellowship of the Ring* is expected to arrive at the end of the week; demand continues to be brisk. Rayner looks forward to seeing the Appendices, which he expects are in the post.

9 December 1954 The English Faculty give an informal farewell dinner for C.S. Lewis at Merton College. Among those present, besides Lewis and his brother Warnie, are Tolkien and his son Christopher, Hugo Dyson, Lord David Cecil, J.N. Bryson, F.P. Wilson, Nevill Coghill, Irvine R. Browning (one of Lewis's students), J.A.W. Bennett, R.E. Havard, and Emrys Jones, Lewis's successor at Magdalen.

13 December 1954 Tolkien writes to Rayner Heppenstall with criticisms of the broadcast of *The Homecoming of Beorhtnoth*. The letter does not survive in the BBC Archive, but apparently included comments that the readers ignored the alliterative metre of the work, and delivered the verse as if it were iambic pentameter. – Heppenstall replies on the same day. He thinks that Tolkien has taken a very negative view of what was done.

16 December 1954 Rayner Unwin writes to Tolkien, asking him to send such material as he has produced for the Appendices so that Allen & Unwin can have something to set in type. Otherwise they will have to consider publishing the first impression at least of *The Return of the King* with only the text and add the Appendices to a later impression.

18 December 1954 L.G. Smith sends Tolkien a proof of an advertisement, presumably for *The Two Towers*, which will appear in twenty papers including the *Manchester Guardian*, the *New Statesman*, and the *Listener*.

20 December 1954 Tolkien writes to Rayner Unwin. 'I have been trying hard; but I have been grievously harried, and also for the last week or more ill' (Tolkien-George Allen & Unwin archive, HarperCollins). He will try to send at least the main matter for the Appendices the next day. – He also writes to Patricia Kirke, who had written to him about *The Lord of the Rings*.

Christmas 1954 Tolkien is ill.

1955

January 1955 Tolkien again takes up the story of *Tal-Elmar*, which he had begun apparently in the early 1950s. He now writes on the manuscript 'Continuation of Tar-Elmar' and the date January 1955. The new manuscript is roughly written: in the first stage of composition it becomes almost illegible, and at the end narrative gives way to discontinuous fragments and queries. Christopher Tolkien will later comment how remarkable it seems that his father should have worked on *Tal-Elmar* when he was under extreme pressure to produce the Appendices for *The Lord of the Rings*.

5 January 1955 Rayner Unwin writes to Tolkien. Houghton Mifflin seem to have accepted most of his corrections to their blurb for *The Two Towers*; he sends a revised copy of the jacket. He asks if Tolkien can send Allen & Unwin any more copy for the Appendices.

13 January 1955 Tolkien attends a Merton College meeting. – Rayner Unwin writes to Tolkien. He has seen Christopher Tolkien in London, who promised to help with the map of Rohan, Gondor, and Mordor if he can.

16 January 1955 Hilary Full Term begins. Tolkien's scheduled lectures for this term are: *Sir Gawain and the Green Knight* on Wednesdays at 11.00 a.m. in the Examination Schools, beginning 19 January; the *Ayenbite of Inwit* on Wednesdays at 12.00 noon in the Examination Schools, beginning 19 January; and Philology: History of English Accidence on Fridays at 12.00 noon in the Examination Schools, beginning 21 January. He will continue to supervise B.Litt. students J.C. Haworth, V.M. Martin and B.D.H. Miller, D.Phil. students R.W. Burchfield, A.D. Horgan, A. Kurvinen, and E.J. Stormon, and probationer student L. Glanville. – The opening of term is difficult for Tolkien: after being ill himself over Christmas, his wife has been seriously ill.

21 January 1955 At an English Faculty Board meeting, in Tolkien's absence, a committee is appointed (not including Tolkien) to consider the syllabus of the Final Honour School and the Preliminary Examination and present a report with recommendations to the Board not later than Michaelmas Term 1956.

25 January 1955 Terence Tiller of the BBC writes to Tolkien. The Third Programme propose to broadcast a radio adaptation of *The Fellowship of the Ring* as six features of forty-five minutes each. Tiller hopes that Tolkien and Allen & Unwin will give them permission to do so. He has been entrusted with the adaptation and production. He would be happy to receive any preliminary suggestions that Tolkien might make, and is willing to submit his draft scripts to Tolkien for approval.

26 January 1955 Tolkien replies to Terence Tiller. His suggestion is 'most interesting and gratifying', but before granting approval asks for a general idea of how the BBC intend to deal with the lengthy narrative in four and a half hours. Although he has his own views on the matter, 'the "adapter" must, I think, work on his own lines. I should like to have some idea of what those are likely to be' (BBC Written Archives Centre). Having discussed the proposal with Rayner Unwin, who visits Tolkien in Oxford this afternoon, Tolkien adds a postscript that his publisher has approved the project, and will deal with the financial arrangements. – Rayner Unwin is apparently accompanied on this visit by his wife Carol and their young son Merlin. It seems likely that Rayner tells Tolkien at this time that as a result of unexpectedly good sales of the first two volumes of *The Lord of the Rings* Allen & Unwin are prepared to at least double the number of pages in *The Return of the King* allowed for the Appendices. *See note*. It may be that on this occasion he delivers to Tolkien a set of page proofs of the volume, excepting the Appendices. (In fact they are not proper page proofs, but cut up galley proofs printed with running heads and page numbers.) Tolkien in turn gives Rayner some material for the Appendices: *The Languages and Peoples of the Third Age* and *On Translations* (which became Appendix F); the Shire Calendar (part of Appendix D); and a page of runes (part of Appendix E). Tolkien has presumably only just finished the papers he hands over, on which he has been working during the Christmas vacation and the early part of the year. He evidently finds it difficult and frustrating to compress the material into the space available.

28 January 1955 Philip Unwin writes to Tolkien. Allen & Unwin have received a formal proposal from the BBC for the dramatization of *The Fellowship of the Ring* intended to be broadcast between April and June 1955. Although by contract both dramatic and broadcasting rights are vested in Allen & Unwin, before signing he wants to be sure that Tolkien approves.

29 January 1955 Tolkien replies to Philip Unwin. He has already been contacted by Terence Tiller and has discussed the matter with Rayner Unwin, who thinks that the broadcast would be good publicity for *The Lord of the Rings*. Tolkien agrees, 'but I think it would be desirable to obtain as much consideration for my own views and taste as it is possible to obtain from that

Corporation. . . . I view the project with deep misgivings, and do not expect to derive anything but pain and irritation from the result. *But so long as I am firmly advised by you that it is a "good thing" for the book*, I am prepared to put up with that' (Tolkien-George Allen & Unwin archive, HarperCollins, italics Tolkien's). Tolkien asks Unwin to wait a few days before granting formal permission, as he hopes to hear more details from Tiller.

2 February 1955 Rayner Unwin writes to Tolkien. The material for the Appendices Tolkien provided is already at the printers. He asks Tolkien to send piecemeal any other matter he completes. – On the same day, Terence Tiller replies to Tolkien that the dialogue of *The Fellowship of the Ring* will be preserved as far as possible, and presented in dramatic form, while a narrator will link dramatized scenes; but 'both narrative and dialogue would therefore need substantial reduction; and I fear that many, but I hope not all, of the songs and poems would need to be excised' (BBC Written Archives Centre). But the BBC will commission specially composed music.

?4 (received 5) February 1955 Tolkien writes to Terence Tiller, giving his approval of the *Fellowship of the Ring* dramatization. He is telling Allen & Unwin to sign the contract. 'I shall, of course, be much interested to see what it comes out like in the script and performance. I shall be happy (as they say, meaning only too ready) to offer any comments or provide any information' (BBC Written Archives Centre). He accepts that most of the 'songs' will have to be cut, but hopes that some will survive. He suggests his own ideas for the Troll-song and Galadriel's lament.

9 February 1955 Tolkien attends a Merton College meeting. As Subwarden he is a member of a committee to consider possible variations in numbers and arrangements of public dinners given by the college; and also a member of a committee to consider what research fellowships should be offered for election in 1955–6. – Tolkien writes to Patricia Kirke, presumably in reply to a letter, advising her of the best time to visit Oxford and where she might stay.

14 February 1955 Terence Tiller, BBC, writes to Tolkien. He will send Tolkien each script of the *Fellowship of the Ring* adaptation as it is completed.

15 February 1955 Tolkien resigns from the Oxford Dante Society.

16 February 1955 Tolkien replies to a letter of appreciation of *The Lord of the Rings* from a Mrs G. Wood. The success of the book has given him hope of being able to publish what he has written about the earlier Ages of his fictional world (i.e. 'The Silmarillion').

17 February 1955 W.N. Beard writes to Tolkien. As a result of an order from Houghton Mifflin for 1,000 further copies of *The Hobbit*, Allen & Unwin will be reprinting. Beard asks for any corrections that Tolkien wishes to be made. Allen & Unwin intend to add information about *The Lord of the Rings* at the end of the last chapter of *The Hobbit*. Rayner Unwin has asked if Tolkien has been able to complete *The Tale of Years*, not to mention the rest of the Appendices and the map.

2 March 1955 Rayner Unwin writes to Tolkien, pleading for the rest of the Appendices, the map, and corrected proofs of *The Return of the King*. If these are not received soon, Allen & Unwin will have to 'yield to the intense pressure that is accumulating and publish without all the additional material' (*Letters*, p. 209).

3 March 1955 Tolkien replies to a fan letter from Dora Marshall. He has been surprised and delighted at the success of *The Lord of the Rings*.

4 March 1955 W.N. Beard sends Tolkien galley proofs of Appendix F (dated 2 March) and of the Shire Calendar. A block is being made of the 'page of runes', presumably the Angerthas table in Appendix E (Tolkien-George Allen & Unwin archive, HarperCollins).

6 March 1955 Tolkien writes to Rayner Unwin, agreeing to 'make do with what material I can produce' in short order.

I now wish that no appendices had been promised! For I think their appearance in truncated and compressed form will satisfy nobody: certainly not me; clearly from the (appalling mass of) letters I receive not those people who like that kind of thing – astonishingly many. . . . The demands such people make would require a book at least the size of Vol. I.

In any case the 'background' matter is very intricate, useless unless exact, and compression within the limits available leaves it unsatisfactory. It needs great concentration (and leisure), and being completely interlocked cannot be dealt with piecemeal. I have found that out, since I let part of it go.

But I am now in receipt of galleys of the material you took away, and that gives me some indication of *space*. I calculate that the items on 'languages' and on 'translation' will occupy at least 8 pages of Vol. III [in fact they will fill 12 pages as published].

That being more or less so, I think I can manage to compress into the remaining space – allowing pages for the blocks – 1) The Tale of Years, and chronology of the Great Years and after. 2) Some abbreviated comments on the alphabets and spellings. 3) Some short comments on the Calendars. 4) And I hope some further information clamoured for about the Houses of Eorl, Durin, and the Rulers of Gondor.

I need hardly say that I have laboured at these things with all available time, and the effort to do what is a full-time job in itself on top of the labours in what is a critical time in the history of the university, the English School, and the College, has pretty nearly broken me!' [Tolkien-George Allen & Unwin archive, HarperCollins, partly printed in *Letters*, p. 210]

(It is perhaps significant that for the first time, a chronology of 'the Great Years and after' is mentioned in association with *The Tale of Years*. It seems likely that this section was written only when more space was allowed for the Appendices.) – Tolkien also writes to W.N. Beard, commenting that he has been ill, and though now up again he is almost incapacitated with lumbago and confined to quarters, and has no copy of the revised *Hobbit* at hand. Therefore he cannot check for corrections, but the only important one is the change from 'present' to 'guess' on p. 87. He approves putting a notice about *The Lord of the Rings* in *The Hobbit*. He thanks Beard for the galley proofs, and asks if he is correct in assuming that these, excluding a page of Calendar, will occupy about 8 pages as typeset. – He also writes to Philip Unwin that he has no objection to the BBC proposal.

9 March 1955 W.N. Beard replies to Tolkien. He is correct in his estimate of the pages the galleys will take. – Philip Unwin writes to Tolkien. Allen & Unwin have signed a contract with the BBC on condition that Tolkien has the right to approve the text of the dramatization.

10 March 1955 Tolkien takes part in the re-election of E.O.G. Turville-Petre to the Vigfússon Readership in Ancient Icelandic Literature and Antiquities for seven years from 1 October 1955.

11 March 1955 Tolkien attends an English Faculty Board meeting. From this date the first Board meeting of term is held at 2.25 p.m., and the second at 3.30 p.m. It is reported that the board of electors to the O'Donnell Lecturership in Celtic Studies (of which Tolkien is a member) have appointed Sir Cyril Fox as O'Donnell Lecturer for 1955–6. The Applications Committee has accepted Tolkien's probationer student, L. Glanville of Somerville College, as a full B.Litt. student to work on 'a new edition of the Middle English romance "The Weddyng of Syr Gawen and Dame Ragnell"'. Tolkien remains her supervisor, and is also appointed supervisor in place of C.L. Wrenn of probationer student D.C. Levinson of St Anne's College.

12 March 1955 Hilary Full term ends.

14 March 1955 Tolkien attends a Merton College meeting at 10.00 a.m. in the Common Room. The report of the committee on research fellowships is presented.

22 March 1955 Rayner Unwin writes again to ask if Tolkien can return the corrected proofs of *The Return of the King*, which can then go to press, and such parts of the Appendices he has been able to complete. He hopes that the map can follow a day or two later if need be. He fears a loss of good will if the publication of *The Return of the King* is delayed much longer.

?Late March–?11 April 1955 Tolkien is presumably working on the material that W.N. Beard will send to the printer on 12 April. This probably includes greatly emending a typescript of part of the chronology of the Third Age from *The Tale of Years* written in the 'staccato' mode which Rayner Unwin had advised (22 October 1954) so that it approaches the published form, then making the typescript for the whole *Tale of Years* from which Appendix B will be printed. Tolkien may be able to keep this shorter, as he is now assured of space to include what will become Appendix A. For *The Realms in Exile* section in Appendix A Tolkien returns to the greatly abridged version of *The Heirs of Elendil* made in the autumn of 1954 and begins to expand it again to reach the published text. For Appendix A he makes three versions of the text that begins *The Númenórean Kings (i) Númenor*, giving a brief description of events in the First Age and the choices of Elrond and Elros. This is followed by a very short history of Númenor, replaced in the published text by the longer version written while trying to reduce *The Tale of Years*. Much of the information in the next three sections will derive from the various texts of *The Heirs of Elendil*. Tolkien may have begun by making yet another version, in which sections concerning Arvedui are greatly expanded. For *(ii) The Realms in Exile* he lists the kings, chieftains, and stewards of those realms. The text of *Eriador, Arnor, and the Heirs of Isildur* is apparently composed *ab initio* in the typescript that went to the printer, though preparatory material may have been lost.

Tolkien begins to introduce the story of Aragorn and Arwen near the end of this when mentioning King Elessar's visits to Annúminas, but abandons it after a while and types a replacement page. In contrast, the section *Gondor and the Heirs of Anárion* is achieved with much retyping and replacement of pages, as new elements enter. When Tolkien makes his abortive attempt to introduce *The Tale of Aragorn and Arwen* into *Eriador, Arnor, and the Heirs of Isildur*, what he writes, as far as it goes, is a reduced version of the earlier text and very close to that published as Appendix A (v). He then makes a typescript with only a brief summary of Aragorn's part in the War of the Ring, with the heading 'Here follows a part of the Tale of Aragorn and Arwen'. Tolkien begins a typescript of *The House of Eorl* with the last of the three versions written in 1948–9 before him, expanding it as he works. Only one page of this survives, but Christopher Tolkien thinks that others have been lost, and that it is unlikely that his father composed the rest of the section *ab initio* in the typescript that went to the printer.

Though Tolkien originally intended *The Quest of Erebor* to be part of *Durin's Folk* in what became Appendix A, he finds that it takes up too much space. He does make another, shorter manuscript, telling the story in a more tightly constructed form (*Unfinished Tales*, pp. 321–6), possibly an attempt to reduce it to a length suitable for the Appendix, but even this proves too long. The final typescript of *Durin's Folk* includes only a brief version, but takes up material from other notes, including information attributed to Gimli about Dwarf-women. Tolkien uses engagement calendar pages for 30 January–12 February 1955 for early drafts of the introduction to Appendix E; some other material published in this Appendix on consonants, vowels, and accents and on scripts had been included in early versions of Appendix F.

April 1955 W.H. Auden, who has been sent a proof of *The Return of the King*, writes to Tolkien with questions about the book. Tolkien will write a long reply which unfortunately does not survive.

5 April 1955 Tolkien returns to Allen & Unwin marked proofs of pp. 1–192 of *The Return of the King*.

6 April 1955 Tolkien returns to Allen & Unwin marked proofs of pp. 193–311 of *The Return of the King*, with two more corrections for the pages he sent the previous day. He asks to have the corrections back so that he can keep his record of alterations intact.

Easter 1955 (Easter Sunday is 10 April) Tolkien spends a few days in the Isle of Wight and attends Easter service at Quarr, a 20th-century Benedictine house on the site of an old Cistercian Abbey.

c. **11 April 1955** Tolkien sends to Allen & Unwin additional copy for the Appendices.

12 April 1955 W.N. Beard sends to the printer the corrected proofs for *The Return of the King*, pp. 1–311 plus Appendix F, and copy for Appendices A, B, and E.

14 April 1955 Tolkien writes to Rayner Unwin. He encloses seven more corrections for the page proofs of *The Return of the King*, six close together in Book VI, Chapter 2, and one not so urgent but desirable in Book VI, Chapter 6. 'The map is hell! I have not been as careful as I should in keeping track of distances. I think a large scale map simply reveals all the chinks in the armour – besides being obliged to differ somewhat from the printed small scale version, which was semi-pictorial. May have to abandon it for this trip!' (*Letters*, p. 210).

16 April 1955 The Committee of the Early English Text Society, in Tolkien's absence but with the assistance of a report by him, discuss an edition of the *Bibliotheca Historica* of Diodorus Siculus.

Mid-April 1955 Tolkien and his son Christopher work intensively to produce a large scale map of Rohan, Gondor, and Mordor. In April 1956 he will write in a draft letter to H. Cotton Minchin:

> I remember that when it became apparent that the 'general map' would not suffice for the final Book [i.e. volume of *The Lord of the Rings*], or sufficiently reveal the courses of Frodo, the Rohirrim, and Aragorn, I had to devote many days, the last three virtually without food or bed, to drawing re-scaling and adjusting a large map, at which [Christopher] then worked for 24 hours (6 a.m. to 6 a.m. without bed) in re-drawing just in time. Inconsistencies of spelling are due to me. It was only in the last stages that (in spite of my son's protests: he still holds that no one will ever pronounce *Cirith* right, it appears as *Kirith* in his map, as formerly also in the text) I decided to be 'consistent' and spell Elvish names and words throughout without *k*. [*Letters*, p. 247]

This process also entailed re-reading the book in its entirety.

18 April 1955 Tolkien writes to Rayner Unwin. He is sending separately by registered post a map for *The Return of the King* which Christopher has redrawn from Tolkien's own draft large scale map. It can be reproduced the same size as the general map, and should replace that in the third volume. The scale is 5 times enlarged from that of the general map.

19 April 1955 Rayner Unwin writes to assure Tolkien that the alterations he sent will be incorporated in *The Return of the King*.

21 April 1955 Tolkien attends a Merton College meeting. – *The Two Towers* is published in the United States.

24 April 1955 Trinity Full Term begins. Tolkien's scheduled lectures for this term are: *Sir Gawain and the Green Knight* on Wednesdays at 12.00 noon in the Examination Schools, beginning 27 April; and the *Ayenbite of Inwit* on Thursdays at 12.00 noon in the Examination Schools, beginning 28 April. He will continue to supervise B.Litt. students L. Glanville, V.M. Martin, and B.D.H. Miller, D.Phil. students R.W. Burchfield, A.D. Horgan, A. Kurvinen, and E.J. Stormon, and probationer student D.C. Levinson.

28 April 1955 P.H. Newby writes to Tolkien. The BBC are considering whether to broadcast a talk by someone who identifies the author of *Pearl* and *Sir Gawain and the Green Knight* as Hugh Mascy, and the dead child as Margery Mascy. He asks Tolkien if this is a new theory.

29 April 1955 Tolkien attends an English Faculty Board meeting, at which he is elected to the nominating committee for the Diploma in Celtic Studies.

?May 1955 Tolkien replies to a letter from Harvey Breit, who is writing a piece about Tolkien and his books for the *New York Times Book Review*. The article by Breit, published on 5 June ('Oxford Calling'), will distort some of the information provided by Tolkien.

2 May 1955 Tolkien writes to Miss Turnbull. He is now putting final touches on the third volume of *The Lord of the Rings* (evidently in Appendices D and E).

4 May 1955 R.M. Dawkins dies.

5 May 1955 W.N. Beard writes to Tolkien. He is sending galley proofs of Appendices A, B, and E (still lacking some elements), and an intended revision of Appendix F (in fact he sends another proof identical to that of 2 March). He still needs copy for the matter to accompany the alphabets, and the Shire Calendar, and the correct sequence of the Appendices. – Presumably after receiving this letter Tolkien makes the typescript from which Appendix D is printed, with no additional text, only rough notes, between it and the earlier versions made in 1948. He prefaces it with one of the proofs of the Shire Calendar he had been sent. The typescript is rough with many emendations, showing the pressure under which he is working.

12 May 1955 Tolkien apparently writes to Rayner Unwin on this date, commenting on the last material for the Appendices that he is now or will be sending to Allen & Unwin. He probably also makes suggestions as to what might be omitted if there is not enough space for everything, such as the Bolger and Boffin family trees, and asks for a copy of the latest *Hobbit* and the Houghton Mifflin *Fellowship of the Ring*. – Tolkien replies to P.H. Newby's letter of 28 April by telephone. – Newby writes to Tolkien on the same day, confirming what they discussed. He encloses a letter from Ormerod Greenwood and asks Tolkien to say if he has a case for his identification of the author of *Pearl* and *Sir Gawain*. The BBC had broadcast some months earlier a talk by Thurston Dart, which identified the composer of a medieval mass as John Lloyd by methods similar to Greenwood's; he sends Tolkien the text of that talk. He is arranging for Tolkien to be paid a consultant's fee and the cost of the phone call. Apparently Newby also sends Tolkien a copy of his own recently published book, *Picnic at Sakkara*. He reminds Tolkien that the latter has promised to have lunch with Newby when Tolkien is next in London. – On this date Newby also writes an internal BBC memo, justifying Tolkien's fee by arguing that he would 'have to consider a very detailed argument running to about two thousand words, and we are asking him to say whether he thinks the proposed speaker has a reasonable case' (BBC Written Archives Centre).

13 May 1955 Ronald Boswell, Talks Booking Manager for the BBC, writes to Tolkien, offering a consultant's fee of three guineas plus reimbursement of the cost of his phone call to Newby.

14 May 1955 Tolkien writes to Boswell, accepting the consultant's fee and stating the cost of the telephone call at four shillings and sixpence.

14–15 May 1955 From midnight to 2.00 a.m. Tolkien writes a long letter to P.H. Newby, commenting on Greenwood's identification of the author of *Pearl* and *Sir Gawain*. He dislikes Greenwood's stress on numerology, and though there is some matter in his argument worthy of consideration, and his identification is more probable than others, Tolkien does not find it exciting or significant. He thinks that Thurston Dart's piece is much superior, and he is intrigued by a philological point in it (chiefly the relationship of *fludd* to *Lloyd* in the context of a surname), which he discusses in great detail. (Greenwood's argument will be laid out in an introduction to his translation of *Sir Gawain and the Green Knight* published in 1956, and others will take up the question in later years.)

16 May 1955 Tolkien sends his letter to P.H. Newby with a covering note, saying that he has done what he can 'in a late session far from books of learning. . . . I look forward to two things: a break in my present 14-hour day which will give me a chance of reading your *Picnic*; and a chance of lunching with you in town' (BBC Written Archives Centre). – Later that day he sends Newby a postcard correcting one of the points Tolkien made about the Dart text.

17 May 1955 Ronald Boswell, BBC, informs Tolkien that he will be sending a cheque for the full amount. – Possibly on this date Tolkien writes to W.N. Beard and encloses marked proofs of parts of the Appendices (presumably following on those sent by Beard on 5 May) and final copy for *The Return of the King*. – He receives a gift of wine or sherry from his correspondent Miss Turnbull of Whitby, Yorkshire.

18 May 1955 Tolkien attends a Merton College meeting. As Sub-warden he is appointed member of a committee to review the system of guest nights and common room rights. – P.H. Newby writes to Tolkien, expressing gratitude for Tolkien's very full notes. – W.N. Beard writes to Tolkien. He is sending proofs of the map. He acknowledges Tolkien's letter with 'proofs etc.' (Tolkien-George Allen & Unwin archive, HarperCollins).

19 May 1955 Tolkien writes to W.N. Beard. The proof of the map 'looks well', but 'the intended scale on my original draft was 1 millimetre = 1 mile; and that seems to have been preserved pretty well in C.J.R.T.'s [Christopher

Tolkien's] drawing. Your scale is short by ½ *millimetre* in 60; or 3 mm. in the total breadth of the map. At least I have checked this on 3 of such instruments as I possess – 2 of them good mathematical protractors. The inaccuracy will be reduced of course in the block' (Tolkien-George Allen & Unwin archive, HarperCollins, italics Tolkien's). – Tolkien writes to Miss Turnbull, thanking her for her gift. He finds it appropriate, since he has just sent to Allen & Unwin the last texts for *The Return of the King*.

20 May 1955 W.N. Beard writes to Tolkien. He feels that as a new block of the scale for the map might still be inaccurate, it is best to leave things as they are. Allen & Unwin have sent all of the Appendix matter to the printers, and have dropped the Bolger and Boffin family trees. The printers will add rules and figures to the blocks.

23 May 1955 Tolkien writes to W.N. Beard that if the genealogy of the Dwarves in Appendix A iii gives any trouble for space, the footnote can be dropped or else printed as the first of the short notes that follow, immediately preceding the notes on 'Dís'. He agrees not to worry about the scale on the map, and promises to try to deal with the proofs speedily. He queries and discusses how references to *The Hobbit* are to be given in *The Lord of the Rings*, since the revision to Chapter 5 of *The Hobbit* in 1951 means that the first and second editions have different pagination.

24 May 1955 Rayner Unwin writes to Tolkien. The Appendices will all fit in very well, except for the Bolger and Boffin family trees. He is not eager to omit Tolkien's note on translations unless it proves imperative to save space; 'I confess that I hadn't realised you would be treating the languages and the calendar so fully' (Tolkien-George Allen & Unwin archive, HarperCollins). He has sent Tolkien a copy of the latest printing of *The Hobbit*, and has asked Houghton Mifflin for a copy or copies of their *Fellowship of the Ring*. He probably also now sends Tolkien a draft of Houghton Mifflin's text for the dust-jacket of *The Return of the King*.

25 May 1955 W.N. Beard writes to Tolkien. The footnote to the Dwarf genealogies will fit without difficulty. He favours for references to *The Hobbit* Tolkien's suggestion that they should be to the first edition and, at the first mention, that a footnote state that for second edition page references the reader should add five to all page numbers from 100 onwards. He asks Tolkien to approve such a note drafted by Rayner Unwin.

26 May 1955 Tolkien writes to Rayner Unwin. He returns the Houghton Mifflin draft without comment. He thinks it odd that Houghton Mifflin have sent him six copies of *The Two Towers* but none of *The Fellowship of the Ring*. They had also promised to send him a folder of review clippings, but have not. He finds the printers of *The Return of the King* to be 'pretty good really. The misprints of words are very few and their proofreader even corrects points of Númenórean chronology when I make slips!' He thinks that it will not take long to deal with the remaining page proofs, but warns that he will be away at certain times. 'I shall be away between June 6 and June 13 incl[usive]. . . . To prevent a collapse I am just secretly disappearing without a word to anyone (but now to you)' (Tolkien-George Allen & Unwin archive, HarperCollins). In the event, he has to abandon this plan because of a rail strike between 29 May and 14 June. – After he has written this letter, Tolkien receives one from Rayner enclosing American reviews, and comments on them in a postscript.

1 June 1955 E.H. Wakeham, BBC, writes to inform Tolkien there is to be a repeat broadcast of *The Homecoming of Beorhtnoth Beorhthelm's Son* on 19 June. She will arrange for the appropriate fee to be paid after the broadcast.

3 June 1955 W.H. Auden, who has been asked to give a talk about *The Lord of the Rings* on the Third Programme in October, writes to ask Tolkien if there are any points he would like Auden to make, and if he could supply a few human touches in the form of information about how the book came to be written.

7 June 1955 Tolkien writes at length to W.H. Auden, about himself and about the writing of *The Hobbit* and *The Lord of the Rings*. – Thurston Dart of Jesus College, Cambridge, writes to Tolkien. The BBC have sent him Tolkien's comments. Dart had had to summarize his work for his radio talk (as Tolkien had surmised from its script), and now gives more detail about the point that interested Tolkien.

9 June 1955 English Final Honour School Examinations begin. – In the evening, Tolkien borrows from Edith P.H. Newby's book *Picnic at Sakkara* and goes to sleep 'very late (even for me) as a result' (letter to Newby, 10 June 1955, BBC Written Archives Centre).

10 June 1955 Tolkien writes to P.H. Newby, proposing to lunch with him in London on Friday, 24 June. 'I should just have laid down a tiresome office which has darkened the last two years [presumably the Sub-wardenship of Merton College], and should find myself without Examinations for the first June in years' (BBC Written Archives Centre). In any case, there will be a meeting on 24 June at University College, London which he should attend (presumably of the Early English Text Society Council). – Tolkien writes to Terence Tiller. He would also like to visit Tiller in London on 24 June. – Tolkien writes to Patricia Kirke. If she visits Oxford on a Sunday, they will have to meet after lunch, as he cannot leave his wife alone and she will not accept invitations to eat out.

13 June 1955 P.H. Newby writes to Tolkien. He would be delighted to entertain Tolkien to lunch on 24 June. He suggests that Tolkien come to Broadcasting House at 12.30 p.m., and they can then 'walk down Carnaby Street and get a table at Le Petit Coin de France' (BBC Written Archives Centre).

14 June 1955 Terence Tiller writes to Tolkien. A meeting would be valuable, although he has written only rough drafts of dramatizations of *The Fellowship of the Ring* and for only three of the six programmes. He suggests that he and Tolkien meet during the morning of 24 June.

17 June 1955 At an English Faculty Board meeting, in Tolkien's absence, it is announced that the Applications Committee has accepted his probationer student D.C. Levinson of St Anne's College as a full B.Litt. student to work on 'studies in the treatment of Old Testament themes in the poems of MS. Junius

11, Part I', with Tolkien as her supervisor. – Possibly also in Tolkien's absence, the Committee for Comparative Philology meets on the same day. In its report to the Quinquennial Grant Committee the Committee for Comparative Philology considers the establishment of a Readership in Phonetics a high priority, and also urges the General Board to establish a Readership in General Linguistics. – *The Homecoming of Beorhtnoth Beorhthelm's Son* is rebroadcast in the Third Programme at 10.25 p.m.

18 June 1955 Trinity Full Term ends.

20 June 1955 Tolkien writes to Rayner Unwin. He will be in London on 24 June and would like to 'look in at [the publisher's offices in] Museum Street some time, just to hear how things are going', but probably not until the afternoon. If Rayner will be attending the Trinity College, Oxford celebrations at the end of the week and will have any spare time, Tolkien will be available then, 'except for a stray gaudy or two' (Tolkien–George Allen & Unwin archive, HarperCollins). – Tolkien writes to Terence Tiller. He will try to catch the 9.10 a.m. train, 'an effort for one so used to night-work' (BBC Written Archives Centre), and should arrive just before 11.00 a.m., otherwise just before noon. – Tolkien writes a postcard to P.H. Newby to confirm his appointment on the 24th. – He also writes again to Patricia Kirke. As Edith is going to Ditchling from 21 to 27 June (probably to visit Marjorie Incledon), he will be staying in college during her absence, and can meet Kirke on Sunday the 26th. He offers to meet her train.

21 June 1955 Tolkien attends a Merton College meeting. – Terence Tiller sends a telegram to Tolkien, suggesting that he and Tolkien meet at the BBC Club, 10 Chandos Street, London, shortly after noon on 24 June.

22 June 1955 Encaenia. – Tolkien writes a postcard to Terence Tiller, confirming their appointment. – He also writes to Allen & Unwin to thank them for forwarding a copy of the Houghton Mifflin *The Fellowship of the Ring*. He has noticed that pp. 321–36 in this are missing. – Tolkien writes as well to a reader in response to queries about runes. He distinguishes those in *The Hobbit* from those in *The Lord of the Rings*. The matter will be explained in the third volume of the latter.

22 or 23 June 1955 Tolkien writes to Patricia Kirke, presumably in reply to a letter in which she says that she will come to Oxford on Sunday. Tolkien suddenly realizes that he does not know what she looks like. He remembers an occasion when he missed someone at Cork because neither knew what the other looked like. He will be at Oxford station at 11.15 a.m., on the platform close to the ticket-exit, 'grey haired, unbearded and shall be in blue (corduroy jacket)' (Gerard A.J. Stodolski, *Catalogue 4* (August 1995), item 43). He encloses a photograph of himself torn from the back of the jacket of the American *Fellowship of the Ring*.

23 June 1955 The BBC sends Tolkien an invoice to sign for payment for the repeat broadcast of *The Homecoming of Beorhtnoth*.

24 June 1955 Presumably Tolkien travels by train to London, sees Terence Tiller at the BBC Club at noon, lunches with P.H. Newby at Le Petit Coin de

France, calls at Allen & Unwin in Museum Street, and at 4.30 attends a meeting at University College. He and Rayner Unwin discuss 'The Silmarillion'; in a letter to Naomi Mitchison on 29 June he will write: 'I think "A and U" may now take the "earlier history" in some form. When I was in town last Friday they seemed willing to envisage a book about as long as Vol. I [of *The Lord of the Rings*]' (*Letters*, p. 217).

28 June 1955 Rayner Unwin writes to Tolkien. *The Lord of the Rings* is to be broadcast in a schools programme on BBC radio in 1956.

29 June 1955 Tolkien writes to Naomi Mitchison. He has had 'a very gruelling time, with far more work than I could really cope with, *plus* Vol. III. I am feeling as flat as a burst tyre . . .' (*Letters*, p. 217). He has been told that he will receive the final proofs for *The Return of the King* tomorrow. – Tolkien writes, or completes, a two-paragraph preface for the Modern English translation of *The Ancrene Riwle* by his former student M.B. Salu.

30 June 1955 Tolkien writes to Houghton Mifflin. They should not blame him for what Harvey Breit wrote in the *New York Times Book Review*: the answers he sent to Breit made sense. He encloses a note about himself and his writings, which the publisher may use in future if they are asked for information. In it he mentions that he still hopes to finish his poem *The Fall of Arthur*.

2 July 1955 Tolkien receives proofs of the Appendices sent by the printers, Jarrold & Sons, on 29 June but delayed in the post.

***c.* 2 July 1955** Finding a problem in proof with the table of values to accompany the drawn table of runes in Appendix E, Tolkien writes about it to Jarrold & Sons (see further, entry for 15 July).

4 July 1955 W.N. Beard writes to Tolkien. The printers have promised to complete production of *The Return of the King* in time for publication in the last days of September, if they have the Appendix proofs returned by 8 July.

5 July 1955 Tolkien writes to W.N. Beard. The proofs did not arrive until 2 July. It is putting on pressure to ask him to check 103 pages of closely printed matter and many references quickly. 'Fortunately the work has been done well, and there is as far as I can see at first reading little needing correction. However, they have left p. 402 blank except for the numerals, and I do not feel inclined to pass that "carte blanche".' He has had no final page proof of the narrative (pp. 1–312) and would like to see one to be sure that all of the alterations he sent in have been included. He also needs a copy to check the footnote references to pages in vol. III in the Appendices.

> I think the best I can do is to send the marked proofs to you *tomorrow*, Wed[nesday], at whatever cost of sleep. (I unfortunately lost 3 days of leisure and am not now so free!) The blanks on p. 402 I will fill in by hand. But I shall *want a revise of that*. And I do want a final revised set of the pages of the narrative of Vol. III. I do not anticipate that any of the references to it will be wrong, or at least no more so than can be dealt with by a letter. *But I want to see it in its final state*. [Tolkien-George Allen & Unwin archive, HarperCollins]

6 July 1955 W.N. Beard writes to Tolkien. The proofs from Jarrold's had been delayed in the post. Allen & Unwin have not asked for a revised proof of the narrative of *The Return of the King*, and there will be no further proofs, but Jarrold's have been asked to send Tolkien a copy of the unrevised page proof for him to check the page references. Tolkien will see a revise of the Appendix pages but must deal with them quickly. – P.H. Newby writes to Tolkien. He enjoyed their meeting, but had forgotten to ask if Tolkien would be interested in giving a talk on the Third Programme on Joseph Wright, to mark the centenary of his birth in 1855. Newby thinks that Wright was one of several distinguished philologists who had not been educated in the normal way.

14 July 1955 Tolkien writes to P.H. Newby. He knew Joseph Wright very well, and is in fact the executor of his estate. But he does not want to broadcast about him while his widow, Elizabeth, is alive. He does not know of any other philologists who came from an illiterate background as Wright did. – W.N. Beard sends Tolkien proofs of the second block of the Angerthas table, and says that Rayner Unwin is not happy with it. He asks if they should they make a new block from Tolkien's original art.

15 July 1955 Tolkien writes to W.N. Beard. The remaining parts of the Appendices, particularly the Angerthas tables in Appendix E, 'have got into rather a mess. Partly owing to my inexperience. We should probably have saved time and money, if I had been able to come up and go through the material with Production before it went to Jarrolds.' He had intended the table opposite the drawn chart of runes 'to be an ingenious device (!) whereby the "values" of the decorative Runes could be *printed* as a key without injuring the appearance of the more carefully drawn "Angerthas", and without having to have another block. The symbols chosen were therefore not strictly "phonetic", but such as I imagined were within the compass of a non-specialized fount.' When he received the proof, however, the table of values was blank except for reference numerals. He wrote to the printer about it, but 'owing to the pressure put on me I could not wait for their answer. The page I sent in (filling in the blanks by hand) was merely *a direction for printing*, and quite unsuitable for a block. Blocks are as unkind even to a carefully done page as neon-lighting to the human face; and this scruffy page, of course, looks frightful.' Tolkien encloses three alternatives for Beard's consideration. He also notes that some pages have been placed out of order, and that there is an error in his calculations in the appendix on calendars. 'I have devised a form which will I think fit the space and only affect 5 or 6 lines of the text.' He again expresses a desire to check that the further corrections he has sent have been incorporated in the narrative by seeing a revised proof. Most of them were the result of his work preparing a draft for the map that Christopher made, and he has 'somehow lost, mislaid, or destroyed all record of them at this end; and the labour of rechecking all distances with map and text would be formidable (and time-taking)'. He asks if it is really impossible for him to have a complete copy of *The Return of the King* before finally 'giving the word go'. But he advises Beard not to 'brood on it! I am going abroad on July 30, and want to clear everything this week' (Tolkien-George Allen & Unwin archive, HarperCollins).

***c.* 16 July 1955** W.N. Beard telephones Tolkien to say they have decided to have the Angerthas table of values in a printed form rather than as a block.

18 July 1955 W.N. Beard sends Tolkien final proofs of pp. 305–416 of *The Return of the King* (the gatherings which include the Appendices), with queries by the printer's reader.

20 July 1955 Tolkien receives the proofs from W.N. Beard. – A member of Allen & Unwin's staff, hoping for a blurb, writes to ask Tolkien if he would read a proof copy of Naomi Mitchison's *To the Chapel Perilous*.

?20–?22 July 1955 Tolkien marks the final *Return of the King* proofs and annotates the printer's queries. Among his latter notes is one replying to a query about the spelling *nought* v. *naught*: 'I do not mind! English has hesitated between a/o in this word for 1200 years & I fear I do still . . .' (quoted in Sotheby's, *English Literature and History, Private Press and Illustrated Books, Related Drawings and Animation Art*, London, 21–22 July 1992, p. 97).

22 July 1955 Tolkien writes to W.N. Beard. He is returning the material he received on 20 July in a separate parcel. He does not understand, since the corrected page proofs and extra corrections were sent to the printer in April, why I should now receive Queries, raised by the head reader in the course of his "*final reading of the main text*" that are not based on the final text, but on one that does not incorporate numerous (and some extensive) revisions. Errors are almost certain to occur, or to have occurred, at some of these points. The compositors always make mistakes in setting from my handwriting!' He is also disturbed that on the pages on which the reader has written queries 'there remain *errors* . . . that are neither queried nor corrected. For instance the heading *House* [rather than Houses] of Healing throughout Bk. V, Ch. 8 in spite of the chapter title.' He has very little time left before he goes abroad, and cannot deal with anything which arrives after the 27th.

> Not being satisfied nor indeed (frankly) wholly reassured, I have made out a list of all the emendations, insertions, and corrections of the main text which do *not* yet appear in the proofs. I have made this list as clear as I can, and I hope it will be carefully checked with the text. It contains all those corrections that I have noted as previously sent in (though I have an uneasy feeling that it is not complete, and that some adjustments were made, when the new Map was made). To these are added a few – marked * – that are fresh, or to which I have no note indicating that they had been sent in.

(Tolkien's copy of this list is preserved at Marquette University both as a manuscript and a typescript. In the manuscript, the existing text is written in black ink and the desired text in red.) He thinks that the marked proofs of the Appendices have now been set in order, with only two bad pages and the matter of the Angerthas table of values remaining. He sends corrections to four lines on p. 386, concerning calendars, 'which should set things right, and which should according to my knowledge and arithmetic (neither v[ery] g[ood]) stand the test of those critics who will work it out for themselves.' He is anxious about the Angerthas tables. 'I should perhaps have used a proper phonetic notation throughout, which would have been intelligible to those most interested; but I have had so many enquiries from people to whom phonetic symbols would have been "darker" than the *Angerthas* that I tried to do without' (Tolkien–George Allen & Unwin archive, HarperCollins, partly printed in *Letters*, p. 222).

23 July 1955 Tolkien replies to Allen & Unwin that he would be delighted to read *To the Chapel Perilous*, though he will not have much time to look at it before he goes abroad.

25 July 1955 Tolkien posts the proofs of the Appendices and the reader's queries to Allen & Unwin. – Rayner Unwin writes to Tolkien. He has sent a copy of the Appendices and the *Return of the King* map to Terence Tiller.

26 July 1955 Tolkien replies to a fan letter, chiefly commenting on the word *dwarves*.

27 July 1955 Tolkien writes to Rayner Unwin. 'I leave the North Kingdom [England] for a rapid excursion to Gondor [Italy] on Saturday morning, but shall, I hope, be back by August 16' (Tolkien–George Allen & Unwin archive, HarperCollins). – Tolkien writes to Terence Tiller. He is sorry that there has been such a delay since their meeting in sending him anything that might prove useful to his scripts. – Tolkien replies to a fan letter from a Miss Judson of Tunbridge Wells, remarking on his laborious work on *The Return of the King* in boiling down material for the Appendices. – Allen & Unwin agree that Tolkien's reading of *To the Chapel Perilous* can await his return from holiday. (In the event, Tolkien does not review the book.)

28 July 1955 Tolkien replies to a letter from a Mrs Dixey in South Africa. He does not think that he will write any more about Hobbits, but because of the success of *The Lord of the Rings*, which has surprised his publishers as well as himself, he thinks that Allen & Unwin may now publish his legends of the First and Second Ages. – Tolkien replies to a letter written in March by Jennifer Brookes-Smith. He tells her how busy he has been, but is now off on holiday to 'Gondor ... Pelargir and Lossarnach, i.e. Italy: Venice and Assisi (Christie's, *20th Century Books and Manuscripts*, London, 2 December 2003, p. 25).

29 July 1955 Tolkien writes to Rayner Unwin, thanking him for forwarding four copies of the Houghton Mifflin '*Lord of the Rings*' (presumably *The Fellowship of the Ring* only). He has received the copy of Mitchison's *To the Chapel Perilous*, which is going to put him 'in a v[ery] awkward hole' as he despairs 'of finding any formula that will mitigate the intensity of my distaste sufficiently to avoid offence' (Tolkien–George Allen & Unwin archive, HarperCollins). – Terence Tiller writes to Tolkien. He hopes to send at least the first three scripts for the BBC *Fellowship of the Ring* shortly after Tolkien's return.

30 July 1955 Edith Tolkien leaves home early to join three friends on a Mediterranean cruise. – Tolkien and his daughter Priscilla travel by train from

Oxford to Paddington Station, London, cross London to Victoria Station, and have lunch before catching the boat train for a visit to Italy. They have a calm Channel crossing on a French boat, the *Côte d'Azur*, but the voyage is 'rather spoiled by the French Police, who made us stand in a long tiresome queue filling in a questionnaire and having our passports visaed'. At Calais they board a train for Italy, and have a good dinner en route. 'At some point . . . our carriage was converted into "couchettes", three on either side. We had the two bottom ones: stuffier and more draughty, but easier to get out of. . . . Since undressing was impossible, I should have preferred to sit in a seat all night, without the turmoil, discomfort and "homelessness" of the processes of conversion from a compartment to couchettes and back again.' When they reach Paris their carriage is shunted and hooked to the Simplon-Orient Express. (These quotations, and others concerning Tolkien's visit to Italy, are from his *Giornale d'Italia*, a typescript in the Tolkien Papers, Bodleian Library, Oxford.)

31 July 1955 As the train nears Lake Geneva fog hides the scenery, but the weather clears enough for 'wonderful views before we reached Brig' in Switzerland. 'There we were turned out, and obliged to look for seats in another carriage of the same train, already packed.' Tolkien finds one for Priscilla, but has to stand most of the way to Milan himself. At Vallorbe he manages

> by standing in a polyglot queue to get two cups of coffee off a stall on the platform. Carrying them (blazing hot liquid in cardboard cups) along a long quai was a difficult feat. But we got neither food, wash nor drink again from there to Venice! – except for a single lunch-packet for one, which I managed to get at Domodossola. We shared its excellent contents: some chicken, a little ham and salami, two rolls, a piece of cheese and some fruit, and a minute bottle of wine; and that saw us through.

They find Milan's huge railway station 'hot smoky and stuffy under its great roof', after which they have lovely views while crossing Lombardy. 'It all seemed to me oddly familiar and expected (I suppose from seeing so many pictures) and much less "foreign" than parts of Ireland. It was not very hot. We got a view of Verona, and some marvellous glimpses of Lake Garda.' The train arrives in Venice over an hour and a half late, at 7.35 p.m. Tolkien and Priscilla take a *vaporetto* (water bus) and make their way to their hotel, the Albergo Antico Panada, near the Piazza San Marco (St Mark's).

> We barely waited to wash before indulging in a 'fabulous' dinner, selected from an enormous menu: even the reduced version for those on '*pensione*' closely covered a foolscap page. From an English point of view the cheapest thing is wine; and the ordinary unnamed table wine, *rosso* or *bianco*, seemed excellent. We took it by the litre, though I found it most refreshing diluted. Our first feast contained among other things, ham and melon, roast veal and stuffed tomatoes, Bel Paese, real Pêche Melba,

and abundant fruit. We arrived just at peach time, and I ate more peaches in fourteen days than in all my days before together.

They are joined at 10.30 p.m. by Christopher Tolkien and his wife Faith, who are already in Venice. The four of them talk until late.

1 **August 1955** Tolkien finds his way to St Mark's and hears part of a Mass in a side chapel before having a late breakfast. He and Priscilla fill the rest of the morning wandering near by. 'The external beauty of Venice is even greater than I expected, and quite different. Owing perhaps partly to the weather (pale blue sky and much light cloud) it is much paler and less hard and clear in colour than I expected: black, white, pale pink, grey. Actually I found the teeming internationalism of the Piazza rather exciting: English (even American) lost in a torrent of German, French, Serb, Italian and (I suppose) local dialect.' They meet Christopher and Faith for lunch, then take the boat from the Fondamenta Nuova to Torcello.

We were fortunate in going early by an ordinary 'bus', for we arrived before the trips [tourist parties] – two great boat-loads; and so we saw the churches in peace. The little round church of Santa Fosca could have been beautiful, but was rather sad, dusty, and neglected. But the cathedral was beautiful and what was left of its Byzantine carving and mosaics lovely. It was here that in a corner, neglected except by excursionists, centuries past its days of wealth, that I first had the feeling that haunted me during the rest of my short visit to Italy: that of having come to the heart of Christendom; an exile from the borders and far provinces returning home, or at least to the home of his fathers. This had little to do with 'art' or formal beauty. Neglected or broken, adorned or overlaid, and despite the behaviour either of the people of the land or of *turisti*, I felt a curious glow of dormant life and Charity – especially in the chapels of the Blessed Sacrament (often commonplace or tawdry in their gear).

On their way back to the boat they stop at a *trattoria* for a draught of peach-juice. They encounter beggars, including an old crone and many small boys; Tolkien and Priscilla give them some coins, 'and we were amused and not at all pained to find them (crone and all) on our boat, returning to Venice with our *soldi*'. Later they sit in the Campo di San Giovanni e Paolo listening to bells and watching passers-by, and ride in a gondola: 'round the small back canals until darkness fell: sinister & strange in deep canyons of towering decaying buildings with rotting windows, black and silent. (But we had already learned that the outward appearance of ruin was no certain evidence of what was to be found inside).' Tolkien is pleased to be free in Venice, with its water rather than roads, 'of the cursed disease of the internal combustion engine of which all the world is dying'. Their *gondoliere* averts perils by crying out at corners and junctions, though they have a close call with a heavy commercial power barge. Their dinner is in the garden of a *trattoria* in the Campo San Tomà:

A lovely meal under vines and fig trees lit with lamps beneath. Infested by cats, busy with their own affairs, fighting desperate duels (in the intervals of furtive begging) with invaders from over the walls. . . .

We made the acquaintance of a charming Italian, Sr. Gardin, who had some English but was incredibly gracious and patient with our attempts upon his own language. I received a linguistic shock at the discovery that, contrary to legend and my belief, Italians . . . dislike exaggeration, superlatives, and adjectives of excessive praise. But they seem to answer to colour and poetic expression, if justified.

Signor Gardin escorts them back to their hotel. 'We go he said "by boat and feet": he seemed enormously diverted by the fact that the English say "on foot". After receiving much instruction in Italian it was difficult to resist the professional temptation to inform him that "foot" was dative plural. It was resisted, and we parted friends.'

2 August 1955 Tolkien and Priscilla meet Christopher and Faith on the Rialto Bridge, and travel by gondola to the island of Murano, where they visit two glass factories. Tolkien finds most of the products remarkably vulgar and tasteless. 'A gesture of dismissal at some monstrous bloated floreated jug only led to a show-case of filthy Disney figures and Mickey-mice. Yet there was some lovely glass to be found, beautiful in shape and colour. . . . But it was beyond our purses as a rule.' They are entertained by one of the *maestri* blowing and shaping vases and animal figures with speed and dexterity. They return to Venice for lunch with Christopher and Faith, and in the afternoon, under darkening skies, all four visit 'S. Giorgio' (presumably San Giorgio Maggiore), which Tolkien finds 'hideous'. He is delighted to return to the Campo S. Tomà, where they spend the evening, 'drinking and talking outside the *trattoria*, and later having a magnificent *cena* [supper] in the *giardino* [garden] behind.' It rains and thunders nearly all night.

3 August 1955 The rain continues until almost noon; Tolkien and Priscilla have no umbrellas or raincoats. In the morning, with difficulty, they find their way to the Teatro La Fenice and buy tickets for an open air opera performance of *Rigoletto* in the Campo Sant'Angelo on the following evening. They again lunch with Christopher and Faith, and in the afternoon visit St Mark's, but find the interior largely hidden by scaffolding. Later all four go to 'the great church of the Frari', the Franciscan Chiesa di Santa Maria Gloriosa dei Frari (St Mary of the Friars). Tolkien supposes that this was once beautiful, but it is now 'deformed by additions and by monuments (of doges and other notables), many of which are of a tastelessness on a crushing scale hardly to be rivalled in Westminster Abbey.' He remarks particularly on 'the preposterous monument to a 17th century Doge over the north door' which is 'beaten only by the appalling Canova monument'. He finds 'the whole place deeply depressing, though a few old men collected chairs in the middle of the nave and had a pleasant evening chat.' He thinks the *Assumption*, painted by Titian behind the high altar, pleasantly lit; and its lovely red and golden colours are most beautiful as colour – to me especially from the distance of the west door! It has nothing whatever to say to me about the Assumption: which means that with that in mind it is offensive (to me). One begins to yearn for a picture not directly concerned with religion. Can a picture concerned with religion be satisfactory on one side only? Spiritual but bad art; great art but irreligious? I find it impossible to disentangle the two. Easier perhaps for the irreligious. I am thinking, of course, only of any one individual beholder. My religious feelings and ideas are no doubt as ignorant as my artistic ones – to speak of one such beholder.

After dining at the same *trattoria*, Tolkien and Priscilla say goodbye to Christopher and Faith, who are leaving for Florence the next day, and return to their hotel. It is a 'beautiful balmy night . . . . Venice seemed incredibly, elvishly lovely – to me like a dream of Old Gondor, or Pelargir of the Númenorean Ships, before the return of the Shadow. A *serenata* floated by, with music and singing, and many pink and golden lamps, as we stood on the landing stage.' Tolkien suffers, however, from mosquito bites, 'devoured, and blistered, face, arms and legs'.

4 August 1955 In the morning, Tolkien and Priscilla spend two hours in the Gallerie dell'Accademia with its 'many marvellous things from the 14th century onwards. I as a rule like pictures (especially Italian pictures) the earlier the better. I saw many that I had never seen before even in reproduction, and many that were either intensely interesting, or moving (or both) – notably the Tintorettos. But we saw too many for memory or emotion to keep a firm hold. For some reason I was much moved by Bassano's St Jerome.' They leave 'feeling sated (not unpleasantly – in fact the sensation is rather like leaving the theatre after a tragedy)' and eat lunch at a nearby *trattoria*. Then they sit for a while outside the church of S. Trovaso and watch some Italian children playing. In mid-afternoon they return to their hotel to write postcards. They have an early pre-opera dinner, but a violent thunderstorm arrives: 'A rather wretched evening of waiting with ever-waning hope. There was one great crack over us at which all the lights went out for a moment. We waited till after 22.30 before we at last gave up hope. The opera was a wash-out literally. NO performance on Friday, our last day in Venice. Disappointed, and annoyed at waste of money and effort.'

5 August 1955 Tolkien is kept awake much of the night by the thunderstorm, and by the noise of a gramophone or radio being played just across the alley from his hotel. He wakes, tired, to 'a marvellous sparkling fresh morning, like blue and gold soda-water'. In the morning, they visit the Doge's Palace and the international exhibition *Giorgione e i giorgioneschi*.

Many wonderful pictures, and many (to me) detestable. If all the Giorgiones are correctly ascribed, he had a range of styles and of goodness and of badness, that is incredible. . . . By 12.30 I was more than sated, and while P[riscilla] went back to look a second time at some favourites, I wandered in the palace, and looked out from the western arcade over the piazza and the lagoon and the Giudecca. Everything glittering. Heart-rendingly lovely after so short a stay, so soon to end. Still no hard or deep colours. Clear but pale sky, glass-grey glinting water, light olive-green-ness.

They eat an enormous lunch at their hotel, and are shown by the proprietor a notice in the local newspaper that a special performance of *Rigoletto* is to be given that evening at 9.00 p.m., for which tickets for the washed-out perform-ance of the previous evening are valid. Tolkien sleeps part of the afternoon so that he will be able to enjoy the opera, while Priscilla goes out on her own. After dinner they make their way to the Campo Sant'Angelo 'in a night of vel-vet indigo and white stars'. They are among the first to arrive at the venue, of perhaps more than 1,000 all told. The performance begins late, and does not end until half past midnight.

The chairs were quite comfortable (plus a welcome cushion at the rather exorbitant hire of 100 lire each). My first experience of opera in Italy, under a perfect night, with an eager and concentrated audience that *hished* even a shuffling of the feet. During the performance! Plenty of noise in the intervals, while enormous scenes were constructed before our eyes – men walking about with castles and cottages and arches, and great hammerings – and vendors of *birra* [beer] and *gelati* [ice cream] shouted their wares. . . . I had never seen *Rigoletto* before. We bought a libretto and were able to read it before the acts, which helped a great deal. It is a good dramatic plot, though both the handling by Piave and Verdi's music dragged in places. Not the fault of the performers. They not only (to my inexperienced ears) sang beautifully, but acted well, and were a delight to look at. The star was supposed to be the Rigoletto, though the name means nothing to me: Dino Dondi was billed for the Thursday, but it may not have been the same on Friday [*see note*]. He was a huge man (not fat), and not really very convincing as a hunchback, though all the more credible as the father of the beautiful Gilda. Far the best I thought was the Duca. I have never before in opera had the for-tune to see a young man who *looked* young gallant handsome and wilful, was beautifully dressed, acted excellently and sang superbly. He swept both P[riscilla] and me off our feet, together with Gilda and Maddalena, though we knew all about his wickedness. The moment when his voice in the background is heard repeating the *la donna è mobile*, just as Rigoletto is gloating over his supposed mantled corpse, is or was on this occasion, a great dramatic thrill. This is a lot for one to say, who is not dramatic or operatic in taste.

– Rayner Unwin writes to Tolkien, sending three small queries from the printer which must be answered before *The Return of the King* can go to press.

6 August 1955 Tolkien and Priscilla breakfast at 8.00 a.m., pay their bill, and go by boat to Santa Lucia Station where they board a train for Florence. They hope to have a few hours in that city, but due to a mistake in their itinerary (by their travel organizer, Pickfords) their train arrives later than expected, and they have only a glimpse of the Duomo before catching the train to Terentola. There they have 'a breathless rush in which a tired but determined little porter managed to insert us, by the skin of our teeth (and toes), into a small Diesel-engine train as it moved off'. At Perugia they change trains again and have an hour's wait before boarding a train which takes them to Assisi.

> Though we had some very beautiful views and glimpses of Italy, I found the journey tiring and heady, especially owing to the innumerable tunnels. Added to which our mosquito bites were becoming very nasty. I had a vast blister developing on my right leg. Thank heavens for Dettol and Calamine! . . . I got a bottle of Orvieto [white wine] and of minerale [mineral water] at Venice, and these together with four rolls filled with ham provided by Zini [the proprietor of their hotel in Venice], kept us going. We had nothing, having no time or chance of getting it, between 12 noon and our arrival, about 20.00, at the Suore Collatine in Assisi, except an ice for P[riscilla] and a minerale for me during our wait at Perugia.

They see a blood-red sunset as their bus climbs the winding road to the town. They make their way to the convent where they are to stay, and their porter protests that they have over-tipped him. Tolkien finds that the convent provides a great contrast to the near luxury of their lodging in Venice:

> We are housed in big rather bare rooms in what appears to be a kind of farm-house away in the largish garden and grounds of the convent. Our first meal to which we went at once, was in a bare room attached to the convent, amongst many guests, mostly anything but 'well-to-do', and nearly all, like the sisters, French-speaking. . . .
> I find the attempt to switch from my embryonic Italian to my weak French destroys both; but P[riscilla] seems to get on famously. . . .

From his window he has 'a wide view of the plain below with hills and mountains in the distance', but there are holes in the netting over the window, and as the room 'appears to be above fowl-houses, and a large huddle of cages for pigeons and rabbits, the flies are a pest'. Tolkien and Priscilla go for a short stroll after supper, and she tends his blistered mosquito bite before he goes to bed. During the night mosquitoes get into his room through the holes in the netting.

7 August 1955 Tolkien is met, on this Sunday morning, with 'a tremendous babel of bells at 5.30. In Assisi one might say that some times all the bells are ringing, and at all times some bells are ringing. I slept blissfully (the air is lovely) from about 0.45 to 6, and lazed till 7.20.' He and Priscilla find that they are too late to attend the last Mass at the nearby church of San Pietro. Instead they first have breakfast, and after a stroll in the garden go to high Mass in the upper church at San Francesco at 10.00 a.m. This is 'marvellously sung by the friars in the choir in the beautiful church ablaze with Giotto frescoes; but it was spoiled a little by the bad habit of the friars of not stopping sightseers while Mass is going on. . . . Mass was over at 10.50, and we visited the lower church. Outside a blaze of white light; inside cool dark and enchanting.' As they return to the convent they visit the church of San Pietro; Tolkien loves its 'bareness and antiquity'. They eat lunch at the convent: 'plenty to eat, though of course neither of the abundance nor quality of Venice. Vermicelli soup, galantine, stewed meat and potatoes, melon and pears, home-baked bread, red wine.' They take a siesta under a tree in the garden, but are driven indoors by rain and write some postcards. Later they go out so that Tolkien can post a card to Edith. They meet their porter, who insists on buying them a coffee,

in settlement of his over-payment, I suppose. The coffee, as usual, very good and very strong. I offered him some cigarettes which he accepted, and then in return insisted on leading us up winding alleys and flights of steps to the Cathedral of San Ruffino. A beautiful ancient façade, but inside sombre and lugubrious baroque: much of it actually hideous, though we could hardly see anything on that occasion because of the darkness. The porter seemed to know a great deal about it, but (he is a very devout man) was particularly anxious for us to visit the tiny side-chapel where there is the very old and primitive image of Our Lady with Christ dead upon her knees: Madonna del Pianto (I think): evidently much venerated, and *molto molto antico*, as the porter told us in a vast whisper with unusual emphasis.

They return to the convent to escape more rain, and look out from the window 'at the sombre wet misty landscape, while a pandemonium arises from the little piazza of San Pietro just below. It is alas! a parking place and haunt of those horrible afflictions in narrow streets: the *autobus* and the *autopulman*.' In the evening the weather is still bad, but at 7.10 they go downhill to San Pietro to attend Benediction, 'wickedly (and vainly) intending to miss *rosario*'. They find the church almost empty, and discover that they have misread the noticeboard and that on *giorni feriali* (Sundays of no special eminence) *rosario* and Benediction are at 7.30 p.m., by which time others have arrived.

We had rosary, very well said, and entirely in Latin to my pleasure and surprise: it seemed altogether familiar to the people, though most were poor (to all appearances). The Litany of Loretto, also in Latin. There was a small organ and the congregation sang, in this small bright corner of the large austere dark church. It was homelike and delightfully familiar. Indeed when one of the ladies persistently outstripped the others, the organist exclaimed *scusi, signora!*, and she fell silent.

After dinner, the rain having stopped, Tolkien and Priscilla sit 'in the dark on the garden wall looking over the lamp-lit plain and listening to the cicalas [cicadas] thrilling, in competition with motor-horns and tripper-shouts. We thought also to cheat the mosquitoes in the cool. Indeed it soon became so chilly that we had to go in. But the mosquitoes do not mind cold food any more than other Italians, so they ate us. My room is full of flies.'

8 August 1955 Tolkien and Priscilla attend Mass in the Basilica of San Francesco before breakfast. They spend most of the morning visiting the Basilica. Tolkien hears most of another Mass at the Tomb of St Francis, 'beautifully said. . . . A large pilgrimage came in, but behaved devoutly. All the same it seemed odd when the server deserted the priest just before the Post-Communion and went off to sell candles, while his place was taken by an Italian in dungarees.' Tolkien spends much of his time in the upper church looking at the frescoes attributed to Giotto. Not all of them please him. 'The general effect is (now) perhaps too red: ochre, brick-red, scarlet, crimson. But the blues have evidently faded and changed most. The blue with gold stars of the roof has gone a brilliant green in irregular seaweed-like patches.' He thinks most of the frescoes in the lower church lovely. He and Priscilla return to the convent for lunch just as a storm breaks, and stay indoors during the afternoon. At about 5.30 p.m., when the weather clears, they visit the church of Santa Chiara, and see the body of St Clare and other relics, including the cross that spoke to St Francis: 'The piping voice of the little Poor Clare behind the grille, describing the relics was rather terrifying; like the voice of a little tired (veiled) ghost, doing duty on earth, an immeasurable distance away from its real habitation.' They decide to stay for Benediction, which they think will be at 6.15 p.m.

At 18.30 a friar and two acolytes came and said rosary (badly), and the litany, and then presto! a microphone appeared, and after it a young smiling fattish smooth (clean-shaven) friar. At once he began an impassioned sermon. Hardly any of it was intelligible to us: it seemed an endless and hardly modified sequence of shouting and gesturing. On and On. 5 minutes. 10 minutes, 15, 25, 30; still on, and our supper time came. Still on. Looking wildly round my heart failed: I could see no hope of escape or dare to attempt flight. But at last a huge woman (in sandals with large bare feet and long white toe-nails) rose with the look of an outraged dragon and removed herself. So encouraged P[riscilla] got up, and I followed, and we fled by a side door on to the piazza, scorched by looks such as in England might be turned on any one getting up and leaving in the middle of a soliloquy by a star Shakespearean actor. Without Benediction and much shattered we returned to dinner, late.

They later discover the friar is a famous orator, Padre Cristoforo Cecci.

9 August 1955 After breakfast Tolkien and Priscilla visit the church of San Damiano, 'based on the chapel that our Lord in a vision commanded Francis to repair', and which later became the first house of the Poor Clare nuns. He finds that on one of the walls of St Clare's tiny garden

> is inscribed in antique latinate Italian ... St Francis' Hymn to the Sun, supposed to have been composed in the gardens below. The sun was burning on the wall. A wonderful place to read the words. All San Damiano I found enchanting or moving – even though it shows one of the worst examples of the vile and superstitious habit (certainly NOT encouraged by the Church!) of writing names on walls, on lovely frescoes, and even on crucifixes (unless protected by wire gauze). ... In St Clare's Oratory a notice said pointedly that scribbling on walls and sacred objects will not attract the attention of the saints but arouse their indignation. But even this notice was scribbled on.
>
> We walked round the lovely little cloister ... and looked into the refectory, where a vase of flowers is still set on the table at the place where St Clare sat. I felt the whole place more soaked with a sense of the personality of St Clare, and of St Francis, than anywhere else in Assisi, even the tombs.

In the afternoon, misled by their guidebook, Tolkien and Priscilla take a long walk to the Public Gardens, which they find dreary, and the site of a Roman Amphitheatre, where nothing is still visible. Later they meet their 'pet porter', who guides them on a visit to the Rocca Maggiore and tells them the names of some of the plants and flowers along the way. Tolkien finds the castle ruins 'very large and impressive'. They climb the highest tower and have a magnificent view. – Tolkien receives from Allen & Unwin a proof page from Appendix E with two queries but no covering note. He worries that he has had no letter or card from Edith.

10 August 1955 Tolkien goes to early Mass at San Pietro. It is a fine fresh day. After breakfast he and Priscilla spend the morning visiting the Capella dei Pellegrini, having refreshments in the vine-arbour of a café on the Piazza San Francesco, walking along a cypress-lined road to the cemetery, and wandering through narrow streets. They have a good lunch of aubergines (eggplant). Tired, they take a long siesta. Tolkien is pleased to receive a card from Edith at last. He writes letters to her and to Allen & Unwin, and posts them in the Piazza Communale. After dinner he and Priscilla go into the convent garden on a 'brilliant night', but the wind is too cold.

11 August 1955 In the morning, Tolkien and Priscilla go shopping and 'discover the natural law that "the nearer the Saint, the higher the prices"'. When he returns to the Convent for lunch Tolkien finds Rayner Unwin's letter of 5 August. He writes a reply to W.N. Beard, answering the printer's queries as best he can, but cannot be sure of his response until he can consult his notes in England. Later Tolkien and Priscilla do more shopping and visit the Foro Romano and the church built above the Tempio di Minerva. They sit in the Piazza Communale listening to the town band, but as it is the *festa* of San Ruffino and the vigil of Santa Chiara, instead of light and merry music the band play 'a Marcia Sinfonica (dreary); Dal Nuovo Mondo (on indifferent brass!), and Werther'. On the way back to the convent 'there was an international University Tours convoy bedevilling the narrow ways to the basilica. A great autopulman like a tank belched smoke and oil over shops and wayfarers, and we only escaped being befouled by flying up some steps.' In the evening, Tolkien and Priscilla go for a walk and find many of the towers and façades floodlit for the vigil, 'and the streets in many places were like a small-scale St Giles [fair in Oxford] with booths and stalls marked out and a clutter of goods and small lorries, waiting for the morning'.

12 August 1955 The weather for the feast of Santa Chiara is wet and gloomy. Tolkien and Priscilla decide to attend High Mass in the church of Santa Chiara; she gets the last seat left, while Tolkien retires to a corner 'where a ledge on the base of a pillar gave me some chance of an occasional leg-rest'. Beginning at 10.35 a procession of friars, halberdiers, trumpeters, guards, and officials enters, followed by the celebrant, Cardinal Micara.

> The great choir of friars sang magnificently, to my thinking, with enormous controlled power – capable of lifting the roof even of Santa Chiara instantaneously and without effort. Mass was over about 12.15. No sermon! It was a little spoiled for us ... by the ceaseless passage of long streams of people going down to the Tomb and up again. ... There were a great many children. ... I was startled when, just as the choir crashed into the Patrem Omnipotentem of the Creed, a large Italian woman shouted out *Giorgio*! with a force that must have reached the Cardinal in spite of the choir. But it had no effect on Giorgio. He had to be fetched – from the Tomb, while his small sister sat on the floor at my feet and played with a toy. ...
>
> Personally I found the fanfare of trumpets at the first Elevation very impressive and not at all improper at so high a ceremony. But it was a pity that Cardinal Micara had not a note of music, and could not even manage the Pater Noster. The end was rather straggling. No one stops to the bitter end of a Mass any more than of an opera, it seems. The outgoing procession had to fight its way, and really needed the halberdiers. But they had already filtered out to the great doors.

In mid-afternoon Tolkien and Priscilla pay farewell visits to the basilicas and other places in Assisi. Tolkien buys some biscuits to sustain them on their journey home. They have their last meal in the convent refectory, pay their bill, and pack. Tolkien is afflicted by 'a bite on my face and blistered legs, and a swollen fist; so that at least one may look forward to parting with mosquitoes. But in spite of them and the far worse motors [motorcars] it has been an experience of overwhelming delight. I wish I could have come to Italy long ago and learned Italian while there was still a chance of doing it properly.'

13 August 1955 Tolkien and Priscilla rise at 5.15 a.m. At 6.25 the taxi they have ordered takes them to the railway station on a 'sad grey morning'. Their departure is too early for breakfast at the convent, but they are able to obtain coffee and chocolate at the station. At Terentola they have a long wait as their train to Florence is running late. They arrive in Florence twenty minutes after the time their train to Milan was due to leave, but after a few frantic minutes find that it is an hour late. In Milan a Cook's guide, 'a huge burly man with a queer (but not Italian) English accent' takes immediate charge of them, and of two young Englishmen, and marches them to platform 6 in spite of their protests.

We soon discovered that he was trying the Italian manoeuvre of going to the place where the train comes in and boarding it 'unofficially' (from either the proper or the forbidden side) as soon as it stopped. However the train came in again very late, and by that time hosts of others (mainly Italian) were assembled for the same purpose. The rain began to pour down, and leaked in spouts through the roof. Conversation with the Cook's guide revealed him as a Welshman from Cardiff – it seemed odd to exchange a few words in Welsh under the dome of Milan station! But thank heaven for the Welsh, and seemingly for football. He must once have been a redoubtable forward. Only his prowess saved us from disaster. I have never seen anything like it: this great bullock laden with the luggage of four persons, charging the packed train, through a wild mob of besiegers trying to get in, and passengers trying to get out, down a blocked corridor, ejecting people right and left like a bulldozer. He actually got *four* seats, three of them corners, before the assaulting forces knew what had happened to them. I never saw what happened to him. He was swallowed in a human turmoil; but if they were trying to lynch him, I am certain that they did not succeed. *Cymru am byth* ['Wales for ever']!

After that: late, late, and later, all the way along. Cloud, mist, and rain spoiling nearly all the views of lakes and mountains. After 9 p.m. (for 8.12) we were tipped out at Brig into the wet and dark, and waited ages for the appearance of our coach with the couchettes. But in a way the lateness was an advantage, as they promptly turned the compartments into sleepers, and there was nothing to do save go to bed. . . . Food (and drink) was a problem all the way along. A cup of coffee and a biscuit or two at Assisi in the early morn. Nothing more till I managed to get 2 rolls and a small bottle of Chianti at Florence, which we had before Milan. We could have got something there, but did not expect the dislocation that was to follow. We got nothing more until after vain attempts at each stop I got two lunch-packets at Domodossola which gave us the most welcome meal of all (unless it was our first dinner at Venice). We ate it in a halt before entering the tunnel. For each: a small bottle of red wine, ham and salami, part of a chicken, 2 rolls, cheese, 2 plums, peach (or pear). Famine prices, but worth it. From that time (about 7 p.m. Saturday) until midday on Sunday, when we got on the boat, we had nothing to drink, and only a biscuit or two to eat.

14 August 1955 Their train reaches Paris late, and there is no restaurant car on the train to Calais. A Global Tours party blocks the corridor, whose guide uses one of the lavatories, and the only other washing place not a lavatory, as a store for his group's extra baggage. 'Protests to the Wagon-lit man were treated contemptuously; though I had the pleasure of mining my way into one lavatory, and turning all his stacks upside down (carefully burying his satchel and papers).' When Tolkien and Priscilla at last get on the boat at Calais they go straight to the dining room and have a good meal and a bottle of wine. Getting off the boat when it arrives proves 'horrible. I should think about 2000 people (it felt like 3000) with only one gangway; and the whole thing bedevilled by another abomination, called Hotel Plan. They parked all their mountains of luggage in all the accesses to the gangway. It took half an hour of struggle to extricate ourselves.' They clear Customs and finds seats on their train. 'England basking in sun! It looked lovely. Is there anything that we should call "country" outside this island? It seems so much less crowded and noisy on return.' At Victoria Station a porter gets them a taxi, and they reach Paddington with nearly an hour to wait before their train. 'No dining-room open. I queued for two cups of tea, while P[riscilla] telephoned Edith. We then treated ourselves to two first class tickets, and finished the journey like VIPs in a carriage to ourselves, with a really clean lavatory next door, done up in primrose, and actually supplied with hot water, and soap. The first hot wash since Venice.' When they arrive in Oxford, only seven minutes late, they are met by their neighbour Miss Brockett with her car, and are home just after 8.00 p.m.: '37 and a half hours from door to door'.

15 August 1955 Tolkien probably telephones W.N. Beard, as promised in his letter of 11 August, presumably after looking at his proofs of the Appendices. – He writes to Christopher and Faith Tolkien, describing his time in Italy since they parted. 'I am typing out a diary. I remain in love with Italian, and feel quite lorn without a chance of trying to speak it!' (*Letters*, p. 223).

Late August 1955 Having found on his return from Italy, or received soon after, a letter from Terence Tiller on how he intends to dramatize *The Fellowship of the Ring*, Tolkien writes to him, suggesting several alterations. Tiller replies, accepting all or most of these, and saying that the use of music will add much to the broadcasts. He asks Tolkien what accents the various characters should have. He also invites him to come to London on 12 November, probably to attend a rehearsal. (Neither letter is present in the BBC archive.)

6 September 1955 Tolkien completes a form applying for membership in the Society of Authors. In a covering letter to the Society he apologizes for not answering an invitation for membership he had received five years earlier; from the date, he had received it as he was about to move house, and it has only now come to light.

7 September 1955 Tolkien replies to a letter from Richard Jeffery (written at least in part in Tengwar) asking for a translation of one of Treebeard's songs in *The Lord of the Rings* and explanation of various words and names.

8 September 1955 Tolkien replies to a letter from a Mrs Souch, explaining why *The Return of the King* had not been published in the spring: he had written the narrative long ago, but providing material for the Appendices proved a long and difficult task.

9 September 1955 Tolkien writes to John Sparrow, concerning subscriptions and membership in the Ad Eundem club.

10 September 1955 Tolkien writes to Terence Tiller, thanking him for accepting the suggested alterations. Tolkien looks forward with interest to the result, 'and to the effect of the use of music'. In regard to accents, Tolkien says what he thinks should be done, 'though I quite understand that the need for characterization, and making different speakers audibly recognizable, may well override my opinion. Also the skill of the actors may be inadequate to deal in nuances.' He stresses particularly that 'the Hobbit "gentry"', Frodo, Merry, and Pippin, 'should *not* be made rustical in actual tones and accents. . . . But Sam *and Butterbur* . . . may well be characterized by speaking with a "country accent" of some kind' (BBC Written Archives Centre). He suggests that the pronunciation of *r* might be a main characterizing detail. He will endeavour to come to London on 12 November.

11 September 1955 Tolkien writes to Hugh Brogan, who has queried the use of 'Núminor' by C.S. Lewis in *That Hideous Strength*. He also answers a query about the shape of the world in the Third Age: 'I am afraid that was devised "dramatically" rather than geologically, or paleontologically. I do sometimes wish that I had made some sort of agreement between the imaginations or theories of the geologists and my map a little more possible' (*Letters*, p. 224).

17 September 1955 Tolkien attends an Early English Text Society Council meeting at Magdalen College, Oxford.

18 September 1955 Hugh Brogan writes to Tolkien, with apologies for being 'impertinent, stupid, or sycophantic' in his letter in December 1954 criticizing the archaic narrative style of parts of *The Two Towers* (quoted in *Letters*, p. 225). – Tolkien, who still has not answered Brogan's earlier letter, begins a draft letter explaining the difference between 'archaism' and 'tushery'. In the event, he abandons the letter and sends Brogan instead a brief note saying that the matter of archaism 'would take too long to debate' in a letter, and must wait until they next meet (*Letters*, p. 225).

21 September 1955 Terence Tiller writes to Tolkien, sending copies of the six scripts for *The Fellowship of the Ring*. He is afraid that Tolkien will be at first 'a little shocked at the extent of the cutting: six half hours are pitifully brief'. (At some point which cannot be determined, the length of each pro-gramme has been cut from the forty-five minutes mentioned in Tiller's letter of 25 January to only thirty minutes.) Despite telescoping and simplification, Tiller hopes that the main themes of the work have not been 'totally obscured or mutilated' (BBC Written Archives Centre).

27 September 1955 Tolkien writes to Terence Tiller. He apologizes for not replying sooner, but felt that he should consider the scripts with care. 'I am quite unable to judge of its effect on the air (especially without any notion of the music); but I do not think that with the time at your disposal you could have done better. Granted that the procedure is really a good thing – about which I had and have my doubts.' He is interested in what Tiller has included and what he has cut but even more in 'the fact that the inevitable reduction of background and detail had tended to reduce the whole thing, making it much more of a "fairy-tale" in the ordinary sense. The hobbits seem sillier and the others more stilted. . . . Anyway, as an author, I was comforted by being con-firmed in my opinion that there are actually few, if any, unnecessary details in the long narrative! The loss of any of them deprives the story of some sig-nificance at some later point' (BBC Written Archives Centre). He offers minor criticisms and corrects a few misprints or errors in the typescript. He would like to be present at a rehearsal. (Also in the BBC archive is a manuscript page by Tolkien, possibly from this date, suggesting two alternatives to Tiller's treat-ment of the description of the Ringwraiths at Weathertop – spoken either by the narrator or by Frodo – the first of which was accepted.) – While working on his forthcoming O'Donnell Lecture (*English and Welsh*), Tolkien has evi-dently asked someone at Merton College for information about laws made by Henry VIII and earlier rulers against the use of Welsh. 'John' at Merton Col-lege now writes to Tolkien, providing as much information as he has been able to find.

28 September 1955 Tolkien replies to a Miss Perry, to whom he must have lent a proof of *The Return of the King*, and with whom he seems to have exchanged several letters. He acknowledges the return of the proof and hopes that they might meet some time.

29 September 1955 Philip Unwin writes to Tolkien. A reader has pointed out what he thinks is a discrepancy in *The Two Towers*, in regard to references to the 'second' and 'third' days of Entmoot.

30 September 1955 Tolkien writes to Philip Unwin. The reader is correct; the discrepancy noted is the result of Tolkien having to extend Entmoot to fit events elsewhere. He asks when *The Return of the King* will be published: 'I shall be murdered if something does not happen soon' (Tolkien-George Allen & Unwin archive, HarperCollins). He also asks if it would be possible, in a reprint of *The Return of the King*, to include an errata slip covering the whole of *The Lord of the Rings*, as in addition to the Entmoot error he or diligent readers have found a few others.

5 October 1955 Tolkien attends a Merton College meeting.

6 October 1955 Terence Tiller writes to Tolkien. Every excision or shortcut in his scripts for *The Fellowship of the Ring* has been painful, but he thinks that the actors will make a difference. The broadcasts will begin on 13 November and continue weekly, with a repeat each week.

7 October 1955 Philip Unwin writes to Tolkien. *The Return of the King* will be published on 20 October, but as they have bound all 7,000 copies printed, it is too late to include an errata slip.

9 October 1955 Michaelmas Full Term begins. Tolkien's scheduled lectures for this term are: Phonology: English Verbs on Wednesdays at 11.00 a.m. in the Examination Schools, beginning 12 October; *The Owl and the Nightingale* on Thursdays at 12.00 noon in the Examination Schools, beginning 13 October; the 'Pardoner's Tale' and Prologue by Chaucer on Fridays at 12.00 noon in the Schools, beginning 14 October; and *English and Welsh* (the O'Donnell Lecture) on 21 October. He will continue to supervise B.Litt. students L. Glanville, D.C. Levinson, V.M. Martin, and B.D.H. Miller, as well as G.M.G. Evans whose B.Litt. thesis has been referred back, and D.Phil. students R.W. Burchfield, A.D. Horgan, A. Kurvinen, and E.J. Stormon.

12–20 October 1955 Tolkien is laid up with a throat problem which makes lecturing impossible until 21 October.

12 October 1955 Tolkien writes to Philip Unwin. He 'will go through the Vols. and pick out the few "errors" of importance, in the hope that a slip can be inserted in a reprint'. He begs Unwin not to fail to publish *The Return of the King* on 20 October, as on 21 October he is to give the overdue first O'Donnell Lecture and 'I must hope that a large part of my audience will be so bemused by sitting up late the night before that they will not so closely observe my grave lack of equipment as a lecturer on a Celtic subject' (Tolkien-George Allen & Unwin archive, HarperCollins; partly printed in *Letters*, p. 227). He asks to be reminded to whom he had asked Allen & Unwin to send copies when the earlier volumes of *The Lord of the Rings* came out, as he might want to revise the list.

14 October 1955 At an English Faculty Board meeting, in Tolkien's absence, he is again co-opted to the Standing Committee on Monographs. The Applications Committee has granted his B.Litt. student B.D.H. Miller of New College permission to become an advanced student (D.Phil.) with the same topic (an edition of 'Dame Sirith') and with Tolkien continuing as his supervisor. Tolkien is also appointed supervisor to probationer B.Litt. student W.O. Evans of Merton College, to work on a Middle English subject.

20 October 1955 *The Return of the King* is published.

21 October 1955 Though suffering from laryngitis, Tolkien delivers the first O'Donnell Lecture, *English and Welsh*, at 5.00 p.m. in the Examination Schools, Oxford.

22 October 1955 Tolkien receives his author's copies of *The Return of the King*. He inscribes one to his son Michael, and possibly also inscribes and posts other presentation copies. – Tolkien writes to Miss Judson, who has written again. Tolkien has had a large number of letters, but very few from people like Miss Judson, with an interest in languages. – Tolkien writes to a Mr Mitchell, who has already read *The Return of the King* and expressed his approval.

24 October 1955 Tolkien writes to Katharine Farrer. He has been surprised and pleased by the reception of *The Lord of the Rings*, but still feels the picture 'incomplete without something on Samwise and Elanor [as in the deleted Epilogue], but I could not devise anything that would not have destroyed the ending, more than the hints (possibly sufficient) in the appendices' (*Letters*, p. 227).

25 October 1955 Philip Unwin writes to Tolkien. He comments on three good reviews and says that sales of *The Return of the King* are already approaching 5,000 copies, and a reprint has been ordered. He sends a list of four people Tolkien had asked to have complimentary copies. – Later the same day Philip Unwin writes again, to say that the BBC Home Service will review *The Lord of the Rings* in the programme 'Talking of Books' on 30 October.

27 October 1955 Rayner Unwin, who has returned after a long absence abroad, writes to Tolkien. He too mentions satisfactory reviews. He asks:

> Before you take your well earned rest may I breathe the word of future plans? We did briefly discuss the Silmarillion and I think we agreed that the time was ripe for its appearance providing it was in good shape and I hope that over the next few months you may have the leisure to prune and prepare this book to meet a public that doubtless awaits it.
>
> We also talked briefly about your essay on Fairy Stories which Mrs Farrer and others are most anxious to see in print again. . . . I . . . feel convinced that it could be reprinted as a small book by itself if you felt that you could expand it, even if discursively, to about half its size again, and remould it out of the framework of a lecture into a long essay. [Tolkien-George Allen & Unwin archive, HarperCollins]

30 October 1955 Tolkien is staying in Cambridge, in a house without radio, and unable to listen to Arthur Calder-Marshall discuss *The Hobbit* and *The Lord of the Rings* in 'Talking of Books'.

November 1955 M.B. Salu's translation of *The Ancrene Riwle*, with a preface by Tolkien, is published.

2 November 1955 Tolkien attends a Merton College meeting.

7 November 1955 Terence Tiller writes to Tolkien. Rehearsals for the first part of *The Fellowship of the Ring* will take place at Grafton Studio, Euston Road, London on 12 November, 10.30 a.m.–5.30 p.m., and on 13 November, 10.30 a.m.– 4.00 p.m., followed by the actual recording from 4.00 to 4.45 p.m.

10 November 1955 Tolkien writes to Terence Tiller. He will not be able to attend the rehearsals as he feels exhausted and not well, but he will be home by about 11.00 a.m. on Saturday (12 November), so can be telephoned if needed. – Tolkien writes to Lord Halsbury, who has suggested publishing *The Silmarillion* by subscription, that the success of *The Lord of the Rings* makes that unnecessary. The publishers are now pressing for it, and as soon as he can find time Tolkien intends 'to try to set the material in order for publication. Though I am rather tired, and no longer young enough to pillage the night to make up for the deficit of hours in the day'. He offers to let Halsbury see some of the 'Silmarillion' material 'before it is properly shaped or revised, bearing in mind that it is likely to be much altered in detail & presentation – and certainly in style' (*Letters*, p. 228).

11 November 1955 In the evening, Tolkien attends a dinner of The Society hosted by John Sparrow in his lodgings at All Souls College, Oxford. Fifteen members are present. Sparrow addresses them on 'some human aspects of Mark Pattison'. Pleading ill health, R.W. Chapman submits his resignation as Secretary. After discussion, the members agree that it should no longer be obligatory upon the host of the dinner (a point often ignored) to read a paper; instead he should have the option of initiating a general discussion on some topic close to himself.

14 November 1955 Rayner Unwin writes to Tolkien. He suggests that now that *The Lord of the Rings* is well established, they should remove the blurbs on the dust-jackets (by Mitchison, Hughes, and Lewis) which have been criticized by reviewers. But he has been unable come up with an alternative, and wonders if Tolkien has any ideas. – The first part of the radio adaptation of *The Fellowship of the Ring*, 'The Meaning of the Ring', is broadcast in the Third Programme at 10.10 p.m. Tolkien evidently listens to most, probably all, of the broadcasts, and will comment on them in letters.

15 November 1955 The first part of the BBC *Fellowship of the Ring* is rebroadcast at 6.40 p.m.

16 November 1955 Tolkien listens to a talk by W.H. Auden on *The Lord of the Rings* on the BBC radio programme 'Talking of Books'. Auden says that if someone dislikes the work, 'I shall never trust their literary judgement about anything again' (*Letters*, p. 229).

18 November 1955 Terence Tiller writes to Tolkien that he will be welcome at the later rehearsals.

20 November 1955 Tolkien listens to a discussion of the dramatization of *The Fellowship of the Ring* on the BBC radio programme 'The Critics' at 12.10 p.m.

21 November 1955 The second part of *The Fellowship of the Ring*, 'Black Riders and Others', is broadcast in the Third Programme at 9.50 p.m.

23 November 1955 The second part of the BBC *Fellowship of the Ring* is rebroadcast at 7.00 p.m.

24 November 1955 The Committee on Monographs of the Oxford English Faculty Board produces a report with this date. The Committee consists of Tolkien, F.P. Wilson, and Helen Gardner.

29 November 1955 The third part of *The Fellowship of the Ring*, 'Aragorn', is broadcast in the Third Programme at 7.10 p.m.

30 November 1955 Tolkien writes to Molly Waldron, who has written to him about *The Lord of the Rings* and the BBC *Fellowship of the Ring*. He thinks the book 'quite unsuitable for "dramatization"', and have not enjoyed the broadcasts – though they have improved' (*Letters*, p. 228). – The third part of the BBC *Fellowship of the Ring* is rebroadcast at 9.40 p.m.

?December 1955 Tolkien receives a letter from Michael Straight, who is to write a review of *The Lord of the Rings* for the *New Republic*, asking questions about the book. Tolkien makes extensive drafts for his reply. He hopes that Straight has *enjoyed* the book, 'for it was written to *amuse* (in the highest sense): to be readable. There is *no* 'allegory', moral, political, or contemporary in the work at all' (*Letters*, p. 232). *See note.*

?Beginning of December 1955 Tolkien is interviewed for the magazine *Picture Post* by Tim Raison.

2 December 1955 Tolkien attends an English Faculty Board meeting at 3.30 p.m. The Committee on Monographs presents its report. Tolkien states that he has decided not to publish his O'Donnell Lecture for 1954–5 at present. The Applications Committee has appointed Tolkien to supervise the B.Litt. thesis of F.E. Richardson of St Hugh's College, who is to work on an edition of *Sir Eglamour of Artois*, and to be an examiner with G.V. Smithers of the D.Phil. thesis of B.D.H. Miller. In a letter to Naomi Mitchison on 8 December Tolkien will say: 'I have now got a pestilent doctorate thesis to explore, when I would rather be doing something less useful' (*Letters*, p. 229). – Tolkien writes to *Elizabeth Jennings, whom he has known since she was a child (and whose family had been a recipient of one of his author's copies of *The Hobbit*). He congratulates her on the publication of her book of poetry, *A Way of Looking*, and on its reception. He mentions that it is reviewed together with Auden's *Shield of Achilles* in the same issue of *Time and Tide* in which his own poem *Imram* is printed, and that Auden has sent him an inscribed copy of his book. – Tolkien writes, and possibly at the same time sends a registered packet, to Tim Raison of *Picture Post*.

3 December 1955 Michaelmas Full Term ends. – Tolkien's poem *Imram* is published in *Time and Tide* for 3 December.

4 December 1955 Hugh Brogan writes to Tolkien, wondering if in some of his (Brogan's) comments on *The Lord of the Rings* he might have given a wrong impression of his 'real admiration for your great book' (quoted in *Letters*, p. 230). – The fourth part of *The Fellowship of the Ring*, 'Many Meetings', is broadcast in the Third Programme at 9.30 p.m.

5 December 1955 Tolkien attends a Merton College meeting. – The fourth part of the BBC *Fellowship of the Ring* is rebroadcast at 6.35 p.m.

6 December 1955 Rayner Unwin writes to Tolkien. Mr Raison of *Picture Post* has rung and is happy about his interview. Rayner has asked the printer Purnell & Sons to send Tolkien a copy of 'the big map', presumably the fold-out map of Middle-earth from *The Lord of the Rings*; and promises to have some cranberries sent to him also. – Edith Tolkien writes to Rayner Unwin. As the mother of three Oratory School Old Boys she would like to give the School library a set of *The Lord of the Rings*. Her son Michael, who is Second Master at the School, is indignant that the volumes are not already in the library.

7 December 1955 Tolkien writes to Tim Raison of *Picture Post*.

8 December 1955 Tolkien writes to Terence Tiller. He is sorry that he has not been able to attend any of the rehearsals: he was ill at the critical moment and took some time to recover, 'finding it difficult to cope with the ordinary business of term made worse by enforced neglect'. He comments on reviews of the broadcasts, and on letters he has received about them. He liked Glóin's 'foreign accent – though it was perhaps a bit heavily laid on', and thinks Tiller's cutting down of the Council of Elrond 'masterly', but considers it a pity 'that the preliminary announcer (unless I misheard) called Goldberry "Bombadil's *daughter*" (!) and asserted that the evil willow was an ally of Mordor. Mordor is not the master of all things hostile to the "humane"; and, so to say, there is much that seems evil to us that is not in league with the Devil'. He will continue to listen with great interest, and hopes to see Tiller again. He thinks that *The Two Towers* might 'go even better in this form' (BBC Written Archives Centre). – Tolkien writes to Naomi Mitchison, apologizing for not having written before, and for having felt too exhausted to repay her for her blurb and reviews of *The Lord of the Rings* in the matter of *To the Chapel Perilous*. He thinks 'poorly of the broadcast adaptations. Except for a few details I think they are not well done, even granted the script and the legitimacy of the enterprise (which I do not grant). But they took some trouble with the names.' He is 'sorry about my childish amusement with arithmetic; but there it is: the Númenórean Calendar was just a bit better than the Gregorian: the latter being on average 26 secs [seconds] fast p.a. [per annum], and the N[úmenórean] 17.2 secs slow', illustrating the amount of study and calculation that Tolkien put into Appendix D of *The Lord of the Rings* (*Letters*, p. 229). – Tolkien writes to Rayner Unwin. He received the map yesterday 'and was rather mystified; but guessed it had something to do with Raison. As he has not replied to a letter of last Friday, nor acknowledged a registered packet, I wrote to him. I am anything but happy about the interview, or "Picture Post" in general, and I find Mr Tim Raison's happiness rather ominous. I can only hope I shall have some chance of seeing what he is up to before it [the interview] appears.' He comments on the BBC broadcasts, the discussion of them on 'The Critics', and the 'Talking of Books' programme in which W.H. Auden appeared. He agrees with the 'critics' about the radio adaptation of *The Fellowship of the Ring*, but was annoyed that they had discussed the book after confessing that none had read it. He thought Auden 'rather bad . . . and deplored his making the book "a test of literary taste"'. He missed the programme 'Talking of Books' with Arthur Calder-Marshall, which he understands has been the best so far, and asks Rayner if it would be possible to obtain a script. His correspondence 'is now increased by letters of fury against the critics and the broadcast'. He hopes 'in this vacation to begin surveying the "Silmarillion"; though evil fate has plumped a doctorate thesis on me' (Tolkien-George Allen & Unwin archive, HarperCollins, partly printed in *Letters*, p. 229). He asks Rayner to charge the books requested by Edith to his account; the master in charge of the School library considers *The Lord of the Rings* 'nonsense', but Michael thinks that the Head Master will not refuse gift copies. Tolkien says that he met the Headmaster of Eton, who told him that *The Lord of the Rings* is very popular in that school; and he has also had a letter of appreciation from Sir Ernest Barker (a retired Professor of Political Science).

9 December 1955 Tolkien is invited to the St Thomas Feast, a celebratory dinner to which dons at New College, Oxford invite guests.

11 December 1955 The fifth part of *The Fellowship of the Ring*, 'The Moria Gate', is broadcast at 8.00 p.m.

12 December 1955 Tolkien writes to L.G. Smith in the publicity department of Allen & Unwin, thanking him for letting him see proofs of an advertisement and leaflet. Tolkien assumes that 'it was "for information only", and that criticism or alteration would be unwelcome, and ineffectual anyway, at such a late stage'. He is sorry, however, that Smith picked one quotation by W.H. Auden; for although 'Auden's support has been most welcome . . . I do not think it right or fair to make any work, new or old, and especially new, a "test of literary judgement". I have an uneasy consciousness of the hopeless untrustworthiness of my own literary judgement by such tests' (Tolkien-George Allen & Unwin archive, HarperCollins). – Tolkien writes to David I. Masson, who has had a letter published in the *Times Literary Supplement* in which he criticized some aspects of its review of *The Return of the King*. – Terence Tiller writes to Tolkien. He has had few letters about the broadcasts, and takes responsibility for the statement that Goldberry is Tom's daughter. 'But who *is* she?' – The fifth part of the BBC *Fellowship of the Ring* is rebroadcast at 6.20 p.m.

14 December 1955 Tolkien writes to Hugh Brogan. He can stand criticism 'even when stupid, or unfair, or even (as I occasionally suspect) a little malicious. . . . But you are welcome to let your pen run as it will (it is horrible writing letters to people with whom you have to be "careful"), since you give me such close attention, and sensitive perception' (*Letters*, p. 230). – Rayner Unwin writes to Edith Tolkien. A set of *The Lord of the Rings* has been sent to the Oratory School.

15 December 1955 Tolkien writes to Terence Tiller. He had forgotten that not everything known about Tom Bombadil from the poem published in 1934 is included in *The Fellowship of the Ring*. 'Authors are no doubt often peevish folk! Still I must say that I should like to have the thing continued – if you are the producer' (BBC Written Archives Centre).

16 December 1955 Tolkien writes to a Mr Capan, declining an invitation to talk to the Cambridge University English Club. It is difficult for him to travel to Cambridge during term, and has no time to prepare a paper or address for the Club.

18 December 1955 The sixth part of *The Fellowship of the Ring*, 'The Breaking of the Fellowship', is broadcast at 7.20 p.m.

21 December 1955 Elizabeth Jennings has written to Tolkien, commenting on W.H. Auden's poetry, and has sent him a copy of *A Way of Looking*, her first book of poetry, just published. Tolkien replies with a four-page letter in which he comments in detail on some of Jennings' poems, on the appreciation on the dust-jacket, and on Auden and his poetry. In discussing her poem *New*

Worlds he says that he does not think 'it was *hope* that made (makes: it is very real to me) Atlantis real. "Hope" maybe imparts such reality as "countries in space" may possess for the mind. But to me Atlantis is a myth of regret' (British Library MS Add. 52599). – The sixth part of the BBC *Fellowship of the Ring* is rebroadcast at 7.20 p.m.

28 December 1955 Rayner Unwin writes to Tolkien. In the week before Christmas, sales of his books were spectacular, particularly in London. He encloses two copies of *The Return of the King* for Tolkien to autograph for the John Wilson family of Bumpus, the famous London bookshop. Rayner sends his suggested revisions for the blurb for *The Lord of the Rings*, and will try to obtain a copy of the Calder-Marshall script. The cranberries to be sent to Tolkien arrived just before Christmas.

?Late 1955 or ?1956 Tolkien writes a six-page letter to G.E. Selby, who has read *The Lord of the Rings*. Tolkien says that it is not a trilogy, nor an allegory, and comments on reviews, Frodo's failure, the Elvish languages, and the poem *Errantry*.

Late 1955 or early 1956 Tolkien is probably interviewed again by Anthony Price for an article, 'With Camera and Pen', published in the *Oxford Times* for 27 January 1956.

1956

1956–1958 Priscilla Tolkien attends the London School of Economics, earning certificates in Social Science and Applied Social Studies.

?1956 Tolkien visits Lord David Cecil at his home in Oxford to meet his teenage son, Hugh Cecil, who has greatly enjoyed *The Lord of the Rings*. He signs Hugh's copies of the three volumes, and when asked which works of folklore have been his inspiration, mentions 'Norse and Teutonic legends, including Siegfried', and the *Kalevala* (quoted in Christie's, *20th Century Books and Manuscripts*, London, 2 December 2004, p. 47)

1956 Tolkien writes a poem, **Cat*, to amuse his granddaughter Joanna (Joan Anne), daughter of his son Michael. Her mother has several cats.

5 January 1956 Tolkien writes to Rayner Unwin. He has returned the signed volumes for John Wilson, and encloses a short note of good wishes to Wilson for his birthday, which he asks Rayner to address. Having made a copy for himself, he returns the script of the Calder-Marshall broadcast Rayner has sent him. He has 'had *no time at all* for "The Silmarillion". But perhaps term will be easier, once the administrative rush is over and lectures are in order.' He has received the cranberries (about 4½ pounds). Rayner has presumably told him that *Picture Post* have decided not to publish an article; Tolkien remarks that he would not have spent so much time with Mr Raison, if he had known the article to be only a possibility. In regard to a new blurb for the *Lord of the Rings* dust-jacket, he asks if anything at all is necessary.

The usual answer in writing, when a thing won't come right, is to leave it out altogether! I have looked through the 30 reviews of any length that I have seen of vol. iii, and the bad or less good ones do not seem to have produced any sticking phrase of abuse, being mostly concerned to damn with faint praise, or loftily patronizing. Anyway I do not think I can improve on your effort in this direction. If one merely wants a blurb of phrases of praise there are plenty which make me blush to read, and I would rather leave the selection to you.

Houghton Mifflin have sent him a book of carols 'illustrated with distressing vulgarity' (Tolkien–George Allen & Unwin archive, HarperCollins). He has also received some drawings from an artist who hopes that they might be used in an illustrated edition. – *The Return of the King* is published in the United States.

11 January 1956 Tolkien attends a Merton College meeting.

14 January 1956 Tolkien writes a letter to Peter Alford, commenting on the BBC production of *The Fellowship of the Ring*. – He drafts a long reply to an appreciative letter from a Mr Thompson. Commenting on his works, published and unpublished, Tolkien says that he has 'long ceased to *invent* . . . I wait till I seem to know what really happened. Or till it writes itself.' After the success of *The Lord of the Rings* 'I am being positively *bullied* to put *The Silmarillion* into form, and anything else!' (*Letters*, pp. 231–2).

15 January 1956 Hilary Full term begins. Tolkien's scheduled lectures for this term are: the 'Pardoner's Tale' and Prologue by Chaucer on Wednesdays at 12.00 noon in the Examination Schools, beginning 18 January; and *The Owl and the Nightingale* on Wednesdays at 12.00 noon in the Examination Schools, beginning 18 January. (So says the *Oxford University Gazette*, with no later correction of the duplicated scheduling.) Tolkien continues to supervise B.Litt. students G.M.G. Evans, L. Glanville, D.C. Levinson, V.M. Martin, and F.E. Richardson, D.Phil. students R.W. Burchfield, A.D. Horgan, and A. Kurvinen, and probationer B.Litt. student W.O. Evans.

20 January 1956 Tolkien attends an English Faculty Board meeting.

c. 22 January 1956 Tolkien writes to Rayner Unwin. He has at last found time to compile a list of errors of copy or of setting in *The Lord of the Rings*. He has now heard from Tim Raison that *Picture Post* have dropped their planned story. He asks that a copy of *The Fellowship of the Ring* be sent to his cousin Marjorie Incledon. Fan mail continues to arrive, though not much from America, but Michael Straight has sent him two copies of his review in the *New Republic*, one of which he offers to Rayner.

23 January 1956 Rayner Unwin writes to Tolkien. The corrections will be incorporated as each volume is reprinted. He has not heard when Houghton Mifflin will publish *The Return of the King*. The *Fellowship* is being sent to Miss Incledon as requested. Rayner would indeed like a copy of the review in the *New Republic*.

?Late January 1956 Tolkien sees W.H. Auden's review of *The Return of the King* ('At the End of the Quest, Victory') in the *New York Times Book Review* for 22 January 1956. Probably when he first reads this he writes a lengthy comment, which he will rewrite at a later date.

Late January–early February 1956 Tolkien is twice laid up with illness.

31 January 1956 Milton Waldman dines with Tolkien. In the course of conversation he mentions that *The Hobbit* would be a very desirable addition to Collins' Fontana paperback series. Tolkien refers him to Allen & Unwin.

5 February 1956 Robert Burchfield, now Secretary of the Early English Text Society, writes to Tolkien. Burchfield would like to present to the EETS Council at their next meeting a progress report on Tolkien's edition of the *Ancrene Wisse*.

6 February 1956 Rayner Unwin forwards to Tolkien a reader's letter suggesting corrections to *The Return of the King*.

15 February 1956 Rayner Unwin writes to Tolkien. Collins have asked if Allen & Unwin will let them publish *The Hobbit* in their Fontana series. Rayner does not support the idea, as the hardcover edition is still selling well. He queries how Tolkien would like his income from *The Lord of the Rings* to be paid to obtain the most advantageous tax position.

?Mid-February 1956 Tolkien writes to Peter Alford, giving details of the titles considered for the six books of *The Lord of the Rings*.

18 February 1956 Tolkien writes to Rayner Unwin. In regard to the proposed Fontana *Hobbit*, he would be interested if the scheme were to offer any hope of immediate profit, but would not go against Rayner's advice or interests since he owes so much to Allen & Unwin. He has not yet received a statement of account for 1955, and is concerned about his tax position. – In a second letter to Rayner Unwin on this date, Tolkien dismisses most of the suggested corrections to *The Return of the King* as pedantic.

23 February 1956 The Electors to the Readership in Textual Criticism, including Tolkien, meet.

28 February 1956 Rayner Unwin writes to Tolkien. He advises against agreeing to a Fontana edition of *The Hobbit*; the royalty Collins offer is small, and it is not worth risking a loss of sales of the Allen & Unwin hardback. Allen & Unwin's accounts for 1955 will not be ready until April.

29 February 1956 Tolkien writes to Rayner Unwin, leaving the Fontana decision to him. He asks for a rough figure of the profits on *The Lord of the Rings* in advance of final accounts. 'I am much harassed with professional concerns, and I have not had a chance of turning, as is my chief desire, to the *Silmarillion*. It needs prolonged concentration. But I hope at last to do something this vacation' (Tolkien-George Allen & Unwin archive, HarperCollins). – Tolkien declines an invitation to speak at the Oxford University English Club in Trinity Term, for lack of time.

Early March 1956 Peter Goolden's manuscript for *The Old English Apollonius of Tyre* is destroyed in a fire at University College, London. He has another copy of his thesis at the Bodleian Library, but has to start over on revision.

2 March 1956 Tolkien and G.V. Smithers examine B.D.H. Miller of New College, Oxford *viva voce* on his D.Phil. thesis *Dame Sirith* at 2.30 p.m. in the Examination Schools.

7 March 1956 Tolkien replies to a letter from a Mr Durden, a reader in California. It is unlikely that he will write anything about events later than those in *The Lord of the Rings*, but he hopes to publish legends of the First and Second Ages.

9 March 1956 Tolkien attends an English Faculty Board meeting.

10 March 1956 Hilary Full Term ends.

12 March 1956 Tolkien attends a Merton College meeting. – Mrs S. Newman of the foreign rights department, George Allen & Unwin, writes to Tolkien. She has concluded an agreement for a Dutch edition of *The Lord of the Rings* and asks if Tolkien can supply biographical and bibliographical information for the Dutch publisher; otherwise she will refer them to *Who's Who*.

c. **13–20 March 1956** Tolkien is on holiday in Sidmouth.

15 March 1956 Rayner Unwin writes to Tolkien. His share in the profits on *The Lord of the Rings* for 1955 will be over £3,000, in addition to royalties due on *The Hobbit* and *Farmer Giles of Ham. See note.*

18 March 1956 Tolkien replies to a letter from a Mr Sam Gamgee of London, who has asked how Tolkien came to choose the name 'Sam Gamgee' in *The Lord of the Rings*. Tolkien explains the background to the name and offers to send Gamgee signed copies of the three volumes.

19 March 1956 Tolkien writes to Christopher and his wife Faith about the real Sam Gamgee, and the good news from Allen & Unwin on forthcoming payments.

21 March 1956 Tolkien writes to Rayner Unwin. He is 'agreeably surprised' at the amount of royalties he will receive, but realizes that income tax is going to be a problem. 'So much so, that if there was any security for such continued sales, it would evidently pay me to retire (and write more!).' *See note.* – Tolkien writes to Mrs Newman at Allen & Unwin. Even though the project is obviously far advanced, he cannot find any previous mention in his correspondence of a Dutch edition of *The Lord of the Rings*. He asks for more information, in particular whether the edition is to be a translation, which he thinks hardly likely 'in view of the bulk and difficulty of the work' (Tolkien-George Allen & Unwin archive, HarperCollins). He asks for examples of the biographical and bibliographical information required. – Robert Burchfield meets or telephones Tolkien, who promises to hand over his transcript of the *Ancrene Wisse* at or just after the meeting of the Early English Text Society Council on 23 March, as well as any observations on the manuscript and its history that he has collected.

22 March 1956 Ronald and Edith Tolkien celebrate their Ruby Wedding Anniversary with all of their children, daughters-in-law, and grandchildren present.

23 March 1956 Tolkien attends an Early English Text Society Council meeting at Magdalen College. He shows his transcript of the *Ancrene Wisse* and proposes to revise it during the summer, so that the text will be ready by Michaelmas Term 1956. This is probably the occasion described by Burchfield in 1989:

> Against all precedents he had set out the text line-by-line with the original manuscript. We [the EETS Council] loved it. We gazed with amazement at the way he had hand-drawn, in a most elegant manner, the large initial letters of the words at the beginning of sections and paragraphs. He had turned his task into something resembling that of the original scribe. As in so much of his work, he had left the twentieth century behind. ['My Hero: Robert Burchfield on J.R.R. Tolkien', *The Independent Magazine*, 4 March 1989, p. 50]

Since Tolkien feels unable to write an introduction, it is agreed that this should be done by N.R. Ker, but he cannot begin work on it until October. In other business, Tolkien thinks that W. Meredith Thompson's edition of *Þe Wohunge ure Lauerd* and other pieces should now be accepted for publication, and offers to read through its notes and help the editor make them conform with the requirements of the Society.

26 March 1956 Mrs Newman writes to Tolkien. Allen & Unwin have been making all possible efforts to sell foreign rights. She asks for confirmation that Tolkien wants them to do this. The Dutch edition is to be a translation, with an advance on royalties of £40.

28 March 1956 Tolkien writes to Patricia Kirke. He is harassed not only by ill health and professional duties, but also 'by the endless concerns of the additional role of author, involved with Income Tax, agreements, translation rights, and the clamour for more'. He will put aside such concerns for a few days to celebrate Easter, but while he approves 'in the abstract of the reform of the liturgy ... one feels a little dislocated and even a little sad at my age to know that the ceremonies and modes so long familiar and deeply associated with the season will never be heard again!' (Gerard A.J. Stodolski, *Catalogue 299*, [June 1999], item 29). He has been reading about the 'Holy Shroud' (of Turin).

30 March 1956 Sam Gamgee of London writes to Tolkien with information about the Gamgee family.

April 1956 Tolkien drafts a long reply, and probably sends a letter, to Joanna de Bortadano, saying that *The Lord of the Rings* is not an allegory, and that its real theme is Death and Immortality.

?Early April 1956 H. Cotton Minchin writes to Tolkien about *The Lord of the Rings*, apparently suggesting an additional volume with more information about Middle-earth.

3 April 1956 Tolkien replies to Mrs Newman. He would like her to continue her efforts in regard to foreign editions. But as the author he feels a

> deep and immediate concern in *translation*. And this one is, unfortunately, also a professional linguist, a pedantic don, who has wide personal

connexions and friendships with the chief English scholars of the continent. . . .

The translation of *The Lord of the Rings* will prove a formidable task, and I do not see how it can be performed satisfactorily without the assistance of the author. (By 'assistance' I do not, of course, mean interference, though the opportunity to consider specimens would be desirable. My linguistic knowledge seldom extends, beyond the detection of obvious errors and liberties, to the criticism of the niceties that would be required. But there are many special difficulties in this text. To mention one: there are a number of words not to be found in the dictionaries, or which require a knowledge of older English. On points such as these, and others that would inevitably arise, the author would be the most satisfactory, and the quickest, source of information.) That assistance I am prepared to give, promptly, if I am consulted.

I wish to avoid a repetition of my experience with the Swedish translation of *The Hobbit*. . . . I regard the text (in all its details) of *The Lord of the Rings* far more jealously. No alterations, major or minor, re-arrangements, or abridgements of this text will be approved by me – unless they proceed from myself or from direct consultation. . . . [Tolkien-George Allen & Unwin archive, HarperCollins, partly printed in *Letters*, pp. 248–9]

6 April 1956 Tolkien writes to Rayner Unwin. He is glad that Allen & Unwin rejected a proposal (whose author has also written directly to Tolkien) for an adaptation of *The Lord of the Rings* for schoolchildren. 'Except under duress, I will not tolerate the abridgement or re-arrangement of this book. . . . "Broadcasting" is rather different; it is at least temporary, and one is pitied rather than blamed for its defects.' In regard to translation of *The Lord of the Rings*,

I have already been compelled by correspondents abroad to consider the difficulties involved, and my own views. . . . I am concerned, of course, to protect myself as far as possible from liberties and misrepresentation, but I am most concerned to be helpful. This text presents several special problems, to some of which it is probable that I alone hold the key. It seems to me very desirable from all points of view that some degree of consultation with the author should be provided for.

The Appendices present a separate problem; and in their case at any rate reduction or even omission in parts might be a reasonable process. Only Appendix A v [the *Tale of Aragorn and Arwen*] . . . is really essential to the story. However views may differ. . . . I fear the 'General Linguistics' experts are already busy with the Elvish tongues, and I shall inevitably be obliged to provide more information than appears in the book.

He hopes to produce something else soon, though he 'cannot now do much until the long vacation, which (so far) I have kept free from any serious commitments or travels, except ancient debts. The E(arly) E(nglish) Text S[ociety] will I fear demand a long overdue pound of flesh [*Ancrene Wisse*]' (Tolkien-George Allen & Unwin archive, HarperCollins). Tolkien also discusses income tax concerns, and asks to be sent a set of *The Lord of the Rings* and a copy of *The Hobbit*.

9 April 1956 Mrs Newman writes to Mr D. de Lange at Het Spectrum, the Dutch publisher, quoting Tolkien's comments on translation.

11 April 1956 Tolkien replies to a letter from a Mrs M. Wilson. He says that *The Lord of the Rings* was not written for children, and thinks it a pity if children read it too soon. 'I am a very "unvoracious" reader, and since I can seldom bring myself to read a work twice I think of the many things that I read – too soon! Nothing, not even a (possible) deeper appreciation, for me replaces the bloom on a book, the freshness of the unread' (*Letters*, p. 249).

12 April 1956 Tolkien replies to a letter from a Mr Earle. He comments on *The Lord of the Rings* and its sources, and on the origins of the name *Tolkien*.

13 April 1956 Rayner Unwin writes to Tolkien, enclosing a copy of Mrs Newman's letter to de Lange. He apologizes for not informing Tolkien when the Dutch translation rights were sold. In the normal course of events authors are not told of such things, but in future Allen & Unwin will keep Tolkien informed.

16 April 1956 Tolkien drafts, then writes, a five-page letter in reply to H. Cotton Minchin. 'I once had myself the idea of preparing a special volume of material for "specialists"', but production costs made it impossible. Although it might now be practicable, 'the chief objection is the labour involved (on my part), and the weight of other duties which demand most of my time. My professional and philological colleagues and critics are scandalized by my disgraceful excursion into "literature".... The many unfinished and long-promised professional commitments and works are being demanded with increasing pressure' (finished letter, Christie's, *Valuable Printed Books and Manuscripts*, London, 26 November 1997, p. 110). In draft, Tolkien continues:

> My plans for the 'specialist volume' were largely linguistic. An index of names was to be produced, which by etymological interpretation would also provide a quite a large Elvish vocabulary....
>
> But the problems (delightful if I had time) which the extra volume will set, will seem clear if I tell you that while many like you demand *maps*, other wish for *geological* indications rather than places; many want Elvish grammars, phonologies, and specimens; some want metrics and prosodies – not only of the brief Elvish specimens, but of the 'translated' verses in less familiar modes, such as those written in the strictest form of Anglo-Saxon alliterative verse.... Musicians want tunes, and musical notation; archaeologists want ceramics and metallurgy. Botanists want a more accurate description of the *mallorn*, of *elanor, niphredil, alfirin, mallos*, and *symbelmynë*; and historians want more details about the

social and political structure of Gondor; general inquirers want information about the Wainriders, the Harad, Dwarvish origins, the Dead Men, the Beornings, and the missing two wizards (out of five). It will be a big volume, even if I attend only to the things revealed to my limited understanding! [*Letters*, pp. 247–8; *see note*]

– Mrs Newman sends Tolkien a letter from D. de Lange (not preserved in the Allen & Unwin archive) in which he evidently suggests that he and the author should meet.

19 April 1956 Tolkien attends a Merton College meeting.

20 April 1956 Tolkien replies to the Rev. Paul Spilsbury, who had written about *The Lord of the Rings*. – Mrs Newman sends Tolkien a proposal for a French translation of *The Hobbit* by L.A. Dickson.

22 April 1956 Trinity Full term begins. Tolkien's scheduled lectures for this term are: *Sawles Warde* on Wednesdays at 12.00 noon in the Examination Schools, beginning 25 April; and the 'Pardoner's Tale' by Chaucer (concluded) on Fridays at 12.00 noon in the Examination Schools, beginning 27 April. He continues to supervise B.Litt. students G.M.G. Evans, L. Glanville, D.C. Levinson, V.M. Martin, and F.E. Richardson, D.Phil. students R.W. Burchfield, A.D. Horgan, and A. Kurvinen, and probationer B.Litt. student W.O. Evans.

23 April 1956 C.S. Lewis marries Joy Gresham (*née* Davidman), a divorced American, in the Oxford registry office, to enable her to stay in Britain. The marriage is kept secret from most of Lewis's friends, including Tolkien.

27 April 1956 Tolkien attends an English Faculty Board meeting. He is appointed to the Nominating Committee for the Honour School, Group B6, and Preliminary Examinations in place of C.L. Wrenn until 1957. (Wrenn is to be on sabbatical leave from Michaelmas Term 1956 to Michaelmas Term 1957.)

?Late April 1956 Tolkien sends best wishes to his granddaughter Joanna (Joan Anne), elected May Queen at Checkendon Primary School.

29 April 1956 Tolkien writes to Rayner Unwin. He has neglected the *Pearl* and *Sir Gawain* translations, but *Ancrene Wisse* must take precedence in matters 'professional'. He would be grateful for any advice about income tax. He is being 'honoured/or pestered by would-be illustrators' and asks if he is right in thinking that an illustrated edition of *The Lord of the Rings*, 'even more costly', is not being contemplated; he has replied to such letters 'that I am not myself eager to have an illustrated edition, and that the immediate need, when possible or suitable, is for a cheaper edition' (Tolkien-George Allen & Unwin archive, HarperCollins). – Tolkien writes to Mrs Newman. He looks forward to meeting de Lange, and has written to L.A. Dickson. – Tolkien replies to Rosfrith Murray, who has written asking for information about Shakespeare, and about Chapman's *Tragedy of Gowrie*. He will try to find an expert such as F.P. Wilson to help her, as he himself knows little about the matter.

1 May 1956 Rayner Unwin writes to Tolkien, with a statement of royalties and shared profits owed him for 1955, and a cheque for more than £3,500. He agrees that a cheaper edition of *The Lord of the Rings* is needed rather than a more expensive illustrated edition, and feels that 'illustration is such a personal matter in the case of your book that for the few it would please many more would be unnecessarily irked by the artist's interpretation' (Tolkien-George Allen & Unwin archive, HarperCollins). – At Rayner's request Mr Knight, Secretary of Allen & Unwin, sends Tolkien advice about income tax. – Mrs Newman writes to Tolkien concerning Dickson's proposal. Allen & Unwin have made many unsuccessful efforts to obtain a contract for a French edition of *The Hobbit*, and are discussing a possible German edition.

14 May 1956 With support by Tolkien and C.L. Wrenn, the Delegates of Oxford University Press approve publication of *The Old English Apollonius of Tyre*, ed. Peter Goolden, in the *Oxford English Monographs*.

16 May 1956 Tolkien attends a Merton College meeting.

28 May 1956 Mrs Newman writes to Tolkien, forwarding a letter from Het Spectrum dated 24 May. The Dutch translation of the first half of *The Fellowship of the Ring* is nearly finished; the translator has not experienced particular difficulties, but has transformed a few names into Dutch with equivalent meanings or associations. It is suggested that Tolkien provide a list of points in the first volume where he thinks the translator might go astray, and the Dutch translator will send him his solutions. Mrs Newman has seen a sample of Dickson's French translation, which she thinks of poor quality.

7 June 1956 English Final Honour School Examinations begin.

11 June 1956 W.H. Auden gives his inaugural lecture as Professor of Poetry at Oxford. Rachel Trickett, a fellow don, will recall that Tolkien was present when

> Auden astonished and horrified the undergraduates in the audience by saying that the only part of the English syllabus that had been of any use to him at all as a practising poet was Old English. And as the undergraduates were beginning their endless agitation to get Old English dropped from the syllabus, this was a shattering blow to them. And he said, 'I can remember hearing Professor Tolkien reading *Beowulf* which was one of the great experiences in my undergraduate days.' I can see Tolkien now executing a little dance as we walked across New College Quad for a party afterwards for Auden and saying, 'He paid me a compliment, he paid me a compliment!' [Marion E. Wade Center, Wheaton College, Wheaton, Illinois]

See note. – Alina Dadlez, Allen & Unwin, writes to Tolkien. She encloses a list of Dutch versions of the place names on the maps to look at and, she hopes, approve. The translator has finished the first half of *The Fellowship of the Ring*, but foresees that he might need help from Tolkien in the second part. Dadlez asks if she may give the Dutch publishers Tolkien's address.

12 June 1956 Tolkien receives the Dutch list of names. Probably on this date, he writes on the letter from Alina Dadlez that she may provide his address, and returns it to her.

15 June 1956 Tolkien attends an English Faculty Board meeting. The Board expresses its appreciation of C.H. Wilkinson (to whom *Farmer Giles of Ham* had been dedicated) on his retirement as a University Lecturer. The Applications Committee has accepted W.O. Evans of Merton College as a full B.Litt. student working on 'the five virtues of Gawayn's shield and their contemporary equivalents', with Tolkien as his supervisor. – Tolkien may also have attended a meeting of the Committee for Comparative Philology at 5.00 p.m. in the Delegates Room of the Clarendon Building.

16 June 1956 Trinity Full Term ends.

17 June 1956 D.C. Corner, of the University College of North Staffordshire, writes to Tolkien, enclosing a copy of an Economics examination paper in which one question concerns the Shire and the consumption of 'necessities' by Hobbits. (The commodities are 'pipe tobacco', beer, 'waybread', and 'Brandywine water'.)

19 June 1956 Tolkien attends a Merton College meeting.

20 June 1956 Encaenia.

29 June 1956 Rayner Unwin writes to Tolkien. The latter has not yet commented on the list of names for the Dutch translation, and Het Spectrum urgently need his approval of the names that are to appear on the maps.

3 July 1956 Tolkien writes a card to Rayner Unwin. The list of names had arrived during his most crowded period of the year. If the Dutch translator 'was up to his job, a glance should have been sufficient; but a glance was sufficient to show me that I should have to give careful consideration to the whole business and to each item. That I have only just found time to do' (Tolkien-George Allen & Unwin archive, HarperCollins). – Later that day Tolkien writes, or begins to write, a long letter to Rayner Unwin. The matter of the Dutch translation 'is (to me) important; it has disturbed and annoyed me greatly, and given me a great deal of unnecessary work at a most awkward season'. He asks that his views be transmitted to Het Spectrum 'in such a tone and form as your experience suggests is likely to be effective without being too upsetting'. He does not understand how either Het Spectrum or the Allen & Unwin Foreign Rights staff could expect the Dutch versions of his place-names to have his approval.

> Very slight acquaintance with the book, its structure (or with me), should warn any one that I should regard it as an intolerable impertinence, and also stupidly unperceptive. . . .
>
> *In principle* I object as strongly as is possible to the 'translation' of the *nomenclature* at all (even by a competent person). I wonder why a translator should think himself called on or entitled to do any such thing. That this is an 'imaginary' world does not give him any right to remodel it according to his fancy, even if he could in a few months create a new coherent structure which it took me years to work out. . . .
>
> But, of course, if we drop the 'fiction' of long ago, 'The Shire' is based on rural England and not on any other country in the world – least

perhaps of any in Europe on Holland, which is topographically wholly
dissimilar. . . . After all the book is English, and by an Englishman, and
presumably even those who wish its narrative and dialogue turned into
an idiom that they understand, will not ask of a translator that he should
deliberately attempt to destroy the local colour. . . .

I am sure the correct . . . way is to leave the maps and nomenclature
alone as far as possible, but to substitute for some of the least-wanted
Appendices a glossary of names (with meanings but no [references]). I
could supply one for translation.

May I say at once that I will *not* tolerate any similar tinkering with the
personal nomenclature. Nor with the name/word *Hobbit*. . . . [Tolkien-
George Allen & Unwin archive, HarperCollins; partly printed in *Letters*,
pp. 249–51]

He encloses 'in justification of my strictures a detailed commentary on the
[translator's] lists', eight manuscript pages. These elaborate upon notes he has
made on six typed pages of English names on the 'Een Deel van de Streek' (the
Shire Map) and the 'Grote Kaart' (the general map of Middle-earth) with their
proposed Dutch equivalents. He asks Rayner Unwin if it would be possible to
provide him with copies of the Dutch translator's list, without his corrections
or notes, so that he can annotate it for his own purposes (he may be thinking
of future translations). He has had no time to make typed copies of his comments, but thinks it too much to ask Allen & Unwin to produce a typescript.

5 July 1956 Tolkien writes to Allen & Unwin, thanking Mrs Newman and
Mr Knight for their letters and informing them that he will be away until 20
July. He asks them to send a set of *The Lord of the Rings* to Mrs D.E. Sykes.

c. **6–20 July 1956** Tolkien is in the Republic of Ireland, staying part of
the time with Professor J.J. Hogan in Dublin. He is possibly acting as Extern
Examiner for the National University of Ireland. *See note.*

6 July 1956 Rayner Unwin writes to Tolkien. A Norwegian publisher is
showing interest in *The Lord of the Rings*.

9 July 1956 Rayner Unwin, having read Tolkien's long letter and enclosures, writes a sympathetic reply. He sends him two typed copies of the Dutch
lists and (after all) of Tolkien's comments, together with his suggestion for a
temperate covering letter.

13 July 1956 Tolkien writes to Rayner Unwin from the Royal Marine Hotel,
Dun Laoghaire, Co. Dublin. He is grateful for Rayner's sympathy and approves
his suggested letter, but cannot send it until he has had time to correct the
typescript of his comments, 'a v[ery] gallant and substantially successful effort'
(Tolkien-George Allen & Unwin archive, HarperCollins). He expects to stay in
Dun Laoghaire until 18 July.

c. **14–18 July 1956** Tolkien's comments on the Dutch names, with Rayner's
letter, are sent to Het Spectrum.

26 July 1956 Tolkien drafts, and probably sends, a letter to Miss J. Burn in
reply to one of her own. He explains that it was quite impossible for Frodo to

surrender the Ring, and that 'I am not writing the *Silmarillion*, which was long ago written; but trying to find a way and order in which to make the legends and annals publishable' (*Letters*, p. 252).

27 July 1956 Tolkien writes a letter to Amy Ronald similar to his draft of 26 July. She too has written to him about Frodo's failure. He mentions that he once met Walter de la Mare, 'many years ago, and we had little to say' (*Letters*, p. 253).

28 July 1956 Tolkien attends a Merton College meeting, and is appointed a member of a committee to consider the emoluments of college officers.

30 July 1956 Rayner Unwin copies to Tolkien replies received from D. de Lange of Het Spectrum. De Lange accepts many of Tolkien's comments, but argues that just as Westron names in the Allen & Unwin edition of *The Lord of the Rings* have been 'translated into English,' so in the Dutch edition they must be 'translated into Dutch'. He cites Tolkien's introduction to Appendix E and 'On Translation' in Appendix F as justification. He encloses a long list of emended translations of names for Tolkien's consideration. Rayner also sends news of a proposed Swedish translation and asks Tolkien to let him know if he approves. (Although Rayner Unwin in his letters to Het Spectrum tries to support Tolkien, the only concession he will be able to obtain is the use of 'Hobbit' – originally rejected because it sounded unmistakably English – rather than the publisher's choice, 'Hobbel'.)

9 August 1956 By now Allen & Unwin have received a cablegram from Het Spectrum saying that the Dutch publisher must go ahead with their translation of *The Lord of the Rings* after 15 August whether or not Tolkien has replied to their latest list of names. Rayner Unwin evidently informs Tolkien by telephone, Tolkien promises to write to Het Spectrum that day, and Allen & Unwin cable that answer to Het Spectrum. Rayner sends copies of both cables to Tolkien. (There is no copy of Tolkien's reply to Het Spectrum in the Tolkien-George Allen & Unwin archive.)

11 August 1956 Robert Burchfield, Early English Text Society, writes to Tolkien. As C.T. Onions does not want an EETS Council meeting in September, Burchfield has drafted a letter to the Council members making several proposals, which he will send out next week. He comments on inaccuracies in W. Meredith Thompson's *Wohunge*, and hopes that Tolkien's work on the *Ancrene Wisse* is going smoothly.

17 September 1956 Terence Tiller, BBC, writes to Tolkien. The BBC wish to adapt for the Third Programme *The Two Towers* and *The Return of the King* in six episodes. Since the allotted time is so limited, the cuts to these volumes will have to be far more drastic than for *The Fellowship of the Ring*. The BBC propose to broadcast the series from mid-November to late December. (Tolkien will subsequently agree, but his reply is not in the BBC archive.)

?Autumn 1956 Tolkien writes to Anne Barrett at the Houghton Mifflin Company. He will publish 'The Silmarillion' if he can, but I am not allowed to get at it. I am not only submerged (sans secretary) under business of the [*Lord of the Rings*], but also under professional business – one of the ways of making us professors 'go quietly' with practically no pension, is to make our last two or three years of office intolerably laborious – ; while the appearance of the L.R. has landed me in the pincers. Most of my philological colleagues are shocked (cert[ainly] behind my back, sometimes to my face) at the fall of a philological into 'Trivial literature'; and anyway the cry is: 'now we know how you have been wasting your time for 20 years'. So the screw is on for many things of a more professional kind long overdue. Alas! I like them both, but have only one man's time. Also I am getting rather ripe, if not actually decrepit! . . . With the retirement this summer of Sir John Beazley, and Lord Cherwell, I am left the senior professor of this ancient institution, having sat in a chair here since 1925 – or 31 years, though no one seems to observe the fact. [*Letters*, p. 238]

10 October 1956 Tolkien attends a Merton College meeting.

14 October 1956 Michaelmas Full Term begins. Tolkien's scheduled lectures for this term are only *Sir Gawain and the Green Knight* on Wednesdays and Fridays at 11.00 a.m. in the Examination Schools, beginning 17 October. He continues to supervise B.Litt. students G.M.G. Evans, W.O. Evans, L. Glanville, D.C. Levinson, and F.E. Richardson, and D.Phil. students R.W. Burchfield, A.D. Horgan, and A. Kurvinen.

16 October 1956 Alina Dadlez, Allen & Unwin, writes to ask Tolkien to confirm that he has heard nothing more about the French translation of *The Hobbit* which L.A. Dickson had been going to submit for Tolkien's approval. Dadlez has had another enquiry for French translation rights.

17 October 1956 Tolkien replies to Alina Dadlez. He has heard nothing more from L.A. Dickson.

18 October 1956 Tolkien attends a meeting of the O'Donnell Trustees and representatives of the universities of Edinburgh, Wales, and Oxford, at the Senate House, University of London, to discuss the O'Donnell Lecture Scheme.

19 October 1956 Tolkien attends an English Faculty Board meeting at 2.15 p.m. in the Board Room of the Clarendon Building. Tolkien is elected to replace F.P. Wilson on the Standing Committee on Matters Referred by the General Board, and to the Standing Committee on Monographs (on which he had been previously a co-opted member) until Michaelmas Term 1957. The Applications Committee has appointed him director of studies of recognized student W. Swieczkowski, graduate in English of the Catholic University of Lublin, Poland.

22 October 1956 Tolkien attends a Merton College meeting.

1 November 1956 Terence Tiller sends Tolkien copies of the first three scripts of his continuation of *The Lord of the Rings*. He has been 'forced on many occasions to script his own narration, rather than use Tolkien's' (BBC

Written Archives Centre, Caversham). He asks what accents the various races of the book should have. He will be rehearsing and pre-recording the six programmes in Studio Piccadilly Two during the period 18 November to 7 December 1956.

2 November 1956 Tolkien writes to Terence Tiller. He hopes to study the scripts during the weekend. He gives advice on accents.

5 November 1956 Tolkien writes an eight-page letter in reply to queries sent him by a Mr Britten, mainly concerning 'The Silmarillion'.

6 November 1956 Tolkien writes to Terence Tiller. He has not had time 'for more than two rapid readings of the 3 episodes. . . . I am not offering any criticism of detail. The objects you had in making this version seem fairly clear, and (granted their value or legitimacy) I do not think they could have been much better achieved' (*Letters*, p. 254). But he asks: Why such a treatment? And what value can it have? He thinks the book not suitable for dramatic representation, but if attempted it would need a lot of space. – Tolkien also writes to a Mr Hill, declining an invitation from the Bodley Club, since he is already committed to two dinners during the same week, and will probably have to drop one of those for digestive reasons.

7 November 1956 Tolkien attends a Merton College meeting.

18 November 1956 Tolkien travels to London on business connected with the University of London.

19 November 1956 The first part of the radio adaptation of *The Two Towers* and *The Return of the King*, 'Fangorn', is broadcast in the BBC Third Programme at 10.30 p.m.

20 November 1956 Tolkien probably attends the Boar's Head Dinner at Merton College, Oxford.

22 November 1956 Tolkien accepts an invitation from Miss Stanley-Smith of the Deddington Library, Oxfordshire, to make a speech at the opening of the new library on 14 December, and to lunch with her first. He asks how long his speech should be. He accepts her offer to send a car, and says that he often visited Deddington before the war, when he himself had a car. – 'Fangorn' is rebroadcast in the BBC Third Programme at 7.50 p.m.

23 November 1956 In the evening, Tolkien attends a dinner of The Society hosted by Thomas Armstrong at Christ Church, Oxford. Ten members are present. Armstrong considers certain words (*colour, texture, melodies, harmony, counterpoint*) frequently employed in the discussion of music and poetry.

24 November 1956 Tolkien writes to Rayner Unwin, probably in reply to a letter no longer in the files. He has not been consulted on any point of the Dutch *Lord of the Rings* other than nomenclature, so any 'howlers' are the fault of the Dutch translator. He asks Rayner to send one of his five author's copies to his friend, Professor Dr P.N.U. Harting in Amsterdam, whom he intends to ask for his view of the translation. He himself does not have the time to scrutinize the book, but in any case doubts that criticism would do any good. 'I still think the "translation" of the nomenclature a primary blunder, indicative of a wrong attitude; and as I was not able to carry that point, I do not suppose I should be more successful on other points' (Tolkien-George Allen & Unwin archive, HarperCollins). He has taken the same view of the BBC adaptations, that is, there is no point in criticizing scripts in detail. He notes that the bust Christopher Tolkien's wife, sculptress Faith Tolkien, has made of him is about to be unveiled.

26 November 1956 The second part of the radio adaptation of *The Two Towers* and *The Return of the King*, 'Rohan and Isengard', is broadcast in the BBC Third Programme at 10.40 p.m.

28 November 1956 Rayner Unwin writes to Tolkien. He hopes that four complimentary copies of the Dutch *Fellowship of the Ring* are on their way to Tolkien and one to Prof. Harting. He entirely agrees with Tolkien's comments on translation and on the broadcasts, but thinks that the latter have introduced *The Lord of the Rings* to a wider audience.

29 November 1956 'Rohan and Isengard' is rebroadcast in the BBC Third Programme at 6.45 p.m.

2 December 1956 The third part of the BBC radio adaptation of *The Two Towers* and *The Return of the King*, 'Into the Dark', is broadcast in the Third Programme at 8.45 p.m.

7 December 1956 Tolkien attends an English Faculty Board meeting. The report of the committee on the syllabus set up on 21 January 1955 is received, and it is agreed to refer it to the Faculty for observations. Some of its suggestions are aimed at lightening linguistic study imposed on those taking Course III, which is mainly Literature. Course I should remain primarily Linguistic, but the Board members think that Course II, which is primarily medieval, should be planned to make it possible for candidates with literary interests to study Old and Middle English without neglecting everything after 1400 or 1550. F.P. Wilson reports on behalf of the Standing Committee on Monographs that Miss Cecily Clark's edition of the *Peterborough Chronicle* is at the press, and should be published in 1957. A report of the meeting of the O'Donnell Trustees on 18 October is also presented. – 'Into the Dark' is rebroadcast in the BBC Third Programme at 7.20 p.m.

8 December 1956 Michaelmas Full Term ends.

9 December 1956 The fourth part of the BBC radio adaptation of *The Two Towers* and *The Return of the King*, 'The Siege of Gondor', is broadcast in the Third Programme.

10 December 1956 Tolkien attends a Merton College meeting. – Alina Dadlez writes to Tolkien. She is sending him the one complimentary copy of the Dutch *Fellowship of the Ring* she has received, and has reminded Het Spectrum that more copies are due.

12 November 1956 'The Siege of Gondor' is rebroadcast in the BBC Third Programme at 6.15 p.m.

14 December 1956 Tolkien makes a speech at the dedication of the new library in Deddington. He says that few things are more heartening in the present shadow under which people live than the growth of the public library system, and declares: 'Books are besieged by a great many embattled enemies, but from them comes the food of the mind. It is not good for the stomach to be without food for a long period and it is very much worse for the mind' ('Deddington Court Now Library', *Oxford Mail*, 15 December 1956, p. 1). Christine Hole, an authority on English folklore and witchcraft, thanks Tolkien for his speech, but chides him for making the public wait so long between volumes of *The Lord of the Rings*. Tolkien explains that because he has no secretary he had to type his own manuscripts and correct his own proofs, and is thus forgiven.

15 December 1956 Tolkien writes to Amy Ronald, discussing Frodo's attitude towards weapons. As a Roman Catholic Tolkien does 'not expect "history" to be anything but a "long defeat" – though it contains (and in a legend may contain more clearly and movingly) some samples or glimpses of final victory' (*Letters*, p. 255).

16 December 1956 Tolkien writes to Rayner Unwin. His first impressions of the Dutch *Fellowship of the Ring* are very favourable, 'except for the jacket, which among other sins got my initials wrong!' (Tolkien-George Allen & Unwin archive, HarperCollins). – The fifth part of the radio adaptation of *The Two Towers* and *The Return of the King*, 'Minas Tirith and Mount Doom', is broadcast in the BBC Third Programme at 5.25 p.m.

?17 and 18 December 1956 Tolkien is in Cambridge, possibly working on the *Ancrene Wisse* or attending an Ad Eundem dinner.

18 December 1956 'Minas Tirith and Mount Doom' is broadcast in the BBC Third Programme at 7.10 p.m.

19 December 1956 Tolkien writes to Miss Stanley-Smith, in reply to her thanks for his attendance at the dedication of Deddington Library. Until her letter arrived he had been unhappy with his performance on the occasion.

23 December 1956 The sixth part of the BBC radio adaptation of *The Two Towers* and *The Return of the King*, 'Many Partings', is broadcast in the Third Programme.

24 December 1956 Tolkien learns of the marriage of C.S. Lewis to Mrs Joy Gresham, a patient in the Churchill Hospital, Oxford, from a notice in *The Times*.

27 December 1956 'Many Partings' is rebroadcast in the BBC Third Programme at 6.00 p.m.

28 December 1956 Alina Dadlez sends Tolkien three more copies of the Dutch *Fellowship of the Ring*.

?Late December 1956 or early January 1957 William Ready, Director of Libraries at Marquette University, Milwaukee, Wisconsin, who is building the University's research collections, asks Bertram Rota, a distinguished London bookseller, to approach Tolkien to see if he is willing to sell the manuscripts of *The Hobbit* and *The Lord of the Rings*. Ready admires the latter (see *Libraries and archives). – Rota writes to Tolkien in this regard, and Tolkien replies before 10 January.

1957

10 January 1957 Bertram Rota writes to William Ready. Tolkien seems willing to consider the sale of his manuscripts, but has asked what amount Marquette University is willing to offer. Tolkien has sent a rough list of *The Hobbit* and *The Lord of the Rings* material which he might sell, to enable Marquette to judge what might be a suitable price. Rota thinks it necessary to offer Tolkien a substantial sum, and suggests a minimum of £1,000 with the final sum to be decided when Rota has examined the documents on offer. – On the same day, Rota writes to inform Tolkien that he has sent the information to Ready.

14 January 1957 At a special meeting in Tolkien's absence, the English Faculty Board considers a petition signed by twenty-seven members of the Faculty expressing their view that the Merton Professorship of English Literature should be offered to C.S. Lewis. (Tolkien is not one of the signatories, but his son Christopher is.) The Board agrees that since the intention of the petition has been fulfilled – presumably to show the Faculty's appreciation of Lewis – there is no need for further action.

15 January 1957 Tolkien is interviewed in London by Ruth Harshaw for a broadcast in the United States (on 9 March 1957). In 'When Carnival of Books Went to Europe', *American Library Association Bulletin* 51 (February 1957), she will write that she had difficulty in understanding Tolkien, and said in desperation: 'I do appreciate your coming up from Oxford so that I might record you, Professor Tolkien, but I can't understand a word you say.' Amused, he replied: 'A friend of mine tells me that I talk in shorthand and then smudge it.' – Rayner Unwin forwards to Tolkien a letter from Caroline Everett, a student at Florida State University, who asks various questions as research for her M.A. thesis on Tolkien.

17 January 1957 Tolkien attends a Merton College meeting.

18 January 1957 Bertram Rota receives a letter from William Ready, suggesting that he tell Tolkien that Marquette University expects to be able to offer not less than £1,000, and perhaps as much as £1,250 for his papers, and that a definite offer will be made after Rota has inspected them. Rota immediately writes to inform Tolkien of this offer, and says that he is willing to come to Oxford to inspect the papers.

20 January 1957 Hilary Full term begins. Tolkien's scheduled lectures for this term are: *Sir Gawain and the Green Knight* (continued) on Wednesdays and Fridays at 11.00 a.m. in the Examination Schools, beginning 23 January; and the Old English *Exodus* on Thursdays at 11.00 a.m. in the Examination Schools, beginning 24 January. Tolkien also prepares for students attending the lectures a modern English translation and an edition of the Old English *Exodus*, incorporating 'the emendations and punctuations favoured by me in the lectures to the class' – though 'I have not had time to complete revision of text & translation' (Tolkien Papers, Bodleian Library, Oxford). There are probably only a few copies of these, as he asks that they be circulated as quickly as possible and returned to him. J.S. Ryan, who attends these lectures, will record that there were only about eight or ten students in the course, but several of Tolkien's academic colleagues also were present, including Alistair Campbell, J.A.W. Bennett, Eric Dobson, Pamela Gradon, Elaine Griffiths, Douglas Gray, and Bruce Mitchell. – Tolkien continues to supervise B.Litt. students W.O. Evans, L. Glanville, and F.E. Richardson, and D.Phil. students R.W. Burchfield, A.D. Horgan, and A. Kurvinen. In C.L. Wrenn's absence, Tolkien is now also supervising the B.Litt. thesis of J. Ross of St Anne's College, a critical edition of the Middle English poem 'On God Ureisun of Ure Lefdi' from MS Cotton Nero A. XIV, with a study of the earliest English Marian poetry.

25 January 1957 Tolkien attends an English Faculty Board meeting. Dorothy Whitelock has resigned her University Lecturership in English Language with effect from 30 September 1957, and the General Board has given the Faculty Board leave to fill the post. The matter is referred to a committee consisting of the Tolkien, J.N. Bryson, Eric Dobson, and the chairman (F.P. Wilson), with the power to advertise the post if they see fit, and to make recommendations to the board for an appointment. Tolkien's student D.C. Levinson is granted a B.Litt. certificate.

30 January 1957 Rayner Unwin forwards to Tolkien letters from Het Spectrum (apparently from or on behalf of Max Schuchart, the Dutch translator), and from J.W. Pownall-Gray of the Savile Club, expressing his enthusiasm for *The Lord of the Rings*. Rayner hopes to be in Oxford in a week or two, and would like to visit Tolkien and learn how *The Silmarillion* is progressing. – Father Alexander Jones of St Joseph's College, Upholland, writes to Tolkien. He asks if Tolkien would be willing to take part in an English translation of *La Bible de Jérusalem*, considered the best Catholic edition of the Bible. Jones has read *The Lord of the Rings* and longs to have an English Bible translation from its author. He offers Tolkien a wide choice of books. He hopes that Tolkien might agree to undertake a considerable amount, but will be grateful even if he only takes on a small book of the Bible, such as Jonah (see *The Jerusalem Bible*).

February or early March 1957 The English Faculty Board meets to discuss the report of the committee on the reform of the syllabus.

Early February 1957 Tolkien replies to Father Alexander Jones. He has many commitments, and is no French scholar, but is willing to submit a sample for the *Jerusalem Bible* project.

3 February 1957 Tolkien writes to Rayner Unwin. He returns the letter from Het Spectrum and encloses a reply to be forwarded. He has answered queries from Max Schuchart concerning *The Two Towers*, and commented on points arising from Tolkien's reading of the Dutch *Fellowship* which, he regrets, has not proceeded very far. 'I hope I have been sufficiently polite. After all, they cannot expect me not to notice actual errors – and a close examination would show these to be fairly numerous; whereas only a thorough knowledge of Dutch (which I do *not* possess) would enable me to appreciate any positive virtues.' Prof. Harting, however, finds it better than he expected, on the whole readable though he has noticed many minor slips and does not think much of the verse. Tolkien says that he is 'having a rather troublesome time, and with one professor [Wrenn] in America and another [Wilson] retiring (involving me in all the difficulties of an election) I have more to do than can be managed. I have not got near *The Silmarillion* for months. It cannot be "interleaved": it needs sole and concentrated attention' (Tolkien-George Allen & Unwin archive, HarperCollins). He would like to see Rayner in Oxford, but if possible he should avoid Wednesdays, Thursdays, and Fridays.

4 February 1957 Tolkien writes directly to Max Schuchart, concerning additional points in the Dutch translation of *The Fellowship of the Ring*.

7 February 1957 Tolkien takes part in the election of the Merton Professor of English Literature. Nevill Coghill is elected to the chair, with effect from 1 October 1957. – Rayner Unwin writes to Tolkien. He has forwarded Tolkien's letter to Het Spectrum. He hopes to visit Oxford by car on Tuesday, 12 February, and asks to call on Tolkien at 9.30 or 10.00 a.m. on his way into the city (Sandfield Road leads off of the main road into Oxford from the east).

9 February 1957 Tolkien writes to Rayner Unwin. He will be at home on 12 February. About 10.00 a.m. would be fine for Rayner to visit.

12 February 1957 In the morning, Rayner Unwin visits Tolkien in Oxford. On 1 March Tolkien will apologize for being 'tired, bothered, and confused' on the occasion. 'I was having, and am having, a very bothersome (and extremely laborious) term; but I seem to be regaining control.' They discuss, or attempt to discuss, 'The Silmarillion', but Tolkien forgets that 'the main matter' is 'all neatly in a case where it had been packed for safe custody when I was away' (Tolkien-George Allen & Unwin archive, HarperCollins). They also discuss the sale of his manuscripts to Marquette.

14 February 1957 Father Alexander Jones replies to Tolkien. He primarily wants someone able to write good English, and only secondarily with a knowledge of French.

***c.* 14–19 February 1957** Tolkien makes and sends to Father Alexander Jones a sample translation from *Isaiah* (1:1–31).

20 February 1957 Father Alexander Jones writes to Tolkien. The sample translation is exactly what is wanted. He is sending Tolkien the Book of Jonah. He is having difficulty in writing guidelines for translators, and asks for Tolkien's views. – On the same day Jones writes another letter, commenting in detail on Tolkien's Isaiah text.

***c.* 20 February–6 March 1957** Tolkien translates Jonah for *The Jerusalem Bible* and sends the result to Father Alexander Jones, with comments on translating.

23 February 1957 In the evening, Tolkien attends a dinner of The Society hosted by G.F. Hudson at St Anthony's College, Oxford. Nine members are present. Hudson reads a paper about William Jones, orientalist and jurist.

Early March 1957 Tolkien is approached to take part in an unscripted two-way transatlantic discussion with John McCaffery in New York, in the series *WNYC Book Festival*.

1 March 1957 Tolkien writes to Rayner Unwin, enclosing letters from Bertram Rota for Stanley Unwin to review. He is inclined to negotiate, but has to take into account how a sale might affect his income tax. He hopes to return to 'The Silmarillion' 'soon, if the philological harpies will leave me alone. But I have to face almost a "Court Martial" by the other directors of the Early English Text Society at their meeting on 19 March' (Tolkien-George Allen & Unwin archive, HarperCollins). – Tolkien writes to Viscount Monckton, a fellow member of the Ad Eundem dining club. As secretary of the Oxford branch, Tolkien apologizes for delaying a dinner and then giving short notice. He tries to make amends by giving early notice of likely dates for the next two dinners. He asks Monkton to suggest other dates if these are not suitable for him.

4 March 1957 Viscount Monckton replies to Tolkien. At the moment all except one of the dates Tolkien mentioned are possible.

5 March 1957 Rayner Unwin writes to Tolkien. He will show the Rota correspondence to his father when Stanley Unwin returns from abroad later in the week.

7 March 1957 Father Alexander Jones writes to Tolkien, thanking him for his translation and comments. He agrees with what Tolkien has said about archaisms.

***c.* 8–11 March 1957** Tolkien writes to Father Alexander Jones, regretfully supporting the use of 'you' in *The Jerusalem Bible* rather than 'thou'.

12 March 1957 Tolkien returns a signed contract to the BBC, who are arranging the interview with John McCaffery. He has no objection to the procedure mentioned in case of a defective telephone recording, which is to be made in London. *See note.* – Father Alexander Jones writes to Tolkien, returning his Jonah translation with comments. He asks Tolkien to send it back, corrected, at his leisure. He sends Tolkien *Joshua* to work on when he has time. – Rayner Unwin writes to Tolkien, returning the Rota correspondence. Stanley Unwin thinks the offer very generous. Tolkien should probably accept if his income tax advisors think that it will be treated as a capital gain and not income. But Rayner asks exactly how much, and what, Tolkien is offering: 'Is it just the typescript of *The Lord of the Rings* with hand-writing insertions and corrections? Or is a large portion in your own hand?' (No answer by Tolkien to these questions is preserved in the Allen & Unwin archive. In his *George Allen & Unwin: A Remembrancer* Rayner Unwin wrote that his father assumed that what Tolkien was selling would be a straightforward typescript with manuscript corrections.)

15 March 1957 Tolkien attends an English Faculty Board meeting. The report on the revision of the syllabus is received, and the matter referred to the members of the Board on the syllabus committee. The Applications Committee has appointed Tolkien supervisor of recognized student H.J.O. Voitl, Dr. Phil. Freiburg, working on 'history of the development of the English language with special reference to the 15th, 16th & 17th centuries'. He has also been appointed examiner, with Ursula Mary Brown, of the B.Litt. thesis of J.F.

Kiteley of Wadham College on 'Characterisation in *Sir Gawain and the Green Knight*'. – Tolkien completes and returns a form for his election to the Royal Society of Literature. – Bertram Rota writes to William Ready, reporting that Tolkien is willing to negotiate the sale of manuscripts as long as the price paid would not be regarded by Inland Revenue as 'income'.

16 March 1957 Hilary Full Term ends. – Officers of the Ad Eundem dining club, including Tolkien, possibly meet to discuss dates for future dinners.

18 March 1957 Tolkien attends a Merton College meeting.

19 March 1957 Because of a sore throat, Tolkien sends his apologies for not attending an Early English Text Society Council meeting. Norman Davis is chosen as the new Director of EETS. The Council approves A.H. Smith's proposal that the Society needs a constitution; R.W. Burchfield is asked to draw up a rough plan and circulate it to members. The Council members discuss proposed publications, including Mrs M.Y. Offord's edition of *The Parlement of the Thre Ages* (the subject of the B.Litt. thesis she produced under Tolkien's supervision). Some members feel that this is not a real advance on the Gollancz edition, but it is agreed that J.A.W. Bennett will give a second opinion. (It will be published by the Society in 1959.) Burchfield's offer of an edition of the *Ormulum* is accepted.

21 March 1957 Tolkien writes to Katharine Farrer. 'I believe you have been much concerned with the troubles of poor Jack [C.S.] Lewis. Of these I know little beyond the cautious hints of the discreet [R.E.] Havard. When I see Jack he naturally takes refuge in "literary" talk (for which no domestic griefs and anxieties have yet dimmed his enthusiasm)' (*Letters*, p. 256). – C.S. Lewis and Joy Gresham, who is thought to be near death from cancer, are married again in a Church of England ceremony at her hospital bedside.

***c.* 23–26 March 1957** Tolkien has a brief holiday away in Canterbury, to try to recover his health.

26 March 1957 Robert Burchfield writes to tell Tolkien what was decided at the Early English Text Society Council meeting on the 19th. He asks if Tolkien has had time to examine a specimen homily for P. Clemoes' edition of *Ælfric: Catholic Homilies*, and if so, if he would return it with comments. Burchfield wants Clemoes to get on with the edition, but if there is any chance of him having the benefit of Tolkien's comments he will wait a few weeks before contacting him. (Clemoes, a perfectionist, continued to revise his work until his death. His text of the first series of Ælfric's homilies was completed by Malcolm R. Godden and published at last in 1997–2000.) He asks when Tolkien will be able to let the EETS have his edition of *Ancrene Wisse*; the Council and all Middle English scholars are longing for it to appear. He repeats an offer to verify any points of Tolkien's transcription against the manuscript, if Tolkien is not able to do this himself in Cambridge. Neil Ker is ready to write an introduction.

?End of March 1957 Tolkien begins to draft a reply to Robert Burchfield's letter of 26 March, but never completes it. He is beginning to feel my age, and last term seemed terribly laborious. What with [Peter Goolden's] *Apollonius* left on me by [C.L.] Wrenn and a third lecture [presumably on *Exodus*] requiring much more work than I expected and so on, I arrived at the end rather staggered. I suppose too that the professorial and lecturership elections (the latter still unconcluded), with their dreadful mixture of personal embarrassment and public responsibility, had also weighed on one. Anyway I felt ill all last week, and had, with me a frequent sign of exhaustion, a frightful throat, and could not speak for two or three days.

Having spent four days in Canterbury with fine weather, he now feels recovered, and will make *Ancrene Wisse* 'a first charge on what time is left' before the beginning of Trinity Term. He has spent several weeks, over the years, with the *Ancrene Wisse* manuscript in Cambridge. 'But work put aside, as you know, has practically to be done over again. And notes, clear at the time, do not seem so when taken up again. Also I am not at home in such work. However, I can I think present a fair text (by transferring all my notes and corrections from my working copy to the spare typescript made from photostats) by the end of this vacation' (Tolkien Papers, Bodleian Library, Oxford). He would like to check some points in the manuscript again, but if that should mean further delay in completing the edition, he will accept Burchfield's offer of assistance. He has searched everywhere, but cannot find Clemoes' specimen.

29 March 1957 Tolkien writes to Max Schuchart, expressing his preference for not translating names in *The Lord of the Rings*, commenting on some of Schuchart's proposed translations, and suggesting which parts of the Appendices might be omitted from the Dutch *Return of the King*.

9 April 1957 Tolkien replies to a letter from a Mr Hayward, who has expressed his pleasure in *The Lord of the Rings*.

23 April 1957 Tolkien returns to the Royal Society of Literature a signed undertaking to observe the Society's regulations.

24 April 1957 Tolkien writes to his grandson, Michael George, with the news that he has just been elected a Fellow of the Royal Society of Literature. He has had to swot at Dutch to read the translation of *The Lord of the Rings*, and is at present is immersed in Hebrew, as he hopes when he retires to be part of a new Bible-translation team (for *The Jerusalem Bible*), and has passed the test with a version of the Book of Jonah. This morning he hears on the radio of the death of Roy Campbell.

25 April 1957 Tolkien attends a Merton College meeting.

28 April 1957 Trinity Full Term begins. Tolkien's scheduled lectures for this term are: the Old English *Exodus* on Wednesdays at 11.00 a.m. in the Examination Schools, beginning 1 May; and The Language of Chaucer on Fridays at 11.00 a.m. in the Examination Schools, beginning 3 May. He continues to supervise B.Litt. students W.O. Evans, L. Glanville, F.E. Richardson, and J. Ross, and D.Phil. students A.D. Horgan and A. Kurvinen. – Tolkien and Edith lunch with George and Moira Sayer.

2 May 1957 Rayner Unwin writes to Tolkien, sending him accounts and a cheque for royalties and profits for 1956. Tolkien's books are selling steadily, not only in Britain but around the world.

3 May 1957 Tolkien attends an English Faculty Board meeting. F.P. Wilson points out that since his retirement will be effective from 30 September 1957, the Board will be without a chairman until the first meeting of Michaelmas Term. It is agreed to ask Professor Tolkien to act as chairman during this interval. Eric Dobson is elected to replace Tolkien on the nominating committee for the Honour School, Group B6, and Preliminary Examinations. The report of the committee on the University Lecturership in English Language (which includes Tolkien), recommending the appointment of M.E. Griffiths to the Lecturership, is received, and her appointment for five years from 1 October 1957 agreed subject to the approval of the General Board and Congregation.

5 May 1957 Bertram Rota visits Tolkien, first in his room at Merton College and then, after lunch in Oxford, for the afternoon at Sandfield Road. He inspects the manuscripts, etc. of *The Hobbit* and *The Lord of the Rings* that Tolkien is willing to sell and, since there is more to the papers than expected, makes an offer of £1,250 on behalf of Marquette University. Tolkien accepts. He tells Rota that he has consulted his publishers, the Society of Authors, his solicitor, and his accountant about the offer. He does not want the payment made at once, and would like part of it to be held in U.S. dollars, as he is considering accepting the offer of an expenses-paid trip to New York to give lectures. Rota urges him to accept, and to visit Marquette University while in America. Tolkien does not want to hand over the papers immediately, but would like to keep them for a short time while he searches for additional material which he will include without extra charge. He shows Rota two typescripts of *Farmer Giles of Ham*, and his unpublished illustrated story *Mr. Bliss*, which he has unearthed while looking for the other material. He indicates that he is willing to sell these also. – That evening Rota writes to William Ready, reporting the day's events. He thinks that he will be able to collect the papers from Tolkien in June. (Tolkien includes illustrations and dust-jacket designs in the material to be sold, but in the event, almost of all these will be retained by him.) Rota suggests that Ready offer Tolkien another £250 for *Farmer Giles of Ham* and *Mr. Bliss*, making £1,500 in all.

7 May 1957 Tolkien attends the Perne Feast in Cambridge, and cancels Oxford lectures so that he can stay a couple of nights and spend some time with the *Ancrene Wisse* manuscript at Corpus Christi College.

c. 9–13 May 1957 William Ready replies to Bertram Rota, agreeing to a revised offer. He also evidently expresses an interest in purchasing Tolkien's library if he does not have space for it when he has to vacate his Merton College room on retirement in 1959. – Rota presents the £1,500 offer to Tolkien, who accepts it.

9 May 1957 Tolkien writes to Rayner Unwin. If he had had any idea of the amount of his literary earnings, he would seriously have thought of retiring that July instead of accepting an extra two years' tenure and paying heavy taxation on his total income. His professional duties allow him little time for work on 'The Silmarillion'; he has not touched it since last autumn. He has not been well, and arthritis makes sitting for a long time painful.

10 May 1957 The members of the Committee for Comparative Philology meet at 5.00 p.m. in the Delegates Room of the Clarendon Building.

13 May 1957 Bertram Rota writes to William Ready, informing him that Tolkien has accepted the revised offer, and has also found the original manuscript of *Farmer Giles of Ham* which he will include at no additional cost. Although Tolkien's library is not very large, it is probably first-rate in his field, containing many works difficult to obtain. Rota will try to prepare the way for its purchase later.

21 May 1957 Robert Burchfield, Early English Text Society, writes to Tolkien, inviting him to an event, but the invitation is misplaced and Tolkien does not reply.

22 May 1957 Tolkien attends a Merton College meeting. – Rayner Unwin sends Tolkien photographs of illustrations of characters from *The Lord of the Rings* by J.W. Pownall-Gray.

28 May 1957 Rayner Unwin writes to Tolkien, forwarding a letter from Voorhoeve & Dietrich Boekhandel, a bookseller in Rotterdam, inviting Tolkien to visit Holland. Rayner suggests that if Tolkien does not want to go, he might consider making a tape recording of himself reading a passage or two from his books, with an introductory word of greeting to Dutch readers. – Robert Burchfield writes to Mabel Day, discussing the four *Ancrene Riwle* projects that have not been completed for the Early English Text Society (Tolkien is not the only culprit). He thinks that at the next EETS Council meeting they should fix a deadline for the delivery of the typescripts, and if they do not arrive, allocate the tasks to new editors.

?Early June 1957 Tolkien writes a letter of reference for a former student, F.E. Richardson, whose B.Litt. has just been granted and who has applied for an Assistant Lecturership at Trinity College, Dublin.

7 June 1957 Tolkien hands over to Bertram Rota material for *The Hobbit*, *Farmer Giles of Ham*, and *Mr. Bliss*, but not for *The Lord of the Rings*, which he feels still needs to be put in order.

9 June 1957 Tolkien writes to William Ready. He apologizes for not replying to a letter from him, or to an invitation from the director of the Marquette Department of English to visit the University, pleading 'overwork, difficult domestic and academic circumstances, and the necessity of coping (or trying to cope) with a now very large mail, as well as heavy professional work and duties, without *any secretary!*' (quoted in Ready, *The Tolkien Relation* (1968), pp. 59–60). – Tolkien writes to the director of the Marquette Department of English, accepting his invitation, but Tolkien will not be able to get a leave of absence from Oxford until spring 1958.

13 June 1957 English Final Honour Examinations begin.

16 June 1957 Tolkien writes to Rayner Unwin. Term has been wearying, and he has arthritis in his right hand. He is not against an expenses-paid trip to Holland if the dates fit. He thinks that a visit might be less trouble than preparing tape recordings. 'So far as I can see, I am likely to be in Oxford, except for very short absences, for the rest of the year. My wife and I were actually supposed to be flying to U.S.A. and back between August 11 and 26; but as domestic affairs seem to have made that impossible for my wife, I expect the whole thing will fall through. I should be relieved, really, as if I do not get on with the *Silmarillion* this Long Vac. it will still further postpone it' (Tolkien-George Allen & Unwin archive, HarperCollins). He has mixed feelings about Pawnall-Gray's illustrations, and suggests that Rayner make a polite reply on his behalf.

17 June 1957 Rayner Unwin writes to Tolkien. Allen & Unwin have received an inquiry from Al Brodax about making an animated motion picture of *The Lord of the Rings*. Rayner thinks that such a film would be 'almost inevitably tasteless and a travesty of the book' but there could be 'big money' involved (Tolkien-George Allen & Unwin archive, HarperCollins). – In a second letter the same day Rayner Unwin says that he will make suitable replies to Voorhoeve en Dietrich and Pawnall-Gray. – William Ready sends Tolkien a short story he has written.

19 June 1957 Tolkien writes to Rayner Unwin. He is happy to leave the matter of the film to Allen & Unwin, since they are also much involved. 'Personally, I should welcome the idea of an animated motion picture, with all the risk of vulgarization; and that quite apart from the glint of money, though on the brink of retirement that is not an unpleasant possibility. I think I should find vulgarization less painful than the sillification achieved by the B.B.C.' (*Letters*, p. 257). He would like to learn more about the project. He has plans to fly to New York on 11 August, though that is not certain because of Edith's health: she is not well enough to accompany him, and he cannot leave her alone. But if he does go to New York, he might be able to meet Brodax. He expects to go to the United States early in 1958, if he can get leave from Oxford, as Marquette University has offered to pay his travel expenses and $600 per lecture.

20 June 1957 In reply to a telephone call from Robert Burchfield, who has had no replies to his letters of 24 March and 21 May on Early English Text Society business, Tolkien writes to apologize for his acute 'state of disorganization and muddle'. His wife remembers perfectly Burchfield's invitation of 21 May, and suggests that she handle his calendar from now on. Pain from arthritis in his right hand makes it difficult to hold a pen; 'typing (using only one finger on the right) seems to be possible without pain, as long as it does not go on too long. A hindrance and I have no time at the moment for any treatment.' He has begun a letter to Burchfield regarding the *Ancrene Wisse*: 'What I have to do should not now take very long, if only I concentrate on it. I shall be overjoyed to have the help of [Neil] Ker, or rather to hand over the matter, which he will do so much better than I to him' (Early English Text Society archive). – Father Alexander Jones writes to Tolkien, asking to visit so that he can ask Tolkien something about *The Jerusalem Bible* before he meets with the French editor and the publisher.

c. **21–24 June 1957** Tolkien replies to Father Alexander Jones.

21 June 1957 Tolkien attends an English Faculty Board meeting. The Applications Committee has appointed him director of studies of recognized student Y. Inokuma of the University of the Sacred Heart, on 'The Characteristics of English Children's Literature'.

22 June 1957 Trinity Full Term ends. – Tolkien replies to a letter from a Mr Schiller, who has sent him a paper he has written on *Sir Gawain and the Green Knight*. Tolkien does not have time to discuss it properly, but makes some remarks about metrical practice and rules.

22–24 June 1957 Tolkien stays in Merton College; presumably Edith is out of town.

24 or 25 June 1957 Tolkien replies to Caroline Everett's letter. He is sorry to find himself the subject of a thesis, and does not feel inclined to provide biographical detail, as he doubts its relevance to criticism; but he does so anyway. *See note.*

25 June 1957 Tolkien attends a Merton College meeting. – He replies to a letter from a Major Bowen, giving some details about Sauron and the Ainur. – Father Alexander Jones writes to Tolkien. He asks if 2 July would be suitable for a visit.

26 June 1957 Encaenia. – Tolkien writes to Father Alexander Jones. He will be free on 2 July, and suggests what they might do.

27 June 1957 Father Alexander Jones writes to Tolkien. He is delighted at the suggested programme, if it will not be too much trouble for Tolkien and his wife.

29 June 1957 In the evening, Tolkien attends a dinner of The Society hosted by Nevill Coghill in a restaurant, followed by discussion in his rooms at Exeter College. Five members are present.

2 July 1957 Father Alexander Jones visits Tolkien in Oxford.

3 July 1957 Father Alexander Jones writes to thank Tolkien for his entertainment and sums up their discussions. Tolkien has evidently told him that he will not be able to do much for *The Jerusalem Bible* until his retirement in 1959, but during the next two years might be able to do Jonah, Joshua, and Judges, and perhaps even 1 and 2 Samuel. Even after his retirement he does not want to take on any official editorship, but would be willing to comment occasionally on texts (apparently he was asked to become an editor for the *Bible*). He thinks that the literary editorship of the *Bible*, as well as the scriptural, should be left to Jones.

4 July 1957 Alina Dadlez, George Allen & Unwin, writes to ask what Tolkien would like her to do with complimentary copies of the Dutch *Two Towers* she has just received.

9 July 1957 Tolkien writes to Viscount Monckton, who has written to say he cannot attend the Ad Eundem dinner on 13 July. Tolkien says that the most likely date of the next dinner is 14 December, and reminds Monckton about his subscription.

13 July 1957 Tolkien presumably attends the Ad Eundem dinner in Oxford.

18 July 1957 Jerome W. Archer, director of the Department of English at Marquette, sends an official invitation to Tolkien and his wife to visit the University in spring 1958.

26 July 1957 Tolkien writes to the Secretary of Faculties of the University of Oxford, requesting a leave of absence in Hilary and Trinity Terms 1958. He wishes to accept a number of invitations to lecture and visit scholars abroad, in particular in Sweden and the United States, in early 1958. – Tolkien writes to Alina Dadlez, apologizing for his delay in replying. He has been having difficulties with Max Schuchart's translation of *The Return of the King*, 'especially the Appendices, one of which I have had to re-write' (Tolkien-George Allen & Unwin archive, HarperCollins). He would like one copy of the Dutch *Two Towers* to be sent to Prof. Harting, another to Alistair Campbeil, and the rest to himself.

30 July 1957 Rayner Unwin writes to Tolkien. The Dutch copies have been dealt with as Tolkien requested. Allen & Unwin are planning to issue the three volumes of *The Lord of the Rings* as a boxed that autumn as a sales device.

5 August 1957 Tolkien writes two letters to Jerome W. Archer at Marquette University. The first is a formal acceptance of, and gratitude for, the invitation to visit Marquette in spring 1958 and the proposed financial arrangements. He will do his best to arrange matters. In the second letter he explains that his real doubt as to whether he will be able to visit is personal:

> Continuous over-work since 1951 has begun to tell on me; and I am feeling rather exhausted. I have recently been ill; and I am obliged to cancel plans for travel this vacation. . . .
>
> Leave of absence will, however, I hope, enable me to clear off before next spring some of the things that are now harassing me; and I am now making preliminary plans for the use of the time, and am trying to fix some dates. [Special Collections and University Archives, John P. Raynor, S.J., Library, Marquette University]

He asks how long Marquette University would like him to stay. Assuming that he does get leave of absence, such a visit would have to be fitted into the period 7 April to 31 May. He does not think that he will find time or material for more than one lecture of a serious kind, suitable for publication, but does not object to lecturing several times.

6 August 1957 Tolkien writes to William Ready of his hope to visit Marquette, and comments on a short story Ready has sent him. He hopes to finish organizing the *Lord of the Rings* papers soon.

27 August 1957 C.L. Wrenn sends to D.M. Davin at Oxford University Press Peter Goolden's edition of *The Old English Apollonius of Tyre*, now complete and ready for press. He complains that Tolkien had the manuscript for a year and did nothing with it, and that the matter should have been dealt with at once, as a German work with the same text was published in 1956. 'It does seem hard that Goolden, the Editor, should suffer all this delay merely because

T[olkien] is busy with other (less academic) matters' (Oxford University Press archives).

29 August 1957 Rayner Unwin writes to inform Tolkien that he has won the International Fantasy Award. An invitation is being sent for him to attend a luncheon on 10 September at which the award will be presented. He explains that the award trophy is in the form of a rocket incorporating a Ronson lighter.

31 August 1957 Tolkien writes to Rayner Unwin from The Red House, Canterbury. If an invitation has been sent, it is probably waiting for him at Merton College. He does not 'want a Ronson lighter, still less a rocket; but I think it would be a mistake to be stuffy. . . .' He comments that he did not go to New York after all, because he discovered that the group that had invited him were 'reincarnation cranks', and as a result did 'a little work' during August. 'Canterbury is made crowded & uncomfortable by Cricket' (Tolkien-George Allen & Unwin archive, HarperCollins).

2 September 1957 Tolkien returns to Oxford from Canterbury. – Sir William Craigie dies.

4 September 1957 Forrest J. Ackerman, acting for a company interested in making an animated film of *The Lord of the Rings*, visits Tolkien in Oxford, accompanied by several other men and women. They miss the train and take a taxi all the way from London. Since they have to catch the 5.35 p.m. train back to London, there is no time to discuss financial matters. Tolkien is shown specimen drawings by Ron Cobb, which he thinks admirable, as well as some colour photographs, and is given a copy of the proposed story-line. – Tolkien writes to Rayner Unwin, describing the visit of Ackerman and company and promising to send Rayner the story-line when Tolkien has had time to consider it. He is keeping 10 September free but has still not received an invitation to the International Fantasy Award luncheon. – Philip Unwin phones Tolkien. Having made enquiries, he has learned that there has been a delay in sending the invitations to the luncheon, but Tolkien's is being posted that day. Unwin confirms that the lunch will be held on 10 September at the Criterion Restaurant, Piccadilly Circus, London.

5 September 1957 Rayner Unwin writes to Tolkien. He is surprised and delighted that Forrest J. Ackerman made such a good impression. Stanley Unwin will also be present at the lunch on 10 September.

6 September 1957 Tolkien writes a letter to Forrest J. Ackerman, to be sent when he receives Ackerman's address. It will never be sent, but Tolkien will incorporate part of its contents in a letter written the following year.

7 September 1957 Tolkien writes to Rayner Unwin. He has posted the story-line to him this day. It is

on a much lower level of art and perceptiveness than the pictorial material. It is in some points bad, and unacceptable, but is not irremediable, if the author of it (a certain Morton Grady Zimmerman) is open to criticism and direction. The ending is badly muffed ... it reads like a production of haste, after a single reading, & without further reference to text. . . . Mr Ackerman's line of talk was that a big object to the group was "pleasing the author". I have indicated to him that will not be easy.

Quite crudely: displeasing the author requires a cash equivalent! Only the prospect of a very large financial profit would make me swallow some of the things in this script! . . .

An *abridgement* by selection with some good picture-work would be pleasant, & perhaps worth a good deal in publicity; but the present script is rather a *compression* with resultant over-crowding and confusion, blurring of climaxes, and general degradation: a pull-back towards more conventional 'fairy-stories'. People gallop about on Eagles at the least provocation; Lórien becomes a fairy-castle with 'delicate minarets', and all that sort of thing.

But I am quite prepared to play ball, if they are open to advice – and if you decide that the thing is genuine, and worthwhile. [Tolkien-George Allen & Unwin archive, HarperCollins; partly printed in *Letters*, p. 261]

10 September 1957 Tolkien attends the luncheon at the Criterion Restaurant, London, which is the climax of the Fifteenth World Science Fiction Convention. *The Death of Grass* by John Christopher is the runner-up to Tolkien for the International Fantasy Award; tied for third place are William Golding's *The Lord of the Flies* and Frank Herbert's *Dragon in the Sea*. The chairman at the lunch is Arthur C. Clarke, and the speakers include Stanley Unwin and Clemence Dane. In his acceptance speech Tolkien says: 'I have never stopped a rocket before, they had better not know about this in Oxford' ('Fantasy Award to Professor Tolkien', *The Bookseller*, 14 September 1957, p. 1074). On 11 September it will be said in the *Oxford Mail* that Tolkien 'sees the funny side of a Professor of English, "who should be doing learned works", winning such an award. "But of course my answer is that it [*The Lord of the Rings*] *is* learned work"' ('Fantasy of the Year', p. 4, italics added). – Tolkien deposits the award trophy in the window of Allen & Unwin's premises at 40 Museum Street. Tolkien and Stanley Unwin discuss the proposed film and agree on a policy: '*Art or Cash*. Either very profitable terms indeed; or absolute author's veto on objectionable features or alterations' (letter to Christopher and Faith Tolkien, 11 September 1957, *Letters*, p. 261).

11 September 1957 Tolkien writes to Christopher and Faith Tolkien. He describes the award luncheon and presentation. 'The speeches were far more intelligent' than the rocket-lighter trophy, 'especially that of the introducer: Clemence Dane, a massive woman of almost Sitwellian presence' (*Letters*, p. 261). He also comments on the visit from Forrest J. Ackerman and associates.

13 September 1957 Tolkien travels to Belgium and stays with Simonne d'Ardenne at Solwaster.

?Mid-September 1957 Since he has heard nothing further from Forrest J. Ackerman, Tolkien sends the letter he had written to him on 6 September to Rayner Unwin for him to forward to Ackerman if he should contact Rayner.

17 September 1957 Tolkien writes from Solwaster to Robert Burchfield. He has got his dates wrong, and only just realized that he should be attending an Early English Text Society Council meeting on 18 September.

19/20 September 1957 Tolkien arrives back in Oxford at about midnight and spends the night at Merton College.

26 September 1957 Jerome W. Archer, Marquette University, writes a formal letter to Tolkien expressing pleasure at his acceptance of the invitation. He also sends an 'informal note', suggesting that Tolkien stay on campus for about a week, preferable 20–26 April 1958, but the following two weeks would also be suitable. During the week they would like Tolkien to present the one lecture he would regard as suitable for publication, and also one or two lectures of a lighter character, which could be on *The Lord of the Rings*.

30 September 1957 Rayner Unwin, on his return from Scandinavia, writes to congratulate Tolkien on his 'rocket'. While in Stockholm Rayner learned that the Swedish translation of *The Fellowship of the Ring* is nearly complete, and he has persuaded one publisher in Norway to read the book.

1–18 October 1957 Tolkien is acting chairman of the English Faculty Board.

4 October 1957 Rayner Unwin writes to Tolkien. Allen & Unwin have still not heard from Ackerman.

9 October 1957 Tolkien attends a Merton College meeting.

11 October 1957 D.M. Davin, Oxford University Press, writes to Tolkien about Goolden's *Old English Apollonius of Tyre*.

13 October 1957 Michaelmas Full Term begins. Tolkien's scheduled lectures for this term are: *Sawles Warde* on Wednesdays at 11.00 a.m. at Merton College, beginning 16 October; and Some Middle English Dialects on Fridays at 11.00 a.m. at Merton College, beginning 18 October. He continues to supervise B.Litt. students W.O. Evans (whose thesis has been referred back), L. Glanville, and J. Ross, and D.Phil. students A.D. Horgan and A. Kurvinen. In a letter to P.H. Newby on 8 February 1958 Tolkien will comment that Michaelmas Term 'was crushing, as I tried to clear up things before going on leave' (BBC Written Archives, Reading).

16 October 1957 Tolkien attends an Applications Committee meeting, and is appointed supervisor of probationer B.Litt. student V.A. Kolve of Jesus College, to work on a medieval English Literature subject, and of advanced student M.C. Seymour of St Edmund Hall, who is working on *A Study of the Inter-relationship of the English Versions of Mandeville's Travels*. – Helen Gardner, with Tolkien and F.P. Wilson an editor of the *Oxford English Monographs*, speaks with Tolkien about Goolden's *Old English Apollonius of Tyre*. They discuss whether a note from the *Monographs* editors is necessary to explain the special circumstance of its publication when a German edition has already appeared.

18 October 1957 Tolkien chairs an English Faculty Board meeting at 2.15 p.m. in the Board Room of the Clarendon Building. Lord David Cecil is elected chairman. Tolkien is re-elected to the Standing Committee on Applications until Michaelmas Term 1959; to the Standing Committee on Matters Referred by the General Board until Michaelmas Term 1959; and to the Standing Committee on Monographs until Michaelmas Term 1959. 'It is agreed to recommend that Tolkien be granted sabbatical leave for Hilary and Trinity Terms 1958 in order to visit Sweden and the United States, and to inform the General Board that no additional teaching' need be provided (Oxford University Archives FA 4/5/1/2). – Rayner Unwin writes to Forrest J. Ackerman, asking if he is still interested in the film project, and saying that he has been holding a letter of comment from Tolkien to give him if he should visit Allen & Unwin.

21 October 1957 Bertram Rota writes to Tolkien, urging him to gather together the *Lord of the Rings* papers and give him a date for collecting them.

22 October 1957 The Visitatorial Board approves Tolkien's request for leave during Hilary and Trinity Terms 1958. – L.G. Smith, George Allen & Unwin, writes to ask Tolkien if he could make use of any of the facsimile reproductions used in the prospectus for *Early English Manuscripts in Facsimile*.

27 October 1957 Tolkien replies to D.M. Davin, Oxford University Press. Tolkien examined Dr Josef Raith's edition of the Old English *Apollonius of Tyre* before allowing Goolden's edition to go forward. Apart from sympathy with Goolden, whose work missed priority due to misfortune, Tolkien feels that there are features in his edition which are not in Raith's, it is far more suitable for the use of most English students, and it was 'plainly not based on or cribbed from the Munich edition' (Oxford University Press archives). But he supposes that there should be a note to this effect in the volume. He has drafted one and sent it to Goolden for approval.

31 October 1957 Tolkien probably attends a meeting of the English Faculty as a whole at 8.30 p.m. in the Summer Common Room, Magdalen College. Elaine Griffiths is elected chairman. The meeting makes elections and discusses lecture forecasts, reports of examiners, and proposals for changes in the syllabus. (There is probably at least one such meeting each term, but this is one of the very few for which a record survives.) – Elizabeth Wright writes to Tolkien, asking him to deal with a letter she has received from the bank. Tolkien continues to be an executor of her late husband Joseph Wright.

?November 1957–?October 1972 Tolkien doodles on newspapers, usually while doing the crossword, and also makes occasional drawings on sheets or scraps of paper, altogether numbering in the hundreds. *See note.*

c. **November 1957** Priscilla Tolkien is ill with mumps. Her mother nurses her, though Edith herself is in poor health.

1 November 1957 In the evening, Tolkien attends a dinner of The Society hosted by J.T. Christie, the Principal of Jesus College, Oxford, in his lodgings. Eight members are present. Christie reads a paper concerning A.E. Housman's *A Shropshire Lad*. Nevill Coghill proposes, and Tolkien seconds, the nomination of Jonathan Wordsworth for membership in The Society.

6 November 1957 Tolkien attends a Merton College meeting.

7 November 1957 Tolkien attends a Special Meeting of the English Faculty Board at 2.15 p.m. in the Board Room of the Clarendon Building. Lord David Cecil is in the chair. The recommendations of members of the Faculty Board on the syllabus committee for changes in regulations are amended and adopted. It is agreed to hold a further special meeting in Hilary Term 1958 to deal with amendments in the set books. On Tolkien's motion, it is agreed to put forward the name of Professor Stanley Rypins of Brooklyn College for an award under the Fulbright programme for 1959–60, as a research worker.

10 November 1957 Robert Burchfield, Early English Text Society, sends Tolkien a print of the last leaf of *Beowulf* to be used in a forthcoming reprint of Zupitza's edition of the text. He asks for news about *Ancrene Wisse*.

13 November 1957 Tolkien attends a meeting of the Board of Electors to the O'Donnell Lecturership in Celtic Studies. They elect C.L. Wrenn to the lecturership for 1957/8, and agree to meet in future in Hilary Term to consider the election of a lecturer for the following academic year.

14 November 1957 Rayner Unwin writes to Tolkien. He asks how matters stand between him and Voorhoeve & Dietrich in regard to their invitation to Tolkien to visit Holland. Rayner has heard nothing more from Ackerman.

15 November 1957 P.H. Newby, BBC, writes to ask Tolkien if he is still interested in broadcasting. He suggests that Tolkien might give a talk on the Third Programme on 'the seriousness of fairy tales'.

17 November 1957 Tolkien replies to a letter from Dr Herbert Schiro. He says that there is '*no* "symbolism" or conscious allegory' in *The Lord of the Rings*, but that does not mean 'no applicability'. It is not so much about 'Power and Dominion' as about 'Death and the desire for deathlessness' (*Letters*, p. 262).

20 November 1957 In the evening, Bertram Rota, who has written to Tolkien several times and unsuccessfully tried to contact him by phone, at last finds him at home when he telephones. Tolkien explains that professional and family affairs have kept him busy, and that he has kept putting off writing in the hope of having more definite news, but has still not found time to put the *Lord of the Rings* papers in order or to search for more material. Only he can put the papers in order, and date and explain them; he promises to do this soon. Tolkien is doubtful about whether he will be able to visit the United States and Marquette University.

21 November 1957 Tolkien probably attends a meeting of the entire English Faculty at 8.30 p.m. at St Anne's College.

25 November 1957 Rayner Unwin writes to Tolkien. Allen & Unwin have received five copies of the Dutch *Return of the King*, and asks if they should do as they did last time, and send three to Tolkien, and one each to Harting and Campbell.

?End of November 1957 Cees Ouboter of Voorhoeve & Dietrich writes to Tolkien, asking him to visit Rotterdam to attend a literary luncheon in January.

Late 1957 Lord Halsbury, invited by Tolkien to read parts of 'The Silmarillion' in manuscript, writes one or more appreciative letters.

6 December 1957 Tolkien attends an English Faculty Board meeting. Helen Gardner presents a report from the Committee on Monographs. Miss Clark's edition of The *Peterborough Chronicle* will appear shortly; Goolden's edition of the *Old English Apollonius of Tyre* and Mr Story and Miss Gardner's edition of the *Sonnets of William Alabaster* are passing through the press. During Tolkien's absence on sabbatical leave C.L. Wrenn is to replace him on the Standing Committee on Applications, as interviewer of research students, and on the Standing Committee on Matters Referred by the General Board. The Applications Committee has appointed substitute supervisors for four of Tolkien's post-graduate students during his absence: Miss C.L. Morrison for Inokuma; J.A.W. Bennett for Kolve; G.V. Smithers for Seymour; and E.J. Dobson for Voitl. As no substitutes are noted as being appointed for Tolkien's other students, either he continues to supervise them even though on leave, or they are allowed to work without supervision for the two terms.

Early December 1957 Rayner Unwin visits Tolkien in Oxford. The main purpose of the visit is apparently to discuss 'The Silmarillion'. Tolkien wants to show him Lord Halsbury's last letter, but cannot find it. Rayner borrows some of the 'Silmarillion' material. He passes to Tolkien a package from Almqvist & Wiksell, the publishers of the Swedish translation of *The Lord of the Rings*.

7 December 1957 Tolkien writes to Rayner Unwin. As soon as Rayner left after his visit, Tolkien found Lord Halsbury's letter 'in full view', and has since received another fourteen-page letter from him. Tolkien quotes extracts and says:

> I now see quite clearly that I must, as a necessary preliminary to 'remoulding' ['The Silmarillion'], get copies made of all copyable material. And I shall put that in hand as soon as possible. But I think the best way of dealing with this (at this stage, in which much of the stuff is irreplaceable sole copies) is to install a typist in my room in college, and not let any material out of my keeping, until it is multiplied. I hope that, perhaps, then your interest will be sufficient for you to want at least a sketch of the remaining part. [*Letters*, p. 262]

The package from Sweden contained a letter in Swedish from the translator of *The Lord of the Rings*, Åke Ohlmarks, and a nine-page foolscap list of names he has altered. Tolkien has tried to translate the letter, and is not impressed by Ohlmarks, who asserts the 'antipathy' of the Swedish language to borrowing foreign words and yet used many in his letter.

> I find this procedure puzzling, because the letter and the list seem totally pointless unless my opinion and criticism is invited. But if this is its object, then surely the timing is both unpractical and impolite, presented together with a pistol: 'we are going to start the composition now'. Nei-

ther is my convenience consulted: the communication comes out of the
blue in the second most busy academic week of the year. I have had to sit
up far into the night even to survey the list. Conceding the legitimacy or
necessity of translation (which I do not, except in a limited degree), the
translation does not seem to me to exhibit much skill, and contains a fair
number of positive errors. [*Letters*, p. 263]

He is also sure that Ohlmarks has not read the Appendices. Tolkien criticizes the translation generally and specifically, and summarizes his replies to
Almqvist & Wiksell and Ohlmarks. In his letter to Almqvist he has said that he
feels he should have been consulted earlier, and that he dealt with Ohlmarks'
list as well as time allowed; and although he is not troubling them directly with
any detailed criticisms, he insists that the word *hobbit* should not be altered.
He has sent Ohlmarks a detailed criticism of his list, and 'told him that though
unconvinced by his arguments, I conceded the legitimacy of translating names
that are cast in modern English form, and are or are meant to have an intelligible meaning for mod[ern] English readers; but all other names should be
left alone – if they are not in English there is no reason why they sh[oul]d be
Swedish. I have insisted upon *hobbit*.' Even though he probably has no real
power in the matter, he hopes that his protest will be effective, and that it can
be arranged, when negotiating further translations, that he be consulted at an
early stage.

I see now that the lack of an 'index of names' is a serious handicap in
dealing with these matters. If I had an index of names ... it would be
a comparatively easy matter to indicate at once all names suitable for
translation (as being themselves according to the fiction "translated"
into English), and to add a few notes on points where (I know now)
translators are likely to trip. So far, though both eager to translate the
toponymy into other terms, and deliberately to efface the reference to
England (which I regard as integral and essential), neither appear to be
at all conversant with English toponymy, or even to be aware that there is
anything to know. ...

This 'handlist' would be of *great* use to me in future corrections and in
composing an index (which I think should replace some of the present
appendices); also in dealing with *The Silmarillion* (into which some of
the L.R. has to be written backwards to make the two coherent). Do you
think you could do anything about this? [Tolkien-George Allen & Unwin
archive, HarperCollins, partly printed in *Letters*, pp. 262–4]

Tolkien must turn his attention to the *Poema Morale* in six manuscripts. –
Michaelmas Full Term ends.

9 December 1957 Tolkien attends a Merton College meeting.

12 December 1957 Rayner Unwin writes to Tolkien. He agrees that it would
be wise to stipulate in future agreements the use of *hobbit*, and that in 'trans-

lation' proper names of topographical words should be arranged to Tolkien's satisfaction at an early stage. If the list of names Tolkien needs is a job that 'could be done rather as an index is done without very much judgement, but a good deal of donkey work', Allen & Unwin can have this made by one of their regular indexers. Rayner is reading with greatest interest 'Silmarillion' papers Tolkien has lent him. He encloses a copy of a letter he has just received from Forrest J. Ackerman and his proposed reply, which he will send to Ackerman if Tolkien approves. This includes the suggestion that Tolkien would be willing to give some general advice on broader issues, and to annotate briefly points in the story-line to which he objects. Rayner acknowledges to Tolkien that if he agrees, this will make some demands on his time but, if the film project comes off, it would 'be under your care more than is usual' (Tolkien-George Allen & Unwin archive, HarperCollins). He asks whether Tolkien has decided to visit Holland.

13 December 1957 Tolkien writes to Rayner Unwin. He has written to Voorhoeve & Dietrich that he cannot manage the visit to Holland. He is now officially on leave, but has 'to hold a delayed examination on Jan. 7th [possibly the *viva voce* examination eventually held on 20 January] and shall alas! be fully occupied, apart from Christmas, with that. Also, while my domestic circumstances make absence at that time difficult, I myself feel the strain of so many interwoven activities, and I think I must stay at home and not fritter away any surviving energies.' The index he needs is a matter of 'pure "donkey-work" . . . an alphabetical list of all proper names of persons, places, or things . . . in the *text* (including Foreword and Prologue, but *not* the Appendices)'. His 'own experience with donkey-work of this kind (I have made a good many glossaries) is that the more mechanical and the less selective one can be in the process of extracting the references, the quicker and more accurately is this process completed'.

He approves Rayner's letter to Ackerman. He thinks that the artist Ron Cobb and the model-maker Jon Lackey have real talent, but does not think that 'the visual art' for the proposed film to be 'of such a superlative order that it could carry the stupidity and vulgarities of the script. . . . Either the script-writer must be humble and co-operative, or his "visual" colleagues must go unpublished. . . . If there is to be dialogue &/or narrative transitions, the word of the text must be closely followed'. His main criticism of the project is that

> the chief and special talent of the group obviously lies, and will lie, in the *scenic*, & pictorial. The script-writer should consider this. On the contrary, he wants feverish action, and simply cuts out parts in which climate and scenery are the chief interest, such as 'The Ring Goes South' or 'The Great River'. . . .
>
> Grateful as I am, & should be, for the abundance of people who profess enjoyment of *The Lord of the Rings*, I wish that the commonest reaction of admirers was not the desire to tinker with it! [Tolkien-George Allen & Unwin archive, HarperCollins]

c. **13 December 1957** Tolkien writes to Cees Ouboter of Voorhoeve & Dietrich. His own and his wife's poor health have prevented him writing sooner. Unfortunately he will not be able to come to Holland in January.

Mid-December 1957 Before he receives Tolkien's letter, Cees Ouboter writes again. He wishes to postpone Tolkien's visit as he has been unable to make arrangements for January.

17 December 1957 Simonne d'Ardenne writes in her Christmas card that she hopes to visit Tolkien at the end of January.

19 December 1957 Tolkien writes to Cees Ouboter. He cannot give a definite answer but would very much like to visit Holland. The period between 24 March and 2 April 1958 would suit him best. He is supposed to be visiting Sweden in March, 'though this is now highly improbable' (quoted in René van Rossenberg, 'Tolkien's Exceptional Visit to Holland: A Reconstruction', *Proceedings of the Tolkien Centenary Conference 1992* (1995), p. 303).

24 December 1957 Rayner Unwin writes to Tolkien, asking if he knows a fan who might be interested in compiling the *Lord of the Rings* index. Otherwise, Allen & Unwin will use one of their regular indexers.

31 December 1957 Rayner Unwin writes to Tolkien. He returns 'the rough draft of a part of your *Silmarillion*', which is 'in a state where it is a bit uncompromising for the general reader'. He found that

> this batch of typescript, like the early books of the Bible was of mixed literary value. Some scenes and incidents are vivid and beautiful, others such as the chapter 'Of Beleriand and Its Realms' remind me of the Book of Numbers though instead of names it was topography that was present in a somewhat undigested form. I was not attracted by the rather rudimentary narrative form that inserts itself at irregular intervals, "Quoth Aelfwinë", nor of the variable archaism of language, particularly of the heavy use of the second person singular verb. I felt that this gave a somewhat precious feeling to the narrative.

He thinks that a big map or maps would be necessary, 'also now and then some simplification of the telling of the story. Many readers who love the simple music and magic of the tales of other days will get very confused if they do not have a story or narrative thread to guide them. After a cursory reading I was far from clear about the "Who's Who" of the participants of the story' (Tolkien-George Allen & Unwin archive, HarperCollins). Nonetheless his appetite has been whetted for the complete work.

1958

c. **1958** Tolkien begins **The New Shadow*, a sequel to *The Lord of the Rings*, but soon abandons it. He will later recall that it 'proved both sinister and depressing' and was 'not worth doing' (letter to Colin Bailey, 13 May 1964, *Letters*, p. 344). His first attempt covers only two sides of a sheet. This is followed by a second manuscript, occupying only eight pages in *The Peoples of Middle-earth*, which extends as far as the story ever goes. Tolkien then makes a typescript which ends at the same point.

January–Mid-February 1958 Tolkien and Cees Ouboter continue to correspond about arrangements for Tolkien's proposed visit to Rotterdam. In his letters Tolkien shows 'considerable anxiety about travelling alone' (René van Rossenberg, 'Tolkien's Exceptional Visit to Holland: A Reconstruction', p. 303).

January 1958 Exeter College announces that Tolkien has been made an Honorary Fellow.

14 January 1958 Rayner Unwin writes to Tolkien. He has found an indexer for *The Lord of the Rings*, and will tell her that Tolkien wants 'an index in two parts, one of proper names and one of geographical and topographical names, that it should be double spaced and include everything without any selectivity' (Tolkien-George Allen & Unwin archive, HarperCollins). He congratulates Tolkien on his Honorary Fellowship, and sends him a copy of the latest letter from Forrest J. Ackerman.

19 January 1958 Hilary Full Term begins. Tolkien has no lectures this term, as he is on sabbatical leave.

20 January 1958 Tolkien and U.M. Brown examine J.F. Kiteley of Wadham College *viva voce* at 11.00 a.m. in the Examination Schools on his B.Litt. thesis *Characterisation in Sir Gawain and the Green Knight*.

22 January 1958 Despite the fact that Tolkien is on sabbatical leave, the *Oxford University Gazette* lists him as supervisor of B.Litt. students W.O. Evans, L. Glanville, and J. Ross, and D.Phil. student A. Kurvinen. It may be that he continues to supervise, perhaps at less frequent intervals, or else his students are able to work by themselves for two terms. – Alina Dadlez of George Allen & Unwin writes to Tolkien. She has received five complimentary copies of the German *Hobbit* from Paulus Verlag, and asks if she should send them all to Tolkien. Allen & Unwin are hoping to find a German publisher for *The Lord of the Rings*.

26 January 1958 Father Alexander Jones sends Tolkien the first draft of a translation of most of the Book of Job for *The Jerusalem Bible* and asks for comments.

27 January 1958 Rayner Unwin writes to Tolkien. Work has begun on the index to *The Lord of the Rings*.

8 February 1958 Tolkien writes to P.H. Newby. He has found Newby's letter of 15 November 1957 'in a pile, and I am afraid that having no recollection of answering it is sufficient proof that I never did. I shall have to get a secretary (though I cannot afford one): I am nearly buried in paper.' He is supposed to be finishing overdue works and travelling while on leave, but will probably have to cancel the visits and might not get much work done, as his wife has to have an operation. This will mean several weeks in hospital and then convalescence. He is still interested in broadcasting but doesn't 'feel like "fairy-stories" at present' (BBC Written Archives, Reading).

11 February 1958 P.H. Newby writes to Tolkien. He is sorry to hear of Edith's illness. He asks Tolkien to lunch with him if he comes to London.

13 February 1958 Edith is admitted to hospital for an operation. In the meantime, Tolkien stays at Merton College. – Bertram Rota writes to William Ready at Marquette University, who is still waiting for the *Lord of the Rings* papers. Tolkien has contacted Rota and explained that problems arising from his wife's ill health have prevented him from organizing the *Lord of the Rings* papers as he had promised. If all goes well with the operation, Tolkien promises to give that task priority. Rota hopes to collect the papers on 1 March, and will pay Tolkien the money he has been holding pending delivery. – At a special meeting of the English Faculty Board, in Tolkien's absence, changes to the syllabus are agreed, to take effect for the Preliminary Examination from 1 October 1958 and for the Final Honour School from 1 October 1960.

15 February 1958 Robert Burchfield writes to Tolkien. He is sorry to hear that Edith is not well. He hopes for an encouraging message about the *Ancrene Wisse*.

?20 February 1958 Tolkien writes to Cees Ouboter. He confirms that he will attend a reception in Rotterdam on 28 March. – Tolkien phones or writes to Bertram Rota. His wife has had her operation, and the surgeon has found no cause for alarm. – Tolkien attends a paper, 'Barbarians and Citizens', given at St Anne's College by his son Christopher, now a university lecturer at Oxford.

20 February 1958 Alina Dadlez sends Tolkien five complimentary copies of German *Hobbit*.

21 February 1958 Tolkien writes to his son Christopher. He comments on 'Barbarians and Citizens' and expresses the pleasure it gave him to hear it. – Bertram Rota writes to William Ready that he still hopes to collect the *Lord of the Rings* papers on 1 March.

22 February 1958 Rayner Unwin writes to Tolkien. He asks if Tolkien would like Allen & Unwin to book his passage to Holland.

26 February 1958 Tolkien writes to Rayner Unwin. He apologizes that 'the confusion and anxiety of my days since the beginning of the year have landed me in so many neglects and discourtesies'. He has been anxious about Edith's health since the end of November; his daughter had needed nursing while suffering with mumps, and not until she had recovered would Edith agree to see a doctor. She has now had a serious operation and is still in a nursing home. He is staying in college, but

> I have had so many things to see to and so much anxiety that I have become snowed up with neglected letters. I have not unnaturally been unwell myself though 'going to bed' is not possible. I have had to cancel all tours (Sweden, Finland, USA etc. [*see note*]), since it is clear that my wife will need extended convalescence, and I cannot leave her. I am afraid that, even with the release from tours and lectures, the prospects of connected work look dim. I feel exhausted anyway.

> But I have kept Holland on the map. My daughter will be at home

... so that if my wife continues to improve (she is making fair but slow progress) I hope to be able to leave on March 27 and return on Monday 31st. [Professor] Harting desires to take me to Amsterdam after the show to exhibit me to further fans. [Tolkien-George Allen & Unwin archive, HarperCollins]

He welcomes Rayner's offer to make his travel arrangements, but suggests that he wait a few days. He expects Edith to be able to leave the nursing home on 4 March, and he will then take her to Bournemouth and stay there until Priscilla is able to come to Oxford to be with her mother. He asks Rayner to thank Alina Dadlez for the copies of the German *Hobbit* which he has not had time to look at.

1 March 1958 Bertram Rota collects the *Lord of the Rings* papers from Tolkien in Oxford. Tolkien still has not been able to find time to put them in order.

4 March 1958 Rayner Unwin writes to Tolkien. Allen & Unwin will make his travel arrangements for the Dutch visit. Rayner assumes that Tolkien would prefer the night boat to The Hook of Holland rather than travel by air. He asks for the dates and route Tolkien wishes to travel.

7 March 1958 Tolkien writes to Rayner Unwin from the Hotel Miramar, Bournemouth. As Edith seems to be doing well, he thinks it safe for Allen & Unwin to make the arrangements for his visit to Holland. He expects to return to Oxford on 17 March and could leave on 27 March for Rotterdam and return overnight 31 March–1 April from Amsterdam.

c. **8 March 1958** Tolkien writes to Professor Harting in Amsterdam, and to Voorhoeve & Dietrich in Rotterdam, confirming his visit to Holland.

11 March 1958 Rayner Unwin writes to Tolkien. He has made the travel reservations, and will send the tickets and sailing berth accommodation in a few days. He encloses a list of queries from the indexer, who has almost completed her work.

12 March 1958 From the Hotel Miramar, Bournemouth, Tolkien returns the indexer's queries to Rayner Unwin, with notes and replies. He is grateful for the indexer's care and thought. He encloses a proposal he has received from ABC Television for a programme on 16 March, a date he cannot make, and asks Rayner's advice.

14 March 1958 Rayner Unwin writes to Tolkien. He is very much in favour of Tolkien accepting the proposal from ABC Television if they offer him another date.

15 March 1958 Hilary Full term ends.

17 March 1958 Tolkien and Edith return to Oxford from Bournemouth.

18 March 1958 Tolkien writes to Voorhoeve & Dietrich with various questions about his visit.

19 March 1958 Rayner Unwin sends Tolkien the tickets and reservations for the visit to Holland.

20 March 1958 Tolkien writes to Rayner Unwin. He asks for more information about the travel timetable. Edith is still very weak. Tolkien is very busy, and practically tied to the house until Priscilla arrives. A friend has sent him a copy of the programme for Rotterdam, expressing alarm at 'Maggot-soup' (in fact, mushroom soup named for Farmer Maggot in *The Lord of the Rings*) on the dinner menu. The friend has also sent him a copy of a long review in Dutch, which Tolkien describes as 'rather an extreme example of its kind, and I thought rather naïf in its almost explicit avowal that the critic has waded through all three volumes of [*The Lord of the Rings*] in the vain hope of finding descriptions of excretion or copulation; and being cheated decided this was not high-class literature!' (Tolkien-George Allen & Unwin archive, Harper-Collins). – Tolkien writes to Cees Ouboter, thanking him for a letter which answered many questions. He tells Ouboter what ferry and train he will be taking.

22 March 1958 Professor Jongkees writes to Tolkien, sent to Amsterdam to await his arrival.

25 March 1958 Tolkien writes to Allen & Unwin, thanking them for the travel timetable he has received.

27 March 1958 Tolkien travels to London. He takes the 7.30 p.m. boat train from Liverpool Street Station to Harwich, to connect with the night ferry *SS Duke of York*. – Rayner Unwin writes to Tolkien. Ackerman and Zimmerman have been given a free option on the film rights of *The Lord of the Rings* for six months, during which time Zimmerman will try to produce a story-line more agreeable to Tolkien. This option will run from the date Zimmerman receives Tolkien's comments on, and objections to, the first story-line. Rayner points out the financial advantages to Tolkien if a film is eventually made, and returns the story-line which has been at Allen & Unwin since the autumn of 1957.

28 March 1958 The *SS Duke of York* arrives at the Hook of Holland early in the morning. Tolkien travels by train to Rotterdam Central Station, arriving at 7.28 a.m. in sunshine. Cees Ouboter of Voorhoeve & Dietrich, waving a copy of *The Lord of the Rings* to identify himself, meets him on the platform. *See note.* Ouboter introduces Tolkien to Mr Jo van Rosmalen, head of the publicity department of the Dutch publishers Het Spectrum, who will look after him. Rosmalen offers Tolkien coffee, but Tolkien prefers Dutch cold beer. Wanting to see Rotterdam, they walk through the city, which still shows the scars of the Second World War, together with (as Tolkien will describe it) much 'gigantic and largely dehumanised reconstruction' (letter to Rayner Unwin, 8 April 1958, *Letters*, p. 265). He asks Rosmalen the Dutch names of the trees and flowers they see during the walk. At about 1.00 p.m. they arrive at the bookshop of Voorhoeve & Dietrich. Tolkien has something to eat and talks with the staff and with customers. In mid-afternoon he is taken to his hotel to rest for half an hour, then he and Rosmalen again walk through the streets until it is time for the 'Hobbit Maaltijd' at 5.30 p.m. at the Flev-restaurant. All 200 places have been booked. The proceedings begin at 6.00 p.m. when everyone is seated, Tolkien and other special guests at a high table.

During the evening, interspersed between courses, there are nine speeches, all in English and each restricted to five minutes. The courses have been given names inspired by *The Lord of the Rings*: 'Egg-salad à la Barliman Butterbur', 'Vegetables of Goldberry', 'Ice and Fruits of Gildor', 'Maggot soup' (which causes some confusion and hilarity). Although it is a Friday, the organizers have obtained a dispensation from the Roman Catholic diocese of Rotterdam for the guests to eat meat: 'Fricandeau à la Gimli'. The hall is hung with posters advertising 'Pipe-weed for Hobbits' supplied by the Dutch tobacco company Van Rossem, which has also provided 'free tobacco in beautiful Delft blue porcelain jars and old-fashioned clay pipes to all the gentlemen present' (René van Rossenberg, 'Tolkien's Exceptional Visit to Holland: A Reconstruction', p. 307). Tolkien signs autographs. At the end of the banquet he makes a speech, starting with a greeting in Dutch, and continuing with a parody of Bilbo's speech at the 'long-expected party', including some phrases in Elvish. After answering questions and talking with some of the attendees, Tolkien returns to his hotel.

29 March 1958 Tolkien's friend Piet Harting takes him first to The Hague, where they visit the Mauritshuis, then to Amsterdam where they have dinner with a small group, mainly Amsterdam professors of various faculties.

30 March 1958 Palm Sunday. Tolkien spends time visiting Amsterdam, probably including the Rijksmuseum.

31 March 1958 Tolkien sees more of Amsterdam, and visits the University where 'we picked up a number of students of the English department, and made an extremely hobbit-like expedition to Wynand Fockink', a distillery (letter to Rayner Unwin, 8 April 1958, Tolkien-George Allen & Unwin archive, HarperCollins). In the evening, Tolkien travels by train to the Hook to take the night ferry back to England. – At an Early English Text Society Council meeting, in Tolkien's absence, the Council regrets that Tolkien has not replied to requests for information about the progress of his *Ancrene Wisse*. It is reluctantly decided to inform Tolkien that if he is not able to deliver his transcript to the Society by 30 June 1958, the Council will issue a facsimile of the manuscript rather than an edition. Neil Ker has agreed to write a short palaeographical introduction. M.Y. Offord's edition of the *Parlement of Thre Ages* has been accepted, and specimen printed pages are approved.

1 April 1958 Tolkien returns to Harwich and, as he later writes to Rayner Unwin, 'the branch of box-tree that I brought back so intrigued the Customs official that more usual "loot" such as Bols or cigars seemed to have no interest for him' (letter to Rayner Unwin, 8 April 1958, Tolkien-George Allen & Unwin archive, HarperCollins). He takes the train to Liverpool Street Station and from there a taxi to Paddington and manages to catch the 9.45 a.m. fast train from Paddington to Oxford.

2 April 1958 Tolkien writes a letter of thanks to Cees Ouboter. – He replies to a letter from Professor Jongkees received in Amsterdam. He regrets that he was not able to meet him. – Tolkien writes to Peter Alford, describing the dinner in Rotterdam and enclosing a copy of the menu and programme, with manuscript alterations.

4 April 1958 Robert Burchfield writes to Tolkien, reporting the decision of the Early English Text Society Council on 31 March.

8 April 1958 Tolkien writes to Rayner Unwin, whose letter about Ackerman and Zimmerman arrived in his absence. Since his return, 'various domestic events (such as the visit of a grand-daughter, now 13), and the liturgical occupations of Holy Week, which began for me with *Palmzondag* [Palm Sunday] in Amsterdam, have prevented me from settling down to Zimmerman until now' (Tolkien-George Allen & Unwin archive, HarperCollins). He describes his visit to Holland at length. – In an enclosed second letter to Rayner Unwin, Tolkien deals with the Zimmerman story-line. He is 'entirely ignorant of the process of producing an "animated picture" from a book, and of the jargon connected with it'. He wonders about the function of a 'story-line'. He is not concerned so much about expressions in the document which may be 'simply directions to picture-producers', but as it stands the story-line 'is sufficient to give me grave anxiety about the actual *dialogue* that (I suppose) will be used. I should say Zimmerman, the constructor of this s-l., is quite incapable of excerpting or adapting the 'spoken words' of the book. He is hasty, insensitive, and impertinent.' Tolkien continues with general criticism in the same vein. He will send Rayner his remarks and comments on the story-line as soon as possible. Nothing will go to Ackerman except through Rayner. 'I could make an abridged synopsis, redivided for scenes, myself with less labour than will be needed in commenting on this stupid script!' (Tolkien-George Allen & Unwin archive, HarperCollins, partly printed in *Letters*, pp. 266–7).

10 April 1958 Tolkien writes to Cees Ouboter. There is no intended 'message' in *The Lord of the Rings*. – Rayner Unwin writes to Tolkien. He too is ignorant of the function of the story-line. He suggests that the matter be clarified with Zimmerman. Tolkien should 'correct the obvious inaccuracies both of name and of action in Mr. Zimmerman's story-line and indicate in general terms whether you think he has gone off the rails in the necessary process of reducing the bulk of your narrative to the relatively small compass of animated feature' (Tolkien-George Allen & Unwin archive, HarperCollins).

?11 April–*c.* 21 April and *c.* 28 April–5 May 1958 Tolkien works on the Zimmerman story-line. He begins a letter to Forrest J. Ackerman, in part based on the letter he wrote on 6 September 1957 but did not send. He regrets that the story-line is not on the same level as the conceptual art he was shown. He has no clear idea of how long the film is expected to be,

but some idea of the length aimed at, and the reasons for reduction of the original (whether artistic, practical, or financial), is really necessary for a general criticism.

The Lord of the Rings is arranged in 6 sections or 'books'. Each section consists of a series of chapters or scenes; and the placing in sequence of these, as also of the sections themselves, is the result of purpose and thought. *In the author's opinion this arrangement cannot be altered without serious damage....*

The 'interleaving' of the events in the two main threads, Frodo-Sam and the War, which was deliberately avoided in the original with good reason, produces a jumble, that would be bewildering to any viewers not well acquainted with the book. The latter would not recognize the story as the one that I have told at all: the events, the characters, and the moral significance have all been altered and distorted. . . .

I pass over the major matter: that the most important part of the whole work, the journey through Mordor and the martyrdom of Frodo, has been cut in preference for battles; though it is the chief point of the Lord of the Rings that the battles were of subordinate significance. [author's italics]

The story-line gives him the impression that it is the 'product of a hasty reading of the original, which has failed to appreciate the tone and significance of the narrative. It appears to be based primarily on the memory of this reading (altered by the adapter's private imagination)'. Granting 'the necessity for drastic reduction, I think that Mr. Z. is often mistaken in the methods that he employs for shortening. One may cut, or one may compress. In general, he prefers the more dangerous method of compression.' Tolkien also works on a page-by-page analysis of the story-line, in which there has been 'constant needless alteration of points of detail' (Special Collections and University Archives, John P. Raynor, S.J., Library, Marquette University; see further, *Adaptations).

16 April 1958 Rayner Unwin writes to Tolkien. Allen & Unwin's agent in Hollywood has reported that Ackerman has agreed that should he wish to extend the six-month option, which starts upon receipt of Tolkien's comments on the story-line, he will pay $500 for a second six months.

c. **21–28 April 1958** Various troubles, including a week suffering with laryngitis, interrupt Tolkien's work on the story-line.

27 April 1958 Trinity Full Term begins. Tolkien has no scheduled lectures, as he is on sabbatical leave.

28 April 1958 Two busts, including one of Tolkien, sculpted by his daughter-in-law, Faith (Christopher's wife), have been accepted for the Royal Academy's summer exhibition in London. Faith visits the Academy (on 'varnishing day') and telephones Tolkien to say that his bust has been well placed in Room 1.

29 April 1958 Tolkien writes to Rayner Unwin. His work on the story-line had been nearly finished more than a week ago when various troubles interrupted it. He hopes to send his comments at the end of the week. He informs Rayner about the bust at the Royal Academy.

?Early May 1958 Robert Murray writes to Tolkien, asking for comment on 'holy' words, in particular 'the original meaning of, and relationships between, the various words for "holy" in the Indo-European languages' (Humphrey Carpenter, *Letters*, p. 267).

1 May 1958 Rayner Unwin writes to Tolkien. He is delighted to hear about the bust and will go to Room 1 first when he attends the Private View at the Royal Academy on 2 May.

2 May 1958 At an English Faculty Board meeting, C.L. Wrenn is appointed to replace Tolkien on the Nominating Committee for the Diploma in Celtic Studies.

4 May 1958 Tolkien writes a long letter to Robert Murray in response to his request for information about 'holy words'.

c. 5 May 1958 Tolkien faints and, in falling, breaks his spectacles and hurts his face. His collapse is due to a nervous condition resulting from stress. His doctor wants him to go into a nursing home, but he refuses because of his domestic situation. He is forbidden to write or read, and indeed for some time does not feel able to do so. At some date before 16 May he and Edith go to stay at the Hotel Miramar, Bournemouth.

8 May 1958 T.W. Earp dies.

9 May 1958 Rayner Unwin writes to Tolkien. The head of the agency in Hollywood to whom they have entrusted negotiations with Zimmerman and Ackerman will visit Allen & Unwin towards the end of May. Rayner wants to show him Tolkien's annotations to the story-line, and if possible let him take them back to the United States. He asks if Tolkien can provide the annotations by 22 May.

15 May 1958 Rayner Unwin writes to Tolkien, sending the index of proper names in *The Lord of the Rings* with queries from the indexer, who had to rush the work to completion because she is near the end of pregnancy.

16 May 1958 Tolkien writes to Rayner Unwin from the Hotel Miramar, Bournemouth. His face is healing, and he is beginning to feel able to read and write. He has not been able to complete his work on the story-line but will, on his return to Oxford on 20 May (if not before), return the original with enough matter for Rayner to be able to deal with it.

> I shall, of course, be only too pleased if you will edit it or tone it down to make the pill more swallowable.
>
> The vital point is (if possible) to secure a revision of the story-line, with the object of removing its more wanton divergences from the book. Especially (for instance) reduction of eagles to their proper place; and amendment of such gross vulgarizations as the fairy-castle and minarets intruded into Lórien: and restoration of the vital scene at the end of the Ring in Chamber of Fire. In general the story-line writer should allow the *pictorial artists* more scope.

He encloses 'two sheets of the commentary I was making' – presumably the letter to Forrest J. Ackerman begun in April or early May – to give an idea of his 'general drift and tone. It is my intention to proceed to offer some examples of *drastic cuts* that I should tolerate (in lieu of jumbled compression); and to offer specific comments page by page on the story-line' (Tolkien–George Allen

& Unwin archive, HarperCollins). ABC Television have again invited him to appear on one of their programmes and he has reluctantly consented.

20 May 1958 Tolkien returns to Oxford from Bournemouth.

22 May 1958 Rayner Unwin writes to Tolkien. He expresses his sympathy and approves Tolkien's suggested reply to Ackerman. It needs no alteration.

23 May 1958 Tolkien sees his doctor, who pronounces him fit again.

26 May 1958 Tolkien is driven at high speed to ABC Television's studio at Aston, Birmingham. The programme *The Book Man*, broadcast at 2.30 p.m., evidently features the fulfilment of the wish by the winner of a competition to meet and talk with an author he has enjoyed. Tolkien likes the winner, Hal Coomer from Macclesfield, but thinks that he is treated badly by ABC who have promised him a copy of the work to be discussed, but give him only *The Return of the King*. Coomer apparently asks Tolkien to sign the book. Tolkien returns by train with 'Bulldog Drummond and Inspector Webb', presumably actors who played those characters on television or radio (Tolkien-George Allen & Unwin archive, HarperCollins).

27 May 1958 Tolkien writes to Rayner Unwin. He found the index compiled (by Mrs Nancy Smith) awaiting him when he returned to Oxford. He encloses a letter for her and a sheet of answers to her queries. He asks Rayner to let him know when her baby is born, so that he can send her greetings and congratulations. Since his return he has been

> entangled in a mesh woven of bothers about Irish exam-papers, and endeavours to complete my letter and notes on the 'Story-line'. (I do not seem to have got either straightened out yet). In the latter task I have already found the *Index* useful. It will, of course, be still more useful later on when I at last get some time (unbroken by catastrophes) to take up the *Silmarillion* etc. with concentration. Also I think some specific use should be made of it in some later edition and/or revision of *The* [*Lord of the Rings*]. . . . My impression (from v[ery] many letters) is that every part of the Appendices has found some readers' interest; but all miss an *index* (with indications of the meaning of names in other tongues). Some of what exists could be dropped without any damage at all, I think. I should say (1) most of Appendix D (other than [the Shire Calendar]); probably most of App. E II, and most of F II, for a start, possibly some 15 pages. If the *Silmarillion* could be finished A3 (i) and probably (v) would also be unnecessary.

The story-line seems worse to him the more he looks at it. Wherever he can, Zimmerman

> presents scenes of confused and violent action (difficult to depict) and cuts out the scenic effects and the sense of space that could be so well represented. Everything is 'soon' or 'close' for him, and though all scales of time and space have disappeared in the 'synopsis' (!), I calculate that

all the 'story' he produces would hardly have occupied a month, or required a space much bigger than the Shire. I have nearly completed my notes. They are too numerous (and sometimes too long), and also betray my exasperation too freely. I will try to get a more moderate form typed shortly. [Tolkien-George Allen & Unwin archive, HarperCollins]

He suggests that if Allen & Unwin's agent arrives before he has finished, the agent could be given 'my truncated letter' (the 'two sheets of commentary' of 16 May), with a promise of detailed notes to follow. Tolkien gives an account of his appearance on the ABC Television programme. He wants to give Hal Coomer the first two volumes of *The Lord of the Rings*, and asks Rayner to arrange this.

29 May 1958 Rayner Unwin writes to Tolkien. He will seriously consider the question of incorporating the index in *The Lord of the Rings* and possibly dropping parts of the Appendices, but wonders if it would not be best done to coincide with the publication of *The Silmarillion*. Nothing more has been heard from the agent in Hollywood; if he does not come, Rayner will send Tolkien's first two pages of comments to Forrest J. Ackerman and say that further considerations will follow. He is arranging for copies of *The Fellowship of the Ring* and *The Two Towers* to be sent to Hal Coomer.

30 May 1958 Rayner Unwin sends Tolkien's unfinished letter to Forrest J. Ackerman of April or early May to Allen & Unwin's agent in Hollywood.

1 June 1958 Tolkien writes to Hal Coomer. He has asked Allen & Unwin to send him the first two volumes of *The Lord of the Rings*. He will also send Coomer a label, or possibly two, with his signature and greetings to place in the books that are being sent by Allen & Unwin.

2 June 1958 Tolkien writes to Rayner Unwin. A decision on the Appendices can wait. Przemysl Mroczkowski, the head of the English department at Lublin, Poland, who has nearly completed a year in Oxford as a visiting scholar, is interested in translating *The Hobbit* and *The Lord of the Rings* into Polish. Although Mroczkowski is a very good English scholar, Tolkien has no idea of his skill with Polish, and has told him that it is up to Allen & Unwin to arrange contracts for translation.

9 June 1958 Tolkien writes a letter to Forrest J. Ackerman to accompany his lengthy commentary on the Zimmerman story-line. He is sorry if Zimmerman or others feel 'irritated or aggrieved by the tone of many of my criticisms. . . . But I would ask them to make an effort of imagination sufficient to understand the irritation (and on occasion the resentment) of an author, who finds, increasingly as he proceeds, his work treated as it would seem carelessly in general, in places recklessly, and with no evident signs of any appreciation of what it is all about.' He quotes an extract from an essay by C.S. Lewis, 'On Stories' (1947), criticizing a film version of *King Solomon's Mines* which substituted a subterranean volcanic eruption and an earthquake for the simple entombment of the heroes in a rock chamber. Lewis speculated that 'the scene in the original' may not have been 'cinematic', and therefore the filmmaker 'was right, by the canons of his own art, in altering it. *But it would have been better not to have chosen in the first place a story which could be adapted to the screen only by being ruined.* Ruined, at least for me' (italics added by Tolkien). Tolkien comments that these 'are my sentiments and opinions too' (Special Collections and University Archives, John P. Raynor, S.J., Library, Marquette University; partly printed in *Letters*, p. 270).

10 June 1958 Edgar Carter of H.N. Swanson, Allen & Unwin's agents in Hollywood, sends Forrest J. Ackerman Tolkien's comments on the story-line (the two-page unfinished letter of April or early May). He promises to send Tolkien's complete analysis as soon as he receives it.

12 June 1958 English Final Honour School Examinations begin.

13 June 1958 Robert Burchfield, Early English Text Society, writes to Tolkien. He reminds him that 30 June, the deadline for delivery of his transcript of the *Ancrene Wisse*, is fast approaching.

16 June 1958 Tolkien writes to Rayner Unwin, returning the Zimmerman story-line to Rayner Unwin, together with a lengthy commentary (partly printed in *Letters*, pp. 271–7) and the covering letter to Forrest J. Ackerman dated 9 June. He has made copies of both for himself. 'I do not want . . . to kill the project, which I think promised well on the pictorial side; but there is a limit to one's endurance. I fear that close study of "Z" causes me to think that he is probably *not* a person of sufficient competence in this line to do a tolerable job.' He fears that at times his comments show his annoyance, but he has no time to rewrite them. 'If you think the stuff is too stiff, and tantamount to saying NO; please do what you will with it. But . . . I think you will probably agree that we could not accept it as it stands without compensation in cash far beyond the means of these people!' (Tolkien-George Allen & Unwin archive, HarperCollins).

19 June 1958 Rayner Unwin, having returned from a trip to Poland, writes to Tolkien that two Polish publishers are interested in *The Hobbit* and *The Lord of the Rings*. Half of the payments for translation rights cannot be transferred out of Poland, but Allen & Unwin usually adjust the amount asked so that the 50% transferable into sterling is not too insignificant. He hopes to make agreements with Iskry for *The Hobbit* and Czytelnik for *The Lord of the Rings*.

20 June 1958 At a meeting of the English Faculty Board, in Tolkien's absence, he is re-elected to the board of electors for the Jesus Professorship in Celtic, and to the electors to the O'Donnell Lecturership in Celtic Studies until Michaelmas Term 1963. But since Tolkien is to retire in 1959, the Board chooses new electors for other positions: Eric Dobson succeeds Tolkien as an elector for the Rawlinson and Bosworth Professorship; Basil Willey as an elector for the Merton Professorship of English Literature; and C.L. Wrenn as an elector for the Taylorian Professorship of German Language and Literature.

21 June 1958 Trinity Full Term ends.

22 June 1958 Tolkien writes to Robert Burchfield. He asks him to ring him on 23 June, preferably in the morning between 10.00 a.m. and 12.30 p.m. He presumably asks for an extension of his deadline for *Ancrene Wisse*.

24 June–2 July 1958 Tolkien travels to Ireland to act as Extern Examiner for the National University of Ireland.

July 1958 Lionel Stanley, a devoted fan and amateur photographer, visits Tolkien at Merton College and takes several photographs of him: two portraits, two of him in his study at Merton, two in the Fellows' Quadrangle, and two under trees in the college grounds. Later he will send Tolkien the negatives.

August 1958 Tolkien works hard to finish his edition of the *Ancrene Wisse*. He will write in a letter of 14 October 1958 that he 'was all through August working long hours, seven days a week, against time, to finish a piece of work' (letter to Rhona Beare, *Letters*, p. 278)

6 August 1958 Rayner Unwin writes to Tolkien, asking 'tenderly' about the status of 'The Silmarillion'.

?Late August–?early September Rhona Beare sends writes to Tolkien with a series of questions about *The Lord of the Rings*, so that she can give his answers to fellow enthusiasts.

?30 August 1958 George Sayer stays with C.S. Lewis in Oxford while both Lewis's wife Joy and brother Warren are away. In the evening, R.E. Havard drives Tolkien to Lewis's home, picks up Lewis and Sayer, and drives them to Studley Priory, at that time Lewis's favourite country hotel.

> While Jack was paying the bill after a hilarious dinner, we talked a little about his health. Tolkien was gloomy about the terrible strains and anxieties Jack was suffering: Warren's drunkenness, two rather difficult boys, and 'a strange marriage' to 'a sick and domineering woman'. It turned out that what worried him most was that she was a divorcee. He did not accept my argument that she could not have been divorced, since as a Christian she had never been married. However, the reappearance of Jack forestalled a discussion of this question. [Sayer, *Jack: A Life of C.S. Lewis* (2nd edn. 1994), p. 375]

3 September 1958 Tolkien gives his typescript of the *Ancrene Wisse* to Robert Burchfield, with the first page of a memorandum letter to the Early English Text Society Council, presumably urging that the *Ancrene Wisse* should be printed line-by-line.

4 September 1958 Robert Burchfield sends Tolkien's typescript of the *Ancrene Wisse* to Oxford University Press.

c. 4–8 September 1958 Tolkien completes his memorandum letter to the Early English Text Society Council with three more pages.

8 September 1958 Robert Burchfield writes to Tolkien about *Ancrene Wisse* and its printing. The printer has agreed to produce two specimens of the same passage by 27 September. In the first he will try to do as Tolkien wants: preserve the lines of the (prose) manuscript, and 'attempt to produce an even right hand margin by varying (within limits) the spacing between words, and by over-running (without counting the over-runs as lines) where there is much Latin'. In the second, the text will be printed continuous, but with an apostrophe inserted within the printed lines to indicate the end of manuscript lines. Burchfield favours the second format, which the Society has used in publishing other manuscripts of the *Ancrene Riwle*, and lists his reasons: consistency; the Society might one day produce a facsimile edition which would show the original line-by-line in a more pleasing format; Tolkien's proposed layout would look ugly; and 'the more important line-end features (errors, unusual forms) can be dealt with in the introduction'. He continues with comments and suggestions on the representation of capitals, underlinings, and other details, and wonders if such slight details as 'a blue spot on outer left margin' need be noted (Tolkien Papers, Bodleian Library, Oxford). He asks to keep Tolkien's text a while longer to show to Dr Onions.

?9–?20 September 1958 Tolkien drafts a reply to Robert Burchfield (three typed pages) in which he counters each of the points made against Tolkien's preferred format. Burchfield is, 'of course', entitled to his 'views and prejudices. If I think you wrong, and your arguments sometimes confused and inconsistent, your remarks are helpful, and they are made with your usual courtesy. . . .' The series, he notes, 'is already inconsistent . . . There is no virtue in mere consistency as such: it may become mere persistence – in error. We are not dealing with consistent documents'. In response to the suggestion that the Society might produce a facsimile one day: 'I thought that scholars were so hungry for a printed version "A" [the *Ancrene Wisse* manuscript from Cambridge] that if I did not produce mine tout de suite, I was to be sacked.' He rejects the criticism of 'ugliness' and thinks that what Burchfield really means is 'not in conformity with the practice of modern presses in general, and of the Clarendon Press in particular'. He declares that important line-end features cannot be dealt with in the introduction to the book, and gives his reasons. He then discusses other details mentioned by Burchfield, agreeing with his suggestion for the representation of coloured initials, but adding: 'I toyed with the idea of open forms in outline for red; and black for blue. But I expect that, even if practical, is the unnecessary niggling of a man who has pored over a single document too long. I do wish, though, that something could be done about that wretched "thorn"' (the Anglo-Saxon character as represented in the font to be used). He thanks Burchfield for a correction and remarks: 'I have transcribed the reproduction (in many cases several times). The transcript has been compared with the original twice (with a magnifying glass). The final form submitted was compared with the reproduction. But I still find errors. Depressing.' He discusses the layout of various references on the page. Burchfield should keep the transcript and show it to the Council at the meeting to be held on 27 September, which he cannot attend. He is at present 'sinking under a tide of theses and scripts', but once term begins he intends 'to compose the introductory matter – within the limits of my competence. I should prefer to do this. But the result will need a lot of correction, and supplementing I fear' (Tolkien Papers, Bodleian Library, Oxford). He finishes with comments about a text prepared by W. Meredith Thompson which Burchfield has sent him. – Tolkien alters his draft memorandum to the Early English Text Society Council in the light of Burchfield's letter of 8 September. He produces ten typescript pages, reproducing folios 12b–17a of the *Ancrene Wisse* manuscript, as if printed, but with large initials drawn in, plus other typed specimen layouts indicating the various ways the manuscript might be printed, both in a line-by-line format (which he wants) and as a solid block with an apostrophe marking line-ends (which he rejects – if printed as a solid block, line-ends should not be indicated). In his memorandum he says that these specimens 'are only intended as an illustration of what seems to me desirable, and I hope possible. But if the unaccommodating typewriter can make a fair job of it, a compositor with far more adaptable means of expansion and contraction at his disposal, may perhaps do better – if he will try.' He discusses at length how to deal with short or long lines, and the overruns necessitated by the latter, and still obtain a straight right edge, which is what the Council wants. He feels that the text of the *Ancrene Wisse* 'could be printed line by line *and* with a straight right edge, with little trouble, granted the willing co-operation of the compositor'. He admits that printing the text as a block would save space: the manuscript has 6539 lines, which if printed in a block would probably take 6421 lines, needing about 184 pages at 35 lines per page (or 189 at 34 lines per page); if set line-by-line, the overruns might bring the total number of lines to about 6866. He calculates the number of pages required for this if printed 34 or 35 lines per page (197 or 202 pages), concluding that the line-by-line method would require approximately 13 more pages than printing the text as a solid block. He leaves it to the Council to decide if these extra pages are 'too costly'. Some members of the Council having objected to the 'ugliness' of a line-by-line format, Tolkien criticizes 'the general unloveliness of the versions [of the *Ancrene Riwle*] so far printed' and thinks that some of their 'least lovely features ... have no utility' (Tolkien Papers, Bodleian Library, Oxford).

11 September 1958 Robert Burchfield writes to Tolkien. When he showed Tolkien's transcription of the *Ancrene Wisse* to C.T. Onions, the latter was impressed, and supported Tolkien's view that it should be printed line-by-line. Burchfield would now like to show it to J.A.W. Bennett. He asks by what date Tolkien needs it returned.

17 September 1958 Alina Dadlez, George Allen & Unwin, writes to Tolkien. Agreement has been reached with Czytelnik for a Polish translation of *The Lord of the Rings*. Czytelnik have signed a contract for *The Fellowship of the Ring* only, and have options on the other volumes. They have been informed of Tolkien's wish that the word *Hobbit* should be retained, and that he 'should be consulted by the translator about geographical and proper names, etc. and they have promised to comply with these conditions' (Tolkien-George Allen & Unwin archive, HarperCollins).

22 September 1958 Tolkien writes to Robert Burchfield, asking him to present Tolkien's apologies for absence at the Council meeting. Probably referring to his long letter and memorandum, he comments: 'Like the advertisement of soap I expect that you find I produce *too much* or *too little* (or nil);

but I both hope and intend to conclude this affair as soon as possible' (Early English Text Society archive).

23 September 1958 Tolkien takes his granddaughter Joanna to her school, St Mary's Abbey, Oulton, Staffordshire, where Christopher Wiseman's sister, the Reverend Mother Mary St John, is headmistress. – He then continues to Ireland to act as Extern Examiner for the National University of Ireland.

24 September 1958 Robert Burchfield writes to Tolkien. He sends some specimens produced by Oxford University Press, the best the printer could do at short notice. He has not attempted to achieve a justified right margin. The Council will have to consider the difference in cost between a version set ragged right and one with a straight right edge; the latter would naturally be more costly. 'At the meeting members of the Council will have to imagine the aesthetic appeal of spaced out lines. They will have your several pages of specially prepared typescript for comparison too, and also cyclostyled [mimeographed] copies of your memo . . .' (Tolkien Papers, Bodleian Library, Oxford).

24 September–7 October 1958 Tolkien will write to Robert Burchfield on 8 October that during this time he covers 1,500 miles. 'On Sept. 24th I was involved in an alarming tempest at sea, and began to think I should suffer the fate of Lycidas King. I arrived 5 hours overdue in Dublin at noon on 25th, rather battered; and I have since crossed Eire (E–W, and N–S) about 6 times, read 130 lbs (avd [avoirdupois]) of theses, assisted in the exams of 4 colleges, and finally presided at fellowship-vivas in Dublin before re-embarking (doubled up with lumbago)' (Early English Text Society archive).

27 September 1958 The Early English Text Society Council meets. The members discuss a specimen page of *Ancrene Wisse*, and Tolkien's transcript is displayed. It is decided to print the edition line-by-line and to have a justified right margin, spacing out words or running over lines as needed, provided that the cost of printing is not excessive. – Immediately after the meeting, Robert Burchfield writes to inform Tolkien of the decision. The Printer will be asked for a specimen page with the right-hand margin justified, and for an estimate of the difference in cost between justified and unjustified margins. He lists various points of presentation decided at the meeting and sends Tolkien a fresh copy of the specimen, asking him to adjust text and footnotes in accordance with the decisions made. He apologizes for having inflicted his personal views upon Tolkien, and says that he is delighted that Tolkien's colleagues on the Council supported him.

3 October 1958 In Cork Tolkien finds Burchfield's letters of 24 and 27 September waiting for him.

7 October 1958 Tolkien returns from Ireland to Oxford. He will write to Robert Burchfield on 8 October: 'My train broke down at Leamington, and I arrived home late to find it more or less in ruins. None of the time-schedules had been adhered to, and I came on a lot of unsupervised hobbits smoking in the garage, while the house had neither gas, water, cooking facilities or lavatories [he and Edith are evidently having work done in their house]. Into this chaos my wife arrived two hours later. My whole attention is for the moment concentrated on 'domestic affairs'; I have exhausted my vocabulary, and nearly fused the telephone-wires' (Early English Text Society archive).

8 October 1958 Tolkien writes to Robert Burchfield, thanking him for his trouble and begging him not to apologize. He had every right to express his views – 'to a friend after all, not a stranger; and if my pleasure in controversy led me into any intemperate expressions, forget them!' (Early English Text Society archive). He will deal with the specimens as soon as possible; he is 'at the moment very tired, and my domestic affairs [are] in chaos', as he describes.

12 October 1958 Michaelmas Full Term begins. Tolkien's only scheduled lectures for this term are *Sir Gawain and the Green Knight* on Wednesdays and Fridays at 11.00 a.m. in the Examination Schools, beginning 15 October. He continues to supervise B.Litt. students W.O. Evans, L. Glanville, and J. Ross, D.Phil. students A. Kurvinen and M.C. Seymour, and probationer B.Litt. student V.A. Kolve.

14 October 1958 Tolkien belatedly writes a twelve-page reply to Rhona Beare. His draft for the letter includes further material not included in the letter sent.

17 October 1958 Tolkien attends an English Faculty Board meeting. The Applications Committee has appointed him supervisor of two probationer B.Litt. students: R.J. Jones of St Hugh's College, who is to work on a medieval English Literature subject, and D.J. Tittensor of Merton College, who is to work on a Middle English philology subject.

24 October 1958 The Committee for Comparative Philology meets at 5.00 p.m. in the Delegates Room, Clarendon Building.

25 October 1958 Tolkien replies to a letter from Deborah Webster (later Deborah Webster Rogers, author of a Ph.D. thesis on Tolkien and C.S. Lewis in relation to their medieval sources). He does not like to give facts about himself, because he thinks 'the contemporary trend in criticism with its excessive interest' in details of an author's life only distracts attention from the author's works. But he does discuss some points, including possible influences of his religion on *The Lord of the Rings*, and ends with a sketch of his personal tastes:

I am in fact a *Hobbit* (in all but size). I like gardens, trees and un-mechanized farmlands; I smoke a pipe, and like good plain food (unrefrigerated), but detest French cooking; I like, and even dare to wear in these dull days, ornamental waistcoats. I am fond of mushrooms (out of a field); have a very simple sense of humour (which even my appreciative critics find tiresome); I go to bed late and get up late (when possible). I do not travel much. I love Wales (what is left of it, when mines, and the even more ghastly sea-side resorts, have done their worst), and especially the Welsh language. But I have not in fact been in W[ales] for a long time (except for crossing it on the way to Ireland). I go frequently to Ireland (Eire: Southern Ireland) being fond of it and of (most of) its people; but the Irish language I find wholly unattractive. [*Letters*, pp. 288–9]

– Tolkien replies to a letter from George Engle (later the lawyer Sir George Engle). If there is a new edition of *The Lord of the Rings*, an index will replace part of the Appendices. Much more could go if he could find time to prepare the First and Second Age material for publication, but his professional colleagues, since discovering how he has been wasting time, are applying pressure for him to produce long promised works.

26 October 1958 Tolkien writes a letter to Mrs L.M. Cutts. He thinks that any analysis of the sources of *The Lord of the Rings* would be very complex, and probably not worth doing, but gives a few examples.

27 October 1958 Dr Küntzel of Almqvist & Wiksell/Gebers writes to Tolkien. He explains various problems that have delayed the publication of the Swedish translation of *The Fellowship of the Ring*.

30 October 1958 The English Faculty meet at 8.30 p.m. at St Anne's College, Oxford.

November 1958 Peter Goolden's edition of *The Old English Apollonius of Tyre*, with a prefatory note by Tolkien, is published. In his preface Goolden says that he is indebted to his editors, 'especially Professor J.R.R. Tolkien who kindly suggested revisions in presentation and style' (p. vi).

?Late 1958 A.C. Nunn writes to Tolkien, pointing out a contradiction in Gollum's claim that the Ring was his 'birthday present' and the statement in the first chapter of *The Lord of the Rings* that 'Hobbits give presents to other people on their own birthdays'.

4 November 1958 Rayner Unwin writes to Tolkien. He hopes to come to Oxford on Wednesday, 12 November, and would like to see Tolkien at some convenient time.

5 November 1958 Bonamy Dobrée writes to Tolkien. He is the editor of the series *Writers and their Work*, published by the British Council 'for the use and edification of foreign students of English, and amateurs of its literature'. He asks Tolkien if he would write on *Beowulf* for the series. They need 'someone with knowledge, with lore of the subject-matter, and who can write' (National Archives, Kew, BW 2/650). He gives details of the usual format, contents, length (10,000 words maximum, excluding bibliography), intended audience, and the fee to be paid.

6 November 1958 Tolkien writes to Rayner Unwin. He asks if Rayner could lunch with him in college at 1.00 p.m. on 12 November, but in a postscript notes that he has been summoned to a college meeting at 2.00 p.m. that day, which will make lunch impossible. They will have meet at 11.55 a.m. at the Examination Schools, or after 3.00 p.m.

7 November 1958 Tolkien replies to Bonamy Dobrée. He is very attracted by the proposal to write on *Beowulf*, and will accept if the matter is not urgent. He has other unfulfilled commitments which he needs to deal with before he retires, and in particular the introduction to his edition of the *Ancrene Wisse*. He will have no time to deal with *Beowulf* until the following term. 'I do not think I should take very long, once I started (though I am a slow composer). The bibliography would be my chief headache. I have not kept up' (National

Archives, Kew, BW 2/650). He would like to see Dobrée, if he is ever in Oxford, but cannot easily get away himself, mainly because of his wife's health.

10 November 1958 Edith Tolkien has a serious fall at home and breaks her arm. – Rayner Unwin writes to Tolkien. He will see him on 12 November at 3.00 p.m., at Merton College. – Bonamy Dobrée writes to Tolkien. There is no great urgency for *Beowulf.* He is pleased that Tolkien is willing to take it on.

12 November 1958 Tolkien attends a Merton College meeting at 2.00 p.m. – He presumably meets Rayner Unwin at Merton at 3.00 p.m.

18 November 1958 L. Brander of the British Council sends Tolkien a formal commissioning letter for *Beowulf.*

?Late November 1958 Tolkien writes to either Bonamy Dobrée or L. Brander. He explains that because of his wife's accident he will be unable to write on *Beowulf* for the British Council. He notes on Brander's letter 'Cancelled', which he later interprets as meaning that he wrote a letter to this effect. But no such letter is received by the British Council.

5 December 1958 Tolkien attends an English Faculty Board meeting. Helen Gardner reports on behalf of the Standing Committee on Monographs on progress of works being prepared for publication.

6 December 1958 Michaelmas Full Term ends.

?Late 1958–?early 1959 Tolkien drafts, and perhaps sends, a long reply to A.C. Nunn. To account for the discrepancy of present-giving among Hobbits in *The Lord of the Rings*, he devises much detail about Hobbit customs which does not appear elsewhere (see *Letters*, pp. 289–96).

?Late 1958–?mid-1960 Tolkien returns to 'The Silmarillion' to prepare it for publication. He apparently does little sustained work on it during 1958, but with secretarial assistance begins to make progress in 1959. *See note.*

Tolkien's various secretaries make a number of typescripts from existing manuscripts or typescripts, and incorporate any emendations made to them. Tolkien uses some of these as the basis of further significant work. He emends others more casually at various times, sometimes in different ways on the top and carbon copies.

A major new element now introduced is that the children of Finwë, the ruler of the Noldor, do not have the same mother. Tolkien inserts into the old text of the *Quenta Silmarillion* a rider with the new story of the 'death' of Fëanor's mother, Míriel, after his birth, and the refusal of her spirit to return to her body; Finwë's second marriage, to Indis of the Vanyar; and Fëanor's resentment of his half-brothers. At about the same time, he inserts similar entries into the *Annals of Aman* which predate an amanuensis typescript made in this period. In association with this new material, Tolkien writes an independent text on the nature of the Eldar, their marriage laws and customs, and the meaning to the Elves of death, immortality, and rebirth: a completed manuscript, *Laws and Customs among the Eldar*, is revised in a partial typescript made in 1959 or later. Presumably between the manuscript and typescript of *Laws and Customs among the Eldar* Tolkien types (on his older typewriter) a new chapter, 'Of Finwë and Míriel', for the *Quenta Silmarillion*. He decides not to use this, however, and makes two successive typescripts (1959 or later) to replace the sixth chapter and part of the seventh chapter of the existing *Quenta Silmarillion* ('Of Fëanor and the Silmarilli, and the Darkening of Valinor' and 'Of the Flight of the Noldor') subdivided into new chapters: 'Of Finwë and Míriel', 'Of Fëanor and the Unchaining of Melkor', 'Of the Silmarils and the Unrest of the Noldor', 'Of the Darkening of Valinor', 'Of the Rape of the Silmarils', and 'Of the Thieves' Quarrel'.

Tolkien rewrites part of the chapter of the *Quenta Silmarillion* entitled 'Of the Naugrim and the Edain'. He gives the first version, which deteriorates into confusion, the title 'Of Aulë and the Dwarves', and inscribes it 'Amended Legend of the Origin of the Dwarves'. He inserts the following fair copy into the *Quenta Silmarillion* as a separate chapter, 'Concerning the Dwarves'. He also makes a new version of the second part of the original chapter, with the title 'Of the Coming of Men into the West and the Meeting of the Edain and the Eldar'. In this the Edain reach Beleriand much earlier, which requires changes in chronologies and the making of new genealogies.

Tolkien makes emendations on an amanuensis typescript of the first chapter of the *Quenta Silmarillion*, 'Of the Valar', and then himself makes two successive typescripts (1959 or later) introducing changes and new subsections, 'Of the Maiar' and 'Of the Enemies', but decides that these should be a separate work with the title *Valaquenta*. Elsewhere in the *Quenta Silmarillion* he makes only a few emendations.

The tragic story of Húrin and Morwen, and of their children Túrin and Nienor, becomes of increasing importance to Tolkien in his later years. Christopher Tolkien will write that for his father this story became 'the dominant and absorbing story of the end of the Elder Days, in which complexity of motive and character, trapped in the mysterious workings of Morgoth's curse, sets it altogether apart'. The narratives that result show a greater confidence and immediacy, 'as if the focus of the glass by which the remote ages were viewed had been sharply changed' (*The War of the Jewels*, pp. viii–ix).

Tolkien returns to the *Narn i Chîn Húrin*, writing an extensive text of the earlier history of Túrin up to his time in Nargothrond. He makes important changes in the story and introduces much new material, but never completes or develops what he writes into a finished form. The texts become increasingly scrappy, and in the later parts exist only in discontinuous fragments and outlines. Tolkien also writes an 'introductory note' to the *Narn* in two versions, a clear manuscript followed by a typescript, then a typescript which describes its writing and transmission. Associated with this work, he makes several plot-synopses arranged in annalistic form.

Tolkien writes the story of Húrin in a substantial text, *The Wanderings of Húrin*. This describes Húrin's return to Hithlum after his release by Morgoth and his adventures in Brethil, and was probably intended to continue with his journeys to Nargothrond and Doriath. The original draft deteriorates towards the end, and Tolkien begins a new draft from part way through the story. He then makes a typescript (1959 or later). When his ideas for the story and the social organisation of the Men of Brethil change as he types, he adapts the typescript with extensive manuscript emendations and replaces substantial passages with new typescript. *See note.*

22 December 1958 Tolkien writes to his grandson Michael George, enclosing a book token for Christmas. 'I hope it will come in time, but I have been having a very difficult and laborious period.' It has been raining in Oxford: 'We are as sodden as old blotting paper down here' (British Library MS Add. 71657).

1959

1 January 1959 Rayner Unwin forwards a letter from a Spanish admirer, and wishes Tolkien a Happy New Year.

12–16 January 1959 At some time during this period Tolkien visits a colleague of P.H. Newby while she is convalescing in Oxford. They talk about many things, including Irish culture in the Dark Ages, the role of the BBC Third Programme in combating the narrowness of culture today, and ideas for radio talks that Tolkien might give.

12 January 1959 Simon Mario Reuel Tolkien, son of Christopher and Faith Tolkien, is born. – Norman Davis is elected to succeed Tolkien as Merton Professor of English Language and Literature.

15 January 1959 Tolkien attends a Merton College meeting.

18 January 1959 Hilary Full Term begins. Tolkien's only scheduled lectures for this term are on *Sawles Warde*, on Fridays at 11.00 a.m. in the Examination Schools, beginning 23 January. He continues to supervise B.Litt. students W.O. Evans and J. Ross, D.Phil. students A. Kurvinen and M.C. Seymour, and probationer B.Litt. students R.J. Jones and D.J. Tittensor. V.A. Kolve is now a B.Litt. student supervised by Miss Lea. By 13 March Tolkien will help R.J. Jones to choose the thesis topic *Sir Kaye in Medieval Arthurian Literature*, but Jones's work will be supervised by G.V. Smithers.

21 January 1959 Rayner Unwin writes to Tolkien. He asks him to inscribe copies of *The Fellowship of the Ring* for two booksellers who have been enthusiastic in selling *The Lord of the Rings*.

23 January 1959 Tolkien attends an English Faculty Board meeting.

28 January 1959 Rayner Unwin writes to Tolkien. He asks if the Professor Davis who has been elected to succeed Tolkien is the one with whom Rayner had English Language tutorials at Oriel College, Oxford in about 1948.

29 January 1959 Tolkien returns the copies of *The Fellowship of the Ring*, autographed, to Rayner Unwin, with a letter. He has not been able to work seriously on 'The Silmarillion', or on anything else, and probably will not until his retirement. Het Spectrum have told him that they are translating *The Hobbit* into Dutch, but he has heard nothing more about the Swedish translation.

30 January 1959 The Committee for Comparative Philology meets at 5.00 p.m. in the Delegates Room of the Clarendon Building. – Rayner Unwin writes to Tolkien. Allen & Unwin have sold Polish translation rights to *The Hobbit*.

4 February 1959 Tolkien writes to Rayner Unwin. Norman Davis had indeed been Rayner's tutor in 1948. Tolkien urges Rayner to send congratulations to Davis, and is himself very pleased by the appointment. – Charles Lewis of George Allen & Unwin writes to Tolkien. The publishers have received a request for *The Hobbit* to be serialized in edited pictorial form in a children's paper called *Playhour*, samples of which Lewis encloses. If Tolkien agrees, the publisher of *Playhour* is willing to discuss details with him and submit drafts for his approval.

6 February 1959 Tolkien writes to Rayner Unwin, enclosing a letter dated 3 December 1958 which he has found among his neglected fan mail, from someone who wants to make a motion picture of *The Hobbit* in four sections, lasting nine to ten hours. Tolkien has replied that the matter is in the hands of Allen & Unwin.

7 February 1959 Tolkien writes to Charles Lewis at Allen & Unwin. He agrees to the *Playhour* proposal in principle, and would be pleased to discuss details with any representatives if they wish to see him, but is content to wait and see drafts. 'I really only feel anxious about one point: the dwarves should not be made ridiculous in the Disney manner (nor "Hobbits")' (Tolkien-George Allen & Unwin archive, HarperCollins).

10 February 1959 Charles Lewis writes to Tolkien. A representative of *Playhour* wants to arrange a meeting with Tolkien in Oxford to discuss illustrations, text, etc. for the adaptation of *The Hobbit*. Lewis has given her Tolkien's address. An appointment will be made for 26 February.

11 February 1959 Rayner Unwin writes to Tolkien. He looks with trepidation on the proposal to film *The Hobbit*, which would 'incarcerate us in our local Odeons [cinemas] for nine or ten hours' (Tolkien-George Allen & Unwin archive, HarperCollins).

14 February 1959 Rayner writes to Tolkien. He has heard that Ackerman and company have decided not to take up their option on the film rights of *The Lord of the Rings*. Swanson, the agent for Allen & Unwin, has asked if Tolkien wants his notes on the story-line returned.

?Mid-February 1959 Tolkien writes to Bertram Rota, asking for the balance of the payment for the manuscripts sold to Marquette University, which has been held for his use during a planned visit to America in 1959. Edith's health will not permit him to travel. – Rota asks Tolkien to write a formal request for payment to be forwarded to Marquette. Tolkien does so by 21 February.

c. 24 February–?mid-March 1959 Tolkien falls ill and is admitted to hospital. He undergoes surgery for appendicitis.

24 February 1959 Tolkien authorizes his secretary, Miss A.M. Hope, to collect any letters or parcels sent to him at Merton College. – Miss Hope writes to Rayner Unwin. Tolkien has asked her to let Rayner know that he is in hospital and will not be able to see the representative from *Playhour* on 26 February as scheduled. He is prepared to let the magazine serialize *The Hobbit*, but would like Rayner to deal with the matter, and asks to see specimens of the pictures before they are agreed to. He also would like the notes he made on the Zimmerman story-line returned.

5 March 1959 Tolkien writes to William Ready at Marquette University, in reply to a letter of 24 February, thanking him for arranging payment for the manuscripts. He comments on his appendicitis, 'but it does not seem to be the only thing that is the matter'. Having received a copy of Ready's novel *The Poor Hater* just before his collapse, he hopes 'to recover sufficient concentration soon to be able to read it, among other things' (Department of Special Collections and University Archives, John P. Raynor, S.J., Library, Marquette University).

14 March 1959 Hilary Full Term ends.

?Mid-March–25 March 1959 Tolkien convalesces after his surgery, probably in Bournemouth.

18 March 1959 At a meeting of the Early English Text Society Council, in Tolkien's absence, it is decided to print 2,000 copies of *Ancrene Wisse* rather than the usual EETS run of 1,000 copies. It is agreed that Tolkien should be asked to supply his brief introduction by the Feast of Corpus Christi (28 May).

22 March 1959 Robert Burchfield writes to inform Tolkien of the decisions made at the Early English Text Society meeting, and sends him the approved specimen (with the right margin justified). He warns Tolkien that as the text is going to the printer immediately, proofs might be ready in a few weeks.

24 March 1959 *Joy Hill, Rayner Unwin's secretary, forwards to Tolkien a letter in which a reader of *The Lord of the Rings* asks about its languages and writing systems, and thinks that Tengwar has a superficial resemblance to Arabic and Southern Indian script.

25 March 1959 Tolkien returns to Oxford from his convalescence.

30 March 1959 Robert Burchfield writes to Tolkien. The latter's transcript of *Ancrene Wisse* is with the printer. Proofs should begin to arrive in June or July, and when corrected should be returned to Burchfield. Members of the Early English Text Society Council will also receive proofs, and will forward any comments to Burchfield to be sent on to Tolkien.

?April 1959 Tolkien ponders underlying theoretical or philosophical concepts in 'The Silmarillion' and begins to explore them in writing. In any event, he will wrap several short pieces of this sort in a newspaper dated April 1959. *See note.* Already in the mid-1940s he had considered whether to make Arda a round world from the beginning, but rejected the idea, at least temporarily; now 'he had come to believe . . . that the cosmos of the old myth was no longer valid; and at the same time he was impelled to try to construct a more secure "theoretical" or "systematic" basis for elements in the *legendarium* that were not to be dislodged' (Christopher Tolkien, *Morgoth's Ring*, p. 369). Closely linked with the shape of Arda is the question of whether the Sun and Moon were mythically created from the fruit and flower of the Two Trees, or if they had existed long before life in Middle-earth, and if the latter, why the light of the Two Trees was significant. Tolkien now makes notes on the problem on two slips of paper which he pins to the amanuensis typescripts of the *Annals of*

Aman. He seems to decide that despite the loss of some dramatic moments in the story, he cannot retain the 'astronomically absurd business of the making of the Sun and the Moon' (*Morgoth's Ring*, p. 370) and he would have to explain 'The Silmarillion' as a Mannish work in which Mannish myths and cosmic ideas were blended and confused with the 'true' account of events learned long ago by the Edain from the Elves.

But Tolkien's conceptions are still in flux, a state reflected in the texts later published as 'Myths Transformed' in *Morgoth's Ring*, and are often ambiguous, allusive, and sometimes illegible as Tolkien writes quickly to record his thoughts. In one text he considers how the Elves could still be 'Star-folk' if the Sun is coeval with the Earth: he makes an outline of how the story might be retold, and writes a section of narrative. He also considers how to preserve the significance of the light of the Two Trees if they do not precede the Sun and Moon, and discusses the Dome that Varda raised over Aman to protect the land from the defiled light of the sun. But he does not develop most of these ideas further. Christopher Tolkien will suggest that 'it seems at any rate arguable that while committed in mind to the abandonment of the old myth of the origin of the Sun and the Moon my father left in abeyance the formulation and expression of the new. It may be, though I have no evidence on the question one way or the other, that he came to perceive from such experimental writing . . . that the old structure was too comprehensive, too interlocked in all its parts, indeed its roots too deep, to withstand such a devastating surgery' (*Morgoth's Ring*, p. 383).

Tolkien also writes a four-page essay, *Some Notes on the 'Philosophy' of the Silmarillion*, and begins an expanded, twelve-page (but unfinished) version entitled **Notes on Motives in the Silmarillion*. In these he compares Morgoth with Sauron, and discusses the nature of Evil and the actions and motives of Manwë and the Valar. In **Melkor Morgoth*, he decides that Melkor must be made much more powerful, and considers consequent changes in the story. He begins a short essay on Orcs ('their nature and origin require more thought', *Morgoth's Ring*, p. 409), as well as a separate related note written quickly in pencil.

5 April 1959 Robert Burchfield writes to Tolkien. Professor Dickins has reported a difference between the *Ancrene Wisse* manuscript and the specimen produced by the printer, and also a printer's error in the specimen.

6 April 1959 Tolkien writes to Burchfield. Although he is not yet fully recovered from his illness, he is making good progress. He will try to complete an introduction to the *Ancrene Wisse* by 28 May, though it might be 'pretty sketchy'. He hopes that he 'shall have your sympathy in the troubles which have befallen me since I made a determined effort to clear up *Ancrene Wisse*. If I had been able to carry straight on I could have done the introduction more easily, but owing to the illnesses of my wife and myself I have not been able to look at it since the beginning of last September' (Tolkien Papers, Bodleian Library, Oxford). The discrepancy noted by Dickins is the result of a error made by Tolkien when typing from his original transcript. Tolkien comments that this is a warning that he must check the proofs against the facsimile. – Tolkien writes to Joy Hill. He tells her how to reply to the letter she had forwarded, pointing out that both the languages and scripts are invented. 'But it is impossible at this date to devise either a language or a script that has no resemblance in style or detail to others that have been in actual use or still are.' He is feeling better, but is 'appalled by the accumulation of neglected business' (Tolkien-George Allen & Unwin archive, HarperCollins).

12 April 1959 Tolkien writes to Peter Sutcliffe at Oxford University Press, regarding a list of suggested corrections sent by a reader for the Tolkien-Gordon edition of *Sir Gawain and the Green Knight*. These include some that Tolkien had not noticed before. He has accumulated a considerable number of corrections which might be incorporated in a reprint, though what is really required is a complete revision.

17 April 1959 In response to a request by Walter Allen to contribute to a symposium to be published in a children's book supplement of the *New Statesman*, Tolkien drafts a lengthy reply, but eventually sends only a brief letter to say that he has just returned from convalescence and cannot produce any copy by 19 April (presumably the deadline given him).

20 April 1959 Tolkien receives a letter from the Clarendon Press. They will not consider revising his and E.V. Gordon's edition of *Sir Gawain and the Green Knight* until current stocks are exhausted, in about three years.

22 April 1959 Joy Hill returns to Tolkien his notes on the film story-line, which have been recovered from Forrest J. Ackerman.

23 April 1959 Tolkien attends a Merton College meeting. – Charles Lewis of George Allen & Unwin sends Tolkien a letter from an American who has made a dramatization of *The Hobbit*, which the Yale Drama School would like to perform. The adapter offers to pay a royalty, subject to Tolkien's approval of the adaptation.

26 April 1959 Trinity Full Term begins. Tolkien's only scheduled lectures for this term are on *Sawles Warde*, on Wednesdays at 11.00 a.m. in the Examination Schools, beginning 29 April. His valedictory address is scheduled for Friday, 5 June at 11.00 a.m. in the Examination Schools, but the time and place will change. He continues to supervise B.Litt. student J. Ross, D.Phil. students A. Kurvinen and M.C. Seymour, and probationer B.Litt. student D.J. Tittensor.

30 April 1959 Tolkien writes to Charles Lewis. Lewis's letter arrived 'just at the outbreak of term, coinciding with the departure to more profitable fields of my part-time secretary [Miss Hope], leaving my papers in unwonted tidiness (which means I cannot readily discover the ones I want).' The adapter of *The Hobbit* sent him a copy of the play some time ago, but since the accompanying letter said nothing about performances or even asked his opinion, he has done nothing about it. He admits to a prejudice against dramatization and any kind of 'children's theatre', but might change his mind if the adaptation were 'good of its kind'. The present effort, however, seems to him 'a mistaken attempt to turn certain episodes of *The Hobbit* into a sub-Disney farce for rather silly children. . . . At the same time, it is entirely derivative.' He 'would rather not be associated with such stuff', but if the Yale Drama School is an official department of the University, he wonders if he should, 'as a university man, waive my objections. I would do so *on the understanding (or undertaking)* that the performance of this play is part of the normal processes of Drama School (sc. in the teaching and practice of drama-writing); and that the permission for performance does not imply approval of the play for publication, sale, or performance outside the Yale School. But it is probably better simply to say NO' (Tolkien-George Allen & Unwin archive, HarperCollins). He asks about the status of the *Hobbit* adaptation in *Playhour*.

1 May 1959 Tolkien attends an English Faculty Board meeting.

6 May 1959 Tolkien replies to a letter from a student at Harvard University who is writing his undergraduate thesis on Tolkien. Tolkien does not approve of research on living authors, but is willing to answer pertinent questions on his work, not about his life, if the process does not take too long. – Charles Lewis writes to Tolkien. He has sent a reply to the American adapter of *The Hobbit*, outlining Tolkien's reasons for rejecting the dramatization, but saying that Tolkien would not object to the performance of the play by the Yale Drama School only. Lewis hopes to hear from *Playhour* shortly.

8 May 1959 Tolkien sends a letter and cheque to Miss Hope, his departed secretary. He is grateful for her help, especially in beginning to put his papers in order.

26 May 1959 Tolkien replies to a letter from a Miss Robinson. He is glad that she wrote to him only about enjoying *The Lord of the Rings*, and not about interpretation of the work.

28 May 1959 Charles Lewis writes to Tolkien. The adapter of *The Hobbit* for the Yale Drama School has requested the return of her manuscript.

1 June 1959 A child sends Tolkien a fan letter written in the Angerthas runic script, which Tolkien transliterates (and presumably answers).

4 June 1959 Maria Skibniewska, who is translating *The Lord of the Rings* into Polish, writes to Tolkien with queries.

5 June 1959 Tolkien delivers his valedictory address to the University of Oxford at 5.00 p.m. in the Hall at Merton College, to a capacity audience. Tolkien enters in full spate, shouting the opening lines of *Beowulf*. The *Oxford Mail* will report on 6 June that 'this was a strictly academic farewell ... and a very vigorous one. The Professor re-fought, with gusto, some of the historic battles of the English Faculty. Even that warlike corner of the learned world has seen few more redoubtable guerrillas, and his resounding denunciation of old errors, alternating with deflating asides, or melodramatic declamation in Anglo-Saxons [*sic*] proved yesterday that he takes ample vigour to his retirement' ('Tolkien's Farewell', p. 4). One text of the address will be published in 1979, in *J.R.R. Tolkien, Scholar and Storyteller: Essays in Memoriam*, ed. Mary Salu and Robert T. Farrell; an alternate version will be published in *The Monsters and the Critics and Other Essays* (1983).

11 June 1959 English Final Honour School Examinations begin.

18 June 1959 Tolkien writes to Rayner Unwin. He would like to see Rayner soon to discuss something. Although he himself is more or less recovered, it would not be easy for him to come to London because of Edith's poor health. 'I have come to the end of my last term as Professor, though I do not actually hand over to my successor until September 30th; but my sins of omission in the past are still pursuing me. However, my chief need in the future will be financial and I feel inclined to give priority to any work likely to add to my much reduced income' (Tolkien-George Allen & Unwin archive, Harper-Collins). Tolkien will refuse the University pension, take the lump sum offered, and invest it in a trust managed by his bank.

19 June 1959 Tolkien attends his final English Faculty Board meeting at 3.30 p.m. in the Board Room, Clarendon Building, with Lord David Cecil in the chair. A B.Litt. certificate is granted to W.O. Evans whom Tolkien has supervised. R.B. Mitchell is appointed to replace Tolkien as supervisor of D.J. Tittensor. – Tolkien types a two-page reply to a fan letter, answering queries about *The Lord of the Rings*.

20 June 1959 Trinity Full Term ends.

23 June 1959 Tolkien attends a Merton College meeting.

Summer 1959 Having lost his room in Merton College on his retirement, Tolkien has to find space for the books he has kept there. Since his study-bedroom at home is already full, he decides to convert the garage into an office and library. Even so, he has to sell some of his books. It takes several months to sort everything out. – After his retirement, Tolkien finds himself isolated. Sandfield Road is some two miles from the centre of Oxford. He no longer has frequent meetings with his colleagues and friends at work or socially, and he misses their company and intellectual conversation.

24 June 1959 Encaenia.

27 June–2 July 1959 Tolkien is in Ireland as Extern Examiner for the National University of Ireland.

July 1959 James Reeves of the publisher William Heinemann, to whom P.H. Newby had lent the BBC copy of Tolkien's translation of *Sir Gawain and the Green Knight*, contacts Tolkien to say that Heinemann would like to publish it in their *Poetry Bookshelf* series. Tolkien having asked what sort of book is proposed, Reeves replies that 'we would like you to feel that this is *your* book, to edit as you think best' (quoted by Tolkien in a letter to Rayner Unwin, 27 August 1959, Tolkien-George Allen & Unwin archive, HarperCollins). Reeves offers useful suggestions as to matters which might be touched on in a brief introduction.

1 July 1959 Alina Dadlez of George Allen & Unwin forwards to Tolkien a letter from Mrs Skibniewska, the Polish translator. Allen & Unwin have recently sold Hebrew translation rights to *The Hobbit*.

3 July 1959 Tolkien replies to Alina Dadlez. He will try to answer Mrs Skibniewska as soon as possible. 'A proper answer will of course need a sketch of the general policy for her to follow (if she agrees), and that will require some thinking out. Though I have thought about the difficulties of name-translation in a language quite alien to English, which is a rather different situation to that presented by the Dutch translation.' He asks if Dadlez thinks that 'it would be useful if I cast my remarks in a form generally suitable? For instance, it might be then available for a Hebrew translation. Translators are of course of very different kinds. Not all are as humble as the Polish lady. I had an acrimonious correspondence with a very conceited Swede; in the end, of course, one gives way on the principle that any translation is better than none' (Tolkien-George Allen & Unwin archive, HarperCollins).

5 July 1959 Tolkien writes to Patricia Kirke. He comments on the chaos that resulted from losing his college room. Apparently he has found a successor to Miss Hope, possibly Elisabeth Lumsden, who is certainly his secretary in June 1960.

7 July 1959 Alina Dadlez writes to Tolkien. It would be very useful if he were to draft some general remarks and instructions for all future translators of *The Lord of the Rings*.

22 July 1959 Rayner Unwin forwards to Tolkien a letter from Robert Gutwillig, who is interested in making a film of *The Lord of the Rings*. He represents the Herb Jaffe Literary and Dramatic Agency of New York.

23 July 1959 A.R. Beal of William Heinemann writes to Tolkien about publishing his translation of *Sir Gawain and the Green Knight*.

27 July 1959 Tolkien replies to Robert Gutwillig. He has 'given a considerable amount of time and thought to' a film of *The Lord of the Rings*, 'and have already some ideas concerning what I think would be desirable, and also some notion of the difficulties involved, especially in the inevitable compression' (Tolkien-George Allen & Unwin archive, HarperCollins). But as Allen & Unwin are equally concerned, he is sending them a copy of his letter. – Tolkien writes to Rayner Unwin, enclosing a copy of Gutwillig's letter and his own reply. – A.R. Beal writes again to Tolkien, sending him a contract. In a covering letter he draws Tolkien's attention to the standard clause in the contract relating to the publisher's right of first refusal of the author's next work.

28 July 1959 Rayner Unwin writes to Tolkien, thanking him for sending a copy of the letter from Robert Gutwillig, who has already phoned Allen & Unwin.

29 July 1959 Robert Gutwillig writes to thank Tolkien for his most encouraging letter.

1 August 1959 Robert Murray, having been ordained a Catholic priest on 31 July, says his first Mass in St Aloysius Church in Oxford. He will later recall that Tolkien 'was proud to serve my first mass in 1959 (in full academic dress, excitement making him clumsy as a boy)' (*The Tablet*, 15 September 1973, p. 880). Christopher Tolkien is also present.

4 August 1959 Tolkien writes to Rayner Unwin.

I have got myself into a mess, owing to distractions and incompetence. . . . I was on the point of signing a contract with Heinemanns for the inclusion in their 'Poetry Bookshelf' of my translation of *Sir Gawain and the Green Knight*, when, observing in their Clause 15 the usual reference to giving the publishers first refusal of next or further works, I realised that my agreement with you contains a similar clause. . . . I really do not know how I came to do this, since I know that you would probably be perfectly willing to publish this translation, alone or with others, if I would only put it into order.

He thinks it 'high time *Sir Gawain* was published' and asks if Rayner would welcome it. He does not think it will delay work on 'The Silmarillion', as 'there are two things I must clear off and out of my mind before I give whole-hearted attention to my own stories: the *Ancrene Wisse*, the text of which, delayed by the [printers'] strike, will now shortly be coming in proof; and this business of *Sir Gawain*' (Tolkien-George Allen & Unwin archive, HarperCollins). In fact, the strike will prevent proofs of *Ancrene Wisse* from reaching him until February 1960. – Tolkien writes to A.R. Beal at Heinemann's. On reading his letter drawing his attention to the contract clause requiring first refusal, he has remembered that his contract with Allen & Unwin contains a similar clause, and they would probably consider that it covered his translation of *Sir Gawain*.

c. **5–11 August 1959** Tolkien helps his daughter Priscilla find a place to live in Oxford.

5 August 1959 Rayner Unwin writes to Tolkien. Allen & Unwin certainly want his *Sir Gawain and the Green Knight*, alone or with other translations.

7 August 1959 A.R. Beal writes to Tolkien. He appreciates Tolkien's position, but hopes that as *Sir Gawain* was commissioned for a specific series, Allen & Unwin will not raise any objections.

11 August 1959 Tolkien writes to A.R. Beal. He does not think that Allen & Unwin are willing to release *Sir Gawain*, and suggests that Beal contact Rayner Unwin. – Tolkien writes to Rayner Unwin. He cannot settle down to *Sir Gawain* and his other translations immediately, but thinks that it would be helpful if Rayner could visit him to discuss an agreement and the form of such a book. He hopes that Rayner can deal with Mr Beal, and encloses copies of Beal's latest letter and his own reply. 'It is not strictly true that the book was "commissioned", since the translation was known to be in existence' (Tolkien-George Allen & Unwin archive, Harper Collins). He has replied to a correspondent, who has been told by a bookseller that *Farmer Giles of Ham* is out of print, that he believes this to be incorrect.

12 August 1959 Tolkien replies to the Deputy Registrar, University of Madras, who has written to inform him (without any previous consultation) that he has been appointed a member of the University's Board of Examiners. Tolkien thanks him for the honour, but points out that he is now retired, and that it would be a good idea to consult the person involved before making such an appointment.

13 August 1959 Rayner Unwin writes to Tolkien. He will deal with Mr Beal. He suggests that he visit Tolkien at about 10.00 a.m. on 19 August to discuss *Sir Gawain*. – Sam Gelfman, of Herb Jaffe Associates, a colleague of Robert

Gutwillig, writes to Tolkien that he will be in London in September and will contact him.

16 August 1959 Tolkien writes to Rayner Unwin. He will be delighted to see him on Wednesday morning. Mr Roberts and Miss Clowes have contacted him in connection with the *Playhour* project, and propose to visit him some time that same morning with drawings, but it does not matter if their visit and Rayner's overlap.

19 August 1959 Rayner Unwin visits Tolkien. They discuss agreements for the publication of various works. Rayner agrees that these should not contain definite delivery dates, though Tolkien gives Rayner some idea of when he thinks they might be completed. Rayner will write to him the following day, summarizing their discussion: 'Unofficially I gather that you are likely to have *Sir Gawain* and possibly the expanded version of [*On*] *Fairy Stories* ready by about the end of the year, and *The Silmarillion*, we can hope for at about the end of 1960' (Tolkien-George Allen & Unwin archive, HarperCollins). They also discuss clearing rights to *On Fairy-Stories* with Oxford University Press, and agree that if Blackwell will release *Pearl* it could be published with *Sir Gawain*. – Later in the morning, Mr Roberts and Miss Clowes visit Tolkien.

20 August 1959 Rayner Unwin writes to Tolkien, enclosing three signed agreements. He also encloses a draft of a letter for Tolkien to send to Oxford University Press about *On Fairy-Stories*, and (presumably also agreed on 19 August) a note about the assessment of literary property for death duties.

23 August 1959 Tolkien writes to Rayner Unwin. He has sent the letter to Oxford University Press, but has not yet arranged to see Basil Blackwell about *Pearl*. When those matters are cleared up, 'I shall know where I stand; though standing will be about all I can manage, I fear, for some weeks. There will not be much room to sit! My study will be in the hands of the carpenter, my refuge in college closed, and the house upheaved by the transference of my daughter's furniture and belongings to her new abode in Oxford. Then comes the business of the National University of Ireland.' He has now resigned from the Irish appointment in future. He found the artist's work for the *Playhour Hobbit* 'at worst tolerable, at best very good', but declined to write the 'potted "story" under the pictures' (Tolkien-George Allen & Unwin archive, HarperCollins).

24 August 1959 Tolkien sees Basil Blackwell, who relinquishes any rights in Tolkien's translation of *Pearl*. On 25 August 1959 Tolkien will write to Rayner Unwin:

> As for the matter of my default and the cost of the abortive setting-up, [Blackwell] refuses to consider it. I feel a little better about this, for yesterday I tracked down in Christopher [Tolkien]'s library the lost galleys. Inspection showed them to have been of an astonishing badness; so that the cost of correction of about a thousand fatuous mistakes (from reasonable copy), which would have arisen if I had proceeded with the publication, was at any rate spared! [Tolkien-George Allen & Unwin archive, HarperCollins]

25 August 1959 Tolkien writes to Rayner Unwin about his successful meeting with Basil Blackwell, from whom he learned that Allen & Unwin are agents for the Levin and Münksgaard corpus of Icelandic literary monuments, which began to appear about 1930. Tolkien subscribed to the first six volumes, but could not afford to continue. Since neither he nor Christopher can now find room for these, he is considering trying to sell them. He asks Rayner if they are saleable. He has lost his glasses and broken his spare pair, and can hardly see if what he has typed to Rayner is legible. – John Brown of Oxford University Press writes to Tolkien. They consider *On Fairy-Stories* to be his property. – Rayner Unwin writes to Tolkien. He has had a letter from Mr Beal, 'who seems to think that Mr James Reeves has been more than a little responsible for ushering your *Gawain* into print and should consequently receive acknowledgement and, it is suggested, a fee' (Tolkien-George Allen & Unwin archive, HarperCollins).

27 August 1959 Tolkien writes to Rayner Unwin. Oxford University Press has disclaimed any rights in *On Fairy-Stories*. He does not think that the BBC has any publication rights to his translation of *Sir Gawain*, or of his introduction to it, and since the Clarendon Press is not considering a revised edition of the Tolkien-Gordon edition of *Sir Gawain and the Green Knight* in the near future, there should be no objection to his indicating his personal views in an introduction to the translation. In regard to Heinemann, he agrees that he has put them and James Reeves 'to a certain amount of unnecessary trouble', but cannot see what Reeves has done to earn a fee. Allen & Unwin knew of the translations long ago 'without the necessity of any midwifery by Reeves'. Reeves might be basing his claim on the reply he made to Tolkien's query as to the nature of the book he envisaged. The three suggestions he had made as to matters which might be touched on in an introduction were obvious points, which Tolkien had dealt with in his introduction and epilogue to the broadcast and which Reeves had probably seen. 'If you think a fee is justified on these grounds, or merely on the grounds of courtesy and saving my damaged face, please pay one – and debit me with the amount. But I think it is a case for "farthing" damages, if any.' He apologizes again for his odd behaviour in even considering the Heinemann offer.

> I suppose that the best form of amends would be to get *Gawain* and *Pearl* into your hands as soon as possible. The spirit is indeed willing; but the flesh is weak and rebellious. It has contracted lumbago, from amongst its weapons of delay – with the colourable excuse that an old man, robbed of helpers by mischance, should not shift bookcases and books unaided. Every book and paper I possess is now on the floor, at home and in college, and I have only a table to type on. When the turmoil will subside, I do not know for certain; nor in what state of weariness I shall then be. [Tolkien-George Allen & Unwin archive, HarperCollins]

– Rayner Unwin writes to Tolkien. He is delighted to hear of Basil Blackwell's generosity regarding *Pearl*.

31 August 1959 Rayner Unwin writes to Tolkien. He has sent a letter to Mr Beal which he thinks will settle the matter with Heinemann's.

?Autumn 1959–?beginning of 1960 On 9 December 1959 Tolkien will write to Rayner Unwin: 'with the help of my secretary I have been charging well ahead with the reconstruction of the Silmarillion etc.' (Tolkien-George Allen & Unwin archive, HarperCollins). Although he acquired a new secretary by early July, it seems unlikely that he does much writing until he has reorganized his garage as an office and library. Subsequent to writing *Laws and Customs among the Eldar*, Tolkien's ideas on Elvish rebirth and reincarnation change. He begins a new typescript text, *The Converse of Manwë and Eru*, but abandons it before it is finished, then writes a second, fuller form after a few pages.

He writes the *Athrabeth Finrod ah Andreth* for which some preliminary drafting exists, possibly based on a lost earlier version. In this the Elf Finrod and the mortal woman Andreth discuss the different fates of Elves and Men, the original design of Eru for Mankind, and its perversion by Morgoth. The debate proper is preceded by an introductory section. The first part considers the slowness of change in Aman which accords with the Elvish speed of 'growth' but which would be a curse not a blessing to a man. Tolkien detaches this as a separate work with the title *Aman*. The second part of the introductory section briefly describes the Elvish view of Men, and the background of the participants in the debate. Tolkien emends his manuscript and makes minor changes to the second of two amanuensis typescripts made from it, omitting the introductory text. He roughly drafts an emended version of the second part of introductory text, and makes a typescript and attaches these to the beginning of the second typescript and its carbon. After some rough drafting, he types (in top copy and carbon) a lengthy commentary on the *Athrabeth* (as Tolkien usually referred to the work) with numbered notes longer than the commentary. To one of them he attaches the *Tale of Adanel* recounting the legend of Melkor's Deception and the Fall of Man. He also makes a manuscript glossary or brief index of names and terms used in the *Athrabeth* proper, with definitions and some etymological information. Miscellaneous notes and short texts show that Tolkien is devoting a great deal of thought to the matters discussed in these papers. The text and the commentary are preserved in a folded newspaper of January 1960.

Tolkien develops his ideas of Elvish rebirth further in a rough manuscript, *Reincarnation of Elves*, written after the *Athrabeth* but before the commentary to that work.

7 September 1959 Tolkien writes to Bonamy Dobrée, probably having just received a letter from him expressing impatience at not hearing any news about Tolkien's essay on *Beowulf* for the British Council or any response to the letter he sent to Tolkien on 10 November 1958. Tolkien says that he had written, withdrawing from the project because his wife had had a serious accident, on that very day. There is no hope that he could undertake such a work for a very long time.

9 September 1959 Sam Gelfman visits Tolkien in the afternoon. They discuss a projected film of *The Lord of the Rings*. Tolkien finds him intelligent and reasonable, and tells him that the business arrangements would be in Allen & Unwin's hands. – Alina Dadlez of Allen & Unwin writes to Tolkien, asking if he has had time to draft some instructions for the Polish translator of *The Lord of the Rings*. She encloses a copy of a letter from the Polish publishers.

11 September 1959 Tolkien replies to Alina Dadlez. He has neglected Mrs Skibniewska's letter because of domestic troubles, and does not have the time to write a lot of notes for her use.

> As a general principle for her guidance, my preference is for as little translation or alteration of any names as possible. As she perceives, this is an English book and its Englishry should not be eradicated. That the Hobbits actually spoke an ancient language of their own is of course a pseudo-historical assertion made necessary by the nature of the narrative. . . . My own view is that the names of persons should all be left as they stand. I should prefer that the names of places were left untouched also, including Shire. The proper way of treating these I think is for a list of those that have a meaning in English to be given at the end, with glosses or explanation in Polish. I think a suitable method or procedure would be that which was followed in the Dutch and Swedish versions, with Mrs. Skibniewska making a list of all the names in the book which she finds difficult or which she might for any reason wish to alter or translate. I will then be very happy to annotate this list and criticise it. [Tolkien-George Allen & Unwin archive, HarperCollins, partly printed in *Letters*, p. 299]

– Tolkien writes to Rayner Unwin of his meeting with Sam Gelfman.

14 September 1959 Rayner Unwin forwards to Tolkien a letter from Ejnar Munksgaard offering to buy back the six volumes of the Icelandic Corpus.

18 September 1959 Tolkien replies to Rayner Unwin. Munksgaard's offer is not good enough.

22 September–8 October 1959 Tolkien visits Ireland as an Extern Examiner for the last time.

3 October 1959 At a meeting of the Early English Text Society Council, in Tolkien's absence, the question of the introduction to his edition of *Ancrene Wisse* is held over until the March 1960 meeting. Professor d'Ardenne is to be invited to submit her transcript of MS Bodley 34 for consideration.

9 October 1959 A letter from Eric Rogers, addressed to 'any Professor of English Language' at Oxford, has been passed to Tolkien despite the fact that he is now retired. In reply to the question of whether it is correct to say 'a number of office walls *has* been damaged', or '*have* been damaged', Tolkien writes: 'The answer is that you can say what you like. Pedantry insists that since *number* is a singular noun, the verb should be singular, (has). Common sense feels that since the *walls* is plural, and are really concerned, the verb should be plural (have). You make take your choice' (*Letters*, p. 300).

14 October 1959 Charles Lewis, George Allen & Unwin, writes to Tolkien. An admirer has asked whether it would constitute a breach of copyright if she were to register a litter of Siamese kittens under names taken from *The Lord of the Rings*.

15 October 1959 Tolkien replies to a letter from Naomi Mitchison. Now that he is retired, despite having belonged to the Federated Superannuation Scheme for universities, things would be meagre without income from his books.

16 October 1959 Tolkien replies to Charles Lewis. He considers that 'Siamese cats belong to the fauna of Mordor' (*Letters*, p. 300, incorrectly dated 14 October). – At an English Faculty Board meeting, appointments are made to replace Tolkien on various committees. The Board agrees to the chairman's motion to send a letter of appreciation to Professor Tolkien on his retirement from his professorship and from the Board.

22 October 1959 At the request of the English Faculty Board, D.M. Hawke, University Registrar, sends a letter to Tolkien expressing the Board's appreciation for his 'long and invaluable service' both as Merton Professor of English Language and Literature and as a member of the Board, and its 'regret that it will not in future have the benefit of your wise advice and unsparing help in its deliberations. It wishes at the same time to express its sense of the distinction which your wide, meticulous, and imaginative scholarship has brought to the faculty and to the University' (quoted in *Letters*, pp. 300–1).

24 November 1959 Tolkien replies to D.M. Hawke. He is 'deeply grateful to the Board of the Faculty of English for the extremely generous terms in which they have addressed me', and notes that 'one result of retirement that I never expected is that I actually miss the meetings of the Board. Not, of course, the agenda, but the gathering together of so many dear friends' (*Letters*, p. 301). This letter will be read to the Faculty Board at its next meeting on 4 December.

27 November 1959 In the evening, Tolkien hosts a dinner of The Society at Merton College. Eight members are present.

3 December 1959 Rayner Unwin writes to Tolkien, forwarding a letter from the Librarian of the Central Lending Library of Scunthorpe, and three lists she has made of names, places, and words in *The Lord of the Rings*. She has asked if Allen & Unwin would consider including this material in the book, but Rayner thinks that it would serve no purpose since they already have an index to be included at some point. As an alternative, she asks if she may produce the lists as a supplementary service to readers. Rayner does not object to this, but thinks that Tolkien might glance through the lists as a check against the index. He asks Tolkien how his three projects are progressing, and if he will finish *Sir Gawain* by the end of the year as he hoped.

9 December 1959 Tolkien writes to Rayner Unwin. The lists seem sufficiently accurate and complete to be useful to readers, and he sees no reason why 'Scunthorpians' should not benefit from them. He asks Rayner to tell the librarian that he appreciates her work and would like to keep the lists (carbon copies) for a little while 'as I should then be able to make them perhaps a little more useful by some corrections in the "tentative vocabulary". I think this is a remarkable performance, especially considering the very scanty information provided in the book about the languages concerned'. If she could spare him another carbon copy, he could retain one and return the other with corrections and suggestions. 'Her work is not of the same kind as the admirable index which you had prepared, but the linguistic analysis will prove a valuable addition to that.' He has 'become immersed again in work in which you are interested', but in the wrong order.

> With the help of my secretary I have been charging well ahead with the reconstruction of the Silmarillion etc. Your letter comes as a timely if unwelcome jerk on the reins. Quite clearly I must take up *Gawain* immediately. I shall not manage it before Christmas; but I recently ordered and inspected the material and I do not think that the actual text of the translation of *Gawain* and of *Pearl* now need very much work. I shall be able to let you have the text of the two poems soon after Christmas; they can I think be set up separately. I am still a little uncertain about the other matter to add to them by way of introduction or notes. I think very little, since people who buy the translations will probably belong to one of two classes: those who just want the translation, and those who have access to editions and other full treatments of the problems presented by the poems. [Tolkien-George Allen & Unwin archive, HarperCollins, partly printed in *Letters*, p. 301]

– Possibly in response to the lists sent by the Scunthorpe librarian, but certainly at about this time, Tolkien begins, but does not complete, an analysis of all fragments of other languages found in *The Lord of the Rings* (see *The War of the Ring*, p. 20).

10 December 1959 Rayner Unwin writes to Tolkien. He will write to the Librarian at Scunthorpe. He still wants to include an index in *The Lord of the Rings* when the publication of *The Silmarillion* makes it possible to omit a large part of the Appendices. Four thousand sets of *The Lord of the Rings* have been sold at a low price to the Readers' Union for distribution as a special choice to their members.

11 December 1959 Tolkien writes to Peter Sutcliffe at Oxford University Press about his and E.V. Gordon's edition of *Sir Gawain and the Green Knight*. He will send some corrections for a reprint, all minor. 'I am afraid any attempt to emend the book as a whole would be a major operation, requiring the rewriting of nearly everything except the text, and though I think I could do this and should like to do it, I cannot possibly do so for some time' (Oxford University Press archives). *See note.*

17 December 1959 Tolkien writes to Rayner Unwin, sending a letter he has received from a schoolteacher. She wants to produce dramatized episodes of *The Lord of the Rings* linked by a narrator as a sort of pageant on Speech Day. He has told her that he has no personal objection so long as it is for a particular occasion and is not published or repeated, but that Allen & Unwin must be consulted. – Rayner Unwin writes to Tolkien, enclosing two sets of a revised list sent by the Scunthorpe Librarian, and asking him to return the two sets he already has.

18 December 1959 Tolkien writes to Rayner Unwin, returning the one original list he received from the Scunthorpe Librarian. He will let her have an annotated copy in due course.

23 December 1959 Rayner Unwin writes to Tolkien. He has no objection to the adaptation of *The Lord of the Rings* as a pageant play for the school.

?End of 1959–?March 1960 Tolkien writes *Essekenta Eldarinwa* or **Quendi and Eldar*. He begins the work with much preliminary manuscript drafting, sometimes in multiple versions and often differing from the finished version. He then makes a typescript and carbon copy of nearly fifty closely typed pages, and a manuscript introductory page describing the contents: 'Enquiry into the origin of the Elvish names for Elves and their varieties clans and divisions: with Appendices on their names for the other Incarnates: Men, Dwarves and Orcs; and on their analysis of their own language, Quenya: with a note on the 'Language of the Valar'. As is his custom in these late writings, Tolkien includes notes of varying length to explain more fully points made in the text. To both copies he adds a separate eight-page typescript, the *Ósanwe-kenta* or *Communication of Thought* (in relation to which he also makes some manuscript etymological notes), and a four-page typescript, **Orcs*. He corrects both copies carefully and almost identically, and places one in a newspaper dated March 1960.

Tolkien also makes and emends a separate typescript and carbon copy of the **Cuivienyarna*, a legend of the awakening of the Three Clans of the Elves, referred to in *Quendi and Eldar*. He notes on one copy that it was 'written (in style and simple notions) to be a surviving Elvish "fairytale" or child's tale, mingled with counting-lore' (*The War of the Jewels*, p. 421).

He writes as well four Elvish genealogies, mainly concerned with the descendants of Finwë, which are accompanied by notes dated December 1959, and probably also similar genealogies of the Edain. Other works which date to about this period are *Concerning Galadriel and Celeborn*, a short and roughly composed document which is an important source of information for events in the Second Age, with emendations made at various times; and *The Elessar*, a rough four page manuscript in the first stage of composition, with some later pencilled emendations (see **The History of Galadriel and Celeborn and of Amroth King of Lórien*).

1960

1960 Tolkien begins a revision of *The Hobbit*, but gets no further than emendations to Chapter 1 and a substantial new section for Chapter 2. – Tolkien dates thirty newspaper doodles, and fourteen on other papers, to 1960. Another fifty-eight extant doodles are on newspapers from that year. (The more significant of these, mainly those in some way identified with the *legendarium*, together with undated drawings which seem to be contemporary with them and related in subject matter, are entered in the **Chronology** under the relevant dates.)

19 January 1960 C.H. Wilkinson dies.

21 January 1960 Alina Dadlez writes to Tolkien. The Swedish *Fellowship of the Rings* has been published, and Ohlmarks' translation has been praised.

26 January 1960 Rayner Unwin writes to Tolkien, sending a translation of a major review of the Swedish *Fellowship of the Ring*. He asks for a recent photograph of Tolkien.

February 1960 A doodle by Tolkien on a newspaper is dated 'February 1960' and inscribed 'Num[enórean] Ceramic Grass Pattern'.

1 February 1960 Rayner Unwin writes to Tolkien, asking if he has finished with the lists made by the Scunthorpe librarian.

3 February 1960 Tolkien attends a meeting of the electors to the O'Donnell Lecturership in Celtic Studies. Mrs N.K. Chadwick, F.B.A., or failing her Mrs R. Bromwich or failing her Dr H.P.R. Finberg is elected to the Lecturership for the year 1960–1.

4 February 1960 This date is stamped by Oxford University Press on signature B of the proofs of Tolkien's edition of the *Ancrene Wisse*.

7 February 1960 Robert Burchfield writes to Tolkien. The next Early English Text Society Council meeting will be on 19 March. He reminds Tolkien that he should wait until he has a complete corrected set of proofs and then return them to him, and not to the printer; but if there are any serious faults in the first section, Tolkien should let him know. He asks for Tolkien's text for his introduction, which ought to go to press in a few weeks.

9 February 1960 Tolkien writes to Rayner Unwin. Both he and his secretary have been ill, and he is trying to put things in order again. He encloses the only recent non-copyrighted photographs he has of himself, taken in the Fellows' Quadrangle of Merton College in July 1958 by Leslie Stanley. On receiving Rayner's letter of 1 February, he

> did sit down promptly and dutifully to the Scunthorpe lists, but I found
> that any attempt to correct them or explain them landed me in difficulty
> and actually revealed many points in the general structure of names,
> etc. I will send them back fairly soon with only minor notes. Time has
> not been wasted. I have done a great deal of work on the Silmarillion
> largely as a consequence of thinking about the points raised. I think the
> Silmarillion might now be described accurately as "in an active state of

preparation" – thanks largely to my present secretary. [Tolkien-George Allen & Unwin archive, HarperCollins]

– Tolkien writes to Alina Dadlez. The news of the Swedish translation cheered him when ill.

11 February 1960 Rayner Unwin writes to Tolkien. He is delighted with the news about 'The Silmarillion', and asks if Tolkien has deferred work on *Sir Gawain* and *Pearl*. He is sure that the Scunthorpe librarian will await the annotations patiently, but Tolkien should not spend too much time on the matter, but give it to 'The Silmarillion'. He thinks the photographs excellent.

12 February 1960 Tolkien writes to Rayner Unwin. He has set *Sir Gawain* and *Pearl* aside until he and his secretary have got 'all the present *Silmarillion* material typed out and arranged'. This is nearly done, but a few days ago 'the proofs of the *Ancrene Wisse*, more than a year delayed by printing strikes and other troubles, began suddenly to descend on me. At any rate I am in for a Middle English interval evidently' (Tolkien-George Allen & Unwin archive, HarperCollins). He is glad that the photographs he sent are suitable, and asks that the photographer be acknowledged. – Alina Dadlez writes to Tolkien. Het Spectrum have asked to borrow the original *Hobbit* maps, as they are having difficulty reproducing from a copy of the book. Does Tolkien still have the originals? Allen & Unwin are about to conclude a contract for a Swedish *Hobbit* with Rabén & Sjögren, associates of Kooperativa Förbundet who published the earlier Swedish edition.

15 February 1960 Tolkien writes to Alina Dadlez. He has not had time to look, but thinks that he has the originals of the two maps for *The Hobbit*. He hopes to find and send them in a few days. He is glad that there is to be a Swedish *Hobbit*, but remarks that Kooperativa Förbundet had taken 'impertinent and unwarranted liberties with the text' in the earlier edition. He hopes that the new edition will not have the same 'frightful' illustrations 'quite out of tune with the tone of the text' (Tolkien-George Allen & Unwin archive, Harper-Collins). He has received a schoolteacher's dramatized version of *The Lord of the Rings*, prepared for a school performance. He finds it harmless and suitable for its purpose. Unless Allen & Unwin wish to see the script, he will send it back, agreeing to a single performance, and not ask for a fee.

19 February 1960 Rayner Unwin writes to Tolkien. If the dramatization has Tolkien's blessing, it also has Allen & Unwin's.

20 February 1960 In the evening, Tolkien attends a dinner of The Society hosted by F.J. Witts at Magdalen College. Eleven members are present. Witts introduces as a topic for discussion the relationship of medical science and practice to new vehicles of mass entertainment and instruction.

23 February 1960 Tolkien writes to Alina Dadlez. He has found the original drawings of the two maps, as well as the slip for the runes on *Thror's Map* which had been overlooked at the time, so that they had been reproduced from clumsy art. He is sending these by registered post, but since they are now valuable, he would like them returned, and they are not to be marked.

26 February 1960 Alina Dadlez writes to Tolkien, acknowledging receipt of the maps. She has discovered, however, that Allen & Unwin can send Het Spectrum some unfolded *Hobbit* endpapers instead. If they decide to do this, she will return the original maps to Tolkien by registered post. Rabén & Sjögren have told her that they will use a new Swedish translation of *The Hobbit* and not include the old illustrations. The contract, as usual, provides that the word *Hobbit* not be translated. She is sending Tolkien separately five copies of the Swedish *Fellowship of the Ring*.

29 February 1960 Tolkien writes to Rayner Unwin. He repeats the information in his letter of 12 February about the photographs. Since he has not had a reply, he wonders if his letter reached Rayner. He asks if Rayner would

> have any objection to me publishing any separate or minor items belonging to the Ring cycle? I am frequently asked for small minor contributions and offered good terms for them. The things I have in mind are not integral parts of the Silmarillion, and for some of them it is very likely that no place will be found in that work, but I suppose I could publish them without in any way affecting the question of their inclusion in the major work if necessary. [Tolkien-George Allen & Unwin archive, HarperCollins]

March 1960 Tolkien dates a drawing of a Númenórean helmet on a newspaper 'March 1960'. On the same piece of paper, he writes that the helmet belongs to a 'captain of the Uinendili'. The *Uinendili* or Guild of Venturers founded by Aldarion are mentioned in the unfinished story **Aldarion and Erendis* which Tolkien is probably writing at this time. This story is developed in a series of five plot-outlines, each beginning in annal form and moving into narrative. The last version is a sixty-page manuscript which ends abruptly. Some rough notes and jottings, made at different times and often contradictory, give some indication of how the story might have been continued. – Other works dealing with Númenor are probably contemporary with *Aldarion and Erendis*: **A Description of the Isle of Númenor*, together with a rapid sketch map of the island; several closely related genealogical tables of the earlier generations of the Line of Elros; and **The Line of Elros: Kings of Númenor*, listing the rulers of Númenor from Elros to the Downfall, their dates, and the principal events in their lives.

1 March 1960 Tolkien writes to Alina Dadlez. She acted correctly in providing in the contract for the Swedish *Hobbit* that the word *Hobbit* should not be translated, but since, after acrimonious correspondence, he had to allow another word in the Swedish *Lord of the Rings*, the same word should probably be used in the new Swedish *Hobbit*. He received five copies of the Swedish *Fellowship of the Ring* last year, so now has ten copies. – Stanley Unwin replies to Tolkien's letter to Rayner. Minor items belonging to the Ring cycle might be published as Tolkien suggests, but with a note that they are taken from *The Silmarillion*, for which they would be advance publicity.

2 March 1960 Tolkien replies to Stanley Unwin. The value of minor items as publicity material has occurred to him, and he will see that if any such items are published they will be presented 'more or less as "trailers"' (Tolkien-George Allen & Unwin archive, HarperCollins).

9 March 1960 Tolkien so dates a doodle entitled 'Númenórean Ceramic Pattern' on a newspaper. – Alina Dadlez writes to Tolkien. Since Het Spectrum are able to work from unbound endpapers, she is returning the *Hobbit* maps to Tolkien separately by registered post. She has passed Tolkien's comment on the word *Hobbit* to Rabén and Sjögren. She asks if he received the first five copies of the Swedish *Fellowship of the Ring* direct from the publisher. As no copies had been received at Allen & Unwin, she had asked for them and the publisher sent a second set, assuming that the first had been lost. She asks Tolkien to send the extra five copies either to the Swedish publisher with a note, or to her and she will return them. – Rayner writes to Tolkien, with apologies for not having answered Tolkien's letter of 12 February.

10 March 1960 Among Tolkien's papers is an invitation to a lecture on this date (the Feast of St Thomas Aquinas) at Blackfriars at 6.15 p.m., 'The Coming General Council of the Church: Everybody's Concern', given by the Very Rev. Fr. Jerome Hamer, O.P., S.T.M.

19 March 1960 At a meeting of the Early English Text Society Council, in Tolkien's absence, it is thought desirable that copy for the introduction of his edition of the *Ancrene Wisse* should be received by 1 September.

31 March 1960 On a newspaper dated 31 March 1960 Tolkien makes various doodles, including flowers and a pattern which may be a precursor of a heraldic device for Fingolfin.

?April 1960 Tolkien writes to the editor of the fanzine *Triode*, who had sent him a copy of the issue for January 1960, which contained an article, 'No Monroe in Lothlorien', on the possibility of a film of *The Lord of the Rings*. Tolkien says that from his experience with scripts and 'story-line' he feels that 'only an overwhelming financial reward could possibly compensate an author for the horrors of the conversion of such a tale into film' (*Triode* 18 (May 1960), p. 27).

20 April 1960 This date is stamped by Oxford University Press on signatures C–G of the proofs of Tolkien's edition of *Ancrene Wisse*.

25 April 1960 Rayner Unwin writes to Tolkien. He does not want to disturb Tolkien's work on 'The Silmarillion', but asks what the position is in regard to the lists made by the Scunthorpe librarian.

1 May 1960 Robert Burchfield, Early English Text Society, writes to Tolkien. While discussing with Professor d'Ardenne her companion volume to the facsimile of Bodleian MS 34, the Society asked her if she still intended to offer one day what they had understood to be her edition of *St Katherine*. She replied 'that certain parts are ready. . . . But then she speaks of it as *your* edition: "You should enquire whether Prof. Tolkien is still contemplating an edition of St. Katherine"' (Tolkien Papers, Bodleian Library, Oxford). He asks if *St Katherine* is to be edited jointly by Professor d'Ardenne and Tolkien, or by Tolkien alone. Council Members have sent him a few points on the *Ancrene*

Wisse proofs which he will send to Tolkien when he has gathered them together. He encloses a memo about Heywood's *Dialogue of Proverbs* (possibly being considered as a future Society publication).

2 May 1960 Tolkien drafts a letter to someone who was unable to attend the next Ad Eundem dinner at Oxford. He has been tempted to change the date to suit the people he would like to see at the dinner, but has not done so.

5 May 1960 Tolkien writes to Rayner Unwin. He has done nothing about the Scunthorpe lists for a long time.

> When I first worked at it, it revealed to me that a good deal of work on the nomenclature and linguistic elements in *The Lord of the Rings* was needed, and I have done that. But to deal with the Scunthorpe indices would either mean voluminous notes (for which I have not time) or a few casual corrections (which now seem niggardly after so much delay). It will have to be the latter, and I will see to it.

Because of various domestic troubles he has had very little connected time for work of any kind for some weeks. 'I do give all the time I possibly can to the books which I have promised to you, though I begin to feel depressed by the amount of work still to do and the difficulty of getting any time for concentration' (Tolkien-George Allen & Unwin archive, HarperCollins).

12 May 1960 This date is stamped by Oxford University Press on signature H of the proofs of Tolkien's edition of *Ancrene Wisse*.

14 May 1960 Robert Burchfield writes to Tolkien about the *Ancrene Wisse* proofs. He has marked on a proof of pp. 1–96 a few probable printer's errors noted by Council members. In addition, parts of pp. 18–21 have been collated with the manuscript in Cambridge and some points made.

30 May 1960 This date is stamped by Oxford University Press on signature I of the proofs of Tolkien's edition of *Ancrene Wisse*.

?May–?June 1960 C.L. Wrenn collects from Tolkien the tape recorder bought in 1953 for the use of Tolkien and the English Faculty. This will be deposited in the English Faculty Library.

Early June 1960 Edith Tolkien, who has been in poor health, is admitted to hospital 'under grave suspicion which mercifully proved unfounded, though the actual conditions revealed are not proving easy to alleviate' (letter to Rayner Unwin, 31 July 1960, Tolkien-George Allen & Unwin archive, Harper-Collins). In a letter to Jane Neave of 18 July 1962 Tolkien will refer to Edith having been diagnosed with 'an internal complaint, small internal lesions (I gather), which cause pain, often incalculably, either by strain, or vibration, or by digestive irritations' (*Letters*, p. 316). – While in the Acland Nursing Home Edith meets C.S. Lewis's wife, Joy, who is also a patient. On one occasion when he visits Edith in hospital, Tolkien bumps into Lewis, and he is introduced to Joy. Walter Hooper thinks that this is the only occasion on which Tolkien and Joy met.

?Early or mid-June 1960 Simonne d'Ardenne is in Oxford. She visits the Tolkien family, and also sees Robert Burchfield and Norman Davis. In an undated letter following her visit, she will ask if Tolkien approves her decision to give the Early English Text Society the unsold copies of her *Edition of the Liflade ant te Passiun of Seinte Iuliene*. She suggests that she and Tolkien could compile a page or two of corrigenda. She is going to prepare an edition of *Seinte Katerine*, on which she expects that they will both work, and which will be published under both their names. The Early English Text Society has also agreed to an edition of *Sawles Warde*, which she also sees as a joint work. She reminds Tolkien to give his secretary his notes on *The Owl and the Nightingale*, which he had promised to give to d'Ardenne; these are to be entered under his name in a forthcoming edition (apparently never published).

5 June 1960 Robert Burchfield writes to Tolkien, forwarding queries on pp. 113–28 of the *Ancrene Wisse* proofs. He asks what Tolkien would like to have as a frontispiece to the book. He reminds Tolkien that the Council had requested the introduction by 28 May 1959, and with the printing of the text so far advanced it is now urgently needed. He asks how likely it is that Tolkien can send it in the next few weeks.

8 June 1960 This date is stamped by Oxford University Press on signatures K–P of the proofs of Tolkien's edition of *Ancrene Wisse*.

8–9 June 1960 Tolkien so dates doodles related to heraldic devices (*Artist and Illustrator*, fig. 184) on a newspaper of 25 April 1960.

16 June 1960 Simonne d'Ardenne writes in reply to an answer from Tolkien (not seen) to her previous letter. She will have to return the notes on *The Owl and the Nightingale* untouched, as she has not had time to look at them. She plans to return to Oxford when he has had time and opportunity to work on *Sawles Warde* and *Seinte Katerine*.

17 June 1960 Tolkien dates a doodle of an iris-like flower on a newspaper (*Pictures*, no. 43). – Robert Burchfield writes to Tolkien, forwarding notes on the proof of *Ancrene Wisse* sent by two members of the Council. He reminds Tolkien that he has not yet replied to Burchfield's letter of 5 June.

21 June 1960 Tolkien dates a sheet on which he has drawn paisley designs and 'sunburst' motifs similar to the heraldic devices he will draw later in the year.

22 June 1960 Encaenia. – Rayner Unwin writes to Tolkien. He is coming to Oxford for a Trinity College 'gaudy' on Friday 24 June. He asks if he may see Tolkien at any time before 11.00 a.m. on that date to discuss things with him.

24–29 June 1960 On four sheets of paper Tolkien draws eleven triangles filled with geometric patterns, in ink and coloured pencil. During the summer months he will draw some related doodles on newspapers.

24 June 1960 In the morning, in his capacity as Honorary Director of the Early English Text Society, Norman Davis visits Tolkien. The latter tells Davis that he is unable to write the introduction to *Ancrene Wisse* and will give him the notes he has assembled over the years, to be passed to Neil Ker to use if he wishes. – Later that day, Robert Burchfield writes to Ker, saying that the introduction will be his responsibility. He also tells him that Tolkien, who has been ill, is still not well enough to correct the proofs of the text and has agreed that Davis should do this against Tolkien's photostats. Davis will collect the material from Tolkien next week. – Possibly Tolkien also sees Rayner Unwin in the morning.

27 June 1960 Tolkien writes to his grandson, Michael George. He gives him advice on how to cope with stress towards the end of his school career. He tells him what scholarships are available for English students at Oxford, and the requirements of the English School. He advises him not to enter the History School if he intends eventually to switch to English.

30 June 1960 Robert Burchfield notes in a memo that Norman Davis rang to report that he had collected the photostats of folios 60–end of the *Ancrene Wisse* from Tolkien, but Tolkien has retained the earlier part to correct and suggested that he and Davis have a race to see who finishes first. Tolkien has not been able to find the notes he had made for the introduction. He would like folios 1r and 69r reproduced for the frontispiece.

4 July 1960 Alina Dadlez writes to Tolkien. She is sending him copies of the Dutch *Hobbit* (Prisma-boek paperback).

7 July 1960 Tolkien writes to Alina Dadlez. The Prisma *Hobbit*s have arrived safely. As far as he has been able to examine the text, the translation seems to have been done very well.

9 July 1960 An Ad Eundem dinner takes place in Cambridge. – Leonard Rice-Oxley dies.

?11–?16 July 1960 Tolkien is away from Oxford. Since he visits Hereford on 15 July he is probably staying nearby, perhaps with his brother Hilary.

14 July 1960 Joy Davidman Gresham Lewis dies.

15 July 1960 Tolkien and his son Christopher visit Hereford Cathedral library, unannounced. They are researching John Joscelyn, whom Tolkien thinks might have some connection with the *Ancrene Wisse* manuscript.

19 July 1960 Canon Morton, the Librarian at Hereford Cathedral library, writes to Tolkien. After Tolkien and Christopher left, they found an entry in the Chapter Act Book concerning John Joscelyn.

20 July 1960 Rayner Unwin writes to Tolkien, forwarding a query from Het Spectrum. They would like to know if he received a letter from pupils at a school in Deurne which they sent him some time ago. He has not replied to it.

?29–?31 July 1960 Tolkien is probably in Cambridge.

31 July 1960 Tolkien writes to Canon Morton, Hereford Cathedral, to thank him for his kindness and to explain his interest in John Joscelyn. – Tolkien writes to Rayner Unwin. He did receive the letter from schoolchildren forwarded by Het Spectrum. He does not think he has answered 'my part-time and not very efficient at business but a good typist, and critical' is away for some weeks.

> I am in fact utterly stuck – lost in a bottomless bog, and anything that could cheer me would be welcome. The crimes of omission that I com-

mitted in order to complete [*The Lord of the Rings*] are being avenged.
The chief is the *Ancrene Riwle*. My edition of the prime [manuscript, i.e.
Ancrene Wisse] should have been completed *many* years ago! I did at
least try to clear it out of the way before retirement, and by a vast effort
sent in the text in Sept. *1958*. But then one of the misfortunes that attend
on delay occurred; and my [manuscript] disappeared into the confusion of the Printing Strike. The proofs actually arrived at the beginning
of *this* June, when I was in full tide of composition for the Silmarillion,
and had lost the threads of the M[iddle] E[nglish] work. I stalled for a
while, but I am now under extreme pressure: 10 hours hard per diem day
after day, trying to induce order into a set of confused and desperately
tricky proofs, and notes. And then I have to write an introduction. (And
then there is *Sir Gawain*). Until the proofs of the *text* at least have gone
back, I cannot lift my head. I hope this will be accomplished in the next
2 weeks. Then I should more than welcome a talk. And I have specimens
of rewriting or addition that I should like you to see. Let me know your
dates! . . .

PS. Actually any time would do. Confound the proofs. I think a break
wd. do them good! [Tolkien-George Allen & Unwin archive, Harper-
Collins, partly printed in *Letters*, pp. 301–2]

8 August 1960 Rayner Unwin writes to Tolkien. He hopes that Tolkien will
be able to clear his academic commitments and be free to resume work on *The
Silmarillion* and *Sir Gawain*. He suggests a visit to Tolkien in early September,
as Rayner is temporarily without a car.

9 August 1960 Norman Davis forwards to Tolkien some collations for the
Ancrene Wisse sent by Bruce Dickins. He looks forward to seeing Tolkien the
next day (probably socially).

16 August 1960 Norman Davis sends Tolkien a report on the reading of a
passage in a text of the *Ancrene Riwle*.

17 August 1960 Neil Ker writes to Tolkien, commenting on points in the
manuscript of the *Ancrene Wisse*.

18 August 1960 Neil Ker writes to Tolkien, commenting on the use of colour by the rubricator in the *Ancrene Wisse* manuscript.

24 August 1960 Tolkien delivers his section of the proofs of *Ancrene Wisse*
to Robert Burchfield at his home in Walton Crescent, Oxford. In a covering
letter he mentions having found many errors and omissions, made by himself,
in the footnotes, which also needed correction to satisfy criticisms made by
Neil Ker. Except for large initials, he feels that copy has been faithfully ren-
dered in the book. Although many line over-runs could have been avoided, he
has seldom interfered unless an extra line was actually required. He encloses
a note of points he is especially curious about in the Titus manuscript of the
Ancrene Riwle. He appends a note on a two-line 'thorn': 'a hideous and totally
inaccurate letter, apparently derived (clumsily) from later debased hands –
inexcusable' (Early English Text Society archive).

?c. 25 August–?1 September 1960 Tolkien visits his son John in Staffordshire.

30 August 1960 Tolkien writes a two-page letter from Stoke-on-Trent to George Lewis Hersch. He comments, concerning invented languages, that 'much is only in my head, but even such parts as are in writing are complex, long and technical treatises on the historical connexion between Quenya and Sindarin, and their derivation from a common origin'. Tolkien thinks that Hersh, a zoologist, might be interested in a description of the flora and fauna of Númenor, 'limited of course to my own simple-mindedness and ignorance, and also by the necessary suppositions that are derived from documents of a merely descriptive and unscientific kind, and finally by the "mythological" ingredient'. But he discovered, when he turned his mind on Númenor, that its 'shadow' cast on *The Lord of the Rings* was 'thus dispelled and must again have its background of the half-known and unknown'. That is his 'great difficulty': in *The Lord of the Rings*, the matter of 'The Silmarillion' was used as history and background; but in *The Silmarillion* 'Thangorodrim *visited* will lose all that effect' (Michael Silverman, *Catalogue No. 2* (1998), item 43). He is visiting his son after spending fifty-six hours at his desk per week for several weeks, working on the *Ancrene Wisse*. – David H. Jones writes to Tolkien, asking permission to base an operetta for children on *The Hobbit*.

31 August 1960 Rayner Unwin writes to Tolkien. He will visit him at about 10.15 a.m. on 7 September.

4 September 1960 Paul Banham of Salt Lake City, Utah, writes to Tolkien. He asks on behalf of a sick and depressed friend who has presented him and many others with copies of *The Hobbit*, for a page of manuscript or drawing from that work. He adds to his plea that he himself was once a student at an institution near Merton College.

5 September 1960 Tolkien writes to Rayner Unwin. He has been laid up for some days, but would like to see him on Wednesday.

7 September 1960 Rayner Unwin visits Tolkien. He is lent some 'Silmarillion' manuscripts to read.

9 September 1960 Tolkien writes to Rayner Unwin, sending the letter from David H. Jones which he had forgotten to give to Rayner on Wednesday. While he is 'prejudiced against operettas in general and the use of The Hobbit for this purpose in particular', he would not 'disapprove out of hand' until he has seen what is produced (Tolkien–George Allen & Unwin archive, HarperCollins). But he suspects that the writer will be put off by the financial arrangements Allen & Unwin might wish to make.

10 September 1960 Tolkien sends Paul Banham a (then) unpublished drawing of the Lonely Mountain for his friend (*Artist and Illustrator*, fig. 136).

12 September 1960 Tolkien writes to his son Christopher. He has just received a copy of *Studies in Words* by C.S. Lewis, on which he comments unfavourably. He had written for Lewis 'a long analysis of the semantics and formal history of *BHŪ with special reference to φύσις' (*Letters*, p. 302), but Lewis has used little of it in his book.

15 September 1960 Rayner Unwin writes to Tolkien, acknowledging receipt of Jones's letter. He will deal with it.

20 September 1960 Rayner Unwin writes to Tolkien. He will 'look in' on him on 22 September to return the manuscripts he borrowed. – Rayner's letter having reached Tolkien the same day, he replies at once. He will be delighted to see Rayner. He is still laid up (with fibrositis) and will be having appointments for medical treatment in the near future. – Tolkien writes to Robert Burchfield. He cannot attend the Early English Text Society Council meeting the following day.

22 September 1960 Rayner Unwin presumably returns some of the 'Silmarillion' manuscripts to Tolkien.

27 September 1960 Tolkien undergoes treatment for fibrositis. – Robert Burchfield writes to Tolkien. Neil Ker has finished his part of the introduction to *Ancrene Wisse*. A copy will be sent to Tolkien in a few days for his comments, and if Tolkien wishes, he can prepare a supplementary note on any points not covered to his satisfaction. The corrected proofs have been returned to the printer. Revises should start to arrive in November. 'Your notes on capitals were handed in with the proofs, and their man [at the printer] told me on the telephone that he found your instructions "very clear"' (Tolkien Papers, Bodleian Library, Oxford). Burchfield and Ker think that small capitals should be used in certain places, and have tried to mark all such on the proofs. The negatives of the two frontispiece illustrations have arrived and been sent to the printer. Burchfield asks if he may keep Tolkien's photostats of the *Ancrene Wisse* manuscript a little longer.

1 October 1960 Robert Burchfield writes to Tolkien, answering some of his queries about the Titus manuscript of the *Ancrene Riwle*. He encloses a note from Neil Ker on some points in the *Ancrene Wisse* footnotes.

11 October 1960 Robert Burchfield writes to Tolkien, sending Ker's introduction to *Ancrene Wisse*. He asks for any comments to be sent to Ker or himself, and if Tolkien intends to contribute a supplementary introduction. He encloses information about forthcoming Early English Text Society publications and recent sales.

21 October 1960 Alina Dadlez sends Tolkien five copies of the Polish *Hobbit*.

24 October–early November 1960 Tolkien and Edith stay at the Hotel Miramar in Bournemouth.

25 October 1960 Elisabeth Lumsden, Tolkien's secretary, writes to Alina Dadlez to acknowledge the copies of the Polish *Hobbit*. – She also writes to Rayner Unwin to ask on Tolkien's behalf the name of the current editor of the magazine *Time and Tide*. Tolkien wants to offer him a short piece he has written, 'a sort of satirical fantasy' (Tolkien-George Allen & Unwin archive, HarperCollins; this is probably the still unpublished *Bovadium Fragments*, see *Environment).

30 October 1960 Robert Burchfield writes to Tolkien. The Early English Text Society want to know if he intends to contribute any additional material to the introduction to *Ancrene Wisse*, otherwise they will send Ker's introduction to the printer at once. The introduction must go to the printer by the beginning of January 1961. The printer is substituting a slightly darker set of small bold capitals for ones that Tolkien found unsatisfactory in the proofs.

November and December 1960 Tolkien dates various finished drawings of Númenórean artefacts, heraldic devices, and flowers to November and December 1960 or specific dates within those months. Probably most of his drawings of heraldic devices were done in this period. Some are quite rough but others are drawn and coloured with exquisite detail. They include a sheet with finished devices for Beren and Finrod, a device labelled 'Finwë > Lúthien > Finarphin', plus two sketchy devices, one of which may be an early version of that for Gil-galad (Beren and Finrod devices reproduced in *Pictures*, no. 47); a sheet with preliminary designs for devices for Fëanor and Eärendil; other sheets with devices for Finwë and Elwë (*Artist and Illustrator*, fig. 191); for Finarphin and Fingolfin (*Artist and Illustrator*, fig. 192); for Eärendil and Fëanor (both devices reproduced in *Pictures*, no. 47); for the House of Haleth (*Pictures*, no. 47); for Hador (*Pictures*, no. 47); for Melian (*Artist and Illustrator*, fig. 193); for Finwë and the High Kings of the Noldor (*Pictures*, no. 47); two devices for Lúthien (*Artist and Illustrator*, figs. 194, 195); a sheet with finished and unfinished devices and ?tiles – including a device for Beor and or Haleth (the device reproduced *Pictures*, no. 47); an 'Ancient emblem representing one derivation of the Silmarils from the light of the Trees upon Ezellohar' (*Pictures*, no. 47) (Tolkien Drawings, Bodleian Library, Oxford); and a decorative floral alphabet (*Artist and Illustrator*, fig. 197).

5 November 1960 On a copy of *The Times* (for 7 October 1960) Tolkien draws a design which resembles looping decorative belts. These seem closely related to several more finished, undated drawings (one partly reproduced in *Pictures*, no. 44), one of which is inscribed 'The belt of two & fifty shields' (Tolkien Drawings, Bodleian Library, Oxford).

10 November 1960 Tolkien writes to his cousin, Dorothy Wood, and her husband Leslie. He apologizes for not writing earlier. Despite his retirement, he has been very busy and in ill health.

14, 15, 16, 17 November 1960 Tolkien dates four sheets of finished decorative borders incorporating both floral and geometrical motifs (some reproduced in *Pictures*, nos. 44, 45). Other, undated drawings probably belong to the same time. Some similar finished borders are drawn on newspapers dating from August to October 1960.

16 November 1960 Norman Davis lunches with Tolkien. Later he phones Robert Burchfield to say that he thinks there is no prospect of Tolkien sending anything for the *Ancrene Wisse* introduction. Neil Ker's introduction therefore should be sent to the printer.

23 November 1960 Tolkien writes to Alina Dadlez, thanking her for the Polish *Hobbit*. He hopes to get comments on the translation from his friend Professor Mroczkowski of Cracow. The illustrations are 'Mordoresque'. He encloses a letter he has received from a woman who had proposed long ago to translate *The Hobbit* and *The Lord of the Rings* into Japanese. He had advised that she find a likely publisher in Japan who could then approach Allen & Unwin. Her letter complains that someone else is preparing a translation for the publisher Iwanami. Tolkien asks if Iwanami have approached Allen & Unwin.

24 November 1960 Tolkien dates on an envelope some elaborate doodles and patterns that seem related to his heraldic devices.

28 November 1960 Joy Hill writes to Tolkien. The BBC intends to serialize *The Hobbit* on radio in the *Children's Hour* series in January 1961.

30 November 1960 Alina Dadlez writes to Tolkien. Iwanami have a formal option on *The Hobbit*.

4–9 and 7–9 December 1960 Tolkien dates two related drawings, the first of which is inscribed 'Númenórean carpet' (*Artist and Illustrator*, fig. 187, first only; *Pictures*, no. 46). These incorporate versions of the decorative borders he drew during November.

6 December 1960 Robert Burchfield writes to Tolkien. The printer proposes to use the bold caps shown in enclosed specimen pages, if Tolkien approves. He asks Tolkien to reply as soon as possible if he does not like them. If Burchfield hears nothing, he will assume that Tolkien is satisfied, and the printer will begin to substitute the new characters next week. Burchfield encloses a memo about a related matter and asks for a reply.

7 December 1960 Joy Hill, Allen & Unwin, writes to Tolkien. David Davis will read *The Hobbit* in thirteen weekly instalments on BBC radio beginning Wednesday, 4 January 1961 at 5.40 p.m. in the *Adventures in English* programme. The producer of the BBC Schools Department is considering *The Hobbit* for dramatization in the 1961–2 academic year.

8 December 1960 Burchfield has had a reply from Tolkien by letter or phone to his letter of 6 December. He now writes to the printer that Tolkien is delighted with the new boldface capitals, and the way is clear for the preparation of revises. – Rayner Unwin writes to Tolkien. Puffin Books (an imprint of Penguin Books) would like to publish a paperback edition of *The Hobbit* in 30,000 copies, without the pictures. Rayner is reluctant to agree, as the paperback would affect sales of the Allen & Unwin hardback (*c.* 3,400 copies in 1959).

10 December 1960 Tolkien replies to Rayner Unwin. He leaves the decision about a Puffin *Hobbit* to him. The chances of profit or loss seem about equal. 'If you wish to know my personal feelings: I am no longer able to ignore cash-profit, even to the odd £100, but I do share your reluctance to cheapen the old Hobbit. Unless the profit or advantage is clear, I would rather leave him to amble along' (*Letters*, p. 302). He points out that, although its pictures could be dispensed with, in places the text of *The Hobbit* would be unintelligible without *Thror's Map*. Tolkien's secretary (presumably still Elisabeth Lumsden) has practically deserted him to nurse a sick mother, and he has not been able to find a satisfactory substitute.

10–13 December 1960 Tolkien dates a drawing, which he describes as a 'Númenórean tile from Elenna preserved in Gondor. Pattern derived from Gondolin, Idril's device or Cornflower pattern, Menelluin' (*Pictures*, no. 46; Tolkien Drawings, Bodleian Library, Oxford). An undated sheet with similar patterns, finished and unfinished, is closely connected with this drawing and the one made on 14 December (*Artist and Illustrator*, fig. 188).

14 December 1960 Tolkien dates a drawing (*Artist and Illustrator*, fig. 189), inscribed 'Idril's device. The "Cornflower" pattern Menelluin. Origin of (often debased) Númenórean circular patterns' and 'Inlaid plaque preserved from Gondolin & descending from Eärendil to Númenor, whence it was saved by Elendil & taken to Gondor'.

14 December 1960 or later On an envelope postmarked 13 December Tolkien draws several devices for Eärendil and Gil-galad (*Artist and Illustrator*, fig. 190).

15 December 1960 Robert Burchfield writes to Tolkien, sending him matter for preliminaries in *Ancrene Wisse*. They cannot use the standard prefatory note because of Tolkien's different editorial conventions, and asks him to make any necessary alterations or additions and return the revised version as soon as possible. Neil Ker's introduction was sent to the printer a week ago.

29 December 1960 Rayner Unwin writes to Tolkien. Nothing has been decided about the proposed Puffin *Hobbit*. Allen & Unwin are trying to get a higher royalty. Rayner is leaving on a three-month trip to the Middle East and India.

31 December 1960 Tolkien replies to a letter from Professor L.W. Forster. He comments on influences on *The Lord of the Rings*, in particular those of the two World Wars.

1961

?1961 Tolkien is sent a copy of Burton Raffel's *Poems from the Old English* and an article by him. He makes extensive critical comments.

5 January 1961 Tolkien replies to a letter from a Mrs E.C. Ossendrijver in the Netherlands. He comments on the name *Númenor*, his 'own invention'. He is 'now under contract engaged (among alas! other less congenial tasks) in putting into order for publication the mythology and stories of the First and Second Ages – written long ago, but judged hardly publishable, until (so it seems) the surprising success of *The Lord of the Rings*, which comes at the end, has provided a probably demand for the beginnings' (*Letters*, p. 303).

6 January 1961 Stanley Unwin writes to Tolkien. Penguin Books have made a revised offer, and want to print 35,000 copies of *The Hobbit*. They will ask Pauline Baynes for a cover illustration.

7 January 1961 Tolkien writes to Stanley Unwin. He is sure that the negotiations for the Puffin *Hobbit* are in the best possible hands. He is pleased to hear that Pauline Baynes is to produce the cover art, and would like to see the design in advance. He asks for her address, as he has mislaid it. He would like to see Unwin again, 'but with my wife's ill health, slowly deteriorating, I am very much tied, and indeed seldom go away, or even out for long' (Tolkien-George Allen & Unwin archive, HarperCollins).

9 January 1961 Stanley Unwin writes to Tolkien. Penguin Books have agreed to pay a higher royalty for *The Hobbit*. The maps will be included, but not the illustrations.

13 January 1961 Alina Dadlez writes to Tolkien. Cytelnik, the Polish publisher preparing a translation of *The Fellowship of the Ring*, has asked for a contract for *The Two Towers* and an option on *The Return of the King*. A contract has been signed with Compania General Fabril Editora of Buenos Aires for Spanish language rights in *The Lord of the Rings*, and they have also asked for a contract for *The Hobbit*. The Swedish publisher of *The Lord of the Rings*, Gebers, wants to omit the Appendices as they think they give the work a 'scholarly' appearance. Allen & Unwin are trying to place the Norwegian and German rights for *The Lord of the Rings*.

14 January 1961 Tolkien begins to draft a reply to Alina Dadlez with unfavourable comments about the cover of the Swedish *Fellowship of the Ring*, omitted from the letter he will send on 16 January.

16 January 1961 Tolkien writes to Alina Dadlez. He is giving careful consideration to the Swedish request to omit the Appendices. He asks for her views, as they might help him 'to form a cooler opinion'. Does she think that the Appendices in any way impede sales? He observes that 'readers' tastes have little to do with reviewers' opinion'. His 'immediate impression is that the Swedish publishers in fact merely want to cut down immediate costs'. While on the subject of Swedes, when Allen & Unwin are negotiating contracts for translations he wishes it to be clear that no biographical or critical material on himself by the translator should be included without his permission. 'The five pages of impertinent nonsense inserted by Mr. Ohlmarks in the beginning of Volume I . . . could well have been spared' (Tolkien-George Allen & Unwin archive, HarperCollins). As soon as he hears from Dadlez by telephone or letter, he will send a considered reply.

18 January 1961 Alina Dadlez writes to Tolkien. She thinks that he should either compromise with Gebers and tell them which parts of the Appendices he considers essential, or agree to their omission from *The Return of the King* in consideration of their undertaking to publish them in a separate volume. But if the latter course is agreed, she thinks that Gebers should be asked to add a note, perhaps drafted by Tolkien, at the end of *The Return of the King* about the proposed volume and explaining the nature of the Appendices. She will bear in mind Tolkien's request about the inclusion of biographical or critical material in translations.

24 January 1961 Tolkien replies to Alina Dadlez. He had not realized that Gebers were considering publishing the Appendices independently. He had already thought that some note should be included in vol. 3 if the Appendices were omitted. He and Allen & Unwin might agree to Gebers omitting the Appendices 'on condition that, in fairness to author and purchasers, any omission shall be recorded in a footnote at the end of Vol. iii'. He suggests wording for the note. If Gebers are considering a separate volume, for the sake of its bulk they will want to omit all of the Appendices.

> I have no objection (in any case) to the omission of C, D (except for the Shire Calendar . . .), E ii and F ii. Omission of the remainder would be, in different degrees, damaging to the book as a whole. . . . I feel strongly that the absolute minimum is retention of . . . 'Of Aragorn and Arwen', and the Shire Calendar: two items essential to the understanding of the main text in many places. . . .
>   I do not believe that [the Appendices] give the work a 'scholarly' . . . look, and they play a major part in producing the total effect. . . . Actually, an analysis of many hundreds of letters shows that the Appendices have played a very large part in readers' pleasure, in turning library readers into purchasers (since the Appendices are needed for reference), and in creating a demand for another book. A sharp distinction must be drawn between the tastes of reviewers . . . and of readers! I think I understand the tastes of simple-minded folk (like myself) pretty well.

He asks what the position is regarding the sale of the English edition in countries where a translation has been published. He is interested because 'the original is my only protection against the translators. I cannot exercise any control over the translation of such a large text, even into the few languages that I know anything about; yet the translators are guilty of some very strange mistakes.' He lists some of those made by Ohlmarks in his translation. He does not object to a biographical notice appearing in the books, 'but it should be correct, and it should be pertinent. I think I must ask to be allowed to see anything of this kind in future, before it is printed. Or alternatively I will draw up a brief statement which I will submit to you as a possible hand-out in case of any demand for such material.' Ohlmarks, he says, prefers 'his own fancy to facts, and [is] very ready to pretend to knowledge which he does not possess'. It is 'improper of Messrs. Gebers and of Ohlmarks to preface to my work such stuff, without warning or consultation' (Tolkien-George Allen & Unwin archive, HarperCollins, partly printed in *Letters*, pp. 304–5). He offers to send a copy of Ohlmarks' foreword, if Allen & Unwin do not have a copy of the Swedish edition.

26 January 1961 This date is stamped by Oxford University Press on signature A (Ker's introduction) of the proofs of *Ancrene Wisse*.

?Late January–first half of February 1961 Tolkien writes a lengthy commentary on Neil Ker's introduction to *Ancrene Wisse*, disagreeing with him on many points. He begins to draft a letter, probably to Robert Burchfield, explaining his opinions and seeking advice on how to deal with the matter, since he does not wish to offend Ker, or appear to insist that Ker change the expression of his own opinion, in his own introduction. The whole occupies some twenty pages, closely typed and handwritten. Burchfield's letter of 19

February 1961 will indicate that Tolkien sent six typed pages of notes (not in the Early English Text Society archive).

7 February 1961 Alina Dadlez writes to Tolkien. The Swedish publishers will include the minimum of Appendices as required by Tolkien (in fact, they will include *The Tale of Aragorn and Arwen* and the whole of Appendix D, not just the Shire Calendar), and will insert a footnote in vol. 3 about the other Appendices being omitted. Unfortunately a foreword by Ohlmarks has already been printed in the second volume. Dadlez would be interested to read Ohlmarks' earlier foreword, but does not understand Swedish. An publisher in Argentina has asked if Tolkien could write a biographical notice for their translation of *The Lord of the Rings*.

9 February 1961 Tolkien replies to Alina Dadlez. He is distressed to learn of Ohlmarks' foreword. 'I must say I think his habit of reviewing the book as well as translating it is impertinent, especially without consulting me, and I hope I shall not have to suffer this treatment in any other language.' He asks if Dadlez could obtain some Swedish reviews from Gebers. He will send her a copy of the first note by Ohlmarks, with a translation, after he has seen the second. Since he is 'at present working against time with the proofs and prefaces to a "learned work"' (Tolkien-George Allen & Unwin archive, HarperCollins), he will let the publisher in Argentina make up its own notice, but would like to see a draft of it before it is printed.

13 February 1961 Eric Dobson writes to Tolkien about some presentation given by the latter (probably a talk to a society). Dobson is constantly using the transcript of the British Museum Cotton MS Cleopatra text of the *Ancrene Riwle*, and could easily check anything for Tolkien.

15 February 1961 Tolkien attends a meeting of the electors to the O'Donnell Lecturership in Celtic Studies.

16 February 1961 Alina Dadlez writes to Tolkien. Gebers have asked if Tolkien would mind if, in place of a footnote about the excluded Appendices, a loose card were inserted in each copy, listing the exclusions and announcing an eventual separate volume of Appendices if there is a demand. Or, they might include a footnote and insert a card for the reader to order the eventual extra volume. She thinks that some information about the omitted material should appear in the book itself. She has asked Gebers for some Swedish reviews, and the Argentinian publishers to let Tolkien see a draft of the biographical notice.

Mid-February 1961 Tolkien writes to A.H. Smith, University College, London, asking about the British Museum MS Cotton Cleopatra *Ancrene Riwle* manuscript, an edition of which Smith is preparing for the Early English Text Society. – Smith replies that he is sending Tolkien a set of prints from the manuscript, and if there are any doubtful points he could check the original in the British Museum.

19 February 1961 Robert Burchfield writes to Tolkien. He has summarized the main points in Tolkien's six pages of notes on Ker's introduction to *Ancrene Wisse*, and entered on a spare proof the changes that Tolkien proposed. He is sending the summary and proof to Ker, and suggesting that when Ker has incorporated Tolkien's points, the Early English Text Society should ask for a revised proof, 'so that duplication and/or conflicts of view can be avoided as far as possible between his part and yours. This will not affect the timing of your introduction. I am assuming that it will reach me at the end of February as we have agreed' (Tolkien Papers, Bodleian Library, Oxford). (This last sentence suggests that after receiving Tolkien's letter, Burchfield had discussed the matter with him.) Burchfield then considers various typographical points. – On the same day, Burchfield writes to Neil Ker that Tolkien has sent 'some complex material' on his introduction and has decided to write a supplemental introductory note himself. He thinks it a pity that Tolkien did not make his objections when Ker's introduction was in typescript rather than in proof.

20 February 1961 Alina Dadlez sends Tolkien reviews of the Swedish *Two Towers*. She asks if he has received his complimentary copies of the book.

23 February 1961 Tolkien writes to Alina Dadlez. He agrees to either of Gebers' suggestions about the Appendices, but prefers the second. He asks her to thank Gebers for the reviews, though he thinks that he too should write to them. He would like some reviews of the first volume. He has received six copies of the Swedish *Two Towers*, but has not looked at Ohlmarks 'second outburst. I feel I cannot just now take any more' (*Letters*, p. 305). He encloses a copy of Ohlmarks' foreword with a translation, eight closely typed pages – four for the translation and four of detailed comment. – Tolkien writes to Robert Burchfield. 'Poor Ker will feel a bit inundated. I gave him a lot of notes when he called for the photostats. . . . I hope Ker is not making too many alterations in his stuff, for of course, many of the points could hardly be treated in his Introduction, and if treated at all will have to be treated by me in mine. I am working at it, but making heavy weather and am rather tired' (Early English Text Society archive). He has revised the prefatory note, and encloses a draft. He asks Burchfield about a reading in the *Ormulum*.

26 February 1961 Robert Burchfield writes to Tolkien, sending the *Ormulum* reading requested. He looks forward to receiving Tolkien's revised, double-spaced prefatory note. 'As I said on the telephone, either of the two versions you sent seems acceptable (I should rather say "both are admirable")' (Tolkien Papers, Bodleian Library, Oxford).

27 February 1961 Tolkien writes to Robert Burchfield, thanking him for the *Ormulum* information and commenting on it. He remarks that Burchfield had not observed a serious omission in the prefatory note: 'No thanks expressed for the man to whom I have given the most trouble: R.W.B. [Robert W. Burchfield]' (Early English Text Society archive). – Neil Ker writes to Tolkien, thanking him for going through the proof so carefully and saving him from errors, some serious. He hopes that some of what Tolkien has put down will come in his part of the introduction. He would not like to see some of it under his name, because he could not have said it himself. He discusses some of the points and various changes he has made, or might make, and asks if he can keep Tolkien's photostats a little longer.

28 February 1961 Robert Burchfield writes to Neil Ker. He has had two talks on the telephone with Tolkien, the second a few minutes ago, concerning their respective introductions. – Ker writes to Tolkien. Burchfield has the photostats of the *Ancrene Wisse*, which Ker proposes to collect on Friday and bring them to Tolkien.

2 March 1961 Tolkien writes to thank Robert Burchfield for sending a reference. He encloses the revised prefatory note, and suggests that it should not be set until he has seen a draft of Ker's revision. 'If you and [Norman] Davis would prefer to hide your blushes under the partial anonymity of Honorary Secretary and Honorary Director please do so. I prefer the real names because many will not know to whom titles belong and I owe you both a personal debt ...' (Early English Text Society archive). – A.H. Smith replies to a letter in which Tolkien told him that the photostats of the Cleopatra manuscript Smith had sent were incomplete. He has another set in the country, but cannot collect them until 11 March; he will send them then, if that is not too late. He repeats his offer to check any points in the actual manuscript in the British Museum.

7 March 1961 Tolkien writes to A.H. Smith. 11 March will be soon enough. He hesitates to ask him to take time to visit the British Museum. If Smith sends the photostats, Tolkien can probably deal with the points he lists. But there is one point holding up his introduction which he would like Smith to check in Joscelyn's manuscript Old English dictionary in the Museum. Tolkien is unable to consult it personally: 'I am very much tied; and I am obliged to take my wife away for a rest and recuperation on March 20' (Tolkien papers, Bodleian Library, Oxford). – Robert Burchfield writes to Tolkien. He has received the prefatory note and Ker's corrected proof. He notes one or two changes he has made to the prefatory note, mainly for consistency. 'I propose to keep the return-proof of NRK's introduction here, and also the typescript of your Prefatory Note, until your introduction arrives. Then they can all go to the Printer together. You will forgive the poor Hon. Sec. if he says that your introd[uction] cannot come too soon' (Early English Text Society archive). – Burchfield also writes to Neil Ker, mentioning that Tolkien's introduction has been 'faithfully promised' before Norman Davis leaves for New Zealand on 10 March, but he does not think that it will be finished.

8 March 1961 Joy Hill writes to Tolkien. Stanley Unwin has signed the contract for the Puffin *Hobbit*. Joy encloses Pauline Baynes' cover design for Tolkien's approval.

11 March 1961 Helen Darbishire dies.

13 March 1961 Tolkien writes to Joy Hill, returning Pauline Baynes' cover design. He likes it very much. He also encloses a letter to be forwarded to Kaye Webb, the Puffin Books editor.

15 March 1961 Alina Dadlez writes to Tolkien, sending reviews of the Swedish *Fellowship of the Ring*. She expresses her shock at seeing how Åke Ohlmarks has distorted the facts. She will show Tolkien's translation and comments to Rayner Unwin on his return from the Middle East.

18 March 1961 Tolkien writes to Robert Burchfield. He is aware that 'if I had not had other urgent matters on hand at the time when [Ker] sent in his first draft and had given it proper attention at once, I could have saved a lot of trouble. I think he (and you) have taken my belated criticism very kindly. I am accommodating my remarks to his amended form'. He then comments that Ker's statement that the manuscript has sustained little damage since it was written is hardly accurate:

> Four pages have demonstrably been torn out or removed. I can hardly blame Ker (though he ought perhaps to have wondered about the short quire), since long acquaintance with the text did not reveal this to me until a few days ago, when I was writing a section on the reliability of the scribe and his text, and dealing with his more serious omissions by jumping forward. I had naturally noticed, though it is not immediately obvious, that there is an anacolouthon between the end of f. 14b and beginning of f. 15, but I had supposed that it was due to one of these jumps. However, consideration of the other versions, especially the French, showed that the missing matter was of great length; what is more calculation showed that it required precisely 4 × 28 A lines (that is 4 pages) to accommodate it. This taken with the fact that the break occurs at the centre of the only short quire (8 leaves for 10) is sufficient proof that the central sheet of the quire (or two added leaves) has been lost. . . .
>
> I regret that the pleasure of the discovery was soon changed to shame at my own ignorance and chagrin: for [scholar G.C.] Macaulay had already noticed this.

Tolkien hopes to find room for a note in the revises, and will deal with it in the introduction. He continues:

> My dear Hon. Sec. I am very sorry indeed. I cannot send you copy yet for my Introduction. Most of it is in existence now, but very rough. I had every intention of completing it before Davis went away; but it has not proved possible, in spite of cracking labour. I am now (temporarily, I hope) at the end of my physical and mental tether. I must rest or bust. I have been under continuous pressure of many kinds since I recovered from a near breakdown last autumn; and I am now in a nervous condition in which I cannot concentrate or get a sentence right, or sleep properly. Also I can get small relief, as I am tied. My wife is nearly always ill with rare intervals; and I am under orders to take her away. I am going on Monday next until the Thursday before Easter. A temporary respite, which I hope will enable me to rest and sleep enough to complete my stuff for you soon after I return. Beyond that the future is rather dark. I have no idea how I shall organize my affairs, if my wife continues slowly, as is likely, to get worse. And I have other heavy contracts overdue; not to mention endless warfare with publishers and translators, and a very

large correspondence.... And for some weeks I have only had occasional help from my secretary – owing to her domestic troubles. It has not been possible to replace her, an educated part-time sec[retary] now well acquainted with my business.

He asks for Burchfield's help with two things. First, since A.H. Smith has not replied to his request to look up some points on Joscelyn's Anglo-Saxon dictionary, he needs someone to look at the manuscript in the British Museum. Second,

> I have lost heart and confidence in any of the stuff that I am painfully producing from a welter of notes made at different times. Easy enough to unload them on you or Davis in unpublishable notes; not so easy to organize for print. I send you the only part of my Introduction that I have so far succeeded in getting into printable form, or so I thought. It now seems to me rather silly. It is the larger part of the section on the Marginalia [apparently on the Nota].... I should welcome an opinion from someone outside my isolation whether this piece seems worth writing or printing. A frank opinion would not wound, as I am quite prepared to tear it up. And all the rest – which will certainly be no better. Indeed if my delay makes grave difficulties, I think the volume had better proceed without me. [Tolkien Papers, Bodleian Library, Oxford]

19 March 1961 Tolkien writes to Neil Ker, telling him of the missing pages.

20–30 March 1961 Tolkien and Edith stay at the Hotel Miramar, Bournemouth. Tolkien later writes to Robert Burchfield that he had slept and done little else. 'We had marvellous weather. A cold North wind is marvellous in Bournemouth: it brings sun, and there is plenty of shelter' (7 April 1961, Tolkien Papers, Bodleian Library, Oxford). During their stay, Tolkien and Edith are visited by Rosfrith Murray, daughter of James Murray of the *Oxford English Dictionary*, and they in turn visit her at home in Ringwood during their return journey to Oxford.

22 March 1961 Joy Hill writes to Tolkien. The Puffin *Hobbit* is to be published in October.

27 March 1961 Robert Burchfield writes to Tolkien, sending him the names of two people who could do research for him in the British Museum, and commenting on nota signs (marginalia). The next Early English Text Society Council meeting will be on 29 April.

31 March 1961 Neil Ker writes to Tolkien. He is thankful that Tolkien noticed the missing pages, and to have been referred to Macaulay.

Late March or beginning of April 1961 Tolkien receives a reminder from the publishers of *The Jerusalem Bible* that his contribution, the Book of Jonah, is due.

Early April 1961 Tolkien spends a day or two completing Jonah for *The Jerusalem Bible*.

4 April 1961 Robert Burchfield, who has seen or written to Mrs Offord, one of the two people he suggested to do research in the British Museum, informs Tolkien that she would be delighted to help.

7 April 1961 Tolkien writes to Robert Burchfield. He has written to Mrs Offord, whom he knows, having once been her B.Litt. supervisor. He is encouraged by Burchfield's remarks on his work on nota-signs. He will send a copy to Ker. 'Forgive my chattiness. . . . I am rather isolated, and it is a relief to chat even by way of typewriter to someone who has any interest in the work' (Tolkien Papers, Bodleian Library, Oxford).

8 April 1961 Tolkien writes to Neil Ker about later hands in the *Ancrene Wisse* manuscript. He asks for information about Wigmore Abbey and its history. – Yvonne Offord sends Tolkien the results of her research at the British Museum. She also gives him the name of someone who could answer any palaeographical queries.

11 April 1961 Tolkien writes to Joy Hill. He would like to know which edition of *The Hobbit* is being used for the Puffin Books edition. It should be the sixth impression (2nd edn. 1954). The note at the beginning is not necessary, but two errors need correcting. Since time might be important, he has also written directly to Puffin editor Kaye Webb.

17 April 1961 Joy Hill replies to Tolkien. The Puffin *Hobbit* is being printed from the second edition, twelfth impression (1961), to which all necessary corrections have been made.

25 April 1961 Tolkien sends his translation of the Book of Jonah to the publisher of *The Jerusalem Bible*.

26 April 1961 This date is stamped by Oxford University Press on signatures B and C of the revised proofs of Tolkien's edition of *Ancrene Wisse*.

29 April 1961 Tolkien attends an Early English Text Society Council meeting at Magdalen College, Oxford. It is noted that the Society's version of Simonne d'Ardenne's edition of *Seinte Iuliene* will be published soon. Also, as Tolkien's *Ancrene Wisse* and the Titus manuscript are in press, the end of the scheme to publish all the extant versions of the *Ancrene Riwle* is in sight. – Neil Ker writes to Tolkien, approving his piece on marginalia.

3 May 1961 Joy Hill writes to Tolkien. The BBC Schools Department plan a four-part dramatization of *The Hobbit* on 5, 12, 19, and 26 October. She has asked for copies of the script for Tolkien to see. She thinks that this will increase sales.

4 May 1961 Rayner Unwin writes to Tolkien. He encloses a cheque Tolkien asked for by telephone this morning. 'You know you have only to ask if you want any of the money that is owing to you' (Tolkien-George Allen & Unwin archive, HarperCollins). This is an advance on royalties and profits for 1960, due at this time of the year.

5 May 1961 Tolkien writes to Rayner Unwin. He thanks him for the cheque and explains that his difficulty was caused by 'Income Tax delayed from a time when "The Lord of the Rings", plus a salary, put me in the Surtax class – out of which I have now fallen' (Tolkien-George Allen & Unwin archive, Harper-

Collins). – Tolkien writes to Joy Hill. He hopes that any increased sales of *The Hobbit* as a result of the BBC dramatization will not all be copies of the Puffin edition.

12 May 1961 This date is stamped by Oxford University Press on signatures D and E of the revised proofs of the *Ancrene Wisse*. – Rayner Unwin writes to Tolkien. Gebers, the Swedish publisher, is sending him a book in Swedish containing an essay on *The Lord of the Rings* by Erik Ryding. They would have omitted Ohlmarks' preface from *The Return of the King*, but as it was already at press they had only been able to exclude certain passages. In future editions they will include only material written or approved by Tolkien.

?13–?16 May 1961 Tolkien visits Cambridge.

14 May 1961 Tolkien finds *The Lord of the Rings* 'well entrenched' in Cambridge. 'I spent the whole of Sunday in the company of what appears to be quite a large Club in Queens' College devoted to my works. I was of course more pleased by the wealth of information and knowledgeable criticism that was brought to bear on my work than by incense. The idea of having a separate "fan" volume was welcomed with applause' (letter to Rayner Unwin, 16 May 1961, Tolkien-George Allen & Unwin archive, HarperCollins).

16 May 1961 Tolkien writes to Rayner Unwin. He will probably be able to read Ryding's essay. He cannot understand why Ohlmarks had not consulted him about the biographical material in the course of their considerable correspondence.

17 May 1961 Robert Burchfield writes to Tolkien. C.T. Onions has objected to Tolkien's use of 'altered from' instead of 'altered to' in some of the footnotes in the *Ancrene Wisse*.

19 May 1961 Rayner Unwin sends Tolkien five illustrations of *The Lord of the Rings* by a Dutchman, Cor Blok. If Tolkien likes them, Rayner will encourage the man from Het Spectrum who is coming over this year to bring the rest of Blok's 300 pictures with him.

20 May 1961 Tolkien types multiple draft replies (five pages) to Robert Burchfield. In these he discusses in great detail the point made by Onions, but suggests that it be dealt with by removing the word 'altered'. (The letter finally sent is not in the Early English Text Society archive.)

23 May 1961 Tolkien writes to Rayner Unwin. He finds the Cor Blok drawings he has just received most attractive, though four are bad as illustrations. He would like to see others in the hope that some will be as good as *The Battle of the Hornburg*. He will return them under separate cover.

24 May 1961 Rayner Unwin replies to Tolkien. He thinks that Blok's drawings have 'a curious charm' (Tolkien-George Allen & Unwin archive, HarperCollins). He will suggest that the Het Spectrum director bring the rest of the pictures with him to show Tolkien.

25 May 1961 Tolkien forwards to Rayner Unwin a letter from a girl in the USA. She complains that *Farmer Giles of Ham* is out of print there. He is inclined to send her a copy, and asks Rayner to do this at his expense.

26 May 1961 Robert Burchfield writes to Tolkien. Onions has been pursuing the point with Early English Text Society editors, the Clarendon Press, and the printer without any success.

30 May 1961 Tolkien writes to Allen & Unwin, thanking them for a further cheque and a statement of accounts. – Rayner Unwin writes to Tolkien. He confirms that Houghton Mifflin have let *Farmer Giles of Ham* go out of print. He has been trying to interest some other American publisher. – This date is stamped by Oxford University Press on signatures F and G of the revised proof of *Ancrene Wisse*.

8 June 1961 Tolkien replies to a letter from Rhona Beare. He answers various questions about *The Lord of the Rings*, mainly concerning his invented languages. – This date is stamped by Oxford University Press on signatures H and I of the revised proofs of *Ancrene Wisse*.

21 June 1961 Encaenia.

4 July 1961 Rayner Unwin writes to Tolkien. He asks when the Dutch publisher can visit him to show him the rest of Cor Blok's illustrations and retrieve the first five. – Joy Hill sends Tolkien the four scripts by Sam Langdon dramatizing *The Hobbit*, and a letter from Miss Doolan of the Schools Broadcasting Department.

5 or 6–15 July 1961 Tolkien and Edith stay in Bournemouth.

12 July 1961 Joy Hill writes to Tolkien. *Pamela Chandler, a well-known portrait photographer, would like to photograph him.

18 July 1961 Tolkien writes to Joy Hill. He apologizes for not answering her letters before. The person who was supposed to forward all correspondence to Bournemouth had sent only the bills and circulars. He asks her to pass on to Miss Doolan the comments he has made on the scripts (which he presumably returns). He thinks that Sam Langdon has done a respectable job, within the destructive limits in which he was obliged to work. – This date is stamped by Oxford University Press on signatures B and C of the proofs of Frances M. Mack's edition of *Ancrene Riwle* (British Museum MS Cotton Titus D. XVIII) for the Early English Text Society, which are sent to Tolkien, as a member of the EETS Council, for comment.

18 or 19 July 1961 Joy Hill, anxious about the BBC scripts, telephones Tolkien.

20 July 1961 Joy Hill writes to Tolkien. She has now received the BBC scripts. She explains the sales advantages and publicity to be expected from such a serialization.

24 July 1961 Pamela Chandler writes to Tolkien. She asks whether he would prefer her to photograph him in her studio in London or in Oxford.

27 July 1961 This date is stamped by Oxford University Press on signatures K–N of the revised proofs of Tolkien's edition of the *Ancrene Wisse*.

28 July 1961 Tolkien writes to Pamela Chandler. He asks her to come to Oxford, explaining that he is not very mobile and is having treatment for fibrositis and arthritis.

31 July 1961 Rayner Unwin writes to Tolkien. He suggests a meeting on 4 August, at 9.45 or 10.00 a.m.

2 August 1961 Tolkien writes to Rayner Unwin. He would be delighted to see him on 4 August. 10.00 a.m. would be best, as the son who is spending a holiday with him (probably John) is leaving that day at 9.45. – Tolkien writes to Pamela Chandler. He will be free to be photographed on the morning of 17 August.

4 August 1961 Rayner Unwin presumably visits Tolkien in the morning.

10 August 1961 Norman Davis talks to Tolkien about the *Ancrene Wisse*.

14 August 1961 Norman Davis calls on Tolkien in the evening to discuss the *Ancrene Wisse*.

17 August 1961 Pamela Chandler photographs Tolkien in his garage-study, and Tolkien and Edith at their garden gate.

18 August 1961 Robert Burchfield writes to Tolkien. Norman Davis has sent him a note by Tolkien on the title and arrangement of the first five pages of *Ancrene Wisse*. This means that the pages will have to be re-imposed. He encloses a proof on which Tolkien should mark this change. Two more Early English Text Society titles are ready for press, and Tolkien will be aware that the Titus proofs have begun to appear. Burchfield sends him a proof of an article by C.A. Ladd on the *Ancrene Riwle* which is to appear in *Notes and Queries* (August 1961), though he is not sure that Tolkien will agree with it.

***c.* 20 August 1961** Tolkien drafts a three-page reply to Robert Burchfield. His note to Norman Davis had been only a suggestion, but he is pleased that Burchfield seems to think it important enough to make the change. He has read the section of the Titus edition with care, 'as befits one who has received many valuable suggestions from other members of the Council'. There is not much comment he can offer, but he asks to have another copy on which to send in suggestions, since 'I have defaced the pages that I have received with many notes, since they happen to cover what I consider the most important passages in the textual criticism of the A[ncrene] R[iwle]. . . .' He is held up in the correction of his own revises, as he has received only up to p. 192. 'The matter of capitals has proved difficult and costly in time', partly because of inconsistency and confusion resulting from changes he had made, but 'made worse by corrections in the proofs' which 'appear to have been made partly in deference to Ker's remarks in his Introduction. . . . But these remarks are in my opinion misleading, defective, or simply wrong as a description of the facts of the [manuscript] . . . and of its usage.' He is 'under treatment for arthritis and fibrositis, which makes the long desk hours (their chief cause) painful. . . . The A[ncrene] W[isse] is only one of my troubles . . . made worse by the long delay between copy and first proofs, in which I had to turn to other matters, and lost the threads. As I have now lost the threads of my other work' (Tolkien Papers, Bodleian Library, Oxford). He also comments on Ladd's article.

29 August 1961 Robert Burchfield writes to Tolkien. He hopes that Tolkien will return all of the revises of *Ancrene Wisse* soon after the remainder (pp. 192–222) arrive.

14 September 1961 This date is stamped by Oxford University Press on signature D of the proofs of Frances M. Mack's edition of *Ancrene Riwle*, sent to Tolkien for comment.

15 September 1961 This date is stamped by Oxford University Press on signature O of the revised proof of the *Ancrene Wisse*.

16 September 1961 This date is stamped by Oxford University Press on signatures E–G of the proofs of Frances M. Mack's edition of *Ancrene Riwle*, sent to Tolkien for comment.

22 September 1961 This date is stamped by Oxford University Press on signature H of the proofs of Frances M. Mack's edition of *Ancrene Riwle*, sent to Tolkien for comment. The rest of the signatures are not date-stamped, but presumably arrive soon after.

25 September 1961 Hilary Box, of George Allen & Unwin, writes to Tolkien. The Puffin *Hobbit* is to be published on 26 October. She sends him four advance copies, with a fifth which she asks him to sign for Sir Allen Lane, head of Penguin Books.

27 September 1961 Tolkien replies to a letter from his former colleague M.R. Ridley, some part of which was written in Tengwar. Tolkien finds Ridley's use of Tengwar better than that of other correspondents who use this script. He also signs slips of paper for Ridley to insert in his volumes of *The Lord of the Rings*. On one slip he writes three words from Galadriel's song of farewell, *Namárië*, and in his letter corrects its translation in the published text. – Tolkien's fan mail includes a number of letters written in Tengwar or runes, often from children. He cannot leave their transliteration to a secretary and has to do it himself. He himself sometimes gives up when the writer has not fully mastered the script.

30 September 1961 Tolkien receives from Pamela Chandler proofs of the photographs she had taken, and shows them to several people.

Autumn 1961 (before 15 November) The woman who for eight years has provided domestic help at 76 Sandfield Road can no longer continue because of ill health. It is not easy to find a replacement, which means extra work for Edith and Tolkien.

?Early October 1961 Jane Neave writes to Tolkien. She asks 'if you wouldn't get out a small book with Tom Bombadil at the heart of it, the sort of size of book that we old 'uns can afford to buy for Christmas presents' (quoted in *Biography*, p. 244). – Norman Davis writes to Robert Burchfield. Tolkien now says that he does not think that he will be able to produce a satisfactory introduction for *Ancrene Wisse*, except for what he has done already (which Burchfield thinks out of proportion. Tolkien may have more to say when Davis sees him on 10 October.

1 October 1961 Tolkien writes to Pamela Chandler. Her photographs have been generally approved. He asks for finished copies of all but three.

4 October 1961 Tolkien replies to Jane Neave. Her idea for a book with Tom Bombadil is 'a good one, not that I feel inclined to write any more about him. But I think that the original poem . . . might make a pretty booklet of the kind you would like if each verse could be illustrated by Pauline Baynes' (*Letters*, p. 308). He offers to send a copy of the poem to Jane if she has not seen it. – Tolkien replies to Hilary Box, thanking her for the copies of the Puffin *Hobbit* and returning the signed copy for Sir Allen Lane.

9 October 1961 Pamela Chandler writes to Tolkien, giving details of print sizes. She tells him to keep the proofs as long as he likes.

10 October 1961 Norman Davis sees Tolkien. He records in a memo that Tolkien 'now thought he would have to give up the idea of an Introd[uction] on the scale he had hoped, & just "knock out a brief note of two or three pages"' (Early English Text Society archive).

11 October 1961 Tolkien writes to Rayner Unwin. He tells him of the suggestion by Jane Neave ('a kind enthusiast'). The Tom Bombadil poem is 'very pictorial', and if Pauline Baynes 'could be induced to illustrate it, it might do well' (Tolkien-George Allen & Unwin archive, HarperCollins). If Rayner is interested, Tolkien will have copies made so that one might be sent to Miss Baynes. – Tolkien writes to Pamela Chandler. He will be sending some orders for prints shortly, and looks forward to seeing the pictures of himself and Edith. – This date is stamped by Oxford University Press on signature P of the revised proof of Tolkien's edition of the *Ancrene Wisse*.

17–31 October 1961 Tolkien and Edith stay at the Hotel Miramar, Bournemouth.

18 October 1961 Rayner Unwin writes to Tolkien . 'It would be enchanting to have an illustrated Tom Bombadil' (Tolkien-George Allen & Unwin archive, HarperCollins). He asks if it is as long as *Farmer Giles of Ham*. He would like to see the text. Stanley Unwin has met an American, Edmund Fuller, who has written in praise of Tolkien in the United States. If Tolkien can spare Fuller a quarter of an hour of his time, it might be worthwhile.

21 October 1961 At a meeting of the Early English Text Society Council, in Tolkien's absence, it is decided that the corrected proofs of the *Ancrene Wisse* must be returned by the end of November, as well as copy for an introduction to supplement that written by Neil Ker. Although it is not recorded in the minutes of the meeting, on 23 January 1962 Robert Burchfield will inform Norman Davis that no provision has been made to send further proofs to Tolkien, which Burchfield believes was the view of the EETS Council at its October meeting.

22 October 1961 Tolkien writes to Rayner Unwin, sending a copy of the poem *The Adventures of Tom Bombadil*. It is short but might make an inexpensive 'gift book'. He found Pamela Chandler, the photographer, a very charming person, though she 'inflicted such blistering lights on me, & held the poses until I was nearly stunned. So that I felt like a boiled or grilled owl, and I think look rather like one in most of the resulting pictures' (Tolkien-George Allen & Unwin archive, HarperCollins). He has had correspondence with Edmund Fuller, but they have been unable to find a suitable time for him to visit Tolkien.

29 October 1961 Robert Burchfield writes to Tolkien. The corrected revises of *Ancrene Wisse* and copy for the introduction (longer or shorter version) should be returned by 30 November. If Tolkien cannot complete his introduction by then, the Society will publish the book with just Ker's introduction. He encloses details of a few doubtful readings in the revises.

31 October 1961 Tolkien and Edith return to Oxford. Tolkien is suffering from a throat infection and cold, and has to stay indoors for several days.

November 1961 The electors to the Vigfússon Readership in Ancient Icelandic Literature and Antiquities (including Tolkien) agree by correspondence to re-elect E.O.G. Turville-Petre to the post.

2 November 1961 Rayner writes to Tolkien. Since *The Adventures of Tom Bombadil* is so short, Tolkien might collect together enough of these occasional verses to make a book, not just the ones in *The Lord of the Rings* and *The Hobbit*.

?3–15 November 1961 In response to Rayner Unwin's request, Tolkien makes 'a search as far as time allowed' and has 'copies made of any poems that might conceivably see the light or (somewhat tidied up) be presented again'. He will later comment that he enjoyed himself 'very much digging out these old half-forgotten things and rubbing them up. All the more because there are other and duller things I ought to have been doing' (letters to Rayner Unwin and Jane Neave, 15 and 22 November, *Letters*, p. 309). The 'rubbing up' indicates that he emends or revises at least some of the poems.

4 November 1961 Tolkien writes to Joyce Reeves (the children's author Joyce Gard). He enjoyed the book she sent to him (*Woorroo*, 1961).

6 November 1961 Alina Dadlez sends Tolkien five copies of the Swedish *Return of the King*.

13 November 1961 Tolkien writes to Kenneth R. Brooks, thanking him for a copy of his book, *Andreas and the Fates of the Apostles*. Brooks had worked on the text as a D. Phil. student under Tolkien. He asks Brooks for a signed slip to insert in his copy. He will buy one or two copies for presents.

14 November 1961 Alina Dadlez sends Tolkien five copies of the Swedish *Farmer Giles of Ham*.

15 November 1961 Tolkien writes to Rayner Unwin. He explains that the 'elderly lady' who had suggested the Tom Bombadil book had been thinking of something like the Beatrix Potter books. He sends copies of some poems which might be suitable. 'The harvest is not rich, for one thing there is not much that really goes with Tom Bombadil' (Tolkien-George Allen & Unwin archive, HarperCollins, partly printed in *Letters*, p. 309). He sends *Errantry, The Man in the Moon Came Down Too Soon, Perry-the-Winkle, The Dragon's Visit, The Sea-Bell,* and *The Hoard*. – Tolkien writes to Jane Neave. Allen & Unwin want a bigger book than she, or he, intended. He sends her copies of poems (probably the same as sent to Rayner Unwin, plus *Princess Mee*, perhaps found after Tolkien wrote to Rayner). He asks which she thinks might go with *The Adventures of Tom Bombadil*. – K.R. Brooks sends Tolkien the requested signed slip.

18 November 1961 Tolkien writes to Rayner Unwin. He has found another poem (*Princess Mee*) which might also be considered for the book. – Rayner Unwin writes to Tolkien. He is sending the poems to Pauline Baynes to see if they interest her. He thinks that 'it would be wise to include most, if not all, those you have sent us as very small books tend to look horribly expensive' (Tolkien-George Allen & Unwin archive, HarperCollins).

22 November 1961 Tolkien writes a long letter to Jane Neave. He thanks her for returning the poems, and at length discusses writing for children. – Rayner Unwin writes to Tolkien. He has sent the extra poem to Pauline Baynes.

23 November 1961 Tolkien writes to Pauline Baynes. He hopes that the poems Rayner Unwin has sent will amuse her, and that at least some will inspire her as an artist. When the idea of a book about Tom Bombadil with pictures was suggested, he immediately thought of her. He is delighted with her cover for the Puffin *Hobbit*.

?Late November 1961 Pauline Baynes writes to Tolkien. She likes the poems and would enjoy illustrating them. She describes them as 'dream-like – to be *felt* rather than seen' (quoted by Tolkien in a letter to Rayner Unwin, 8 December 1961, Tolkien-George Allen & Unwin archive, HarperCollins), and evidently makes some comment on the problem posed by the varying styles and content of the poems. She wonders if her ideas would agree with Tolkien's.

?December 1961 Cor Blok visits Tolkien in Sandfield Road and shows him illustrations of *The Lord of the Rings*. 'Tolkien gave Blok the impression of an absent-minded professor, although Blok thought Tolkien was acting the part. For about an hour and a half they talked in Tolkien's untidy study, mainly about art and Tolkien's opinion of illustrating his own work. Tolkien showed Blok his own drawings and watercolours . . . and mentioned his dissatisfaction with them. Tolkien did like Blok's work very much' (René van Rossenberg, 'Dutch Tolkien Illustrators', *Tolkien Collector* 3 (May 1993), p. 18).

1 December 1961 Rayner Unwin writes to Tolkien. He has been trying to generate interest in a television programme on Tolkien and his writings. Christopher Burstall of BBC Television might get in touch with him.

2 December 1961 In the evening, Tolkien attends a dinner of The Society hosted by J.B. Joll at St Antony's College, Oxford. Twelve members are present. Joll opens a discussion on the request by undergraduates to participate in government of the University; this devolves into sometimes heated discussions on the subject of undergraduate morals.

6 December 1961 Tolkien replies to Pauline Baynes. He is delighted that she is interested in the poems. Except for *The Sea-Bell* they were 'conceived as a series of very definite, clear and precise, pictures – fantastical, or nonsensical perhaps, but not dreamlike! And I thought of you, because you seem able to produce wonderful pictures with a touch of "fantasy", but primarily bright and clear visions of things that one might really see.' He hopes that she will accept the commission, but comments: 'Alas! you put your finger unerringly on a main difficulty: they are *not* a unity from any point of view, but made at different times under varying inspiration' (*Letters*, p. 312).

7 December 1961 Alina Dadlez sends Tolkien four copies of the Polish *Fellowship of the Ring*. The other volumes will be published in 1962 and 1963.

8 December 1961 Tolkien writes to Rayner Unwin. For the past few weeks he has been without secretarial help, 'and also recently ill with influenza'. He has heard from Mr Burstall at the BBC, who will probably visit him next week. 'I am sure I shall loathe the whole thing but I am very willing to suffer in a good cause.' He has also heard from Pauline Baynes, though he did not feel entirely happy with her view that the poems are 'dream like', but he agrees 'heartily with her feeling that all the pieces are very different' (Tolkien-George Allen & Unwin archive, HarperCollins). He thinks that perhaps *The Sea-Bell* ought to be omitted from the collection.

13 December 1961 Rayner Unwin writes to Tolkien. Allen & Unwin need all the poems Tolkien can find to make a book of reasonable size. He encloses a letter from their Hollywood agent, Swanson, reporting that Rembrandt Films is interested in making cartoon films of *The Hobbit*. Rayner reminds Tolkien of the policy he had agreed years ago with Stanley Unwin: cash or kudos. He wants to query certain points in the proposed contract.

14 December 1961 Tolkien writes to Rayner Unwin. He leaves it to him to deal with the contract offered by Rembrandt Films.

> I clearly understand that one must either turn the matter down or put up with the many objectionable things that they are sure to perpetrate in their production. I am sure advice or argument would be quite unavailing (except to make them throw the whole thing up) and I have no time for either. In any case I do not feel so deeply about The Hobbit; and anyway since I am now mainly dependent for my support on my earnings as an author I feel justified in sinking my feelings in return for cash.

The poetry book is turning into something quite different from the small book he had contemplated, with illustrations as important as the verses.

> Looking out, furbishing up, or re-writing of further items to go with *Tom Bombadil* and *Errantry*, took a lot of work and caused the Clarendon Press to rampage [i.e. the Oxford University Press has complained about delays in completing work on the *Ancrene Wisse*]. If you really want more poems, whether suitable or not to go with Tom, I can find a number, and am prepared to let the Clarendon Press rampage while I do so, if you really think stuff of this sort is publishable and saleable. [Tolkien-George Allen & Unwin archive, HarperCollins]

Today he received a letter from someone who wishes to produce a play of *The Hobbit* next summer. Tolkien supposes that there is no harm in agreeing to this, if there will be only 'one or a very short series of performances'.

15 December 1961 Robert Burchfield writes to Tolkien. He and Norman Davis had not pressed for the return of the *Ancrene Wisse* proofs last week as they knew that Tolkien had influenza. They are now awaiting the corrected proofs for the text, and will need to consult the Council to find out if they are willing to extend the time limit for the introduction. Burchfield reminds Tolkien that over 500 members and a greater number of non-members are waiting for this book, and printers do not like to leave type standing too long (i.e. metal type set up for printing).

20 December 1961 Rayner Unwin writes to Tolkien. Allen & Unwin are going ahead with Rembrandt Films with certain precautionary provisos. Tolkien will receive a minimum advance of $7000. Rayner will send him copies of the relevant letters, but there is no need for him to acknowledge them. He is sorry if he is 'warping your original intention' for Tom Bombadil, but production costs make books of fewer than sixty-four pages seem very expensive. 'What we have in mind is a flat volume about the same outside dimensions as *The Lord of the Rings* but of 64 pages with board covers, illustrations in litho[graphy]'. He hopes to send a mock-up soon. He would welcome any additional poems Tolkien can send. 'I would suggest, however, that you don't start the Clarendon Press rampaging until we have got out some figures. . . . Incidentally I am disturbed that the Clarendon Press are still rampagable. I thought you had pretty well cleared them out of the way by now' (Tolkien-George Allen & Unwin archive, HarperCollins). He has given permission for the *Hobbit* play.

21 December 1961 Joy Hill writes to Tolkien. She is sending him a copy of *School Magazine* from New South Wales, with an article and an extract from *The Hobbit*, for which a fee has been paid.

26 December 1961 Robert Burchfield writes to Tolkien. He has heard good news that Tolkien has undertaken to return the proofs of the *Ancrene Wisse* text by 21 January. He encloses two memos about Early English Text Society matters.

28 December 1961 Tolkien writes to Pauline Baynes. He thanks her for her Christmas card and hopes that she is still interested in illustrating the poems. When looking at the Swedish translation of *Farmer Giles of Ham* he had been 'again struck by the enormous importance (to that little squib) of your work' (courtesy of Mrs Pauline Gasch). He mentions three beautiful birches in his garden which he has grown from seedlings.

29 December 1961 Tolkien replies to several letters from a Miss Perry. He can no longer remember addresses, and his papers are in a confused state, but 'recently I found someone willing to go through the confusion; and she had special orders to look out for certain addresses. Just before Christmas she unearthed yours' (Michael Silverman, *Catalogue Nine* (1993), p. 32 and pl. 8).

30 December 1961 Tolkien writes to Rayner Unwin. He has not yet had time to look for more poems.

I am still in trouble with the Clarendon Press. The *Ancrene Wisse* with its 234 closely written [manuscript] pages, its textual problems, its marginalia, and the attached Elizabethan matter, has proved a much greater task than I expected. It has been made more time-consuming by difficulties at the Press. My [manuscript] disappeared into the confusion caused by the printers' strike, and came out again only after a long delay, badly mishandled. The revises have been slowly coming back, again mishandled – causing me a great deal of close work, largely owing to the well-meaning but unwarranted interference of an Early English Text Soc[iety] official. I have still a quire or two of these revises to put into order. The absolute closing date (they say) is Jan. 21. For the Revises! I have still to get the Introduction typed.

A few days earlier, needing to look up a passage in *The Hobbit*, he had picked up a copy of the Puffin edition and found that changes had been made in the text: *dwarfs* instead of *dwarves*, *dwarfish* instead of *dwarvish*, *elfish/ Elfish* instead of *elvish/Elvish*). 'Penguin Books had, I suppose, no licence to edit my work, and should have reproduced faithfully the printed copy; and at least out of courtesy to Allen and Unwin and myself should have addressed some enquiry before they proceeded to correct the text' (Tolkien-George Allen & Unwin archive, HarperCollins, partly printed in *Letters*, p. 313). He would not have signed a copy of the book for Sir Allen Lane had he noticed this before. He realizes that nothing can be done, but thinks that Penguin Books should be informed that the changes have not passed unobserved. He lists the few errors he found in the setting (obviously having been through the whole text), as well as an error taken up from the text they used. He asks Rayner to thank Joy Hill for the *School Magazine*, and comments on the article.

1962

First half of 1962 Tolkien engages a new secretary, Anne Slim.

4 January 1962 Rayner Unwin writes to Tolkien. Allen & Unwin have licensed only one printing of the Puffin *Hobbit*. The additional correction Tolkien has noticed will be made in the next Allen & Unwin printing.

12 January 1962 Rayner Unwin writes to Tolkien, sending a specimen page for the *Adventures of Tom Bombadil* collection with cost estimates. If Allen & Unwin print 10,000 copies with 64 pages, with the same trim size as *The Lord of the Rings* and with the contents divided about equally between Tolkien's text and the illustrations, the book could be sold probably at 12s 6d. Allen & Unwin need to use all of the material Tolkien has already sent to fill the volume, 'though substitutions in order to make a more unified whole are still entirely allowable' (Tolkien-George Allen & Unwin archive, HarperCollins). Rayner has had some encouraging correspondence with the Hollywood agent.

16 January 1962 Tolkien replies to Rayner Unwin. He likes the specimen page, and wants Pauline Baynes to illustrate the book. He will reconsider the poems already sent and try to find more; he can probably do so in the following week, as he hopes to return corrected proofs of *Ancrene Wisse* on 20 January and 'pack off the visitors who have descended upon me (as usual at the most awkward time) on Tuesday [23 January]' (Tolkien-George Allen & Unwin archive, HarperCollins).

18 January 1962 David Nichol Smith dies.

23 January 1962 Tolkien writes to Robert Burchfield, transmitting the proofs of *Ancrene Wisse* with a typed statement which indicates his displeasure with amendments made to the revised proof. He apologizes for the delay in providing corrections, but 'the delay in receiving the last two sections of the Revises also proved troublesome. Though I made notes on an old proof, while my mind was on the matter, it proved necessary in the end to correct these pages afresh.' He is grateful to the reader who spotted so many minor errors and typographical inconsistencies, and for his helpful queries.

> But I find that in the Revises one or more other hands have been busy, not offering queries, but making independent editorial changes, or cancelling my instructions. This is surely irregular? In any case I view the procedure with displeasure.
>
> The object . . . was no doubt benevolent, though I have not discovered what its precise aim was. If it was either to assist me, or to reduce some inconsistencies to order, it failed in both objects.

Alterations in one hand are mainly to capitals, but were done inconsistently, and made worse by another hand haphazardly cancelling some of these alterations. 'But I find the assumption of editorial function in other matters, as in the alteration or re-writing of my footnotes, even more objectionable. Even if the changes happen to be justified, I think I should be accorded the courtesy of a by-your-leave enquiry. And unless I am denied the right of dissent, a query would prove more economical in proof-corrections.' He summarizes his decisions about the use of capitals made at various times when preparing the work for publication.

> I will not here argue the decision to dismiss all small capitals from the text. It is based on a reconsideration line by line of the whole work. In the Revises as now returned all alterations or restorations affecting capitals are marked in *green*. If these seem numerous, the challenge of the busy hands is primarily responsible. I was given no explanation of their objects or principles, to justify their behaviour. If only to try and discover them, I was obliged to undertake a survey of "capitals" and their forms and functions in the [manuscript], which I had thought (mistakenly) could safely be left to the Palæographical Introduction.
>
> I hope these green directions will be respected; at least not changed without query. [Early English Text Society archive]

In the process of writing this letter, Tolkien makes fourteen pages of typed and manuscript drafts, more forceful than the final statement. These include:

I have had to do a good deal of work on this Introduction, to prevent it from being worse than it is, though I had hoped to turn to it for help and instruction; but I did not bother about the matter of capitals. I supposed that K[er] might be trusted here, where nothing linguistic or textual was likely to arise. . . . [Ker's] errors are not of great moment, having little or no textual bearings – as long as my transcript is left alone. . . . [Tolkien Papers, Bodleian Library, Oxford]

– Robert Burchfield writes to Tolkien. He is sorry that Tolkien does not entirely approve of the changes made by Ker, whom he is sure acted with good intentions. Opinions differ in matters involving capitalization. The printer will be asked to follow Tolkien's instructions in all parts of the edition for which he is responsible. He thinks, as a consequence, that Neil Ker may want to make one or two changes to his introduction, so that it agrees with what is printed. In regard to the alterations, no discourtesy to Tolkien was intended, but in the interest of speed, it was felt that no harm would result from making changes in the proofs, as Tolkien would see every alteration in the revises and be free to cancel or modify them as he wished.

c. **24 January 1962** Tolkien drafts a reply to Robert Burchfield (the final letter is not in the Early English Text Society archive). He does not understand how the procedure followed for *Ancrene Wisse* could have been expected to save time.

The alterations were often to all appearances casual, leaving similar or identical things at other points in the [manuscript] untouched. They were in three inks, and some not readily distinguishable from my own hand – needing reference to a second set of proofs, which was more or less fully corrected. And I was totally in the dark as to why or by whom they had been made. . . . I should have been informed that this procedure was going to be adopted, or at least that it had been. . . .

Now I will retire to the salutary recollection of my own faults and the trouble I have given. . . . I will say no more, except to assure you, that it is NOT to correction and advice that I object. I need them both. . . . But one is entitled to know who one is dealing with, and also to some reasons. If I had received Ker's notes for the revision, I should have welcomed them with the gratitude they deserve. [Tolkien Papers, Bodleian Library, Oxford]

24 January 1962 Oxford University Press date-stamps the proofs of Tolkien's essay *English and Welsh* for the volume of O'Donnell Lectures, *Angles and Britons*.

?Late January 1962 Tolkien drafts five pages for a letter to Neil Ker. 'May I thank you, belatedly, for corrections in the revision of the Proofs, which appear in the Revises? I was not informed of their (ultimate) origin, and in a letter to Burchfield I rather testily described them as "unauthorized"' (Tolkien

Papers, Bodleian Library, Oxford). He hopes that no similar changes based on his notes have been introduced into Ker's pages. He then explains at length why he decided to make certain changes.

25 January 1962 Rayner Unwin writes to Tolkien. He has received a fulsome apology from Penguin Books for their changes to the *Hobbit* text. They will restore Tolkien's spellings if a reprint is licensed. Already 20,000 of the 35,000 copies they printed have been sold. Rayner asks about the poems Tolkien had promised to look for. – William L. Snyder of Rembrandt Films writes to Tolkien. He has reached an agreement with Allen & Unwin's agent. He assures Tolkien that the filmmakers will treat his work with the respect it deserves. Although there is no clause in the film contract which requires Tolkien's services as an advisor, Snyder hopes that he might be free to call on Tolkien from time to time.

29 January 1962 Robert Burchfield writes to Tolkien. Neil Ker has adjusted his introduction slightly to avoid any conflict with the new readings Tolkien introduced in the revises. All of the proofs are to return to the printer on 30 January. – Burchfield writes to Oxford University Press, explaining the state of the proofs. He asks for new revises, but it has been decided that these should not be sent to Tolkien.

1 February 1962 Tolkien replies to a letter from the Dutch artist Cor Blok. He is interested to hear of an exhibition Blok is planning. He would like to buy two pictures by Blok based on *The Lord of the Rings*, *The Battle of the Hornburg* and *The Dead Marshes*. – Robert Burchfield sends Tolkien a copy of the frontispiece for *Ancrene Wisse*.

2 February 1962 Tolkien writes to Robert Burchfield, thanking him for his letters. The first, of 23 January, had astonished and perturbed him: 'if I had fully understood the situation earlier I should have spoken less testily, and also probably acted differently in places. But do not imagine me brooding in dudgeon. Any trouble that I have been given is small in comparison with the trouble that I have given to you and others.' He notes that the proofs had been sent back, but after receiving Burchfield's first letter

> I had to think again about one or two points; and also I came across some notes for Revise that were overlooked in the final rush. In that same rush I also neglected to make my spare Revises a perfect record of changes made in the copy returned. I wonder if [it] is still possible to see that certain changes are made before the Revises are dealt with, or that one or two small changes are cancelled? (Some of them may have been made, and not properly recorded.)
>
> I have put them on a separate sheet so they can be sent to the Press, if approved. [Tolkien Papers, Bodleian Library, Oxford]

5 February 1962 Tolkien writes to Rayner Unwin. His time has been occupied with 'lingering guests' and *Ancrene Wisse*, but 'I have raked over my collection of old verses; there are some that might be made use of with a thorough re-handling. I am too tired to do that now and am going away on Thursday under medical advice for one week' (Tolkien–George Allen & Unwin archive, HarperCollins). He encloses four poems: *Firiel*, *Shadow-Bride*, *Knocking at the Door*, and *The Trees of Kortirion*, though he thinks the latter 'too long and too ambitious'. He suggests that one or two poems from *The Lord of the Rings* might be included, such as *Oliphaunt* and *The Man in the Moon Stayed Up Too Late*. He asks for a list of the poems he has already sent. He encloses (as he thinks) a copy of the letter from Mr Snyder; Tolkien has replied that he would be pleased to see him. – While considering poems for inclusion in the proposed book, Tolkien probably revises *The Trees of Kortirion* and *The Little House of Lost Play: Mar Vanwa Tyaliéva*.

6 February 1962 Tolkien realizes that he did not enclose the letter from Mr Snyder with his letter to Rayner Unwin, and sends it now with a note. – This date is stamped on two ?revised proof pages of *English and Welsh*.

8–16 February 1962 Tolkien stays at the Hotel Miramar, Bournemouth.

8 February 1962 Rayner Unwin writes to Tolkien. He will read all of the poems and consider which, if any, should be discarded, and will then contact Pauline Baynes. The film contract for *The Hobbit* has run into 'a slight snag concerning copyright' and discussions are 'back in the melting pot again' (Tolkien–George Allen & Unwin archive, HarperCollins). Within the next month, Rayner and Tolkien will discuss the validity of the American copyright of *The Hobbit*, which has been called into question.

11 February 1962 Neil Ker writes to Tolkien, discussing proposed changes to *Ancrene Wisse*. When he receives a proof, he will work carefully through Tolkien's notes. He apologizes for what has happened. He had not expected that the changes he made would go so far without Tolkien seeing them.

12 February 1962 Rayner Unwin writes to Tolkien. He asks if he might call on him on 19 February at about 10.00 a.m., to discuss an idea he has about the poems. He lists the poems he has received, and agrees that *The Trees of Kortirion* does not fit, but thinks that one or two poems from *The Lord of the Rings* could be included.

13 February 1962 Tolkien writes to Rayner Unwin. He will be delighted to see him on 19 February.

18 February 1962 Tolkien writes to the University of Wales Press. He has found it necessary to make considerable alterations or excisions to page proofs of his essay *English and Welsh* in four places (pp. 13, 33, 37, and 38) and hopes that these will not prove too troublesome. He encloses the marked proofs.

19 February 1962 Rayner Unwin visits Tolkien in Oxford to discuss the book of poems.

26 February 1962 A Mrs Newdigate writes to Tolkien, asking if a Braille version of *The Lord of the Rings* might be produced.

c. 26 February–1 March 1962 Tolkien replies to Mrs Newdigate. He is agreeable to her request, but any arrangements must be made with Allen & Unwin.

28 February 1962 Rayner Unwin writes to Tolkien. The contract with Rembrandt Films has been sorted out. He sends Tolkien documents in quadruplicate to sign. Allen & Unwin are negotiating for another book club *Hobbit*.

1 March 1962 Tolkien forwards Mrs Newdigate's letter to Rayner Unwin. He is returning the Rembrandt contract documents separately.

2 March 1962 Joy Hill, in Rayner Unwin's absence, writes to Tolkien. Mrs Newdigate has been referred to the Royal National Institute for the Blind.

6 March 1962 Mahmoud Manzalaoui, who reviewed *The Lord of the Rings* in the *Egyptian Gazette* and received a letter from Tolkien, is in Oxford on sabbatical leave. He contacts Tolkien by sending him an offprint of his article 'Lydgate and English Prosody' from *Cairo Studies in English*.

21 March 1962 Rayner Unwin writes to Tolkien. Rembrandt Films 'have woken up at last about the equivocal copyright position [of *The Hobbit*] in the U.S.A. and are trying out a little last minute bargaining' (Tolkien-George Allen & Unwin archive, HarperCollins). He has heard from Nelson that their edition of *Farmer Giles of Ham* is selling well in the United States.

29 March 1962 Rayner Unwin writes to Tolkien. Allen & Unwin has come to a form of agreement with Rembrandt Films by making compromises. He encloses forms for Tolkien to sign or initial.

?End of March–3 April 1962 Tolkien stays in Bournemouth. The visit is evidently unplanned: on 31 March he writes to Rayner Unwin: 'I was obliged to come away for a few days – at an awkward time' (Tolkien-George Allen & Unwin archive, HarperCollins).

31 March 1962 Tolkien writes to Rayner Unwin from Bournemouth. He has initialled and signed the various amendments to the contract, and presumably returns them.

?Beginning of April 1962 Edith Tolkien has another fall in the garden. No bones are broken, but she is badly scratched from clutching at a rose bush, strains her shoulder, and suffers shock.

3 April 1962 Henry Lewis, who is reading the proofs of *English and Welsh*, writes to Tolkien, querying the Welsh form Tolkien gives for a Gallo-Roman name. – Taylor F. Campbell, a bookseller in Richmond, Virginia, writes to Tolkien. He has been unable to get any information for a customer from either Houghton Mifflin or a public library about *The Lord of the Rings*. He thinks that it is a compilation of *The Fellowship of the Ring*, *The Two Towers*, and *The Return of the King*. In an undated draft reply to this letter, Tolkien will comment that Houghton Mifflin must have answered the inquiry in their sleep. The draft is written on the back of a copy of *Cat*, the poem written for his granddaughter in 1956 which he is considering for the *Adventures of Tom Bombadil* collection.

5 April 1962 Tolkien replies to Henry Lewis. He accepts the form of the name suggested.

6 April 1962 Tolkien writes to George Sayer. He had planned to visit Sayer in Malvern, but cannot do so because he is unwilling to leave Edith after her fall.

9 April 1962 Tolkien replies to another letter he has received from Cor Blok. He is pleased that Blok has reserved for him the pictures he requested.

12 April 1962 Tolkien writes to Rayner Unwin. He has given every moment he can spare to the poems for the *Adventures of Tom Bombadil* collection, but has lost confidence in them.

> The various items . . . do not really 'collect'. The only possible link is the fiction that they come from the Shire from about the period of *The Lord of the Rings*. But that fits some uneasily. I have done a good deal of work, trying to make them fit better: if not much to their good, I hope not to their serious detriment. You may note that I have written a new *Bombadil* poem [*Bombadil Goes Boating*], which I hope is adequate to go with the older one, though for its understanding it requires some knowledge of the *L.R.* . . .
>
> I have placed the 16 items in an order: roughly Bilboish, Samlike, and Dubious. Some kind of order will be necessary, for the scheme of illustration and decoration. But I am not wedded to this arrangement. I am open to criticisms of it – and of any of the items; and to rejections. Miss Baynes is free to re-arrange things to fit her work, if she wishes.
>
> Some kind of foreword might possibly be required. The enclosed is not intended for that purpose! Though one or two of its points might be made more simply. But I found it easier, and more amusing (for myself) to represent to you in the form of a ridiculous editorial fiction what I have done to the verses, and what their references now are. [Tolkien-George Allen & Unwin archive, HarperCollins, partly printed in *Letters*, p. 315]

He encloses a copy of Campbell's letter. He finds it incredible that Houghton Mifflin do not know the titles of the books they publish. He receives numerous complaints from the USA that booksellers do not know, will not find out, and are unwilling to order a copy anyway. He forgot, in the rush, to note some details of the film contract, and asks Rayner for information. He wishes to give a set of *The Lord of the Rings* to an Oxford lorry driver who has become engrossed in the book while on probation, and asks for the books to be sent to him (Tolkien) and debited to his account. He will take the set to the man in person.

19 April 1962 Tolkien replies to a letter from a woman in Pittsburgh, Pennsylvania. He does not 'approve of research into living authors; it is too much like vivisection' (Tolkien-George Allen & Unwin archive, HarperCollins), and he is very busy. Answers to the questions asked by the writer can be found in *Who's Who*. – Rayner Unwin writes to Tolkien. He thinks that Tolkien has 'fashioned and shaped' the poems 'very promisingly' (Tolkien-George Allen & Unwin archive, HarperCollins). He approves the fictional scholarship of the introduction. As there are now more poems than before, he is obtaining a new estimate of printing costs. He also gives some details of the film contract.

26 April 1962 Rayner Unwin writes to Tolkien. Rembrandt Films have signed the contract. Rayner asks if Tolkien has an example of W.H. Auden's signature which Allen & Unwin could reproduce in a book by Auden that they are publishing in their Unwin Books series.

1 May 1962 Tolkien writes to Rayner Unwin. He is pleased that Rayner was amused by the introduction. He would like to read though the text of the poems and introduction again, to check for errors, before they go to the printer. He is glad that Rembrandt Films have signed, and looks forward to receiving the first instalment of the fee. He is sending Rayner by registered post his copy of *The Shield of Achilles* which contains Auden's signature. 'I am now pushing along with *Gawain* and *Pearl* and have now revised Fit 1 of *Gawain*' (Tolkien-George Allen & Unwin archive, HarperCollins). He asks if Rayner has the address of critic Edmund Fuller. – Tolkien writes to Paul Bibire, a schoolboy. He responds to questions about the English syllabus at Oxford.

5 May 1962 Rayner Unwin writes to Tolkien. He plans to publish 10,000 copies of *The Adventures of Tom Bombadil and Other Verses from the Red Book* in time for Christmas. Royalties will begin at a lower rate because of the cost of illustration.

7 May 1962 Joy Hill writes to Tolkien, asking him for a 200-word description of the *Adventures of Tom Bombadil* collection for advance publicity.

8 May 1962 Tolkien writes to Rayner Unwin. He agrees to the terms of the contract for *The Adventures of Tom Bombadil and Other Verses from the Red Book*. He wants to make one change to the description of the kingfisher in *Bombadil Goes Boating*, 'since alas! the birds have not got scarlet crests in our region; & though I suppose one could create a new species or variety, the flora & fauna are meant to be strictly Oxford & Berks' (Tolkien-George Allen & Unwin archive, HarperCollins). Both Edith and Tolkien's secretary are ill.

9 May 1962 Joy Hill writes to Tolkien. Allen & Unwin have offered Pauline Baynes the commission to illustrate the *Adventures of Tom Bombadil* collection. They assume that Tolkien will let them know what change is to be made to *Bombadil Goes Boating*, and look forward to receiving the signed contract. They hope that at the same time he will send the blurb and introduction. *The Shield of Achilles* is being returned with Joy's letter.

11 May 1962 Tolkien writes to Joy Hill, returning the signed contract for *The Adventures of Tom Bombadil and Other Verses from the Red Book*. He will deal with the other matters over the weekend.

14 May 1962 Tolkien replies to a letter from Cor Blok, in which he had told of a successful exhibition at The Hague, and that he is sending Tolkien the two pictures he wishes to buy, as well as *Dunharrow* as a present. – Tolkien writes to Joy Hill. He returns the corrected introduction, and a list of corrections to the *Bombadil* poems. The idea of writing a blurb makes his heart sink, but he encloses a note of about a hundred words: 'If this seems to be a good line to take, I could, I suppose, puff it out a bit, unless someone else could be induced to do this' (Tolkien-George Allen & Unwin archive, HarperCollins). He encloses an acknowledgement for a cheque and accounts. The signature on the acknowledgement is marked by Allen & Unwin to be used in the *Festschrift* *English and Medieval Studies Presented to J.R.R. Tolkien.*

15 May 1962 Joy Hill writes to Tolkien, thanking him for returning the contract and sending him a copy.

17 May 1962 Alina Dadlez sends Tolkien five copies of the Polish translation of *Farmer Giles of Ham.* – Joy Hill writes to Tolkien. She has passed his corrections to Allen & Unwin's editorial department together with his blurb, which they will use as the basis for a draft to be sent to him for approval. Pauline Baynes has accepted the commission. Allen & Unwin will have the poems set in type at once and send the artist a rough pull.

18 May 1962 Joy Hill writes to Tolkien. She is sending him Cor Blok's illustrations of *The Battle of the Hornburg, The Dead Marshes II,* and *Dunharrow.*

?20–?26 May 1962 Tolkien is away from Oxford, possibly staying in Bournemouth.

28 May 1962 Tolkien writes to Joy Hill. He should have acknowledged the Cor Blok pictures earlier, but they arrived as he was about to go away, and he has not been well since his return. He is a little disappointed, since he thought that he had asked for *The Dead Marshes I* but has been sent *The Dead Marshes II.* He will have to take the matter up with Blok, which is difficult since Blok has given Tolkien *Dunharrow,* one of his best pictures. – Tolkien writes to Alina Dadlez, thanking her for the copies of the Polish *Farmer Giles of Ham.*

29 May 1962 Joy Hill writes to Tolkien. There was no other version of the *Dead Marshes* among the pictures she received from Blok. Some of Blok's drawings may be exhibited at the Bear Lane Gallery, Oxford, at Christmas.

31 May 1962 Kenneth Sisam writes to Tolkien. He asks if Tolkien has any essential corrections for the glossary (or elsewhere) in *Fourteenth Century Verse and Prose.* He has heard that Tolkien might help out in the Oxford English School while C.L. Wrenn is on sabbatical leave during Michaelmas Term 1962 and Hilary Term 1963.

?June 1962 Tolkien is visited by the composer Thea Musgrave, who wants to write a musical dramatic work for amateurs based on *The Lord of the Rings,* with the text adapted by the Scottish author and poet Maurice Lindsay. Tolkien will describe her visit in a letter to Rayner Unwin on 21 July: 'I had the impression of a small kettle on the boil, without any certainty of tea, or much water' (Tolkien-George Allen & Unwin archive, HarperCollins). He tells Rayner that although he is not excited about the project, he told Musgrave that he would await further developments with interest.

8 June 1962 Rayner Unwin sends Tolkien a slightly emended version of his blurb for the *Adventures of Tom Bombadil* collection for approval. He asks if Tolkien has kept any fan letters from which Allen & Unwin could extract names and addresses of readers to send information about the new book.

13 June 1962 Ronald Eames, Allen & Unwin, sends Tolkien galley proofs for *The Adventures of Tom Bombadil and Other Verses from the Red Book.*

18 June 1962 Tolkien writes to Ronald Eames. He will correct the proofs as soon as possible, but cannot do so immediately. He will take them away with him and hopes to return them from Staffordshire later in the week. – Tolkien writes to Rayner Unwin. He returns the copy of the proposed blurb. He thinks that references in it to *The Faerie Queene*, Malory, and Ariosto had better be cut out, as they aroused hostility when they were published in *The Lord of the Rings* and are not applicable to the present book. He will be away from 20 June to 15 July, but letters can be sent to his secretary, Mrs Slim, who will try to make a list of addresses from his fan mail.

19 June 1962 Pauline Baynes, who has received the galley proofs for *The Adventures of Tom Bombadil and Other Verses from the Red Book*, writes to Tolkien. Ronald Eames has suggested that she visit Tolkien to discuss the illustrations, but she does not think it necessary to take up his time. Instead, she asks him to tell her if he has any strong feelings about anyone or anything, and then give her a free hand. This letter is forwarded to Tolkien on 23 June.

20–28 June 1962 Tolkien stays with his son John in Staffordshire.

21 June 1962 Tolkien writes to Ronald Eames. He is returning the corrected galley proofs separately. He lists the few corrections in case of postal accident or delay. – Rayner Unwin writes to Tolkien. He will adapt the blurb in accordance with Tolkien's suggestions. There is no immediate urgency for the list of fan mail addresses. He has dealt with a person who wrote to both Tolkien and Allen & Unwin on 14 June, seeking permission for plays and musicals.

?25 June 1962 Tolkien replies to Pauline Baynes. He immediately thought of her when his aunt raised the possibility of an illustrated book containing the poem *The Adventures of Tom Bombadil*.

> I have vivid visual pictures of those pieces that are narrative, but I cannot communicate them. Nor will they be the same as those awakened in the minds of readers. But I believe that yours will be of the order and mode which I should like, and will in fact probably enrich my own imagination. . . .
>
> You may, perhaps, like or wish to consult when you have really begun, and your own ideas and visions are forming; but in the meanwhile I do not think I have anything useful – general or particular to say. Apart from the indications given in the 'preface' – including the point that though on the surface 'lighthearted' these things have a serious undercurrent, and are not meant at any point to be merely comic. . . . [courtesy of Mrs Pauline Gasch]

He lists changes and corrections he has made to the galley proofs.

29 June 1962 Rayner Unwin writes to Tolkien. He understands that Tolkien has met Thea Musgrave and given her his blessing. He thinks that the fees offered are low, and that Tolkien should have the right to approve Lindsay's libretto.

2–10 July 1962 Tolkien and Edith stay at the Hotel Miramar, Bournemouth.

2 July 1962 Pauline Baynes writes to Tolkien. She appreciates a free hand with the *Adventures of Tom Bombadil* collection, but it makes her nervous. 'This is the sort of commission that *every* artist would give his all for' (Tolkien Papers, Bodleian Library, Oxford).

3 July 1962 Alina Dadlez writes to Tolkien, sending a copy of a letter from a publisher in Argentina with questions about translating *The Hobbit* into Spanish.

?Mid-July 1962 Jane Neave writes to Tolkien. He has sent her a cheque, but she wonders if the money should not rather be spent on a wheelchair for Edith.

18 July 1962 Tolkien replies to Jane Neave. He asks her to cash the cheque and spend it on herself. Edith does not need a chair, and he could afford it if she did. It is astonishing that instead of trying to live on an inadequate pension, he has an abundance which enables him to give instead of receive. 'Saving universal catastrophe, I am not likely to be hard up again in my time.' Both he and Edith are in better health this year. Edith still does 'all the cooking, most of the housework, and some of the gardening. I am afraid that this often means rather heroic effort; but of course, within limits, that is beneficial. Still it is hard being attacked in two different ways at once – or three. Great increase in weight due to operations. Arthritis, which is made more painful and acute by the weight; and an internal complaint, small internal lesions . . . which cause pain . . .' (*Letters*, p. 316). He gives a progress report on the *Adventures of Tom Bombadil* collection. He is putting his translations of *Sir Gawain* and *Pearl* in order, with notes and a brief preface, before returning to work on 'The Silmarillion'. He gives some background information about *Pearl*, and promises a copy of his translation as soon as he can get one made. Meanwhile he encloses a sheet with a copy of the opening stanza in the original and translation.

20 July 1962 Tolkien writes to Alina Dadlez. He apologizes for not replying sooner, but mail had not been forwarded despite his arrangements. The most important point to make to the translator of *The Hobbit* into Spanish is that if he uses *gnomos* for dwarves, it must not be used in the phrase 'the elves that are now called gnomes'. He wishes '*hobbit* to remain untranslated (as a protection against the private fancies of translators . . .). In a Latin language *hobbits* looks dreadful . . .' (Tolkien-George Allen & Unwin archive, HarperCollins). If he had been consulted earlier, he would have agreed to some naturalization of the form in Spanish, such as *hobitos*.

21 July 1962 Tolkien writes to Rayner Unwin. He hopes to have a list of addresses made from his fan mail before the end of August. 'I am without any help at all at the moment, but I am expecting to find someone with more time and more competence (for my purposes) in a day or two.' In regard to Thea Musgrave's project, he would certainly wish to see what Maurice Lindsay writes as a libretto. He has received two visits from Edmund Fuller (but gives no indication when). In regard to his standing in for C.L. Wrenn for two terms, he notes that it is 'pleasant but inopportune in view of all that I have on hand, to be temporarily dusted and taken off the shelf' (Tolkien-George

Allen & Unwin archive, HarperCollins). – Tolkien writes to Pauline Baynes. The pleasure and enthusiasm in her letter of 2 July was welcome, since he had begun to lose confidence in the verses.

25 July 1962 Rayner Unwin writes to Tolkien. Allen & Unwin are working hard to publish *The Adventures of Tom Bombadil and Other Verses from the Red Book* for Christmas, but much depends on Pauline Baynes. He wonders if Tolkien will be able to put *Gawain* and *Pearl* in shape before he is again occupied with academic duties.

?Late July 1962 Pauline Baynes writes to Tolkien. She notes that the typescript of the title poem in the book describes a peacock's feather in Tom's hat, but the galley proofs have 'a swan-wing feather'.

27 July 1962 Tolkien is interviewed in the BBC's Oxford studio by Alan Blaikley for the programme *Writing for Children*.

31 July 1962 Rayner Unwin writes to Tolkien. He would like to visit him to show him the first of Pauline Baynes' pictures for *The Adventures of Tom Bombadil and Other Verses from the Red Book*.

1 August 1962 Tolkien writes to Pauline Baynes. He had made a few changes to the poems since they were sent to her. In the pre-*Lord of the Rings* poem, Tom had worn a peacock's feather, but in rewriting he changed this to the more appropriate swan-wing feather. In *Bombadil Goes Boating* this is replaced by a kingfisher feather, the blue feather mentioned in *The Lord of the Rings*. He explains some of the allusions made in the poem.

2 August 1962 Rayner Unwin visits Tolkien in Oxford and shows him some of Pauline Baynes' drawings, possibly including her design for the dust-jacket of the *Adventures of Tom Bombadil* collection.

3 August 1962 Tolkien writes to Pauline Baynes. He is delighted with the pictures Rayner Unwin showed him yesterday. 'I do not think that they could have been more after my own heart. I am not surprised: I felt certain that anything you produced would delight me – and make me deeply envious of your skill' (courtesy of Mrs Pauline Gasch). He looks forward to seeing more. – Rayner Unwin writes to Tolkien. He hopes to have the *Adventures of Tom Bombadil* dust-jacket at the printer in a day or two, and Pauline Baynes will try to finish the illustrations within a fortnight. He encloses a copy of an article in *English* by Hugo Dyson (probably mentioned during their meeting on 2 August). He invites Tolkien to lunch with his father and himself, and 'to spare an hour either before or afterwards to shake hands quite informally with some of our salesmen and Sales Manager who will have the task of selling *Tom Bombadil*, and who, of course, are more than familiar with you by name already' ('Tolkien-George Allen & Unwin archive, HarperCollins). He suggests either 22 August or 5 September as possible dates.

9 August 1962 Tolkien replies to Rayner Unwin. 22 August suits him. He would have replied earlier, but he is 'much harried – not to mention cloud-burst on Monday night & flooded "study"' (Tolkien-George Allen & Unwin archive, HarperCollins).

14 August 1962 Rayner Unwin writes to Tolkien. He is looking forward to lunch on 22 August. The Sales Manager and some of the sales representatives have asked if they might have a half-hour chat about *The Adventures of Tom Bombadil*, *The Lord of the Rings*, etc.

16 August 1962 Tolkien writes to Rayner Unwin. The only possible train on 22 August is the 10.39 a.m. which arrives in Paddington Station at 11.55 a.m. He will probably arrive at Allen & Unwin's offices by 12.30 p.m. He wants to be back in Oxford by 7.00 p.m., so he will aim to return by the 4.30 p.m. train and avoid the rush hour.

17 August 1962 The University of Wales Press sends Tolkien revised proofs of *English and Welsh*. He is asked to return the marked set with reader's queries as soon as possible.

?Late August 1962 Tolkien lends a set of proofs of *English and Welsh* to his Aunt Jane Neave.

22 August 1962 Tolkien has lunch with Stanley and Rayner Unwin, and meets with the Allen & Unwin sales staff. He probably lends Rayner a copy of part of his translation of *Pearl*, and gives him the list of fan mail addresses. Rayner shows him Pauline Baynes' six full-page illustrations for the *Adventures of Tom Bombadil* collection. 'Father and I gave him lunch beforehand. It was a strange encounter. I sat between them, feeling that both were being quirky and old. They wanted to appreciate each other, but they found each others conversation baffling. However, elaborate courtesy prevailed throughout, and I tried to act as an interpreter between the two men' (Rayner Unwin, *George Allen & Unwin: A Remembrancer* (1999), p. 114).

27 August 1962 Rayner Unwin sends Tolkien Pauline Baynes' full-page *Adventures of Tom Bombadil* pictures. Since only five have been allowed for in the book, Tolkien is asked to decide which one should be excluded.

28 August 1962 Rayner Unwin writes to Tolkien. He has read the *Pearl* translation and likes it.

29 August 1962 Tolkien writes to Rayner Unwin about the illustrations for the *Tom Bombadil* collection, which he has now considered carefully:

> Pauline rather carries one away at first sight; but there is an illustrative as well as a pictorial side to take into account.
> The choice for discard must lie between the *Dragon* and *The Man in the Moon*. *Cat* is one of the best, though as an illustration, it misses a main point in not making one of the 'thought-lions' engaged in *man*-eating. I think the sentence of omission must fall on the *Dragon*.
> I hope this will not pain you. It pains me. But in spite of the excellent Worm it fails badly on the young warrior. This is an archaic and heroic theme . . . , but the young person, without helm or shield, looks like a Tudor lackey with some elements of late mediaeval armour on his legs. I understand the pictorial difficulties; but of course no dragon, however decrepit would lie with his head away from the entrance. [Tolkien-George Allen & Unwin archive, HarperCollins]

He is glad that Rayner likes *Pearl*, and encloses a copy of his translation of the remaining (still unrevised) thirty-one stanzas. He has received revises from the University of Wales Press which have proved troublesome.

30 August 1962 Rayner Unwin writes to Tolkien. He is returning Tolkien's fan mail folder, which Allen & Unwin staff have copied. 'I think we can cut our correspondence with the British public if on the next printing of *The Fellowship of the Ring* we omit the sentence about the Index of Proper Names which never went into the Appendix as was intended. Are you agreeable?' (Tolkien-George Allen & Unwin archive, HarperCollins).

?Summer–early Autumn 1962 Allen & Unwin sends C.S. Lewis a copy of *The Adventures of Tom Bombadil and Other Verses from the Red Book*, with a request for a 'puff'. Lewis writes to Tolkien that he has explained to Allen & Unwin that a blurb from him would 'probably do the book no good and might do it harm' (quoted in A.N. Wilson, *C.S. Lewis: A Biography* (1990), p. 294). Lewis praises the poems and suggests one emendation.

5 September 1962 Tolkien writes to Miss Stella Hillier, Features Organizer for the BBC, thanking her for a copy of the proposed talk on *Writing for Children*. He is returning it with a few corrections and the signed contract.

6 September 1962 Stella Hillier, BBC, writes to Tolkien. The transcript of the talk sent to Tolkien was made direct from the recorded tape. The errors he notes will be omitted from the broadcast.

8–9 September 1962 Tolkien writes to Jane Neave, replying to comments on *English and Welsh* and explaining some of the things mentioned in the paper. 'I was a bit afraid that I had overstepped the mark with that lecture: much of it rather dull except to dons' (*Letters*, p. 319). He encloses a copy of *Leaf by Niggle* made specially for her, and gives the background to its writing.

11 September 1962 Ronald Eames, Allen & Unwin, sends Tolkien proofs of the cover for the *Adventures of Tom Bombadil* volume. The same picture is to appear on the binding and the dust-jacket.

12 September 1962 Tolkien writes to Ronald Eames. He is a little disappointed in the dust-jacket design. 'As produced, and visually divided, the picture in colour and general effect is not as pleasing as it appeared at first. Alas! it is only now, too late, that I observe ... that the picture should have been reversed: with Bombadil on the front, and the Ship sailing left, westward!' He hopes that something can still be done about its 'heavy fat-serifed lettering' (added by the publisher, not the artist), which he finds 'very displeasing and at odds with the style of the picture' (Tolkien-George Allen & Unwin archive, HarperCollins). He also criticizes the placing of his name.

14 September 1962 Ronald Eames replies to Tolkien. It is indeed too late to consider a revision to the dust-jacket art, or to alter the lettering, as in a four-colour print that would involve making a new black plate of the entire illustration. This would be not only expensive but time-consuming, and Allen & Unwin are working to a very tight schedule. It is because of the time factor that they did not submit type pulls to Tolkien. If time permits, they might revise the lettering on a reprint (but this is never done).

15 September 1962 Tolkien addresses a conference of school librarians in Oxford, and shows them the dust-jacket for *The Adventures of Tom Bombadil and Other Verses from the Red Book.*

17 September 1962 Alina Dadlez writes to Tolkien. She forwarded his comments on translating *The Hobbit* into Spanish to Compania General Fabril Editora in Argentina. They are unable to find the quotation cited by him in the copy of *The Hobbit* they are using. Also they point out that as *h* is mute in Spanish, perhaps they should spell 'Hobbit' *jobito*, and the plural *jobitos*, for *hobito* would be pronounced *obito*.

18 September 1962 Alina Dadlez sends Tolkien four copies of the Polish translation of *The Two Towers.*

19 September 1962 Tolkien writes to Alina Dadlez. He gave the wrong reference in *The Hobbit* because he had used an older edition. He would prefer *hobitos* 'since it preserves to the eye more relationship to the original word. I do not much mind the *h* being "mute". I am sure many hobbits drop their *h*s like most rural folk in England' (Tolkien-George Allen & Unwin archive, HarperCollins). – Ronald Eames writes to Tolkien. He is sending a copy of the paste-up of the *Adventures of Tom Bombadil* volume. On receiving it, Tolkien will telephone Eames, approving the layout but querying the inclusion of all six full-page illustrations, including the one with the dragon.

24 September 1962 Ronald Eames writes to Tolkien. As agreed by telephone, Allen & Unwin are proceeding with production. 'We have agreed to retain the dragon illustration which does not entirely meet with your approval at least for the first printing' (Tolkien-George Allen & Unwin archive, Harper-Collins). He apologizes that Tolkien was not informed that space had been found to include the extra illustration without adding to the cost. (The full-page illustration for *The Hoard* in fact will be retained in all future printings.)

30 September 1962 Robert Burchfield writes to Oxford University Press. The Early English Text Society particularly want Tolkien's *Ancrene Wisse* to be published in 1962 to coincide with the presentation to Tolkien in December of a volume of essays to mark his seventieth birthday.

4 October 1962 This date is stamped on proofs of the preliminaries, table of contents, and introductions of Frances M. Mack's edition of *Ancrene Riwle*, sent to Tolkien for comment.

6 October 1962 Robert Burchfield writes to Tolkien. His edition of the *Ancrene Wisse* will be published in December. Bound copies should be ready by 28 November. Tolkien will receive twelve author's copies, plus his copy as a member of the Early English Text Society around the date of publication. If he would like additional copies, he will be able to obtain them at a reduced rate.

7 October 1962 Material from an interview with Tolkien is included in *Writing for Children*, introduced by Alan Blaikley, broadcast on the BBC Home Service from 10.10 to 10.50 p.m.

9 October 1962 Rayner Unwin writes to Tolkien, sending a transcript of a talk on the Belgium Third Programme, presumably discussing one or more of Tolkien's works.

14 October 1962 Michaelmas Full Term begins. Tolkien is acting as a substitute for C.L. Wrenn during the latter's absence on sabbatical leave. Tolkien's scheduled lectures for this term are: *Beowulf* on Tuesdays and Thursdays at 11.00 a.m. in the Examination Schools, beginning 16 October.

15 October 1962 Rayner Unwin again asks Tolkien's opinion on dropping the note about the index of proper names from the next printing of *The Fellowship of the Ring*. He also asks about progress on *Sir Gawain and the Green Knight* and *Pearl*.

18 October 1962 Joy Hill writes to Tolkien. During BBC radio schools programmes on 30 October and 6 November a Dr V.W. Turner will be talking about *The Lord of the Rings*. A fee will be paid for quotations used.

19 October 1962 Rayner Unwin writes to Tolkien. *The Adventures of Tom Bombadil and Other Verses from the Red Book* will be published on 22 November.

26 October 1962 Rayner Unwin writes to Tolkien. He is sending an advance copy of the *Adventures of Tom Bombadil* volume. There is 'obviously too heavy a weight of illustrations on pages 50 and 51, but this was inevitable as we printed second colour only on one [side of each] sheet. In the event of a reprint would we have your permission to move the order of the poems a little to get the picture of the cat on the same opening as the poem and away from the large Fastitocalon drawing?' (The full-page illustration for *Cat* has been placed on p. 50, bisecting *Fastitocalon* and opposite the major picture for that poem.) Orders for the book are 'rolling in nicely' (Tolkien-George Allen & Unwin archive, HarperCollins).

31 October 1962 Robert Burchfield writes to Tolkien. The *Ancrene Wisse* will be published on 20 December.

2 November 1962 Tolkien writes to Rayner Unwin. The *Adventures of Tom Bombadil* volume, which he has received this morning, 'looks a very pretty book'. He agrees with the suggested change in order of the poems. 'The thing started, as you know, with my nonagenarian aunt. I think it would give her very great pleasure if a complimentary copy could be sent to her as from the firm and not from me.' Allen & Unwin may charge it to his account or take it out of his author's copies. Tolkien asks Rayner to recommend a press cuttings agency for him to subscribe to; he missed a piece by Stanley Unwin in the *Sunday Times*, which Tolkien gave up taking after the paper changed hands. He has completed his translations of *Pearl* and *Sir Gawain*, but they need a final revision before being sent to Allen & Unwin. '*Pearl* in particular has been subjected to a good deal of criticism, much of which is justified, by an expert in this field. These translations are of course on my list as the most urgent task before me, but the return to lecturing this term has proved a much greater burden than I expected. It has taken much more work than I guessed to shake the dust of seventeen years off matter which I once thought I knew.' (Tolkien had last lectured on *Beowulf* in Trinity Term 1946.) He agrees to drop the sentence about an index from *The Fellowship of the Ring*. 'An index is very much needed, but it must, I suppose, wait until it becomes necessary to consider issuing *The*

Lord of the Rings in some different form. In which case . . . part of the Appendices to Volume 3 might disappear' (Tolkien-George Allen & Unwin archive, HarperCollins). (In the event, the sentence is never removed from the original Foreword.)

6 November 1962 Rayner Unwin writes to Tolkien. He will have the printer rearrange the poems in the *Adventures of Tom Bombadil* volume, since a reprint will probably be needed. He anticipates sales of 5,000 copies by publication day. An advance copy has been sent to Jane Neave. He gives Tolkien the name of a press cuttings agency, and encloses a photographic copy of the feature in the *Sunday Times* to which Stanley Unwin contributed (presumably 'Publishers' Pick I', 16 September 1962). In this 'publishers were invited to pick one Autumn publication that they thought particularly highly of and *Tom Bombadil*' led off the list. He is sorry that Tolkien was unable to complete his work on *Sir Gawain* and *Pearl* before the start of term.

9 November 1962 Tolkien writes to Rayner Unwin, thanking him for a copy of the article in the *Sunday Times*. 'Please thank your father for his words; if I fail to become a conceited old man he will at least have done his best.' Soon he will send a list of people whom he wants to receive copies of *The Adventures of Tom Bombadil* over and above his author's copies. He would be grateful if Allen & Unwin could send them and debit his account. – Tolkien learns of the imminent publication of *English and Medieval Studies*, a *Festschrift* in honour of his seventieth birthday, with contributions by many of his colleagues and former students. This has been kept secret by the editors Norman Davis and C.L. Wrenn, and by Rayner Unwin, who has organized the printing and publishing by Allen & Unwin. Rayner Unwin on ?19 November:

> The 'gunpowder plot', in which you have been implicated, was exposed almost (Nov. 9) on the correct date. My spies and agents failed me, or I should have become aware of it some time ago. But benevolent as this was in object – to 'blow me up' in NED [*New English Dictionary*, i.e. **Oxford English Dictionary*, sense 23 not 24! – it came as a shock. That I should be treated to a 'festschrift' had never occurred to me! I must say that it was a very great added pleasure that 'Allen & Unwin' had taken it on. [Tolkien-George Allen & Unwin archive, HarperCollins]

After 9 November 1962 Tolkien writes to C.S. Lewis, asking him to attend the dinner to mark the publication of the *Festschrift*.

14 November 1962 Tolkien writes to Cotton Minchin. Philip Toynbee's comments in the *Observer* for 6 August 1961, that Tolkien's 'Hobbit fantasies' though once 'taken very seriously indeed by a great many distinguished literary figures. . . . have passed into a merciful oblivion', has caused so much angry reaction 'that the noise was nearly as good as a new book' (quoted in Christie's, *Valuable Printed Books and Manuscripts*, London, 26 November 1997, p. 110). – Percy Simpson dies.

?19 (received 20) November 1962 Tolkien writes to Rayner Unwin. He would like twenty-four copies of *The Adventures of Tom Bombadil and Other Verses from the Red Book* in addition to those due to him as its author. 'Apart from the convenience of Christmas, the list of those to whom I feel I must send a copy has been enlarged by recent events' (Tolkien-George Allen & Unwin archive, HarperCollins). He also asks Allen & Unwin to send copies directly to five people outside England, and encloses their addresses. He has found lecturing again to be rather too much for him and had to take all last week off but is now better.

20 November 1962 Rayner Unwin writes to Tolkien. He admits having aided and abetted the production of the *Festschrift*. Copies of the *Adventures of Tom Bombadil* volume have been sent to Tolkien and the five addresses he had given. – C.S. Lewis writes to Tolkien. He will not be able to attend the *Festschrift* dinner for health reasons.

21 November 1962 Tolkien replies to an enquiry, explaining briefly the relationship between Sindarin and Welsh.

22 November 1962 *The Adventures of Tom Bombadil and Other Verses from the Red Book* is published in Britain.

28 November 1962 Tolkien writes to Stanley Unwin. Christopher Burstall of the BBC 'has returned the charge, and reluctantly, & chiefly because I believe you would wish it, I have agreed to come up to town on Monday Dec. 10th, and be put on the mat or in the armchair, or whatever they do and talk (or answer questions) about myself & work.' He thinks he will not be wanted until the afternoon, and wonders if he could call at Unwin's office in Museum Street and 'waste a little of your time beforehand'. He comments on two reviews of the *Adventures of Tom Bombadil* collection, in the *Times Literary Supplement* and *The Listener*: 'was agreeably surprised. I expected remarks far more snooty and patronizing. Also I was rather pleased, since it seemed that the reviewers had both started out not wanting to be amused, but had failed to maintain their Victorian dignity intact.' He has received 'a "manifesto" of congratulation signed by nine men from Winchester (College): evidently not put off by waggery' (Tolkien-George Allen & Unwin archive, HarperCollins).

29 November 1962 Rayner Unwin writes to Tolkien. He is delighted that Tolkien has agreed to appear on BBC television, and asks if he can see him when he comes to London to be interviewed.

3 December 1962 Stanley Unwin writes to Tolkien. He finds some reviews of the *Adventures of Tom Bombadil* collection puzzling, but on the whole excellent.

5 December 1962 Ronald and Edith attend a small dinner party at Merton College, arranged by Norman Davis, during which Tolkien is presented with a specially bound copy of the *Festschrift*. The frontispiece is a photograph of Tolkien taken by Pamela Chandler, with a facsimile of his signature. In the following days, Tolkien will writes letters of appreciation to all twenty-two contributors in which, as he will comment in a letter to Pauline Baynes, he has to show that he has looked at their work.

6 December 1962 Alina Dadlez sends Tolkien five copies of the Swedish translation of *The Hobbit*.

7 December 1962 Tolkien writes to Rayner Unwin, confirming a telephone conversation. Rayner apparently asked him to autograph copies (?of the *Festschrift* or of the *Adventures of Tom Bombadil* volume) during his London visit. Tolkien has discovered that he is to be at the BBC before lunch. He will try to make a quick visit to Allen & Unwin before going to the BBC, but if there is not enough time, he could make another visit later to autograph copies. Can he get more copies of the *Festschrift*? In particular, he wants to send a copy to former Oxford visiting scholar Przemysl Mroczkowski in Krakow. – Tolkien writes to Stanley Unwin. He has to postpone their planned meeting, so that he can be at the BBC before lunch. – Tolkien's edition of the *Ancrene Wisse* is published by the Early English Text Society. – Anne Slim, who had been Tolkien's secretary during at least part of the time *The Adventures of Tom Bombadil and Other Verses from the Red Book* was being prepared for press, writes to thank him for sending her a copy of the book.

8 December 1962 Michaelmas Full Term ends.

10 December 1962 Tolkien is interviewed in London by John Bowen for a BBC television.

12 December 1962 The interview is broadcast on BBC TV's *Bookstand* (10.15–10.45 p.m.), produced by Christopher Burstall. The section on Tolkien begins with John Bowen reading a poem from *The Lord of the Rings*; this is followed by the recorded interview, almost eight minutes, in which Bowen and Tolkien discuss the latter's work.

16 December 1962 Tolkien writes to Simonne d'Ardenne to thank her for her contribution to the *Festschrift*.

19 December 1962 Tolkien writes to his son Michael. Allen & Unwin have paid him some royalties in advance of the usual May date because *The Adventures of Tom Bombadil and Other Verses from the Red Book* has sold so well (nearly 8,000 copies before publication) and it is already being reprinted. He comments that even on a minute initial royalty he is making more on verse than is usual for anyone but John Betjeman.

20 December 1962 Rayner Unwin writes to Tolkien. A bookseller has suggested that Allen & Unwin celebrate the tenth anniversary of the publication of *The Fellowship of the Ring* by producing a six-volume *Lord of the Rings* in a somewhat de luxe format, which might appeal to an untapped market. Rayner is not entirely convinced but asks Tolkien for his reactions to a choice of illustrator: 'So far we have Mr. Blok and Pauline Baynes who seem to have something of the spirit of your writing in their art' (Tolkien-George Allen & Unwin archive, HarperCollins).

23 December 1962 Tolkien writes to Pauline Baynes. The *Adventures of Tom Bombadil* volume is selling very well, in large part, he thinks, due to her illustrations and dust-jacket.

24 December 1962 C.S. Lewis writes to Tolkien. He thanks Tolkien for a letter, probably one of those that Tolkien wrote to contributors to the *Festschrift*.

29 December 1962 Pauline Baynes writes to Tolkien. She is glad that the *Adventures of Tom Bombadil* book is doing well.

Late 1962 or early 1963–spring 1964 The next secretary to work for Tolkien is Naomi Collyer, beginning probably from very late 1962 or early 1963. She will later write:

> I first met Professor Tolkien in 1962. Just married, I was looking for part-time work, and the Professor needed someone to cope with the fan mail, which was piling up unanswered while he tried to pursue the many strands of his creative work – sorting of material for the *Silmarillion* (for example at that time he was torn between his prose and verse versions of the story of Beren and Lúthien), polishing his translations of *Pearl* and *Sir Gawain*, and corresponding with publishers about *Tree and Leaf*, then just in the press [in fact, not until 1963 or 1964]. I worked primarily in his well-known garage-library, where surrounded with texts ranging from huge Anglo-Saxon [manuscripts] in facsimile to brand new copies of his own works, and looking out over the beautiful garden, I typed his courteous replies to his fans all over the world. It was not long however before I started a family and gave up work. ['Recollections of Professor J.R.R. Tolkien', *Arda* 5 (1988, for 1985), p. 1]

Late 1962–early 1963 'Deep in the winter of 1962–3' Christopher Tolkien persuades his father to call on C.S. Lewis at The Kilns, his home in Oxford. According to the account given by Christopher Tolkien to A.N. Wilson: 'It was an awkward meeting, like an encounter between estranged members of a family. Neither Tolkien nor Lewis had much to say to one another' (*C.S. Lewis: A Biography*, p. 294).

1963

c. **1963** Tolkien drafts a long reply in response to a letter concerning Faramir and Éowyn.

Early 1963 Jane Neave dies.

3 January 1963 John F. Avedon visits Tolkien. At the age of eleven, he is already an aspiring writer, and Tolkien is his inspiration. His father, a fashion photographer shooting autumn collections in Europe,

> insists that John meet the creator of Middle Earth. So, having learned it was Tolkien's birthday, he bought a cake, drove John out to Oxford 'and to my complete chagrin and humiliation', his son recalls, rang the doorbell. Remarkably, his father's ploy worked. Although the great author made a stab at pretending to be indisposed with a terrible cold,

he quickly warmed to his visitors and invited them to his study for half an hour of chat about writing. [Donald G. McNeil, Jr., 'Heirs', *People*, 26 November 1984, p. 79]

– Austin Farrer writes to Tolkien, thanking him for a copy of the *Adventures of Tom Bombadil* volume.

20 January 1963 Hilary Full Term begins. Tolkien's scheduled lectures for this term are: *The Freswæl* (Episode and Fragment), Courses I and III on Tuesdays at 11.00 a.m. in the Examination Schools, beginning 22 January.

28 January 1963 Austin Olney, of the Houghton Mifflin Company, writes to Tolkien, suggesting a sumptuous illustrated edition of *The Hobbit*. He wants to commission an artist.

?February or March 1963 Tolkien writes to Austin Olney, giving permission for the illustrated *Hobbit*.

13 February 1963 Tolkien replies to a letter from a Miss Allen, answering queries about *The Mewlips*.

15 February 1963 Rayner Unwin writes to Tolkien. He is coming to Oxford on 22 February, and asks if 10.00 a.m. would be a good time to visit.

17 February 1963 Tolkien replies to Rayner Unwin. He would be delighted to see him on 22 February. 'I have been almost completely knocked out by the weather, but am beginning to revive' (Tolkien-George Allen & Unwin archive, HarperCollins).

21 February 1963 Tolkien replies to a letter of appreciation of *The Lord of the Rings* from a Mrs Gill. He is glad that she found 'pleasure and encouragement' in it, 'especially in this dreadful winter' (eBay, December 2003).

22 February 1963 Rayner Unwin visits Tolkien in the morning. Tolkien apparently requests four more copies of *The Adventures of Tom Bombadil and Other Verses from the Red Book*.

25 February 1963 Rayner Unwin returns the draft of *Pearl* to Tolkien. He hopes that *Pearl* and *Sir Gawain* will be ready for Allen & Unwin to begin production this spring. He has arranged for four copies of the *Adventures of Tom Bombadil* collection to be sent to Tolkien.

16 March 1963 Hilary Full Term ends.

?Late March–1 April 1963 Tolkien is on holiday (possibly in Bournemouth), but it is spoiled because he is ill with bronchitis.

20 March 1963 Alina Dadlez writes to Tolkien. She is sending him five copies of the Portuguese translation of *The Hobbit*. She apologizes that the word *hobbit* has been translated in this.

23 March 1963 Two anthropologists, Anneke C. Kloos-Adriaansen and P. Kloos, write to Tolkien about his sources and inspiration for *The Hobbit* and *The Lord of the Rings*.

1 April 1963 Rayner Unwin writes to Tolkien, sending a letter to Mr Snyder of Rembrandt Films which Tolkien is to sign.

5 April 1963 Tolkien writes to Rayner Unwin. He has signed the letter to Mr Snyder, and returns it to Rayner. 'His request seems to me quite reasonable, but I join you in hoping that he will not multiply delays. Good or bad, I should like to see the product, but at the present rate that seems unlikely to be possible until the present decade is nearly out.' He tells Rayner about his spoiled holiday. He is 'still unwell and confined to quarters' (Tolkien-George Allen & Unwin archive, HarperCollins).

17 April 1963 Tolkien writes to Rayner Unwin. 'I am now recovering, at any rate from the effects of the drugs if not entirely from the disease, but morale remains shattered.' He asks Rayner's advice about giving permission for a photocopy of *On Fairy-Stories*. 'My recollection is that the [Oxford University Press] had resigned all interest in the matter and that I am the owner of the copyright' (Tolkien-George Allen & Unwin archive, HarperCollins).

18 April–end of August 1963 Tolkien is afflicted with fibrositis in his right side and arm, which makes writing or typing difficult. His condition gradually improves, but he will tell Stanley Unwin on 5 October 1963: 'It was not until the end of August that I got relief from the trouble with my shoulder and arm. I found not being able to use a pen or pencil as defeating as the loss her beak would be to a hen' (*Letters*, p. 248).

18 April–6 May 1963 Tolkien begins to type a long reply to Anneke C. Kloos-Adriaansen and P. Kloos, but pain from fibrositis forces him to abandon the letter.

25 April 1963 Rayner Unwin writes to Tolkien. He would like to be able to publish *Sir Gawain and the Green Knight* and *Pearl* for Christmas.

28 April 1963 Trinity Full term begins. C.L. Wrenn is back in Oxford, and Tolkien is no longer lecturing.

6 May 1963 Tolkien finishes his letter to Anneke C. Kloos-Adriaansen and P. Kloos.

11 May 1963 Tolkien attends an Early English Text Society Council meeting at Magdalen College, Oxford. This is the last EETS meeting he will attend until 1972.

16 May 1963 Bruce Mitchell, who had not been invited to contribute to the seventieth birthday *Festschrift*, writes to Tolkien. He encloses an offprint of his article '"Until the Dragon Comes": Some Thoughts on *Beowulf*', as a personal tribute to Tolkien.

23 May 1963 Tolkien writes to Bruce Mitchell. 'The faintest cloud upon my gratitude for the magnificent tribute of the *Festschrift* . . . was its exclusions: inevitable, I suppose, for reasons of cost and size. . . . I shall keep your offprint tucked into the *Festschrift*.' He encloses a note, sketching his thoughts on the article. He would like to write more, but is 'under an interdict: not to use my right arm at all if possible, nor to bend over a desk. Typing is less trying than writing' (Tolkien Papers, Bodleian Library, Oxford).

29 May 1963 F.P. Wilson dies.

11 June 1963 Rayner Unwin writes to Tolkien. He hopes that the lack of letters from Tolkien in the past few weeks means that Tolkien is busy with *Sir Gawain* and *Pearl*, but they have missed the Christmas season for 1963. 'An otherwise slightly snooty review' of the *Festschrift* in the *Cambridge Review* suggests that Tolkien 'would be better complimented, and the public would be better edified, by the issue of a collection [of] Professor Tolkien's own previously uncollected writings' (Tolkien-George Allen & Unwin archive, HarperCollins). Rayner asks if Tolkien would consider letting his son Christopher compile such a collection.

14 June 1963 Rayner Unwin writes to Tolkien, in response to a letter (not now in the Tolkien-George Allen & Unwin archive at HarperCollins) or to a telephone call. He is sorry to hear about his troubles and hopes that he can do something to help him. He asks if Tolkien could see him if he comes to Oxford on 21 June, perhaps at 10.00 a.m.

21 June 1963 Rayner Unwin visits Tolkien in Oxford. They discuss the publication of *On Fairy-Stories*.

25 June 1963 Tolkien replies to a letter from Rhona Beare. He explains about the Cirth and other matters in *The Lord of the Rings*. 'I hope you will forgive pencil and a crabbed and not too legible hand. I am (temporarily, I hope) deprived of the use of my right hand and arm, and am in the early stages of teaching my left hand. Right-handed pens increase the crabbedness, but a pencil accommodates itself' (*Letters*, p. 325).

26 June 1963 Encaenia.

3 July 1963 Rayner Unwin writes to Tolkien. He has had an estimate made for publishing *On Fairy-Stories* in its present form. Having re-read it, he thinks that Tolkien probably would not feel inclined 'to expand what is already a well conceived and well rounded thesis'. Very little change is needed except on the first page, and one deletion. If this is acceptable to Tolkien, Allen & Unwin would be happy to produce the essay in their 'U Books' paperback series. 'Alternatively, it could be expanded if you honestly felt you could find the time and new material to do the job, or it could be produced as a completely separate half of a book which could also include *Leaf by Niggle*.' If it is published in the 'U Books' series, the contract Tolkien signed in 1959 would have to be modified, as royalties differ on paperbacks. Allen & Unwin would need Tolkien to supply 'a suitably terse and pithy blurb . . . and some suggestion as to a suitable cover illustration that would conform with the general pattern of the series. We try to have a fairly striking detail, or simple complete object of some artistic worth which has a sort of relationship to the title of the book depicted on each cover' (Tolkien-George Allen & Unwin archive, HarperCollins). He suggests that an illustration from one of Andrew Lang's fairy books might be suitable. If Tolkien does not like the idea, he should ignore Rayner's 'musings', but Rayner is anxious to publish something by Tolkien at regular intervals.

8 July 1963 *Angles and Britons*, containing Tolkien's O'Donnell Lecture, *English and Welsh*, is published.

12 July 1963 Rayner Unwin writes to Tolkien. He encloses a new contract to replace that signed for *On Fairy-Stories* in 1959. It is clear that they have had further contact since Rayner's letter of 3 July, and have already decided that *On Fairy-Stories* and *Leaf by Niggle* should be published together. Rayner asks if Tolkien has cleared the copyright for *Leaf by Niggle* with the *Dublin Review*.

Allen & Unwin think that the book will sell best as a paperback, but propose to produce a small clothbound library edition as well. He again asks Tolkien about a possible illustration for the cover.

15 July 1963 C.S. Lewis enters the Acland Nursing Home in Oxford for an examination. While there, he has a heart attack and goes into a coma. Over the next two weeks in the Acland he will improve and have many visitors, including Tolkien.

Early August 1963 Tolkien discovers among correspondence neglected because of his arm, and replies to, a letter from Scott, Foresman and Company seeking permission to use a Tolkien item in an anthology. They have his permission, but all such matters including the question of fees are dealt with by Allen & Unwin.

9 August 1963 Tolkien writes to Rayner Unwin. He encloses the new contract for *On Fairy-Stories* and *Leaf by Niggle*, duly signed, and the letter from Scott, Foresman and Company with a summary of his reply. He does not know if the *Dublin Review* still exists, and is uncertain about the copyright position. His arm is better but still painful, and he is allowed to write and type again. – Rayner Unwin writes to Tolkien. The Northern Ireland Region radio are interested in broadcasting *Farmer Giles of Ham*, read in four parts, in one of their children's programmes.

13 August 1963 Rayner Unwin writes to Tolkien, sending his copy of the agreement for the publication of *On Fairy-Stories* and *Leaf by Niggle*, signed by Allen & Unwin.

18 August 1963 Tolkien writes to his grandson Michael George, who has written to Tolkien while on holiday. Tolkien himself finds it almost impossible to write while away from home. He is looking forward to seeing Michael George in September, but at the moment is kept busy with visitors from America, Finland, Belgium, Poland, and so on. – Tolkien's son John arrives to stay with his parents for a week.

19–24 August 1963 At some time during this period Tolkien expresses a wish to see C.S. Lewis, who has recovered and left hospital. John Tolkien drives his father to The Kilns, where Tolkien and Lewis talk for about an hour. Among the subjects they discuss is the *Morte d'Arthur*.

20 September 1963 Tolkien drafts a letter in reply to Colonel Worskett, a reader of *The Lord of the Rings*. Professional tasks, neglected while preparing *The Lord of the Rings* for publication, have held up further writing about his imaginary world, but 'that will be over, for the present, when my translation of *Sir Gawain and the Green Knight* goes to press: soon, I hope. Then I shall return to the task of putting in order all or some of the legends of the earlier ages . . .' (*Letters*, p. 333). He writes at length about the Ents and how he might bring them into the earlier legends. At the end of the draft he pencils a note that in the opinion of some, the Ents had been created at the request of Yavanna after Eru gave life to the Dwarves created by Aulë.

?Autumn 1963 Tolkien writes a brief text, *Of the Ents and the Eagles. It is undated, and cannot have been written before 1958-9, but seems closely related to the note at the end of the draft letter to Colonel Worskett.

22 September–c. 3 October 1963 Tolkien replies to a letter from Eileen Elgar. His letter of six typed sides, noted as begun on 22 September, evidently took some time to complete. The envelope is postmarked 3 October 1963. The letter differs considerably from the draft published in *Letters*, pp. 325-33. Tolkien answers questions about *The Lord of the Rings*, in particular about Frodo's failure.

24 September 1963 Rayner Unwin writes to Tolkien. He is leaving for two months in the Far East. He hopes that Tolkien will give his 'earnest and immediate attention to the small problem of recasting the first two paragraphs of your essay *On Fairy-Stories* and providing us with perhaps another paragraph or two by way of a unifying introduction to our proposed paperback edition of that essay and *Leaf by Niggle*' (Tolkien-George Allen & Unwin archive, HarperCollins). This needs to be done fairly soon if the book is to be published in the spring. Ronald Eames will send Tolkien some ideas of leaf illustrations that might be used on the cover.

?5–22 October 1963 Tolkien and Edith stay at the Hotel Miramar, Bournemouth. Tolkien does not feel well for much of the time.

5 October 1963 Tolkien writes to Stanley Unwin in Rayner's absence. He sends the revisions to *On Fairy-Stories* requested for the new book.

> I should like to have your approval (or censure) especially of the Introductory Note.
>
> Rayner wished for a paragraph or two to justify the issue of the two pieces under one cover. I hope I have done this well enough, in not too solemn a manner. Perhaps with too little solemnity?
>
> While I was composing the note it occurred to me that it might be suitable to have a common title ... *Tree and Leaf*, with reference to the passage at the top of page 73 in the Essay, and to the "key-word" *effoliation* at the end, p. 84. [Tolkien-George Allen & Unwin archive, HarperCollins; page references are to *Essays Presented to Charles Williams* = pp. 52 and 66 in *Tree and Leaf*, 1988 edn.]

He asks if Unwin thinks that any acknowledgements are due to the previous publishers of the works. He is uncertain about the first publication dates of both works.

7 October 1963 Joy Hill writes to Tolkien. Houghton Mifflin have sent a photostat of a sample illustration by Virgil Finlay whom they are considering as illustrator for the proposed new edition of *The Hobbit*. They are not entirely pleased with Finlay's characterization of Bilbo, but if Allen & Unwin and Tolkien approve this general approach, they are sure that they can work out the details. If Tolkien does not like it, they will look elsewhere. Associated Redifusion have enquired about a ten- to fifteen-minute dramatization of a short extract from *The Hobbit* for a schools programme, but Joy Hill considers the fee they offer insufficient. She asks if Tolkien has any objection to the idea.

8 October 1963 Stanley Unwin writes to Tolkien. He notes that in the revised text of *On Fairy-Stories* Tolkien has not made the deletion suggested by Rayner Unwin on 3 July. Otherwise, he approves what Tolkien has done.

9 October 1963 Blackwell's Bookshop sends Tolkien a copy of a letter from a customer who has just ordered three sets of *The Lord of the Rings*, and three copies of *The Hobbit*, a repeat of several similar orders.

10 October 1963 Christopher Tolkien is elected to a fellowship at New College, Oxford.

11 October 1963 Tolkien writes to Stanley Unwin from the Hotel Miramar, Bournemouth. He remembers Rayner suggesting the deletion: Allen & Unwin should duly make it. He is not very well, but 'received today a tonic better than ozone or doctors' medicaments in the shape of news' of Christopher's election as a Fellow of New College (Tolkien-George Allen & Unwin archive, Harper-Collins). – Tolkien writes to Joy Hill. He is inclined to let Houghton Mifflin 'get on with' their de luxe *Hobbit*,

> according to their own taste and estimate of what is attractive. It would take too long for you or for me to exercise any real or effective criticism of the illustrations for an American edition. And I (at any rate) should probably be wrong, for the purpose. As for the specimen [by Virgil Finlay] – though it gives prospects of a general treatment rather heavier and more violent and airless than I should like – I thought it was good, and actually I thought Bilbo's rather rotund and babyish (but anxious) face was in keeping with his character (up to that point). After the horrors of the 'illustrations' to the translations, Mr Finlay is a welcome relief. As long (as seems likely) as he will leave 'humour' to the text, and pay reasonable attention to what the text says, I shall I expect be quite happy. One point: if he includes any illustration of *Gollum*, it should be noted that G. is *not* a monster, but a slimy little creature not larger than Bilbo.

He returns the illustration and asks if Joy could send him a copy of what he has written about it. He has no objection to the Associated Rediffusion proposal. He asks her to 'forgive this dreadful scrawl. This small and otherwise v[ery] comfortable hotel is deficient in places for writing' (Tolkien-George Allen & Unwin archive, HarperCollins).

14 October 1963 Tolkien visits Eileen Elgar, with whom he has corresponded about his books and who lives near the Hotel Miramar. She is stone-deaf. Tolkien will remark in a letter to his grandson, Michael George, on 16 October: 'Conversation by writing pad is defeating' (*Letters*, p. 336).

15 October 1963 At lunch Tolkien rescues an old woman choking on a whiting-bone and gets her to a doctor. In the afternoon, he entertains 'another deaf old lady', 'almost the last of the children of the great Sir James Augustus Henry Murray' of the *Oxford English Dictionary*. 'She is on mother's side a

Ruthven and has been researching for years into the Gowrie conspiracy. As my knowledge of Scottish History is v[ery] small I find it difficult to follow who murdered whom, or why' (letter to Michael George Tolkien, 16 October 1963, *Letters*, p. 336).

16 October 1963 Tolkien writes to Michael George from the Hotel Miramar, recounting the events of the previous days. He tells his grandson, who is studying English at St Andrews, to get a good tweed jacket made for himself, and he will pay for it. 'I was not well when I came away and I have been rather ill (until yesterday); but there is a very good doctor here . . . and he seems to have done good. However I do not feel much inclined for work (which is in any case very difficult in a hotel)' (British Library MS Add. 71657).

21 October 1963 Tolkien writes a lengthy reply to a Mrs Munby, who has asked several questions about *The Lord of the Rings* on behalf of her son. Tolkien says that 'it is not possible to represent an "imaginary" world, and have answers for all the questions that may be asked about it' (quoted in Sotheby's, *Literature and Illustration*, London, 11–12 July 2002, p. 372).

22 October 1963 Tolkien and Edith return to Oxford. – *The Adventures of Tom Bombadil and Other Verses from the Red Book* is published in the United States.

23 October 1963 Alina Dadlez sends Tolkien four copies of the Polish translation of *The Return of the King*.

24 October 1963 Professor E.J. Dobson gives a lecture to the Society for the Study of Mediæval Languages and Literature (of which Tolkien is a member), '*Ancrene Wisse*: Observations on Date and Authorship'.

28 October 1963 Joy Hill writes to Tolkien. Houghton Mifflin report that their pre-publication sales of *The Adventures of Tom Bombadil and Other Verses from the Red Book* were over 3,000 copies. They have enquired about *The Silmarillion*.

29 October 1963 Tolkien replies to a letter (written on 27 May) from a reader in Michigan seeking permission to set some of Tolkien's poems to music. Tolkien grants this on his part, but points out that for any publication which includes the words, permission from Allen & Unwin will also be needed. – Joy Hill writes to Tolkien. Houghton Mifflin are sending him five copies of their edition of *The Adventures of Tom Bombadil and Other Verses from the Red Book*.

?Late October–?early November 1963 Anthony Curtis, who had been a student in the English School at Oxford in the mid-1940s, interviews both Tolkien and C.S. Lewis for an article. He describes Tolkien as puffing at his pipe as he describes his current writing, which 'deals with an earlier period and concerns a more rational, humanoid type of creature [than the Hobbits] and the powers of evil. The problem is to get across a whole mythology which I've invented before you get down to the stories. For instance you can't expect people to believe in a flat earth any more. Half way through the elves discover the world is round.' The work also contains much about immortality: 'You see both the idea of death and the thought of immortality on earth – Swift's struldbugs [in the third book of *Gulliver's Travels*] – are equally intolerable' ('Hobbits and Heroes', *Sunday Telegraph*, 10 November 1963, p. 16). Although Curtis may have misunderstood some of what Tolkien said, such as Elves being more 'rational' and 'humanoid' than Hobbits, this interview shows clearly topics which are uppermost in Tolkien's mind at this time, and that he still intends to change his cosmology. Recalling this interview years later, and repeating some of his article, Curtis will write that Tolkien 'spoke without any self-consciousness of a set of events which in his mind seemed to exist with as much reality as the French Revolution or the Second World War' ('Remembering Tolkien and Lewis', *British Book News*, June 1977, p. 30).

Late October 1963 Michael Tolkien, now a schoolmaster at the Oratory School, Woodcote, writes to his father. He is depressed, not well, and refers to his 'sagging faith' (quoted in *Letters*, p. 337).

1 November 1963 Tolkien replies to his son Michael. He hopes that the depression 'is partly due to [his] ailment. But I am afraid it is mainly an occupational affliction [of a teacher], and also an almost universal human malady (in any occupation) attaching to your age.' For 'sagging faith' he recommends frequent Communion, and writes at length on the issue. 'Though always Itself, perfect and complete and inviolate, the Blessed Sacrament does not operate completely and once for all in any of us. Like the act of Faith it must be continuous and grow by exercise.' He himself has 'got over my complaints for the present and feel as well as my old bones allow. I am getting nearly as unbendable as an Ent. My catarrh is always with me (and will be) – it goes back to a nose broken (and neglected) in schoolboy Rugby.' In regard to Michael George, who at university has complained about learning Old English, Tolkien 'cannot (of course) understand why Anglo-Saxon should seem difficult – not to people able to learn any language (other than their own) at all.' He warns Michael not to speak to him about Income Tax 'or I shall boil over. They had *all* my literary earnings until I retired. And now, even with the concession ... that Earned Income does not pay Surtax (within my limits of earning), I am being mulcted next January of such a sum as will cripple my desire to distribute some real largesse to each of you. However, I will do something ... ' (*Letters*, pp. 336–41). – Tolkien writes to Alina Dadlez. He thinks the covers of the Polish *Return of the King* are of a 'Mordor hideousness' (Tolkien-George Allen & Unwin archive, HarperCollins), but he understands from Professor Mroczkowski that the treatment of the text is not akin to the cover. He asks if some of the royalties from the Polish editions cannot be transferred outside of Poland (then behind the Iron Curtain). If so, he wonders if it might be possible for him to use the monies, if any, through an agent.

7 November 1963 Alina Dadlez replies to Tolkien's query. Over £76 in royalties are being held in Poland in blocked zlotys.

***c*. 15 November 1963** Tolkien writes a note about *On Fairy-Stories* as it is to appear in *Tree and Leaf*: 'I think that the subheadings 1–5 *Fairy-story, Origins, Children, Fantasy, Recovery* etc. should probably (like the last, *Epilogue*) *not* be numbered. I think their presence is of assistance, but numeration exaggerates their importance and rigidity' (Tolkien-George Allen & Unwin archive, HarperCollins).

15 November 1963 Tolkien writes to Joy Hill. She can tell Houghton Mifflin that '*The Silmarillion* is nearer to completion than it was, but still has a long way to go' (Tolkien-George Allen & Unwin archive, HarperCollins).

19 November 1963 Joy Hill writes to Tolkien. The interview with Anthony Curtis published in the *Sunday Telegraph* on 10 November has resulted in many enquiries. The fan mail list which she keeps is now quite large.

22 November 1963 C.S. Lewis dies.

26 November 1963 Tolkien attends the funeral of C.S. Lewis accompanied by his son Christopher. Many other Inklings are present. – Later Tolkien writes to his daughter Priscilla, thanking her for a letter of sympathy.

> So far I have felt the normal feelings of a man of my age – like an old tree that is losing all its leaves one by one: this feels like an axe-blow near the roots. Very sad that we should have been so separated in the last years; but our time of close communion endured in memory for both of us. I had a mass said this morning, and was there, and served; and Havard and Dundas Grant were present. The funeral at Holy Trinity, the Headington Quarry church, which Jack attended, was quiet and attended only by intimates and some Magdalen people including the President. Austin Farrer read the lesson. The grave is under a larch in the corner of the church-yard. Warnie [Lewis] was not present, alas! I saw Owen Barfield, George Sayer and John Lawlor . . . among others. [*Letters*, p. 341]

– Tolkien writes to his grandson Michael George, in reply to a letter. He is glad that the tweed jacket turned out well. Since Michael George will be twenty-one in January, Tolkien would like to mark that occasion by helping him purchase a cello.

28 November 1963 Tolkien writes to George Sayer. He remarks on the obituaries for C.S. Lewis and other comments in the press. Years ago he had refused an invitation to write an obituary for Lewis (probably for *The Times*) on religious grounds: 'A Catholic could not possibly say anything sincere about Jack's books without giving widespread offence' (quoted in Christie's, *20th-Century Books and Manuscripts*, 16 November 2001, p. 22).

?Late November–?early December 1963 Tolkien drafts a belated reply to a letter from his son Michael. 'Jack Lewis's death on the 22nd has preoccupied me. It is also involving me in some correspondence, as many people still regard me as one of his intimates. Alas! that ceased to be so some ten years ago. We were separated first by the sudden apparition of Charles Williams, and then by his marriage. . . . But we owed each a great debt to the other' (*Letters*, p. 341).

30 November 1963 A memorial service for C.S. Lewis is held at Magdalen College. Tolkien is not among those listed in the *Oxford Mail* as being present, but the list is not complete. – Soon after Lewis's death Tolkien begins to keep a diary, as he had not done for years, but tends to make entries only when he is feeling unhappy or depressed. One entry is quoted in *Biography* (p. 242): 'Life is grey and grim. I can get nothing done, between staleness and boredom (confined to quarters), and anxiety and distraction. What am I going to do? Be sucked down into residence in a hotel or old-people's home or club, without books or contacts or talk with men? God help me!' Many of the diary entries are written in an improved version of the 'New English Alphabet' of his own invention (see *Writing systems).

Late 1963 Soon after Lewis's death both Tolkien and his wife are taken ill. Edith remains unwell through Christmas.

December 1963 Merton College bestows an Emeritus Fellowship on Tolkien.

4 December 1963 Tolkien writes to Allen & Unwin. He asks them to send a set of *The Lord of the Rings* to his granddaughter Joanna as a birthday and Christmas present. – Tolkien writes a three-page letter to a Miss Clark. He comments on some of his works, and on his designs for the dust-jackets of *The Lord of the Rings*.

?10 (received 11) December 1963 D.E. Roberts of Fleetway Publications writes to Tolkien, reminding him of an aborted project discussed years earlier, for a picture version of *The Hobbit* in a juvenile publication. He would now like to serialize *The Hobbit* in a paper called *Princess*, in the form of full-colour pictures with captions to be edited from Tolkien's text. Two artists would share the job. If Tolkien is agreeable to the project, Roberts will send sample pictures of characters with captions for the first instalment.

11 or 12 December 1963 Tolkien replies to D.E. Roberts. He agrees in principle to his proposal, but matters concerning rights and fees must be dealt with by Allen & Unwin.

12 December 1963 Tolkien writes to Allen & Unwin, enclosing a copy of Roberts' letter and summarizing his reply. Tolkien thinks that the fee offered for the adaptation is reasonable, and that such a publication is unlikely to affect ordinary sales. He is prepared to look at the sample pictures and captions. For the moment, his only anxieties are that they spell his name correctly (Roberts had misspelled it 'Tolkein') and that Gollum is not depicted as a monster.

?Mid-December 1963 Mrs Nancy Smith, the compiler of the index for *The Lord of the Rings* in 1958, now living with her husband in the United States, writes to Tolkien. She has been asked to give a talk to a group of Tolkien fans on 8 January 1964 and asks for information about himself and his writings. She is uncertain of Tolkien's current address, and therefore sends her letter via Christopher Tolkien, a close friend of her husband.

18 December 1963 Joy Hill writes to Tolkien. She will contact Mr. Roberts.

20 December 1963 Rayner Unwin, just returned from the Far East, writes to Tolkien. He likes the title *Tree and Leaf*, and wants to consult Tolkien about the cover design. He suggests some tree or leaf, or both, perhaps from a medieval manuscript, or perhaps Tolkien himself has made a drawing of a tree that would be appropriate. He is also pleased that the interview printed in the *Sunday Telegraph* suggests Tolkien is getting on with *The Silmarillion*.

23 December 1963 Tolkien writes to Rayner Unwin. Medieval manuscripts

are not (in my not very extensive experience) good on trees. I have among my 'papers' more than one version of a mythical 'tree', which crops up regularly at those times when I feel drawn to pattern-designing. They are elaborated and coloured and more suitable for embroidery than printing; and the tree bears besides various shapes of leaves many flowers small and large signifying poems and major legends.

I have made a hasty reduction of this pattern into leafy-terms. If you think that something of this sort might do, I will do the design again more carefully, and larger. (Four times larger? – at present it could approx[imately] be accommodated on the cover as it stands). Unless you think it had better be given to someone of more skill & firmer line.

He hopes that Rayner approves the prefatory note to *Tree and Leaf*. He acknowledges that 'the *Silmarillion* is growing in the mind (I do not mean getting larger, but coming back to leaf & I hope flower) again. But I am still not through with *Gawain* etc. A troublous year, of endless distraction and much weariness, ending with the blow of C.S.L.'s death' (Tolkien-George Allen & Unwin archive, HarperCollins; partly printed in *Letters*, p. 342).

24 December 1963 Tolkien attends a family party at Christopher Tolkien's house, and is given the letter from Nancy Smith. – Rayner Unwin writes to Tolkien. Penguin Books have again asked to reprint *The Hobbit*. He encloses figures which show a decline in sales of the Allen & Unwin hardback while the Puffin edition was available. He thinks that the payments for the Puffin copies more or less compensated for this decline, so he will do whatever Tolkien decides.

25 December 1963–2 January 1964 Tolkien writes a long reply to Nancy Smith. He hopes that her index will be used some day in a new edition of *The Lord of the Rings*, or perhaps in a fourth volume. He and his publishers have been astonished at the success of the books.

28 December 1963 Tolkien replies to Rayner Unwin. He leaves the Puffin Books decision to him, but is against agreeing unless they are prepared to correct the text. He objects to the number of misprints the edition contained, and the 'impertinent alteration of my usage in an enormous number of cases. . . . My only copy, carefully corrected, is out on loan, but it will reach me by Monday or Tuesday, and I can send it to you if that will be useful' (Tolkien-George Allen & Unwin archive, HarperCollins). Since his granddaughter has not received the set of *The Lord of the Rings* he promised, he assumes his letter of 4 December did not reach Allen & Unwin. He asks Rayner to see that a set is sent. (The publisher will note on this sheet that the earlier letter was never received.)

31 December 1963 Rayner Unwin writes to Tolkien. In regard to a design for the cover of *Tree and Leaf*, he asks if Tolkien could 'redraw the tree to about double the size – four times would be excessive – using either Indian ink or, if you prefer, a hard firm pencil. If it were possible for you to make the design a little less square and rather more elongated it would be an advantage and if you could put your initials on the drawing that would add to its charm' (Tolkien-George Allen & Unwin archive, HarperCollins).

1964

1964 Tolkien looks at such *Lord of the Rings* papers as had not gone to Marquette University. It is probably at this time that he writes beside a note, 'Adventures . . Stone Men', made in August 1939: 'Thought of as just an "adventure". The whole of the matter of Gondor (Stone-land) grew from this note' (*The Return of the Shadow*, p. 379).

Early 1964 Christopher Tolkien and his wife separate. Their marriage will end in divorce.

?2 January 1964 The Rev. Denis Tyndall writes to Tolkien, recalling the days when they were both at King Edward's School, Birmingham.

3 January 1964 Tolkien writes to Michael George, thanking him for a letter and enclosing a cheque to pay for a cello. 'I am pretty well, but Grannie [Edith] is very poorly indeed today, which has rather overshadowed my "festa" [birthday]. . . . I had a pretty good post-bag this morning, and was additionally astonished to see that "The Times" had noted my birthday' (British Library MS Add. 71657). He hopes that his translations of *Sir Gawain and the Green Knight* and *Pearl* will be published in 1964.

7 January 1964 Tolkien writes to Rayner Unwin. He has not yet had time to redraw the tree for the cover of *Tree and Leaf*, but hopes to do so today. His granddaughter has now received her set of *The Lord of the Rings*.

8 January 1964 Tolkien writes to Rayner Unwin, sending a redrawn design for *Tree and Leaf*. If it is of no use, he will try again.

9 January 1964 Tolkien replies to the Rev. Denis Tyndall. He reminisces in turn about their time at King Edward's School. – Joy Hill writes to Tolkien. Associated Rediffusion will be presenting *The Hobbit* in their schools programme *Story Box* on 4 March, with a repeat broadcast two days later.

10 January 1964 Tolkien writes to the Royal Society of Literature, declining a request to write an obituary of C.S. Lewis for their journal *Report*. He suggests that Owen Barfield do so instead. Tolkien long ago resigned from writing Lewis's obituary for *The Times*. 'I feel his loss so deeply that I have since his death refused to write or speak about him' (quoted in Martin Bentham, 'Literary Greats Exposed as Gossips and Snipes', *Sunday Telegraph*, 7 February 1999). – Rayner Unwin writes to Tolkien about his cover design for *Tree and Leaf*: 'Lovely Tree. Thank you' (Tolkien-George Allen & Unwin archive, HarperCollins).

18 January 1964 Tolkien replies to a letter from Justin Arundale, a reader aged 10, who wants to know when *The Silmarillion* will be published. Tolkien regrets that this will not be for some time.

27 January 1964 Ronald Eames writes to Tolkien, enclosing proofs of *Tree and Leaf*, with the corresponding typescript. He asks Tolkien to mark corrections to printer's errors in a different colour to any changes he makes to the text, and to return the marked proof by 10 February if possible. (This letter will be forwarded from Sandfield Road to the Hotel Miramar on 31 January.)

End of January 1964 *Letters to Malcolm* by C.S. Lewis is published. Tolkien buys it probably on or soon after publication. On 11 November 1964 he will write in a letter to David Kolb: 'I personally found *Letters to Malcolm* a distressing and in parts horrifying work. I began a commentary on it, but if finished it would not be publishable' (*Letters*, p. 352). A.N. Wilson will note in his *C.S. Lewis: A Biography* (1990, pp. xvii, 289–90) that among the comments Tolkien wrote in his copy were that the book was not 'about prayer, but about Lewis praying', and 'But the whole book is *always interesting*. Why? Because it is about Jack, by Jack, and that is a topic that no one who knew him well could fail to find interesting even when exasperating.' Wilson will feel that Tolkien found distasteful the idea of 'an "unqualified" Protestant layman taking upon himself a teaching office in a matter so delicate as how we should pray'.

29 January–10 February 1964 Tolkien and Edith stay at the Hotel Miramar, Bournemouth.

2 February 1964 Tolkien writes to Ronald Eames from the Hotel Miramar. He received the proofs for *Tree and Leaf* on 1 February and will correct them today.

3 February 1964 Tolkien writes to Ronald Eames, enclosing the proofs of *Tree and Leaf*. He has made no alterations. He queries the cover/title-page which does not include his tree design. In regard to the facsimile of his signature on the title-page: 'I do not and never have used the signature "Ronald Tolkien" as a "public" or auctorial signature, and I do not think it suitable for this purpose' (Tolkien-George Allen & Unwin archive, HarperCollins). A facsimile of the author's signature is a feature of the title-page of books in Allen & Unwin's 'U Books' series. 'Ronald Tolkien' was presumably taken from one of Tolkien's letters to Rayner; this will be changed to another signature, 'J.R.R. Tolkien'. – Tolkien writes again to Ronald Eames. Since posting the proofs, he has noticed a possible erroneous date. 'If this alteration is derived from the corrections sent in by me, then *stet*' (Tolkien-George Allen & Unwin archive, HarperCollins).

4 February 1964 Ronald Eames sends Tolkien proofs of the dust-jacket for the hardback edition of *Tree and Leaf*.

5 February 1964 Ronald Eames writes to Tolkien. The tree design is intended for the cover of the paperback edition, not the title-page. He hopes to send a proof of the cover soon. He asks Tolkien to supply a more suitable version of his signature for the title-page.

6 February 1964 Ronald Eames writes to Tolkien. The date in the proof, queried by Tolkien on 3 February, is from a correction Tolkien made.

7 February 1964 Tolkien writes to Ronald Eames, enclosing specimen signatures. He thinks that his ordinary signature is more appropriate, but the matter is not important enough for production to be delayed or any serious expense incurred. He leaves it to Allen & Unwin's discretion. The proofs of the dust-jacket have not reached him in Bournemouth.

11 February 1964 Ronald Eames writes to Tolkien. Allen & Unwin will use one of the specimen signatures he sent. He encloses a further proof of the dust-jacket.

21 February 1964 Ronald Eames sends proofs of the paperback cover for *Tree and Leaf.*

22 February 1964 Tolkien writes to Ronald Eames. He approves the cover proofs. While glancing at the book this morning, he noticed an error which had escaped him before. He expects that it is too late to correct it.

25 February 1964 Rayner Unwin forwards to Tolkien a letter from Houghton Mifflin. They are now considering Maurice Sendak to illustrate their proposed new edition of *The Hobbit.* Rayner will be in Oxford on 28 February, and asks if he may call on Tolkien at about 10.30 a.m.

28 February 1964 Presumably Rayner Unwin visits Tolkien.

5 March 1964 Tolkien replies to a letter from Eileen Elgar. He answers queries about some of the poems in *The Adventures of Tom Bombadil and Other Verses from the Red Book.* Also he encloses a nine-page manuscript giving an outline of 'The Silmarillion', with a family tree entitled 'Kinship of the Half-elven' (reproduced in Sotheby's, *English Literature and English History*, London, 6–7 December 1984, lot 276, and in *Beyond Bree*, May 1985, p. 4).

16 March 1964 Joy Hill writes to Tolkien, enclosing a pamphlet produced by the BBC for use with a schools programme. It includes a poem from the *Adventures of Tom Bombadil* collection.

15 April 1964 Rayner Unwin writes to Tolkien. Allen & Unwin will probably have to discontinue the slipcased sets of *The Lord of the Rings.* They have never charged extra for the slipcase, and the price of the set no longer covers the cost. However, they are considering the publication of a de luxe edition, bound in good buckram, with gilt top edges, coloured endpapers, and headbands, in a better quality slipcase with a full-colour wraparound design, perhaps by Pauline Baynes. It would be sold only as a set, for five guineas. The old edition will continue to be sold, but without a box. Rayner asks if Tolkien approves. He also asks about the status of *Sir Gawain and the Green Knight* and *Pearl.*

17 April 1964 Naomi Collyer, Tolkien's secretary, sends Rayner Unwin a promised list of addresses of 205 people who have recently written fan letters to Tolkien.

?Late April or (probably early) May 1964 Naomi Collyer, expecting a baby, resigns as Tolkien's secretary. Tolkien will not find a replacement for some time, and for much of May is unable to deal with correspondence or even keep it in order. – Tolkien drafts a letter to Cor Blok, in reply to his of 27 April, but does not make a copy to send. He will eventually do so on 22 August.

13 May 1964 Tolkien begins a reply to a letter from Colin Bailey. After writing one paragraph, he leaves the letter unfinished, but will take it up again on 6 June.

15 May 1964 Martin Blackman, Publicity Manager for Allen & Unwin, writes to Tolkien. He asks if Allen & Unwin could borrow material – perhaps a page of manuscript, doodles, or drawings – for their display at the World Book Fair in London.

21 May 1964 Joy Hill writes to Tolkien. Houghton Mifflin have asked to pay Allen & Unwin a lower royalty on the de luxe illustrated *Hobbit* so as to give a small royalty to the artist, Maurice Sendak.

28 May 1964 – Tolkien writes to Rayner Unwin, one of the first letters he has written in weeks. 'The events and troubles of this year have defeated me, and I began to think finally. I am at last recovering health and some kind of mental equilibrium. As I have no secretary, and my typewriter (symbolically) broke down completely after typing two lines', he is dealing in this letter with various outstanding questions from Allen & Unwin. He hopes that Rayner has assumed rightly that he agrees to the discontinuation of the boxed sets and the production of a de luxe *Lord of the Rings*. He thinks that a scenic design would be best, and Pauline Baynes has a good scenic imagination. 'Personally I should make the eruption of Mount Doom the central motif' (Tolkien-George Allen & Unwin archive, HarperCollins). He agrees to a reduced royalty on the Houghton Mifflin illustrated *Hobbit* subject to Allen & Unwin's advice. He will look out for some material for the Publicity Manager for the World Book Fair. There is to be an exhibition in The Hague in 1965 dealing with invented languages and alphabets, and Cor Blok has asked him to lend material. He apologizes for his scrawl, but arthritis is affecting him more and more. – *Tree and Leaf* is published.

29 May 1964 Rayner Unwin writes to Tolkien. He hopes that Tolkien can overcome his problems and not give in to despair. In the absence of a secretary he should not hesitate to scribble only brief replies to Allen & Unwin's enquiries. The material for the World Book Fair is needed by 2 June.

31 May 1964 Tolkien replies to a letter from Jane Sibley, a reader in Connecticut. He explains why the runes in *The Hobbit* differ from those in *The Lord of the Rings*.

1 June 1964 Tolkien writes to Martin Blackman, Allen & Unwin, sending material for display at the World Book Fair: three 'facsimiles' from the 'Book of Mazarbul' in *The Lord of the Rings*, a sketch of a cover design for *The Return of the King*, the drawings *Old Man Willow*, *Moria West Gate*, and *Barad-dûr*, specimens of Elvish script, and two pieces of manuscript draft (from 'Shelob's Lair' and 'The Muster of Rohan'). He asks the date of the World Book Fair.

4 June 1964 Martin Blackman writes to Tolkien. The material arrived too late to include as much as Allen & Unwin would have liked, but they are using one of the 'Book of Mazarbul' pages and returning the rest. They would be delighted if Tolkien could visit the Fair, and can send him a complimentary ticket. It runs from 10 to 20 June.

6 June 1964 Tolkien continues his letter to Colin Bailey begun on 13 May. He mentions his abandoned sequel to *The Lord of the Rings* (*The New Shadow*) and discusses the word *Númenor*. Professional tasks have occupied him, but 'in a month or two' he hopes to get back to 'The Silmarillion', much of which 'is now in type' (i.e. typescript; Marion E. Wade Center, Wheaton College, Wheaton, Illinois).

9 June 1964 Tolkien writes to Martin Blackman. He thanks him for the offer of a complimentary ticket to the World Book Fair. The only day he might be able to come to London is Tuesday, 15 June, but as even that is uncertain, he thinks it hardly fair to ask for a ticket. He asks him to pass to the appropriate department a request for a copy of *Tree and Leaf*. He is beginning to receive letters about it, some pointing out errors and misprints.

15 June 1964 Tolkien nonetheless visits the World Book Fair at Earl's Court in London. A correspondent will later mention that his father met Tolkien at the Fair.

24 June 1964 Encaenia.

27 June 1964 A nine-year-old girl in Australia writes a letter in runes to Tolkien, which he transliterates before drafting a short reply.

?July 1964 Tolkien's 'secretary' (possibly Joy Hill) signs a reply from Tolkien to Colin Smythe, declining a request for an article for a student newspaper.

3 July 1964 In the evening, Tolkien attends a dinner of The Society hosted by Patrick Gardiner at Magdalen College. Nine members are present. Gardiner begins a discussion on complementary studies in schools of art.

10 July 1964 Tolkien posts a letter to Christopher Bretherton.

12 July 1964 A schoolboy at St Marylebone Grammar School, London, writes to Tolkien. A group of boys at the school would like to make a tape recording of all or most of *The Lord of the Rings*. Tolkien will reckon that a reading would probably take forty hours.

?13 July 1964 Christopher Bretherton replies to Tolkien's letter. Tolkien will receive Bretherton's letter on 14 July.

?15 July 1964 (postmark) Tolkien finds an unfinished letter to Miss J.L. Curry begun in April but then neglected. He now completes it, apologizing for the delay. He expresses his dislike of Disney's films: 'Though in most of the "pictures" proceeding from his studios there are admirable or charming passages, the effect of all of them is to me disgusting. Some have given me nausea' (quoted in Sotheby's, *English Literature, History, Children's & Illustrated Books & Drawings*, London, 10 July 2001, p. 123). He criticizes Disney's business practices, and would not have given a film proposal from Disney any consideration at all.

16 July 1964 Tolkien replies to the letter of ?13 July from Christopher Bretherton. He does 'not regard typing as a discourtesy. Anyway, I usually type, since my "hand" tends to start fair and rapidly fall away into picturesque inscrutability. Also I like typewriters; and my dream is of suddenly finding myself rich enough to have an electric typewriter built to my specifications, to type the Fëanorian script' (*Letters*, p. 344). In a lengthy letter he says how noisy Sandfield Road had become, and gives much information about his writings, and some biographical details.

22 July 1964 Rayner Unwin writes to Tolkien. 'The Bath Song' (*The Lord of the Rings*, Book I, Chapter 5) has been reprinted in a school magazine in New South Wales. Rayner asks if Tolkien has made any progress with his writing.

31 July 1964 Rayner Unwin visits Tolkien. He shows him Pauline Baynes' design for the slipcase for the de luxe *Lord of the Rings*. Rayner will write to Pauline Baynes that Tolkien 'was enchanted and said you had exactly his eye for landscape and asked if, when we had finished using it for technical reproduction, he could have your original on permanent loan in his study' (George Allen & Unwin archive, University of Reading). – Tolkien replies to a letter from Jared C. Lobdell about a proverb used in *The Lord of the Rings*.

?August 1964 Notes on both sides of a calendar leaf for 2–8 August indicate that Tolkien is again considering early versions of the *Pater Noster*.

2 August 1964 Tolkien sends Rayner Unwin the letter from St Marylebone Grammar School, which he forgot to give him on his visit. He dislikes the proposal and the idea of having such a series of tapes in existence and out of control, but imagines that the project will not be completed, and as long as no public use of it is made, it could do little harm.

> I wish that 'Copyright' could protect *names*, as well as extracts. It is a form of invention that I take a great deal of trouble over, and pleasure in; and really it is quite as difficult (often more so) as, say, lines of verse. I must say I was piqued by the 'christening' of that monstrous 'hydrofoil' *Shadowfax* – without so much as 'by your leave' – to which several correspondents drew my attention (some with indignation). I am getting used to *Rivendells*, *Lóriens*, *Imladris* etc. as house-names – though maybe they are more frequent than the letters which say 'by your leave'. [*Letters*, p. 349]

He wants to write to Stanley Unwin for his eightieth birthday, but has forgotten the date.

7 August 1964 Tolkien writes to Anne Barrett at Houghton Mifflin. He enjoyed Charles Williams' company, but they had little in common. In regard to a proposed blurb for *Tree and Leaf*,

> I am afraid that difficulty really arises from the juxtaposition of two things that only in fact touch at a corner, so to speak. I do not think I was responsible for the proposed association, and anyway it came up at a time of great troubles and distractions for me. Myself, I had for some time vaguely thought of the reprint together of three things that to my mind really do flow together: *Beowulf: The Monsters and the Critics*; the essay *On Fairy-stories*; and *The Homecoming of Beorhtnoth*. [*Letters*, pp. 349–50]

– Rayner Unwin writes to Tolkien. He has dealt with the proposal from St Marylebone Grammar School. Stanley Unwin's birthday is on 19 December.

10 August 1964 Tolkien replies to a letter from Miss Carole Ward, a freelance writer who has suggested a serialization of *The Lord of the Rings* on BBC 2. He is averse to any dramatization of his works, especially *The Lord of the Rings*. Because of its length, it would have to be severely cut and edited, damaging or even destroying 'a complicated but closely-woven story' (quoted in Christie's, *20th-Century Books and Manuscripts*, London, 6 December 2002, p. 21). He advises Ward to contact Allen & Unwin.

11 August 1964 *The Horn Book*, a journal devoted to children's literature, plans to publish *On Fairy-Stories* by permission of Oxford University Press, without reference to Tolkien. Having heard of this, Tolkien writes to Ruth Viguers, editor of the *Horn Book*. In the event, the journal does not proceed with publication.

13 August 1964 Joy Hill writes to Tolkien. Mr Roberts of Fleetway Publications now proposes that instead of publishing *The Hobbit* in *Princess* in cartoon form, they would like to serialize it in ten or twelve instalments, each of about 3,500 words, accompanied by three or four illustrations by Ferguson Dewar. She encloses some of Dewar's sketches for the illustrations, and asks if Tolkien approves of such a serialization. If so, Joy intends to ask for a higher fee than that offered, with no syndication rights. For convenience, she encloses a business reply label for Tolkien to return the sketches.

14 August 1964 Tolkien replies to Joy Hill. He agrees to the serialization on the terms she proposes. Criticizing the drawings would probably not achieve anything, 'though I should myself wish at least that Gandalf were less fussy and over-clad and had some dignity. He should *not* be styled "magician" but "wizard".' Although he chose to use the form 'dwarves' in *The Hobbit*, he thinks that the correct form 'dwarfs' might be used in *Princess* instead. He has heard of an unfortunate schoolmaster who corrected a child for using 'dwarves', and was then shown *The Hobbit*. 'I am all in favour of spelling being taught, and do not wish a master's authority to be damaged by the quirks of a professor!' (Tolkien-George Allen & Unwin archive, HarperCollins).

16 August 1964 Tolkien replies to a letter from Carey Blyton, who has asked permission to compose a work based on *The Hobbit*. Tolkien feels honoured to have inspired a composer. 'I have long hoped to do so, and hoped also that I might perhaps find the result intelligible to me, or feel that it was akin to my own inspiration. . . .' He himself has 'little musical knowledge' (*Letters*, p. 350).

19 August 1964 Joy Hill writes to Tolkien. Mr Roberts has agreed to her terms. She will forward Tolkien's comments and see that he receives a copy of each issue of *Princess*. Allen & Unwin are on the point of authorizing the Southern Rhodesian Broadcasting Corporation to serialize *The Hobbit*. The fee is small, but the book will get free publicity in *Young Rhodesia* magazine in connection with the broadcast.

c. **21 August 1964** Tolkien is away from Oxford for a few days, probably in Bournemouth.

22 August 1964 Tolkien replies at last to a letter from Cor Blok of 27 April. He discusses the proposed exhibition in The Hague with which Blok is involved, and what Tolkien might be able to contribute, if his reply has not come too late.

27 August 1964 Joy Hill writes to Tolkien. Carole Ward has been in touch with her also. She read Tolkien's reply to Joy, who 'noted what you say but I must say I feel very sceptical about the whole idea' (Tolkien-George Allen & Unwin archive, HarperCollins). Allen & Unwin have also had enquiries about such a serial from ITV.

28 August 1964 Tolkien writes to E. Rasdall, sending an autographed copy of the *Adventures of Tom Bombadil* volume (which he probably has been asked to sign). He would prefer to answer personally most of the letters he receives from writers who appreciate his works, but it is no longer possible. Correspondence has become a chief cause of delay of *The Silmarillion*.

29 August 1964 Tolkien replies to a letter from a child in Sweden, who has asked if he can visit Tolkien while his family is in England at the end of September. Tolkien drafts a reply on the envelope that he will be away in October and is very busy.

30 August 1964 Tolkien writes to Anne Barrett at Houghton Mifflin. He comments on an article about C.S. Lewis by a former pupil in *The Reporter*, presumably sent by Barrett to Tolkien. – Tolkien writes to L. Sprague de Camp. De Camp has sent Tolkien a copy of *Swords and Sorcery*, an anthology of heroic fantasy he has edited, with works by Poul Anderson, H.P. Lovecraft, Robert Howard, Henry Kuttner, Lord Dunsany, Clark Ashton Smith, C.L. Moore, and Fritz Leiber. Tolkien comments that 'all the items seem poor in the subsidiary (but to me not unimportant matters of nomenclature. Best when inventive, least good when literary or archaic' (quoted in letter by L. Sprague de Camp, *Mythlore* 13, no. 4, whole no. 50 (Summer 1987), p. 41).

1 September 1964 Professor Clyde S. Kilby of Wheaton College, Illinois has tea with R.E. Havard, who lives at 28 Sandfield Road near Tolkien. Later, encouraged by Havard, Kilby visits Tolkien at home. They talk for some time in Tolkien's garage-study, and Tolkien invites Kilby to return on 4 September.

2 September 1964 Michael di Capua of Pantheon Books, New York, writes to Tolkien. He asks if Tolkien would consider writing a short preface for a new edition of George MacDonald's fairy-tale 'The Golden Key', which is to be illustrated by Maurice Sendak.

4 September 1964 Clyde Kilby visits Tolkien in the morning. Edith Tolkien shows him upstairs to Tolkien's 'main office, a room crowded with a large desk, a rotating bookcase, wall bookcases, and a cot. . . . While he talked he stood up and walked about or else sat on his cot' (Kilby, *Tolkien & The Silmarillion* (1976), pp. 11–12, using *cot* in the sense 'a small folding bed'). – Joy Hill writes to Tolkien. Allen & Unwin have had an inquiry from someone who wants to produce a puppet version of one of Tolkien's books for television.

7 September 1964 Tolkien replies to Michael di Capua. He would like to write a preface to 'The Golden Key', 'but I am unfortunately very hard pressed at present, being involved in a contract overdue owing to recent illness and troubles; and I cannot lay this aside now until it is finished. So I am obliged, before agreeing, to ask what approximate number of words you have in mind, and (more important) what is the deadline: when at latest must you receive my contribution?' (Tolkien Papers, Bodleian Library, Oxford).

8 September 1964 Tolkien receives proofs of the Houghton Mifflin edition of *Tree and Leaf*, with a short deadline for their return. – Cor Blok writes to Tolkien. The exhibition will not take place until May 1965, but they need to settle on what will be included by November. He suggests what Tolkien might contribute. The exhibition will include sections on script and language.

10 September 1964 Tolkien writes to Houghton Mifflin in regard to the proofs of their edition of *Tree and Leaf*. He finds the block on 'p. iii . . . very distasteful', and wonders 'if it could not perhaps be reconsidered, or omitted. The lettering is, to my taste, of a bad kind and ill-executed. . . . The fat and apparently pollarded trunk, with no roots, and feeble branches, seems to me quite unfitting as a symbol of Tale-telling, or as a suggestion of anything that Niggle could possibly have drawn!' (*Letters*, pp. 351–2). The reference is presumably not to the title-page device (p. iii as published), but to the dust-jacket art.

11 September 1964 Tolkien replies to several letters from Joy Hill. In regard to Carole Ward's proposal, he repeats for emphasis that he does not favour dramatization of his works. 'I do not expect anything tolerable . . . nor anything sufficiently profitable for either publisher or author to be interested.' In regard to the proposal that one of his works be performed by puppets, 'I hope we never hear any more about them'. He wonders if Rembrandt Films will actually produce anything; 'what on earth or in America it will be like; and whether I shall ever see it?' He complains of the cost of returning the proofs of *Tree and Leaf* to Houghton Mifflin to make their deadline.

> I had to correct their setting, and compare it with 'copy' (our paperback) and the original text. In this process I discovered a very large number of misprints and errors in the paperback. (I did not see any proofs of this.) Would it be useful, if I sent in a list of these – probably exhaustive, since I took some trouble – in case a reprint may be called for? [Tolkien-George Allen & Unwin archive, HarperCollins]

18 September 1964 Joy Hill writes to Tolkien. 'Quite frankly I just cannot see any of the ideas of these television people coming off and I take it all with a large pinch of salt.' She writes to tell Tolkien about such things as Rayner Unwin likes to keep Tolkien informed. Allen & Unwin would indeed like a list of misprints and errors for *Tree and Leaf*. The serialization of *The Hobbit* in *Princess* is to commence on 10 October. – Mabel Day dies.

23 September 1964 Michael di Capua writes to Tolkien. He is delighted that Tolkien is willing to write a preface to 'The Golden Key'. He suggests 1

February 1965 for delivery but, if Tolkien cannot manage that, asks him to suggest another date. The preface should be about 800 to 1,500 words in length. Tolkien might find it best to address what he writes to an adult reader, assuming that a child who does not understand the preface would skip it.

29 September 1964 Tolkien attends the Merton Septcentenary Dinner. During the evening he talks to Burke Trend, Secretary to the Cabinet, who tells him that he and most of the Cabinet are fans of *The Lord of the Rings*, as are Members of Parliament on both sides of the House of Commons.

9 October 1964 Rayner Unwin writes to Tolkien. He reports on the progress of the Rembrandt Films *Hobbit*. After solving some problems, Aubrey Menen is writing the screenplay, and production might begin in spring 1965. Rayner asks again if Tolkien has made progress on his translations of *Sir Gawain and the Green Knight* and *Pearl*. 'I am so anxious to get these into print and I do feel that now it only takes a comparatively short heave to get the prefatory paragraphs into shape. Could you not do this fairly quickly?' (Tolkien-George Allen & Unwin archive, HarperCollins).

?Early November 1964 Clyde S. Kilby writes to Tolkien. The illustrated manuscript of *Mr. Bliss* at Marquette University having come to his attention, he asks about the possibility of its publication in the United States. He also asks if Tolkien is willing to sell more of his manuscripts, and if he would agree to an American paperback edition of *The Lord of the Rings*, with the publication of which Kilby apparently wishes to be involved.

11 November 1964 Tolkien replies to Clyde S. Kilby. He is prepared to consider the publication of *Mr. Bliss* in the USA, but would like more information about the method of printing and terms. He does not feel inclined to sell any more manuscripts. Allen & Unwin probably are not disposed at present to consider a paperback edition of *The Lord of the Rings*, and if they were, would probably offer it to the Houghton Mifflin Company in the first instance. – Tolkien writes to David Kolb, S.J. He comments on C.S. Lewis's 'Narnia' books and *Letters to Malcolm*.

16 November 1964 Michael di Capua writes to Tolkien. He has had no reply to his letter of 23 September and fears that it has gone astray. He repeats that text in the present message.

19 November 1964 Tolkien's new secretary, Mary E. Hares, writes to Michael di Capua. Tolkien did write in response to di Capua's letter of 23 September. (No copy of that reply, however, is preserved in the Tolkien Papers at Oxford.) Tolkien is willing to deliver the preface to 'The Golden Key' by the beginning of February.

24 November 1964 Tolkien attends the final lecture in a series given by Robert Graves, Professor of Poetry at Oxford. He will describe the occasion to his son Michael in a letter of 9–10 January 1965:

> It was the most ludicrously bad lecture I have ever heard. After it he [Graves] introduced me to a pleasant young woman who had attended it: well but quietly dressed, easy and agreeable, and we got on quite well. But

Graves started to laugh; and he said: 'it is obvious neither of you has ever heard of the other before'. Quite true. And I had not supposed that the lady would ever have heard of me. Her name was Ava Gardner, but it still meant nothing, till people more aware of the world informed me that she was a film-star of some magnitude, and that the press of pressmen and storm of flash-bulbs on the steps of the Schools were not directed at Graves (and cert[ainly] not at me) but at her. [*Letters*, p. 353]

?Late November 1964–?mid-February 1965 Tolkien works on a preface to 'The Golden Key'. In the end, however, as he will later note on the carbon copy of the letter written on 19 November,

the project fizzled out. It was in the course of trying to write an intro-duction (aimed at children!) to 'The Golden Key' – after re-reading that (and much also of G[eorge] MacDonald's) that I found how greatly selec-tive memory had transmuted his 'F[airy] Stories' & how much I disliked them now. I think in any case I [should] have abandoned the effort. But [*Smith of Wootton Major*] arose out of my attempt (I tried to give an exemplar of 'fairy' magic). [Tolkien Papers, Bodleian Library, Oxford]

In another account he says that

when striving to say some useful things in a preface, I found it necessary to deal with the term 'fairy'. . . .
   In the course of this I tried to give an illustration of 'Faery', and said: 'this could be put into a short story like this' – and then proceeded in what is a first version of *Smith of W.M.* pp. 11–20. There I stopped, real-izing that the 'short story' had developed an independent life and should be completed as a thing in itself. [Tolkien Papers, Bodleian Library, Oxford]

When he realizes that *Smith of Wootton Major* has an independent life, Tol-kien makes this into a separate work through a combination of typescript and manuscript, with emendations. One typescript bears the title *The Great Cake*. While the work is in progress, Tolkien produces time-schemes and other material about the characters and story, for his use as background reference. By mid-February 1965 at the latest, he completes *Smith of Wootton Major* (as finally entitled) and begins to lend a typescript to relatives and friends.

26 November 1964 Tolkien is interviewed at 76 Sandfield Road by Irene Slade for the BBC radio programme *Reluctant Olympians*, in the series *A World of Sound* to be broadcast in January. He is also interviewed for about half an hour by Denys Gueroult, the programme's producer, using a midget recorder. This is intended to be a trial run for an official interview to be placed in the BBC's Sound Archives. Tolkien autographs Gueroult's copies of *The Hobbit* and *The Return of the King*.

30 November 1964 Rayner Unwin writes to Tolkien. Longmans Green would like to publish an edition of *The Hobbit* for schools. Allen & Unwin themselves

> have a small school book department but it would probably do less than justice to *The Hobbit* and we are inclined to sub-contract under quite advantageous terms.... One of the advantages in this arrangement, which would yield you a royalty and would not interfere in any way with bookshop sales, is that we would be able to run on ourselves a large printing fairly cheaply of *The Hobbit* in our paperback 'U Book' format which could take the place for at least a limited period of the Puffin Book edition and yield you rather better rewards. [Tolkien-George Allen & Unwin archive, HarperCollins]

Allen & Unwin would print 20,000 copies of the paperback and hope to sell it at 7s 6d. The box makers for the de luxe *Lord of the Rings* are working very slowly, but Rayner hopes to have some sets available before Christmas. The boxed set will sell for 6 guineas, and with the newest reprint the price of the individual volumes will have to rise from 21s to 25s.

19 December 1964 Stanley Unwin turns eighty. Tolkien attends a celebration of the event on this date or very close to it, and meets Joy Hill for the first time.

29 December 1964 Tolkien forwards to Allen & Unwin a letter written on behalf of a woman in Nairobi who wishes to produce a puppet version of *The Hobbit*. He has replied that all such matters are in Allen & Unwin's hands, and as far as he is concerned, he has no objection as long as the adapter adheres to her intention not to alter or add to the original story. – Denys Gueroult, BBC, writes to Tolkien. He has asked the BBC Contracts Department to contact Tolkien in connection with the interview he recorded on 26 November. 'I am, as you know, very interested in recording in greater detail your views on many aspects of "The Lord of the Rings" for our Sound Archives. If you have a morning or an afternoon free in the next fortnight I would be happy to come to Oxford again and we could perhaps record in the BBC studio' (BBC Written Archives Centre).

30 December 1964 Mary Hares, Tolkien's secretary, sends a letter dictated by him to Denys Gueroult. He would be glad to make a recording for the Sound Archives but cannot find time in the next fortnight. He asks Gueroult to suggest a later date.

31 December 1964 Joy Hill sends Tolkien copies of the later issues of *Princess* with the latter half of *The Hobbit* serial. She will write to the woman in Nairobi about the puppet play.

1965

January 1965 Tolkien's secretary makes a typescript of his unfinished story *Aldarion and Erendis*. Soon afterward, Tolkien begins to type a fuller version, with the title *Indis i · Kiryamo 'The Mariner's Wife': A Tale of Ancient Númenórë, which Tells of the First Rumour of the Shadow*, but abandons it after two pages.

1 January 1965 Tolkien's interview with Irene Slade is broadcast on the BBC Home Service as part of *Reluctant Olympians*, 9.05–9.30 a.m. The programme is concerned with 'the more easily understandable worlds that have been created by authors whose books have a particular appeal to the young' (*Radio Times*, 24 December 1964, p. 44). – Mary Herring, BBC Talks Booking Manager, writes to Tolkien concerning his interview with Denys Gueroult. She outlines terms, and notes that a recording of the interview is to be placed in the BBC's Recorded Programmes Permanent Library. If Tolkien finds the terms acceptable, he should sign a copy of her letter and return it.

3 January 1965 Tolkien celebrates his seventy-third birthday.

4 January 1965 Tolkien continues to celebrate his birthday. 'Owing to the real day [3 January] being a Sunday, it began on January 2nd and ended on the 4th, when we had a party (now an annual event) on the day between my birthday and the birthday of my friend and successor, Norman Davis's wife' (letter to Michael George Tolkien, 6 January 1965, British Library MS Add. 71657). – Mary Hares returns Tolkien's signed declaration to the BBC. – Denys Gueroult writes to Tolkien. He asks if Tolkien is free to be interviewed either during the week beginning 18 January, or the following week.

5 January 1965 Tolkien replies to Denys Gueroult. He suggests 18, 19, or 20 January in the morning for the interview.

5 or 6 January 1965 Tolkien to his great surprise receives a warm fan letter from Iris Murdoch.

6 January 1965 Tolkien writes to Michael George, who is studying English at the University of St Andrews. He is sorry that his translations of *Sir Gawain and the Green Knight* and *Pearl* will not be out in time to assist him,

> largely owing, in addition to the natural difficulty of rendering verse into verse, to my discovering many minor points about words, in the course of my work, which lead me off. *Pearl* is, of course, about as difficult a task as any translator could be set. It is impossible to make a version in the same metre close enough to serve as a 'crib'. But I think anyone who reads my version, however learned a Middle English scholar, will get a more direct impression of the poem's impact (on one who knew the language). [*Letters*, p. 352]

He might be able to lend Michael George some proofs or a typescript during the next vacation. He sends him a copy of his essay 'Ofermod' from *The Homecoming of Beorhtnoth Beorhthelm's Son*.

8 January 1965 Denys Gueroult writes to Tolkien. He has made arrangements for the interview to take place in the BBC Oxford studio on 20 January. He suggests that they meet in the foyer of the Randolph Hotel in Beaumont Street at 10.45 a.m. on that day. – C.T. Onions dies.

9–10 January 1965 Tolkien writes to his son Michael. He comments on the deaths of Onions and of T.S. Eliot, and on other matters.

11 January 1965 Mary Hares writes to Denys Gueroult. Tolkien will meet him in the Randolph Hotel as suggested.

13 January 1965 Tolkien attends the funeral service for C.T. Onions in the chapel of Magdalen College.

19 January 1965 Tolkien replies to a letter from Miss A.P. Northey, who has asked about the fate of Shadowfax in *The Lord of the Rings*. Tolkien assures her that Shadowfax went into the West with Gandalf.

20 January 1965 Tolkien meets Denys Gueroult in the foyer of the Randolph Hotel. He is interviewed in the BBC studio in Oxford for nearly two hours.

22 January 1965 Denys Gueroult writes to thank Tolkien for the interview. When the tapes have been edited, he will try to arrange a meeting for Tolkien to hear them. – Austin Olney, Houghton Mifflin, writes to Rayner Unwin. Several American publishers have enquired about permission to publish paperback editions of Tolkien's works, but because of a legal technicality, the status of Tolkien's copyrights in the United States is uncertain. He thinks it unlikely that any reputable publisher would issue Tolkien's works without permission, but if new material were added to them it would be possible to obtain secure copyright for the new editions. He suggests that new material might include a short introduction to each volume. (See further, *Ace Books controversy.)

2 February 1965 Rayner Unwin writes to Tolkien. 'A very complicated business connected with Houghton Mifflin and the copyright situation in the U.S.A. for *The Lord of the Rings* and *The Hobbit* has cropped up which I feel I ought to explain to you in person' (Tolkien-George Allen & Unwin archive, HarperCollins). He suggests that he come to Oxford on 8 February and see Tolkien at 3.00 or 4.00 p.m. – Rayner Unwin writes to Austin Olney. He doubts that Tolkien would wish to write new introductions 'or could be persuaded to'. He wonders if such corrections as are made could 'be fitted in towards the end of chapters so as to make as little disturbance as possible in the typesetting' (George Allen & Unwin archive, University of Reading).

3 February 1965 Tolkien writes to Rayner Unwin. He will be delighted to see him on 8 February. 3.00 p.m. would be best, since 'I may be required to help entertain a visitor (of wealth and eccentricity) who is staying with us, as 4 p.m. approaches' (Tolkien-George Allen & Unwin archive, HarperCollins).

8 February 1965 Rayner Unwin visits Tolkien in the afternoon. He explains the need for new editions of *The Hobbit* and *The Lord of the Rings* to ensure secure American copyright. Tolkien agrees to help produce technically new editions.

11 February 1965 Austin Olney writes to Rayner Unwin. He suggests that adding an index to *The Return of the King* might be sufficient for that volume.

16 February 1965 Rayner Unwin writes to Tolkien. Houghton Mifflin have suggested that the addition of the promised index of proper names to *The Lord of the Rings* would help to secure copyright. He assumes that Tolkien has a copy (or both copies) of the index made by Nancy Smith, and asks if Tolkien would be willing to let Houghton Mifflin have a copy, and if he thinks it accurate enough to use. – Austin Olney writes to Rayner Unwin. He suggests that W.H. Auden be asked to write a foreword to either *The Hobbit* or *The Lord of the Rings*.

23 February 1965 Tolkien writes to Rayner Unwin. He had been sent only the carbon copy of the index in May 1958. It is sixty-seven pages and, printed in two columns, probably would occupy thirty or more pages. He has found it accurate but thinks that it needs considerable editing to make it suitable and to provide the kind of information readers want. 'My late secretary (alas!) could have done this, or most of it. I should myself be delighted to edit it. *But*, as you know, I cannot take it up immediately: not unless the copyright matter is so urgent that it must be an absolute priority.' (Tolkien presumably wishes to complete his work on *Sir Gawain* and *Pearl* first.)

> There is also another point. I should be reluctant to see the American edition adorned with an *index*, unless and until ours [the Allen & Unwin edition] is similarly furnished. (Or unless we could put on sale an index). I take it that the inclusion of an *index* might entail the cutting out of some of the *Appendices*, and that would require consideration. [Tolkien-George Allen & Unwin archive, HarperCollins]

He will be absent from Sandfield Road from 4 to 26 March, and from Oxford from 8 March, but will take *The Hobbit* and *The Lord of the Rings* away with him to work on the revision.

25 February 1965 Joy Hill writes to Tolkien. Rayner Unwin is away in Pakistan. Austin Olney will be in London in about two weeks, when the copyright question no doubt will be discussed.

1 March 1965 Marjorie Incledon, Tolkien's cousin, writes to him. She is returning the copy of *Smith of Wootton Major* he has lent her. She describes it as enchanting.

4 March 1965 *Tree and Leaf* is published in the United States.

4–8 March 1965 Tolkien stays elsewhere in Oxford, probably at Merton College.

6 March 1965 In the evening, Tolkien hosts a dinner of The Society at Merton College. Ten members are present. According to the minutes, 'the host, to the great satisfaction of his guests, delivered himself of a vigorous, instructive and entertaining philological medley. Discussion of this, and general conversation, were entertained until 11.40 p.m.' (Bodleian Library, Oxford, MS Eng. d.3529).

8–26 March 1965 Tolkien and Edith stay at the Hotel Miramar, Bourne-mouth. During the visit he probably meets Eileen Elgar again, and lends her *Smith of Wootton Major*.

8 March 1965 Rayner Unwin writes to Tolkien. If the index needs work, Tolkien should leave it for a while and 'concentrate first on the more modest proposal of making certain changes to the actual text and I am sure that by the time you are back at the end of March will be time enough for Houghton Mif-flin'. He will discuss the matter in detail with Austin Olney. Meanwhile, any minor changes that Tolkien can make to *The Hobbit* and *The Lord of the Rings* which would make new and copyrightable editions would be welcome, but 'please don't forget that now the text of *Pearl* is complete and *Gawain* virtually so, one small heave and we have another book ready for the press. If you could get it to us in a month or two we would catch this Christmas for publication' (Tolkien-George Allen & Unwin archive, HarperCollins). – The composer Donald Swann writes to Allen & Unwin. On his way home from Australia, he set six songs from *The Lord of the Rings* to music (**The Road Goes Ever On: A Song Cycle*), and now seeks formal permission to do so. If they or Tolkien would like to hear the songs, he would be pleased to play them. He would like Tolkien's advice on a few matters, in particular on the correct pronunciation of Elvish.

10 March 1965 Joy Hill replies to Donald Swann. Neither Tolkien nor Allen & Unwin object to his setting the songs. Joy Hill offers to forward a letter to Tolkien.

22 March 1965 Joy Hill writes to Tolkien, sending a copy of Donald Swann's letter. She has talked with Swann: he plans a cycle of five songs to be performed by a baritone, suitable for inclusion in a concert. If Tolkien agrees to the project, Allen & Unwin will make a financial agreement with Swann. He is eager to meet Tolkien, not only to play his compositions to him, but also to raise one or two points. He is willing to come to Oxford.

30 March 1965 Eileen Elgar writes to Tolkien. As he asked, she comments on *Smith of Wootton Major*, the typescript of which she will return to him by post tomorrow.

13 April 1965 Donald Swann writes to Joy Hill. He has to be in Oxford on the morning of 30 May. He would be glad if he and his wife could visit Tolkien in the afternoon. He asks if Tolkien has a piano.

14 April 1965 Rayner Unwin writes to Tolkien. He asks if he may call on him on 21 April at about 3.00 p.m. He has 'wind of some possible secretarial help which we might have a brief word about' (Tolkien-George Allen & Unwin archive, HarperCollins). He has heard from Donald Swann, who wonders if he could visit Tolkien in the afternoon of 30 May and play his song settings to him. Does Tolkien have a piano? To save Tolkien writing a letter, Rayner encloses a note which needs only two ticks by way of reply, and a stamped addressed envelope.

21 April 1965 Rayner Unwin possibly visits Tolkien in Oxford, unless the latter has already gone out of town (see following entry).

c. **23 April 1965** Tolkien is away from Oxford. It may be that he and Edith are in Bournemouth for a few days.

23 April 1965 Joy Hill, having discussed the matter with Tolkien, writes to Donald Swann. Tolkien will be delighted to meet him and hear his compositions. Although Tolkien does not have a piano, there is one at his daughter's house in Oxford, where it might be possible to meet. A date cannot be settled until Tolkien returns to Oxford. (Edith is prevented by arthritis from playing her piano, which she has given to Priscilla.)

27 April 1965 Alina Dadlez, Allen & Unwin, writes to Tolkien. She is sending four copies of a reprint of the Polish translation of *Farmer Giles of Ham*.

28 April 1965 Austin Olney writes to Rayner Unwin. He has heard that Ace Books of New York, believing that copyright in *The Lord of the Rings* has been lost in the United States, intend to publish an unauthorized paperback edition.

?May 1965 Ace Books publish an unauthorized edition of *The Fellowship of the Ring*.

?Early May 1965 W.H. Auden writes to Tolkien. He asks if it was not heretical to have, in the Orcs of Tolkien's mythology, an entire race that is irredeemably wicked.

6 May 1965 Austin Olney writes to Tolkien, explaining the Ace Books problem. He suggests that to ensure copyright with a new edition of *The Lord of the Rings* Tolkien should write a new introduction to each volume or, if he cannot manage this, W.H. Auden or someone else should be asked to do so. A complete index to all three volumes should be added to each volume. If Tolkien cannot deal with the index, he knows an American couple eager to do the work. He also suggests that Tolkien add paragraphs at the end of chapters where space is available.

11 May 1965 Tolkien replies to Austin Olney. He agrees to provide new material and revisions for *The Hobbit* and *The Lord of the Rings*. This will put great pressure on Tolkien at a time when he has no secretarial help, and other matters are put aside. – Tolkien fills in this date and the name of the recipient on a printed form reply to a letter of appreciation. This will not be sent, however, until 4 October 1965, when Tolkien discovers it in a pile of neglected papers.

12 May 1965 Tolkien replies to W.H. Auden. He is not a sufficient theologian to say whether his depiction of the Orcs is heretical, but points out that Frodo says that Orcs are not evil in origin. 'I was just sending into press a revision of my translation of *Gawain* together with one of *Pearl* when a desperate problem of U.S.A. copyright fell on me, and I must now devote all the time I have to produce a revision of both *The Lord of the Rings* and *The Hobbit* that can be copyrighted and, it is hoped, defeat the pirates' (*Letters*, p. 355).

13 May 1965 Joy Hill writes to Tolkien, asking if he has been able to find out if it is convenient to meet Donald Swann at Priscilla's house in the afternoon of 30 May.

14 May 1965 Tolkien talks with Joy Hill by telephone. He is still not sure about 30 May. She will send him a form letter to sign and return when he knows. – Rayner Unwin writes to Tolkien, urging him to provide Houghton Mifflin with the material they want as soon as possible. He encloses specimen pages in various typefaces for *Pearl* and *Sir Gawain*, and gives his personal choice. 'But we would willingly be influenced by your own feelings and alterations can of course be easily experimented with at this stage. Did you I wonder manage to complete the transcription of corrections of the later fits of *Gawain* during these last two or three weeks? We shall look forward to having the rest of this typescript and the brief prefatory remark as soon as you can' (Tolkien-George Allen & Unwin archive, HarperCollins).

?16 (received 17) May 1965 Tolkien writes to Joy Hill, returning her form letter. He can meet Donald Swann at Priscilla's house on 30 May at 3.00 p.m. But if Swann will meet him at the gate of Merton College at about 12.50 p.m., he can provide parking for his car and take him to the Eastgate Hotel (a few yards away) for lunch at 1.00 p.m. He draws a map for Swann, showing how to get to Priscilla's house.

17 May 1965 Joy Hill presumably telephones Donald Swann when she receives Tolkien's letter. She writes to Tolkien that Swann and his wife will be delighted to accept his invitation to lunch.

18 May 1965 Austin Olney writes to Tolkien. Houghton Mifflin are negotiating with two reputable reprint houses to licence paperback editions of Tolkien's works. He asks for the new material by July.

19 May 1965 Rayner Unwin writes to Tolkien. He returns *Smith of Wootton Major* which Tolkien has lent him, and wishes there was more like it. He wonders if anything 'equally alluring' is buried in Tolkien's papers. He urges him not to bury this one, 'but keep it right on the surface so that if the spirit moves you to write three or four others we might make a little collection of them' (Tolkien-George Allen & Unwin archive, HarperCollins).

20 May 1965 Tolkien writes to Rayner Unwin. He has nothing similar to *Smith of Wootton Major* among his papers.

> There is a lot of unfinished material there, but everything belongs definitely to the *Silmarillion* or all that world. To which I should now be in only a few days returning, if it were not for this infernal copyright business. I shall be sending you the remainder of the text of *Gawain* and my comments on specimen pages you sent me, to reach you I hope by Monday next. I cannot produce the prefatory note or the commentary until the revision of *The Lord of the Rings* is finished. I shall have to work hard to get it to Boston [Houghton Mifflin] by July 1. . . .
>
> P.S. I am now inserting in every note of acknowledgement to readers in U.S.A. a brief note informing them that *Ace Books* is a pirate, and asking them to inform others. [*Letters*, pp. 355–6]

21 May 1965 Tolkien writes to Michael George. He hopes that the translations of *Pearl* and *Sir Gawain* will be published before Christmas. They are primarily aimed at those ignorant of Middle English, 'but I may have room to include a few notes for "scholars" on words and text – since I have naturally made a good many minor discoveries in the course of translation'. He complains that 'the American copyright laws are full of holes and these rogues . . . have, or think they have, found one' (British Library MS Add. 71657).

25 May 1965 Tolkien writes to Rayner Unwin. 'I ran into some unexpected difficulties at the end of *Sir Gawain*, which I found had been less carefully revised than the rest. I am now within three stanzas of the end. . . .' He comments on the specimen pages and the possible problem of over-runs. 'I have therefore gone through the text and tried to make sure that no lines . . . will be of excessive length.' The roman numerals marking rhyme-groups in *Pearl* might be put in the left margin 'immediately before the Arabic stanza numeral. If that causes difficulty where both numerations increase . . . then I think we will abandon the Roman numerals altogether rather than disturb the equal distribution on the page. Each rhyme-group will be clearly marked by the black capital at the beginning.' He is

> not relishing the task of 're-editing' *The Lord of the Rings*. I think it will prove very difficult if not impossible to make any substantial changes in the general text. Volume I has now been gone through and the number of necessary or desirable corrections is very small. I am bound to say that my admiration for the tightness of the author's construction is somewhat increased. The poor fellow (who now seems to me only a remote friend) must have put a lot of work into it. I am hoping that the alteration of the introductions, considerable modifications of the appendices and the inclusion of an index may prove sufficient for the purpose.

He repeats that he is including a note that the Ace Books edition 'is piratical and issued without the consent of my publishers or myself and of course without remuneration to us' in all replies or acknowledgements to fan letters from America, and asks if Rayner thinks that this might be useful if done on a larger scale (Tolkien-George Allen & Unwin archive, HarperCollins; partly printed in *Letters*, p. 356). – Tolkien writes a note to Donald Swann, and sends it (with a covering letter) to Joy Hill to forward.

26 May 1965 Tolkien writes in his diary: 'Worked all day (save rest of 2 hrs in afternoon) at Gawain – am now on last stanza & bothered with *bot vnhap ne may hit*' (quoted in a note of diary entries written by Humphrey Carpenter, in the Tolkien Papers, Bodleian Library, Oxford). – Rayner Unwin, about to leave for the United States, writes to Tolkien. He will discuss the Ace Books matter with Houghton Mifflin during his visit. Tolkien should send the remainder of the *Sir Gawain* text and his comments to Ronald Eames at Allen & Unwin.

28 May 1965 Tolkien writes in his diary: 'I worked as much as I could all day save rest in afternoon at *bot vnhap ne may hit*. (Decided error was *non* for *man*). Went to bed v[ery] late' (Tolkien Papers, Bodleian Library, Oxford). (In the Tolkien-Gordon edition of *Sir Gawain and the Green Knight*, the full line reads: 'For non may hyden his harme, bot vnhap ne me hit'.)

30 May 1965 Donald Swann and his wife lunch with Tolkien, and probably Edith and Priscilla as well, at the Eastgate Hotel in Oxford. In the afternoon, they go to Priscilla's house, where Swann sings the six Tolkien poems he had set to music, accompanying himself on the piano. Tolkien approves five of the settings, but objects to the music for *Namárië*. He hums a Gregorian chant to show how he imagines the poem sung. Swann will rewrite the music, incorporating Tolkien's theme.

31 May 1965 Tolkien writes in his diary: 'Spent (or wasted) most of available time on *bot vnhap ne may hit*. . . . Went to bed ridiculously late' (Tolkien Papers, Bodleian Library, Oxford).

?Early June 1965 Donald Swann writes to Tolkien. He thanks him for lunch and for receiving himself and his wife. He asks some questions about the chant for *Namárië*. He and his partner Michael Flanders will be performing in Oxford in September. He offers to provide tickets for Tolkien, Edith, and Priscilla.

June–early July 1965 Houghton Mifflin sends several letters and cables to Tolkien asking when they may expect the promised material.

2 June 1965 Tolkien writes in his diary: 'Still working at *vnhap*' (Tolkien Papers, Bodleian Library, Oxford).

3–4 June 1965 Tolkien writes in his diary: 'Have at last finished *vnhap* & can now go on to [*The Lord of the Rings*]. . . . Sat up late finishing *vnhap*: it is now 3 a.m. Friday' (Tolkien Papers, Bodleian Library, Oxford).

7 June 1965 Tolkien replies to Donald Swann. 'I tried to make some notes on the "chant" which might assist you. But they are too elaborate (though reduced). I send them in case any items are either useful or interesting . . .' (Marion E. Wade Center, Wheaton College, Wheaton, Illinois). In response to the offer of tickets, he and Edith could make any day in the week 13–18 September. Although Edith usually avoids going out in the evening, she will break the rule if there are no early performances. Priscilla is not sure what she will be doing on those dates.

11 June 1965 Ronald Eames, Allen & Unwin, writes to Tolkien. He is sending revised specimen pages for *Sir Gawain* and *Pearl*. These incorporate the suggestions he made in his letter of 25 May.

c. 14 June 1965 Allen & Unwin consult with Tolkien, probably by telephone, about cover art for their 'U Books' edition of *The Hobbit*. He suggests that they use his drawing *Death of Smaug* (*Artist and Illustrator*, fig. 137), which he will look for among his papers.

14 June 1965 Joy Hill writes to Tolkien. She has introduced Donald Swann to a friend of hers, a music student with a baritone voice, called William Elvin (here spelled 'Elvine'). Donald Swann thinks his voice ideal. They will practice together and hope to let Tolkien hear the song cycle again. Swann wants to plan some concerts at which they will perform it. Allen & Unwin are looking forward to seeing the dragon picture when Tolkien has looked it out. – C.A. Furth writes to Tolkien. Allen & Unwin are now completing arrangements with Longmans for their edition of *The Hobbit*. They assume that Tolkien will accept the same royalty for the 'U Books' edition of *The Hobbit* as he receives for the paperback *Tree and Leaf* in the same series.

18 June 1965 Joy Hill writes to Tolkien. She has heard Donald Swann record a talk for a radio programme, *Home This Afternoon*. He gave *The Lord of the Rings* some good publicity, and sang and played one of his six songs.

19 June 1965 Tolkien writes to Joy Hill. He is constantly in touch with Swann. 'William Elvine' is 'a name of good omen!' He encloses 'a crude drawing (all I can find) of my attempt to catch a glimpse, beyond my skill of the death of Smaug. . . . It might help, inspire, imitate? an artist such as P[auline D[iana] B[aynes] to do something' (Tolkien-George Allen & Unwin archive, HarperCollins). – Tolkien writes to Ronald Eames, at least in draft (no final letter survives in the Tolkien-George Allen & Unwin archive). He sends the text of Fits II–IV of *Sir Gawain and the Green Knight* and approves the revised specimen pages. He was delayed by the American copyright problem and by the discovery that he had revised the later parts of *Sir Gawain* less carefully before they were typed. He has now corrected them as best he can. He would like the size of two initials to be increased, and asks if it would be possible to print them in a second colour.

21 June 1965 Joy Hill writes to Tolkien. St Edward's School, Oxford, have asked permission to mount a performance of one of his works. She asks how she should reply, and encloses a form response for Tolkien to complete.

23 June 1965 Encaenia. – Tolkien replies to C.A. Furth. He leaves the proposals for the paperback *Hobbit* in Allen & Unwin's hands, as they are 'better able to judge what is good for the book and its sales than I am'. Remembering what happened with the Puffin *Hobbit*, however, he is anxious that nothing similar should happen with the Longmans/Allen & Unwin edition. He suggests that a general direction be issued that no changes should be made other than those authorized by him.

> I have already and recently re-read *The Hobbit* in various forms down to a copy of the second edition, and have notes ready, but it is much simpler to indicate required corrections on a printed copy. The minor errors that still survive, or have later appeared, are very few. But since in effect a new [edition] (for U. Books) is being re-set, I think the time has come to make a few alterations (in 6 places) which I have prepared: their object is to correct a small discrepancy; to make the note on *Thrain*, which was still necessary in the Puffin version, unnecessary; and to bring *The Hobbit* in line with *The Lord of the Rings* where needed. The changes are in each case very small in extent. . . .
>
> The maps will, I suppose, be included in some way similar to that adopted in the Puffin [edition]. The proper place for the dwarf-chart of the Mountain [*Thror's Map*] is, of course, between the present pages 32, 33; but that is probably impossible in such an edition. The 'Wilderland Map' is desirable (but not essential, I think). I hope it can be better reproduced than in the 'Puffin'.

He thinks the loss of runes from the cover regrettable, as his fan mail proves that young readers like them. 'I should be pleased to supply some new material of similar sort to be included in a new cover, if that were acceptable to the designer.' Since this is to be a 'school' edition, he thinks that it should include a note on the spelling 'dwarves', and suggests wording for it.

> These very small alterations are all that is *necessary*, I think, though much more could be introduced with advantage. Those that I here refer to are insufficient for the purposes of Houghton Mifflin and the copyright business. What view do you take of a divergence of text between the English and American editions? Should the 'revisions' which I shall be sending to Houghton Mifflin before the end of July, be made with any reference to the present proposals for re-setting as an 'Unwin Book' – in which case they must be cut to a minimum – or in any other future edition by Allen & Unwin? . . .
>
> (I have now some secretarial assistance, but that is wholly occupied with the rush job on *The* [*Lord of the Rings*]). [Tolkien-George Allen & Unwin archive, HarperCollins]

– Ronald Eames writes to Tolkien. Allen & Unwin can now obtain costings for publishing the translations. They can make the two initials larger, and will consider the possibility of printing them in a second colour. The format of the 'U Books' *Hobbit* will not allow them to reproduce the whole of *Death of Smaug*.

28 June 1965 Ronald Eames writes to Tolkien. He has discussed the *Hobbit* cover design with Rayner Unwin, who agrees that it would be excellent to reproduce Tolkien's drawing of Smaug. It will leave no room on the front cover for runes, but they might find space on the back if Tolkien could let them have the material. (In the event, no runes will be included.) He asks for an explanatory sentence about the drawing to put on the back cover. – Rayner Unwin, who has returned from the USA, writes to Tolkien. He thinks that Longmans will do a decent job with their *Hobbit*, but he will pass on the gist of Tolkien's letter. He will send Tolkien a copy of Allen & Unwin's latest printing of *The Hobbit* in which he can mark any corrections or emendations necessary, and will let Tolkien see a proof of the new typesetting. He approves Tolkien's other suggestions, including the note on the spelling of *dwarves*.

> I would have thought that the English and American editions of *The Hobbit* ought to be the same and although I realise you will be making certain changes in addition to the half dozen necessary corrections for the benefit of Houghton Mifflin I think that we had better wait and incorporate the Houghton Mifflin changes in our new edition together with Longmans. . . . Surely, another half dozen *un*necessary corrections added to the half dozen necessary ones would be sufficient both for Houghton Mifflin's copyright purposes and for us? [Tolkien-George Allen & Unwin archive, HarperCollins]

30 June 1965 Joy Hill writes to Tolkien. She repeats her query about the St Edward's School proposal.

?July 1965 Ace Books publish unauthorized editions of *The Two Towers* and *The Return of the King*.

c. 6–16 July 1965 Tolkien stays at the Hotel Miramar, Bournemouth.

9 July 1965 Tolkien writes to Joy Hill. He has

> been grievously pressed. I was in fact obliged to break off and come away last week as I felt on edge: I could not sleep or think or force myself to attempt to cope.
>
> A change of scene and a few days somnolent idleness have I think mended matters, and I am now getting on again. My secretary interpreted my orders very literally, and did not send your letter, or Mr Rayner's on, though I thought I had exempted anything from A. and U. from being temporarily impounded, until yesterday. [Tolkien-George Allen & Unwin archive, HarperCollins]

He finds projects such as that suggested by St Edward's School annoying and distressing; and though he has a soft heart, he thinks that the answer had better be No. He sends Joy a neglected letter from a schoolmaster who (apparently) wants to adapt one of Tolkien's works for the stage. Tolkien thinks that Allen & Unwin would be better than he at pouring cold water on the project.

14 July 1965 Rayner Unwin writes to Tolkien. In Joy Hill's absence he has dealt with both letters about dramatizations, and would willingly deal with any other letters Tolkien sends to him with the briefest scribble in the margin to indicate his wishes.

Mid-July 1965 Zillah Sherring writes to Tolkien. She has bought a second-hand copy of *The Fifth Book of Thucydides* with some strange inscriptions written in it and Tolkien's name on the flyleaf. She asks if he is responsible for the inscriptions, and sends a transcript of the longest.

16 July 1965 Baillie Knapheis (see *Christopher Tolkien), now Tolkien's secretary, writes to Rayner Unwin, sending a copy of a letter written by Nan C. Scott of Kansas to Tolkien, and a letter to Scott from Donald A. Wollheim of Ace Books. When Scott had received a letter from Tolkien in which he complained about the Ace piracy, she wrote to her local bookshop objecting to their selling the Ace edition. The shop sent her letter to Ace Books, and she received a letter from Donald Wollheim. In this, dated 2 July 1965, Wollheim declares that Tolkien's books are in the public domain in the USA and blames Houghton Mifflin for that fact. Although Ace Books, he says, have done nothing illegal or illicit, they would be willing to offer Tolkien some sort of royalty or honorarium if he were to contact them. Wollheim suggests that as Nan Scott is in contact with Tolkien, she should ask him to contact Ace Books.

20 July 1965 Tolkien replies to Zillah Sherring. He confirms that the copy of *The Fifth Book of Thucydides* had once belonged to him. The inscriptions are in Gothic, 'or what I thought was Gothic or might be' (*Letters*, p. 357). He explains his early interest in the language, translates the inscription, and comments on his errors.

21 July 1965 Tolkien writes to Nan C. Scott. He expresses his gratitude for the information she has sent and for her campaign against the Ace Books edition. 'I have been taken off all my other work and driven nearly over the edge by the attempt to get an *authorized* paperback by Ballantine Books produced as soon as possible' (*Letters*, p. 273). – Rayner Unwin sends Austin Olney, Houghton Mifflin, Tolkien's new Foreword for *The Fellowship of the Ring*. Tolkien has promised to send corrections for that volume by the end of the week.

25 July 1965 Tolkien sends Houghton Mifflin the 'Note on the Shire Records' to be placed at the end of the Prologue of *The Lord of the Rings*.

Late July 1965 W.H. Auden writes to Tolkien. He asks him to contribute to a *Festschrift* for Nevill Coghill on his retirement, and if Tolkien has heard of the forming of a 'New York Tolkien Society' (*Fandom).

28 July 1965 Tolkien writes to Austin Olney. He sends the 'proposed corrections, additions, alterations' required for *The Fellowship of the Ring* and apologizes for the delay.

> I ran into some difficulties with the maps. I have finally decided, where this is possible and does not damage the story, to take the *maps* as 'correct' and adjust the narrative. I do not suppose that it is intended or possible to correct the *maps* at this stage.
>
> The *small map* 'Part of the Shire' is most at fault and much needs correction (and some additions), and has caused a number of questions to be asked. The chief fault is that the Ferry at Bucklebury and so Brandy Hall and Crickhollow have shifted about 3 miles too far north (about 4 mm.). This cannot be altered at this time, but it is unfortunate that Brandy Hall clearly on the river-bank is placed so that the main road runs in front of it instead of behind. There is also no trace of the wood described at top of p. 99 [2004 edn., p. 90]. I have had simply to disregard these map-errors. If it were possible to make the small minimal changes (marked in green) it would be a great improvement, but perhaps unnecessary for most readers? [Tolkien-George Allen & Unwin archive, HarperCollins; partly printed in *Letters*, p. 358]

31 July 1965 Tolkien writes to Austin Olney, sending corrections for *The Two Towers* and three additions or alterations.

August 1965 While revising *The Lord of the Rings* Tolkien looks at and partly revises the amanuensis typescript of *The Heirs of Elendil*, made *c.* 1959. He adds a section expanding the account of events leading to the kin-strife in Gondor. In a slightly abridged form, this will appear in Appendix A in the Ballantine Books edition (1965) and the Allen & Unwin second edition (1966). He also looks at the elven genealogies he made in 1959, and writes a note that the best solution to the problem of Gil-galad's parentage is to make him the son of Orodreth. Probably he also writes a long note to elucidate the passage in *The Two Towers* in which Faramir mentions Gandalf's several names (bk. IV, ch. 5). He finds the typescript of *The New Shadow*, abandoned several years before, and sits up until 4.00 a.m. reading and thinking about it.

2 August 1965 Austin Olney writes to Tolkien. Ballantine Books have forestalled an unauthorized edition of *The Hobbit* by quickly producing their own (unrevised) paperback. Olney sends a copy of the cover, with art by Barbara Remington. He is anxiously awaiting the rest of the revisions for *The Lord of the Rings*.

3 August 1965 Tolkien writes to the Librarian at Marquette University about the *Lord of the Rings* papers he sold to them.

> I am now engaged in a revision of *The Lord of the Rings* and in the process I have been unable to find some of the material that I wish to refer to. I believe that the papers I sent you have been sorted and arranged. It would be a great courtesy on your part if you could in the first instance let me know briefly what they are. Ultimately I should like to have photostatic copies of items that I need urgently. I am especially anxious, for example, to find a copy of an elaborate plan drawn up in columns, recording the place and actions of each major character on every day during the period occupied by the story. [Special Collections and University Archives, John P. Raynor, S.J., Library, Marquette University]

According to his recollection, Marquette were to have all written or typewritten material, but not pictorial matter. He has found more written matter which he thinks should go to them, and will look into this when he has completed his revision.

4 August 1965 Tolkien writes to W.H. Auden. He is 'grieved' that he has nothing to contribute to the Nevill Coghill *Festschrift*, but quotes a clerihew he had once written about him. He has heard about the New York Tolkien Society. 'Real lunatics don't join them, I think. But still such things fill me too with alarm and despondency' (*Letters*, p. 359).

***c.* 6–9 August 1965** Tolkien receives the cover of the Ballantine Books *Hobbit* sent by Austin Olney, and writes a short note to Olney expressing his opinion of it. He will summarize the note in a letter to Rayner Unwin on 12 September:

> I think the cover ugly; but I recognize that a main object of a paperback cover is to attract purchasers, and I suppose that you are better judges of what is attractive in USA than I am. I therefore will not enter into a debate about taste – (meaning though I did not say so: horrible colours and foul lettering) – but I must ask this about the vignette: what has it got to do with the story? Where is this place? Why a lion and emus? And what is the thing in the foreground with pink bulbs? I do not understand how anybody who has read the tale (I hope you are one) could think such a picture would please the author. [*Letters*, p. 362]

6 August 1965 Tolkien replies to a correspondent. 'The goodness of the West and the badness of the East has no modern reference. The concept came about through the necessities of narrative' (Tolkien-George Allen & Unwin archive, HarperCollins). C.S. Lewis's references to *Numinor* derive from hearing Tolkien read his works.

13 August 1965 Austin Olney writes to Rayner Unwin. He has received Tolkien's letter about the cover art for the Ballantine Books *Hobbit*. Unlike Tolkien, everyone in the Houghton Mifflin office approves of it.

16 August 1965 An unrevised paperback edition of *The Hobbit* is published by Ballantine Books.

18 August 1965 Austin Olney writes to Tolkien. It is too late to change the maps in the Ballantine Books edition of *The Lord of the Rings*, as they have been prepared in advance. Houghton Mifflin are still awaiting the textual changes for *The Return of the King*. The first two volumes are already set in page form. As soon as they receive the index from Tolkien, they will begin to replace the hardcover page references with those for the paperback.

19 August 1965 Tolkien writes to Rayner Unwin, enclosing two letters. He received one, from the Library of Congress, 'this morning', concerning registration of *The Lord of the Rings* for copyright. 'Should not the works previously published in the United States have already been entered in Library of Congress?' His secretary discovered the second letter, neglected, asking permission to make and sell small bronze figures of characters from (presumably) *The Lord of the Rings*. The writer's 'feeling of moral obligation rightly prompted him to seek my permission, but he appears to ask also for my blessing (unrecompensed)' (Tolkien-George Allen & Unwin archive, HarperCollins).

24 August 1965 Tolkien writes to Rayner Unwin, sending the revised and corrected *Hobbit* text.

> I have (I hope) resisted the inclination to 'improve' *The Hobbit* – except for removing the 'author-to-reader' asides, in some places: very irritating to intelligent children (as some have said). There are some corrections due to the actual errors and discrepancies in the tale itself; some that try to make things clearer. But since in order to spot these things – including printer's errors that still survive! – one has to read the whole with line-to-line care, it seemed to me a pity not to get rid of a few happy-go-lucky passages that are quite out of joint. *The Hobbit* is taken as a prologue to *The* [*Lord of the Rings*] and though no one expects consistency between the two to be exact, it is a pity that some passages in *The* [*Hobbit*] should be completely impossible in *The* [*Lord of the Rings*]. I hope you will agree, for instance, that the alterations in Ch. II provide that the journey as far as the first troll-adventure though suitably rapid and understated now could be a quick glance at the same country that is described in the long work. [Tolkien-George Allen & Unwin archive, HarperCollins]

25 August 1965 Rayner Unwin writes to Tolkien. He is passing the corrected *Hobbit* to Allen & Unwin's printers immediately, and sending a duplicate to Houghton Mifflin. He assumes that the Library of Congress request is a result of either Houghton Mifflin or Ballantine Books filing new editions. He is returning the document to Tolkien so that he can complete it. – Baillie Knapheis writes on Tolkien's behalf to the Director of Libraries at Marquette University, acknowledging receipt of an inventory of their Tolkien manuscripts.

26 August 1965 Tolkien writes to Paula Iley, a young friend of the Tolkien family, who has sent him some of her poems to read. Tolkien writes a five-page commentary on them, emphasizing the importance of the technical aspects of verse. – Alina Dadlez writes to Tolkien. She is sending him five copies of *The Hobbit* in Spanish, published by Compania General Fabril Editora of Buenos Aires. The same company will publish *The Lord of the Rings*.

29 August 1965 Betty Ballantine of Ballantine Books sends Tolkien photographic copies of two articles in American papers about the Ace Books affair.

31 August 1965 Tolkien sends the revisions of *The Return of the King* to Houghton Mifflin by airmail.

Early September 1965 Dick Plotz, 'Thain' of the Tolkien Society of America, writes to Tolkien. He tells Tolkien of the founding of the Society and its activities, and asks Tolkien to become a member. He asks various questions, including C.S. Lewis's use of *Numinor*.

?1–?7 September 1965 Tolkien spends seven days in Ireland, mainly in the extreme west of the country. He travels for the first time by air, flying from Birmingham to Dublin. He is accompanied by his son Christopher, who drives him across Ireland to Galway.

1 September 1965 Rayner Unwin writes to Tolkien. Betty Ballantine, during a visit to Allen & Unwin, told him that copies of the Ace Books edition have been found on sale in Canada, where Tolkien's books are certainly protected by copyright. Allen & Unwin are taking this up with their Canadian agents and hope to have copies seized, with attendant publicity. To enable Allen & Unwin to do this, Rayner asks Tolkien to sign a document clarifying their position. In addition, as a further step against Ace, Allen & Unwin will license Ballantine Books to sell their edition in Canada until the end of 1966.

7 September 1965 Austin Olney writes to Tolkien, acknowledging receipt of corrections and alterations to both *The Hobbit* and *The Return of the King*, and the index for the latter. He is sending them immediately to Ballantine Books.

11 September 1965 Tolkien writes to Rayner Unwin, enclosing the document sent him on 1 September, now with his signature. He also sends photographic copies of the articles sent to him by Betty Ballantine. He finds one of them of interest ('The War over Middle-earth' by Joseph Haas, *Chicago Daily News*, 7 August 1965, p. 7), since it quotes statements from Donald Wollheim, which it would appear have been made publicly elsewhere, and have succeeded in confusing the issue. I do not much like being regarded as a dear old septuagenarian whose pure creative soul has been darkened and shocked by becoming involved in a dog-fight; and even so I cannot see what injustice is done to the dear old thing, if his watch-dog offers battle when a pariah tries to rob his larder. But I do not think Mr. Joseph Haas would have taken this line, if he had not believed the Wollheim statement that I was offered some remuneration *before* publication of the paperback was put in hand.

I do not believe that any such letter was ever written to me. I certainly never received one. . . . I should think that in any legal proceedings the doubt that could be cast on the veracity of this statement might assist in showing Ace Books to be in fact pariahs who had originally no intention of doing more than purloin something that seemed to be unguarded.

After commenting about Houghton Mifflin's part in the affair, he makes the telling point that when Donald Wollheim wrote to Nan C. Scott on 2 July, he made no mention of having offered Tolkien an 'honorarium' before publication. 'That they did not do so, seems to me proof that they never wrote to me. . . . The lying embroidery about an unanswered offer is a counter to the discovery that many people are not going to be appeased by talk of legalities and the "public domain".' He asks Rayner to return the articles, as he wants to send them to a Society which had asked for facts about "this dispute"' (Tolkien-George Allen & Unwin archive, HarperCollins).

?11 or 12 September 1965 Betty Ballantine telephones Tolkien. They have a long conversation, much of it apparently about the cover of the Ballantine Books *Hobbit*. In a letter to Rayner on 12 September Tolkien will write that she seemed impermeable to his objections: 'I should judge that all she wanted was that I should recant, be a good boy and react favourably', and when he repeated his objections 'her voice rose several tones and she cried: "But the man hadn't TIME to read the book!"' . . . With regard to the pink bulbs she said as if to one of complete obtusity: "they are meant to suggest a Christmas tree"' (*Letters*, p. 363).

12 September 1965 Tolkien replies to Dick Plotz. He found his letter 'amid a mountain of mail' on his return from Ireland. He feels it would not be suitable for him to

become a 'member' of a society inspired by liking for my works and devoted (I suppose) to study and criticism of them, as at least part of their activities.

I should, however, be pleased to be associated with you in some informal capacity. I should, for instance, be willing to offer any advice that you wished to seek, or provide information not yet in print – always with the proviso (especially with regard to 'information') that the plea: *Engaged on the matter of the Eldar and of Númenor* [i.e. *The Silmarillion*]:

would be accepted without offence as an adequate excuse for an inadequate answer to enquiries.

He thinks it a mistake for members of the Tolkien Society of America to take the names of characters in the story, and suggests that instead that they might take the title of '"Member for Some-place-in-the-Shire", or in Bree' and offers to provide additional Shire place-names. He explains the problems he faces in writing the 'Silmarillion', and answers Plotz's query about C.S. Lewis. He mentions that he is 'in an interim between part-time secretaries for a few days' (*Letters*, pp. 359, 360, 362). – Tolkien writes to Rayner Unwin, expressing his opinion of the cover of the Ballantine edition of *The Hobbit* and giving an account of his telephone conversation with Mrs Ballantine.

> I begin to feel that I am shut up in a madhouse. Perhaps with more experience you know of some way out of the lunatic labyrinth. I want to finish off *Gawain* and *Pearl*, and get on with the *Silmarillion* and feel that I cannot deal with H[oughton] M[ifflin] or Ballantine Books any more. Could you suggest that I am now going into purdah (to commune with my creative soul), the veil of which only you have the authority to lift – if you think fit? [*Letters*, p. 363]

14 September 1965 Tolkien writes to Donald Swann, thanking him for sending tickets to the performance on 18 September. As Priscilla will be away at that time, Tolkien has asked Dr Havard to go with Edith and himself. – Rayner Unwin writes to Tolkien. He feels guilty that Tolkien has 'been drawn into these aggravating copyright matters to such an extent and now that you have done everything that we have all been asking you to do I think that you can reasonably say that your part of the innings is closed.' He will tell Houghton Mifflin that all queries must be funnelled through Allen & Unwin in the future.

> I will weed them out and if there is anything that simply must have your attention, I will come to you with it, but otherwise I will do my best to fend off. It is far more important for us all that you should have a clear run to get on with *Gawain* and *Pearl* and then *The Silmarillion*. In this connection any correspondence either from fans or anyone else connected with the copyright business that you get and want to pass on we will take over and answer.

He will ask Houghton Mifflin to persuade Ballantine Books 'to get someone who has at least read the books to sketch out some alternative cover designs for future printings which I will ask to have submitted here and will bring for you when I next call' (Tolkien-George Allen & Unwin archive, HarperCollins). *See note.* He has written to Mr. Joseph Haas to set the record straight.

16 September 1965 Tolkien writes to his grandson Michael George. But for the Ace Books problem, *Sir Gawain* and *Pearl* by now would be reaching proof stage. He has just finished all that he needs to do to deal with Ace Books, and after a brief respite will return to his translations. He comments on his 'holiday (or high-speed raid) in Ireland' at the beginning of September. He has 'a good many friends' there, 'and am treated as sort of Irish-by-adoption, sealed by the possession of a Dublin degree' (British Library MS Add. 71657).

18 September 1965 Tolkien and Edith, accompanied by R.E. Havard, attend a performance of Donald Swann and Michael Flanders' *At the Drop of Another Hat* at the New Theatre, Oxford. Afterwards, they visit the performers backstage.

21 September 1965 Rayner Unwin writes to Tolkien. He now has all of the material for the revised *Hobbit*, and both Allen & Unwin and Longmans can proceed with their editions. They will replace the first blurb on the 'U Books' cover with one that Rayner has drafted and Tolkien approved. Rayner asks if there is any chance of Tolkien finishing *Sir Gawain* and *Pearl*. – Joy Hill writes to Tolkien, sending a batch of answered fan mail. She has heard no more from the film producer who was in touch with Tolkien and Allen & Unwin.

29 September 1965 A young physicist attending a conference in Oxford visits Tolkien, and tells him that the University of California at Berkeley has boycotted all Ace Books productions.

29–30 September 1965 Tolkien writes to Rayner Unwin. He encloses a 'troublesome letter' from the author of a projected fantasy of 100,000 words who has asked for his opinion, and asks Rayner to deal with it (Tolkien-George Allen & Unwin archive, HarperCollins). He encloses a letter from Clyde S. Kilby about Ace Books, and the Haas article. He suggests that Rayner inform Kilby of the true facts.

30 September 1965 Rayner Unwin writes to Tolkien, summarizing an agreement for using the Longmans typesetting of *The Hobbit* also for the 'U Books' edition. He asks Tolkien to sign a document agreeing to a scale of royalties.

October 1965 The revised edition of *The Lord of the Rings* is published in three paperback volumes by Ballantine Books. – *Winter's Tales for Children I*, including two poems by Tolkien, *Once upon a Time and *The Dragon's Visit* (revised), is published by Macmillan, London. An American edition will also be published in 1965 by St Martin's Press, New York.

4 October 1965 Tolkien writes to Rayner Unwin, returning the signed agreement. – While trying to clear up papers before going away, Tolkien finds a reply to a fan letter, dated 11 May 1965 but never sent. He adds a manuscript apology and explanation to the letter before posting it.

5 October 1965 Rayner Unwin writes to Tolkien. He encloses the outside cover of a Het Spectrum catalogue announcing a paperback edition of the Dutch translation of *The Lord of the Rings*.

c. **5–15 October** Tolkien is away from Oxford, possibly in Bournemouth. He develops a poisoned left arm, which is treated with penicillin. It is better by the time he returns home to find a heap of letters awaiting him.

20 October 1965 Tolkien replies to a letter from Clyde S. Kilby, who has sent a copy of 'The Candy Covered Copyright' by David Dempsey (*Saturday Review*, 2 October 1965). Tolkien has received and read a copy of *Light on C.S. Lewis* (1965), ed. Jocelyn Gibb.

25 October 1965 Rayner Unwin writes to Tolkien, forwarding a letter 'which is one of a constant stream of fan mail that we have been blindly forwarding to you. I thought it worth asking whether you would like us, in order to relieve some of the pressure on you, to try to deal with some of this mail rather than forward it automatically' (Tolkien-George Allen & Unwin archive, HarperCollins); in fact, Allen & Unwin are already answering some of Tolkien's fan mail, as shown by Joy Hill's letter of 21 September. Rayner has heard that Maurice Sendak, whom Houghton Mifflin have proposed to illustrate *The Hobbit*, has called the Ballantine *Lord of the Rings* covers 'atrocious'.

30 October 1965 Tolkien replies to a letter from Michael George. He has decided not to complicate matters for his grandson by sending him any of Tolkien's notes for *Beowulf*, *Sir Gawain and the Green Knight*, or *Pearl* before Michael George has his final examinations. 'But for the piracy campaign, my translations of G[awain] and P[earl] might have been out this Christmas. . . .' He thinks that he and Edith are unlikely to move from Oxford:

> Anywhere in sight of the sea proves too vastly expensive, while the service problem (our chief trouble) is as bad or worse than here. I am not 'rolling in gold', but by continuing to work I am (so far) continuing to have an income about the same as a professor-in-cathedra, which leaves me with a margin above my needs nowadays. If I had not had singular good fortune with my 'unprofessional' work, I should now be eking out a penurious existence on a perishable annuity of not 'half-pay' but more like ¼ pay. [*Letters*, p. 363]

His 'campaign' in the USA has gone well. Negative publicity about Ace Books has assisted sales of the authorized paperback of *The Lord of the Rings*. – Tolkien replies to a letter from J.L.N. O'Loughlin. He has read article by O'Loughlin, which he finds plausible, but does not have time to comment on it in detail. (This may be a reference to an introduction or essay in *Odham's Dictionary of the English Language*, ed. A.H. Smith and J.L.N. O'Loughlin (1965).)

2 November 1965 Rayner Unwin writes to Tolkien. Houghton Mifflin have heard that an American bookshop has been extracting an unofficial royalty from purchasers of the Ace Books edition and will send Tolkien the money thus collected.

3 November 1965 Alina Dadlez sends Tolkien copies of Het Spectrum's one-volume hardback edition of the Dutch *Lord of the Rings*, and of the three-volume paperback edition under their 'Prisma' imprint.

6 November 1965 Tolkien writes to Rayner Unwin. He is glad to hear that the Ballantine Books *Lord of the Rings* is doing well. He would like to see copies 'and observe what Ballantine Books have made of the "corrections and additions". I made these as clear as I could, but they would require careful handling.' He accepts Rayner's offer to deal with fan mail and send him only those letters that need his attention. 'I have given fan mail special attention in the last few months, since I have used the replies to letters of all sorts as a means for disseminating a note on Ace Books. With some widespread effect. But there is no need for that any longer, I think.' He encloses two letters he has received, one without name or address, and the other talking in 'a windy way about films and television', which he has acknowledged and said that he was sending it to Allen & Unwin (Tolkien-George Allen & Unwin archive, Harper-Collins).

8 November 1965 Tolkien writes to Alina Dadlez at Allen & Unwin. He likes Cor Blok's cover designs for the Dutch editions, and is pleased that the text has been corrected in places, though he has not had the time to examine it carefully. He mentions only the correcting of the translation of *Golden Perch*. He wonders how the Dutch paperback price compares with the American. – Tolkien writes to Rayner Unwin. In regard to *Sir Gawain and the Green Knight* and *Pearl*,

> I am doing what I can [with these] in what now seem very short days. (What I need is domestic rather than secretarial assistance!) It was rather disastrous that I had to put them aside, while I had them fully in mind. The work on the 'revision' of *The Lord of the Rings* took me clean away, and now I find work on anything else tiresome.
>
> I am finding the selection of notes, and compressing them; and the introduction difficult. Too much to say, and not sure of my target. The main target is, of course, the general reader of literary bent with no knowledge of Middle English; but it cannot be doubted that the book will be read by students, and by academic folk of 'English Departments'. Some of the latter have their pistols loose in the holsters.
>
> I have, of course, had to do an enormous amount of editorial work, unshown, in order to arrive at a version; and I have, I think, made important discoveries with regard to certain words, and some passages. . . . The exposition of these points, of course, must await articles in the academic journals; but in the meanwhile I think it desirable to indicate to those who possess the original texts where and how my readings differ from the received.

He asks how much space he will be allowed in addition to that for the texts, and if it would be possible to include a stanza from each poem in the original Middle English, which would help him 'make clearer and shorter any remarks on the relationship of the version to the original in style, language and metre etc. I shall need to make a few alterations in the texts as sent in, especially in the First Fit of *Gawain*, which was over hasty' (Tolkien-George Allen & Unwin archive, HarperCollins; partly printed in *Letters*, p. 364).

11 November 1965 Rayner Unwin writes to Tolkien. He is sending proofs of the Longmans edition of *The Hobbit* with Tolkien's revisions. This is the same setting of the text which Allen & Unwin will be using for their 'U Books' paperback, with different preliminaries and cover. As a result of the corrections Tolkien has made, the old explanatory note is no longer necessary, which leaves a blank page. Should the note Tolkien wrote about the spelling 'dwarves' for the Longmans edition be placed on this page? Rayner suggests wording to describe Tolkien's cover art, *Death of Smaug*. Does Tolkien approve, and can he date the drawing?

12 November 1965 Rayner Unwin writes to Tolkien. He hopes that despite having to look at proofs of *The Hobbit*, Tolkien will soon finish *Sir Gawain* and *Pearl*, and be free soon to return to *The Silmarillion*.

19 November 1965 Clyde S. Kilby writes to Tolkien, offering to come to Oxford to help him, in any way possible, with *The Silmarillion*. – In the evening, Tolkien attends a dinner of The Society hosted by John Bryson at Balliol College. Ten members are present, now including Christopher Tolkien as well. Bryson speaks on Swinburne and the Old Mortality Society, illustrated with photographs of the original members and a copy of its rare *Undergraduate Papers* (1857–8).

Late November and early December 1965 On 18 December Tolkien will write of this period to Clyde S. Kilby:

> When your letter [of 19 November] came to me I was rather burdened and distracted. My wife's health for more than a month has given me much anxiety (it necessitated my going twice to the South coast in the autumn with much loss of time, but became worse with the early onset of winter). A competent part-time secretary after giving me much assistance with Ballantine business, departed. And I was suddenly presented with the necessity of revising and correcting proofs of *The Hobbit* for new editions. [Marion E. Wade Center, Wheaton College, Wheaton, Illinois]

30 November 1965 Joy Hill writes to Tolkien, with news about Donald Swann. Sir Thomas Armstrong, Principal of Royal Academy of Music, approves of William Elvin.

1 December 1965 Tolkien writes to Joy Hill. He used to know Sir Thomas Armstrong well, and sometimes meets him still (in gatherings of The Society). He thanks Joy for dealing with his fan mail. – Tolkien replies to a letter from Peter H. Salus of Queen's College. He hopes in due course to replace the indices in the Ballantine Books *Lord of the Rings* with more complete versions giving etymological information. Only he can do this, since it requires, among other things, a deep knowledge of the Elvish languages; but he is too busy at present to put that information in order for the general public.

2 December 1965 Alina Dadlez writes to Tolkien. She is sending him a presentation copy of the Japanese *Hobbit* published by Iwanami Shoten, with graceful inscriptions in English and Japanese by the translator and the illustrator. – Rayner Unwin writes to Tolkien. Longmans have sent the drawing for their *Hobbit* cover. He asks Tolkien to draft two lines of runes to be included, possibly saying: 'This school book edition is published by Longmans Green and Company'.

6 December 1965 Tolkien writes to Rayner Unwin, returning the Longmans drawing with suggestions for runes. He queries the apparent omission of both maps, and points out that if *Thror's Map* is omitted, the words in the text 'Look at the map at the beginning of the book' are meaningless. The letter is signed for him by 'P.M.J.', i.e. Phyllis M. Jenkinson, who by now is his secretary. She will remain Tolkien's secretary until he moves to Poole in July 1968. Miss Jenkinson had previously spent eleven years assisting Lord David Cecil. – Tolkien replies to a letter from G.S. Rigby. There is a lot of theology included in *The Lord of the Rings*.

7 December 1965 Alina Dadlez writes to Tolkien with the price of the Dutch paperback *Lord of the Rings*.

9 December 1965 Tolkien writes to thank William McCullam of Ohio, who has sent him a 'royalty' for the Ace Books *Lord of the Rings*. – Tolkien writes to Jane Dixon of Ohio, who has sent him a copy of the *Saturday Review* article about the Ace Books affair. He thanks her for efforts on his behalf, and reassures her that neither he nor his publishers have any intention of allowing Walt Disney to make a film of his works. – Tolkien replies to a letter from a Miss Jaworski. He is not interested in drama and does not want his work dramatized. – Tolkien replies to a reader in New Jersey. He is interested in her comments on the climax of *The Lord of the Rings*. He apologizes for a short reply: 'If I answered all the letters I receive as they deserved, I should write nothing else' (Special Collections and University Archives, John P. Raynor, S.J., Library, Marquette University).

10 December 1965 Tolkien writes to Rayner Unwin, returning the proofs and printer's copy of the proposed 'U Books' and Longmans editions of *The Hobbit*. 'I think this revision (in its way) important and I was unwilling to release the stuff till I had done what I could. As far as I am concerned, it is now "go ahead" – except in one point: The "blurb". In so far as my "imprimatur" is required or desired, I can only withhold it. I can think of only one just adjective: fatuous' (Tolkien-George Allen & Unwin archive, HarperCollins). He encloses his replies to the printer's queries.

13 December 1965 Rayner Unwin writes to Tolkien. He sends for Tolkien's consideration a draft blurb for the Allen & Unwin hardback edition of *The Hobbit* which they will have to reprint soon, with an increase in the price.

15 December 1965 Tolkien writes to Rayner Unwin. There had not been much to correct in *The Hobbit*, but he made a few further alterations, devised to fit available space. He agrees that there is no longer any need to include the note that explained the change in Bilbo's story, and the two Thrains, but the space could well be used for notes answering questions most often asked by readers. I have devised a page, which I enclose for you to make use of, if you wish. It was arranged to provide some runic matter for the boys [i.e. young male readers who like runes], if the Map was not included in the paperback. But it will suit any edition that includes the Map, if the last part (marked off by red brackets) is omitted. The information provided should forestall letters asking for a full alphabet of runes. It should also make the map more intelligible, since the marking of the compass point in runes, and with East at the top has puzzled young readers. (Incidentally the Map, though accurate enough, would be more useful if the position of the ruined bridge at the beginning of the first great bend in the river was indicated by \\, as I think I have shown in pencil on the map in the printer's copy.).

He cannot remember exactly when he made the sketch *Death of Smaug*, but it was probably *c.* 1936. He comments at considerable length and in detail on the proposed 'blurb' for the 'U Books' edition. He does not want to hurt the feelings of the writer, but hopes that Rayner will agree that 'this will not do. Apart from its unfortunate style, it misrepresents the story, and the way in which it is presented.' He likes Rayner's blurb for the hardback received that morning, and asks if it could be used also on the paperback. He forgot to return the six pages of preliminaries for the Longmans edition, which he now encloses. He asks Rayner to thank Miss Dadlez for sending a presentation copy of the Japanese *Hobbit*. He has only just had time to look through it. He finds the pictures 'in many ways astonishing' (Tolkien–George Allen & Unwin archive, Harper-Collins; partly printed in *Letters*, p. 365). He asks Rayner to send a set of the de luxe *Lord of the Rings* in the Pauline Baynes box to Hugh Brogan, a fan since he was a small boy and now a don at St John's College, Cambridge. He sends Rayner his best wishes for Christmas and the New Year, and asks him to mark the New Year by dropping 'Professor' and using the less formal 'Tolkien'.

17 December 1965 Donald A. Wollheim writes to Tolkien. He asserts that Ace Books have no legal obligation to pay Tolkien anything, but if Tolkien would communicate with them directly, they will inform him what royalties they are prepared to pay. If he is unable to accept such royalties because of a commitment to another publisher, they are willing to pay full royalties to establish an annual science-fantasy award, to be known as the Tolkien Award, with the Science Fiction Writers of America acting as judges. (This is clearly in response to criticism of the Ace Books edition in 'The Tolkien Affair: An Editorial', *SFWA* [Science Fiction Writers of America] *Bulletin* 1, no. 3 (November 1965).)

18 December 1965 Tolkien replies to Clyde S. Kilby. He is overwhelmed by Kilby's offer. He explains his uncertainties about *The Silmarillion*. He has been writing it since 1916–17 and it 'is now in a confused state having been altered, enlarged, and worked at, at intervals between then and now. If I had the assistance of a scholar at once sympathetic and yet critical, such as yourself, I feel I might make some of it publishable. It needs the actual *presence* of a friend and adviser at one's side, which is just what you offer.' He hopes to be able to return to it soon. He would not be able to offer Kilby lodging in Oxford but Kilby could have access to all the material and Tolkien would be able to 'benefit by your opinion and assistance, specially with regard to the main problem: in what mode to present it. Discussion would be (for me) great encouragement and help' (Marion E. Wade Center, Wheaton College, Wheaton, Illinois; partly printed in *Letters*, p. 366).

24 December 1965 Tolkien receives Donald A. Wollheim's letter.

27 December 1965 W.H. Auden and Peter H. Salus attend a meeting of the New York Tolkien Society the previous evening. During this meeting, according to a report in the *New Yorker* ('The Elvish Mode', 15 January 1966, pp. 24–5), Auden comments that Tolkien lives in 'a hideous house – I can't tell you how awful it is – with hideous pictures on the walls'.

28 December 1965 W.H. Auden writes to Tolkien. He has agreed to produce, together with Peter H. Salus, a short book on Tolkien for a series entitled *Christian Perspectives*.

29 December 1965 Tolkien drafts a reply to Donald A. Wollheim. He would be interested to hear what royalties Ace Books are now prepared to pay. He has sent a copy of Wollheim's letter to Allen & Unwin, and would be obliged if Ace Books would communicate their terms to them. – Tolkien writes to Rayner Unwin, enclosing a copy of Wollheim's letter and his draft reply. He deduces that Ace Books want to continue to publish their edition, and hope to appease hostility towards them by making a payment. He wonders how acceptance of 'royalties' and so virtual 'authorization' of the Ace Books edition would affect the position in Canada. He has no interest in establishing a Tolkien Award. Ace Books

seem now very anxious to present themselves with clean hands to SFWA and others (having washed them after dinner if not before). But I cannot think that many writers would be much appeased by such a method of employing money due to him and his publishers. What would a skipper say to a pirate who (spying an ominous sail and ensign on the horizon) said "Shake hands! If you feel sore about this, I can assure you that we will spend all the profits of our loot on a hostel for poor sailors'?

He thinks they should either refuse to treat with Ace or to countenance their edition; or accept the royalties, if adequate, on copies what already distributed, provided no more printed. He leaves the decision to Allen & Unwin, but notes, if he refuses the payment offered, that he will need to publish his reasons. He is confined at home with a devastating cold, and none of these letters will go off today. He is not sure 'how long an air-borne virus remains active after leaving a human carrier; but I have taken almost operational care to prevent breath and hands from coming in contact with them' (Tolkien-George Allen & Unwin archive, HarperCollins).

Mid-1960s Tolkien begins two translations of the opening verse of *Gloria in Excelsis Deo* (*Luke* 2:14; see *Alcar mi Tarmenel na Erun: The Gloria in Excelsis Deo in Quenya*).

1966

1966 *The Jerusalem Bible* is published, including Tolkien's translation of Jonah (revised by others before publication). – Tolkien is visited by his former student Alan Bliss. Bliss has presented a paper, 'Hengest and the Jutes', after which he was told by colleagues that nearly all of his conclusions had been anticipated years earlier, by Tolkien in lectures. Bliss discusses this during his visit, and a few days later receives a letter from Tolkien saying that the latter is unlikely to be able to publish the material in the near future. He offers to lend all of his papers to Bliss to use them as he wishes. Tolkien wants to put them in some order before handing them over, but never does so; in fact, it is not until after Tolkien's death that Christopher Tolkien passes the papers to Bliss. They will later be edited , who edits them and they are published in 1982 by Allen & Unwin as *Finn and Hengest: The Fragment and the Episode*. – Probably during this year Oxford University Press decides that a revision of the Tolkien-Gordon edition of *Sir Gawain and the Green Knight* cannot wait any longer, and as Tolkien does not have the time to deal with it, he evidently agrees that Norman Davis, his successor in the Merton Chair of English Language and Literature, should undertake the task. In his introduction to the revised edition Davis will write that 'J.R.R. Tolkien, long ago my teacher and now my much honoured friend, has allowed me a free hand in revising his work and has generously given me the use of his later notes. Many of these I have incorporated' (1967, p. v).

3 January 1966 Rayner Unwin writes to Tolkien. He thinks that they should not reject Donald Wollheim's offer out of hand, and suggests some changes in Tolkien's reply. – Austin Olney writes to Rayner Unwin. As yet neither Tolkien nor Allen & Unwin have received copies of the Ballantine Books edition of *The Lord of the Rings*, but these are being sent together with a master set of proofs on which all corrections made in the Ballantine edition (except for the Appendices and maps) are marked.

4 January 1966 Rayner Unwin telephones Tolkien, asking to see the *SFWA Bulletin*. Tolkien will post it later in the day. – Stanley Unwin writes to Tolkien. It is too late for Unwin to wish Tolkien a happy birthday, but he sends best wishes for 1966.

7 January 1966 Tolkien replies briefly to a long letter from Benjamin P. Indick. He cannot reply as his letter deserves, since 'if I am ever to produce any more of the stories which you ask for, that can only be done by failing to answer letters' (*Letters*, p. 366). – Donald A. Wollheim writes to Tolkien. He wishes to deal directly with Tolkien, not with Allen & Unwin, whom he blames for vicious attacks upon Ace Books. But he encloses a carbon copy of his letter for Tolkien to send to his publisher should he wish to do so. Wollheim repeats his position that Tolkien's works are in the public domain in the USA, and that Ace Books are doing only what most other American publishers do. He offers Tolkien a royalty of 2%, half of the usual rate, but if Tolkien opts for income to be used to establish a Tolkien Award, Ace Books will pay full royalties. – Tolkien replies to a letter from a Roger Shaw, who had suggested that the landscape of *The Lord of the Rings* was inspired by that of Iceland. Tolkien has never been to Iceland, but knows its landscapes from photographs. The name *Midgewater Marshes*, however, was taken from Icelandic 'Mývatn' (a name which appears in *Hrafnkels Saga*).

10–14 January 1966 At some time during this week, Joy Hill telephones Tolkien to say that they have agreed terms and royalties with Donald Swann for his song cycle.

11 January 1966 Rayner Unwin writes to Austin Olney. Allen & Unwin have received the Ballantine sets, and the proofs with corrections.

14 January 1966 Tolkien writes to Donald A. Wollheim. He says that his only publisher is Allen & Unwin, who deals on his behalf in all negotiations with publishers in foreign countries. He has sent them Wollheim's letter of 7 January, since they have interest in profits derived from *The Lord of the Rings*. He is not in favour of establishing an award. – Tolkien writes to Rayner Unwin, enclosing Wollheim's letter and a copy of his reply. – Tolkien is evidently not feeling well, and decides to make an unplanned stay in Bournemouth. He takes his letter to Rayner with him, adding the address 'Hotel Miramar, Bournemouth' at the top and a note at the bottom: 'I am feeling tired and unwell. I fear this break was necessary. I have not in fact sent the letter to Wollheim, and shall not until I hear that you think it suitable and undamaging' (Tolkien-George Allen & Unwin archive, HarperCollins). He probably does not post this immediately, as it will not reach Allen & Unwin until 18 January.

14–31 January 1966 Tolkien and Edith stay at the Hotel Miramar, Bournemouth. Both fall ill with influenza. Tolkien takes with him to Bournemouth W.H. Auden's recently published book of poetry, *About the House*, sent to him by its author. He will later tell Auden: 'I took it up to read one night when I was about to get into a warm bed (about midnight). At 2.30 a.m. I found myself, rather cold, still out of bed, reading and re-reading it' (23 February 1966, *Letters*, pp. 367–8).

17 January 1966 Rayner Unwin writes to Tolkien. Figures provided by Houghton Mifflin show that the Ballantine Books *Hobbit* and *Lord of the Rings* are selling well and replacing the Ace Books *Lord of the Rings*. He sends a copy of Edmund Fuller's review of *The Lord of the Rings* in the *Wall Street Journal*. He hopes to be in Oxford on 24 January, and would like to see Tolkien in the afternoon.

18 January 1966 Joy Hill writes to Tolkien. The possibility of producing a long-playing record with Swann's song cycle, and with Michael Flanders reading extracts from Tolkien's works, is being considered. She is pursuing the idea with various people. She has been visited by someone from the Canadian Broadcasting Corporation who would like to do a programme on Tolkien.

19 January 1966 Rayner Unwin writes to Tolkien. He has revised and strengthened Tolkien's letter to Donald Wollheim, and asks him to post it if he approves. Rayner hopes that Ace Books might raise the payment offered, but he thinks that they should take anything if Wollheim gives an undertaking not to reprint. Without that, he would not accept a penny. Having one or two questions he would like to discuss with Tolkien, Rayner asks if he may visit him in Oxford on 2 February.

20 January 1966 Tolkien receives Rayner Unwin's letter at 2.00 p.m., signs the revised letter to Wollheim at once, and catches the 2.15 p.m. post. The revised version says that Tolkien has consulted Allen & Unwin, who have agreed that if Ace Books give a clear undertaking not to reprint the unauthorized *Lord of the Rings*, Allen & Unwin will waive claims on any payments made by Ace to Tolkien. He is not in favour of a Tolkien award: 'You can perhaps explain why a Tolkien award should be considered twice as deserving as the living author.' (Tolkien-George Allen & Unwin archive, HarperCollins). – Tolkien writes to Rayner Unwin, with thanks for waiving any claim to payments from Ace Books. It will be convenient for Rayner to visit him in Oxford on 2 February. He is

> not very well, since the infection my wife, and later I, picked up has now settled in weak spots: my throat, and my shoulders and neck. But though virtually confined to quarters by the weather ... we are living in the height of comfort in what is practically our private house – a chef and a number of servants that we know personally to wait on us two and 3 others. ...
>
> I am not entirely idle. I find that in the quiet and relief from chores, and also the absence of too voluminous notes, my mind is working again on the problems before me. [Tolkien-George Allen & Unwin archive, HarperCollins]

– Alina Dadlez writes to Tolkien. She is sending him the four copies of the Japanese *Hobbit* owed to him. – The *Daily Telegraph*, which Tolkien reads every morning, reports the remarks that Auden is said to have made to the New York Tolkien Society about Tolkien's hideous house, previously published in the *New Yorker*.

24 January 1966 Rayner Unwin writes to Tolkien, sending some American reviews of *The Lord of the Rings*, and a cutting of the *New Yorker* article. – Rayner Unwin writes to Austin Olney, Houghton Mifflin. The corrections for the Appendices cannot be found. Rayner will have to ask Tolkien to read the Ballantine Books printed Appendices to check if Allen & Unwin may use them for copy.

27 January 1966 In Tolkien's absence, Phyllis Jenkinson writes to Rayner Unwin, acknowledging receipt of a set of the Ballantine Books *Lord of the Rings*. – Donald A. Wollheim replies to Tolkien, enclosing copies of an agreement Ace Books are willing to make with him. They offer 'to pay a royalty of

4 per cent. on all copies of their edition sold, and not to reprint it when it is exhausted (without my consent)' (Tolkien to W.H. Auden, 23 February 1966, *Letters*, p. 367). A condition of the agreement is that Tolkien sign an acceptable letter or statement which Ace Books can make public, in which he accepts the 'voluntary' offer and recognizes that Ace Books have 'no legal obligation' to pay royalties (Tolkien-George Allen & Unwin archive, HarperCollins). Tolkien is also to undertake to inform his correspondents that he has come to an agreement with Ace Books.

?Early February 1966 Tolkien is interviewed by John Ezard for an article in the *Oxford Mail*. He 'is soon likely to sign a "peace treaty" in an international publishing war which has delayed him for over six months in writing a new book', though the 'terms of an agreed statement' still have to be worked out. Completing *The Silmarillion* has been delayed not only by the Ace Books affair, but also by his wife's illness and their inability to get domestic help. For various reasons he can now spend only three or four hours per day writing, compared with ten hours previously. 'If I lived until I was 90 and could work every day, the stories I have in my head would make another four or five books' ('Successor to the Hobbits at Last', *Oxford Mail*, 11 February 1966, p. 11 of the late final edn.). At this meeting or soon after, Tolkien invites Ezard to his Golden Wedding anniversary party at Merton.

February–early March 1966 Tolkien and Edith make arrangements to celebrate their Golden Wedding on 22 March. – Ballantine Books publish in the United States a revised edition of *The Hobbit*.

2 February 1966 Rayner Unwin visits Tolkien in Oxford. Probably at this meeting Tolkien shows Rayner the letter and proposed agreement he has received from Donald Wollheim. Either during this meeting or in correspondence no longer in the files, Tolkien and Rayner agree to accept the offered agreement, but apparently decide to suggest an 'agreed statement' to be attached to the letter suggested by Wollheim. Also during this meeting Rayner probably tells Tolkien that the emended sheets for the Appendices sent to Ballantine Books cannot be found, and asks him to check the accuracy of the Appendices and index as printed in the Ballantine Books edition.

c. **2–26 February 1966** Tolkien spends much time checking the Appendices and index in a copy of the Ballantine Books *Return of the King* and making emendations so that it can be used as copy-text for the new Allen & Unwin edition. In early February he records in his diary that he found more errors in the Ballantine Appendices than he expected. He writes a report that (at first reading) the resetting appeared to have been done with care, most of its errors having arisen from dealing with his corrections and emendations.

I have now revised all that follows the end of the narrative in vol. III: Appendices, and Index. I have only paid strict attention to alterations of AU [Allen & Unwin text], and errors in unaltered passages have only been observed by the way. . . .

It is unfortunate that the emended sheets for the Appendices are not available, since I was very hard pressed for time at this point. Emendation of the Appendices though desirable, in view of my own reconsiderations and criticisms by keen-eyed critics, required much work and calculation; and I appear, by reference to the B [Ballantine] text, not in my check-copy to have taken the same care as elsewhere to distinguish between changes sent to HM [Houghton Mifflin], those suggested but reserved for possible inclusion in a new AU edition, and those few discovered as necessary after I had sent the sheets to USA. In consequence some of the work has had to be done again. I have taken the B text as basic, and have in general contented myself with correcting errors in it, avoiding the introduction of serious discrepancies between B and a new AU.

The Index appears to have been a good piece of work for its limited object (largely owing to the care of the N. Smith index). I sent it off under time-pressure without revision, supposing (foolishly) that the material would be used, but not the 'asides' in the first person.

I now suggest different headings. . . .

He adds two entries to the index and checks it for errors and wrong spellings, but not the actual references except where other errors are involved.

After writing this, Tolkien looks again at the Ballantine Books setting, and on 26 February adds a note at the end of the report:

Closer scrutiny has revealed many more errors, several omissions, and some confused entries. I have in the event done much alteration and correction – making, I think, the index more useful and informative within its limits. I now send on typed sheets all the proposed changes, since the margins in B make it impossible to record them in the copy of B that I have; I have thus also a copy for me to retain for reference. [Tolkien-George Allen & Unwin archive, HarperCollins]

9 February 1966 Austin Olney writes to Rayner Unwin. Ballantine Books would like to publish a 'Tolkien reader' later in the year. They suggest that it contain *Farmer Files of Ham, The Adventures of Tom Bombadil and Other Verses from the Red Book, Tree and Leaf*, possibly something new, and essays and articles on Tolkien.

10 February 1966 Tolkien writes to Donald A. Wollheim, enclosing two signed copies of the proposed agreement, and a copy of the agreed statement which he will make public when he is assured it is acceptable. – Tolkien writes to Rayner Unwin. He has sent the agreement and their proposed statement to Donald Wollheim. His secretary is reading *The Hobbit* and has found five errors in the latest version which he seems to have missed. 'At any rate they are not emended in the check-copy I have of corrections and additions sent to you for your use and the Ballantine paperback.' He sends a list.

11 February 1966 John Ezard's interview, 'Successor to the Hobbits at Last' is published in the *Oxford Mail*.

14 February 1966 Phyllis Jenkinson writes to Rayner Unwin on Tolkien's behalf, sending an extract from a fan letter which suggests that someone has read *The Hobbit* in Finnish. – Rayner Unwin writes to Tolkien, sending a batch of answered fan mail.

15 February 1966 Rayner Unwin writes to Austin Olney. Because of the lost corrections and changes to the Appendices, and because the existing plates are worn, so that changes to the text will stand out, Allen & Unwin have decided to reset the Appendices for their second edition of *The Lord of the Rings*.

16 February 1966 Donald A. Wollheim writes to Tolkien, acknowledging receipt of the agreement. He points out that Tolkien forgot to date it. He asks him to confirm that it was signed on 10 February, the same day as the covering note. But he finds the 'agreed statement' unacceptable.

17 February 1966 Tolkien writes to Michael George. He invites him to attend his and Edith's Golden Wedding celebrations, but will understand if, with finals so close, Michael George does not want to take time away from his studies. Michael George having been provisionally accepted by Merton College as a postgraduate student, Tolkien explains the Oxford B.Litt.

19 February 1966 Tolkien writes to Donald A. Wollheim. He will have a copy made of their agreement, and send it to him signed and dated. He sends

> a copy of the letter you proposed to me, duly signed, without the attachment of my 'agreed statement'. With regard to paragraph 4 of the agreement, I shall endeavour to fulfil this in suitable terms of my own, in keeping with the key-word 'amicable'; and I expect that any statements on your part will have the same tone – having regard to the fact that the agreement is made between Ace Books and *myself* and my publishers are not concerned. [Tolkien-George Allen & Unwin archive, HarperCollins]

21 February 1966 Tolkien writes two Donald A. Wollheim the two copies of the agreement signed and dated as promised. – Rayner Unwin writes to Tolkien. The corrections he sent will be incorporated in the Longmans and 'U Books' editions of *The Hobbit*.

22 February 1966 Rayner Unwin writes to Tolkien. They will enquire into the Finnish *Hobbit*; if it exists, it is unauthorized. – Joy Hill writes to Tolkien, sending the dates of some of Donald Swann's performances of the Tolkien song cycle. She encloses a fan letter she cannot answer.

23 February 1966 Tolkien writes to Joy Hill. He will deal with a runic letter from Lisbon. He has been informed that an FM station in New York broadcast an hour of readings of verses from *The Lord of the Rings*, including songs, with background music by Alan Hovhanness and Benjamin Britten. – Tolkien writes to Donald Swann with news of the FM radio broadcast, as Swann's intended exclusive rights in certain songs are affected. Ace Books 'have agreed to pay a royalty on all copies sold, and stop publication when stocks are exhausted' (Marion E. Wade Center, Wheaton College, Wheaton, Illinois). – Tolkien writes to W.H. Auden. He regrets that Auden has signed a contract to write a book about him:

> I regard such things as premature impertinences; and unless undertaken by an intimate friend, or with consultation of the subject (for which I have at present no time), I cannot believe that they have a usefulness to justify the distaste and irritation given to the victim. I wish at any rate that any book could wait until I produce the *Silmarillion*. I am constantly interrupted in this – but nothing interferes more than the present pother about 'me' and my history.

He has received some reports of Auden's visit to the New York Tolkien Society. 'I cannot say that the (I imagine garbled) notices of your remarks or of [Peter H.] Salus' gave me much pleasure' (*Letters*, p. 367). Upon receiving this letter, Auden will decide not to continue with the book.

24 February 1966 Joy Hill writes to Tolkien. Allen & Unwin will investigate the New York radio broadcast.

25 February 1966 Donald A. Wollheim writes to Tolkien, enclosing royalty statements for the Ace Books *Lord of the Rings*, and a cheque.

28 February 1966 Stanley Unwin writes to Tolkien and Edith. It would be a privilege for him to participate in the celebration of their Golden Wedding on 23 March.

1 March 1966 Rayner Unwin writes to Tolkien and Edith, with thanks for their invitation to be at home with them at Merton College on 23 March.

?2 March 1966 By previous arrangement, Tolkien is interviewed across the Atlantic on the telephone by Henry Resnik for the *Saturday Evening Post* ('The Hobbit-Forming World of J.R.R. Tolkien', 2 July 1966). Tolkien says that he and Edith take three newspapers, and he reads newspapers every day. Resnik will later tell the Tolkien Society of America that he and Tolkien spoke for half an hour. Clyde S. Kilby will later report that Tolkien did not like the article when it appeared, and had finally hung up on Resnik.

2 March 1966 Tolkien writes to Donald A. Wollheim, thanking him for his letter, statement, and cheque. – In the evening, Tolkien attends a dinner of The Society hosted by John Sparrow in the Wharton Room at All Souls College, Oxford. Thirteen members are present. Sparrow again reads a paper on Mark Pattison. – Roger Verhulst of Wm. B. Eerdmans Publishing Company writes to Tolkien. Eerdmans have obtained rights for an American paperback edition of *Essays Presented to Charles Williams*, and W.H. Auden has agreed to write *J.R.R. Tolkien in Christian Perspective* for their series *Contemporary Writers in Christian Perspective*. The first volume in the series will be *Charles Williams in Christian Perspective* by Mary Shideler. Since Tolkien was a friend of Williams, Verhulst is sending an uncorrected proof copy, and hopes that if Tolkien approves of the work, he will write a blurb.

4 March 1966 Tolkien writes to Rayner Unwin, enclosing his recent correspondence with Ace Books. His secretary having failed to make copies of the Ace royalty statements as asked, Tolkien copies selective information by hand on the verso of the letter.

5 March 1966 Tolkien writes to Rayner Unwin. 'I trust that I do not sound too cordial in my final reply to Wollheim. I had agreed to be "amicable" – but not juicy. . . . His letter is so comically reminiscent of Dan Russel to Chanteclere: com doun and I vil telle thee what I mente. (He could, of course, have approached me from the beginning with his flatter, but he is not quite as clever as the Fox)' (Tolkien-George Allen & Unwin archive, HarperCollins; the allusion is to 'The Nun's Priest's Tale' in Chaucer's *Canterbury Tales*). He has no intention of agreeing to any reprint of the Ace Books edition, but thinks that he should not say so now. He encloses photostats of the *Lord of the Rings* index supplied to Houghton Mifflin, and a typed copy of his primary corrections to it as it appears in the Ballantine Books edition. He has more to send, and a few textual corrections, but may not do so until 9 March. Donald Swann has just telephoned and offered to perform, with William Elvin, the song cycle at Tolkien's party on 23 March. – An hour after writing this letter, Tolkien goes out of town. – Tolkien also writes a personal note to Rayner Unwin, reminding him that he is invited to the Golden Wedding lunch on 22 March as well as to the party on 23 March.

5–8 March 1966 Tolkien is away from Oxford, probably in Bournemouth.

7 March 1966 Joy Hill writes to Tolkien, sending a letter from Austin Olney who is investigating the New York broadcast.

9 March 1966 Tolkien writes a letter to Rayner Unwin but does not send it until ?14 March. He asks Rayner to deal with some of the more annoying and troublesome letters among those he found awaiting him on his return, including one from a woman who wants to 'Easternise' his stories, and the letter from Eerdmans. The latter puzzles him, as Oxford University Press had disclaimed rights to *On Fairy-Stories* in 1959, and had let the book go out of print. He wonders if there is any way to prevent the publication of the book by Auden. He is grateful for Auden's supportive reviews of *The Lord of the Rings*, but incensed by his remarks as recently reported in newspapers. 'I should like to be free from distractions. But if his nonsense were enlarged to the size of a pamphlet, I should find it impossible to ignore' (Tolkien-George Allen & Unwin archive, HarperCollins). – Tolkien replies to Roger Verhulst at Eerdmans, with some remarks concerning his relationship with Charles Williams, but presumably declining to comment on Shideler's book. He explains that although he owes a debt of gratitude to Auden, he does not think that Auden knows him well enough to write a book about him. – Rayner Unwin writes to Tolkien. The text proper of the new Allen & Unwin edition of *The Lord of the Rings* is straightforward, but its Appendices and index may present problems. He spent the previous evening 'carefully correlating the text references in the Ballantine appendices with the page numbers of the English edition. There were, I am afraid, a number of bloomers which I think have occurred in the sheer mechanics of transcription.' He has not yet checked the index, partly because he is half expecting some further additions from Tolkien, and because he feels that they ought to have a reset text before accepting the pagination of the index as automatically correct. But 'there is nothing, however, that I don't think cannot be done here, and I will do it myself if I am around' (Tolkien-George Allen & Unwin archive, HarperCollins).

11 March 1966 Tolkien writes to George Sayer. He was about to ask Allen & Unwin to send Sayer a set of the de luxe *Lord of the Rings* in the Pauline Baynes box, but he wonders if he would not prefer a copy of the new edition, to be published in the autumn, instead, as it will incorporate additions and corrections. He sends news about the capitulation of Ace Books under the pressure of public opinion, and the publication history of *Essays Presented to Charles Williams* in light of Eerdmans' plans to reprint it.

?14 (received 15) March 1966 Tolkien adds a manuscript addition to his letter to Rayner Unwin typed on 9 March. He apologizes for the delay in posting it; he has been waiting to complete work on the index. His secretary is typing it now, and Rayner will receive it soon.

17 March 1966 Tolkien writes to Donald Swann. Merton College has given leave for the hire of a piano. 'The room will probably not be very suitable. . . . It is low-ceilinged and curtains with stuffed furniture; but that is necessary for an assembly containing a fair number of elderly folks.' If Swann arrives before 5.30 p.m., he can inspect it. Tolkien will be in college from about 5.00 p.m. He has had a small notice typed so that he will not have to make an announcement: 'At about 6 p.m. Mr Donald Swann and Mr William Elvin have kindly offered to give a short recital of songs composed by Mr Swann to words from *The Lord of the Rings*' (Marion E. Wade Center, Wheaton College, Wheaton, Illinois). – Rayner Unwin writes to Tolkien. He has investigated the question of *Essays Presented to Charles Williams* and the Eerdmans reprint. Originally proceeds from the book went to Charles Williams' widow. The Eerdmans reprint 'is not piracy but at worst a misunderstanding' about the reprint rights to *On Fairy-Stories* (Tolkien-George Allen & Unwin archive, HarperCollins). He thinks that it might be difficult to prevent Eerdmans publishing a book on Tolkien by W.H. Auden, but suggests that Tolkien see if he can persuade Auden against the project, or at least ask to see the work before it is set in type.

18 March 1966 Austin Olney writes to Rayner Unwin. Ballantine Books now suggest that *The Tolkien Reader* contain *The Adventures of Tom Bombadil and Other Verses from the Red Book*, *Tree and Leaf*, *Farmer Giles of Ham*, *English and Welsh*, an essay on *Beowulf*, and *Mr. Bliss*. Since W.H. Auden has declined to write an introduction, they are considering Clyde S. Kilby or Dick Plotz.

19 March 1966 Tolkien writes to Michael George. He will miss him at the celebrations, but thinks that his grandson has made the right decision to stick with his studies. He is glad to hear from Norman Davis that Merton College has accepted Michael George as a prospective B.Litt. student, provided that he earns a good B.A. degree.

?20 March 1968 Donald Swann telephones or writes to Tolkien. He wants to be sure the piano will be tuned for the occasion. He cannot stay for dinner after the performance. He also makes some suggestion about publicity, and raises the question of the correct pronunciation of Elvish, in particular in Galadriel's lament (*Namárië*).

21 March 1966 Tolkien writes to Donald Swann. While he welcomes well-informed publicity, he is trying to keep the Golden Wedding celebrations free from photographers. He is about to go into Oxford and will look in at the piano hire firm to make sure the piano is tuned. He gives some advice for William Elvin on Elvish pronunciation and accent. Unfortunately, Tolkien has developed laryngitis. – Tolkien writes to George Sayer. He is delighted that Sayer is coming to the party on 23 March.

22 March 1966 Ronald and Edith Tolkien's actual Golden Wedding anniversary. They have a small lunch party at 12.30 p.m. at Merton College for about twelve family members and close friends, among them Hilary Tolkien and Rayner Unwin. Stanley and Rayner Unwin send them fifty golden roses.

23 March 1966 Ronald and Edith continue to celebrate their Golden Wedding anniversary with a party at Merton College from 5.30 to 7.00 p.m. Donald Swann and William Elvin perform Swann's song cycle of Tolkien poems. Among the guests are Stanley and Rayner Unwin, George Sayer, Joy Hill, John Ezard, colleagues, and other friends. Rayner Unwin will recall that 'Tolkien actively relished the occasion. . . . I still remember the relish with which Tolkien inspected the label on the wine that was being served and declared it to be Pouligny Montrachet' (*George Allen & Unwin: A Remembrancer* (1999), pp. 122–3). Neither Tolkien nor Edith feel 'very well, nor as gay as we should have wished; but we swam home on champagne, and retain the most golden recollections of the kindness showered on us' (letter to Donald Swann, 28 March 1966, Marion E. Wade Center, Wheaton College, Wheaton, Illinois). – Possibly at the party Swann asks further about Elvish pronunciation.

24 March 1966 Edith is not well after all the excitement. Tolkien fears that they will have to delay a planned departure for Bournemouth. – Tolkien writes to George Sayer. This morning he received from the Sayers a gift of coffee.

25 March 1966 Edith is better. After some last-minute packing, she and Tolkien are driven to Bournemouth. They take the Unwins' golden roses with them.

25 March–4 April 1966 Tolkien and Edith stay at the Hotel Miramar, Bournemouth.

28 March 1966 Tolkien writes to Donald Swann. He thanks him 'for gracing our "party", and raising it far above the level of college receptions' (Marion E. Wade Center, Wheaton College, Wheaton, Illinois). He has tried to find a tape recorder in Bournemouth on which to record Galadriel's lament. If the matter is urgent, he will make more enquiries. If it can wait until he returns home, he will make a tape then. He encloses some notes in advance of a tape.

29 March 1966 Rayner Unwin writes to thank Tolkien and Edith for their hospitality. He reminds Tolkien that he had mentioned to him (probably in person) that Houghton Mifflin and Ballantine Books want to publish a 'so-called *Tolkien Reader*' with *The Adventures of Tom Bombadil and Other Verses from the Red Book*, *Tree and Leaf*, *Farmer Giles of Ham*, and a 'curious rag-bag of your other writings, learned and otherwise, which they have heard about. They list an essay entitled *English and Welsh*, and an essay on Beowulf (I suppose they mean *Beowulf: The Monsters and the Critics*), and a story called *Mr. Bliss* that you are alleged to have written for some Christmas supplement.' He asks for Tolkien's opinions on the inclusion of these or anything else in *The Tolkien Reader*. Rayner is not keen to allow *Smith of Wootton Major* to be launched 'as a minor part of a mixed-up paperback because I feel that it might well stand, if not on its own, at least as a substantial part of a smaller book of two or three stories'. He understands that Ballantine Books want to include 'some scrap of novelty' (Tolkien-George Allen & Unwin archive, Harper-Collins). He thinks it unwise of them to include academic works, and feels that a collection of Tolkien's writings on *Beowulf* and allied subjects would be worth compiling as a book for Allen & Unwin. Ballantine have sent a list of articles that might be included and ask if Tolkien approves any of them. – Edith Tolkien writes to Stanley Unwin, thanking him for attending the party, and for the roses. She has given Ronald his message and he promises to send some manuscripts when he returns home.

Spring 1966 Tolkien receives the first of two visits from Nan C. Scott, who had supported him in his campaign against Ace Books. She is accompanied by her husband. They are making an extended stay in England while William O. Scott is on sabbatical leave, and Nan Scott is attending acting classes in London. They talk with Tolkien in his garage-study. On their first visit, when Nan Scott tells Tolkien that she has just begun to read Charles Williams' books, he describes them as 'dreadful'. On one or both of these visits, the Scotts take photographs of Tolkien. One taken by William Scott of his wife standing with Tolkien in the garden at 76 Sandfield Road will be first published with the article 'A Visit with Tolkien' by Nan C. Scott in *The Living Church*, 5 February 1978. The photograph and article (retitled 'Tolkien: Hobbit and Wizard') will be reprinted in *Eglerio!: In Praise of Tolkien*, ed. Anne Etkin (1978); this will also contain a photograph of Tolkien leaning on his gate, taken by Nan C. Scott.

?April 1966 Tolkien sends a few revisions to *The Lord of the Rings* to Ballantine Books, including the addition to the Took and Brandybuck family trees of Estella Bolger, sister of Fredegar and later wife of Meriadoc Brandybuck. The trees will be emended in the third Ballantine printing of *The Return of the King* (June 1966).

?Early April 1966 Mother Mary Anthony, of the English Department of Rosemont College, Pennsylvania, writes to Tolkien. She is evidently writing a lecture about Charles Williams, and asks various questions about him.

5 April 1966 Joy Hill writes to Tolkien. The New York radio programme had been broadcast by a non-commercial university network. They did phone

Houghton Mifflin to tell them that they were doing the programme, and they gave the Ballantine Books *Lord of the Rings* credit. Allen & Unwin are therefore not asking any fees, but have asked to be contacted if the network wishes to broadcast any further programmes. Presumably without consulting Tolkien, Joy has sent *The Lord of the Rings* to Walt Disney to see if the studio might be interested in a film adaptation, but they have replied that this would be too costly an enterprise.

6 April 1966 Phyllis Jenkinson sends Rayner Unwin some letters for Allen & Unwin to deal with.

8 April 1966 Tolkien writes to W.H. Auden. If his letter of 23 February seemed 'a little tart', it was as a reaction to remarks Auden and Peter H. Salus were reported to have made to the New York Tolkien Society. Not only were some of those about Tolkien and his writings incorrect, but the ones about Tolkien's house were reported in the English papers 'and exposed my wife and myself to a certain amount of ridicule' (*Letters*, p. 368). – Tolkien writes to Roger Verhulst of Eerdmans. Judging by Auden's reported remarks, he does not think his proposed book (evidently now abandoned) would have had much value without personal consultation with the subject, for which Tolkien has no time at present.

12 April 1966 Tolkien replies to Mother Mary Anthony. He has little personal knowledge of Charles Williams' 'biographical or mental history'. He 'had no personal discussions with him about literature. His work gave me no pleasure. . . . But I found him a pleasant companion socially' (Marion E. Wade Center, Wheaton College, Wheaton, Illinois). He asks for a copy of her lecture on Williams.

19 April 1966 Rayner Unwin writes to Tolkien. He is about to leave on a visit to Canada. He encloses a proposed modification of the dust-jacket design for *The Lord of the Rings* which he hopes that Tolkien will like. 'It is a little bolder than the old one and more in line with current jackets but, at the same time, it is in no way revolutionary', and would distinguish the revised edition from the original (Tolkien-George Allen & Unwin archive, HarperCollins). Unsure what to do about a blurb, he asks if Tolkien would like to write a new one, unless he is content to keep the old blurb. Ballantine Books would like a decision on *The Tolkien Reader* soon. Rayner thinks that apart from the three existing books, he should agree to the inclusion in this of very little new, and nothing of great importance like *Smith of Wootton Major*. He hopes that neuritis is no longer affecting Tolkien's arm (perhaps mentioned at the anniversary party or by phone), and that, by the time Rayner returns from Canada, Tolkien will have written the preface for *Pearl* and *Sir Gawain and the Green Knight*. – Joy Hill writes to Phyllis Jenkinson. The letters Jenkinson sent to Rayner Unwin have been passed to Joy, since she deals with rights. She suggests that similar letters should be sent direct to her in future.

25 April 1966 Tolkien writes to Rayner Unwin. Though he would like to spend time on the proposed new jacket design, 'I think I had better not'.

My chief criticism is that the Rings and fire-letters, if used at all, should not be so much reduced. If used, the fire-letters should be legible and seen to correspond to the inscription in Vol. I, Ch. 2. On the new scale the designer appears to have found this impossible, though what you sent me is probably only a sketch to show the general layout. If you want to use a small ring as a motif on the back, I suggest that the letters should be reduced simply to a red flame flaring up round the small ring.

He will not attempt to write a new blurb. Allen & Unwin can continue to use the old one. He had not realized that the Americans were waiting for him to produce new material for *The Tolkien Reader*. 'If the Reader is to be of use (e.g. stopping people attributing views to me that I don't hold), I personally should wish to include the poem "The Homecoming of Beorhtnoth", with the accompanying essay on "Heroism" ["Ofermod"] – this is very germane to the general division of sympathy exhibited in *The Lord of the Rings*' (Tolkien-George Allen & Unwin archive, HarperCollins). A nosy bibliographer having unearthed *Songs for the Philologists*, one or two of its poems might do for the *Reader*.

27 April 1966 Tolkien writes a short reply, typical of many at this period, to A.E. Couchman, who has asked about 'Gods' in *The Lord of the Rings*.

28 April 1966 Philippe Halsman telephones Tolkien to make an appointment to take photographs to illustrate an article for the *Saturday Evening Post* (presumably the Resnik interview). Tolkien refuses testily, annoyed at the interruption. Halsman then contacts Allen & Unwin and speaks to Joy Hill, who rings Tolkien. – Ronald Eames, Allen & Unwin, replies to Tolkien in Rayner Unwin's absence. He confirms that what was sent was a rough sketch and the rings and fire-letters would be clearer in the finished dust-jacket design, but he agrees that the size of the ring and lettering on the front should be increased, and the lettering around the ring on the spine reduced to a red flame.

29 April 1966 Tolkien writes to Joy Hill in regard to their telephone conversation the previous day. 'Please note that if any enquiries of this kind come through your hands, I will not submit, at any rate to being photographed, for such a purpose. I have written a polite and, I hope, soothing letter to Jeanette Wagner, the Senior Editor of Saturday Evening Post, and I hope that no real damage is done to this line of publicity' (Tolkien-George Allen & Unwin archive, HarperCollins).

3 May 1966 Joy Hill writes to Tolkien. Mr Halsman was sent by the *Saturday Evening Post* to photograph the Prime Minister and Tolkien; the former agreed while Tolkien did not. Joy is asking Pamela Chandler to send the *Saturday Evening Post* a selection of her photographs of Tolkien. Donald Swann has made an experimental tape recording of the song cycle which can be played to recording companies. Joy sends details of the first public performances of the cycle, and could arrange for Tolkien and his wife to attend one if they wish. She now has a tape of the New York radio programme, and since its producers want to repeat it she will ask for a payment. Donald Swann is to play part of the song cycle on *Today* (an early morning radio programme). Either she or Donald will let Tolkien know the time.

6 May 1966 Tolkien writes to Joy Hill. If Donald Swann's concert on Sunday, 12 June, at Watford is in the afternoon, he and Edith would like to attend. His daughter Priscilla might accompany them or go alone. His wife listened to the *Today* programme but it was 'far too early for me' (Tolkien-George Allen & Unwin archive, HarperCollins).

***c.* 8 May 1966** Norman Davis writes to Tolkien on behalf of the English Faculty of Oxford University. They wish to acquire a bust of Tolkien by Faith Tolkien to place in a prominent position in the English Faculty Library.

9 May 1966 Joy Hill writes to Tolkien. Rayner Unwin has written from Canada asking if Tolkien could send Allen & Unwin copies of *The Homecoming of Beorhtnoth Beorhthelm's Son* and the essay 'Heroism' which would probably do for the *Tolkien Reader* and be more suitable than Old English versions of popular songs from *Songs for the Philologists*. But if this is going to be a trouble for Tolkien, he should probably just say that he has nothing suitable. Joy encloses a letter which she is unable to answer, and asks if Tolkien or Miss Jenkinson could telephone brief replies. Since interest in Tolkien in America is spreading, she suggests for his own protection that he remove his telephone number from *Who's Who* and perhaps go ex-directory.

10 May 1966 Tolkien writes to Joy Hill, giving some details of *The Homecoming of Beorhtnoth*. He thinks that Rayner Unwin should look at before Tolkien does anything. He has only one copy of *Essays and Studies* in which the work was published, and is reluctant to lend it. If Rayner cannot get a copy otherwise, he will have a typed copy made. Tolkien will consider Joy's suggestions about his telephone number. 'With regard to the letter you enclosed, I consider this equal in impertinence to the worst I have received. The answers to most of the questions are in the book (in spite of his boasts this young fellow evidently reads with little attention or understanding), while question 8 should surely be referred to a bookseller. Personally, if received direct, I should not have answered it at all' (Tolkien–George Allen & Unwin archive, Harper-Collins). – Tolkien writes to Norman Davis. Both he and Faith feel much honoured. He offers to present the bust to the Faculty, and, since a plaster bust would be fragile, to have it cast in bronze. He has already consulted Faith about how to get this done. – Tolkien replies to a letter from Pamela Chandler. He would like to see the photographs she took of him and Edith in the garden. He and Edith are going away on 14 May until immediately after Whitsuntide.

12 May 1966 Joy Hill writes to Tolkien. Donald Swann's concert on 12 June is to be in the evening. Rayner Unwin and his wife hope to attend. She sends a copy of the programme and a form for Priscilla to complete if she wants tickets. – Joy writes a second letter. She has borrowed a copy of *Essays and Studies* (with *Beorhtnoth*) from the London Library for Rayner to read on his return. She feels that Tolkien really ought to go ex-directory, and mentions that a very determined American, who is very keen to meet him, has turned up at Allen & Unwin. She has given him vague answers, but he could get the information he needs from *Who's Who*. – With the growth of the Tolkien cult, particularly in the USA, Tolkien suffers from uninvited callers, people trying to take photographs of him in the privacy of his home, and telephone calls from strangers, some in the middle of the night from people who do not realize the time difference between England and the USA. – A woman in Massachusetts writes a long letter to Tolkien, putting forward a theory about the Middle English poems *Pearl, Patience, Purity*, and *Sir Gawain and the Green Knight*.

13 May 1966 Tolkien writes to Joy Hill. He is sending a request for two seats for the Donald Swann concert, which he hopes to attend. He has received a letter from a woman asking about the possibility of translating *The Lord of the Rings* into German. He asks Joy if a German translation is being considered. A sample translation of the very difficult preliminary verses shows care and skill.

14 May–?late May 1966 Tolkien and Edith are away from Oxford.

16 May 1966 Joy Hill writes to Tolkien. The prospective translator has been referred to the German publishers Ernst Klett, who are considering whether to publish *The Lord of the Rings*.

?Mid-May 1966 Nancy Smith, compiler of the index to *The Lord of the Rings*, writes to Tolkien. She warns him that she has allowed some paragraphs from the letter Tolkien wrote to her at Christmas 1963 to be included in an issue of *The Diplomat*, a magazine which is also publishing several items devoted to him and his works.

25 May 1966 Tolkien writes to Michael George, with best wishes and prayers for his final examinations. – Rayner Unwin writes to Tolkien. He is sending pre-publication copies of the Longmans and 'U Books' editions of *The Hobbit*. He apologizes for a silly slip in Tolkien's new preface (made by Longmans) which will be corrected in the next reprint. Allen & Unwin urgently need the index material for the new edition of *The Return of the King*. Rayner will come to Oxford if Tolkien wants to discuss it. *The Homecoming of Beorhtnoth* will do admirably for *The Tolkien Reader*; he has ascertained from the English Association that Tolkien owns the reproduction rights.

?Late May–?early July 1966 Tolkien is working on *The Lord of the Rings* for the new Allen & Unwin edition. Some time in June, Tolkien records in his diary that he is attempting to complete this revision and 'cannot leave it while it is all in my mind. So much time has been wasted in all my work by this constant breaking of threads' (quoted by Douglas A. Anderson, 'Note on the Text' preceding *The Fellowship of the Ring*, 2004 edn., p. xiii).

27 May 1966 Tolkien writes to Joy Hill. The Donald Swann concert at Watford is too late in the day for himself and his wife, but he would like two tickets, for Priscilla and a friend. – Tolkien writes to Rayner Unwin. He would like to see Rayner if he can spare the time. Rayner may inform Ballantine Books that Tolkien agrees to the inclusion of *The Homecoming of Beorhtnoth* in *The Tolkien Reader* if they wish.

30 May 1966 Tolkien replies to the woman in Massachusetts regarding *Sir Gawain*, etc. He regrets that he is very busy on other projects and has no time to consider the points she has made. – Tolkien writes to Nancy Smith about *The Diplomat*. He hopes that 'the matter will not be as distasteful and erroneous as most articles so far have been' (quoted in Christie's, *Fine Printed Books and Manuscripts*, New York, 24 May 2002, p. 282).

?Late Spring or early summer 1966 Daphne Castell, who for a short time had been a postgraduate student supervised by Tolkien, writes to ask if she may interview him. He apparently agrees, but asks her to indicate in advance the questions she will be asking. In one of three articles based on this interview, she will write that Tolkien

> talks very quickly, striding up and down the converted garage which serves as his study, waving his pipe, making little jabs with it to mark important points; and now and then jamming it back in and talking round it. It is not always easy to hear him; and one dare not miss anything, for he has the habits of speech of the true story-teller, and seldom indulges in the phrase-ridden and repetitive ways most people use nowadays. Every sentence is important, and lively, and striking. ['The Realms of Tolkien', *New Worlds* 50 (November 1966), p. 144]

Asked about Queen Berúthiel, he tells Castell a detailed story which she describes in her *New Worlds* article. *See note.* Later she will send him a transcript of the interview, on which Tolkien makes notes, and a typescript of one of her articles.

June 1966 Nan C. Scott and William O. Scott visit Tolkien in Oxford a second time. During this visit, according to Nan Scott, Tolkien 'expressed distaste for C.S. Lewis's "Narnia" books because of their allegorical nature. Even more limiting than religious allegory, a narrow political interpretation of literature was his especial detestation; and he spoke with scorn of critics who tried to reduce the War of the Rings to an analog of World War II with Hitler as Sauron, the Dark Lord' ('A Visit with Tolkien', *The Living Church*, 5 February 1978, p. 12). – The Longmans school edition of *The Hobbit*, in their *Heritage of Literature* series, is published. (The British Library deposit copy will be stamped on 6 June.)

1 June 1966 Rayner Unwin sends Tolkien an offprint of an article by Peter Beagle which Ballantine propose using as an introduction to the *Tolkien Reader*, unless Tolkien objects. – Joy Hill writes to Tolkien. She will arrange for two tickets for the Flanders-Swann performance for Priscilla and her friend. Michael Flanders is enjoying reading *The Lord of the Rings*, and considering including *I Sit beside the Fire* in the American run of *At the Drop of Another Hat*.

7 June 1966 Rayner Unwin writes to ask Tolkien if it would be convenient for Rayner to call on him in Oxford on 13 June at about 10.00 a.m.

9 June 1966 Tolkien replies to Rayner Unwin. He will expect him at 10.00 a.m. on Monday the 13th.

10 June 1966 In the evening, Tolkien attends a dinner of The Society hosted by Lord David Cecil at Christ Church, Oxford. Eleven members are present.

13 June 1966 Rayner Unwin visits Tolkien in Oxford. The main topic of conversation is probably the Allen & Unwin second edition of *The Lord of the Rings*. – Jack Beale, BBC, writes to Joy Hill. The Drama Department would like to broadcast a radio adaptation of *The Hobbit* in eight 30-minute episodes.

14–15 June 1966 Tolkien is consulted about the BBC dramatization.

16 June 1966 Stanley Unwin signs a contract for the BBC dramatization of *The Hobbit*, to take place within one year. Joy Hill sends it to the BBC, apologizing for the delay while it was shown to Tolkien.

?16 or 17 June 1966 Clyde S. Kilby arrives in England to help Tolkien with 'The Silmarillion'. He first visits Rayner Unwin in London, who urges him to persuade Tolkien to write a brief preface to *Pearl* and *Sir Gawain and the Green Knight*. After settling in Pusey House in Oxford, he telephones Tolkien.

?16 or 17 June–?beginning of September 1966 Clyde S. Kilby stays in Oxford and visits Tolkien in Sandfield Road two or three times per week, for one to three hours each time, 'periods solidly filled with talk, nearly all his. . . . One often felt that his words could not pour out fast enough – there was a sense of the galloping on of all his ideas at once, along with kaleidoscopic facial changes' (Kilby, *Tolkien & The Silmarillion*, p. 24). He is 'warmly welcomed into the Professor's upstairs quarter. . . . He was in process of revising *The Two Towers*. He began our new association by showing me boxes of manuscripts – poetic, scholarly, creative.' When he finds Tolkien looking here and there for portions of 'The Silmarillion', Kilby offers to put his papers in order, 'a proposal he quickly rejected on the ground that *then* he should never find anything' (p. 19). They usually work in Tolkien's upstairs room, but sometimes in his garage-study. 'When the weather was warm, we might go out into the garden. On our first visit there he took me round the garden and gave me the personal history of nearly every plant, and even the grass . . . and pointed out the trees he himself had planted. . . . He spoke of birds, saying that a certain blackbird was now tame enough to eat out of Mrs. Tolkien's hand' (pp. 25–6). 'It would be satisfying to record that I always found him busy at his writing,' Kilby will recall, 'but that is not true. I did find him sometimes working at his Elvish languages, an activity which seemed endlessly interesting to him. I think he did a good deal of reading of detective stories and science-fiction' (p. 26). Kilby quickly discovers that Tolkien needs encouragement rather than negative criticism, and that 'any discussion of his most deeply private world was simply impossible for him' (p. 34). Kilby therefore begins to write out his comments and attach them to manuscripts. Christopher Tolkien will note that on the back of the slip on which Kilby wrote comments and criticisms of *The Wanderings of Húrin*, Tolkien rejected most of what he said (*The War of the Jewels*, p. 310). Kilby will record that 'sometimes [Tolkien] could rise from a chair only with real effort, and then would remain standing rather than sit again. . . . He said it was no longer possible for him to walk far. He reminisced about earlier years when he could ride his bicycle up the long, steep Headington Hill between his home and the university' (p. 27). 'On more than one occasion' Kilby finds Tolkien 'unable to answer specific questions about the contents of *The Silmarillion*. . . .

For a man of his age it was a superlunary task to set about integrating the three ages of Middle Earth [sic] into one whole.' Kilby takes to his room portions of 'The Silmarillion' handed to him, and tries 'to judge them individually and in relation to each other'. In hopes of encouraging Tolkien 'to go on with the composition, I pointed out with serious concern that I had found nothing about Tom Bombadil, the Ents and Entwives, the making of the Palantíri, etc.' (pp. 44–5). Kilby has no more success with *Pearl* and *Sir Gawain*. 'My various reminders and coaxings [to write a brief preface to the translations, as asked by Rayner Unwin] were accepted seriously, yet at the end of the summer Tolkien almost triumphantly said, "Well, I didn't write it!" One day, earlier in the summer, he had said, in some exasperation, . . . that he *couldn't* write it until the thing came "rightly" to him' (p. 19). Kilby finds that Tolkien has three sorts of replies to his fan mail: 'a) a purely form letter, b) a form letter he personally signs, and infrequently c) a response dictated to his secretary' (p. 21).

17 June 1966 Allen & Unwin write to Houghton Mifflin. Tolkien is still completing his revision of *The Return of the King*.

22 June 1966 Encaenia.

End of June 1966 Tolkien hears of successful examination results achieved by his grandson Michael George. He wires his congratulations.

24 June 1966 Rayner Unwin writes to Tolkien. He reckons that the index in the first printing of the new edition will be a stop-gap 'and the finer version will have to await the next printing' (Tolkien-George Allen & Unwin archive, HarperCollins). The woman who is typing the index has raised some queries. Rayner reminds Tolkien that he has promised to let Allen & Unwin have a copy of his notes for indexing more logically the three main characters Gandalf, Aragorn/Strider, and Éomer.

30 June 1966 The 'U Books' paperback edition and Allen & Unwin third hardback edition of *The Hobbit* are published.

2–?13 July 1966 Tolkien and Edith stay at the Hotel Miramar, Bournemouth, to rest and recover their health.

6 July 1966 Tolkien writes to Michael George. He is sorry not to have followed his telegram sooner with a letter, but he has been suffering 'bouts of pressure on several fronts at once: [*The Lord of the Rings*], Silmarillion, Gawain & Pearl, and Income Tax' (British Library MS Add. 71657). He hopes that Michael George will be able to live in college for his first postgraduate year at Merton.

?12 July 1966 Tolkien writes to Clyde S. Kilby, thanking him for his help. He and Edith will be returning to Oxford tomorrow, and he will get in touch with Kilby as soon as possible.

16 July 1966 K.B. McFarlane dies.

18 July 1966 Tolkien replies to a letter from a Mrs Webster at Pate's Junior School, Cheltenham. She has adapted some scenes from *The Lord of the Rings* for performance by her pupils, and invites him to attend a performance. He tells her that technically it is not he, but Allen & Unwin, who give permission for use of his work in a public performance. He is unable to attend, not only because he is busy, but because his wife has other engagements, but he asks her to give his best wishes to all of the cast. Clyde Kilby, on Tolkien's suggestion, will attend one of the performances.

19 July 1966 Joy Hill writes to Tolkien. She confirms that an appointment has been made for Mr Cater of the *Daily Express* to interview Tolkien on 2 August at 11.00 a.m. She has spoken to Tolkien on the telephone about the need for him to apply for membership in the Performing Rights Society, since Donald Swann will be performing his setting of Tolkien's poems. Joy now sends him a membership application form as promised. She asks for some brief biographical material, and a photograph to help her deal with enquiries.

21 July 1966 Joy Hill writes to Phyllis Jenkinson. She and Rayner Unwin have devised a letter to send to people who wish to set Tolkien's poems to music. She would like to help by dealing with more letters so that Miss Jenkinson and Tolkien can get on with *The Silmarillion*. (As a result of Tolkien's suddenly increased popularity, his fan mail and requests to adapt, or set to music, or otherwise use his writings now involve a considerable amount of work for him, his secretary, and Joy Hill as well as others at Allen & Unwin.)

22 July 1966 Tolkien attends an evening meeting at Wadham College arranged by Walter Hooper for people who had been friends of C.S. Lewis. Among those present are Warnie Lewis, Hugo Dyson, Colin Hardie, Austin Farrer, R.E. Havard, Owen Barfield, and Clyde S. Kilby. Warnie Lewis will record in his diary that 'Tollers is putting on weight', and that he left at about 7.00 p.m. 'in company with Tollers, who struck me as having had as much sherry as was good for him, and told me some fantastic story about how he had once emptied a sauce boat of melted butter over [Maurice] Bowra's head' (Marion E. Wade Center, Wheaton College, Wheaton, Illinois).

23 July 1966 Tolkien travels to Cambridge to attend an Ad Eundem dinner in the evening. – Phyllis Jenkinson writes to Joy Hill, welcoming her help and enclosing for her to deal with a letter from *Life* magazine, on which Tolkien has written comments.

24 July 1966 Tolkien returns to Oxford.

25 July 1966 Tolkien writes to Joy Hill. He will prepare a brief biographical note for her as soon as possible. He has no recent photographs except those by Pamela Chandler. Some time ago he had sent Allen & Unwin a photograph taken by Mr Leslie Stanley, who had given permission for it to be used in return for acknowledgement. If Allen & Unwin still have it, they could use it with that proviso. His appointment with Mr. Cater of the *Daily Express* and

the fact that Professor Kilby is in Oxford ('helping' with *The Silmarillion*), seems very quickly to have leaked out, and I was rung up by John Ezard of the Oxford Times. He was very perturbed about the Daily Express and also very anxious to make a story about Kilby. To the latter I objected very strongly. I intend in due course to make such acknowledgements of any help Kilby gives me as may become due; but though he is a pleasant and modest man, I must be on my guard against any attempt by him or others to represent him as my particular agent and go-between in the United States.

He asks her to tell Rayner Unwin that he is now working on *Sir Gawain and the Green Knight*. He would like Allen & Unwin to return the typed text of at least the Third Fit 'into which I am (in the process of considering my notes) obliged to introduce a number of alterations. It would save time to make these on a clean copy; my carbon of this Fit has now become rather illegible' (Tolkien-George Allen & Unwin archive, HarperCollins).

26 July 1966 Tolkien is interviewed by John Ezard of the *Oxford Times* at 10.30 am. Probably at this time, Tolkien lends him *Smith of Wootton Major* to read. In an undated letter Ezard will thank him for the loan and comment on the story. An article by Ezard, including a quote from the as yet unpublished story, will appear in the *Oxford Mail* for 3 August 1966. – Joy Hill writes to Tolkien. Allen & Unwin have no photograph by Leslie Stanley. The only photographs they have are those by Pamela Chandler, one of Tolkien as a young man, and one taken at Merton College. 'That Professor Kilby was coming to Oxford was known in America before it was known here and was in fact announced in one of the Tolkien Society of America journals. The papers here heard through their New York offices' (Tolkien-George Allen & Unwin archive, HarperCollins). Joy encloses the whole of the *Sir Gawain* typescript. – Joy Hill writes to Phyllis Jenkinson. She will deal with *Life*. She encloses a request from *Holiday* magazine for 250 words from Tolkien. – Joy Hill writes to a professor in London who is preparing a lecture on Tolkien. She provides brief information about Tolkien's parents. Tolkien has asked not to be visited for this purpose.

27 July 1966 J.S. Ryan, a former student of Tolkien, together with Hans-Jörg Modlmayr, visit him without an appointment. Tolkien talks with them and shows them translations of his works.

29 July 1966 Tolkien writes to Joy Hill. He has received the typescript of *Sir Gawain* and hopes to send the revision soon. The Leslie Stanley photograph of him had been used in the *Concise Encyclopaedia of Modern World Literature* (ed. Geoffrey Grigson, 1963). – Tolkien writes to Michael George. He is sorry that Michael George will not be living in college after all. He gives him advice about buying a typewriter, and offers to lend him his own 'Imperial "Good Companion": a light portable machine' which he occasionally uses when away from home; this has a special keyboard incorporating useful philological signs and letters. He also has 'a much larger machine (a Remington Rand 'Noiseless')' (British Library MS Add. 71657). He discusses the etymology of *Mirkwood* at length. – Joy Hill writes to Michael Flanders. Every week, journalists are arriving from the USA hoping to interview Tolkien, and 'he is becoming thoroughly pestered'. Allen & Unwin have put an end to interviews and 'have taken over all Tolkien's mail (except his personal correspondence)' (George Allen & Unwin archive, University of Reading).

?Early August 1966 Mrs L. Young de Grummond, University of Southern Mississippi, writes to Tolkien. She asks if he could contribute a manuscript or illustration to a collection of children's books she plans to form.

1 August 1966 Tolkien writes to Clyde Kilby. One of his sons (?John or Christopher) is taking him to lunch on 4 August and would like Kilby to join them.

2 August 1966 Tolkien is interviewed at 11.00 a.m. by William Cater for the *Daily Express* ('Lord of the Hobbits', 22 November 1966, p. 10). In 1977 Cater will recall that

[Tolkien] was wandering up and down, endlessly striking matches to light the pipe he was never without, and talking through it, and round it, and sometimes *to* it, and to me, and frequently over my head, about that long-awaited next book. . . .

You must imagine this punctuated and interrupted by diggings into a tobacco pouch, by puffings and pauses, the scraping of matches and rattlings of a matchbox, and the old man's sudden grin which would charm birds off trees. ['The Filial Duty of Christopher Tolkien', *Sunday Times Magazine*, 25 September 1977]

3 August 1966 John Ezard's mainly biographical article, 'The Hobbit Man', appears in the *Oxford Mail*.

4 August 1966 Joy Hill writes to Tolkien. In future she will forward to him only letters received via Allen & Unwin that are of a personal nature.

5 August 1966 The Allen & Unwin editorial department writes to Tolkien, sending proofs of the *Lord of the Rings* index.

Before 7 August 1966 Joy Hill speaks with Tolkien by telephone. John Ezard wants to interview him again, and the *Sunday Times* also wants an interview. She has arranged for Pamela Chandler to take more photographs.

7 August 1966 Tolkien is photographed by Pamela Chandler. She takes three rolls of colour film of Tolkien alone, and with Edith, in his garage-study, and in the garden at Sandfield Road.

8 August 1966 Tolkien writes to Joy Hill. He has had no confirmation from the *Sunday Times* or Ezard, and 'with the *Sunday Times* I must really finally close down. I can't take any more.' He sends 'a little packet for your delectation' and asks if it would be possible to patent the word *Hobbit* which would 'at least prevent people sticking this label on disgusting objects, or on any objects, without some compensation' (Tolkien-George Allen & Unwin archive, Harper-Collins). Clyde S. Kilby will recall: 'A problem that was bothering him when I was with him involved an American manufacturer who proposed to exploit the Hobbit image by making dolls, T-shirts and the like. This manufacturer declared his intention of going ahead with or without permission but offered some remuneration for the privilege. Again I felt it was simply a legal matter that need not at all trouble Tolkien the writer' (*Tolkien & The Silmarillion*, p. 32). – Joy Hill writes to Tolkien. His membership application has been sent to the Performing Rights Society. She is preparing for submission to Stanley and Rayner Unwin proposals for the best way of protecting Tolkien commercially (the use of his characters in books, of the Elvish languages, etc.).

9 August 1966 Philip Norman interviews Tolkien for an hour and a half for an article to appear in a future colour supplement of the *Sunday Times*. Norman will report that when asked about the delay in publishing *The Silmarillion* Tolkien said: 'Most of the time I'm fighting against the natural inertia of the lazy human being. The same old university don who warned me about being useful round the house, once said, "It's not only interruptions, my boy; it's the fear of interruptions"' ('The Hobbit Man', *Sunday Times Magazine*, 15 January 1967, p. 34). – Joy Hill writes to Tolkien. She had impressed upon Philip Norman on 5 August that he must confirm his appointment. She agrees that Tolkien must now shut himself away from journalists, photographers, and fans, and suggests again that he make his phone number ex-directory and remove his address from the next *Who's Who*. She points out that it is not possible to copyright or patent the phrase 'The Hobbit', but it could be registered as a trademark.

10 August 1966 Clyde Kilby finds Tolkien working on *Sir Gawain and the Green Knight*. Tolkien assures Kilby that he expects to finish it soon.

15 August 1966 Tolkien replies to Mrs L. Young de Grummond. He is not able to contribute to her collection because he is too busy to look through his material, and in any case he has 'practically decided . . . to bequeath all that I still retain to my literary executor for benefit of my own family' (Tolkien-George Allen & Unwin archive, HarperCollins). – Joy Hill writes to Tolkien. Stanley Unwin has been looking into various ways of protecting Tolkien's interests. She has had a letter from Leslie Stanley listing the photographs he took of Tolkien: the Merton photograph she mentioned previously is one of these. She has had a long visit from Theodore Denis, an American composer referred to Tolkien by Mr P.A. Brunt of Oriel College, Oxford. He will send a score and tape.

?Mid-August 1966 Donald Swann writes to Tolkien. He is leaving on 6 September on an American tour of *At the Drop of Another Hat* with Michael Flanders. They hope to include a Tolkien song in their performance.

18 August 1966 Tolkien works on *Sir Gawain and the Green Knight*. – Phyllis Jenkinson writes to Joy Hill. Tolkien is particularly anxious to patent the word *Hobbit*. He does not like any of the photographs taken when he was young.

19 August 1966 Rayner Unwin writes to Tolkien. He would like to call on Tolkien on 24 August at about 10:00 a.m. It will be mainly a social visit, but he would like to collect any comments Tolkien might wish to make about the enclosed copy of Philip Norman's article for the *Sunday Times*, which Rayner thinks is muddled in places. He hopes that 'the collar in which you are constricted is not proving too burdensome' (Tolkien-George Allen & Unwin archive, HarperCollins). By now Tolkien's doctor had prescribed a cervical collar to ameliorate muscular spasm.

24 August 1966 Rayner Unwin visits Tolkien in the morning and collects his comments on Philip Norman's article. Tolkien lends him *The Bovadium Fragments*. Clyde Kilby will later comment that this was among shorter pieces Tolkien gave him to read also, and asked if Kilby thought them publishable.

25 August 1966 Tolkien works on *Sir Gawain*. He tells Clyde Kilby that Rayner Unwin expects it to be finished by 15 September. – Rayner Unwin writes to Tolkien. He has forwarded Tolkien's comments to Philip Norman. He read *The Bovadium Fragments* with pleasure on his way back to London, and thinks that Tolkien should publish it in the *Oxford Magazine*.

26 August 1966 Tolkien writes to thank a Mrs Webster of Gloucestershire for an album of photographs of her school's performance of scenes from *The Lord of the Rings*. He will show them to Clyde Kilby, who was present at the occasion.

29 August 1966 Tolkien replies to a letter from Donald Swann. Although neither he nor his wife are very well, both are arthritic, and he is 'supposed to be wearing a kind of rubber dog collar' but seldom does, they hope to sail from Southampton on 15 September on a cruise that will take them as far as the Aegean Sea. He would be very pleased for Flanders and Swann to include one of his songs in their revue. He suggests an alteration of 'butterfly' to 'dragonfly' in *I Sit beside the Fire*, to reduce a clash with Michael Flanders' 'Sloth' (Marion E. Wade Center, Wheaton College, Wheaton, Illinois). He hopes that Donald and his wife Janet will visit the Tolkiens in Oxford when Donald returns from the USA.

?End of August or beginning of September 1966 Clyde Kilby will recall that one day towards the end of summer 'I found Tolkien in very low spirits. He said he was too tired to think about anything. He had been up during the night with Mrs Tolkien and said he was going to bed for some rest' (*Tolkien & The Silmarillion*, p. 28).

September 1966 *The Tolkien Reader* is published.

12 September 1966 Tolkien writes to Michael George. He encloses a brush for cleaning typefaces on the typewriter Tolkien has lent him. He and Edith are busy packing for their cruise.

14 September 1966 Pamela Chandler visits Tolkien in the morning. – Tolkien and Edith begin their journey to Southampton in wind and rain. During the night, which they spend en route, this becomes a howling gale.

15 September 1966 Tolkien and Edith ride through the New Forest in sunshine to Southampton to board a Royal Mail Lines ship for a Mediterranean cruise. The ship sails at 12.49 p.m. 'with merry music – into nearly 17 days of unbroken sunshine (and moon light). The Bay of Biscay was like a blue lake, and the Mediterranean also – the only clouds and haze were over the distant shores' (Tolkien, letter to Clyde S. Kilby, 11 October 1966, Marion E. Wade Center, Wheaton College, Wheaton, Illinois). Unfortunately, on the first day Edith slips and falls heavily, hitting her head and knees and damaging the leg already under treatment. She will need attention from the ship's surgeon for most of the cruise. Although the organizers of the cruise provide carrying chairs and stalwart men, she will find it difficult to disembark, and more so to get around on shore. In consequence, she and Tolkien do very little sightseeing. On most days the ship offers passengers films, bingo, and dancing, as well as other entertainment. On the first evening there is a performance of light music.

16 September 1966 The ship passes through the Bay of Biscay.

17 September 1966 The Captain's cocktail party, followed by a gala dinner and dance.

18 September 1966 Sunday. At 4.30 a.m. the ship passes Gibraltar and enters the Mediterranean. The Captain officiates at divine service. In the evening there is a 'Book Dinner'.

19 September 1966 At 8.05 a.m. the ship arrives at Barcelona. Passengers may spend the day ashore.

20 September 1966 The ship leaves Barcelona before dawn. During the day there is a 'Race Meeting' on F Deck.

21 September 1966 At 7.31 a.m. the ship arrives at Civitavecchia, where passengers may spend the day ashore. Probably because of Edith's injury, Tolkien does not take the opportunity to visit Rome.

22 September 1966 The ship leaves Civitavecchia just after midnight. At 2.45 p.m. it passes Stromboli, an active volcano. At 5.30 p.m. the ship passes through the Straits of Messina. *See note.*

23 September 1966 During the afternoon the ship passes to the south of Greece, clearing Cape Matapan at 2.40 p.m. In the late afternoon there is a bridge drive. In the evening, the ship sails through the Cyclades.

24 September 1966 At 7.56 a.m. the ship arrives at Izmir in Turkey, where passengers may disembark. Edith is carried ashore so that she and Tolkien are able to see a little of the port. The ship leaves at 8.07 p.m.

25 September 1966 Sunday. The Captain officiates at divine service. At 12.30 p.m. the ship passes to the south of Cape Matapan. In the afternoon, there is a water polo match between passengers and officers, and in the evening a quiz.

26 September 1966 During the day there is a 'Frog Race Meeting' on deck.

27 September 1966 At 8.35 a.m. the cruise ship arrives at Venice, where the passengers again may go ashore. In the evening, there is a cabaret show. – Joy Hill writes to Phyllis Jenkinson, enclosing all of the material Allen & Unwin have received from the Performing Rights Society.

28 September 1966 Tolkien goes ashore in Venice and attends 8.00 a.m. Mass in St Mark's. The ship leaves at 12.07 p.m. In the late afternoon there is a children's fancy dress tea party, and in the evening a fancy dress dinner and dance.

29 September 1966 At 12.30 p.m. the ship rounds the heel of Italy. There is a concert in the evening. – Joy Hill writes to Phyllis Jenkinson. She thinks that all Performing Rights forms had better be dealt with through Allen & Unwin. She asks her to tell Tolkien on his return that she has duly sent a telegram in his name to Donald Swann and Michael Flanders for their opening night in

Boston, Massachusetts. Allen & Unwin have sold an extract from *The Lord of the Rings* to a Fleetway Magazine for their Christmas number.

30 September 1966 On the cruise ship there are aquatic sports in the morning and a concert in the evening. At 3.00 p.m. the ship passes Cape Bon on the Tunisian Coast.

October 1966 *Tolkien on Tolkien*, which contains extracts (with transcription errors) from Tolkien's letter to Nancy Smith of 25 December 1963, and from the autobiographical material he sent to Houghton Mifflin in 1955, is published in the October 1966 issue of *Diplomat*.

1 October 1966 On the cruise ship during the day there is a return polo match and a race meeting on deck. – John Tolkien is appointed Rector of the Church of Our Lady of the Angels and St Peter in Chains, Stoke-on-Trent.

2 October 1966 Sunday. The Captain officiates at divine service. At midday the ship passes Europa Point, the southernmost tip of Gibraltar, and cruises round Gibraltar Bay. In the late afternoon there is a progressive whist drive, and in the evening a concert of light music. At 11.00 p.m. the ship rounds Cape St Vincent, the south-western point of Portugal.

3 October 1966 The ship arrives at Lisbon at 8.16 a.m. in heavy rain. Some passengers, including Tolkien, are suffering from a throat infection. Tolkien and Edith have friends in Lisbon, Francis Stilwell and his wife. They were intending to show the Tolkiens around Lisbon, but because of the bad weather the Stilwells come aboard ship and lunch with the Tolkiens. In the evening, there is folk dancing. – Donald Swann writes to Tolkien and Edith from Boston, with news of the American tour, in particular the reception of *I Sit beside the Fire*. He has lunched with Austin Olney of Houghton Mifflin, who may publish Swann's settings of Tolkien songs. Swann is therefore considering a setting of *Errantry*, perhaps as a duet.

4 October 1966 The cruise ship leaves Lisbon at 3.17 a.m. and travels north through a rough sea with frequent rain squalls. In the evening, there is a farewell dinner and dancing.

5 October 1966 The weather improves as the ship passes through the Bay of Biscay.

6 October 1966 The ship arrives late in Southampton during the morning and, according to Tolkien, 'the precious "dockers" made this an excuse to refuse to assist in landing the luggage, so that disembarkation was confused and further delayed' (letter to Clyde Kilby, 11 October 1966, Marion E. Wade Center, Wheaton College, Wheaton, Illinois). He finds a mound of correspondence awaiting him.

7 October 1966 Pamela Chandler visits Tolkien. They discuss gardening, botany, and *English and Medieval Studies Presented to J.R.R. Tolkien* in which one of Chandler's photographs was used as a frontispiece.

8 October 1966 Donald Swann writes to Joy Hill. Houghton Mifflin have agreed to publish his songs as a book. He suggests various ideas for it: runic signs for illustrations; perhaps the first line of each song in Tengwar or runes; an extract from a glossary Tolkien has sent him for *Namárië*. He himself will write a preface describing how he came to set Tolkien's poems to music, and advice on how they might be sung.

10 October 1966 Rayner Unwin writes to Tolkien. Dick Plotz of the Tolkien Society of America wants to come to England and interview Tolkien for an article in the magazine *Seventeen*. The next time that Rayner visits Tolkien he will bring him a parcel from America with a jar of mushrooms and a message in the form of a scroll. He has heard that a woman arrested in Seattle for growing marijuana signed in at the police station in Elvish.

11 October 1966 Tolkien writes to Clyde Kilby, thanking him for his help during the summer.

> It was among the many evil effects of 'Ace Books' that the 'Gawain' business was not concluded, so that I was not able to give an undivided mind to the *Silmarillion*. But I became so involved in it again, and so re-energized and enheartened by you, that it made tinkering with *Gawain* and *Pearl* as unappetizing, not to say revolting, as eating a cold dinner already rejected. . . . In fact I am now still at it – as I failed to send in the stuff before sailing. [Marion E. Wade Center, Wheaton College, Wheaton, Illinois]

He describes the cruise. He and Edith are both still tired, but their former 'help' has returned to work for them. – Joy Hill writes to Phyllis Jenkinson. She is sure that there is a mound of paperwork awaiting Tolkien's attention, but asks Jenkinson to put the Performing Rights Society material somewhere near the top for Tolkien's signature. Tolkien should be told that Allen & Unwin intend to change their agreement with Donald Swann to give him exclusive use of the poems for a specific period of time. Rayner Unwin has signed a contract with the BBC for readings of Tolkien's works on the radio in 1967; the Canadian Broadcasting Corporation are interested in the same sort of idea.

12 October 1966 Tolkien sends the signed Performing Rights Society documents to Joy Hill. He did not return them immediately because they had required some consideration. If Donald Swann sets *Errantry*, the documents might need a little modification; perhaps they should provide for this. He complains that the documents have misspelled 'Tolkein' in one place and 'Revel' instead of 'Reuel' in each instance. – An artist in Kansas City, Missouri writes to Tolkien, asking permission to send for his consideration sketches he has made of characters from Tolkien's works. He mentions the possibility of syndicating to Sunday newspapers a serialization, lasting several years, of *The Hobbit* and *The Lord of the Rings* illustrated in full colour.

13 October 1966 Tolkien writes to Rayner Unwin. As a result of her fall at the start of the cruise, Edith will need lengthy treatment for her leg. He finds being interviewed a bore and a nuisance, but feels that he should meet Dick Plotz since he owes the Tolkien Society of America gratitude for helping with the Ace Books affair. He will give Plotz two hours, but there is to be no photography. He would like two copies of *The Adventures of Tom Bombadil* *and Other Verses from the Red Book* to be sent with an enclosed note to Francis Stilwell and his wife in Portugal. Referring to the mention of marijuana in Rayner's letter of 10 October, Tolkien does not like being associated with the drug traffic or drug taking. – Rayner Unwin writes to Tolkien. Ernst Klett have made a firm offer for a German translation of *The Lord of the Rings*, and want Tolkien to see some specimens. Separately he sends him cuttings from American newspapers, and a report from America on registration of proper names (such as *hobbit*).

14 October 1966 Tolkien writes to Donald Swann. He has considered whether *Errantry* might be abbreviated for performance, 'but its metrical scheme, with its trisyllabic near-rhymes, makes this very difficult. It is of course a piece of verbal acrobatics and metrical high-jinks' (*The Treason of Isengard*, p. 85). – Phyllis Jenkinson writes to Joy Hill, enclosing four letters. One is from a woman who also rang Tolkien, much to his annoyance, and whom he referred to Joy.

17 October 1966 Tolkien replies to the artist in Missouri. He does not have 'the time or, in fact, the competence to judge either the merit or the sales prospects of such a series as you indicate' (Tolkien-George Allen & Unwin archive, HarperCollins). Allen & Unwin deal with such matters; he is forwarding the letter to them. If the artist wishes to send any preliminary sketches, they should go to Allen & Unwin. – Tolkien writes to Rayner Unwin. He would like to see specimens of the German translation of *The Lord of the Rings*. He leaves it to Rayner to decide if it is worthwhile pursuing the possibility of obtaining patents. – Tolkien replies to a letter of appreciation of *The Hobbit* from children at a primary school in Acocks Green, Birmingham. He tells them about the much longer *Lord of the Rings*. When he lived at Sarehole as a child he used to walk to Acocks Green to visit an uncle.

18 October 1966 Rayner Unwin writes to Tolkien. He has just received photostats of *Mr. Bliss* from Marquette University. Copies of the *Adventures of Tom Bombadil* volume have been sent to the Stilwells. He will write to Dick Plotz. – Alina Dadlez writes to Tolkien, sending specimens of a German translation of *The Lord of the Rings* from the woman referred to in Tolkien's letter of 13 May. Klett, however, have not confirmed that she has been chosen as the translator of their edition.

19 October 1966 Joy Hill writes to Tolkien. She has adjusted the Performing Rights Society documents to allow for modification and/or rearrangement of *Errantry*, but Tolkien will have to sign them again. The woman who had telephoned Tolkien has now visited Joy and been told that she must look elsewhere for her non-commercial film project. – Rayner Unwin writes to Tolkien. He has told *Seventeen* magazine that Tolkien will see Dick Plotz for two hours only, and there is to be no photography. They have suggested 27, 28, or 31 October or 1 November for the interview. He has heard more from the patent agent, but it does not seem to get them any further.

21 October 1966 Tolkien writes to Rayner Unwin. He can see Dick Plotz on 1 November between 10.30 a.m. and 12.30 p.m. The other dates are not available. – Tolkien writes to Alina Dadlez. He has considered the specimens of German translation 'sufficiently to form a poor opinion of them' (contrary to his opinion of the translator's work expressed on 13 May 1966).

24 October 1966 Tolkien writes to Alina Dadlez. 'I had cherished special hopes with regard to a translation of *The Lord of the Rings* into German, believing that in Germany more people could be found with a knowledge of English studies, and the general Germanic field, than elsewhere. But I am disappointed with this version. It seems to me in general unskilful, so far as my knowledge of modern German allows me to judge.' The translator does not appear to have read *The Hobbit* or Appendix F (on translation) in *The Lord of the Rings*. Tolkien comments on her inconsistent system of translation of nomenclature, and finds her translations of verses 'clumsy and defective'.

> *Gamgie*, for instance . . . is not a phonetic rendering of *Gamgee*. If altered at all, it should be *Gamdschie*. The name and its pronunciation is entered in the Shorter Oxford Dictionary [i.e. *The Shorter Oxford English Dictionary*]. It means *cottonwool*. It is derived from the surname *Gamgee*, a medical family. It is still current, if locally. The name is not common, but probably more so than Tolkien. It appears in telephone directories, certainly in those of the London area. I am inclined to think that (for a translator resident in England at any rate) such name-lists might be remembered as useful – not to mention reference to good dictionaries offering a wide range of the vocabulary of 'modern' literary English plus some dialect, such as the Shorter Oxford, 2 vols, but not bulky.

He has 'made a number of notes on various points which I won't trouble you with now. In any case I have not had time to study the material with sufficient care to justify any attempt to influence the German publishers in their choice.' He notes that the translator has used the old (first) edition, and thinks that it would be better to use the forthcoming new edition. 'Of course if the German or publishers in any other country wish or intend to use the Index, the whole matter of nomenclature will be much easier to deal with. A copy could be provided in which all names could be marked that I wish left unchanged in form and spelling. . . . I should be perfectly willing to give my advice or opinion on the few remaining names that offer any difficulty' (Tolkien-George Allen & Unwin archive, HarperCollins). –The Director of the Junior Theatre in Wallingford, Pennsylvania writes to Tolkien. She would like his permission to mount a dramatization of *The Hobbit* for their April show.

?Late October 1966 Tolkien writes to Donald Swann. He comments on visual taste at Houghton Mifflin, in particular on the cover of the American edition of *Tree and Leaf*. – Possibly by now Tolkien has written, or begun to write, an essay on the content and meaning of *Smith of Wootton Major*, with initial remarks similar to some made at Blackfriars on 26 October.

26 October 1966 Tolkien reads *Smith of Wootton Major* at 8.15 p.m. at Blackfriars, St Giles', Oxford. Even though it is a very wet evening, over 800 people attend, more than the Refectory can hold: arrangements have to be made to relay the reading to those in the passages outside. The event is arranged by the Prior of Blackfriars and the Master of Pusey House.

27 October 1966 The Allen & Unwin second edition of *The Lord of the Rings* is published. – Alina Dadlez writes to Tolkien. Klett have decided not to use the translator whose work Tolkien criticized.

28 October 1966 Tolkien replies to a letter from Michael George. Since he is finding the typewriter so useful, Tolkien will give it to him as a coming-up gift. He tells him about the reading at Blackfriars, and comments on 'research' and modern literature. He and Edith hope that Michael George and Irene Ferrier (Michael George's future wife) will lunch with them soon at the Eastgate Hotel in Oxford. Edith is better, 'but her legs are painful, and she gets about with more difficulty than before we went away. She will be having some more treatment as soon as we return [from another stay in Bournemouth] on November 18' (British Library MS Add. 71657). – Rayner Unwin writes to Tolkien, confirming Dick Plotz's visit on 1 November, at 10.30 a.m.

?Late October or early November 1966 Gene Wolfe of Hamilton, Ohio writes to Tolkien. He asks about the etymology of *orc* and *warg*.

1 November 1966 Dick Plotz visits Tolkien at 10.30 a.m. Tolkien enjoys talking with him, and finds that his main interest is linguistic. Plotz asks Tolkien to sign the Allen & Unwin second edition *Lord of the Rings* Rayner Unwin has given him. Tolkien has not yet received a copy himself, and on opening it a misprint on the first page catches his eye. He gives Plotz a copy of the latest hardback *Hobbit* in which the coloured plates have reappeared. Plotz will describe the interview in *Seventeen* for January 1967 that precisely on time,

> Professor Tolkien opened the door, greeted me, came outside and shut the door behind him. He led me to a sort of garage attached to the house which can only be entered from outdoors. . . .
> He took out a pipe as he entered his study, and all during the interview he held it clenched in his teeth, lighting and relighting it, talking through it; he never removed it from his mouth for more than five seconds. . . .
> I tried out a few set questions I had prepared and found very quickly that Professor Tolkien had little taste for straight question-and-answer interviewing. He was always responsive and fascinating in what he said, but he was dizzyingly roundabout. As soon as he expressed one idea, it suggested another to him, and he was constantly making connections and going off in new directions. . . . I stopped trying to ask him questions and settled down to a conversation rather than an interview. ['J.R.R. Tolkien Talks About the Discovery of Middle-earth, the Origins of Elvish', p. 92]

Tolkien tells him that one of the snags delaying publication of *The Silmarillion* is its quasi-biblical style, which Tolkien considers 'his best, but his publishers disagree. Another problem is that of finding a story line to connect all the parts. At the moment, Professor Tolkien is considering making use of Bilbo again ... perhaps *The Silmarillion* will appear as his research in Rivendell' (p. 118). Tolkien and Plotz discuss Elvish languages, and Tolkien promises to send Plotz information about declensions in Quenya, which he will do some time in 1966–7 (the so-called 'Plotz declensions').

4 November 1966 Tolkien writes to Rayner Unwin. He describes Plotz's visit. He would like a set of the new edition of *The Lord of the Rings*, and a copy of the latest hardback edition of *The Hobbit* to replace his copy which he gave to Plotz.

7 November 1966 Tolkien replies to Gene Wolfe, explaining the real world etymology of *orc* and *warg*. – Tolkien replies briefly to a letter from an American who enclosed a proposal by his son and another American teenager for a film of *The Hobbit*. Tolkien is forwarding the proposal to Allen & Unwin. – Phyllis Jenkinson writes to Joy Hill, sending the film proposal, its covering letter, and a copy of Tolkien's reply.

8–18 November 1966 Tolkien and Edith stay at the Hotel Miramar, Bournemouth.

9 November 1966 Rayner Unwin writes to Tolkien. He has asked that a set of *The Lord of the Rings* and a replacement *Hobbit* be sent to Tolkien immediately.

13 November 1966 Donald Swann writes to Tolkien. He gives more news of the tour and the reception of *I Sit beside the Fire*. He has suggested to Austin Olney that each song in the planned book of the song cycle might have its first line written out in Elvish lettering, or even translated into Elvish. He wonders if Tolkien might write out the words for an illustrator to copy. Olney has agreed to decorative lettering in principle. The book might also include all or part of the glossary that Tolkien wrote out for *Namárië* in three coloured inks. Swann himself will write an introduction, and invites Tolkien to add introductory words of his own. He has been working on the setting of *Errantry*, and asks if, during his brief time at home over Christmas, he and his wife may visit Tolkien on the morning of 20 December at about 11.00 to 11.30 a.m. for an hour, drive him to a piano, and play him the song; he does not think that there will be time for lunch. In a postscript, Swann wonders about the word *melody*.

15 November 1966 Joy Hill writes to Tolkien, returning the Performing Rights Society documents to him again and asking him to initial the places where his (misspelled) name has been corrected.

18 November 1966 Tolkien replies to Donald Swann. He and Edith will be delighted to welcome Swann and his wife on the morning of 20 December. They may be able to have the use of a good piano in the house next door, but Tolkien will deal with that as soon as he returns home from Bournemouth. If there is any possibility of them having lunch in or near Oxford, he would like to be host. He is sending Swann a copy of his poem *Once upon a Time*. In regard to *melody*, Tolkien comments:

Only a few weeks ago I became interested in it – coming at it through the name *Philomel* . . . in one of J.I.M. Stewart's (Michael Innes) murder-stories. I found the puzzle, when looked into, much more complicated and less soluble than the murder. Since the investigation needs at least the help of a musician, and probably one who knows something about (the theories concerning) ancient Greek music, I put it aside. I am always doing this, and my room is like a jackdaw's nest, full of discarded invasions onto other peoples' condemned property. [Marion E. Wade Center, Wheaton College, Wheaton, Illinois]

19 November 1966 Tolkien probably attends the Boar's Head Dinner in Merton College Hall.

22 November 1966 The bronze bust of Tolkien, made from Faith Tolkien's plaster version, is installed in the English Faculty Library at 6.00 p.m. The English Faculty invite members of the Tolkien family to the ceremony. – Tolkien writes to Walter Hooper, thanking him for a copy of *Of Other Worlds: Essays and Stories by C.S. Lewis*, which Hooper has edited. Tolkien has read it with great interest. – Joy Hill writes to Tolkien. She is delighted that he is willing to see Charlotte and Denis Plimmer on 30 November at 10.00 a.m. (for an article to be published in the *Sunday Telegraph*, the arrangements probably made by telephone on this day or soon before).

23 November 1966 Tolkien telephones Joy Hill. He is being awarded the A.C. Benson Silver Medal for outstanding services to literature by the Royal Society of Literature.

24 November 1966 An announcement appears in *The Times* that the Royal Society of Literature has awarded the Benson Silver Medal to Dame Rebecca West and Professor J.R.R. Tolkien, after a lapse of fourteen years since the last award. (The dies to cast the medals were lost in the war. The Society has only now given up hope that they might turn up, and has commissioned new designs.)

27 November 1966 A brief interview, 'Tolkien Talking', appears in the *Sunday Times*.

28 November 1966 Tolkien replies to a letter from Clyde Kilby. Edith is still having treatment for her leg. Tolkien has not yet returned to work on *The Silmarillion*.

29 November 1966 Phyllis Jenkinson writes to Joy Hill, sending four letters with Tolkien's comments (for Joy to use in replying), and a fifth with a copy of Tolkien's reply.

30 November 1966 Tolkien is interviewed in the morning by Charlotte and Denis Plimmer. – Tolkien replies to a letter from Stanley Unwin. It was 'one of the most fortunate chances of my life that put me in touch with you' (Tolkien–George Allen & Unwin archive, HarperCollins). – Tolkien writes to Pamela Chandler. He asks about large photos of himself and Edith which they have ordered to give as Christmas presents.

7 December 1966 Tolkien writes to R.A.E. Baldick at Merton College, Oxford. Although he does not make much use of the Senior Common Room facilities, he encloses a donation for the Christmas box for the Common Room servants. – A young writer in London sends Tolkien a synopsis of his idea for a continuation of *The Lord of the Rings*, and three sample chapters. This could be altered to suit any ideas that Tolkien may have. He hopes for Tolkien's comments soon, and a chance to meet and discuss the matter and financial arrangements.

9 December 1966 Alina Dadlez writes to Tolkien. Allen & Unwin have sold the Danish translation rights for *The Lord of the Rings* to Gyldendal. She has asked them to consult Tolkien on nomenclature, and they have agreed.

12 December 1966 Tolkien writes to Joy Hill, sending the young writer's proposal for a continuation of *The Lord of the Rings*. He describes it as an 'impertinent contribution to my troubles' and asks about the legal position. He has informed the writer that he is forwarding his letter and enclosures to Allen & Unwin. Tolkien suggests that a letter from Allen & Unwin might be more effective than one from himself. He once received 'a similar proposal, couched in the most obsequious terms from a young woman, and when I replied in the negative, I received a most vituperative letter' (*Letters*, p. 371). – Tolkien writes to Alina Dadlez. He is pleased to hear about the proposed Danish translation. He has begun

to prepare an annotated name list based on the index: indicating those names that were to be left unchanged and giving information of the meaning and origin of those that it was desirable to render into the language of translation, together with some tentative advice on how to proceed. I hope soon to complete this and be able to send you a copy or copies for the use of translators appointed by the Danish publishers or the German publishers. [Tolkien-George Allen & Unwin archive, Harper-Collins; see *The Nomenclature of The Lord of the Rings*]

13 December 1966 Edith Tolkien writes to Clyde S. Kilby, thanking him for offering the Tolkiens a turkey for Christmas. They no longer have a turkey at Christmas, as none of the family are present, but do have a small one for Tolkien's birthday on 3 January. – Paddy Roberts, Chairman of the Songwriters Guild of Great Britain and Vice-Chairman of the Performing Rights Society, writes to welcome Tolkien as a member of the latter. He sends him the relevant forms in case he would like to consider joining the Songwriters Guild as well.

14 December 1966 Tolkien writes to Rayner Unwin, asking advice about a letter he has received from PEN (*Societies and clubs), asking him to contribute a manuscript to benefit the International Writers Fund. He is a member of PEN, but not eager to donate anything at the moment, 'since my income tax agents are busy reviewing and arranging all my property with a view to immediate tax and also to will-making, and I am at present considering the advisability of presenting all manuscripts of published work to my son Christopher' (Tolkien-George Allen & Unwin archive, HarperCollins). He sends a list of people to whom he would like copies of books sent. – Tolkien inscribes a copy of the Japanese *Hobbit* to Father Hugh Maycock, and writes a brief note to accompany it. – Rayner Unwin writes to Tolkien, forwarding a letter. He notes that the volume of Tolkien's fan mail intercepted by Allen & Unwin is growing mightily. He congratulates Tolkien on the award of the Benson Silver Medal.

Late December 1966 Otto B. Lindhardt of the Danish publisher Gyldendals Bibliotek writes to Tolkien. He is looking forward to publishing his work.

20 December 1966 Donald Swann and his wife Janet visit the Tolkiens and possibly lunch with them. Swann plays his setting of *Errantry*. At this meeting Tolkien and Swann agree on the production of a long-playing record with Swann and Elvin performing the song cycle on one side and Tolkien reading poems on the other. Swann probably also shows Tolkien his draft foreword for the book of the song cycle. They also discuss possible decorations or embellishments. In a letter to Joy Hill on 20 January 1967 Swann will say that he asked Tolkien if providing decorations for the book would upset his work on *The Silmarillion*, and Tolkien said no, that he was excited and felt creative, and at that showed Swann a folder of drawings.

21 December 1966 Rayner Unwin writes to Tolkien. He is unable to advise about the International Writers Fund. He has despatched the books as Tolkien requested.

22 December 1966 Jan Howard Finder, an instructor at the University of Illinois, Chicago, writes to ask permission to produce *The Hobbit* as a children's serial for school radio. He gives details and offers to send a copy of the adaptation of the first chapter. He has already written to Allen & Unwin. – Joy Hill writes to Austin Olney at Houghton Mifflin. Tolkien and Swann have agreed on a long-playing record with the song cycle on one side and Tolkien reading on the other.

25–26 December 1966 Tolkien and Edith travel to Abingdon on Christmas Day with some friends of Christopher, and stay in a hotel. They spend 26 December with Christopher and his son Simon.

28 December 1966 Joy Hill writes to Tolkien, asking if he owns the copyright in *Beowulf: The Monsters and the Critics*. She has received a request to reprint it. She encloses a letter to Tolkien from the Songwriters Guild.

29 December 1966 Tolkien writes to Joy Hill. He is not sure about ownership of the copyright in *Beowulf: The Monsters and the Critics*. He was paid an honorarium and has always supposed that he has some rights and is free to reprint it in a collection of his writings or otherwise. Since he does not at present intend to write words for songs, he does not think it worthwhile to join the Songwriters Guild of Great Britain. He sends her a letter already answered, with a copy of his reply, and two letters with his comments on how to deal with them. 'I am becoming snowed up again.' In regard to the suggestion of a radio adaptation of *The Hobbit* for children, he writes on that letter: 'Don't like it. Would stop it if I could. Don't want to see the script, would only give me the horrors. Have not answered it myself' (Tolkien-George Allen & Unwin archive, HarperCollins). He has not yet written to Donald Swann. – Tolkien replies to William Foster, who has asked to interview him for *The Scotsman*. Tolkien has had 'a surfeit of visits and interviews during the present year. I have found none of them pleasant, nearly all of them a complete waste of time, even from the point of view of sales.' Even though '*The Scotsman* is a highly reputable paper', Tolkien is 'desperately in need of time, and I have with the assent of my publishers decided in no circumstances to give any more interviews until I have brought out another book' (*Letters*, p. 372). See further, however, entry for Early 1967. – Joy Hill writes to Tolkien, asking for a specimen signature needed by the Performing Rights Society.

30 December 1966 Joy Hill writes to Tolkien, sending a copy of Dick Plotz's article in *Seventeen*. – The owner of a bar on Pensacola Beach, Florida writes to Tolkien c/o Ballantine Books. He has christened his establishment 'Hobbit' and would like permission to display the Ring verse on an inside wall.

?Late 1966 Tolkien is approached to make a contribution to an issue of *Shenandoah: The Washington and Lee University Review* which is to be a 'A Tribute to Wystan Hugh Auden on His Sixtieth Birthday'. Tolkien writes a poem, **For W.H.A.*, in Old and Modern English.

1967

From 1967 Telephone calls between Tolkien and either Rayner Unwin or Joy Hill at Allen & Unwin become increasingly frequent. Subjects discussed by phone subsequently appear in letters.

1967 Five newspaper doodles are dated by Tolkien to this, and forty-one others are on newspapers dating to 1967. Nine other doodles can be dated to 1967. – Tolkien writes a note in which he takes an entirely different view of the meaning of Gandalf's words, 'in the South Incánus', and of the etymology of the name *Incánus*, from that taken in a note written in 1966, before the publication of the second edition of *The Lord of the Rings* (see entry for August 1965).

Early 1967 Tolkien is interviewed by William Foster for *The Scotsman*. Although he had politely refused in a letter dated 29 December 1966, he has evidently relented. In his article, 'A Benevolent and Furry-footed People', *Week-end Magazine*, 25 March 1967, Foster will report that Tolkien's patience with his cult status is wearing thin, especially with fans or reporters who turn up unannounced on his doorstep. He describes Tolkien's converted garage: tacked to the window-sill is a map of Middle-earth showing the routes of two hobbit expeditions, and a list of Tolkien's engagements carefully written in blue-black ink. Tolkien gets up at 8.30 every morning, and sometimes goes to bed at 2.30 a.m., working away steadily on *The Silmarillion*, but admits that he finds it exhausting. Most of his time is fighting against the natural inertia of a lazy human being.

1 January 1967 Tolkien and Edith enjoy a turkey provided by Clyde Kilby, served with cranberry sauce, the cranberries given by another American.

2 January 1967 Tolkien writes to Joy Hill. He encloses the specimen signature she has requested, as well as two letters from a 'patent ass' (Tolkien-George Allen & Unwin archive, HarperCollins). – Tolkien replies to Otto B. Lindhardt, Gyldendals Bibliotek. 'Experience in attempting to help translators or in reading their versions has made me realise that the nomenclature of persons and places offers particular difficulty', but is important 'since it was constructed with considerable care, to fit with the supposed history of the period described. I have therefore recently been engaged in making, and have nearly completed, a commentary on the names in this story, with explanations and suggestions for the use of a translator, having especially in mind Danish and German' (Tolkien-George Allen & Unwin archive, HarperCollins). He would be pleased to send a copy to Gyldendal's translator. – Stanley Unwin writes to congratulate Tolkien on reaching the dignified age of 75. He sends his and Rayner Unwin's best wishes. – Joy Hill writes to Tolkien. She wishes him a happy birthday, and says that Dick Plotz has organized a special birthday greeting. She has sent him a copy of the *Children's Treasury of English Litera-ture*, published by Paul Hamlyn, an anthology which includes the first chapter of *The Hobbit*. She will consult Stanley Unwin about the copyright of *Beowulf: The Monsters and the Critics*. She asks if Miss Jenkinson could include a note of its length with her next batch of letters. Joy is unhappy about the foreword Donald Swann is writing for the planned Houghton Mifflin volume of the song cycle, but cannot interfere as it is not an Allen & Unwin publication. (Possibly Tolkien has spoken to her about it. In a letter to Austin Olney on 17 January she will say that Tolkien has read the foreword and is going to make some comments, but she does not know if he has done so.) She has dealt with or will deal with various letters sent by Tolkien. – Pamela Chandler writes to Tolkien. She has been asked to illustrate the article by Charlotte and Denis with some natural pictures of a day in Tolkien's life.

3 January 1967 Tolkien celebrates his seventy-fifth birthday. He receives many cards, letters and telegrams. – Edith Tolkien writes to Pamela Chandler. Tolkien agrees to be photographed, but not until February. Edith is still unable to walk, and is having treatment twice a week.

5 January 1967 Tolkien writes to Joy Hill. He will pass *The Children's Treasury of Literature* to his youngest grandson, aged 8 (Christopher's son Simon). He finds 'a great many' of its illustrations 'very good, including some of the modern ones', but those for the *Hobbit* extract seem 'vulgar, stupid and entirely out of keeping with the text' (collection of René van Rossenberg). He informs Joy of the length of *Beowulf: The Monsters and the Critics* as published for the British Academy. – Tolkien replies to a letter from Clyde Kilby, which mentions the Tolkien issue of *Diplomat*. Tolkien thinks that it is probably best that he does not see it, as he finds such things disturbing, 'and the best thing is to get on with my work without bothering what people say' (Marion E. Wade Center, Wheaton College, Wheaton, Illinois).

10 January 1967 Tolkien writes to Michael George. He has a copy of the new edition of *The Lord of the Rings* as a gift for his birthday. He has heard that Michael's sister Joanna and her husband Hugh Baker are coming to Oxford on Friday. She is expecting a child, so 'I shall, all being well, as I expected, reach the eminent position of great-grandfather in the course of the year' (British Library MS Add. 71657).

11 January 1967 Tolkien replies to a letter from R.B. McCallum, Master of Pembroke College, who has written concerning the College's financial needs. Tolkien's income has been much exaggerated by the press, and he does not have much surplus. He will keep Pembroke in mind in his will.

12 January 1967 Austin Olney writes to Joy Hill, sending a sample sketch by Maurice Sendak for Houghton Mifflin's proposed illustrated *Hobbit*.

13 January 1967 Tolkien is presumably visited by his granddaughter Joanna and her husband Hugh Baker.

15 January 1967 Philip Norman's article, 'The Hobbit Man', is published in the *Sunday Times Magazine*, and in the *New York Times Magazine* as 'The Prevalence of Hobbits'.

16 January 1967 Tolkien writes to Joy Hill. He found Philip Norman's article less bad than it might have been. 'I was rung up last night near bedtime by a woman who didn't give her name; she had just herself been rung up by the *New York Times*. They appear to have been interested in film and television reproduction, especially after a long article on me in their paper' (Tolkien-George Allen & Unwin archive, HarperCollins). He hopes that Houghton Mifflin can send him a copy of the article. He has completed, and Miss Jenkinson has typed, a commentary on the names in *The Lord of the Rings*. He has only a top copy and a carbon. He asks if Joy could arrange for more copies to be made.

17 January–1 February 1967 Tolkien and Edith stay at the Hotel Miramar, Bournemouth.

17 January 1967 Joy Hill writes to Phyllis Jenkinson. Joy has had a letter from Austin Olney, who says that Tolkien promised Donald Swann that he would look out for 'embellishments' for the song cycle book. She asks if Miss Jenkinson knows if Tolkien did this. Olney would like the material by 1 March.

18 January 1967 Donald Swann writes to Tolkien. He hears that Tolkien has been in touch with Swann's wife Janet and their children in the past few weeks. Austin Olney would be delighted to have Tolkien embellish the song book, if he feels that it would not disturb other work. Swann has altered the setting of one line of *Errantry*. He encloses a copy of his revised foreword for the book; Tolkien may ask for alterations to be made. It is planned to print, near a translation of *Namárië*, the manuscript Tolkien sent to Swann, and which Tolkien wants to revise or copy, concerning words and accentuation of the poem (presumably the glossary referred to in previous correspondence). Austin Olney seems amenable to any kind or extent of decoration. Swann hopes that Joy Hill can take photocopies of any originals, and be responsible for sending any material to the USA.

?Late January or early February 1967 In an undated draft for a letter to Donald Swann, possibly a reply to Swann's letter of 18 January, Tolkien writes that the text of *Namárië* 'should be given set out plain (in addition to the words fitted to music)' according to the Allen & Unwin revised second edition, noting where that differs from the Ballantine Books edition. He asks if Swann thinks that 'a text such as I sent you, with scansion marks, and stress-marks, and pause-signs is really required in a book in which the *Lament* is set to music? Anyway the elementary remarks on metre might be cut down' (Tolkien Papers, Bodleian Library, Oxford).

19 January 1967 Joy Hill writes to Tolkien. Charlotte and Denis Plimmer have sent one copy of their draft article which Allen & Unwin had to return to them. Joy thinks that it is better than anything that has yet appeared, but it has to be cut. No date has been set for its publication. Joy has had an offer from the Canadian Broadcasting Corporation to read *The Lord of the Rings* in approximately thirty-nine episodes for a fee of $500 per volume. She is investigating the length of each episode. Allen & Unwin would like to have Tolkien's commentary on names; they can make further copies photographically.

21 January 1967 Phyllis Jenkinson writes to Joy Hill, sending a copy of the commentary on nomenclature, and *Lord of the Rings* index. She knows nothing about embellishments for the song book, and will write to ask Tolkien.

23 January 1967 Rayner Unwin writes to Tolkien. Ian Ballantine, of Ballantine Books, is coming to England in mid-February and would like to see Tolkien. Rayner thinks that Tolkien should agree to do so. Rayner wants to visit Tolkien himself, as soon as he has returned to Oxford, to discuss various things. 'If you thought it would be better to kill two birds with one stone I could escort Mr Ballantine to you and escort him away again' (Tolkien-George Allen & Unwin archive, HarperCollins).

24 January 1967 Rayner Unwin writes to Austin Olney. He will show Maurice Sendak's sketch to Tolkien when the latter returns to Oxford early in February. He will also 'try to take up with Tolkien the business of the embellishments [to *The Road Goes Ever On: A Song Cycle*]. His calligraphic hand is not so firm as it used to be, and whatever he does would have to be accurately redrawn, I suspect' (George Allen & Unwin archive, University of Reading).

26 January 1967 Joy Hill writes to Phyllis Jenkinson. She should tell Tolkien that the *New York Times Magazine* article is a reprint of the Philip Norman article in the *Sunday Times*. She thanks her for 'the last two batches of horrors. I must say the multi-coloured envelopes at least make me answer the letter since the longer they sit on my desk the dizzier I feel' (Tolkien-George Allen & Unwin archive, HarperCollins).

Late January 1967 William Ready, formerly Director of Libraries at Marquette University, now at McMaster University, Hamilton, Canada, writes to Tolkien. He is writing a book about Tolkien.

29 January 1967 Tolkien replies to a letter from Humphrey Carpenter, asking permission for himself and Paul Drayton to use *The Hobbit* as a basis for a children's musical play. He agrees, but points out that Allen & Unwin's consent is also needed. He would like to see Carpenter again but he is very busy at the moment.

31 January 1967 Joy Hill writes to Tolkien. Since the publication of *The Homecoming of Beorhtnoth* in *The Tolkien Reader*, Allen & Unwin have been receiving enquiries about publication rights. Joy asks if Tolkien would like Allen & Unwin to deal with these rights on the same basis that they deal with his other published works. If so, she asks him to sign a duplicate copy of the letter to this effect.

February 1967 L. Sprague de Camp (a writer of science fiction and fantasy) visits Tolkien with Alan Nourse (also a writer of science fiction) during a short stay in London on their way back to the United States from India. De Camp and Tolkien had corresponded, and on this occasion Tolkien 'kindly invited me out for an afternoon. We drank beer in his garage (converted to a storage library) and talked about everything under the sun. . . . [Tolkien] conceded that the curious lack of large wild life in Middle-earth (e.g. no mammoths or sabre-toothed cats) was a reflection of his own background of the English countryside . . .' (letter to the editor, *Andúril* 1 (April 1972), pp. 8–9).

2 February 1967 Tolkien replies to William Ready. 'I dislike being written about, and the results to date have caused me both irritation and distaste.' He has vetoed a book (by Auden) planned by the publisher Eerdmans, but 'will not attempt to do the same with regard to your project. But I hope you will make it literary (and as critical of that aspect as you like) and not personal. I have no inclination, and in fact must refuse, to provide information about myself, family and family origin' (quoted in Ready, *The Tolkien Relation* (1968), pp. 55–6). – Donald Swann writes to Joy Hill about plans for the long-playing record. He would like William Elvin to work for a few hours with Tolkien.

6 February 1967 Tolkien reads the draft article by Charlotte and Denis Plimmer. He objects to parts of it, and telephones Joy Hill in the morning to say so. He refuses to be photographed for the article. He tells Joy that he has some problem with his eyes. – After the telephone call, Joy Hill re-reads the article and writes to Tolkien that she does not think he comes out badly in it. Both Stanley and Rayner Unwin see nothing wrong with the article. They all think that it is better than anything else that has been written about Tolkien so far. She told the Plimmers before the interview that if Tolkien asked to see the article and asked them to make changes to it, they must agree to his wishes; but it seems that he did neither, and it is now more difficult to ask for changes. She understands his feelings;

> but when an author is acclaimed in the way you have been acclaimed, when an author's books sell at the fantastic proportion yours sell and when you are the only English author to appear in the list of America's bestsellers this year, you do become a target for press, radio and television. . . . When a writer reaches the stature that you have now attained then the public want to know more. We protect you a good deal from the press but no publisher in their senses would want to turn down the

chance of a large illustrated article devoted to one author in the *Weekend Telegraph*. . . . If there is a cause for complaint about some point which is totally inaccurate then I will make that complaint but if the article can do good, to cross swords with the press can do harm all round. [Tolkien–George Allen & Unwin archive, HarperCollins]

Joy was responsible for suggesting to the *Telegraph*, when they asked about photographs, that Tolkien would probably agree to another sitting with Pamela Chandler. – Tolkien writes to Pamela Chandler. He feels that he cannot spare the time, nor 'tolerate any further photographs of myself in my own home'. He finds the Plimmers' article 'ill-written, though more pretentious, in fact actually little better than other recent interviews. Much of it I resent as an impertinent intrusion into my privacy' (Pamela Chandler archive).

8 February 1967 Tolkien writes to Charlotte and Denis Plimmer about their article.

It is evident that I presented some difficulties to you during the interview: by my swift speech (which is congenital and incurable), my discourtesy in walking about, and my use of a pipe. No discourtesy was intended. I suffer from arthritis and my knees give me pain if I sit for long. It is one alleviation of being interviewed if I can stand. I should forgo smoking on these occasions, but I have found being interviewed increasingly distasteful and distracting, and need some sedative. . . .

There are one or two points I should prefer to see altered, and some inaccuracies and misunderstandings that have, no doubt partly by my own fault, crept into the text. . . . I am a pedant devoted to accuracy, even in what may appear to others unimportant matters.

He will send detailed comments in a few days. He will not agree to be photographed. 'I regard all such intrusions into my privacy as an impertinence, and can no longer afford the time for it. The irritation it causes me spreads its influence over a far greater time than the actual intrusion occupies. My work needs concentration and peace of mind' (*Letters*, pp. 372–3). – Tolkien writes to someone in Spain who wishes to translate one or more of his works into Spanish, referring him to Allen & Unwin. – Tolkien replies to a letter from Colin Manlove: '*The Lord of the Rings* was a deliberate attempt to write a large-scale adult fairy-story' (quoted in Manlove, *Modern Fantasy: Five Studies* (1975), p. 158).

10 February 1967 Joy Hill writes to Tolkien. A publisher in Argentina was granted world rights for Spanish translations of *The Hobbit* and *The Lord of the Rings*, but she will investigate the matter and reply to the person who wrote to Tolkien.

?15 February 1967 Tolkien sends Charlotte and Denis Plimmer a ten-page typescript commenting on their article.

16 February 1967 Tolkien writes to Charlotte and Denis Plimmer. He asks them to excise a sentence from the commentary that is on its way to them. – Rayner Unwin visits Tolkien, perhaps accompanied by Ian Ballantine (who certainly visits Tolkien by 28 February). They discuss the one-volume paperback of *The Lord of the Rings* that Allen & Unwin are now planning. They need any corrections to the 1966 second edition as soon as possible to incorporate in the new setting. They would like a cover design from Tolkien, but if he does not have time to make one, Allen & Unwin will use Pauline Baynes' design for the box of the de luxe set, and might need to borrow her original painting from Tolkien. Rayner also raises matters relating to the book of the Swann song cycle: he asks for specimens of Elvish script suitable for embellishing the binding, and for the note on Elvish accentuation which Tolkien sent to Swann and then retrieved. (Tolkien will look for this, but cannot find it.) Rayner and Tolkien agree that *Mr. Bliss* should probably not be published. Rayner shows Tolkien the sample illustration by Maurice Sendak for the proposed Houghton Mifflin illustrated *Hobbit*. Rayner will write to Austin Olney on 20 February that Tolkien was not 'wildly happy about the proportions of the figures' in the Sendak drawing, and that he claimed that he could easily produce some Elvish calligraphy for the song book.

17 February 1967 Rayner Unwin writes to Tolkien, summarizing their discussions of the previous day.

Late February and March 1967 Tolkien spends time on corrections and emendations for the one-volume paperback *Lord of the Rings*, which are also to be incorporated in reprints of the three-volume hardback second edition. He makes several changes in references to the *palantíri*, and while working on these, writes notes and background material on the *palantíri* later published in *Unfinished Tales* (**The Palantíri*).

20 February 1967 Tolkien writes to Clyde Kilby. He thanks him for sending a copy of *Science Is a Sacred Cow* (presumably the book by Anthony Standen, first published 1950). Tolkien intends to go away for three days, and will take the book with him. – Rayner Unwin writes to Austin Olney, reporting on relevant matters dealt with during his visit to Tolkien. Although Tolkien said that he could easily produce some Elvish calligraphy, Rayner doubts that he will do so by Olney's 1 March deadline. He suggests that if Olney has heard nothing by that date, he should go ahead without the calligraphy.

21 February 1967 Austin Olney sends Joy Hill a rough dummy spread for *The Road Goes Ever On: A Song Cycle*. He explains where he would like to place decorations, some of which could be repeated. If Tolkien cannot manage to produce these, Houghton Mifflin will ask another artist. – Tolkien's poem *For W.H.A.* is published in the Winter 1966 issue of *Shenandoah: The Washington and Lee University Review*, 'A Tribute to Wystan Hugh Auden on His Sixtieth Birthday'.

23 February 1967 Rayner Unwin sends Tolkien a revised agreement for publication of *The Silmarillion*, to cover a point raised during a discussion by Tolkien with his solicitor. (Tolkien is making his will, and arranging for his son

Christopher to deal with *The Silmarillion* after his death.) Rayner also sends a list of questions which Andrew Salkey, an interviewer for a possible BBC broadcast, would like to ask him.

24–27 February 1967 Tolkien had intended to be away from Oxford, but this is apparently postponed. Edith has contracted mumps.

27 February 1967 Donald Swann writes to Rayner Unwin. Tolkien has still not produced the accentuation notes, nor the requested translation of the verse *A Elbereth Gilthoniel.*

28 February 1967 Rayner Unwin writes to Tolkien. He encloses colour photographs of people dressed as *Lord of the Rings* characters at the World Science Fiction Convention. Ian Ballantine was delighted by his reception. Austin Olney and Donald Swann are waiting anxiously for the embellishments and the note on accentuation. – Iris Goldsworthy, of the London office of Caedmon Records, writes to Tolkien, presumably c/o Allen & Unwin. Her firm (a specialist in spoken word recordings) would like to record Tolkien reading some of his work, especially *The Hobbit*. If he is interested, they would like him to provide a sample recording of his voice.

?Early March 1967 Oxford University Press sends Tolkien proofs of his and E.V. Gordon's edition of *Sir Gawain and the Green Knight*, as revised by Norman Davis.

1 March 1967 Tolkien and Rayner Unwin speak by telephone. Rayner has presumably rung to remind Tolkien that 1 March had been set as the deadline for delivery of the embellishments for the song book. Tolkien promises to send something before 3 March. – While they are talking, Donald Swann rings Allen & Unwin and speaks to Joy Hill. She will later write to tell him of Tolkien's promise. – Austin Olney writes to Rayner Unwin. Donald Swann thinks that Tolkien is too bogged down to do anything about the embellishments, and that Olney should perhaps look for an American artist to provide them. But it would be helpful to have ideas from Tolkien on what should be included.

3 March 1967 In the evening, Tolkien attends a dinner of The Society hosted by J.T. Christie at Jesus College, Oxford. Nine members are present. Christie reads a paper on Richard Bentley and his revisions of Horace.

6 March 1967 Rayner Unwin writes to Austin Olney. Tolkien has said that he will produce the calligraphy by the end of the week, but Rayner doubts this. There are also various other things that Donald Swann needs, 'all of which it seems virtually impossible to extract' (George Allen & Unwin archive, University of Reading). – Joy Hill replies to Mrs Goldsworthy of Caedmon Records. She explains that Allen & Unwin have Tolkien's instructions to open mail addressed to him. She does not think that Tolkien would agree to read the whole of *The Hobbit* for a recording, but the possibility that he will record some of his poetry is already being considered.

c. **7–13 March 1967** Tolkien and Edith stay at the Hotel Miramar, Bournemouth. Tolkien will write to Rayner Unwin on 14 March: 'I was unable to get on with work at Bournemouth, although I took some with me. My wife was ill and I was uncomfortably housed. On arrival we found that we were landed in the middle of a (mild) dysentery plague which struck down one by one guests and staff', though he and Edith were spared (Tolkien-George Allen & Unwin archive, HarperCollins).

14 March 1967 Tolkien writes to Rayner Unwin. He would rather be spared another interview, and is unhappy with the list of proposed questions from Mr Salkey. 'I am very bad at these things. Recent results have made me feel sore and ill-tempered. . . . I find it difficult to make people realise the amount of disquiet and dislocation of thought that this form of publicity afflicts me with' (Tolkien-George Allen & Unwin archive, HarperCollins). Tolkien has just recovered from an attack of crippling lumbago. – Tolkien writes to Alina Dadlez. He encloses a letter from a German apparently proposing an illustrated edition of *The Lord of the Rings*. It is not clear if he is proposing himself as the artist, or if it is the English edition or the German edition that he thinks should be illustrated. 'As far as an English edition goes,' Tolkien writes, 'I myself am not at all anxious for *The Lord of the Rings* to be illustrated by anybody whether a genius or not' (Tolkien-George Allen & Unwin archive, HarperCollins).

15 March 1967 Tolkien and Edith attend the Senior Proctor's lunch at Merton College. In a letter to Donald Swann, Tolkien will say that they enjoyed it, 'and from a far table where she was in the company of Nevill Coghill [Edith] occasionally waved a glass of '59 back at me' (20 March 1967, Marion E. Wade Center, Wheaton College, Wheaton, Illinois). – Alina Dadlez writes to Tolkien. She returns his commentary on the *Lord of the Rings* index. Allen & Unwin have made several photocopies, which are being sent to publishers preparing translations of *The Lord of the Rings*.

16 March 1967 Rayner Unwin apparently talks with Tolkien by telephone before writing to Austin Olney. Tolkien '*says* that he will give the *Song Book* material top priority and will let me have something this week. I think he will honestly try to do so and when it comes I think it will be far more elaborate and probably rather more enchanting than we had either of us envisaged, but that is the nature of the man.' If Tolkien does not produce anything, Olney must go ahead without it, 'but I would be very careful indeed about Elvish or Runic inscriptions without the author's guiding hand. . . . I would underdecorate rather than risk the numerous pitfalls into which the uninitiated in Elvish can fall.' He is still trying to extract the material Donald Swann wants. 'Perhaps I am the least surprised of all about these alarms and delays – I have been experiencing them since I was eleven years old' (George Allen & Unwin archive, University of Reading). – Donald Swann writes to Tolkien. He had hoped to decorate the pages of the song book with Tolkien's Elvish script and drawings, but does not want this to be a burden for Tolkien rather than a pleasure. If Tolkien is too busy to do this and to supply a translation for *A Elbereth Gilthoniel*, he should not worry. As for the accentuation sheet for *Namárië* of which Tolkien had hoped to make a better copy, Swann thinks that the original would do.

17 March 1967 Alina Dadlez writes to Tolkien. She has replied to the writer from Germany, and has sent the German publisher a photocopy of Tolkien's commentary on the index, with the request that their translator should follow his instructions regarding nomenclature and contact Tolkien only if there are problems.

20 March 1967 Tolkien writes to Donald Swann. He thanks him for not cursing him

> as a dilatory old dog, miner of friendship and destroyer of business. The truth is I cannot do two things at the same time, nor anything perfunctorily. This business of the Elvish Songs, and versions, and examples of Elvish Script is just precisely what I like doing; but unfortunately it *has* come at the wrong time. In that, in spite of every kind of interruption and distraction I am desperately trying to get off and out my '*Gawain and the Pearl*' – and I have now slapped on my table the proofs of the revised edition of the M[iddle] E[nglish] Text of *Gawain* [i.e. the revision by Norman Davis of the Tolkien-Gordon edition], which has to be considered in itself and in the rendering. I have tried to sit on two stools and have of course slumped between them, and given no pleasure to anybody.

Today, however, he completed two 'brochures', one for *Namárië* and one for *A Elbereth Gilthoniel* (and for illustration, Sam's invocation to Elbereth). 'Both contain text, literal version, notes on metre, pronunciation, and on words and mythology and what not.' The latter also has metrical versions. 'Use what you like of it. . . . These, with some calligraphic (?) specimens, possibly usable for décor, I am sending *direct to you* tomorrow, expressed' (Marion E. Wade Center, Wheaton College, Wheaton, Illinois). He hopes that Austin Olney can arrange to have them photographed for Tolkien's records of his own work. Tolkien has also been in contact with Janet Swann, and protests that *he* had wanted to entertain *them* (the Swanns) on 1 May. – Rayner Unwin writes to Tolkien. He has been approached by someone who wants to record Tolkien reading selections from *The Hobbit* and *The Lord of the Rings*. Rayner understands that this person is a colleague of a former student of Tolkien. The decision is up to Tolkien, but Allen & Unwin feel that Caedmon Records are probably better equipped for such a project.

21 March 1967 Tolkien writes to Donald Swann, sending the background material for *The Road Goes Ever On: A Song Cycle*. In a covering letter he says that since he had to redo a page of the decorative matter, spoiled 'by a clumsy botch and error', he will send it by the next post. 'It consists of [Galadriel's] Lament and Chant both written out in a fair Elvish book-hand, rubricated' (Marion E. Wade Center, Wheaton College, Wheaton, Illinois). – Rayner Unwin rings Tolkien. He is told that Tolkien has just posted the material wanted for the song book. Rayner cables Houghton Mifflin that the material had been sent.

22 March 1967 Tolkien and Edith celebrate their fifty-first wedding anniversary. – Tolkien writes to Donald Swann. He sends

> two 'calligraphic' transcripts of the Lament and Chant – alas poor. My old hand is no longer much skilled. Also I made some blunders imperfectly emended. Use them on any part that may be useful. They would give 'fans' some exercise in reading Elvish script. The Lament is in the Standard (Third Age) Quenya spelling described on page III 399 [of *The Return of the King*]. . . . The Chant is in the Sindarin mode used in the inscription on the Gate of Moria in Vol. I.

He asks forgiveness for 'imperfections, delays, etc.' (Marion E. Wade Center, Wheaton College, Wheaton, Illinois).

24 March 1967 Tolkien receives a letter from W.H. Auden, thanking him for his contribution to *Shenandoah* and praising Tolkien's poem *The Sea-Bell*. Auden encloses a typescript of his and Paul B. Taylor's translation of 'The Song of the Sibyl' from the *Elder Edda*.

27 March 1967 Donald Swann writes to Tolkien. He is thrilled with the second package which arrived this morning, and which has been sent on to Houghton Mifflin. He hopes that they use it suitably. Austin Olney wants to weave Elvish writing around the music throughout the book. He might want also to print part or whole of the final manuscript, but Swann points out that the attraction of Tolkien's notes for the back of the song book lies in their handwriting, layout, and scholarship, not only in their meaning. William Elvin is now learning *Errantry*. When Swann next sees Tolkien, he would like to discuss how best to coach Elvin, or Elvin could come and sing the songs to Tolkien. Swann is determined that the songs be recorded with correct inflection, etc.

28 March 1967 Rayner Unwin writes to Tolkien. The film rights of *The Hobbit* are confused. Allen & Unwin dispute that Rembrandt Films have fulfilled their contract by submitting, before the date their option expired, a film of only ten to twelve minutes. Rayner warns Tolkien not to let himself be recorded on tape without making the same demand as for a film: cash or kudos.

29 March 1967 Tolkien writes to W.H. Auden. He thanks him for his letter, and the typescript. If he can find it, he will send him something he wrote years ago 'when trying to learn the art of writing alliterative poetry: an attempt to unify the lays about the Völsungs from the Elder Edda, written in old eight-line fornyrðislag stanza' (*Letters*, pp. 378–9; see *Northernness).

30 March 1967 Joy Hill writes to Tolkien. She encloses his translation and notes on *Namárië* and *A Elbereth Gilthoniel*, together with a typed version which has not yet been copy-edited. Houghton Mifflin are delighted with the material, and would like to include Tolkien's notes as an appendix to the song book.

?End of March 1967 Humphrey Carpenter visits Tolkien at Sandfield Road, and is received in the converted garage-study. (Carpenter will describe the meeting in *Biography*.) Tolkien is trying to clear up an apparent contradiction in a passage in *The Lord of the Rings* which has been pointed out by a reader, and the matter is urgent as a revised edition is about to go to press.

April 1967 or later A sketch on an April newspaper is inscribed 'The Flame-thorn'. Another, of scrolling stems (also on an April newspaper), is similar to various undated finished drawings by Tolkien of grasses, rushes, and reeds in the manner of oriental bamboo paintings (e.g. *Artist and Illustrator*, p. 6).

?1–?14 April 1967 Tolkien and Edith stay at the Hotel Miramar, Bournemouth.

1 April 1967 Donald Swann writes to Rayner Unwin. He and Austin Olney have been assuming that Tolkien has no objection to the reproduction of his manuscripts in the book, but Swann has never asked him directly. He asks Rayner to check this with Tolkien, perhaps by phone.

3 April 1967 Phyllis Jenkinson sends to Rayner Unwin copies of *The Lord of the Rings* with corrections entered by Tolkien for the one-volume edition. He has not yet done anything to the index and the Appendices, since those will not be included in the one-volume edition. But he has prepared the text to suit both the one-volume edition and a future revision of the three-volume edition and will deal with the index and Appendices in due course. Tolkien has his own fully corrected copies, but would like to have back those he is sending when the printers have finished with them.

4 April 1967 Rayner Unwin writes to Tolkien. Donald Swann thinks that Houghton Mifflin may wish to produce Tolkien's glosses and designs as written in his own handwriting, and therefore wants to check that Tolkien has no objection. Unless he hears to the contrary, Rayner will assume that Tolkien does not object.

6 April 1967 Joy Hill writes to Tolkien. *The Lord of the Rings* is being transcribed into Braille and made into a talking book for the blind.

10 April 1967 Rayner Unwin writes to Donald Swann. He has checked that Tolkien has no objections to his manuscript glosses, etc. being reproduced.

12 April 1967 Tolkien writes to Donald Swann. Before leaving Oxford for Bournemouth, he began a reply to Swann's last letter, but it became very long as it was difficult to make the points clear. It would be easier to discuss these when they next meet.

The intentionally 'calligraphic' pages, in formal and decorative scripts, were intended to be reproduced. (Though I now fear that a photographic copy may be a necessity to ensure that I have not made errors in them. A characteristic I did not mention was my inability (in spite of care) to produce 'copy' without auctorial errors! I have not received a copy of the calligraphic pages, but alas! I find there are errors *of mine* (a few) in the Commentaries.)

He cannot visualize what is meant by Olney's suggestion of 'weaving the Elvish writing round the music'. It might be decorative, but the result might be absurd

> unless the designers are fully aware of the actual meaning of the lines, words, or other elements so used. My notion was these pages providing 'authoritative' examples of the use of the scripts would face the pages on which the song-texts (in modern alphabet) were contained, so providing a 'crib' for the instruction of script-fans (most of whom are much at sea in the matter). If I were producing a text (in say Russian or Greek or other in our roman script) with a roman transcription fitted to music, and a text in the original letters, I should much prefer the latter to be produced organically, by itself with its own grace, rather than interwoven or scattered about.
>
> I am convinced that they are not fit for reproduction by 'photography' as they stand; and also are in many points not really suitable for printing as they stand. . . . They were written under too much pressure to be (in pen-terms) well written; or indeed as far as matter goes, well arranged for publication. After consultation with you I am perfectly willing (I should love doing it) to re-write, both in handwriting and in matter, what is suitable of this matter. To use the stuff I sent to you as it stands would court disaster. If 'reproduced' it would evidently be largely illegible; if printed it would be likely to be largely nonsensical.

The typescript made from the commentaries sent to him by Austin Olney contains so many errors that they are reduced to nonsense. He cites a few examples.

> What is needed is 'copy' in a larger and clearer script . . . *or*, and I think this alone would really work, a carefully *typed copy* (typed on this side) with instructions that it must be printed precisely as per copy supplied. Some reductions would have to be made. And some alterations. For instance 'phonetic' instructions were aimed at you (and Elvin) who speak the same language. They would be useless or confusing to U.S.A. readers. [Marion E. Wade Center, Wheaton College, Wheaton, Illinois]

17 April 1967 Tolkien replies to a letter from J.D. Gilbert of London. He thinks that one reason that some books, read and enjoyed in childhood, later lose their charm is that an inexperienced young reader does not notice that they are badly written.

21 April 1967 Austin Olney speaks by telephone with Donald Swann, who has just received Tolkien's letter of 12 April. He then writes to Tolkien. The typed copy sent earlier had been only roughly transcribed. He is now enclosing a more final arrangement of the material for the appendix (not necessarily free from errors), so that Tolkien can judge better. Donald Swann has suggested that rather than set them in type, Tolkien might like to rewrite his comments in his own manuscript, making modifications as he sees fit. Houghton Mifflin would be happy for Tolkien to do this, but they need copy in a week. He encloses photographic copies of very rough sample pages, both for the music and the text of the song book. Houghton Mifflin intend to run Tolkien's original manuscript consecutively as a decorative border along the top and bottom of each page, increased in size and in a second colour. – John Leyerle, a former student of Tolkien and now a professor in Toronto, writes to Tolkien. He is preparing some early English texts for a large anthology being edited by Northrop Frye, and asks if he may include Tolkien's translations of *The Owl and the Nightingale* and *Sir Gawain and the Green Knight*.

Between 21 and 28 April 1967 William Ready delivers Leyerle's letter by hand to Tolkien. He spends about an hour and a half talking with Tolkien, mainly (Tolkien will recall) about himself. Ready will later claim that he spent hours interviewing Tolkien, which Tolkien will refute in several letters.

24 April 1967 Rayner Unwin forwards Austin Olney's letter to Tolkien, sent via Allen & Unwin. Allen & Unwin, who are to publish the British edition of *The Road Goes Ever On: A Song Cycle*, would welcome the inclusion of appendices in Tolkien's facsimile handwriting. Rayner asks if it is really necessary for Tolkien to rewrite the material.

26 April 1967 Rayner Unwin writes to Tolkien. At Tolkien's request, Allen & Unwin have been trying to sell *Smith of Wootton Major* (apparently, that is, in the magazine market). *Redbook* have offered $2,000 for a single use in their Christmas 1967 issue, but want some cuts to be made, either by Tolkien or with his approval. Would Tolkien be willing to make some reduction himself, or authorize someone else to make it? Rayner points out that once the story has been published, there will be pressure for it to appear in a more permanent form. He thinks that they should anticipate this by producing it as a small Christmas gift book, with embellishments by Pauline Baynes. Allen & Unwin and Donald Swann have put together a scheme for a long-playing record to be produced by Caedmon, which (as discussed earlier) will have the song cycle performed by Swann and Elvin on one side, and Tolkien reading some of his poems on the other. The recording people are willing to come to Tolkien in Oxford. Rayner gives details of the terms offered, and thinks that the record will be an excellent link with the song book.

27 April 1967 Rayner Unwin writes to Tolkien. He has heard that the official presentation to Tolkien of the Benson Silver Medal by the Royal Society of Literature will take place on 19 July. He asks Tolkien to have a celebratory lunch with him before the event.

28 April 1967 Tolkien replies to John Leyerle. He has at present given up the task of translating *The Owl and the Nightingale*. His translations of *Sir Gawain and the Green Knight* and *Pearl* are to be published soon by Allen & Unwin. But he thinks that he could find 'the reasonably successful translation of *Sir Orfeo*' he made some years ago, and might be willing to submit it for use in Leyerle's anthology, subject to suitable commercial arrangements. – Allen

& Unwin have either received a letter from Tolkien (now missing), or Rayner Unwin or Joy Hill has been in contact with him by telephone. Joy Hill writes to Donald Swann that Tolkien has agreed to the long-playing record project. She asks Swann to discuss it with Tolkien in more detail when they meet on 1 May. – Joy Hill writes to the senior editor of *Redbook* that Tolkien is not willing for *Smith of Wootton Major* to be cut.

1 May 1967 Donald and Janet Swann celebrate Janet's birthday by entertaining Ronald, Edith, Christopher, and Priscilla Tolkien and R.E. Havard at the Eastgate Hotel. Swann and Tolkien discuss the song book and the record project. At this meeting Tolkien probably gives Swann some new notes and translations. – Tolkien forwards to Joy Hill a cable he has received concerning film rights.

2 May 1967 Joy Hill writes to Tolkien, sending William Elvin's address. A representative from Caedmon will deliver a recording machine to Tolkien by the end of the week, which he can keep (and presumably use for practice) until he makes the actual recording.

8 May 1967 Caedmon Records write to Tolkien, giving the terms of the proposed contract for the Swann/Elvin/Tolkien album.

9 May 1967 Tolkien replies to Oscar Morland. He thanks him for copies of indexes of *The Lord of the Rings* Morland has compiled privately. He thinks that they will be of use when he can find time to correct and improve the existing index.

10 May 1967 Austin Olney writes to Donald Swann. The new notes and translations have arrived. He is not sure that it will be possible to have facsimiles of Tolkien's handwriting, as there are reproduction problems. He does not think that there is sufficient difference between English and American pronunciation to require a footnote. Houghton Mifflin have photostatted the Elvish characters in a larger size from Tolkien's hand for the decorations.

11 May 1967 A.H. Smith dies.

12 May 1967 John Masefield dies.

15 May 1967 A pupil at Cherry Creek High School, Englewood, Colorado, sends Tolkien a letter in Tengwar, which Tolkien transliterates, then writes a correct version at the bottom of the letter.

Mid-May–*c.* 24 May 1967 Tolkien and Edith stay at the Hotel Miramar, Bournemouth.

18 May 1967 Joy Hill writes to Tolkien. *Redbook* has agreed to print *Smith of Wootton Major* in full in their Christmas issue for the agreed sum. Joy encloses a manual for the Philips cassette recorder Tolkien is using for practice.

***c.* 19 May 1967** Rayner Unwin sends Tolkien the Caedmon contract to sign.

***c.* 20–23 May 1967** Tolkien writes to Rayner Unwin, returning the contract. He is mastering the tape recorder.

25 May 1967 Rayner Unwin writes to Tolkien. Since Tolkien has omitted one signature, Rayner returns the Caedmon contract with a reply paid envelope. When Tolkien has decided whether 14 or 15 June, and whether morning or afternoon, would suit him best for the recording, he should let Rayner know, and Rayner will make the arrangements. Pauline Baynes has agreed to illustrate *Smith of Wootton Major*. Rayner sends for Tolkien's comments a draft he has written for advance publicity for that work.

?Early June 1967 Donald Swann writes to Tolkien. He encloses a copy of the cover for the song book. He comments unfavourably on the form of 't' used.

8 June 1967 Rayner Unwin writes to Tolkien. A Caedmon recording technician will be at Sandfield Road on 15 June, arriving probably between 3.00 and 4.00 p.m.

9 June 1967 Tolkien replies to a letter from the publisher Victor Gollancz. He refuses a request to write a recommendation for a book by a Professor (?M.K.) Joseph. He is too busy, and is not attracted by the book.

12 June 1967 In the morning, Joy Hill and Tolkien speak by telephone. Tolkien probably asks if the recording technician could arrive earlier. – Joy Hill then telephones Mrs Goldsworthy at Caedmon Records, and writes to Tolkien. Caedmon's producer and engineer will leave London as soon as they can on 15 June, but probably will not arrive until about 4.00 p.m. 'All they need is a small place in your study and a power point into which they can plug their cables. I assure you that everything will be done with the least possible fuss' (Tolkien-George Allen & Unwin archive, HarperCollins).

14 June 1967 Tolkien replies to a letter from a Sister Anne in St Louis, Missouri. He has no intention of writing a sequel to *The Lord of the Rings*.

15 June 1967 In late afternoon Tolkien records poems which will be included on the record album *Poems and Songs of Middle Earth* (*sic*), and others not issued until 2002 (see *Recordings). He will write to Donald Swann on 19 June: 'Personally I rather enjoyed the recording as the two men, Blackler and the machine operator, were helpful and appreciative' (Marion E. Wade Center, Wheaton College, Wheaton, Illinois). Joy Hill will report to Austin Olney on 19 June that Tolkien read through the whole of *The Adventures of Tom Bombadil and Other Verses from the Red Book*, plus some Elvish. *See note.* While reading *The Sea-Bell*, he discovers an error in the collection.

?16–?19 June 1967 Joy Hill telephones Tolkien to find out how the recording went. She asks him what works he read.

18 June 1967 Tolkien, Edith, and Priscilla have a meal at the inn at Roke to celebrate Priscilla's birthday. (This is probably the Home Sweet Home at (Roke) Wallingford, where they will also eat on Christmas Day.)

19 June 1967 Tolkien writes to Donald Swann. He thanks him for the book cover. He has compared the form of 't' used there with photographs and specimens of genuine manuscripts. – Joy Hill writes to Tolkien. She had not managed to catch on the telephone the titles of the Elvish poems he read for the recording. She asks him to write them at the foot of her letter and return it in a prepaid envelope.

21 June 1967 Tolkien writes to Rayner Unwin. He encloses a proposal (with no further details) that he has received from 'two obviously incompetent young boys or men, who should be prevented if possible from proceeding with their work and, at any rate, publishing any of it'. He comments on an article on his created languages by C.J. Stevens forwarded to him by Rayner (presumably a typescript or other advance copy of 'Sound Systems of the Third Age of Middle Earth', which will be published in the *Quarterly Journal of Speech* 54, no. 3 (October 1968)). Tolkien thinks it useless, because there is insufficient linguistic material in *The Lord of the Rings* for such an enquiry.

> This of course is intentional and necessary in presenting a work that must stand or fall primarily as a narrative. . . . It should have be clear . . . that the sound system and structure and history of these languages must have been worked out in great detail. The only possible answer would be to publish in as succinct a form as possible a grammar and analysis of the two Elvish languages and their relationship. I should, of course, very much enjoy doing this, and indeed hope to do something of the kind before I lay down the pen. But now is not the time. [Tolkien-George Allen & Unwin archive, HarperCollins]

He would like to see Rayner soon, and among the matters he would like to discuss is the settlement of his copyrights before a possible change in the law.

23 June 1967 Tolkien writes to Joy Hill. The two pieces of Elvish sent for *The Road Goes Ever On: A Song Cycle* have no titles, but 'can be called for convenience "A Elbereth" and "Namárië" (Farewell)' (Tolkien-George Allen & Unwin archive, HarperCollins). – Rayner Unwin writes to Tolkien. He will deal with 'the extraordinarily inept request of the two Californian youths' (Tolkien-George Allen & Unwin archive, HarperCollins). He suggests that he visit Tolkien on 3 July at 10.00 a.m.

24–26 June 1967 Tolkien is away from Oxford.

27 June 1967 Tolkien writes to Rayner Unwin. He will be delighted to see him on 3 July at 10.00 a.m. He encloses a letter he has received which contains a poem inspired by his writings, on which Tolkien comments unfavourably. Tolkien asks Rayner to deal with it.

28 June 1967 Joy Hill telephones Tolkien in the morning. The Literary Society of the University of Birmingham has invited him to address them. Tolkien tells her to decline. – Joy Hill writes to Tolkien. She has talked with Mrs Goldsworthy of Caedmon Records, who want to present Tolkien with a tape recorder of his choice. Mrs Goldsworthy has written to him enclosing brochures of different models. Joy suggests that he ring her when he has made a choice, and she will make the arrangements. – Ronald Eames, Allen & Unwin, sends Tolkien proofs of *Smith of Wootton Major* and his typescript. He asks Tolkien to try to fit any alterations into the same space, and if possible to return the proofs by 14 July.

30 June 1967 Tolkien receives the brochures about tape recorders. He telephones Joy Hill to suggest that she make the choice for him. – She decides on the Philips Automatic Family De Luxe model, and rings Mrs Goldsworthy of Caedmon Records to inform her of the choice. – Joy Hill writes to Tolkien to confirm their conversation and explain her choice. The BBC will broadcast some of the songs from the long-playing record when it is released. – Donald Swann visits Rayner Unwin in London. Both have received photocopies from Austin Olney of the lettering and decorations that Houghton Mifflin have commissioned from Samuel Hanks Bryant. Rayner writes to Olney that he liked 'the Roman style calligraphy' in an earlier sample (possibly the 'Forum' typeface used in the published book), but neither he nor Swann like the new version.

July 1967 Tolkien's grandson Michael George and Irene Ferrier are married in St Andrews.

3 July 1967 Rayner Unwin visits Tolkien in Oxford. They discuss the new sample Austin Olney has sent; Tolkien dislikes it. Tolkien probably asks Rayner's advice about buying a new portable typewriter.

5 July 1967 Rayner Unwin sends Tolkien a prospectus for Olivetti typewriters. Joy Hill is scornful about their quality, and recommends the slightly heavier but much sturdier Olympic. Rayner offers to meet Tolkien's train from Bournemouth on 19 July.

10 July 1967 Tolkien thanks Rayner Unwin and Joy Hill for their advice about the choice of a typewriter. He rang British Railways to try to find out about a new fast service from Bournemouth to London 'and was treated with the expectable discourtesy. A raucous voice refused to answer any questions about the new service and shouted out the times of a few trains taking nearly all of them three hours, and then rang off.' He will make further enquiries when he arrives in Bournemouth. 'I must say I look forward to your entertainment of me much more than the R[oyal] S[ociety of] L[iterature]. I hope you were merely teasing me when you suggested I might have to make a speech, of any kind' (Tolkien-George Allen & Unwin archive, HarperCollins).

11 July 1967 Rayner Unwin writes to Tolkien. He is sending him the matter Tolkien wrote for *The Road Goes Ever On: A Song Cycle*, now set in type. Houghton Mifflin would like it corrected and returned as soon as possible. Rayner apparently has been negotiating changes with Austin Olney:

I am happy to say that we have won nine-tenths of the battle with the lettering and the concerted onslaught of yourself, Donald Swann, and myself has brought back the rather pleasant Roman lettering and ousted the very unpleasant quasi-Elvish lettering on the Song Book. The only last enclave of somewhat bad taste Donald Swann will be writing to you about. It is the calligraphic doodles that occur from time to time at the end of songs etc. [i.e. flourishes drawn with a pen by Samuel Hanks Bryant, intended to relieve large blank spaces that occurred when music did not entirely fill a page]. On the telephone Swann and I agreed that we would not bitterly object to these as we had wrung so many concessions from Houghton Mifflin already but if you feel strongly you have only to say so and we will support you, but in that case I suggest we send a page or two of your scrapbook with your own doodles as substitute material. [Tolkien-George Allen & Unwin archive, HarperCollins; Tolkien Papers, Bodleian Library, Oxford]

12–13 July 1967 Tolkien replies to a letter from Donald Swann. If Swann and Rayner Unwin 'are prepared to break off the battle and let Olney have his, or Bryant's, tasteless squiggles or equivalent spacefillers, then I capitulate', but he makes some reservations about the indiscriminate use of the letter 'T'. 'I really am very annoyed about this business: changing a lay-out already approved, and wasting our time arguing about it.' Tolkien feels that the flourishes are unsuitable for the text.

> I was at first greatly alarmed when I looked at Bryant's work; but I have since concluded that these four pages were simply reproductions of his proposals *all* in his hand. The 'elvish' decorations begin by being inaccurate and end in mere nonsense. I hope this is no indication of how they may appear in the final stage.
>
> I also hope that with the reduction of his 'decoration' to a few space-filling squiggles we are rid of Bryant and his unwanted cooperation.... 'Elvish' may be no more than a teenage lark, but it is treated seriously in this book, and ridiculous stuff scattering vowel-signs as mere ornament makes the whole thing seem silly. [Marion E. Wade Center, Wheaton College, Wheaton, Illinois]

Rayner has suggested that if Tolkien wants to veto these, he should send doodles of his own to replace them. Tolkien would have liked to provide such tailpieces if he had known they were wanted, but there is no time now. He thinks that he may have made a mistake in his Elvish, and asks Swann to check the reproduction. Tolkien does draw a calligraphic design of his initials and Swann's, intended for the book, but it is too late to be included.

13 July 1967 Tolkien writes to Rayner Unwin. He hopes to return the proofs of the material for *The Road Goes Ever On: A Song Cycle* later that day. His notes 'have been vetted by someone of great competence and keen eye, and difficulties are mainly due to my own inaccuracies (in hastily produced copy).... I do not so violently object to the squiggles as to set myself up (at this stage) against a professional squiggler. But of course if any space-fillers are needed they should be something more suitable to the text and music. But I cannot help that now' (Tolkien-George Allen & Unwin archive, HarperCollins). He tells Rayner that in addition to everything else, he is busy clearing part of his dilapidated house for decorators to work in during his absence.

15–30 or 31 July 1967 Tolkien and Edith stay at the Hotel Miramar, Bournemouth.

16 July 1967 Tolkien makes inquiries at Bournemouth station concerning train service to London. – Tolkien writes to Rayner Unwin. On 19 July he will take the 10.40 a.m. train to London, due at Waterloo Station at 12.20 p.m.

19 July 1967 Tolkien takes the train from Bournemouth to London. He lunches with Rayner Unwin, who shows him Pauline Baynes' drawings for *Smith of Wootton Major*. Tolkien probably gives Rayner a correction for the Tengwar in *The Road Goes Ever On: A Song Cycle*, which Rayner will send to Austin Olney the next day. At a reception in the evening, Lord Butler, the President of the Royal Society of Literature, presents Tolkien and Dame Rebecca West with the A.C. Benson Silver Medal. In his speech Tolkien comments that 'though *The Lord of the Rings* has had many astonishing results, I think that receiving this silver medal is the most astonishing as it is the most delightful' (Royal Society of Literature, *Report* (1966–7), p. 37).

20 July 1967 Ronald Eames, Allen & Unwin, writes to Pauline Baynes. Tolkien is delighted with her drawings for *Smith of Wootton Major*, but has vetoed the use of a second colour. 'He has a strong feeling for the whole of the text appearing in simple black and white which he found so successful with "Farmer Giles"' (George Allen & Unwin archive, University of Reading).

21 July 1967 Tolkien writes to Rayner Unwin. He thanks him for his kindness on 19 July. 'I am singularly fortunate in having such a friend. I feel, if I may say so, that our relations are like that of Rohan and Gondor, and (as you know) for my part the oath of Eorl will never be broken, and I shall continue to rely on and be grateful for the wisdom and courtesy of Minas Tirith' (*Letters*, p. 379).

23 July 1967 Donald K. Fry of the University of Virginia writes to Tolkien. He asks permission to include *Beowulf: The Monsters and the Critics* in a volume of *Beowulf* essays he is editing for Prentice-Hall. If Tolkien agrees, he will work out permission to reprint with the copyright holder, whom he assumes is the British Academy, and pay the normal rate.

24 July 1967 Rayner Unwin writes to Tolkien, sending a spare print from a transparency, 'which will be of use for minor publicity purposes' (Tolkien-George Allen & Unwin archive, HarperCollins). This is probably of Pauline Baynes' design for the de luxe *Lord of the Rings* box, which is to be reproduced also on the long-playing record sleeve and the one-volume paperback cover.

25 July 1967 Joy Hill writes to Tolkien. There is a delay in the production of the type of tape recorder she chose for him, but he will get one as soon as possible after the 30th. The Philips representative in the Oxford area will telephone him, and bring him the machine when it is convenient for Tolkien. – P.H. Newby sends a memo to Terence Tiller at the BBC. Tolkien has sent *Smith of Wootton Major* to the BBC for consideration, stipulating that it must not be cut, and that he is prepared to read it himself. Neither Newby nor Tiller are impressed by the story.

August 1967 Tolkien draws a doodle, labels it *Mordor Special Mission Flying Corps Emblem*, and sets beside it the Eye of Sauron (see *Artist and Illustrator*, fig. 185). – Tolkien drafts a long reply to a Mr Rang about his nomenclature. He rejects Rang's assumptions as to its origins. In the end, Tolkien will send 'only a brief (and therefore rather severe) reply', as he notes at the top of the letter (*Letters*, p. 379).

1 August 1967 Tolkien and Joy Hill talk by telephone. Probably they discuss the desire by Houghton Mifflin to have a different title for *Smith of Wootton Major*.

2 August 1967 Tolkien writes to Joy Hill. He encloses two items which he thinks should have been returned with the proofs from Houghton Mifflin. He cannot understand why Houghton Mifflin should want to change the title *Smith of Wootton Major* of the story, 'though doubtless the mild joke of the title, vaguely suggesting a school story, is lost on an American' (Tolkien-George Allen & Unwin archive, HarperCollins). No one from Philips has yet contacted him. – Tolkien writes to Donald K. Fry. He gives permission for *Beowulf: The Monsters and the Critics* to be included in Fry's anthology. He is glad of Fry's courtesy in writing: the essay has been printed several times without Tolkien's permission being asked. – Tolkien writes to the Royal Society of Literature to obtain another copy of their *Essays for Divers Hands*, n.s. 29 (1958), which contains an essay by Morchard Bishop, 'John Inglesant and Its Author'. Tolkien comments that the public interest in J.H. Shorthouse's *John Inglesant* (1880, 1881) has similarities to his own experience. The essay had warned him not to make Shorthouse's mistake of spending too much time trying to explain his book.

4 August 1967 Charles A. Huttar, who has had some correspondence with Tolkien, is in Oxford. He telephones Tolkien, asking to visit him; Tolkien agrees. When Huttar arrives in Sandfield Road, however, Tolkien and Edith are just getting into a taxi. Tolkien explains that when he spoke on the phone, he had forgotten a doctor's appointment. He shows Huttar into his garage-study, where Huttar waits until Tolkien returns. They talk for a while. Huttar, who is in the early stages of planning a *Festschrift* for Clyde S. Kilby (eventually published in 1971 as *Imagination and the Spirit: Essays in Literature and the Christian Faith presented to Clyde S. Kilby*), asks Tolkien if he would be able to contribute. Tolkien has nothing suitable, and needs to devote his time to 'The Silmarillion'. He gives Huttar an autographed Dutch *Hobbit*.

5 August 1967 Donald K. Fry writes to Tolkien. He is shocked that no other users of *Beowulf: The Monsters and the Critics* have made any payment to Tolkien. He has offered a fee to the British Academy (the original publisher), and offers an even higher payment to Tolkien. He has heard that Tolkien is writing a sequel, or perhaps 'prequel' to *The Lord of the Rings*. He hopes that Tolkien will excuse his pun. (This is the earliest use of *prequel* that we have seen, presumably originated by Fry. All examples of its use by Tolkien appear to postdate this letter.)

7 August 1967 Ronald Eames, Allen & Unwin, writes to Tolkien. He sends page proofs of *Smith of Wootton Major* with the illustrations in position, together with the corrected galley proofs. He hopes that Tolkien can return the corrected proofs within the present week, as the production schedule is tight.

8 August 1967 Joy Hill writes to Tolkien. She will telephone Mrs Goldsworthy about the tape recorder. She is dealing with Humphrey Carpenter's request for the musical dramatization of *The Hobbit*. She has an idea for stock replies which Tolkien could tick, for use by Miss Jenkinson in responding to letters.

9 August 1967 Immediately after breakfast, without having made an appointment, a young man brings Tolkien the Philips tape recorder. He is not prepared to demonstrate it, but Tolkien thinks that the instructions are adequate. – Tolkien writes to Ronald Eames, returning the page proofs of *Smith of Wootton Major*. He retains the galley proofs and loose illustrations. He comments on the 'rather alarming publication date (1567)' (Tolkien-George Allen & Unwin archive, HarperCollins), and otherwise finds only three corrections needed to the text. But he has problems with two of the illustrations (as illustrations of his text, not as art), in particular their placement. He suggests exchanging the frontispiece with another picture. – Having missed the post, Tolkien rings Joy Hill and gives her a message for Eames about placing of the pictures in *Smith of Wootton Major*. – Tolkien writes to Joy Hill. Miss Jenkinson is willing to collaborate in a more complete list of items for a stock letter. He encloses two manuscripts he has received, and asks if they are worth doing anything about. – Tolkien writes to thank Donald K. Fry for his letter and the proposed fee, and uses the term *prequel*.

10 August 1967 Joy Hill writes to Tolkien. She has given Ronald Eames his message, and will get in touch with Miss Jenkinson about compiling a card of itemized answers to letters.

c. **12–18 August 1967** Tolkien and Edith stay at the Hotel Miramar, Bournemouth.

15 August 1967 Ronald Eames writes to Tolkien. He is sorry that Tolkien is unhappy about the placement of the pictures. He proposes a different rearrangement to that suggested by Tolkien, since he is reluctant to move the frontispiece which had been planned as a single design with the title-page (i.e. a double-page spread). He sends a new proof so that Tolkien can see what he suggests. If he hears nothing in two days, he will assume that Tolkien approves. He also encloses proofs of the cover.

16 August 1967 Joy Hill writes to Tolkien. W.H. Auden has agreed to write liner notes for the sleeve of the Caedmon long-playing record.

17 August 1967 Tolkien writes to Ronald Eames. He entirely approves of the new layout, and thinks the jacket 'both a good illustration and attractively striking' (Tolkien-George Allen & Unwin archive, HarperCollins). (In the event, *Smith of Wootton Major* will be published in Britain with an illustrated binding, but not a dust-jacket.)

?Mid-August 1967 Mr S.E.O. Joukes of Antwerp in Belgium writes to Tolkien. He wants to call his newborn daughter *Ioreth*, but has encountered difficulty with government officials because it is not a recognized name. He asks Tolkien to explain its meaning.

18 August 1967 Joy Hill sends Tolkien correspondence from Harper & Row asking for an account of his 'interior literary history' (Tolkien-George Allen & Unwin archive, HarperCollins).

19 August 1967 Phyllis Jenkinson writes to Joy Hill. She likes the idea of an itemized card for replying to letters. Possibly assisted by Tolkien, she lists phrases for inclusion.

22 August 1967 Tolkien's first great-grandchild, Mandy, daughter of Joanna and Hugh Baker, is born.

24 August 1967 Joy Hill writes to Tolkien. She has sold *The Hobbit* to the BBC for a serial dramatization in the Home Service. Broadcasts are to begin on 2 December.

c. 25 August 1967 Tolkien begins a long letter to his son Michael. He describes his visit to Switzerland in 1911, and discusses trends in the Catholic Church. He does not finish the letter and when he finds it again on 11 October 1968 he writes on the top 'Not sent or finished for reasons forgotten' (*Letters*, p. 391).

25 August 1967 Tolkien writes to Joy Hill about the Harper & Row proposal. He does 'not have the time to deal with any account of my interior literary history'. In any case, 'there is a particular reason for not publishing anything at the present time: my work is not finished; an account of its progress and genesis is quite impossible without reference to *The Silmarillion* and all that, which preceded what is published' (Tolkien-George Allen & Unwin archive, HarperCollins). He can understand people's interest: he would like to know how author Mary Renault would answer the same question. Not long ago he received fan mail from her. – Joy Hill writes to Tolkien. She has given permission for Humphrey Carpenter to perform *The Hobbit* in New College at Christmas, subject to various stipulations. She asks Tolkien to sign and return a form for the Performing Rights Society in connection with this musical performance.

27 August 1967 With assistance, Tolkien spends 'some time making recordings and investigating the capabilities of the Philips machine'. He finds it easy to use, but his recordings are not very good. He suspects that 'the microphone provided is not equal in quality to the machine. Recordings that I made nine or ten years ago when reproduced by it were very superior to those made direct' (letter to Joy Hill, 30 August 1967, Tolkien-George Allen & Unwin archive, HarperCollins). It will be useful for practising, however.

28 August 1967 Tolkien replies to Mr S.E.O. Joukes. He would be pleased for him to use the name *Ioreth* for his daughter, but points out that as it means 'old woman' in Elvish, it is perhaps not very suitable. He does not think that the name occurs outside *The Lord of the Rings*. He has had a similar query from the Netherlands about *Arwen*, in which case he was able to give not only the Elvish meaning but to point out that it has a meaning in Welsh.

28 August 1967 An American writes to Tolkien with an idea for making an animated film of Tolkien's stories. He asks permission to telephone Tolkien on 7 September, at 6.00 p.m. British time.

30 August 1967 Tolkien writes to Joy Hill. He has signed the form for the Performing Rights Society and sent it on. He is pleased that W.H. Auden has agreed to write the liner notes for the Caedmon record. He lends Joy a copy of *Shenandoah* with the poem he wrote for Auden.

?Late summer 1967 Tolkien receives Humphrey Carpenter, and Paul Drayton who is writing the music for their dramatization of *The Hobbit*, not in the garage but in Edith's sitting room. – Tolkien begins a letter to Clyde S. Kilby. He mentions Charles Huttar's recent visit, and apologizes in advance for not contributing to the *Festschrift* to be presented to Kilby. 'My work has proceeded hardly at all (in plain truth) during the past year. I have been so distracted by business and family affairs (interlocked), and my dear wife's health, which does not improve, that there seems little time for concentration: except at night, and I can no longer burn so much of the wrong end of the candle as I used to' (Marion E. Wade Center, Wheaton College, Wheaton, Illinois). He does not finish the letter, and will enclose it in its unfinished state with a letter written at the beginning of December.

?Early September 1967 William Luther White, chaplain at Illinois Wesleyan University, who is writing a book on C.S. Lewis, writes to Tolkien. He asks about the origin of the name *Inklings*.

1 September 1967 Rayner Unwin writes to Tolkien. He has dealt with the Harper & Row proposal.

5 September 1967 Rayner Unwin sends Tolkien various letters from their American agent, Mr Swanson. MGM Records want to record *Farmer Giles of Ham*, preferably read by Tolkien. Rayner knows that Tolkien does not object to this (presumably it has been discussed already, at a meeting or by telephone), except for the precious time it involves. If Tolkien does not want to spare the time, the reading probably could be done by someone else. Rayner encloses Swanson's suggested reply, and asks if Tolkien approves, or would like it emended in any way. Swanson has also written about an offer for film rights of *The Lord of the Rings*. Rayner asks for a decision as to whether they should proceed. – H.M. Houseman, Clarendon Press, writes to Tolkien. He is sending an advance copy of the new edition of *Sir Gawain and the Green Knight*, revised by Norman Davis. Tolkien is entitled to three further free copies, which they will be happy to distribute if Tolkien will send a presentation list of names.

7 September 1967 In the evening, Tolkien probably receives a telephone call from the American interested in making an animated film.

8 September 1967 Tolkien replies to H.M. Houseman. He would like one more free copy of *Sir Gawain and the Green Knight* for himself, and asks that the other two be sent to Christopher Tolkien and Simonne d'Ardenne. – Tolkien probably rings Rayner Unwin to give his decisions on answers to Swanson, and mentions the letter he has received from the American. – Tolkien writes to Rayner Unwin, enclosing the 'effusive letter' from the American who wishes to make an animated film of Tolkien's works. There are many things in it which Tolkien finds attractive, but Rayner will know best how to deal with it. He would like to know more about the writer of the letter and his associate. He asks to have the letter back eventually for his records; it is too long to spend time copying it.

9 September 1967 Rayner Unwin writes to Tolkien. He has written to Swanson, telling him to go ahead with MGM's proposal for recording Tolkien reading *Farmer Giles of Ham*. He encloses details of another project, suggested by St Martin's Press.

?10 September 1967 Tolkien writes to St. Martin's Press, declining their suggestion.

11 September 1967 Tolkien replies to William Luther White, with information about the origins of the Inklings. – Rayner Unwin writes to Tolkien. He returns the letter from the American filmmaker, which he has copied. He has written to the correspondent that he should get in touch with Swanson, as Allen & Unwin's American agent. He thanks Tolkien for writing to St Martin's Press. He is 'not surprised you declined the invitation but very touched by the manner in which you have done so' (Tolkien-George Allen & Unwin archive, HarperCollins). Rayner also advises Tolkien in regard to a request to reprint his verses on W.H. Auden (as published in *Shenandoah*), and the fee that should be asked.

18 September 1967 Rayner Unwin writes to Tolkien. He encloses a draft translation of *Leaf by Niggle* made by Margaret Carroux, who is translating *The Lord of the Rings* into German. She has asked if Tolkien could glance at this, to judge her quality as a translator of his work. She would like to consult Tolkien in Oxford during the latter half of October or in November. Rayner asks Tolkien to let him know when he will be away from Oxford during that period. They will inform Frau Carroux and leave it to her to arrange her visit. – Christopher Tolkien, divorced from his first wife, marries Baillie Klass (formerly Tolkien's secretary Baillie Knapheis).

19 September 1967 Tolkien writes to Alina Dadlez, Allen & Unwin. He encloses a letter he has received from someone interested in translating one of his works into French. He has told the prospective translator that Allen & Unwin are responsible for dealing with translation rights, and that the first step is to find a French publisher.

21 September 1967 Tolkien is taken ill with a virus infection.

25 September 1967 Phyllis Jenkinson writes to Rayner Unwin. She acknowledges his letter of 18 September and its enclosure, the draft translation of *Leaf by Niggle*. At present Tolkien feels too ill to do anything. He will be going to Bournemouth for the last half of October.

26 September 1967 Rayner Unwin writes to Phyllis Jenkinson. He will contact Margaret Carroux and explain the situation. He has passed to Tolkien's solicitor, F.R. Williamson, an important document from Swanson about film rights of *The Lord of the Rings*. Mr Williamson will be getting in touch with Tolkien soon.

27 September 1967 Joy Hill writes to Phyllis Jenkinson. The Canadian Broadcasting Corporation want to film Mary Quant, Winston Churchill (the younger), and Tolkien. They have asked her to learn if Tolkien is willing. BBC

Television (*24 Hours*) would also like to film him, for an item to go out on the programme either when *Smith of Wootton Major* is published or when the long-playing record *Poems and Songs of Middle Earth* is released in Britain next year.

29 September 1967 F.R. Williamson visits Tolkien. – Phyllis Jenkinson writes to Joy Hill. Tolkien was a little better yesterday, but is much worse this morning, and the doctor's report is not encouraging. It might be some weeks before he is fit again. In the meantime, he is getting more and more depressed. Various worries, domestic and financial, had affected his health even before his illness, and these do not help his recovery. He cannot deal with anything at the moment. She presumes that the BBC does not need an immediate reply, and asks how soon the CBC require an answer. – According to a letter Tolkien writes to Clyde S. Kilby at the beginning of December 1967, his illness is so serious that his doctor (R.E. Havard) visits him daily for a month. The illness leaves him 'an emaciated wreck'. It is eight weeks before he can walk about. His 'wife was in some ways the chief sufferer, since my children were abroad, and she had to do the nursing (to the great increase of her arthritic affliction) for three weeks' (Marion E. Wade Center, Wheaton College, Wheaton, Illinois).

?Beginning of October 1967 Rayner Unwin writes to Edith Tolkien. He expresses his and his father's sympathy, and their best wishes for Tolkien's recovery.

2 October 1967 Joy Hill writes to Phyllis Jenkinson. She is upset to hear how ill Tolkien is. They should forget about the Canadian Broadcasting Corporation, who are in England only for a week. There is no need to hurry a reply to the BBC. – Probably on this day Rayner Unwin sends Tolkien a letter of sympathy and best wishes from his father and himself for Tolkien's recovery.

4 October 1967 Edith Tolkien writes to Rayner Unwin. 'Ronald is a little better, though still has a good deal of pain in his eyes, ears, head and neck. The temperature has been most persistent for nearly a fortnight – so he's weak and Dr Havard won't let him get up – except to just come down for lunch (as stairs and carrying trays are dreadfully difficult for me)' (Tolkien-George Allen & Unwin archive, HarperCollins). If he is fit to travel, they will go to Bournemouth on 13 October. Tolkien will be looked after there, and she will get some rest. Miss Jenkinson is helping as far as she can with letters, but other business will have to wait.

11 October 1967 Phyllis Jenkinson writes to Joy Hill. Tolkien is much better, but because of a fluctuating temperature is still not allowed to get up and dress, though he comes down for meals. The doctor thinks that he will be able to travel to Bournemouth on Friday by car if he is well wrapped up and goes straight to bed on arrival. Mrs Tolkien is very tired and not too well, and needs a rest.

13 October 1967 Tolkien and Edith are driven to the Hotel Miramar, Bournemouth.

13 October–14 November 1967 Tolkien and Edith stay at the Hotel Miramar. For the first week, Tolkien stays in bed.

24 October 1967 Tolkien is still weak and suffering from headaches, and has problems with his eyes. He goes out for the first time (excluding the drive to Bournemouth) in nearly five weeks.

25 October 1967 Joy Hill writes to Phyllis Jenkinson. She has had a letter from someone at Towson State College, Baltimore, saying that he wrote to Professor Tolkien on 20 September, inviting him to some festival in America, and has had no reply. She has written to him, politely declining the invitation on Tolkien's behalf.

26 October 1967 Joy Hill forwards to Phyllis Jenkinson a copy of a letter from Houghton Mifflin. A correspondent has pointed out some possible errors in *The Lord of the Rings* (one is probably the two different birthdates given for Sam Gamgee).

29 October 1967 Phyllis Jenkinson writes to Joy Hill. She expects Tolkien to be away for another fortnight. She has forwarded Houghton Mifflin's letter to him, and asked him to scribble down on Joy's covering letter what she should say about the query if he does not feel up to answering it himself.

30 October 1967 Tolkien writes to Joy Hill. He cannot answer the query from Houghton Mifflin, as he does not have the necessary books in Bournemouth. He has 'ceased to bother about these minor "discrepancies", since if the genealogies and calendars etc. lack verisimilitude it is in their general excessive accuracy; as compared with real annals or genealogies! But errors in the text are another matter' (Tolkien-George Allen & Unwin archive, HarperCollins). Tolkien notes the one referred to in the letter from Houghton Mifflin, and will look into it when he can. He himself found an error in *The Sea-Bell* while making the recording of it. *See note.* He is recovering at last, slowly, and is ordered by the doctor to remain in Bournemouth until mid-November. – Phyllis Jenkinson writes to Allen & Unwin, acknowledging receipt of six copies of *Smith of Wootton Major*.

Autumn 1967 The record *Poems and Songs of Middle Earth* is issued in the United States. On one side, Donald Swann and William Elvin perform Swann's song cycle of Tolkien's poems, and on the other, Tolkien reads some of his verses.

31 October 1967 *The Road Goes Ever On: A Song Cycle* is published in the United States. – Joy Hill writes to Phyllis Jenkinson. She wants to come to Oxford as soon as possible after Tolkien's return, to persuade him to take part in a BBC programme.

1 November 1967 Barbara Remington, who painted the cover art for the Ballantine *Hobbit* and *Lord of the Rings* which Tolkien disliked so much, sends a letter to Tolkien with an olive branch attached. She explains that the publisher was trying to get the books out as fast as possible because of competition, and did not give her time to read them. She had to produce the *Hobbit* cover in only three hours, and was then instructed to put an animal (the offending lion) in an empty space. She has since been enthralled by *The Lord of the Rings* and is distressed that her cover illustrations do not do it justice.

8 November 1967 Tolkien writes to Amy Ronald. He is sorry that he was too ill to see her when she was in Oxford. 'I am afraid this malady which reduced me to a shape resembling the last emaciated state of Gollum has interfered abominably with work' (quoted in Christie's, *Autograph Letters and Printed Books, including First Editions*, London, 19 May 2000, p. 37). He thanks her for flowers she sent. He will send her a copy of *Smith of Wootton Major*.

9 November 1967 *Smith of Wootton Major* is published by George Allen & Unwin. Allen & Unwin have shipped 17,000 copies to their outlets around the world.

10 November 1967 Clyde S. Kilby writes to Professor and Mrs Tolkien. He is sorry to hear that Tolkien is ill. He has heard that *Smith of Wootton Major* is about to be published. – A professor from Florida writes to Tolkien. He and an associate want to use Tolkienian names on land being developed on Florida's Wakulla River.

14 November 1967 Tolkien and Edith return to Oxford.

16 November 1967 Edith writes to Pamela Chandler. Tolkien is better, but still cannot do very much and is easily tired. She herself can hardly walk because of arthritis. – Joy Hill writes to Tolkien. Allen & Unwin have shipped a further 3,000 copies of *Smith of Wootton Major* in the first week since publication. She would like to come to Oxford to see Tolkien on 22 November to discuss some matters, and to bring with her Pauline Baynes' original painting for the de luxe box, which has been returned by Caedmon Records.

17 November 1967 Phyllis Jenkinson writes to Joy Hill. Tolkien will be very pleased to see her on 22 November.

22 November 1967 Joy Hill visits Tolkien in Oxford. She returns Pauline Baynes' painting. During their meeting Tolkien asks her to get some cards he can enclose with presentation copies of *Smith of Wootton Major*.

23 November 1967 Joy Hill writes to Tolkien. She encloses a copy of the December 1967 issue of *Redbook* with *Smith of Wootton Major*, and the cards he requested. She suggests that he give her a list of people to whom he might want a copy of a new publication to be sent. Three complimentary copies of *Poems and Songs of Middle Earth* have been shipped to Tolkien from New York; the British version will not be issued until 1968. Alina Dadlez has asked Joy to tell Tolkien that Margaret Carroux wants to know if it would be convenient for her to visit Tolkien some time between 10 and 20 December. – Clyde Kilby writes to Tolkien. He has asked Joy Hill to send him a copy of *Smith of Wootton Major*. He reminds Tolkien that he is interested in obtaining one of his manuscripts for the collection at Wheaton College, and expresses an interest in *Smith of Wootton Major*.

24 November 1967 *Smith of Wootton Major* is published in the United States. – Tolkien writes to Terence Pratchett (later himself a prominent fantasy author), thanking him for the first letter Tolkien has received about *Smith of Wootton Major*. 'You evidently feel about the story very much as I do myself' (Tolkien-George Allen & Unwin archive, HarperCollins). – Tolkien writes to the professor in Florida, giving permission to use names from his books in the planned land development. – Joy Hill writes to Tolkien. *Poems and Songs of Middle Earth* will probably not be issued in Britain until March 1968 because of a royalty problem. – With another letter of the same date, Joy Hill returns the copy of *Shenandoah* Tolkien had lent her.

27 November 1967 Tolkien writes to Joy Hill. He thinks that it would be simpler if he were to send out most of the copies of *Smith of Wootton Major* since he is in close touch with a large number of the intended recipients. He encloses a list of thirteen names, together with cards, of those to whom he would like Allen & Unwin to send copies. He wonders if copies could not be sent from Houghton Mifflin to the three American addresses. He encloses a second list of ten names to whom future publications should be sent, since he owes them 'a considerable amount for help, encouragement and gifts' (Tolkien-George Allen & Unwin archive, HarperCollins): Simonne d'Ardenne, George Sayer, Austin and Katharine Farrer, the Reverend Mother Prioress of Oulton Abbey, K.M. Briggs, Professor Dr P.N.U. Harting of Amsterdam, the Earl of Halsbury, Professor Clyde Kilby, Edmund Fuller, and W.H. Auden. He is willing to meet Frau Carroux, and suggests the most suitable dates and times. – Rayner Unwin, who has just returned from the United States, writes to Tolkien. He thinks that agreement is close with United Artists for the *Lord of the Rings* film rights.

29 November 1967 Rayner Unwin writes to Tolkien. He encloses a communication he has just received from Swanson about the film rights. He thinks that the proposals are acceptable.

?Late November 1967–January or February 1968 Phyllis Jenkinson is not able to work for Tolkien, as she has to take care of her sick father. She is thus occupied by 15 December 1967, and returns to work for Tolkien at some date between 7 January and 19 February 1968.

c. **3 December 1967 (postmark)** Tolkien writes to Clyde Kilby. He encloses the letter he began some time ago (?late summer 1967). He discusses the possible sale of *Smith of Wootton Major* material to Wheaton College, and lists it in detail. He needs to consult his legal advisors about taxation on such a sale, and also take into account that the papers might be a valuable part of his heirs' inheritance. He asks what Wheaton College might be prepared to pay for them. Eerdmans have sent him two copies of C.S. Lewis's *Letters to an American Lady*, which he finds deeply interesting.

5 December 1967 Edith Tolkien writes to Pamela Chandler. Tolkien is much better, but still cannot do much and is easily tired.

6 December 1967 Joy Hill writes to Tolkien. She encloses the first 110 pages of the German translation of *The Lord of the Rings*, and confirms that Margaret Carroux will visit him on the morning of 13 December.

8 December 1967 Rayner Unwin writes to Tolkien. For some time, the Dramatic Publishing Company of Chicago has persisted in requesting permission to publish an adaptation of *The Hobbit* for the amateur stage. Tolkien does not want to agree, but the validity of his American copyright in *The Hobbit* is still at issue, and the Company will publish even if Tolkien and Allen & Unwin do not sign an agreement; in that case, no payment will be made, nor will there be any possibility of control over the product. The Company has promised to show the dramatization to Tolkien before it is printed, but (Rayner writes) 'whether they will accept any criticism or whether their work is capable of criticism is another matter' (Tolkien-George Allen & Unwin archive, Harper-Collins).

9 December 1967 Clyde S. Kilby writes to Tolkien, thanking him for a copy of *Smith of Wootton Major*. He offers Tolkien a turkey for Christmas or for his birthday. He has heard that William Ready's book on Tolkien is to be published soon.

Mid-December 1967 Towards the end of Christmas term a performance of the musical adaptation of *The Hobbit* by Humphrey Carpenter and Paul Drayton is given by New College School. Tolkien, Edith, and Priscilla attend the final night. Carpenter watches Tolkien during the performance, and notices that he smiles a lot, and seems to appreciate the boy's performance, but apparently shows disapproval when the adaptation departs from the original. Tolkien brings some autographed copies of *The Hobbit* to be auctioned, as well as copies of the American edition of *Smith of Wootton Major* which he gives to Carpenter and Drayton. He also gives a copy of *The Hobbit*, inscribed 'From J.R.R. Tolkien to Bilbo Baggins', to the boy who plays Bilbo. Tolkien autographs books for most of the actors, but no arrangements are made for him to meet the technical crew or to sign books for them.

?Mid-December 1967–?beginning of January 1968 Ken Jackson, technical director at the performance of *The Hobbit*, writes to Tolkien on behalf of the technical crew.

12 December 1967 Tolkien writes to Roger Lancelyn Green, thanking him for a review of *Smith of Wootton Major*. He describes the work as 'an old man's book, already weighted with the presage of "bereavement"' (*Letters*, p. 389).

13 December 1967 Margaret Carroux probably visits Tolkien in the morning.

14 December 1967 Tolkien rings Joy Hill. They discuss who is to be sent copies of *The Road Goes Ever On: A Song Cycle*. Probably they also talk about Carey Blyton's *Hobbit* overture, a copy of which Tolkien lends to Joy together with related correspondence. – Tolkien sends Christmas greetings to Rosfrith Murray, with a copy of the Houghton Mifflin *Smith of Wootton Major*. He prefers this to the Allen & Unwin edition, though he does not like the photograph of himself (by Roger Hill) on the back of the dust-jacket.

15 December 1967 Joy Hill writes to Tolkien. She returns Carey Blyton's *Hobbit* overture and related correspondence. She has written to Mr Blyton herself, since she knows that Tolkien is without Miss Jenkinson. She has received, and replied to, a letter from a Dutchman who wants to compose some chant music. After Tolkien rang her on 14 December, she looked at the list of people who are to receive complimentary copies of future publications, and thinks that Houghton Mifflin could send copies of *The Road Goes Ever On: A Song Cycle* to the three Americans since their edition has already been published. If Tolkien would like to sign three of his small cards and send them to Joy, she will arrange the matter.

19 December 1967 Rayner Unwin sends Tolkien more correspondence about negotiations with United Artists for the *Lord of the Rings* film rights.

20 December 1967 Stanley Unwin writes to thank Professor and Mrs Tolkien for the colour photograph.

25 December 1967 Tolkien, Edith, Priscilla, and a Slovak friend of Priscilla have a pleasant feast at the Home Sweet Home at (Roke) Wallingford. Late on Christmas night, both Tolkien and Edith feel unwell. He will describe this as 'a mild variety of virus' in a letter to Donald Swann on 30 December (Marion E. Wade Center, Wheaton College, Wheaton, Illinois), and as influenza to Clyde Kilby on 7 January.

28 December 1967 Alina Dadlez writes to Tolkien. She is sending him four complimentary copies of the Swedish pocket book edition of *The Lord of the Rings*.

30 December 1967 Tolkien writes to Donald Swann. He apologizes for his delay in replying to a long letter from Swann. His illness has left him lazy: 'The habit of doing nothing and being pampered is easily acquired and not easy to give up!' (Marion E. Wade Center, Wheaton College, Wheaton, Illinois). He has now more or less recovered after the virus he picked up on Christmas day, but Edith is not well, and her arthritis is worse than it was. He asks Swann and his wife to be their guests at the Hotel Miramar for a night or two in January, the only way they have of properly entertaining real friends.

1968

***c.* 1968** Tolkien writes an essay, **Eldarin Hands, Fingers & Numerals*, along with related texts (*'Synopsis of Pengoloð's *Eldarinwe Leperi are Notessi*', *'Variation D/L in Common Eldarin').

1968 Tolkien finds and reads his unfinished tale *Tal-Elmar*, written in the mid-1950s. He notes that

> it was begun without much consideration of geography (or the situation as envisaged in *The Lord of the Rings*). But either it must remain as a separate tale only vaguely linked with the developed *Lord of the Rings* history, or – and I think so – it must recount the coming of the Númenóreans (Elf-friends) *before the Downfall*, and represent their choice of permanent havens. So the geography must be made to fit with the mouths of Anduin and the Langstrand. [*The Peoples of Middle-earth*, p. 422]

There is no evidence that he adds anything to it.

?Early 1968 Wheaton College, probably through Clyde S. Kilby, makes an offer for the *Smith of Wootton Major* papers.

1 January 1968 The turkey ordered by Clyde Kilby arrives. – Rayner Unwin writes to Tolkien. As Tolkien knows, Allen & Unwin have been making enquiries about the making of a film in which Tolkien is willing to take part 'based on a walk and talk around Middle Earth [sic] associations of Oxford'. Allen & Unwin is not really well equipped to commission and sell such a film, but a BBC producer is interested in making a similar film. Rayner encloses the proposal. Tolkien would be asked to co-operate in the filming for at least two half days, and at most two full days. No preliminary work would be required, and the interviews 'would be largely determined as the spirit moves you'. In addition to a fee of £250 Tolkien would receive further payments for repeat showings in Great Britain, and for showings elsewhere in the world. Rayner recommends this as 'the least painful way of putting yourself on record for posterity and giving yourself a let-out for future importunate film-makers' (Tolkien-George Allen & Unwin archive, HarperCollins). He suggests that Allen & Unwin should act as his agents in this matter, and if Tolkien agrees to the project, to write them a note to that effect.

2 January 1968 Father John Tolkien comes to stay with his parents. His arrival is delayed because he also has had influenza. The turkey sent by Clyde Kilby is cooked, and all toast Kilby's health.

4 January 1968 Tolkien replies to Ken Jackson. He encloses some signed programmes and stick-in autographs for the technical crew at the December production of *The Hobbit*, whose importance he recognizes.

7 January 1968 Tolkien writes to Clyde Kilby. He describes his various contacts with William Ready, but stresses that the latter knows 'no more about me than is common knowledge, and of my "biography" nothing. He is I think a genuine (and intelligent) liker of my works, but I suspect . . . not unwilling to turn a penny on the basis of a somewhat remote connexion while my vogue lasts' (Marion E. Wade Center, Wheaton College, Wheaton, Illinois).

c. **8–9 January 1968** Tolkien looks at *The New Shadow*, his aborted sequel to *The Lord of the Rings*. He probably makes a third and final typescript, changing the name of the young man to *Saelon* and making some alterations of the wording, but not the story. On an envelope postmarked 8 January 1968 he roughs out a passage which would follow the point reached by this typescript.

9–23 January 1968 Tolkien and Edith stay at the Hotel Miramar, Bournemouth. They take with them their grandson Simon, who has been ill with influenza over Christmas.

12 January 1968 Tolkien and Edith celebrate Simon's ninth birthday.

17 January 1968 Joy Hill writes to Tolkien. She encloses some reviews of *The Road Goes Ever On: A Song Cycle* provided by Houghton Mifflin, which has already sold about 15,000 copies. Allen & Unwin have sold about 23,000 copies of *Smith of Wootton Major*. Joy is delighted to hear from Rayner Unwin that Tolkien thinks favourably of the BBC project.

18 January 1968 Donald Swann and his wife stay as Tolkien and Edith's guests at the Hotel Miramar. The length of their stay is not clear, but Tolkien will later write to Rayner Unwin (on 2 December 1968) that on 18 January Swann 'did a solo performance on the piano more astonishing and diverting than on any stage' (Tolkien-George Allen & Unwin archive, HarperCollins).

– Rayner Unwin writes to Tolkien concerning royalties on the Allen & Unwin edition of *The Road Goes Ever On: A Song Cycle*.

25 January 1968 Joy Hill writes to Tolkien. She will telephone tomorrow as arranged. Leslie Megahey, the director of the proposed BBC Television programme on Tolkien, spent an afternoon with her and seems to have some excellent ideas.

26 January 1968 Joy Hill rings Tolkien. They discuss the BBC programme. – After ringing the BBC, she writes to Tolkien. She hopes to have the contract for the film this afternoon. She and Leslie Megahey will come to Oxford on 30 January.

29 January 1968 Tolkien writes to W.H. Auden. He mentions his poem *Völsungakviða en nýja*, and possibly sends him a copy. – Tolkien replies to a letter from Ken Jackson, who has asked permission to name his house 'Bag End'. Although, as Tolkien explains, Jackson has no obligation to ask permission, the courtesy is appreciated. The name is not Tolkien's invention, but the local name for the house in which his Aunt Jane Neave lived for a time.

30 January 1968 According to plans outlined in Joy Hill's letter of 26 January, Leslie Megahey drives her to Oxford. She arrives at Sandfield Road at about 10.40 a.m. Leslie Megahey joins her and Tolkien a little later, having first visited a local researcher. Tolkien possibly accepts Megahey's invitation that they lunch with him and continue to discuss the film. Joy probably brings with her a statement authorizing Allen & Unwin to act as his agents in negotiations with the BBC; Tolkien signs and dates it. Tolkien and Joy Hill also discuss a proposed reception to launch the publication of *The Road Goes Ever On: A Song Cycle*.

31 January 1968 Joy Hill writes to Tolkien. She enjoyed her visit. Both Donald Swann and William Elvin are free on 14 March, the date suggested for the reception. She now has to consider where to hold it. Mr Megahey will have a car during the filming. His assistant will drive Tolkien to wherever he is needed at the right time.

End of January 1968 Father John Tolkien comes to Oxford on indefinite sick leave.

Early February 1968 It is decided to hold the reception for the publication of *The Road Goes Ever On: A Song Cycle* at Crosby Hall in Chelsea.

2 February 1968 Tolkien begins to transliterate a fan letter written in Tengwar. He gives up because, as he scribbles on the letter, it is 'hopelessly inaccurate & confused'. In his reply he tells the writer that it would take too long to decipher, and explains that he has 'a very large post-bag and letters must be legible to a secretary who cannot be expected to decipher even accurate Elvish' (Tolkien-George Allen & Unwin archive, HarperCollins). – The BBC send Tolkien the contract for filming, which is specified to take place between 5 and 9 February, partly at his home.

5–9 February 1968 The BBC shoot the film that will be aired as *Tolkien in Oxford*. Tolkien will describe his feelings in a letter to Donald Swann on 29 February:

I am merely impressed by the complete 'bogosity' of the whole performance. The producer, a very nice, very young man, and personally
equipped with some intelligence and insight, was nonetheless already
so muddled and confused by BBCism that the last thing in the world he
wished to show was me as I am/or was, let alone 'human or lifesize'. I was
lost in a world of gimmickry and nonsense, as far as it had any design
designed it seemed simply to fix the image of a fuddy not to say duddy
old fireside hobbitlike boozer. Protests were in vain, so I gave it up, &
being tied to the stake stayed the course as best I could. I am told that
the picture results were v[ery] g[ood] – at which my blood runs cold:
it means they've got what they wanted, and that my histrionic tempera-
ment (I used to like 'acting') betrayed me into playing ball (the ball
desired) to my own undoing. I was not lifted up in a helicopter, though
I am surprised one was not substituted for an eagle: they appeared completely confused between ME and my story, and I was made to attend
a firework show: a thing I have not done since I was a boy. [*Letters*, pp.
389–90]

Tolkien is accompanied to the bonfire and fireworks at the Dragon School by
Faith Tolkien and her son Simon. According to an article by Anthony Wood
in the *Oxford Mail* ('Fireworks for the Author – and B.B.C. 2 Viewers', 9 February, p. 10) Tolkien arrives late because the car sent to fetch him was caught
in a traffic-jam, and he was not very enthusiastic. During the making of the
programme John Wyatt, the BBC's chief cameraman, takes several still photographs of Tolkien.

7 February 1968 Twenty-four 'Friends' at the *Encyclopaedia Britannica*,
Chicago, send Tolkien a Valentine wish and the programme of their Second
Annual Hobbit Day celebrations held on 13 December 1967.

8 February 1968 Alina Dadlez sends Tolkien five copies of a paperback of
the Dutch translation of *Smith of Wootton Major*. This is a special edition produced by the publisher, Het Spectrum, for presentation at Christmas. They will
publish a hardcover edition in a few months' time. She also sends the proposed
cover for the Italian translation of *The Lord of the Rings*.

9 February 1968 Joy Hill writes to Tolkien. She asks if he has arranged to
stay with Donald Swann on 14 March before the reception.

***c.* 11 February 1968** Tolkien dines at Exeter College to meet a number of
fans, including one of the English dons.

12 February 1968 Tolkien writes to Donald Swann. He hopes to see him
on 14 March, but cannot come to the performance of *The Road Goes Ever On*
at the Camden Festival in the evening of 15 March. 'It is quite impossible for
Edith to come to London, and still more to stay a night. . . . I am sending Edith
down to Bournemouth on March 14th and myself coming to London, but I feel
I must return to Bournemouth that night' (Marion E. Wade Center, Wheaton
College, Wheaton, Illinois). Joy Hill would like to arrange for part of the proceedings at Crosby Hall to be televised, but Tolkien dislikes the idea. He asks if

Swann feels the same. – Tolkien writes to Joy Hill, probably enclosing a guest list for the reception.

13 February 1968 Tolkien writes to Joy Hill. He asks her to add his daughter, Priscilla, to the list of invitations for 14 March. He has just learned that she can attend.

?13 February 1968 Donald Swann writes to Joy Hill. Since he knows that Tolkien is against television, he will not press for coverage of the Camden Festival performance.

14–26 February 1968 Tolkien, Edith, and their son John stay at the Hotel Miramar, Bournemouth.

15 February 1968 Joy Hill writes to Tolkien. If he tells her the time of his arrival at Paddington Station on 14 March, she will meet him there. Stanley Unwin would like Tolkien to lunch with him at the Reform Club. Joy has a variety of plans for the afternoon. She will tell him about these next week, and he can then choose. She needs Christopher's address for his invitation.

19 February 1968 Tolkien writes to Alina Dadlez. He is horrified by the cover proposed for the Italian translation of *The Lord of the Rings* 'based on and even degraded from the frightful Ballantine cover' (Tolkien-George Allen & Unwin archive, HarperCollins), but is comforted by a letter from someone he knows, and whose opinion he respects, praising the Italian translation. He sends the letter for her to see, and asks for its return. – Tolkien writes to Joy Hill. He is having 'a difficult time with two invalids [Edith and John], and work is at a standstill' (Tolkien-George Allen & Unwin archive, HarperCollins). He thinks that the only possible train for him on 14 March is the 10.22 a.m. from Oxford. He gives her Christopher's address. – Tolkien writes to Rayner Unwin. He asks for advice about a letter he has received asking for permission to reprint two poems in a limited edition to be signed by Tolkien.

20 February 1968 Tolkien writes to Stanley Unwin. He is looking forward to having lunch with him 'My wife's health seems to be deteriorating and Bournemouth has so far failed to have its usual recuperative effect.' His son, however, is improving. 'I cannot do much work here, but I can do nothing at home in the present circumstances' (Tolkien-George Allen & Unwin archive, HarperCollins). – Tolkien writes to Walter Hooper, who has asked about C.S. Lewis's poem 'We were talking of dragons, Tolkien and I'. Tolkien explains a possible 'remote source' of the lines (*Letters*, p. 389). – Rayner Unwin writes to Tolkien. Marquette University has invited Tolkien to visit Boston and Milwaukee, expenses paid. Rayner thinks that the object of the visit to Milwaukee would be the conferment of an honorary degree. If Tolkien wishes to excuse himself, he should write a note, and Allen & Unwin will tell Marquette of his decision. Rayner forwards a letter from Houghton Mifflin with some questions: Tolkien should return it if he does not want to reply.

22 February 1968 Rayner Unwin replies to Tolkien's letter of 19 February. He thinks the terms offered are reasonable, if Tolkien is prepared to sign his name 150 times. Tolkien should first learn if the publisher produces attractive books, and then ask to see a draft contract. Allen & Unwin will willingly look over this to see that his interests are protected: the two poems requested might be needed one day for Tolkien's collected works.

26 February 1968 Joy Hill writes to Tolkien. The invitations have been sent. Rayner Unwin would like to borrow Pauline Baynes' painting used on the sleeve of the *Poems and Songs of Middle Earth* record (presumably to be displayed at the reception for *The Road Goes Ever On: A Song Cycle*). Joy would like to come to Oxford to discuss the arrangements for 14 March, and suggests 29 February, morning or afternoon. She is away tomorrow, but Tolkien could ring her on 28 February.

27 or 28 February 1968 Tolkien presumably rings Allen & Unwin to say that 29 February is not a suitable time for Joy Hill to visit him.

28 February 1968 Joy Hill visits Tolkien in Oxford. They discuss arrangements for the reception, and how Tolkien might spend his time in London. He vetoes the suggestion that he might spend the afternoon making some 'tapes' for the BBC radio programme *Woman's Hour*.

29 February 1968 Tolkien writes to Donald Swann. He describes his experiences with the BBC for *Tolkien in Oxford*, and discusses arrangements for the reception. On 14 March he will travel to London in the morning and lunch with Stanley Unwin, but will be left to his own (or Joy Hill's) devices after lunch.

> I wonder if it would bore you, if I visited you? If there is any corner (in 40 Museum Street? [the offices of Allen and Unwin]) where an old boozy hobbit could snooze for a bit, that would suit me. But then I might stalk forth like an Ent refreshed, with a *hoom* and a *ha* and descend on you? You need not take any notice of me. I should feel safe for a bit. La Gioconda [Tolkien's occasional nickname for Joy Hill] had various nefarious plans for using me when she called here on Wednesday. . . . I turned them down flat . . . but goodness knows what she will think up next.

It is sad that Edith cannot be present at the reception, but he is against her making the effort as he is sure she would suffer for it, 'but, being a gallant member of the brave sex, she may yet decide to risk it! If so all my arrangements will have to be modified' (Marion E. Wade Center, Wheaton College, Wheaton, Illinois). – Joy Hill writes to Tolkien to confirm the arrangements made the previous day. He will arrive at Paddington at 12.25 p.m., and lunch with Stanley Unwin at the Reform Club. During the afternoon Joy will take him to Battersea, where Donald Swann lives. Tolkien is scheduled to arrive at Crosby Hall at 5.00 p.m. She has reserved a first class seat for him on the 8.30 p.m. train from Waterloo, arriving at Bournemouth at 10.10 p.m.

1 March 1968 Tolkien telephones Joy Hill. Edith has decided to attend the reception. – Joy Hill writes to Tolkien. She has booked a second seat on the 8.30 p.m. train from Waterloo to Bournemouth. She will arrange for Edith, Priscilla, and Miss Jenkinson to be met at Paddington at 4.30 p.m. on 14 March and taken straight to Crosby Hall. She will see that Edith has a comfortable chair in the hall while Tolkien meets the press in the gallery. She warns Tolkien that there may be a television camera crew filming Donald Swann and William Elvin, but he will be involved only if the producer perhaps asks him to shake Donald's hand at the end of the performance. – Rayner Unwin, who is about to depart on a foreign business trip, writes to Tolkien. He has been looking over the prepared copy for the planned one-volume paperback edition of *The Lord of the Rings*, and thinks that the last paragraph at the end of the Foreword, about changes in the second edition and the new index (which is not to be included in the one-volume edition), should be replaced with a paragraph explaining that the Appendices can be found in the hardback edition. He also proposes to omit any blurb.

3 March 1968 Joy Hill writes to Tolkien, sending a revised and fuller timetable for 14 March.

4 March 1968 Tolkien replies to Rayner Unwin. He understands that it is not possible to bind a paperback with the number of pages required by the inclusion of the Appendices and index, but if is not too late, he makes a plea to include the *Tale of Aragorn and Arwen*. He suggests a different substitute paragraph at the end of the Foreword. He points out that most of his fan mail refers to the Appendices, and asks if it might pay to publish them separately.

> I could revise these and clarify the points which I now know require improvement or revision. I could also excise a good deal of the less useful or well considered parts. This would not hold up my work, since (once *Gawain* is out of the way) I should have to do precisely this revision for the purpose of integrating the early legends ['The Silmarillion'] with *The Lord of the Rings*. I have in fact done work of this kind already. It occurs to me that it might be possible to keep the appendices separate from the main story in any future edition of the hardback form that may be required. [Tolkien-George Allen & Unwin archive, HarperCollins]

He agrees to dropping the blurb. – Donald Swann writes to Tolkien. He commiserates with him on his treatment by the BBC, but suggests that it may turn out better than Tolkien fears. Swann and his wife have a room where Tolkien can rest during the afternoon of 14 March before they all go to Crosby Hall. He offers to collect Tolkien after his lunch with Stanley Unwin and drive him to his home in Battersea.

6 March 1968 Tolkien writes to his grandson Michael George. He offers to lend him the tape recorder given him by Caedmon Records. He comments on the superior quality of the tapes made on his previous tape recorder (provided by the University, and returned when he retired), 'when my voice was good or at any rate better than now'. Also tapes are perishable even with care – 'I have had to have some re-played and renewed.' John is better, and will return to work in a few days. Edith has a cold, but 'all being well we are both going to London on March 14 to a great A[llen] & U[nwin] jamboree' (British Library MS Add. 71657).

14 March 1968 Allen & Unwin hosts a reception at Crosby Hall, Chelsea, to launch the publication of their edition of *The Road Goes Ever On: A Song Cycle*. Tolkien travels from Oxford to London in the morning, and lunches with Stanley Unwin. After the lunch, Tolkien goes to Donald Swann's home in Albert Bridge Road, Battersea; he teaches Swann a version of demon patience that he has invented. At 4.50 p.m. Joy Hill comes to collect them, and she, Tolkien, and the Swanns drive to Crosby Hall, arriving at 5.00. From 5.15 until the reception begins at 5.45, Tolkien meets and talks to members of the press. At 6.45 Stanley Unwin introduces Donald Swann and William Elvin, who perform the song cycle. Joy Hill will write to Ian Ballantine on 18 March that 'the B.B.C. came along and filmed Donald Swann playing the song cycle and Professor Tolkien sitting in a chair listening but he flatly refused to be interviewed' (George Allen & Unwin archive, University of Reading). At 7.50 Tolkien and Edith leave for Waterloo Station to take the 8.30 p.m. train to Bournemouth. Among the guests invited by Tolkien for this occasion are Sir Thomas Armstrong (Principal of the Royal Academy of Music), Carey Blyton (composer of *Hobbit* overture), Nevill Coghill, Mr and Mrs Michael Flanders, and the Earl of Halsbury. Also present, invited by Allen & Unwin, are several of Tolkien's European publishers, and over one hundred members of the press, the BBC, and booksellers. Rayner Unwin will recall that this 'was the only book trade occasion that Tolkien ever attended, and the last time my father and Tolkien met' (*George Allen & Unwin: A Remembrancer*, p. 123). *See note.*

Late evening on 14 March–early April (before 8 April) 1968 Tolkien and Edith stay at the Hotel Miramar, Bournemouth.

19 March 1968 Joy Hill writes to Tolkien. Donald Swann's concert on 15 March at the Camden Festival went very well. He is to be interviewed by the BBC on Friday.

22 March 1968 Joy Hill writes to Tolkien. Swann's interview for the BBC will be broadcast on 25 March in the programme *Woman's Hour*. – Charlotte and Denis Plimmer's article, 'The Man Who Understands Hobbits', is published in the *Daily Telegraph Magazine*.

25 March 1968 Joy Hill replies to a postcard from Tolkien. The broadcast of Swann's interview has been postponed until 26 March. Rayner Unwin and Donald Swann have been interviewed for the BBC programme *The World at One*.

26 March 1968 Rayner Unwin writes to Tolkien. He has seen a galley proof of William Ready's forthcoming book on Tolkien, *The Tolkien Relation*. 'He has got several facts wrong and many speculations would I believe anger you.' He thinks that there is little they can do about it, and presumes that Tolkien has no particular desire to see galley proofs. He notices that the book is dedicated to Tolkien, and comments that he had always thought that one should get permission to do that, 'but obviously I am as old fashioned as he frequently accuses you of being' (Tolkien-George Allen & Unwin archive, HarperCollins).

28 March 1968 Alina Dadlez writes to Tolkien. She is sending him five copies of the Danish translation of *The Fellowship of the Ring*.

30 March 1968 The film *Tolkien in Oxford* is broadcast on BBC2 as part of the programme *Release* from 9.50 to 10.35 p.m. Also on the programme is a film on the sculptress Barbara Hepworth. The blurb for the Tolkien film in the *Radio Times* of 28 March has said:

A film about *The Lord of the Rings*: In Europe and in Asia it is a school set book. In America it's a craze bigger than Batman: one million copies sold in 1967 alone. In Britain a lot of people have never even heard of it. J.R.R. Tolkien, seventy-six, retired Oxford don, talks about his major work. Readers in Oxford try to explain the phenomenon of the lord of the hobbits, the orcs, and the elves. A literary masterpiece or a pleasant donnish joke? [p. 7]

5 April 1968 Colin Smythe, a London publisher, writes to Tolkien. He would like to publish a Tolkien poem.

8 April 1968 Tolkien writes to the President of the Tolkien Society of America about the forthcoming William Ready 'biography'. He does not want to advertise the book by making a public protest, but would like it made known to members of the Society that 'this book is bogus'. Ready 'has neither the authority nor the knowledge to write such a book. He visited me recently for about an hour and talked mostly about himself. My agents have read the proofs and report that it is a piece of word-spinning, inaccurate even in many points among the little information it provides' (quoted in Ed Meskys, 'Tolkien Notes from All Over', *Tolkien Journal* 3, no. 3, whole no. 9 (late summer 1968), p. 3).

10 April 1968 Tolkien writes to Colin Smythe. He does not think that there is any difficulty in offering a single poem for publication. He suggests that he consider the two already published in *Winter's Tales for Children I*, though perhaps he is interested only in something new.

11 April 1968 Colin Smythe replies to Tolkien. He will look at *Winter's Tales for Children I* but hopes that Tolkien will have a new poem for him to publish in the not too distant future.

13 April 1968 Tolkien writes to Clyde S. Kilby. The publisher Geoffrey Bles has sent him a copy of *A Mind Awake*, an anthology of writings by C.S. Lewis. This has reminded him 'of many good things that are scattered throughout Lewis's works'. He has not yet replied to Wheaton's offer for the *Smith of Wootton Major* manuscripts, because he has not made up his mind whether to sell them, and has been advised not to sell anything while 'the difficult arrangements I am making for the safeguarding of what little I can of my property are still incomplete. The recent budget in England has made things even more difficult' (Marion E. Wade Center, Wheaton College, Wheaton, Illinois).

17 April 1968 Donald and Janet Swann write to Tolkien and Edith. Swann comments on *Tolkien in Oxford*. He was generally not impressed, but thinks that it was unable to spoil Tolkien's personality. – A master at King Edward's School, Birmingham, writes to Tolkien. He asks permission for a dramatization of *The Lord of the Rings*, concentrating on Frodo, to be performed by the Junior Dramatic Society.

19 April 1968 Tolkien replies to the master at King Edward's School, Birmingham. He dislikes dramatizations of his work, but he is not so bigoted as to try to prevent a project which the master and many of the children will no doubt enjoy. But he must also get permission from Allen & Unwin, to whom Tolkien is sending the original letter.

23 April 1968 Rayner Unwin writes to Tolkien. He reminds him that reluctantly they have been forced to agree to licence the Dramatic Publishing Company of Chicago to produce a dramatic version of *The Hobbit* for amateur use, restricted to the USA. As agreed, the Company have now sent the typescript, which Rayner encloses for Tolkien to see before publication. 'It will not please you but we never supposed for a moment that it would. All that one could hope to do is remove the more offensive excrescences (why should poor Bifur be a candy bar eater?). Anything more fundamental would involve you in re-writing which would be a great mistake and a waste of time.' Since the contract allows only a short time for comment, Rayner asks that Tolkien, in the next ten days, 'skim through it making any changes that are absolutely necessary and comparatively simple and thereafter forget it as quickly as you can' (Tolkien-George Allen & Unwin archive, HarperCollins).

24 April 1968 Joy Hill writes to Tolkien. She encloses a copy of her letter to the master at King Edward's School. Allen & Unwin have received many similar requests in the past six months.

?Late April 1968 Tolkien is interviewed in Oxford by Keith Brace for an article, 'In the Footsteps of the Hobbit' which will appear in the *Birmingham Post* on 25 May. This will be concerned mainly with Tolkien's early life and his Birmingham connections.

29 April 1968 Rayner Unwin replies to Tolkien's letter of 4 March. Allen & Unwin will include the *Tale of Aragorn and Arwen* as the only appendix in the one-volume paperback *Lord of the Rings*. He thinks that to encourage sales of the hardbound edition, which still sells well, it would be sensible to keep the additional material contained in the appendices only obtainable in that edition, so that interested paperback readers might buy the hardback later. He would like to see what happens before making a decision about a separate paperback of the appendices or any other alternative.

30 April 1968 Tolkien writes to Rayner Unwin, returning the script of the Dramatic Publishing Company's *Hobbit* play. He cannot cope with it. He also encloses a letter from UNICEF asking for something to publish, with a copy of his original reply. He had considered sending them a story (*The Sellic Spell*), but having now received another letter making it clear that they reserve the right to cut the work in any way they choose, he has decided to say that he has nothing suitable. He has received more accounts from Ace Books, which show that the stock of their edition of *The Lord of the Rings* is now exhausted.

Spring 1968 The album *Poems and Songs of Middle Earth* is issued in Britain.

?Early May 1968 Nicholas Thomas of the City Museum and Art Gallery, Birmingham, writes to Tolkien. He encloses a brochure about Sarehole Mill, which is now a museum.

2 May 1968 Tolkien writes to Time-Life International, who have asked to photograph him while working. Since he never works 'while being photographed, or talked to, or accompanied by anybody in the room', 'a photograph of me pretending to be at work would be entirely bogus' (*Letters*, p. 390). – Rayner Unwin writes to Tolkien. He will go through the dramatization of *The Hobbit* as best he can. Allen & Unwin have received, unsolicited from a reader, part of 'an alphabetical list of characters, places, and events in *The Lord of the Rings* which she is compiling, giving a brief summary under each entry together with page references' (Tolkien-George Allen & Unwin archive, HarperCollins). She asks if Allen & Unwin are interested in publishing it. Rayner sends the material to Tolkien and asks if it is worth encouraging the project.

3 May 1968 Phyllis Jenkinson writes to Joy Hill, presumably responding to a letter or telephone call. Tolkien does not think that correspondence he has read in *The Times* about the proposed paperback *Lord of the Rings* is worth bothering about. He does want to see the British version of *Poems and Songs of Middle Earth*.

6 May 1968 Tolkien replies to the letter from Nicholas Thomas. Sarehole Mill dominated his childhood. If subscriptions to the Appeal for the Mill are still welcome, he would like to subscribe.

6–21 May 1968 Tolkien and Edith stay at the Hotel Miramar, Bournemouth.

7 May 1968 Joy Hill writes to Phyllis Jenkinson. An English pressing of *Poems and Songs of Middle Earth* was posted to Tolkien on 3 May. –Stanley Unwin signs a contract with the BBC for a radio dramatization of *The Hobbit*, to be broadcast towards the end of 1968 (i.e. the dramatization originally planned for 1967, postponed several times).

8 May 1968 Rayner Unwin sends H.N. Swanson, Allen & Unwin's American agent, his comments on the dramatization of *The Hobbit* to be forwarded to the Dramatic Publishing Company. Tolkien has asked Rayner to reply on his behalf.

It would be useless to pretend that he likes this dramatization. As, however, it is presented to him virtually as force majeure he has confined his comments and corrections to the very minimum, and only to those cases where the adapter has departed from the text of *The Hobbit* and, without any dramatic necessity, intruded his own invention. It is a regrettable fact that the adapter seems very insensitive indeed to the characters in the original work and to the diction and manner of expression that is used. [George Allen & Unwin archive, University of Reading]

9 May 1968 Phyllis Jenkinson writes to George Burke Johnston of Virginia, acknowledging in Tolkien's absence receipt of his booklet *The Poetry of J.R.R. Tolkien. See note.*

14 May 1968 Tolkien writes to Rayner Unwin. He thanks him for dealing with 'that shocking "dramatization" of *The Hobbit*'. The compiler of the list of characters, etc. might be encouraged, as 'her work seems careful and well-expressed. So long as she realizes that it is a work in which I must cooperate eventually. It needs among other things explanation of the meaning and structure of the names. If she likes to proceed, I should be glad; but I cannot turn aside for the moment, as I am in last throes of *Gawain* and *Pearl*.'

> I have not had, and did not expect to have, a restful stay here. Edith was very bad when I felt obliged to leave home again (with Gawain text etc. which I have hardly had a moment to attend to). Since part of the malady is immobility . . . I have been ramping round this large (but in part very beautiful) conurbation. The red light is on. I shall get nothing effectively done in the wretched condition of Sandfield Road. The shift must be now or never.
>
> I have discovered a very admirable and commodious bungalow in the borough of Poole. . . . It is quite possible that I shall have bought it before I return next week. Edith is recovering as she always does here and under better and more up to date treatment is already improving in mobility, as I myself feel very energetic (as usual here). [George Allen & Unwin archive, University of Reading]

Tolkien asks for three copies of the paperback *Hobbit*. – Rayner Unwin writes to Tolkien, returning the UNICEF correspondence and *The Sellic Spell*. He thinks that the story might be worth publishing with suitable companions.

15 May 1968 Alina Dadlez writes to Tolkien, She encloses a copy of a letter from M. André Bay of Éditions Stock, who are preparing a French edition of *The Hobbit*. He thinks that the word *Hobbit* might have the wrong connotation in French, for reasons he dare not explain, and asks if it could be replaced by *Hopin*. Dadlez asks Tolkien if he agrees. – Tolkien replies to Alina Dadlez, apparently on the same day. He must accept 'the objections of those who know more of the depths of the colloquial language!' (Tolkien-George Allen & Unwin archive, HarperCollins). He is willing to accept *Hopin*.

20 May 1968 Rayner Unwin writes to Tolkien. He hopes that the bungalow 'proves all that you desire.' (Tolkien-George Allen & Unwin archive, Harper-Collins). He is glad to hear that *Sir Gawain* and *Pearl* are nearly finished, and hopes that once they are out of the way Tolkien will be able to return to *The Silmarillion*.

24 May 1968 Tolkien writes to George Burke Johnston. He thanks him for *The Poetry of J.R.R. Tolkien* and explains the slang meaning of a word in *The Stone Troll*. He will be moving from Oxford soon.

27 May 1968 The Dramatic Publishing Company write to Rayner Unwin. They insist that they know better than he what is needed for a dramatic publication, and that many famous authors have been pleased with dramatizations made of their works. They agree, however, to make some changes. They enclose the entry they have prepared for the *Hobbit* dramatization in their catalogue, which says that it has Tolkien's approval and is published with his authorization.

28 May 1968 Phyllis Jenkinson writes to Joy Hill, presumably in response to a suggestion made in a letter or by telephone. 'Tolkien does *not* feel disposed to sign dozens of labels as this would obviously continue *ad infinitum*. He does not mind doing a few from time to time for the fans I deal with who have actually bought his book' (Tolkien-George Allen & Unwin archive, HarperCollins). – Rayner Unwin writes to Tolkien. He has heard of two more books planned on Tolkien: one from Twayne Publishers, and one from Ballantine. He has requested to see proofs of both. *See note.*

29 May 1968 Joy Hill writes to Phyllis Jenkinson. She made the suggestion of labels after receiving a rather nice letter from a child. After more thought, she has decided against having an answer card for dealing with stock questions from fans, as that might create a bad image.

1 June 1968 Michael Kilgarriff writes to Tolkien. He has adapted *The Hobbit* for the forthcoming dramatization on BBC radio. He enjoyed the work, and hopes to meet Tolkien some time during the production.

4 June 1968 Tolkien writes to Clyde S. Kilby. He is moving from Oxford to the South Coast. His new address will not be made public except to a few close and trusted people; his contact address will be c/o Messrs Allen & Unwin. William Ready had 'the impertinence' to send him an inscribed copy of his book, *The Tolkien Relation*. He refutes Ready's claim that he spent hours interviewing Tolkien. He made only a short visit, and talked mainly about himself.

> I can now see his difficulty. If he had brought out a notebook and informed me of his object, I should have shown him out. He therefore had to rely on his own memory of the few remarks I made about my personal history. These he appears to have embroidered with wholly illegitimate deductions of his own and the additions of baseless fictions. I have now made up my mind not to see anybody from your country whom I do not already know, nor anybody from any Press in any country. [Marion E. Wade Center, Wheaton College, Wheaton, Illinois]

– Tolkien writes to Colin Smythe. He thinks that he can find a poem for him to publish, about 'Westernesse'.

5 June 1968 Colin Smythe replies to Tolkien. He would be delighted to be able to publish the poem that Tolkien offers.

13 June 1968 Alina Dadlez writes to Tolkien. She is sending him a copy of the second edition of the German translation of *The Hobbit*, published by Paulus Verlag, with a new dust-jacket.

17 June 1968 In the afternoon, Tolkien falls while running downstairs in his house in Sandfield Road and injures his leg. He will later write: 'I was picked up off the floor of the hall and transported to the Nuffield [Orthopaedic Centre] as I was and never went back again – never saw my room, or my house again' (letter to Michael Tolkien, October 1968, *Letters*, p. 395).

17 June–mid-July Tolkien is in hospital. He is unable to pack, or supervise the packing of, his books and papers for the move to Poole. He is still in hospital when the actual move takes place.

18 June 1968 Tolkien undergoes an operation in the Nuffield Orthopaedic Centre.

19 June 1968 Rayner Unwin writes two letters to Tolkien. He has obtained an assurance from the American publisher of *The Tolkien Relation* that it will not be offered to any English publisher. Swanson has sent the proposed contract for the film rights of *The Lord of the Rings*, and that the same film company has bought the rights to *The Hobbit* from their previous owner. He has sent the contract to Tolkien's legal advisor. He has also received a long letter from the Dramatic Publishing Company, objecting to many of the changes Rayner suggested, but they have 'deleted a lot of the worst excesses and infelicities' (Tolkien-George Allen & Unwin archive, HarperCollins). Rayner assumes that Tolkien wants no part in the matter, and will battle on in Tolkien's name unless he hears from him to the contrary. – Phyllis Jenkinson writes to Rayner Unwin to inform him of Tolkien's accident. Tolkien is worrying about the moving of his books. Edith hopes that Christopher will be able to return from a visit to France earlier than planned to help deal with them.

20 June 1968 Rayner Unwin writes to H.N. Swanson. He has discussed with Tolkien the changes the Dramatic Publishing Company are willing to make, and since these alterations have satisfied many of the points raised, the publication can go ahead. 'Neither Professor Tolkien nor I are concerned about the process of dramatization so long as it is a dramatization of the book in question and that intrusions from elsewhere conform to the spirit and style of the original.' Tolkien has commented on the advertisement that 'he agrees the publication is with his authorization . . . he would not wish it to be said that the dramatization has his *approval*' (George Allen & Unwin archive, University of Reading). – Joy Hill writes to Tolkien, sending a copy of a letter from the Performing Rights Society about 'The Ballad of Bilbo Baggins' which Tolkien has evidently asked to have investigated. *See note.*

c. 21 June 1968 Stanley and Rayner Unwin each writes to Tolkien, expressing regret for his accident.

21 June 1968 Rayner Unwin writes to Tolkien. The University of Notre Dame Press has announced the publication of a collection of essays, *Tolkien and the Critics*, ed. Neil D. Isaacs and Rose A. Zimbardo.

25 June 1968 Tolkien is asked his opinion about *The Lord of the Rings* as an adult animated television series.

26 June 1968 Tolkien dictates letters to Miss Jenkinson, which she signs for him. One is to thank Stanley Unwin for his letter of sympathy. Another is to Rayner Unwin. In the latter, he notes that he is recovering and hopes to be on crutches about 8 July. He is now able to do a certain amount of business and can be contacted by letter or telephone at the hospital. Among the many things the accident has caused him to neglect is the matter of William Ready's book. He encloses a copy of a letter from a reader, Bonniejean Christensen, to Dr Robert R. Kirsch of the *Los Angeles Times*, which she has sent to Tolkien, and in which she criticizes Ready's book in great detail. Tolkien comments that it reveals Ready as a charlatan, although Christensen 'doesn't of course know of the enormity and the nonsense when he speaks about my private life and family affairs' (Tolkien–George Allen & Unwin archive, HarperCollins). Tolkien's solicitor wants him to consult an American lawyer about the film contract. – Phyllis Jenkinson writes to Colin Smythe. Because of Tolkien's accident there will be some delay in sending the poem.

28 June 1968 Joy Hill writes to Tolkien. In response to Phyllis Jenkinson's telephone call, she has ordered six copies of *Smith of Wootton Major* to be sent to Miss Jenkinson's home. (Tolkien probably wants these to give to staff at the hospital.) The photographs of him taken by John Wyatt, the BBC cameraman, are very good. – Rayner Unwin writes to Tolkien. The first printing of the one-volume paperback of *The Lord of the Rings* will be 50,000 copies. He has received a massive draft contract for the film rights.

1 July 1968 Phyllis Jenkinson writes to Rayner Unwin. Tolkien has asked her to tell Rayner that he will be at the hospital until at least 10 July.

?Early July 1968 Edith moves from Sandfield Road and stays at the Hotel Miramar. Her health making it impossible for her to direct the removal men, they take advantage, placing furniture in the wrong rooms and piling boxes and crates containing books and other items in a vast heap in the garage.

4 July 1968 Joy Hill writes to Tolkien. She encloses a proof copy of *Waes*, a historical fantasy by David Grant, which she hopes Tolkien might like. Miss Dadlez has asked her to tell Tolkien that she is signing a contract for a Romanian translation of *The Hobbit*. – Joy Hill writes to Phyllis Jenkinson. She encloses photostats of correspondence with the Performing Rights Society. She and Rayner Unwin agree that 'The Ballad of Bilbo Baggins' does not infringe any rights.

5 July 1968 Leslie Megahey visits Tolkien in hospital. He brings with him six further copies of *Smith of Wootton Major* and three of the paperback *Hobbit* requested by Tolkien, with Joy Hill's letter of 4 July.

7–13 July 1968 During this week, Christopher and Baillie Tolkien visit Edith. They stay a night at the Hotel Miramar and approve the bungalow.

10 July 1968 Brian Sibley writes to Tolkien. He greatly enjoyed *Smith of Wootton Major*. He asks for an inscription to place in his copy of *The Road Goes Ever On: A Song Cycle*. (Much later, Sibley will dramatize *The Lord of the Rings* and other works by Tolkien for BBC radio.)

16 July 1968 Tolkien leaves hospital, still in a plaster cast from foot to waist. He is driven to the Hotel Miramar.

18 July 1968 Edith Tolkien writes to Rayner Unwin.

It *has* been a hectic & worrying time – with so much to do & arrange, both at Oxford & here, but it was a great relief to sell the Sandfield Rd. house, & now to have the 3 day move behind me.

The Bungalow remains in chaos – just as the movers left it – but it's going to be charming, *when* we get straight. There's a very nice garden – & lots of roses – & a gate leading into Branksome Chine & to the sea.

Tolkien is 'getting about with elbow crutches – but is soon tired with the effort. Yes – he does get impatient, & feels so frustrated when there is so much to do. . . . The surgeon says he *may* walk by Xmas' (Tolkien-George Allen & Unwin archive, HarperCollins). Tolkien would be cheered by a visit, if Rayner can spare the time. Miss Jenkinson has been a great help. – Rayner Unwin writes to Tolkien. He sends a list of queries from proofreaders who have been making a careful comparison of the new reset paperback *Lord of the Rings* with the three-volume hardback edition. He asks for Tolkien's comments. The paperback will be published in October, and the Allen & Unwin sales department have suggested that, to build up substantial initial sales, booksellers who pre-order one hundred or more copies should get an extra free copy signed by Tolkien.

19 July 1968 Edith Tolkien replies to Rayner Unwin's letter, as Tolkien is still unable to write. All of Tolkien's books are in crates in the garage at the bungalow, and they can't find anything, not even a copy of *The Lord of the Rings* to consider the proofreaders' queries. Tolkien is willing to sign copies of the paperback for publicity purposes. He would like Rayner to ring him. 10.00 a.m. would be a good time. – Rayner Unwin writes to Edith, asking if it would be convenient for him to visit them in Bournemouth on 25 July for lunch. – Tom Clarke, Assistant Editor for *Queen* magazine, writes to Tolkien. They are planning a photographic feature on writers and their relationship with their fictional characters, and would like to photograph Tolkien as Gandalf with a number of models in other relevant roles. – A librarian in Boston writes to Tolkien, asking permission to make a photocopy of *Songs for the Philologists*.

22 July 1968 Edith Tolkien writes to Rayner Unwin. 25 July will be convenient for his visit. – Ian Curtis, a producer for BBC Television, writes to Tolkien. The BBC are considering a new series of portraits of distinguished academic figures. Curtis asks if he and a colleague can visit Tolkien next week.

25 July 1968 The publisher Macmillan & Co. sends Tolkien a proof copy of Kevin Crossley-Holland's translation of *Beowulf*. If Tolkien likes it and Bruce Mitchell's editorial contribution, he is asked to provide a quote to be used in publicity.

?Late July 1968 Tolkien receives a request from a Californian to use his 'Elvish battle cry' 'A Elbereth Gilthoniel' and certain place-names from *The Lord of the Rings* in a story he is writing. At some date Tolkien will scribble on the letter: 'It is *not* a battle cry and I should strongly object to its use in a story by another author.' He regards the use of his names 'as an impertinence and not a compliment' (Tolkien-George Allen & Unwin archive, HarperCollins).

30 July 1968 John Tolkien comes to Poole to help his parents settle into their new home at 19 Lakeside Road. Tolkien will later write that John wears himself out in getting the chief living-rooms and the garden into order. On John's arrival, or the next day, Edith moves from the Miramar to her new home. Tolkien stays at the hotel.

31 July 1968 Tolkien visits the bungalow to have supper with Edith and John. – Joy Hill writes to Tolkien, sending him two letters to sign. She will inform reference books that they should remove his Oxford address. She forwards a message from Leslie Megahey that he will have a reproduction of a photograph of Simon Tolkien made (presumably from the photos taken by John Wyatt in February) when he returns to his office.

3 August 1968 Tolkien writes a long letter to Joy Hill. He is still at the Hotel Miramar, feeling much better, but

> pretty completely frustrated. (I am ceasing to notice the great weight of plaster, but a straight unbendable leg makes all things difficult; dressing is a problem, and [I] cannot ride in a car, except laid out on the back seat.) Even with great effort I cannot do anything useful to reorder the complete confusion of my books files and papers – mostly still quite inaccessible. Also – a natural result this and the shock of the accident – I still find concentration even on simple letters very difficult. And crutches give me stiff tired hands. With the help of my eldest son, who is occupying my bedroom in Lakeside Road, the house is now domestically almost in order and quite habitable. But my own room, and the prospective library remain in piled disorder; and after nearly 3 weeks of negotiations I have still not managed to get anything done about it. B[ournemou]th is at the height of its season, and also engaged in a frenzy of building, public and private, so that architects, carpenters, and furniture-heavers are hard to discover. [collection of René van Rossenberg]

So far he has informed only Allen & Unwin, his family and a few close friends, his bank, trustees and lawyers, and Oxford University Registry and his colleges of his new address, and has asked all of these to refer enquirers to him c/o Allen & Unwin. *Who's Who* is the only British reference book that needs to be altered, but the Royal Society of Literature should probably be informed to use the Allen & Unwin address. Houghton Mifflin could probably inform any American reference sources. He encloses the letter from Macmillan & Co. and the proof copy of Crossley-Holland's translation of *Beowulf*, and asks Joy to explain that he cannot deal with it because of his accident.

4 August 1968 Donald Swann, and probably his wife, visit Tolkien and Edith.

7 August 1968 Tolkien writes to a Mrs Ogden, presumably at the Nuffield Orthopaedic Centre. He asks how long he will need to stay in hospital when he returns on 8 September for an appointment with his specialist on 9 September. He needs to arrange for someone to stay with his wife in his absence. – Joy Hill writes to Tolkien. She sends him copies of letters she has written to Macmillan & Co. and to Kevin Crossley-Holland, and a letter to the Royal Society of Literature about his change of address for him to sign. An American magazine has discovered *Goblin Feet*: Joy asks if it is Tolkien's work, and if she should she give permission to reprint it for a fee.

c. 8 or 9 August 1968 Mrs Ogden replies to Tolkien. He will need to stay in hospital for a fortnight, not only for the fitting of a new support for his leg, but also to restore strength to the leg which has been in plaster.

By 9 August 1968 Tolkien has found some domestic help. This is probably Mrs Parke, who will act as driver and general help for several hours a week for much of the time that Tolkien lives in Poole.

c. 9–10 August 1968 When Tolkien receives the letter from Mrs Ogden he tries to arrange to obtain treatment for his leg at a hospital in Bournemouth as an outpatient. There is no room at the Hotel Miramar for Edith, and no family member who is free to stay with her in Tolkien's absence.

12 August 1968 Tolkien writes to Joy Hill.

Most of my time and such energy as I have is still occupied in the endlessly frustrated task of getting any one to do anything. At last, after almost one month, men are actually beginning to erect my bookshelves. I am physically very tired, since the ordinary things of daily life are exhausting. Dressing and undressing are the equivalent to an hour's hard work; and 100 yds on crutches equals . . . a four mile walk for the uninjured. Both my hands are permanently weary. My doctor diagnoses me as still suffering from shock, and recommends a period of quiet – about as useful as advising a poor pensioner to go on a sea-cruise. [collection of René van Rossenberg]

He sends a few letters, some with notes, for Joy to deal with. He would like a copy of the paperback *Lord of the Rings*. He has not forgotten that he is to sign copies for publicity use. (With this letter, Tolkien begins to address Joy Hill as 'Joy' rather than 'Miss Hill'.) – Joy Hill writes to Tolkien. She sends a copy of John Wyatt's photograph of him, which they are using to promote the paperback *Lord of the Rings*.

16 August 1968 Tolkien moves from the Hotel Miramar to his new home in Lakeside Road, Poole.

17 August 1968 A reader in California writes to Tolkien. He sends questions about Wizards, Frodo's journey into the West, and the competing claims of Tom Bombadil and Treebeard to be 'Eldest'.

20 August 1968 Joy Hill writes to Tolkien. He will be sent a paperback *Lord of the Rings* as soon as copies arrive, probably next week.

21 August 1968 Tolkien writes to Stanley Unwin. 'I am beginning to feel that the forcible damming up of the stream may soon release a good head of water to set the wheels turning again – as soon as I have anywhere to write in peace' (Tolkien-George Allen & Unwin archive, HarperCollins).

26 August 1968 Joy Hill writes to Tolkien. She encloses a letter from President Johnson's daughter, whom Joy has told that she may send her copy of *The Hobbit* to be autographed by Tolkien. Joy suggests that after Tolkien has returned from the hospital, she should visit him, and they should look at the long letter with biographical information that he sent to Houghton Mifflin in 1955, with other biographical material she has on hand, and prepare a biographical note for Houghton Mifflin and Tolkien's foreign-language publishers. The BBC are finally going to broadcast *The Hobbit* beginning at the end of September. Joy is sending him the artwork for a reprint of *The Hobbit* recently issued by Longmans, now in their *Pleasure in Reading* series.

27 August 1968 Joy Hill writes to the librarian in Boston on Tolkien's behalf. Tolkien has given permission for him to make a photocopy of *Songs for the Philologists*, provided that he inserts a note explaining that it is full of errors. Tolkien has corrected and revised the sections of this book for which he was responsible. When he has unpacked his library, he will be happy to send the correspondent a corrected copy.

28 August 1968 Tolkien writes to Joy Hill. 'There are 48 crates of books to get up on shelves, and all is at moment still in confusion. It is like a jigsaw trying to clear the boxes and still find room to store the empties till they are fetched away. I can still not find my papers and required files and other missing items. Also I fear that in spite of care I have miscalculated the required book space and shall have to get rid of many books' (collection of René van Rossenberg). – Joy Hill writes to Tolkien. Allen & Unwin hope to have copies of the paperback *Lord of the Rings* next week.

?Late August 1968 Tolkien scribbles answers to or comments on the questions in the 17 August letter from a fan. From these he drafts a letter to be typed by Joy Hill.

8–20 September 1968 Tolkien returns to hospital in Oxford to have his plaster removed and his leg strengthened. He is supplied with a pair of crutches and a brace and caliper. Also he is treated for a blood condition that is a result of his long immobility.

***c.* 11 September 1968** Margaret Carroux writes to Tolkien. She consults him about various difficulties with her translation of *The Lord of the Rings* into German, in particular problems with Tolkien's poetry.

20 September 1968 A.V. Hall, manager of Parker and Son, an Oxford bookshop, writes to Tolkien. They are planning an extensive display for the publication of the paperback *Lord of the Rings* and the Caedmon recording. Tolkien is asked if he would undertake a short autograph session.

27 September 1968 Joy Hill writes to Tolkien. She explains the arrangements for signing the paperback *Lord of the Rings* on 3 October. She has been in touch with John Powell, who is producing the BBC dramatization of *The Hobbit*; he is sending a spare script. *See note.*

29 September 1968 Tolkien replies to Margaret Carroux, with whom he has corresponded since her visit to Oxford on 13 December 1967. He refers to specimens of verse she has sent him, and encourages her:

I should certainly not have taken the trouble that I took with your specimens, if I had not felt that you had the sympathy and understanding required, and only needed a little help and some encouragement to persevere in what is a very difficult task.

And I, of course, assumed that the translation would be by one hand throughout. The verses are an integral part of the narrative (and of the delineation of the characters) and not a separable 'decoration' like pictures by another artist. For success a separate translator of the verses would need to have a detailed knowledge of the whole original text, and of the prose version. It seems to me highly improbable that such a special 'lyric-writer' would bother to acquire this knowledge. Discrepancies of various kinds would certainly be introduced, unless he/she was much more conscientious than any pictorial illustrator that I have had to do with. [Tolkien-George Allen & Unwin archive, HarperCollins]

He hopes that Carroux will be able to continue her efforts. He is willing to assist her with other pieces of verse than those he has already seen. – Tolkien writes to Joy Hill, sending his reply to Frau Carroux for Joy to post. He also forwards to Joy a letter which the publisher Jonathan Cape had sent to him with a copy of the book *Musrum* by Eric Thacker and Anthony Earnshaw. Cape is presumably seeking words of approval to use for publicity. Tolkien does not like the book at all, and has had difficulty in writing a reply which does not seem rude. He asks Joy's opinion of a non-committal reply that the book 'is quite outside the range of my interests and I do not feel moved to say anything at all about it' (Tolkien-George Allen & Unwin archive, HarperCollins). – Tolkien replies to a letter from Billy Callahan, a schoolboy in Philadelphia. He does not have a photograph to send, but as some compensation is sending three signatures which Billy can put in his books if he wishes. (The letter will be reproduced in *Wisterian*, the newspaper of La Salle College High School, 20 December 1968, p. 3). – The first part of the BBC adaptation of *The Hobbit*, 'An Unexpected Party', is broadcast on Radio 4 at 8.30 p.m.

1 October 1968 Tolkien talks with Joy Hill by telephone about various matters. – George D. Astley, the Registrar of the Society of Authors, sends an appeal for a donation. When he gets it, Tolkien writes a note (probably to Rayner Unwin) on the envelope asking for advice. He has received useful and prompt advice from the Society in the past. – The first part of the BBC *Hobbit* is rebroadcast at 3.00 p.m.

2 October 1968 Joy Hill writes to Tolkien. She comments on his letter about *Musrum*, and returns statements of sales from Ace Books which belong in Tolkien's files.

3 October 1968 Martin Blackman, Allen & Unwin home trade manager, brings to the Hotel Miramar at about 11.00 a.m. one hundred copies of the paperback *Lord of the Rings* for Tolkien to sign. He collects them later in the day. He also delivers a note from Joy Hill, dated 1 October, transmitting an item 'with the very best wishes of the Directors and Staff of Allen & Unwin.

I hope the mounting and framing are to your liking' (Tolkien-George Allen & Unwin archive, HarperCollins). (This may be the photograph of Simon Tolkien taken by John Wyatt.)

6 October 1968 The second part of the BBC adaptation of *The Hobbit*, 'Out of the Frying Pan into the Fire', is broadcast on Radio 4 at 8.30 p.m.

8 October 1968 The second part of the BBC *Hobbit* is rebroadcast at 3.00 p.m.

10 October 1968 Allen & Unwin's one-volume paperback edition of *The Lord of the Rings* is published.

11 October 1968 and ?later that month On 11 October Tolkien finds the unfinished letter to his son Michael begun some time after 25 August 1967. He now continues this, describing his reactions to the recent move. He had known exactly where everything was in his study at Sandfield Road, but he never saw it again after his fall.

> In addition to the shock of the fall and the operation, this has had a queer effect. It is like reading a story and coming to a sudden break (where a chapter or two seems missing): complete change of scene. For a long time I felt that I was in a (bad) dream and should wake up perhaps and find myself back in my old room. It also made me feel restless & uncomfortable – and 'suspicious'. I could not mentally settle in the new home, as if it was something unreal & might vanish! Also I am still – since no one seems able to help me, and I have been too lamed to help myself for long without weariness – searching for vanished or scattered notes; and my library is still a wilderness of disordered books. [*Letters*, pp. 395–6]

13 October 1968 The third part of the BBC adaptation of *The Hobbit*, 'Riddles in the Dark', is broadcast on Radio 4 at 8.30 p.m. – Stanley Unwin dies.

c. **14–18 October 1968** Joy Hill stays at the Hotel Miramar and helps Tolkien set up an office and library in his new home. In 1990 she will write: 'One day as I picked up a pile of books in my arms and put them on the shelf, something dropped out from between two of them. It was an exercise book: just the covers with a single sheet between, and on the page, a poem. [Tolkien] asked what it was; I gave it to him and he read it aloud. It was *Bilbo's Last Song*' (*The Times*, 10 December 1990, p. 16). *See note.* Tolkien will write to Rayner Unwin that during this visit Joy Hill 'in her efforts to arouse me from a lethargy of despair, and of bodily weariness since I was still under thrice-weekly painful treatment, showed special anxiety that any "compositions", shall we say, of my own should be collected and stored safely' (2 December, Tolkien-George Allen & Unwin archive, HarperCollins). She takes some items back to London to show Rayner Unwin.

?Mid-October 1968 Tolkien receives a pompous letter from a student in Illinois, aged between thirteen and eighteen, seeking help for a school project. When he receives it, Tolkien scribbles various critical remarks on it and drafts a reply.

Mid-October 1968–?November 1971 Joy Hill makes many visits to Tolkien in Lakeside Road, most only for a day, but on occasion for a longer period, during which Joy stays at the Hotel Miramar. In an article published in 1974 it will be said that Joy used to visit Tolkien every month after he moved to Poole,

> laden with fan letters and the presents people sent – a bottle of claret, a tapestry, Hobbit drawings, a silver goblet . . . a large quantity of mushrooms. . . . The ceremony of present opening was always the first event of the visit. Then they would get to work, and often fierce argument over office practices, as when he wanted to file all amusing letters under 'A'. . . .
>
> 'He dominated the visit [Joy recalled]: you talked about what he wanted to talk about. You'd think, "Perhaps I could ask him so-and-so today," and you'd never get the opportunity; so the things you were desperate to know, you never found out. But on the other hand you might be going for a walk, and you'd get a fantastic nonstop half-hour lecture on Frodo's moral failure or the origins of a certain word. Or perhaps one on how you were a stupid girl to sit in the sun and how much better it was to have a white skin than a sunburnt one.' [Janet Watts, 'Bilbo Sings Again', *The Guardian*, 19 September 1974]

15 October 1968 The third part of the BBC *Hobbit* is rebroadcast at 3.00 p.m.

20 October 1968 The fourth part of the BBC adaptation of *The Hobbit*, 'Strange Lodgings', is broadcast on Radio 4 at 8.30 p.m.

22 October 1968 The fourth part of the BBC *Hobbit* is rebroadcast at 3.00 p.m.

23 October 1968 Joy Hill writes to Tolkien. 'The luxury of last week is like a dream' (Tolkien-George Allen & Unwin archive, HarperCollins). She has nearly completed an index of all of the things she put in the cupboard in Tolkien's study.

27 October 1968 The fifth part of the BBC adaptation of *The Hobbit*, 'Barrels Out of Bond', is broadcast on Radio 4 at 8.30 p.m.

28 October 1968 Rayner Unwin writes to Tolkien. He suggests a contribution to the Society of Authors of around £50.

29 October 1968 The fifth part of the BBC *Hobbit* is rebroadcast at 3.00 p.m.

30 October 1968 Rayner Unwin writes to Tolkien. Mr Sachler, who supervised the recording of *Poems and Songs of Middle Earth*, is in England again until Christmas, and would like to make another recording of Tolkien. The impending film contract prevents any recording of *The Lord of the Rings* and *The Hobbit*, but *Smith of Wootton Major* would be possible if Tolkien is interested.

3 November 1968 The sixth part of the BBC adaptation of *The Hobbit*, 'A Warm Welcome', is broadcast on Radio 4 at 8.30 p.m.

5 November 1968 The sixth part of the BBC *Hobbit* is rebroadcast at 3.00 p.m.

10 November 1968 The seventh part of the BBC adaptation of *The Hobbit*, 'The Gathering of the Cloud[s]', is broadcast on Radio 4 at 8.30 p.m.

12 November 1968 The seventh part of the BBC *Hobbit* is rebroadcast at 3.00 p.m.

14 November 1968 Tolkien writes to Joy Hill. He has booked a room for her at the Hotel Miramar for the night of 23 November. – In the afternoon, four bottles of port and three of sherry are delivered, a gift to Tolkien from Amy Ronald. – Tolkien writes a letter of thanks to Amy Ronald. 'We are fairly snug now in our new home, having learned to manage the central heating that was unfamiliar' (*Letters*, p. 396).

16 November 1968 Tolkien sends Joy Hill a mixed lot of letters to deal with. One is to The Society, explaining that he has moved and must reluctantly resign. He would like Joy to post this, to avoid a Bournemouth postmark. Another letter (probably in this group) is to the Dean of Queen's College, Cambridge, who had been hoping to bring members of a society, the Ring Readers, to Oxford to meet Tolkien.

17 November 1968 The eighth part of the BBC adaptation of *The Hobbit*, 'The Clouds Burst', is broadcast on Radio 4 at 8.30 p.m.

19 November 1968 Tolkien writes to Mrs Ogden (presumably at the Nuffield Orthopaedic Centre). He had been unable to return to Oxford on 28 October. He will try to return the pair of crutches lent to him (and the brace and caliper also, if wanted) as soon as possible. He is now walking without a stick, but awkwardly, as his knee does not bend easily. He finds the therapy tiring and painful. – The eighth part of the BBC *Hobbit* is rebroadcast at 3.00 p.m.

23–24 November 1968 Joy Hill stays the night at the Hotel Miramar, and probably helps Tolkien on 23 and 24 November.

29 November 1968 Tolkien writes to Joy Hill. He thanks her for all her work and kindness. He wonders if he should continue his subscription to a press cutting agency, since they seem to miss many references to him, rather than to his works. Allen & Unwin already gets those cuttings that refer to his works. He sends Joy a cheque for her expenses for the previous weekend. Edith has been ill, and he himself has not felt well. 'My leg has (I think) missed the red lamp, and also it has been impossible to go for walks in dark, wet, stuffy days. In addition the artillery away west have been firing away continuously from dawn to dusk making one only too reminded of war' (collection of René van Rossenberg). – Rayner Unwin writes two letters to Tolkien. One concerns an unacceptable point in the film rights contract proposed by United Artists. If Tolkien agrees with the enclosed letter, written by Rayner on his behalf, he should sign it and send it to Swanson. The other letter also mentions United Artists, and a list of Tolkien's unpublished works made by Joy Hill.

2 December 1968 Tolkien writes to Rayner Unwin. He has signed and sent the letter to Swanson, but is not at all confident that United Artists will concede the point. He comments on the

> appalling year, 1968, which began in January with the breakdown of Edith's failing health, after the strains of nursing me at the end of the previous year, and the collapse of my son John who took refuge with us on the very near verge of a nervous breakdown – and proceeded to the present chaos. I seem to have spent most of my time in the Miramar Hotel, where 'work' of any real kind, and the control of correspondence, was impossible.

He comments of the list of his unpublished works, made by Joy Hill 'in her efforts to arouse me from a lethargy of despair, and of bodily weariness since I was still under thrice-weekly painful treatment'. Joy is anxious that his unpublished works should be collected, catalogued, and safely stored. 'The things she brought to you (there are others such as *The End of Bovadium* [i.e. *The Bovadium Fragments*]) I have no intention of publishing now (if ever) or of allowing them to get in the way of my proper work.' Nothing fills him 'with greater longing than the thought of being able to spend some uninterrupted hours at a desk in an ordered library again – but the bedevilment of my books has been appalling, and I am still unable to find most of those that I most need!' (Tolkien-George Allen & Unwin archive, HarperCollins).

29 December 1968 Tolkien replies to a letter from a correspondent who has asked about similarity of some of Tolkien's names to those of William Blake. By chance, just before he received the letter, he had been reading his 1919 diary in which he had noted on 21 February of that year he had been reading part of Blake's prophetic books for the first time, and himself discovered the similarity. His own *orc* is borrowed from Old English *orc* 'demon', which is supposedly derived from Latin *Orcus* which Blake probably knew, 'and also supposed to be unconnected with *orc* the name of a marine animal. But I recently investigated *orc* and find the matter complex' (Tolkien-George Allen & Unwin archive, HarperCollins). – Austin Farrer dies.

31 December 1968 Tolkien writes to Joy Hill. He encloses forms he has been asked to sign. He asks her to post his letter of 29 December; he answered the query to prevent his being associated with Blake, whose works he detests. He is 'snowed up' with late Christmas, New Year, and birthday post, most of which needs no answer. He hopes that the contract with United Artists will be concluded soon, supposing that this would prevent any possibility of a film of his work being produced with designs by Heinz Edelmann. Tolkien refers to Edelmann's 'sinister plans', and describes some of his pictures (possibly from the Beatles' *Yellow Submarine*) as 'the lowest point in foul vulgarity' (collection of René van Rossenberg). (Joy Hill will add a note to this letter, after it reaches her desk, that the film contract would not prevent United Artists from licensing a production with whomever they chose.) Tolkien encloses a communication from the Performing Rights Society, and thinks that it might be best if they were asked to send everything to Allen & Unwin.

1969

***c.* 1969 and later** Tolkien is 'moved to write extensively, in a more generalised view, of the languages and peoples of the Third Age and their interrelations, closely interwoven with discussion of the etymology of names' (*The Peoples of Middle-earth*, p. 293). This work involves him in a close study of which elements had been 'fixed' by publication, and which could be changed or have a different origin. But these philological investigations often involve much historical writing, and even complete stories, for at this stage linguistic development and history become increasingly intertwined. Usually he composes these works *ab initio* on a typewriter, though he may ponder them for a long time before putting words to paper. Some end in 'chaotic and illegible or unintelligible notes and jottings' (*The Peoples of Middle-earth*, p. 294), while the rest are not necessarily finished, and there is no subsequent development or refining of texts. Since they are basically etymological, they are extremely discursive as one point leads to another, and are often interspersed with many, sometimes lengthy notes explaining or expanding on particular points. For much of this late work Tolkien uses scrap paper from Allen & Unwin with dates 'some from 1967, the great majority from 1968, and some from 1970' (p. 293), but on at least some occasions the paper is not used until two years later.

Several works are typed or written on the blank versos of cyclostyled sheets of a BBC script of *The Hobbit* from autumn 1968. In **The Shibboleth of Fëanor* Tolkien seeks to record the part played in the divisions among the Noldorin princes in Valinor by a difference in pronunciation of a single consonantal element in Quenya. This includes three extensive notes: on the reasons for the change in pronunciation, on Mother-names, and on the names of the descendants of Finwë, King of the Ñoldor. Tolkien does not finish composing this last, long item on the typewriter, but drafts notes in manuscript concerning the names of the sons of Fëanor and the story of his two youngest sons. Versos are also used for philological writing on the names *Galadriel, Celeborn,* and *Lórien* (see **The History of Galadriel and Celeborn and of Amroth King of Lórien*).

Tolkien makes various manuscript notes, and then begins to type an essay on the Common Eldarin root ȝOR and its descendants, including the Quenya derivative *óre* (**Notes on Óre*), but does not proceed very far. Some time after writing *The Shibboleth of Fëanor* he gives further consideration to the etymology of the name *Elros* and of associated names such as *Elwing*, already discussed in the third note to the earlier work. Now in a series of typescripts, to which Christopher Tolkien has given the name **The Problem of Ros*, he devises a solution which satisfies him, then realizes that it contradicts a statement already in print. The texts also include in passing an elaborate discussion of the intermingling of Elven and Mannish languages, and much background history.

Some of the works that belong to this late period, but cannot be more precisely dated, give more details of matters mentioned in *The Lord of the Rings*. Tolkien makes a rough typescript of **The Disaster of the Gladden Fields* in the first stage of composition, and begins but does not complete a fair copy typescript incorporating many changes. Associated material gives information about measurement in Númenór (**Númenórean Linear Measures*) and the heights of various races. In **The Battles of the Fords of Isen* Tolkien not only provides a detailed account of events dealt with only briefly in *The Lord of the Rings*, but also writes about the military organization of the Rohirrim and the history of Isengard. In a long note he gives some account of the history of Calenardhon, the arrival of the Rohirrim, their history, and Saruman's settlement at Isengard. Other late texts with no indications of date which may be assigned to the period 1969 or later are an essay on the Silvan Elves and Silvan Elvish; a discussion of the boundaries of Lórien (perhaps included in the texts on the Silvan Elves); and a discussion of linguistic and political interrelations in Middle-earth (see **The History of Galadriel and Celeborn and of Amroth King of Lórien*).

?1969 or later Tolkien drafts a reply to a letter he has received, written in a formal, pseudo-diplomatic style as from 'King Ephedolos', asking questions about *The Lord of the Rings* and 'The Silmarillion'. Tolkien's reply is in the same style, and is sent to Joy Hill to deal with and post. Tolkien will describe the letter as 'cracked', but confesses that 'this kind of thing amuses me, since I may be considered rather cracked myself in similar ways. . . . "Playing the game" with readers of this sort (if not too time-wasting) is perhaps worthwhile, if only as a means of keeping interest in the L.R. alive among the less fantastical (or drugged) young folk' (quoted in Sotheby's, *English Literature and History, Private Press and Illustrated Books and Related Drawings*, London, 14–15 December 1992, p. 75).

1969 *The Image of Man in C.S. Lewis* by William Luther White is published. Printed in this is the complete letter that Tolkien wrote to White on 11 September 1967, including his Oxford address and private telephone number. It is fortunate that, by now, these are no longer current.

2 January 1969 Tolkien writes to his son Christopher. 'My library is now in order; and nearly all the things that I thought were lost have turned up. (Also some things which I thought were lost before the move!) . . . I have horrible arthritis in the *left* hand, which cannot excuse this scrawl, since, mercifully, my right is not yet affected!' (*Letters*, p. 397). – Tolkien replies to a letter from Amy Ronald. He explains his names and the different ways that family and friends address him.

3 January 1969 Rayner Unwin sends Tolkien greetings on his birthday.

7 January 1969 Tolkien writes to his grandson Michael George. He is much better.

Just after Christmas my surgeon paid me a farewell visit, released me from 'treatment' exercises and all that; and even my walking-stick has gone back to its proper place: the hall-stand. But my right leg remains 'entish' (not very bendable). The surgeon says that I shall gain a few, perhaps 20 degrees, more flexion in time – which will enable [me] to surmount the chief remaining obstacles: walking *down* steps in normal fashion, and kneeling.

He worked hard 'to reduce the chaos of my books and papers to order before 1968 passed. The basic chaos created by removers had been made far worse by "helpers", and in the end every single book, file and [manuscript] had to be moved and replaced. I have not yet in fact completed the task, but my study-office is at least useable and habitable' (British Library MS Add. 71657). Allen & Unwin are in constant touch with him by telephone. *See note.* – Joy Hill writes a memo to Rayner Unwin. Tolkien is furious because he hears that the Beatles (whom he loathes) are planning to make a film of *The Lord of the Rings*.

20 January 1969 Rayner Unwin writes to Tolkien. He doubts that the Beatles are really involved with plans for a film of *The Lord of the Rings*; 'however this may be, I think it is one of the wearisome things that we shall all of us, doubtless be subjected to as a price of the film contract once it is made! This is part of the show business world. I am perfectly certain that we shall both of us dislike intensely every manifestation of what is done to *The Lord of the Rings*.' But he reminds Tolkien of their agreement: that if a film brings cash, they will waive any kudos. He points out that whatever a film is like, 'the book remains inviolable and that is the main thing. What they do with the property in other media will, I regret to say, be entirely their responsibility from an aesthetic point of view, will only vary in degrees between bad at best and execrable at the worst' (Tolkien-George Allen & Unwin archive, HarperCollins).

25 February 1969 Joy Hill writes to Colin Smythe. Tolkien cannot send a poem at the moment, as he is working on 'The Silmarillion'.

28 February 1969 Rayner Unwin writes to Tolkien. The expected film contract has still not arrived, due to negotiations regarding rights to *The Hobbit*. He is delighted to hear from Joy Hill that Tolkien is back at work and that his papers and books are now in reasonable order. Allen & Unwin abandoned the old three-volume de luxe set of *The Lord of the Rings* in the Pauline Baynes slipcase because it did not sell well; but they now find a certain demand for them, and are thinking of producing a single volume on the best quality India paper with the Appendices and folding maps. Tolkien may be asked in the near future if he has any ideas about embellishments, heraldic or otherwise, that might be used on the binding case or on blank pages.

?Early March 1969 Ian Bishop of the University of Bristol writes to Tolkien. Bishop had been a B.Litt. student working on *Pearl* in the early 1950s, supervised first by Gervase Mathew and then by Tolkien. He sends a copy of his book, *Pearl in Its Setting: A Critical Study of the Structure and Meaning of the Middle English Poem* (1968), which contains an acknowledgement to Mathew and Tolkien: 'To both of these scholars I am indebted for their great kindness and encouragement at that time [when Bishop was working towards his B.Litt.]; had it not been for the interest which they took in my work then, the present study would probably never have been begun' (p. vii).

3 March 1969 Adam Reuel Tolkien, son of Christopher and Baillie Tolkien, is born.

6 March 1969 Joy Hill replies to Colin Smythe, who has written to her recounting the history of his attempt to obtain a Tolkien poem to publish. She has spoken to Tolkien, who says that the material he has is not suitable, and he is too busy to write anything new.

15 March 1969 Tolkien writes to Amy Ronald. He thanks her for the gift of five bottles of alcoholic beverages. He is not getting much done, and neither he nor his wife is in good health. He sends her a copy of a new French edition of *The Hobbit*.

?16–19 March 1969 Amy Ronald writes to Tolkien. She had ordered *six* bottles to be delivered to him.

18 March 1969 Tolkien replies to Ian Bishop. He thanks him for the copy of his book and comments on it. He asks about an article published by Bishop some years before, to which Bishop refers ('The Significance of the "Garlande Gay" in the Allegory of *Pearl*', *Review of English Studies*, n.s. 8 (1957), pp. 12–21). He tells Bishop that his translation of *Pearl* should appear soon.

20 March 1969 Tolkien writes to Amy Ronald. He gave the wrong number in his letter, possibly because he 'had appropriated the Courvoisier to my sole usage' (quoted in Sotheby's, *Autograph Letters and Printed Books, including First Editions*, London, 19 May 2000, p. 37).

21 March 1969 The actor James Cairncross writes to Tolkien, asking him to autograph a copy of *The Lord of the Rings* for Cairncross to give to actress Judi Dench. He and Dench sustained themselves on a tough tour of Ghana and Nigeria by reading *The Hobbit*. Tolkien will draft a reply for Joy Hill to send. He cannot undertake to sign and return books, as he gets so many requests, but encloses an adhesive insertion slip. (The letter from Cairncross is forwarded to Tolkien by Merton College. The writer, however, knows that Tolkien is now living in the area of Bournemouth, having learned of it through the son of Lord David Cecil. Tolkien will note on the letter that some who know his address 'are being culpably careless' in revealing it (Tolkien-George Allen & Unwin archive, HarperCollins).)

22 March 1969 Ian Bishop sends Tolkien a spare offprint of the article he had asked about. Tolkien will reply with thanks, probably soon after Bishop's letter is received.

15 April 1969 Rayner Unwin writes to Tolkien. He is looking forward to seeing Tolkien on 18 April, apparently at the same time as Tolkien's solicitor, F.R. Williamson. Rayner will be coming to Bournemouth by train.

17 April 1969 Catherine Mary, daughter of Michael George and Irene Tolkien, and Tolkien's great-grand-daughter, is born.

18 April 1969 Rayner Unwin visits Tolkien at Lakeside Road. They discuss the film contract, and the forthcoming India paper *Lord of the Rings*.

21 April 1969 Rayner Unwin writes to Tolkien. He is sending Tolkien a set of maps, including the map of the Shire, so that he can indicate any corrections that need to be made for the India paper edition. He looks forward to receiving 'any rough emblem or heraldic device that you may be inspired to create that would serve as a blocking device' (Tolkien-George Allen & Unwin archive, HarperCollins) for the cover of the proposed de luxe *Lord of the Rings*. He hopes to be able to give Tolkien more information about the film contract in a few days.

23 April 1969 Tolkien writes to Michael George and Irene. He sends his love, good wishes, and congratulations on the birth of their daughter.

?Early May 1969 Camilla Unwin, Rayner's daughter, writes to Tolkien. As part of a school project she asks him 'What is the purpose of life?' (quoted in *Letters*, p. 399).

16 May 1969 Rayner Unwin writes to Tolkien. After several hectic transatlantic telephone calls, progress has been made on the film contract.

20 May 1969 Tolkien writes at length to Camilla Unwin. He treats her question seriously, and has obviously thought carefully about his reply.

23 May 1969 F.R. Williamson telephones Tolkien. The film contract has been agreed, and should be ready for signing next month.

24 May 1969 Tolkien writes to Rayner Unwin, enclosing Camilla's letter and his reply. 'If you write for children at all, I think you should not fob them off with something conventional. Better to shoot above their heads than that.' He feels that Rayner should approve his reply before it goes to Camilla. 'It is probably rather absurd, even silly in the circumstances. But it is probably the first time I have attempted to write what might be called a "sermon"' (Tolkien-George Allen & Unwin archive, HarperCollins). If Rayner thinks it is ridiculous, he should put it aside and tell Camilla that Tolkien had no time to answer her.

28 May 1969 Tolkien replies to a request to use 'Rivendell' for the name for a house. He gives his permission, but explains that *Rivendell* is not an exact translation of *Imladris*. He provides Tengwar versions of both 'Rivendell' and 'Imladris' in various modes.

30 May 1969 Rayner Unwin writes to Tolkien. Tolkien has excelled himself in his reply to Camilla. He hears from Joy Hill that Tolkien is working diligently. He would like to visit soon to hear 'how your mind and pen are getting round to refashioning *The Silmarillion*' (Tolkien-George Allen & Unwin archive, HarperCollins).

31 May 1969 C.L. Wrenn dies.

12 June 1969 M.R. Ridley dies.

20 June 1969 Rayner Unwin writes to Tolkien. He understands that Tolkien's solicitor will be bringing the film contract for his signature at about the same time as he receives Rayner's letter. He advises that if the press manage to contact him, he should say 'that you have no objection to people going to the film but you yourself go very little and would anyway regard the book that you had written as preferable to any interpretation in [any] other medium'

(Tolkien-George Allen & Unwin archive, HarperCollins). He encloses Tolkien's original drawing for the binding of the India paper *Lord of the Rings* (an unused design for *The Return of the King* dust-jacket) and a redrawn and slightly simplified version. It will be produced in silver and gold on a black ground. If Tolkien approves, he should keep his original and return the redrawn artwork. Does he think that some explanation of the device should appear in the preliminaries? If so, would he draft it and give it to Joy Hill. – Probably at about this time Tolkien writes a letter about the proposed film, an extract from which is quoted by Joy Hill to another enquirer: 'No film nor any "version" in another medium could appear satisfactory to any devoted and attentive reader. On the other hand some of the greater pictorial and dramatic scenes could, with modern resources, be a moving experience. All possible precautions have been taken that the story should be presented without serious mutilation and without alteration or alterations' (*Carandaith* 2, no. 1 (January 1970), p. 67).

c. **23 June 1969** Paul Bibire writes to Tolkien. He has passed the Bachelor of Philosophy examination in Old English at Oxford. He asks Tolkien if the River Glanduin is the same as the Swanfleet.

30 June 1969 Tolkien replies to Paul Bibire. He confirms that the Glanduin is the same river as the Swanfleet, but also gives much information about the names and the history of the region. He is, after a year, much recovered from his accident and 'I can walk about fairly normally now, up to two miles or so (occasionally), and have some energy. But not enough to cope with both continued composition and the endless "escalation" of my business' (quoted in *The Rivers and Beacon-hills of Gondor*, in *Vinyar Tengwar* 42 (July 2001), p. 7).

?Early Summer 1969 Rayner Unwin has the idea of issuing a poster-map of Middle-earth based on the large map in *The Fellowship of the Ring* and *The Two Towers*. He presumably seeks Tolkien's approval of the project, and offers the commission to Pauline Baynes.

July 1969 and later His interest piqued, Tolkien types a thirteen-page historical and etymological essay, with a manuscript note on the name *Belfalas*. He gives it a brief title, *Nomenclature*, but Christopher Tolkien will later call it *The Rivers and Beacon-hills of Gondor*. During its writing, Tolkien conceives the idea that the tomb of Elendil is on Halifirien, from which proceeds *Cirion and Eorl and the Friendship of Gondor and Rohan*, written in part on the blank versos of a script for the BBC *Hobbit*. At some time after typing *The Rivers and Beacon-hills of Gondor*, Tolkien adds a note that a discussion of the Eldarin number system in the essay is too complicated; and as an offshoot, he writes a short tale, *Part of the Legend of Amroth and Nimrodel Recounted in Brief* (see *The History of Galadriel and Celeborn and of Amroth King of Lórien*).

4 July 1969 Rayner Unwin visits Tolkien. They discuss various matters, including the forthcoming India paper edition of *The Lord of the Rings*. Tolkien gives Rayner sheets of corrections to that work, and tells Rayner that he would like to have, for his own use, an index of foreign words used in *The Lord of the Rings*.

8 July 1969 Tolkien, who has not been feeling well, is visited and examined by his doctor. Denis Tolhurst diagnoses an inflamed or diseased gall-bladder, and orders Tolkien to avoid all fats, including butter, and all alcohol.

9 July 1969 Rayner Unwin writes to Tolkien. He returns the sheets of corrections, which have been incorporated in the new edition. He recommends someone who could compile the list of foreign words in *The Lord of the Rings* that Tolkien wants.

***c*. 10 July 1969** Tolkien telephones Rayner Unwin. He has found more errors in *The Lord of the Rings* which need correction.

12–*c*. 18 July 1969 Priscilla Tolkien visits her parents.

16 July 1969 Royd, son of Joanna and Hugh Baker, is born, Tolkien's third great-grandchild.

***c*. 18–19 July** Edith Tolkien writes to Rayner Unwin. She encloses a snapshot taken during his visit. Tolkien is reading a book sent him by Rayner. He is to be X-rayed on Monday and Thursday.

18 July 1969 Tolkien writes to Richard L. Hoffman of Queens College, City University of New York. He thanks him for an offprint of an article he has written ('The Theme of Judgment Day 11' from *English Language*). He will not send the letter until 1 August.

21 July 1969 Tolkien is X-rayed.

24 July 1969 Tolkien is X-rayed a second time. The radiologist develops the plates and tells him that they will be sent to his doctor, but his gall-bladder looks all right, and no gallstones or growths are visible. Tolkien is advised to have a good lunch. – Joy Hill telephones to hear the result of the X-rays.

25 July 1969 Rayner Unwin writes to Edith Tolkien. He hopes that Tolkien's tests have been reassuring.

28 July 1969 Edith Tolkien writes to Rayner Unwin. She and her husband are very thankful and relieved that the results of the tests were negative. Ronald is much better and back at work. They think it must have been a virus.

29 July 1969 Tolkien is visited by Dr Tolhurst. Tolkien no longer has to keep to his prescribed diet, but butter and alcohol are still recommended only 'in moderation'.

31 July 1969 Tolkien replies to a letter from his son Christopher, received today. Tolkien is beginning

> to feel a bit desperate: endlessly frustrated. I have at last managed to release the demon of invention only to find myself in the state of a man who after a strong draught of a sleeping potion is waked up and not allowed to lie down for more than a few consecutive minutes. Neither in one world or another. Business – endless – lies neglected, yet I cannot get anything of my real work finished. Then came this last stroke of malice. I was assailed by very considerable pain, and depression, which no ordinary remedy would relieve.

Although he has now recovered, life is not easy. Their domestic help is ill, and 'Mummy is ailing, and I fear slowly "declining". Also I feel very cut off' (*Letters*, p. 401).

1 August 1969 Tolkien adds a note to his letter of 18 July to Richard L. Hoffman and dates it. He has not been able to send the letter until now because of illness.

c. **20 August 1969** Pauline Baynes and her husband Fritz Gasch visit the Tolkiens in Lakeside Road and lunch with them at the Hotel Miramar. The main reason for their visit is the poster map of Middle-earth for which she is to do the artwork. Pauline leaves a photocopy of the general map from the published *Lord of the Rings* for Tolkien to annotate.

28 August 1969 Tolkien writes to Pauline Baynes. 'I am afraid the enclosed (your map) will not be very intelligible. If you cannot make use of it, get me another and I will try to do better. But I would prefer to leave it to you to make as attractive a poster (as you can I am sure): and am only really anxious personally that *names* should be spelt right' (Marion E. Wade Center, Wheaton College, Wheaton, Illinois). He thinks that the only error on the printed map is *Enedwaith* for *Enedhwaith*, but *Kiril* should be spelt *Ciril*. Because the river names in Gondor are not very legible, he lists them, and notes that 'Lefnui' is misplaced: the name should be closer to the river. At some point, he gives Pauline some extra names to enter on the map.

Late August 1969 C.P. Hartley, President of the PEN English Centre, writes to Tolkien, who is a member of the international writers group. Hartley asks for a contribution to the cost of extending the Centre's buildings. Joy Hill evidently shows the letter to Tolkien, and notes on it that he is not able to do anything at the moment. Other letters to members of his family indicate that at this time, Tolkien is setting up a trust for their benefit, and this temporarily restricts what he can dispose of for other purposes.

September 1969 Pauline Baynes evidently sends another photocopied map to Tolkien, probably for clarification of Tolkien's intentions. – Priscilla Tolkien is taken ill. As soon as she can be moved by car, Tolkien brings her to Bournemouth and puts her under the care of a specialist. He is alarmed by some of her symptoms. At the same time, Edith again is ill, and Tolkien himself has 'an acutely painful arm which makes writing difficult and typing almost so' (letter to Pauline Baynes, 1 October 1969, Marion E. Wade Center, Wheaton College, Wheaton, Illinois).

4 September 1969 Rayner Unwin writes to Tolkien. Rayner has had a visit from John Leyerle, to whom Tolkien wrote on 28 April 1967 that he might be able to provide him with specimens of Early or Middle English verse in translation, for an anthology. Leyerle has told Rayner that he thinks that Tolkien might also have a verse translation of *Beowulf*. Rayner points out that even fragments of translations by Tolkien have a value, and feels that if Tolkien grants the use of any fragments to Leyerle, it should be on a commercial basis. If Tolkien has anything substantial, Allen & Unwin would like to publish it themselves, and the copyright and rights would be clearly established.

8 September 1969 Rayner sends Tolkien an invitation to lecture at the Cheltenham Festival. He expects Tolkien's reply to be No.

October 1969 or later Tolkien writes a long essay with no title but with the explanatory note: 'an extensive commentary and history of the interrelation of the languages [and writing systems of Dwarves and Men] in *The Silmarillion* and *The Lord of the Rings*, arising from consideration of the Book of Mazarbul, but attempting to clarify and where necessary to correct or explain the references to such matters scattered in *The Lord of the Rings*, especially in Appendix F and in Faramir's talk in LR II' (*The Peoples of Middle-earth*, p. 295; see **Of Dwarves and Men*). He composes the first three and half pages in manuscript, then types the remaining twenty-four and a half pages, using Allen & Unwin scrap paper of various dates through September 1969. While writing, he realizes that his 'Book of Mazarbul' pages for *The Lord of the Rings* are not really facsimiles, since their runes and Tengwar transliterate English (as representing Common Speech), and not the 'real' Common Speech. Tolkien also makes a rough synopsis of the essay, with the title *Dwarves and Men*.

1 October 1969 Tolkien writes to Pauline Baynes. He returns the photocopy of the map, with some comments. He has decided that the spelling *Enedwaith* should not be changed. He apologizes for being dilatory, and explains about illness in his family.

Late October or beginning of November 1969 Pauline Baynes and her husband Fritz Gasch visit Tolkien and Edith. They take with them the finished painting for the poster *A Map of Middle-earth*, along with gifts: a poinsettia, chocolates, some cakes, and a book which Pauline has just illustrated, *Kitchen Essays* by Lady Jekyll.

November 1969 Possibly at this time, Tolkien makes one of his most beautiful drawings, *The Hills of the Morning* (*Artist and Illustrator*, fig. 1). It seems to be dated 'Nov. 1969', but the date in pale orange pencil is rubbed and not absolutely clear. Stylistically the drawing seems closer to the heraldic drawings made in late 1960.

?Early November 1969 Amy Ronald sends Tolkien a copy of *Wild Flowers of the Cape Peninsula* by Mary Matham Kidd. – Tolkien has been invited to take part in, or attend, a programme devoted to himself and his writings, entitled 'An Afternoon in Middle-earth', to be held at the Studio Theatre, Midlands Arts Centre, Cannon Hill, on the afternoon of 30 November. He now writes to decline the invitation, and comments on his connections with the West Midlands. Part of his letter will be published in the programme for the event.

3 November 1969 Joy Hill telephones Tolkien in the evening. She is about to collect the artwork for the poster from Pauline Baynes.

16 November 1969 Tolkien writes to Amy Ronald. He has enjoyed *Wild Flowers of the Cape Peninsula*. 'All illustrated botany books (or better, contact with an unfamiliar flora) have for me a special fascination' (*Letters*, p. 402). He comments at length on flowers and gardening.

25 November 1969 Tolkien writes to his son Michael. He wishes that he had time to produce an elementary grammar and vocabulary of Quenya and Sindarin. He is 'having to do some work on them, in the process of adjusting "the Silmarillion and all that" to [*The Lord of the Rings*]. Which I am labouring at, under endless difficulties: not least the natural sloth of 77+' (*Letters*, p. 403).

Late November or early December 1969 Christopher and Baillie Tolkien, their son Adam, and Christopher's son Simon visit Tolkien and Edith. They stay at the Hotel Miramar for a weekend.

15 December 1969 Tolkien replies to a letter from Christopher. He comments that 'dull stodges' are often more educable than corrupted higher intelligences (*Letters*, p. 403). – Robert Burchfield, who is working on the supplement to the *Oxford English Dictionary*, writes to Tolkien. He asks for information about the origins of the word *hobbit*, and encloses draft entries for the *Dictionary*.

19 December 1969 Rayner Unwin writes to Tolkien. He is delighted to hear from Joy Hill that Tolkien is being very single-minded about his work on *The Silmarillion*. 'I suggested to her that as soon as you have reached a sort of "natural break" that might indicate the end of a publishable volume I would be delighted to come down to Bournemouth, read it, discuss it, and make all suitable preparations for ushering the most anticipated book in England into the world' (Tolkien-George Allen & Unwin archive, HarperCollins).

Christmas 1969 Priscilla Tolkien spends nearly a week with her parents, probably staying at the Hotel Miramar.

31 December 1969 Tolkien writes a long letter to his cousin Dorothy Wood. He describes the move to Poole and the difficulties caused by his fall. So far, his new address has remained a secret. He discusses family history, including the origin of the name *Tolkien*.

1970

c. **1970** Tolkien has an amanuensis typescript, with carbon copy, made from *Of Meglin* written in 1951, taking up most of the emendations made to the manuscript (see **Of Maeglin: Sister-son of Turgon, King of Gondolin*).

1970 or later Tolkien adds two manuscript notes to the essay on Orcs he wrote *c.* 1959 (**Orcs*, Text X of *Morgoth's Ring*).

1 January 1970 Tolkien writes to his son Michael. He asks him to pray that his father has time to put some of 'The Silmarillion' into readable form. He would also like to record his memories of his childhood and his close relatives.

I am *not* getting on fast with *The S[ilmarillion]*. The domestic situation, Mummy's gallant but losing fight against age and disability (and pain), and my own years – and all the interruptions of 'business' do not leave much time. I have in fact so far been chiefly employed in trying to co-ordinate the nomenclature of the very early and later parts of the *Silmarillion* with the situation in [*The Lord of the Rings*]. 'Stories' still sprout in my mind from names; but it is a very difficult and complex task. [*Letters*, p. 404]

7 January 1970 Tolkien writes to his grandson Michael George. He is distressed to hear that his cello has been deliberately damaged. He comments on the etymology of the name *Catherine*, the name of Michael George's daughter. He and Edith are going to stay at the Hotel Miramar for a few days, since their domestic help has been ill for some weeks and won't return for some time. (Presumably this is still Mrs Parke.)

10–?12 January 1970 Tolkien and Edith stay at the Hotel Miramar with their grandson Simon.

?Early February 1970 Philip Smith, a creative bookbinder, writes to Tolkien. He has devised a special binding technique for a copy of *The Lord of the Rings* and, wanting to give the process an appropriate name, enquires what 'open-ended' might be in Quenya.

4 February 1970 Edith Tolkien writes to Pauline Baynes and Fritz Gasch. She thanks them for sending her flowers. She had been feeling ill when they arrived, but they cheered her a great deal. 'Ronald is working away at the "Silmarillion" but gets very tired' (private collection). Joy Hill has just telephoned them.

12 February 1970 Tolkien replies to Philip Smith. He is honoured that Smith has devised a special binding for *The Lord of the Rings*. 'But I am afraid that "open-ended" . . . is not within the range of my knowledge of Quenya' (Tolkien-George Allen & Unwin archive, HarperCollins; the copy is marked as 'dictated [presumably to Joy Hill] and signed in his absence').

16 February 1970 Tolkien talks by telephone with Joy Hill. One topic of their conversation is Philip Smith's letter.

19 February 1970 Rayner Unwin writes to Tolkien. He is looking forward to accompanying him to Nottingham in May, where Tolkien is to receive an honorary degree. Rayner has been leaving him undisturbed, as he understands that Tolkien is immersed in 'The Silmarillion'. He is willing to come at any time to read or discuss 'The Silmarillion' in whole or in part. If it still likely to take a considerable time to complete, perhaps they should consider whether there is 'some fragment complete in itself which does not fit into the framework of the whole' which might form a little book on its own, like *Smith of Wootton Major*, to help keep Tolkien 'in the eye of the public'. (Tolkien-George Allen & Unwin archive, HarperCollins).

?April 1970 Edith Tolkien falls in the bath and hurts her arm. After some time when it is still painful, she sees a doctor, who finds that she has cracked her shoulder. He gives her an injection, and prescribes tablets and heat treatment. She has to keep her arm in a sling, which prevents her doing much, and the pain hinders her from sleeping. – Rayner Unwin spends a weekend in Bournemouth, probably at the Hotel Miramar. He and Tolkien discuss various matters, especially 'The Silmarillion'.

?12 (received 13) April 1970 Tolkien writes to T.A. Shippey, commenting on his paper 'The Author as Philologist' which he has sent to Tolkien.

19 April 1970 Tolkien and Edith lunch at the Hotel Miramar (possibly with Rayner Unwin). They are told that Tolkien's cousin, Dorothy Wood, has been enquiring about the availability of a room some time in June.

22 April 1970 Tolkien writes to his cousin Dorothy Wood. He has heard about her enquiries at the Hotel Miramar. He looks forward to seeing her soon.

***c.* 30 April–5 May 1970** Edith stays at the Hotel Miramar to allow her to rest and be cared for while Tolkien is in London and Nottingham. Tolkien stays there also, except on 1 and possibly 2 May.

1 May 1970 Tolkien travels to London and stays the night. – Vera Chapman writes to inform him of the existence of the (British) Tolkien Society, which she helped to found in late 1969. She describes the Society's aims, and asks if Tolkien would agree to be its Chief Patron.

2 May 1970 Rayner Unwin accompanies Tolkien to Nottingham, where he is to receive an Honorary D.Litt. Tolkien and the other honorees are entertained to lunch in the Portland Building before the ceremony. The occasion is unfortunately marred by noisy student demonstrations aimed at another recipient, Sir Frederic Seebohm, Chairman of Barclays Bank which has alleged connections with Rhodesia. The lunch is interrupted by a band, and the procession to the Trent Building for the ceremony has to pass through lines of students holding placards and handing out leaflets, and shouting 'Sieg heil!' and 'British Imperialism out!' The shouts and banging of dustbin lids outside during the ceremony often drown the Public Orator's voice, made worse during his oration for Tolkien because the public address system breaks down.

7 May 1970 Edith Tolkien writes to Pauline Baynes. Her arm is still not right, and the doctor says that she may need to be X-rayed and see a surgeon. Tolkien has been working steadily for some time, presumably on 'The Silmarillion'.

13 May 1970 Rayner Unwin writes to Tolkien. Ian Ballantine will be in England next week and hopes to see Tolkien during his stay. He would come to Bournemouth, and it would be nice if Tolkien could arrange a lunch at the Miramar. Rayner is about to go to Scotland, so he will leave it to Joy Hill and Ballantine to make the arrangements.

?Third week of May 1970 Ian Ballantine probably visits Tolkien in Bournemouth.

End of May or early June 1970 Tolkien's cousin Dorothy Wood stays at the Hotel Miramar and visits the Tolkiens. On one day they lunch with her at the Hotel.

10 June 1970 Rayner Unwin sends Tolkien a proof of *Red Moon and Black Mountain* by Joy Chant, and asks him to write a sentence of commendation if he likes it.

22 July 1970 Rayner Unwin's secretary sends a second copy of *Red Moon and Black Mountain*, as Tolkien has not received the first.

27 July 1970 Rayner Unwin sends Tolkien six copies of the poster *Map of Middle-earth*. When Tolkien receives them, he notices a misprint.

?Mid-August 1970 Tolkien is sent, or Joy Hill brings him, copies of *A Map of Middle-earth* to sign. He finds that their surface will not take ordinary ink.

24 August 1970 Tolkien writes to Robert Burchfield. In the course of a recent clear-up he has discovered in his files Burchfield's letter of 15 December 1969, still unanswered. He remembers Norman Davis reminding him about it, but it has been a difficult year, and he has neglected many matters that could not be dealt with by his secretary at Allen & Unwin. 'I suppose that nothing can now be done about the draft entries that you sent me', but if it is not too late, 'I will at once send my comments. The definition [of *hobbit*] as it stands is erroneous' (Oxford University Press archives). He has not succeeded in finding a suitable secretary locally.

27 August 1970 Robert Burchfield writes to Tolkien. There is still time to change the entry for *hobbit*. Tolkien should send his comments. – Rayner Unwin writes to Tolkien. He apologizes for the problem of the maps. Tolkien was using a water-based ink, but with experimenting they find that an oil-based German black ink called Pelikan works: perhaps he could try this the next time someone from Allen & Unwin visits him. It would be difficult to correct the misprint, as it would mean altering all four colour plates.

?Late summer or autumn 1970 Tolkien writes to a Mr Wood. He returns, as requested, three cards with his signature, and explains that the design on the binding of the India paper edition is a simplified version of a design originally made for *The Return of the King*.

c. 3 September 1970 Tolkien gives Joy Hill a manuscript of the poem *Bilbo's Last Song*, with its copyright, but requests her not to publish or sell it until after his death. She will later explain in her article 'Echoes of the Old Ringmaster' that when she visited Tolkien, taking parcels sent by fans, he and she tried to guess what was in them. 'One day, as he cut the string on a packet, he said: "If I find this is a gold bracelet studded with diamonds, it is to be yours". Of course it wasn't, but the bracelet became a joke between us.' Much later, on another visit, 'he said: "We've opened all the parcels and there was no gold bracelet for you. . . . I've decided this [*Bilbo's Last Song*] is going to be your bracelet"' (*The Times*, 10 December 1990, p. 16). *See note.*

11 September 1970 Tolkien writes to Robert Burchfield. He is 'anxious that the meaning [of *hobbit*] intended by me should be made clear'. With the prospect of the inclusion of *hobbit* in the new supplement to the *Oxford English Dictionary*, he has been investigating the matter, and 'as all lexicographers know' things usually turn out to be less simple than expected. He will write a long letter on the subject soon, but at present 'I am having the matter of the etymology: "Invented by J.R.R. Tolkien": investigated by experts' (*Letters*, pp. 404–5). In the meantime, he suggests two forms of definition, depending on whether or not evidence of prior use is found.

14 September 1970 Robert Burchfield replies to Tolkien. He has made slight alterations to Tolkien's suggested entries, and looks forward to receiving his promised letter.

24 October 1970 Princess Margrethe of Denmark writes to Tolkien. She has enjoyed *The Lord of the Rings* very much, and encloses copies of illustrations she has made for it.

31 October 1970 Tolkien writes to Amy Ronald. He thanks her for her gift (apparently a voucher for alcohol). He has bought burgundy, port, sherry, liqueurs, and champagne. 'I like port (v[ery] much) as a mid-morn[ing] drink: warming, digestible, and v[ery] good for my throat, when taken (as I think it should be) by itself or with a dry biscuit, and NOT after a full meal, nor (above all) with dessert!' (*Letters*, p. 405).

11 November 1970 Rayner Unwin writes to Tolkien. The *Map of Middle-earth* has been a great success. He would like to publish a companion poster map for *The Hobbit*. Pauline Baynes is willing to produce the artwork. She would use the *Hobbit* map-endpapers and Tolkien's own pictures as a guide, but 'doubtless . . . you could give her as you did in the case of the *Middle-earth* map some further information on these points' (Tolkien-George Allen & Unwin archive, HarperCollins).

22 November 1970 Tolkien writes to Neil Ker, thanking him for an offprint of an article on A.S. Napier. He has found it interesting, and it confirms his guess that it was probably the influence of L.R. Farnell, then Rector of Exeter College, that allowed Tolkien to keep his Classical Exhibition when as an undergraduate he transferred to the Oxford English School.

16 December 1970 An edited version of Denys Gueroult's 1965 interview with Tolkien is broadcast for the first time on BBC Radio 4, in the programme *Now Read On*, 9.00–9.45 p.m. The *Radio Times* for 10 December 1970 describes the programme as including 'J.R.R. Tolkien talking about the world of *The Hobbit* and *The Lord of the Rings* both in paperback' (p. 45).

17 December 1970 *Now Read On* is rebroadcast on Radio 4 at 3.45 p.m.

18 December 1970 Tolkien writes to Joy Hill. He asks her to send a card and a copy of *A Map of Middle-earth* to Mrs Eileen Elgar. He does not want the postmark to reveal that he is now living near her. The manageress of the laundry that the Tolkiens use rang up today to ask if he is the Tolkien interviewed in the BBC broadcast. Tolkien comments: 'There's fame for you' (collection of René van Rossenberg).

30 December 1970 Rayner Unwin writes to Tolkien. He has heard that Tolkien may visit Oxford in the New Year; if he stays any length of time, Rayner may come and see him there. Allen & Unwin have been licensing Ballantine Books to export their editions of Tolkien to Canada, to discourage illegal importation of the Ace Books copies, but Allen & Unwin now want to license a Canadian firm to produce their own edition. Since the Ballantine copies have carried a notice that they are published with Tolkien's consent, the Canadian firm wants a similar notice for their edition. He suggests a suitable wording. He also encloses a letter from Dick Plotz.

1971

?1971 Tolkien takes up *Of Meglin* in the amanuensis typescript and carbon copy. He gives the top copy the title *Of Maeglin: Sister-son of Turgon, King of Gondolin*, and writes on the first page that the text is 'an enlarged version of the coming of Maeglin to Gondolin, to be inserted in [Fall of Gondolin] in its place' (*The War of the Jewels*, p. 317). This seems to indicate that he still hopes to complete at length the retelling of the Fall of Gondolin, which he began with *Of Tuor and His Coming to Gondolin*. He emends both the top copy and the carbon, but in different ways, and makes a few emendations also to the manuscript of 1951. In addition, he inserts in the top copy a great deal of new manuscript material, including a lengthy section on the flight of Maeglin and Aredhel, and Eöl's pursuit. Tolkien also writes other separate but related and overlapping material, including notes on names and geography, calculations of times and distances on horseback, notes on Eöl's history, and a discussion of the motives of Celegorm and Curufin towards Eöl, and of their other actions. He also marks on photocopies of the relevant part of his 'Silmarillion' map new or changed features arising from his work on the story of Maeglin, and dates two of these '71' (i.e 1971).

1971 Tolkien adds a note about the name *Atalantë* to one of the copies of the amanuensis typescript of the *Akallabêth*.

8 January 1971 Tolkien writes to Roger Lancelyn Green. Tolkien's claim to have invented the word *hobbit* rests solely on his recollection of the occasion of the invention, and he had not then any knowledge of *Hobberdy* etc. (for house-sprites, though he has recently investigated this in depth). Since the name is to be included in the *Second Supplement* to the *Oxford English Dictionary*, he needs to justify his claim. In 1938 a writer to *The Observer* suggested that the name might have occurred much earlier in a collection of fairy-stories; but Tolkien has been unable to discover any such collection, despite recent intensive research. He asks Green, as 'the most learned of living scholars in this region' (*Letters*, p. 407), if he knows of any prior use of *hobbit* or a similar name, and if he can identify a collection Tolkien remembers having read in childhood, which included the story *Puss Cat Mew*, of which he was very fond. – Tolkien also writes to his grandson Michael George. Tolkien's work has not been going well, but prospects look better as it appears that both he and Edith will be getting a great deal more (both domestic and secretarial?) help. Secretarial help possibly is provided by Jocelyn Tolhurst, the wife of Tolkien's doctor.

From 11 January 1971 Tolkien and Edith stay at the Hotel Miramar for a while with their grandson Simon.

25 January 1971 Tolkien replies to a letter from Mrs Ruth Austin. He 'owes much' of the 'character of Galadriel to Christian and Catholic teaching and imagination about Mary', but actually she had been 'a leader in the rebellion against the Valar' (*Letters*, p. 407).

4 February 1971 Tolkien replies to a letter from P. Rorke, S.J., who has made reference to the 'glittering caves' in *The Lord of the Rings*. Tolkien comments that the caves of Helm's Deep were inspired by those in the Cheddar Gorge.

13 February 1971 Rachel Clare Reuel Tolkien, daughter of Christopher and Baillie Tolkien, is born.

18 March 1971 Tolkien writes to William Cater. 'As far as my work goes, things are looking more hopeful now than they have done for some time and it is possible that I may be able to send an instalment of the *Silmarillion* to Allen & Unwin later this year' (*Letters*, p. 408). – Tolkien replies to a letter from the BBC, who wish to use one of his poems in a broadcast. He refers them to Allen & Unwin.

7 April 1971 Tolkien signs a form reply to a reader. He is 'inundated with correspondence', and if he is to 'concentrate on [*The Silmarillion*] I must beg to be excused from answering questions' (reproduced in the fanzine *Amon Dîn* 2, no. 1 (21 January 1973), p.2).

21 April 1971 Rayner Unwin writes to Tolkien. He encloses something sent by Dick Plotz, who will be visiting England with his wife at the end of August and hopes to see Tolkien.

May 1971 During this month Tolkien does not do 'a stroke of "writing"', as he will write to his son Christopher on 2 June (*Letters*, p. 408).

?4–?9 May 1971 Tolkien's cousin, Dorothy Wood, stays at the Hotel Miramar. During this time, or just before, Ronald and Edith send her flowers and a greetings telegram for her eightieth birthday.

22 May 1971 Graham Tayar writes to Tolkien. He asks about the names *Gamgee* and *Gondor*.

25 May 1971 Lord Snowdon, accompanied by a senior journalist from *The Times*, spends several hours photographing Tolkien for an article to be published in the *Sunday Times* to mark Tolkien's eightieth birthday. He takes several photographs in the wooded Branksome Chine behind Lakeside Road. One of these, with Tolkien seated among the exposed roots of a tree, will be published with the article in the *Sunday Times Magazine* on 2 January 1972 (pp. 24–5), and become well known. They also drive to a more isolated and exposed section of cliff, where Lord Snowdon photographs Tolkien silhouetted against the sea. One of the latter photographs will be reproduced on the cover of 1997 HarperCollins paperback edition of *The Monsters and the Critics and Other Essays*.

26 May 1971 Tolkien writes to Dorothy Wood. He has asked Allen & Unwin to send her a copy of the India paper *Lord of the Rings*. He describes being photographed by Lord Snowdon, and comments that they 'had much in common – especially a devotion to trees' (quoted in Sotheby's, *English Literature, History, Children's Books, Illustrations and Photographs*, London, 8 July 2004, p. 232).

?Late May 1971 Tolkien and Edith spend a week at Sidmouth, staying at the Belmont Hotel. Tolkien will later write to Christopher:

Neither M[ummy] nor I have eaten so much in a week (without indigestion) for years. In addition our faithful cruise-friends (Boarland) of some six years ago, who recently moved to Sidmouth, and were so anxious to see us again that they vetted our rooms [at] the Belmont, provided us with a car, and took us drives nearly every day. So I saw again much of the country you (especially) and I used to explore in the old days of poor JO, that valiant sorely-tried old Morris [car]. . . . An added comfort was the fact that Sidmouth seemed practically unchanged. . . . [begun about 2 June 1971, *Letters*, p. 408]

***c*. 2 June 1971** Tolkien begins a letter to Christopher. He describes the visit to Sidmouth.

4–5 June 1971 Tolkien replies to Graham Tayar. His questions touch on a matter 'of great interest: the nature of the process of "linguistic invention" (including nomenclature) in general, and in *The Lord of the Rings* in particular. It would take too long to discuss this – it needs a long essay which I have often in mind but shall probably never write' (*Letters*, p. 409). He mentions that he has no secretary at home.

10 June 1971 Tolkien continues his letter to Christopher, begun *c*. 2 June. Both he and Edith have been ill, 'afflicted with what may be either a "virus", or food-poisoning. . . . I am longing to see you. . . . What I personally need, prob[ably] more than anything, is two or three days general consultation and interchange with *you*.' He regrets that because of the move to Poole 'we are separated by a distance too great for swift interchange, and I am so immoveable' (*Letters*, p. 409).

20 June 1971 An Australian writes to Tolkien, putting forward a theory that it might be possible to date *Sir Gawain and the Green Knight* by the words used for certain pieces of armour.

17 July 1971 Tolkien writes to Roger Lancelyn Green. He explains about journeys by Frodo and others into the West. Frodo and 'other mortals . . . could only dwell in *Aman* for a limited time. . . . The *Valar* had neither the power nor the right to confer "immortality" upon them. Their sojourn was a "purgatory", but one of peace and healing and they would eventually pass away (*die* at their own desire and of free will) to destinations of which the Elves knew nothing' (*Letters*, p. 411).

?Late July 1971 Tolkien suggests to Joy Hill that he would like to read books that Rayner Unwin has written, and intends this to be an order to purchase them. He will write to Rayner on 24 July: 'I have recently become conscience-stricken: feeling that authors ought to *buy* their fellow-labourers' works, and aware that I am parsimonious in that respect (which ill befits me). Alas! I am also very slothful in reading!' (Tolkien–George Allen & Unwin archive, HarperCollins).

21 July 1971 Rayner Unwin writes to Tolkien. He would like to visit Tolkien and Edith on 5 August. He would arrive in time to take Tolkien and Edith to lunch, and could chat with Tolkien during the afternoon.

24 July 1971 Tolkien writes to Rayner Unwin. 5 August will suit himself and Edith admirably, but *they* want to give *him* lunch at the Miramar. Tolkien regrets that because of Rayner's greater responsibilities following Stanley Unwin's death (his 'accession to the throne'), he sees him less frequently. Edith 'is now so immobile, except with pain and effort, that it is no longer a question of avoiding steps and stairs, but even of any distance to be walked (on two sticks) indoors. At [the Miramar] we can arrange for this to be as short as possible' (Tolkien-George Allen & Unwin archive, HarperCollins). He thanks Rayner for sending him inscribed copies of two books he has written.

5 August 1971 Rayner Unwin visits Tolkien at Lakeside Road and lunches with Tolkien and Edith at the Hotel Miramar. They discuss the *Hobbit* map, the proposed Allen & Unwin schools edition of *The Hobbit* to replace that licensed to Longmans, and interviews to mark Tolkien's eightieth birthday. Tolkien objects to an abridged edition of *The Hobbit* being considered by Allen & Unwin. He is not willing to give any interviews, especially with the BBC, in connection with his birthday or any other event; Rayner will suggest in an internal memo that Tolkien might be persuaded if approached tactfully: 'What he would like to do is ramble and not be bound into opinions about things that he does not want to talk about' (Tolkien-George Allen & Unwin archive, HarperCollins). Tolkien wants three further copies of an English/German parallel text edition of *Farmer Giles of Ham*, published in 1970. He has no objection to the proposed publication of Italian translations of *Tree and Leaf* and *Beowulf: The Monsters and the Critics* together in one volume.

11 August 1971 Rayner Unwin writes to thank Tolkien for a delightful day. 'I have written to Pauline Baynes encouraging her to come with Fritz and the *Hobbit* map when it is at the stage prior to completion so that you can talk over points with her which she might otherwise miss. I told her to entitle it in the cartouche "There and Back Again, A map of Bilbo's Journey through Eriador and Rhovanion"' (Tolkien-George Allen & Unwin archive, HarperCollins).

20 August 1971 Carole Batten-Phelps writes to Tolkien about her delight in *The Lord of the Rings*. Apparently she was introduced to it through classes or lectures given by M.R. Ridley.

25 August 1971 Tolkien replies to a letter from Robert H. Boyer. He explains his acquaintance with W.H. Auden, and regards him 'as one of my great friends although we have so seldom met except through letters and gifts of his works' (*Letters*, p. 412).

26 August 1971 Kenneth Sisam dies.

9 September 1971 Tolkien adds this date to a newspaper doodle of no great significance. It is the latest surviving dated or datable newspaper doodle.

15 September 1971 Rayner Unwin writes to Tolkien. Dick Plotz and his wife came to see him. He thinks that they considered him a poor substitute for Tolkien (whom they did not visit). They gave Rayner on behalf of the author, Robert Foster, a privately printed *Guide to Middle Earth*, which Rayner thinks will amuse Tolkien. 'It is in fact an extension of your Index of Proper Names' (Tolkien-George Allen & Unwin archive, HarperCollins). Rayner encloses an agreement for Tolkien to sign concerning the royalty to be paid on the new *Hobbit* map. Everyone who has seen the map has been delighted with it.

Autumn 1971 Tolkien drafts a reply to Carole Batten-Phelps. He knew M.R. Ridley well at Oxford. He was deeply moved by her comments on the sanity and sanctity of *The Lord of the Rings*.

Autumn (before 29 October) 1971 Pauline Baynes and her husband Fritz Gasch visit Tolkien to show him her finished painting for the *Hobbit* poster map.

?October 1971 Tolkien drafts a reply to a letter from Peter Szabó Szentmihályi. He has no time to provide biographical detail, and does not approve of literary biography, or of affixing labels to writers.

?Early October 1971 The poet and critic Anthony Thwaite writes to Tolkien. He encloses a letter from Yoko Inokuma, whose translation of *Smith of Wootton Major* into Japanese is to be published soon. She is now working on a translation of *On Fairy-Stories*, and has some queries for Tolkien.

Early October 1971 Tolkien feels ill, but recovers. He and Edith stay for a while at the Hotel Miramar, and his illness returns. Nonetheless he goes to Oxford to attend the autumn Fellows' Dinner at Merton College, and presumably stays in Merton. He feels ill during the visit, and on his return feels so bad that he has to spend most of the day in bed and is unable to eat anything. In a letter to his son Michael in January 1972, he will say that he lost over a stone (fourteen pounds) during this illness, and did not fully recover until Christmas.

16 October 1971 Tolkien replies to Anthony Thwaite. He remembers Mrs Inokunia from the time she spent at Oxford studying 'fairy-stories', and corresponded with her for a while after she returned to Japan. He will do what he can to assist her.

17 October 1971 Tolkien writes to Rayner Unwin. He tells him about Mrs Inokuma, and assumes that Allen & Unwin already know about her translation of *Smith of Wootton Major*. Some of her queries about *On Fairy-Stories* will not be difficult to answer, but others are more problematical. But if she is making a translation which will be published, perhaps he should try to do more. He has been ill. He thinks he has now recovered, but is looking rather emaciated. He and Edith have decided to cancel a visit to Sidmouth which should have begun on 20 October. Rather late, he returns the agreement for the *Hobbit* map.

19 October 1971 William Cater writes to Tolkien, probably to ask for an interview for an article to be published to mark Tolkien's eightieth birthday.

25 October 1971 Rayner Unwin writes to Tolkien. Allen & Unwin hope to publish the *Hobbit* map before Christmas. A contract has been signed with Fukuinen Shoten for a Japanese translation of *On Fairy-Stories*; if Mrs Inokuma is working for them (she is) then any help would probably be gratefully received.

27 October 1971 Tolkien replies to a request to reprint *Goblin Feet*. 'I wish the unhappy little thing, representing all that I came (so soon after) to fervently dislike, could be buried for ever' (quoted in *The Book of Lost Tales, Part One*,

p. 32). He adds, on an approximate copy he makes of the letter sent, that the poem was reprinted in 1920 in *The Book of Fairy Poetry*, edited by Dora Owen, with an illustration by Warwick Goble 'who accorded my "poem" a picture (as bad as it deserved)' (Tolkien-George Allen & Unwin archive, HarperCollins).

28 October 1971 Tolkien decides that he must formalize his gift of *Bilbo's Last Song* to Joy Hill. He writes her two letters, and a note to place with the poem.

28 October 1971 Tolkien replies to a letter asking about runes.

?Early November 1971 A Miss Morley writes to Tolkien at his Poole address. She offers her secretarial services, and notes that she has a knowledge of Finnish and Finland.

1 November 1971 Tolkien replies to William Cater. He probably sets a date for an interview.

8 November 1971 Tolkien replies to Miss Morley. Allen & Unwin provide him with a secretary who deals with most of his correspondence. Only a small amount needs personal answers or decisions from him. Very little comes to him direct, since his address is no longer public. A secretary cannot help him in the writing on which he is now engaged, since 'I cannot dictate it, nor indeed compose any matter of the sort without a pen in hand. My first (written) drafts are generally beyond a secretary's (and sometimes of my own) power of accurate decipherment, and I always use a typewriter myself for their revision' (Dominic Winter Book Auctions, *Printed Books, Maps & Ephemera*, 15 December 2004, Lot 378). He has never mastered Finnish.

18 November 1971 William Cater interviews Tolkien. The result will be published in the *Sunday Times* on 2 January 1972 ('The Lord of the Legends').

19 November 1971 During the night, Edith Tolkien falls ill with an inflamed gall-bladder.

?21–29 November 1971 Edith is in hospital. Tolkien will write to William Cater on 29 November that 'her courage and determination . . . carried her through to what seemed the brink of recovery, but a sudden relapse occurred which she fought for nearly three days in vain' (*Letters*, p. 415).

29 November 1971 In the morning, Edith dies in hospital. – Tolkien writes to William Cater. 'She died at last in peace. I am utterly bereaved, and cannot yet lift up heart, but my family is gathering round me and many friends' (*Letters*, p. 415).

30 November 1971 Priscilla Tolkien writes to Dorothy Wood, informing her of Edith's death. Tolkien adds a postscript.

2 December 1971 A Requiem Mass is said for Edith Tolkien at 9.00 a.m. at the Church of the Sacred Heart, Bournemouth. At 1.15 p.m. she is buried in Wolvercote Cemetery, Oxford.

11 December 1971 Tolkien replies briefly to a letter of condolence from George Sayer, no doubt one of many.

12 December 1971 Tolkien writes to the directors and staff of George Allen & Unwin. He thanks them for their kind messages of sympathy and beautiful flowers in memory of his wife.

14 December 1971 Tolkien writes to Sister Linthune. He encloses an inscribed copy of *Smith of Wootton Major* and asks her to accept it 'as an (inadequate) memento and token of my gratitude to you' (Ulysses, *Catalogue 24: Modern First Editions & Illustrated Books*, November 1993, p. 68). Sister Linthune presumably cared for Edith in hospital.

15 December 1971 Priscilla Tolkien replies to a letter of condolence from Dorothy Wood. She notes that her father has started to write a letter to Dorothy and has spoken of her to Priscilla.

20 December 1971 Tolkien writes on a compliments slip to accompany a signed letter he is sending Joy Hill to post for him: '9.35 a.m. Dec. 20. Have just spent about 10 hours sorting and packing. All being well I leave 19 L[akeside] R[oad] for Priscilla's at 12.30' (collection of René van Rossenberg).

20–23 December 1971 Tolkien stays in Oxford with Priscilla.

23–31 December 1971 Tolkien stays with his son John at Northcote House, 104 Hartshill Road, Stoke-on-Trent.

24 December 1971 Tolkien writes to Eileen Elgar. He expresses his desolation at Edith's death. He wonders if he shall ever write again. 'She was my *Lúthien Tinúviel*, with her river [*sic*? as transcribed, for "raven"] hair and fair face and bright starry eyes' (quoted in Sotheby's, *English Literature and English History*, London, 6–7 December 1984, lot 273). Among other matters, he thinks that the *Hobbit* poster map by Pauline Baynes is better than *A Map of Middle-earth*; he is glad that Mrs Elgar has enjoyed the Narnia books of C.S. Lewis, though he himself does not like them, merely a difference in taste; and he comments on the naming of pets after Hobbits. He thinks *Bilbo* a good name for an animal. His brother Hilary has a young dog which is called *Bilbo* when it is good, but *Baggins* when it is bad.

25 December 1971 *Attacks of Taste*, compiled and edited by Evelyne B. Byrne and Otto M. Penzler, is published, including a letter from Tolkien. The editors wrote to various people of note, asking which books influenced them as teenagers. Tolkien mentions *Flowers of the Field* by C.A. Johns.

26 December 1971 Tolkien writes to Joy Hill. He wore a gift from her on Christmas Day 'with dazzling effect'. Signing himself 'J.R.R.T.', he notes that his contemporaries used to write his initials as 'JR²T' and pronounce them 'to rhyme with *dirt*' (collection of René van Rossenberg).

31 December 1971–before 24 January 1972 Tolkien stays with Priscilla in Oxford, and begins to look for a new home. He does not want to live alone in Poole.

1972

1 January 1972 Tolkien is included in the New Year's Honours List. He is awarded the CBE (Commander of the Order of the British Empire) for services to English Literature.

2 January 1972 H.T. Wade-Gery dies.

3 January 1972 Tolkien reaches his eightieth birthday. His friends give him a party. Hilary Tolkien is among those present. The directors and staff of Allen & Unwin send him a birthday card three feet high, which they have all signed. The Tolkien Society send congratulations and a gift of tobacco.

?Early 1972 Tolkien visits Christopher Wiseman, who now lives at Milford-on-Sea near Bournemouth. Wiseman has recently married a second time, after the death of his first wife.

Mid-January 1972 Christopher Tolkien writes to the Warden of Merton College. He explains that his father is looking for somewhere to live in Oxford and asks if the College has anything available. The Warden calls a special meeting of the Governing Body, which unanimously votes that Tolkien should be invited to become a Residential Fellow. The Warden writes to Tolkien, offering him a set of rooms in a College house in Merton Street, and the services of a scout and his wife to look after him. Tolkien accepts.

By 24 January–1 February 1972 Tolkien stays with his son Christopher at West Hannay, near Oxford.

24 January 1972 Tolkien writes to his son Michael, telling him of Merton's offer and describing its advantages. As a result of Edith's death 'I do not feel quite "real" or whole, and in a sense there is no one to talk to. . . . I still often find myself thinking "I must tell E. about this" – and then suddenly I feel like a castaway left on a barren island under a heedless sky after the loss of a great ship' (*Letters*, p. 416).

30 January 1972 Tolkien writes to his grandson Michael George. He describes the advantages of being a Residential Fellow at Merton. The only disadvantage is that he will no longer be as protected from intrusive fans and the press; but he will be able to see many of his old friends.

31 January 1972 Tolkien officially takes possession of a flat in 21 Merton Street, though he will not move there until mid-March.

1 February–13 March 1972 For much of this period Tolkien stays at the Hotel Miramar to deal with the sale of 19 Lakeside Road and of items of furniture for which there will be no room in his new home, and the packing of his papers and books.

2 February 1972 Tolkien writes to Dorothy Wood about his forthcoming visit to Buckingham Palace to receive the CBE. He is disappointed that the Queen Mother, whom he has seen several times, may be making the presentations rather than Queen Elizabeth, whom he has seen only once, at a distance. 'I am one of her devoted subjects and greatly admire her, though her voice is not one of her graces' (quoted in Sotheby's, *English Literature, History, Children's Books, Illustrations and Photographs*, London, 8 July 2004, p. 232). (In the event, Queen Elizabeth will make the presentation.)

6 February 1972 Tolkien writes to Vera Chapman and the Tolkien Society, thanking them for their good wishes and gift.

7 March 1972 Rayner Unwin writes to Tolkien. He explains arrangements he has made, or is making, for Tolkien's visit to London to receive the CBE at Buckingham Palace. He is arranging a dinner party for the evening before the ceremony, and has booked rooms at Brown's Hotel for Tolkien, John, and Priscilla.

13 March 1972 Tolkien moves to Oxford from Poole. He rides with the three removal men in their pantechnicon. He inscribes copies of *The Lord of the Rings* and *The Hobbit* for one of them, Fred Archer. – Rayner Unwin writes to Tolkien about the royalty to be paid on Allen & Unwin's schools edition of *The Hobbit*.

13 March 1972–31 August 1973 Tolkien lives at 21 Merton Street, Oxford. He is looked after by the scout Charlie Carr and his wife, who live in the basement flat. They bring him breakfast in his rooms, and sometimes cook lunch or supper for him if he does not feel well or does not want to eat in college or at the nearby Eastgate Hotel. According to an interview with Carr after Tolkien's death, Tolkien keeps regular habits. He always has breakfast at 9.00 a.m. On Sundays a taxi collects him at 10.20 a.m. to take him to St Antony's Church, Headington. After attending the service he visits Edith's grave at Wolvercote Cemetery, then returns home for lunch. Tolkien still has many old friends and colleagues in Oxford, and also the company of the other Fellows at Merton. He pays frequent visits to West Hannay where Christopher and Baillie live with their two children.

?Mid-March 1972 Tolkien is interviewed for an article in the *Oxford Mail*, and photographed in the gardens of Merton College by Athar Chaudry. In the anonymous article published on 22 March Tolkien is quoted as saying that 'coming back to Oxford is like returning to a metropolis from a desert island. . . . I've come here hoping for a time of peace, without interruptions, in which to pick up the threads of my work, including the revision of *The Silmarillion*. . . . I hope before very long to begin publishing this in parts' ('Tolkien Seeks the Quiet Life in Oxford', p. 10). His presence in Oxford is known, but he tries to keep his exact address as secret as possible, and asks that his mail be addressed to Merton College, not to 1 Merton Street.

16 March 1972 Tolkien writes to Rayner Unwin. He is still settling in, but hopes to have his flat in order in a few days, except for recalling his books from store. – The *Oxford University Gazette* announces that Tolkien has been made an Honorary Fellow of Pembroke College.

Second half of March 1972 Tolkien attends a Merton gaudy. As Roger Lancelyn Green will recall, it is the last time that he sees Tolkien. After dinner, 'Tolkien and I sat talking on a sofa in the Senior Common Room until nearly two o'clock in the morning. And finally Tolkien said: "I wish we could go on talking till morning – but I'm supposed to go to bed early. Old age, you know!"' (Green, 'Recollections', *Amon Hen* 44 (May 1980), p. 8). At the same gaudy, Stephen Medcalf asks Tolkien if is true that some aspects of the Ents were modelled on C.S. Lewis. Tolkien replies indignantly: 'Lewis had nothing at all to do with the Ring' (quoted in Medcalf, '"The Language Learned of Elves": Owen Barfield, *The Hobbit*, and *The Lord of the Rings*', *Seven* 16 (1999), p. 31).

21 March 1972 The Congregation of Oxford University approves a proposal to confer on Tolkien an honorary degree of Doctor of Letters. – Rayner Unwin writes to Tolkien to confirm arrangements for 27–28 March. He reminds Tolkien that if he has been sent a car sticker for admission to Buckingham Palace, he should bring it with him.

22 March 1972 Tolkien writes to Rayner Unwin. He expects to arrive at Brown's Hotel in London at about 5.00 p.m. on 27 March. He has to show a letter to gain admission to the Palace.

27 March 1972 Tolkien, John, and Priscilla arrive at Brown's Hotel in London. At about 7.00 p.m. they go to the Garrick Club, where Rayner Unwin and his wife Carol give them a dinner party. The others present are Lord and Lady Halsbury, Sir Burke Trend, and Donald and Janet Swann. Rayner will write in his *George Allen & Unwin: A Remembrancer* (1999): 'Tolkien sparkled. In the atmosphere of the club, surrounded by friends and, for a brief time, free from the multifarious concerns that all too easily overwhelmed him, he was animated and delighted all of us by the pleasure he took in our company and by his keen anticipation of the ceremony in store for him next day' (p. 133). Rayner will also recall that Tolkien chose for his meal smoked salmon, a kipper, and stilton cheese (p. 45).

28 March 1972 As arranged by Rayner Unwin, a car collects Tolkien, John, and Priscilla from Brown's Hotel at 9.45 a.m. and drives them to Buckingham Palace. Tolkien receives his CBE medal from Queen Elizabeth II. 'Inside the Palace the ceremonies were, especially for "recipients", accompanied by some tedium (with a few touches of the comic). But I was very deeply moved by my brief meeting with the Queen, & our few words together. Quite unlike anything that I had expected' (letter to Rayner Unwin, 30 March 1972, *Letters*, p. 418).

30 March 1972 Tolkien writes to Rayner Unwin. He thanks him for all his arrangements and describes his impressions of the two days in London. He asks: 'Would it be possible for you to use my Christian name? I am now accepted as a member of the community here – one of the habits of which has long been the use of Christian names, irrespective of age or office – and as you are now a v[ery] old friend, and a very dear one, I should much like also to be a "familiaris"' (*Letters*, p. 418).

?Late March or April 1972 Tolkien writes some notes for Joy Hill. She has evidently asked how to reply to a letter from someone asking for a list of works by or about Tolkien. Bibliographies have been compiled and some published, but he cannot help, as his books and papers are still in store. He suggests that she contact the Tolkien Society.

?April 1972 Tolkien dines with a friend, and finds that Humphrey Carpenter is also a guest. In fact, Carpenter, who wants to persuade Tolkien to agree to be interviewed or to read from one of his books on Radio Oxford, has asked a mutual friend to invite them both to dinner to enable him to broach the matter in an informal atmosphere. Tolkien suggests that Carpenter take him out to dinner and ask him again.

14 April 1972 Joy Hill, presumably after a visit to Oxford, writes a memo to Rayner Unwin. Tolkien would like to meet the Allen & Unwin staff at Museum Street and Hemel Hempstead to thank them for his birthday present.

20 April 1972 Tolkien attends an Early English Text Society Council meeting at Merton College – Rayner Unwin writes to Tolkien. An appropriate time for him to meet the Allen & Unwin staff would be when their salesmen, 'who virtually live in a world of your making during their work-life, assemble for a briefing session at Hemel Hempstead on 13th and 14th July'. Rayner will arrange for Tolkien to be driven from Oxford and, as well as meeting the salesmen, Tolkien can 'walk round the various departments, seeing as many of the individuals in our business as you wished' (Tolkien–George Allen & Unwin archive, HarperCollins). Rayner suggests that Tolkien could meet the staff at Allen & Unwin's Museum Street offices the next time he visits London.

27 April 1972 Tolkien writes to Rayner Unwin. He can make either date for the visit to Hemel Hempstead, but would prefer 14 July. He sees no hope of getting his books and papers in order, and in place, before the end of May.

May 1972 C.V.L. Lycett, who had been at King Edward's School with Tolkien, writes to him reminiscing about school days.

1 May 1972 Humphrey Carpenter takes Tolkien to dinner at The Bell at Charlbury. Carpenter will later comment: 'I was very lucky because it turned out to be exactly the sort of food [Tolkien] liked – plain English cooking. I remember we had cutlets – lamb cutlets with paper frills on the bone, a detail you never see nowadays. He was absolutely thrilled with this.' Tolkien is still bereaved after Edith's death, but also merry. He and Carpenter talk about a variety of things, including his disapproval of the revised Catholic liturgy and 'the Marx Brothers, of whom he surprisingly proved to have been a fan, once upon a time. I remember him standing with his coattails against the great big open fire. He was drinking brandy and warming himself by the fire' ('". . . One Expected Him To Go On a Lot Longer": Humphrey Carpenter Remembers J.R.R. Tolkien', *Minas Tirith Evening-Star* 9, no. 2 (January 1980), p. 12). At the end of the evening, Carpenter raises the question of a radio broadcast, and with some reluctance Tolkien agrees. The broadcast is to take place a few days later.

3 May 1972 Tolkien writes to Graham Tayar, accepting an invitation to dine with the London Old Edwardians.

c. 4 May 1972 Tolkien rings Radio Oxford the day before he is to be recorded: he has changed his mind about the interview. – Humphrey Carpenter telephones Tolkien about this, but Tolkien is not persuaded. (The interview never takes place.)

14 May 1972 Tolkien replies to a letter from Jonathan Wordsworth, an Oxford don. He hopes to dine with The Society on 7 June. He has sent a card of acceptance to David Cecil. Such occasions, he says, are one of the attractions of living in Oxford again.

18 May 1972 Tolkien replies to a letter from Michael Salmon. He explains that 'every extra task however small diminishes my chance of ever publishing

The Silmarillion'. He cannot 'spend time making any comments on myself or my works' (*Letters*, p. 418).

23 May 1972 Tolkien writes to Sir Patrick Browne. 'Being a cult figure in one's own lifetime I am afraid is not all pleasant. However I do not find that it tends to puff one up; in my case at any rate it makes me feel extremely small and inadequate. But even the nose of a very modest idol . . . cannot remain entirely untickled by the sweet smell of incense!' (*Letters*, p. 418). He intends to be at the Ad Eundem gathering on 30 July, and hopes to see Sir Patrick then.

25 May 1972 Tolkien replies to a letter from a Mr Wrigley, who has commented on the search by academics for the sources of *The Lord of the Rings*. To Tolkien's mind 'it is the particular use in a particular situation of any motive, whether invented, deliberately borrowed, or unconsciously remembered that is the most interesting thing to consider' (*Letters*, p. 418).

?By early June 1972–August 1973 Tolkien asks Naomi Collyer, who had been his secretary some years earlier, if she will help him with his correspondence, since her children are now at school. They work in his room in Merton Street with two windows overlooking the Botanic Garden. There is a desk before each window; she sits on the left. She will later describe the routine:

> Our work was undertaken in a very light-hearted manner. We always enjoyed a chat before we got down to letters, and the Professor loved to tell me of things that had amused him. He had a rich fund of stories, some of which I never heard the crucial point of, because his pipe got in the way of his words, but I had to laugh anyway because his humour was so infectious.
>
> Some of the letters were dealt with quickly in one or two sentences, but others the Professor would take great time and trouble over. . . . He dictated his replies at a tremendous rate (the words battling with the pipe) and then there would be a great upheaval as we looked for another missing letter he wanted to answer. It was always at the bottom of some pile of papers and scraps. . . . Then as I typed he would sit at the other desk . . . puffing away at his pipe and pondering, gazing out of the window, or perhaps into the past; I would hear him murmur to himself "Yes . . . yes." ['Recollections of Professor J.R.R. Tolkien', *Arda* 5 (1988, for 1985), p. 2]

She works for Tolkien until his death.

3 June 1972 Oxford University confers upon Tolkien an honorary Doctorate of Letters. The ceremony takes place in the Sheldonian Theatre, with the Vice-Chancellor, Sir Alan Bullock, presiding. Colin Hardie, the Public Orator, makes a speech in Latin, referring to *The Lord of the Rings* as well as to Tolkien's academic achievements.

?6 June 1972 Tolkien replies to a letter from Father Douglas Carter. He comments on the Entwives and on the Greek language.

6 June 1972 H.S. Bennett dies.

7 June 1972 In the evening, Tolkien attends a dinner of The Society hosted by Lord David Cecil at New College, Oxford. Sixteen members are present, including Christopher Tolkien. The Secretary will record that the meeting is particularly notable for Tolkien's return after a long absence.

13–20 June 1972 Tolkien visits his brother Hilary, who lives near Evesham. On this (or on another visit in the summer of 1972 or 1973) 'the two old brothers watched cricket and tennis on television, and drank whisky' (Humphrey Carpenter, *Biography*, p. 254).

c. **13 June 1972** Joy Hill writes to the Tolkien Society. Tolkien has done no work on 'The Silmarillion' since Edith's death, and at present is busy putting his library in order.

20 June 1972 Tolkien probably attends an Ad Eundem meeting and dinner.

21 June 1972 Tolkien takes part in Encaenia.

27 June 1972 Tolkien attends a reception at Allen & Unwin's Museum Street offices in London, beginning at noon. He meets staff and invited guests, among whom are Ian and Betty Ballantine and Vera Chapman, founder of the Tolkien Society. Chapman speaks to Tolkien, who agrees to be Honorary President of the Society. He tells her that he has been greatly distressed by the theft of his CBE medal and some of his wife's jewellery from his rooms in Merton Street.

29 June 1972 In a leader entitled 'Forestry and Us', p. 18, the *Daily Telegraph* refers to 'a kind of Tolkien gloom' with reference to plantations made by the Forestry Commission.

30 June 1972 Tolkien writes to the *Daily Telegraph* in reply to 'Forestry and Us'.

Summer 1972 One day Rayner Unwin fetches Tolkien from Oxford and drives him to have lunch with Rayner and his wife at their home in Little Missenden, Buckinghamshire. – Artist Ted Nasmith writes to Tolkien. He sends him photographs of his drawings, inspired by *The Lord of the Rings*. Tolkien will reply that Bilbo in the 'Unexpected Party' is too childlike.

4 July 1972 Tolkien's letter is published in the *Daily Telegraph*, there entitled *Beautiful Place Because Trees Are Loved*. 'I feel that it is unfair to use my name as an adjective qualifying "gloom", especially in a context dealing with trees' (p. 16). – Rayner Unwin writes to Tolkien. He confirms arrangements for Tolkien's visit to Hemel Hempstead on 14 July. He hopes that 'the lumbago cure was permanently successful' (Tolkien-George Allen & Unwin archive, HarperCollins; perhaps mentioned by Tolkien during his visit of 27 June). While sorting papers, Rayner has come across a 1937 reader's report on *The Lost Road*. He asks if this ever progressed beyond two chapters, and if it still exists, if Rayner may read it.

11 July 1972 Tolkien writes to Rayner Unwin. 'A chapter or two' of *The Lost Road* exists, or did exist when Tolkien lived in Poole, but he has not seen it since his move. When he finds it, he will let Rayner see it.

11 and 13 July 1972 Tolkien begins a letter to his son Christopher. He explains the inscription he would like to place on the stone on Edith's grave, and how she inspired the story of Lúthien.

I should like ere long to have a long talk with *you*. For if as seems probable I shall never write any ordered biography – it is against my nature, which expresses itself about things deepest felt in tales and myths – someone close in heart to me should know something about things that records do not record: the dreadful sufferings of our childhoods, from which we [Tolkien and Edith] rescued one another, but could not wholly heal the wounds that later often proved disabling; the sufferings that we endured after our love began – all of which (over and above our personal weaknesses) might help to make pardonable, or understandable, the lapses and darknesses which at times marred our lives – and to explain how these never touched our depths nor dimmed our memories of our youthful love. For ever (especially when alone) we still met in the woodland glade, and went hand in hand many times to escape the shadow of imminent death before our last parting. [*Letters*, pp. 420–1]

14 July 1972 A car sent by Allen & Unwin collects Tolkien from Oxford at 10.00 a.m. and drives him to their offices and warehouses at Hemel Hempstead. Tolkien will describe his visit to Christopher on 15 July:

I paid a kind of official visitation, like a minor royalty, and was somewhat startled to discover the *main* business of all this organization of many departments (from Accountancy to Despatch) was dealing with my works. I was given a great welcome (& v[ery] g[ood] lunch) and interviewed them all from board-room downwards. 'Accountancy' told me that the sales of *The Hobbit* were now rocketing up to hitherto unreached heights. Also a large single order for copies of *The* [*Lord of the Rings*] had just come in. When I did not show quite the gratified surprise expected I was gently told that a single order of 100 copies used to be pleasing (and still is for other books), but this one for *The L.R.* was for 6,000. [*Letters*, p. 421]

During the visit, he signs copies of his books for members of the staff. At the end he is driven back to Oxford in time for dinner in hall at Merton.

15 July 1972 Tolkien continues his letter to Christopher. He describes his visit to Hemel Hempstead.

27 July 1972 Tolkien has decided to donate to *Help the Aged*, in memory of Edith, the desk she had given him in 1927. He writes a certificate of authentication to go with the desk when it is sold at Sotheby's. He used this desk while writing and illustrating *The Hobbit*, and when he wrote much of *The Lord of the Rings*.

31 July 1972 Tolkien writes to Joy Hill. He authorizes her 'in future (until & unless otherwise advised by me) to reply in a polite *negative* to all enquiries or requests for *interviews, attending or speaking at meetings,* [or] *lecturing* without referring to me'. Periodically she may send him a list of names, and if he knows any of the writers he might ask to see their letters. 'I *must* clear my time and attention from all side issues. I am now longing to get back to my work; and when at last my rooms are reasonably uncluttered, and my books off the ground, and my typewriter is going again, I shall be obdurate. If I have any strength left. One thing I am alas now sure of: it will not run to v[ery] many hours a day (or night)' (collection of René van Rossenberg).

3 August 1972 Tolkien travels to Stoke-on-Trent. Although he had been advised to change trains at Stafford, the inspector on the train insists that he must change at Birmingham. 'I got out at B'ham and found it impossible: tired and with luggage I was supposed to climb a bridge and go to the far side of the huge station and to the end of a long platform and catch the connexion. A kindly ticket-collector' sees his distress and tells him to get back on the train and change at Stafford, where he will not have to change platforms (letter to Joy Hill, 4 August 1972, collection of René van Rossenberg). John meets him at Stoke. – Tolkien writes to Dorothy Wood, mainly about family matters. He also comments on the diminishing state pension. This is one of several letters he and his cousin exchange during this summer.

3–16 August 1972 Tolkien stays with his son John in Stoke-on-Trent.

4 August 1972 Tolkien writes to Joy Hill. He thanks her for dealing with the certificate for the desk. He is very tired. 'I am beginning to feel anxious, as my strength and resilience has been so severely taxed since March and is waning. I begin to feel that when at last, if ever, I break through the endless entanglements and delays that prevent me from returning to my "work", I shall be finally exhausted.' But he is now being 'pampered' by John and his housekeeper (collection of René van Rossenberg).

14 August 1972 Richard Jeffery writes to Tolkien. He asks several questions about Quenya and Sindarin names. Tolkien will compose a reply at intervals, but not complete it until 17 December.

17 August 1972 Joy Hill visits Tolkien in Oxford. They lunch together at the Eastgate Hotel.

22–29 August 1972 Tolkien stays at Sidmouth for a week with his daughter Priscilla and grandson Simon.

?Summer 1972 Ballantine publishes *The J.R.R. Tolkien Calendar 1973* with ten colour illustrations by Tolkien, a colour photograph of him by John Wyatt, and Pauline Baynes' *Map of Middle-earth* and *There and Back Again* (the *Hobbit* poster map). Three of Tolkien's illustrations are published for the first time: *Old Man Willow, Moria Gate* (cut in half and used as two pictures), and *Barad-dûr* (*Artist and Illustrator*, figs. 147–149, 145).

17 September 1972 Tolkien writes to his cousin Marjorie Incledon. Although he appreciates all that Merton College has done for him, 'nonetheless – I often feel very lonely, and long for a change! After term (sc. when the undergraduates depart) I am all alone in a large house with only the caretaker & his wife far below in the basement, and since I am (especially on my return to Oxford) a marked man, and troubled with many intruders and some nefarious persons, I live behind locked doors.' He is still not fully settled in, but in 'considerable confusion' (*Letters*, pp. 421–2). ('Nefarious persons' may be a reference to the theft of his CBE medal and Edith's jewellery.) – Tolkien writes to Dorothy Wood. He will be staying at the Hotel Miramar for three nights in October. He looks forward to seeing her there.

?October 1972 Humphrey Carpenter, who has read of the forthcoming sale of Tolkien's desk for charity, again approaches Tolkien about being interviewed for Radio Oxford, with the desk as a primary topic. Tolkien agrees, but cancels on the day of the interview.

10 October 1972 Rayner Unwin writes to Tolkien. Ballantine Books want to reprint their *Tolkien Calendar* for 1974, with some variation to distinguish it from the 1973 *Calendar*. They 'wondered whether you could ring round any particular dates which were auspicious for you. Or for the inhabitants of Middle-earth!' (Tolkien-George Allen & Unwin archive, HarperCollins).

11 October 1972 Tolkien attends a meeting of the Fellows of Merton College.

12 October 1972 Tolkien writes to Rayner Unwin. He thanks him for two copies of the Ballantine *Tolkien Calendar*, which he had not seen. He thinks it well produced, but wonders why the colours seem to have been deliberately changed. 'The picture for September seems to me rather poor: the bottom end of the following picture for October which was cut off and not meant to be used' (*Moria Gate*, i.e. the West-gate, see *Artist & Illustrator*, figs. 148, 149). He could supply a new illustration to replace it. He is against events in his life being mixed up with the events of the story, with the exception of the publication dates of *The Hobbit* and of *The Fellowship of the Ring*. He suggests that Ballantine Books use pp. 372–6 in *The Return of the King* ('The Great Years' in *The Tale of Years*, Appendix B) to choose dates to put in the calendar.

14–17 October 1972 Tolkien stays at the Hotel Miramar, Bournemouth. Dorothy Wood also stays there during at least part of the time.

?Mid–late October 1972 Tolkien's son John visits his father for five days in Oxford. Tolkien will write to Humphrey Carpenter on 31 October: 'I found myself very heavily occupied in filling his few days with me to give him the most pleasurable time I could' (University Archives, *Catalogue 116* (1994), p. 18).

20 October 1972 Rayner Unwin writes to Tolkien. He thinks that the colour separation and printing of the Ballantine calendar could have been done better.

26 October 1972 Tolkien draws and dates a heavy and inelegant version of his 'Tree of Amalion' on the back of an invitation card for an event on 6 July 1972, and two small doodles on the front. Possibly at about the same time, he draws on the back of an invitation to a party on 12 October a decorative paisley motif.

31 October 1972 Tolkien writes 'a charming note' in reply to 'a rather cross letter' from Humphrey Carpenter, sent after Tolkien cancelled the second arrangement for a broadcast at short notice ('". . . One Expected Him To Go On a Lot Longer": Humphrey Carpenter Remembers J.R.R. Tolkien', *Minas Tirith Evening-Star* 9, no. 2 (January 1980), p. 13). The reason Tolkien gives for the second cancellation is that his son John 'came to visit me for five very full days . . . the first time the poor man had been able to visit Oxford since he was ordained' (University Archives, *Catalogue 116* (1994), p. 18). *See note.*

Michaelmas Term 1972 On one evening during this term Tolkien attends a dinner of The Society hosted by Angus Macintyre at Magdalen College. Thirteen members are present, including Christopher Tolkien. The host reads a paper on the role of the war artist. The company adjourn just before midnight.

1 November 1972 Rayner Unwin writes to Tolkien. *Oz* magazine is advertising the Ballantine Books edition of *The Lord of the Rings* to its readership in the UK. This is an infringement of copyright, which Rayner is sure is being done without Ballantine's knowledge. (Ballantine Books are not licensed to sell their edition in the UK, in competition with Allen & Unwin.) Allen & Unwin's solicitors have written to *Oz*, and intend also to write to Customs and Excise. – The desk given to Tolkien by his wife in 1927, and on which wrote *The Hobbit* and much of *The Lord of the Rings*, is sold at Sotheby's together with his explanatory letter. It fetches £340. (This desk is now in the Marion E. Wade Center, Wheaton College, Wheaton, Illinois.)

?Early November 1972 Mrs Meriel Thurston writes to Tolkien. She asks permission to use *Rivendell* as the name of her herd, and other of Tolkien's invented names for individual cows and bulls.

3 November 1972 Tolkien writes to Graham Tayar. Ill health now prevents him from keeping his engagement to dine with the London Old Edwardians. Later, with the help of Tayar, he will record a short speech to be played to the Old Edwardians on the occasion.

7 November 1972 Tolkien writes to Rayner Unwin. He leaves the *Oz* matter in his hands. But he has learned of another form of piratical operation: 'Many of our "public schools" are filled with the most degraded posters purporting to be illustrations of *The Lord of the Rings*. I provided Miss Hill with a copy of a fearful thing bearing in enormous letters GOLLUM which I believe she has sent to United Artists. These things appear to be produced in America. . . . They are even on sale in reputable bookshops like Blackwell's' (Tolkien-George Allen & Unwin archive, HarperCollins). – Tolkien writes to Dorothy Wood. He is now in better health.

9 November 1972 Tolkien replies to Mrs Meriel Thurston. He is 'quite willing that you should use the name of Rivendell as a herd prefix, though in my ignorance I don't think the actual valley of Rivendell would have been suitable for herd breeding' (*Letters*, p. 422). He will be interested to hear what names she chooses. The Elvish word for 'bull' is *mundo*.

13 November 1972 Rayner Unwin writes to Tolkien. *Oz* have apologized, after Allen & Unwin issued a writ. They will try to suppress the posters.

21 November 1972 Tolkien writes to Sterling Lanier, who has received a prize he finds useless. A fan once sent Tolkien a drinking goblet 'engraved with the terrible words seen on the Ring. I of course have never drunk from it, but use it for tobacco ash' (*Letters*, p. 422).

23 November 1972 Tolkien replies to Edmund Meskys, who has written to ask about Elvish numerals and duodecimals.

I did devise numeral signs to go with the Fëanorian alphabet accommodated to both a decimal nomenclature and a duodecimal, but I never used them and no longer have an accurate memory of them. I am afraid the folder containing the numeral systems is not available and may be locked away in a strongroom. I remember that the numerals were written according to a positional system like the Arabic, beginning at the left with the lowest number and rising to the highest on the right. [*Letters*, pp. 422–3]

28 November 1972 In the morning, a representative of an Oxford housing association phones to ask if they can name the Common Room in some new flats in St Clements after Edith Tolkien. Tolkien writes to say that he would be pleased for them to do this.

30 November 1972 Tolkien replies to another letter from Meriel Thurston. He is 'rather against giving strictly human and noble names to animals' (*Letters*, p. 423), such as *Elrond* and *Glorfindel*. He suggests some more suitable ones.

Late November–December 1972 Tolkien signs a copy of the India paper edition of *The Lord of the Rings* for Andrew Warde, and also writes in it the poem 'Tall ships and tall kings' in red and blue ink.

November and December 1972 and later Tolkien writes various short texts, some at least developing queries raised in letters. He intersperses the main texts with notes written in italic script to distinguish them. These include two versions of a text considering whether Glorfindel of Gondolin and Glorfindel of Rivendell are one and the same (see *Glorfindel*); two versions of a discussion of the question of Elvish reincarnation, in which Tolkien changes his former ideas, and leads eventually to a discussion of the 'reincarnation' of Dwarves (see *'Elvish Reincarnation'*); a brief *Note on the Landing of the Five Wizards and Their Functions and Operations* (see *The Five Wizards*), which arises from Tolkien's consideration of the matter of Glorfindel; some rough notes on the Istari; and a brief manuscript, *Círdan* (on the verso of one of the pages of the second text on Glorfindel), which adds interesting details to his story.

December 1972 or later Tolkien writes a note on the Elvish strain in Men being indicated by beardlessness, and in this connection mentions the House of Dol Amroth. Perhaps at the same time, he draws a genealogy of the line of Dol Amroth with a note on the marriage of Galador, the first Lord, with the Elven-lady Mithrellas.

13 December 1972 Tolkien replies to a letter from Lyle Leach, who has asked for help with an academic project concerning Tolkien's works. 'I should not feel inclined to help in this destructive purpose, even if it did not seem to me that this exercise was supposed to be your own private work without assistance' (*Letters*, p. 424).

17 December 1972 Tolkien completes a reply to the letter by Richard Jeffery written on 14 August. 'I am an old man, and slower at work than I used to be; but I am still burdened with a great many affairs, that constantly interrupt my efforts to publish at least some of my other legends. I have also often been unwell during the last 3 months.' Jeffery's questions are all interesting, but 'satisfactory answers require in many cases reference to linguistic and legendary matters that would take far too long to deal with in a letter' (*Letters*, p. 424). Nonetheless, he writes at considerable length, noting he has been composing his answer at intervals.

Christmas 1972 Tolkien stays with his son John in Stoke-on-Trent. John is a victim of the influenza epidemic. Tolkien, who has had an anti-influenza vaccination, is also affected, but only mildly.

1973

?Beginning of 1973 Donald and Janet Swann write to Tolkien. They would like to come to Oxford to see him and Priscilla, at some date after 24 January.

?Early January–?May 1973 Tolkien begins to suffer from severe indigestion. He will write to Christopher Wiseman on 24 May 1973: 'I have had a longish bout of poor health since my 81st birthday (a mere sequel in time & not due to the party!). After having my inside X-rayed extensively (with on the whole v[ery] g[ood] reports) I am now deprived of the use of *all* wines, and on a somewhat restricted diet; but am allowed to smoke & consume the alcoholic products of barley, as I wish' (*Letters*, p. 429).

3 January 1973 Tolkien celebrates his eighty-first birthday with a party.

8 January 1973 Tolkien writes to Donald and Janet Swann. He will try to find a date that suits everyone, and ring them on 25 January. He is free in the period 26 January–7 February, except 3 February. He wants to be the host, and suggests the Eastgate Hotel as a reasonable restaurant.

Late January–early February 1973 Presumably Donald and Janet Swann come to Oxford and lunch with Tolkien and Priscilla.

8 February 1973 According to *The Times* of 9 February ('Staying Home', in 'The *Times* Diary'), ill health keeps Tolkien from travelling to Paris to receive his prize for *The Lord of the Rings* as France's best foreign novel of the year. *See note.*

12 February 1973 Tolkien declines a request to write a foreword to a book. He explains that he is not well.

6 March 1973 Tolkien replies to a letter from Mrs Catherine Findlay. He explains the name *Galadriel*.

8 March 1973 Tolkien replies to a letter from Mrs E.R. Ehrardt. He rejects her comments on the meaning of the name 'Tolkien'. – Tolkien writes to Clyde S. Kilby. Poor health prevents him accepting an invitation (presumably to Wheaton College). 'I have been in medical hands recently and have had some severe advice with regard to my future conduct' (Marion E. Wade Center, Wheaton College, Wheaton, Illinois).

9 April 1973 W.H. Lewis dies.

20 April 1973 Tolkien writes to Denis Tolhurst in Bournemouth. He refers to an imminent family gathering.

?Late April 1973 Tolkien writes to a Mr Hodgson, who has asked for a handwritten copy of the 'Road Goes Ever On' verse. Tolkien asks if he wants the version in *The Fellowship of the Ring*, or would he like the copy to be in Tolkien's normal hand but carefully, or something more calligraphic. He warns that 'my ageing hands are now losing their steadiness, and such moderate skill as I ever had' (Phillips, *Books, Maps & Manuscripts*, 24 March 2000, p. 73). In reply, Hodgson asks for a calligraphic version, which Tolkien send but omits to sign it as requested. Hodgson sends it back for a signature.

3 May 1973 Tolkien's election as an Honorary Fellow of Merton College is published in newspapers. He was previously an Emeritus Fellow.

7 May 1973 Tolkien writes again to Mr Hodgson. He returns the calligraphed verse with his signature and an inscription.

8 May 1973 In the morning, Tolkien visits the exhibition *Craftsman's Art* at the Victoria and Albert Museum. He is photographed with the Duke of Edinburgh and Philip Smith. The Duke had been presented with a copy of *The Lord of the Rings* bound by Smith and autographed by Tolkien.

12 May 1973 Tolkien attends an Early English Text Society Council meeting at Lady Margaret Hall at 2.15 p.m.

16–22 May 1973 Tolkien stays in Bournemouth, presumably at the Hotel Miramar. He will later write to his son Christopher that he 'returned [to Oxford] much the better. I had some good plain food, a room with a private balcony, and saw a good deal of my dear friends the Tolhursts; and I had good weather (which Oxford did *not* get' (*Letters*, p. 430). While there, he presents the Tolhursts with an inscribed copy of the India paper *Lord of the Rings*.

18 May 1973 R.B. McCallum dies.

24 May 1973 In the afternoon, Tolkien votes in the election held in the Sheldonian Theatre for the new Professor of Poetry. According to Martin Halsall, 'Sheer Poetry as Green Velvet Sets the Scene', *Oxford Mail*, 25 May 1973, p. 13: 'Professor J.R.R. Tolkien arrived in style, doffing his mortar board to friends, pausing to autograph a copy of *The Hobbit* and twinkling in the sunshine with allusions to Milton. He ... voted for [John] Jones. "It's high time the chair came back to what it was originally intended for, scholars interested in poetry, but not practising poets, who are not in general very good lecturers on the subject."' John Wain, however, is elected to the Chair. – During the voting Tolkien meets Elaine Griffiths and accepts a long-standing invitation to visit her. She drives him to her home in Hinton Waldrist. He tells her that

Eilert Ekwall was wrong about the etymology of that name (presumably in his *Concise Oxford Dictionary of English Place-names*). When they arrive, she asks him what he would like to drink; he asks for whisky. He wanders around her garden and tells her the botanical name of a weed that he finds. – Tolkien writes to Christopher Wiseman, telling him that he is now settled in at Merton, and forwarding the contents of a letter he has received from one of their contemporaries at King Edward's School. – Tolkien writes to the Kings Arms, Chipping Campden, confirming rooms he has booked for himself and his son John at the end of June and beginning of July.

29 May 1973 (postmark) Tolkien replies to a letter from Christopher, who is in France. Priscilla has just returned from a very successful holiday in Crete. Since Easter he has been subject to 'unending pressure: social, literary, professional & financial' (*Letters*, p. 430). He mentions the recent deaths of W.H. Lewis, Tom Dunning (T.P. Dunning, a former student), R.B. McCallum, and Rosfrith Murray.

5 June 1973 Tolkien writes to Ungfrú Aðalsteinsdottir. He is pleased to hear that *The Hobbit* is being translated into Icelandic. – Tolkien writes to James A.H. Murray, a grandson of Sir James A.H. Murray of the *Oxford English Dictionary*, inviting his to visit him in his 'guarded' rooms in Merton Street, where he can show him some pictures and a tapestry inspired by *The Lord of the Rings*. His rooms are guarded because, since the secret of his whereabouts became known, 'I have been assailed by hosts of people, and worse, have been invaded by criminals, so that I live behind locked doors, and under the eye of the local C.I.D' (quoted in Sotheby's, *English Literature, History, Private Press & Children's Books*, London, 12 December 2002, p. 239). *See note.*

24 June 1973 Tolkien writes to Dorothy Wood. His health is not good, and he is forbidden to drink wine. He is not allowed to live in peace, but suffers from the constant attention of journalists, and others writing about him, tourists who regard him as one of the sights of Oxford, and criminals who believe false accounts of his wealth. – Tolkien replies to a request to inscribe a copy of the India paper *Lord of the Rings* with the same poem ('Tall ships and tall kings') which he had inscribed in a copy for Andrew Warde in 1972. He is willing to do so, but does not have time at the moment, as he is going away into the country for a short rest. In the meantime, he is returning the book, signed, and later will write the poem on a loose leaf. – Tolkien declines an invitation to dinner, but suggests luncheon. He has to avoid heavy evening meals.

25 June–3 July 1973 Tolkien and his son John stay at the Kings Arms, Chipping Campden.

Early July 1973 Joy Hill telephones Tolkien several times, and worries when she has no reply. When she eventually makes contact, Tolkien tells her that he had been having a marvellous time watching Wimbledon tennis on Charlie Carr's television.

5 July 1973 Tolkien writes to Basil Blackwell, recalling that Blackwell had been his first publisher (of *Goblin Feet* in *Oxford Poetry 1915*).

8 July 1973 Tolkien, in response to a request from Canon Norman Power, sends him a signature on adhesive paper which he can put in a book for a Mrs Ellwood. He comments on his childhood in Birmingham. He sends Canon Power a spare copy of *Essays by Diverse Hands* 13, issued by the Royal Society of Literature, which has an account of J.H. Shorthouse.

c. 10–17 July 1973 Tolkien travels to Edinburgh with his daughter Priscilla. They stay for a week with his former student Angus McIntosh, now Professor of English, and his wife Barbara.

12 July 1973 Edinburgh University confers on Tolkien an honorary degree of Doctor of Letters.

15 July 1973 Tolkien autographs a copy of *The Lord of the Rings*, probably for Angus McIntosh's son.

20 July 1973 Tolkien attends an Ad Eundem dinner at St John's College, Cambridge. His host is Professor Glyn Daniel.

26 July 1973 Lord Halsbury visits Tolkien. They discuss 'The Silmarillion', and Galadriel. A few days later, Tolkien will write to him:

> When you were here . . . I became again vividly aware of your invigorating effect on me: like a warm fire brought into an old man's room, where he sits cold and unable to muster courage to go out on a journey that his heart desires to make. For over and above all the afflictions and obstacles I have endured since *The Lord of the Rings* came out, I have lost confidence. May I hope that perhaps, even amid your own trials and the heavy work which must precede your retirement, you could come again before so very long and warm me up again? I particularly desire to hear you read verse again, and especially your own: which you make come alive for me. [4 August 1973, *Letters*, pp. 430–1]

?August 1973 Tolkien lunches with Robert Murray (and possibly others). Murray will recall that

> Ronald was maintaining with great vigour over the luncheon table that one of the greatest disasters of European history was the fact that the Goths turned Arian: but for that, their languages, just ready to become classical, would have been enriched not only with a great bible version but also, on Byzantine principles, with a vernacular liturgy, which would have served as a model for all the Germanic peoples and would have given them a native Catholicism which would never break apart. And with that he rose and in splendidly sonorous tones declaimed the Our Father in Gothic. ['A Tribute to Tolkien', *The Tablet*, 15 September 1973, pp. 879–80]

August 1973 Tolkien adds a note to the typescript of the *Annals of Aman* about Galadriel fighting in defence of Alqualondë. He also writes a rough note giving a new version of the story of Galadriel and Celeborn, their motives and actions, probably his last writing for the *legendarium*. These changes in his conception of Galadriel would have entailed a considerable amount of rewriting of the existing narrative of 'The Silmarillion', had he been able to continue it. – Marjorie Incledon visits and stays with Tolkien.

4 August 1973 Tolkien writes to Lord Halsbury. He thanks him for a gift of whisky Halsbury is sending. When Halsbury retires, he will ask for his help: 'Without it, I begin to feel that I shall never produce any part of *The Silmarillion*.' He means to deal immediately with Galadriel, and with the question of Elvish child-bearing. Galadriel was 'unstained' (*Letters*, p. 431): she reached Middle-earth independently, and had no part in Fëanor's revolt.

9 August 1973 Tolkien visits the Botanic Garden, Oxford, with his grandson Michael George. Michael George photographs him standing next to one of his favourite trees, a *Pinus Nigra*. This is probably the last photograph of Tolkien to be taken.

17 August 1973 Tolkien replies to a letter about *The Lord of the Rings*. His view of his books is rather different from that of the letter-writer. 'It is enough for me that people enjoy *Lord of the Rings* as a story without forming detailed comparisons between Middle-earth and the world today' (Tolkien-George Allen & Unwin archive, HarperCollins).

25 August 1973 Tolkien writes to Glyn Daniel, thanking him for a delightful dinner in Cambridge. He has suffered no ill effects, and most of the restrictions on his diet have now been lifted.

?Late August 1973 Joy Hill visits Tolkien for the last time. When she arrives, instead of settling down to work, he first offers her a drink, and then says that they will go for a long walk. He tells her that they are going to see all his favourite trees. They visit the Botanic Garden, then walk by the river to look at willows, then visit the Botanic Garden again. He asks her to bring a camera on her next visit in September, to take some photographs for him. – Tolkien meets Priscilla, who has just returned from a holiday in Salzburg. She gives him a bottle of Austrian liqueur and a box of *Mozartkugeln*. After his death, she will find that he has eaten all of the chocolates, but did not have time to drink the liqueur.

28 August 1973 Tolkien is driven to Bournemouth by a Mr Causier in a hired car. Causier's wife and son go with them. They have lunch at the Red Lion in Salisbury. Tolkien is to stay with Dr and Mrs Tolhurst. The Causiers drop Tolkien off while they look for lodgings for themselves, and Tolkien wanders around Bournemouth doing some shopping and having his hair cut. At about 4.45 p.m. he makes his way to the Hotel Miramar, where he hopes to meet the Causiers. He finds that he has lost his bank card and some money, but is recognized by the person on the desk at the hotel and made welcome. He has tea there. He is told that if he wants to stay at the Miramar, they have a room available from 4 September. He takes a taxi to the Tolhursts' house at 22 Little Forest Road. Their son telephones the Red Lion and finds that Tolkien has left his bank card there. The Causiers bring his luggage during the evening, and tell him that they have found rooms for themselves.

29 August 1973 Tolkien writes to Priscilla. He recounts his adventures of the previous day, and says that he has decided to stay at the Hotel Miramar from 4 to 11 September. He wishes to visit various people in Bournemouth, as well as Christopher Wiseman.

30 August 1973 Tolkien joins in celebrations for Mrs Tolhurst's birthday, but does not feel well, and does not eat much though he drinks a little champagne. During the night he is in pain.

31 August 1973 Tolkien is taken to a private hospital, where he is diagnosed as suffering from an acute bleeding gastric ulcer. John and Priscilla are summoned, but Michael and Christopher are in Switzerland and France respectively. At first the reports are optimistic.

1 September 1973 Tolkien develops a chest infection.

2 September 1973 John Ronald Reuel Tolkien dies early this Sunday.

6 September 1973 A Requiem Mass is held for Tolkien in the Church of St Anthony of Padua in Headington, Oxford. The prayers and readings have been chosen by his son John, who says Mass with the assistance of Tolkien's friend Robert Murray and the parish priest, Mgr Doran. Tolkien is buried beside Edith in the corporation cemetery at Wolvercote in the section reserved for members of the Catholic Church. The grave is marked with a grey slab of Cornish granite, inscribed: 'Edith Mary Tolkien, Luthien, 1889–1971. John Ronald Reuel Tolkien, Beren, 1892–1973'.

Michaelmas Term 1973 At a dinner of The Society this term, the Secretary expresses sadness at Tolkien's death. He notes that Tolkien had been a member of The Society for thirty-seven years, and was pleased to have been to two of its dinners in the final year of his life.

17 November 1973 A memorial service for Tolkien is held at noon in Merton College Chapel. The Reverend Mark Everitt, the Chaplain, officiates. The lessons are read by Nevill Coghill and John Tolkien. Oxford University is represented by the Pro-Vice Chancellor, Mr J.B. Bamborough, and the Proctors, and Merton College by the Warden and Fellows. Among those present are members of Tolkien's family, representatives of the English Faculty, the Early English Text Society (Norman Davis and his wife), the Oxford University Catholic Chaplaincy, the Newman Trustees, Pembroke College, Exeter College, Campion Hall, and the Tolkien Society; Lord Halsbury, Simonne d'Ardenne, Mr and Mrs Rayner Unwin, Joy Hill, and many former students, colleagues, secretaries, and friends.

NOTES

31 January 1892 Humphrey Carpenter, *Biography*, p. 13, states that Tolkien was christened on this date; but in a letter to Nancy Smith, 25 December 1963–2 January 1964 (Special Collections and University Archives, John P. Raynor, S.J., Library, Marquette University), Tolkien dates his baptism to 8 January 1892. The correct date is 31 January, according to the baptismal records of Bloemfontein Cathedral.

1898–1899 On 23 December 1963 Tolkien wrote to Nancy Smith that he was 'somewhere about six years old' when he wrote about a 'green great dragon' (*Letters*, p. 221); but in his letter to *W.H. Auden of 7 June 1955 he said that he was 'about seven' (*Letters*, p. 214), and he gave this age also in a letter of 26 August 1965 to Paula Iley. In the letters to Smith and Iley he said that he had tried to write verses about a dragon, while he told Auden that it was a 'story'.

?1900 The 'small book' has long been said (even in our *Reader's Companion*, p. 18) to be *Celtic Britain* by John Rhys, first published in 1882. But this is by no means 'professedly for the young', and there are now second thoughts whether Tolkien recalled correctly, so long after the fact. *Ond*, however, does appear to be a source for the name *Gondor* ('stone-land') in *The Lord of the Rings*.

Autumn term 1910 'Nominally under the control of an assistant master,' the School library 'was in practice administered chiefly by a number of senior boys who were granted the title of Librarian' (Humphrey Carpenter, *Biography*, p. 45). At this time the head Librarian was W.H. Payton.

June or July 1911 The manuscript of this poem is dated both 'July 1911' and 'June or July 1911'. It may be an odd coincidence, or a matter of Tolkien writing (later?) '1911' for '1912', that the subject for the 1912 Sir Roger Newdigate Prize at Oxford was 'Richard before Jerusalem'.

21 June 1911 In his letter to Michael, *c.* 25 August 1967, Tolkien recalled that he 'was one of 12 [cadets]' sent from King Edward's School (*Letters*, p. 391). The *King Edward's School Chronicle* for July 1911, however, reporting on the event soon after it occurred, records only eight.

August–early September 1911 Humphrey Carpenter writes (*Biography*, p. 50) that Tolkien

> and his brother Hilary were among a party organised by a family named Brookes-Smith, on whose Sussex farm Hilary was now working, having left school early to take up agriculture. There were about a dozen travellers: the Brookes-Smith parents, their children, Ronald and Hilary Tolkien and their Aunt Jane (now widowed), and one or two unattached schoolmistresses who were friends of Mrs Brookes-Smith.

Colin Brookes-Smith, whose parents organized the 1911 visit to Switzerland, suggests however in an unpublished account that Ronald and Hilary came to know the Brookes-Smiths through their Aunt Jane Neave, whom the Brookes-Smith parents had already met in St Andrews. He writes that his parents were then living in Sussex, in a country house at Hurst Green, but makes no mention of a farm or of Hilary until noting that in 1913 his parents bought two farms at Gedling, including Phoenix Farm to which Hilary came to live; nor does he mention Jane Neave at Gedling, though Humphrey Carpenter places her there by September 1914 (*Biography*, p. 71). Colin Brookes-Smith describes sixteen members of the tour party when it stopped for a photograph on the Aletsch Glacier in Switzerland, including a Swiss guide and a Swiss nanny.

10 November 1911 At this time Oxford University also required students to take a second compulsory examination, in Holy Scripture, which included the Greek text of two of the Gospels. We have found no record of Tolkien having taken this examination; it may be that his passing mark in Scripture Knowledge (Greek Text) in the Oxford and Cambridge Higher Certificate in July 1910 fulfilled the requirement.

Hilary Term 1913 No term card survives in the Tolkien Papers for the Apolausticks after Michaelmas Term 1912, though that organization was still active on 31 May 1913 when they met for a dinner. The *Stapeldon Magazine* records three meetings of the Exeter College Essay Club during Hilary Term 1913 but gives no details, and unfortunately no minutes of the Club survive from Tolkien's time until 1914. Former Exeter College Archivist Lorise Topliffe, in her *Tolkien as an Undergraduate, 1911–1915* in the *Exeter College Association Register 1992*, writes of the Essay Club that 'in [Hilary Term] 1913 papers on "The poetry of Wilde" and "Rossetti as poet and artist" were being presented' (p. 36).

28 February 1913 When Tolkien enlisted in the Army in 1915 he stated that he joined the King Edward's Horse in *October* 1911 and resigned in *January* 1913. It may be that in both cases the paperwork was postdated; the length of service noted in the discharge certificate, 1 year 93 days, agrees however with the dates in the certificate.

March 1913 The 'alpha' mark was reported as 'α+' by Joseph Wright on 22 June 1925 in his letter of support for Tolkien's application for the Rawlinson and Bosworth chair of Anglo-Saxon at Oxford, and by Tolkien to his son Christopher in a letter of 2 January 1969 (*Letters*, p. 397). The examiner's mark book for Tolkien preserved in the Oxford University Archives (EX 2/2/23), however, records a mark of only 'α', not 'α+'. That was enough, even so, to save Tolkien's 'bacon', as he put it in his letter of 2 January 1969, 'by squeaking into a "second" instead of merited "third", with the consequence that I did not lose my "exhibition", and was allowed by a generous college . . . to transfer to "English". . . .' In *Biography*, p. 62, Humphrey Carpenter reports that Tolkien 'achieved a "pure alpha", a practically faultless paper, in his special subject, Comparative Philology'.

?17–?19 December 1913 Tolkien saw Gilson, Smith, and Wiseman in Birmingham on 15–16 December, but apparently did not at that time, or before, tell them of his engagement. The wording of Wiseman's postcard of 20 December, and of Gilson's letter of 4 January, each sending congratulations, strongly suggests that each friend had heard the news since his last meeting with Tolkien (i.e. 16 December) – and at least in Gilson's case, only the bare fact of the engagement: he hopes that Tolkien will tell him the name of his intended. Humphrey Carpenter says in *Biography*, p. 68, that despite their division between Oxford and Cambridge,

> the four [T.C.B.S.] friends occasionally met, but Tolkien had never mentioned to them the existence of Edith Bratt. Now that the time was approaching for her reception into the Catholic Church they had decided to be formally betrothed, and he would have to tell his friends. He wrote to Gilson and Wiseman, very uncertain as to what to say, and not even telling them his fiancée's name; clearly he felt that it all seemed to have little to do with the male comradeship of the T.C.B.S.

Carpenter presumably did not say that Tolkien also wrote to Smith because no letter of congratulations from Smith is present in the small (and undoubtedly incomplete) archive of T.C.B.S. correspondence among Tolkien's papers. It may be that Tolkien told Smith the news in person (they were both at Oxford from Michaelmas Term 1913), but wrote to Gilson and Wiseman (at Cambridge); or he wrote to Smith, but Smith's reply has been lost, or else Smith delivered congratulations only in person.

According to John Garth in *Tolkien and the Great War*, Tolkien 'appears to have told Smith, who apparently passed the news on to Gilson and Wiseman' (p. 33). Garth also writes that 'there is no evidence for [Carpenter's] view that JRRT wrote directly to RQG and CLW with news of his engagement' (p. 320). But Carpenter was given unrestricted access to all of Tolkien's papers, and may have found evidence for his statement in a source other than the T.C.B.S. papers seen by Garth. Equally there is no certain evidence for Garth's assumption that Tolkien informed Gilson and Wiseman through Smith, neither of whom indicate in their messages of congratulations to Tolkien that they had heard the news from Smith, as would seem natural given that circumstance.

Michaelmas Term 1914 We have preferred the form 'St John Street', as in the *Blue Guide* to Oxford, Hibbert's *Encyclopaedia of Oxford*, etc. *Biography* and other sources have it as 'St John's Street'.

22 November 1914 These quotations are from the earliest extant version of Tolkien's essay on the *Kalevala*, written in ink over an earlier, erased pencil version. (A similar quotation in *Biography*, p. 59, is from a revised typescript of the essay made in the early 1920s.) He begins by stating that he is reading this essay, which has previously been read before a different society, as a stop-gap for a speaker who has been unable to appear. In a later note Tolkien says that he read this paper to the Sundial Society in November 1914 and to the Exeter

Essay Club in (February) 1915, which suggests that the extant ink text is that read to the latter group. Internal evidence shows that the ink version cannot be earlier than the beginning of the First World War. For further discussion, see entry for *Kalevala* in **Reader's Guide**.

?10 (possibly, less likely 17) March 1915 Most of G.B. Smith's surviving letters to Tolkien are headed only with the day of the week. We have assigned likely dates of writing according to our interpretation of internal evidence and the relation of letters one to another. In a few instances, John Garth has assigned different dates to Smith's letters in *Tolkien and the Great War* (2003).

8–9 July 1915 This section of *The Book of Ishness* (19v–23r as originally constructed) contains four watercolours on successive rectos, three with carefully placed inscriptions written on the facing versos: 'ILLUSTRATION to SEA-SONG of an ELDER Day' facing *Water, Wind & Sand*; no inscription facing *Tanaqui*; 'The Shores of Faery' facing the watercolour of Kôr framed by the two trees; and 'ILLUSTR. to "MAN in MOON"' above the last four lines of the second verse of the poem *Why the Man in the Moon Came Down Too Soon* and the illustration (*Artist and Illustrator*, fig. 4). The words 'The Shores of Faery' are centred on the page like the other two inscriptions, from which one may easily infer that they are meant to be the title of the facing picture. Below these words Tolkien wrote out the earliest extant version of the poem now known as *The Shores of Faery*; but the verses appear not to have been written at the same time as the title phrase with which they are associated, perhaps only by proximity. They are not centred under the title, and are written less carefully: Tolkien found that he did not have enough space for the last five lines, and placed them in a second column to the extreme right of the page. Indeed, from this evidence it seems that the picture *The Shores of Faery* may have preceded the poem of the same title, or at least preceded its earliest extant manuscript: for that appears to be a fair copy, which implies the existence of earlier workings (now lost).

In *Artist and Illustrator*, p. 47, we rashly stated that the date written on the fair copy manuscript of the poem was 'mistakenly assigned' by Tolkien; in the first reprint of our book this was emended to 'elsewhere assigned'. We felt, however, that since the earliest surviving version of the poem in *The Book of Ishness* was written opposite a painting dated 10 May 1915 which depicts many of the elements mentioned in the verses, both picture and poem might have been produced at roughly the same time in May, and that the July dates on subsequent versions might reflect revision rather than original composition. On re-examination of the physical evidence, this still seems possible, even likely; and certainly Tolkien was pondering many of the elements of the poem already in May, in order to depict them visually. But for simplicity's sake in **Chronology** we have recorded the painting of the watercolour under its own date, and the writing of *The Shores of Faery* separately, in the entry for 8–9 July 1915, accepting Tolkien's dating for this as we have for other poems – positive evidence, after all, reinforced by the July date on the later typescript, whereas the manuscript in *The Book of Ishness* bears no date.

19 October 1915 According to J.C. Latter, *The History of the Lancashire Fusiliers, 1914–1918* (1949), the 13th Battalion moved to Rugeley Camp in November 1915 and to Brocton Camp in December 1915; and yet Tolkien was evidently at Rugeley Camp, specifically at the part known as Penkridge Bank, at a slightly earlier date. It may be that he was in an advance party, and for that reason was not able to meet Gilson, Smith, and Wiseman on 23–24 October. In any event he seems to have returned before long to Whittington Heath, Lichfield, to which address Smith and Gilson subsequently sent letters.

November 1915–early 1916 J.S. Ryan recalled that Tolkien 'attended his troops' cutting up of a poached deer from the Pennine Uplands' in a lecture on *Sir Gawain and the Green Knight* delivered at Oxford in Hilary Term 1955, at which Ryan was present as a student ('The Origin of the Name Wetwang', *Amon Hen* 63 (August 1983), p. 13, n. 13.

7 June 1916 A brief account of the soldier's life at Étaples is given by Malcolm Brown in *Tommy Goes to War* (1978; reissue 1999, 2001): '"Eat-apples", or "E-taps", as it was variously known to the Tommy [ordinary soldier], had enough facilities to cope with 100,000 men: here too in the sand dunes near the railway was the notorious "Bullring" training ground' (p. 26). Men were given rigorous training, taught to fight with the bayonet, to march in formation, to deal with a poison gas attack, etc.

In the British Army of the First World War, the *division* was the largest tactical unit. It comprised a headquarters, three *infantry brigades*, and other troops of all sorts, more than 18,000 men and 5,000 horses when fully established. An infantry brigade, in turn, consisted of a headquarters and four *battalions*. In 1914 a full infantry battalion comprised 1,007 men (of whom 30 were officers) and 56 horses; it was further divided into four *companies*, each company into four *platoons*, and each platoon into four *sections*. In practice during the war, it was rare for any battalion to be at full strength. A *regiment* is an 'administrative family' of infantry battalions, such as the Lancashire Fusiliers.

June–October 1916 In Tolkien's war service diary an asterisk, used thirteen times, probably marks attendance at Mass or some service; it appears for seven Sundays (2, 9, 23 July, 6, 13 August, 17 September, 1 October) as well as Tuesday, 27 June; Monday and Tuesday, 14 and 15 August (Vigil and Feast of the Assumption); Saturday, 19 August; Wednesday, 27 September (that evening Tolkien left for the trenches); and Thursday, 2 November (All Souls' Day). Tolkien never marked Sundays thus when he was in the front line; but against this interpretation, he did write 'mass' for Sunday, 10 September; perhaps he was able to attend Mass in the village church at Beauval where he was billeted. A 'cross potent' – four equal arms with a bar at the end of each arm – is used eight times: two Sundays and four Saturdays, as well as Friday, 22 September, and Wednesday, 1 November (All Saints' Day). In only one case (other than on 9 September, when Tolkien definitely attended Mass the next day) is it not associated with an asterisk on the same or the following day.

8–10 July 1916 Tolkien's diary entry and the fact that he was not involved at the front line might suggest that he was in B or D Company, who were kept behind the lines to act as carrying parties for rations and ammunition. The Tolkien Papers in the Bodleian Library, however, provide considerable evidence that Tolkien was in A Company. John Garth notes in *Tolkien and the Great War* (2003) that when the 11th Lancashire Fusiliers left Bouzincourt on 6 July their 'signal officer, W.H. Reynolds, went to run communications at their trench headquarters, but Tolkien did not go with him. Instead he stayed put at Bouzincourt, along with the signal office running communications for the whole 25th Division' (p. 158).

7 August 1916 This entry, and those for 10 August and 7–12 September 1916, are based in part on the printed orders received by Tolkien for these dates, preserved in the Tolkien Papers, Bodleian Library, Oxford, and are meant to convey how specific were the instructions that governed Tolkien's movements and actions.

6 September 1916 The Battalion diary says that the relief and move to Bouzincourt took place on 5 September, but Tolkien's diary records that he spent the nights of 1–5 September at Ovillers-La Boiselle, and that the night of 6 September was his first at Bouzincourt. The records of the 74th Infantry Brigade state that the brigade was relieved by the 33rd Infantry Brigade on 6 September, and that the 11th Battalion went to Bouzincourt on that date. – The letter is preserved in the Tolkien Papers at the Bodleian Library, Oxford, and is partly reproduced in *Life and Legend*, p. 35. Its envelope, also preserved, is addressed 'To the Second in Command A C[ompan]y' of the 11th Lancashire Fusiliers. Thomas Gaskin, who was killed on 16 July 1916, seems to have been the batman to the addressee. Tolkien was not himself the second in command, but may have been asked to answer this letter because correspondence of this sort was a common responsibility of officers.

18 October 1916 The 11th Battalion received the following order (Operation Order No. T26) concerning the pending attack on Regina Trench (preserved in the National Archives, Kew, WO 95/2246–7):

The Battalion will take part in an attack to be made by 74th Inf. Bde. [Infantry Brigade] in conjunction with other troops on the flanks.

Objective – Regina Trench from R.23a.2.4½. to R.22.b.4.4.

The 18th Division will attack simultaneously on the right and 9th L.N.L1 [Loyal North Lancashires] on the left.

At zero hour artillery rolling barrage will start from 100 to 150 yards in front of Hessian Trench and roll towards the objective.

The attack will be made in three waves as under and will follow the artillery barrage as close as possible.

1st Wave. 2 companies in line, 'B' Coy. on the right and 'C' Coy. on the left. One L.G. [Lewis gun] will be in the centre of each Coy. and one on either flank of the wave with platoon bombers. Each man in first wave will carry 2 grenades in side pockets.

2nd Wave. 'A' Company in line extended across whole Battalion front. Each man to carry 5 grenades No. 5 and pick or shovel strapped on the back (proportion of 1 pick to 3 shovels). 2 L.G.s. on flanks with platoon bombers. Half Bn. [Battalion] bombers on extreme right flank.

3rd Wave. 'D' Company in line extended across whole Battalion front. Each man to carry 5 grenades. The following details will advance with this line:

Bn. snipers 2 to each L.G. and Vickers Gun.
2 reserve L.Gs.
Half Bn. bombers on extreme right flank.
'C' Detachment signallers.
1 Stokes Gun on each flank.
2 Vickers Guns.

Junction of Kendal Sap with Regina Trench will mark division between 'B' and 'C' Companies.

As soon as the objective is gained all the L.Gs. will push forward 100 to 150 yards in front of the trench, each accompanied by 2 snipers carrying tools, where they will consolidate in shell holes.

The bombers will bomb down Regina Trench eastwards until in touch with the 18th Division who are bombing westwards up that trench.

The V.Gs. [Vickers guns] will take up suitable positions in or behind the captured line.

In case of troops on the flanks failing to gain their objective defensive flanks will at once be formed by L.Gs. and bombers.

As soon as the objective is occupied all men not actually required for consolidation etc. in Regina Trench will commence work on C.Ts [communications trenches] back to Hessian Trench as follows:

All available men of 'B' and right half of 'A' deepening and Kendal Sap. All available men of 'C' and left half of 'A' on C.T. from suitable point in front line to existing trench at R22.d.4.9.

EQUIPMENT

Battle with 2 sandbags rolled on back of belt, unexpended days ration, 1 days rations and the iron rations. Filled waterbottles.

Grenades carried by men other than Bn. or platoon bombers will not be used without orders but will be collected and dumps formed in suitable places in captured trench.

2 dumps one in each Company frontage will be formed in Hessian [to] contain the reserves of ammunition and supplies. Police and Pioneers will be detailed to take charge of these under the B.S.M. [Brigade Sergeant Major] and be prepared to carry forward supplies as required.

Bn. H&Q [Battalion headquarters] will be situated at R.22.d.9.9. in Hessian Trench.

Frequent messages and reports are to be sent back.

Prisoners to be sent back overland as soon as possible to Hessian Trench whence they will be dealt with by 2nd R.I.R. [Royal Irish Rifles].

Red flares will be carried in the proportion of 1 to every 3 men and will be burnt in answer to signals on the klaxon horn by areoplane [sic] by men in the captured trench.

One red flag per platoon and by Bn. bombers will be carried.

White tapes to mark the line of advance will be laid on either flank in the night 18/19 inst from Hessian Trench towards the objective on previously obtained compass bearings.

Zero hour will be notified later and watches synchronised at 9.0 a.m.

L.G. Bird, Lieut. Colonel,
Commanding 11th Bn. The Lancashire Fusiliers

21 October 1916 Following the attack on Regina Trench by the 11th Battalion, the following report was written by Lt. Col. Bird (preserved in the National Archives, Kew, WO 95/2246–7):

The objective assigned to this Battalion was from R2 3.a.20.4.5 to R22. b.4.4. Assembly trench was that portion of Hessian Trench opposite to the objective.

The Battalion had been previously formed up at Ovillers Post in order in which it was to attack on the afternoon of 20th as follows:

1st Wave. 'B' Company in line on the right, 'C' Company in line on the left.

2nd Wave. 'A' Company in line, with half Bn. [Battalion] bombers on either flank.

3rd Wave. 'D' Company in line with 2 reserve Lewis Gun teams in addition to Company Guns.

The 2nd and 3rd waves were then closed on the 1st wave. The Battalion paraded in this order when proceeding to the trenches, the whole line being split up into four parties irrespective of Companies and marched via Ovillers and 'K' dump where bombs, sandbags, etc. were issued, thence via Centre Way and Lancs Trench into Hessian Trench.

The last party arrived about 3.0 a.m. in the Assembly trench where work on improving trench and means of exit was carried out for the remainder of the night. By daybreak 21st everything was in readiness for the attack.

At zero hour 12.6 p.m. 21st when the first barrage opened, the leading wave went over the parapet, and moved up close to the barrage followed at about 30 yards distance by 2nd and 3rd waves. One section of 74th M.G. [machine gun] Company being in the centre of the 3rd wave. Two Stokes Guns of 74th T.M. [trench mortar] Battery were concentrated on strong point on our extreme right.

All waves followed the lifts of the barrage closely.

On the final barrage lifting off Regina Trench, the leading wave rushed the trench, whereupon the majority of the garrison surrendered. The enemy however showed fight in two portions of the trench, namely on the extreme right, where about 30 men under an Officer resisted with rifle fire and bombs. A Lewis Gun was brought into action on the parapet against them, and a bombing party worked down the trench, led by 2nd Lieut. R.K. Beswick. The enemy were also attacked by a bombing party of the 8th Norfolks on our right.

After about half the enemy party had been killed and wounded the remainder surrendered, and were sent back across No Man's Land to Hessian Trench. The bombing party then advanced and gained touch with the 8th Norfolks.

The other party, numbering about 12 held out at about R22.b.6.3. After several had been killed the remainder surrendered.

This completed the capture of the whole objective, time being about 12.50 p.m. the left bombing party being in touch with the 9th L.N. Lancs. [Loyal North Lancashires].

During this fighting, visual messages were sent back to the signal station in Hessian Trench asking for more bombs. Large numbers of enemy stick grenades were found in the trench and were used against them.

Lewis Gun teams and snipers were then pushed out about 50 to 70 yards in front of the captured position, five posts in all being established along the Battalion front. Some of the more advanced posts had to be slightly withdrawn owing to their coming under our own barrage, which was placed closer to our trench than had been expected.

Supplies of bombs were brought over by parties of 2nd R.I.R. [Royal Irish Rifles] under Lieut. Leach, No Man's Land being traversed several times.

The enemy's artillery fire was slow in opening and all waves got across, most of the casualties suffered being due to the leading wave keeping rather too close under the first barrage.

The enemy appeared to be taken by surprise as none of them had their equipment on.

Work of consolidating the position was at once put in hand.

The enemy did not commence to shell the captured position heavily till the following morning, but from this time until about 4.0 p.m. when the Battalion was relieved by 7th Queens R. & W. [Royal West] Surrey Regt. [Regiment] he shelled the trench consistently with 77 M/M [77 mm shells] and 4.2 [4.2-inch mortars] doing a considerable amount of damage to the trench and causing some casualties.

I regret to report that Lieut. R.F. Mackinnon commanding 'D' Coy. and 2nd Lieut. A.H. Bradbeer 3rd Manchester Regt. attached to this Bn. were killed whilst crossing No Man's Land.

Operation orders are attached, and recommendations will follow.

Lieut. Colonel,
Commanding 11th Bn. The Lancashire Fusiliers

9 November 1916 Tolkien's war service diary places him at the 1st Southern General Hospital on 9 November. The Medical Board report of 2 December 1916 gives the date of his admission as 10 November, perhaps counting from his first full day as a patient. (The same report states that he remained at the Red Cross Hospital at Le Touquet for nine days, while Tolkien's diary indicates ten, from 29 October to 7 November inclusive.)

End of 1916–first half of 1917 In later years Tolkien said that *The Fall of Gondolin* was the first tale in his mythology to be written; and so it seems to be, if one discounts *The Cottage of Lost Play* as not strictly a 'tale'. But *The Cottage of Lost Play* was certainly in existence by mid-February 1917, when Edith Tolkien made a fair copy, while revisions to *Sea-Song of an Elder Day* in spring or summer 1917, which connect that poem with the story of Tuor, would seem to reflect work on *The Fall of Gondolin* in the first half of 1917. Tolkien does not appear to have been occupied with any other part of his mythology until the episode in Roos in late May or early June 1917 inspired *The Tale of Tinúviel* (*'Of Beren and Lúthien'). For further arguments on dating, see **Reader's Guide**, various entries.

27 February 1917 Humphrey Carpenter's account of Tolkien's movements during 1917 and the first half of 1918 disagrees on several points with Tolkien's Army medical record, which was not yet open to consultation in the Public Record Office when Carpenter was writing the *Biography*. He says (p. 95):

Towards the end of his sick leave at Great Haywood he was taken ill again. He got better after a few weeks and was posted temporarily to Yorkshire. Edith and her cousin Jennie packed their belongings and followed him north, moving into furnished lodgings a few miles from his camp, at Hornsea. But after he had returned to duty he went sick once more, and was put into a Harrogate sanatorium. . . . By April he was passed fit again.

The official record however indicates no point when Tolkien might have been considered fit enough to be posted to Yorkshire until after he had been treated at Harrogate.

19 April 1917 Humphrey Carpenter writes in *Biography*, pp. 95–6, that by April 1917 Tolkien 'was passed fit again and was sent for further training at an army signalling school in the North-East. There was a good chance that if he passed an examination he might be appointed Signals Officer at the Yorkshire camp, a post that would probably keep him from the trenches. He sat the examination in July, but failed. A few days later he was taken ill again.' Tolkien's official Army record (concerned only with his fitness for duty and his place of posting, and not with his duties) does not mention signals training at this time; the *Service Record of King Edward's School, Birmingham during the War 1914–1919* (1920, p. 143), however, includes a cryptic note concerning Tolkien: 'July 1917 Lt., Signal Dépôt'.

?Late May–?early June 1917 Internal evidence in *The Tale of Tinúviel* and in later retellings suggests that the visit to the wood near Roos took place in early summer, probably in late May or early June. The flowering season for hemlocks and other umbellifers in England at its widest range is May to September. Tolkien also mentions chestnut trees in flower and white moths fluttering: chestnut trees usually flower in late May or early June, and moths are unlikely to be active outside the warmer months. In *The Tale of Tinúviel* Tolkien actually states that Beren first saw Tinúviel 'on a time of June' (*The Book of Lost Tales, Part Two*, p. 10). As for external evidence, Tolkien was certainly with the Humber Garrison between mid-April and mid-August 1917, except for a period at a signalling school.

Humphrey Carpenter in *Biography*, p. 97, dates the incident in Roos after the birth of the Tolkiens' first child on 16 November 1917, and, despite Tolkien's statement to Christopher Bretherton, places the writing of *The Tale of Tinúviel* after *The Tale of Turambar*, thus presumably in 1918. It seems unlikely, however, that Edith would have danced on the windy east coast of England in the middle of winter 1917–18, while still recovering from a difficult birth.

c. 22 November 1917 Carpenter states in *Biography*, p. 97, that after the christening of John Tolkien 'Edith brought the child back to Yorkshire, moving into furnished rooms at Roos', after which he dates the episode of Edith dancing in the wood (see entry for Late May–early June 1917). It seems almost certain that Edith, John, and Jennie Grove returned to Yorkshire to be close to Tolkien, but we have found no specific evidence of a move between ?late September 1917, when Edith and Jennie went to Cheltenham, and spring (?May) 1918, when Edith, John, and Jennie moved to Gipsy Green in Staffordshire.

Spring (?May) 1918 The connection between the names *Gipsy Green* and *Fladweth Amrod* is suggested by John Garth in *Tolkien and the Great War*.

10 March 1920 In an interview conducted shortly after Tolkien's death Nevill Coghill recalled that it was he, as Secretary of the Exeter College Essay Club, who had asked Tolkien to read a paper, and that when told that its subject would be 'the fall of Gondolin' he spent weeks fruitlessly trying to find a reference to it. But according to the Exeter College archives, Coghill was elected to the Essay Club only on 27 February 1920, and held no office. Unless he completely misremembered the circumstances, more than fifty years later, it seems likely that Coghill met Tolkien not long before the meeting and asked him what he would be reading for the occasion, but was not involved in its planning. Tolkien's introduction of course states that it was only as a last resort that he read *The Fall of Gondolin*, in lieu of the expected critical paper.

1 October 1920 Humphrey Carpenter states in *Letters*, p. 437, note 46, that Tolkien's salary appears to have been £500, but Leeds University records show that it was in fact £600.

March 1921 Humphrey Carpenter states in *Biography*, p. 103, that Tolkien did not find temporary accommodation for his family 'until the beginning of 1921'. Christopher Tolkien, however, informs us that his father took furnished rooms at 5 Holly Bank more specifically in March 1921, and that his family moved there after the Leeds spring vacation.

Hilary Term 1926 In *Biography* Humphrey Carpenter describes a meeting of the Kolbítar in John Bryson's rooms in *Balliol* College, Oxford, and in *The Inklings* he describes Bryson as the English tutor at Balliol during the time of the Kolbítar. In fact Bryson did not move to Balliol, as a Fellow, until after the outbreak of the Second World War. The Kolbítar probably met in his rooms in the High Street, Oxford, which his obituary in the London *Times* (20 August 1976) mentions were a popular meeting place for his friends in the 1920s and 1930s.

5 June 1926 After examiners have read and considered a written thesis they then examine the candidate orally (*viva voce*), in public, and in particular ask for elaboration on any weak or confused points.

?Late 1920s or 1930s T.A. Shippey refers to these poems in *J.R.R. Tolkien: Author of the Century* (2000), p. 278, but there is no basis for the title *Sigurðarkviða hin nyja*. See instead his *Road to Middle-earth* (1982, 2nd edn. 1992), p. 277.

4 November 1927 The Applications Committee decides most matters concerning research students: whom to accept as a probationer, B.Litt., or D.Phil. student, the allocation of supervisors and examiners, approval of the subjects of theses, requests to prolong or interrupt residence while working on a thesis, etc. The members usually meet a day or so before the Board meetings, but sometimes earlier the same day, and report their decisions at the general meeting for the Board to affirm. No minutes are kept, so one cannot be certain which Committee meetings Tolkien attended.

Summer 1928 Humphrey Carpenter suggests in *Biography* that *Mr. Bliss*, in which the title character has misadventures with a car, dates from 1932 when Tolkien bought his first car and proved to be a hazardous driver. Joan (Mrs Michael) Tolkien, however, in 1982 stated in a letter to the *Sunday Times* that *Mr. Bliss* was written for Tolkien's three sons in 1928, and that Mr Bliss's car was inspired by a toy owned by Christopher. Of course the story may not have been written down immediately, but it seems more suitable to the ages of the boys in 1928 than in 1932. See further, the entry for *Mr. Bliss* in **Reader's Guide**.

26 April 1931 At the beginning of the academic year Tolkien projected two further series of lectures for Trinity Term 1931, which were not given: The Germani: Problems of Gothic Philology, and Introduction to the *Elder Edda*.

8 October 1933 From this point the *Oxford University Gazette* lists continuing postgraduate students at the beginning of each term.

?Michaelmas Term 1933 On 11 September 1967 Tolkien recalled that Tangye Lean's Inklings 'soon died . . . but C.S. L[ewis] and I at least survived. Its name was then transferred (by C.S.L.) to the undetermined and unelected circle of friends who gathered about C.S.L., and met in his rooms in Magdalen' (letter to William Luther White, *Letters*, p. 388). Humphrey Carpenter notes in *The Inklings* that although Tolkien seems to imply in this letter that the transfer of the name 'Inklings' from Tangye Lean's group to the 'circle of friends' around Lewis 'took place as soon as Tangye Lean's club broke up, which would be in about 1933 [when Tangye Lean graduated]', 'there is no record of precisely when this happened – if indeed it was a precise event and not a gradual process' (p. 67). In 1990 Owen Barfield recalled in a memoir that he could not agree with the statement in *Brothers and Friends* (which he wrongly ascribed to Walter Hooper) that the 'probable' date of the beginning of the latter Inklings was 1933. There were, he recalled, 'quite a few meetings – enough to constitute a "series" – in Lewis's room in the twenties between Lewis, Tolkien, and myself, sometimes together with Colin Hardie, and at least one with Nevill Coghill. I think it was these foregatherings that ultimately turned into the Inklings, though it may well be that the name was not adopted until 1933' ('The Inklings Remembered', *The World & I* (April 1990), p. 548).

26 March 1934 Tolkien and the Lewis brothers met regularly in early 1934 to read the four operas of Wagner's *Der Ring des Nibelungen*, in preparation for a planned attendance of the complete cycle at Covent Garden in London along with their friends Owen Barfield and Cecil Harwood. In the event, Harwood failed to book their seats. Priscilla Tolkien recalls, however, that her father and C.S. Lewis once attended a performance of one of the operas, possibly *Siegfried*, at Covent Garden, where they found themselves to be almost the only members of the audience in their part of the theatre not in evening dress.

11 June 1935 Priscilla Tolkien believes, though she is not certain, that her father was unable to attend the funeral of Father Francis, but was represented there by his son John.

?Early 1936 Accounts vary regarding the circumstances by which Susan Dagnall learned of *The Hobbit* and came to borrow the typescript for consideration by George Allen & Unwin. See further, entry for *The Hobbit* in **Reader's Guide**.

16 January 1936 On 30 August 1937 (see entry) Mabel Day informed Tolkien that according to Dr Pollard, he seems never to have received Tolkien's letter arguing in favour of line-by-line presentation. It may be that Tolkien wrote two drafts of the letter, but never posted a final version.

13 February 1937 In her letter of 23 January 1937 Susan Dagnall arranged to meet Tolkien in company with C.A. Furth. Since Furth met with Tolkien on 27 February, however, it seems likely that he did not accompany Dagnall earlier in the month.

?9 July 1937 Tolkien speculated some thirty years after the fact that his sketch *Death of Smaug* (*Artist and Illustrator*, fig. 137) dated from around 1936. We have suggested in *Artist and Illustrator* that it may have been drawn earlier, as an aid to working out the climax of Chapter 14 of *The Hobbit*; but it also seems possible that the sketch dates instead from July 1937, and was an abandoned attempt by Tolkien to develop one of the colour illustrations he produced at that time.

2 October 1937 *The Loom of Language: A Guide to Foreign Languages for the Home Student* by Frederick Bodmer, edited and arranged by Lancelot Hogben, was published by Allen & Unwin in 1943.

15 December 1937 The reviewer's exact words were: 'The few pages of (presumably) prose transcript from the original are immeasurably better in every way [than the *Lay of Leithian*]; the tale here proceeds at a stinging pace and is told with a picturesque brevity and dignity that holds the reader's interest in spite of its eye-splitting Celtic names' (Tolkien-George Allen & Unwin archive, HarperCollins). It is not clear what these 'few pages' were. Humphrey Carpenter suggested in *Biography* that they were included to give Allen & Unwin's reader the end of the story of the unfinished poem, which Christopher Tolkien accepted in his note at the end of *The Lays of Beleriand* (p. 365). But there is apparently no surviving suitable prose account of the end of the story of Beren and Lúthien which fits this description. Neither the synopses that accompanied the writing of the *Lay of Leithien*, nor the draft that declined into a scrawl from which the final *Quenta Silmarillion* version was made, seems a suitable candidate. Tolkien could not have detached a part of the *Quenta Silmarillion* for that purpose, since the end of the story was written only during the time that the *Lay of Leithian* and the *Quenta Silmarillion* were with Allen & Unwin. It may be that he sent part of the *Quenta Noldorinwa* or part of his first, abandoned attempt to write the tale for the *Quenta Silmarillion*; or it could be that the pages in question no longer exist.

22 December 1937 A first printing of *The Hobbit* inscribed to K.M. Kilbride and with an added manuscript verse by Tolkien in Anglo-Saxon (partly derived from one in *The Lost Road*) was sold by Sotheby's New York on 13 December 2002. Either Kilbride managed to find a first printing to send to Tolkien, or Tolkien somehow still had a copy to spare.

14 February 1938 In *Amon Hen* 28 (August 1977), and again in the souvenir book of the 1992 Tolkien Centenary Conference, Canon N.S. Power recalled the delight with which *Farmer Giles of Ham* was greeted by the members of the Lovelace Society, and how after the reading there was a round of port and a discussion. 'One undergraduate asked about the truth underlying all legends – he referred especially to Dragons – and Tolkien said, "Yes – there was always a kernel of fact behind a legend." He pulled out of a pocket . . . a *leprechaun's shoe!*' It measured about six to seven inches and was very green, as if lizard's skin, with a long thin pointed toe. 'I still don't know how serious Tolkien was, or what the shoe was really. He *seemed* quite serious' (*Amon Hen* 28, p. 18). The minutes of the Lovelace Society record that Power was indeed present on the occasion; but they also record that there was neither criticism nor discussion following Tolkien's story, at least not as part of the official meeting.

10 February 1939 There is no record in the Allen & Unwin archives that Tolkien sent his publisher any typescript of *The Lord of the Rings* as completed to this date. Such evidence as there is suggests that he did no more work on *The Lord of the Rings* until August 1939.

August–autumn 1939 Of his father's work on *The Lord of the Rings* in the latter part of August through autumn 1939, Christopher Tolkien writes (**The Treason of Isengard* (1989), p. 5):

> I doubt that it would be possible to deduce a perfectly clear and coherent, step-by-step chronology of this period in the narrative evolution, or to relate precisely the development of the early chapters of what became Book II to the new work on Book I; for my father moved back and forth, trying out new conceptions and then perhaps abandoning them, and producing such a tangle of change as cannot always be untied.

– In his Foreword to the second edition of *The Lord of the Rings* (1965) Tolkien said that in writing the story he suffered delays because of his academic duties, which were

> increased by the outbreak of war in 1939, by the end of which year the tale had not yet reached the end of Book I. In spite of the darkness of the next five years I found that the story could not now be wholly abandoned, and I plodded on, mostly by night, till I stood by Balin's tomb in Moria. There I halted for a long while. It was almost a year later when I went on and so came to Lothlórien and the Great River late in 1941.

'This can only mean,' as Christopher Tolkien has said, 'that the story was broken off in Moria late in 1940.' But Tolkien's letter to Stanley Unwin on 19 December 1939 clearly indicates that he was at work on 'The Mines of Moria' in 1939, from which Christopher Tolkien has convincingly argued that the hiatus in writing must have begun instead in 1939 rather than 1940. 'I feel sure, therefore, that – more than a quarter of a century later – [my father] erred in his recollection of the year' (Christopher Tolkien, *The Return of the Shadow*, p. 461) – a memory, perhaps, of his revision of the Moria episode rather than its initial writing. (See further, entry for Late August 1940–?late 1941.)

15 October 1939 At the end of Trinity Term 1939 Tolkien was scheduled to give the following lectures in Michaelmas Term 1939: Old English Verse: Metre, Style, and Diction on Tuesdays and Thursdays at 11.00 a.m. in the Examination Schools, beginning 17 October; and The *Fréswæl* (Episode and Fragment) (i.e. the 'Finn episode' in *Beowulf* and *The Fight at Finnesburg*) on Tuesdays and Thursdays at 12.00 noon in the Examination Schools, beginning 17 October. According to the *Oxford University Gazette* for 8 September, however, the schedule of lectures for Michaelmas Term was cancelled, and we have found no revised schedule in subsequent numbers of the *Gazette*. Alan Bliss has recalled specifically that Tolkien's lectures on the *Fréswæl* were cancelled for this term. The fact that Tolkien's lectures scheduled for Hilary Term 1940 include '*Exodus* (2)', that is, a continuation of lectures on the Old English *Exodus*, could mean that he began a course on that work during Michaelmas Term 1939.

23 November 1939 C.S. Lewis, Charles Williams, C.L. Wrenn, and Williams' colleague Gerard Hopkins began to read *Irene Iddesleigh* when they met the previous week. According to Walter Hooper, it became a customary feature of Inklings meetings to bet that no one could read a passage from the writings of Amanda M'Kitterick Ros (1860–1939), the 'World's Worst Writer', with a straight face (C.S. Lewis, *Collected Letters*, vol. 2 (2004), p. 294, n. 168).

6–12 June 1940 It is traditionally a bad omen for a wild bird to enter a house.

Late August 1940–?late 1941 On the question of a hiatus in the writing of *The Lord of the Rings* since autumn 1939, Christopher Tolkien comments (*The Treason of Isengard*, p. 67) that 'it may be much oversimplified to suppose that nothing at all was done' in this period; and yet no relevant papers exist that are dated between autumn 1939 and the 'New Plot' of 26–27 August 1940. Nor can it be said with certainty how far Tolkien progressed with the book in the period August–autumn 1940, or which work was done during the Christmas vacation 1940–1, or at some other time or times before late 1941, except that some revisions may be dated to no earlier than February and March 1941 (see further, entry and note for Late 1941–1942). That a gap in the writing occurred in autumn 1940 is evident from Tolkien's comment in a letter to his son Michael on 2 January 1941, that he 'got as far as getting my story out again'. The next clearly datable part of the *Lord of the Rings* manuscripts belongs to the winter of 1941–2.

In *The Treason of Isengard*, p. 129 ff., Christopher Tolkien places the writing of the fifth version of 'The Council of Elrond' during this period, though not necessarily immediately following the writing of the fourth. Later, however (see *The War of the Ring* (1990), p. 149), he found evidence that the fifth version might have been made subsequent to 1944. But other indications, such as the name *Ond* changed to *Ondor*, support an earlier date, before the name became *Gondor* in 1942 – though Tolkien was not always consistent in making emendations. Also, some of the new material in the fifth version is written on the examination scripts sent from the United States (see entry for 5 August 1940), which had been almost exhausted by the time Tolkien came to write 'Farewell to Lórien' (published bk. II, ch. 8), of which chapter Christopher Tolkien made a typescript in August 1942.

In regard to the 'facsimiles' of the Book of Mazarbul, Christopher Tolkien recalls seeing his father make the finished versions in 20 Northmoor Road, therefore between early 1941, when he made the earlier versions, and March 1947, when the Tolkiens left Northmoor Road for Manor Road.

27 July 1941 This date is wrongly given as 29 July in Charles Williams, *To Michal from Serge* (2002).

Late 1941–?January 1942 In his Foreword to the second edition of *The Lord of the Rings* (1965) Tolkien said that in writing the story, having 'halted for a long while' at Balin's tomb in Moria, 'it was almost a year later when I went on and so came to Lothlórien and the Great River late in 1941.' Manuscript and textual evidence appears to confirm this date. – In *Artist and Illustrator* the present authors dated the drawing *The Forest of Lothlorien in Spring* to 'probably around late 1940 . . . [when Tolkien] began to write of the dream-like land of the Elves east of Moria, and the resemblance of the title border of the drawing to that of *Spring 1940* [*Artist and Illustrator*, fig. 3] further suggests that it dates from early in that decade' (p. 164). The latter point, however, now seems weak evidence on which to pin a date, and in any case the chronology at this point is reasonably clear in pointing to 1941 rather than 1940.

?February–?Midsummer 1942 In his Foreword to the second edition of *The Lord of the Rings* (1965) Tolkien says that in 1942 he 'wrote the first drafts of the matter that now stands as Book III, and the beginnings of Chapters 1 and 3 of Book V. . . .' After 9 February 1942 the next datable manuscript related to *The Lord of the Rings* is a letter of 31 July 1942, on the back of which Tolkien drafted a passage for Book III, Chapter 8 ('The Road to Isengard').

?April 1942 Although Tolkien wrote to his Aunt Jane Neave on 8–9 September 1962 that *Leaf by Niggle* 'was written (I think) just before the [Second World] War began, though I first read it aloud to my friends early in 1940' (*Letters*, p. 320), and in his introductory note to *Tree and Leaf* (1964) he recalled that it was written in the period 1938–9, it seems certain that he was referring to *Leaf by Niggle* in a postcard he wrote to the poet Alan Rook on 21 April 1943, in which he hopes that Rook will one day (metaphorically) paint a 'great picture', and promises to send him a story relevant to 'pictures' that Tolkien 'wrote this time last year' (reproduced on eBay online auctions, October 2001).

7 June 1944 Marquette University (*Libraries and archives) holds typescripts made by Tolkien at this time of all of the chapters of Book IV of *The Lord of the Rings* except for 'The Black Gate Is Closed'. Of that chapter *only* there is a carefully written manuscript. It seems that both Tolkien's own typewriter and Christopher Tolkien's typewriter, which he had left behind while in the R.A.F., broke around this time. In a letter to Stanley Unwin of 29 June 1944 Tolkien remarked: 'It is frightfully difficult and/or expensive getting anything typed in this town, and when my typewriter broke down nobody would repair it' (*Letters*, p. 86). On 27 June he wrote to Christopher: 'I managed to get the typewriter (yours) repaired: so I can now get on on my own' (courtesy of Christopher Tolkien). By 7 July he was using his own 'Hammond' typewriter again.

10 October–?end of October 1944 Tolkien says in his Foreword to the second edition of *The Lord of the Rings* that as well as writing the first drafts of Book III at the end of 1942, he also began to write Chapters 1 and 3 of Book V ('Minas Tirith' and 'The Muster of Rohan'). Christopher Tolkien, however, has found nothing relating to Book V which might have been written in 1942, and taking this together with Tolkien's remark in his letter of 12 October 1944 that he had actually begun Book V, thinks that his father's memory erred when writing the new Foreword in 1966 (and evidently also when writing to his Aunt Jane Neave in 1962: see *Letters*, p. 321), and that the beginnings of Book V should be placed instead in October 1944. This view seems to be confirmed by the mention in one of the drafts for 'Minas Tirith' of Faramir, who did not enter the story until 1944.

?27 November 1944 In *Inklings*, pp. 121–2, Humphrey Carpenter writes: "'This morning I reached Magdalen at 11 a.m.,'" Tolkien recorded one Monday morning . . .' which he identifies as a quotation from a letter to Christopher Tolkien dated 29 November 1944; but that date was a Wednesday.

?Christmas 1944 C.S. Lewis describes this occasion in his introduction to *Arthurian Torso* (1948), and says that it took place 'in vacation' (p. 2). Williams' letters to his wife seem to indicate that he may have begun to write *The Figure of Arthur* by 6 December 1944, was definitely working on it on 30 December, and had done a little more by 3 February 1945. He wrote five chapters before his death in May 1945. His reading of the first two chapters therefore could have taken place in Easter vacation 1945, but the Christmas vacation of 1944 seems more likely.

Christmas 1945–August 1946 In regard to Tolkien's statement that he had written 'three parts' of *The Notion Club Papers* during 'a fortnight of comparative leisure', Christopher Tolkien concludes in *Sauron Defeated* that the quantity of material constituting *The Notion Club Papers*, or associated with that work, could not possibly have been written in so short a time. He argues that during the 'fortnight' around Christmas 1945 his father wrote the first two manuscripts of Part One and the manuscript of Part Two (as far as it proceeds); and that the rest of the work (the later versions of the both parts of *The Notion Club Papers*, the work on the Adunaic language, and *The Drowning of Anadûnê*) was written during the first part of 1946. The fact that Tolkien read *The Drowning of Anadûnê* to Christopher in summer 1946, and to the Inklings on 22 August 1946, supports the view that he continued to work on that tale into the middle of the year.

c. **23 September 1946–?October 1947** One of the differences between 'The Story Foreseen from Forannest' (mentioned later in this entry) and the final text reveals that Tolkien wrote this outline before he wrote the latter part of 'The Siege of Gondor'; but it is also clear that it was written after the initial drafting for 'The Ride of the Rohirrim'. From this Christopher Tolkien believes that his father probably worked on the two chapters simultaneously, moving back and forth between them.

14 August–14 September 1948 Christopher Tolkien has mentioned, when recounting the slim evidence for the chronology of the writing of *The Lord of the Rings* in its later period, that there are 'two pages on which my father made a list of candidates for an academic post with notes on their previous experience. Against several of the names he noted both date of birth and present age, from which it is clear that the year was 1948' (*Sauron Defeated*, p. 12). On the versos of these leaves is drafting for 'The Land of Shadow' and 'The Tower of Kirith Ungol'. These pages are presumably notes made by Tolkien in April 1948 when considering candidates for the Chair of Education at the Institute of Education, London; see entries for 10 and 12 April 1948, above. It seems likely, however, that Tolkien did not return to *The Lord of the Rings* as early as April 1948, but instead wrote Book VI during the summer vacation, beginning perhaps even before he moved to Woodcote for a month.

27 October 1949 This letter is given in full in the Lewis *Collected Letters*, vol. 2 (2004), pp. 990–1, with the date 27 October 1949. Carpenter cites it in *Inklings*, p. 277, as written on 21 October 1949. The phrase 'If I include none of my adverse criticisms . . .' as quoted in *Biography* seems correct in context, whereas 'If I include more of my adverse criticism . . .' given in *Collected Letters* does not.

4 April 1950 Lewis dated the diary entry from which this note is drawn as 'Saturday 4 April', but in 1950 4 April was a Tuesday.

26 January 1951 A recognized student at Oxford is one who is not a member of a college or the University, but is placed under an academic advisor.

Late July–15 August 1951 Tolkien later incorrectly inscribed one of these drawings 'Aug. 1952'. We, in *J.R.R. Tolkien: Artist and Illustrator*, and Humphrey Carpenter in *Biography*, did not question this date, but when we tried to fit the holiday into the present chronology we found no gap unaccounted for in August 1952, or indeed during the summer vacation 1952. Priscilla Tolkien, however, has a clear memory of the holiday, just after her final examinations at Oxford, and was able to confirm that it took place in 1951, not 1952.

26 October 1951 We could find no examiners' report for T.J. Grace in the Oxford University Archives, or notification of a viva date in the *Oxford University Gazette*, but the examination was evidently completed by 17 April 1952.

?Late 1951–?early 1952 Christopher Tolkien dates this revision of the 'earliest' *Annals of Valinor* to 1951 or later in *The Shaping of Middle-earth*, p. 282, since it has 'Melkor' and not 'Melko', a change which appears in a list headed 'Alterations in last revision 1951'. Tolkien often wavered over changes of name, however, and Christopher Tolkien notes in *The Lost Road and Other Writings*, p. 338, a use of 'Melkor' in the conclusion of the *Quenta Silmarillion* written at the end of 1937. It may be significant that Tolkien lectured on the glosses in the Vespasian Psalter in the 1930s and the first half of the 1940s, while he was Professor of Anglo-Saxon, but not after 1945.

7 December 1951 Burchfield continued to be listed as a D.Phil. student under Tolkien until Hilary Term 1957, later than the dates given in this statement, but it may be that the listings in the *Oxford University Gazette* continued for the maximum period that the regulations allowed a student to work on the degree, even though he was no longer actually working.

Late August 1952 In both his sleeve notes for the Caedmon LPs and his enlarged account of Tolkien's visit in the 1992 *Proceedings* Sayer suggests that it was the making of the recordings that inspired Tolkien to contact Rayner

Unwin again about *The Lord of the Rings*. But this account is contradicted by material in the Tolkien-George Allen & Unwin archive, HarperCollins, and by correspondence between Tolkien and the Sayers sold at Christie's South Kensington in 2001.

16 October 1953 According to the Oxford University Archives, the Applications Committee on this occasion also appointed Tolkien the supervisor of B.Litt. student J. Bruhn, who was working on *The Conception of National Socialism in English Literature and Public Opinion from the Foundation of the NSDAP to the Occupation of Czechoslovakia (1919–March 1939)*. This, however, was not listed in the *Oxford University Gazette*, and it seems a strange subject for Tolkien to supervise. We suspect that there is an error in the official record.

18 May 1954 This seems to be the meeting described by Humphrey Carpenter in *The Inklings*, pp. 229–30. He comments that F.P. Wilson and David Cecil, the Professors of English Literature, did not share the view held by Tolkien and by C.S. Lewis that Victorian literature should be excluded from compulsory examinations in the Oxford English School, so as to leave room for Old English and medieval studies; and at about this time a committee was established, 'which also included Humphry House and Helen Gardner' besides Professors Wilson and Cecil, to consider possible changes to the syllabus.

As Professor of English Language and Literature, Tolkien was an inevitable choice to be a fifth member of the committee, and he was eventually persuaded by his colleagues on it that the time had come to restore Victorian literature to the syllabus, and indeed to extend the period of study into the twentieth century. This was what the committee recommended to the full Faculty in their report.

Lewis was still passionately devoted to the syllabus that he and Tolkien had created. He was now deeply upset that Tolkien had deserted their cause.... Before the Faculty meeting which was to vote on the report, he campaigned energetically; and at the meeting he made an impassioned speech championing the present syllabus and opposing any changes. He achieved his aim, for the proposals were voted down for the time being, despite opposition led by David Cecil.... Moreover, among those who voted against them was Tolkien, for Lewis had persuaded him to change his mind; so the Faculty was presented with the spectacle of Tolkien voting in the full meeting against proposals which he himself had helped to draft in committee.

Carpenter gives no date for this meeting. T.A. Shippey in *The Road to Middle-earth* (p. 22) dates it to 1951, possibly because in the paragraph preceding those quoted above Carpenter discussed the Professorship of Poetry election of 1951. The present writers kept Carpenter's account in mind while searching the Oxford University Archives, but found no other occasion which corresponds as closely as that of May 1954. The only discrepancy between the two is that Helen Gardner was not a member of the committee set up by the Faculty Board to consider the matter (see entry for 12 March 1954). Carpenter's account clearly depends on the memories of one or more of those present at the Faculty meeting, who may have conflated memories of this meeting with other attempts to make changes in the syllabus. In 1952 Helen Gardner and Humphry House proposed that the Preliminary Examination (not the Final Honour Examination) be revised, but no committee was formed, nor was there a meeting of the Faculty. In 1955, after C.S. Lewis had left Oxford University for Cambridge, Helen Gardner (but not Tolkien) was a member of a committee formed to discuss both the preliminary and final examinations.

Carpenter does not explain that the proposal to make Victorian literature a compulsory subject applied only to Course III, for students whose main interest was literature (see *Oxford English School), and not to those who chose to concentrate on Old and Middle English, and Philology. A similar suggestion that the nineteenth century should be compulsory for Course III students was made during the reform of the English School syllabus at the beginning of the 1930s, in which Tolkien and Lewis took a prominent part. On one document of that time (see entry for 22 May 1931) is a note: 'Professor Tolkien would agree to the modification but considers it a matter primarily for the decision of those mainly concerned with the direction of the work in modern literature' (Oxford University Archives FA 4/5/2/3). If this was still Tolkien's view in 1954, it would explain why he voted against the proposed change when the views of the majority of the Faculty became clear.

Carpenter's account has been cited as evidence of a growing rift between Tolkien and Lewis, or as one of the reasons for it. At this time, however, Tolkien had been supporting Lewis in his election to the chair of Medieval and Renaissance English at Cambridge, and only the day before the Faculty meeting had visited Lewis and persuaded him to accept.

9 September 1954 Evidence suggests that Margaret Douglas actually typed only Book IV, not the whole of *The Two Towers*. – Part of the enclosure is published in *Letters*, p. 185, erroneously dated to 18 September. The error apparently arose because, in the Allen & Unwin files, the pages that had been sent with Tolkien's letter of 9 September became attached to his later letter of 18 September, to W.N. Beard. In the latter Tolkien says that he has had no response to the answers and queries he had enclosed with the letter sent on 9 September, and in case Rayner is away, summarizes them from memory. This summary agrees with the four sides of comments now attached to the letter of 18 September.

26 January 1955 Rayner Unwin told Tolkien in June 1954 that Allen & Unwin intended to make *The Return of the King* the same length as *The Two Towers*, which would have allowed about 44 pages for the Appendices; and on 22 October 1954 he told Tolkien that *The Tale of Years* was too long. Tolkien told Rayner on 9 September 1954 that one of his problems was selection from 'too abundant matter' (Tolkien-George Allen & Unwin archive, HarperCollins), and undoubtedly the need to compress, which he always found difficult, made his work on the Appendices slow even in the face of frequent inquiries by his publisher. Sales of *The Fellowship of the Ring* were so good that a first reprint was ordered in September 1954, and another already in December, while a second printing of *The Two Towers* was commissioned in November 1954, two weeks after first publication. In addition, Tolkien and Allen & Unwin received a great deal of mail from readers, many of them asking questions which related to material that might be included in the Appendices.

When *The Return of the King* was published, the Appendices occupied not 44 but 104 pages. Allen & Unwin must have looked at the sales of *The Fellowship of the Ring* and *The Two Towers* and realized that they could increase the size of the third volume not only with no danger of a loss, but with the advantage that Tolkien might thereby produce the Appendices more quickly. There is nothing in the surviving Allen & Unwin correspondence with Tolkien which mentions this increase of space for the Appendices, so it was probably settled during a meeting between Tolkien and Rayner Unwin, most probably on 26 January 1955; or possibly, though less likely, by the telephone (at about this time even so).

5 August 1955 Michaël Devaux has established from the archives of La Fenice, Venice, that Dino Dondi did sing the part of Rigoletto in the performance Tolkien attended. Other members of the cast were Antonioli Doro (Duca – the Duke of Mantua), Renata Ferrari Ongaro (Gilda), Agostino Ferrin (Sparafucile), Tina Pradella (Maddalena).

?December 1955 Tolkien's final letter to Michael Straight is not extant, but it seems almost certain that one is sent, even if not at the length of the drafts, since Straight in his review cites *On Fairy-Stories* to which Tolkien refers in the drafts, and seems to know facts about Tolkien's life which would not have been generally known (e.g. that he had been on the Western Front in the First World War, and that the snowstorm in the high pass was inspired by a visit to Switzerland). *Letters*, pp. 232–7, includes the undated drafts, and suggests that they were written in January or February 1956. But since Straight's review appeared in the *New Republic* for 16 January 1956, it must have been written by early January at the latest, more likely by the beginning of that month.

15 March 1956 According to *Biography*, p. 224, the payment from Allen & Unwin for 1955 was over £3,500.

21 March 1956 Tolkien's professorial salary, advertised as £2,500 on his retirement in 1959, together with his literary earnings would have come to some £6,000. Out of this, he and Edith being a married couple without dependants, Tolkien would have paid about one-half in income tax, plus payments for National Insurance. On an income of £3,500 he would have paid just over a third in income tax. In 1956, apart from excise duties on alcohol and tobacco products, there was no Value Added Tax or Sales Tax.

16 April 1956 There is no evidence that Tolkien seriously considered producing such a 'specialist' volume, or even that he discussed the idea with Rayner Unwin. The index he mentions is that which was promised for *The Return of the King* and abandoned in autumn 1954. The list of requested information is interesting for the light it throws on Tolkien's fan mail.

11 June 1956 In a letter to *The Times*, published on 17 November 1965 ('Is Beowulf Needed?', p. 13), Helen Gardner remarked of Auden's enthusiasm for Old English poetry that when she and he were undergraduates at Oxford, the only prescribed Old English texts were passages from Sweet's *Anglo-Saxon Reader*.

c. **6–20 July 1956** Tolkien is not recorded in the University calendar as acting as an Extern Examiner in 1956, but neither is he so recorded for 1958 or 1959, yet correspondence provides evidence that he was certainly an Examiner in those years.

12 March 1957 The contract and a memorandum say that the first broadcast of the interview was to be on 27 March 1957, and to last about eight minutes. A letter from the Houghton Mifflin Company to George Allen & Unwin on 1 April, however, says that the interview will be broadcast on 10 April, during the Fifth Annual WNYC Book Festival; and it is listed in the radio programme of the *New York Times* for that date, one of several connected with the Festival. The proposed broadcast on 27 March may have been postponed.

24 or 25 June 1957 *Letters* dates Tolkien's letter to 24 June, Everett's thesis to 25 June.

?November 1957–?October 1972 Among the Tolkien Papers in the Bodleian Library, Oxford are some 200 pages or scraps torn from newspapers on which Tolkien doodled. These vary from a single simple pattern to multiple designs of varying complexity on the same page. Those newspapers that can be dated range from November 1957 to September 1967, with a few dated by Tolkien himself from February 1960 to 9 September 1971. Where Tolkien gives a date on a dateable newspaper it is usually two or three months later than that of the issue date of the paper. Presumably he kept crosswords for when he had leisure or was in the mood to solve them. The items in the Bodleian suggest that 1960 and 1967 were years in which Tolkien was particularly attracted to this type of doodling, but this may be only a matter of chance survival.

Closely related to the newspaper doodles are about as many drawings (if one counts rectos and versos separately) – from the simplest sketch to finely finished work – made on sheets or scraps of paper, blotting paper, envelopes, letters, etc.; and even fewer of these are, or can be, dated. Such dates as there are range from June 1960 to October 1972, with 1960 and 1967 again the years with the most dated items. Tolkien seems to have developed most of his finished drawings from doodles, redrawn as heraldic motifs, flowers, or artefacts associated with his mythology.

Five doodles survive on newspapers from November 1957, and might have been made then, or early in 1958.

In the **Chronology** we have noted more significant and definitely dated items under the correct date, and only briefly note at the beginning of a year less significant items dated to that year, or on datable newspapers.

26 February 1958 The cancelled visit to the United States was that to Marquette University. We have been unable to find any information about the proposed visits to Sweden and Finland.

28 March 1958 René van Rossenberg, in 'Tolkien's Exceptional Visit to Holland: A Reconstruction', *Proceedings of the J.R.R. Tolkien Centenary Conference 1992* (1995), states that Tolkien arrived at the Hook at about 9.30 a.m. He has told us that this was based on the memories of those who met Tolkien at Rotterdam central station. 7.28 a.m. is the time given for arrival at the station (only a short journey from the Hook) in the itinerary Allen & Unwin sent to Tolkien.

?Late 1958–?mid-1960 Comments in Tolkien's letters support the conclusion that although he did some work on 'The Silmarillion' before 1959, there were long periods in which he hardly touched it, and apparently it was not until 1959 that he was able to do any sustained writing or revision. On 5 January 1956 he had had 'no time at all' for it; on 29 February 1956 he had 'not had a chance of turning' to it; in ?Autumn 1956 'I am not allowed to get at it' (*Letters*, p. 238); on 3 February 1957 'I have not got near the *Silmarillion* for months'; on 9 May 1957 'I have had to lay it aside since last autumn', and while he remains in office 'it is practically impossible to get any connected time to spend on it' (*Letters*, p. 256). He wrote to Rayner Unwin on 31 August 1957 that he had done 'a little work' during that month, probably on 'The Silmarillion'. His comment in a letter of 7 December 1957, that he sees clearly 'that I must, as a necessary preliminary to "re-moulding", get copies made of all copyable material' (*Letters*, p. 262), suggests that not much systematic work had yet been done.

Although during Hilary and Trinity Terms 1958 Tolkien was free of professorial duties, he spent much time on *Ancrene Wisse*, and on his comments on the Zimmerman story-line for the *Lord of the Rings* film. His wife's poor health, apart from her operation in the spring and accident in late autumn, meant that he had to undertake more domestic duties, and he himself was not in good health for much of the year. On 27 May 1958 he wrote to Rayner Unwin that Mrs Smith's index would be useful 'when I at last get some time (unbroken by catastrophes) to take up the *Silmarillion* etc. with concentration'. On 6 November 1958 he wrote to Rayner: 'I have been having a foul time all this year – rising crescendo to a climax during October; but I am surviving though "the Matter of Middle-earth" has had to be shelved, I fear.' On 29 January 1959 he had 'not had any chance of doing serious work on the "Silmarillion", or any other such work. I fear it is unlikely I shall have time to do this until I retire at the end of next term.' (Quotations above not attributed to *Letters* are from the Tolkien-George Allen & Unwin archive, HarperCollins.)

Christopher Tolkien assumes (*Morgoth's Ring*, pp. 142, 300) that his father obtained a secretary soon after mentioning the idea in his letter of 7 December 1957, and therefore Christopher assigned to 1958 the beginning of the 'remoulding' referred to in that letter, and a considerable amount of new writing for, and revision of, 'The Silmarillion' to the end of the 1950s and 1960; but he notes that there is very little evidence for more precise dating, other than that some of his father's typescripts can be dated to January 1959 *or later* since they were made on a typewriter that Tolkien first used in that month (typescripts noted as 1959 or later). (See *Morgoth's Ring*, p. 300.)

The one piece of evidence for Tolkien doing some work on 'The Silmarillion' late in 1958 has to be weighed against his statements noted above. In his late work on the *Quenta Silmarillion* he introduced elements also found in the unsent draft continuation of his letter to Rhona Beare of 14 October 1958. The matter in the draft, unlike that in the letter sent, was not written in answer to specific questions from Beare. It begins with a summary of his Creation myth; then, while writing on the different fates of Elves and Men, he refers, almost in passing, to the 'strange case of an Elf (Míriel mother of Fëanor) that tried to *die*' and 'refused rebirth' (*Letters*, p. 286). This does not seem likely to be an idea which has just occurred to Tolkien, but rather to a story already developed in more detail, even if perhaps not yet written down. Then, to illustrate the fact that even the Valar can fall, he describes the making of the Dwarves by Aulë in considerable detail. According to Christopher Tolkien, the account in the draft letter 'belongs with the first or draft text' made for incorporation in the *Quenta Silmarillion* during this period (*The War of the Jewels*, p. 213).

The extracts from Tolkien's letters listed above, however, do not suggest that much work was done in 1958, and the earliest mention we have seen of Tolkien having a secretary is a letter to Rayner Unwin of 24 February 1959, signed by 'A.M. Hope, Secretary'. It may be that she began work only after Tolkien's pessimistic forecast in his letter of 29 January 1959. On 30 April 1959 Tolkien commented to Charles Lewis at Allen & Unwin that Lewis's letter written on 23 April had coincided with the departure of Tolkien's part-time secretary. On 8 May 1959 Tolkien sent a letter to his former secretary, Miss Hope, thanking her 'for the all help that you have given me, especially in *beginning* the task of putting my papers into order' (Michael Silverman, *Catalogue Eleven* (1994), p. 33, emphasis ours). This presumably refers to work on 'The Silmarillion', and suggests that the ordering of papers has not proceeded very far. It is not until 9 December 1959 that Tolkien's correspondence with Rayner Unwin suggests that any real progress has been made: 'With the help of my secretary I have been charging well ahead with the reconstruction of the *Silmarillion* etc.' (*Letters*, p. 301). On 12 February 1960 he wrote to Rayner that he had deferred work on *Sir Gawain and the Green Knight* and *Pearl* until 'we [i.e. he and his then secretary, Elisabeth Lumsden] get all the present *Silmarillion* material typed out and arranged. This is nearly complete' (Tolkien-George Allen & Unwin archive, HarperCollins). In June 1960, when he is 'in full tide of composition for the *Silmarillion*' (*Letters*, p. 302), he has to turn his attention to the *Ancrene Wisse* proofs.

Specifically in regard to *The Wanderings of Húrin*, although some of the draft and preliminary workings are on the backs of documents dated 1954 or 1957, this gives only a date *post quem* for the writing. The typescript was made on the typewriter that Tolkien began to use in 1959. Christopher Tolkien states that 'the work can be placed with fair certainty towards the end of the 1950s' (*The War of the Jewels*, p. 258).

?April 1959 The dates of newspapers used by Tolkien in which to wrap some of his writings are not necessarily reliable indicators of the enclosed works. Such evidence, however, tends to be consistent with other evidence for dating that exists. Dated doodles drawn by Tolkien near newspaper crossword puzzles are usually two or three months later than the date of the paper.

11 December 1959 The mention of a reprint of *Sir Gawain and the Green Knight* seems strange, since in April Tolkien had been informed that the Press had enough stock to last three years. Perhaps Tolkien noted some necessary corrections while working on his translation of *Sir Gawain*. Someone at Oxford University Press noted on the letter: 'Norman Davis thinks a lot should be done [with the edition] & hopes some time to get T[olkien]'s permission to do it for him. But I don't think T will agree. He is more likely to go on saying he will do it himself & do nothing. But you will need, even to get the few corrections promised here, to follow up in about a week from now with another request!' (Oxford University Press archives).

14 September 1965 Rayner Unwin's reference to cover designs for 'the books', plural, suggests that by now at least he, and possibly Tolkien also, has seen sample covers for the Ballantine Books *Lord of the Rings*. For these Barbara Remington painted a single picture which was divided across the three volumes. Part of the cover for *The Fellowship of the Ring* was similar to the vignette on the Ballantine *Hobbit*, with 'pink bulbs' and emus (but no lion).

?Late Spring or early summer 1966 The story of Queen Berúthiel told to Daphne Castell is similar to the 'primitive' outline Christopher Tolkien describes in *Unfinished Tales*, pp. 401–2, n. 7. The latter also probably dates from this period, though it differs in some details.

22 September 1966 Later in 1966, according to Dick Plotz, Tolkien told him that he had seen Mount Doom. 'At night the boat he was on went past Stromboli which was spewing fire. He said he's never seen anything that looked so much like Emyn Anar' ('An Edited Transcript of Remarks at the December 1966 TSA [Tolkien Society of America] Meeting', *Niekas* 19 (Spring 1967), p. 40). The abstract of the ship's log provided to the passengers at the end of the cruise specifically mentions passing Stromboli on 22 September at 2.45 p.m., when it was certainly not night, and the weather was noted as 'partly cloudy, fine and sunny'. The log gives no indication of the return route between the 'heel of Italy', rounded at 12.30 p.m. on 29 September, and Cape Bon on the coast of Tunisia passed at 3.00 p.m. on 30 September. The most logical route would be south of Sicily; a possible if unlikely route through the narrow Strait of Messina (which one would certainly expect to be noted in the log) and then north of Sicily might have allowed a second view of Stromboli in the distance, and at night, but in that case the ship would probably have passed a considerable distance north of Cape Bon.

We are informed by Arden R. Smith that *Emyn Anar* ('the Hills of the Sun') does not appear in Tolkien's writings (compare, as Sindarin names for Mount Doom, *Orodruin* and *Amon Amarth*).

15 June 1967 Recordings by Tolkien of only eight out of the sixteen poems in *The Adventures of Tom Bombadil and Other Verses from the Red Book* have been issued to date.

30 October 1967 On p. 60 of *The Adventures of Tom Bombadil and Other Verses from the Red Book*: 'men that meet' should be 'men that I meet'. This was corrected some time after the second printing.

14 March 1968 We have found no confirmation that Edith Tolkien attended the event, but neither have we found any evidence that she did not.

9 May 1968 Johnston's booklet was published in Blacksburg, Virginia by White Rhinoceros Press in 1967, slightly revised from its appearance in *The Tolkien Papers*, i.e. *Mankato Studies in English* 2 (February 1967).

28 May 1968 The Ballantine book is *Tolkien: A Look Behind 'The Lord of the Rings'* by Lin Carter, first published in March 1969. The book from Twayne, New York, may have fallen through or been much postponed: the first book Twayne published on Tolkien was *J.R.R. Tolkien* by Deborah Webster Rogers and Ivor A. Rogers, in 1980.

20 June 1968 The song 'The Ballad of Bilbo Baggins', as performed by Leonard Nimoy, the actor who played 'Mr Spock' on *Star Trek*, is famous in Tolkien fan circles as an embarrassing relic of the sixties.

27 September 1968 Since the broadcasts began on 29 September, and this is the only mention in the Allen & Unwin archives of a script being sent to Tolkien, it seems that he did not want to be involved with the production, or circumstances did not permit it. Later he used the blank versos of part of the script for work on 'The Silmarillion'. We have found no comments by Tolkien on the broadcasts, nor any evidence that he listened to them.

c. 14–18 October 1968 As noted earlier, *Bilbo's Last Song (at the Grey Havens)* is a revision of Tolkien's *Vestr um haf* (Old Norse 'west over sea') from the 1920s or 1930s.

7 January 1969 From this point, because of frequent phone calls, and matters raised or dealt with during Joy Hill's visits, the written material in the Tolkien-George Allen & Unwin archive at HarperCollins becomes more fragmentary. In addition, the general Allen & Unwin archive has not been preserved beyond 1967.

c. 3 September 1970 In 'Echoes of the Old Ringmaster' Joy Hill says that the gift took place after Tolkien returned to Oxford in 1972, or rather that he then recorded his wish that that poem and copyright should be given to her after his death. However the sale of Joy Hill's Tolkien collection at Sotheby's London on 14 December 1992 included a letter and a note dated 28 October 1971 recording the gift of the poem and its copyright on (approximately) 3 September 1970.

31 October 1972 Humphrey Carpenter wrote on Tolkien's letter, in regard to the latter's reference to 'the first time the poor man [his son John] had been able to visit Oxford since he was ordained', that John in fact had been ordained just after the war, and had visited Oxford many times since. Carpenter was correct; but it seems likely that Tolkien was simply muddled, and meant to write that it was John's first visit since Tolkien had returned to live in Oxford.

8 February 1973 We have seen no mention of a planned visit by Tolkien to Paris. Possibly when he was invited, he wrote to say that his health prevented him from attending.

5 June 1973 In an undated draft memo from Tolkien to Joy Hill (1972 or 1973) he pleads with her to 'try to stop this disastrous leaking of the number of the house in which I have rooms. I do not know how it has occurred and reached writers unknown to me. It is contrary to my wishes & orders & has already as you know given me serious trouble – now increased by the return of the undergrad[uate] population (who leave all doors to the street open)' (Tolkien-George Allen & Unwin archive, HarperCollins).

Family Trees

THESE GENEALOGICAL CHARTS illustrate the family lines of George William Tolkien, paternal great-grandfather of J.R.R. Tolkien; John Benjamin Tolkien, paternal grandfather; John Suffield, father and son, Tolkien's maternal grandfather and great-grandfather; Arthur and Hilary Tolkien, father and brother of our subject; and Tolkien himself, to the level of his great-grandchildren. We are indebted to Priscilla Tolkien for much of the information concerning her family in more recent times. Earlier data has been gleaned from various documents, especially the Census records at the National Archives, Kew. Queried birth dates are based on current ages reported in Census data. Those wishing to pursue Tolkien's family history further are advised that official records, such as Census forms, sometimes badly misspell names, or those who have made indexes to the records have misread them, making retrieval of pertinent records difficult; and that some genealogical lists posted to the Internet concerning the Tolkiens and Suffields mistakenly include persons not in the same line of descent as our subject (though they may be more distantly related).

George William Tolkien (?1784–1840) = Eliza Lydia Murrell (?1787–1863)

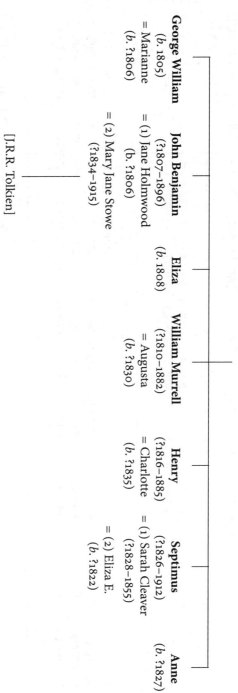

George William
(b. 1805)
= Marianne
(b. ?1806)

John Benjamin
(?1807–1896)
= (1) Jane Holmwood
(b. ?1806)
= (2) Mary Jane Stowe
(?1834–1915)

Eliza
(b. 1808)

William Murrell
(?1810–1882)
= Augusta
(b. ?1830)

Henry
(?1816–1885)
= (1) Sarah Cleaver
(?1828–1855)
= (2) Eliza E.
(b. ?1822)

Septimus
(?1826–1912)
= Charlotte
(b. ?1835)

Anne
(b. ?1827)

[J.R.R. Tolkien]

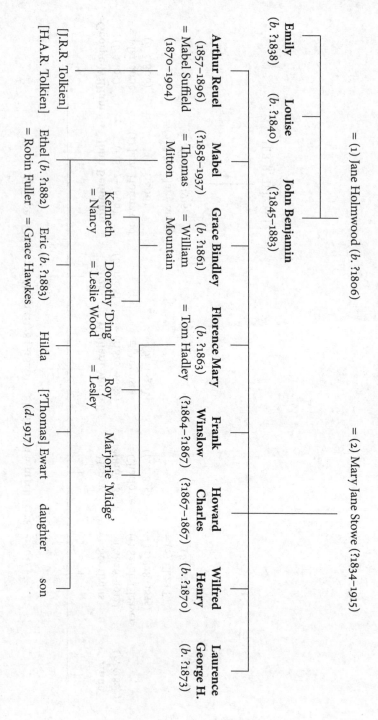

John Benjamin Tolkien (?1807–1896)

= (1) Jane Holmwood (b. ?1806)　　　= (2) Mary Jane Stowe (?1834–1915)

Emily
(b. ?1838)

Louise
(b. ?1840)

John Benjamin
(?1845–1883)

Arthur Reuel
(1857–1896)
= Mabel Suffield
(1870–1904)

Mabel
(?1858–1937)
= Thomas
Mitton

Grace Bindley
(b. ?1861)
= William
Mountain

Florence Mary
(b. ?1863)
= Tom Hadley

Frank
Winslow
(?1864–?1867)

Howard
Charles
(?1867–1867)

Wilfred
Henry
(b. ?1870)

Laurence
George H.
(b. ?1873)

[J.R.R. Tolkien]
[H.A.R. Tolkien]

Ethel (b. ?1882)
= Robin Fuller

Eric (b. ?1883)
= Grace Hawkes

Hilda

[?Thomas] Ewart
(d. 1917)

daughter

son

Kenneth
= Nancy

Dorothy 'Ding'
= Leslie Wood

Roy
= Lesley

Marjorie 'Midge'

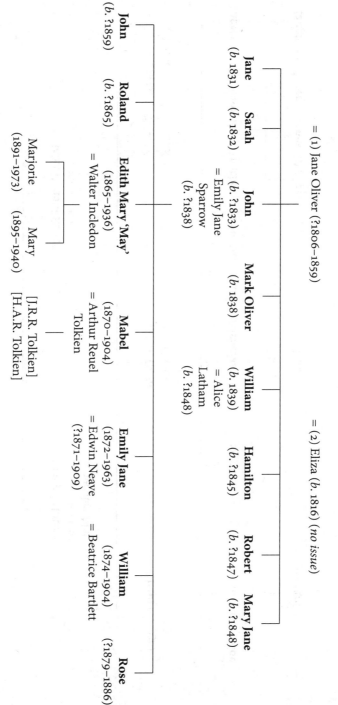

John Suffield (1802–1891)

= (1) Jane Oliver (?1806–1859)   = (2) Eliza (b. 1816) (no issue)

- John (b. ?1859)
- Jane (b. 1831)
- Sarah (b. 1832)
- John (b. ?1833) = Emily Jane Sparrow (b. ?1838)
- Mark Oliver (b. 1838)
- William (b. 1839) = Alice Latham (b. ?1848)
- Hamilton (b. ?1845)
- Robert (b. ?1847)
- Mary Jane (b. ?1848)

- Roland (b. ?1865)
- Edith Mary 'May' (1865–1936) = Walter Incledon
- Mabel (1870–1904) = Arthur Reuel Tolkien
- Emily Jane (1872–1963) = Edwin Neave (?1871–1909)
- William (1874–1904) = Beatrice Bartlett

- Marjorie (1891–1973)
- Mary (1895–1940)
- [J.R.R. Tolkien]
- [H.A.R. Tolkien]
- Rose (?1879–1886)

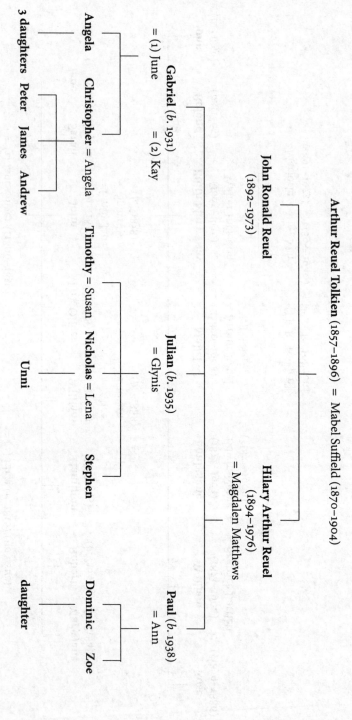

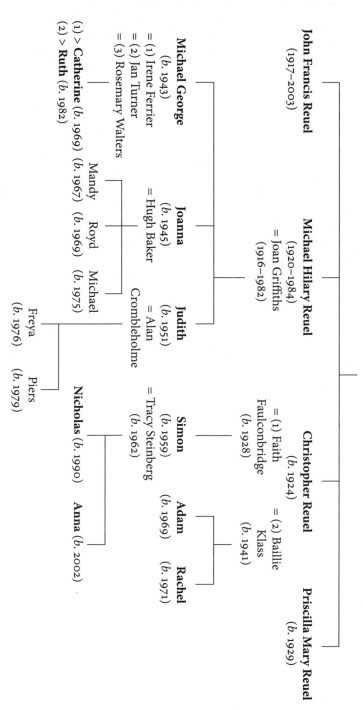

John Ronald Reuel Tolkien (*b.* 1892–1973) = Edith Bratt (*b.* 1889–1971)

John Francis Reuel
(1917–2003)

Michael Hilary Reuel
(1920–1984)
= (1) Joan Griffiths
(1916–1982)

Christopher Reuel
(*b.* 1924)
= (1) Faith
Faulconbridge
(*b.* 1928)
= (2) Baillie
Klass
(*b.* 1941)

Priscilla Mary Reuel
(*b.* 1929)

Michael George
(*b.* 1943)
= (1) Irene Ferrier
= (2) Jan Turner
= (3) Rosemary Walters

Joanna
(*b.* 1945)
= Hugh Baker

Judith
(*b.* 1951)
= Alan
Crombleholme

Simon
(*b.* 1959)
= Tracy Steinberg
(*b.* 1962)

Adam
(*b.* 1969)

Rachel
(*b.* 1971)

(1) > **Catherine** (*b.* 1969)
(2) > **Ruth** (*b.* 1982)

Mandy
(*b.* 1967)

Royd
(*b.* 1969)

Michael
(*b.* 1975)

Freya
(*b.* 1976)

Piers
(*b.* 1979)

Nicholas (*b.* 1990)

Anna (*b.* 2002)

Bibliographies

THE PUBLISHED WRITINGS OF J.R.R. TOLKIEN

Listed here are all of the books and separate publications by Tolkien, and those edited, translated, or with a significant contribution by Tolkien, published to date, and his primary contributions to periodicals published during his lifetime. For the first category, we have described only the most significant editions and printings, always including the first editions published in Britain and the United States. The arrangement in each section is alphabetical by title of the book or periodical, except for the *History of Middle-earth* series, which is arranged in order of publication.

Since Tolkien's death, miscellaneous texts and extracts, especially linguistic texts, tables, etc., have appeared in periodicals, notably *Mythlore*, *Parma Eldalamberon*, and *Vinyar Tengwar*. The most substantive of these are listed below in section VII. Although some numbers of *Parma Eldalamberon* are books in themselves, for convenience we have treated them as periodicals.

Tolkien contributed, often without credit, to many more writings than are cited in sections II and III below, in so far as he helped colleagues and students with their work, at the least providing information, suggestions, and corrections. Some of this activity is described in other parts of the *Companion and Guide*.

For additional and fuller bibliographical descriptions and notes, and lists of minor writings (such as letters and extracts) by Tolkien published in books and periodicals, see *J.R.R. Tolkien: A Descriptive Bibliography* by Wayne G. Hammond with the assistance of Douglas A. Anderson (1993, 2nd edn. forthcoming), and addenda and corrigenda to the *Descriptive Bibliography* in the occasional magazine *The Tolkien Collector*, edited and published by Christina Scull (begun 1992). The *Descriptive Bibliography* and *Tolkien Collector* are here abbreviated **DB** and **TC**, and cited by entry and issue numbers respectively. Notes on the manuscript and printing history, contents, and reprints of Tolkien's works may be found in individual entries in the **Reader's Guide**.

I. BOOKS AND SEPARATE PUBLICATIONS BY J.R.R. TOLKIEN, PUBLISHED IN HIS LIFETIME

The Adventures of Tom Bombadil and Other Verses from the Red Book. Illustrated by Pauline Baynes. London: George Allen & Unwin, 1962; Boston: Houghton Mifflin, 1963. A later edition (London: Unwin Paperbacks, 1990; Boston: Houghton Mifflin, 1991) was illustrated by Roger Garland. Contains sixteen poems by Tolkien: *The Adventures of Tom Bombadil, Bombadil Goes Boating, Errantry, Princess Mee, The Man in the Moon Stayed Up Too Late, The Man in the Moon Came Down Too Soon, The Stone Troll, Perry-the-Winkle, The Mewlips, Oliphaunt, Fastitocalon, Cat, Shadow-Bride, The Hoard, The Sea-Bell, The Last Ship*. DB A6.

An Application for the Rawlinson and Bosworth Professorship of Anglo-Saxon in the University of Oxford by J.R.R. Tolkien, Professor of the English Language in the University of Leeds, June 25, 1925. Privately printed for the author, 1925. DB Dii1.

Beowulf: The Monsters and the Critics. London: Humphrey Milford, 1937. Later published in vol. 22 (1937) of the annual *Proceedings of the British Academy*. Compare *Beowulf and the Critics*, in section II below. DB A2.

Farmer Giles of Ham. Illustrated by Pauline Baynes. London: George Allen & Unwin, 1949; Boston: Houghton Mifflin, 1950. A later edition (London: Unwin Paperbacks, 1990; Boston: Houghton Mifflin, 1991) was illustrated by Roger Garland. The fiftieth anniversary edition (London: HarperCollins; Boston: Houghton Mifflin, 1999) includes a facsimile of the 1949 text and pictures, a transcription of the earliest extant version of *Farmer Giles of Ham*, Tolkien's notes for an abandoned sequel, an added map by Pauline Baynes, and an introduction and notes to the volume by Christina Scull and Wayne G. Hammond. DB A4; TC 22 (1999 edn.).

The Hobbit, or, There and Back Again. London: George Allen & Unwin, 1937; Boston: Houghton Mifflin, 1938. The first Allen & Unwin printing contained ten illustrations by Tolkien, in black and white; of these, *Mirkwood* was printed as a halftone plate. Four colour illustrations by the author (omitting *Bilbo Woke Up with the Early Sun in His Eyes*) were added in the second Allen & Unwin printing (1937), the new colour frontispiece replacing the same subject (*The Hill*) in pen and ink. *Mirkwood* was omitted with the third Allen & Unwin printing. The first printing of the Houghton Mifflin edition also included four colour illustrations by Tolkien (but with *Bilbo Woke*, omitting *Bilbo Comes to the Huts of the Raft-Elves*) as well as *Mirkwood*, but the latter was redrawn (not by Tolkien) and printed in line rather than halftone.

A revised edition of *The Hobbit*, most notably including changes to Chapter 5, was first published by George Allen & Unwin and Houghton Mifflin in 1951. The first paperback edition of the work was published in 1961 by Penguin (Puffin) Books, Harmondsworth, Middlesex. The first American paperback edition was published in 1965 by Ballantine Books, New York. Further revised editions include: New York: Ballantine Books, 1966; London: Unwin Books, 1966; London: George Allen & Unwin, 1966; Boston: Houghton Mifflin, 1967; London: George Allen & Unwin, 1978; Boston: Houghton Mifflin, [1985]; London: HarperCollins, 1995; London: Collins, 1998; Boston: Houghton Mifflin, 1999;

Boston: Houghton Mifflin, 2001. Other notable editions include that produced for the fiftieth anniversary, with a foreword by Christopher Tolkien (London: Unwin Hyman, 1987; Boston: Houghton Mifflin, 1987); *The Annotated Hobbit*, with an introduction and notes by Douglas A. Anderson (Boston: Houghton Mifflin, 1988; London: Unwin Hyman, 1989; 2nd edn., Boston: Houghton Mifflin, 2002; London: HarperCollins, 2003); and editions illustrated by Eric Fraser (London: Folio Society, 1979), Michael Hague (London: George Allen & Unwin, 1984; Boston: Houghton Mifflin, 1984), and Alan Lee (London: Harper-Collins, 1997; Boston: Houghton Mifflin, 1997). *The Hobbit* has been frequently reprinted and reset, with and without illustrations, and with a complicated history of textual errors and correction. See further, *The Annotated Hobbit*; DB A3; TC 11, p. 9; 17, pp. 5–6; 22, p. 5; 25, p. 7; 26, p. 9.

The Lord of the Rings. London: George Allen & Unwin, 1954–5; Boston: Houghton Mifflin, 1954–6 (3 vols.). *The Lord of the Rings* has been reset and reprinted numerous times, and has a complicated history of revision, errors, and corrections, of which only highlights may be given here. An unauthorized paperback edition was published in 1965 by Ace Books, New York (3 vols.). A revised, authorized paperback edition was published later in 1965 by Ballantine Books, New York (3 vols.). A second hardback edition, revised, was issued by George Allen & Unwin in 1966, and Houghton Mifflin, 1967. It was further revised in the second British printing (1967), but not in the American edition until 1987. The latter introduced additional corrections, and included a note on the text by Douglas A. Anderson. The text of the edition issued for Tolkien's centenary, illustrated by Alan Lee (London: HarperCollins; Boston: Houghton Mifflin, 1991), was derived largely from the first (1 vol.) British paperback edition (London: George Allen & Unwin, 1968) and the India paper edition (London: George Allen & Unwin, 1969), in a line of descent lacking the revisions and corrections applied to the second (hardback) edition (1966–7). A further corrected edition, but with numerous new errors introduced, was published in London by HarperCollins and in Boston by Houghton Mifflin in 1994 and 1999 respectively (with misleading dates printed on the copyright page), with a revised note by Anderson. The fiftieth anniversary edition of 2004 (HarperCollins; Houghton Mifflin) was extensively corrected by Wayne G. Hammond and Christina Scull with the advice of Christopher Tolkien; further corrections were made, and a new index introduced, in printings of 2005. Most of these emendations were documented by Hammond and Scull in *The Lord of the Rings: A Reader's Companion* (2005). DB A5; TC 9, pp. 6–7; 20, p. 8.

A Middle English Vocabulary. Oxford: Clarendon Press, 1922. Also published together with *Fourteenth Century Verse and Prose*; see section IV, below. DB A1.

Smith of Wootton Major. Illustrated by Pauline Baynes. London: George Allen & Unwin, 1967; Boston: Houghton Mifflin, 1967. A later edition (London: Unwin Hyman, 1990; Boston: Houghton Mifflin, 1991) was illustrated by Roger Garland. An 'extended edition', edited by Verlyn Flieger, including related material from Tolkien's papers, was published by HarperCollins, London, in 2005. DB A9.

The Tolkien Reader. New York: Ballantine Books, 1966. Reprints *The Homecoming of Beorhtnoth Beorhthelm's Son, On Fairy-Stories, Leaf by Niggle, Farmer Giles of Ham,* and *The Adventures of Tom Bombadil and Other Verses from the Red Book,* with a general prefatory note by Peter S. Beagle and illustrations (for *Farmer Giles of Ham* and the *Adventures of Tom Bombadil* collection) by Pauline Baynes. DB A8.

Tree and Leaf. London: George Allen & Unwin, 1964; Boston: Houghton Mifflin, 1965. Revised versions of *On Fairy-Stories* and *Leaf by Niggle,* with an introductory note by the author. A new edition (London: Unwin Hyman, 1988; Boston: Houghton Mifflin, 1989) also contains the poem *Mythopoeia,* and a preface by Christopher Tolkien incorporating his father's original introduction. Yet another edition (London: HarperCollins, 2001) adds *The Homecoming of Beorhtnoth Beorhthelm's Son* to the volume. DB A7.

II. BOOKS AND SEPARATE PUBLICATIONS BY J.R.R. TOLKIEN, PUBLISHED POSTHUMOUSLY

Beowulf and the Critics. Edited by Michael D.C. Drout. Tempe, Arizona: Arizona Center for Medieval and Renaissance Studies, 2002. Lecture materials from which *Beowulf: The Monsters and the Critics* was derived. TC 26, p. 6.

Bilbo's Last Song. Boston: Houghton Mifflin, 1974; London: George Allen & Unwin, 1974. First published as a poster. The Allen & Unwin edition features an illustration by Pauline Baynes. Set to music in *The Road Goes Ever On: A Song Cycle,* 2nd edn. (1978); see pt. IV, below. Later published in book form (London: Unwin Hyman, 1990; Boston: Houghton Mifflin, 1990) with illustrations by Pauline Baynes. A later edition (London: Hutchinson, 2002; New York: Alfred A. Knopf, 2002) omits part of the Baynes art. DB A11; TC 26, pp. 6–7.

The Father Christmas Letters. London: George Allen & Unwin, 1976; Boston: Houghton Mifflin, 1976. Partly reprinted as *Letters from Father Christmas* (London: CollinsChildren'sBooks, 1995; Boston: Houghton Mifflin, 1995), as facsimiles of letters with envelopes, with three previously unpublished pictures. Revised and enlarged as *Letters from Father Christmas* (London: HarperCollins, 1999; Boston: Houghton Mifflin, 1999; and again, from the same publishers in 2004). See further, the section on the 'Father Christmas' letters in PUBLISHED ART BY J.R.R. TOLKIEN, below. DB A14; TC 11, pp. 8–9; 22, pp. 5–6.

Letters of J.R.R. Tolkien. Edited by Humphrey Carpenter, with the assistance of Christopher Tolkien. London: George Allen & Unwin, 1981; Boston: Houghton Mifflin, 1981. The original index was replaced in the HarperCollins, 1999 and Houghton Mifflin, 2000 paperback printings with a new, expanded index by Christina Scull and Wayne G. Hammond. DB Di1; TC 20, p. 6.

Mr. Bliss. London: George Allen & Unwin, 1982; Boston: Houghton Mifflin, 1983. DB A18.

The Monsters and the Critics and Other Essays. Edited by Christopher Tolkien. London: George Allen & Unwin, 1983; Boston: Houghton Mifflin, 1984. Reprints *Beowulf: The Monsters and the Critics, On Translating Beowulf* (i.e. *Prefatory Remarks on Prose Translation of 'Beowulf'), On Fairy-Stories*, and *English and Welsh*. Also contains, previously unpublished, *Sir Gawain and the Green Knight* (Tolkien's W.P. Ker Lecture), *A Secret Vice*, and *Valedictory Address to the University of Oxford* (edited from a different manuscript than that published in *J.R.R. Tolkien: Scholar and Storyteller*; see section V, below). DB A19.

Pictures by J.R.R. Tolkien. Foreword and notes by Christopher Tolkien. London: George Allen & Unwin, 1979; Boston: Houghton Mifflin, 1979. A second, revised edition was issued by the same publishers in 1992. DB Ei2; TC 1, p. 4; 2, p. 9.

Poems and Stories. Illustrated by Pauline Baynes. De luxe edition, London: George Allen & Unwin, 1980. Trade edition, London: HarperCollins, 1992; Boston: Houghton Mifflin, 1994. Reprints *The Adventures of Tom Bombadil and Other Verses from the Red Book, The Homecoming of Beorhtnoth Beorhthelm's Son, On Fairy-Stories, Leaf by Niggle, Farmer Giles of Ham*, and *Smith of Wootton Major*. DB A16; TC 1, p. 5; 7, p. 6.

Roverandom. Edited, with an introduction and notes, by Christina Scull and Wayne G. Hammond. London: HarperCollins, 1998; Boston: Houghton Mifflin, 1998. TC 17, p. 9; 18, p. 8.

The Silmarillion. Edited by Christopher Tolkien. London: George Allen & Unwin, 1977; Boston: Houghton Mifflin, 1977. Reprinted with illustrations by Ted Nasmith, London: HarperCollins, 1998; Boston: Houghton Mifflin, 1998. Reprinted with corrections, London: HarperCollins, 1999; Boston: Houghton Mifflin, 2001. DB A15; TC 20, pp. 9–10; 22, p. 7.

Tales from the Perilous Realm. London: HarperCollins, 1997. Reprints *Farmer Giles of Ham, Leaf by Niggle, Smith of Wootton Major*, and *The Adventures of Tom Bombadil and Other Verses from the Red Book*. TC 16, pp. 6–7.

Unfinished Tales of Númenor and Middle-earth. Edited by Christopher Tolkien. London: George Allen & Unwin, 1980; Boston: Houghton Mifflin, 1980. DB A17.

III. THE HISTORY OF MIDDLE-EARTH

The Book of Lost Tales, Part One. Edited by Christopher Tolkien. London: George Allen & Unwin, 1983; Boston: Houghton Mifflin, 1984. *The History of Middle-earth*, vol. 1. DB A21.

The Book of Lost Tales, Part Two. Edited by Christopher Tolkien. London: George Allen & Unwin, 1984; Boston: Houghton Mifflin, 1984. *The History of Middle-earth*, vol. 2. DB A22.

The Lays of Beleriand. Edited by Christopher Tolkien. London: George Allen & Unwin; Boston: Houghton Mifflin, 1985. *The History of Middle-earth*, vol. 3. DB A23.

The Shaping of Middle-earth: The Quenta, the Ambarkanta and the Annals, Together with the Earliest 'Silmarillion' and the First Map. Edited by Christopher Tolkien. London: George Allen & Unwin; Boston: Houghton Mifflin, 1986. *The History of Middle-earth*, vol. 4. DB A24.

The Lost Road and Other Writings: Language and Legend before 'The Lord of the Rings'. Edited by Christopher Tolkien. London: Unwin Hyman; Boston: Houghton Mifflin, 1987. *The History of Middle-earth*, vol. 5. DB A25.

The Return of the Shadow: The History of The Lord of the Rings, Part One. Edited by Christopher Tolkien. London: Unwin Hyman; Boston: Houghton Mifflin, 1988. *The History of Middle-earth*, vol. 6. DB A26.

The Treason of Isengard: The History of The Lord of the Rings, Part Two. Edited by Christopher Tolkien. London: Unwin Hyman; Boston: Houghton Mifflin, 1989. *The History of Middle-earth*, vol. 7. DB A27.

The War of the Ring: The History of The Lord of the Rings, Part Three. Edited by Christopher Tolkien. London: Unwin Hyman; Boston: Houghton Mifflin, 1990. *The History of Middle-earth*, vol. 8. DB A28.

Sauron Defeated: The End of the Third Age (The History of The Lord of the Rings, Part Four), The Notion Club Papers, and The Drowning of Anadûnê. Edited by Christopher Tolkien. London: HarperCollins; Boston: Houghton Mifflin, 1992. *The History of Middle-earth*, vol. 9. DB A29.

Morgoth's Ring: The Later Silmarillion, Part One: The Legends of Aman. Edited by Christopher Tolkien. London: HarperCollins; Boston: Houghton Mifflin, 1993. *The History of Middle-earth*, vol. 10. TC 5, p. 6.

The War of the Jewels: The Later Silmarillion, Part Two: The Legends of Beleriand. Edited by Christopher Tolkien. London: HarperCollins; Boston: Houghton Mifflin, 1994. *The History of Middle-earth*, vol. 11. TC 9, pp. 8–9.

The Peoples of Middle-earth. Edited by Christopher Tolkien. London: HarperCollins; Boston: Houghton Mifflin, 1996. *The History of Middle-earth*, vol. 12. TC 14, pp. 7–8.

IV. BOOKS EDITED, TRANSLATED, OR WITH A CONTRIBUTION
BY J.R.R. TOLKIEN, PUBLISHED IN HIS LIFETIME

The Ancrene Riwle. Translated by M.B. Salu. London: Burns & Oates, 1955; Notre Dame, Indiana: University of Notre Dame Press, 1956. Contains a preface by Tolkien, p. v. DB B23.

Ancrene Wisse: The English Text of the Ancrene Riwle. Edited by J.R.R. Tolkien. London: Published for the Early English Text Society by the Oxford University Press, 1962. DB B25.

Angles and Britons: O'Donnell Lectures. Cardiff: University of Wales Press, 1963. Contains *English and Welsh* by Tolkien, pp. 1–41. DB B26.

Attacks of Taste. Compiled and edited by Evelyn B. Byrne and Otto M. Penzler. New York: Gotham Book Mart, 1971. Contains a statement by Tolkien on the books he loved when he was a teenager, p. 43. DB B29.

Beowulf and the Finnesburg Fragment: A Translation into Modern English Prose by John R. Clark Hall. New edition, revised by C.L. Wrenn. London: George Allen & Unwin, 1940. Contains *Prefatory Remarks on Prose Translation of 'Beowulf'* by Tolkien, pp. viii–xli. The remarks were reprinted in *The Monsters and the Critics and Other Essays* (1983) as *On Translating Beowulf*. DB B17.

Essays and Studies by Members of the English Association, vol. 14. Collected by H.W. Garrod. Oxford: Clarendon Press, 1929. Contains the essay *Ancrene Wisse and Hali Meiðhad* by Tolkien, pp. 104–26. DB B12.

Essays and Studies 1953. Collected for the English Association by Geoffrey Bullough. London: John Murray, 1953. Contains *The Homecoming of Beorhtnoth Beorhthelm's Son* by Tolkien, pp. 1–18. DB B21.

Essays Presented to Charles Williams. Edited by C.S. Lewis. London: Oxford University Press, 1947. Contains *On Fairy-Stories* by Tolkien, pp. 38–89. DB B19.

Fourteenth Century Verse & Prose. Edited by Kenneth Sisam. Oxford: Clarendon Press, 1921 (i.e. 1922). Some copies were published with *A Middle English Vocabulary* by Tolkien; see section I, above. DB B3.

The Jerusalem Bible. London: Darton, Longman & Todd; Garden City, N.Y.: Doubleday, 1966. Tolkien contributed a translation of the Book of Jonah, revised by others before publication. DB pp. 278–9.

Leeds University Verse 1914–24. Compiled and edited by the English School Association. Leeds: At the Swan Press, 1924. Contains three poems by Tolkien, *An Evening in Tavrobel*, p. 56; *The Lonely Isle*, p. 57; and *The Princess Ní*, p. 58. DB B5.

Þe Liflade ant to Passiun of Seinte Iuliene. Edited by S.R.T.O. d'Ardenne. Liège: Bibliothèque de la faculté de philosophie et lettres de l'Université de Liège; Paris: E. Droz, 1936. Reissued with corrigenda, Oxford: Early English Text Society, 1961. Tolkien was a silent joint editor with his student Simonne d'Ardenne. DB p. 278.

A New English Dictionary on Historical Principles (*Oxford English Dictionary*). Oxford: Clarendon Press, 1921–6 for the fascicles concerned. Tolkien contributed to, at least, the entries for *wag, walrus, wampum, warm, wasp, water, wick* (*lamp*), and *winter*. DB p. 278.

A New Glossary of the Dialect of the Huddersfield District by Walter E. Haigh. London: Oxford University Press, 1928. Contains a foreword by Tolkien, pp. xiii–xviii. DB B11.

A Northern Venture: Verses by Members of the Leeds University English School Association. Leeds: Swan Press, 1923. Contains three poems by Tolkien, *Tha Eadigan Saelidan: The Happy Mariners*, pp. 15–16; *Why the Man in the Moon Came Down Too Soon*, pp. 17–19; and *Enigmata Saxonica Nuper Inventa Duo*, p. 20. DB B4.

The Old English Apollonius of Tyre. Edited by Peter Goolden. Oxford: Oxford University Press, 1958. *Oxford English Monographs*. Contains, p. iii, a preface by Tolkien, who was also a general editor for the series. DB B24.

Oxford Poetry 1915. Edited by G.D.H. Cole and T.W. Earp. Oxford: B.H. Blackwell, 1915. Contains *Goblin Feet* by Tolkien, pp. 64–5. DB B1.

Pearl. Edited by E.V. Gordon [and Ida L. Gordon]. Oxford: Clarendon Press, 1953. Tolkien contributed notes, corrections, and a small part of the introduction ('Form and Purpose', pp. xi–xix). DB B22.

Realities: An Anthology of Verse. Edited by G.S. Tancred. Leeds: At the Swan Press, 1927. Contains *The Nameless Land* by Tolkien, pp. 24–5. DB B9.

The Reeve's Tale: Version Prepared for Recitation at the 'Summer Diversions'. Oxford: Privately printed, 1939. Edited from Chaucer's *Canterbury Tales* and with an introduction by Tolkien. DB B16.

Report on the Excavation of the Prehistoric, Roman, and Post-Roman Site in Lydney Park, Gloucestershire by R.E.M. Wheeler and T.V. Wheeler. Oxford: Printed at the University Press for the Society of Antiquaries, 1932. Contains the essay *The Name 'Nodens'* by Tolkien, as Appendix I, pp. 132–7. DB B13.

The Road Goes Ever On: A Song Cycle. Poems by J.R.R. Tolkien, music by Donald Swann. Boston: Houghton Mifflin, 1967; London: George Allen & Unwin, 1968. Second edition, Boston: Houghton Mifflin, 1978; London: George Allen & Unwin, 1978. Third edition, London: HarperCollins, 2002. The first edition contains seven poems set to music. A setting by Swann of Tolkien's *Bilbo's Last Song* was added to the second edition, and a setting of *Lúthien Tinúviel* to the third edition. DB B28; TC 26, pp. 14–15.

Sir Gawain and the Green Knight. Edited by J.R.R. Tolkien & E.V. Gordon. Oxford: Clarendon Press, 1925. Second edition, revised by Norman Davis, Oxford: Clarendon Press, 1967. DB B7.

Sir Orfeo. Oxford: [Reproduced by the] Academic Copying Office, 1944. Edited by Tolkien for instruction of Navy and Royal Air Force cadets. DB B18. Reprinted, with an introduction and notes by Carl F. Hostetter, in *Tolkien Studies* 1 (2004), pp. 85–123.

Songs for the Philologists by J.R.R. Tolkien, E.V. Gordon and others. London: Privately printed in the Department of English at University College, 1936. Contains thirteen poems by Tolkien: *From One to Five*, p. 6; *Syx Mynet*, p. 7; *Ruddoc Hana*, pp. 8–9; *Ides Ælfscyne*, pp. 10–11; *Bagme Bloma*, p. 12; *Eadig Beo Þu!*, p. 13; *Ofer Widne Garsecg*, pp. 14–15; *La Huru*, p. 16; *I Sat upon a Bench*, p. 17; *Natura Apis*, p. 18; *The Root of the Boot*, pp. 20–1; *Frenchmen Froth*, pp. 24–5; and *Lit' and Lang'*, p. 27. DB B16.

A Spring Harvest by Geoffrey Bache Smith. London: Erskine Macdonald, 1918. Contains a prefatory note by Tolkien, p. 7, and was co-edited by him with Christopher Wiseman. DB B2.

Transactions of the Philological Society. London: Published for the Society by David Nutt (A.G. Berry), 1934. Contains the essay *Chaucer as a Philologist: The Reeve's Tale* by Tolkien, pp. 1–70. DB B14.

Winter's Tales for Children 1. Edited by Caroline Hillier. Illustrated by Hugh Marshall. London: Macmillan, 1965; New York: St Martin's Press, 1965. Contains two poems by Tolkien: *Once upon a Time*, pp. 44–5, and *The Dragon's Visit*, pp. 84, 86–7. DB 27.

The Year's Work in English Studies, vol. 4 (for 1923). Edited for the English Association by Sir Sidney Lee and F.S. Boas. London: Oxford University Press, 1924. Contains a review essay, *Philology: General Works*, by Tolkien, pp. 20–37. DB B6.

The Year's Work in English Studies, vol. 5 (for 1924). Edited for the English Association by F.S. Boas. London: Oxford University Press, 1926. Contains a review essay, *Philology: General Works*, by Tolkien, pp. 26–65. DB B8.

The Year's Work in English Studies, vol. 6 (for 1925). Edited for the English Association by F.S. Boas and C.H. Herford. London: Oxford University Press, 1927. Contains a review essay, 'Philology: General Works', by Tolkien, pp. 32–66. DB B10.

V. BOOKS EDITED, TRANSLATED, OR WITH A CONTRIBUTION BY J.R.R. TOLKIEN, PUBLISHED POSTHUMOUSLY

Finn and Hengest: The Fragment and the Episode. Lecture notes by J.R.R. Tolkien. Edited by Alan Bliss. London: George Allen & Unwin, 1982; Boston: Houghton Mifflin, 1983. DB B36.

J.R.R. Tolkien, Scholar and Storyteller: Essays in Memoriam. Edited by Mary Salu and Robert T. Farrell. Ithaca, N.Y.: Cornell University Press, 1979. Contains *Valedictory Address to the University of Oxford, 5 June 1959* by Tolkien, pp. 16–32, edited from a different manuscript than that published in *The Monsters and the Critics and Other Essays* (see section II, above). DB B34.

The Old English Exodus. Text, translation, and commentary by J.R.R. Tolkien. Edited by Joan Turville-Petre. Oxford: Clarendon Press, 1981 (i.e. 1982). DB B35.

Sir Gawain and the Green Knight, Pearl and Sir Orfeo. Translated by J.R.R. Tolkien. Edited with a preface and notes by Christopher Tolkien. London: George Allen & Unwin, 1975; Boston: Houghton Mifflin, 1975. DB B30.

A Tolkien Compass. Edited by Jared Lobdell. La Salle, Illinois: Open Court, 1975. Contains *Guide to the Names in The Lord of the Rings* by Tolkien, i.e. *Nomenclature of The Lord of the Rings*, pp. 153–201. DB B31. The *Nomenclature* was re-edited by Wayne G. Hammond and Christina Scull in *The Lord of the Rings: A Reader's Companion* (2005), pp. 750–82.

VI. CONTRIBUTIONS BY J.R.R. TOLKIEN TO PERIODICALS, PUBLISHED IN HIS LIFETIME

In addition to these writings (limited here to those intended by their author for publication), Tolkien contributed an early version of *Shadow-Bride* to a periodical possibly titled *Abingdon Chronicle*; and possibly other (unsigned) reports and articles to the *King Edward's School Chronicle* in 1910–11.

Bulletin of the Modern Humanities Research Association, London

Henry Bradley, 3 Dec., 1845–23 May, 1923. October 1923, pp. 4–5. DB C15.

Catholic Herald, London

The Name Coventry. 23 February 1945, p. 2. Letter to the editor. DB Dii4.

Chronicle of the Convents of the Sacred Heart, Roehampton

Firiel. 4 (1934), pp. 30–2. Illustrated by an unidentified artist. DB C25.

Daily Telegraph, London

Beautiful Place Because Trees Are Loved. 4 July 1972, p. 16. Letter to the editor. DB Dii20.

Dublin Review, London

Leaf by Niggle. January 1945, pp. 46–61. DB C32.

English Studies, Amsterdam

'Iþþlen' in Sawles Warde. 28 (December 1947), pp. 168–70. Written with S.R.T.O. d'Ardenne. DB C34.

The Gryphon, Leeds

The Clerke's Compleinte. n.s. 4 (December 1922), p. 95. Poem. Signed 'N.N.' A revised manuscript of the poem was printed in facsimile in 'The Clerkes Compleinte Revisited', *Arda 1986* (1990), pp. 1–13. DB C11.

Iúmonna Gold Galdre Bewunden. n.s. 4 (January 1923), p. 130. A revised version was published in the *Oxford Magazine*; see below. DB C12.

Light as Leaf on Lindentree. n.s. 6 (June 1925), p. 217. DB C18; A23.

Inter-University Magazine, Oxford

The Grey Bridge of Tavrobel. Issue unknown, [?mid-1920s], p. 82. DB, p. 344.

Tinfang Warble. Issue unknown, [?mid-1920s], p. 63. DB, p. 344.

King Edward's School Chronicle, Birmingham

Acta Senatus. n.s. 26 (March 1911), pp. 26–7. Unsigned. DB C5.

The Battle of the Eastern Field. n.s. 26 (March 1911), pp. 22–6. With mock comments signed 'G.A.B.' DB C4.

Debating Society. n.s. 26, no. 183 (November 1910), pp. 68–71; n.s. 26, no. 184 (December 1910), pp. 94–5; n.s. 26, no. 185 (February 1911), pp. 5–9; n.s. 26, no. 187 (June 1911), pp. 42–5. DB C1–3, 7.

Editorial. n.s. 26 (June 1911), pp. 33–4; n.s. 26 (July 1911), pp. 53–4. Unsigned. DB C6, 8.

Oxford Letter. n.s. 28, no. 202 (December 1913), pp. 80–1. Signed 'Oxon'.

Medium Ævum, Oxford

Sigelwara Land [Part 1]. 1, no. 3 (December 1932), pp. 183–96. DB C23.

Sigelwara Land [Part 2]. 3, no. 2 (June 1934), pp. 95–111. DB C28.

The Microcosm, Leeds

The City of the Gods. 8 (Spring 1923), p. 8. DB C13.

The Observer, London

Letter to the editor. 20 February 1938, p. 9. DB Dii3.

Oxford Magazine, Oxford

The Adventures of Tom Bombadil. 15 February 1934, pp. 464–5. DB C27.

The Dragon's Visit. 4 February 1937, p. 342. DB C29.

Errantry. 9 November 1933, p. 180. DB C24.

Iumonna Gold Galdre Bewunden. 4 March 1937, p. 473. DB C31.

Knocking at the Door: Lines Induced by Sensations when Waiting for an Answer at the Door of an Exalted Academic Person. 18 February 1937, p. 403. Signed 'Oxymore'. DB C30.

Looney. 18 January 1934, p. 340. DB C26.

The Oxford English School. 29 May 1930, pp. 778–80, 782. DB C21.

Progress in Bimble Town. 15 October 1931, p. 22. Signed 'K. Bagpuize'. DB C22.

Radio Times, London

A Fourteenth-Century Romance. 4 December 1953, p. 9. DB C36.

Review of English Studies, London

The Devil's Coach-Horses. 1 (July 1925), pp. 331–6. DB C19.

Some Contributions to Middle-English Lexicography. 1 (April 1925), pp. 210–15. DB C17.

Shenandoah: The Washington and Lee University Review, Lexington, Va.

For W.H.A. 18 (Winter 1967), pp. 96–7. DB C39.

Stapeldon Magazine, Oxford

Adventures in Unnatural History and Medieval Metres, being the Freaks of Fisiologus: (i) Fastitocalon, (ii) Iumbo, or ye Kinde of ye Oliphaunt. 7 (June 1927), pp. 123–7. Signed 'Fisiologus'. DB C20.

From the Many-willow'd Margin of the Immemorial Thames. 4 (December 1913), p. 11. Signed 'J'. DB C9.

The Happy Mariners. 5, no. 26 (June 1920), pp. 69–70. DB C10.

Studia Neophilologica, Uppsala

MS. Bodley 34: A Re-Collation of a Collation. 20, nos. 1–2 (1947–8), pp. 65–72. Written with S.R.T.O. d'Ardenne. DB C35.

Sunday Times, London

Research v. Literature. 14 April 1946, p. 3. TC 7, p. 22.

Time and Tide, London

Imram. 3 December 1955, p. 1561. Illustrated by Robert Gibbings. DB C37.

Times Literary Supplement, London

Holy Maidenhood. 26 April 1923, p. 281. Unsigned. DB C14.

Triode, Manchester, England

Letter to the editor. 18 (May 1960), p. 27. DB Dii8.

Welsh Review, Cardiff

The Lay of Aotrou and Itroun. 4 (December 1945), pp. 254–66. DB C33.

Yorkshire Poetry, Leeds

The Cat and the Fiddle: A Nursery-Rhyme Undone and Its Scandalous Secret Unlocked. 2 (October–November 1923), pp. 1–3. DB C16; A5, 6, 27.

Mythlore

'The "Gondolinic Runes": Another Picture' by Paul Nolan Hyde. 18, no. 3, whole no. 69 (Summer 1992), pp. 20–5. Includes a table of 'Gondolinic Runes' by Tolkien.

'Narqelion: A Single, Falling Leaf at Sun-fading' by Paul Nolan Hyde. 15, no. 2, whole no. 56 (Winter 1988), pp. 47–52. Includes the poem *Narqelion* by Tolkien.

Parma Eldalamberon

'Addendum to *The Alphabet of Rúmil* and *The Valmaric Script*'. 15 (2004), pp. 85–8. Edited by Arden R. Smith.

'*The Alphabet of Rúmil: Documents by J.R.R. Tolkien*. 13 (2001), pp. 3–89. Edited by Arden R. Smith.

'Early Noldorin Fragments'. 13 (2001), pp. 91–165. Edited by Christopher Gilson, Bill Welden, Carl F. Hostetter, and Patrick Wynne.

'Early Qenya Fragments'. 14 (2003), pp. 3–34. Edited by Patrick Wynne and Christopher Gilson.

'Early Qenya Grammar'. 14 (2003), pp. 35–86. Edited by Carl F. Hostetter and Bill Welden.

'Early Qenya Pronouns'. 15 (2004), pp. 41–58. Edited by Christopher Gilson.

'Early Runic Documents'. 15 (2004), pp. 89–121. Edited by Arden R. Smith.

'English–Qenya Dictionary'. 15 (2004), pp. 65–84. Edited by Arden R. Smith and Christopher Gilson.

'Index of Names for *The Lay of the Children of Húrin*'. 15 (2004), pp. 59–64. Edited by Bill Welden and Christopher Gilson.

I·Lam na·Ngoldathon: The Grammar and Lexicon of the Gnomish Tongue. 11 (1995). Edited by Christopher Gilson, Patrick Wynne, Arden R. Smith, and Carl F. Hostetter.

'Name-list to *The Fall of Gondolin*'. 15 (2004), pp. 19–30. Edited by Christopher Gilson and Patrick H. Wynne.

Names and Required Alterations. 15 (2004), pp. 5–18. Edited by Patrick H. Wynne.

Qenyaqetsa: The Qenya Phonology and Lexicon; Together with The Poetic and Mythologic Words of Eldarissa. 12 (1998). Edited by Christopher Gilson, Carl F. Hostetter, Patrick Wynne, and Arden R. Smith.

'Sí Qente Fëanor'. 15 (2004), pp. 31–40. Edited by Christopher Gilson.

The Valmaric Script: Documents by J.R.R. Tolkien. 14 (2003), pp. 89–134. Edited with introduction and commentary by Arden R. Smith.

Vinyar Tengwar

Ae Adar Nín: The Lord's Prayer in Sindarin. 44 (June 2002), pp. 21–30, 38. Edited with notes and analysis by Bill Welden.

'*Alcar mi Tarmenel na Erun*: The *Gloria in Excelsis Deo* in Quenya'. 44 (June 2002), pp. 31–7. Edited with notes and analysis by Arden R. Smith.

'The Bodleian Declensions: Analysis' by Patrick Wynne, Christopher Gilson, and Carl F. Hostetter. 28 (March 1993), pp. 8–34. Includes the earliest extant chart of Quenya noun declensions by Tolkien.

'A Brief Note on the Background of the Letter from J.R.R. Tolkien to Dick Plotz Concerning the Declension of the High-elvish Noun' by Jorge Quiñonez. 6 (July 1989), pp. 13–14. Includes a transcription of the 'Plotz declension' (of Quenya *cirya* and *lasse*), with notes by Tolkien. Parts of this were published earlier, in *Tolkien Language Notes* 2 (1974) and *Beyond Bree* for March 1989.

'*Eldarin Hands, Fingers & Numerals* and Related Writings'. 47 (February 2005), pp. 3–42, and 48 (December 2005), pp. 4–34. Edited by Patrick H. Wynne.

'The *Entu, Ensi, Enta* Declension: A Preliminary Analysis' by Christopher Gilson. With an introduction by Carl F. Hostetter. 36 (July 1994), pp. 7–29. Reproduces and transcribes a Quenya 'declensional paradigm' by Tolkien.

Etymological Notes on the Ósanwe-kenta. 41 (July 2000), pp. 5–6. Edited with notes by Carl F. Hostetter.

From Quendi and Eldar, Appendix D. 39 (July 1998), pp. 4–20. Edited with introduction, glossaries, and additional notes by Carl F. Hostetter.

From The Shibboleth of Fëanor. 41 (July 2000), pp. 7–10. Notes excluded from *The Shibboleth of Fëanor* in *The Peoples of Middle-earth.* Edited with notes by Carl F. Hostetter.

Notes on Óre. 41 (July 2000), pp. 11–19. Edited with notes by Carl F. Hostetter.

Ósanwe-kenta. 39 (July 1998), pp. 21–34

The Rivers and Beacon-hills of Gondor. 42 (July 2001), pp. 5–31.

'Trees of Silver and of Gold: A Guide to the Koivienéni Manuscript' by Patrick Wynne and Christopher Gilson. 27 (1993), pp. 7–42. Reproduces the recto of this manuscript by Tolkien, containing a sentence in Quenya and its translation.

'"Words of Joy": Five Catholic Prayers in Quenya'. 43 (January 2002), pp. 4–38, and 44 (June 2002), pp. 5–20. Edited by Patrick Wynne, Arden R. Smith, and Carl F. Hostetter.

PUBLISHED ART BY J.R.R. TOLKIEN

Following is a list of pictorial art by J.R.R. Tolkien published to date. It includes the author's own illustrations, maps, and plans for his stories, separate paintings and drawings, and formal calligraphy. Titles supplied by Tolkien are given in *italics*. Titles in quotation marks are given as previously used in *J.R.R. Tolkien: Artist and Illustrator* by Wayne G. Hammond and Christina Scull (1995); *Pictures by J.R.R. Tolkien*, edited by Christopher Tolkien (1979; 2nd edn. 1992); and *J.R.R. Tolkien: Life and Legend* by Judith Priestman (Bodleian Library, 1992). Some untitled works, such as the 'heraldic' devices related to Tolkien's mythology, have been most readily identified by a descriptive phrase. By and large, these titles or phrases are arranged either alphabetically within each section or subsection, or in order according to the story for which the pictures were made; and in most sections, it has seemed best to group related pictures together.

After most titles we have cited by figure number a reproduction in *J.R.R. Tolkien: Artist and Illustrator* (here abbreviated *Artist*) or in *Pictures by J.R.R. Tolkien* (abbreviated *Pictures*), or both. The first of these books is to be preferred for clarity of image, fidelity of colour, and attention to scale; it is also more commonly found in libraries and bookshops, whereas *Pictures* is out of print. Some of Tolkien's published art, however, is in neither of these sources, and sometimes a reproduction elsewhere is superior – say, reproduced in colour rather than in black and white; in such cases, we have cited other locations where pictures may be found. Among these, *J.R.R. Tolkien: Life and Legend* is cited as *Life and Legend*, and *The Invented Worlds of J.R.R. Tolkien: Drawings and Original Manuscripts from the Marquette University Collection* (Patrick and Beatrice Haggerty Museum of Art, 2004) is cited as *Invented Worlds*. Citations to Tolkien's own works are to the first edition unless otherwise stated.

References to *Pictures by J.R.R. Tolkien* apply to both the first and second editions unless otherwise noted. Where illustrations are printed in *Pictures* on both pages of an opening, **A** refers to a black and white plate on the left-hand page, and **B** to a colour plate on the right. We have omitted from this list reproductions of pictures by Tolkien coloured by H.E. Riddett.

I. TOPOGRAPHICAL AND FAMILY ART

'Alder by a Stream'. *Artist*, fig. 7.
Caerthilian Cove & Lion Rock. *Artist*, fig. 20.
'Code-letter to Father Francis Morgan'. Recto, *Life and Legend*, p. 17, and *Invented Worlds*, p. 24; verso, *The Tolkien Family Album*, p. 22.
The Cottage, Barnt Green. *Artist*, fig. 18.
Cove near the Lizard. *Artist*, fig. 21.
Foxglove Year. *Artist*, fig. 17.

Gipsy Green. Artist, fig. 22.

High Life at Gipsy Green. Artist, fig. 23.

Keystone of Door and *Gargoyles, South Side, Lambourn. Artist,* fig. 13.

King's Norton from Bilberry Hill Artist, fig. 16.

Lambourn, Berks. Artist, fig. 11.

Lyme Regis Harbour from the Drawing Room of the Cups Hotel. Artist, fig. 8.

'Mountain Landscape'. *Artist,* fig. 53.

New Lodge, Stonyhurst. Artist, fig. 28.

Oh to Be in Oxford (North) Now That Summer's There. Artist, fig. 25.

Pageant House Gardens, Warwick. Artist, fig. 14.

Phoenix Farm, Gedling. Artist, fig. 15.

'Quallington Carpenter' Eastbury Berkshire. Artist, fig. 12.

Ruins at West End of Whitby Abbey. Artist, fig. 10.

Sea Weeds and Star Fishes. Life and Legend, pp. 12–13.

'Ship at Anchor'. *Artist,* fig. 6.

Spring 1940. Artist, fig. 3.

Summer in Kerry. Artist, fig. 29.

They Slept in Beauty Side by Side. Artist, fig. 4.

'Three Sketches', including a view of 22 Northmoor Road, Oxford.
    Artist, fig. 77.

'The Tolkien Family and Jennie Grove'. *Artist,* fig. 24.

Tumble Hill near Lyme R[egis]. Artist, fig. 27.

Turl Street, Oxford. Artist, fig. 19; see also Miscellaneous Art,
    Exeter College Smoker.

'Two Boys at the Seaside'. *Artist,* fig. 5.

View from Mr. Wallis' Broad Street, Lyme. Artist, fig. 26.

What Is Home without a Mother (or a Wife). Life and Legend, p. 14.

Whitby, view with swing bridge. *Artist,* fig. 9.

'Sketch of Whitby'. *Life and Legend,* p. 19.

II. THE 'FATHER CHRISTMAS' LETTERS

This series of elaborate letters and pictures, in decorative envelopes, was sent to the Tolkien children between 1920 and 1943 by their father in the guise of Father Christmas, the North Polar Bear, or the elf Ilbereth. It has been published in several editions, each of which differs in contents and format.

The Father Christmas Letters (1976) includes most of the major illustrations, but fewer reproductions of envelopes and of the letters themselves than in the 1999 and 2004 editions. In general, the 1976 colours are more accurate, and some items are not included elsewhere: the first page of the 1933 letter (p. 4); part of the 1932 letter (p. 6); a stamp from one of two 1924 envelopes (p. 6, top right; this appears on the envelope in *Artist,* fig. 65); a reproduction of 'Love from Father Christmas | 1926' from the verso of the 1926 drawing (p. 11); and a final foliage decoration from the 1938 letter (p. 43).

Letters from Father Christmas (1995) contains ten facsimile envelopes with facsimiles of eight letters and two pictures, with other pictures on intervening pages. Although not as complete as other editions, its colour is generally more accurate than in the 1999 and 2004 editions. Three pictures which were not in the 1976 edition are included: 'North Polar Bear helping Father Christmas with the Cooking' from 1931; *A Merry Christmas 1940, A Happy New Year 1941* (*Artist*, fig. 70); and 'View of the heavens' from ?1933. All of these are in the 1999 edition. The reproductions of eight out of the ten facsimile envelopes are partially hidden by panels with printed text, and all have had the date of the postmark removed (since the letters inside the envelopes generally are not of the same date as the postmarks). None of these appear in the 1976 edition; all are reproduced in the 1999 edition, except for the 1924 envelope (one of two), which is reproduced as fig. 65 in *Artist*. The eight facsimile letters are each of one page only, sometimes cropped or with paragraphs relocated; only the 1920 letter was reproduced in 1976. Three do not appear in the 1999 or 2004 editions: parts of the letters for 1930, 1933, and 1937.

Letters from Father Christmas (1999) includes the largest number of reproductions of pictures, envelopes, and letters, but the colour printing of some of the items, mainly letters and envelopes, tends to be inaccurate, and pages are cluttered by details in the margins and silhouettes behind printed text.

Letters from Father Christmas (2004) is a reduction both in the number of pages and physical size from the 1999 edition. The layout of illustrations and text is similar, but with fewer distracting details. The number of pages was reduced by omitting almost all of the envelopes: nine are reproduced on the back of the dust-jacket, too small to be seen clearly, and some of the stamps are reproduced much enlarged on pp. 2–3. Some letters are also omitted, but the only picture lost is the pencil sketch of Father Christmas in his sleigh (p. 62 in the 1999 edn.). The quality of colour reproduction is similar to that in 1999.

The items published in *Artist and Illustrator* and *Pictures* are (in chronological order):

> 1932 *A Merry Christmas*. *Artist*, fig. 63.
> *Me and My House*. *Artist*, fig. 64.
> Envelope, 1924. *Artist*, fig. 65. This is not shown completely in any
>   edition of *The Father Christmas Letters*. Its 'stamp' is reproduced
>   in the 1976 edition.
> 1928 *A Merry Christmas from Father Christmas and P.B. 1928*. *Pictures*,
>   no. 39.
> 1931–32 *N.P.B. Karhu*. *Artist*, fig. 66.
> 'Cave Paintings'. *Artist*, fig. 67.
> *Christmas 1933*. *Artist*, fig. 68.
> *Rhyme*, first page. *Artist*, fig. 69.
> *A Merry Christmas 1940, A Happy New Year 1941*. *Artist*, fig. 70.

III. THE HOBBIT

The first edition of *The Hobbit* (George Allen & Unwin, 1937) contained a large number of illustrations, including *The Hill* in black and white and *Mirkwood* as a separate plate. The latter appeared also in the second Allen & Unwin printing (1937), which introduced colour plates. The first American printing (Houghton Mifflin, 1938) included a selection of colour plates slightly different from that of the British edition, and a version of *Mirkwood* redrawn by another artist. Some of the subsequent printings and editions of *The Hobbit* have included various combinations of pictures by Tolkien.

ILLUSTRATIONS (IN STORY ORDER)

The Hill: Hobbiton. Artist, fig. 92.
'Sketch for *The Hill*'. *Artist*, fig. 93.
The Hill: Hobbiton. Artist, fig. 94.
'Sketch for *The Hill*'. *Artist*, fig. 95.
'Sketch for *The Hill*'. *Artist*, fig. 96.
The Hill: Hobbiton across the Water. Artist, fig. 97; *Pictures*, no. 1A (2nd edn. only; in the 1st edn. a tracing of this drawing was published in error).
The Hill: Hobbiton-across-the Water. Artist, fig. 98; *Pictures*, no. 1B.
Bag End Underhill. Artist, fig. 90.
One Morning Early in the Quiet of the World. Artist, fig. 89.
Gandalf. Artist, fig. 91.
Trolls' Hill. Artist, fig. 99.
The Three Trolls Are Turned to Stone. Artist, fig. 100; *Pictures*, no. 3A.
The Trolls. Artist, fig. 102; *Pictures*, no. 2A.
'Sketches of Dwarves Marching, and Smaug'. *Artist*, fig. 103.
Riding Down into Rivendell. Artist, fig. 104.
Rivendell Looking West. Artist, fig. 105; *Pictures*, no. 4.
Rivendell Looking East. Artist, fig. 106; *Pictures*, no. 5.
Rivendell, sketch. *Artist*, fig. 107.
Rivendell, finished art. *Artist*, fig. 108; *Pictures*, no. 6.
The Mountain-Path. Artist, fig. 109; *Pictures*, no. 7A.
The Misty Mountains Looking West from the Eagles' Eyrie towards Goblin Gate. Artist, fig. 110.
The Misty Mountains Looking West from the Eyrie towards Goblin Gate. Artist, fig. 111; *Pictures*, no. 8A.
Bilbo Woke Up with the Early Sun in His Eyes. Artist, fig. 113; *Pictures*, no. 9.
Firelight in Beorn's House. Artist, fig. 115.
Beorn's Hall. Artist, fig. 116; *Pictures*, no. 10A.
Mirkwood. Artist, fig. 88; *Pictures*, no. 37A.
'Entrance to the Elvenking's Halls'. *Artist*, fig. 117.
Entrance to the Elvenking's Halls. Artist, fig. 118.
'Entrance to the Elvenking's Halls'. *Artist*, fig. 119.

'The Elvenking's Gate', unfinished painting. *Pictures*, no. 11.

Gate of the Elvenking's Halls. *Artist*, fig. 120.

The Elvenking's Gate, finished art. *Artist*, fig. 121; *Pictures*, no. 12A.

Sketch for the Forest River. *Artist*, fig. 122; *Pictures*, no. 13.

'Sketch for *Bilbo Comes to the Huts of the Raft-elves*'. *Artist*, fig. 123.

Bilbo Comes to the Huts of the Raft-elves. *Artist*, fig. 124; *Pictures*, no. 14.

Esgaroth. *Artist*, fig. 126.

Lake Town. *Artist*, fig. 127; *Pictures*, no. 15A.

The Lonely Mountain and map of the Long Lake. *Artist*, fig. 128.

'Schematic drawing of the Lonely Mountain'. *The Hobbit*, fiftieth
    anniversary edn., p. 12 (George Allen & Unwin, 1987); unnumbered
    (Houghton Mifflin, 1987).

The Front Gate. *Artist*, fig. 130; *Pictures*, no. 16A.

The Back Door. *Artist*, fig. 131.

View from the Back Door. *Artist*, fig. 132.

Conversation with Smaug. *Artist*, fig. 133; *Pictures*, no. 17.

'Smaug Flies around the Lonely Mountain'. *Artist*, fig. 134.

The Front Door. *Artist*, fig. 135.

The Lonely Mountain. *Artist*, fig. 136.

Smaug Flies round the Mountain. *Pictures*, no. 18.

Death of Smaug. *Artist*, fig. 137; *Pictures*, no. 19.

The Coming of the Eagles. *Artist*, fig. 138.

The Hall at Bag-End. *Artist*, fig. 139; *Pictures*, no. 20A.

MAPS

'Earliest manuscript of *The Hobbit* with earliest version of Thror's Map',
    two pages. *The Hobbit*, fiftieth anniversary edn., pp. ii–iii (George Allen
    & Unwin, 1987); unnumbered (Houghton Mifflin, 1987); in colour,
    Invented Worlds, p. 9.

Thror's Map, Copied by B. Baggins. *Artist*, fig. 85.

Thror's Map, printed proof with corrections. *Artist*, fig. 86.

Wilderland, preliminary art. *Artist*, fig. 84.

Wilderland, final art. *Artist*, fig. 87.

BINDING AND DUST-JACKET

The Hobbit, design for upper binding. *Artist*, fig. 140.

The Hobbit, design for spine and lower binding. *Artist*, fig. 141.

The Hobbit, original binding, based on Tolkien's designs. *Artist*, fig. 142.

The Hobbit, preliminary dust-jacket design. *Artist*, fig. 143 (black and
    white); detail in colour in Steve Schultz, 'Hobbits in the House',
    Marquette: The Magazine of Marquette University 19, no. 4
    (Fall 2001), pp. 16–17.

The Hobbit, dust-jacket design. *Artist*, fig. 144.

IV. THE LORD OF THE RINGS

ILLUSTRATIONS (IN STORY ORDER)

'Brandywine Ferry'. *Artist*, fig. 146.

Old Man Willow. *Artist*, fig. 147; *Pictures*, no. 21.

Moria Gate, upper section. *Artist*, fig. 148; *Pictures*, no. 22B.

Moria Gate, lower section. *Artist*, fig. 149; *Pictures*, no. 24 (1st edn.),
   23 (2nd edn.).

'Doors of Durin'. *Artist*, fig. 150; *The Treason of Isengard*, showing more
   of the surrounding manuscript, p. 182; *Biography*, plate 12.

'Doors of Durin'. *Artist*, fig. 151; in colour, *Invented Worlds*, p. 13.

'Doors of Durin'. *Artist*, fig. 152.

'Doors of Durin'. *Artist*, fig. 153.

'Doors of Durin', redrawn by blockmaker. *Artist*, fig. 154; *Pictures*, no. 22A.

One Page of the Book of Moria. First page, second version. *Artist*, fig. 155.

A Page of the Book of [Moria] > *[Mazarbul]*. First page, third version.
   Marquette: The Magazine of Marquette University 19, no. 4 (Fall 2001),
   p. 18; *Invented Worlds*, p. 6.

First page of the 'Book of Mazarbul', final version. *Pictures*, no. 23 I
   (1st edn.), 24 I (2nd edn.).

Second page of the 'Book of Mazarbul', final version. *Pictures*, no. 23 II
   (1st edn.), 24 II (2nd edn.).

Third page of the 'Book of Mazarbul', final version. *Artist* 156; *Pictures*,
   no. 23 III (1st edn.), 24 III (2nd edn.).

'Dimrill Dale and Mountains of Moria'. *Artist*, fig. 158.

The Forest of Lothlorien in Spring. *Artist*, fig. 157; *Pictures*, no. 25.

G-rune on Sam's box. *The Treason of Isengard*, p. 274.

Rauros Falls and the Tindrock. *Artist*, fig. 159.

Sketch-plan of the scene of the Breaking of the Fellowship. *The Treason
   of Isengard*, p. 383.

[*Fangorn Forest*, see *Taur-na-Fúin* in section V, below]

'Helm's Deep'. *Artist*, fig. 160.

Helm's Deep and the Hornburg. *Artist*, fig. 161; *Pictures*, no. 26.

Orthanc (1). *Artist*, fig. 162.

'Orthanc "2", "3" and "4"'. *The War of the Ring*, p. 33.

'Orthanc II', plans. *Sauron Defeated*, p. 139.

'Orthanc III'. *Pictures*, no. 27a (part only); *Sauron Defeated*, p. 139.

Isengard/Nan Curunír. *Artist*, fig. 163.

Isengard and Orthanc. *Artist*, fig. 164; in colour, *Invented Worlds*, p. 10,
   and large detail on wrappers.

'Minas Morgul Gate'. *Artist*, fig. 170; *The Treason of Isengard*, whole page
   with more of surrounding manuscript, p. 342.

'Two Early Sketches of Kirith Ungol'. *The War of the Ring*, p. 108.

'Third Sketch of Kirith Ungol', on manuscript page. *The War of the Ring*, p. 114.

Shelob's Lair. *Artist*, fig. 171; *Pictures*, no. 28.

'Kirith Ungol'. *Artist*, fig. 172; *The War of the Ring*, p. 204.

'Kirith Ungol'. *Artist*, fig. 173.

Plan of Shelob's Lair. *The War of the Ring*, p. 201.

Plan of tunnel at Kirith Ungol. *The War of the Ring*, p. 225.

'Minas Tirith'. *Artist*, fig. 167; *The War of the Ring*, whole page with surrounding text, p. 261.

Stanburg or *Steinborg*. *Artist*, fig. 168; *Pictures*, no. 27B.

'Minas Tirith'. *Artist*, fig. 169.

Sketches of Dunharrow. *The War of the Ring*, p. 239.

Dunharrow. *Artist*, fig. 166; *Pictures*, no. 29.

'Dunharrow I'. *Sauron Defeated*, p. 140.

'Dunharrow II'. *Sauron Defeated*, p. 141.

'Three Sketches of Dunharrow'. *Artist*, fig. 165.

Starkhorn, Dwimerberg and Irensaga. *The War of the Ring*, p. 314.

'Tower of Kirith Ungol'. *Artist*, fig. 174.

Mordor Special Mission Flying Corps Emblem. *Artist*, fig. 185.

Orodruin, Mount Doom. *Pictures*, no. 30A.

Barad-dûr. *Artist*, fig. 145; *Pictures*, no. 30B.

Drawing of Crown of Gondor. *Letters of J.R.R. Tolkien*, p. 281.

Plan of Farmer Cotton's House. *Artist*, fig. 175.

DUST-JACKET DESIGNS

The Fellowship of the Ring. *Artist*, fig. 176.

The Fellowship of the Ring. *Artist*, fig. 177.

The Fellowship of the Ring. *Life and Legend*, p. 2.

The Two Towers. *Artist*, fig. 178.

The Two Towers. *Artist*, fig. 179.

The Two Towers. *Artist*, fig. 180 (the true background colour is brown, not green).

The Return of the King. *Artist*, fig. 181.

The Return of the King. *Artist*, fig. 182.

The covers or jackets of at least four three-volume editions of *The Lord of the Rings* reproduce Tolkien's own designs (*Artist*, figs. 177, 180, 182): Harper-Collins paperback 1997; HarperCollins hardcover with dust-jacket, 1998; Quality Paperback Book Club 2001; HarperCollins hardcover with dust-jacket, 2005. In all cases, Tolkien's own lettering has been replaced or relocated. For all HarperCollins editions, the positioning of the three smaller rings has been changed on *The Fellowship of the Ring*, on all three paint has been retouched, and the central ring motif has been strengthened. The 1997 and 1998 covers were printed on glossy paper, but for 2005 a matte paper was used, as would have been the case had Tolkien's designs been adopted in 1954–5. Only on the Quality Paperback Book Club covers do Tolkien's actual drawings appear not retouched: on the pale cover of *The Fellowship of the Ring* can be seen even more clearly than in the smaller reproduction in *Artist* the faint pencil lines with which Tolkien marked out the design, and the holes made by a compass.

MAPS AND PLANS

'First Map' of Middle-earth. *Life and Legend*, p. 63; redrawn by Christopher Tolkien, *The Treason of Isengard*, pp. 302–3, 305, 308–9, 314, 317, 319.

Map of the Shire. The Return of the Shadow, frontispiece.

Plan of Bree. *The Return of the Shadow*, p. 335.

Sketches of road between Weathertop and Rivendell. Redrawn by Christopher Tolkien, *The Return of the Shadow*, p. 201.

The Earliest Map of the Lands South of the Map of Wilderland in *The Hobbit. The Return of the Shadow*, p. 439.

Sketch-plan of the scene of the Breaking of the Fellowship. *The Treason of Isengard*, p. 383.

Map of Frodo's Journey to the Morannon. Redrawn by Christopher Tolkien, *The War of the Ring*, p. 117.

Map of Minas Morghul and the Cross-roads. *The War of the Ring*, p. 181.

Map of Anórien and Minas Tirith. Catalogue of an Exhibit of the Manuscripts of JRRT (Marquette University Memorial Library, 1984), p. 21.

Map of the White Mountains and South Gondor. Redrawn by Christopher Tolkien, *The War of the Ring*, p. 269.

Minas Tirith and Mindolluin. *The War of the Ring*, p. 280; in colour, *Invented Worlds*, p. 23.

Plan of Minas Tirith. *The War of the Ring*, p. 290.

Harrowdale. *The War of the Ring*, p. 258.

Starkhorn, Dwimerberg and Irensaga. *The War of the Ring*, p. 314.

Plan of Farmer Cotton's House. Artist, fig. 175.

RELATED CALLIGRAPHY

'Title page for *The Lord of the Rings*'. *The Manuscripts of J.R.R. Tolkien* (Marquette University Memorial Library, 1984), p. 27.

Inscriptions in Cirth and Tengwar. *The Lord of the Rings*, title-spread.

'Draft of Ring Inscription'. *The Manuscripts of J.R.R. Tolkien* (Marquette University Memorial Library, 1984), p. 27.

Ring inscription. *The Lord of the Rings*, bk. I, ch. 2. A preliminary version was mistakenly printed in the fiftieth anniversary edition (2004).

Early version of inscription on Balin's tomb. Drawn by Tolkien, *The Treason of Isengard*, p. 186.

Inscription on Balin's tomb. Drawn by Tolkien, *Life and Legend*, p. 88.

Inscription on Balin's tomb. Redrawn by blockmaker, *The Lord of the Rings*, bk. II, ch. 4.

A Elbereth Gilthoniel, Namárië, brief extracts from *The Lord of the Rings*. *Les Aventures de Tom Bombadil* (Christian Bourgois, 1975), pp. 4–5.

Namárië, in Tengwar. *The Road Goes Ever On: A Song Cycle*, dust-jacket and headings.

King's Letter, first and third versions. *Sauron Defeated*, pp. 130–1.

King's Letter, second version. *Artist*, fig. 199.

Beginning of *The Adventures of Tom Bombadil* in 'pointed' Tengwar. *Pictures*, no. 48 (bottom left).

Beginning of *The Adventures of Tom Bombadil* in 'decorated verse-hand' Tengwar. *Pictures*, no. 48 (bottom right).

Beginning of *Errantry* in 'pointed' Tengwar. *Pictures*, no. 48 (top).

V. MR. BLISS

All of the extant artwork and the written text for this story are reproduced in *Mr. Bliss* (George Allen & Unwin, 1982; Houghton Mifflin, 1983), excepting a few minor preliminary drawings. *Artist and Illustrator* includes (in story order):

'Mr Bliss Collides with Mr Day'. *Artist*, fig. 80.
'Archie, Teddy, and Bruno'. *Artist*, fig. 81.
'Party at the Bears' House'. *Artist*, fig. 82.
'Mr Bliss on the Hillside'. *Artist*, fig. 83.

VI. ROVERANDOM

All of the art for this story is reproduced in *Roverandom* (1998) and in *Artist and Illustrator* (in story order):

House Where 'Rover' Began His Adventures as a 'Toy'. Artist, fig. 73.
'Rover Arrives on the Moon'. *Artist*, fig. 74.
Lunar Landscape. Artist, fig. 72.
The White Dragon Pursues Roverandom and the Moondog. Artist, fig. 75.
The Gardens of the Merking's Palace. Artist, fig. 76.

VII. ART RELATED TO 'THE SILMARILLION'

ILLUSTRATIONS

Glórund Sets Forth to Seek Túrin. Artist, fig. 47; *Pictures*, no. 38.
Gondolin & the Vale of Tumladin from Cristhorn. Artist, fig. 58; *Pictures*, no. 35A.
Halls of Manwë on the Mountains of the World above Faerie. Artist, fig. 52; *Pictures*, no. 31.
The Hills of the Morning. Artist, fig. 1 (frontispiece).
The Man in the Moon. Artist, fig. 45.
Mithrim. Artist, fig. 46; *Pictures*, no. 32.
Nargothrond, unfinished watercolour. *Pictures*, no. 33.
'Nargothrond', with slender arched bridge. *Artist*, fig. 57.
Nargothrond, with timbered doors. *Artist*, fig. 56; *Pictures*, no. 34A.
The Shores of Faery. Artist, fig. 44.
Tanaqui. Artist, fig. 43.
Taur-na-Fúin. Artist, fig. 54; *Pictures* 37B. Later entitled: *Fangorn Forest*.
The Vale of Sirion. Artist, fig. 55; *Pictures* 36A.
I Vene Kemen. The Book of Lost Tales, Part One (George Allen & Unwin, 1983), frontispiece and p. 84; (Houghton Mifflin, 1984), p. 84 only; *Life and Legend*, p. 70.
Water, Wind & Sand. Artist, fig. 42.

HERALDIC DEVICES

Bëor. *Pictures*, no. 47.
Beren and Finrod Felagund. *Pictures*, no. 47.
Earendel and Gil-galad (2). *Artist*, fig. 190; *Pictures*, no. 47 (one of Gil-galad only).
Eärendil and Fëanor. *Pictures*, no. 47.
Eärendil. *The Silmarillion Desk Calendar 1979*, February.
Finarphin and Fingolfin. *Artist*, fig. 192; *Pictures*, no. 47 (Fingolfin only).
Finwë and Elwë. *Artist*, fig. 191; *Pictures*, no. 47 (Elwë only).
Finwë. *Pictures*, no. 47.
Hador. *Pictures*, no. 47.
House of Haleth. *Pictures*, no. 47.
Idril (4). *Artist*, fig. 188.
Idril. *Artist*, fig. 189; *Pictures*, no. 47.
Lúthien Tinúviel. *Artist*, fig. 194; *Pictures*, no. 47.
Lúthien Tinúviel. *Artist*, fig. 195; *Pictures*, no. 47.
Melian. *Artist*, fig. 193; *Pictures*, no. 47.
The Silmarils. *Pictures*, no. 47.

Tavrobel (Great Haywood), Kortirion (Warwick), and Celbaros (Cheltenham). 'Early Noldorin Fragments', *Parma Eldalamberon* 13 (2001), pp. 93–6.

Unidentified device. *The Silmarillion Desk Calendar 1979*, June.

MAPS

'The earliest map'. Redrawn by Christopher Tolkien, *The Book of Lost Tales, Part One*, p. 81.

First 'Silmarillion' map. *Life and Legend*, p. 89 (in part); *The Shaping of Middle-earth*, between pp. 220 and 221 (George Allen & Unwin edn., in colour; Houghton Mifflin edn., in black and white).

Westward extension of the first 'Silmarillion' map. *The Shaping of Middle-earth*, p. 228.

Eastward extension of the first 'Silmarillion' map. *The Shaping of Middle-earth*, p. 231.

Diagram I illustrating *The Ambarkanta*. *The Shaping of Middle-earth*, p. 243.

Diagram II illustrating *The Ambarkanta*. *The Shaping of Middle-earth*, p. 245.

Diagram III illustrating *The Ambarkanta*. *The Shaping of Middle-earth*, p. 247.

Map IV illustrating *The Ambarkanta*. *The Shaping of Middle-earth*, p. 249.

Map V illustrating *The Ambarkanta*. *The Shaping of Middle-earth*, p. 251.

Second 'Silmarillion' map. Earliest state, copied by Christopher Tolkien, *The Lost Road and Other Writings*, pp. 408–11; as later emended, copied by Christopher Tolkien, *The War of the Jewels*, pp. 182–5, 331.

MISCELLANEOUS

Númenórean carpet. *Pictures*, no. 46 (bottom left).

Númenórean carpet (*Akallabêth*). *Artist*, fig. 187; *Pictures*, no. 46 (bottom right).

Númenórean helmet, redrawn. *Unfinished Tales* (1980), dust-jacket.

Númenórean tile. *Pictures*, no. 46 (top).

Pilinehtar. *Pictures*, no. 45 (centre).

RELATED CALLIGRAPHY

Page from the *Dangweth Pengoloð*. *Artist*, fig. 198.

Page from the *Lay of Leithian Recommenced*. *The Lays of Beleriand*, George Allen & Unwin, 1985, frontispiece (colour); Houghton Mifflin, 1985, p. [i] (black and white).

Arundel Lowdham's fragments from *The Notion Club Papers*. *Sauron Defeated*, two colour plates preceding the half-title.

Title-page for *The Notion Club Papers*, and title inscription in foreword. *Sauron Defeated*, pp. 154–5.

Pages from Edwin Lowdham's manuscript (*The Notion Club Papers*), in Tengwar. *Sauron Defeated*, pp. 319–21.

First page of *The Tale of Years*. *Morgoth's Ring*, frontispiece.

VIII. MISCELLANEOUS ART

PICTURES

Afterwards. *Artist*, fig. 31.

Before. *Artist*, fig. 30.

Beyond. *Artist*, fig. 39.

Chequers Clubbe Binge June 1914. *Life and Legend*, p. 26.

'Dragon and Warrior'. *Artist* 49; *Pictures*, no. 40.

'Dragon Coiled around a Tree'. *Pictures*, no. 40.

Eeriness. *Artist*, fig. 40.

End of the World. *Artist*, fig. 36.

Exeter College Smoker Nov. 19th 1913. *Life and Legend*, p. 26; *The Tolkien Family Album*, p. 32. See also section I, *Turl Street, Oxford*.

'Gnarled Tree'. *Artist*, fig. 129.

Goosegrass. *Artist*, fig. 2.

Grownupishness. *Artist*, fig. 35.

Hringboga Heorte Gefysed (Coiled Dragon). *Artist*, fig. 48; *Pictures*, no. 40 (top).

The Land of Pohja. *Artist*, fig. 41.

Maddo. *Artist*, fig. 78.

Moonlight on a Wood. *Artist*, fig. 61.

The Misty Mountains. *Artist*, fig. 200.

'Northern House'. *Artist*, fig. 38.

Owlamoo. *Artist*, fig. 79.

A Shop on the Edge of the Hills of Fairy Land. *Artist*, fig. 71.

Thought. *Artist*, fig. 33.

'Three Sketches' (with giant and ogre). *Artist*, fig. 77.

'Trees in Moonlight'. *Life and Legend*, p. 5.

Undertenishness. *Artist*, fig. 34.

Wickedness. *Artist*, fig. 32.

The Wood at the World's End. *Artist*, fig. 60.

Wudu Wyrtum Faest (Grendel's Mere). *Artist*, fig. 50.

Wudu Wyrtum Faest (Grendel's Mere). *Artist*, fig. 51.

Xanadu. *Artist*, fig. 37.

PATTERNS

Belt designs. *Pictures*, no. 44 (centre).
Doodles. *Life and Legend*, p. 82.
Doodles on *Daily Telegraph* page. *Artist*, fig. 184.
Doodles on newspapers. *Pictures*, no. 43.
Flowering tree with a bird. *Pictures*, no. 42.
Frieze. *Pictures*, no. 44 (top right).
Frieze. *Pictures*, no. 44 (top left).
Frieze. *Pictures*, no. 45.
Friezes. *Pictures*, no. 44 (bottom two).
Grasses. *Artist*, fig. 196.
Paisley shape. *Pictures*, no. 44 (top right).
Paisley shape. *Pictures*, no. 44 (bottom left).
Patterns. *Artist*, fig. 183.
Patterns on envelope. *Artist*, fig. 186.
Plant. *Pictures*, no. 45 (top left).
Plant. *Pictures*, no. 45 (bottom left).
Spiral. *Pictures*, no. 44 (top left).
Sun motif (similar to Finwë device). *Pictures*, no. 44 (bottom right).
Sun motifs (similar to Finwë device). *Catalogue of an Exhibition of Drawings by J.R.R. Tolkien* (Ashmolean Museum and National Book League, 1976), preceding section on *The Lord of the Rings*.
Three friezes. *Artist*, fig. 59; *Pictures*, no. 42 (two only).
Tree of Amalion. *Artist*, fig. 62; *Pictures*, no. 41b (upper left).
Tree of Amalion. *Pictures*, no. 41A.
Tree of Amalion. *Pictures*, no. 41B (lower left).
Tree of Amalion. Upper cover of George Allen & Unwin paperback editions of *Tree and Leaf*, 1964–c. 1973.
Tree with flowers. *Pictures*, no. 41B (right).
Two flowers. *Pictures*, no. 42 (left and right).
Willow-like tree. *Pictures*, no. 45 (top right).

CALLIGRAPHY

First page of *Doworst*. *A Elbereth Gilthoniel* (newsletter of the Fellowship of Middle Earth, Monash University) 1, no. 2 (summer 1978), p. 3.
'Floral Alphabet'. *Artist*, fig. 197.

POETRY BY J.R.R. TOLKIEN

Following are lists of poems known to have been written by Tolkien, arranged by title and by first line. For those that have been published, the place and page(s) of first publication are given; for poems published with notes or commentary, or with illustrations, the stated range of pages generally includes such features. With very few exceptions (reflecting quirks of publication), entry is according to latest title; variant titles, and earlier or later versions, are noted when appropriate, and fuller information is given under a selected principal version in the title index. Untitled poems are listed in the title index by first line (in quotation marks). An asterisk (*) indicates that a descriptive entry for the poem may be found, under the title so marked, in the **Reader's Guide** volume of the *Companion and Guide*.

Because the published treatment of draft or alternate versions of poems ranges between full text at one extreme, and mere mention of variant words or lines at the other, we have partly sacrificed consistency of approach for the sake of clarity, e.g. omitting separate entry of first lines for poems where little or nothing else has been published, and (generally in the title index) concentrating information about versions under single entries rather than treat each version as a distinct poem.

BY TITLE

'A Elbereth Gilthoniel'. *The Lord of the Rings*, bk. II, ch. 1. An earlier version, beginning 'Elbereth Gilthoniel sir evrin pennar oriel', was published in *The Return of the Shadow*, p. 394. A variant, beginning 'A! Elbereth Gilthoniel', is in *The Lord of the Rings*, bk. VI, ch. 9. Earlier versions of the latter were published in *Sauron Defeated*, p. 112. See also *The Road Goes Ever On: A Song Cycle*, pp. 63–6 (1st. edn.), pp. 72–4 (2nd and 3rd edn.).

Adventures in Unnatural History and Medieval Metres, Being the Freaks of Fisiologus see *Fastitocalon*; and *Iumbo, or Ye Kinde of ye Oliphaunt*

*The Adventures of Tom Bombadil. *Oxford Magazine*, 15 February 1934, pp. 464–5. A later version with the same title was published in *The Adventures of Tom Bombadil and Other Verses from the Red Book*, pp. 11–16.

Ælfwine's Song Calling upon Eärendel see *The Nameless Land*

'Alive without breath'. *The Hobbit*, ch. 5. An extended version was published in *The Lord of the Rings*, bk. IV, ch. 2.

'All that is gold does not glitter'. *The Lord of the Rings*, bk. I, ch. 10, and bk. II, ch. 2. Earlier versions were published in *The Treason of Isengard*, pp. 49, 50, 77, 78.

'Annon edhellen, edro hi ammen!' *The Lord of the Rings*, bk. II, ch. 4.

Aotrou and Itroun see *The Lay of Aotrou and Itroun*

'Arísath nú Ridend míne!' *The War of the Ring*, p. 389.

'Arise, arise, Riders of Théoden!' *The Lord of the Rings*, bk. V, ch. 5. Cf. *The War of the Ring*, p. 385.

'Arise now, arise, Riders of Théoden!' *The Lord of the Rings*, bk. III, ch. 6.

'As I was sitting by the way'. *The Return of the Shadow*, p. 98.

As Light as Leaf on Lindentree see *Light as Leaf on Lindentree*

As Two Fair Trees. Nine lines published in *Biography*, p. 74.

Bagme Bloma. Songs for the Philologists, p. 12. A version corrected and revised by Tolkien was published in *The Road to Middle-earth* by T.A. Shippey, pp. 226–7 (1st edn. 1982), 303–4 (2nd edn. 1992).

The Ballad of St Brendan's Death see *Imram*

The Battle of the Eastern Field. King Edward's School *Chronicle*, March 1911, pp. 22–6.

'Be he foe or friend, be he foul or clean'. *Morgoth's Ring*, p. 112.

Beowulf. Unfinished verse translation into Modern English. Unpublished.

The Bidding of the Minstrel, from the Lay of Eärendel. *The Book of Lost Tales, Part Two*, pp. 269–71. Its earliest finished text was called (apparently) *The Minstrel Renounces the Song*. Later called *Lay of Eärendel*, and finally *The Bidding of the Minstrel, from the Lay of Eärendel*.

Bilbo's Last Song (At the Grey Havens). First published as a poster, later in book form. Adapted from *Vestr um Haf*.

'Bless the water O my feet and toes!' *The Return of the Shadow*, p. 102.

Bombadil Goes Boating. The Adventures of Tom Bombadil and Other Verses from the Red Book, pp. 17–23.

'A box without hinges, key or lid'. *The Hobbit*, ch. 5.

The Brothers in Arms (or *The Brothers-in-Arms*). Unpublished.

The Bumpus see *Perry-the-Winkle*

Cat. The Adventures of Tom Bombadil and Other Verses from the Red Book, p. 48 (first British printing, with illustration on p. 50), pp. 50–1 (second British printing, first American printing).

The Cat and the Fiddle: A Nursery-Rhyme Undone and Its Scandalous Secret Unlocked see *The Man in the Moon Stayed Up Too Late*

The Children of Húrin. Two versions of an unfinished alliterative poem. *The Lays of Beleriand*, pp. 3–130. The typed text of the first version had the title *The Golden Dragon*, emended to *Túrin Son of Húrin & Glorund the Dragon*; the second version was called *Túrin*, emended to *The Children of Húrin*. Two sections of the poem were separately developed: one text begins 'The high summer / waned to autumn, // and western gales', a second with greater changes is called *Storm over Narog*, and a third, with few further changes, is *Winter Comes to Nargothrond*; see *The Lays of Beleriand*, pp. 127–9. Another version of *The Children of Húrin*, with the same title, unpublished, is in rhyming couplets.

'Chip the glasses and crack the plates!' *The Hobbit*, ch. 1.

The City of the Gods. *The Microcosm*, Spring 1923, p. 8. Earlier called *Kôr: In a City Lost and Dead*.

'Clap! Snap! the black crack!' *The Hobbit*, ch. 4.

The Clerke's Compleinte. *The Gryphon*, December 1922, p. 95. Cf. later manuscript facsimile in *Arda 1986* (1990), pp. 2–3.

A Closed Letter to Andrea Charicoryides Surnamed Polygrapheus, Logothete of the Theme of Geodesia in the Empire, Bard of the Court of Camelot, Malleus Malitiarium, Inclinga Sum Sometimes Known as Charles Williams. *The Inklings*, pp. 123–6.

'Cold be hand and heart and bone'. *The Lord of the Rings*, bk. I, ch. 8. A brief comment on the first version was published in *The Return of the Shadow*, p. 127.

'The cold hard lands'. *The Lord of the Rings*, bk. IV, ch. 2. An earlier version was published in *The War of the Ring*, p. 111.

Companions of the Rose. Unpublished.

Completorium. Unpublished. Earlier called *Evening*.

Consolatrix Afflictorum see *Stella Vespertina*

Copernicus and Ptolemy (or *Copernicus v. Ptolemy*). Unpublished. Earlier called *Dark*.

Courage Speaks with the Love of Earth (or *Courage Speaks with a Child of Earth*) see *The Two Riders*

The Dale-lands. Unpublished. Earlier called *The Dale Lands*.

'Dar fys ma vel gom co palt 'Hoc'. *Biography*, p. 36, with English translation ('There was an old man who said "How'). Cf. *A Secret Vice* in *The Monsters and the Critics and Other Essays*, p. 203.

Dark see *Copernicus and Ptolemy*

Dark Are the Clouds about the North. Unpublished.

Darkness on the Road. Unpublished.

The Death of St Brendan see *Imram*

'Dir avosaith a gwaew hinar'. *A Secret Vice,* in *The Monsters and the Critics and Other Essays,* p. 217.

'Dr U.Q. Humphrey'. *The Inklings,* p. 177.

'Down the swift dark stream you go'. *The Hobbit,* ch. 9.

*Doworst. First page only published in *A Elbereth Gilthoniel!* (newsletter of the Fellowship of Middle Earth), [?Summer 1978]. Later called *Visio Petri Aratoris de Doworst.*

'The dragon is withered'. *The Hobbit,* ch. 19.

*The Dragon's Visit. Oxford Magazine, 4 February 1937, p. 342. One of the *Tales and Songs of Bimble Bay.* A later version with the same title was published in *Winter's Tales for Children I,* pp. 84, 86–7.

A Dream of Coming Home. Unpublished.

Eadig Beo Þu! Songs for the Philologists, p. 13. A version corrected and revised by Tolkien was published in *The Road to Middle-earth* by T.A. Shippey, pp. 228–9 (1st edn. 1982), 304–5 (2nd edn. 1992).

Tha Eadigan Saelidan: The Happy Mariners see *The Happy Mariners*

*Éalá Éarendel Engla Beorhtast. The Book of Lost Tales, Part Two, pp. 267–9, with variant readings of the earliest version, *The Voyage of Éarendel the Evening Star.* An intermediate version was called *Éalá Éarendel Engla Beorhtast 'The Last Voyage of Eärendel'.*

Earendel see *Earendel at the Helm*

*Earendel at the Helm. A Secret Vice, in *The Monsters and the Critics and Other Essays,* pp. 216–17, 220. English version (in verse) of *Earendel,* a poem in Quenya with English prose translation, also in *A Secret Vice,* p. 216.

'Eärendil was a mariner'. *The Lord of the Rings,* bk. II, ch. 1. See *The Treason of Isengard,* ch. 5, for the evolution of the poem relative to **Errantry;* and see also *The Short Lay of Eärendel: Eärendillinwë.*

Elf Alone. Unpublished. Earlier called *The Lonely Harebell.*

'An Elven-maid there was of old'. *The Lord of the Rings,* bk. II, ch. 6. Earlier versions were published in *The Treason of Isengard,* pp. 223–4.

*Elvish Song in Rivendell. The Annotated Hobbit, rev. and expanded edn., pp. 92–3.

Enigmata Saxonica Nuper Inventa Duo. Two riddles in Old English ('Meol-chwitum sind marmanstane', 'Hæfth Hild Hunecan hwite tunecan') in *A Northern Venture*, p. 20.

'Ents the earthborn, old as mountains'. *The Lord of the Rings*, bk. III, ch. 10.

'Ere iron was found or tree was hewn'. *The Lord of the Rings*, bk. III, ch. 8.

Errantry. Oxford Magazine, 9 November 1933, p. 180. A later version with the same title was published in *The Adventures of Tom Bombadil and Other Verses from the Red Book*, pp. 24–7. See also early versions and evolution, relative to *Eärendil Was a Mariner*, in *The Treason of Isengard*, ch. 5.

Eruman beneath the Stars see *Habbanan beneath the Stars*

Evening see *Completorium*

An Evening in Tavrobel. Leeds University Verse 1914–24, p. 56. Earlier called *Two Eves in Tavrobel.*

'An eye in a blue face'. *The Hobbit*, ch. 5. (But see *Letters*, p. 123.)

A Faërie: Why the Man in the Moon Came Down Too Soon see *The Man in the Moon Came Down Too Soon*

'Faithful servant yet master's bane'. *The Lord of the Rings*, bk. 5, ch. 6.

The Fall of Arthur. Unpublished, except for brief extracts in *Biography*, p. 169.

'Far over the misty mountains cold'. *The Hobbit*, ch. 1.

'Farewell! farewell, now hearth and hall!' *The Return of the Shadow*, pp. 300–1. See 'Farewell we call to hearth and hall!'

'Farewell sweet earth and northern sky'. *The Silmarillion*, p. 178.

'Farewell we call to hearth and hall!' *The Lord of the Rings*, bk. 1, ch. 5. An earlier version, beginning 'Farewell! farewell, now hearth and hall!' was published in *The Return of the Shadow*, pp. 300–1.

Fastitocalon. Stapeldon Magazine, June 1927, pp. 123–5. Published as one of two parts of *Adventures in Unnatural History and Medieval Metres, being the Freaks of Fisiologus*. Precursor of the poem by the same title in *The Adventures of Tom Bombadil and Other Verses from the Red Book.*

Fastitocalon. The Adventures of Tom Bombadil and Other Verses from the Red Book, pp. 49, 51 (first British printing), pp. 48–9 (second British printing, first American printing). A related poem, by the same title, was published earlier in the *Stapeldon Magazine.*

'Fela bið on Westwegum werum uncúðra'. *The Lost Road* in *The Lost Road and Other Writings*, pp. 44, 55, 103–4, 203.

Ferrum et Sanguis. Unpublished.

'Fifteen birds in five firtrees'. *The Hobbit*, ch. 6.

'Fil me a cuppe of ful gode ale'. *Sauron Defeated*, p. 245.

'The finest rockets ever seen'. *The Lord of the Rings*, bk. II, ch. 7.

Firiel see *The Last Ship*

Flight of the Gnomes see *The Flight of the Noldoli from Valinor*

The Flight of the Gnomes as Sung in the Halls of Thingol see *The Flight of the Noldoli from Valinor*

*The Flight of the Noldoli from Valinor. *The Lays of Beleriand*, pp. 131–41. Earlier versions were *The Flight of the Gnomes as Sung in the Halls of Thingol* and *Flight of the Gnomes*.

*For W.H.A. In Old English and Modern English. *Shenandoah*, Winter 1967, pp. 96–7.

The Forest-walker. Unpublished. Earlier called *The Forest Walker*.

A Fragment of an Epic: Before Jerusalem Richard Makes an End of Speech. Unpublished.

Frenchmen Froth. *Songs for the Philologists*, pp. 24–5.

'From dark Dunharrow in the dim morning'. *The Lord of the Rings*, bk. V, ch. 3.

From Iffley. The first stanza, beginning **'From the many-willow'd margin of the immemorial Thames'*, was published in the *Stapeldon Magazine*, December 1913, p. 11.

From One to Five. *Songs for the Philologists*, p. 6.

*'From the many-willow'd margin of the immemorial Thames'. *Stapeldon Magazine*, December 1913, p. 11. First stanza of *From Iffley*; the second stanza is unpublished. Later revised as *Valedictory*.

Gawain's Leave-taking. *Sir Gawain and the Green Knight, Pearl and Sir Orfeo*, p. 149.

G.B.S. Unpublished. Earlier called *GBS*.

The Gest of Beren Son of Barahir and Lúthien the Fay Called Tinúviel the Nightingale see *Lay of Leithian*

'Get out, you old Wight! Vanish in the sunlight!' *The Lord of the Rings*, bk. 1, ch. 8.

'Gil-galad was an Elven-king'. *The Lord of the Rings*, bk. 1, ch. 11.

*Glip. *The Annotated Hobbit*, rev. and expanded edn., p. 119. One of the *Tales and Songs of Bimble Bay*.

Goblin Feet. Oxford Poetry 1915, pp. 64–5.

The Golden Dragon see *The Children of Húrin*

'Gondor! Gondor, between the Mountains and the Sea!' *The Lord of the Rings*, bk. 3, ch. 2. An earlier version, beginning 'Ondor! Ondor! Between the Mountains and the Sea', was published in *The Treason of Isengard*, pp. 395–6.

The Grey Bridge of Tavrobel. Inter-University Magazine, [?mid-1920s], p. 82.

The Grimness of the Sea see *The Horns of Ylmir*

Gunnar's End. Unpublished. Translation of brief passage from the Norse *Atlakviða* into Old English verse.

Guðrúnarkviða en nýja ('The New Lay of Gudrún'). Unpublished.

Habbanan beneath the Stars. The Book of Lost Tales, Part One, pp. 91–2. Later called *Eruman beneath the Stars*.

'Hæfth Hild Hunecan hwite tunecan' see *Enigmata Saxonica Nuper Inventa Duo*

The Happy Mariners. Stapeldon Magazine, June 1920, pp. 69–70. Later revised as *Tha Eadigan Saelidan: The Happy Mariners*, in *A Northern Venture*, pp. 15–16. A much later revision was published in *The Book of Lost Tales, Part Two*, pp. 273–7, with the first version.

'He knows Tom Bombadil, and Tom's name will help you'. *The Return of the Shadow*, p. 130.

'Hey! Come derry dol! Hop along, my hearties!' *The Lord of the Rings*, bk. I, ch. 6.

'Hey! Come merry dol! My darling!' *The Lord of the Rings*, bk. I, ch. 6.

'Hey dol! merry dol! ring a dong dillo!' *The Lord of the Rings*, bk. I, ch. 6.

'Hey! now! Come hoy now! Whither do you wander?' *The Lord of the Rings*, bk. I, ch. 8.

'Ho! Ho! Ho! to the bottle I go'. *The Lord of the Rings*, bk. I, ch. 4. An earlier version, beginning 'Ho! ho! ho! To my bottle I go', was published in *The Return of the Shadow*, p. 91.

'Ho! Tom Bombadil, Tom Bombadillo!' *The Fellowship of the Ring*, bk. I, ch. 7, 8. An earlier version, beginning 'Ho! Tom Bombadil! Whither do you wander?' was published in *The Return of the Shadow*, p. 123.

The Hoard. The Adventures of Tom Bombadil and Other Verses from the Red Book, pp. 53–6. An earlier version, *Iúmonna Gold Galdre Bewunden*, was published in *The Gryphon*, January 1923, p. 130. Another version, *Iumonna*

Gold Galdre Bewunden, was published in the *Oxford Magazine*, 4 March 1937, p. 473. *Beowulf and the Critics* (see **Beowulf: The Monsters and the Critics*) includes an intermediate version of the poem, pp. 110–12.

*The Homecoming of Beorhtnoth Beorhthelm's Son. Essays and Studies 1953, pp. 1–18. Alliterative verse-drama, published with introduction and afterword. Part of an earlier version, in rhyming verse, was published in *The Treason of Isengard*, pp. 106–7.

'Hop along, my little friends, up the Withywindle!' *The Lord of the Rings*, bk. I, ch. 6.

The Horns of the Host of Doriath. Unpublished. An earlier version was called *The Trumpets of Faery*.

The Horns of Ulmo see *The Horns of Ylmir*

*The Horns of Ylmir. *The Shaping of Middle-earth*, pp. 213–18. Earlier versions were called *The Grimness of the Sea* (unpublished), *The Tides*, *Sea Chant of an Elder Day*, *The Horns of Ulmo*. An extract from *The Tides* was published in *The Shaping of Middle-earth*, p. 214. Extracts from *Sea Chant of an Elder Day* were published in *Biography*, pp. 73–4; *The Shaping of Middle-earth*, p. 214; and *Artist and Illustrator*, pp. 45–6. Notes on *The Horns of Ulmo* were published in *The Shaping of Middle-earth*, p. 215.

'Hwaet! Éadweard cyning Ælfredes sunu'. *Sauron Defeated*, pp. 271–2.

'Hwaet! we Inclinga'. *The Inklings*, pp. 176–7.

'Hwaet! wé on geárdagum of Gársecge'. *Sauron Defeated*, p. 273.

'I had an errand there: gathering water-lilies'. *The Lord of the Rings*, bk. I, ch. 7.

'I sang of leaves, of leaves of gold, and leaves of gold there grew'. *The Lord of the Rings*, bk. II, ch. 8. The earliest version was published in *The Treason of Isengard*, p. 284.

I Sat upon a Bench. Songs for the Philologists, p. 17.

'I sit beside the fire and think'. *The Lord of the Rings*, bk. II, ch. 3. Part of an earlier version was published in *The Treason of Isengard*, p. 173.

Ides Ælfscyne. Songs for the Philologists, pp. 10–11. A version corrected and revised by Tolkien was published in *The Road to Middle-earth* by T.A. Shippey, pp. 229–31 (1st edn. 1982), 306–7 (2nd edn. 1992).

'Ilu Ilúvatar en karé eldain a fírimoin'. *The Lost Road* in *The Lost Road and Other Writings*, pp. 63, 72.

*Imram. Time and Tide, 3 December 1955, p. 1561. An intermediate version, *The Death of St Brendan*, was published in *Sauron Defeated*, pp. 261–4, with variant readings for the earliest version, *The Ballad of St Brendan's Death*.

'In Dwimordene, in Lórien'. *The Lord of the Rings*, bk. III, ch. 6.

'In the willow-meads of Tasarinan I walked in the Spring'. *The Lord of the Rings*, bk. III, ch. 4. Differences in an earlier version are noted in *The Treason of Isengard*, p. 420, n. 6.

'In western lands beneath the Sun'. *The Lord of the Rings*, bk. VI, ch. 1. An earlier version, beginning 'I sit upon the stones alone', was published in *Sauron Defeated*, pp. 27–8.

'It cannot be seen, cannot be felt'. *The Hobbit*, ch. 5.

Iumbo, or ye Kinde of ye Oliphaunt. One of two parts of *Adventures in Unnatural History and Medieval Metres, being the Freaks of Fisiologus*. *Stapeldon Magazine*, June 1927, pp. 125–7. Precursor of *Oliphaunt*.

Iúmonna Gold Galdre Bewunden, Iumonna Gold Galdre Bewunden see *The Hoard*

'I've got a very Briny Notion'. *The Notion Club Papers* in *Sauron Defeated*, p. 224.

'J.R.R. Tolkien'. *Letters*, p. 398.

'The King beneath the mountains'. *The Hobbit*, ch. 10.

King Sheave. *The Lost Road* in *The Lost Road and Other Writings*, pp. 86–92.

Knocking at the Door see *The Mewlips*

Kôr: In a City Lost and Dead see *The City of the Gods*

Kortirion among the Trees see *The Trees of Kortirion*

La, Húru. *Songs for the Philologists*, p. 16.

The Last Ark. Two versions in English, in *A Secret Vice* in *The Monsters and the Critics and Other Essays*, pp. 214–15, 221–3. Cf. *Oilima Markirya*, versions in Quenya. The earlier title of one of the English versions is *The Last Ship*, not related to the poem of that name published in *The Adventures of Tom Bombadil and Other Verses from the Red Book*.

The Last Ship. *The Adventures of Tom Bombadil and Other Verses from the Red Book*, pp. 61–4. An earlier version, *Firiel*, was published in the *Chronicle of the Convents of the Sacred Heart*, 1934, pp. 30–2.

The Lay of Aotrou and Itroun. *Welsh Review*, November–December 1945, pp. 254–66.

Lay of Eärendel see *The Bidding of the Minstrel*

The Lay of Eärendel. *The Lays of Beleriand*, pp. 141–4.

Lay of Leithian. The first version, called *The Gest of Beren Son of Barahir and Lúthien the Fay Called Tinúviel the Nightingale*, was published in *The Lays of Beleriand*, pp. 150–329; and later revisions with the title *Lay of Leithian*, pp. 330–63. A slightly emended section was published in *The Silmarillion*, p. 171.

The Lay of the Children of Húrin see *The Children of Húrin*

The Lay of the Fall of Gondolin. *The Lays of Beleriand*, pp. 144–9.

'Lazy Lob and crazy Cob'. *The Hobbit*, ch. 8.

'Learn now the lore of Living Creatures!' *The Lord of the Rings*, bk. III, ch. 4.

'Legolas Greenleaf long under tree'. *The Lord of the Rings*, bk. III, ch. 5. An earlier version, beginning 'Greenleaf, Greenleaf, bearer of the elven-bow', was published in *The Treason of Isengard*, p. 431.

Light as Leaf on Lindentree. *The Gryphon*, June 1925, p. 217. An alliterative introduction begins ''Tis of Beren Ermabwed brokenhearted'. Early versions were called *Light as Leaf on Lind*, *As Light as Leaf on Lindentree*, and *As Light as Leaf on Lind* (emended to *Linden-tree*); see *The Lays of Beleriand*, pp. 120–3. Later versions were published in *The Return of the Shadow*, pp. 179–82, and *The Lord of the Rings*, bk. I, ch. 11 ('The leaves were long, the grass was green').

Lit' and Lang'. *Songs for the Philologists*, p. 27.

The Little House of Lost Play: Mar Vanwa Tyaliéva. *The Book of Lost Tales, Part One*, pp. 27–32. Included there are an earlier version, *You & Me and the Cottage of Lost Play*, pp. 28–30, and notes of emendations for an intermediate version, *Mar Vanwa Tyaliéva, The Cottage of Lost Play*.

The Lonely Harebell see *Elf Alone*

The Lonely Isle. *Leeds University Verse 1914–24*, p. 57. An earlier version, unpublished, was called *Tol Eressëa*.

'Long live the Halflings! Praise them with great praise!' *The Lord of the Rings*, bk. VI, p. 4. Earlier versions were published in *Sauron Defeated*, pp. 46–7.

Looney see *The Sea-Bell*

'The Lord of the Rings'. *Biography*, p. 223.

Magna Dei Gloria. Unpublished.

The Man in the Moon Came Down Too Soon. *The Adventures of Tom Bombadil and Other Verses from the Red Book*, pp. 34–8. The earliest workings were called *Why the Man in the Moon Came Down Too Soon (An East Anglian Phantasy)*, and the first finished text *A Faërie: Why the Man in the Moon Came Down Too Soon*. A later version, *Why the Man in the Moon*

Came Down Too Soon, was published in *A Northern Venture*, pp. 17–19. A still later version with this title was published in *The Book of Lost Tales, Part One*, pp. 204–6.

*The Man in the Moon Stayed Up Too Late. *The Lord of the Rings*, bk. I, ch. 9, without title, and *The Adventures of Tom Bombadil and Other Verses from the Red Book*, so titled, pp. 31–3. An earlier version, *The Cat and the Fiddle: A Nursery-Rhyme Undone and Its Scandalous Secret Unlocked*, was published in *Yorkshire Poetry*, October–November 1923, pp. 1–3, and the first manuscript version in *The Return of the Shadow*, pp. 145–7.

Mar Vanwa Tyaliéva, The Cottage of Lost Play see *The Little House of Lost Play: Mar Vanwa Tyaliéva*

May-day. Unpublished. Earlier called *May Day, May Day in a Backward Year*.

A Memory of July in England. Unpublished.

'Meolchwitum sind marmanstane' see **Enigmata Saxonica Nuper Inventa Duo*

The Mermaid's Flute. Unpublished.

*The Mewlips. *The Adventures of Tom Bombadil and Other Verses from the Red Book*. pp. 45–6. An earlier version, *Knocking at the Door*, was published in the *Oxford Magazine*, 18 February 1937, p. 403.

The Minstrel Renounces the Song see *The Bidding of the Minstrel*

'Mr Neville Judson Coghill'. *Letters*, p. 359.

'Mr Owen Barfield's'. *The Inklings*, p. 177.

'Monath módaes lust mith meriflóda'. *The Notion Club Papers* in *Sauron Defeated*, p. 243. A variant, 'Monath módes lust mid mereflóde', was published on p. 272. See also *The Lost Road and Other Writings*, p. 84, and *Sauron Defeated*, pp. 287–8.

Monoceros, the Unicorn. Unpublished.

Morning see *Morning Song*

Morning Song. Unpublished. Earlier called *Morning-song*. An earlier version, also unpublished, was called *Morning*.

Morning Tea. Unpublished.

'Mourn not overmuch! Mighty was the fallen'. *The Lord of the Rings*, bk. V, ch. 6.

*Mythopoeia. *Tree and Leaf*, 1988 edn., pp. 97–101. Earlier called *Nisomythos: A Long Answer to Short Nonsense*. A variant first line, 'He looks at trees and labels them just so', is quoted on p. 7. An extract was published earlier in *On Fairy-Stories*.

Namárië. *The Lord of the Rings*, bk. II, ch, 8, emended slightly in the 2nd edn. See also *The Road Goes Ever On: A Song Cycle*, pp. 58–62, 68 (1st edn.), 66–70, 76 (2nd and 3rd editions).

*The Nameless Land. *Realities*, pp. 24–5. Later version, *The Song of Ælfwine (on Seeing the Uprising of Eärendel)* and *The Song of Ælfwine on Seeing the Uprising of Eärendil*, with the intermediate title *Ælfwine's Song Calling upon Eärendel*, were published in *The Lost Road and Other Writings*, pp. 100–104.

*Narqelion. Published in 'Narqelion: A Single, Falling Leaf at Sun-fading' by Paul Nolan Hyde, *Mythlore*, Winter 1988, pp. 47–52. Four lines, inaccurately transcribed, were earlier published in *Biography*, p. 76. See also *Vinyar Tengwar*, April 1999, pp. 5 (photograph) and 8.

Natura Apis. *Songs for the Philologists*, p. 18.

The New Lemminkäinen. Unpublished.

*Nieninque. *A Secret Vice*, in *The Monsters and the Critics and Other Essays*, pp. 215–16.

Nisomythos: A Long Answer to Short Nonsense see *Mythopoeia*

Now and Ever see *The Two Riders*

'Now let the song begin! Let us sing together'. *The Lord of the Rings*, bk. I, ch. 6.

'O Naffarinos cutá vu navra cangor'. *A Secret Vice* in *The Monsters and the Critics and Other Essays*, p. 209.

'O Orofarnë, Lassemista, Carnimirië!' *The Lord of the Rings*, bk. III, ch. 4.

'O slender as a willow-wand! O clearer than clear water!' *The Lord of the Rings*, bk. I, ch. 7.

'O! Wanderers in the shadowed land'. *The Lord of the Rings*, bk. I, ch. 6. Earlier versions, beginning 'O Wanderers in the land of trees' and 'O! Wanderers in the shadow-land', are noted in *The Return of the Shadow*, pp. 112, 114–15.

'O! What are you doing'. *The Hobbit*, ch. 3.

Ofer Widne Garsecq. *Songs for the Philologists*, pp. 14–15. A version corrected and revised by Tolkien was published in *The Road to Middle-earth* by T.A. Shippey, pp. 231–3 (1st edn. 1982), 308–9 (2nd edn. 1992).

Oilima Markirya. Two versions in Quenya, in *A Secret Vice* in *The Monsters and the Critics and Other Essays*, pp. 213–14, 220–3. Cf. **The Last Ark*, versions in English.

'Old fat spider spinning in a tree!' *The Hobbit*, ch. 8.

Old Grabbler. Unpublished. One of the *Tales and Songs of Bimble Bay*. Earlier called *Poor Old Grabbler*.

'Old Tom Bombadil is a merry fellow'. *The Lord of the Ring*, bk. I, ch. 7, 8.

*Oliphaunt. *The Lord of the Rings*, bk. IV, ch. 3, without title, and *The Adventures of Tom Bombadil and Other Verses from the Red Book*, p. 47, so titled. A related poem, *Iumbo, or Ye Kinde of Ye Oliphaunt*, was published earlier in the *Stapeldon Magazine*.

*Once upon a Time. *Winter's Tales for Children* 1, pp. 44–5.

'Ónen i-Estel Edain, ú-chebin estel anim'. *The Lord of the Rings*, Appendix A.

'Our dear Charles Williams many guises shows'. *The Inklings*, pp. 123–6.

'Out of doubt, out of dark to the day's rising'. *The Lord of the Rings*, bk. VI, ch. 6.

Outside. Unpublished.

*Over Old Hills and Far Away. *The Book of Lost Tales, Part One*, pp. 108–10. Earlier readings are noted on p. 110.

'Over the land there lies a long shadow'. *The Lord of the Rings*, bk. V, ch. 2. Related poems and earlier versions were published in *The War of the Ring*, pp. 300, 302, 305, 307, 311.

The Owl and the Nightingale. Unpublished. Unfinished translation into Modern English.

*Pearl. Translation into Modern English in *Sir Gawain and the Green Knight, Pearl and Sir Orfeo*, pp. 89–122.

*Perry-the-Winkle. *The Adventures of Tom Bombadil and Other Verses from the Red Book*, pp. 41–4. An earlier version (unpublished) was called *The Bumpus*, one of the *Tales and Songs of Bimble Bay*.

The Pool of the Dead Year. Unpublished.

Poor Old Grabbler see *Old Grabbler*

*Princess Mee. *The Adventures of Tom Bombadil and Other Verses from the Red Book*, pp. 28–30. Greatly rewritten from *The Princess Ní*.

*The Princess Ní. *Leeds University Verse 1914–24*, p. 58. Later greatly rewritten as *Princess Mee*.

*Progress in Bimble Town. *Oxford Magazine*, 15 October 1931, p. 22. One of the *Tales and Songs of Bimble Bay*.

Reginhardus the Fox. Unpublished.

'The Rev. Mathew (Gervase)'. *The Inklings*, p. 186.

Rhyme. The 'Father Christmas' letters, letter for 1938.

A Rime for My Boy. Unpublished.

'The Road goes ever on and on'. Variant texts in *The Lord of the Rings*, bk. I, ch. 1 (Bilbo), bk. I, ch. 3 (Frodo), and bk. VI, ch. 6 (Bilbo). Earlier versions were published in *The Return of the Shadow*, pp. 47, 53, 240, 246, 278, 284, 324.

'Roads go ever ever on'. *The Hobbit*, ch. 19.

'Roll – roll – roll – roll'. *The Hobbit*, ch. 9.

The Root of the Boot see *The Stone Troll*

Ruddoc Hana. *Songs for the Philologists*, pp. 8–9.

The Ruined Enchanter: A Fairy Ballad. Unpublished.

'(Said I) / "Ho! Tom Bombadil'. *The Return of the Shadow*, pp. 115–16. Precursor of *Bombadil Goes Boating*.

'The sales of Charles Williams'. *The Inklings*, p. 187.

The Sea-Bell. *The Adventures of Tom Bombadil and Other Verses from the Red Book*, pp. 57–60. An earlier version, *Looney*, was published in the *Oxford Magazine*, 18 January 1934, p. 340.

Sea-Chant of an Elder Day see *The Horns of Ylmir*

Sea-Song of an Elder Day see *The Horns of Ylmir*

'Seek for the Sword that was broken'. *The Lord of the Rings*, bk. I, ch. 2. Earlier versions were published in *The Treason of Isengard*, pp. 128, 146.

Shadow-Bride. *The Adventures of Tom Bombadil and Other Verses from the Red Book*, p. 52. An earlier version was apparently published in the 1920s, in an unidentified magazine possibly called *Abingdon Chronicle*.

The Shores of Faery. The earliest extant version was published in *Biography*, pp. 76–7, with errors of transcription, and more faithfully in *Artist and Illustrator*, pp. 47–8 (and p. 66, n. 31), excepting one error of punctuation. A later version with the same title was published in *The Book of Lost Tales, Part Two*, pp. 271–3, with notes of emendations from the first version.

The Short Lay of Eärendel: Eärendillinwë. The further development and final form of the poem which evolved from *Errantry* to 'Eärendil was a mariner' in *The Lord of the Rings*, bk. II, ch. 1. Emendations to the two texts that followed that published in *The Lord of the Rings*, *The Short Lay of Eärendel* and *The Short Lay of Eärendel: Eärendillinwë* were published in *The Treason of Isengard*, pp. 102–5. The complete text of *The Short Lay of Eärendel: Eärendillinwë* was published in *Reader's Companion*, pp. 210–13.

'Silver flow the streams from Celos to Erui'. *The Lord of the Rings*, bk. V, ch. 9.

'Sing all ye joyful, now sing all together!' *The Hobbit*, ch. 19.

'Sing hey! for the bath at close of day'. *The Lord of the Rings*, bk. I, ch. 5. An earlier version, beginning 'O! Water warm and water hot!' was published in *The Return of the Shadow*, p. 98.

'Sing now, ye people of the Tower of Anor'. *The Lord of the Rings*, bk. VI, ch. 5.

*Sir Gawain and the Green Knight. Modern English translation in *Sir Gawain and the Green Knight, Pearl and Sir Orfeo*, pp. 25–88.

*Sir Orfeo. Modern English translation in *Sir Gawain and the Green Knight, Pearl and Sir Orfeo*, pp. 125–37.

The Sirens. Unpublished.

'Snow-white! Snow-white! O Lady clear!' *The Lord of the Rings*, bk. I, ch. 3. Earlier versions were published or noted in *The Return of the Shadow*, pp. 59, 68, beginning 'O Elberil! O Elberil!' and 'O Elbereth! O Elbereth!'

The Song of Ælfwine (on Seeing the Uprising of Eärendel), The Song of Ælfwine on Seeing the Uprising of Eärendil see *The Nameless Land*

*A Song of Aryador. *The Book of Lost Tales, Part One*, pp. 138–9.

A Song of Bimble Bay. Unpublished. One of the *Tales and Songs of Bimble Bay*.

The Song of Eriol see *The Town of Dreams and the City of Present Sorrow*

The Sorrowful City see *The Town of Dreams and the City of Present Sorrow*

Sparrow Song (Bilink). Unpublished. Earlier called *Sparrow-song*.

Stella Vespertina. Unpublished. Earlier called *Consolatrix Afflictorum*.

'Still round the corner there may wait' see 'Upon the hearth the fire is red'

*The Stone Troll. *The Lord of the Rings*, bk. I, ch. 12, without title, and *The Adventures of Tom Bombadil and Other Verses from the Red Book*, pp. 39–40, so titled. An earlier version, *The Root of the Boot*, was published in *Songs for the Philologists*, pp. 20–1.

Storm over Narog see *The Children of Húrin*

The Story of Kullervo. Unpublished. Prose tale which includes much verse; see **The Kalevala*.

Sunset in a Town. Unpublished.

The Swallow and the Traveller on the Plains. Unpublished. Earlier called *Thoughts on Parade*.

Syx Mynet. *Songs for the Philologists*, p. 7.

Tales and Songs of Bimble Bay see **The Dragon's Visit, *Glip, *Perry-the-Winkle, Old Grabbler, *Progress in Bimble Town, A Song of Bimble Bay*.

'Tall ships and tall kings'. *The Lord of the Rings*, bk. III, ch. 11.

The Thatch of Poppies. Unpublished.

'There was an old man who said 'How' see 'Dar fys ma vel gom co palt 'Hoc'

'There was an old priest naméd Francis'. *The Tolkien Family Album*, p. 22.

'Thirty white horses on a red hill'. *The Hobbit*, ch. 5. Cf. *Letters*, p. 123.

'This thing all things devours'. *The Hobbit*, ch. 5.

Thoughts on Parade see *The Swallow and the Traveller on the Plains*

'Three Rings for the Elven-kings under the sky'. *The Lord of the Rings*, preliminaries, bk. I, ch. 2, etc. Earlier versions were published in *The Return of the
Shadow*, pp. 258, 259, 269.

'Through Rohan over fen and field where the long grass grows'. *The Lord of the
Rings*, bk. III, ch. 1.

'Thus cwæth Ælfwine Wídlást'. *The Lost Road* in *The Lost Road and Other
Writings*, pp. 44, 55. Also published as 'Þus cwaeÞ Ælfwine Wídlást' in
Quenta Silmarillion, in *The Lost Road and Other Writings*, p. 203, and as
'Þus cwæð Ælfwine Wídlást Éadwines sunu' in *The Notion Club Papers*, in
Sauron Defeated, pp. 245, 288.

The Tides see *The Horns of Ylmir*

Tinfang Warble. Inter-*University Magazine*, [?mid-1920s], p. 63.

'To Isengard! Though Isengard be ringed and barred with doors of stone'. *The
Lord of the Rings*, bk. III, ch. 4, 9.

'To the Sea, to the Sea! The white gulls are crying'. *The Lord of the Rings*, bk.
VI, ch. 4.

Tol Eressëa see *The Lonely Isle*

'Tom's country ends here: he will not pass the borders'. *The Lord of the Rings*,
bk. I, ch. 8.

The Town of Dead Days: An Old Town Revisited see *The Town of Dreams and
the City of Present Sorrow*

The Town of Dreams: An Old Town Revisited see *The Town of Dreams and the
City of Present Sorrow*

The Town of Dreams and the City of Present Sorrow. *The Book of Lost Tales,
Part Two*, pp. 295–300. The title on the earliest drafts was *The Wanderer's
Allegiance*, later subdivided into three parts, subtitled 'Prelude', 'The Inland
City', and 'The Sorrowful City'. The overall title was possibly changed to
The Sorrowful City. The only other copy of the complete poem has the over-
all title *The Town of Dreams and the City of Present Sorrow*, with subtitles

'Prelude', 'The Town of Dreams', and 'The City of Present Sorrow'. A part of 'The City of Present Sorrow' was treated as a separate poem, with the title *The Sorrowful City*, changed to *Wínsele wéste, windge reste réte berofene*. A section of 'The Town of Dreams' was also treated as a separate poem, in two versions called *The Town of Dreams: An Old Town Revisited* and then *The Town of Dead Days: An Old Town Revisited*. The 'Prelude' became the beginning of a new poem, *The Song of Eriol*.

*The Trees of Kortirion. *The Book of Lost Tales, Part One*, pp. 39–43. Two earlier versions, called *Kortirion among the Trees*, were published in the same volume, pp. 33–9.

The Trumpets of Faery see *The Horns of the Host of Doriath*

Túrin see *The Children of Húrin*

Túrin Son of Húrin & Glórund the Dragon see *The Children of Húrin*

Two Eves in Tavrobel see *An Evening in Tavrobel*

The Two Riders. Unpublished. Earlier versions (unpublished) were called *Courage Speaks with the Love of Earth*, *Courage Speaks with a Child of Earth*, and *Now and Ever*.

'Under the Mountain dark and tall'. *The Hobbit*, ch. 15.

'Upon the hearth the fire is red'. *The Lord of the Rings*, bk. 1, ch. 3. Earlier versions were published in *The Return of the Shadow*, pp. 57, 67.

'Úþwita sceal // ealdgesægenum'. *Henry Bradley. 3 Dec., 1845–23 May, 1923* in *Bulletin of Modern Humanities Association*, October 1923, p. 5.

Valedictory see *From the Many-willow'd Margin of the Immemorial Thames*

Vestr um Haf. Unpublished. Adapted as **Bilbo's Last Song*.

Visio Petri Aratoris de Doworst see *Doworst*

'Voiceless it cries'. *The Hobbit*, ch. 5.

Völsungakviða en nýja ('The New Lay of the Völsungs'). Unpublished.

The Voyage of Earendel the Evening Star see *Éalá Éarendel Engla Beorhtast*

'Wake now my merry lads! Wake and hear me calling!' *The Lord of the Rings*, bk. I, ch. 8.

The Wanderer's Allegiance see *The Town of Dreams and the City of Present Sorrow*

'We come, we come with roll of drum: ta-runda runda runda rom!' *The Lord of the Rings*, bk. III, ch. 4. Earlier versions were published in *The Treason of Isengard*, pp. 420–1.

'We heard of the horns in the hills ringing'. *The Lord of the Rings*, bk. V, ch. 6. An earlier version, beginning 'We heard in the hills the horns ringing', was published in *The War of the Ring*, p. 371.

'What has roots as nobody sees'. *The Hobbit*, ch. 5. A later version was published in *The Return of the Shadow*, pp. 263.

'When evening in the Shire was grey'. *The Lord of the Rings*, bk. II, ch. 7. Earlier versions, beginning 'When morning on the Hill was bright', were published in *The Treason of Isengard*, pp. 264, 266.

'When spring unfolds the beechen leaf, and sap is in the bough'. *The Lord of the Rings*, bk. III, ch. 4. Part of an earlier version was published in *The Treason of Isengard*, p. 421.

'When the black breath blows'. *The Lord of the Rings*, bk. V, ch. 8.

'When winter first begins to bite'. *The Lord of the Rings*, bk. II, ch. 3.

'Where now are the Dúnedain, Elessar, Elessar?' *The Lord of the Rings*, bk. III, ch. 5. Earlier versions were published in *The Treason of Isengard*, pp. 431, 448.

'Where now the horse and the rider? Where is the horn that was blowing?' *The Lord of the Rings*, bk. III, ch. 5.

Why the Man in the Moon Came Down Too Soon see *The Man in the Moon Came Down Too Soon*

'Wilt thou learn the lore // that was long secret'. *Unfinished Tales*, pp. 395–6.

'The wind so whirled a weathercock'. Preface to *The Adventures of Tom Bombadil and Other Verses from the Red Book*, p. 7.

'The wind was on the withered heath'. *The Hobbit*, ch. 7.

Winsele wéste, windge reste réte berofene see *The Town of Dreams and the City of Present Sorrow*

Winter Comes to Nargothrond see *The Children of Húrin*

Wood-sunshine. Six lines in *Biography*, p. 47.

'The world was young, the mountains green'. *The Lord of the Rings*, bk. II, ch. 4. Earlier readings were published in *The Treason of Isengard*, pp. 183–4.

You & Me and the Cottage of Lost Play see *The Little House of Lost Play: Mar Vanwa Tyaliéva*

A! rundamāra-nundarūn tahōra-mundakumbalūn. Intermediate version of the marching song of the Ents in *The Lord of the Rings*, bk. III, ch. 4. *The Treason of Isengard*, pp. 420–1.

A! the Trees of Light, tall and shapely. *The Flight of the Noldoli from Valinor*, in *The Lays of Beleriand*, pp. 131–41.

A Elbereth Gilthoniel. *The Lord of the Rings*, bk. II, ch. 1.

Again this year, my dear Priscilla. Rhyme in the 'Father Christmas' letters, letter for 1938.

Ai! laurië lantar lassi súrinen. *Namárië*, in *The Lord of the Rings*, bk. II, ch. 8.

Ai lintulinda Lasselanta. *Narqelion*, extract in *Biography*, p. 76.

Alive without breath. *The Hobbit*, ch. 5. An extended version was published in *The Lord of the Rings*, bk. IV, ch. 2.

All that is gold does not glitter. *The Lord of the Rings*, bk. I, ch. 10, and bk. II, ch. 2.

Annon edhellen, edro hi ammen! *The Lord of the Rings*, bk. II, ch. 4.

Arísath nú Ridend míne! *The War of the Ring*, p. 389.

Arise, arise, Riders of Théoden! *The Lord of the Rings*, bk. V, ch. 5. Cf. *The War of the Ring*, p. 385.

Arise now, arise, Riders of Théoden! *The Lord of the Rings*, bk. III, ch. 6.

As I was sitting by the way. *The Return of the Shadow*, p. 98.

At last out of the deep sea he passed. *Imram*, in *Time and Tide*, 3 December 1955, p. 1561. The first line is identical for earlier versions, *The Ballad of St Brendan's Death* and *The Death of St Brendan*, published in *Sauron Defeated*, pp. 261–4.

Be he foe or friend, be he foul or clean. *Morgoth's Ring*, p. 112.

Bimble Bay has a steep street. *Progress in Bimble Town*, in the *Oxford Magazine*, 15 October 1931, p. 22.

Bless the water O my feet and toes! *The Return of the Shadow*, p. 102.

A box without hinges, key or lid. *The Hobbit*, ch. 5.

Brunaim bairiþ Bairka bogum. *Bagme Bloma* in *Songs for the Philologists*, p. 12.

Chip the glasses and crack the plates! *The Hobbit*, ch. 1.

Clap! Snap! the black crack! *The Hobbit*, ch. 4.

Cold be hand and heart and bone. *The Lord of the Rings*, bk. I, ch. 8.

The cold hard lands. *The Lord of the Rings*, bk. IV, ch. 2. An earlier version with the same first line was published in *The War of the Ring*, p. 111.

Come home, come home, ye merry folk! *Elvish Song in Rivendell* in *The Annotated Hobbit*, rev. and expanded edn., pp. 92–3.

Come sing ye light fairy things tripping so gay. *Wood-sunshine*, extract in *Biography*, p. 47.

Dar fys ma vel gom co palt 'Hoc. *Biography*, p. 36, with English translation ('There was an old man who said "How").

Day is ended, dim my eyes. *Bilbo's Last Song (At the Grey Havens)*.

The days are numbered; the kings are sleeping. *The War of the Ring*, p. 305. See 'Over the land there lies a long shadow'.

Dir avosaith a gwaew hinar. *A Secret Vice*, in *The Monsters and the Critics and Other Essays*, p. 217.

Dr U.Q. Humphrey. *The Inklings*, p. 177.

Down the swift dark stream you go. *The Hobbit*, ch. 9.

The dragon is withered. *The Hobbit*, ch. 19.

The dragon lay on the cherry trees. *The Dragon's Visit* in the *Oxford Magazine*, 4 February 1937, p. 342.

Eadig beo Þu, goda mann! *Eadig Beo Þu!* in *Songs for the Philologists*, p. 13.

Eala hu is wynsum þeos woruld to-niht. *La, Húru* in *Songs for the Philologists*, p. 16.

Éarendel arose where the shadow flows. *Éalá Éarendel Engla Beorhtast* in *The Book of Lost Tales, Part Two*, pp. 267–9.

Earendel sprang up from the Ocean's cup. *The Voyage of Éarendel the Evening Star*, earliest version of *Éalá Éarendel Engla Beorhtast* in *The Book of Lost Tales, Part Two*: see variant readings, p. 268.

Eärendil was a mariner. *The Lord of the Rings*, bk. II, ch. 1. Also the first line of *The Short Lay of Eärendel: Eärendillinwë*, the further development and final form of the poem which evolved from *Errantry*; the complete text was published in *Reader's Companion*, pp. 210–13.

East of the Moon, West of the Sun. *The Shores of Faery*, later version, in *The Book of Lost Tales, Part Two*, pp. 271–2.

Elbereth Gilthoniel sir evrin pennar oriel. *The Return of the Shadow*, p. 394. See 'A Elbereth Gilthoniel'.

Elfstone, Elfstone, bearer of my green stone. *The Treason of Isengard*, pp. 431, 448. See 'Where now are the Dúnedain, Elessar, Elessar?'

An Elven-maid there was of old. *The Lord of the Rings*, bk. II, ch. 6.

Ents the earthborn, old as mountains. *The Lord of the Rings*, bk. III, ch. 10.

Ere iron was found or tree was hewn. *The Lord of the Rings*, bk. III, ch. 8.

Eressëa! Eressëa! *The Song of Ælfwine on Seeing the Uprising of Eärendil* in *The Lost Road and Other Writings*, pp. 100–104. See *The Nameless Land.

An eye in a blue face. *The Hobbit*, ch. 5.

Faithful servant yet master's bane. *The Lord of the Rings*, bk. 5, ch. 6.

Far over the misty mountains cold. *The Hobbit*, ch. 1.

Farewell! farewell, now hearth and hall! *The Return of the Shadow*, pp. 300–1. See 'Farewell we call to hearth and hall!'

Farewell sweet earth and northern sky. *The Silmarillion*, p. 178.

Farewell we call to hearth and hall! *The Lord of the Rings*, bk. 1, ch. 5.

The fat cat on the mat. *Cat in *The Adventures of Tom Bombadil and Other Verses from the Red Book*, p. 48 (first British printing), p. 51 (second British printing, first American printing).

Fela bið on Westwegum werum uncúðra. *The Lost Road* in *The Lost Road and Other Writings*, pp. 44, 55, 103–4, 203.

Fifteen birds in five firtrees. *The Hobbit*, ch. 6.

Fil me a cuppe of ful gode ale. *The Notion Club Papers* in *Sauron Defeated*, p. 245.

The finest rockets ever seen. *The Lord of the Rings*, bk. II, ch. 7.

Firiel looked out at three o'clock. *Firiel* in *The Chronicle of the Convents of the Sacred Heart*, 1934, pp. 30–2. Revised, with the same first line, as *The Last Ship*, in *The Adventures of Tom Bombadil and Other Verses from the Red Book*, pp. 61–4.

From dark Dunharrow in the dim morning. *The Lord of the Rings*, bk. V, ch. 3.

*From the many-willow'd margin of the immemorial Thames. *Stapeldon Magazine*, December 1913, p. 11. First stanza of a two-stanza poem, *From Iffley*, published without title.

Get out, you old Wight! Vanish in the sunlight! *The Lord of the Rings*, bk. 1, ch. 8.

Gil-galad was an Elven-king. *The Lord of the Rings*, bk. 1, ch. 11.

Gondor! Gondor, between the Mountains and the Sea! *The Lord of the Rings*, bk. 3, ch. 2.

The grass was very long and thin. **Light as Leaf on Lindentree*, in *The Gryphon*, June 1925, p. 217. Introduced by non-rhyming verse, "Tis of Beren Ermabwed brokenhearted'.

Greenleaf, Greenleaf, bearer of the elven-bow. *The Treason of Isengard*, p. 431. See 'Legolas Greenleaf long under tree'.

Grey as a mouse. **Oliphaunt*, in *The Lord of the Rings*, bk. IV, ch. 3.

Hæfth Hild Hunecan hwite tunecan. One of two riddles published as **Enigmata Saxonica Nuper Inventa Duo* in *A Northern Venture*, p. 20.

Halt! What do you want? Hell take you! Speak! **The Homecoming of Beorhtnoth Beorhthelm's Son*, in *Essays and Studies 1953*, pp. 1–18.

He knows Tom Bombadil, and Tom's name will help you. *The Return of the Shadow*, p. 130.

Here many days once gently past me crept. *The Town of Dreams* in *The Book of Lost Tales, Part Two*, pp. 296. See **The Town of Dreams and the City of Present Sorrow*.

Hey! Come derry dol! Hop along, my hearties! *The Lord of the Rings*, bk. I, ch. 6.

Hey! Come merry dol! My darling! *The Lord of the Rings*, bk. I, ch. 6.

Hey dol! merry dol! ring a dong dillo! *The Lord of the Rings*, bk. I, ch. 6.

Hey! now! Come hoy now! Whither do you wander? *The Lord of the Rings*, bk. I, ch. 8.

Hi grornodon, gnornodon. *Ruddoc Hana* in *Songs for the Philologists*, pp. 8–9.

The high summer / waned to autumn, // and western gales. *The Lays of Beleriand*, p. 128. Early version of *Winter Comes to Nargothrond*; see **The Children of Húrin*.

Ho! ho! ho! To my bottle I go. *The Return of the Shadow*, p. 91. See 'Ho! Ho! Ho! to the bottle I go'.

Ho! Ho! Ho! to the bottle I go. *The Lord of the Rings*, bk. I, ch. 4.

Ho, rattles sound your warnote! **The Battle of the Eastern Field* in *King Edward's School Chronicle*, March 1911, pp. 22–6.

Ho! Tom Bombadil, Tom Bombadillo! *The Fellowship of the Ring*, bk. I, ch. 7, 8.

Ho! Tom Bombadil! Whither do you wander? *The Return of the Shadow*, p. 123. See 'Ho! Tom Bombadil, Tom Bombadillo!'

Hop along, my little friends, up the Withywindle! *The Lord of the Rings*, bk. I, ch. 6.

Hwaet! Éadweard cyning Ælfredes sunu. *The Notion Club Papers* in *Sauron Defeated*, pp. 271–2.

Hwaet! we Inclinga. *The Inklings*, pp. 176–7.

Hwaet! wé on geárdagum of Gársecge. *The Notion Club Papers* in *Sauron Defeated*, p. 273.

I am off down the road. *Goblin Feet* in *Oxford Poetry 1915*, pp. 64–5.

I had an errand there: gathering water-lilies. *The Lord of the Rings*, bk. I, ch. 7.

I know a window in a western tower. *The Happy Mariners* in *The Stapeldon Magazine*, June 1920, pp. 69–70. A much later version reads (capitalized) 'Western tower'.

I sang of leaves, of leaves of gold, and leaves of gold there grew. *The Lord of the Rings*, bk. II, ch. 8. The earliest version, with the same first line, was published in *The Treason of Isengard*, p. 284.

I sat on the ruined margin of the deep-voiced echoing sea. *The Tides*, extract in *The Shaping of Middle-earth*, p. 214. See *The Horns of Ylmir*.

I sat upon a bench and I up and I sang. *I Sat upon a Bench* in *Songs for the Philologists*, p. 17.

I sit beside the fire and think. *The Lord of the Rings*, bk. II, ch. 3.

I sit upon the stones alone. *Sauron Defeated*, pp. 27–8. See 'In western lands beneath the Sun'.

I walked by the sea, and there came to me. *The Sea-Bell* in *The Adventures of Tom Bombadil and Other Verses from the Red Book*, pp. 57–60.

Ilu Ilúvatar en karé eldain a fírimoin. *The Lost Road* in *The Lost Road* in *The Lost Road and Other Writings*, pp. 63, 72.

In a dim and perilous region, down whose great tempestuous ways. *Sea Chant of an Elder Day*, extracts in *Biography*, pp. 73–4; *The Shaping of Middle-earth*, p. 214; and *Artist and Illustrator*, pp. 45–6. See *The Horns of Ylmir*.

In a summer season when sultry was ye sun. *Doworst*, the first page of which was published in *A Elbereth Gilthoniel!* (newsletter of The Fellowship of Middle Earth), [?Summer 1978], p. 3.

In Britain's land beyond the seas. *The Lay of Aotrou and Itroun* in *Welsh Review*, November–December 1945, pp. 254–66.

In days of yore out of the deep Ocean. *King Sheave* in *The Lost Road*, in *The Lost Road and Other Writings*, pp. 86–92.

In Dwimordene, in Lórien. *The Lord of the Rings*, bk. III, ch. 6.

In Habbanan beneath the Stars. **Habbanan beneath the Stars* in *The Book of Lost Tales, Part One*, pp. 91–2.

In the Lay of Leithian, // Release from Bondage. Introduction in alliterative verse to *As Light as Leaf on Lindentree*, published in *The Lays of Beleriand*, pp. 120–1. See **Light as Leaf on Lindentree*.

In the vales of Aryador. **A Song of Arydor* in *The Book of Lost Tales, Part One*, pp. 138–9.

In the willow-meads of Tasarinan I walked in the Spring. *The Lord of the Rings*, bk. III, ch. 4.

In unknown days my fathers' sires. Prelude to **The Town of Dreams and the City of Present Sorrow* in *The Book of Lost Tales, Part Two*, p. 295–8. The first section, with the same first line, was reused as the beginning of *The Song of Eriol*, in *The Book of Lost Tales, Part Two*, pp. 298–300.

In western lands beneath the Sun. *The Lord of the Rings*, bk. VI, ch. 1.

The Indic oliphaunt's a burly lump. *Iumbo, or Ye Kinde of Ye Oliphaunt*, one of two parts of *Adventures in Unnatural History and Medieval Metres being the Freaks of Fisiologus* in the *Stapeldon Magazine*, June 1927, pp. 125–7.

It cannot be seen, cannot be felt. *The Hobbit*, ch. 5.

It was early and still in the night of June. **Over Old Hills and Far Away* in *The Book of Lost Tales, Part One*, pp. 108–10.

I've got a very Briny Notion. *The Notion Club Papers* in *Sauron Defeated*, p. 224.

J.R.R. Tolkien. *Letters*, p. 398.

Kildo kirya ninque. *Oilima Markirya* in *A Secret Vice*, in *The Monsters and the Critics and Other Essays*, pp. 220–1. See **The Last Ark*.

The King beneath the mountains. *The Hobbit*, ch. 10.

A king there was in days of old. **Lay of Leithian* (*The Gest of Beren and Lúth-ien*), second typescript version, in *The Lays of Beleriand*, pp. 154 ff. (see also pp. 150–4, 157). This is also the reading of the first line of the poem as revised *c.* 1950, see *The Lays of Beleriand*, pp. 351 ff.

A king there was in olden days. **Lay of Leithian* (*The Gest of Beren and Lúth-ien*), first typescript version, in *The Lays of Beleriand*, p. 158 (see also pp. 154, 157).

A king was in the dawn of days. **Lay of Leithian* (*The Gest of Beren and Lúth-ien*), first manuscript version, in *The Lays of Beleriand*, p. 157.

Lazy Lob and crazy Cob. *The Hobbit*, ch. 8.

Learn now the lore of Living Creatures! *The Lord of the Rings*, bk. III, ch. 4.

The leaves were long, the grass was green. *The Lord of the Rings*, bk. I, ch. 11. See *Light as Leaf on Lindentree*.

The leaves were long, the grass was thin. *The Return of the Shadow*, pp. 180–2. See *Light as Leaf on Lindentree*.

Legolas Greenleaf long under tree. *The Lord of the Rings*, bk. III, ch.5.

Little Princess Mee. *Princess Mee* in *The Adventures of Tom Bombadil and Other Verses from the Red Book*, pp. 28–30.

Lo! the flame of fire and fierce hatred. *Lay of Eärendel* in *The Lays of Beleriand*, pp. 141–4.

Lo! the golden dragon // of the God of Hell. *The Children of Húrin*, first version (*Túrin Son of Húrin & Glórund the Dragon*), in *The Lays of Beleriand*, pp. 6 ff.

Long live the Halflings! Praise them with great praise! *The Lord of the Rings*, bk. VI, p. 4.

Look, there is Fastitocalon! *Fastitocalon* in *The Adventures of Tom Bombadil and Other Verses from the Red Book*, pp. 49, 51 (first British printing), pp. 48–9 (second British printing, first American printing).

The Lonely Troll he sat on a stone. *Perry-the-Winkle* in *The Adventures of Tom Bombadil and Other Verses from the Red Book*, pp. 41–4.

The Lord of the Rings. *Biography*, p. 223.

Lo! young we are and yet have stood. *As Two Fair Trees*, extract in *Biography*, p. 74.

The Man in the Moon had silver shoon. *The Man in the Moon Came Down Too Soon* in *The Adventures of Tom Bombadil and Other Verses from the Red Book*, pp. 34, 36–8. An earlier version with the same first line, *Why the Man in the Moon Came Down Too Soon*, was published in *A Northern Venture*, pp. 17–19. A revised version, also with this first line, was published in *The Book of Lost Tales, Part One*, pp. 204–6.

Man kiluva kirya ninqe. *Oilima Markirya* in *A Secret Vice*, in *The Monsters and the Critics and Other Essays*, pp. 213–14. See *The Last Ark*.

Men kenuva fáne kirya. *Oilima Markirya*, alternate version, in *A Secret Vice*, in *The Monsters and the Critics and Other Essays*, pp. 221–2. See *The Last Ark*.

Meolchwitum sind marmanstane. One of two riddles published as *Enigmata Saxonica Nuper Inventa Duo* in *A Northern Venture*, p. 20.

Mr Neville Judson Coghill. *Letters*, p. 359.

Mr Owen Barfield's. *The Inklings*, p. 177.

Monath módaes lust mith meriflóda. *The Notion Club Papers* in *Sauron Defeated*, p. 243, translated as 'My soul's desire over the sea-torrents' (p. 244).

Monað modes lust mid mereflode. *The Lost Road* in *The Lost Road and Other Writings*, p. 84. See also *Sauron Defeated*, pp. 272.

Mourn not overmuch! Mighty was the fallen. *The Lord of the Rings*, bk. V, ch. 6.

My soul's desire over the sea-torrents. *The Notion Club Papers* in *Sauron Defeated*, p. 244. Translation of 'Monath módaes lust mith meriflóda' in *Sauron Defeated*, pp. 243, 287–8.

N·alalmino lalantila. *Narqelion* in 'Narqelion: A Single, Falling Leaf at Sunfading' by Paul Nolan Hyde, *Mythlore* 56, Winter 1988, pp. 47–52. Four lines (inaccurately transcribed) were earlier published in *Biography*, p. 76. See also *Vinyar Tengwar*, April 1999, pp. 5 (photograph) and 8.

The Night is still young and our drinks are yet long. *Natura Apis* in *Songs for the Philologists*, p. 18.

Nine for the Elven-kings under moon and star. First complete version of the Ring-verse for *The Lord of the Rings*, in *The Return of the Shadow*, pp. 259, 269. See 'Three Rings for the Elven-kings under the sky'.

Norolinde pirukendea. *Nieninque* in *A Secret Vice*, in *The Monsters and the Critics and Other Essays*, pp. 215–16, 220.

Now let the song begin! Let us sing together. *The Lord of the Rings*, bk. I, ch. 6.

Now Lords and Ladies blithe and bold. *Gawain's Leave-taking* in *Sir Gawain and the Green Knight, Pearl and Sir Orfeo*, p. 149.

O agéd city of an all too brief sojourn. *The Sorrowful City* in *The Book of Lost Tales, Part Two*, p. 298. See *The Town of Dreams and the City of Present Sorrow*.

O ancient city on a leaguered hill! *The Trees of Kortirion* in *The Book of Lost Tales, Part One*, pp. 39–43.

O Elbereth Gilthoniel. *The Lord of the Rings*, bk. IV. ch. 10, changed to 'A Elbereth Gilthoniel' in the 2nd edn.

O Elbereth! O Elbereth! *The Return of the Shadow*, p. 68. See 'Snow-white! Snow-white! O Lady clear!'

O fading town upon a little hill. *Kortirion among the Trees*, first version, in *The Book of Lost Tales, Part One*, pp. 33–6. See *The Trees of Kortirion*.

O fading town upon an inland hill. *Kortirion among the Trees*, revised version, in *The Book of Lost Tales, Part One*, pp. 36–9. See **The Trees of Kortirion*.

O glimmering island set sea-girdled and alone. **The Lonely Isle* in *Leeds University Verse*, p. 57.

O Naffarinos cutá vu navra cangor. *A Secret Vice* in *The Monsters and the Critics and Other Essays*, p. 209.

O Orofarnë, Lassemista, Carnimirië! *The Lord of the Rings*, bk. III, ch. 4.

O slender as a willow-wand! O clearer than clear water! *The Lord of the Rings*, bk. I, ch. 7.

O the hoot! O the hoot! **Tinfang Warble* in *Inter-University Magazine*, [?mid-1920s], p. 63.

O! The Princess Ní. **The Princess Ni* in *Leeds University Verse*, p. 58.

O! Wanderers in the shadowed land. *The Lord of the Rings*, bk. I, ch. 6.

O! Water warm and water hot! *The Return of the Shadow*, p. 98. See 'Sing hey! for the bath at close of day'.

O! What are you doing. *The Hobbit*, ch. 3.

Old Fastitocalon is fat. **Fastitocalon*, one of two parts of *Adventures in Unnatural History and Medieval Metres being the Freaks of Fisiologus* in the *Stapeldon Magazine*, June 1927, pp. 123–5.

Old fat spider spinning in a tree! *The Hobbit*, ch. 8.

Old Tom Bombadil is a merry fellow. *The Lord of the Ring*, bk. I, ch. 7, 8.

Old Tom Bombadil was a merry fellow. **The Adventures of Tom Bombadil* in *Oxford Magazine*, 15 Feb 1934, pp. 464–5. A later version with the same title and first line was published in *The Adventures of Tom Bombadil and Other Verses from the Red Book*, pp. 11–16.

The old year was turning brown; the West Wind was calling. **Bombadil Goes Boating* in *The Adventures of Tom Bombadil and Other Verses from the Red Book*, pp. 17–23.

On the cherry-trees the dragon lay. **The Dragon's Visit* in *Winter's Tales for Children 1*, pp. 84–7.

Once there were two little groups. *Lit' and Lang'* in *Songs for the Philologists*, p. 27.

Once upon a day on the fields of May. **Once upon a Time* in *Winter's Tales for Children 1*, pp. 44–5.

Ondor! Ondor! Between the Mountains and the Sea. *The Treason of Isengard*, pp. 395–6. See 'Gondor! Gondor, between the Mountains and the Sea!'

One old man of Durham. *From One to Five* in *Songs for the Philologists*, p. 6.

Ónen i-Estel Edain, ú-chebin estel anim. *The Lord of the Rings*, Appendix A.

Our dear Charles Williams many guises shows. *The Inklings*, pp. 123–6.

Out of doubt, out of dark to the day's rising. *The Lord of the Rings*, bk. VI, ch. 6.

Out of the mountain shall they come their tryst keeping. *The War of the Ring*, pp. 300, 302. See 'Over the land there lies a long shadow'.

Over the land there lies a long shadow. *The Lord of the Rings*, bk. V, ch. 2.

Pearl of delight that a prince doth please. **Pearl*, Modern English translation in *Sir Gawain and the Green Knight, Pearl and Sir Orfeo*, pp. 89–122.

The places where the Mewlips dwell. *Knocking at the Door* in the *Oxford Magazine*, 18 February 1937, p. 403. See **The Mewlips*.

The Rev. Mathew (Gervase). *The Inklings*, p. 186.

The Road goes ever on and on. Variant texts in *The Lord of the Rings*, bk. I, ch. 1 (Bilbo), bk. I, ch. 3 (Frodo), and bk. VI, ch. 6 (Bilbo).

Roads go ever ever on. *The Hobbit*, ch. 19.

Roll – roll – roll – roll. *The Hobbit*, ch. 9.

A sable hill, gigantic, rampart-crowned. **The City of the Gods* in *The Microcosm*, Spring 1923, p. 8. An earlier version with the same first line, *Kôr: In a City Lost and Dead*, was published in *The Book of Lost Tales, Part One*, p. 136.

(Said I) / 'Ho! Tom Bombadil. *The Return of the Shadow*, pp. 115–16.

The sales of Charles Williams. *The Inklings*, p. 187.

San ninqeruvisse lútier. *Earendel* in *A Secret Vice*, in *The Monsters and the Critics and Other Essays*, p. 216. See **Earendel at the Helm*.

Seek for the Sword that was broken. *The Lord of the Rings*, bk. I, ch. 2.

The shadows where the Mewlips dwell. **The Mewlips* in *The Adventures of Tom Bombadil and Other Verses from the Red Book*, pp. 45–6.

Silver flow the streams from Celos to Erui. *The Lord of the Rings*, bk. V, ch. 9.

Sing all ye joyful, now sing all together! *The Hobbit*, ch. 19.

Sing hey! for the bath at close of day. *The Lord of the Rings*, bk. I, ch. 5.

Sing now, ye people of the Tower of Anor. *The Lord of the Rings*, bk.VI, ch. 5.

Sing us yet more of Eärendel the wandering. **The Bidding of the Minstrel, from the Lay of Eärendel* in *The Book of Lost Tales, Part Two*, pp. 269–71.

Snow-white! Snow-white! O Lady clear! *The Lord of the Rings*, bk. I, ch. 3.

Still round the corner there may wait. *The Lord of the Rings*, bk. VI, ch. 9. See 'Upon the hearth the fire is red'.

The summer slowly // in the sad forest. *Winter Comes to Nargothrond* in *The Lays of Beleriand*, p. 129. See **The Children of Húrin*.

Syx mynet lufige ic. *Syx Mynet* in *Songs for the Philologists*, p. 7.

Ta-rūta dūm-da dūm-da dūm / ta-rāra dūm-da dūm-da būm! Earliest version of the marching song of the Ents in *The Lord of the Rings*, bk. III, ch. 4. *The Treason of Isengard*, p. 420.

Tall ships and tall kings. *The Lord of the Rings*, bk. III, ch. 11.

Þa ær ic wæs cniht, þa com ic on pliht. *Ides Ælfscyne* in *Songs for the Philologists*, pp. 10–11.

Þa ofer widne garsecg weow unwidre ceald. *Ofer Widne Garsecg* in *Songs for the Philologists*, pp. 14–15.

There is an inn, a merry old inn. **The Man in the Moon Stayed Up Too Late* in *The Lord of the Rings*, bk. I, ch. 9, without title, and *The Adventures of Tom Bombadil and Other Verses from the Red Book*, so titled, pp. 31–3.

There lingering lights do golden lie. **The Nameless Land* in *Realities*, pp. 24–5.

There lingering lights still golden lie. *The Song of Ælfwine (on Seeing the Uprising of Eärendel)* in *The Lost Road and Other Writings*, pp. 100–2. See **The Nameless Land.*

There was a gallant passenger. Intermediate text between **Errantry* and 'Eärendil was a mariner', in *The Treason of Isengard*, pp. 91–4.

There was a man who dwelt alone. **Shadow-Bride* in *The Adventures of Tom Bombadil and Other Verses from the Red Book*, p. 52.

There was a merry messenger. Early versions of **Errantry*, in *The Treason of Isengard*, pp. 89, 91.

There was a merry passenger. **Errantry* in the *Oxford Magazine*, 9 November 1933, p. 180.

There was an old man who said 'How. English version of the poem 'Dar fys ma vel gom co palt 'Hoc', in *Biography*, p. 36.

There was an old priest naméd Francis. *The Tolkien Family Album*, p. 22.

There were elves olden and strong spells. *Iúmonna Gold Galdre Bewunden* in *The Gryphon*, January 1923, p. 130. See **The Hoard.*

There's an old grey bridge in Tavrobel. **The Grey Bridge of Tavrobel* in *Inter-University Magazine*, [?mid-1920s], p. 82.

They say there's a little crooked inn. *The Cat and the Fiddle : A Nursery-Rhyme Undone and Its Scandalous Secret Unlocked* in *Yorkshire Poetry*, October–November 1923, pp. 1–3. The earliest, manuscript version, with the same first line, was published in *The Return of the Shadow*, pp. 145–7. See **The Man in the Moon Stayed Up Too Late*.

Thirty white horses on a red hill. *The Hobbit*, ch. 5.

This thing all things devours. *The Hobbit*, ch. 5.

Though Frenchmen froth with furious sound. *Frenchmen Froth* in *Songs for the Philologists*, pp. 24–5.

Three Rings for the Elven-kings under the sky. *The Lord of the Rings*, preliminaries, bk. I, ch. 2, etc. An earlier version with the same first line was published in *The Return of the Shadow*, pp. 258, 259.

Through Rohan over fen and field where the long grass grows. *The Lord of the Rings*, bk. III, ch. 1.

Thus cwæth Ælfwine Wídlást. *The Lost Road* in *The Lost Road and Other Writings*, pp. 44, 55. Also published as 'Þus cwaeÞ Ælfwine Wídlást' in *Quenta Silmarillion*, in *The Lost Road and Other Writings*, p. 203, and as 'Þus cwæð Ælfwine Wídlást Éadwines sunu' in *The Notion Club Papers*, in *Sauron Defeated*, pp. 245, 288.

'Tis of Beren Ermabwed brokenhearted. Alliterative introduction to **Light as Leaf on Lindentree* in *The Gryphon*, June 1925, p. 217. See also *The Lays of Beleriand*, pp. 120–1.

'Tis the time when May first looks toward June. **An Evening in Tavrobel* in *Leeds University Verse 1914–24*, p. 56.

To Isengard! Though Isengard be ringed and barred with doors of stone. *The Lord of the Rings*, bk. III, ch. 4, 9.

To the Sea, to the Sea! The white gulls are crying. *The Lord of the Rings*, bk. VI, ch. 4.

Tom's country ends here: he will not pass the borders. *The Lord of the Rings*, bk. I, ch. 8.

A troll sat alone on his seat of stone. *The Root of the Boot* in *Songs for the Philologists*, pp. 20–1. See **The Stone Troll*.

Troll sat alone on his seat of stone. **The Stone Troll* in *The Lord of the Rings*, bk. I, ch. 12, without title, and *The Adventures of Tom Bombadil and Other Verses from the Red Book*, so titled, pp. 39–40.

'Twas a very quiet evening once in June. Earlier version of **Over Old Hills and Far Away*; see variant readings in *The Book of Lost Tales, Part One*, p. 110.

'Twas in the Land of Willows where the grass is long and green. *The Horns of Ylmir in The Shaping of Middle-earth, pp. 215–18. The first line later began 'It was' (p. 218).

Twelve for Mortal Men doomed to die. Early version of the Ring-verse, in The Return of the Shadow, p. 269. See 'Three Rings for the Elven-kings under the sky'.

Under the cliffs of Bimble Bay. *Glip in The Annotated Hobbit, rev. and expanded edn., p. 119.

Under the Mountain dark and tall. The Hobbit, ch. 15.

Upon the hearth the fire is red. The Lord of the Rings, bk. 1, ch. 3.

Úþwita sceal // ealdgesægenum. Henry Bradley. 3 Dec., 1845–23 May, 1923 in Bulletin of Modern Humanities Association, October 1923, p. 5.

Voiceless it cries. The Hobbit, ch. 5.

Wake now my merry lads! Wake and hear me calling! The Lord of the Rings, bk. I, ch. 8.

We come, we come with roll of drum: ta-runda runda runda rom! The Lord of the Rings, bk. III, ch. 4.

We heard in the hills the horns ringing. The War of the Ring, p. 371. See 'We heard of the horns in the hills ringing'.

We heard of the horns in the hills ringing. The Lord of the Rings, bk. V, ch. 6.

We knew that land once, You and I. *The Little House of Lost Play: Mar Vanwa Tyaliéva in The Book of Lost Tales, Part One, pp. 30–1

We often read and written find. English translation of *Sir Orfeo in Sir Gawain and the Green Knight, Pearl and Sir Orfeo, pp. 125–37.

West of the Moon, East of the Sun. *The Shores of Faery, earliest version, in Biography, pp. 76–7, with errors of transcription; published with the first lines emended from the manuscript (to 'East of the Moon / West of the Sun') in Artist and Illustrator, pp. 47–8 (and see p. 66, n. 31).

Whanne that Octobre mid his schoures derke. *The Clerke's Compleinte in The Gryphon, December 1923, p. 95.

What has roots as nobody sees. The Hobbit, ch. 5. A later version is published in The Return of the Shadow, pp. 263.

When evening in the Shire was grey. The Lord of the Rings, bk. II, ch. 7.

When morning on the Hill was bright. The Treason of Isengard, pp. 264, 266. See 'When evening in the Shire was grey'.

When spring unfolds the beechen leaf, and sap is in the bough. *The Lord of the Rings*, bk. III, ch. 4.

When the black breath blows. *The Lord of the Rings*, bk. V, ch. 8.

When the land is dark where the kings sleep. *The War of the Ring*, p. 307. See 'Over the land there lies a long shadow'.

When the Moon was new and the sun young. *Iumonna Gold Galdre Bewunden* in the *Oxford Magazine*, 4 March 1937, p. 273. See *The Hoard.

When spring unfolds the beechen leaf, and sap is in the bough. *The Lord of the Rings*, bk. III, ch. 4.

When the siege and the assault had ceased at Troy. English translation of *Sir Gawain and the Green Knight* in *Sir Gawain and the Green Knight, Pearl and Sir Orfeo*, pp. 25–88.

When winter first begins to bite. *The Lord of the Rings*, bk. II, ch. 3.

Where have you been; what have you seen. *Looney* in the *Oxford Magazine*, 18 January 1934, p. 340. See *The Sea-Bell.

Where now are the Dúnedain, Elessar, Elessar? *The Lord of the Rings*, bk. III, ch. 5.

Where now the horse and the rider? Where is the horn that was blowing? *The Lord of the Rings*, bk. III, ch. 5.

A white horse in the sun shining. *Earendel at the Helm* in *A Secret Vice, The Monsters and the Critics and Other Essays*, pp. 216–17, 220.

A white ship one saw, small like a butterfly. *The Last Ark*, alternate version, in *A Secret Vice* in *The Monsters and the Critics and Other Essays*, pp. 220–1.

Who shall see a white ship. *The Last Ark* in *A Secret Vice*, in *The Monsters and the Critics and Other Essays*, pp. 214–15.

Wilt thou learn the lore // that was long secret. *Unfinished Tales*, pp. 395–6.

The wind so whirled a weathercock. Preface to *The Adventures of Tom Bombadil and Other Verses from the Red Book*, p. 7.

The wind was on the withered heath. *The Hobbit*, ch. 7.

With the seething sea // Sirion's waters. Untitled adaptation from *The Children of Húrin*, related to *Winter Comes to Nargothrond*, in *The Lays of Beleriand*, pp. 129–30.

The world was young, the mountains green. *The Lord of the Rings*, bk. II, ch. 4.

Woruldbúendra sum bið wóðbora. *For W.H.A. in *Shenandoah*, Winter 1967, pp. 96–7.

Ye Gods who girt // your guarded realms. *The Children of Húrin, second version, in The Lays of Beleriand, pp. 95–130.

You & me – we know that land. You & Me and the Cottage of Lost Play in The Book of Lost Tales, Part One, pp. 28–30. See *The Little House of Lost Play: Mar Vanwa Tyaliéva.

You look at trees and label them just so. *Mythopoeia in Tree and Leaf, 1988 edn., pp. 97–101.

TRANSLATIONS OF TOLKIEN'S WORKS

Following is a list of Tolkien's works with the languages into which they have been translated, as known to us in June 2006. Included are only complete or nearly complete translations (e.g. a substantial abridgement of *The Lord of the Rings*, or a translation which omits the Appendices), but not extracts (such as those that have appeared in fan magazines and art collections, and individual poems taken from larger works).

Works included in collections such as *Tree and Leaf* and *The Monsters and the Critics and Other Essays* are dealt with individually. Poems included in *The Hobbit*, *The Lord of the Rings*, *The Adventures of Tom Bombadil*, and *The History of Middle-earth* are not listed separately.

An asterisk before the name of a language indicates that more than one independent translation exists; in this regard we have not counted revisions to existing translations.

The Adventures of Tom Bombadil and Other Verses from the Red Book. Bulgarian, Chinese, Czech, Danish, Dutch, French, German, Hebrew, Hungarian, *Italian, Japanese, *Polish, Portuguese (European), Russian, Serbian, Spanish, Swedish.

Beowulf: The Monsters and the Critics. French, German, Italian, Polish, Russian, Spanish, Swedish.

Bilbo's Last Song. Dutch, Finnish, French, German, Italian, Japanese, Russian.

The Book of Lost Tales (*Part One* and *Part Two*). Czech, French, German, Hungarian, Italian, *Polish, Russian, Spanish, Swedish.

The Dragon's Visit. Russian.

English and Welsh. French, Italian, Polish, Spanish, Swedish.

Farmer Giles of Ham. Aragonese, Basque, *Bulgarian, Catalan, Chinese, *Czech, Danish, *Dutch, Estonian, Faeroese, Finnish, French, German, Greek, Hebrew, *Hungarian, Icelandic, Indonesian, *Italian, Japanese, Norwegian, *Polish, Portuguese (European), *Russian, Serbian, Slovenian, Spanish, Swedish, Turkish, Valencian.

Farmer Giles of Ham (earlier version of text). French.

Farmer Giles of Ham (50th anniversary edition, with earliest version and synopsis for sequel). Italian, Portuguese (Brazilian).

The Father Christmas Letters (1976 format). Czech, Danish, Dutch, French, German, Greek, Italian, Japanese, Polish, *Russian, Spanish, Swedish. See also *Letters from Father Christmas*.

Goblin Feet. Russian.

The Hobbit. Armenian, Belarusian, Breton, *Bulgarian, Catalan, *Chinese, Croatian, Czech, Danish, Dutch, Esperanto, Estonian, Faeroese, *Finnish, French, Galician, *German, Greek, *Hebrew, Hungarian, *Icelandic, Indonesian, Italian, *Japanese, *Korean, Latvian, Lithuanian, Luxemburgian,

Moldavian, *Norwegian, *Polish, Portuguese (Brazilian), Portuguese (European), *Romanian, *Russian, Serbian, Slovak, Slovenian, *Spanish, *Swedish, Thai, *Turkish, Ukrainian.

The Homecoming of Beorhtnoth Beorhthelm's Son. *Czech, Dutch, French, Italian, Japanese, *Russian, Spanish, Swedish.

Imram. Norwegian, Russian.

The Lay of Aotrou and Itroun. Russian, Serbian.

The Lays of Beleriand. French, Spanish.

Leaf by Niggle. Bulgarian, Catalan, Chinese, *Czech, *Danish, *Dutch, Estonian, Finnish, French, German, Greek, Hebrew, *Hungarian, Italian, Japanese, Norwegian, *Polish, Portuguese (European), *Russian, Serbian, Slovenian, Spanish, Swedish, Turkish.

Letters from Father Christmas (edn. with facsimiles). Japanese.

Letters from Father Christmas (enlarged edn. 1995). Polish.

Letters from Father Christmas (2004 edn.). Dutch, Finnish, German, Turkish.

Letters of J.R.R. Tolkien. Dutch, French, German, Italian, Polish, Portuguese (Brazilian), Russian, Spanish.

The Lord of the Rings. Albanian, Armenian (possibly *The Fellowship of the Ring* only), Basque, Bulgarian, Catalan, Chinese, Croatian, Czech, Danish, Dutch, Esperanto, Estonian, Faroese, Finnish, French, Galician, *German, Greek, Hebrew, Hungarian, Icelandic, Indonesian, Italian, Japanese, Korean, Latvian, Lithuanian, *Norwegian, *Polish, *Portuguese (Brazilian), Portuguese (European), Romanian, *Russian, Serbian, Slovak, *Slovenian, Spanish, *Swedish, Thai, Turkish, *Ukrainian.

The Lost Road and Other Writings. Spanish.

Mr. Bliss. Danish, Dutch, Finnish, German, Italian, Japanese, Korean, Spanish, Swedish.

The Monsters and the Critics and Other Essays. See under constituent parts: *Beowulf: The Monsters and the Critics*; *Prefatory Remarks on Prose Translation of 'Beowulf'* (= *On Translating Beowulf*); *Sir Gawain and the Green Knight*; *On Fairy-Stories*; *English and Welsh*; *A Secret Vice*; *Valedictory Address*.

Morgoth's Ring. Spanish.

Mythopoeia. Danish, Finnish, French, Hebrew, Hungarian, Italian, Japanese, *Norwegian, Polish, Russian, Serbian, Spanish.

On Fairy-Stories. Czech, *Danish, Dutch, Finnish, *French, German, Greek, Hebrew, Hungarian, Italian, *Japanese, Norwegian, *Polish, *Russian, Serbian, *Spanish, Swedish.

On Translating Beowulf see *Prefatory Remarks on Prose Translation of 'Beowulf'*

The Peoples of Middle-earth. Spanish.

Pictures by J.R.R. Tolkien. French, Italian, Spanish.

Prefatory Remarks on Prose Translation of 'Beowulf' (= *On Translating Beowulf*). French, German, Italian, Polish, Russian, Spanish, Swedish.

The Return of the Shadow. Spanish.

The Road Goes Ever On: A Song Cycle. German, Russian (part).

Roverandom. Bulgarian, Catalan, Chinese, Croatian, Czech, Danish, Dutch, Estonian, Finnish, French, German, Greek, Hungarian, Italian, Japanese, Latvian, Norwegian, Polish, Romanian, *Russian, Serbian, Spanish, Turkish.

Sauron Defeated. Spanish (in two volumes).

A Secret Vice. French, German, Italian, Polish, Russian, Spanish.

The Shaping of Middle-earth. Spanish.

The Silmarillion. Bulgarian, Catalan, *Czech, Danish, Dutch, Estonian, Finnish, French, German, Greek, Hebrew, Hungarian, Icelandic, Italian, Japanese, Korean, Norwegian, Polish, Portuguese (Brazilian), Portuguese (European), Romanian, *Russian , Serbian, Slovak, Spanish, Swedish.

Sir Gawain and the Green Knight (lecture). French, German, Italian, Polish, Russian, Spanish.

Sir Gawain and the Green Knight, Pearl and Sir Orfeo. Japanese, Polish.

Smith of Wootton Major. Afrikaans, Bulgarian, Catalan, Chinese, *Czech, Danish, *Dutch, Estonian, Finnish, *French, German, Greek, Hebrew, *Hungarian, Italian, Japanese, Norwegian, *Polish, Portuguese (European), *Russian, Serbian, Slovenian, Spanish, Swedish, Turkish, Valencian.

Smith of Wootton Major (2005 expanded edn.). Italian.

The Treason of Isengard. Spanish.

Tree and Leaf see *On Fairy-Stories, Leaf by Niggle.*

Unfinished Tales. Bulgarian, Catalan, Czech, Danish, Dutch, Finnish, French, German, Greek, Hebrew, Hungarian, Italian, Japanese, Norwegian, *Polish, Portuguese (European), Russian, Spanish, Swedish.

Valedictory Address to the University of Oxford (*Monsters and the Critics* version). French, German, Italian, Polish, Spanish.

The War of the Jewels. Spanish

The War of the Ring. Spanish.

The following translations are known to be forthcoming as of June 2006:

Beowulf: The Monsters and the Critics. Czech, Portuguese (European).

English and Welsh. Czech, Portuguese (European).

The Hobbit. Irish.

Leaf by Niggle. Portuguese (Brazilian).

The Lord of the Rings. Arabic.

Mister Bliss. Russian, Turkish.

On Fairy-Stories. Portuguese (Brazilian), Portuguese (European).

Prefatory Remarks on Prose Translation of 'Beowulf'. Czech, Portuguese (European).

Roverandom. Latvian.

A Secret Vice. Czech, Portuguese (European).

Sir Gawain and the Green Knight (lecture). Czech, Portuguese (European).

Valedictory Address to the University of Oxford (*Monsters and the Critics* version). Czech, Portuguese (European).

Works Consulted

FOLLOWING is a list of the books, articles, Web pages, and other materials used in the writing of *The J.R.R. Tolkien Companion and Guide* – among much else examined in the course of research – exclusive of works by Tolkien himself, which are listed separately (but occasionally cross-referenced from authors below), and writings mentioned in passing in entries in the **Reader's Guide**. Some of these resources are cited in the text as notable references or sources of quotations; others, cited only below, have provided general background and historical or chronological data. A dagger (†) preceding an entry indicates that we consider the source to be particularly useful for an appreciation of Tolkien's life and works. Although any such selection must be subjective, and necessarily omits much that is of interest and value, we hope that we have made it less according to taste or critical preference than by good judgement informed by decades of study. Many of the works so marked, it will be noticed, are collections of notable essays, some of which are also cited individually in this list. To these we would also add, for the study of Tolkien's invented languages, the journals *Parma Eldalamberon* and *Vinyar Tengwar*.

Some journals and newsletters listed here are (or were) connected with societies of Tolkien enthusiasts: *Amon Hen* and *Mallorn* (Tolkien Society); *Angerthas* (Arthedain, the Tolkien Society of Norway); *Anor* (Cambridge Tolkien Society); *Arda* (Arda-sällskapet and Tolkiensällskapet Forodrim, Sweden); *Beyond Bree* (American MENSA Tolkien Special Interest Group, published by Nancy Martsch); *Carandaith* (Australian Tolkien Society); *Inklings-Jahrbuch* (Inklings Gesellschaft für Literatur und Ästhetik, Germany); *Lembas* (Unquendor Tolkien Genootschap, the Dutch Tolkien Society); *Minas Tirith Evening-Star* (American Tolkien Society); *Mythprint* and *Mythlore* (Mythopoeic Society); *Orcrist* (University of Wisconsin Tolkien Society, Madison); *Parma Eldalamberon* and *Vinyar Tengwar* (Elvish Linguistic Fellowship); *The Southern Star* (Southfarthing Fellowship, Brighton); *Tolkien Journal* (Tolkien Society of America). *The Tolkien Collector* is an occasional publication of Christina Scull.

Corporate authors whose names include personal names, e.g. 'George Allen & Unwin', are alphabetized by the (first) surname. Dates and page numbers of newspaper and journal contributions are given when known, but we have not always been able to examine the original publication.

PUBLISHED SOURCES

'The Ace-Ballantine Storm of Competition over "Tarzan" and J.R.R. Tolkien Paperbacks'. *Book Production Industry*, September 1967.

Agøy, Nils Ivar. 'The Fall and Man's Mortality: An Investigation of Some Theological Themes in J.R.R. Tolkien's "Athrabeth Finrod ah Andreth"'. In Agøy, *Between Faith and Fiction*, pp. 16–30.

——, ed. *Between Faith and Fiction: Tolkien and the Powers of His World*. Arda Special 1. Oslo: Arthedain; Upsala: Arda-society, 1998.

Alderson, Brian. Review of *Smith of Wootton Major*. *Children's Book News*, January/February 1968.

Alexander, Peter. *Roy Campbell: A Critical Biography*. Oxford: Oxford University Press, 1982.

†Allan, Jim, ed. *An Introduction to Elvish*. Hayes, Middlesex: Bran's Head Books, 1978.

Allen, Carleton Kemp. 'College Life'. In *Handbook to the University of Oxford*, pp. 101–23.

George Allen & Unwin. *Fifty Years of Publishing Books That Matter*. London: George Allen & Unwin, 1964.

——. *Summer Announcements*. London: George Allen & Unwin, 1937.

Amis, John. 'Donald Swann'. *The Independent*, 25 March 1994, p. 30.

Anderson, Douglas A. 'Christopher Tolkien: A Bibliography'. In Flieger and Hostetter, *Tolkien's Legendarium*, pp. 247–52.

——. '"An Industrious Little Devil": E.V. Gordon as Friend and Collaborator with Tolkien'. In Chance, *Tolkien the Medievalist*, pp. 15–25.

†——. Introduction and notes to *The Annotated Hobbit* by J.R.R. Tolkien. Rev. and expanded edn. Boston: Houghton Mifflin, 2002.

——. 'J.R.R. Tolkien and W. Rhys Roberts's "Gerald of Wales on the Survival of Welsh"'. *Tolkien Studies* 2 (2005), pp. 230–4.

——. 'R.W. Chambers and *The Hobbit*'. *Tolkien Studies* 3 (2006), pp. 137–47.

——. 'Scholar Guest of Honor: Christopher Tolkien, Biographical and Bibliographical Sketch'. *The XVIIIth Mythopoeic Conference* [souvenir programme]. Milwaukee: Mythopoeic Society, 1987. pp. 8–9, 12.

'Andrew Lang's Unrivalled Fairy Stories: Oxford Professor's St Andrews Address'. *St Andrews Citizen*, 11 March 1939, p. 6.

Angles and Britons: O'Donnell Lectures. Cardiff: University of Wales Press, 1963.

'Another Book Still Awaits Completion'. *Oxford Times*, 7 September 1973, p. 6. Note on *The Silmarillion*.

Apeland, Kaj André. 'On Entering the Same River Twice: Mythology and Theology in the Silmarillion Corpus'. In Agøy, *Between Faith and Fiction*, pp. 44–51.

Armstrong, Helen. 'Good Guys, Bad Guys, Fantasy and Reality'. In Reynolds and GoodKnight, *Proceedings of the J.R.R. Tolkien Centenary Conference 1992*, pp. 247–52.

Ashmolean Museum and National Book League. *Catalogue of an Exhibition of Drawings by J.R.R. Tolkien.* Oxford: Ashmolean Museum; London: National Book League, 1976.

Atkins, Philip, and Michael Johnson. *A New Guidebook to the Heart of Oxford.* Stonefield, Oxfordshire: Dodo Publishing, 1999.

Attebery, Brian. *Strategies of Fantasy.* Bloomington: Indiana University Press, 1992.

Attenborough, Philip. 'Rayner Unwin'. *The Independent,* 23 December 2000, p. 4.

Auden, W.H. 'At the End of the Quest, Victory'. *New York Times Book Review,* 22 January 1956, p. 5. Review of *The Return of the King.*

——. 'Good and Evil in *The Lord of the Rings*'. *Tolkien Journal* 3, no. 1 (1967), pp. 5–8.

——. *Making, Knowing and Judging.* Oxford: Clarendon Press, 1956.

——. 'The Quest Hero'. *Texas Quarterly* 4, no. 4 (Winter 1961), pp. 81–93. Reprinted in Isaacs and Zimbardo, *Tolkien and the Critics,* pp. 40–61.

——. 'A World Imaginary, but Real'. *Encounter* 3 (November 1954), pp. 59–60, 62.

Baedeker, Karl. *Switzerland and the Adjacent Portions of Italy, Savoy, and Tyrol: Handbook for Travellers.* 24th edn. Leipzig: Karl Baedeker, 1911.

Baker, Chris. *The Long, Long Trail: The British Army in the Great War of 1914–1918. www.1914-1918.net/index.htm.*

Baker, D.C. Review of *The Old English Exodus. English Language Notes* 21, no. 3 (March 1984), pp. 58–60.

Baker, Peter S., ed. *Beowulf: Basic Readings.* New York: Garland, 1995. Reissued by Garland in 2000 as *The Beowulf Reader.*

Baldwin, Edea A. 'The Flag of Middle-earth: Tolkien's Use of Chesterton to Illustrate Hope and Despair in *The Lord of the Rings*'. 2003. *www.much-ado. net/flourish&blotts/main.php?p=tolkien.*

Barfield, Owen. *A Barfield Reader.* Ed. G.B. Tennyson. Hanover, New Hampshire: Wesleyan University Press/University Press of New England, 1999.

——. *A Barfield Sampler.* Ed. Jeanne Clayton Hunter and Thomas Kranidas. Albany: State University of New York Press, 1993.

——. 'Foreword'. *Seven* 1 (1980), p. 9.

——. 'The Inklings Remembered'. *The World & I* (April 1990), pp. 548–9.

Barnfield, Marie. 'Celtic Influences on the History of the First Age'. *Mallorn* 28 (September 1991), pp. 2–6.

——. 'More Celtic Influences: Númenor and the Second Age'. *Mallorn* 29 (August 1992), pp. 6–13.

——. 'The Roots of Rivendell'. *Þe Lyfe ant þe Auncestrye* 3 (Spring 1996), pp. 4–18.

——. 'Túrin Turambar and the Tale of the Fosterling'. *Mallorn* 31 (December 1994), pp. 29–36.

†Battarbee, K.J., ed. *Scholarship & Fantasy: Proceedings of The Tolkien Phenom-enon, May 1992, Turku, Finland*. Turku: University of Turku, 1993. *Anglicana Turkuensia* 12.

Baxter, John. 'The Tolkien That Should Remain Decently Buried'. *Australian*, 11 February 1984. Review of *The Book of Lost Tales, Part One*.

Beach, Sarah. 'A Myth for Angle-land: J.R.R. Tolkien and Creative Mythology'. *Mythlore* 15, no. 4, whole no. 58 (Summer 1989), pp. 31–6.

Beagle, Peter S. 'A Fantasy Feast from Middle-earth'. *San Francisco Examiner*, 19 October 1980, pp. A13–14. Review of *Unfinished Tales*.

Beatie, Bruce. 'The Tolkien Phenomenon: 1954–1968'. *Journal of Popular Culture* 3, no. 3 (Spring 1970), pp. 689–703.

Bender, Donald. 'And Tolkien Begat the Silmarillion'. *Independent Berkeley Gazette*, 14 October 1977, p. 23. Review of *The Silmarillion*.

Walter R. Benjamin Autographs. *The Collector* 910 (1985).

Bennett, J.A.W. 'Charles Talbut Onions, 1873–1965'. *Proceedings of the British Academy* 65 (1979), pp. 743–58.

——. *Chaucer at Oxford and at Cambridge*. Toronto: University of Toronto Press, 1974.

——. 'Clive Staples Lewis (1898–1963)'. Rev. Emma Plaskitt. *Oxford Dictionary of National Biography*. Online edn.

Bentham, Martin. 'Literary Greats Exposed as Gossips and Snipes'. *Sunday Telegraph*, 7 February 1999.

Benton, Jill. *Naomi Mitchison: A Biography*. London: Pandora Press, 1990.

Bergman, Frank. 'The Roots of Tolkien's Tree: The Influence of George MacDonald and German Romanticism upon Tolkien's Essay "On Fairy-Stories"'. *Mosaic* 10, no. 2 (Winter 1977), pp. 5–14.

Bertenstam, Åke. 'Some Notes on the Reception of *The Hobbit*'. *Angerthas* 23 (16 August 1988), pp. 16–17, 20–5.

†—— (as Åke Jönsson). *En Tolkienbibliografi 1911–1980: verk av och om J.R.R. Tolkien = A Tolkien Bibliography 1911–1980: Works by and about J.R.R. Tolkien*. Rev. edn. Uppsala: Jönsson, 1986. Supplements have been published in *Arda*.

Bibire, Paul. 'By Stock or by Stone: Recurrent Imagery and Narrative Pattern in *The Hobbit*'. In Battarbee, *Scholarship & Fantasy*, pp. 203–15.

——. 'Sægde se þe cuþe: Tolkien as Anglo-Saxonist'. In Battarbee, *Scholarship & Fantasy*, pp. 111–31.

'Big Reduction in Paper Supply'. *The Times* (London), 15 April 1940, p. 8.

Birmingham Oratory. *The Birmingham Oratory. www.birmingham-oratory. org.uk/index.htm*.

†Birzer, Bradley J. *J.R.R. Tolkien's Sanctifying Myth: Understanding Middle-earth*. Foreword by Joseph Pearce. Wilmington, Delaware: ISI Books, 2002.

Bishop, Ian. *Pearl in Its Setting: A Critical Study of the Structure and Meaning of the Middle English Poem*. Oxford: Basil Blackwell, 1968.

Bissett, William. 'Elizabeth Jennings'. *Dictionary of Literary Biography 27: Poets of Great Britain and Ireland, 1945–1960.* Ed. Vincent B. Sherry, Jr. Detroit: Gale Research, 1984. pp. 163–70.

Bjork, Robert E., and John D. Niles, eds. *A Beowulf Handbook.* Lincoln: University of Nebraska Press, 1997.

Björkman, Måns. *Amanye Tenceli. at.mansbjorkman.net/.*

Blackburn, Bonnie, and Leofranc Holford-Strevens. *The Oxford Companion to the Year.* Oxford: Oxford University Press, 1999.

Blackwelder, Richard E. 'Dissertations from Middle-earth'. *Beyond Bree,* March 1990, pp. 4–5.

——. 'The Great Copyright Controversy'. *Beyond Bree,* September 1995, pp. 1–7.

——. *A Tolkien Thesaurus.* New York: Garland, 1990.

Bliss, A.J., ed. *Sir Orfeo.* Oxford: Oxford University Press, 1954.

Blomfield, Joan. 'The Style and Structure of *Beowulf*'. *Review of English Studies* 14 (1938), pp. 396–403.

Bloomfield, Leonard. 'Why a Linguistic Society'. *A Leonard Bloomfield Anthology.* Abridged edn. Ed. Charles F. Hockett. Chicago: University of Chicago Press, 1987. pp. 68–9. Originally published in *Language* 1 (1925).

Bodleian Library. *Drawings for 'The Hobbit' by J.R.R. Tolkien.* Oxford: Bodleian Library, 1987.

Bonhams. *Printed Books & Maps.* Auction catalogue (online). 24 February 2004. *www.bonhams.com.*

Bonjour, Adrien. *The Digressions in Beowulf.* Oxford: Basil Blackwell, 1950. *Medium Ævum Monographs* 5.

——. 'Monsters Crouching and Critics Rampant: or The *Beowulf* Dragon Debated'. *PMLA* 68 (March 1953), pp. 304–12.

Bowra, C.M. *Memories, 1898–1939.* London: Weidenfeld & Nicholson, 1966.

Boyd, J. 'Joseph Wright'. *Dictionary of National Biography 1922–1930.* pp. 923–5.

Brace, Keith. 'In the Footsteps of the Hobbits'. *Birmingham Post Midland Magazine,* 25 May 1968.

Bradfield, J.C. *A Dictionary of Quenya and Proto-Eldarin and Ante-Quenya.* Cambridge: J.C. Bradfield, 1982; rev. 1983.

Bratman, David S. 'A History of Tolkien Fandom'. *Gemini* 1, no. 2 (June 1976), pp. 13–19.

——. 'Hugo Dyson: Inkling, Teacher, Bon Vivant'. *Mythlore* 21, no. 4, whole no. 82 (Winter 1997), pp. 19–34.

——. 'In Search of the Shire: Tolkien and the Counties of England'. *Mallorn* 37 (December 1999), pp. 5–13.

——. 'The Literary Value of *The History of Middle-earth*'. In Flieger and Hostetter, *Tolkien's Legendarium,* pp. 69–91.

——. 'R.B. McCallum: The Master Inkling'. *Mythlore* 23, no. 3, whole no. 89 (Summer 2001), pp. 34–42.

——. Review of *The Book of Lost Tales, Part Two. Mythprint* 21, no. 12, whole no. 55 (December 1984), pp. 2–3.

——. Review of *The Lays of Beleriand*. *Mythprint* 22, no. 12, whole no. 67 (December 1985), pp. 2–3.

——. 'The Years' Work in Tolkien Studies 2001–2002'. *Tolkien Studies* 2 (2005), pp. 289–315.

Brazier, Reginald H., and Ernest Sandford. *Birmingham and the Great War, 1914–1919*. Birmingham: Cornish Brothers, 1921.

Brett, Cyril. Review of *Sir Gawain and the Green Knight* (ed. Tolkien and Gordon). *Modern Language Review* 22 (October 1927), pp. 451–8.

Brierly, J.L., and H.V. Hodson. 'The Constitution of the University'. *Handbook to the University of Oxford*, pp. 79–100.

Briggs, Julia. *A Woman of Passion: The Life of E. Nesbit, 1858–1924*. Harmondsworth: Penguin, 1989.

Briggs, K.M. Review of *Tree and Leaf*. *Folklore* 75 (Winter 1964), pp. 293–4.

Brock, M.G., and M.C. Curthoys, eds. *The History of the University of Oxford, Vol. VII: Nineteenth-Century Oxford, Part 2*. Oxford: Clarendon Press, 2000.

Brogan, Hugh. *The Life of Arthur Ransome*. London: Jonathan Cape, 1984.

——. 'Why Hobbits?' *Cambridge Review*, 23 January 1965, pp. 205–6.

——. 'Tolkien's Great War'. *Children and Their Books: A Celebration of the Work of Iona and Peter Opie*. Ed. Gillian Avery and Julia Briggs. Oxford: Clarendon Press, 1989. pp. 351–67.

Brooks, Paul. *Two Park Street*. Boston: Houghton Mifflin, 1986.

Brown, Arthur. 'Professor Albert Hugh Smith (1903–1967)'. *Proceedings of the Ninth International Congress of Onomastic Sciences*. Comp. J. McN. Dodgson and A.D. Mills. Ed. H. Draye. Louvain: International Centre of Onomastics, 1969. pp. 8–22.

Brown, Malcolm. *The Imperial War Museum Book of the Somme*. London: Pan Books, 2002.

——. *Tommy Goes to War*. New edn. Additional research by Shirley Seaton. Stroud, Gloucestershire: Tempus, 2001.

Brown, Ursula, ed. *Þorgils saga ok Hafliða*. Oxford: Oxford University Press, 1952. *Oxford English Monographs*.

Brunsdale, Mitzi M. 'Norse Mythological Elements in *The Hobbit*'. *Mythlore* 9, no. 4, whole no. 34 (Winter 1983), pp. 49–50.

Buechner, Frederick. 'For Devotees of Middle-Earth'. *New York Times Book Review*, 16 November 1980, pp. 15, 20.

Burchfield, R.W. 'My Hero: Robert Burchfield on J.R.R. Tolkien'. *Independent Magazine* (London), 4 March 1989, p. 50.

——. 'The *OED*: Past and Present'. *Unlocking the English Language*. New York: Hill and Wang, 1992. pp. 188–97.

Burkitt, M.C. *Prehistory: A Study of Early Cultures in Europe and the Mediterranean Basin*. 2nd edn. Cambridge: At the University Press, 1925.

Burns, Marjorie J. 'Echoes of William Morris's Icelandic Journals in J.R.R. Tolkien'. *Studies in Medievalism* 3, no. 3 (Winter 1991), pp. 367–73.

——. 'J.R.R. Tolkien and the Journey North'. *Mythlore* 15, no. 4, whole no. 58 (Summer 1989), pp. 5–9.

——. 'Norse and Christian Gods: The Integrative Theology of J.R.R. Tolkien'. In Chance, *Tolkien and the Invention of Myth*, pp. 163–78.

†——. *Perilous Realms: Celtic and Norse in Tolkien's Middle-earth.* Toronto: University of Toronto Press, 2005.

Caldecott, Stratford. *The Power of the Ring: The Spiritual Vision behind The Lord of the Rings.* New York: Crossroad, 2005.

Caluwé-Dor, Juliette de. 'Bibliographie de S.R.T.O. d'Ardenne'. *Revue des langues vivantes* 35 (1969), pp. 456–60.

Campbell, Roy. *Light on a Dark Horse: An Autobiography (1901–1935).* Chicago: Henry Regnery, 1952.

'Canon Adam Fox'. *The Times* (London), 19 January 1977, p. 16.

'Canterbury Tale and Ballet: Oxford Performances of Summer Diversions'. *Oxford Mail*, 29 July 1939, final page.

Carpenter, Humphrey. *The Envy of the World: Fifty Years of the BBC Third Programme and Radio 3, 1946–1996.* With research by Jennifer Doctor. London: Weidenfeld and Nicolson, 1996.

†——. *The Inklings: C.S. Lewis, J.R.R. Tolkien, Charles Williams, and Their Friends.* London: George Allen & Unwin, 1978.

†——. *J.R.R. Tolkien: A Biography.* London: George Allen & Unwin, 1977. First published in the United States as *Tolkien: A Biography* (Boston: Houghton Mifflin, 1977). A revised edn. appeared in 1987 (London: Unwin Paperbacks).

——. 'Learning about Ourselves: Biography as Autobiography' (conversation with Lyndall Gordon). *The Art of Literary Biography.* Ed. John Batchelor. Oxford: Clarendon Press, 1995. pp. 267–79.

——. '". . . One Expected Him To Go On a Lot Longer": Humphrey Carpenter Remembers J.R.R. Tolkien', *Minas Tirith Evening-Star* 9, no. 2 (January 1980), pp. 10–13.

——. *OUDS: A Centenary History of the Oxford University Dramatic Society, 1885–1985.* Oxford: Oxford University Press, 1985.

——. *W.H. Auden: A Biography.* London: George Allen & Unwin, 1981.

—— and Mari Prichard. *The Oxford Companion to Children's Literature.* Oxford: Oxford University Press, 1984.

——, George Sayer, and Clyde S. Kilby. 'A Dialogue: Discussion . . . Recorded Sept. 29, 1979, Wheaton, Illinois'. *Minas Tirith Evening-Star* 9, no. 2 (January 1980), pp. 14–18, 8.

Carter, Lin. *Imaginary Worlds.* New York: Ballantine Books, 1973.

——. *Tolkien: A Look Behind 'The Lord of the Rings'.* New York: Ballantine Books, 1969.

Carter, Terry. *Birmingham Pals: 14th, 15th & 16th (Service) Battalions of the Royal Warwickshire Regiment: A History of the Three City Battalions Raised in Birmingham in World War One.* Barnsley, South Yorkshire: Pen & Sword, 1997.

Castell, Daphne. 'The Realms of Tolkien'. *New Worlds* 50 (November 1966), pp. 143–54.

Catenian Association. Web site. *thecatenianassociation.org*.

Cater, William. 'The Filial Duty of Christopher Tolkien'. *Sunday Times Magazine*, 25 September 1977.

——. 'Lord of the Hobbits'. *Daily Express* (London), 22 November 1966, p. 10.

——. 'The Lord of the Legends'. *Sunday Times* (London), 2 January 1972, pp. 24, 27–8.

Cavaliero, Glen. *Charles Williams: Poet of Theology*. Grand Rapids, Michigan: William B. Eerdmans, 1983.

Cecil, David. 'Oxford's Magic Circle'. *Books and Bookmen* 24, no. 4 (January 1979), pp. 10–12.

—— and Rachel Trickett. 'Is There an Oxford "School" of Writing?' *Twentieth Century*, June 1955, pp. 559–70.

Ch., M. 'A Faery-like Loveliness'. *Hindustani Times*, 23 June 1968. Review of *The Road Goes Ever On: A Song Cycle*.

Chabot, Caroline. 'Raymond Wilson Chambers (1874–1942)'. *Moreana* 24, no. 93 (February 1987), pp. 69–82, and no. 94 (June 1987), pp. 83–96.

Chambers, R.W. Review of *Beowulf: The Monsters and the Critics*. *Modern Language Review* 33, no. 2 (April 1938), pp. 272–3.

Chambers Biographical Dictionary. 5th edn. Edinburgh: Chambers, 1990.

Chance, Jane. *The Lord of the Rings: The Mythology of Power*. Rev. edn. Lexington: University Press of Kentucky, 2001.

——. *Tolkien's Art: A Mythology for England*. Rev. edn. Lexington: University Press of Kentucky, 2001.

†——, ed. *Tolkien and the Invention of Myth: A Reader*. Lexington: University Press of Kentucky, 2004.

†——, ed. *Tolkien the Medievalist*. London: Routledge, 2003.

—— and Alfred K. Siewers, eds. *Tolkien's Modern Middle Ages*. New York: Palgrave Macmillan, 2005.

—— and David D. Day. 'Medievalism in Tolkien: Two Decades of Criticism in Review'. *Studies in Medievalism* 3, no. 3 (Winter 1991), pp. 375–87.

Chapman, R.W. 'George Stuart Gordon'. *Dictionary of National Biography, 1941–1950*. pp. 307–9. Farrer obit *The Times* 30 December 1968, p. 10.

Chapman, Vera. 'Reminiscences: Oxford in 1920, Meeting Tolkien and Becoming an Author at 77'. In Reynolds and GoodKnight, *Proceedings of the J.R.R. Tolkien Centenary Conference 1992*, pp. 12–14.

'Characters, 1911–12'. *King Edward's School Chronicle* n.s. 27, no. 193 (June 1912), pp. 39–41.

Chaucer, Geoffrey. *The Works of Geoffrey Chaucer*. Ed. F.N. Robinson. 2nd edn. Boston: Houghton Mifflin, 1961.

Chavasse, Fr. Paul. *The Birmingham Oratory Church: A History and Guide*. Birmingham: Clarkeprint, [c. 1980].

Chesterton, G.K. *The Ballad of the White Horse*. 10th edn. London: Methuen, 1928. First published 1911.

——. *The Coloured Lands*. Introduction by Maisie Ward. London: Sheed & Ward, 1938.

——. *The Everlasting Man*. London: Burns & Oates, 1974. First published 1925.

——. *Heretics*. London: John Lane, the Bodley Head, 1905.

——. *Orthodoxy*. Ed. Craig M. Kibler. Lenoir, North Carolina: Reformation Press, 2002. First published 1908.

——. *The Outline of Sanity*. London: Methuen, 1926.

Christensen, Bonniejean. *Beowulf and The Hobbit: Elegy into Fantasy in J.R.R. Tolkien's Creative Technique*. Ph.D. dissertation, University of Southern California, 1969. Condensed as 'Tolkien's Creative Technique: *Beowulf* & *The Hobbit*' in *Orcrist* 7 (Summer 1973), pp. 16–20. See also her address with the same title published in *Mythlore* 15, no. 3, whole no. 57 (Spring 1989), pp. 4–10.

——. 'Gollum's Character Transformation in *The Hobbit*'. *A Tolkien Compass*. Ed. Jared C. Lobdell. La Salle, Illinois: Open Court, 1975. pp. 9–28.

——. 'Report from the West: Exploitation of *The Hobbit*'. *Orcrist* 4 = *Tolkien Journal* 4, no. 3, whole no. 13 (1969–70), pp. 15–16.

Christie's. *Autograph Letters and Printed Books, including First Editions*. Auction catalogue. London (South Kensington), 19 May 2000.

——. *Fine Printed Books and Manuscripts*. Auction catalogue. New York, 24 May 2002.

——. *Masterpieces of Modern Literature: The Library of Roger Rechler*. Auction catalogue. New York, 11 October 2002.

——. *20th Century Books and Manuscripts*. Auction catalogue. London (St James's), 2 December 2003.

——. *20th Century Books and Manuscripts*. Auction catalogue. London (St James's), 2 December 2004.

——. *20th-Century Books and Manuscripts*. Auction catalogue. London (South Kensington), 16 November 2001.

——. *20th-Century Books and Manuscripts*. Auction catalogue. London (South Kensington), 6 December 2002.

——. *Valuable Manuscripts and Printed Books*. Auction catalogue. London (St James's), 7 June 2006.

——. *Valuable Printed Books and Manuscripts*. Auction catalogue. London (St James's), 26 November 1997.

Christopher, Joe R. *C.S. Lewis*. Boston: Twayne, 1987.

——. 'Roy Campbell and the Inklings'. *Mythlore* 22, no. 1, whole no. 83 (Autumn 1997), pp. 33–4, 36–46.

——. 'Three Letters by J.R.R. Tolkien at the University of Texas'. *Mythlore* 7, no. 2, whole no. 24 (Summer 1980), p. 5.

Clark, George. *Beowulf*. Boston: Twayne, 1990.

†—— and Daniel Timmons, eds. *J.R.R. Tolkien and His Literary Resonances: Views of Middle-earth*. Westport, Connecticut: Greenwood Press, 2000.

'The *Clerkes Compleinte* Revisited'. *Arda* 1986 (1990), pp. 1–13.

Cofield, David. 'Changes in Hobbits: Textual Differences in Editions of *The Hobbit*'. *Beyond Bree*, April 1986, pp. 3–4.

——. Letter to the editor. *Beyond Bree*, September 1992, p. 8.

Coffin, R.P. 'Social Life and Activities at the University'. In Crosby, Aydelotte, and Valentine, *Oxford of Today*, pp. 151–87.

Coghill, Nevill. *The Collected Papers of Nevill Coghill, Shakespearian & Medievalist*. Ed. Douglas Gray. Brighton: Harvester Press, 1988.

Cohen, Morton. 'Roger Lancelyn Green'. *Independent* (London), 12 October 1987.

Cole, G.D.H., and T.W. Earp, eds. *Oxford Poetry 1915*. Oxford: B.H. Blackwell, 1915.

Coleridge, Samuel Taylor. *Biographia Literaria, or Biographical Sketches of My Literary Life and Opinions*. Ed. with an introduction by George Watson. London: J.M. Dent & Sons, 1956.

'Colin Hardie'. *Times* (London), 20 October 1998, p. 21.

'College Societies: 1. Stapeldon Debating Society'. *Stapeldon Magazine* (Exeter College, Oxford) 3, no. 16 (December 1911), pp. 97–101.

Collins, David R. *J.R.R. Tolkien: Master of Fantasy*. Minneapolis: Lerner Publications, 1992.

Collyer, Naomi. 'Recollections of Professor J.R.R. Tolkien'. *Arda* 5 (1988, for 1985), pp. 1–3.

Como, James T., ed. *C.S. Lewis at the Breakfast Table and Other Reminiscences*. New edn. San Diego: Harcourt Brace Jovanovich, 1992.

The Concise Oxford Dictionary of Current English. 8th edn. Ed. R.E. Allen. Oxford: Clarendon Press, 1990.

The Concise Oxford English Dictionary. 10th edn., rev. Ed. Judy Pearsall. Oxford: Oxford University Press, 2002.

Constable, John. 'C.S. Lewis: From Magdalen to Magdalene'. *Magdalene College Magazine and Record*, n.s. 32 (1987–88), pp. 42–6. Reprinted in *Anor* 26, n.s 1 (1995), pp. 15–19.

Cook, Irene Tolkien. Letter to the Editor. *Amon Hen* 162 (March 2000), pp. 24–5.

Coren, Michael. *J.R.R. Tolkien: The Man Who Created The Lord of the Rings*. Toronto: Stoddardt, 2001.

'The Coronation'. *King Edward's School Chronicle* n.s. 26, no. 188 (July 1911), pp. 59–60.

Corpus Christi College, Oxford. *Biographical Register, 1880–1974*. Comp. by P.A. Hunt. Ed. N.A. Flanagan. Oxford: Corpus Christi College, 1988.

Coulombe, Charles. 'The Lord of the Rings – A Catholic View'. In Pearce, *Tolkien: A Celebration*, pp. 53–66.

†Crabbe, Katharyn W. *J.R.R. Tolkien*. Rev. and expanded edn. New York: Continuum, 1988.

Craigie, W.A. 'Henry Bradley'. *Dictionary of National Biography, 1922–1930*. pp. 103–4.

Cranborne, Hannah, ed. *David Cecil: A Portrait by His Friends*. Stambridge, Wimborne, Dorset: Dovecote Press, 1990.

Croft, Janet Brennan. 'Three Rings for Hollywood: Scripts for *The Lord of the Rings* by Zimmerman, Boorman, and Beagle'. Unpublished paper, presented at the Mythopoeic Society Conference, Ann Arbor, Michigan, July 2004.

†——. *War and the Works of J.R.R. Tolkien*. Westport, Connecticut: Praeger, 2004.

——, ed. *Tolkien on Film: Essays on Peter Jackson's The Lord of the Rings*. Altadena, California: Mythopoeic Press, 2004.

Crosby, L.A. 'The Organization of the University and Colleges'. In Crosby, Aydelotte, and Valentine, *Oxford of Today*, pp. 29–39.

——. 'The Oxford System of Education'. In Crosby, Aydelotte, and Valentine, *Oxford of Today*, pp. 48–52.

——, Frank Aydelotte, and Alan C. Valentine, eds. *Oxford of Today: A Manual for Prospective Rhodes Scholars*. New York: Oxford University Press, 1927.

Cross, F.L., and E.A. Livingstone, eds. *The Oxford Dictionary of the Christian Church*. Oxford: Oxford University Press, 1997.

Crouch, Marcus. Review of *Farmer Giles of Ham*. *Junior Bookshelf*, January 1950, pp. 14–15.

Crowe, Edith L. 'Power in Arda: Sources, Uses and Misuses'. In Reynolds and GoodKnight, *Proceedings of the J.R.R. Tolkien Centenary Conference 1992*, pp. 272–7.

Curry, Patrick. *Defending Middle-earth: Tolkien, Myth and Modernity*. Edinburgh: Floris Books, 1997.

——. 'Tolkien and His Critics: A Critique'. *Root and Branch: Approaches towards Understanding Tolkien*. Ed. Thomas Honegger. Comare Series 2. Zurich: Walking Tree Publishers, 1999. pp. 81–148.

Curtis, Anthony. 'Hobbits and Heroes'. *Sunday Telegraph*, 10 November 1963, p. 16.

——. 'Remembering Tolkien and Lewis'. *British Book News*, June 1977, pp. 429–30.

Curtis, Philip. *A Hawk among Sparrows: A Biography of Austin Farrer*. London: SPCK, 1985.

'Daily Life in Middle Earth'. *The Bookseller*, 3 August 1968, p. 374.

Dale, Alzina Stone. *The Outline of Sanity: A Life of G.K. Chesterton*. Grand Rapids, Michigan: William B. Eerdmans, 1982.

'Dame Helen Gardner: Distinguished Contributions to Literary Studies'. *The Times* (London), 6 June 1986, p. 14.

D'Ardenne, S.R.T.O. 'The Editing of Middle English Texts'. In Wrenn and Bullough, *English Studies Today*, pp. 74–84.

——. 'The Man and the Scholar'. In Salu and Farrell, *J.R.R. Tolkien: Scholar and Storyteller*, pp. 33–7.

—— (as S.T.R.O.), ed. *The Katherine Group*. Paris: Société d'Edition 'Les Belles Lettres', 1977.

——, ed. Þe Liflade ant to Passiun of Seinte Iuliene. See THE PUBLISHED WRITINGS OF J.R.R. TOLKIEN in vol. 1.

—— and E.J. Dobson, eds. Seinte Katerine: Re-Edited from MS Bodley 34 and the Other Manuscripts. Oxford: Published for the Early English Text Society by the Oxford University Press, 1981.

Davenport, Guy. 'The Persistence of Light'. National Review, 20 April 1965, pp. 332, 334.

Davin, Dan. 'Norman Davis: The Growth of a Scholar'. Middle English Studies Presented to Norman Davis in Honour of His Seventieth Birthday. Ed. Douglas Gray and E.G. Stanley. Oxford: Clarendon Press, 1983. pp. 1–15.

Davis, Howard. 'The Ainulindalë: Music of Creation'. Mythlore 9, no. 2, whole no. 32 (Summer 1982), pp. 6–9.

Davis, Norman. 'Dr. Mabel Day: Early English Texts'. The Times (London), 24 September 1964, p. 18.

——. 'J.R.R. Tolkien'. Postmaster (Merton College, Oxford), January 1976, p. 10.

——. 'Jack Arthur Walter Bennett, 1911–1981'. Proceedings of the British Academy 68 (1982), pp. 481–94.

—— and C.L. Wrenn, eds. English and Medieval Studies Presented to J.R.R. Tolkien on the Occasion of His Seventieth Birthday. London: George Allen & Unwin, 1962.

De Camp, L. Sprague. Letter to the editor. Andúril 1 (April 1972), pp. 8–9.

——. Letter to the editor. Mythlore 13, no. 4, whole no. 50 (Summer 1987), p. 41.

'Deaths'. The Times (London), 16 March 1942, p. 6. Notice of the funeral of George S. Gordon.

'Deaths'. The Times (London), 14 October 1950, p. 1. Notice of the funeral of R.F.W. Fletcher.

'Deaths'. The Times (London), 5 July 1952, p. 1. Notice of the death of Susan Grindle née Dagnall.

'Debating Characters'. King Edward's School Chronicle n.s. 26, no. 187 (June 1911), pp. 45–7.

'Debating Society'. King Edward's School Chronicle, n.s. 24, no. 177 (November 1909), pp. 83–4; n.s. 24, no. 178 (December 1909), pp. 94–7; n.s. 26, no. 183 (November 1910), pp. 68–71; n.s. 26, no. 184 (December 1910), pp. 94–5; n.s. 26, no. 185 (February 1911), pp. 5–9; n.s. 26, no. 187 (June 1911), pp. 42–5; n.s. 27, no. 191 (March 1912), pp. 11–16; n.s. 27, no. 193 (June 1912), pp. 36–9; n.s. 28, no. 199 (May 1913), pp. 34–7.

'Deddington Court Now Library', Oxford Mail, 15 December 1956, p. 1.

Denniston, Robin. 'Sir Stanley Unwin'. Oxford Dictionary of National Biography. Online edn.

Derrick, Christopher. 'And See Ye Not Yon Bonny Road?' The Tablet, 10 February 1968, p. 132. Review of Smith of Wootton Major.

Deyo, Steven M. 'Niggle's Leaves: The Red Book of Westmarch and Related Minor Poetry of J.R.R. Tolkien'. Mythlore 12, no. 3, whole no. 45 (Spring 1986), pp. 28–31, 34–7.

†Dickerson, Matthew T. *Following Gandalf: Epic Battles and Moral Victory in The Lord of the Rings*. Grand Rapids, Michigan: Brazos Press, 2003.

'Dictionary Editors'. *Oxford English Dictionary* Web site. *www.oed.com/public/inside/editors.htm*.

Dirda, Michael. 'Under the Big Top and on the Road'. *Washington Post Book World*, 3 May 1998, p. 16. Review of *Roverandom*.

'Dr. C.T. Onions: The Making of O.E.D.' *The Times* (London), 12 January 1965, p. 11.

'Dr. George Gordon, President of Magdalen'. *The Times* (London), 13 March 1942, p. 7.

'Dr. J. Fraser, Professor of Celtic at Oxford'. *The Times* (London), 22 May 1945, p. 7.

'Dr. L.R. Farnell: Ancient Greek Religion'. *The Times* (London), 29 March 1934, p. 16.

'Dr. Percy Simpson, Editor of Ben Jonson'. *The Times* (London), 16 November 1962, p. 15.

'Dr. R.W. Chambers, English at University College, London'. *The Times* (London), 24 April 1942, p. 7.

Dolan, T.P. 'Alan J. Bliss, 1921–1985'. *Medieval English Studies Newsletter* 14 (1986), pp. 6–7.

'Donald Swann'. *The Times* (London), 25 March 1994, p. 21.

Doughan, David. 'Elvish and Welsh'. *Mallorn* 30 (September 1993), pp. 5–9.

——. 'An Ethnically Cleansed Faery?: Tolkien and the Matter of Britain'. *Mallorn* 32 (September 1995), pp. 21–4.

——. 'In Search of the Bounce: Tolkien Seen through Smith'. In *Leaves from the Tree: J.R.R. Tolkien's Shorter Fiction*, pp. 17–22.

——, ed. *Translations of The Hobbit Reviewed*. Quettar Special Publication 2. London: Quettar, 1988.

—— and Julian Bradfield. *An Introduction to the Writing Systems of Middle-earth*. Quettar Special Publication 1. London: Quettar, 1987.

Drabble, Margaret. 'Rebels against Ilúvatar'. *The Listener*, 15 September 1977, p. 346. Review of *The Silmarillion*.

Drawings for 'The Hobbit' by J.R.R. Tolkien. Oxford: Bodleian Library, 1987.

Drayton, Paul, and Humphrey Carpenter. 'A Preparatory School Approach'. *Music Drama in Schools*. Ed. Malcolm John. Cambridge: At the University Press, 1971. pp. 1–19.

Drout, Michael D.C. 'The Rhetorical Evolution of "*Beowulf: The Monsters and the Critics*"'. In Hammond and Scull, *The Lord of the Rings, 1954–2004: Scholarship in Honor of Richard E. Blackwelder*, pp. 183–215.

—— and Hilary Wynne. 'Tom Shippey's *J.R.R. Tolkien: Author of the Century* and a Look Back at Tolkien Criticism since 1982'. *Envoi: A Review Journal of Medieval Literature* 9, no. 1 (Fall 2000), pp. 101–67. A version in electronic form is at *members.aol.com/JamesIMcNelis/9_2/Drout_9_2.pdf*.

—— et al. 'A Bibliography of Scholarly Studies of J.R.R. Tolkien and His Works (through 2000)'. *acunix.wheatonma.edu/mdrout/TolkienBiblio/*.

Duane, Diane. 'The Longest Sunday'. In Haber, *Meditations on Middle-earth*, pp. 117–28.

Dubs, Kathleen E. 'Providence, Fate and Chance: Boethian Philosophy in *The Lord of the Rings*'. In Chance, *Tolkien and the Invention of Myth*, pp. 133–42.

Dunbabin, J.P.D. 'Finance since 1914'. In Harrison, *The History of the University of Oxford, Vol. VIII*, pp. 639–82.

Dundas-Grant, James. 'From an "Outsider"'. In Como, *C.S. Lewis at the Breakfast Table and Other Reminiscences*, pp. 229–33.

Dunsire, Brin. 'Of Ham, and What Became of It'. *Amon Hen* 98 (July 1989), pp. 14–17.

Duriez, Colin. 'Survey of Tolkien Literature'. *Seven* 20 (2003), pp. 105–14.

——. 'Tolkien and the Other Inklings'. In Reynolds and GoodKnight, *Proceedings of the J.R.R. Tolkien Centenary Conference 1992*, pp. 360–3.

E., A.B. 'R.F.W. Fletcher (1890–1950)'. *Oxford Magazine*, 26 October 1950, pp. 62, 64.

'The Earl of Halsbury'. *The Times* (London), 18 January 2000, p. 21.

Eddison, E.R. *The Worm Ouroboros*. Introduced and annotated by Paul Edmund Thomas. New York: Dell, 1991.

——. *Zimiamvia: A Trilogy*. Introduced and annotated by Paul Edmund Thomas. New York: Dell, 1992.

Eden, Bradford Lee. 'The "Music of the Spheres": Relationships between Tolkien's *The Silmarillion* and Medieval Cosmological and Religious Theory'. In Chance, *Tolkien the Medievalist*, pp. 183–93.

'An Edited Transcript of Remarks at the December 1966 TSA [Tolkien Society of America] Meeting'. *Niekas* 19 (Spring 1967), pp. 39–40.

'Editorial'. *King Edward's School Chronicle* n.s. 26, no. 186 (March 1911), pp. 17–18.

Edmonds, E.L. 'C.S. Lewis, the Teacher'. *In Search of C.S. Lewis*. Ed. Stephen Schofield. South Plainfield, New Jersey: Bridge Publishing, 1983. pp. 37–51.

Egan, Thomas M. 'Chesterton and Tolkien: The Road to Middle-earth'. *Seven* 4 (1983), pp. 45–53. Another version of this article was published as 'Tolkien and Chesterton: Some Analogies' in *Mythlore* 12, no. 1, whole no. 43 (Autumn 1985), pp. 29–30, 32–5.

——. 'Fragmentary Glimpses'. *Mythlore* 11, no. 1, whole no. 39 (Summer 1984), pp. 36–7. Review of *Finn and Hengest*.

——. 'Fragments of a World: Tolkien's Road to Middle-earth'. *The Terrier* (St Francis College, Brooklyn, N.Y) 48, no. 2 (Fall 1983), pp. 9–10.

——. 'Tolkien's Fantasy Universe Expands'. *New York City Tribune*, 25 March 1985, pp. 5B–6B.

——. 'Tolkien's Son Compiles Fascinating "Book of Lost Tales, Part I"'. *New York Tribune*, 8 March 1984, p. 5B.

Eiseley, Loren. 'The Elvish Art of Enchantment'. *Horn Book*, August 1965, pp. 364–7.

Ekwall, Eilart. *Concise Oxford Dictionary of Place-names*. 4th edn. Oxford: Clarendon Press, 1960.

'Elaine Griffiths'. *The Times* (London), 13 December 1996, p. 21.

'Elizabeth Jennings'. *Daily Telegraph*, 30 October 2001. *www.dailytelegraph. com/obituary*.

'Elizabeth Jennings'. *The Times* (London), 31 October 2001, p. 19.

Elliott, Ralph W.V. *Runes: An Introduction*. Manchester: Manchester University Press, 1959.

Ellison, John A. 'Editorial'. *Mallorn* 31 [December 1994], p. 5.

——. Review of *The Lays of Beleriand*. *Amon Hen* 75 (September 1985), pp. 11–12.

——. 'Tolkien's Art'. *Mallorn* 30 (September 1993), pp. 21–8.

——. 'The "Why", and the "How": Reflections on "Leaf by Niggle"'. In *Leaves from the Tree*, pp. 23–32.

Elton, Oliver. 'Lascelles Abercrombie'. *Dictionary of National Biography, 1931–1940*. pp. 1–2.

——. 'Lascelles Abercrombie, 1881–1938'. *Proceedings of the British Academy* 25 (1939), pp. 394–421.

'The Elvish Mode'. *New Yorker*, 15 January 1966, pp. 24–5.

Emerson, Oliver Farrar. Review of *Sir Gawain and the Green Knight* (ed. Tolkien and Gordon). *Journal of English and Germanic Philology* 26 (1927), pp. 248–58.

Encyclopædia Britannica. 14th edn. New York: Encyclopædia Britannica, 1938.

'The Epic of Westernesse', *Times Literary Supplement*, 17 December 1954, p. 817. Review of *The Two Towers*.

'Essay Club'. *Stapeldon Magazine* (Exeter College, Oxford) 5, no. 26 (June 1920), p. 87.

'Essay Club'. *Stapeldon Magazine* (Exeter College, Oxford) 7, no. 39 (December 1926), p. 96.

Etkin, Anne, ed. *Eglerio! In Praise of Tolkien*. Greencastle, Pennsylvania: Quest Communications, 1978.

Evans, Jonathan. 'The Dragon-Lore of Middle-earth: Tolkien and Old English and Old Norse Tradition'. In Clark and Timmons, *J.R.R. Tolkien and His Literary Resonances*, pp. 21–38.

Evans, Robley. *J.R.R. Tolkien*. New York: Thomas Y. Crowell, 1971.

Everett, Caroline Whitman. *The Imaginative Fiction of J.R.R. Tolkien*. MA thesis, Florida State University, 1957.

Everett, Dorothy. *Essays on Middle English Literature*. Edited by Patricia Kean. Memoir by Mary Lascelles. Oxford: Clarendon Press, 1955.

——. 'Raymond Wilson Chambers'. *Dictionary of National Biography, 1941–1950*. pp. 145–6.

Exeter College, Oxford. [Oxford: Exeter College, *c.* 1980].

Ezard, John. 'The Hobbit Man'. *Oxford Mail*, 3 August 1966, p. 4.

——. 'Successor to the Hobbits at Last'. *Oxford Mail*, 11 February 1966, p. 11 (late final edn.).

'Fable for To-day'. *Church Times*, 8 October 1954, p. 4. Review of *The Fellowship of the Ring*.

'Fantasy Award to Professor Tolkien', *The Bookseller*, 14 September 1957, p. 1074.

'Fantasy of the Year'. *Oxford Mail*, 11 September 1957, p. 4.

Finseth, Claudia Riiff. 'Tolkien's Trees'. *Mallorn* 35 (September 1997), pp. 37–44.

Firth, C.H. 'Joseph Wright, 1855–1930'. *Proceedings of the British Academy* 18 (1932), pp. 422–38.

Fisher, Matthew A. 'Working at the Crossroads: Tolkien, St. Augustine, and the *Beowulf*-poet'. In Hammond and Scull, *The Lord of the Rings 1954–2004: Scholarship in Honor of Richard E. Blackwelder*, pp. 217–30.

Flieger, Verlyn. 'J.R.R. Tolkien and the Matter of Britain'. *Mythlore* 23, no. 1, whole no. 87 (Summer/Fall 2000), pp. 47–58.

——. 'The Footsteps of Ælfwine'. In Flieger and Hostetter, *Tolkien's Legendarium*, pp. 183–98.

†——. *Interrupted Music: Tolkien and the Making of a Mythology*. Kent, Ohio: Kent State University Press, 2005.

——. 'Pitfalls of Faërie'. *Mythos Journal* 2, no. 1 (Winter 1995), pp. 3–11.

†——. *A Question of Time: J.R.R. Tolkien's Road to Faërie*. Kent, Ohio: Kent State University Press, 1997.

†——. *Splintered Light: Logos and Language in Tolkien's World*. 2nd edn. Kent, Ohio: Kent State University Press, 2002.

——. 'Taking the Part of Trees: Eco-Conflict in Middle-earth'. In Clark and Timmons, *J.R.R. Tolkien and His Literary Resonances*, pp. 147–58.

——. 'A Tale That Grew in the Telling'. In *Selections from the Marquette J.R.R. Tolkien Collection*, pp. 16–19.

——. '"There Would Always Be a Fairy-tale": J.R.R. Tolkien and the Folklore Controversy'. In Chance, *Tolkien the Medievalist*, pp. 26–35.

——. 'Tolkien's Experiment with Time: *The Lost Road*, "The Notion Club Papers", and J.W. Dunne'. In Reynolds and GoodKnight, *Proceedings of the J.R.R. Tolkien Centenary Conference 1992*, pp. 39–44.

——. 'Whose Myth Is It?' In Agøy, *Between Faith and Fiction*, pp. 32–42.

——, ed. *Smith of Wootton Major* by J.R.R. Tolkien. Extended edn. London: HarperCollins, 2005.

†—— and Carl F. Hostetter, eds. *Tolkien's Legendarium: Essays on The History of Middle-earth*. Westport, Connecticut: Greenwood Press, 2000.

—— and T.A. Shippey. 'Allegory versus Bounce: Tolkien's *Smith of Wootton Major*'. *Journal of the Fantastic in the Arts* 12, no. 2 (Spring 2002), pp. 186–200.

Flood, John. 'Power, Domination and Egocentrism in Tolkien and Orwell'. *Mallorn* 34 (December 1996), pp. 13–19.

†Fonstad, Karen Wynn. *The Atlas of Middle-earth*. Rev. edn. Boston: Houghton Mifflin, 1991.

'Football'. *King Edward's School Chronicle* n.s. 24, no. 177 (November 1909), pp. 85–8; n.s. 26, no. 183 (November 1910), pp. 82–4.

'Football Characters'. *King Edward's School Chronicle* n.s. 25, no. 180 (April 1910), pp. 35–6.

'Football Characters 1910–11'. *King Edward's School Chronicle* n.s. 26, no. 187 (June 1911), pp. 49–51.

Foote, Peter. 'Gabriel Turville-Petre, 1908–1978'. *Proceedings of the British Academy* 64 (1978), pp. 467–81.

'Forestry and Us'. *Daily Telegraph*, 29 June 1972, p. 18.

Foster, Michael. 'The Shire and Notting Hill'. *Mallorn* 35 (September 1997), pp. 45–53.

†Foster, Robert. *The Complete Guide to Middle-earth: From The Hobbit to The Silmarillion*. London: George Allen & Unwin, 1978. In this, page references, keyed to the standard hardcover editions of the time, are given within the entries. In the HarperCollins, 2003 edn., the references are gathered awkwardly at the end of the volume.

Foster, William. 'A Benevolent and Furry-footed People'. *Scotsman Week-end Magazine*, 25 March 1967.

Fox, Adam. 'At the Breakfast Table'. In Como, *C.S. Lewis at the Breakfast Table and Other Reminiscences*, pp. 89–95.

Frederick, Candice, and Sam McBride. *Women among the Inklings: Gender, C.S. Lewis, J.R.R. Tolkien, and Charles Williams*. Westport, Connecticut: Greenwood Press, 2001.

Freeman, Gwendolen. Review of *Farmer Giles of Ham. Spectator*, 18 November 1949, p. 718.

Freston, H. Rex. *The Quest of Beauty and Other Poems*. Oxford: B.H. Blackwell, 1915.

Frost, K.T. 'The *Critias* and Minoan Crete'. *Journal of Hellenic Studies* 33 (1913), pp. 189–206.

——. 'The Lost Continent'. *The Times* (London), 19 February 1909, p. 10.

Fulford, Roger, J.C. Masterman, and C.H. Wilkinson. *C.H. Wilkinson, 1888–1960*. Oxford: Oxford University Press, 1965.

Fulk, R.D., ed. *Interpretations of Beowulf: A Critical Anthology*. Bloomington: Indiana University Press, 1991.

Fuller, Edmund. 'The Lord of the Hobbits: J.R.R. Tolkien'. Originally published in *Books with Men behind Them* (1962), reprinted in Isaacs and Zimbardo, *Tolkien and the Critics*, pp. 17–39.

——. 'A Superb Addition to Tolkien's Mythological Realm'. *Wall Street Journal*, 19 September 1977, p. 22. Review of *The Silmarillion*.

Fuller, John. *W.H. Auden: A Commentary*. London: Faber & Faber, 1998.

'Funeral and Memorial Services'. *The Times* (London), 24 May 1945, p. 6. On the requiem Mass for John Fraser.

'Funerals'. *The Times* (London), 22 September 1934, p. 15. On the funeral of F.F. Urquhart.

'Funerals'. *The Times* (London), 14 January 1965, p. 12. On the funeral of C.T. Onions.

Fussell, Paul. *The Great War and Modern Memory*. Paperback edn. New York: Oxford University Press, 1977.

'"Gammer Gurton" at Oxford Diversions: with Chaucer's "Nonnes Preestes Tale," Spoken in Middle English by Prof. J.R.R. Tolkien'. *Oxford Mail*, 4 August 1938, p. 6.

Gang, T.M. 'Approaches to *Beowulf*'. *Review of English Studies* n.s. 3 (1952), pp. 1–12.

Gardner, Helen. 'Clive Staples Lewis, 1898–1963'. *Proceedings of the British Academy* 51 (1965), pp. 417–28.

——. 'Is Beowulf Needed?' *The Times* (London), 17 November 1965, p. 13. Letter to the editor.

†Garth, John. *Tolkien and the Great War: The Threshold of Middle-earth*. London: HarperCollins, 2003.

Gay, David Elton. 'J.R.R. Tolkien and the *Kalevala*: Some Thoughts on the Finnish Origins of Tom Bombadil and Treebeard'. In Chance, *Tolkien and the Invention of Myth*, pp. 295–304.

Gillett, Edward, and Kenneth A. MacMahon. *A History of Hull*. 2nd, expanded edn. Hull: Hull University Press, 1989.

Gilliver, Peter M. 'At the Wordface: J.R.R. Tolkien's Work on the *Oxford English Dictionary*'. In Reynolds and GoodKnight, *Proceedings of the J.R.R. Tolkien Centenary Conference 1992*, pp. 173–86.

†——, Jeremy Marshall, and Edmund Weiner. *The Ring of Words: Tolkien and the* Oxford English Dictionary. Oxford: Oxford University Press, 2006.

Gilson, Christopher. 'Elvish and Mannish'. *Vinyar Tengwar* 33 (January 1994), pp. 10–26.

——. 'Gnomish Is Sindarin: The Conceptual Evolution of an Elvish Language'. In Flieger and Hostetter, *Tolkien's Legendarium*, pp. 95–104.

——. '*Narqelion* and the Early Lexicons: Some Notes on the First Elvish Poem'. *Vinyar Tengwar* 40 (April 1999), pp. 6–32.

—— and Patrick Wynne. 'The Growth of Grammar in the Elven Tongues'. In Reynolds and GoodKnight, *Proceedings of the J.R.R. Tolkien Centenary Conference 1992*, pp. 187–94.

——, Bill Welden, Carl F. Hostetter, and Patrick Wynne, eds. 'Early Noldorin Fragments'. *Parma Eldalamberon* 13 (2001), pp. 92–165.

—— see also THE PUBLISHED WRITINGS OF J.R.R. TOLKIEN in vol. 1

Gleeson, Gill. 'Music in Middle-earth'. *Mallorn* 16 (May 1981), pp. 29–31.

Glenn, Lois. *Charles W.S. Williams: A Checklist*. Kent, Ohio: Kent State University Press, 1975.

Gliddon, Gerald. *The Battle of the Somme: A Topographical History*. Corrected edn. Thrupp, Stroud, Gloucestershire: Sutton, 1996.

Godden, Malcolm. 'From the Heroic to the Allegorical'. *Times Literary Supplement*, 8 July 1983, p. 736.

GoodKnight, Glen. 'Two Decades: Looking Back'. *Mythlore* 13, no. 4, whole no. 50 (Summer 1987), pp. 3–4, 57.

Goolden, Peter, ed. *The Old English Apollonius of Tyre*. Oxford: Oxford University Press, 1958. *Oxford English Monographs*.

Gordon, E.V. *An Introduction to Old Norse*. 2nd edn., rev. A.R. Taylor. Paperback edn., from corrected sheets. Oxford: Clarendon Press, 1981.

——, ed. *The Battle of Maldon*. London: Methuen, 1937.

——, ed. *Pearl*. Oxford: Clarendon Press, 1953.

Gordon, George S. *The Discipline of Letters*. Preface by Mary Gordon. Oxford: Clarendon Press, 1946. Includes 'Andrew Lang', pp. 131–51.

——. *The Letters of George S. Gordon, 1902–1942*. Oxford: Oxford University Press, 1943.

Gordon, I.L., ed. *The Seafarer*. London: Methuen, 1960.

Gordon, Mary C. *The Life of George S. Gordon, 1881–1942*. London: Oxford University Press, 1945.

Graham, Malcolm, and Melanie Williams. *When the Lights Went Out: Oxfordshire 1939 to 1945*. Holton, Oxford: Libraries' Department, Oxfordshire County Council, 1979.

Grahame, Kenneth. *First Whisper of 'The Wind in the Willows'*. Ed., with an introduction, by Elspeth Grahame. Philadelphia: J.B. Lippincott, 1945. First published 1944.

——. 'The Reluctant Dragon'. *Dream Days*. London: Bodley Head, 1973. First published 1898.

——. *The Wind in the Willows*. Introduction by Peter Green. Oxford: Oxford University Press, 1983. First published 1908.

Grattan, J.H.G. Review of *Sir Gawain and the Green Knight* (ed. Tolkien and Gordon). *Review of English Studies* 1, no. 4 (October 1925), pp. 484–7.

Gray, Douglas. 'Eric John Dobson, 1913–1984'. *Proceedings of the British Academy* 71 (1985), pp. 533–8.

——. 'Norman Davis, 1913–1989'. *Proceedings of the British Academy* 80 (1993), pp. 261–73.

——. 'A Tribute to J.A.W. Bennett (1911–1981)'. *Medium Ævum* 50, no. 2 (1981), pp. 205–14.

Green, Peter. *Kenneth Grahame, 1859–1932: A Study of His Life, Work and Times*. London: John Murray, 1959.

——. 'Outward Bound by Air to an Inappropriate Ending'. *Daily Telegraph*, 27 August 1954, p. 8. Review of *The Fellowship of the Ring*.

Green, Roger Lancelyn. *Andrew Lang: A Critical Biography*. Leicester: Edmund Ward, 1946.

——. 'Recollections'. *Amon Hen* 44 (May 1980), pp. 6–8.

——. 'Slicing a Magical Cake'. *Sunday Telegraph*, 3 December 1967. Review of *Smith of Wootton Major*.

——. *Tellers of Tales: Children's Books and Their Authors from 1800 to 1964*. Rewritten and rev. edn. London: Edmund Ward, 1965.

—— and Walter Hooper. *C.S. Lewis: A Biography*. Rev. and expanded edn. London: HarperCollins, 2002.

Green, William H. *The Hobbit: A Journey into Maturity*. New York: Twayne, 1995.

Greene, Deirdre. 'Tolkien's Dictionary Poetics: The Influence of the *OED*'s Defining Style on Tolkien's Fiction'. In Reynolds and GoodKnight, *Proceedings of the J.R.R. Tolkien Centenary Conference 1992*, pp. 195–9.

Greenfield, Stanley B. *A Critical History of Old English Literature*. New York: New York University Press, 1965.

Greenman, David. 'Aeneidic and Odyssean Patterns of Escape and Return in Tolkien's *The Fall of Gondolin* and *The Return of the King*'. *Mythlore* 18, no. 2, whole no. 68 (Spring 1992), pp. 4–9.

Grigorieva, Natalia. 'Problems of Translating into Russian'. In Reynolds and GoodKnight, *Proceedings of the J.R.R. Tolkien Centenary Conference 1992*, pp. 200–205.

Grotta-Kurska, Daniel. *J.R.R. Tolkien: Architect of Middle Earth*. Ed. Frank Wilson. Philadelphia: Running Press, 1976. A 2nd edn., as by Daniel Grotta, and with the title *The Biography of J.R.R. Tolkien: Architect of Middle-earth*, was published by Running Press in 1998, and a 3rd edn. by the same publisher in 1992.

Haas, Joseph. 'War over Middle-earth'. *Chicago Daily News*, 7 August 1965.

Haber, Karen, ed. *Meditations on Middle-earth*. New York: St. Martin's Press, 2001.

Hadfield, Alice Mary. *Charles Williams: An Exploration of His Life and Work*. New York: Oxford University Press, 1983.

Haggard, H. Rider. *The Annotated She: A Critical Edition of H. Rider Haggard's Victorian Romance*. Introduction and notes by Norman Etherington. Bloomington: Indiana University Press, 1991. First published 1887.

——. *Ayesha: The Return of She*. New York: Ballantine Books, 1978. First published 1905.

——. *King Solomon's Mines*. Introduction by Roger Lancelyn Green. London: Collins, 1955. First published 1885.

——. *She and Allan*. New York: Ballantine Books, 1978. First published 1921.

†Patrick & Beatrice Haggerty Museum of Art, Marquette University. *The Invented Worlds of J.R.R. Tolkien: Drawings and Original Manuscripts from the Marquette University Collection*. Milwaukee: The Museum, 2004.

——. *J.R.R. Tolkien: The Hobbit Drawings, Watercolors, and Manuscripts*. Milwaukee: The Museum, 1987.

Halliday, W.R. 'Richard McGillivray Dawkins'. *Dictionary of National Biography 1951–1960*. pp. 287–8.

Halsall, Martin. 'Sheer Poetry as Green Velvet Sets the Scene'. *Oxford Mail*, 25 May 1973, p. 13.

Hammond, Wayne G. 'All the Comforts: The Image of Home in *The Hobbit* and *The Lord of the Rings*'. *Mythlore* 14, no. 1, whole no. 51 (Autumn 1987), pp. 29–33.

——. *Arthur Ransome: A Bibliography*. Winchester: St Paul's Bibliographies; New Castle, Delaware: Oak Knoll Press, 2000.

——. 'The Critical Response to Tolkien's Fiction'. In Reynolds and Good-Knight, *Proceedings of the J.R.R. Tolkien Centenary Conference 1992*, pp. 226–32.

——. 'In Memoriam Joy Hill'. *Beyond Bree*, February 1992, p. 5.

——. 'The Nature of the Beast: Tolkien's Bestiary Poems'. Unpublished essay.

——. 'Pauline Baynes'. *British Children's Writers, 1914–1960*. Ed. Donald R. Hettinga and Gary D. Schmidt. Detroit: Gale Research, 1996. pp. 36–44.

——. 'Special Collections in the Service of Tolkien Studies'. In Hammond and Scull, *The Lord of the Rings, 1954–2004: Scholarship in Honor of Richard E. Blackwelder*, pp. 331–40.

——, ed. *C.S. Lewis & Owen Barfield: A Souvenir Book for the Centenary Celebration Held . . . by the Mythopoeic Society*. Wheaton, Illinois: Mythopoeic Society, 1998.

—— and Christina Scull. 'The History of Middle-earth'. *Seven* 12 (1995), pp. 105–10.

†—— ——. *J.R.R. Tolkien: Artist and Illustrator*. London: HarperCollins, 1995. A corrected paperback edn. was issued by HarperCollins in 1998.

—— ——. 'J.R.R. Tolkien: The Achievement of His Literary Life'. *Mythlore* 22, no. 3, whole no. 85 (Winter 1999), pp. 27–37.

†—— ——. *The Lord of the Rings: A Reader's Companion*. London: Harper-Collins, 2005.

†—— ——, eds. *The Lord of the Rings, 1954–2004: Scholarship in Honor of Richard E. Blackwelder*. Milwaukee: Marquette University Press, 2006.

†——, with the assistance of Douglas A. Anderson. *J.R.R. Tolkien: A Descriptive Bibliography*. Winchester: St Paul's Bibliographies; New Castle, Delaware: Oak Knoll Books, 1993. Addenda and corrigenda have appeared in *The Tolkien Collector*.

Handbook to the University of Oxford. Oxford: Clarendon Press, 1933.

Hardie, Colin. 'A Colleague's Note on C.S. Lewis.' *Inklings-Jahrbuch für Literatur und Ästhetik* 3 (1985), pp. 177–82.

Hargrove, Gene. 'Who Is Tom Bombadil'. *Mythlore* 13, no. 1, whole no. 47 (Autumn 1986), pp. 20–4.

Doris Harris Autographs. *Catalogue 36*. Los Angeles, June 1987.

Harris, John. *The Somme: Death of a Generation*. London: White Lion, 1966.

Harris, Jose. 'The Arts and Social Sciences, 1939–1970'. In Harrison, *The History of the University of Oxford, Vol. VIII*, pp. 217–49.

Harrison, Brian, ed. *The History of the University of Oxford, Vol. VIII: The Twentieth Century*. Oxford: Clarendon Press, 1994.

Harshaw, Ruth. 'Carnival of Books no. 70'. Interview with Tolkien, recorded 15 January 1957. Private transcription from tape recording in the Library of Congress.

——. 'When Carnival of Books Went to Europe'. *American Library Association Bulletin* 51 (February 1957), pp. 117–23.

Hartley, L.P. 'Lord David Cecil'. *Essays & Poems Presented to Lord David Cecil*. Ed. W.W. Robson. London: Constable, 1970. pp. 1–8.

Harvey, David. *The Song of Middle-earth: J.R.R. Tolkien's Themes, Symbols and Myths*. London: George Allen & Unwin, 1985.

Harvey, Paul. *The Oxford Companion to English Literature*. 4th edn., rev. Dorothy Eagle. Oxford: Clarendon Press, 1967.

Havard, Robert E. 'Philia: Jack at Ease'. In Como, *C.S. Lewis at the Breakfast Table and Other Reminiscences*, pp. 215–28.

——. 'Professor J.R.R. Tolkien: A Personal Memoir'. *Mythlore* 17, no. 2, whole no. 64 (Winter 1990), p. 61.

Hawtree, Christopher. 'Robert Burchfield'. *The Guardian*, 7 July 2004. *books. guardian.co.uk/obituaries*.

Heath, Charles H., ed. *Service Record of King Edward's School, Birmingham during the War 1914–1919*. Birmingham: Cornish Brothers, 1920; facsimile reprint, with 1931 additions and corrections, Uckfield, East Sussex: Naval & Military Press, (print-on-demand) 2003.

Heiserman, A.R. Review of *Sir Gawain and the Green Knight* (ed. Tolkien and Gordon, rev. Davis). *Speculum* 44 (June 1969), pp. 176–7.

Heinemann, Fredrik J. 'Tolkien and Old Icelandic Literature'. In Battarbee, *Scholarship & Fantasy*, pp. 99–109.

†Helms, Randel. *Tolkien and the Silmarils*. Boston: Houghton Mifflin, 1981.

——. *Tolkien's World*. Boston: Houghton Mifflin, 1974.

Henderson, Jim. 'Dear PROM: Memories of Plyn'. 2001. *www.prom-aber.com*. On Gwyn Jones.

Henry, Emma. 'A Star on His Brow: The Role of Astronomy in *The Lord of the Rings*'. *The Southern Star* 2 (September 1985), pp. 14–16.

Herbert, Kathleen. Review of *Finn and Hengest*. *Mallorn* 20 (September 1983), pp. 12–13, 22.

'Heroic Endeavour', *Times Literary Supplement*, 27 August 1954, p. 541. Review of *The Fellowship of the Ring*.

Heythrop College Faculty, for Robert Murray. *www.heythrop.ac.uk/fac/murray. html*.

Hibbert, Christopher, ed. *The Encyclopædia of Oxford*. Associate ed. Edward Hibbert. London: Macmillan, 1988.

Hieatt, Constance B. 'The Text of *The Hobbit*: Putting Tolkien's Notes in Order'. *English Studies in Canada* 7, no. 2 (Summer 1981), pp. 212–24.

Hill, Joy. 'Echoes of the Old Ringmaster'. *The Times* (London), 10 December 1990, p. 16.

——. Extract from a letter to the editor. *Carandaith* (journal of the Australian Tolkien Society) 2, no. 1 (January 1970), p. 67.

Hillegas, Mark R., ed. *Shadows of Imagination: The Fantasies of C.S. Lewis, J.R.R. Tolkien, and Charles Williams*. Carbondale: Southern Illinois University Press, 1969.

Melissa and Mark Hime. *Precious Stones*. Booksellers' catalogue. Idyllwild, California, 1980.

Himes, Jonathan B. 'What J.R.R. Tolkien Really Did with the Sampo?' *Mythlore* 22, no. 4, whole no. 86 (Spring 2000), pp. 69–85.

Hindle, Alan. 'Memories of Tolkien'. *Amon Hen* 32 [May 1978], pp. 4–6.

The Historical Register of the University of Cambridge: Supplement, 1911–20. Cambridge: Cambridge University Press, 1922.

Hollis, Richard, and Brian Sibley. *Walt Disney's Snow White and the Seven Dwarfs & the Making of the Classic Film.* New York: Hyperion, 1994.

David J. Holmes Autographs. *Catalogue 37: Books from a Private Library (with Additions).* Philadelphia, December 1991.

Homer. *The Iliad.* Trans. E.V. Rieu. Harmondsworth: Penguin, 1950.

Honegger, Thomas. 'The Man in the Moon: Structural Depth in Tolkien'. *Root and Branch: Approaches towards Understanding Tolkien.* Ed. Thomas Honegger. Zurich: Walking Tree, 1999. *Cormarë Series* 2. pp. 9–76.

——, ed., *Tolkien in Translation.* Zurich: Walking Tree, 2003. *Cormarë Series* 4.

——, ed. *Translating Tolkien: Text and Film.* Zurich: Walking Tree, 2004. *Cormarë Series* 6.

'Honours in English: Final School at Oxford'. *The Times* (London), 3 July 1915, p. 6. Notice of Tolkien's First Class in English Language and Literature.

Hooker, Mark. *Tolkien through Russian Eyes.* Zurich: Walking Tree, 2003. *Cormarë Series* 5.

Hooper, Walter. *C.S. Lewis: A Companion & Guide.* London: HarperCollins, 1996.

Hopkins, G.W.S. 'Charles Walter Stansby Williams'. *Dictionary of National Biography, 1941–1950.* pp. 958–9.

Hopkins, Lisa. 'Female Authority Figures in the Works of Tolkien, C.S. Lewis and Charles Williams'. In Reynolds and GoodKnight, *Proceedings of the J.R.R. Tolkien Centenary Conference 1992,* pp. 364–6.

Hornblower, Simon, and Antony Spawforth, eds. *The Oxford Classical Dictionary.* 3rd edn. Oxford: Oxford University Press, 1996.

Horne, Brian, ed. *Charles Williams: A Celebration.* Leominster, Herefordshire: Gracewing, 1995.

Horobin, S.C.P. 'J.R.R. Tolkien as a Philologist: A Reconsideration of the Northernisms in Chaucer's *Reeve's Tale'. English Studies* (Amsterdam) 82, no. 2 (2001), pp. 97–105.

Hostetter, Carl F. '"Elvish as She Is Spoke"'. In Hammond and Scull, *The Lord of the Rings, 1954–2004: Scholarship in Honor of Richard E. Blackwelder,* pp. 231–55.

——. 'Over Middle-earth Sent unto Men: On the Philological Origins of Tolkien's Eärendel Myth'. *Mythlore* 17, no. 3, whole no. 65 (Spring 1991), pp. 5–10.

—— see also THE PUBLISHED WRITINGS OF J.R.R. TOLKIEN in vol. 1

—— and Arden R. Smith. 'A Mythology for England'. In Reynolds and Good-Knight, *Proceedings of the J.R.R. Tolkien Centenary Conference 1992,* pp. 281–90.

—— and Patrick H. Wynne. 'Addenda and Corrigenda to the *Etymologies'. Vinyar Tengwar* 45 (November 2003) pp. 3–38; 46 (July 2004), pp. 3–34 (with an appendix by Arden R. Smith, below).

———— ————. 'An Adunaic Dictionary'. *Vinyar Tengwar* 25 (September 1992), pp. 8–26.

Houghton, Joe. Review of *Finn and Hengest. Amon Hen* 61 (May 1983), p. 4.

Houghton, John. 'Augustine and the *Ainulindalë*'. *Mythlore* 21, no. 1, whole no. 79 (Summer 1995), pp. 4–8.

Howarth, Janet. 'The Self-Governing University'. In Brock and Curthoys, *The History of the University of Oxford, Vol. VII*, pp. 599–643.

Hughes, Richard. 'Books for Pre-Adults'. *New Statesman and Nation*, 4 December 1937, pp. 944, 946.

Hulbert, J.R. Review of *Sir Gawain and the Green Knight* (ed. Tolkien and Gordon). *Modern Philology* 23 (1925–6), pp. 246–9.

Hume, R.H. 'O.T.C. Annual Camp, Aldershot, 1910'. *King Edward's School Chronicle*, n.s. 26, no. 183 (November 1910), pp. 73–4.

Hunnewell, S. Gary. '"Sauron Is Alive and Well in Argentina": The Evolution of Tolkien's Audience in America'. Unpublished essay, presented at the Marquette University Tolkien Conference on 16 September 1983.

Huttar, Charles A., and Peter J. Schakel, eds. *The Rhetoric of Vision: Essays on Charles Williams*. Lewisburg: Bucknell University Press, 1996.

Hutton, T.W. *King Edward's School, Birmingham, 1552–1952*. Oxford: Basil Blackwell, 1952.

Hyde, Paul Nolan. 'The "Gondolinic Rules": Another Picture'. *Mythlore* 18, no. 3, whole no. 69 (Summer 1992), pp. 20–5.

————. 'Leaf and Key'. *Mythlore* 12, no. 4, whole no. 46, pp. 27–29, 36.

————. 'Mythos: The Daughter of Mountains, the Mother of Pearls'. *Mythlore* 16, no. 1, whole no. 59 (Autumn 1989), pp. 27–33.

————. 'Narqelion: A Single, Falling Leaf at Sun-fading'. *Mythlore* 15, no. 2, whole no. 56 (Winter 1988), pp. 47–52.

Isaacs, Neil D. 'On the Need for Writing Tolkien Criticism'. In Isaacs and Zimbardo, *Tolkien: New Critical Perspectives*, pp. 1–7.

————. 'On the Pleasures of (Reading and Writing) Tolkien Criticism'. In Zimbardo and Isaacs, *Understanding The Lord of the Rings: The Best of Tolkien Criticism*, pp. 1–10.

————. 'On the Possibilities of Writing Tolkien Criticism'. In Isaacs and Zimbardo, *Tolkien and the Critics*, pp. 1–11.

†———— and Rose A. Zimbardo, eds. *Tolkien and the Critics: Essays on J.R.R. Tolkien's The Lord of the Rings*. Notre Dame, Indiana: University of Notre Dame Press, 1968.

†———— ————, eds. *Tolkien: New Critical Perspectives*. Lexington: University Press of Kentucky, 1981.

'J.I.M. Stewart'. *The Times* (London), 16 November 1994, p. 19.

†*J.R.R.T.: A Portrait of John Ronald Reuel Tolkien, 1892–1973*. Video; script by Helen Dickinson. London: Produced for the Tolkien Partnership by Landseer Film & Television Productions, 1992.

Jacobs, Alan. *The Narnian: The Life and Imagination of C.S. Lewis*. San Francisco: HarperSanFrancisco, 2005.

James, Lionel. *The History of King Edward's Horse*. London: Sifton, Praed, 1921.

Jellema, Rod. 'Auden on Tolkien: The Book That Isn't, and the House That Brought It Down'. *W.H. Auden: A Legacy*. Ed. David Garrett Izzo. West Cornwall, Conn.: Locust Hill Press, 2002. pp. 39–45.

Jenkins, R.J.H. 'Richard MacGillivray Dawkins, 1871–1955'. *Proceedings of the British Academy* 41 (1955), pp. 373–88.

Jennings, Elizabeth. *A Way of Looking*. London: Andre Deutsch, 1955.

Jensen, Todd. 'Aragorn and Arthur'. *Beyond Bree*, January 1993, pp. 2–3.

——. 'Arthurian Britain and Middle-earth'. *Beyond Bree*, April 1993, pp. 3–4.

——. 'The Historical Arthur'. *Beyond Bree*, March 1993, pp. 2–3.

——. 'Hobbits at the Round Table: A Comparison of Frodo Baggins to King Arthur'. *Beyond Bree*, September 1988, pp. 9–10.

——. 'Merlin and Gandalf'. *Beyond Bree*, November 1992, pp. 2–5.

——. 'Mordred and Maeglin'. *Beyond Bree*, September 1992, pp. 5–6.

——. 'The Sons of Fëanor and the Sons of Lot'. *Beyond Bree*, July 1992, pp. 1–2.

——. 'Tolkien and Arthurian Legend'. *Beyond Bree*, November 1988, pp. 1–3.

——. 'The Zimmerman Film Treatment of *The Lord of the Rings*'. *Beyond Bree*, December 1995, pp. 7–8.

The Jerusalem Bible. General editor, Alexander Jones. Garden City, New York: Doubleday, 1966.

'John Wain'. *The Times* (London), 25 May 1994, p. 19.

†Johnson, Judith A. *J.R.R. Tolkien: Six Decades of Criticism*. Westport, Connecticut: Greenwood Press, 1986.

Johnson, Robert. 'Prizewinner'. *The Irish Press*, 30 March 1968, p. 6.

Johnston, Edward. *Writing & Illuminating, & Lettering*. London: Pitman, 1977. First published 1906.

Johnston, George Burke. 'The Poetry of J.R.R. Tolkien'. *Mankato State University Studies* 2, no. 2 (February 1967), pp. 63–75. *Mankato Studies in English* 2 ('The Tolkien Papers').

Jones, Leslie Ellen. *J.R.R. Tolkien: A Biography*. Westport, Connecticut: Greenwood Press, 2003.

Jones, Nicolette. 'Tolkien – "He was impossible, but a gent"'. *Publishing News*, 20 February 1987, p. 11.

Jones, R.V. 'Wing Commander A.H. Smith, O.B.E.' *Early English and Norse Studies Presented to Hugh Smith in Honour of His Sixtieth Birthday*. Ed. Arthur Brown and Peter Foote. London: Methuen, 1963. pp. 217–25.

'Kathleen Lea'. *The Times* (London), 21 March 1995, p. 19.

Kay, Guy Gavriel. 'Dug Out of the Dust of Middle-earth'. *Macleans*, 29 January 1981, p. 46.

Keates, Jonathan. 'Just a Bash at Bilbo'. *The Observer*, 15 March 1987. Review of *The Hobbit*.

Kenny, Anthony. *A Path from Rome: An Autobiography*. London: Sidgwick & Jackson, 1985.

Ker, Neil. 'A.S. Napier, 1853–1916'. *Philological Essays: Studies in Old and Middle English Language and Literature in Honour of Herbert Dean Meritt.* Edited by James L. Rosier. The Hague: Mouton, 1970. pp. 152–73.

——. 'Kenneth Sisam, 1887–1971'. *Proceedings of the British Academy* 58 (1972), pp. 409–28.

Kerr, Fergus. 'David James Mathew'. *Dictionary of National Biography, 1971–1980.* Including Gervase Mathew, his brother, p. 584.

Kilby, Clyde S. *Tolkien and the Silmarillion.* Wheaton, Illinois: Harold Shaw, 1976.

'The King in Birmingham: Opening of the New University Buildings'. *The Times* (London), 8 July 1909, p. 12.

Knatchbull-Hugesson, E.H. *Stories for My Children.* London: Macmillan, 1869. 'Ernest' was reprinted in *Alternative Alices: Visions and Revisions of Lewis Carroll's Books,* ed. Carolyn Sigler (Lexington: University Press of Kentucky, 1997). 'Puss-Cat Mew' was reprinted (without illustration) in *Tales before Tolkien: The Roots of Modern Fantasy,* ed. Douglas A, Anderson (New York: Ballantine Books, 2003).

†Kocher, Paul H. *Master of Middle-earth: The Fiction of J.R.R. Tolkien.* Boston: Houghton Mifflin, 1972.

——. *A Reader's Guide to The Silmarillion.* Boston: Houghton Mifflin, 1980.

——. Review of *Sir Gawain and the Green Knight, Pearl and Sir Orfeo. Mythprint* 12, no. 4 (October 1975), pp. 2–4.

König, Helga, and Cordula Schütz, eds. *Kataloge der Universitätsbibliothek Eichstätt,* Bd. 1: *Die Bibliothek der Inklings-Gesellschaft.* Wiesbaden: Harrassowitz Verlag, 2001.

Korn, Eric. 'Doing Things by Elves'. *Times Literary Supplement,* 30 September 1977, p. 1097. Review of *The Silmarillion.*

Kuteeva, Maria. '"Old Human", or "The Voice in Our Hearts": J.R.R. Tolkien on the Origin of Language'. In Agøy, *Between Faith and Fiction: Tolkien and the Powers of His World,* pp. 72–90.

Kuznets, Lois R. 'Tolkien and the Rhetoric of Childhood'. In Isaacs and Zimbardo, *Tolkien: New Critical Perspectives,* pp. 150–62.

Lacy, Norris J., ed. *The New Arthurian Encyclopedia.* New York: Garland, 1996.

Lambert, J.W. 'New Fiction'. *Sunday Times* (London), 8 August 1954, p. 5. Review of *The Fellowship of the Ring.*

Lamont, Claire. 'Mary Madge Lascelles, 1900–1995'. *Proceedings of the British Academy* 111 (2002), pp. 575–91.

Lang, Andrew. *Prince Prigio & Prince Ricardo.* London: J.M. Dent & Sons, 1961. First published separately, 1889 and 1893.

——, ed. *The Blue Fairy Book.* 6th edn. London: Longmans, Green, 1893. First published 1889.

——, ed. *The Lilac Fairy Book.* London: Longmans, Green, 1914. First published 1910.

——, ed. *The Red Fairy Book.* 5th edn. London: Longmans, Green, 1895. First published 1890.

Langer, William L., comp. and ed. *An Encyclopedia of World History*. Rev. edn. Boston: Houghton Mifflin, 1948.

Latter, J.C. *The History of the Lancashire Fusiliers, 1914–1918*. Aldershot: Gale & Polden, 1949.

Lawhead, Stephen. 'J.R.R. Tolkien: Master of Middle-earth'. In Pearce, *Tolkien: A Celebration*, pp. 156–71.

Lawlor, John. *C.S. Lewis: Memories and Reflections*. Dallas: Spence Publishing Co., 1998.

—— and W.H. Auden, eds. *To Nevill Coghill from Friends*. London: Faber, 1966.

Lea, Kathleen M. 'Dame Helen Louise Gardner'. *Dictionary of National Biography 1986–1990*. pp. 153–4.

——. 'Helen Gardner 1908–1986'. *Proceedings of the British Academy* 76 (1990), pp. 395–409.

†*Leaves from the Tree: J.R.R. Tolkien's Shorter Fiction*. London: The Tolkien Society, 1991.

Lee, Billy C. 'The War over Middle Earth'. *Paperback Quarterly* 1, no. 4 (Winter 1978), pp. 37–42.

Lee, Margaret L. 'Middle English'. *The Year's Work in English Studies* 2 (1920–1), pp. 41–53.

University of Leeds Annual Report. 1920–1 to 1923–4.

University of Leeds Calendar. 1920–1 to 1925–6.

Lennie, Campbell. 'Roy Campbell: Poet and Polemicist'. *Book and Magazine Collector* 208 (July 2001), pp. 39–48.

Levick, Barbara, ed. *The Ancient Historian and His Materials: Essays in Honour of C.E. Stevens on His Seventieth Birthday*. Westmead, Farnborough, Hants: Gregg International, 1975.

Levine, Stuart P. *The Importance of J.R.R. Tolkien*. Farmington Hills, Michigan: Lucent Books, 2004.

Lewis, Alex. 'The Lost Heart of the Little Kingdom'. In *Leaves from the Tree: J.R.R. Tolkien's Shorter Fiction*, pp. 33–44.

Lewis, C.S. *All My Road Before Me: The Diary of C.S. Lewis 1922–1927*. Ed. Walter Hooper. London: Fount, 1991.

——. *Collected Letters*, vols. 1–2 (all published to date): *Family Letters, 1905–1931*; *Books, Broadcasts and War, 1931–1949*. Ed. Walter Hooper. London: HarperCollins, 2000, 2004.

——. 'The Dethronement of Power'. *Time and Tide*, 22 October 1955, p. 1373. Review of *The Two Towers* and *The Return of the King*.

——. 'The Gods Return to Earth'. *Time and Tide*, 14 August 1954, p. 1082. Review of *The Fellowship of the Ring*.

——. *Letters of C.S. Lewis*. Ed., with a memoir, by W.H. Lewis. London: Geoffrey Bles, 1966.

——. 'On Stories'. *Essays Presented to Charles Williams*. London: Oxford University Press, 1947. pp. 90–105.

——. *Out of the Silent Planet*. London: John Lane, the Bodley Head, 1938.

——. *A Preface to 'Paradise Lost'*. Oxford: Oxford University Press, 1942.

——. 'Professor Tolkien's "Hobbit"'. *The Times* (London), 8 October 1937, p. 20. Unsigned review of *The Hobbit*.

——. *Surprised by Joy: The Shape of My Early Life*. London: Geoffrey Bles, 1955.

——. *They Stand Together: The Letters of C.S. Lewis to Arthur Greeves (1914–1963)*. Ed. Walter Hooper. London: Collins, 1979.

——. 'A World for Children'. *Times Literary Supplement*, 2 October 1937, p. 714. Unsigned review of *The Hobbit*.

Lewis, W.H. *Brothers and Friends: The Diaries of Major Warren Hamilton Lewis*. Ed. Clyde S. Kilby and Marjorie Lamp Mead. San Francisco: Harper & Row, 1982.

Liberty Historic Manuscripts. Autumn auction catalogue, 1994.

Linley, Steve. 'Farmer Giles: *Beowulf* for the Critics?' *Amon Hen* 98 (July 1989), pp. 11–12.

——. 'Farmer Giles of Ham'. *Anor* 28 (1996), pp. 4–10.

——. 'Tolkien and Haggard: Some Thoughts on Galadriel'. *Anor* 23 (1991), pp. 11–16.

'Literary Society'. *King Edward's School Chronicle* n.s. 26, no. 186 (March 1911), pp. 19–20.

Lobdell, Jared C. 'Mr. Bliss: Notes on the Manuscript and Story'. In *Selections from the Marquette J.R.R. Tolkien Collection*, pp. 5–10.

†——, ed. *A Tolkien Compass*. LaSalle, Illinois: Open Court, 1975. A 2nd edn. was published by Open Court in 2003 with the same contents, except for Tolkien's *Guide to the Names in The Lord of the Rings*.

Location Register of 20th-century English Literary Manuscripts and Letters. www.library.rdg.ac.uk/colls/projects/locreg.html.

'The London Gazette'. *The Times* (London), 17 July 1915, p. 8.

'The London Gazette'. *The Times* (London), 26 November 1917, p. 2.

Lönnrot, Elias. *The Kalevala, or Poems of the Kaleva District*. Trans. with foreword and appendices by Francis Peabody Magoun, Jr. Cambridge, Massachusetts: Harvard University Press, 1963.

——. *Kalevala: The Land of Heroes*. Trans. W.F. Kirby. London: J.M. Dent & Sons, 1907 (1951 printing).

——. *The Old Kalevala and Certain Antecedents*. Trans. by Francis Peabody Magoun, Jr. Cambridge, Massachusetts: Harvard University Press, 1969.

'Lord David Cecil, Eminent Man of Letters'. *The Times* (London), 3 January 1986, p. 10.

Lowe, Shirley. 'Priscilla Tolkien Talks to Shirley Lowe'. *Over 21*, December 1976, pp. 32–3.

Loyn, Henry. 'Dorothy Whitelock, 1901–1982'. *Proceedings of the British Academy* 70 (1984), pp. 543–54.

Lucas, Peter J. Review of *The Old English Exodus*. *Notes and Queries* (June 1983), pp. 243–4.

——, ed. *Exodus*. Rev. edn. Exeter, Devon: University of Exeter Press, 1994.

Luling, Virginia. 'An Anthropologist in Middle-earth'. In Reynolds and Good-Knight, *Proceedings of the J.R.R. Tolkien Centenary Conference 1992*, pp. 53–7.

Lynch, Doris. *J.R.R. Tolkien: Creator of Languages and Legends*. New York: Franklin Watts, 2003.

Lynch, F. Philip. 'F. Francis Xavier Morgan'. *www.birmingham-oratory.org/uk/morgan.htm*.

Maas, Jeremy, et al. *Victorian Fairy Painting*. London: Merrell Holberton, 1997.

Mable, Eileen. 'A Myth for Our Age'. *Church of England Newspaper*, 2 October 1977. Review of *The Silmarillion*.

McCallum, R.B. 'Pembroke 1925–1967'. *Pembroke Record* (1966–7), pp. 13–17.

McCarthy, Chris. *The Somme: The Day-by-Day Account*. London: Brockhampton Press, 1998.

MacCarthy, Fiona. *William Morris: A Life for Our Time*. London: Faber and Faber, 1994.

MacDonald, George. *At the Back of the North Wind*. London: J.M. Dent, 1956.

——. 'The Fantastic Imagination'. *Fantasists on Fantasy: A Collection of Critical Reflections*, ed. Robert H. Boyer and Kenneth J. Zahorski. New York: Avon Discus, 1984. pp. 14–21.

——. *The Light Princess and Other Tales*. Introduction by Roger Lancelyn Green. London: Victor Gollancz, 1961.

——. *Lilith*. Introduction by Lin Carter. New York: Ballantine Books, 1969.

——. *Phantastes*. Introduction by Lin Carter. New York: Ballantine Books, 1970.

——. *The Princess and Curdie*. London: J.M. Dent, 1949.

——. *The Princess and the Goblin*. London: J.M. Dent, 1949.

Mackail, J.W. 'William Morris'. *Dictionary of National Biography*. Vol. 22 (Supplement), pp. 1069–75.

McMeekin, Janet. 'Lady of the Rings'. *Limited Edition: The Magazine of Oxfordshire* 77 (May/June 1993), pp. 12–13.

McNeil, Donald G., Jr. 'Heirs'. *People*, 26 Nov. 1984, pp. 79–81.

Maggs Bros. *Autograph Letters & Historical Documents* (Catalogue 1086). London, 1988.

'Major W.H. Lewis: Soldier and Writer'. *The Times* (London), 16 April 1973, p. 16.

Malory, Thomas. *The Works of Sir Thomas Malory*. Ed. Eugène Vinaver. Oxford: Clarendon Press, 1947.

Manlove, Colin. *Modern Fantasy: Five Studies*. Cambridge: Cambridge University Press, 1975.

Marinatos, Spyridon. 'The Volcanic Destruction of Minoan Crete'. *Antiquity* 13 (1939), pp. 423–39.

Marks, John. *Moseley and Kings Heath on Old Picture Postcards*. Keyworth, Nottingham: Reflections of a Bygone Age, 1991.

Mars-Jones, Adam. 'Hobbit-forming'. *The Observer*, 11 January 1998, p. 18. Review of *Roverandom*.

Marsh, Jan. 'Tolkien's Source-book'. *Daily Telegraph*, 22 September 1977, p. 14. Review of *The Silmarillion*.

Martsch, Nancy. *Basic Quenya*. Sherman Oaks, California: Beyond Bree, 1992.

——. 'The Poetry of J.R.R. Tolkien'. *Beyond Bree*, January 1983, p. 2.

——. 'Tolkien and William Morris'. *Beyond Bree*, September 1997 pp. 6–7.

——. 'Tolkien, Roman Catholicism, and the Birmingham Oratory'. *Beyond Bree*, March 2000, pp. 2–4.

——. 'Tolkien's Reading'. *Beyond Bree*, April 1997, pp. 4–6.

——. 'Tolkien's Reading: "On Fairy-Stories"'. *Beyond Bree*, August 1997, pp. 1–4.

——. 'The Use of Language in Tolkien's Poetry: Part 1 [*The Hoard*]'. *Beyond Bree*, December 2003, pp. 2–4.

——. 'The Use of Language in Tolkien's Poetry: Part 2 [*The Man in the Moon Came Down Too Soon* and *Errantry*]'. *Beyond Bree*, April 2004, pp. 2–4.

——, ed. *List of Tolkienalia*. Sherman Oaks, California: Beyond Bree, 1992.

Mascall, E.L. 'Austin Marsden Farrer, 1904–1968'. *Proceedings of the British Academy* 54 (1968), pp. 435–42.

Masefield, John. *Letters to Reyna*. Ed. William Buchan. London: Buchan and Enright, 1983.

——. *The Old Front Line, or The Beginning of the Battle of the Somme*. London: William Heinemann, 1917.

Masson, David. 'The Lord of the Rings'. *Times Literary Supplement*, 9 December 1955, p. 743.

Mathew, Gervase. 'Orator'. In Como, *C.S. Lewis at the Breakfast Table and Other Reminiscences*, pp. 96–7.

Mathews, Richard. 'The Edges of Reality in Tolkien's Tale of Aldarion and Erendis'. *Mythlore* 18, no. 3, whole no. 69 (Summer 1992), pp. 27–30.

——. *Fantasy: The Liberation of Imagination*. New York: Twayne, 1997.

Medcalf, Stephen. 'The Anxious Longing'. *Times Literary Supplement*, 23–9 December 1988, p. 1414. Review of *The Lost Road and Other Writings*.

——. 'The Coincidence of Myth and Fact'. *Ways of Reading the Bible*. Ed. Michael Wadsworth. Brighton: Harvester Press; Totowa, New Jersey: Barnes & Noble, 1981. pp. 55–78.

——. 'Hugo Dyson'. *Postmaster* (Merton College, Oxford), January 1976, pp. 13–17.

——. '"The Language Learned of Elves": Owen Barfield, *The Hobbit* and *The Lord of the Rings*'. *Seven* 16 (1999), pp. 31–53.

The Mellonath Daeron Index of Certh Specimina. www.forodrim.org/daeron/mdics.html.

The Mellonath Daeron Index of Tengwar Specimina. www.forodrim.org/daeron/mdtci.html.

Menner, Robert J. Review of *Sir Gawain and the Green Knight* (ed. Tolkien and Gordon). *Modern Language Notes* 41 (June 1926), pp. 397–400.

Mertens-Fonck, P. 'Les Études anglaises medievales à Liège'. *Revue des langues vivantes* (Liège) 35 (1969), pp. 452–6.

Merton College Register II, 1891–1989. Oxford: Merton College for private circulation, 1991.

Mesibov, Bob. 'Tolkien and Spiders'. *Orcrist* 4 = *Tolkien Journal* 4, no. 3, whole no. 13 (1969–70), pp. 3–4.

Meskys, Ed. 'Tolkien Notes from All Over'. *Tolkien Journal* 3, no. 3, whole no. 9 (late summer 1968), p. 3.

——. 'Tolkien Fandom'. *The View from Entropy Hall* 12. *www.worldpath.net/~bullsfan/entropy/issues/12.html*.

'Middle Earth Verse'. *Times Literary Supplement*, 23 November 1962, p. 892. Review of *The Adventures of Tom Bombadil and Other Verses from the Red Book*.

Miller, M.G. 'Lice and Men: Trench Fever and Trench Life in the AIF'. 1993. *raven.cc.ukans.edu/~kansite/ww_one/medical/liceand.htm*.

Miller, Miriam Youngerman. 'J.R.R. Tolkien's Merlin: An Old Man with a Staff: Gandalf and the Magus Tradition'. *The Figure of Merlin in the Nineteenth and Twentieth Centuries*. Ed. Jeanie Watson and Marueen Fries. Lewiston, New York: Edwin Mellen Press, 1989. pp. 121–42.

—— and Jane Chance, eds. *Approaches to Teaching Sir Gawain and the Green Knight*. New York: Modern Language Association of America, 1986.

Millett, Bella, and Jocelyn Wogan-Browne, eds. *Medieval English Prose for Women: Selections from the Katherine Group and Ancrene Wisse*. Rev. ed. Oxford: Oxford University Press, 1992.

Millin, Leslie. 'Books'. *Toronto Globe and Mail*, 17 September 1977, p. 37. Review of *The Silmarillion*.

Mills, Beth Ann. Review of *The Lays of Beleriand*. *Library Journal*, December 1985, p. 114.

Mills, Stella M. *The Saga of Hrolf Kraki*. Oxford: Basil Blackwell, 1933.

Mills, T.F. 'A Dictionary of Unit Nomenclature'. *Land Forces of Britain, the Empire and Commonwealth. www.regiments.org/regiments/nomencla.htm*.

Milward, Peter. 'Perchance to Touch: Tolkien as Scholar'. *Mythlore* 6, no. 4, whole no. 22 (Fall 1979), pp. 31–2.

'Miss D[orothy]. Everett: Studies in Medieval English'. *The Times* (London), 23 June 1953, p. 8.

'Miss Edith Wardale: Women's Education at Oxford'. *The Times* (London), 5 March 1963, p. 7.

'Miss Helen Darbishire: Wordsworth and His Circle'. *The Times* (London), 13 March 1961, p. 21.

'Mr C.E. Stevens: Distinguished Ancient Historian'. *The Times* (London), 2 September 1970, p. 4.

'Mr. C.H. Wilkinson: Former Vice-Provost of Worcester College'. *The Times* (London), 21 January 1960, p. 17.

'Mr. Charles Williams'. *The Times* (London), 17 May 1945, p. 7.

'Mr. E.R. Eddison, Civil Servant and Author'. *The Times* (London), 24 August 1945, p. 6. Eddison.

'Mr. H.S. Bennett, Scholar and Administrator'. *The Times* (London), 8 June 1972, p. 18.

'Mr. H.V.D. Dyson'. *The Times* (London), 11 June 1975, p. 17.

'Mr. J.N. Bryson, Teacher and Editor'. *The Times* (London), 20 August 1976, p. 14.

'Mr John Masefield: Writer of Ships and the Sea and Poet Laureate since 1930'. *The Times* (London), 13 May 1967, p. 12.

'Mr. K.B. McFarlane, Medieval Historian'. *The Times* (London), 18 July 1966, p. 12.

'Mr Kenneth Sisam, Publisher and Editor'. *The Times* (London), 28 August 1971, p. 14.

'Mr. L. Rice-Oxley'. *The Times* (London), 11 July 1960, p. 14

'Mr. L. Rice-Oxley'. *The Times* (London), 15 July 1960, p. 15.

'Mr. M.R. Ridley, Lecturer and Editor'. *The Times* (London), 13 June 1969, p. 12.

'Mr. R. Cary Gilson: A Great Birmingham Headmaster'. *The Times* (London), 20 February 1939, p. 14.

'Mr Roger Lancelyn Green: Treasures of Children's Literature'. *The Times* (London), 12 October 1987.

'Mr. Roy Campbell: Poet and Man of Action', *The Times* (London), 25 April 1957, p. 13.

'Mr. T.W. Earp: Art Critic and Author'. *The Times* (London), 9 May 1958, p. 15.

'Mrs. Joan Bennett'. *The Times* (London), 22 July 1986, p. 14.

Mitchison, Naomi. 'Maps of Middle Earth'. *Books and Bookmen*, October 1977, pp. 28–30. Review of *Biography* and *The Silmarillion*.

——. 'One Ring to Bind Them'. *New Statesman and Nation*, 18 September 1954, p. 331. Review of *The Fellowship of the Ring*.

——. 'Why Not Grown-ups Too?' *Glasgow Herald*, 25 November 1967, p. 9. Review of *Smith of Wootton Major*.

Morey, Dom Adrian. *Bartholomew of Exeter, Bishop and Canonist: A Study in the Twelfth Century*. Cambridge: Cambridge University Press, 1937.

Morris, Richard, ed. *An Old English Miscellany*. London: Published for the Early English Text Society by N. Trübner, 1872.

——, ed. *Specimens of Early English*. 2nd edn, rev. Oxford: Clarendon Press, 1898.

Morris, William. *The Earthly Paradise: A Poem*. London: Longmans, Green, 1918. First published 1868–70.

——. *Icelandic Journals*. Introduction by Magnus Magnusson. Foreword by Fiona MacCarthy. London: Mare's Nest, 1996. First published 1911.

——. *The Roots of the Mountains*. North Hollywood, California: Newcastle Publishing Co., 1979. First published 1889.

——. *A Tale of the House of the Wolfings and All the Kindreds of the Mark*. London: Longmans, Green, 1913. First published 1889 (i.e. 1888).

——. *William Morris: Selected Writings and Designs*. Ed. with an introduction by Asa Briggs. Harmondsworth: Penguin Books, 1962.

——. *The Wood beyond the World*. Introduction by Tom Shippey. Oxford: Oxford University Press, 1980.

Morse, Robert. *Bilbo's Birthday and Frodo's Adventure of Faith*. San Jose, California: Writers Club Press, 2002.

——. *Evocation of Virgil in Tolkien's Art: Geritol for the Classics*. Oak Park, Illinois: Bolchazy-Carducci, 1986.

Morus, Iwan Rhys. Letter to the editor. *Amon Hen* 42 (December 1979), p. 18.

——. 'The Tale of Beren and Lúthien'. *Mallorn* 20 (September 1983), pp. 19–22.

Mosley, Charles. *J.R.R. Tolkien*. Plymouth: Northcote House, in association with the British Council, 1997.

Mumby, F.A., and Frances H.S. Stallybrass. *From Swan Sonnenschein to George Allen & Unwin Ltd*. London: George Allen & Unwin, 1955.

Munro, Robert. *Les Stations lacustres d'Europe aux ages de la pierre et du bronze*. Trans. Paul Rodet. Paris: Schleicher frères, 1908.

Murphy, Jan. 'Another Fairy Tale for Adults'. *San Francisco Chronicle*, 10 November 1985. Review of *The Lays of Beleriand*.

Murray, Robert. 'Faith Tolkien: A Theologian among Sculptors'. *The Month*, August 1994, pp. 320–4.

——. 'Sermon at Thanksgiving Service, Keble College Chapel, 23rd August 1992'. In Reynolds and GoodKnight, *Proceedings of the J.R.R. Tolkien Centenary Conference 1992*, pp. 17–20.

——. 'A Tribute to Tolkien'. *The Tablet*, 15 September 1973, pp. 879–80.

'The Musical and Dramatic Society'. *King Edward's School Chronicle* n.s. 27, no. 191 (March 1912), pp. 9–11.

Nagy, Gergely. 'The Great Chain of Reading: (Inter-)textual Relations and the Technique of Mythopoesis in the Túrin Story'. In Chance, *Tolkien the Medievalist*, pp. 239–58.

'Naomi Mitchison'. *The Times* (London), 13 January 1999. Online edn.

Neimark, Anne E. *Myth Maker: J.R.R. Tolkien*. San Diego: Harcourt Brace, 1996.

Nelson, Graham. 'Seed-ground: *Oxford Poetry*, 1910–2000'. *Oxford Magazine*, second week, Trinity Term, 2000, pp. 4–5.

Nesbit, E. *Five Children and It*. London: T. Fisher Unwin, 1902.

Newbold, John. *A History of the Catholic Church in Bromsgrove*. Bromsgrove, Worcestershire: Chris Floate, 1992.

Nichol Smith, David. 'H.C.K. Wyld'. *Oxford Magazine*, 15 February 1945, pp. 149–50.

——. 'Sir Walter Alexander Raleigh'. *Dictionary of National Biography, 1922–1930*. pp. 701–4.

Noad, Charles E. 'The Natures of Tom Bombadil: A Summary'. In *Leaves from the Tree: J.R.R. Tolkien's Shorter Fiction*, pp. 79–83.

——. 'The Early Days of the Tolkien Society'. *A Long-expected Party: Progress Report* 1 (1990), pp. 9–11.

——. 'On the Construction of "The Silmarillion"'. In Flieger and Hostetter, *Tolkien's Legendarium*, pp. 31–68.

——. Review of *The Book of Lost Tales, Part One*. *Mallorn* 21 (June 1984), pp. 11–13.

——. Review of *The Lays of Beleriand*. *Mallorn* 23 (Summer 1986), pp. 14–16.

——. "'Tolkien Reconsidered": A Talk by Humphrey Carpenter Given at the Cheltenham Festival of Literature'. *Amon Hen* 91 (May 1988), pp. 12–14.

Norman, Philip. 'The Hobbit Man'. *Sunday Times Magazine* (London), 15 January 1967, pp. 34–6. Reprinted as 'The Prevalence of Hobbits', *New York Times Magazine*, 15 January 1967, pp. 30–1, 97, 100, 102.

'Note sur les travaux du Congrès'. *Essais de philologie moderne*. Paris: Société d'édition "Les belles lettres", 1953. pp. 9–12.

'Notes and News', *King Edward's School Chronicle* n.s. 26, no. 189 (October 1911), pp. 74–6

Notice concerning E.O.G. Turville-Petre. *Oxford Magazine* 60, no. 5 (13 November 1941), pp. 65–6.

Notice of George Brewerton's retirement. *King Edward's School Chronicle*, 1914, pp. 4–5.

Notice of R.W. Reynolds' retirement. *King Edward's School Chronicle*, November–December 1922, pp. 79–80.

Obituary of George Brewerton. *King Edward's School Chronicle*, March 1929, p. 4.

Obituary of R.W. Reynolds. *Old Edwardians Gazette*, 1948, pp. 9–10

Obituary of Vincent Trought. *King Edward's School Chronicle* n.s. 27, no. 191 (March 1912), p. 4.

'Officers' Training Corps'. *King Edward's School Chronicle*, n.s. 24, no. 177 (November 1909), pp. 80–2.

'Officers' Training Corps'. *King Edward's School Chronicle* n.s. 26, no. 188 (July 1911), pp. 56–7.

'The Officers Training Corps'. *The Times* (London), 3 July 1911, p. 7.

Orchard, Andy. *A Critical Companion to Beowulf*. Cambridge: D.S. Brewer, 2003.

University of Oxford. *The Examination Statutes*. Oxford: Clarendon Press. Volumes for 1912, 1917, 1925, 1937.

——. *Excerpta e Statutis Universitatis Oxoniensis*. Oxonii: E Prelo Clarendoniano, [1930].

——. *Statuta Universitatis Oxoniensis*. Oxonii: E Typographeo Clarendoniano. Volumes for 1912, 1925.

Oxford Dante Society. *Centenary Essays on Dante*. Oxford: Clarendon Press, 1965.

Oxford English Dictionary. Compact edn. Oxford: Oxford University Press, 1971 (1987 issue with supplement, in 3 vols.).

'Oxford Poetry'. *www.gnelson.demon.co.uk/oxpoetry*.

'The Oxford Summer Diversions'. *The Times* (London), 12 July 1938, p. 14.

Oxford University Gazette, 1911–1972.

Oxford University Calendar. 1911–12 to 1965–6.

'Oxford's Sacrifice'. *Oxford Magazine*, 23 February 1917, p. 173. On Geoffrey Bache Smith.

'Oxoniensis'. 'Oxford Letter'. *King Edward's School Chronicle* n.s. 27, no. 196 (December 1912), pp. 84–5.

Pace, David Paul. 'The Influence of Vergil's *Aeneid* on *The Lord of the Rings*'. *Mythlore* 6, no. 2, whole no. 20 (Spring 1979), pp. 37–8.

Palmer, Alan, and Veronica Palmer. *The Pimlico Chronology of British History*. Updated edn. London: Pimlico, 1996.

Palmer, D.J. *The Rise of English Studies*. London: Published for the University of Hull by Oxford University Press, 1965.

Parker, Douglass. 'Hwaet We Holbytla . . .' *Hudson Review* 9 (Winter 1956–7), pp. 598–609.

Parry, Linda, ed. *William Morris*. London: Philip Wilson, in association with the Victoria and Albert Museum, 1996.

'The Past Year at Oxford'. *The Times* (London), 8 October 1925, p. 10.

Patterson, Nancy-Lou. 'An Appreciation of Pauline Baynes'. *Mythlore* 7, no. 3, whole no. 25 (Autumn 1980), pp. 3–5.

——. 'Tree and Leaf: J.R.R. Tolkien and the Visual Image'. *English Quarterly* 7, no. 1 (Spring 1974), pp. 11–26.

Patry, William F. *Copyright Law and Practice. digital-law-online.info/patry/patry1.html*.

Pavlac, Diana Lynne. 'More than a Bandersnatch: Tolkien as a Collaborative Writer'. In Reynolds and GoodKnight, *Proceedings of the Tolkien Centenary Conference 1992*, pp. 367–74.

Pay, Martin D. 'Reviews'. *British Fantasy Society Bulletin* 8, no. 6 (March/April 1981).

Pearce, Joseph. *Bloomsbury and Beyond: The Friends and Enemies of Roy Campbell*. London: HarperCollins, 2001.

——. *Tolkien: Man and Myth*. London: HarperCollins, 1998.

——. *Wisdom and Innocence: A Life of G.K. Chesterton*. London: Hodder & Stoughton, 2001.

†——, ed. *Tolkien: A Celebration: Collected Writings on a Literary Legacy*. London: Fount, 1999.

Pedersen, Holger. *The Discovery of Language: Linguistic Science in the Nineteenth Century*. Bloomington: Indiana University Press, 1962.

Pentikäinen, Juha Y. *Kalevala Mythology*. Expanded edn. Trans. and ed. Ritva Poom. Bloomington: Indiana University Press, 1999.

Petty, Anne C. *Dragons of Fantasy*. Cold Spring Harbor, N.Y.: Cold Spring Press, 2004.

†——. *Tolkien in the Land of Heroes: Discovering the Human Spirit*. Cold Spring Harbor, New York: Cold Spring Press, 2003.

Phelps, Robert. 'For Young Readers'. *New York Times Book Review*, 4 February 1968, p. 26. Review of *Smith of Wootton Major*.

Phillips. *Books, Maps & Manuscripts*. Auction catalogue. London, 24 March 2000.

Piazza, Paul. 'Mosaics from Middle-earth: Fragments of Tolkien's World'. *Washington Post*, 8 December 1980, p. B7.

Pirson, Ron, ed. 'Schuchart vs. Mensink-van Warmelo: Round Two'. *Lembas-extra 2004*. Leiden: Tolkien Genootschap Unquendor, 2004. pp. 75–99.

Plato. *The Dialogues of Plato*. Trans. B. Jowett. New York: Charles Scribner's Sons, 1905. Vol. 2, including the *Timaeus* and *Critias*.

Plimmer, Charlotte, and Denis Plimmer. 'The Man Who Understands Hobbits'. *Daily Telegraph Magazine*, 22 March 1968, pp. 31–3.

Plotz, Richard. 'The Aims of the Society'. *Tolkien Journal* 1 (Spring 1965), p. 1.

——. 'J.R.R. Tolkien Talks about the Discovery of Middle-earth, the Origins of Elvish'. *Seventeen*, January 1967, pp. 92–3, 118.

The Poetic Edda. Trans. with an introduction and explanatory notes by Lee M. Hollander. 2nd edn., rev. Austin: University of Texas Press, 1962; paperback edn., 1994 printing.

Potter, Jane. 'Rayner Stephens Unwin'. *Oxford Dictionary of National Biography*. Online edn.

Power, Norman S. Letter to the editor. *Amon Hen* 28 (August 1977), p. 18.

——. 'Mists of Middle Earth'. *Birmingham Post*, 17 November 1983. Review of *The Book of Lost Tales, Part One*.

——. 'Recollections'. *The J.R.R. Tolkien Centenary Conference* [souvenir book]. [Oxford]: Tolkien Society and Mythopoeic Society, 1992.

Pratchett, Terry. Review of *The Father Christmas Letters*. *Bath and West Evening Chronicle*, 18 September 1976, p. 7.

Prest, John. 'The Asquith Commission, 1919–1922'. In Harrison, *The History of the University of Oxford, Vol. VIII*, pp. 27–43.

Price, Anthony. 'Fairy Story for Grown Ups Too'. *Oxford Mail*, 16 September 1954, p. 4. Review of *The Fellowship of the Ring*.

——. 'With Camera and Pen'. *Oxford Times*, 27 January 1956, p. 8.

†Priestman, Judith. *J.R.R. Tolkien: Life and Legend*. Oxford: Bodleian Library, 1992.

Prince, Alison. *Kenneth Grahame: An Innocent in the Wild Wood*. London: Allison & Busby, 1994.

'Prof. A.H. Smith: English Place Names'. *The Times* (London), 13 May 1967, p. 12.

'Prof A.J. Bliss'. *The Times* (London), 2 December 1985, p. 14.

'Prof Alistair Campbell: Anglo-Saxon at Oxford'. *The Times* (London), 11 February 1974, p. 16.

'Professor C.L. Wrenn: Noted Scholar of Anglo-Saxon'. *The Times* (London), 4 June 1969, p. 12.

'Professor Dorothy Whitelock: Major Contributions to Anglo-Saxon Studies'. *The Times* (London), 17 August 1982, p. 10.

'Professor E.J. Dobson: Studies in English Philology'. *The Times* (London), 5 April 1984, p. 16.

'Professor F.P. Wilson: Elizabethan Literature'. *The Times* (London), 30 May 1963, p. 18.

'Professor G.V. Smithers', *The Times* (London), 24 May 2000, p. 25.

'Prof Gabriel Turville-Petre'. *The Times* (London), 18 February 1978, p. 16.

'Professor H.C.K. Wyld: Contributions to English Philology'. *The Times* (London), 31 January 1945, p. 7.

'Professor Joseph Wright: A Great English Philologist'. *The Times* (London), 28 February 1930, p. 9.

'Professor Leaves Literary Legacy'. BBC News, 10 December 1999. *news.bbc. co.uk*. On Gwyn Jones.

'Professor Nevill Coghill, Notable Popularizer of the Works of Chaucer'. *The Times* (London), 10 November 1980, p. 14.

'Professor Norman Davis'. *The Times* (London), 5 December 1989, p. 18.

Pugh, Dylan. 'The Tree of Tales'. *Mallorn* 21 (June 1984), pp. 36–8.

†Purtill, Richard L. *J.R.R. Tolkien: Myth, Morality, and Religion*. San Francisco: Harper & Row, 1984.

——. *Lord of the Elves and Eldils: Fantasy and Philosophy in C.S. Lewis and J.R.R. Tolkien*. Grand Rapids, Michigan: Zondervan, 1974.

Pyles, Thomas. *The Origins and Development of the English Language*. 2nd edn. New York: Harcourt Brace Jovanovich, 1971.

Pym, Barbara. *A Very Private Eye: An Autobiography in Diaries and Letters*. Ed. Hazel Holt and Hilary Pym. New York: Dutton, 1984.

Quilter, Harry. *What's What*. London: Sonnenschein, 1902.

Quiñonez, Jorge. 'A Brief Note on the Background of the Letter from J.R.R. Tolkien to Dick Plotz Concerning the Declension of the High-elvish Noun'. *Vinyar Tengwar* 6 (July 1989), pp. 13–14.

'R.W. Burchfield 1923–2004'. *Oxford English Dictionary Newsletter*, September 2004. *oed.com/newsletters/2004-09/suppl.html*.

Raeper, William. *George MacDonald*. Tring, Herts: Lion, 1987.

Ransome, Arthur. *Signalling from Mars: The Letters of Arthur Ransome*. Ed. Hugh Brogan. London: Jonathan Cape, 1997.

Raps, Eduard. *Josef Madlener 1881 bis 1967*. Stadt Memmingen, 1981.

Rateliff, John D. '"And Something Yet Remains to Be Said": Tolkien and Williams'. *Mythlore* 12, no. 3, whole no. 45 (Spring 1986), pp. 48–54.

——. '*The Lost Road, The Dark Tower*, and *The Notion Club Papers*: Tolkien and Lewis's Time Travel Triad'. In Flieger and Hostetter, *Tolkien's Legendarium*, pp. 199–218.

——. 'Owen Barfield: A Short Reading List'. In Hammond, *C.S. Lewis & Owen Barfield*, pp. 22–5.

——. '*She* and Tolkien'. *Mythlore* 8, no. 2, whole no. 28 (Summer 1981), pp. 6–8.

Rautala, Helena. 'Familiarity and Distance: Quenya's Relation to Finnish'. In Battarbee, *Scholarship & Fantasy*, pp. 21–31.

Ready, William. *The Tolkien Relation: A Personal Inquiry*. Chicago: Henry Regnery, 1968. Reprinted as *Understanding Tolkien and The Lord of the Rings* (1969).

Reckford, Kenneth. 'Some Trees in Virgil and Tolkien'. *Perspectives of Roman Poetry: A Classics Symposium*. Ed. G. Karl Galinsky. Austin: University of Texas Press, 1974. pp. 57–91.

Reeves, Marjorie. *St Anne's College, Oxford: An Informal History*. Oxford: St Anne's College, 1979.

Reilly, R.J. *Romantic Religion: A Study of Barfield, Lewis, Williams, and Tolkien*. Athens: University of Georgia Press, 1971.

Reilly, Robert J. 'Tolkien and the Fairy Story'. In Isaacs and Zimbardo, *Tolkien and the Critics*, pp. 128–50.

Reinach, Salomon. Part 2 of 'Andrew Lang' by R.S. Rait, *et al. Quarterly Review* (London) 218, no. 435 (April 1913), pp. 309–19.

Kenneth W. Rendell. *Catalogue 248*. South Natick, Massachusetts, 1995.

Resnik, Henry. 'The Hobbit-forming World of J.R.R. Tolkien'. *Saturday Evening Post*, 2 July 1966, pp. 90–92, 94.

——. 'An Interview with Tolkien'. *Niekas* 18 (Spring 1967), pp. 37–47.

'The Rev A.G. Mathew, Scholar and Polymath'. *The Times* (London), 6 April 1976, p. 18.

'Rev A.M. Farrer, Warden of Keble College, Oxford'. *The Times* (London), 30 December 1968, p. 10.

'The Rev. R.F.W. Fletcher'. *The Times* (London), 17 October 1950, p. 8.

Review of *The Adventures of Tom Bombadil and Other Verses from the Red Book*. *Junior Bookshelf*, March 1963.

Review of *Sir Gawain and the Green Knight, Pearl and Sir Orfeo*. *British Book News*, December 1975.

Revue des langues vivantes (1951/2). Special number on Le Congrès du LXe anniversaire des sections de philologie romane et de philologie germanique de l'Université de Liège, 10–12 November 1950.

'Report for 1921'. *Transactions of the Yorkshire Dialect Society*, part 23, vol. 4 (January 1922), p. 5.

Reynolds, Barbara. *Dorothy L. Sayers: Her Life and Soul*. London: Hodder and Stoughton, 1993.

Reynolds, Patricia. 'A History of the Mythopoeic Society'. *A Long-expected Party: Progress Report* 1 (1990), pp. 12–13.

——. 'The Real Tom Bombadil'. In *Leaves from the Tree: J.R.R. Tolkien's Shorter Fiction*, pp. 85–8.

——. *Tolkien's Birmingham*. Milton Keynes: Forsaken Inn Press, 1992.

†—— and Glen H. GoodKnight, eds. *Proceedings of the Tolkien Centenary Conference 1992*. Milton Keynes: Tolkien Society; Altadena, California: Mythopoeic Press, 1995.

Reynolds, William. 'Poetry as Metaphor in *The Lord of the Rings*'. *Mythlore* 4, no. 4, whole no. 16 (June 1977), pp. 12, 14–16.

Richards, Jeffrey. 'Tiptop Tolkien?' *Daily Telegraph*, 1 February 1997, p. 11.

Paul C. Richards Autographs. *Catalogue 228*. Templeton, Massachusetts, 1988.

Richardson, Maurice. 'New Novels'. *New Statesman and Nation*, 18 December 1954, pp. 835–6.

Ricketts, Rita. *Adventurers All: Tales of Blackwellians, of Books, Bookmen, and Reading and Writing Folk*. Oxford: Blackwell's, 2002.

Ridley, M.R. 'The Trials of Teaching in a Secondary Modern School'. *Daily Telegraph*, 28 October 1955, p. 8.

Ring, Jim. *How the English Made the Alps*. London: John Murray, 2000.

Roberts, W. Rhys. 'Gerald of Wales on the Survival of Welsh'. *Transactions of the Honourable Society of Cymmrodorion: Session 1923–1924*. London: Issued by the Society, 1925. pp. 46–60.

Roche, Norma. 'Sailing West: Tolkien, the Saint Brendan Story, and the Idea of Paradise in the West'. *Mythlore* 17, no. 4, whole no. 66 (Summer 1991), pp. 16–20, 62.

Rogers, William N., and Michael R. Underwood. 'Gagool and Gollum: Exemplars of Degeneration in *King Solomon's Mines* and *The Hobbit*'. In Clark and Timmons, *J.R.R. Tolkien and His Literary Resonances*, pp. 121–31.

'Roman Catholic Ceremony at Oxford'. *The Times* (London), 19 May 1936, p. 28.

Rómenna Meeting Report, 26 October 1986, p. 1.

Rosebury, Brian. *Tolkien: A Critical Assessment*. Houndmills, Basingstoke, Hampshire: Macmillan; New York: St Martin's Press, 1992.

†——.*Tolkien: A Cultural Phenomenon*. Houndmills, Basingstoke, Hampshire: Palgrave Macmillan, 2003.

Rossenberg, René van. 'Dutch Tolkien Illustrators'. *Tolkien Collector* 3 (May 1993), pp. 17–19.

——. 'Tolkien and Linguaphone'. *Tolkien Collector* 5 (November 1993), pp. 18–20.

——. 'Tolkien's Exceptional Visit to Holland: A Reconstruction'. In Reynolds and GoodKnight, *Proceedings of the Tolkien Centenary Conference 1992*, pp. 301–9.

Rossiter, Stuart, ed. *England*. 9th edn. London: Ernest Benn, 1980. *Blue Guide*.

'Royal Review at Windsor: The King and Officers Training Corps'. *The Times* (London), 4 July 1911, pp. 9–10.

Royal Society of Literature. *Report*. 1966–7.

——. Web site. *www.rslit.org*.

Rutledge, Fleming. *The Battle for Middle-earth: Tolkien's Divine Design in The Lord of the Rings*. Grand Rapids, Michigan: William B. Eerdmans, 2004.

Ryan, J.S. 'J.R.R. Tolkien: Lexicography and Other Early Linguistic Preferences'. *Mallorn* 16 (May 1981), pp. 9–12, 14–15, 19–22, 24–6.

——. 'J.R.R. Tolkien's Formal Lecturing and Teaching at the University of Oxford, 1929–1959'. *Seven* 19 (2002), pp. 45–62.

——. 'Lexical Impacts'. *Amon Hen* 76 (November 1985), pp. 21–3; and 77 (January 1986), pp. 20–2.

——. 'The Origin of the Name Wetwang'. *Amon Hen* 63 (August 1983), pp. 10–13.

——. *The Shaping of Middle-earth's Maker: Influences on the Life and Literature of J.R.R. Tolkien*. Highland, Michigan: American Tolkien Society, 1992.

Includes 'An Important Influence, His Professor's Wife, Mrs. Elizabeth Mary (Lea) Wright', pp. 34–8; 'J.R.R. Tolkien, C.S. Lewis and Roy Campbell', pp. 25–9; 'Tolkien and George Gordon: or, A Close Colleague and His Notion of "Myth-maker" and of Historiographic Jeux d'esprit', pp. 30–3.

——. *Tolkien: Cult or Culture?* Armidale, New South Wales: University of New England, 1969.

——. 'Two Oxford Scholars' Perceptions of the Traditional Germanic Hall'. *Minas Tirith Evening-Star* 19, no. 1 (Spring 1990), pp. 8–11.

——. 'The Work and Preferences of the Professor of Old Norse at the University of Oxford from 1925 to 1945'. *Angerthas* 27 (May 1990), pp. 4–10. Reprinted in *Angerthas in English* 2 (i.e. *Angerthas* 31), July 1992, pp. 51–8.

Ryder, Rowland. 'Nevill Coghill'. *Exeter College Association Register 1992*, pp. 39–43.

S., P. 'H.F.B. Brett-Smith, 1884–1951, Editor of *The Oxford Magazine*, 1921–2'. *Oxford Magazine*, 1 February 1951, p. 233.

'The Saga of Middle-earth'. *Times Literary Supplement*, 25 November 1955, p. 704. Review of *The Return of the King*.

St. Clair, Gloria. 'An Overview of the Northern Influences on Tolkien's Works'. In Reynolds and GoodKnight, *Proceedings of the J.R.R. Tolkien Centenary Conference 1992*, pp. 63–7.

——. '*Volsunga Saga* and Narn: Some Analogies'. In Reynolds and Good-Knight, *Proceedings of the J.R.R. Tolkien Centenary Conference 1992*, pp. 68–72.

Sakers, Don. 'It Isn't "Lord of the Rings" but It Is Tolkien'. *The Sun* (Baltimore), 25 March 1984, p. C4. Review of *The Book of Lost Tales, Part One*.

Sale, Roger. *Fairy Tales and After: From Snow White to E.B. White*. Cambridge, Massachusetts: Harvard University Press, 1978.

——. 'Tolkien as Translator'. *Parnassus* 4 (1976), pp. 183–91.

——. 'Wonderful to Relate'. *Times Literary Supplement*, 12 March 1976, p. 289.

Salmon, Nicholas, with Derek Baker. *The William Morris Chronology*. Bristol: Thoemmes Press, 1996.

Salo, David. *A Gateway to Sindarin: A Grammar of an Elvish Language from J.R.R. Tolkien's Lord of the Rings*. Salt Lake City: University of Utah Press, 2004.

Salu, Mary, and Robert T. Farrell, eds. *J.R.R. Tolkien: Scholar and Storyteller: Essays in Memoriam*. Ithaca, New York: Cornell University Press, 1979.

Santoski, Taum (T.J.R.). 'The Boundaries of the Little Kingdom'. In *Selections from the Marquette J.R.R. Tolkien Collection*, pp. 11–15.

——. *Catalogue of an Exhibit of the Manuscripts of JRRT*. Milwaukee: Marquette University Memorial Library, Dept. of Special Collections and University Archives, 1983 [i.e. 1984].

Sarehole Mill. Birmingham: Birmingham Museums and Art Gallery, 1986.

Sayer, George. 'George Sayer'. *A Long-Expected Party: Progress Report* 6 (1992), p. 20.

——. *Jack: C.S. Lewis and His Times*. 2nd edn. Wheaton, Illinois: Crossway Books, 1994.

——. 'Recollections of J.R.R. Tolkien'. In Reynolds and GoodKnight, *Proceedings of the J.R.R. Tolkien Centenary Conference 1992*, pp. 21–5.

——. Sleeve notes for *J.R.R. Tolkien Reads and Sings His The Hobbit and The Fellowship of the Ring*. New York: Caedmon Records, 1975. The same text appears on the sleeve of *J.R.R. Tolkien Reads and Sings His Lord of the Rings: The Two Towers/The Return of the King* (Caedmon, 1975).

——. 'Tales of the Ferrograph'. *Minas Tirith Evening-Star* 9, no. 2 (January 1980), pp. 2–4.

Sayers, Frances Clarke. 'Walt Disney Accused'. *Horn Book* 41, no. 6 (December 1965), pp. 602–11.

Schall, James V., S.J., 'On the Realities of Fantasy'. In Pearce, *Tolkien: A Celebration*, pp. 67–72.

Schultz, Jeffrey D., and John G. West, Jr., eds. *The C.S. Lewis Readers' Encyclopedia*. Grand Rapids, Michigan: Zondervan, 1998.

Schultz, Steve. 'Hobbits in the House'. *Marquette Magazine* 19, no. 4 (Fall 2001), pp. 16–19.

Schweicher, Eric. 'Aspects of the Fall in *The Silmarillion*'. In Reynolds and GoodKnight, *Proceedings of the J.R.R. Tolkien Centenary Conference 1992*, pp. 167–71.

Scott, Nan C. 'No "Intermediary"'. *Saturday Review*, 23 October 1965, p. 56.

——. 'A Visit with Tolkien'. *The Living Church*, 5 February 1978, p. 11–12. Reprinted as 'Tolkien: Hobbit and Wizard' in Etkin, *Eglerio!: In Praise of Tolkien*, pp. 77–81.

——. 'War and Pacifism in *The Lord of the Rings*'. *Tolkien Journal* 15 (Summer 1972), pp. 23–5, 27–30.

Scoville, Chester N. 'Pastoralia and Perfectability in William Morris and J.R.R. Tolkien'. In Chance and Siewers, *Tolkien's Modern Middle Ages*, pp. 93–103.

Scull, Christina. 'The Development of Tolkien's *Legendarium*: Some Threads in the Tapestry of Middle-earth'. In Flieger and Hostetter, *Tolkien's Legendarium*, pp. 7–18.

——. 'Dragons from Andrew Lang's Retelling of Sigurd to Tolkien's Chrysophylax'. In *Leaves from the Tree: J.R.R. Tolkien's Shorter Fiction*, pp. 49–62.

——. 'The Fairy Tale Tradition'. *Mallorn* 23 (Summer 1986), pp. 30–6.

——. '*The Hobbit* Considered in Relation to Children's Literature Contemporary with Its Writing and Publication'. *Mythlore* 14, no. 2, whole no. 52 (Winter 1987), pp. 49–56.

——. 'The Influences of Archeology and History on Tolkien's World'. In Battarbee, *Scholarship & Fantasy*, pp. 33–51.

——. 'Margaret Joy Hill, 22 May 1936–21 December 1991'. *Amon Hen* 113 (January 1992), p. 5.

——. 'Open Minds, Closed Minds in *The Lord of the Rings*'. In Reynolds and GoodKnight, *Proceedings of the J.R.R. Tolkien Centenary Conference 1992*, pp. 151–6.

——. 'Rayner Unwin Speaks to the Cambridge Tolkien Society'. *Beyond Bree*, June 1986, pp. 1–2.

——. Review of *The Book of Lost Tales, Part Two*. *Beyond Bree*, November 1984, pp. 2–4.

——. Review of *The Lays of Beleriand*. *Beyond Bree*, November 1985, pp. 1–4.

——. 'Tom Bombadil and *The Lord of the Rings*'. In *Leaves from the Tree: J.R.R. Tolkien's Shorter Fiction*, pp. 73–7.

——. 'What Did He Know and When Did He Know It?: Planning, Inspiration, and *The Lord of the Rings*'. In Hammond and Scull, *The Lord of the Rings, 1954–2004: Scholarship in Honor of Richard E. Blackwelder*, pp. 101–12.

—— and Wayne G. Hammond, eds. *Farmer Giles of Ham* by J.R.R. Tolkien. Fiftieth anniversary edn. London: HarperCollins, 1999.

—— ——, eds. *Roverandom* by J.R.R. Tolkien. London: HarperCollins, 1998.

—— —— see also under *Wayne G. Hammond*

Seddon, Sue. 'The Return of Tolkien'. *Sunday Times* (London), 19 September 1982, pp. 82–3.

Seeman, Chris. 'Tolkien's Revision of the Romantic Tradition'. In Reynolds and GoodKnight, *Proceedings of the J.R.R. Tolkien Conference 1992*, pp. 72–83.

Selections from the Marquette J.R.R. Tolkien Collection. Milwaukee: Marquette University Library, 1987.

Senior, W.A. 'Loss Eternal in J.R.R. Tolkien's Middle-earth'. In Clark and Timmons, *J.R.R. Tolkien and His Literary Resonances*, pp. 173–82.

Shakespeare, William. *The Complete Works of Shakespeare*. Ed. Irving Ribner and George Lyman Kittredge. Waltham, Massachusetts: Ginn, 1971.

Sheppard, Thomas. *Kingston-upon-Hull before, during and after the Great War*. Hull: A. Brown & Sons, 1919.

Shimmin, A.N. *The University of Leeds: The First Half-Century*. Cambridge: Published for the University of Leeds at the University Press, Cambridge, 1954.

Shippey, T.A. (Tom). *Beowulf*. London: Edward Arnold, 1978.

——. 'Blunt Belligerence'. *Times Literary Supplement*, 26 November 1982, p. 1306. Review of *Mr. Bliss*.

——. 'Boar and Badger: An Old English Heroic Antithesis?' *Leeds Studies in English* 16 (1985), pp. 220–39.

†——. *J.R.R. Tolkien: Author of the Century*. London: HarperCollins, 2000.

——. 'Long Evolution: *The History of Middle-earth* and Its Merits'. *Arda* 1987 (1992), pp. 18–43.

——. 'A Look at *Exodus* and *Finn and Hengest*'. *Arda* 3 (1986, for 1982–83), pp. 72–82.

——. 'Orcs, Wraiths, Wights: Tolkien's Images of Evil'. In Clark and Timmons, *J.R.R. Tolkien and His Literary Resonances*, pp. 183–98.

†——. *The Road to Middle-earth*. 2nd edn. London: Grafton, 1992. We have found this the most convenient edition to cite, but our references may be found also in earlier and later editions. Except for a new final chapter, the text of the 1992 edn. is identical to that of the 1st edn. (1982), but

withdifferent pagination. A further 'revised and expanded edition', reset, was published by Houghton Mifflin, Boston, in 2003.

——. 'Structure and Unity'. *A Beowulf Handbook*. Ed. Robert E. Bjork and John D. Niles (1997). pp. 149–74.

——. 'Tolkien and Iceland: The Philology of Envy'. 2002. *www2.hi.is/Apps/ WebObjects/HI.woa/wa/dp?detail=1004508&name=nordals_en_greinar_ og_erindi*.

——. 'Tolkien and the *Gawain*-poet'. In Reynolds and GoodKnight, *Proceedings of the J.R.R. Tolkien Centenary Conference 1992*, pp. 213–19.

——. 'Tolkien and "The Homecoming of Beorhtnoth"'. In *Leaves from the Tree: J.R.R. Tolkien's Shorter Fiction*, pp. 5–16.

——. 'Tolkien as a Post-war Writer'. In Reynolds and GoodKnight, *Proceedings of the J.R.R. Tolkien Centenary Conference 1992*, pp. 84–93.

——. 'Tolkien's Academic Reputation Now'. *Amon Hen* 100 (November 1989), pp. 18–19, 21–2.

——. 'The Versions of "The Hoard"'. *Lembas* 100 (2001), pp. 3–7.

Shorto, Russell. *J.R.R. Tolkien: Man of Fantasy*. New York: Kipling Press, 1988.

Sibley, Brian. 'History for Hobbits'. *The Listener*, 2 October 1980, pp. 443–4.

——. 'The Ring Goes Ever On'. *www.briansibley.com/Broadcasts/RingGoes-EverOn.htm*.

——, et al. *Microphones in Middle Earth: Radio 4's Serial 'The Lord of the Rings'*. Eastleigh, Hants: Ian D. Smith, 1982.

Signalling: Morse, Semaphore, Station Work, Despatch Riding, Telephone Cables, Map Reading. Written by an Officer of the Regular Army. Edited by E. John Solano. London: John Murray, 1915.

Michael Silverman. *Catalogue No. 2*. London, 1998.

——. *Catalogue Nine*. London, 1993.

——. *Catalogue Eleven*. London, 1994.

'Sir Basil Blackwell'. *The Times* (London), 11 April 1984, p. 16.

'Sir Charles Firth'. *The Times* (London), 20 February 1936, p. 16.

'Sir Stanley Unwin: An Influential Publisher', *The Times* (London), 15 October 1968, p. 13.

'Sir William Craigie: Lexicographer and Scholar'. *The Times* (London), 3 September 1957, p. 13.

Sisam, Kenneth. *The Structure of Beowulf*. Oxford: Clarendon Press, 1965 (corrected printing 1966).

——, ed. *Fourteenth Century Verse & Prose*. Oxford: Clarendon Press, 1921.

Sisson, C.J., and H. Winifred Husbands. 'Raymond Wilson Chambers, 1874–1942'. *Proceedings of the British Academy* 30 (1945), pp. 427–45.

Smith, Alan. 'A Shire Pleasure'. *Pipes and Tobacco* 5, no. 4 (Winter 2001).

Smith, Arden R. '*Certhas, Skirditaila, Fuþark*: A Feigned History of Runic Origins'. In Flieger and Hostetter, *Tolkien's Legendarium: Essays on The History of Middle-earth*, pp. 105–11.

——. 'The *Tengwar* in the *Etymologies*'. *Vinyar Tengwar* 46 (July 2004), pp. 29–34.

——. 'Tolkienian Gothic'. In Hammond and Scull, *The Lord of the Rings, 1954–2004: Scholarship in Honor of Richard E. Blackwelder*, pp. 267–81.

——. 'Transitions in Translations'. *Vinyar Tengwar*, various numbers.

——. 'The Túrin Prose Fragment: An Analysis of a Rúmilian Document'. *Vinyar Tengwar* 37 (December 1995), pp. 15–23.

—— see also THE PUBLISHED WRITINGS OF J.R.R. TOLKIEN in vol. 1

—— and Patrick Wynne. 'Tolkien and Esperanto'. *Seven* 17 (2000), pp. 27–46.

Smith, Mark Eddy. *Tolkien's Ordinary Virtues: Exploring the Spiritual Themes of The Lord of the Rings*. Downers Grove, Illinois: InterVarsity Press, 2002.

R.M. Smythe. *Spring Autograph Auction*. Auction catalogue. New York, 10 May 2001.

Some Moseley Personalities, Volume I. Moseley: Moseley Local History Society, 1991.

Sotheby & Co. *Catalogue of Nineteenth Century and Modern First Editions, Presentation Copies, Autograph Letters and Literary Manuscripts*. Auction catalogue. London, 16–17 July 1973.

Sotheby Parke Bernet. *Catalogue of Autograph Letters, Literary Manuscripts and Historical Documents*. Auction catalogue. London, 16 October 1978.

——. *Catalogue of Nineteenth Century and Modern First Editions, Presentation Copies, Autograph Letters and Literary Manuscripts*. Auction catalogue. London, 28–9 July 1977.

Sotheby's. *Autograph Letters and Printed Books, including First Editions*. Auction catalogue. London, 19 May 2000.

——. *Catalogue of Valuable Autograph Letters, Literary Manuscripts and Historical Documents*. Auction catalogue. London, 21–22 July 1980.

——. *English Literature and English History*. Auction catalogue. London, 6–7 December 1984. See also *Beyond Bree*, May 1985, p. 4.

——. *English Literature and History, Private Press and Illustrated Books, Related Drawings and Animation Art*. Auction catalogue. London, 21–22 July 1992.

——. *English Literature, History, & Children's Books & Illustrations*. Auction catalogue. London, 16 December 2004.

——. *English Literature, History, Children's & Illustrated Books & Drawings*. Auction catalogue. London, 10 July 2001.

——. *English Literature, History, Children's Books and Illustrations*. Auction catalogue. London, 16 December 2004.

——. *English Literature, History, Children's Books and Illustrations*. Auction catalogue. London, 12 July 2005.

——. *English Literature, History, Children's Books, Illustrations and Photographs*. Auction catalogue. London, 8 July 2004.

——. *English Literature, History, Fine Bindings, Private Press Books, Children's Books, Illustrated Books, and Drawings*. Auction catalogue. London, 10 July 2003.

——. *English Literature, History, Private Press & Children's Books*. Auction catalogue. London, 12 December 2002.

——. *Fine Books and Manuscripts, including English and American Literature.* Auction catalogue. New York, 16–17 May 1984.

——. *Literature and Illustration.* Auction catalogue. London, 11–12 July 2002.

——. *Valuable Printed Books and Manuscripts.* Auction catalogue. London, 13 December 2001.

Spacks, Patricia Meyer. 'Ethical Pattern in *The Lord of the Rings*'. *Critique* 3 (Spring–Fall 1959), pp. 30–42. Revised as 'Power and Meaning in *The Lord of the Rings*', in Isaacs and Zimbardo, *Tolkien and the Critics*, pp. 81–99.

Spearing, A.C. Review of *Sir Gawain and the Green Knight, Pearl and Sir Orfeo*. *Times Higher Educational Supplement*, 30 January 1976.

'Speech Day', *King Edward's School Chronicle* n.s. 26, no. 189 (October 1911), pp. 71–2.

Spender, Stephen. 'Wystan Hugh Auden'. *Dictionary of National Biography, 1971–1980*. pp. 24–7.

Spurr, Barry. 'Expert beyond Experience'. *Oxford Today* 4, no. 3 (Trinity 1992), pp. 20, 22. Appreciation of Helen Gardner.

'Staying Home'. *The Times* (London), 9 February 1973, p. 14.

Stanley, E.G., and Douglas Gray, eds. *Five Hundred Years of Words and Sounds: A Festschrift for Eric Dobson.* Cambridge: D.S. Brewer; Totowa, New Jersey: Biblio, 1983.

Stapeldon Magazine 3, no. 16 (December 1911)–7, no. 42 (June 1928). Miscellaneous notes and articles.

Stedman, Michael. *La Boisselle, Ovieller, Contalmaison.* London: Leo Cooper, 1997.

——. *Thiepval.* London: Leo Cooper, 1995.

Steele, Robert. *The Story of Alexander.* London: David Nutt, 1894.

Stenström, Anders (Beregond). 'Något om pipor, blad och rökning' ('Some Notes on Pipes, Leaf and Smoking'). *Arda* 4 (1988, for 1984), pp. 32–93. In Swedish, with summary in English.

——. Review of *Finn and Hengest. Amon Hen* 66 (March 1984), pp. 5–7.

Stephens, Meic, comp. and ed. *The Oxford Companion to the Literature of Wales.* Oxford: Oxford University Press, 1986; reprinted with corrections 1990.

Sterling, Grant C. '"The Gift of Death": Tolkien's Philosophy of Mortality'. *Mythlore* 21, no. 4, whole no. 82 (Winter 1997), pp. 16–18, 38.

Stevenson, Jeffrey. 'T.B. or Not T.B.: That Is the Question'. *Amon Hen* 196 (November 2005), pp. 16–21.

Stimpson, Catharine R. *J.R.R. Tolkien.* New York: Columbia University Press, 1969.

Gerard A.J. Stodolski. *Catalogue 4.* Manchester, New Hampshire, August 1995.

——. *Catalogue 299.* Manchester, New Hampshire, June 1999.

†Strachey, Barbara. *Journeys of Frodo: An Atlas of J.R.R. Tolkien's The Lord of the Rings.* London: George Allen & Unwin, 1981.

Stringer, Jenny, ed. *The Oxford Companion to Twentieth Century Literature in English.* Oxford: Oxford University Press, 1996.

Stukeley, William. *Stonehenge: A Temple Restor'd to the British Druids*. London: Printed for W. Innys and R. Manby, 1740.

Sugerman, Shirley, ed. *Evolution of Consciousness: Studies in Polarity*. Middletown, Connecticut: Wesleyan University Press, 1976.

Sutcliffe, Peter. *The Oxford University Press: An Informal History*. Oxford: Clarendon Press, 1978.

Sutherland, James. 'David Nichol Smith'. *Dictionary of National Biography 1961–1970*. pp. 960–1.

——. 'David Nichol Smith, 1875–1962'. *Proceedings of the British Academy* 48 (1962), pp. 449–59.

Swann, Alison. *The Donald Swann Website. www.donaldswann.co.uk.*

Swann, Donald. Foreword to *The Road Goes Ever On: A Song Cycle* by J.R.R. Tolkien and Donald Swann. 2nd edn., rev. Boston: Houghton Mifflin, 1978.

——. *The Space between the Bars: A Book of Reflections*. New York: Simon and Schuster, 1968.

——. *Swann's Way: A Life in Song*. Recorded and ed. Lyn Smith. Rev. paperback edn. London: Arthur James, 1993.

Sweet, Henry. *An Anglo-Saxon Reader in Prose and Verse*. 8th edn., rev. Oxford: Clarendon Press, 1908.

Sykes, Peter. 'Tolkien's Fairies'. *Oxford Mail*, 28 May 1964, p. 6. Review of *Tree and Leaf*.

Tait, William H. Letter to the editor. *Old Edwardians Gazette*, June 1972, pp. 16–17.

Tayar, Graham. 'Tolkien's Mordor'. *The Listener*, 14 July 1977.

'Telling Stories'. *Times Literary Supplement*, 19 June 1948, p. 345. Review of *Essays Presented to Charles Williams*.

Tennyson, G.B. 'Owen Barfield: First and Last Inklings'. *The World and I* 5, no. 4 (April 1990), pp. 541–5.

Thomas, Paul Edmund. 'Some of Tolkien's Narrators'. In Flieger and Hostetter, *Tolkien's Legendarium*, pp. 161–81.

Thompson, Francis. *The Poems of Francis Thompson*. London: Hollis and Carter 1946.

Thompson, George H. 'Early Articles, Comments, Etcetera about J.R.R. Tolkien'. *Mythlore* 13, no. 3, whole no. 49 (Spring 1987), pp. 58–63.

——. 'Early Reviews of Books by J.R.R. Tolkien'. *Mythlore* 11, no. 2, whole no. 40 (Autumn 1984), pp. 56–60; 11, no. 3, whole no. 41 (Winter–Spring 1985), pp. 59–63; 12, no. 1, whole no. 43 (Autumn 1985), pp. 58–63; 12, no. 3, whole no. 45 (Spring 1986), pp. 61–2; 12, no. 4, whole no. 46 (Summer 1986), pp. 59–62; 13, no. 1, whole no. 47 (Autumn 1986), pp. 54–9.

——. 'Minor, Early References to Tolkien and His Works'. *Mythlore*, 14, no. 1, whole no. 51 (Autumn 1987), pp. 41–2, 55.

Thrall, William Flint, and Addison Hibbard. *A Handbook to Literature*. Rev. and enlarged by C. Hugh Holman. New York: Odyssey Press, 1960.

Thwaite, Anthony. 'Hobbitry'. *The Listener*, 22 November 1962, p. 831. Review of *The Adventures of Tom Bombadil and Other Verses from the Red Book*.

Tillotson, Kathleen. 'Helen Darbishire'. *Dictionary of National Biography 1961–1970*. pp. 270–1.

Timmons, Daniel. Introduction to Clark and Timmons, *J.R.R. Tolkien and His Literary Resonances*, pp. 1–10.

——. 'J.R.R. Tolkien: The "Monstrous" in the Mirror'. *Journal of the Fantastic in the Arts* 9, no. 3 (1998), pp. 229–46.

——. *Mirror on Middle-earth: J.R.R. Tolkien and the Critical Perspectives*. Ph.D. thesis, University of Toronto, 1998.

——. 'Tolkien-Related Dissertations and Theses in English'. *Tolkien Collector* 16 (July 1997), pp. 21–6.

Tolkien, Christopher. Foreword to *The Hobbit* by J.R.R. Tolkien. Fiftieth anniversary edn. London: Unwin Hyman, 1987. pp. i–xvi.

——. 'Notes on the Differences in Editions of *The Hobbit* Cited by Mr. David Cofield'. *Beyond Bree*, July 1986, pp. 1–3.

——. *The Silmarillion [by] J.R.R. Tolkien: A Brief Account of the Book and Its Making*. Boston: Houghton Mifflin, 1977.

——. 'The Tengwar Numerals'. *Quettar* (bulletin of the Linguistic Fellowship of The Tolkien Society) 13 (February 1982), pp. 8–9, with remarks by editor Steve Pillinger, p. 7; and 14 (May 1982), pp. 6–7.

Tolkien, Joan. Letter to the editor. *Sunday Times* (London), 10 October 1982, p. 25.

Tolkien, Joanna. 'Joanna Tolkien Speaks at the Tolkien Society Annual Dinner, Shrewsbury, April 16, 1994.' *Digging Potatoes, Growing Trees*, vol. 2. Ed. Helen Armstrong. Telford: The Tolkien Society, 1998. pp. 31–6.

†Tolkien, John, and Priscilla Tolkien. *A Tolkien Family Album*. London: HarperCollins, 1992.

Tolkien, Michael. 'An Interview with Michael Hilary Reuel Tolkien'. Conducted by Derek Mills on Radio Blackburn in December 1975, transcribed by Gary Hunnewell with help from Sylvia Hunnewell. *Minas Tirith Evening-Star* 18, no. 1 = *Ravenhill* 7, no. 4 (Spring 1989), pp. 5–9.

Tolkien, Priscilla. 'Beginnings and Endings'. *PN Review* 31, no. 1 (September–October 2004), pp. 9–10.

——. Foreword. *A Tribute to J.R.R. Tolkien, 3 January 1892–2 September 1973: Centenary*. Ed. Rosemary Gray. Pretoria: Unisa Medieval Association, 1992. pp. vii–x.

——. 'J.R.R. Tolkien and Edith Tolkien's Stay in Staffordshire 1916, 1917 and 1918'. *Angerthas* 34 (July 1993), p. 4–5.

——. 'Memories of J.R.R. Tolkien in His Centenary Year'. *The Brown Book* (December 1992), pp. 12–14.

——. 'My Father the Artist'. *Amon Hen* 23 (December 1976), pp. 6–7.

——. 'News from the North Pole'. *Oxford Today* 5, no. 1 (Michaelmas 1992), pp. 8–9.

——. 'Priscilla Tolkien Talks to Shirley Lowe'. *Over 21*, December 1976, p. 32.

——. 'Talk Given at the Church House Westminster on 16.9.77 by Priscilla Tolkien', *Amon Hen* 29 [?November 1977], pp. 4–6.

Tolkien, Simon. 'My Grandfather'. *The Mail on Sunday*, 23 February 2003.

'The Tolkien Affair: An Editorial'. *SFWA* [Science Fiction Writers of America] *Bulletin* 1, no. 3 (November 1965).

The Tolkien Collector 1–26 ([Autumn] 1992–December 2002).

'Tolkien Fandom'. *en.wikipedia.org/wiki/Tolkien_fandom*.

Tolkien in Oxford. British Broadcasting Corporation, 1968. Video.

'Tolkien Seeks the Quiet Life in Oxford'. *Oxford Mail*, 22 March 1972, p. 10.

†*Tolkien Studies* 1–3 (2004–6).

'Tolkien Talking'. *Sunday Times* (London), 27 November 1966.

'Tolkien's Farewell'. *Oxford Mail*, 6 June 1969, p. 4.

'Tolkien's Will', *The Bookseller*, 5 January 1974

Tolley, Clive. 'And the Word Was Made Flesh'. *Mallorn* 32 (September 1995), pp. 5–14.

——. 'The *Kalevala* and *The Silmarillion*'. *Mallorn* 15 (September 1980), pp. 13–15.

——. 'Tolkien and the Unfinished'. In Battarbee, *Scholarship & Fantasy*, pp. 151–64.

——. 'Tolkien's "Essay on Man": A Look at *Mythopoeia*'. *Inklings-Jahrbuch* 10 (1992), pp. 221–39.

Tolstoy, Nikolai. *The Quest for Merlin*. Sevenoaks: Coronet Books, 1986. First published London: Hamish Hamilton, 1985.

Topliffe, Lorise. 'Tolkien as an Undergraduate, 1911–1915'. *Exeter College Association Register* (1992), pp. 32–8.

Toynbee, Philip. 'Dissension among the Judges'. *The Observer*, 6 August 1961.

Tracey, Gerard. 'Tolkien and the Oratory'. *www.birmingham-oratory.org.uk/tolkien.htm*.

Traversi, Derek. 'The Realm of Gondor'. *The Month*, June 1956, pp. 370–1.

Treharne, Elaine, ed. *Old and Middle English: An Anthology*. Oxford: Blackwell, 2000.

Trott, Anthony. *No Place for Fop or Idler: The Story of King Edward's School, Birmingham*. London: James and James, 1992.

Trowbridge, Clinton W. *The Twentieth Century British Supernatural Novel*. Ph.D. thesis, University of Florida, 1958.

Turner, Allan. *Translating Tolkien: Philological Elements in The Lord of the Rings*. Frankfurt am Main: Peter Lang, 2005. *Duisburg Papers on Research in Language and Culture* 59.

Turner, F.M. 'Religion'. In Harrison, *The History of the University of Oxford, Vol. VIII*, pp. 293–316.

Turville-Petre, G., ed. *Víga-Glúms Saga*. Oxford: Oxford University Press, 1940. *Oxford English Monographs*.

Twiss, E.F. Obituary of Christopher Wiseman. *Old Edwardians Gazette*, April 1988.

'Two Benson Medals after 14 Years'. *The Times* (London), 24 November 1966, p. 14.

Tyack, Geoffrey. *Oxford and Cambridge*. 5th edn. London: A. & C. Black, 1999. *Blue Guide*.

Ulysses. *Catalogue 24: Modern First Editions & Illustrated Books*. London, November 1993.

'University Intelligence'. *The Times* (London), 8 April 1913, p. 6. Notice of Tolkien's Second Class in Classical (Honour) Moderations.

'University News'. *The Times* (London), 22 July 1925, p. 19. Notice of Tolkien's appointment as Rawlinson and Bosworth Professor of Anglo-Saxon.

'University News'. *The Times* (London), 2 January 1958, p. 8. Notice of Tolkien's appointment as Merton Professor of English Language and Literature.

Unwin, David. *Fifty Years with Father: A Relationship*. London: George Allen & Unwin, 1982.

Unwin, Philip. *The Publishing Unwins*. London: Heinemann, 1972.

Unwin, Rayner. 'Allen & Unwin Comments on Tolkien Reprints'. *Publishers Weekly*, 9 May 1966. Also printed in *Tolkien Journal* 2, no. 2 (Astron 1966), p. 5.

——. 'An At Last Finished Tale: The Genesis of *The Lord of the Rings*'. *Lembas-extra 1998*. Leiden: Tolkien Genootschap Unquendor, 1998. pp. 74–84.

——. 'Early Days of Elder Days'. In Flieger and Hostetter, *Tolkien's Legendarium*, pp. 3–6.

†——. *George Allen & Unwin: A Remembrancer*. Ludlow: Privately printed for the author by Merlin Unwin Books, 1999.

——. 'The Hobbit 50th Anniversary' *The Bookseller*, 16 January 1987, pp. 166–7.

——. "Publishing Tolkien". In Reynolds and GoodKnight, *Proceedings of the J.R.R. Tolkien Centenary Conference 1992*, pp. 26–9.

——. 'Taming the Lord of the Rings'. *The Bookseller*, 19 August 1988, pp. 647–50.

Unwin, Stanley. *The Truth about a Publisher: An Autobiographical Record*. London: George Allen & Unwin, 1960.

Van Meurs, J.C. 'Beowulf and Literary Criticism'. *Neophilologus* 39 (1955), pp. 114–30.

Veldman, Meredith. *Fantasy, the Bomb, and the Greening of Britain: Romantic Protest, 1945–1980*. New York: Cambridge University Press, 1994.

Venables, D.R., and R.E. Clifford, *Academic Dress of the University of Oxford*, 8th edn. Oxford: J. & P. Venables, 1998.

The Venerable English College, Rome. www.englishcollegerome.org/pages/frame1. htm.

Venice: An Illustrated Guide-book. Venezia: Renato Borgoni, [*c.* 1960].

Vergil. *Vergil's Works: The Aeneid, Eclogues, Georgics*. Trans. J.W. Mackail. New York: Modern Library, 1934.

'The Very Rev M.C. D'Arcy: Influential English Jesuit'. *The Times* (London), 22 November 1976, p. 14.

'The Vigfússon Readership', *Oxford Magazine* 60, no. 5 (13 November 1941), pp. 65–6.

Vinaver, Eugène. 'Mr Kenneth Sisam: Encouraging True Scholarship'. *The Times* (London), 2 September 1971, p. 14.

Vink, Renée. 'Translation Troubles of an Author: Some Reflections on an Angry Letter by Tolkien'. *Lembas-extra 93/94*. [Leiden]: Tolkien Genootschap 'Unquendor', [?1994]. pp. 45–57.

Wain, John. 'Push Bar to Open'. *Oxford Magazine*, Hilary Term 1988, pp. 3–5.

——. *Sprightly Running: Part of an Autobiography*. London: Macmillan, 1962.

Ward, Maisie. 'Gilbert Keith Chesterton'. *Dictionary of National Biography, 1931–1940*. pp. 171–5.

——. *Gilbert Keith Chesterton*. New York: Sheed and Ward, 1943.

Waterfield's. *Catalogue 176: Oxford, Oxfordshire & the Cotswolds*. Oxford, 1999.

Watson, J.R. 'The Hobbits and the Critics'. *Critical Quarterly* 13, no. 3 (Autumn 1971), pp. 252–8.

Watts, Janet. 'Bilbo Sings Again'. *The Guardian*, 19 September 1974.

Wawm, Andrew. *The Vikings and the Victorians: Inventing the Old North in 19th-Century Britain*. Woodbridge, Suffolk: D.S. Brewer, 2000.

Wayne, Jenifer. *The Purple Dress: Growing Up in the Thirties*. London: Victor Gollancz, 1979.

Webster's Geographical Dictionary. Rev. edn. Springfield, Massachusetts: G. & C. Merriam, 1957.

Weedon, Joan. *Father John Tolkien*. Eynsham: The Churches, 1994.

West, John G., Jr., ed. *Celebrating Middle-earth: The Lord of the Rings as a Defense of Western Civilization*. Seattle: Inkling Books, 2002.

West, Richard C. '"And She Named Her Own Name": Being True to One's Word in Tolkien's Middle-earth'. *Tolkien Studies* 2 (2005), pp. 1–10.

——. 'The Critics, and Tolkien, and C.S. Lewis: Reviews [of William Ready, *The Tolkien Relation*, etc.]'. *Orcrist* 5 = *Tolkien Journal* 4, no. 3, whole no. 14 (1970–1), pp. 4–9.

——. 'Real-world Myth in a Secondary World: Mythological Aspects in the Story of Beren and Lúthien'. In Chance, *Tolkien the Medievalist*, pp. 259–67.

——. 'The Status of Tolkien Scholarship'. *Tolkien Journal* 15 (Summer 1972), p. 21.

†——. 'A Tolkien Checklist: Selected Criticism 1981–2004'. *Modern Fiction Studies* 50, no. 4 (Winter 2004), pp. 1015–28.

†——. *Tolkien Criticism: An Annotated Checklist*. 2nd edn. Kent, Ohio: Kent State University Press, 1981.

——. 'Túrin's *Ofermod*: An Old English Theme in the Development of the Story of Túrin'. In Flieger and Hostetter, *Tolkien's Legendarium*, pp. 233–45.

——. 'W.H. Lewis: Historian of the Inklings and of Seventeenth-century France'. *Seven* 14 (1997), pp. 74–86.

White, Michael. *Tolkien: A Biography*. London: Little, Brown, 2001.

Whitehouse, C.J. and G.P. *A Town for Four Winters*. [Stafford?]: Staffordshire County Council, in association with the authors, 1983.

Who Was Who. Various volumes.

Who's Who. Various volumes.

Who's Who in Oxfordshire. London: 'Who's Who in the Counties', 1936.

Willett, Edward. *J.R.R. Tolkien: Master of Imaginary Worlds*. Berkeley Heights, New Jersey: Enslow, 2004.

Willey, Basil. 'Helen Darbishire, 1881–1961'. *Proceedings of the British Academy* 47 (1961), pp. 401–15.

——. 'Henry Stanley Bennett, 1889–1972'. *Proceedings of the British Academy* 58 (1972), pp. 551–67.

Williams, Charles. *Arthurian Torso*. With commentary by C.S. Lewis. London: Oxford University Press, 1948.

——. *Essential Writings in Spirituality and Theology*. Ed. Charles Hefling. Cambridge, Massachusetts: Cowley Publications, 1993.

——. *The Image of the City and Other Essays*. Ed. Anne Ridler. London: Oxford University Press, 1958.

——. *Letters to Lalage: The Letters of Charles Williams to Lois Lang-Sims*. Commentary by Lois Lang-Sims. Introduction and notes by Glen Cavaliero. Kent, Ohio: Kent State University Press, 1989.

——. *To Michal from Serge: Letters from Charles Williams to His Wife, Florence, 1939–1945*. Ed. Roma A. King, Jr. Kent, Ohio: Kent State University Press, 2002.

Wilson, A.N. *C.S. Lewis: A Biography*. London: Collins, 1990.

Wilson, Edmund. 'Oo, Those Awful Orcs'. *The Nation* 182 (14 April 1956), pp. 312–14. Review of *The Lord of the Rings*.

Winchester, Simon. *The Meaning of Everything: The Story of the Oxford English Dictionary*. Oxford: Oxford University Press, 2003.

Dominic Winter Book Auctions. *Printed Books, Maps & Ephemera*. Auction catalogue. South Cerney, Gloucestershire, 15 December 2004.

Wiseman, Christopher. 'Christopher Luke Wiseman'. *Old Edwardians Gazette*, April 1988, pp. 22, 24.

——. 'Notes and News'. *King Edward's School Chronicle* n.s. 26, no. 189 (October 1911), pp. 74–6.

Wollheim, Donald A. 'The Ace Tolkiens'. *Lighthouse* 13 (August 1965), pp. 16–18.

——. 'No "Intermediary"' (letter to the editor). *Saturday Review*, 23 October 1965, p. 56.

Wood, Anthony. 'Fireworks for the Author – and B.B.C. 2 Viewers'. *Oxford Mail*, 9 February 1968, p. 10.

Wrenn, C.L. 'Sir W. Craigie: Stimulus to Study of Germanic Languages'. *The Times* (London), 9 September 1957, p. 10.

——. *A Study of Old English Literature*. London: George G. Harrap, 1967.

——, ed. *Beowulf with the Finnesburg Fragment*. Rev. by W.F. Bolton. London: George G. Harrap, 1973.

—— and G. Bullough, eds. *English Studies Today*. Oxford: Oxford University Press, 1951.

Wright, Elizabeth Mary. *The Life of Joseph Wright*. London: Oxford University Press, 1932.

Wyllie, J.M. 'Sir William Craigie, 1867–1957'. *Proceedings of the British Academy* 48 (1962), pp. 272–91.

Wynne, Patrick, and Carl F. Hostetter. '"Verbs, Syntax! Hooray!": A Preliminary Assessment of Adunaic Grammar in *The Notion Club Papers*'. *Vinyar Tengwar* 24 (July 1992), pp. 14–38.

—— see also THE PUBLISHED WRITINGS OF J.R.R. TOLKIEN in vol. 1

—— and Christopher Gilson. 'Bird and Leaf: Image and Structure in *Narqelion*'. *Parma Eldalamberon* 3, no. 1, whole no. 9 (1990), pp. 6–19, 22–32.

Yamniuk, Stephanie. 'Klass and Tolkien Families' Program to Help Disadvantaged'. *On Manitoba*, April 2005, p. 29.

Yates, Jessica. 'Appetizers'. *A Long-Expected Party: Progress Report* 6 (Tolkien Society, 1992), pp. 23–6.

——. '"The Battle of the Eastern Field": A Commentary'. *Mallorn* 13 [1979], pp. 3–5.

——. 'The Other 50th Anniversary'. *Mythlore* 16, no. 3, whole no. 61 (Spring 1990), pp. 47–50.

—— (as Jessica Kemball-Cook). Review of *J.R.R. Tolkien: A Biography* by Humphrey Carpenter. *Amon Hen* 26 (May 1977), pp. 11–12.

——. 'Mr. Bliss in Context'. *Amon Hen* 59 (December 1982), pp. 6–7. Review of *Mr. Bliss*.

——. Review of *The Silmarillion*. *British Book News*, January 1978.

——. 'The Source of "The Lay of Aotrou and Itroun"'. In *Leaves from the Tree: J.R.R. Tolkien's Shorter Fiction*, pp. 63–71.

——. 'Tolkien the Anti-Totalitarian'. In Reynolds and GoodKnight, *Proceedings of the J.R.R. Tolkien Centenary Conference 1992*, pp. 233–45.

Yolton, John. 'In the Soup'. *Kenyon Review* (Summer 1965), pp. 565–7. Review of *Tree and Leaf*.

Zettersten, Arne. 'The AB Language Lives'. In Hammond and Scull, *The Lord of the Rings, 1954–2004: Scholarship in Honor of Richard E. Blackwelder*, pp. 13–24.

——. Review of *Ancrene Wisse*. *English Studies* 47 (1966), pp. 290–2.

Zimbardo, Rose A., and Neil D. Isaacs, eds. *Understanding The Lord of the Rings: The Best of Tolkien Criticism*. Boston: Houghton Mifflin, 2004.

Zimmermann, Manfred. 'The Origin of Gandalf and Josef Madlener'. *Mythlore* 23, no. 4, whole no. 34 (Winter 1983), pp. 22, 24.

Zocca, Emma. *Assisi e Dintorni*. 3rd edn. Roma: Istituto Poligrafico dello Stato, 1960.

Blackwell's Bookshops, Oxford
BBC Written Archives Centre, Caversham Park, Reading
University of Birmingham
Bloemfontein Cathedral
Bodleian Library, Oxford
British Library, London
Cambridge University Library
Centre for Oxfordshire Studies, Oxford Central Library
Corpus Christi College, Oxford
Early English Text Society
English Faculty Library, Oxford
English Place-Name Society
Exeter College Library, Oxford
Glasgow University Archive Services
HarperCollins, London
Hið íslenska bókmenntafélag (Icelandic Literary Society)
King Edward's School, Birmingham
Leeds University
Marquette University Libraries, Milwaukee, Wisconsin
Merton College, Oxford
National University of Ireland
Oxford University Archives
Oxford University Press, Oxford
Pembroke College, Oxford
National Archives, Kew (formerly Public Record Office)
National University of Ireland
Reading University Library
University of St Andrews Library
St Anne's College Library, Oxford
Simmons College, Boston, Massachusetts
Society for the Study of Mediaeval Languages and Literature
Society of the Holy Child Jesus
Staffordshire Archives Service
University College, London
Marion E. Wade Center, Wheaton College, Illinois
Worcester College, Oxford

Private collections

INDEX

Although each of the two volumes of *The J.R.R. Tolkien Companion and Guide* may be used independent of the other, they are designed to work in concert. To that end, we have prepared a common index, covering both the **Chronology** (Volume I) and the **Reader's Guide** (Volume II). This division is indicated by one or two asterisks on the title-page of each part, and by the roman numerals I and II below. The following is not meant to trace every mention of every person, place, or title in our text, but to point to those elements most pertinent to Tolkien's life and works, or otherwise likely to be of interest to readers, including the names of authorities and other writers. It follows the rules of style described in our preface, and the alphabetical structure of the Reader's Guide.

Afterwards I 31
Agøy, Nils Ivar II 65, 352
Ainulindalë I 172, 205, 297, 333, 341, 356,
    II 28–32, 80, 81, 295, 520, 565, 595, 606,
    802, 894–902 *passim*, 907, 908, 911,
    1073
Air raid warden duty I 235–6, 248, 257,
    262, 264, 268, 269, 272, 291, 292, II 1089
Aitken, Daniel Ferguson I 141, 142
Akallabêth (*The Downfall of Númenor*)
    I 180, 339, 443, 751, II 33, 66, 68, 370,
    558, 665, 673–8 *passim*, 700, 753, 849,
    896, 897, 900, 907, 911
Alabaster, William I 515
Albert (France) I 83, 94, II 323
Alcar mi Tarmenel na Erun I 651, II 34
Aldarion and Erendis I 556, 627, II 34–5,
    208–9, 665–6, 881, 899, 900, 1065, 1119
Aldershot I 19, 20, II 37
Alderson, Brian II 948
Aletsch glacier I 27, 777, II 993
Alexander the Great II 174
Alexander, B.H. I 420
Alexander, Peter II 146
Alford, Peter I 484, 485, 523, II 223, 224
All Souls College, Oxford I 177, 225, 347,
    479, 657
Allan, Jim II 480, 1130
Allegory I 319, 480, 483, 487, 514, II 24,
    37–41, 89–90, 192, 217, 489, 495, 496,
    533, 752, 821, 839–40, 945–50 *passim*,
    1089, 1097
Allen, Miss I 604
Allen, Carlton Kemp II 724
Allen, Walter I 542, II 164, 396
George Allen & Unwin I 54, 172, 181 etc.,
    II 1, 9, 17, 21, 28, 54, 76, 85, 149, 153, 160,
    200, 203, 248, 250, 277, 284, 285, 289,
    353–4, 361, 364, 366–7, 380, 392, 393–5,
    489–90, 492, 509, 525, 539, 540, 545,
    546, 547, 552, 561, 563, 591, 593, 625, 649,
    668–9, 687, 761, 782–3, 785, 796–7, 803,
    812, 830, 856, 859, 873, 878, 894, 897,
    898, 909, 910, 930–1, 945, 991, 1023,
    1033–4, 1067–9, 1070, 1081–2, 1084,
    1100; *see also (especially)* Beard, W.N.;
    Dadlez, Alina; Eames, Ronald; Furth,
    C.A. (Charles); Hill, M.J. (Joy); Unwin,
    Philip; Unwin, Rayner; Unwin, Stanley
Allenby, Major-General I 33

Allingham, William II 524, 767
Almqvist & Wiksell (Gebers) I 515, 516,
    535, 567, 568, 569, 575, II 1032, 1034, 1035
Alper, Renee II 286
'Alphabet of Dairon', *The* I 172, II 1129
'Alphabet of Fëanor' II 1127
'Alphabet of Rúmil' I 106, 115, 117, 118,
    II 129, 1126–7, 1128
Alps I 27–8
Alton, Mr I 383
Aman I 549, II 41–2, 62, 597, 613, 899
Ambarkanta I 171–2, 205, 356, II 41–3, 80,
    284, 802, 885, 894, 902, 905, 908
Ambleside II 981, 1018
American Hobbit Association II 286
American MENSA II 287
American Tolkien Society II 286
Amiens I 82, II 323
Amis, John, *Amiscellany* II 992
Amon Hen II 287
Ampleforth II 1021
'Amroth and Nimrodel' *see The History
    of Galadriel and Celeborn*
Amsterdam I 521, 522, 523, 524, II 640;
    Rijkmuseum I 523; University I 523;
    Wynand Fockink I 523
'Analysis of fragments of other languages
    found in *The Lord of the Rings*' II 43
Ancrene Riwle I 40, 114, 135, 137, 154, 155,
    157, 161, 171, 173, 175–6, 177, 179, 182, 183,
    197, 198–9, 223, 253, 282, 283, 285, 293,
    317, 334, 348, 384, 392, 398, 459, 478,
    506, 531–2, 569, 571, 574, 576, 577, 578,
    598, II 44–9, 120, 251, 873, 938, 964;
    translation by M.B. Salu I 392, 459,
    478, II 44, 46, 873; *see also Ancrene
    Wisse*
Ancrene Wisse (MS CCCC 402),
    including Tolkien's edition I 155, 173,
    177–83 *passim*, 199, 216, 220, 226, 256,
    282, 285, 287, 293, 297, 299, 301–2,
    309, 313, 331, 340, 387, 388, 391, 399,
    485, 486–7, 489, 490, 494, 498, 503,
    504, 505, 507, 514, 520, 523, 529, 530–2,
    533, 535, 540, 541–2, 546, 550, 554–88
    passim, 598, 599, 602, 799, 800, II 44–8,
    49, 120, 143, 144, 208, 251, 353, 447, 873,
    897, 910, 964, 1100, 1101, 1111–12
Ancrene Wisse and Hali Meiðhad I 148,
    II 44, 49, 446

to Cees Ouboter (in René van Rossenberg, 'Tolkien's Exceptional Visit to Holland: A Reconstruction', *Proceedings of the J.R.R. Tolkien Centenary Conference 1992*, 1995) © The J.R.R. Tolkien Copyright Trust 1995; letter by J.R.R. Tolkien to a class of primary school children (Sotheby's auction catalogue, 16 December 2004) © The J.R.R. Tolkien Copyright Trust 2004; letter by J.R.R. Tolkien to Eileen Elgar (Sotheby's auction catalogue, 6–7 December 1984) © The J.R.R. Tolkien Copyright Trust 1984; letter by J.R.R. Tolkien to Evelyn B. Byrne and Otto M. Penzler (*Attacks of Taste*, 1971) © The J.R.R. Tolkien Copyright Trust 1971; letter by J.R.R. Tolkien to G.E. Selby (Maggs Bros., *Catalogue 1086*) © The J.R.R. Tolkien Copyright Trust 1988; letter by J.R.R. Tolkien to G.E. Selby (Sotheby's auction catalogue, 28–29 July 1977) © The J.R.R. Tolkien Copyright Trust 1977; letter by J.R.R. Tolkien to G.E. Selby (Sotheby's auction catalogue, 16–17 May 1984) © The J.R.R. Tolkien Copyright Trust 1984; letter by J.R.R. Tolkien to George Lewis Hersch (Michael Silverman, *Catalogue No. 2*) © The J.R.R. Tolkien Copyright Trust 1998; letter by J.R.R. Tolkien to George Sayer (Christie's auction catalogue, 16 November 2001) © The J.R.R. Tolkien Copyright Trust 2001; letter by J.R.R. Tolkien to George Sayer (in Sayer, 'Recollections of J.R.R. Tolkien', *Proceedings of the J.R.R. Tolkien Centenary Conference 1992*, 1995) © The J.R.R. Tolkien Copyright Trust 1995; letter by J.R.R. Tolkien to H. Cotton Minchin (Christie's auction catalogue, 26 November 1997) © The J.R.R. Tolkien Copyright Trust 1997; letter by J.R.R. Tolkien to Humphrey Carpenter (University Archives, *Catalogue 116*) © The J.R.R. Tolkien Copyright Trust 1994; letter by J.R.R. Tolkien to J.L.N. O'Loughlin (Paul C. Richards Autographs, *Catalogue 228*) © The J.R.R. Tolkien Copyright Trust 1988; letter by J.R.R. Tolkien to James A.H. Murray (Sotheby's auction catalogue, 12 December 2002) © The J.R.R. Tolkien Copyright Trust 2002; letter by J.R.R. Tolkien to Jane Louise Curry (Sotheby's auction catalogue, 10 July 2001) © The J.R.R. Tolkien Copyright Trust 2001; letter by J.R.R. Tolkien to Jennifer Brookes-Smith (Christie's auction catalogue, 2 December 2003) © The J.R.R. Tolkien Copyright Trust 2003; letter by J.R.R. Tolkien to Joy Hill (quoted in Hammond and Scull, 'Note on the 50th Anniversary Edition', *The Lord of the Rings*, 2004) © The J.R.R. Tolkien Copyright Trust 2004; letter by J.R.R. Tolkien to 'King Ephedolos' (Sotheby's auction catalogue, 14–15 December 1992) © The J.R.R. Tolkien Copyright Trust 1992; letter by J.R.R. Tolkien to L.M. Cutts (Sotheby's auction catalogue, 10 July 2003) © The J.R.R. Tolkien Copyright Trust 2003; letter by J.R.R. Tolkien to L. Sprague de Camp, *Mythlore*, Summer 1987 © The J.R.R. Tolkien Copyright Trust 1987; letter by J.R.R. Tolkien to Milton Waldman, ?late 1951 (in *La Feuille de la Compagnie Cahier d'études tolkieniennes* 2, l'automne 2003) © The J.R.R. Tolkien Copyright Trust 2003; letter by J.R.R. Tolkien to Miss How (Sotheby's auction catalogue, 21–22 July 1980) © The J.R.R. Tolkien Copyright Trust 1980; letter by J.R.R. Tolkien to Miss Jaworski (Sotheby's auction catalogue, 16 October 1978) © The J.R.R. Tolkien Copyright Trust 1978; letter by J.R.R. Tolkien to Miss Morley (Dominic Winter Book Auctions catalogue, 15 December 2004) © The J.R.R. Tolkien Copyright Trust 1978; letter by J.R.R. Tolkien to Miss Perry (Michael Silverman, *Catalogue Nine*, 1993) © The J.R.R. Tolkien Copyright Trust 1978; letter by J.R.R. Tolkien to Mr Hodgson (Phillips auction catalogue, 24 March 2000) © The J.R.R. Tolkien Copyright Trust 2000; letter by J.R.R. Tolkien to Mrs Gill (eBay.com, December 2003) © The J.R.R. Tolkien Copyright Trust 2003; letter by J.R.R. Tolkien to Mrs Munby (Sotheby's auction catalogue, 11–12 July 2002) © The J.R.R. Tolkien Copyright Trust 1981, 2002; letter by J.R.R. Tolkien to Moira Sayer (Christie's auction catalogue, 13 November 2001) © The J.R.R. Tolkien Copyright Trust 2001; letter by J.R.R. Tolkien to Patricia Kirke (Gerard A.J. Stodolski, *Catalogue 4*, 1995) © The J.R.R. Tolkien Copyright Trust 1995; letter by J.R.R. Tolkien to Patricia Kirke (Gerard A.J. Stodolski, *Catalogue 299*, June 1999) © The J.R.R. Tolkien Copyright Trust 1999; letter by J.R.R. Tolkien to Paul Bibire (*Vinyar Tengwar*, July 2001) © The J.R.R. Tolkien Copyright Trust 2001; letter by J.R.R. Tolkien to Peter Alford (Sotheby's auction catalogue, 13 December 2001) © The J.R.R. Tolkien Copyright Trust 2001; letter by J.R.R. Tolkien to the President of the Tolkien Society of America (*Tolkien Journal*, 1968) © The J.R.R. Tolkien Copyright Trust 1968; letter by J.R.R. Tolkien to Professor Jongkees (R.M. Smythe, *Catalogue 10*, 2001) © The J.R.R. Tolkien Copyright Trust 2001; letter by J.R.R. Tolkien to R.W. Burchfield (Christie's auction catalogue, 7 June 2006) © The J.R.R. Tolkien Copyright Trust 2006; letters by J.R.R. Tolkien to R.W. Chapman (*Moreana*, February and June 1987) © The J.R.R. Tolkien Copyright Trust 1987; letter by J.R.R. Tolkien to 'Rosemary' (*Mallorn*, November 1998) © The J.R.R. Tolkien Copy-

For permission to quote from or refer to materials in their possession, we gratefully acknowledge the BBC Written Archives Centre; the Bodleian Library, University of Oxford (Tolkien A4/2, ff. 1–2, 10, 27–37, 39, 42, 44, 62, 104, 107–8, 110, 113, 116–18, 124–7, 145–8, 163–7, 174–5, 178; Tolkien A7/7, ff. 179, 185, 193–200, 208; Tolkien A8/2, ff. 167–9; Tolkien A9/2, ff. 134–7, 139; Tolkien A12/4, ff. 81–2, 87, 116, 120, 121, 124, 126, 128–30, 132, 134, 136, 137; Tolkien A13/1, ff. 81, 83–5, 168, 170; Tolkien A15/2, ff. 149; Tolkien A18/1, ff. 1–4, 8, 15, 18–23, 28, 32, 101–5, 118; Tolkien A19/3, ff. 1–3, 6, 7; Tolkien A22/1, f. 120; Tolkien A27/2, f. 18a; Tolkien A30/1, ff. 107–9, 121; Tolkien A33/1, ff. 301–7; Tolkien A35, f. 127; Tolkien A66, f. 118; Tolkien C6/1, ff. 30–44; Tolkien E16/45, ff. 11, 47, 101–2, 142; MS Tolkien 4, ff. 56–8, 61–3, 66–7, 76; MS Tolkien 6, ff. 2, 19, 22; MS Tolkien 7, ff. 54, 60, 62–3, 65, 67; MS Tolkien 9, ff. 7, 108, 148, 164; MS Tolkien 13/53; MS Tolkien 14, f. 43, 74, 91, 105, 110, 112, 119, 132, 161; MS Tolkien 19, f. 136; MS Tolkien 21, ff. 3, 22–3, 32–5, 37–8, 48, 52–3, 59, 65, 67, 89, 92–3, 95–6, 111, 125–7, 130; MS Dep Monckton vol. 9, nos. 191–2, 332; MS Eng. d.3529; MSS Gilbert Murray 98, f. 15); the British Library (MS Add. 52599, MS Add. 71657, National Sound Archives recordings T1027W and T29866); the Department of Special Collections and University Archives, John P. Raynor, S.J., Library, Marquette University (Tolkien papers); the National Archives, Kew (BW 2/650; WO 95/1574; WO 95/2238; WO 95/2245–7; WO 339/28936; WO 339/34423; census records); the Oxford University Archives (DC 9/1/1–2; DC 10/3/2-3; EX 2/2/2/3; FA 1/1/2–7; FA 4/5/1/1–2; FA 4/5/2/1-12; FA 4/10/1/1; FA 4/10/2/3; FA 9/2/875; UR 3/1/30/1–2; UR 3/6/2/3; UR 6/ASR/1, file 1; UR 6/EL/3, file 1; UR 6/LEM/2, file 1; UR 6/PHI/2, file 1); the University of Reading (George Allen &

Unwin archive); and René van Rossenberg. Quotations from George Allen & Unwin archives were made with permission of HarperCollins, successor to the publishers George Allen & Unwin and Unwin Hyman. Letters by or to Pauline Baynes were quoted with the permission of Mrs Pauline Gasch. Materials from the Pamela Chandler Archive were used with the permission of Mrs Diana Willson. Letters from the Early English Text Society archives were quoted with permission of the Council of the Early English Text Society. Material from the Exeter College Archives has been used with the permission of the Rector and Fellows of Exeter College, Oxford. Quotations from letters by Robert Q. Gilson were made with the permission of Ms Julia Margretts. Materials from the Oxford University Press Archives were quoted by permission of the Secretary to the Delegates of Oxford University Press. Quotations from letters by Christopher Wiseman were made with the permission of Ms Susan Wood.

The majority of quotations from Tolkien's writings have been made with the kind permission of the Tolkien Estate, and are acknowledged in detail in the preceding copyright statement. Quotations from the unrestricted Tolkien Papers in the Bodleian Library, University of Oxford, are documented below; all other citations in this book to the Tolkien Papers, Bodleian Library refer to materials currently with restricted access.

CHRONOLOGY

p. 183, 'our profit' (Tolkien A4/2, f. 10)
p. 184, 'once (lightheartedly) . . . several in use' (Tolkien A18/1, f. 8)
p. 185, 'grieved that . . . you have given' (Tolkien A4/2, f. 27)
p. 379, 'today . . . curious Chaucer usage' (Tolkien A18/1, f. 32)
p. 499, 'the emendations . . . to the class', 'I have not had time . . . translation' (Tolkien A22/1, f. 120)
p. 504, 'beginning to feel . . . two or three days', 'a first charge on what time is left', 'But work put aside . . . of this vacation' (Tolkien A7/7, f. 179)
pp. 531–2, 'of course' . . . (etc., extracts to) 'have no utility' (Tolkien A7/7, ff. 193–200)
p. 533, 'At the meeting . . . of your memo' (Tolkien A7/7, f. 185)
p. 557, 'that certain parts . . . of St. Katherine' (Tolkien A7/7, f. 208)
p. 563, 'Your notes on capitals . . . "very clear"' (Tolkien A4/2, f. 62)
p. 570, 'so that duplication . . . as we have agreed' (Tolkien A4/2, f. 106)
p. 570, 'As I said . . . admirable")' (Tolkien A4/2, f. 107)
p. 571, 'I am very much tied . . . on March 20' (Tolkien A4/2, f. 113)
pp. 572–3, 'if I had not had' . . . (etc., extracts to) 'proceed without me' (Tolkien A4/2, ff. 116–18)
p. 574, 'Forgive my chattiness . . . in the work' (Tolkien A4/2, ff. 124–5)
p. 577, 'as befits one' . . . (etc., extracts to) 'the threads of my other work' (Tolkien A4/2, ff. 146–8)
p. 586, 'I have had to do . . . is left alone' (Tolkien A4/2, f. 157)
p. 586, 'The alterations were . . . they deserve' (Tolkien A4/2, f. 162)
p. 586, 'May I thank you . . . "unauthorized"' (Tolkien A4/2, ff. 163)
p. 587, 'if I had fully understood . . . you and others', 'I had to think . . . if approved' (Tolkien A4/2, f. 178)
p. 594, 'This is the sort . . . give his all for' (MS Tolkien 19, f. 136)
p. 605, 'The faintest cloud . . . less trying than writing' (MS Tolkien 4, f. 76)
p. 623, 'but I am unfortunately . . . receive my contribution?' (MS Tolkien 9, fol. 164)
p. 687, 'should be given . . . might be cut down' (MS Tolkien 21, f. 3)

READER'S GUIDE

p. 40, 'is *not* an allegory . . . hearer or reader' (MS Tolkien 9, f. 108)
p. 45, 'enormous advantages . . . with the manuscript' (Tolkien A7/7, f. 170)
p. 47, 'the place of the line-ending . . . reasonable choice' (Tolkien A7/7, f. 200)
p. 56, 'hoped that some . . . not quite fair' (MS Tolkien 14, f. 105)

p. 224, 'the characters and even the places . . . limitations of plays' (MS Tolkien 6, f. 19)

p. 244, 'As the train . . . silent and furtive' (MS Tolkien 9, f. 7)

p. 254, 'It was fledged . . . mass-production of slaughter' (MS Tolkien 6, f. 22)

p. 255, 'So to save the life . . . just: no' (MS Tolkien 6, f. 22)

p. 255, 'it may have some practical uses . . . like locusts' (MS Tolkien 14, f. 161)

pp. 385–6, 'took long in first writing . . . than the Dragon' (MS Tolkien 21, f. 130)

p. 350, 'an almost perfect blend . . . explicit and revealed' (MS Tolkien 14, f. 119)

p. 457, 'Philology has been dethroned . . . *legend or myth*', 'higher or lower mythology as A.L. called them' (MS Tolkien 14, f. 91)

p. 458, 'six stories from Grimm . . . *The Red Etin*' (MS Tolkien 14, f. 132)

p. 525, 'The roof of Paddington Station . . . dome of heaven' (MS Tolkien 14, f. 110)

p. 555, 'In vain we regret . . . most of their tongue', 'the ruin of Gaul . . . the Cymric speaking peoples' (Tolkien A15/2, f. 149)

p. 567, 'For me at any rate . . . since childhood' (MS Tolkien 14, f. 74)

p. 568, 'get out B.Litt. on Macdonald' (MS Tolkien 14, f. 43)

p. 570, 'a gem – of the kind . . . Second part of Curdie.)' (MS Tolkien 6, f. 2)

p. 570, 'And beside *The Princess and the Goblin* . . . *The Golden Key*' (MS Tolkien 14, f. 119)

p. 570, 'Death is the theme . . . "romance of Lilith"' (MS Tolkien 14, f. 112)

p. 639, 'triumphant formula . . . Phoenix and the Carpet' (MS Tolkien 14, f. 119)

pp. 653–4, 'I must protest . . . impudence of a parasite' (Tolkien A30/1, f. 121)

p. 687, 'Grown-ups writing fairy-stories . . . "marketing problem"' (MS Tolkien 14, f. 119)

pp. 769–70, 'You of course go clean contrary . . . feeling and thought?' (Tolkien A35, f. 127)

p. 770, 'The making of translations . . . no other way', 'First of all . . . humble and loyal allegiance' (Tolkien A30, ff. 107–9)

p. 771, 'I have at present . . . no room to move' (Tolkien A35, f. 127)

p. 815, 'liked my magic . . . strong meat for nurseries' (MS Tolkien 14, f. 105)

p. 943, 'the project fizzed out . . . exemplar of "fairy" magic)' (MS Tolkien 9, f. 148)

pp. 943–4, 'when striving to say . . . thing in itself' (MS Tolkien 9, f. 3)

pp. 944–5, 'I must beg the pardon . . . sincere and humble – dislike' (MS Tolkien 9, f. 108)

p. 958, 'the Catenians . . . domestic commitments' (Tolkien A6/2, f. 145)

pp. 961–2, 'benefit of clergy', 'I wish I could get off as lightly . . . I know better' (Tolkien A13/1, ff. 168, 170)

p. 964, 'as befits . . . of the Council' (Tolkien A4/2, f. 146)

p. 1130, 'I should like to record . . . across the river' (MS Tolkien 14, f. 119).